Harden's

BEST UK RESTAURANTS

2019

INDEPENDENT AND UNBIASED REVIEWS OF OVER 2,800 RESTAURANTS

'IT WILL TELL YOU WHAT DINERS ACTUALLY LIKE, AS OPPOSED TO MERE RESTAURANT CRITICS'
— RICHARD VINES, CHIEF FOOD CRITIC, BLOOMBERG

Put us in your client's pocket!

Branded gift books and editions for iPhone
call to discuss the options on 020 7839 4763.

Follow Harden's on Twitter @hardensbites

© **Harden's Limited 2018**

ISBN 978-0-99294-080-5

British Library Cataloguing-in-Publication data: a catalogue record for this book is available from the British Library.

Printed in Britain by SRP, Exeter

Assistant editors: Bruce Millar, Clodagh Kinsella, Antonia Russell
Designers: (text) Paul Smith, (cover) Egelnick

Harden's Limited
Beta Space, 25 Holywell Row, London EC2A 4XE

Would restaurateurs (and PRs) please address communications to 'Editorial' at the above address, or ideally by email to: editorial@hardens.com The contents of this book are believed correct at the time of printing. Nevertheless, the publisher can accept no responsibility for errors or changes in or omissions from the details given.

◎ Harden's 100

The UK's 100 Best Restaurants for 2019, as dictated by Harden's annual survey of diners

1	Casamia, The General, Bristol (2)	**26**	Morston Hall, Morston (36)
2	Texture, London (33)	**27**	Quilon, London (-)
3	The Araki, London (1)	**28**	Artichoke, Amersham (61)
4	Restaurant Nathan Outlaw, Port Isaac (4)	**29**	Black Swan, Oldstead (8)
5	The Ledbury, London (3)	**30**	Moor Hall, Aughton (30)
6	La Dame de Pic, London (90)	**31**	L'Enclume, Cartmel (18)
7	Fraiche, Oxton (12)	**32**	Yorke Arms, Ramsgill-in-Nidderdale (19)
8	Winteringham Fields, Winteringham (-)	**33**	The Feathered Nest Inn, Nether Westcote (-)
9	Waterside Inn, Bray (7)	**34**	The Walnut Tree, Llandewi Skirrid (-)
10	Hambleton Hall, Hambleton (43)	**35**	The Clove Club, London (10)
11	Core by Clare Smyth, London (-)	**36**	Brat, London (-)
12	Aulis London, London (-)	**37**	Pétrus, London (41)
13	The Five Fields, London (28)	**38**	Midsummer House, Cambridge (21)
14	Bubbledogs, Kitchen Table, London (27)	**39**	Hedone, London (42)
15	Sushi Tetsu, London (16)	**40**	L'Ortolan, Shinfield (-)
16	Le Manoir aux Quat' Saisons, Great Milton (25)	**41**	Hunan, London (56)
17	The Fat Duck, Bray (5)	**42**	Simpsons, Birmingham (-)
18	Restaurant Martin Wishart, Edinburgh (9)	**43**	Mãos, London (-)
19	The Box Tree, Ilkley (39)	**44**	Gareth Ward at Ynyshir, Eglwys Fach (15)
20	Lympstone Manor, Exmouth (54)	**45**	Freemasons at Wiswell, Wiswell (-)
21	Sorrel, Dorking (-)	**46**	Lucknam Park, Colerne (-)
22	Adam's, Birmingham (32)	**47**	Tyddyn Llan, Llandrillo (38)
23	Restaurant Sat Bains, Nottingham (13)	**48**	Hakkasan Mayfair, London (-)
24	Indian Accent, London (-)	**49**	The Sportsman, Seasalter (85)
25	Le Gavroche, London (22)	**50**	The Neptune, Old Hunstanton (44)

Casamia, The General, Bristol

The Araki, London

Texture, London

Restaurant Nathan Outlaw, Port Isaac

◎Harden's 100

The UK's 100 Best Restaurants for 2019, as dictated by Harden's annual survey of diners

51	Raby Hunt, Summerhouse (29)	**76**	Roganic, London (-)
52	Fera at Claridge's, London (-)	**77**	Chez Bruce, London (53)
53	The Castle Terrace, Edinburgh (-)	**78**	Story, London (17)
54	The Clock House, Ripley (-)	**79**	Jikoni, London (-)
55	Andrew Fairlie, Auchterarder (35)	**80**	Hélène Darroze, London (37)
56	Gidleigh Park, Chagford (11)	**81**	Yauatcha W1, London (-)
57	The Square, London (-)	**82**	Marcus, London (75)
58	The Peat Inn, Cupar (94)	**83**	Pollen Street Social, London (77)
59	Purnells, Birmingham (88)	**84**	Elystan Street, London (69)
60	Pied À Terre, London (23)	**85**	Dinings W1, London (-)
61	Lumière, Cheltenham (-)	**86**	Chutney Mary, London (-)
62	Verveine, Milford-on-Sea (-)	**87**	Outlaw's at The Capital, London (-)
63	Min Jiang, London (99)	**88**	Trinity, London (97)
64	Le Champignon Sauvage, Cheltenham (-)	**89**	Duddell's, St Thomas Church, London (-)
65	Cotto, Cambridge (-)	**90**	Roux at the Landau, London (-)
66	Zuma, London (79)	**91**	Le Cochon Aveugle, York (40)
67	Nobu, London (-)	**92**	Trishna, London (64)
68	Amaya, London (-)	**93**	Murano, London (48)
69	The Greenhouse, London (20)	**94**	The Torridon Restaurant, Annat (-)
70	Hide, London (-)	**95**	The Kitchin, Edinburgh (47)
71	Number One, Balmoral Hotel, Edinburgh (-)	**96**	Paris House, Woburn (-)
72	Harrow at Little Bedwyn, Marlborough (83)	**97**	The Ritz, London (45)
73	Lickfold Inn, Lickfold (-)	**98**	The Frog, London (-)
74	La Trompette, London (71)	**99**	Little Fish Market, Brighton (-)
75	Roux at Parliament Square, London (46)	**100**	Wilks, Bristol (65)

EXMOOR CAVIAR
MADE IN ENGLAND

www.exmoorcaviar.com   info@exmoorcaviar.co.uk   tel.: 08454 349 587
563-565 Battersea Park Road London SW11 3 BL, U.K.

 @londonfinefoods   @londonfinefoods   @londonfinefoods

CONTENTS

Ormer, London

Kaia, The Ned, London

Hide, London

RATINGS & PRICES

Ratings

The ratings in this guide are derived statistically and with the judgement of the editors from ratings provided by ordinary diners in the Harden's diner survey. For more details see opposite. Our rating system does not tell you as most guides do that expensive restaurants are often better than cheap ones! What we do is compare each restaurant's performance as judged by the average ratings awarded by reporters in the survey with other similarly-priced restaurants. This approach has the advantage that it helps you find whatever your budget for any particular meal where you will get the best 'bang for your buck'.

The following qualities are assessed:

F — Food
S — Service
A — Ambience

The rating indicates that, **in comparison with other restaurants in the same price-bracket**, performance is…

5 — Exceptional
4 — Very good
3 — Good
2 — Average
1 — Poor

Prices

The price shown for each restaurant is the cost for one (1) person of an average threecourse dinner with half a bottle of house wine and coffee, any cover charge, service and VAT. Lunch is often cheaper. With BYO restaurants, we have assumed that two people share a £7 bottle of off-licence wine.

Small print

Telephone number – including area code.

Map reference – shown immediately after the telephone number.

Full postcodes – for non-group restaurants, the first entry in the 'small print' at the end of each listing, so you can set your sat-nav.

Website and Twitter – shown in the small print, where applicable.

Last orders time – listed after the website (if applicable); Sunday may be up to 90 minutes earlier.

Opening hours – unless otherwise stated, restaurants are open for lunch and dinner seven days a week.

Credit and debit cards – unless otherwise stated, Mastercard, Visa, Amex and Maestro are accepted.

Dress – where appropriate, the management's preferences concerning patrons' dress are given.

SRA Star Rating – the sustainability index, as calculated by the Sustainable Restaurant Association see page 12 for more information.

YOUR CONTRIBUTION

Every year this guide is based on the Harden's annual survey of ordinary diners.

For our 28th survey, the total number of diners who took part numbered 8,000, and, between them, they contributed 50,000 individual reports.

The survey takes place online each year (and in print for a small number of long-term participants), and anyone is free to sign up. Some of our diners (or 'reporters' as we sometimes call them in the text) have been taking part for over 20 years. The survey invites diners to nominate their favourite restaurant, where they had the best meal of the last 12 months and so on. Diners also award marks for Food, Service and Ambience together with leaving a short comment.

We then take the raw feedback and subject it to a rigorous statistical number-crunching exercise. Ratings for highly commented-on restaurants are derived almost entirely by statistical analysis. Where the level of feedback is lower, editorial judgement plays more of a part.

At a time when a recent study suggested that as many as 1/3 of the reviews on TripAdvisor are paid for by the restaurants they cover, we believe there is an ever-greater need for trusted sources such as the Harden's annual diner survey. For while obviously folks can attempt to stuff the Harden's ballot too, the high degree of editorial oversight plus the historical data we have both about the restaurants and also about those commenting makes it much harder to succeed. In this way Harden's can socially source restaurant feedback, but – vitally – curate it fully as we do so. It is this careful curation which provides extra 'value-added' for diners.

How we determine the ratings

In the great majority of cases, ratings are arrived at statistically. This essentially involves 'ranking' the average survey rating each restaurant achieves in the survey – for food, service and ambience – against the average ratings of the other establishments in the same price-bracket.

(This is essentially like football leagues, with the most expensive restaurants going in the top league and the cheaper ones in lower leagues. The restaurant's ranking within its own particular league determines its ratings.)

How we write the reviews

The tone of each review and the ratings are largely determined by the ranking of the establishment concerned, which we derive as described above.

At the margin, we may also pay some regard to the proportion of positive nominations (such as for 'favourite restaurant') compared to negative nominations (such as for 'most overpriced').

To explain why a restaurant has been rated as it has, we extract snippets from survey comments ("enclosed in double quotes"). On well-known restaurants, we receive several hundred reports, and a short summary cannot possibly do individual justice to all of them.

What we seek to do – without regard to our own personal opinions – is to illustrate the key themes which have emerged in feedback from diners on any particular restaurant.

A sea change is taking place in our attitude towards what and how we eat and it's unlikely the tide will turn any time soon. The catalyst? Sir David Attenborough's Blue Planet II series in which he revealed the devastating scale of destruction plastic is wreaking on our precious oceans.

Chefs, restaurateurs and crucially the dining public have responded. In a survey of Harden's diners in January 2018, less than one in five said they were satisfied with the efforts of the restaurants they ate in to protect the environment.

As well as the giant wave of restaurants and bars removing millions of plastic straws, many have gone much further, taking the opportunity to review what single-use plastic items they really need and are on the way to using more sustainable alternatives.

The shift away from stereotypical, meat-centric offerings continues apace too. Record numbers of participants in events like Veganuary have seen a general move towards more dishes celebrating the joys of veg. In that same survey, almost nine out of ten said they wanted restaurants to focus on creating menus that help them to make sustainable choices.

Faced with a full menu of dishes to choose from, it can be hard to use the power of your appetite wisely. That's why, in 2018 the SRA launched One Planet Plate, a movement to put sustainability on the menu. A One Planet Plate is effectively the chef's sustainable special his or her recommendation whether it celebrates local produce, features more veg, has a lower carbon footprint, includes better meat, showcases sustainably sourced seafood, or wastes no food. More than 2,000 restaurants offering these dishes and their recipes can be found at www.oneplanetplate.org.

We've supported the SRA since soon after their launch in 2010 because, like them, we believe in helping diners vote with their forks for a better food future.

Look out for those restaurants in the guide with an SRA Sustainability Rating, either One, Two or Three Stars, achieved by proving they are doing these ten things:

- Support Global Farmers
- Value Natural Resources
- Treat People Fairly
- Feed Children Well
- Celebrate Local
- Source Fish Responsibly
- Serve More Veg & Better Meat
- Reduce Reuse Recycle
- Waste no Food
- Support the Community

w: thesra.org
Twitter: @the_SRA
Instagram: @foodmadegood

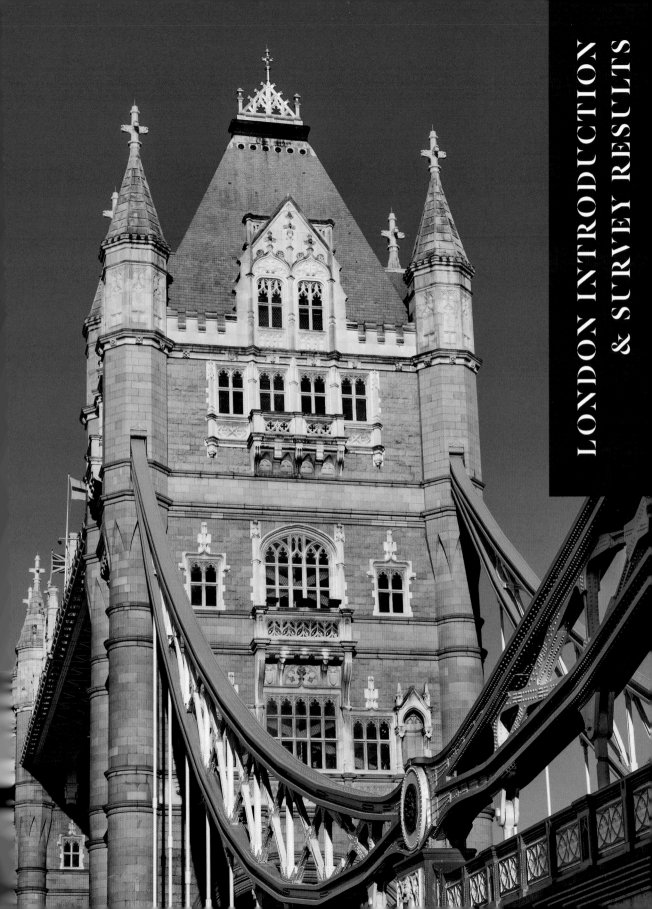

SURVEY MOST MENTIONED

RANKED BY THE NUMBER OF REPORTERS' VOTES

These are the restaurants which were most frequently mentioned by reporters. (Last year's position is given in brackets.)

1	J Sheekey (1)	21	The Cinnamon Club (16)
2	Clos Maggiore (2)	22	La Poule au Pot (22)
3	Chez Bruce (3)	23	Pollen Street Social (20)
4	Le Gavroche (5)	24	Bocca Di Lupo (17)
5	Scott's (4)	25	The Five Fields (32)
6	The Ledbury (6)	26	Enoteca Turi (40)
7	Gymkhana (8)	27	Benares (21)
8	Gauthier Soho (9)	28	Bleeding Heart Restaurant (31)
9	La Trompette (12)	29	Noble Rot (29)
10	The Wolseley (7)	30	Elystan Street (-)
11	Brasserie Zédel (10)	31	Bentley's (33)
12	The River Café (15)	32	Mere (-)
13	Core by Clare Smyth (-)	33	Pied À Terre (37)
14	The Ivy (-)	34	Moro (38)
15	AWong (34)	35	Marcus, The Berkeley (-)
16	The Delaunay (11)	36	Dinner, Mandarin Oriental (18)
17	Andrew Edmunds (13)	37	Gordon Ramsay (24)
18	Trinity (23)	38	Fera at Claridge's (14)
19	Le Caprice (26)	39	Oxo Tower (-)
20	Jamavar (-)	40	The Ritz (-)

J Sheekey

SURVEY NOMINATIONS

Top gastronomic experience

1	The Ledbury (1)
2	Le Gavroche (3)
3	Chez Bruce (2)
4	La Trompette (8)
5	Gauthier Soho (4)
6	Core by Clare Smyth (-)
7	Trinity (-)
8	Pied À Terre (-)
9	The Frog (-)
10	The Five Fields (7)

Best breakfast/brunch

1	The Wolseley (1)
2	The Delaunay (2)
3	Ivy Grills & Brasseries (3)
4	Granger & Co (6)
5	Dishoom (-)
6	Caravan (5)
7	Breakfast Club (10)
8	Côte (Group) (-)
9	The Ivy Café (-)
10	Cecconi's (-)

Most disappointing cooking

1	Ivy Grills & Brasseries (-)
2	Oxo Tower (1)
3	The Ivy (-)
4	Jamie's Italian (-)
5	Alain Ducasse (3)
6	Brasserie Blanc (-)
7	Gordon Ramsay (-)
8	Sexy Fish (2)
9	Chiltern Firehouse (4)
10	Polpo (-)

Most overpriced restaurant

1	The River Café (1)
2	Sexy Fish (2)
3	Oxo Tower (4)
4	Gordon Ramsay (3)
5	The Chiltern Firehouse (6)
6	Ivy Grills & Brasseries (-)
7	Alain Ducasse (7)
8	Le Gavroche (8)
9	Sushisamba (-)
10	Dinner, Mandarin Oriental (5)

Favourite

1	Chez Bruce (1)
2	Barrafina (-)
3	The Ledbury (8)
4	Gauthier Soho (10)
5	The Wolseley (6)
6	Le Caprice (-)
7	Le Gavroche (4)
8	La Trompette (3)
9	J Sheekey (2)
10	The Ivy (-)

Best for business

1	The Wolseley (1)
2	The Delaunay (2)
3	Hawksmoor (Group) (9)
4	Scott's (4)
5	Bleeding Heart (3)
6	Ivy Grills & Brasseries (-)
7	The Don (10)
8	Côte (-)
9	Savoy Grill (7)
10	The Ivy (-)

Best bar/pub food

1	Harwood Arms (2)
2	The Anchor & Hope (1)
3	Bull & Last (3)
4	The Anglesea Arms (4)
5	The Ladbroke Arms (10)
5=	The Wells Tavern (-)
7	The Marksman (9)
7=	Canton Arms (-)
9	Churchill Arms (-)
10	The Cow (-)

Best for romance

1	Clos Maggiore (1)
2	La Poule au Pot (2)
3	Andrew Edmunds (3)
4	Bleeding Heart (5)
5	Le Gavroche (7)
6	Gauthier Soho (4)
7	Chez Bruce (10)
8	Café du Marché (-)
9	Galvin at Windows (-)
10	Galvin La Chapelle (-)

SURVEY HIGHEST RATINGS

FOOD	SERVICE	AMBIENCE	OVERALL
£100+			
1 Texture	1 The Five Fields	1 The Ritz	1 The Ledbury
2 The Araki	2 The Araki	2 Sketch (Lecture Rm)	2 The Five Fields
3 The Ledbury	3 Le Gavroche	3 Le Gavroche	3 The Araki
4 La Dame de Pic London	4 Marianne	4 Pied À Terre	4 Le Gavroche
5 Core by Clare Smyth	5 Core by Clare Smyth	5 Club Gascon	5 Core by Clare Smyth
£75–£99			
1 Sushi Tetsu	1 Noizé	1 L'Escargot	1 Chez Bruce
2 Zuma	2 Chez Bruce	2 Clos Maggiore	2 Sushi Tetsu
3 Trinity	3 Trinity	3 Duck & Waffle	3 Noizé
4 La Trompette	4 Wiltons	4 Bob Bob Ricard	4 Trinity
5 Chez Bruce	5 Hide	5 Min Jiang	5 Roux at the Landau
£60–£74			
1 Brat	1 Brat	1 La Poule au Pot	1 Brat
2 Quilon	2 Cabotte	2 Brat	2 Cabotte
3 Pidgin	3 Oslo Court	3 The Wolseley	3 Jikoni
4 Jikoni	4 Quilon	4 Fredericks	4 Quo Vadis
5 Anglo	5 The Game Bird	5 Quo Vadis	5 Smith'sWapping
£45–£59			
1 AWong	1 Babur	1 The Anglesea Arms	1 Babur
2 Som Saa	2 The Anglesea Arms	2 Andrew Edmunds	2 The Anglesea Arms
3 Jin Kichi	3 The Oystermen	3 José	3 José
4 Babur	4 Lemonia	4 The Wigmore	4 Som Saa
5 José	5 Six Portland Road	5 Babur	5 AWong
£44 or less			
1 Padella	1 Department of Coffee	1 Brasserie Zédel	1 Padella
2 Kiln	2 Paradise Hampstead	2 Padella	2 Department of Coffee
3 Farang	3 Toffs	3 Churchill Arms	3 Paradise Hampstead
4 Department of Coffee	4 Padella	4 Kiln	4 Kiln
5 Tayyabs	5 Ma Goa	5 Paradise Hampstead	5 Brasserie Zédel

SURVEY BEST BY CUISINE

These are the restaurants which received the best average food ratings (excluding establishments with a small or notably local following).

Where the most common types of cuisine are concerned, we present the results in two price-brackets. For less common cuisines, we list the top three, regardless of price.

British, Modern

	£60 and over		Under £60
1	The Ledbury	1	Brat
2	Core by Clare Smyth	2	The Anglesea Arms
3	The Five Fields	3	Lupins
4	Trinity	4	The Dairy
5	The Frog	5	Six Portland Road

French

	£60 and over		Under £60
1	La Dame de Pic London	1	Cigalon
2	La Trompette	2	The Wells Tavern
3	Le Gavroche	3	Casse-Croute
4	Club Gascon	4	The Coach
5	The Square	5	Café du Marché

Italian/Mediterranean

	£60 and over		Under £60
1	Clarkes	1	Padella
2	Murano	2	L'Amorosa
3	The River Café	3	Margot
4	Olivomare	4	Oak
5	Sartoria	5	San Carlo Cicchetti

Indian & Pakistani

	£60 and over		Under £60
1	Indian Accent	1	Lahore Kebab House
2	Jikoni	2	Babur
3	Chutney Mary	3	Ragam
4	Gymkhana	4	Darjeeling Express
5	Amaya	5	Kricket

Chinese

	£60 and over		Under £60
1	Min Jiang	1	A Wong
2	Hunan	2	The Four Seasons
3	Yauatcha	3	Singapore Garden
4	Hakkasan	4	Yming
5	Park Chinois	5	Royal China

Japanese

	£60 and over		Under £60
1	The Araki	1	Takahashi
2	Sushi Tetsu	2	Atari-Ya
3	Dinings	3	Jin Kichi
4	Zuma	4	Tsunami
5	Roka	5	Pham Sushi

British, Traditional

1	St John Smithfield
2	Wiltons
3	Scott's

Vegetarian

1	Vanilla Black
2	Gate
3	Ceremony

Burgers, etc

1	Bleecker Burger
2	Patty and Bun
3	Honest Burgers

Pizza

1	Yard Sale Pizza
2	Pizza East
3	Homeslice

Fish & Chips

1	Bradys
2	Toffs
3	North Sea Fish

Thai

1	Som Saa
2	Kiln
3	Sukho Fine Thai

Steaks & Grills

1	Blacklock
2	Goodman
3	Zelman Meats

Fish & Seafood

1	Texture
2	Angler
3	Outlaws at the Capital

Fusion

1	Twist
2	Bubbledogs (KT)
3	108 Garage

Spanish

1	Barrafina
2	José
3	Cambio de Tercio

Turkish

1	Mangal 1
2	Oklava
3	Le Bab

Lebanese

1	Crocker's Folly
2	Maroush
3	Meza

Kaia, The Ned, London

Outlaws Fish Kitchen, Port Isaac

Celeste at The Lanesborough, London

The Ritz, Palm Court, London

Romulo Café, London

THE RESTAURANT SCENE

Record closures and 'churn'

There are 167 newcomers in this year's guide. Although this is the fourth-best year we have recorded, it is lower than for all three preceding years: significantly down from 2017's record of 200, and taking openings back to pre-2016 levels.

Closures, by contrast, are at a record level. At 117, they are the highest-ever recorded since we started keeping count in 1992, just exceeding the previous record closure-level of 113 in calendar 2003 (recorded in the 2004 guide).

Net openings (openings minus closures) slipped to 50: less than half last year's figure of 115. Since the financial crash of 2008, only one year has seen a weaker level of net openings (2012 at 36).

A further sense of turmoil in the market comes from the ratio of openings to closures. At 1.43:1, only one year has seen a worse performance than this, which was, as above, in 2003/4 (1.2:1) a time when for nearly every restaurant that opened another one closed.

Because Harden's focuses on listing 'indies' over restaurant groups, the above figures almost certainly understate how tough the market is.Although we do rate some bigger groups, we have never sought to track them in our statistics. After a chain becomes more numerous than a couple of spin-offs, it is excluded from our tally. Thus, none of the wellpublicised closures of London branches of Jamie's Italian or Byron, for example, are included in our figures.

What's more, the last year saw a significant number of recently opened restaurants (that had been short-listed for inclusion) come and go before we had a chance to write about them.Allowing for these factors would almost certainly paint a picture of the weakest state of growth in the London restaurant sector in the history of the guide.

This time it's different

It is easy to forget how dire conditions were in 2003. The double whammy of the second gulf war in March and the SARS epidemic in May of that year saw London hotel occupancy rates dive to their lowest levels in recent decades.The knock-on hit to dining out was sufficiently strong to wipe out growth in the restaurant trade.

This time it is not weakness of demand that is hitting the sector, as consumer surveys (for example from Visa) show like-for-like consumer spending on dining-out continuing to increase year-on-year. No, the trade is being squeezed by a large overhang of supply from the restaurant opening boom of the last three years. On top of that it is struggling with huge rates increases. And, as if these challenges were not enough, restaurateurs are also adapting to the cost pressures from Brexit-induced inflation on imported foodstuffs, and Brexit-induced pressures on attracting quality staff.

However, as the numbers above show, openings have far from collapsed and the 'animal spirits' of London's new generation of restaurant entrepreneurs are proving remarkably resilient in the face of this storm system of economic headwinds.

What's hot

Modern British and Italian cuisines remain the most popular for launching a new restaurant, but Japanese newcomers made a stronger showing this year to be the third-mostrepresented cuisine for new arrivals.

Unless you include chicken shops, the shift away from meatbased formulae continued for a second year, with too many cuisines to list ranking higher than those with a primarily steak-led or burger-led offering. In fact – highlighting the increasing popularity of veganism and all things plant-based – purely vegetarian openings were as numerous this year as for those two red meat categories combined.

The hottest of the hot

Every year, we do an editors' pick of the ten most significant openings of the year.This year our selection is as follows:

Aulis London	Indian Accent
Beck at Brown's	Kettners
Brat	Kerridge's Bar & Grill
Cornerstone	Mãos
Hide	Parsons

Prices

The average price of dinner for one at establishments listed in this guide is £55.76 (compared to £53.20 last year). Prices have risen by 4.8% in the past 12 months (up on 3.6% in the preceding 12 months).This rate compares with a general annual inflation rate of 2.4% for the 12 months to August 2018, yet further accelerating the trend seen in the last two years by which restaurant bills have seen price rises running significantly higher than inflation generally.

OPENINGS AND CLOSURES

Openings (167)

Abd El Wahab
Akira at Japan House
Amber
L'Ami Malo
L'Antica Pizzeria da Michele
Ardiciocca
Arlo's (SW11)
Aulis London
Authentique Epicerie & Bar
Babel House
Bagatelle
Bánh Bánh (SW9)
Baptist Grill, L'Oscar Hotel
Beck at Browns
Beef & Brew (N1)
Belmond Cadogan Hotel
Berenjak
Bergen House
Bistro Mirey
Blacklock (EC2)
Bluebird Café White City
Bombay Bustle
Brat
Bryn Williams at Somerset House
Bucket
Buongiorno e Buonasera
Butchies
Caractère
Casa Pastór
Ceremony
Chick 'n' Sours (N1)
Chilly Katz
Chimis
The Chipping Forecast (W1)
Chokhi Dhani London
Chucs Serpentine (W2)
Claw Carnaby
The Coach
Coal Office
Cora Pearl
Cornerstone
Cub
Cut + Grind
Daddy Bao
Delamina (W1)
Din Tai Fung
Dip in Brilliant
Dozo (SW7)
The Drop
The Drunken Butler
The Duke of Richmond
Dynamo (SW17)
Eccleston Place by Tart London

Enoteca Rosso
Essence Cuisine
Evelyns Table at The Blue Posts
Fannys Kebabs
Fayre Share
La Ferme (NW1)
Forest Bar & Kitchen
Freak Scene
The Frog Hoxton (N1)
Gazelle
Genesis
La Goccia
The Good Egg (W1)
Good Neighbour
Granary Square Brasserie
The Greyhound Cafe
Gunpowder (SE1)
Ham
Hans Bar & Grill
The Harlot
Harry's Bar
Harrys Dolce Vita
Hatched (formerly Darwin)
Hicce
Hide
Home SW15
Hovarda
Icco Pizza (NW1)
Ichi Buns
Inko Nito
Ippudo London (WC2)
Jidori (WC2)
Jolene
Jollibee
The Jones Family Kitchen
K10 (EC4)
Kahani
Kanada-Ya (N1)
Kaosarn (SW17)
Kazu
Kerridges Bar & Grill
Kettners
Kudu
Kutir
Kym's by Andrew Wong
Kyseri
Lahpet
Laurent at Cafe Royal
Leroy
Levan
Lina Stores
Linden Stores
Llerena
Lokhandwala
Londrino
Maison Bab
Mamarosa
Mãos

Market Hall Fulham
Melange (NW3)
La Mia Mamma
Mien Tay (SW6)
Native
Neptune, The Principal
Nuala
Nusr-Et Steakhouse
Omars Place
On the Dak
Oval Restaurant
Paladar
Parsons
Passo
Peckham Levels
Purezza
Red Farm
ROVI
Ruya
Sacro Cuore (N8)
Sam's Riverside
San Carlo
San Pietro
Santa Maria (W1)
Sapling
Sargeants Mess
Scarlett Green
Schmaltz Truck
Scully
Sea Garden & Grill
Shu Xiangge Chinatown
Soutine
The Spread Eagle
St Leonards
Stem
Stockwell Continental Street Pizza
Tell Your Friends
temper (WC2)
Terroirs (SE22)
Three Cranes
Tish
Titu
The Trafalgar Dining Rooms
1251
24 The Oval
Two Lights
Vermuteria
Via Emilia
Wahlburgers
Wander
Wellbourne
Wulf & Lamb
Yamabahce
Yen
Zela

Closures (117)

Albion (SE1, E2)
L'Anima
L'Anima Café
Assunta Madre
Aurora
Babaji Pide
Babylon
Barbecoa Piccadilly (W1)
Belpassi Bros
Bó Drake
Brindisa Food Rooms
Bronte
Brown's Hotel, HIX Mayfair
Bukowski Grill (W1, SW9, E1)
Bumpkin (SW3)
Burger & Lobster (WC1)
Cah-Chi (SW18, SW20)
Camino Blackfriars (EC4)
Cau (SE3, SW19, E1)
Cellar Gascon
Charlottes Place
Cheyne Walk Brasserie
Chriskitch (N1)
Cinnamon Soho
Como Lario
Counter Vauxhall Arches
Dandy
Darbaar
The Dock Kitchen
Duckroad
Dukes Brew & Que
Ebury Restaurant
8 Hoxton Square
Ellory, Netil House
Encant
L'Etranger
Eyre Brothers
Falafel King
Flavour Bastard
The Frog E1 (E1)
Gallipoli (N1)
Gay Hussar
Geales Chelsea Green (SW3)
The Gowlett Arms
The Grand Imperial
The Greek Larder
Gul and Sepoy
Hardys Brasserie
HKK
Hush (WC1)
James Cochran N1 (N1)
JAN
Jar Kitchen
Jules
Juniper Tree
Kerbisher & Malt (W5)

Killer Tomato (W12, W10)
Lahore Kebab House (SW16)
Lahpet
Latium
Legs
Lutyens
Madame D's
Marianne
The Magazine Restaurant
The Manor
Massimo, Corinthia Hotel
May The Fifteenth
The Modern Pantry (EC2)
Native
New World
Nirvana Kitchen
Nordic Bakery (W1 x2)
Oliver Maki
One-O-One
The Painted Heron
Paradise Garage
Pizza Metro (W11)
Pizzastorm
Platform1
Pomaio
Popeseye (SW15)
La Porchetta Pizzeria (N1)
La Porte des Indes
QP LDN
Raouls Café & Deli (W11)
Rasa Maricham (WC1)
Rök (EC2)
Royal Exchange Grand Café
Sardo
Sauterelle
Savini at Criterion
Smoking Goat (WC2)
Sosharu
Sree Krishna
Star of India
Summers
Taberna do Mercado
Taiwan Village
Temple & Sons
Test Kitchen
Trawler Trash
Typing Room
Veneta
Villandry (W1, SW1)
Vineet Bhatia London
Walnut Cafe and Dining
Winemakers Deptford
Yalla Yalla (SE10)

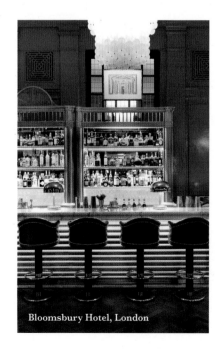

Bloomsbury Hotel, London

Texture, London

A CENA TW1 £50 323

418 RICHMOND RD   020 8288 0108   1–4A

This upmarket Italian, just over the bridge from Richmond in St Margaret's, continues to earn solid local praise for its "good food" and "excellent value"; and is also useful for rugby fans from further afield who want to make a full day of a game at nearby Twickenham. / TW1 2EB; www.acena.co.uk; @acenarestaurant; 11 pm, Sun 10 pm; closed Mon L & Sun D; booking max 6 may apply.

A WONG SW1 £47 553

70 WILTON RD   020 7828 8931   2–4B

"It's hard to get a table, but persevere, you're in for some of the best Chinese cooking in town" at Andrew Wong's Pimlico HQ, which "doesn't look very distinguished, but once the food starts coming, you know you're somewhere special". "Incredible dim sum offers lots of choice and unusual combinations" and – like the "amazing" evening tasting menu – delivers "a taste explosion with every dish". And while the "mind-blowing" cuisine seems "different and contemporary", it still feels authentic in terms of its flavours. "Upstairs feels a bit canteen-like" (and is "noisy and clattery") – you can also eat "in the tucked-away little bar downstairs". As of September 2018, he has also opened a new spin-off City outlet within the Bloomberg HQ (see Kym's). / SW1V 1DE; www.awong.co.uk; @awongSW1; 10 pm; closed Mon L, closed Sun; credit card required to book.

ABD EL WAHAB SW1 £50 333

1-3 PONT ST   020 7235 0005   6–1D

On a well-known Belgravia site that's seen lots of swanky places come and go over the years (including the US steakhouse Palms in recent times), this swish Lebanese is the first non-Middle Eastern branch of a Beirut-based chain that's since spread its wings to Dubai and beyond. Early feedback is up-and-down, but with more positives than negatives. / SW1X 9EJ; www.abdelwahab.restaurant.

THE ABINGDON W8 £65 334

54 ABINGDON RD   020 7937 3339   6–2A

"Always a winner" – this "comfortable" neighbourhood gastropub stalwart in a chichi Kensington backstreet is a case study in consistency. "Very accommodating" staff serve "ever-dependable food" in "agreeable surroundings". "Great for Sunday lunch with children" too. / W8 6AP; www.theabingdon.co.uk; @theabingdonw8; 10.30 pm, Sun & Mon 10 pm.

ABOUT THYME SW1 £56 233

82 WILTON RD   020 7821 7504   2–4B

A "thriving local delight" for many years, this Pimlico stalwart provides "well above average" Spanish food under the eye of popular host Issy ("you never feel rushed out here"). / SW1V 1DL; www.aboutthyme.co.uk; 10.30 pm, Sun & Mon 10 pm; closed Sun.

L'ABSINTHE NW1 £49 233

40 CHALCOT RD   020 7483 4848   9–3B

This "friendly and cheerful" little double-decker bistro on a Primrose Hill corner is "always a good local to go to for steak frites". "The menu doesn't change" and the food is "OK", not more, but that hardly matters: "the place is made by the maître d' and owner, JC" (Burgundian, Jean-Christophe Slowik). / NW1 8LS; www.labsinthe.co.uk; @absinthe07jc; 10 pm, Sun 9 pm; closed Mon, Tue L, Wed L & Thu L.

ABU ZAAD W12 £23 332

29 UXBRIDGE RD   020 8749 5107   8–1C

"Looks a bit cheesy from the outside, but more than makes up once you're in" – this "authentic" Syrian near the top of Shepherd's Bush Market, provides "freshly prepared, generous and delicious Middle Eastern specialities" with "courteous and pleasant service", all at prices that are "excellent value". / W12 8LH; www.abuzaad.co.uk; Mon-Fri 11 pm, Sat & Sun midnight; no Amex.

ADAMS CAFÉ W12 £35 353

77 ASKEW RD   020 8743 0572   8–1B

"A gem for North African food", "off the beaten track" in deepest Shepherd's Bush, this is a "lovely family-run restaurant with super, authentic Tunisian and Moroccan food by night" and "greasy-spoon fare by day". "The hosts epitomise hospitality" and have "maintained high standards for over 25 years". It's "good value, too", with "the bonus of being able to BYO" (although they are now licensed). / W12 9AH; www.adamscafe.co.uk; @adamscafe; 10 pm; closed Mon-Sat L, closed Sun.

ADDIE'S THAI CAFÉ SW5 £35 333

121 EARL'S COURT RD   020 7259 2620   6–2A

"Very authentic" Thai street food – "excellently spiced and at a very reasonable price" – again wins a big thumbs up for this basic canteen in Earl's Court. "It's very cheap, and we're always cheerful after we've eaten there!". No wonder the place is "increasingly packed, but I guess that's part of the (winning) formula". / SW5 9RL; www.addiesthai.co.uk; 11 pm, Sun 10.30 pm; no Amex.

ADDOMME SW2 £53 432

17-21 STERNHOLD AVENUE   020 8678 8496   11–2C

A "tiny, friendly family run pizzeria" next to Streatham Hill station, where "fantastic welcoming owners" Stefano and Nadia are from Capri, and provide "superb Neapolitan style pizzas and bread, plus great pasta dishes" from "very high quality ingredients and dough". / SW2 4PA; www.addomme.co.uk; @PizzAddomme; 11 pm.

THE ADMIRAL CODRINGTON SW3 £58 334

17 MOSSOP ST   020 7581 0005   6–2C

A Chelsea mainstay since the days of the Sloane Ranger Handbook, this backstreet gastroboozer is "fantastic for business lunches but also brilliant for fun socialising". Its food scores are up again this year. / SW3 2LY; www.theadmiralcodrington.co.uk; @TheAdCod; Mon & Tue 11 pm, Wed & Thu midnight, Fri & Sat 1 am, Sun 10.30 pm; No trainers.

AFGHAN KITCHEN N1 £28 422

35 ISLINGTON GRN   020 7359 8019   9–3D

"Still there, still serving excellent food" – this "cheap 'n' cheerful", Islington canteen has seen many of its neighbours come and go. The secret of its success? – a very affordable limited selection of yummy curries. "Easier for take-away than for sit-down as the place is tiny with slightly harassed staff". / N1 8DU; 11 pm; closed Sun & Mon; cash only; no booking.

AGLIO E OLIO SW10 £54 332

194 FULHAM RD   020 7351 0070   6–3B

This "canteen-style Italian" near Chelsea & Westminster Hospital "always hits the spot" with its "simple, peasant-style cooking" – "excellent antipasti and pasta, and a fine selection of secondi if you want one" – although it can get "very noisy". "Always welcoming with kids." Top Menu Tip: "proper fresh zabaglione made to order". / SW10 9PN; www.aglioeolio.co.uk; 10.30 pm.

AKIRA AT JAPAN HOUSE W8 £56

101-111 KENSINGTON HIGH ST
020 3971 4646   6–1A

The Japanese Government's meticulously designed new cultural centre and store – Japan House in Kensington's old Derry & Toms department store – opened in June 2018 and is one of three globally aiming to showcase Nipponese heritage and craft. Its robatayaki and sushi restaurant is brought to us by Akira Shimizu, former chef of Engawa. It's far from being a showcase for budget Japanese dining however! / W8 5SA; www.japanhouselondon.uk; @japanhouseldn; 10.30 pm, Sun 4 pm; closed Sun D.

AL DUCA SW1 £57 222

4-5 DUKE OF YORK ST   020 7839 3090
3–3D

Low-key St James's Italian that's worth knowing about in this posh location. The harsh would say that the food quality is merely "fairly ordinary" or "reliable", but "given its position in the very heart of London, it delivers on value better than some of its central competitors". / SW1Y 6LA; www.alduca-restaurant.co.uk; 11 pm; closed Sun.

AL FORNO £46 234

349 UPPER RICHMOND RD, SW15
020 8878 7522   11–2A | 2A KING'S RD,
SW19   020 8540 5710   11–2B

"Family focused fun" ("expect noise, kids and even old people dancing") is on the menu at these "loud and bubbly" local Italians across south west London. "They can't do enough for you, and the food is pretty good too": a "perfectly respectable selection of standard traditional dishes", led by pasta and particularly pizza. / 10 pm-11 pm.

ALAIN DUCASSE AT THE DORCHESTER W1 £134 223

53 PARK LN   020 7629 8866   3–3A

"I still do not understand why this above other amazing restaurants is one of only three Michelin three-star establishments in London!" The world-famous Gallic chef's luxurious Mayfair outpost is not without a significant number of advocates who hail it as "the best of the best!", with "truly first-class cuisine", "staff who seemingly glide around the floor" and "stunning surroundings". Even they can find it "stupidly expensive" however, and for far too many critics the cooking here is terribly "overrated" and the overall experience "underwhelming compared to other offerings". Top Tip: the best seats in the house are on the 'Table Lumière', surrounded by 4,500 fibre optic cables. / W1K 1QA; www.alainducasse-dorchester.com; 9.30 pm; closed Sat L, closed Sun & Mon; Jacket required.

ALBERTINE W12 £56 445

1 WOOD LN   020 8743 9593   8–1C

This "very buzzy wine bar and bistro" is a "breath of fresh air" in Shepherd's Bush, with "clever, original and inexpensive food" by "the amazing Allegra (McEvedy), who is constantly popping out from the kitchen to check all is well with the world". A refuge from the nearby Westfield shopping centre, it was set up by McEvedy's mother in 1978, and she has retained the charming interior. There's a "huge range of wines from Greece to Morocco, with very strong French selection". / W12 7DP; www.albertinewinebar.co.uk; @AlbertineWine; closed Sat L & Sun; no Amex.

ALCEDO N7 £44 343

237 HOLLOWAY RD   020 7998 7672   9–2D

"Wonderful service from the friendly owner" drives the experience at this bright spark in Holloway – a "decent albeit not outstanding British bistro-style" venue. / N7 8HG; 10 pm.

ALEION N10 £45 333

346 MUSWELL HILL BROADWAY
020 8883 9207   1–1B

"A find in a part of London which has been poorly served by quality restaurants for a long time" – this year-old "small café with a short menu" in Muswell Hill serves "delicious", "fresh" food (from brunch and light lunches to more ambitious fare in the evening) and service is "helpful and friendly" too. / N10 1DJ; www.aleion.co.uk; @Aleion346; Mon-Thu 10 pm, Fri 11 pm, Sat 11.30 pm, Sun 4 pm; closed Sun D.

THE ALFRED TENNYSON SW1 £62 223

10 MOTCOMB ST   020 7730 6074   6–1D

"Craft ales, excellent wines and an interesting menu" are the offer at this plush Belgravia pub. Formerly known as The Pantechnicon Dining Rooms, it has become "much more approachable since its reincarnation". "Upstairs the atmosphere is more gentle for an intimate meal". / SW1X 8LA; thealfredtennyson.co.uk; @TheTennysonSW1; Mon-Fri 10 pm; closed Sat & Sun.

ALI BABA NW1 £26 322

32 IVOR PL   020 7723 5805   2–1A

"Idiosyncratic, different and engaging"; if you're happy to chance it a bit and like Middle Eastern food, this family-run Egyptian – a simple room behind a take-away off Baker Street – is worth a trip and it's not a huge investment: "I have always liked the food even if the ambience is a bit caff-style, but recently for a dinner party I went there, ordered the food, and half an hour later was on my way home with a magnificent spread for the same price as a pizza delivery!" / NW1 6DA; alibabarestaurant.co.uk; @alibabalondon; midnight; cash only.

ALOUNAK £26 333

10 RUSSELL GDNS, W14   020 7603 1130
8–1D | 44 WESTBOURNE GROVE, W2
020 7229 0416   7–1B

Now in their 21st year, this pair of "bustling, tightly packed" BYO Persian cafés in Bayswater and Olympia knock out "cheap but tasty kebabs and other typical Iranian dishes". Not bad for a business that started in a Portakabin next to Olympia Station. / 11.30 pm; no Amex.

ALYN WILLIAMS, WESTBURY HOTEL W1 £104 553

37 CONDUIT ST   020 7183 6426   3–2C

"What a find!". Alyn Williams's "outstanding" dining room hidden away at the back of a luxury Mayfair hotel is "one of the very best restaurants in London" ("and bizarrely underrated"). "It's hard to fault the cooking and staff" – accolades reflected in this year's high ratings – "and there's even plenty of space between the tables". / W1S 2YF; www.alynwilliams.com; @Alyn_Williams; 10.30 pm; closed Sun & Mon; Jacket required.

AMAYA SW1 £85 423

HALKIN ARCADE, 19 MOTCOMB ST
020 7823 1166   6–1D

"Treat yourself – you won't be sorry!" This "dark and luxurious", "fusion-Indian" has a "surprisingly different tapas-style approach that just works". "Subtly-spiced", "wonderfully fragrant" small dishes (many of them from the grill) are prepared in the open kitchen, providing "contemporary food at its best... if at Belgravia prices". "Don't let the staff cajole you into more dishes than you need!". / SW1X 8JT; www.amaya.biz; @theamaya_; 11.30 pm, Sun 10.30 pm; closed Sun L.

AMBER E1 £39

21 PIAZZA WALK   020 7702 0700   12–1A

This bright, attractively decorated, new Middle Eastern café opened in Whitechapel in early 2018. No survey feedback yet, but its modern take on Moorish cuisine looks promising. / E1 8FU; www.thisisamber.co.uk; @ldn.amber.

THE AMERICAN BAR
SW1 £76 **2 5 3**

16 - 18 SAINT JAMES'S PLACE
020 7493 0111 *3–4C*

"Benoit's team provide perfect service" in this "very attractive room" – part of a luxurious St James's hideaway at the end of a cute mews – serving upscale brasserie fare from breakfast on. Top Tip: "the lunchtime food served 'on your lap' is a great partner for the wines on special offer". / SW1A 1NJ; thestaffordlondon.com/the-american-bar; @StaffordLondon; 10 pm; booking L only.

AMETSA WITH ARZAK INSTRUCTION, HALKIN HOTEL SW1 £103 **3 4 2**

5 HALKIN ST 020 7333 1234 *2–3A*

"Very experimental", "highly creative and fun tasting menus" win high praise for this "high-end Basque eatery", and although one or two reporters "expected more given its association with the fabulous Arzak in San Sebastian", most are dazzled by its "skilful and dramatic" cuisine. The very 'boutique-hotel-y' dining room is "clinical", but "what the space lacks in ambience is more than made up for by the terrific attitude of the staff!" / SW1X 7DJ; www.comohotels.com/thehalkin/dining/ametsa; @AmetsaArzak; 10 pm; closed Sun & Mon.

L'AMI MALO E1 £42 **5 4 4**

14 ARTILLERY LANE 020 7247 8595 *13–2B*

"What a refreshing addition to the City restaurant scene!" – "simple but beautifully prepared dishes with wonderful flavours" inspire gushing feedback on this Brêton newcomer: a modern interpretation of a classic French crêperie in the byways just south of Old Spitalfield Market (there's also a 'speakeasy-style' bar at the back, Le Moulin, serving calvados-based cocktails and craft cidres). "Staff seem like they really enjoy working there, and prices are reasonable; I don't want to share my knowledge in the fear that once others discover this gem it'll become over-run!" / E1 7LJ; www.lamimalo.com; @lamimalo; Tue-Thu 9.30 pm, Fri & Sat 10 pm; closed Sun & Mon.

L'AMOROSA W6 £54 **4 4 3**

278 KING ST 020 8563 0300 *8–2B*

"Andy Needham has the right formula" at his "top Italian local with very reasonable prices" near Ravenscourt Park, which is "well worth a detour". "Fine cooking from a limited menu, shows real care given to each dish", and is delivered by "particularly friendly" staff who help foster "a pleasing and lively atmosphere". "If I lived close, I would happily go every week!" / W6 0SP; www.lamorosa.co.uk; @LamorosaLondon; 10 pm; closed Mon & Sun D.

ANARKALI W6 £37 **3 4 3**

303-305 KING ST 020 8748 1760 *8–2B*

This "favourite" fixture of the Hammersmith strip (which opened in 1972) sports a brighter, more modern look than once it did (the '70s-tastic dark glazed frontage is long gone). Praise remains steady for chef Rafiq's deft curries (including "the best bhuna lamb ever"). / W6 9NH; www.anarkalifinedining.com; @anarkalidining; midnight; closed Mon-Sun L; no Amex.

THE ANCHOR & HOPE
SE1 £53 **4 3 3**

36 THE CUT 020 7928 9898 *10–4A*

By a single vote, this "amazing" South Bank boozer finally lost its crown this year as London's No.1 pub (to Fulham's Harwood Arms), but it still remains "the ultimate gastropub" for its huge fan club. It's "cramped", "busy" and "difficult to get a seat" (you can only book for Sunday lunch) but "worth the gamble" thanks to its "changing but always interesting menu at very keen prices", with an emphasis on game, offal and other "thoughtful", hearty British dishes. / SE1 8LP; www.anchorandhopepub.co.uk; @AnchorHopeCut; 10.30 pm, Mon 11 pm, Sun 3 pm; closed Mon L closed Sun D; no Amex; no booking.

ANDI'S N16 £47 **3 3 4**

176 STOKE NEWINGTON CHURCH ST 020 7241 6919 *1–1C*

"The energy bowl is simply gorgeous!" – Great British Menu judge, Andi Oliver's "relaxed and friendly" neighbourhood haunt has proved "a brilliant addition to Stoke Newington Church Street", and is most popular for a "delicious brunch", particularly of the healthy variety. / N16 0JL; www.andis.london; @andisrestaurant; 11.30 pm, Sun 10.30 pm; closed weekday L.

ANDINA £51 **3 3 3**

31 GREAT WINDMILL ST, W1 020 3327 9464 *4–3D* | **157 WESTBOURNE GROVE, W11 020 3327 9465** *7–1B* | **1 REDCHURCH ST, E2 020 7920 6499** *13–1B*

"Bustling, friendly, full of colour and fresh tastes, with lots of fascinating choices (including a whole section of the menu devoted to ceviche)" – these trendily located Peruvians win many upbeat reviews and the general feeling is "they're not a case of style over substance – flavour combinations work well". They are "pricey" though – "while the food was very good, I'm not sure it was great value, probably thanks to the prime location, so I won't rush back". Notting Hill is the latest site with a 'panaderia' (bakery) as well as the 'picanteria'. /

THE ANDOVER ARMS
W6 £51 **2 3 4**

57 ALDENSEY RD 020 8748 2155 *8–1B*

"A proper boozer", lost in the backstreets of Hammersmith, with a quintessentially "cosy and friendly atmosphere, open fireplace, large portions and a great Sunday roast". Fuller's closed it for a refurb and change in management from which it emerged in late September 2018 – we've rated it on the assumption of plus ça change... / W6 0DL; www.theandoverarms.com; @theandoverarms; 10 pm, Sun 9 pm; no Amex.

Andrew Edmunds W1

ANDREW EDMUNDS
W1 £57 **3 4 5**

46 LEXINGTON ST 020 7437 5708 *4–2C*

"Even the plainest of dining partners seems to take on a glow" at this "utterly charming" and amazingly popular veteran – a "Bohemian" old town-house which is "refreshingly constant in the chopping and changing Soho scene" and whose straightforward, notably affordable dishes are perennially "prepared with passion and care". "For a candle-lit supper" it has few equals, as most reporters feel "the cramped conditions only add to the cosy ambience" (although not everyone is wowed by the basement). Top billing goes to the "fantastic wine" – "because of the generosity of the owner, the markups on wines are minimal and it is a very interesting list": "anything on the blackboard deserves attention and, nearly always, consumption!" / W1F 0LP; www.andrewedmunds.com; 10.30 pm; no Amex; booking max 6 may apply.

ANGELUS W2 £75 **3 4 2**

4 BATHURST ST 020 7402 0083 *7–2D*

"An oasis in a part of London ill-served by good restaurants", this attractive Lancaster Gate venue is a "pub converted into an art nouveau bistro" by ex-Gavroche sommelier, Thierry Tomasin "with a wine cellar to match". Tomasin's team provide "great old-fashioned service" ("they welcome you like a regular even if you've never been before") and "though you eat cheek by jowl" the Gallic cuisine "makes it worthwhile". / W2 2SD; www.angelusrestaurant.co.uk; @AngelusLondon; 11 pm, Sun 8 pm.

ANGIE'S LITTLE FOOD SHOP W4 £36 **3 3 3**

114 CHISWICK HIGH RD 020 8994 3931 *8–2A*

"Freshly made divine salads each day, and amazing brunch dishes" (not all of them virtuous) at "reasonable prices" (for Chiswick) make Angie Steele's tightly packed, shabby-chic café "great for snacks and coffee", particularly at weekends. / W4 1PU; www.angieslittlefoodshop.com; 7 pm, Sun 6 pm; L only.

ANGLER, SOUTH PLACE HOTEL EC2 £95 433

3 SOUTH PL   020 3215 1260   13–2A

"One of the best places for lunch in the City" (with "nicely spaced tables so conversations are not overheard") – this "terrific" D&D London operation is the best culinary performer in the group nowadays. "Gary Foulkes is a brilliant fish chef" and tears up the rulebook which says there's no decent cooking in the Square Mile, especially at places with "great views", such as you get at this penthouse perch. "The entrance through the South Place Hotel limits expectations for what lies ahead" and although "it does feel like you're in a hotel" the dining room itself is a "lovely", "light and airy" space. "Get a table on the terrace on a sunny day and enjoy the delicious seafood." / EC2M 2AF; www.anglerrestaurant.com; @Angler_London; 11.30 pm, Sun 10 pm; closed Sat L; may need 8+ to book.

THE ANGLESEA ARMS W6 £57 444

35 WINGATE RD   020 8749 1291   8–1B

"The kitchen is on song" at this "brilliant gastropub" in a side-street near Ravenscourt Park, long known as one of the capital's best, thanks to its "proper" cooking and characterful interior, complete with "roaring fire" in winter, and small outside terrace. Service – historically a weak point – is "attentive and accommodating" too. / W6 0UR; www.angleseaarmspub.co.uk; @_AngleseaArmsW6; Mon-Thu, Sat 10 pm, Sun 9 pm; closed Mon-Thu L, closed Fri; no booking.

ANGLO EC1 £69 542

30 ST CROSS ST   020 7430 1503   10–1A

"If I could give it ten stars I would!" – "Forget the shopfront and the concrete floor" and the "cramped premises" of this Hatton Garden two-year-old. Mark Jarvis's cuisine here is "brilliantly conceived, superbly prepared and keenly priced" and complemented by a "superb wine pairing". Service is "knowledgeable and friendly" and the overall style "relaxed". That it holds no Michelin star is bizarre. / EC1N 8UH; www.anglorestaurant.com; @AngloFarringdon; Tue-Sat, Mon 9.15 pm; closed Mon L, closed Sun; booking max 4 may apply.

ANIMA E CUORE NW1 £48 531

129 KENTISH TOWN RD   020 7267 2410   9–2B

"A hidden gem in Kentish Town" – "don't be put off by the transport caff surroundings, this is Italian cooking at its very best", "prepared with great care in a tiny kitchen by young chefs who work their socks off to produce excellent food". "BYO is the icing on the cake!". There's a Catch 22: "they never answer the phone so it's almost impossible to book, but booking is essential". Top Tip: "strangolapreti (or priest stranglers), gnocchi made from stale bread rather than potatoes". / NW1 8PB; @animaecuoreuk; 9 pm, Sun 2.30 pm.

ANJANAAS NW6 £35 443

57-59 WILLESDEN LANE   020 7624 1713   1–1B

"The food has finesse and is consistently superb at this humble family-run restaurant" – "an excellent Keralan local" that shines even brighter in the still-underprovided 'burb of Kilburn. / NW6 7RL; www.anjanaas.com; Mon-Thu 10.30 pm, Fri & Sat 11 pm, Sun 10 pm.

ANNIES £53 234

162 THAMES RD, W4   020 8994 9080   1–3A | 36-38 WHITE HART LN, SW13   020 8878 2020   11–1A

This pair of "super-reliable locals" near the Thames in Barnes and Strand-on-the-Green, are "just all-round great places for lazy lunch and intimate dinner". "Top service from a very friendly crew" ensures that you "feel very welcome", and "portions are large and full of flavour". / www.anniesrestaurant.co.uk; 10 pm, Sun 9.30 pm.

THE ANTHOLOGIST EC2 £54 233

58 GRESHAM ST   0845 468 0101   10–2C

Well-known bar/café/restaurant, near the Guildhall, whose versatile menu (from breakfast on), attractive interior and handy location make it an ideal City rendezvous. Critics dismiss it as too "average", but, "even when it's heaving, service is efficient, and it continues to produce reliable food day after day". / EC2V 7BB; www.theanthologistbar.co.uk; @theanthologist; 10.30 pm; closed Sat & Sun.

L'ANTICA PIZZERIA NW3 £39 453

66 HEATH ST   020 7431 8516   9–1A

"This tiny authentic pizzeria in Hampstead is simply fantastic!". "Cheerful and good service from the Italian owners ensures a lively atmosphere", while locals rate their wood-fired pizza "among the best in town". / NW3 1DN; www.anticapizzeria.co.uk; @AnticaHamp; 7 pm; Mon-Thu D only, Fri-Sun open L & D.

L'ANTICA PIZZERIA DA MICHELE NW1 £20

199 BAKER ST   020 7935 6458   2–1A

The original London outpost of the famous Naples pizzeria (est 1870, it featured in the film 'Eat, Pray, Love') ceased to trade under this name this year (in Stoke Newington) leaving a single, tourist-friendly outlet on Baker Street. The pizzas in Stokey were generally reckoned "fabulously authentic", but this is a franchise so similarities between locations are looser than might otherwise be the case (hence we've left it unrated). / NW1 6UY; anticapizzeriadamichele.co.uk; @DaMicheleNapoli.

ANTIDOTE WINE BAR W1 £59 223

12A NEWBURGH ST   020 7287 8488   4–1B

Quirky, French-run wine-bar (plus upstairs dining room) tucked away just off Carnaby Street, which has dropped on and off the foodie radar in recent years. Scores currently are well off their highs of a few years ago, but it's still tipped for its wine list and reasonable selection of accompanying nibbles (which incorporate some fairly substantial options). / W1F 7RR; www.antidotewinebar.com; @AntidoteWineBar; 10.30 pm; closed Sun.

APPLEBEE'S FISH SE1 £62 422

5 STONEY ST   020 7407 5777   10–4C

"Fresh off the boats", "simply" and "beautifully cooked" – some of the best seafood in town for a very "reasonable price" is to be found at this "little gem" at Borough Market. "It's bit crowded but the cooking makes up for it". / SE1 9AA; www.applebeesfish.com; @applebeesfish; Mon-Wed 10 pm, Thu-Sat 11 pm; closed Sun; no Amex.

APULIA EC1 £52 332

50 LONG LN   020 7600 8107   10–2B

"The sort of little local you want around the corner" – this southern Italian near Smithfield Market serves "satisfying and appetising Puglian food" at "very sensible prices" – including "fresh homemade pasta in the evenings" and "family dishes using grandmother's recipes". "Freshly made cakes for dessert and a terrific Puglian wine list, too". / EC1A 9EJ; www.apuliarestaurant.co.uk; 11 pm; closed Sun D.

AQUA KYOTO W1 £63 334

240 REGENT ST (ENTRANCE 30 ARGYLL ST)   020 7478 0540   4–1A

The "beautiful top-floor setting in the West End with big outside terrace" creates a vibey environment – "reminiscent of a nightclub" – at this branch of the Hong Kong chain. For somewhere so central (seconds from Oxford Circus), feedback historically has been surprisingly limited and variable, but those who did make the trip this year report "high quality" Japanese sushi and other fare "with an interesting twist on standard dishes". See also Aqua Nueva. / W1B 3BR; www.aqua-london.com; @aqualondon; Mon-Wed 10.30 pm, Thu-Sat 11 pm, Sun 6 pm; closed Sun D.

AQUA NUEVA W1 £68 324

240 REGENT STREET (ENTRANCE 30 ARGYLL ST)   020 7478 0540   4–1A

The Spanish neighbour to Aqua Kyoto shares all the characteristics of this roof-top operation – terraces, clubby decor, dazzlingly central location – and generates even less feedback that its sibling! Such as there is however paints it in a good light this year. / W1B 3BR; www.aqua-london.com; @aquanueva; 1 am, Sun 8 pm.

AQUA SHARD SE1 £104 `1` `1` `3`

**LEVEL 31, 31 ST THOMAS ST
020 3011 1256 10–4C**

"You can't beat the view" from the 31st floor of Western Europe's tallest building: "sitting up in the heavens, overlooking the twinkling lights of London" puts it high on some diners' lists "for a special occasion". Prices at this Hong Kong-owned landmark venture are appropriately "astronomical", but the food is definitely not out-of-this-world and for too many reporters the overall package "can seem poor value for money (even with the special deal!)" / SE1 9RY; www.aquashard.co.uk; @aquashard; 10.45 pm.

AQUAVIT SW1 £77 `2` `2` `2`

**ST JAMES'S MARKET, 1 CARLTON ST
020 7024 9848 4–4D**

"A bit of a goldfish bowl with big windows" – this "awesome-looking" St James's yearling (sibling to one of NYC's most famous restaurants) has yet to reach its full potential. To fans it's "a big, bustling, brassy brasserie with really well-executed Scandi food (and cracking Aquavit)" that's "an excellent place to impress"; to sceptics, it "somehow lacks something" – "it looks beautiful, but feels cold and clinical" and the food is "quite sophisticated, but a bit soulless, mixed in realisation, and not a patch on the one in Manhattan". / SW1Y 4QQ; www.aquavitrestaurants.com; @aquavitlondon.

ARABICA BAR AND KITCHEN SE1 £52 `3` `3` `3`

**3 ROCHESTER WALK 020 3011 5151
10–4C**

"The flavours are amazing" at this modern Levantine outfit on the edge of foodie Borough Market – it has a "real buzz about it" and is "good value" too. / SE1 9AF; www.arabicabarandkitchen.com; @ArabicaLondon; 11 pm, Sun 9 pm; closed Sun D.

THE ARAKI W1 £380 `5` `5` `3`

**UNIT 4 12 NEW BURLINGTON ST
020 7287 2481 4–3A**

"Hands down most memorable restaurant experience of our lives" – Mitsuhiro Araki's Mayfair import from Tokyo (where, as with here, he also held three Michelin stars) offers "the pinnacle of Japanese cuisine": "mind-blowing, mouthwatering food" ("too many amazing dishes to mention") "lovingly handmade in front of you at a tiny 9 seater bar", where "Mr Araki makes you feel like guests in his living room". Is it expensive? Flippin' 'eck it is. But "ignore the price: it's a complete cultural immersion and should be compared to a night in top seats at the opera, not a mere meal!", is the view most folks seem content, nay, ecstatic to take. They say "If you can afford to splash-out, this is a must-try". At the margin are slightly more sceptical types (or maybe just non-billionaires) who find the prices "galling" but ultimately feel it's a Faustian pact that works for them: "It's utterly brilliant and I loved going; but my goodness, it's expensive, at about £40 a mouthful with the same for a modest glass of wine. But I'm so glad

I experienced it. One to save for…" / W1S 3BH; www.the-araki.com; seatings only at 6 pm and 8.30 pm; closed Tue-Sun L, closed Mon.

ARDICIOCCA SW6 £46

**461-465 NORTH END RD 020 3848 6830
6–4A**

Gluten-free pizza and pasta is the promise at this coeliac-friendly, dairy-free, sugar-free Italian on the site near Fulham Broadway vacated by Hanger (RIP). Too few reports as yet for a rating, but such as we have are upbeat: "hope they succeed in a location that's had many failures!" / SW6 1NZ; www.ardiciocca.com; 11 pm.

ARIANA II NW6 £20 `3` `3` `2`

**241 KILBURN HIGH RD 020 3490 6709
1–2B**

"For the money (and the ability to BYO) this place cannot be beat!" – this family-run Afghani in Kilburn provides good "cheap 'n' cheerful" scoff and "particularly good service from the owner"; handy for the Tricycle Theatre. / NW6 7JN; www.ariana2restaurant.co.uk; @Ariana2kilburn; Mon-Thu 11.30 pm, Fri-Sun midnight.

ARK FISH E18 £39 `3` `4` `2`

142 HERMON HILL 020 8989 5345 1–1D

"Shame you can't book" at this South Woodford chippy – it's "a good reliable, casual fish place" that's one of the best options in the area. Owners Mark and Liz Farrell have in their time run legendary chippies (including Lisson Grove's famous Seashell, and Dalston's Faulkners). / E18 1QH; www.arkfishrestaurant.co.uk; 10.30 pm; closed Mon; no Amex; no booking.

ARLO'S £50 `3` `3` `3`

**47 NORTHCOTE RD, SW11 AWAITING TEL
11–2C NEW | 1 RAMSDEN RD, SW12
020 3019 6590 11–2C**

This two-year-old Balham steakhouse, now joined by a branch in Clapham's Northcote Road, is "a must for serious steak fans" – and "the salads are good too". "Friendly, helpful staff and decent wine" contribute to the appeal, and there's an "exceptional value set lunch". What's more, the "light and airy" décor makes a "nice change from exposed brickwork!" /

ARTHUR HOOPER'S SE1 £63 `4` `4` `3`

8 STONEY ST 020 7940 0169 10–4C

"A great new addition to Borough Market" – this "really enjoyable" contemporary wine bar (named for the now-defunct greengrocer's premises that it occupies) wins very consistent praise for its "interesting" Mediterranean dishes and "equally good wine list", with an excellent range by the glass. / SE1 9AA; www.arthurhoopers.co.uk; @arthurhoopers; Mon-Thu 11 pm, Fri & Sat midnight; closed Sun; booking max 6 may apply.

L'ARTISTA NW11 £42 `3` `5` `3`

917 FINCHLEY RD 020 8731 7501 1–1B

"Buzzy pizzeria under the railway arches opposite Golders Green station that's been serving pasta and pizza (mostly pizza) to the locals since forever, and which is always busy, so they must be doing something right!" It's "extremely noisy and cramped", but they are "especially great with children". / NW11 7PE; www.lartistapizzeria.com; 11 pm.

L'ARTISTE MUSCLÉ W1 £48 `2` `2` `5`

1 SHEPHERD MKT 020 7493 6150 3–4B

For a taste of 'la vie en rose', head to this atmospheric Shepherd Market bolthole – "a reminder of bistros in small French towns years ago". "The cooking is simple traditional French, with some depth of flavour", while "the wine is very reasonably priced, especially for Mayfair". / W1J 7PA; @lartistemuscle; 10 pm.

ARTUSI SE15 £48 `4` `3` `3`

161 BELLENDEN RD 020 3302 8200 1–4D

An excellent "cheap 'n' cheerful choice" – this "small neighbourhood place in gentrified Peckham" has won more-than-local renown for its "wonderful modern Italian food, executed with style and elegance". There's a "very good if limited menu (three choices each of starter, main and pudding)" and "lovely staff who are attentive in the right way". / SE15 4DH; www.artusi.co.uk; @artusipeckham; Mon-Wed 11 pm, Thu-Sat midnight, Sun 9.30 pm; closed Mon L.

ASAKUSA NW1 £36 `5` `2` `2`

265 EVERSHOLT ST 020 7388 8533 9–3C

"Top-notch sashimi, tempura and sushi at reasonable prices" inspire the highest praise for this offbeat operation near Mornington Crescent, whose "mock-Tudor-cum-Tyrolean decor is bizarre but doesn't detract from the authentic Japanese cooking". "I'm trying, and failing miserably, to keep it a secret from my friends!". / NW1 1BA; 11.30 pm, Sat 11 pm; closed Mon-Sat L, closed Sun.

ASIA DE CUBA, ST MARTIN'S LANE HOTEL WC2 £82 `2` `2` `3`

45 ST MARTIN'S LN 020 7300 5588 5–4C

This glitzy Cuban-Chinese restaurant and cocktail bar in a boutique hotel near the Coliseum has a "great location" and groovy decor. Verdicts on the main food offering, though, are variable: "first time I've been back for more than a decade, when it first opened: still lovely looking, starters were tasty, mains very ordinary and it was completely overpriced". Top Tip: "afternoon tea with an original twist". / WC2N 4HX; www.morganshotelgroup.com; @asiadecuba; Mon-Fri 9 pm, Sat 9.30 pm, Sun 3 pm.

ASSAGGI W2 £76 3 4 2

39 CHEPSTOW PL 020 7792 5501 7–1B

On the plus-side, this quirky first-floor of a Bayswater pub – "an old favourite" that was re-launched by one of its original owners a couple of years ago – still mostly 'walks the walk', with the "exceptional" cooking and "wonderful personal service" that established it in times gone by as "one of the best Italians in London". Even some fans, though, are losing patience with the "outrageous" pricing nowadays: "very good, but doesn't justify the see-how-much-we-can-get-away-with approach". / W2 4TS; www.assaggi.co.uk; Fri & Sat, Wed & Thu 9.30 pm; closed Sun; no Amex.

ASSAGGI BAR & PIZZERIA W2 £64 4 3 2

39 CHEPSTOW PLACE 020 7792 5501 7–1B

"Quite exceptional pizzas" and a small menu "that changes to reflect seasonal ingredients" are proving a big hit at the street-level bar of this former pub on the Notting Hill-Bayswater border, taken over in recent times by the team who resurrected Assaggi above (see also). Unlike upstairs, here ratings are rock-solid – maybe this is where their focus increasingly lies? / W2 4TS; www.assaggi.co.uk; 10 pm; closed Sun; no booking.

ASTER RESTAURANT SW1 £58 3 2 3

150 VICTORIA ST 020 3875 5555 2–4B

Neither D&D London nor the Nova development are known for their unswerving commitment to interesting cuisine, which makes Helena Puolakka's "unusual", "Scandi-French fusion" venture – "arguably the best new eatery in all these concrete Victoria canyons" – all the more unexpected; and "while it's a bit of a Curate's Egg, it's got a lot going for it" too. On the downside, the design is "a bit soulless", "service can be slow" and "prices are just a bit higher than they should be". But on the bright side, the "roomy" space is "light and airy", and "there's always something interesting on the menu to try". / SW1E 5LB; www.aster-restaurant.com; @AsterVictoria; 10 pm; closed Sun.

L'ATELIER DE JOEL ROBUCHON WC2 £117 2 2 2

13-15 WEST ST 020 7010 8600 5–2B

August 6 2018 saw the passing of Michelin's most fêted chef ever, and where that leaves the London outpost of his global luxury chain – whose "small plates of taste bombs are a little piece of food theatre" – muddies an already-unclear outlook. For most of its lifetime, the assessment of his "intimate" and opulent two-floor venue (plus cocktail bar with roof terrace) in Covent Garden has been that the experience it provides is "an always-exceptional delight" (if a nose-bleedingly expensive one). But "the food has worsened" in the last 2-3 years, and service at times can be "diabolical", while the sense that the place is "horrendously overpriced" has magnified. In the year prior to M Robuchon's death its ratings had staged something of a

comeback on all fronts, so all is by no means lost for whoever takes the business forwards from now on. / WC2H 9NE; www.joelrobuchon.co.uk; @latelierlondon; Sun & Mon 10.30 pm, Tue-Thu 11 pm, Fri & Sat midnight; No trainers.

THE ATLAS SW6 £50 4 4 4

16 SEAGRAVE RD 020 7385 9129 6–3A

"If only all pubs were like this" gastroboozer near West Brompton tube, whose "Med-led" menu "punches over its weight" and which also provides "fabulous wine" and "some of the finest real ale in London". "Now in its 20th year", it finds itself increasingly surrounded by the burgeoning Lillie Square development, but is "still the best place in the area". "The new secluded garden terrace" (much bigger and smarter than the old one) is another reason to visit. / SW6 1RX; www.theatlaspub.co.uk; @theatlasfulham; 10.30 pm, Mon 11 pm, Sun 3 pm.

AUGUSTINE KITCHEN SW11 £52 3 4 3

63 BATTERSEA BRIDGE RD 020 7978 7085 6–4C

«Dix points!» – This "honest local bistro, serving excellent Savoyard fare" has made itself at home just south of Battersea Bridge. Locals value it for "good, reliable, reasonably priced French food, well served in pleasant surroundings". / SW11 3AU; www.augustine-kitchen.co.uk; @augustinekitchen; closed Mon & Sun D.

AULIS LONDON W1 £195 5 5 4

SOHO - ADDRESS ON BOOKING 020 3948 9665 –

"Simon Rogan's development kitchen offers a unique and unforgettable experience" that's "even better than his Claridge's iteration". Its secret location is revealed only on booking, with pre-payment expected (for food and wine pairings). Despite an entry level cost for the evening – wherein two chefs cook for 8 diners in a relatively small room around a chef's table – of upwards of £200 per head, all reporters agree, it's "an all-round exceptional performance". On the menu: new dishes, before they are potentially served at Roganic. / W1; aulis.london; @AulisSimonRogan; Mon-Fri 10 pm, Sat & Sun 9 pm.

AUTHENTIQUE EPICERIE & BAR NW5 £42

114-116 FORTESS RD 020 3609 6602 9–2C

A Tufnell Park wine bar, restaurant, grocery and wine store all rolled into one, featuring a rotating roster of guest chefs and winemakers, which opened in Spring 2018. Alongside food and wine evenings in the wine bar, the attached grocery store offers French delicacies, cheeses and charcuterie, over 400 different vintages and 50 craft beers. / NW5 5HL; authentique-epicerie.com; Tue-Thu, Sun 11 pm, Fri & Sat midnight; closed Mon.

L'AVENTURE NW8 £67 3 4 5

3 BLENHEIM TERRACE 020 7624 6232 9–3A

"Madame Catherine reigns as always with French charm" ("although at times she can be a little touchy") at her St John's Wood stalwart, whose superbly atmospheric quarters are particularly "perfect for an intimate and romantic meal for two". She "keeps high standards" including very "dependable" cuisine bourgeoise (but "some new additions on the menu" might not go amiss). / NW8 0EH; www.laventure.co.uk; 11 pm; closed Sat L.

THE AVENUE SW1 £71 2 2 2

7-9 ST JAMES'S ST 020 7321 2111 3–4D

This "stylish" if "cavernous" modern brasserie – nowadays part of D&D London – trades largely on its Manhattan-esque looks and St James's address, and wins its highest praise from expense-accounters. For folks spending their own cash, the food's not distinguished but not bad, but service can be awful, and management's attempts to pep up the big interior ("blaring muzak", "singer wasn't enough to lift the ambience") don't always go down well. / SW1A 1EE; www.avenue-restaurant.co.uk; @avenuestjames; 10.30 pm, Sun 6 pm; closed Sun D.

AVIARY EC2 £57 2 2 3

10TH FLOOR, 22-25 FINSBURY SQUARE 020 3873 4060 13–2A

"The rooftop views are amazing" from this 10th floor perch on Finsbury Square, which boasts a big outside terrace. Critics feel "you pay for it" when it comes to food though, and argue "it's better as a bar" or for quieter mealtimes like breakfast. / EC2A 1DX; aviarylondon.com; @AviaryLDN; 9.30 pm.

AWESOME THAI SW13 £26 3 4 2

68 CHURCH RD 020 8563 7027 11–1A

"All the classics are nicely done" at this "excellent", "professionally run Thai local" in Barnes, whose brilliant location opposite the popular Olympic Studios cinema ensures that it is "always crowded". / SW13 0DQ; www.awesomethai.co.uk; 10.30 pm, Sun 10 pm; Mon-Thu D only, Fri-Sun open L & D.

LE BAB W1 £44 4 3 3

2ND FLOOR, KINGLY CT 020 7439 9222 4–2B

"Kebabs but not as we know them" – this "fantastic concept" in Kingly Court off Carnaby Street has pimped up the humble skewer to great acclaim. "Good quality fancy kebabs, run by a bunch of public school boys – weird, but enjoyable". / W1B 5PW; www.eatlebab.com; @EatLeBab; 10 pm, Sun 7 pm; booking max 6 may apply.

BABEL HOUSE W1 £83

26-28 BRUTON PLACE   020 7629 5613
3–2B

Inspired by the cuisine of countries bordering the Black Sea – and with a particular focus on the food of Odessa (it's named for that city's famous writer, Isaac Babel, and fresh fish is flown in from Odessa's Pryvoz market), this swanky-looking newcomer set up shop in a super-chichi Mayfair mews in May 2018, just as the survey was coming to a close. Feedback was too sparse for a rating, but the first report is encouraging – "ate just after opening with Ukrainian friends; excellent food; good wine list; will work well once it gets going properly". / W1J 6NG; www.babelhouse.co.uk; @BabelHouseLDN; 12.30 am, Sun 11.30 pm.

BABETTE SE15   £39   334

57 NUNHEAD LANE   020 3172 2450   1–4D

"Welcome to the big plate phenomenon!" – practically the only options are imaginative sharing boards from the blackboard menu at this "excellent French-run neighbourhood spot" – a revamped Old Truman pub in Nunhead. / SE15 3TR; www.babettenunhead.com; @babettenunhead; Wed & Thu 11 pm, Fri & Sat midnight, Sun 7 pm; closed Wed & Thu L, closed Mon & Tue.

BABUR SE23   £57   554

119 BROCKLEY RISE   020 8291 2400   1–4D

"A marvel in a suburban desert" – this Forest Hill "jewel" takes "South London Indian cuisine to a new level and puts it equal with the best in the West End and City". "The cooking is refined and inventive, beautifully spiced and seasoned, and looks as good as it tastes, while service is amiable rather than expert and the decor rather smart". "I've been going there for over 20 years and it remains relevant and delicious with a constantly evolving menu and drinks list". "If you live anywhere remotely within striking distance, you have to try it out!" / SE23 1JP; www.babur.info; @BaburRestaurant; 11.30 pm; closed Sun L.

BACCO TW9   £58   222

39-41 KEW RD   020 8332 0348   1–4A

"An excellent local Italian with gracious service" that's "very convenient to the Orange Tree and Richmond Theatres" – that's how fans think of this "comfortable" and well-established Richmond mainstay. Even they, however, admit "there aren't many good places in the vicinity", and sceptics say it's "OK but nothing special, with food that's presentable but expensive for what it is". / TW9 2NQ; www.bacco-restaurant.co.uk; @BaccoRichmond; 11 pm; closed Sun D.

BAGATELLE W1

34 DOVER ST   020 3972 7000   3–3C

On the former site of Quattro Passi (RIP) – an opening from a swish, well-established international chain with 'clubstaurants' from Dubai to Rio de Janeiro – arrived in Mayfair in Spring 2018. Culinarily speaking it takes its lead from the South of France, with a Provençal-inspired menu. / W1S 4NG; www.bistrotbagatelle.com; @bebagatelle.

BAGERIET WC2   £12   433

24 ROSE ST   020 7240 0000   5–3C

"Cinnamon buns, full of spice and crunchy sugar topping (but not oily) and great for dunking in a coffee" are a highpoint at this "tiny" ("ten people and the place is full") but "welcoming" slice of Sweden, hidden down a Covent Garden alleyway. / WC2E 9EA; www.bageriet.co.uk; @BagerietLondon; 7 pm; closed Sun; no booking.

BALA BAYA SE1   £60   422

OLD UNION YARD ARCHES, 229 UNION ST
020 8001 7015   10–4B

A flavour of Tel Aviv café culture is to be found in a railway arch in Southwark – the first venture of Israeli-born chef Eran Tibi, formerly of Ottolenghi: "great sharing dishes that look as amazing as they taste". Top Tip: "an astonishing cauliflower dish changed my perception of this vegetable". / SE1 0LR; balabaya.co.uk; @bala_baya; 11 pm, Sun 5 pm; closed Sun D.

THE BALCON, SOFITEL ST JAMES SW1   £69   233

8 PALL MALL   020 7968 2900   2–3C

A "very classy set-up" – certainly for a hotel by Trafalgar Square – this all-day Gallic brasserie offers "good-value set menus" and "attentive service in surprisingly comfortable surroundings", which make it a "great West End location for lunch or pre-theatre". Afternoon tea is also a feature here. / SW1Y 5NG; www.thebalconlondon.com; @TheBalcon; 11 pm, Sun 10 pm.

BALTHAZAR WC2   £70   224

4 - 6 RUSSELL ST   020 3301 1155   5–3D

A "terrific buzz" helps justify the presence of Keith McNally's "bustling" NYC import, as does its "handiness for Covent Garden". Opinions differ over its performance relative to the Manhattan original, but there's some agreement that here in WC2 "the service is only just OK, the bistro/brasserie food is very average, but it's the ambience which makes it bearable". Brunch is a good way to give it a whirl. / WC2B 5HZ; www.balthazarlondon.com; @balthazarlondon; Mon-Thu 11.30 pm, Fri & Sat midnight, Sun 11 pm.

BALTIC SE1   £57   343

74 BLACKFRIARS RD   020 7928 1111
10–4A

It's "always fun" to pay a visit to this "interesting" venue – a converted Georgian factory near The Cut, which provides a "buzzy" ("very noisy when full") if slightly "cavernous" backdrop to a meal. On the menu, "hearty, reasonably authentic Mittel-European food" but it's "the amazing list of vodkas" that really gets the party started… / SE1 8HA; www.balticrestaurant.co.uk; @balticlondon; 11.30 pm, Sun 10.30 pm; closed Mon L.

BALUCHI, LALIT HOTEL LONDON SE1   £77   324

181 TOOLEY ST   020 3765 0000   10–4D

The "lovely room" is a highpoint at this former school hall near Tower Bridge (nowadays part of the first European opening from an Indian luxury boutique hotel chain). The food (with inspirations from across India) is on all accounts "beautiful" and "imaginative" too, but "pricey" (some would say "ridiculously expensive") for what it is, especially given service that can prove "lethargic". / SE1 2JR; www.thelalit.com/the-lalit-london/eat-and-drink/baluchi; @TheLalitLondon; 9.30 pm.

BANG BANG ORIENTAL NW9   £37   323

399 EDGWARE RD NO TEL 1–1A

A "fantastic choice of different Asian cuisines" including "all sorts of street food" is available at this vast oriental food court in Colindale: "from Indian and traditional Chinese and Thai to Korean, Filipino, Japanese, Indonesian and more". "Some is toned down for the London market", but the "number of Asian diners is a testament to the authenticity and quality of the food". "Fight for a seat and enjoy the buzz." / NW9 0AS; www.bangbangoriental.com; @bangbangofh; Mon-Thu 10 pm, Fri & Sat 10.30 pm, Sun 9.30 pm.

BÁNH BÁNH   £41   343

46 PECKHAM RYE, SE15   020 7207 2935
1–4D | 326 COLDHARBOUR LANE, SW9
020 7737 5888   11–2D NEW

"Go for the pho and the other Vietnamese specialties… not to mention the spectacular cocktails" – reasons to visit the Nguyen family's "fun, cool, well-priced local" in Peckham Rye. It's only been open a couple of years, and they've already opened a new Brixton sibling too. / www.banhbanh.com; @BanhBanhHQ

BANNERS N8   £51   324

21 PARK RD   020 8348 2930   9–1C

Founded by Juliette Banner nearly 30 years ago, this community-minded Crouch End diner offers an all-day world-food menu and is a local hero for its "great breakfasts" (less so for a visit at other times). / N8 8TE; www.bannersrestaurant.com; 10.30 pm, Mon 11 pm, Sun 3 pm; no Amex.

BAO   £37   433

31 WINDMILL ST, W1   020 3011 1632   5–1A
| 53 LEXINGTON ST, W1 07769 627811 4–2C
| 13 - 23 WESTGATE ST, E8 NO TEL 14–2B

"Oriental steamed buns to die for" explain the "perpetual queue" at these "tiny", "fast 'n' furious" cafés in Soho and Fitzrovia, whose "reinvented Taiwanese street food" ("complex, apparently simple, always daring") includes other intriguing dishes ("like beef cheek and tendon nuggets"), as well as "interesting Taiwanese teas". / W1F Mon-Wed 10 pm, Thu-Sat 10.30 pm, W1T Mon-Sat 10 pm, E8 Sat 4 pm; W1F

& W1T closed Sun, E8 open Sat L only; W1 no bookings, E8 takeout only.

THE BAPTIST GRILL, L'OSCAR HOTEL WC1

2-6 SOUTHAMPTON ROW   020 7405 5555   2-1D

Occupying a once derelict Grade II-listed building by Holborn station (a former HQ of the Baptist Church), this new 39-bedroom luxury hotel opened in mid-summer 2018 and also boasts a mezzanine restaurant & bar (Baptist Bar); and cafe (Café Oscar). The main restaurant, overseen by former Angler chef Tony Fleming, aims for 'a contemporary approach to the traditional grill room'. / WC1B 4AA; www.loscar.com/dining; 11.30 pm.

BAR BOULUD, MANDARIN ORIENTAL SW1   £69   323

66 KNIGHTSBRIDGE   020 7201 3899   6-1D

"A good balance between being casual and fine dining" – this deluxe Knightsbridge diner under the name of the famous NYC chef could be thought of as where the rich go "if you are in the mood for burgers but want the restaurant experience and a good glass of wine" (although the overall menu includes some "seriously accomplished", more 'culinary' options). The space feels like the hotel basement it is, but can develop "a great buzz". / SW1X 7LA; www.barboulud.com; @barbouludlondon; 1 am, Sun midnight; No trainers.

BAR DOURO SE1   £53   443

ARCH 25B FLAT IRON SQUARE, UNION ST 020 7378 0524   10-4B

With its "authentic Portuguese small plates" and "fab list of Portuguese wines", this small blue-and-white-tiled bar near Borough Market "manages, unbelievably, to bring something new to London". It's "a bit hard to find" in the new Flat Iron Square food development – "but worth the search". / SE1 1TD; www.bardouro.com; @BarDouro; 11.30 pm; booking max 4 may apply.

BAR ESTEBAN N8   £48   333

29 PARK RD   020 8340 3090   1-1C

"Definitely a few cuts above your typical tapas", this popular Crouch End spot is "always a joy, with relaxed, affable and attentive staff". Ratings would be even higher but "the food does wobble from time to time". / N8 8TE; www.baresteban.com; @barestebanN8; Mon-Wed 11 pm, Thu-Sat midnight, Sun 9.30 pm; closed weekday L; booking max 8 may apply.

BAR ITALIA W1   £32   335

22 FRITH ST   020 7437 4520   5-2A

"Still the best espresso in the capital", say fans of this 24/7 veteran, now in its 70th year and little changed, and where posing elbow-to-elbow with other late night denizens of Soho, or squeezing in to watch Italian footie, is a London rite of passage. There are light bites, but they aren't the point. / W1D 4RF; www.baritaliasoho.co.uk;

@TheBaristas; 11.30 pm, Sun 10.30 pm; no Amex; no booking.

THE BARBARY WC2   £50   554

16 NEAL'S YARD NO TEL 5-2C

"Believe the hype!" – Palomar's younger sibling in Neal's Yard rocks, from its "exceptional, tasty and distinctive Eastern Mediterranean small plates" to its "exciting atmosphere". Eating is "buzzy, counter-style only" – "get there early if you cannot bear to queue!" / WC2H 9DP; www.thebarbary.co.uk; @barbarylondon; 10 pm, Sun 9.30 pm; no booking.

BARBECOA EC4   £75   222

20 NEW CHANGE PAS   020 3005 8555 10-2B

"The setting overlooking St Paul's is fantastic" but even some praising "decent" cooking at Jamie Oliver's remaining luxury grill leave "feeling like you're being ripped off" and to critics the dishes here are just plain "mediocre and badly served". The swish-looking setting is "just unbelievably noisy – I've been at gigs that were quieter!". Its plush sister venue in Piccadilly closed its doors (after just a year) in February. / EC4M 9AG; www.barbecoa.com; @Barbecoa_london; 9.30 pm.

BARRAFINA   £50   555

26-27 DEAN ST, W1   020 7813 8016   4-1D | 10 ADELAIDE ST, WC2   020 7440 1456 5-4C | 43 DRURY LN, WC2   020 7440 1456 5-2D | COAL DROPS YARD,   N1 AWAITING TEL   9-3C NEW

"The perfect alternative to a trip to Spain!" – in fact "the food is better than in Barcelona" in the branches of the Hart Bros' small chain, which pays homage to that city's Cal Pep with its small (no more than 30 covers) bars in Soho and Covent Garden (and – arriving in autumn 2018, in the trendy new Coal Drops Yard development in King's Cross, alongside a covered and heated terrace separately branded as 'Parrillan'). Confidently 'surfing the Zeitgeist' – no other individual restaurant, never mind group, has ever achieved such an outstanding and consistent level of support in the survey, over many years. There's "no booking and no fuss" – "you often have to queue" (though drinks and nibbles help enliven the experience) and seating is "counter-stye" at the bar ("which works less well for any kind of group, but for couples is ideal"). With its "bold Spanish flavours" the tapas selection is "arguably some of London's best food at any price, and remarkable value" (while by the same token "watching the chefs at work is brilliant" – "there's nothing theatrical, but it's mesmerising seeing experts so engrossed in their stations"). "The wine list is short, punchy and perfectly complements the food", "staff seem to be having as good a time as the clientele" and the overall effect is properly "effervescent". Top Tip: "always go for the daily blackboard specials, especially the fish", which is "cooked to a tee and beautifully seasoned". / www.barrafina.co.uk; 11 pm, Sun 10 pm; no booking, max group 4.

BARRICA W1   £55   332

62 GOODGE ST   020 7436 9448   2-1B

"Really great tapas and a good list of sherries" fit the bill at this "lively if a little cramped" venue in Goodge Street that "feels just like being in Spain". "Everyone we take here adores it." "Can get very busy, so booking is important." / W1T 4NE; www.barrica.co.uk; @barricatapas; Tue-Thu 10 pm, Fri & Sat 10.30 pm, Mon 9.30 pm, Sun 9 pm; closed Sun.

BARSHU W1   £58   422

28 FRITH ST   020 7287 6688   5-3A

"One of Soho's best" – the Sichuan food in this well-known café is "first-rate" – "really spicy and delicious". Much of the menu is not for the faint-hearted, but "it's always possible to avoid overly hot dishes with the aid of the helpful staff". / W1D 5LF; www.barshurestaurant.co.uk; @BarshuLondon; Sun-Thu 11 pm, Fri & Sat 11.30 pm.

BEAN & WHEAT EC1   £29   433

321 OLD ST   020 3802 2190   10-2D

High marks (if from a small fan club) for Adam Handling's new deli-cafe, featuring coffee from independent roasters; and where locally produced bread, and offerings in Kilner jars made from by-products from the kitchen at The Frog help underpin its sustainable aims. Reports were for the original Spitalfields location: it's now moved to this new larger site in Hoxton. / EC1V 9LE; www.beanandwheat.co.uk; @beanandwheat; closed Sat & Sun.

BEARS ICE CREAM W12   £7   333

244 GOLDHAWK RD   020 3441 4982   8-1B

Yummy sprinkles and a mind-numbing array of toppings to decorate the single flavour of Icelandic ice cream draw families to this cute little ice cream parlour on the busy gyratory north of Ravenscourt Park. / W12 9PE; www.bearsicecream.co.uk; @bears_icecream; 8.30 pm; L & early evening only; no booking.

BEA'S CAKE BOUTIQUE WC1   £43   333

44 THEOBALDS RD   020 7242 8330   2-1D

"Fabulously busy… in a good way (as it feels like you have come to the right place)" – this cute tea rooms near Holborn Library spawned a chain of the same name on the back of its inviting-looking cakes and "tasty lunches and snacks" that are "worth a little waiting for". / WC1X 8NW; www.beas.london; @beas_bloomsbury; 7 pm; L & early evening only.

BEAST W1   £117   122

3 CHAPEL PL   020 7495 1816   3-1B

Most reporters are left speechless by the stratospheric prices at this candle-lit surf 'n' turf experience off Oxford Street (part of the Goodman group), where huge portions of Norwegian king crab, Canadian lobster and Nebraskan beef are the building blocks of the small menu. / W1G 0BG; www.beastrestaurant.co.uk; @beastrestaurant; 10.30 pm; closed Sun; may need 7+ to book.

BECK AT BROWNS, BROWNS HOTEL W1 £97 344

BROWNS HOTEL, ALBEMARLE ST 020 7518 4004 3–3C

"Definitely one of London's top Italian restaurants" – Heinz Beck (who has three stars for La Pergola, in Rome, and whose last London venture was at Apsleys, RIP) has achieved a much better showcase for his classic Italian approach at this new incarnation for the main dining room at Mayfair's grand Brown's Hotel. Until recently it traded as Hix Mayfair (now RIP), and the spacious room itself now has a much more "stylish and comfortable" atmosphere than formerly, with bold floral wallpaper above its traditional wood panelling, and feels "so relaxed and convivial". The opening has achieved mixed newspaper reviews and accusations of being over-engineered, but our feedback is much more upbeat. Even fans acknowledge that it's "not cheap", but – by the same token – even the one disappointed reporter who thought the high cost made it "incredibly bad value" acknowledged the food is good. All-in-all, the majority view is that the experience is to be "very highly recommended", not least owing to "a simply scrumptious menu (with plenty of pasta, fish and meat options)", which delivers dishes that are "apparently simple but very skilfully produced, and presented in a stylish yet unfussy manner". A thumbs-up to the "efficient and friendly staff" too, including the "well-informed and helpful sommelier" who presides over an "interesting and long wine list". / W1S 4BP; www.roccofortehotels.com/hotels-and-resorts/browns-hotel/restaurants-and-bars/beck-at-browns; @Browns_Hotel.

Beck at Brown's W1

BEEF & BREW £46 343

33 DOWNHAM RD, N1 020 7254 7858 14–2A NEW | 323 KENTISH TOWN RD, NW5 020 7998 1511 9–2B

"Fantastic beef at affordable prices" and nifty craft beers have carved a local reputation for this "great neighbourhood steak and chips

joint" in Kentish Town – it's "friendly and not too pricey", and with "cool music and vibes". In summer 2018, it opened a new Haggerston spin-off too. / www.beef-and-brew.co.uk; @BeefandBrewLDN.

THE BEGGING BOWL SE15 £45 422

168 BELLENDEN RD 020 7635 2627 1–4D

"As close to the food in Thailand as you're likely to get in London", this "good value" Peckham café has invigorated the southeast London culinary scene in recent years. "Go for the food" even if the no-bookings policy – which irritates some reporters – "can mean a long wait in The Victoria opposite". / SE15 4BW; www.thebeggingbowl.co.uk; @thebeggingbowl; 9.45 pm, Sun 9.15 pm; no booking.

BEIJING DUMPLING WC2 £33 432

23 LISLE ST 020 7287 6888 5–3A

"An impressive choice of dumplings" and other "surprisingly good", "un-gloopy and fresh" dishes make it well worth discovering this small, simple Chinatown café. / WC2H 7BA; 11.30 pm, Sun 10.30 pm.

BELLAMY'S W1 £62 344

18-18A BRUTON PL 020 7491 2727 3–2B

Proprietor Gavin Rankin (ex-MD of Annabel's) "is much in evidence" at this "very discreet and efficient" Mayfair fixture – "a comfortable English take on a Parisian brasserie" that's one of a tiny handful of restaurants ever visited by The Queen (and, fair to say, "a safe place to entertain"). For its traditional following, "this is the sort of restaurant you aspire to go to once a week, for the rest of your life" – a "properly grown-up and elegant" venue, with "impeccable service", offering "good interpretations" of "Anglo-French classic dishes" and "a well-chosen and fairly-priced all-French wine list". / W1J 6LY; www.bellamysrestaurant.co.uk; 10.30 pm; closed Sat L, closed Sun.

BELLANGER N1 £60 223

9 ISLINGTON GRN 020 7226 2555 9–3D

"Pretty much the only 'grown-up' restaurant on Upper Street" – Corbin & King's "elegant" Islington outpost is a "spacious", "clubby and wood lined" operation that makes "a classy destination for anyone at any time – be it for a drink, a snack or a meal" (and is kid- and dog-friendly too). The "unusual and interesting" cuisine – schnitzels, "good tartes flambées, hearty sausages (try the aligot mash), steaks" – aims to recreate that of an Alsatian brasserie and is "decent, if a bit uneven" (ditto the service). "Great range of breakfast options, too, and the atmosphere makes it feel special, whether it's a business meeting or you're lingering at the weekend". / N1 2XH; www.bellanger.co.uk; @BellangerN1; Mon & Tue, Sun 10 pm, Wed-Sat 11 pm.

BELMOND CADOGAN HOTEL SW1

75 SLOANE ST 020 3117 1505 6–2D

Luxury hotel group Belmond (as in Belmond Le Manoir Aux Quat' Saisons) has taken on The Cadogan Hotel, Knightsbridge. A multi-million pound refurb' is in the works, and when it reopens in December 2018 the 54-room hotel will also boast a restaurant with views of Cadogan Place Gardens and wunderkind chef, Adam Handling at the stoves (known as Adam Handling Chelsea, with its own street entrance, and open from breakfast on). Afternoon tea in The Tea Lounge will be another option. / SW1X 9SG; www.belmond.com/hotels/europe/uk/london/belmond-cadogan-hotel; @belmond; 11.30 pm, Sun 10 pm.

BELVEDERE RESTAURANT W8 £69 335

OFF ABBOTSBURY RD IN HOLLAND PARK 020 7602 1238 8–1D

"Difficult to beat for romance" – this "beautiful and elegant" 17th-century ballroom inside Holland Park (with outside terrace) provides one of London's most "delightful and secluded" settings for dinner on a summer's evening or Sunday lunch. Perennially the not-particularly-modern British cuisine is "pretty ordinary", but its ratings batted well above their normal average this year, amidst reports that it was found to be "much better than expected". / W8 6LU; www.belvedererestaurant.co.uk; @BelvedereW8; 11 pm, Sun 3.30 pm; closed Sun D.

BENARES W1 £110 323

12A BERKELEY SQUARE HOUSE, 020 7629 8886 3–3B

"Modern Indian done with style!" Atul Kochhar's swish Mayfair destination in very contemporary, first-floor Berkeley Square premises put in a much stronger showing than in last year's survey. True, "when the dining room is quiet the atmosphere can feel a little strained", but when it fills up it's "much more vibrant", and at its best the cuisine here is "really stunning and beautifully presented". STOP PRESS – in August 2018, Kochhar left the restaurant which he founded, whose cuisine will now be led by Executive Chef Brinder Narula, who has been with the group controlling Benares for three years. / W1J 6BS; www.benaresrestaurant.co.uk; @benaresofficial; 10.45 pm, Sun 9.45 pm; closed Sun L; booking max 10 may apply.

BENTLEY'S W1 £84 343

11-15 SWALLOW ST 020 7734 4756 4–4B

"Top up my bubbles and bring on the gorgeous succulent oysters!" – Richard Corrigan's celebrated, 100-year-old veteran, near Piccadilly Circus, is "an all-time favourite" for many reporters – particularly the "bustling" ground-floor bar – thanks to its "barking fresh seafood" ("a wide variety" incorporating "superbly shucked oysters", an "exceptional seafood platter", dressed crab, and so on). "Downstairs is cosier" and the upstairs dining room can seem "bland" by comparison, but "ideal if you want it to be easier to talk in a bigger group". / W1B

4DG; www.bentleys.org; @bentleys_london; 10.30 pm, Sun 10 pm; No shorts; booking max 8 may apply.

BERBER & Q E8 £48 5 3 5

ARCH 338 ACTON MEWS   020 7923 0829   14–2A

"Hearty… well-seasoned and flavoured… YUMMM!" – "The most delicious selection of smoky grilled meats" can be "a revelation" at Josh Katz's North African-style grill in a funky Haggerstone railway arch… and "the veggie dishes are actually even better (the roast beetroot with whipped feta is to die for!"). "The menu evolves enough to keep things interesting and bring you back for more" and there's "fabulous wine" and spicy cocktails too. / E8 4EA; www.berberandq.com; @berberandq; 11 pm, Sun 9 pm; D only, closed Mon; May need 6+ to book.

BERBER & Q SHAWARMA BAR EC1 £51 4 3 3

EXMOUTH MARKET   020 7837 1726   10–1A

The Tel Aviv-style spit-roasted chicken and lamb, mezze and hummus is "cheap, but very tasty" at this excellent two-year-old Exmouth Market offshoot of Josh Katz's Berber & Q. Primarily walk-in, but you can book for bigger groups. / EC1R 4QL; shawarmabar.co.uk; @berberandq; Mon-Thu 11 pm, Fri & Sat 11.30 pm, Sun 10 pm; closed Mon; no booking.

BERENJAK W1

27 ROMILLY ST AWAITING TEL 5–2A

In conjunction with the successful JKS restaurant empire, Iranian chef Kian Samyani will open this Persian restaurant in Soho in October 2018; named for the toasted rice snack eaten at fairs in Iran, the restaurant will replicate the street food and hole-in-the-wall kebab shop cuisine of the chef's homeland. / W1D 5AL; berenjaklondon.com.

BERGEN HOUSE N16 £45

47 NEWINGTON GREEN   020 7226 2779   1–1C

Joining a growing number of restaurants in Newington Green, this bar-bistro opened in early 2018 and serves steak 'n' chips plus a big selection of hearty sharing plates. Not much feedback yet (hence we've left it unrated) but all positive. / N16 9PX; www.bergenhouse.co.uk; Mon & Tue 9 pm, Fri & Sat 11.30 pm, Wed 10 pm, Thu 11 pm, Sun 5 pm.

BERNARDI'S W1 £64 3 3 3

62 SEYMOUR ST   020 3826 7940   2–2A

"Stylish and cool", this modern Italian on the Marylebone-Bayswater border "surprises with the quality of the food". "There's always a buzz" as well – too much for some, who find "the noise level is unbearable" – and prices are West End-high. / W1H 5BN; www.bernardis.co.uk; @BernardisLondon; 10.30 pm, Sun 9.30 pm.

THE BERNERS TAVERN W1 £75 2 3 5

10 BERNERS ST   020 7908 7979   3–1D

The "awesome" setting of its "beautiful" interior provides one of London's most impressive backdrops for a meal at this grand dining room, north of Oxford Street (recommended for romance, but especially for business). Most reports give a thumbs-up to the "pricey-but-solid" cuisine overseen by Jason Atherton, but – especially at the price – results can be "rather forgettable" (and there were a couple of disastrous meals reported this year). Afternoon teas and Sunday roasts are a recent innovation. / W1T 3NP; www.bernerstavern.com; @bernersTavern; 10.30 pm.

BEST MANGAL £38 4 3 3

619 FULHAM RD, SW6   020 7610 0009   6–4A | 104 NORTH END RD, W14   020 7610 1050   8–2D | 66 NORTH END RD, W14   020 7602 0212   8–2D

"Magic, hearty things are done to all things meaty" at this trio of "glorious" Turkish grills, which have established a strong local following in Fulham over 22 years. "Great kebabs are cooked before your eyes", and there's a "warm welcome". / www.bestmangal.com; midnight, Sat 1 am; no Amex.

BIBENDUM SW3 £132 3 3 4

81 FULHAM RD   020 7581 5817   6–2C

After a year at the stoves, ex-Hibiscus patron, Claude Bosi, is getting more into his stride in this "perennially wonderful dining room", within "the iconic setting of the Michelin building". True, there are still many reporters who are not persuaded by his new regime ("Come back Sir Terence Conran, all is forgiven…") and also many who feel that the "results from the classic French high-falutin' menu are dangerously close to ordinary at this price point" ("only an expense accounter could stomach the stratospheric bill"). Ratings have risen sharply since last year's faltering debut, however, amidst accounts of "a return to form", with "smiling staff gliding about smoothly as though on coasters" and "stunningly crafted dishes with fabulous flavours". / SW3 6RD; www.bibendum.co.uk; @bibendumltd; Wed-Fri 9.45 pm, Sat 10 pm, Sun 9 pm; closed Mon & Tue; booking max 12 may apply.

BIBENDUM OYSTER BAR SW3 £53 3 3 3

MICHELIN HOUSE, 81 FULHAM RD   020 7581 5817   6–2C

(Mostly) upbeat reports again this year on this luxurious café in the beautiful, if echoey tiled foyer of the Michelin Building, where Claude Bosi has added hot items to its traditional offering of cold seafood platters. / SW3 6RD; www.bibendum.co.uk; @bibendumrestaurant; 9.30 pm, Sun 8.30 pm; closed Sun D; no booking.

BIBIMBAP £24 3 2 2

10 CHARLOTTE ST, W1   020 7287 3434   2–1C | 11 GREEK ST, W1   020 7287 3434   5–2A | 39 LEADENHALL MKT, EC3   020 72839165 10–2D

You can find "some of the tastiest street food ever" at these modern Korean canteens in Soho and Fitzrovia. It also has takeaway outlets; three in the City and another in Oxford Street. / 11pm, EC3 3 pm; W1 Sun, EC3 Sat & Sun; no bookings.

BIG EASY £62 2 2 3

12 MAIDEN LN, WC2   020 3728 4888   5–3D | 332-334 KING'S RD, SW3   020 7352 4071   6–3C | CROSSRAIL PL, E14   020 3841 8844   12–1C

"Guilty-pleasure comfort food" served in a "crowded but fun atmosphere" have made this "so authentically American" BBQ and crabshack a King's Road fixture for 27 years (and it underwent a major upgrade in 2018). Now with offshoots in Covent Garden and Canary Wharf, the outfit can seem "very corporate" and is "probably best for large groups or office parties". / www.bigeasy.co.uk; @bigeasytweet; Mon-Thu 11 pm, Fri & Sat 11.30 pm, Sun 10.30 pm.

THE BINGHAM TW10 £69 3 4 5

61-63 PETERSHAM RD   020 8940 0902   1–4A

"A breathtaking panorama overlooking the Thames" helps makes the restaurant of this small boutique hotel "an exceptional choice in Richmond". The cuisine is very "reliable" too, using "fine ingredients", but there's a recurring complaint: "the portions are very small" ("the dining room was full of ladies-who-lunch, and judging by their figures they don't eat that much!"). Top Tip: "the market menu is good value". / TW10 6UT; www.thebingham.co.uk; @thebingham; 11 pm, Sun 10.30 pm; closed Sun D; No trainers.

THE BIRD IN HAND W14 £63 3 2 3

88 MASBRO RD   020 7371 2721   8–1C

"A pub with better pizza than most pizzerias!" sums up the appeal of this converted boozer in the backstreets of Olympia. "Stick to the excellent pizzas", though, "the rest of the food is not amazing and the little tapas never quite hit the mark". Sibling to the Oaks in W2 and W12. / W14 0LR; www.thebirdinhandlondon.com; @TBIHLondon; Mon-Wed 10 pm, Thu-Sat 11 pm; booking weekdays only.

BIRD OF SMITHFIELD EC1 £59 3 3 3

26 SMITHFIELD ST   020 7559 5100   10–2B

"A fine Georgian townhouse in Smithfield with interesting art and a lovely upstairs dining room" hosts Tommy Boland's five-storey venture (with summer roof terrace). Yet again it only inspires limited feedback, but all of it positive for its British fare of some ambition. / EC1A 9LB; www.birdofsmithfield.com; @BirdoSmithfield; Mon-Fri midnight; closed Sat & Sun.

BISTRO AIX N8 £56 2️⃣2️⃣3️⃣

54 TOPSFIELD PDE, TOTTENHAM LN 020 8340 6346 9–1C

A "friendly, retro French bistro sticking unswervingly to the provincial classics" – chef-proprietor Lynne Sanders's smart little venue in Crouch End is "like stepping back in time 30 years". Mixed reports have knocked its ratings this year. Fans reckon it is "always reliable and consistently good", but for a few critics, "the quality has been slipping a bit lately" ("variable, and on our last visit, poor"). / N8 8PT; www.bistroaix.co.uk; @bistroaixlondon; Sun-Thu 11 pm, Fri & Sat midnight; closed Mon-Fri L; no Amex.

BISTRO MIREY SW6 £55 4️⃣4️⃣3️⃣

98 LILLIE RD 020 3092 6969 8–2D

Gerald Mirey and Ko Ito have put down permanent roots in Fulham at this cute little modern bistro, near the top of North End Road's market. Dig beyond the weekend brunch, and the à la carte here is distinctive and very competitively priced, offering fusion dishes underpinned by classic French cuisine with Japanese notes. Alongside the inventive food menu is a list of French wines and Japanese sake (as well as London craft sake Kanpai). / SW6 7SR; www.bistromirey.com; @bistromirey; Wed & Thu 9 pm, Fri & Sat 9.30 pm.

BISTRO UNION SW4 £58 3️⃣3️⃣3️⃣

40 ABBEVILLE RD 020 7042 6400 11–2D

Adam Byatt's "nice local" in Abbeville Road doesn't aim for the culinary fireworks of its stablemate Trinity, but generally delivers enjoyable modern bistro cuisine in a "relaxed" setting. There are a few reporters this year, however, who are "hoping for a return to form" saying that of late it "didn't deliver" as hoped – perhaps a blip. Top Tip: "kids-eat-free Sunday Supper Club". / SW4 9NG; www.bistrounion.co.uk; @BistroUnion; 10 pm, Sun 9 pm; closed Sun L; booking max 8 may apply.

BISTRO VADOUVAN (FRENCH & SPICE) SW15 £57 4️⃣4️⃣3️⃣

30 BREWHOUSE LANE 020 3475 3776 11–2B

"A brilliant combination of flavours" – "predominantly Western but with subtle, Asian-influenced (but not Asian-dominated) spicing" – helps make this "original" yearling "a welcome addition to SW15"; although it has "a great riverside location near Putney Bridge" too. It's the brainchild of Durga Misra and Uttam Tripathy, who both hail from the same town in India (but only met years later at college). / SW15 2JX; bistrovadouvan.co.uk; @BistroVadouvan; 11 pm, Sun 5 pm.

BISTROTHEQUE E2 £64 3️⃣2️⃣4️⃣

23-27 WADESON ST 020 8983 7900 14–2B

Occupying "a great open space", this hip warehouse-conversion in Cambridge Heath has been a "lively" East End feature – particularly for brunch – since 'cool', 'East End' and 'restaurant' first appeared in the same sentence; live music is a regular feature. / E2 9DR; www.bistrotheque.com; @bistrotheque; midnight, Sun 11 pm; closed Mon-Fri L.

BLACK AXE MANGAL N1 £46 4️⃣3️⃣2️⃣

156 CANONBURY RD NO TEL 9–2D

"What can you say? Offal flatbread, blaring hard rock and lurid genitalia painted on the floor – but the food is great" at Lee Tiernan's tiny heavy-metal kebab joint, still taking no prisoners in its third year at Highbury Corner. "Painful seating, but just incredible, confident, stunning cooking". And for those who reckon "Queens of the Stone Age at full volume ruins everything" – Top Tip: "take away!". / N1 \N; www.blackaxemangal.com; @blackaxemangal; 10.30 pm, Sun 3 pm; D only Mon-Fri, Sat L & D, Sun L only; no booking.

BLACK PRINCE SE11 £38 3️⃣3️⃣2️⃣

6 BLACK PRINCE RD 020 7582 2818 2–4D

"Superior pub food (with an outstanding Sunday lunch)" makes it worth remembering this classic Kennington boozer. / SE11 6HS; www.theblackprincepub.co.uk; Sun-Thu midnight, Fri & Sat 1 am.

BLACK ROE W1 £74 3️⃣2️⃣3️⃣

4 MILL ST 020 3794 8448 3–2C

It's "something unique" to its fans, but this Hawaiian-inspired Mayfair three-year-old (speciality poké and other fish dishes) inspires little in the way of feedback. Fans say it can be "outstanding", but toppish prices give rise to some complaint. / W1S 2AX; www.blackroe.com; @blackroe; 11 pm; closed Sun.

BLACKLOCK £44 4️⃣4️⃣4️⃣

24 GREAT WINDMILL ST, W1 020 3441 6996 4–2D | 28 RIVINGTON ST, EC2 020 7739 2148 13–1B NEW | 13 PHILPOT LANE, EC3 020 7998 7676 10–3D

"Simply mouthwatering plates" of "succulent and well-seasoned chops" reward a trip to these "fun" haunts, which in September 2018 added a Shoreditch branch to initial ventures in Soho and the City. It's a case of "simple food but done extremely well" and "if you like meat, this is a good place to share lots of it with friends, and at a very good price too". "OK, so I was sceptical: yet another beards and tatts place, I thought – but the quality is such that I (and my meat-loving wife) discuss little else but when to go next!" / theblacklock.com; @BlacklockChops.

BLANCHETTE £57 2️⃣2️⃣3️⃣

9 D'ARBLAY ST, W1 020 7439 8100 4–1C | 204 BRICK LANE, E1 020 7729 7939 13–1C

"Specialising in Gallic small plates, cheeses and charcuterie" plus dry-aged beef – and with "portions somewhere between tapas and a full plate" – this French-owned duo in Soho (2013) and Brick Lane (2016) have earned quite a culinary reputation, and – though "cramped" and "very noisy" – have a "fun atmosphere". Although praised by their many fans as a "reliable" option, their ratings slipped this year, with various gripes about the tapas-y format: either that it's "expensive", "un-relaxing" or just "doesn't suit this kind of French food". / 11 pm, Sun 9 pm.

BLANDFORD COMPTOIR W1 £60 3️⃣3️⃣3️⃣

1 BLANDFORD ST 020 7935 4626 2–1A

As befits a well-known wine expert, Xavier Rousset's "buzzy" Marylebone bar has a "superbly curated selection of vintages by the glass", but also "excellent", straightforward Mediterranean (primarily Italian) cooking. Top Tip: "very good value set lunch for £20". / W1U 3DA; blandford-comptoir.co.uk; @BlandfordCompt; 10 pm; no Amex.

BLEECKER BURGER £22 5️⃣2️⃣2️⃣

205 VICTORIA ST, SW1 NO TEL 2–4B | UNIT B PAVILION BUILDING, SPITALFIELDS MKT, E1 07712 540501 13–2B | BLOOMBERG ARCADE, QUEEN VICTORIA ST, EC4 020 7929 3785 10–3C

"The best burgers in London" – that's the survey verdict on Zan Kaufman's permanent-now-pop-up chain, now with four outlets including the new Bloomberg arcade and a (May-Sep only) South Bank stall. "Consistently juicy and perfectly cooked burgers and fries are served by friendly, helpful staff who always make you feel welcome". "I eat there any chance I get, they are epic and every bite makes me happy!" /

BLEEDING HEART RESTAURANT EC1 £75 3️⃣3️⃣5️⃣

BLEEDING HEART YD, GREVILLE ST 020 7242 8238 10–2A

That "it's a bit of a maze" adds to the "cosy" and "charming" atmosphere of this intriguing and immensely popular Dickensian cellar, in a "secluded courtyard" on the fringes of the City. Done out in a "conservative", traditional style (with some panelled rooms), it's "a great place to strike a business deal", but likewise smoochy couples also "have a romantic time tucked away in a delightful nook or cranny, somehow isolated from the hubbub and well looked after by the staff". "The French menu is wide-ranging" and quite "traditional". To critics, results can "lack spark", but for most reporters "they get the classics just right". Arguably a bigger deal is the "excellent French-based wine list", also including "interesting choices from the owners' own New Zealand vineyard". / EC1N 8SJ;

bleedingheart.co.uk; @bleedingheartyd; 10.30 pm; closed Sat & Sun.

BLIXEN E1 £47 333

**65A BRUSHFIELD ST   020 7101 0093
13–2C**

This elegant all-day venue in a former bank by Spitalfields Market is inspired by European grand cafés and serves "really good" modern brasserie food. It also has a plant-filled conservatory with a "lovely, nicely cool ambience". / E1 6AA; www.blixen.co.uk; @BlixenLondon; 11 pm, Sun 9 pm.

BLUEBIRD SW3 £74 233

350 KING'S RD   020 7559 1000   6–3C

With its "buzzy ambience" and "stylish interior", this D&D London bar/restaurant prominently situated in a large and elegant building (built in 1923 as a car garage) on the King's Road attracts feedback that's far more good than bad. On the downside, the food is no better than "OK", and the atmosphere can seem "lacking something… perhaps the room is too large". / SW3 5UU; www.bluebird-restaurant.co.uk; @bluebirdchelsea; Wed-Sat 9.30 pm, Sun 3 pm.

BLUEBIRD CAFÉ WHITE CITY W12 £49

**2 TELEVISION CENTRE, 101 WOOD LANE
020 3940 0700   1–2B**

D&D London are rolling out the Bluebird Café concept with this sibling in the former TV Centre at White City: the first eatery to open in the shiny new development. Initial feedback on the food is mostly positive, but its best feature is probably the outside terrace. / W12 7FR; bluebirdcafe.co.uk; @bluebirdcafew12; 10 pm, Sun 9 pm.

BLUEPRINT CAFÉ SE1 £48 224

**28 SHAD THAMES, BUTLER'S WHARF
020 7378 7031   10–4D**

Spectacular first-floor views over the Thames are the primary (some would say only) motivation to visit this D&D London venue on the first floor of the former Design Museum near Tower Bridge. The venue has always tended to score indifferently for its food – even when big name Jeremy Lee was at the stoves – and this profile has persisted since his departure years ago. Heralded chef-patron Mini Patel stepped down in August 2018 having lasted only six months in the role. / SE1 2YD; www.blueprintcafe.co.uk; @BlueprintCafe; 10.30 pm; closed Mon & Sun; no booking.

BOB BOB CITÉ EC3

**122 LEADENHALL ST   020 3145 1000
10–2D**

Tomorrow and tomorrow and tomorrow; we've been billing the arrival of 'BBC' – sibling to Soho's glam Bob Bob Ricard – for over a year now as its opening is pushed back and back. Set to occupy the entire third floor of 'The Cheesegrater', more 'press for Champagne' buttons are promised, alongside a menu

provided by Eric Chavot. When it finally arrives, one thing is certain: it won't be subtle! STOP PRESS: a new, new opening date of January 2019 has been announced. / EC3V 4PE; www.bobbobricard.com; @bobbobcite; Wed-Sat 10 pm, Sun 5 pm.

BOB BOB RICARD W1 £85 335

1 UPPER JAMES ST   020 3145 1000   4–2C

"Who doesn't love a button by the table that is exclusively for ordering Champagne?" And the "matchless", fantasy-plush interior of Leonid Shutov's lavish Soho 'diner' creates a "gorgeous" setting, especially "for a fun date". Eric Chavot's menu of "luxury staples" delivers some "pretty good food", and – while the fact that it's certainly "not a bargain" is a sticking point for a few reporters – most "don't begrudge a penny". / W1F 9DF; www.bobbobricard.com; @BobBobRicard; 11.15 pm, Sat midnight, Sun 11.15 pm; closed Sat L; Jacket required.

BOCCA DI LUPO W1 £62 443

12 ARCHER ST   020 7734 2223   4–3D

"Paradise for Italian food lovers" – Jacob Kenedy's "easygoing" yet "well-run" and immensely popular operation, a short walk from Piccadilly CIrcus, is one of the most culinarily interesting destinations in town (especially of the "reasonably priced" variety). "It's not just your standard Italian trat fayre, yet neither is it merely über-trendy small plates". Instead, an "unrivalled selection of vigorous and distinctive dishes are labelled by region and available in two sizes" (tapas-style or 'main'). "Dishes are from all over Italy, change regularly" and "are often unusual (for example fried calf's foot)". There's also "a terrific Italian wine list (available by the carafe), with knowledgeable advice available at all price levels". "Go early if possible, as it can get too buzzy" and "vibrant" and "is quite packed-in" (although most reporters feel that "the food justifies any lack of comfort"). "Sit at the counter for a bird's-eye-view of the chefs" (although these perches in particular can feel "high, cramped and noisy"). "I think I have eaten over 75 times at Bocca and the food and team there remain at the top of their game – the food is always different and amazingly authentic to its origins". Top Menu Tip: "great puddings including the signature sanguinaccio (blood, pistachio, chocolate)". / W1D 7BB; www.boccadilupo.com; @boccadilupo; 11 pm, Sun 9.30 pm; booking max 10 may apply.

BOCCONCINO W1 £93 322

19 BERKELEY ST   020 7499 4510   3–3C

A modern take on classic Italian cuisine, this Russian-owned joint in a glossy corner of Mayfair is "glitzy and noisy", but the cooking, from fish to pizza, is "credible if overpriced". / W1J 8ED; www.bocconcinorestaurant.co.uk; @BocconcinoUK; 12.30 am, Sun 10.30 pm.

AL BOCCON DI'VINO TW9 £66 445

14 RED LION ST   020 8940 9060   1–4A

"You never know what you're going to eat" at this no-choice Italian feast in Richmond, which has built a loyal following over the last decade. "More than a restaurant, it feels like a holiday in Italy, where you're eating at Nonna's home". Chef Riccardo Grigolo and his team "are so welcoming" and deliver a lengthy Venetian-style meal – "fantastic food that just keeps on coming" and where "every course is delicious". / TW9 1RW; www.nonsolovinoltd.co.uk; @alboccondivino; Tue-Sun 11 pm; closed Tue, Wed L, closed Mon; no Amex.

BODEANS £50 323

**10 POLAND ST, W1   020 7287 7575   4–1C
| 25 CATHERINE ST, WC2   020 7257 2790
5–3D | 4 BROADWAY CHAMBERS, SW6
020 7610 0440   6–4A | 348 MUSWELL HILL
BROADWAY, N10   020 8883 3089   1–1C |
225 BALHAM HIGH ST, SW17   020 8682 4650
11–2C | 169 CLAPHAM HIGH ST, SW4
020 7622 4248   11–2D | 201 CITY RD, EC1
020 7608 7230   13–1A | 16 BYWARD ST,
EC3   020 7488 3883   10–3D**

"If you want a pile of BBQ meat, you won't be disappointed" by these "laid back", "typically American and un-subtle" Kansas City-style BBQs. "No frills", "tender and tasty" food at "decent" prices has proved a recipe for longevity for the group, an early pioneer of London's flesh-plus-fire dining scene. Top Tip: "the pulled pork and burnt ends combo is not to be sniffed at". / www.bodeansbbq.com; 11 pm, Sun 10.30 pm, NW10 pm, Fri & Sat 11 pm; booking: min 8.

BOISDALE OF BELGRAVIA SW1 £68 223

15 ECCLESTON ST   020 7730 6922   2–4B

With its "plush Jockinese decor" and "traditional, meaty Scottish fare" – Ranald Macdonald's long-established Belgravia haunt has become synonymous in some quarters with a very masculine style of dining, buoyed by fine wines and whiskies, plus a cigar terrace and "good jazz". This wasn't a vintage year for its ratings, however – "staff are friendly but can struggle to handle a packed house" and the experience can seem "expensive if you're not booked on a deal". / SW1W 9LX; www.boisdale.co.uk/belgravia; @boisdale; 1 am; closed Sat L, closed Sun.

BOISDALE OF BISHOPSGATE EC2 £73 323

**SWEDELAND COURT, 202 BISHOPSGATE
020 7283 1763   10–2D**

Just off Bishopsgate, this bar (ground floor) and restaurant (basement) is a chip off the original Belgravia block, with plush Caledonian styling and a menu of meaty Scottish fare. Not all reporters are upbeat, but most acclaim it for its "good location" and "food that's good if not cheap". / EC2M 4NR; www.boisdale.co.uk; @Boisdale; 11 pm; closed Sat & Sun.

Bokan E14

BOISDALE OF CANARY WHARF E14 £68 223

CABOT PLACE 020 7715 5818 12–1C

This Boisdale spin-off in Canary Wharf (for a drink, try to grab a seat on the terrace) aims to replicate the Caledonian styling of the Belgravia original, down to the live music and focus on wines and whiskies. When it comes to its traditional, meaty fare, no culinary fireworks were reported this year, but it was consistently well-supported. / E14 4QT; www.boisdale.co.uk/canary-wharf; @boisdaleCW; Mon & Tue 11 pm, Wed-Sat midnight, Sun 4 pm; closed Sat L closed Sun D.

BOKAN E14 £70 333

40 MARSH WALL 020 3530 0550 12–2C

"On a clear day the sights across London are wonderful" on the 37th floor of the recently opened Novotel Canary Wharf. This 65-cover venue still inspires limited feedback, but such as we have praises "beautifully presented dishes, tasty drinks and a great atmosphere". / E14 9TP; bokanlondon.co.uk; @BokanLondon; 10 pm, Sun 9 pm; closed Mon-Thu L.

BOMBAY BRASSERIE SW7 £65 433

COURTFIELD RD 020 7370 4040 6–2B

"Looking very smart" again nowadays, this upmarket "institution" in South Kensington has been run in recent times by luxury Indian chain Taj Hotels and is winning more consistent praise for its "helpful staff and delicious food". It's yet to step back properly onto London's culinary map, however, and even some fans feel "it's still to some extent relying on past glories". / SW7 4QH; www.bombayb.co.uk; @bbsw7; Mon-Fri 11.30 pm, Sat 11 pm, Sun 10.30 pm; closed Mon L.

BOMBAY BUSTLE W1 £68 443

29 MADDOX ST 020 7290 4470 4–2A

"The spicing is fantastic – very authentic", at Samyukta Nair and Rohit Ghai's Mayfair newcomer, on the former site of Hibiscus (RIP), which takes the Mumbai institution of tiffin (and the trains the dabbawalas use to deliver it) as its theme. Many "wonderful" meals are reported in feedback that includes nothing but praise. / W1S 2PA; www.bombaybustle.com; @BombayBustle; Mon-Fri 10 pm, Sat & Sun 9 pm.

BOMBAY PALACE W2 £47 432

50 CONNAUGHT ST 020 7723 8855 7–1D

"The cooking is back on form after a year or two off" (during which the restaurant was closed following a fire), say fans of this Bayswater old-timer, hailing its "excellent food, with fresh spices and not messed about as at many of the newer nouvelle Indians". The interior is a little "dull" but "at least you can hear yourself talk". / W2 2AA; www.bombay-palace.co.uk; @bombaypalaceW2; 1 am.

BON VIVANT WC1 £57 333

75-77 MARCHMONT ST 020 7713 6111 9–4C

"A brave and ambitious attempt to lift culinary standards in a corner of Bloomsbury otherwise only well-served with mid-range chains" – this "very authentic French bistro" is a "very pleasing neighbourhood restaurant". / WC1N 1AP; www.bonvivantrestaurant.co.uk; 10.30 pm.

BONE DADDIES £42 334

NOVA, VICTORIA ST, SW1 NO TEL 2–4B | **14A, OLD COMPTON ST, W1** 020 7734 7492 5–2A | **30-31 PETER ST, W1** 020 7287 8581 4–2D | **46-48 JAMES ST, W1** 020 3019 7140 3–1A | **WHOLE FOODS, KENSINGTON HIGH ST, W8** 020 7287 8581 6–1A | **THE BOWER, BALDWIN ST, EC1** 020 7439 9299 13–1A

The "perfect westernised Japanese food" at former Zuma and Nobu chef Ross Shonhan's "hip" ramen-bar chain "shows how to do fusion": "the soup stock is wonderfully thick and full of flavour, not watery like other places". Top Tip: "soft shell crab ramen". / www.bonedaddies.com; 10 pm, Thu-Sat 11 pm, Sun 9.30 pm; W1 no bookings.

BONHAMS RESTAURANT, BONHAMS AUCTION HOUSE W1 £77 552

101 NEW BOND ST 020 7468 5868 3–2B

Chef Tom Kemble's "excellent cooking" has been blessed by the Tyre Men, and professional service to match makes eating in this "calm and perfect" dining room, at the back of a Mayfair auctioneer, "like a private dining experience" and an excellent business choice. "But the wine is the key factor": the auction house has access to a "fast-changing list" that offers some of the best value in town. / W1K 5ES;
www.bonhamsrestaurant.com; @dineatbonhams; 10 pm; L only, Fri L & D, closed Sat & Sun.

BONNIE GULL £58 533

22 BATEMAN ST, W1D 020 7436 0921 5–2A | **21A FOLEY ST, W1** 020 7436 0921 2–1B

"The perfect seafood restaurant… in Fitzrovia!" – this "tiny", "casual" and "cramped" dining room has won a major following thanks to "straightforward" cooking showing "great attention to detail" – "fish can be tricky in London, but here it works". "The newer shack in Soho is great for a quick bite", too. / www.bonniegull.com; @BonnieGull.

BONOO NW2 £39 443

675 FINCHLEY RD 020 7794 8899 1–1B

"It looks nothing from the modest outside", but this "excellent newcomer" in the "gastronomic desert of Childs Hill" is "always packed" – its "unusual Indian tapas dishes are absolutely superb": "beautifully spiced street food that outstrips more fashionable eateries". / NW2 2JP; www.bonoo.co.uk; @bonoohampstead; 10.30 pm, Sun 9.30 pm.

THE BOOKING OFFICE, ST PANCRAS RENAISSANCE HOTEL NW1 £67 224

EUSTON RD 020 7841 3566 9–3C

The "lovely location" of this all-day operation in the former ticket office at St Pancras station makes it an attractive option for breakfast or afternoon tea ("the pastries are truly exquisite"). For a more substantial meal, feedback is more limited (and mixed). / NW1 2AR; www.bookingofficerestaurant.com; @StPancrasRen; Sun-Wed midnight, Thu-Sat 1 am.

BOOMA SW9 £34 432

244 BRIXTON ROAD 020 7737 4999 11–2D

"Lots of small, tapas-y dishes to share, accompanied by a glass of craft beer" is the formula at this modern Indian café on the northern fringes of Brixton, which delivers "accurate, well-spiced cooking to a higher standard than one might expect". / SW9 6AH; booma-brixton.co.uk; @boomabrixton; Mon-Thu 11 pm, Fri & Sat 11.30 pm, Sun 10 pm; closed Mon-Fri L.

BOQUERIA £49 433

192 ACRE LN, SW2 020 7733 4408 11–2D | **278 QUEENSTOWN RD, SW8** 020 7498 8427 11–1C

"Different and delicious tapas" is bolstered by a "great specials board and cocktails" to win consistent esteem for this Hispanic duo, close together in Battersea and Clapham, where regulars are full of praise for the "welcoming staff" and "buzzy" (if authentically "noisy") atmosphere. /

IL BORDELLO E1 £64 344

**81 WAPPING HIGH ST 020 7481 9950
12–1A**

This "enduringly appealing", "family-run Italian in fashionable Wapping is always packed, so you have to book well ahead". It's "so noisy the children can't be heard", and the "old-style cooking (good pizzas and pasta) means no one leaves hungry" – in fact, "the only fault is that the servings are too large!". / E1W 2YN; www.ilbordello.com; 9.30 pm, Sun 8.30 pm; closed Sat L.

BORO BISTRO SE1 £44 333

**MONTAGUE CL, 6-10 BOROUGH HIGH ST
020 7378 0788 10–3C**

"A real find" in a "lovely setting on the edge of Borough Market", and with "an attractive outside eating area" – this contemporary bistro with is "well worth discovering" for its "great sharing boards and tapas" and a "good selection of beers". / SE1 9QQ; www.borobistro.co.uk; @borobistro; 10.30 pm, Mon & Sun 9 pm; closed Mon & Sun; booking max 6 may apply.

THE BOTANIST £66 222

**7 SLOANE SQ, SW1 020 7730 0077 6–2D |
BROADGATE C!RCLE, EC2 020 3058 9888
13–2B**

Opinions divide on these "spacious" and well-located all-day brasseries in Chelsea (right on Sloane Square) and the City (in Broadgate). Fans vaunt them as "very pleasant" for many occasions, and particularly for a business lunch or "excellent breakfast/brunch". Critics, though, hate them for being "so noisy" and dismiss the food as "overpriced and disappointing". / thebotanist.uk.com; @thebotanistuk; SW1 breakfast 8, Sat & Sun 9, SW1 & EC2 11 pm.

BOUDIN BLANC W1 £65 323

5 TREBECK ST 020 7499 3292 3–4B

Crowded and charming, long-established bistro, which creates a "proper Gallic buzz" in Mayfair's picturesque Shepherd Market. With its "lovely" main dining room and attractive outdoor seating in summer, it used to be a higher profile destination, but its ratings have slightly come off the boil in recent years. It's still pretty popular though, particularly as a business lunching choice. / W1J 7LT; www.boudinblanc.co.uk; Mon & Tue 11 pm, Wed-Sat midnight, Sun 4 pm.

BOULESTIN SW1 £72 232

5 ST JAMES'S ST 020 7930 2030 3–4D

A revival of a venerable name from the 1920s on a classic St James's site (once L'Oranger, RIP), Joel Kissin's bistro rates well for "excellent breakfasts". Beyond that it is "just about OK" but there's an issue: "there's no need to charge their prices". Its trump card is "the courtyard – a hidden joy for al fresco dining in the summer". / SW1A 1EF; www.boulestin.com; @BoulestinLondon; 10 pm; closed Sun; No trainers.

BOWLING BIRD EC1 £34 443

44 CLOTH FAIR 020 7324 7742 10–2B

Excellent but limited feedback on this cute yearling – a straightforward looking operation tucked away down a Smithfield alleyway in a quaint old townhouse that was once Sir John Betjeman's home (and which some older reporters may remember as Betjeman's Restaurant, very long RIP). The small menu, complemented by daily specials, is of diverse inspiration, but the stand-outs are the meat dishes, reflecting chef Emiliano Gallegos's experience at La Pulperia, an Argentinian steakhouse in Paris. / EC1A 7JQ; bowlingbird.com; closed Mon, Sat & Sun.

BOXCAR BUTCHER & GRILL W1 £50 443

23 NEW QUEBEC ST 020 3006 7000 2–2A

From Barry Hirst's Cubitt House group, this Marylebone yearling combines butcher, deli and steakhouse and serves from breakfast onwards. "It does what it says on the tin!" – a short selection of steaks, burgers and other fare offering "top quality meat at a decent price": "given the location, this is great value, fun and quick". / W1H 7SD; boxcar.co.uk; @BoxcarLondon; 10.30 pm, Sun 10 pm.

BOYDS GRILL & WINE BAR WC2 £58 333

**8 NORTHUMBERLAND AVE 020 7808 3344
2–3C**

The potentially "lovely room", just off Trafalgar Square – part of a monumental, much-marbled Victorian hotel (which spent most of the 20th century as part of the MoD) – and "good-value set menu" can make this an "excellent central London location", although its "rather cavernous" nature can mean there's "not a great ambience"; "very nice wine list". / WC2N 5BY; www.boydsbrasserie.co.uk; 10 pm, Sun 12 pm; closed Sun D.

THE BRACKENBURY W6 £58 444

**129-131 BRACKENBURY RD 020 8741 4928
8–1C**

One of London's more accomplished backstreet haunts – this long-established Hammersmith stalwart, buried deep in 'Brackenbury Village', has a convivial style founded in a superior basic formula comprising "a seasonal, well-executed menu, good wine list and knowledgeable staff". The layout is quirky – a u-shaped space with a newish bar area on one side, with the remaining space dedicated to dining; superb summer terrace too. / W6 0BQ; www.brackenburyrestaurant.co.uk; @BrackenburyRest; 10.30 pm; closed Mon & Sun D.

BRACKENBURY WINE ROOMS W6 £58 223

**HAMMERSMITH GROVE 020 3696 8240
8–1C**

"A good range of wines" (served by the glass as well as by the bottle) helps win praise for this attractive Hammersmith corner spot, with deli and wine shop attached (part of a small west London group), and with lovely outside tables in summer. No-one makes exaggerated claims for the cuisine, but for the most part it's well-rated. / W6 0NQ; winerooms.london/brackenbury; @Wine_Rooms; midnight, Sun 11 pm.

BRADLEY'S NW3 £64 222

25 WINCHESTER RD 020 7722 3457 9–2A

This "friendly neighbourhood restaurant" in Swiss Cottage, now closing in on its 30th anniversary, is "good if not brilliant… probably the best in the area". OK, you might not cross town for it, but it's very handy for the Hampstead Theatre, with a "great pre-theatre menu". / NW3 3NR; www.bradleysnw3.co.uk; 10 pm, Sun 2.30 pm; closed Sun D.

BRADY'S SW18 £40 343

39 JEWS ROW 020 8877 9599 11–2B

"The formula of fish 'n' chips and daily fish specials has worked for years and years" for the Brady family's restaurant, which nowadays has "a great location on the river" with "a lovely atmosphere", near Wandsworth Bridge – "less frantic than its original location" which it left behind a few years ago. Top Menu Tip: "everyone comes for the fish but most have a dessert as well!" / SW18 1DG; www.bradysfish.co.uk; @Bradyfish; 9.30 pm, Sun 3.30 pm; closed Tue-Thu L closed Sun D, closed Mon; no booking.

BRASSERIE BLANC £56 222

Even if it's not "the most gastronomic option", Raymond Blanc's contemporary brasserie chain does have fans who laud its "pleasant" branches, and "reliable, routine French cuisine". Critics take a similar view but from a glass-half-empty standpoint: "no big complaints, but the value-for-money is low and service so-so". / www.brasserieblanc.com; most branches close between 10 pm & 11 pm; SE1 closed Sun D, City branches closed Sat & Sun.

BRASSERIE TOULOUSE-LAUTREC SE11 £62 333

**140 NEWINGTON BUTTS 020 7582 6800
1–3C**

Solid all-round ratings (if on limited feedback) for this bravely located Gallic brasserie (and live music venue) convenient for Kennington's cinema museum. / SE11 4RN; www.btlrestaurant.co.uk; @btlrestaurant; Tue-Thu 10 pm, Fri & Sat 10.30 pm, Mon 9.30 pm, Sun 9 pm.

BRASSERIE ZÉDEL
W1 £41 `1``3``5`

20 SHERWOOD ST 020 7734 4888 **4–3C**

"Worth a visit just to look at the main salon" – Corbin & King's "improbably glamorous and huge", Grade I-listed, Art Deco basement is "an extraordinary space that dazzles every newcomer"; and "so handy, being just by Piccadilly Circus tube". "It was a great concept of C & K to try and re-create a proper Parisian brasserie, with menu to match", and by and large they've succeeded. But even some of its greatest fans (of which there are bazillions) would admit that the trade-off is mightily "indifferent" traditional fare and service – which though improved this year – can still be "patchy". Don't be put off though: especially if you're counting the pennies, its low, low prices make it a total "bargain" in the heart of the West End. Top Tips – the set menu is "limited" but "excellent value". Also, "the amazing '30s-style American Bar, and small nightclub called 'The Crazy Coqs'!" (Final note for style anoraks: if you want to be pernickety, "while the basement is genuine Art Deco, the main dining room itself is actually more flamboyant neo-classical. Its only 'real' Art Deco elements are the splendid ceiling lights, added during the last refurbishment.") / W1F 7ED; www.brasseriezedel.com; @brasseriezedel; midnight, Sun 11 pm.

BRAT E1
£61 `5``4``4`

FIRST FLOOR, 4 REDCHURCH ST NO TEL 13–1B

"I just loved everything about it!" – Behind an inconspicuous side-door in Shoreditch, on the panelled first-floor of a converted pub (a pre-gentrification strip club, whose ground floor is nowadays Smoking Goat), chef Tomos Parry (ex-head-chef of Kitty Fishers) "exceeds high expectations" and has a smash hit on his hands, with this "terrific" launch – the survey's highest rated newcomer. The "open plan kitchen approach works well", with the focus on the large grill which produces most of the Basque-influenced cuisine here. "So, obviously you're going to order the turbot" – for which the restaurant is named (look it up) – which is presented whole and "utterly delicious". But "the food is superb throughout and well priced considering its quality and the chef's pedigree".

Brat E1

"Very happy staff", "a lovely atmosphere" and thoughtful wine list complete the picture. / E1 6JJ; www.bratrestaurant.com; @bratrestaurant; Mon-Fri 10 pm, Sat & Sun 9 pm.

BRAVAS E1
£55 `3``4``4`

ST KATHARINE DOCKS 020 7481 1464 **10–3D**

Overlooking the marina at St Katharine Docks, this "cosy and romantic" modern Basque venture serves "brilliant tapas, including some unusual items". "Often busy", it "recently expanded by taking over the sushi bar next door". / E1W 1AT; www.bravasrestaurant.com; @Bravas_Tapas; 11 pm.

BRAWN E2
£63 `4``3``3`

49 COLUMBIA RD 020 7729 5692 **14–2A**

"Put on yer skinnies and wax that beard for this cool-crowd place in hipster central." Ed Wilson's enduring foodie mecca in Bethnal Green is part of the original Terroirs stable that brought natural and biodynamic wines into vogue, and continues to win praise for its "always interesting and well-prepared" dishes and "a great wine list that alone makes it worth a visit". One or two refuseniks feel it falls short, however: "I was expecting / hoping for more". / E2 7RG; www.brawn.co; @brawn49; Mon-Thu 10.30 pm, Fri & Sat 11 pm; closed Mon L, closed Sun; no Amex.

BREAD STREET KITCHEN
EC4 £64 `2``2``3`

10 BREAD ST 020 3030 4050 **10–2B**

"Huge" Gordon Ramsay Group operation in a City mall by St Paul's that wins more enthusiasm for its "buzzing setting" and "really nice warehouse-style modern décor" than for its food, which is at a "reliably good" level for a business lunch, but can otherwise seem "mind-numbingly middle-of-the-road". / EC4M 9AJ; www.breadstreetkitchen.com; @breadstreet; Mon-Wed, Sat midnight, Thu & Fri 1 am, Sun 10 pm.

BREAKFAST CLUB
£41 `3``3``3`

33 D'ARBLAY ST, W1 020 7434 2571 **4–1C** | **2-4 RUFUS ST, N1** 020 7729 5252 **13–1B** | **31 CAMDEN PAS, N1** 020 7226 5454 **9–3D** | **12-16 ARTILLERY LN, E1** 020 7078 9633 **13–2B**

"Breakfast for lunch, breakfast for dinner – and anywhere in between" is the offer – with "really interesting choices" backed up by "speakeasy-style" cocktails – at these "buzzy" cafés which attract "queues out of the door". "I've never been a fan of breakfast but this place has made me think again!" / www.thebreakfastclubcafes.com; @thebrekkyclub; SRA-Food Made Good – 3 stars.

BREDDOS TACOS £48 `3``3``3`

26 KINGLY STREET, W1 4–2B | **82 GOSWELL RD, EC1** 020 3535 8301 **10–1B**

"Brilliant" Mexican-inspired tacos using top-quality British ingredients have taken this operation from a shack in a Hackney car park to a permanent site in Clerkenwell (with a second in Soho). But its marks took a knock across the

board this year amid complaints from erstwhile fans that the food nowadays "lacks a bit of the zing of the street food stall". / breddostacos.com; @breddostacos.

BREW HOUSE CAFÉ, KENWOOD HOUSE
NW3 £31 `2``2``3`

HAMPSTEAD HEATH 020 8348 1286 **9–1A**

For "homemade cakes with good tea and coffee" – or breakfast which "is also excellent" – stroll to the top of Hampstead Heath, to the self-service café within the stable blocks of this English Heritage property: best in summer when you can sit in the marvellous garden. / NW3 7JR; searcyskenwoodhouse.co.uk; @Searcys; closed Mon-Sun D.

BRICIOLE W1
£50 `3``2``2`

20 HOMER ST 020 7723 0040 **7–1D**

"Wonderful, genuine Italian food" justifies a visit to this Marylebone deli-trattoria (an offshoot of Latium, RIP), but at peak times "you have to put up with cramped and noisy surroundings". / W1H 4NA; www.briciole.co.uk; @briciolelondon; Tue-Thu 10 pm, Fri & Sat 10.30 pm, Mon 9.30 pm, Sun 9 pm.

BRICK LANE BEIGEL BAKE
E1 £6 `3``1``1`

159 BRICK LN 020 7729 0616 **13–1C**

"Salt beef and salmon – what more could you ask for?" say fans of the epic filled beigels, sold at prices seemingly unchanged from the 1980s, at this famous, if dead grungy, 24/7 East End bakery. Service is of the unsmiling, Soviet-era variety. / E1 6SB; www.beigelbake.com; @BeigelBake; open 24 hours; cash only; no booking.

BRIGADIERS EC2 £52 `5``4``4`

BLOOMBERG ARCADE, QUEEN VICTORIA ST 020 3319 8140 **10–3C**

Very early feedback is adulatory for the massive menu of flavour-packed Indian BBQ dishes served at this JKS Restaurants (Gymkhana, Hoppers) newcomer (opened in June 2018), which occupies the largest restaurant space in the City's Bloomberg Arcade. A sizeable operation inspired by traditional Indian Army mess halls (well, that's what the press release said) it comprises multiple spaces including several bars (The Tap Room, Blighters) and private rooms (the biggest, The Pot Luck, has its own entrance). / EC2R; www.jksrestaurants.com; @brigadiersldn; 9 pm, Sun 5 pm.

THE BRIGHT COURTYARD
W1 £69 `4``2``2`

43-45 BAKER ST 020 7486 6998 **2–1A**

"Ignore the departure lounge setting (especially if you get exiled to the office block atrium)" – this "new-wave Chinese" in Marylebone is "one of the leading Chinese restaurants in London". Top of the bill is its "unusual dim sum" of "Hong Kong standard". / W1U 8EW; www.lifefashiongroup.com; @BrightCourtyard; 11.30 pm, Sun 10.30 pm.

BRILLIANT UB2   £53   **4 4 3**

72-76 WESTERN RD   020 8574 1928   1–3A

"Straightforward Indian cuisine doesn't come much better" that at this large, legendary, Punjabi venture – lost deep in the 'burbs of Southall – which feels very "unpretentious", but "still maintains its high standards". / UB2 5DZ; www.brilliantrestaurant.com; @brilliantrst; 10.30 pm; closed Mon, Sat L & Sun L.

BRINKLEY'S
SW10   £63   **2 2 3**

47 HOLLYWOOD RD   020 7351 1683   6–3B

A "good", "well-priced" wine list and an "excellent atmosphere" are key to the enduring success of John Brinkley's "neighbourhood stand-by" in a sidestreet near Chelsea & Westminster Hospital. Despite "pretty average cooking" and "pleasant if slow service", it "serves its Chelsea fanbase well (mostly ageing roués on the pull, and with a strong leaning to Eurotrash!)" / SW10 9HX; www.brinkleys.com/brinkleys-restaurant.html; @BrinkleysR; 11 pm, Sun 10.30 pm; closed Mon-Fri L.

BROOKMILL SE8   £54   **3 3 3**

65 CRANBROOK RD   020 8333 0899   1–4D

Gentrified a couple of years ago, this "lively" Deptford gastropub is thriving on its "excellent pub food and great ambience"; cute garden too. / SE8 4EJ; www.thebrookmill.co.uk; @thebrookmillpub; 11 pm, Sun 10.30 pm.

THE BROWN DOG
SW13   £46   **3 3 3**

28 CROSS ST   020 8392 2200   11–1A

You'll need to book for the "great Sunday lunch" at this cute gastropub with a "convivial atmosphere" in the tangle of backstreets comprising Barnes's gorgeous 'Little Chelsea'. "The beef in their Sunday roast is always really tasty", and "my favourite ever roast beef sandwich" also cuts the mustard. A favourite for dog walkers and local families. / SW13 0AP; www.thebrowndog.co.uk; @browndogbarnes; Mon-Thu 10.30 pm, Fri & Sat 11 pm.

BROWN'S HOTEL, THE
ENGLISH TEA ROOM
W1   £76   **3 4 4**

ALBEMARLE ST   020 7493 6020   3–3C

"Home to one of the foremost traditional afternoon teas in London" – this plush hotel lounge wins many nominations as providing one of the finest teatime spreads in town, "boasting an extensive array of teas, plus traditional-with-a-twist sandwiches, scones and cakes that really do melt in the mouth!"; "a thoroughly enjoyable experience". / W1S 4BP; www.roccofortehotels.com; No trainers.

BRUNSWICK HOUSE CAFÉ
SW8   £56   **3 3 5**

30 WANDSWORTH RD   020 7720 2926   11–1D

The "bizarrely brilliant location" of an architectural salvage shop in a grand Georgian mansion on the Vauxhall Cross gyratory provides a "quirky setting for inventive seasonal cooking and cocktails". The food is "unexpectedly lovely": "lunch a bargain and dinner a treat" – "in a unique ambience surrounded by reclaimed chandeliers". ("It's always fun to spot the new arrivals and mentally fit out your dream house!") / SW8 2LG; www.brunswickhouse.co; Mon-Wed 10 pm, Thu-Sat 11 pm; closed Sun D.

BRYN WILLIAMS AT
SOMERSET HOUSE
WC2   £60   **4 4 3**

SOMERSET HOUSE 020 7845 464 2–2D

Welsh chef, Bryn Williams (of Odette's, in NW3 and in North Wales at Porth Eirias) makes a foray into a more central location, in a stately chamber within Somerset House. There's nothing but praise for the "personable" service and "very imaginatively conceived and carefully prepared dishes", but the way it promotes its 'flexitarian' credentials (putting fruit and veg front and centre) can grate – "the menu can seem irritating owing to placing the protein after the veg" and, more seriously, more than one veggie luncher has bizarrely encountered a set menu with no satisfactory veggie alternative ("unheard of in modern veg-friendly civilisation?"). / WC2; www.bryn-somersethouse.co.uk; @bwsomersethouse; 10 pm, Sun 4 pm; closed Sun D.

BUBBLEDOGS W1 £51   **3 4 4**

70 CHARLOTTE ST   020 7637 7770   2–1C

Sandia Chang's "buzzy if slightly cramped" Fitzrovia haunt (a unique double act with husband, James Knappett's fine-dining Kitchen Table, see also) is an unlikely success. As concepts go, hot dogs and Champagne make an "odd couple" – "the dogs are great" "but the real star is the range of fizz – lots of small producers and excellent variety, at good prices". / W1T 4QG; www.bubbledogs.co.uk; @bubbledogsUK; 11 pm; closed Sun & Mon.

BUCKET W2   £46

107 WESTBOURNE GROVE   020 3146 1156   7–1B

On the Bayswater/Notting Hill border, this seafood café opened in May 2018, too late in the day to receive survey feedback. If you fancy sustainably sourced seafood served by the bucket-load (literally, it seems) then it looks worth a try. / W2 4UW; www.bucketrestaurant.com; 11.30 pm, Sun 10.30 pm.

BUEN AYRE E8   £68   **4 3 2**

50 BROADWAY MARKET   020 7275 9900   14–2B

"The best steak ever" (well, nearly) continues to draw enthusiastic fans to this popular little Argentinian parrilla, which is one of the longest standing foodie destinations on Hackney's thriving Broadway Market. / E8 4QJ; www.buenayre.co.uk; Sun-Thu 10 pm, Fri & Sat 10.30 pm; no Amex.

THE BUILDERS ARMS
SW3   £55   **2 2 4**

13 BRITTEN ST   020 7349 9040   6–2C

A super-cute Chelsea backstreet location boosts the attractions of this Geronimo Inns property, whose "reliable pub grub" gives no cause for complaint. Top Tip: "grab a table near the fire" in winter. / SW3 3TY; www.thebuildersarmschelsea.co.uk; @BuildersChelsea; 10 pm, Sun 9 pm; no booking.

THE BULL N6   £53   **3 4 4**

13 NORTH HILL   020 8341 0510   9–1B

"Always of high quality", say fans of the dependable gastrofare at this popular microbrewery-cum-gastropub in Highgate. It's "good with families" too. / N6 4AB; thebullhighgate.co.uk; @Bull_Highgate; 10.30 pm, Mon 11 pm, Sun 3 pm.

BULL & LAST
NW5   £65   **3 3 3**

168 HIGHGATE RD   020 7267 3641   9–1B

"Still setting the standard" for north London gastropubs (amongst which it generates the highest amount of survey feedback) – this "ever-reliable" Kentish Town fixture "has a lovely cosy interior, plus friendly staff" and "a delicious and varied menu". Top Tip: "they produce excellent picnic baskets for taking advantage of a lunch on Hampstead Heath on those warm days". / NW5 1QS; www.thebullandlast.co.uk; @thebullandlast; 10 pm, Sun 9 pm.

BUMPKIN   £57   **2 2 3**

102 OLD BROMPTON RD, SW7 020 7341 0802   6–2B | WESTFIELD STRATFORD CITY, THE ST, E20 020 8221 9900   14–1D

"Buzzy and informal", this pair of farm-to-fork brasseries in South Kensington and Westfield Stratford (shrunk from a mini-chain) "have some interesting English dishes on the menu" which "can be good". But they are "still unbelievably variable", and "can be rather noisy and chaotic". / www.bumpkinuk.com; 11 pm; closed Mon.

BUN HOUSE W1   £14   **4 4 4**

24 GREEK ST   020 8017 9888   5–2A

"Fantastic bao buns" win praise from the small but super-enthusiastic fan club of this year-old Cantonese Soho café on corner of Greek and Old Compton Streets; and "it's such a cute little space" too. Downstairs is a bar, Tea Room, complete with late licence. / W1D 4DZ; www.bun.house; @8unhouse; closed Mon-Sun L.

BUONGIORNO E BUONASERA W1   £35

58 BAKER ST   020 7935 4223   2–1A

Early 2018 opening – a new pizzeria with two branches already in Oxford arrives in Marylebone on Baker Street, serving light, Roman-style pizzas using organic, non-GMO wheat, soy and rice flour. / W1U 7DD; www.buongiornoebuonasera.com; @buongiornoebuonasera

BURGER & LOBSTER   £59   333

HARVEY NICHOLS, 109-125 KNIGHTSBRIDGE, SW1   020 7235 5000 6–1D | 26 BINNEY ST, W1   020 3637 5972 3–2A | 29 CLARGES ST, W1   020 7409 1699 3–4B | 36 DEAN ST, W1   020 7432 4800 5–2A | 6 LITTLE PORTLAND ST, W1 020 7907 7760   3–1C | 18 HERTSMERE RD, E14   020 3637 6709   12–1C | 40 ST JOHN ST, EC1   020 7490 9230   10–1B | BOW BELLS HS, 1 BREAD ST, EC4 020 7248 1789   10–2B

"Does what it says on the tin" – these bustling upscale diners no longer seem quite as novel as they once did but continue to offer "a winning combination of burger and lobster served at a reasonable price point". Under the same ownership as the Goodman steak chain – from autumn 2018, the owners plan a new, more informal spin-off brand, 'Shack by Burger & Lobster', to be launched in Camden. / www.burgerandlobster.com; @Londonlobster; 10.30 pm-11pm, where open Sun 8 pm-10 pm; WC1 & EC2 closed Sun; booking: min 6.

BUSABA EATHAI   £46   212

For a "reliable cheap 'n' cheerful meal, with attractive decor", these Thai canteens still have a big fan club thanks to their well-styled communal interiors and "perhaps-not-wholly-authentic, but tasty" fare ("a good choice, from mild to pretty spicy"). Ratings were more than usually mixed this year, however, especially regarding "chaotic", "disinterested" or even "awful" service. / www.busaba.co.uk; @busabaeathai; 11 pm, Fri & Sat 11.30 pm, Sun 10 pm; W1 no booking; WC1 booking: min 10.

BUTCHIES EC2   £24   322

22 RIVINGTON ST NO TEL 13–1B

Garrett and Emer FitzGerald launched their first permanent venture on the former site of Santo Remedio (RIP) in Shoreditch: a take-away (ground floor) and jammed-in diner upstairs serves premium fried chicken; fair value, but food takes its time coming. / EC2A 3DY; www.butchies.co.uk; @Butchies_London; Mon-Fri 10 pm, Sat & Sun 9 pm.

BUTLER'S RESTAURANT, THE CHESTERFIELD MAYFAIR W1   £84   243

35 CHARLES ST   020 7958 7729   3–3B

"Like an old London club", this traditional Mayfair dining room is "spacious" and "there is absolutely no rush to serve you and get you out". In a similar vein, "you wouldn't necessarily go there for the food", except for the afternoon tea in the adjoining 'Conservatory', go for the classic or novelty-themed version (it's currently 'The Original Sweetshop'). / W1J 5EB; www.chesterfieldmayfair.com; @chesterfield_MF; 12.30 am, Sun 10.30 pm; Jacket required; booking max 8 may apply.

BUTLERS WHARF CHOP HOUSE SE1   £70   324

36E SHAD THAMES   020 7403 3403   10–4D

Created by Sir Terence Conran as part of his '90s 'gastrodrome' overlooking Tower Bridge, this D&D London venue is valued for its "splendid location, especially at night". "Attentive service" makes it business-friendly, and it "lends itself to group bookings with good table sizes". Its wide menu, incorporating lots of steak and grill options, doesn't set the world on fire, but was well-rated this year. / SE1 2YE; www.chophouse-restaurant.co.uk; @BWChophouse; 11 pm.

LA BUVETTE TW9   £48   323

6 CHURCH WALK   020 8940 6264   1–4A

"A feeling of smart cosiness is the best thing" about this "quiet and secluded bistro in central Richmond" (peacefully tucked away beside a churchyard), which makes it "a lovely place for a lunchtime date". If there's a gripe, it is that the "traditional French fare" is "consistent" but, some feel, "not very memorable". / TW9 1SN; www.labuvette.co.uk; @labuvettebistro; 10 pm, Sun 9 pm; booking max 8 may apply.

BY CHLOE WC2

34-43 RUSSELL ST   020 3883 3273   5–2D

The first branch from this US-based vegan chain (a 70-seater, also with 'grab and go') arrived in Covent Garden in Spring 2018, with a big menu from fish 'n' chips developed specially for the UK, to salads, sarnies, burgers and brunch fare. Too little feedback for a rating as yet, although fans say it's "amazing", with service that's "on it". They're already onto number two with a second site near Tower Bridge (at 6 Duchess Walk, One Tower Bridge). / WC2B 5HA; www.eatbychloe.com; @eatbychloe; Sun-Wed 10 pm, Thu-Sat 11 pm; no booking.

BYRON   £36   222

"Once upon a time this chain of posh burger joints stood out from the pack", but – in an ever-moving and competitive market – its troubles in Spring 2018 were well publicised, with five of its 39 restaurants within the M25 (and a total of 16 nationally) having closed. That said, while the view that it is "OK but nothing special" has become widespread nowadays, it still remains one of the most talked-about brands in the survey; ratings improved a smidgeon this year; and a fair few reporters feel that "the business may be in trouble, but the burgers are still the real deal". Top Tip: "love the courgette fries". / www.byronhamburgers.com; most branches 11 pm.

C&R CAFE   £30   422

3-4 RUPERT CT, W1   020 7434 1128 4–3D | 52 WESTBOURNE GROVE, W2 020 7221 7979   7–1B

"Cheap, cheerful and authentic" cafés in Chinatown and Bayswater "popular with Malaysian expats". Most order the "superb noodles", while the "aggressive ginger drinks" offer another blast of southeast Asian flavour. "Not as inexpensive as they used to be, but worth it". / www.cnrrestaurant.com; W1 10 pm, Fri & Sat 11 pm; W2 10.30 pm, Fri & Sat 11 pm, Sun 10 pm; W2 closed Tue.

CABOTTE EC2   £68   454

48 GRESHAM ST   020 7600 1616   10–2C

"If you like Burgundy and are based in the City, it's your Holy Grail!" This year-old, "still relatively undiscovered gem" near the Guildhall ("not traditionally an area which has been over-served with good, regional French food!!") provides "an oasis in the Square Mile", with its combination of "excellent food with a modern twist on classic Burgundian dishes, and a wine list that's heaven for the connoisseur (with plenty on offer for every wallet, City bonus or none)". It's "extremely professionally run, very friendly and authentic". / EC2V 7AY; www.cabotte.co.uk; @Cabotte_; 9.30 pm; closed Sat & Sun.

CACIO & PEPE SW1   £56   332

46 CHURTON ST   020 7630 7588   2–4B

This "friendly and stylish Italian in Pimlico" with "very good pasta dishes" was launched two years ago by Florentine Enrica Della Martira as her first restaurant project. It's rated a "sound choice" with a "menu that changes frequently". Top Tip: "the signature cacio e pepe (pasta with cheese and pepper), served in a parmesan basket". / SW1V 2LP; www.cacioepepe.co.uk; Mon-Thu 10.30 pm, Fri & Sat 11 pm, Sun 10 pm.

CAFÉ BELOW EC2   £44   322

ST MARY-LE-BOW, CHEAPSIDE 020 7329 0789   10–2B

The thousand-year-old crypt of the Bow Bells church provides a "great location" for breakfast and lunch – "you feel so far from the City". It has a "short but excellent menu of hot meals and salads" that are "cheap, tasty, and major on the vegetarian". (Weather permitting, you can eat al fresco in the churchyard here.) / EC2 6AU; www.cafebelow.co.uk; 9.30 pm, Sun 3.30 pm; L only.

CAFÉ DEL PARC N19   £50   453

167 JUNCTION RD   020 7281 5684   9–1C

"A splendid array of fusion tapas" combining Spanish and North African flavours makes this "fun" Archway destination an "absolute north London gem". "The no-choice format of successive dishes works superbly" ("they just bring you a selection, but you can make requests"). / N19 5PZ; www.delparc.com; 10.30 pm; open D only, Wed-Sun; no Amex; booking D only.

CAFÉ DU MARCHÉ
EC1 £58 335

22 CHARTERHOUSE SQ 020 7608 1609 10–1B

"A slice of Paris in a City cobbled lane"; this long-established, "hidden-away gem" – "an attractive, rustic-style dining room with regular live piano music" – has a classic, "very Gallic", "cosy, candlelit, and romantic" ambience of a kind "it's so rare to find nowadays". "The seasonal and all-French menu is packed with classics that are easy choices" and "always well-executed" ("great steaks" in particular). / EC1M 6DX; www.cafedumarche.co.uk; @cafedumarche; 10 pm; closed Sat L, closed Sun.

CAFÉ EAST SE16 £16 522

100 REDRIFF RD 020 7252 1212 12–2B

Possibly "the best pho in London" and "must-have summer rolls" set the standard at this "no frills" Vietnamese canteen in Bermondsey. "There's so much to choose between, all so appetising and delicious" – "there's always a quick turnaround" and it's "great value". / SE16 7LH; www.cafeeastpho.co.uk; @cafeeastpho; Mon, Wed-Sat 10.30 pm, Sun 10 pm; closed Tue; no Amex; no booking.

CAFÉ IN THE CRYPT, ST MARTIN IN THE FIELDS
WC2 £30 214

DUNCANNON ST 020 7766 1158 2–2C

"Plain but well-cooked food at a reasonable price" – "in the beautiful crypt" of St Martin-in-the-Fields – makes this self-service café a useful option for a snack "in the midst of tourist-land". It's right on Trafalgar Square, so "ideal for the National Gallery" – "and the cakes are delicious". / WC2N 4JJ; stmartin-in-the-fields.org/cafe-in-the-crypt; @smitf_london; Mon & Tue 8 pm, Thu-Sat 9 pm, Wed 10.30 pm, Sun 6 pm; L & early evening only; no Amex; may need 5+ to book.

CAFÉ MONICO
W1 £62 234

39-45 SHAFTESBURY AVENUE 020 3727 6161 5–3A

"Slap bang in the middle of Theatreland, this agreeable brasserie is not without a bit of theatre itself" – inspired by an 1877 café of the same name in the area, it has a carefully curated retro vibe and a menu of Franco-Italian classics assembled by Rowley Leigh for the Soho House group, which are "well-priced" ("invaluable given the area") if ultimately rather forgettable. / W1D 6LA; www.cafemonico.com; @cafemonico; Mon-Thu midnight, Fri & Sat 1 am; closed Sun.

CAFE MURANO £69 232

33 ST JAMES'S ST, SW1 020 3371 5559 3–3C | 34 TAVISTOCK ST, WC2 020 3535 7884 5–3D | 36 TAVISTOCK ST, WC2 020 3371 5559 5–3D

"For a handy pre-theatre option, light lunch or mid-afternoon snack; meeting someone for a coffee or glass of bubbles; or for an informal, relaxed business rendezvous", Angela Hartnett's massively popular "relatively casual" spin-offs provide conveniently located venues, which – at their best – deliver a "lovely, regional Italian menu" and "a well-priced, exclusively Italian wine list" in a "pleasantly vibrant" atmosphere. Ratings dipped this year though, with increasing gripes about food that's "decent but lacking that extra sparkle", or decor that's "slightly cramped and nothing special". Higher marks though for the "charming and engaging service". / www.cafemurano.co.uk; 11 pm, Sun 4 pm, Pastificio 9 pm, Sun closed.

CAFÉ SPICE NAMASTE
E1 £56 443

16 PRESCOT ST 020 7488 9242 12–1A

"In an unlikely location" east of the City, Cyrus Todiwala's brightly decorated HQ delivers "time and time again". "No ordinary Indian, the varied food is prepared with panache and extraordinarily skilled mixes of subtle flavours". Service is "excellent" too, and the worst complaint amongst the many reports we receive is that "it's a bit pricey". Events are a regular feature here, and "Cyrus is very informative and entertaining throughout". / E1 8AZ; www.cafespice.co.uk; @cafespicenamast; Wed & Thu 10.30 pm, Fri & Sat 11 pm; closed Mon & Tue & Sun.

CAFFÈ CALDESI
W1 £73 332

118 MARYLEBONE LN 020 7487 0754 2–1A

"Real Italian food" – and "not a giant pepper-grinder in sight" – is on the menu at this "reliably enjoyable" old-school venture in Marylebone ("not too starched, but certainly smart and formal enough"). Downstairs is a wine bar with antipasti, while the upstairs dining room specialises in Tuscan dishes. / W1U 2QF; www.caldesi.com; 10.30 pm; closed Sat L, closed Sun.

LA CAGE IMAGINAIRE
NW3 £48 234

16 FLASK WALK 020 7794 6674 9–1A

Few restaurants enjoy such a picture-book location as this little French restaurant in a gorgeous-looking Hampstead backwater. Over many years, it has never provoked huge feedback, and on occasion the cuisine can seem "tired and unimaginative" but, so long as you go with moderate expectations foodwise, it can provide a "charming" experience. / NW3 1HE; www.la-cage-imaginaire.co.uk; 10.30 pm, Sun 6 pm.

THE CAMBERWELL ARMS
SE5 £54 533

65 CAMBERWELL CHURCH ST 020 7358 4364 1–3C

"Exactly what a good gastropub should be" – Camberwell's sibling to the acclaimed Anchor & Hope offers "outstanding cooking with very fresh ingredients" and "oomph and umami galore". "An upgrade to the interior has kept its neighbourhood boozer charm", and locals are "thankful it's open for lunch once more (if with a somewhat restricted menu)". It gets very busy: be prepared for "noise" and a bit of "jostling". / SE5 8TR; www.thecamberwellarms.co.uk; @camberwellarms; Mon-Wed 11 pm, Thu-Sat midnight, Sun 9.30 pm; closed Mon L & Sun D.

CAMBIO DE TERCIO
SW5 £70 433

161-163 OLD BROMPTON RD 020 7244 8970 6–2B

"Surely among the best Spanish restaurants in London", Abel Lusa's well-regarded (if "pricey") Earl's Court outfit "is getting better and better" – a judgement that is reflected in higher ratings this year. "Very high-class food", including "imaginative, innovative tapas" and an "exceptional tasting menu", is accompanied by an "astonishing range of Spanish wines". / SW5 0LJ; www.cambiodetercio.co.uk; @CambiodTercio; 11.30 pm, Sun & Mon 11 pm.

CAMBRIDGE STREET KITCHEN SW1 £66 233

52 CAMBRIDGE ST 020 3019 8622 2–4B

"A lovely, surprising find" in a Pimlico side street, this "cheerful local" filled with art is a great place to hang out socially – a "real benefit" in an area where most restaurants are "designed just for tourists". / SW1V 4QQ; www.cambridgestreetcafe.co.uk; @TheCambridgeSt; Mon-Wed 5 pm, Thu-Sat 10 pm, Sun 6 pm.

CAMINO £52 332

3 VARNISHERS YD, REGENT QUARTER, N1 020 7841 7330 9–3C | THE BLUE FIN BUILDING, 5 CANVEY ST, SE1 020 3617 3169 10–4A | 2 CURTAIN RD, EC2 020 3948 5003 13–2B NEW | 15 MINCING LN, EC3 020 7841 7335 10–3D

A small group of "buzzy" tapas joints "full of culinary delights" – "and it's possible to eat well without breaking the bank". It caters to a business crowd during the week and families at weekends – "there's always plenty of things on the menu that the kids love". The Blackfriars, Notting Hill and Canary Wharf branches have closed, but a new spot in Shoreditch opened this year. / www.camino.uk.com; 11pm, EC3 Sat 10 pm, Sun 10pm; EC3 closed Sun, EC4 closed Sat & Sun.

CAMPANIA & JONES
E2 £18 434

23 EZRA ST 020 7613 0015 14–2A

"It feels like home… and I want to eat everything on the menu!" – Columbia Road's Campania Gastronomia moved around the corner a year ago into this brilliantly characterful former cowshed, which serves "wonderful and slightly unusual Italian food" (including fresh, homemade pasta) in a supremely "relaxed" atmosphere. / E2 7RH; www.campaniaandjones.com; 11 pm, Sun 6 pm; closed Mon.

CANNIZARO HOUSE, HOTEL DU VIN SW19 £56 ①①④

WEST SIDE, WIMBLEDON COMMON 0871 943 0345 11–2A

A "wonderful orangery" with "lovely views over Wimbledon Common" is let down by "dreadful food" and "indifferent service" at this Hotel du Vin venue. "What a shame to ruin this beautiful location" is typical of many complaints. / SW19 4UE; www.hotelduvin.com/locations/wimbledon; @HotelduVinBrand; Mon-Wed, Sat midnight, Thu & Fri 1 am, Sun 10 pm.

CANTINA LAREDO WC2 £58 ②②②

10 UPPER ST MARTIN'S LANE 020 7420 0630 5–3C

This Theatreland Mexican, part of a US chain, "manages to be both big and stylish" and is a "pretty good option for vegetarians". "The food is very fresh" and "satisfactory without being inspiring", but everyone loves the "fun guacamole made at the table". / WC2H 9FB; www.cantinalaredo.co.uk; @CantinaLaredoUK; Mon-Thu 11.30 pm, Fri & Sat midnight, Sun 10.30 pm.

CANTO CORVINO E1 £78 ③②③

21 ARTILLERY LANE 020 7655 0390 13–2B

This "new-style Italian" by Spitalfields Market features "superb pasta", "first-class ingredients" and a menu that "changes with the seasons". "Maybe a bit 'suits'-dominated, but food, service and style are excellent". Top Tip: "great for Italian brunch". / E1 7HA; www.cantocorvino.co.uk; @cantocorvinoE1; 10 pm; closed Sun.

CANTON ARMS SW8 £51 ④③④

177 SOUTH LAMBETH RD 020 7582 8710 11–1D

"Still one of the best gastropubs", and Stockwell sibling to the famous Anchor & Hope, "this place has nailed it: it's excellent as a pub and brilliant as a bistro". "Innovative dishes of consistent quality" deliver "punchy and intense flavours" and there's "proper drinking ales and pints of quality bitter". Top Tip: "a favourite for Sunday pub lunch". / SW8 1XP; www.cantonarms.com; @cantonarms; 10.30 pm; closed Mon L & Sun D; no Amex; no booking.

CAPRICCI SE1 £55 ③③②

72 HOLLAND ST 020 7021 0703 10–3B

"Don't be put off by the rows of olive oil and Italian delicacies that line the walls of this family-run bistro, just across the road from Tate Modern." "If you're in the vicinity, it serves good, simple Italian food in a small but pleasant location." / SE1 9NX; www.capricciforlondon.co.uk; 10 pm.

LE CAPRICE SW1 £75 ②④④

20 ARLINGTON ST 020 7629 2239 3–4C

"Professional, charming and fun" – this "always elegant and welcoming" stalwart near The Ritz "never fails to turn a meal into a special occasion" and remains one of London's foremost "old favourite" destinations, including for expense accounters (it helps it's "chav-free, unlike The Ivy"). Perhaps it's "not quite what it was" before it was absorbed into Richard Caring's empire, but few would notice given its "polished and discreet" staff and "great buzz". The posh brasserie fare? "predictable but sound". (In 2019, Richard Caring's group is to launch a new spin-off brand, Caprice Café, the first of which will occupy the Mayfair space that's currently trading as Mayfair Garden at 8-10 North Audley Street). / SW1A 1RJ; www.le-caprice.co.uk; @CapriceHoldings; 11 pm; may need 6+ to book.

CARACTÈRE W11

209 WESTBOURNE PARK RD AWAITING TEL 7–1B

The Notting Hill site that was formerly Bumpkin (RIP) has had a change of fortune: Emily Roux (yes, daughter of Michel) and her husband Diego Ferrari (currently head chef at Le Gavroche) have taken it over with a view to creating this October 2018 newcomer with its own, er, character (geddit!). A blend of French and Italian cuisines is promised, but the style is to be simple and seasonal rather than 'fayne dayning'. / W11 1EA; Wed-Fri 11 pm, Sat & Sun midnight.

CARAFFINI SW1 £62 ③⑤④

61-63 LOWER SLOANE ST 020 7259 0235 6–2D

"A great local stalwart that never seems to change" – this "traditional and welcoming" trattoria near Sloane Square particularly benefits from "wonderful" long-serving staff, who provide "the best welcome of any restaurant in London" to regular patrons (including junior members of the party). The fairly old-fashioned cooking is "consistent", if not especially 'foodie'. / SW1W 8DH; www.caraffini.co.uk; 11 pm; closed Sun.

CARAVAGGIO EC3 £62 ③②②

107-112 LEADENHALL ST 020 7626 6206 10–2D

"Ideally located in the City and ideal for business" – a "quality Italian" near Leadenhall Market that thrives as "a good venue for entertaining clients", even if "service is a bit mixed". / EC3A 4DP; www.etruscarestaurants.com; 10 pm; closed Sat & Sun.

CARAVAN £57 ③③③

152 GREAT PORTLAND ST, W1 020 3963 8500 2–1B NEW | 1 GRANARY SQ, N1 020 7101 7661 9–3C | 30 GREAT GUILDFORD ST, SE1 020 7101 1190 10–4B | 11-13 EXMOUTH MKT, EC1 020 7833 8115 10–1A | BLOOMBERG ARCADE, EC4 020 3957 5555 10–3C

A "brilliant option" for brunch – which can be "excitingly different, or traditionally comforting as you choose" – these "vibey", "extremely busy" ("you may have to wait for a table") haunts are "just the job if you're feeling a bit jaded" and "hard to fault" generally. The menu has its wild and wacky moments which are usually "interesting and super-delicious" and "the freshly roasted-on-site coffee is some of the best in London". All its branches are strong performers – especially the Exmouth Market original and well-known Granary Square outlet – and in July 2018 the brand finally reached the West End, in a striking space near Oxford Circus that once housed BBC Radio 1. / www.caravanonexmouth.co.uk; @CaravanResto; 10.30 pm, Sun 8 pm ; closed Sun.

CAROB TREE NW5 £41 ③④②

15 HIGHGATE RD 020 7267 9880 9–1B

"They won't let anyone go hungry!", say fans of this "always crowded" Greek local in Dartmouth Park, where "you're treated as a long lost friend", and which is praised for its "excellent fish and mezze". (One terrible meal was reported here this year – so far it seems like just a blip.) / NW5 1QX; www.carobtree.in; Tue-Fri 11 pm, Sat midnight, Sun 10.30 pm; closed Mon; no Amex.

CAROUSEL W1 £58 ④③④

71 BLANDFORD ST 020 7487 5564 3–1A

"A great concept", this Marylebone venue invites a never-ending roster of top chefs from around the world to prepare their greatest hits at single-sitting dinners. The "always interesting" and "typically high quality" results justify regular visits as "an excellent way to try different food experiences and unusual cuisines". Meanwhile, the versatile in-house kitchen team knock out excellent small plates at lunch times. The gallery upstairs rotates the artists, too. / W1U 8AB; www.carousel-london.com; @Carousel_LDN; Sun-Thu midnight, Fri & Sat 1 am; closed Mon L & Sun L.

CASA BRINDISA SW7 £50 ③③②

7-9 EXHIBITION RD 020 7590 0008 6–2C

From the Spanish food importer of the same name, this Brindisa operation has a very attractive location – near South Kensington tube, with a big outside terrace – "go on a summer's day and watch the world go by". The press of tourists means it doesn't have to try as hard as it might, but its tapas-and-more offering is consistently rated a good "cheap 'n' cheerful" choice. / SW7 2HE; www.brindisatapaskitchens.com/casa-brindisa;

CASA CRUZ W11   £80   1|1|3

123 CLARENDON RD   020 3321 5400   7–2A

It still seems "very popular", but Juan Santa Cruz's "very bling-y" Argentinian hangout on the edge of Notting Hill saw ratings plummet this year. "Starters were great, but main courses slightly disappointing" is about as good as it gets. Others reckon it's "the worst value for money" – "snotty, overpriced, Euroflash with dreadful service". / W11 4JG; www.casacruz.london; @CasaCruzrest; 11 pm, Sun 10.30 pm; closed Mon.

CASA PASTÓR N1

COAL DROPS YARD AWAITING TEL 9–3C

A larger sister restaurant to the Hart Bros' Borough Market taqueria El Pastór arrives, complete with large outside heated terrace (to be known separately as Plaza Pastór), at new canal-side retail development Coal Drops Yard in King's Cross in October 2018. / N1C 4AB.

CASA TUA WC1   £40   4|3|3

106 CROMER ST   020 7833 1483   9–4C

"A lovely, small, cheap 'n' cheerful Italian restaurant" which preserves "a neighbourhood feel" despite being "walking distance from King's Cross". The "authentic food is very fresh", the atmosphere is "relaxed" and "even if service is not fast (Italian) it's invariably friendly". / WC1H 8BZ; www.casatuacamden.com/kings-cross; @casatuagastro.

CASSE-CROUTE SE1   £55   4|4|4

109 BERMONDSEY ST   020 7407 2140   10–4D

"So French you can hardly find it in France!" – you "walk straight into Paris" when you visit this "authentic" Bermondsey bistro south of Tower Bridge, where "everything: wine, waiters, menu, decoration, ambience, whatever – it's all very Gallic". "Simple-but-delicious classics" at "sensible prices" are served by "the friendliest staff" in a "cosy" interior, but, "while squashed, somehow you aren't disturbed by the conversations at adjacent tables". / SE1 3XB; www.cassecroute.co.uk; @CasseCroute109; 10 pm, Sun 4 pm; closed Sun D.

CATFORD CONSTITUTIONAL CLUB SE6   £39   3|4|4

CATFORD BROADWAY   020 8613 7188   1–4D

"Formerly the local Conservative Club and maintaining its 1950s decor", this "vintage-looking" gastropub (run by Antic Pubs) is "a shabby, but charming if cavernous place". "They do a great burger, and other decent grub, and it has a lovely vibe, plus a suntrap garden". / SE6 4SP; catfordconstitutionalclub.com; @CatfordCClub; Tue-Thu midnight, Fri & Sat 1 am, Mon 11 pm; closed Mon-Fri L, closed Sun.

Cecconi's Shoreditch E2

CÂY TRE   £43   3|2|2

**42-43 DEAN ST, W1   020 7317 9118   5–2A |
301 OLD ST, EC1   020 7729 8662   13–1B**

"Vibrant, fresh Vietnamese cooking" is the hallmark of these "buzzy" but basic canteens in Hoxton and Soho. / www.vietnamesekitchen.co.uk; 11 pm, Fri & Sat 11.30 pm, Sun 10.30 pm; booking: min 8.

CECCONI'S   £78   2|2|3

**19-21 OLD COMPTON ST, W1   020 7734 5656
5–2A | 5A BURLINGTON GDNS, W1
020 7434 1500   4–4A | 58-60 REDCHURCH
ST, E2 AWAITING TEL 13–1C NEW | THE
NED, 27 POULTRY, EC2   020 3828 2000
10–2C**

"Brash but fun" Italian bar and brasserie in Mayfair where "the people watching is good", and where "a window table, especially when the front is open in summer, is the best place to be". Service can be "slightly dismissive" and "it's not the greatest food, but it's worth it for the buzz", and particularly popular for business entertaining, notably as "a go-to venue for breakfast with clients". Owned by Soho House, it has been rolled out as a global brand, but how well its expansion goes within London remains to be seen. The year-old venture in The Ned (see also) is a bit of a non-event ("a business Italian with City prices, but nothing exceptional in the food"); and it's still early days for its 'Pizza Bar' in Soho, or its September 2018 opening in Redchurch Street, Shoreditch. /

CECCONI'S AT THE NED EC2   £55   2|2|3

27 POULTRY   020 3828 2000   10–2C

"In the magnificent surroundings of the Lutyens-designed banking hall of the old Midland Bank building", this 3,000 square metre food hall houses seven different restaurants each with about 100 covers. It's easy to feel lost in such a big interior though and these spaces are actually "not that ambient", but are nonetheless very handy for a City rendezvous with OK fare. The top tips are Kaia (Asian-Pacific: "perfect for a quick lunch time meeting"); Malibu Kitchen (Californian: "some unusual and excellent brunch choices"); and Zobler's ('NYC'-Jewish: "comfort food that's easy to eat"). Millie's Lounge (British) also rates mention. Less so Cecconi's, except on business. In each case, go with realistic expectations – otherwise you may sense "too much hype". / EC2R 8AJ; www.thened.com/restaurants/cecconis; @TheNedLondon; 11 pm, Sun 5 pm.

THE CEDAR RESTAURANT   £40   3|3|2

**65 FERNHEAD RD, W9   020 8964 2011
1–2B | 81 BOUNDARY RD, NW8
020 3204 0030   9–3A**

Good all-round standards again win solid ratings for this low-key Lebanese chain in Hampstead, Maida Vale and St John's Wood – open from breakfast on, and "a good place to take the family of a weekend". /

CELESTE AT THE LANESBOROUGH SW1   £133   2|2|4

HYDE PARK CORNER   020 7259 5599   2–3A

This "elegant" dining room with "large and well-spaced tables" and "amazing decor" is the flagship eatery of one of the capital's most luxurious hotels, by Hyde Park Corner, yet it has struggled to catch London's gastronomic imagination. The latest regime, overseen from Paris by multi-Michelin-starred chef Eric Fréchon, continues the trend, but those reporters who have made the trip report an "expensive but well-constructed" menu that "straddles the modern and the traditional". / SW1X 7TA; www.oetkercollection.com/destinations/the-lanes borough/restaurants-bars/restaurants/celeste; @TheLanesborough; 10.30 pm.

CEPAGES W2   £51   4|3|4

**69 WESTBOURNE PARK RD   020 3602 8890
7–1B**

"A fabulous little local French restaurant/ bistro/wine bar" on the borders of Bayswater and Notting Hill that's "always busy". "There's a great wine list which you can sit and work your way through with a selection of good, reasonably priced light dishes or more substantial fare." / W2 5QH; www.cepages.co.uk; @cepagesWPR; 11 pm, Sun 10 pm; closed Mon-Fri L.

CEREMONY NW5   £53   3|4|3

131 FORTESS RD   020 3302 4242   9–1C

"A wonderful new opening that happens to be vegetarian, with cracking cocktails, all in Tufnell Park!"; a "hip" formula that's helped this brick-walled ("noisy") newcomer earn stonking reviews from reporters (and many newspaper reviewers) for its "exceptional veggie food (even for meat lovers who need a big feed)", served by "staff who seem to enjoy what they do". Not quite everyone agrees though, depriving it of a higher rating: niggles include "small portions" or "bland dishes" all at "fine dining prices". / NW5

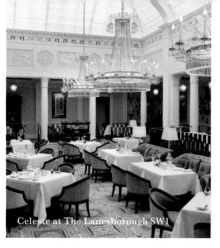
Celeste at The Lanesborough SW1

2HR; www.ceremonyrestaurant.london; Tue-Thu 11 pm, Fri & Sat 11.30 pm, Sun 10 pm; closed Tue-Sat L, closed Mon.

CERU SW7 £34 432

7-9 BUTE ST   020 3195 3001   6–2C

A "different and very refreshing" formula combining "helpful service" and "consistently delicious and inventive Levantine food" all at affordable prices for the area wins enthusiasm for this "cheerful" café in the heart of South Kensington's French quarter. (A second branch has just opened in Soho at 11 D'Arblay Street, W1.) / SW7 3EY; www.cerurestaurants.com; @cerulondon; 2 am, Sun midnight.

CEVICHE £59 534

17 FRITH ST, W1   020 7292 2040   5–2A
| ALEXANDRA TRUST, BALDWIN ST, EC1
020 3327 9463   13–1A

"The flavours are like being back on Lake Titicaca" – Martin Morales's Peruvian operation with venues in Soho and Old Street "delivers a gastronomical explosion on the palate", with "really flavoursome and unusual combinations of ingredients" including "fish like no other". They "may not have a Michelin star, but can't be beaten although others try". Top Tip: pisco sour cocktails. / www.cevicheuk.com; @cevicheuk; W1D 11.30 pm, Sun 10.15 pm, EC1V 10.45 pm, Fri & Sat 11.30 pm, Sun 9.30 pm.

CHAI THALI NW1 £34 333

CENTRO 3, 19 MANDELA ST   020 7383 2030
9–3C

"Cute and cheerful!" pan-Indian street food and bar operation in a new development near Mornington Crescent. All reports are upbeat, if with a caution that you should "pick your way through the menu carefully to have a better-than-standard curry house experience". / NW1 0DU; chaithali.com; @ChaiThaliCamden; 11 pm.

CHAMPOR-CHAMPOR SE1 £54 333

62 WESTON ST   020 7403 4600   10–4C

"Thai-Malaysian cooking with a twist" (the name means 'mix 'n' match') results in "seriously tasty food" at this "charming", if "unprepossessing-looking" little outfit, tucked away behind the Shard and near Guy's Hospital. Scores have ebbed and flowed here over many years, but for the most part "the quality is still high". / SE1 3QJ; www.champor-champor.com; @ChamporChampor; 10 pm; D only.

CHARLOTTE'S £56 333

6 TURNHAM GREEN TER, W4
020 8742 3590   8–2A

"Smart and reliable bistro" (with a cosy, little gin bar) near Turnham Green tube that offers "a menu of crowd-pleasers, cooked with care and a little flair". Part of the Ealing-based Charlotte's Place group, it is "far better than expected from a neighbourhood warhorse". / www.charlottes.co.uk; W4 midnight, Sun 11 pm, W53 10 pm, W5 11.30 pm.

CHELSEA CELLAR SW10 £41 444

9 PARK WALK   020 7351 4933   6–3B

"A small, very welcoming Southern Italian" near the Chelsea & Westminster Hospital, which has become an "absolute local favourite" thanks to its "very appealing and romantic" interior; a very good menu of antipasti plates, home made pasta and daily specials; plus "a selection of good and inexpensive wines from Puglia chosen by the two charming owners". / SW10 0AJ; www.thechelseacellar.co.uk; midnight; closed Tue-Sat L, closed Sun & Mon.

CHETTINAD W1 £38 422

16 PERCY ST   020 3556 1229   2–1C

"Don't be deceived by its average curry house appearance" – "excellent southern Indian food" is to be found at this Fitzrovia fixture. "Dhosas are as good as can be found in Kerala" and "there is (fortunately) little sign of adulteration to suit British tastes". / W1T 1DT; www.chettinadrestaurant.com; @chettinadlondon; Mon & Tue 8 pm, Thu-Sat 9 pm, Wed 10.30 pm, Sun 6 pm; no Amex.

CHEZ ABIR W14 £41 342

34 BLYTHE RD   020 7603 3241   8–1D

Small Lebanese café lost in the backstreets immediately behind Olympia. Known mainly to a faithful local crowd since the days of its redoubtable but endearingly chaotic former owner, "it maintains the standards set by Marcelle: the big difference is in the improved reliability of the service!" / W14 OHA; www.chezabir.co.uk; Mon-Thu 10 pm, Fri & Sat 10.30 pm, Sun 9.30 pm; closed Mon.

CHEZ BRUCE SW17 £83 554

2 BELLEVUE RD   020 8672 0114   11–2C

"The perfect neighbourhood restaurant... I just wish it was actually in my neighbourhood!" – Bruce Poole's "consistently exceptional" legend by Wandsworth Common is, for the 14th year, the survey's No. 1 favourite: "it simply never lets you down". "The attention to detail is wonderful", but "there is nothing flashy or pretentious" about the place. Service is "delightful, chatty enough and knowledgeable", "without ever verging on the fussy or obsequious"; and "there are always gorgeous surprises from the regularly changing, seasonal menu" of "flawless modern European cooking" ("filled with delicate flavours, but also packing a punch!"). Save a little space for the "epic cheese board", which is arguably "the best in town". There is little but a hymn of praise in the huge volume of reports we receive: "on our visit Gordon Ramsay was dining and even he found nothing to complain about!" / SW17 7EG; www.chezbruce.co.uk; @ChezBruce; Sun-Thu 9.30 pm, Fri & Sat 10.30 pm.

CHEZ ELLES E1 £54 445

45 BRICK LN   020 7247 9699   13–2C

"So you're in Paris and the food's great, the wine yummy and it feels intimate but not too packed. No you're not: you're in Brick Lane, and at half the cost!" – that's the gist of all feedback on this "lovely", "very friendly", "very quaint and authentic" East End bistro. / E1 6PU; www.chezellesbistroquet.co.uk; 10.30 pm; closed Tue, Wed L, closed Sun & Mon.

CHICAMA SW10 £65 424

383 KING'S RD   020 3874 2000   6–3C

"Fantastic Peruvian fish, both raw and cooked" – prepared "either incredibly simply or with great imagination" – is the draw to this King's Road yearling from the team behind Pachamama. It's "fun", if "sometimes very noisy", and you really have to like fish! – "otherwise the choice is oddly limited". / SW10 0LP; www.chicamalondon.com; @chicamalondon; midnight; closed Sun.

CHICK 'N' SOURS £42 433

1 EARLHAM ST, WC2   020 3198 4814
5–2B | 62 UPPER ST, N1   020 7704 9013
9–3D NEW | 390 KINGSLAND RD, E8
020 3620 8728   14–2D

"Sublimely juicy chicken with absurdly crunchy coating" – "like KFC pimped to the max" with "must-have dips such as Kewpie mayo and Sriracha sour cream" – have won high ratings for this free-range chicken and sour cocktails duo in Haggerston and Covent Garden (and from September 2018 in Islington too). "It's so good I can't stop going back!". / www.chicknsours.co.uk; @chicknsours.

CHIK'N W1 £37 322

134 BAKER ST   020 7935 6648   2–1A

"Not in the least bit healthy, but love the Korean BBQ and 'hot chick' sandwiches in particular" – this diner-style, grab-and-go yearling near Baker Street scores an enthusiastic thumbs-up (if from quite a small fan club). / W1U 6SH; www.chikn.com; @lovechikn; Mon-Thu 11 pm, Fri & Sat midnight; no booking.

CHILLI COOL
WC1 £34 `4` `2` `1`

15 LEIGH ST   020 7383 3135   2–1D

"Wonderful, spicy" Sichuan cooking, "shabby" surroundings and "authentic service-without-a-smile" – make an outing to this "very low dive" in Bloomsbury a "fun" culinary treat. "The unremarkable exterior does not prepare you for some of the most genuine food ever" and "you'll leave with perfectly tingling pepper-and-chilli lips". / WC1H 9EW; www.chillicool.co.uk; 10.15 pm; no Amex.

CHILLY KATZ W6

LYRIC SQUARE NO TEL 8–2C

Chef Phil Harrison and fashion designer Vera Thordardottir, the team behind Goldhawk Road's 'Bears Ice Cream', launched this funky-looking hole-in-the-wall on Hammersmith's Lyric Square in spring 2018, serving weird-sounding hot dogs (From Reykjavik with Love, Truffle Dog…) / W6 0NB; chillykatz.co.uk; @chillykatz; no booking.

THE CHILTERN FIREHOUSE
W1 £99 `1` `1` `3`

1 CHILTERN ST   020 7073 7676   2–1A

Fans still "love, love, love" this beautiful-crowd Marylebone haunt which occupies a gorgeous building, complete with "lovely terrace" ("it makes me feel like I'm on holiday… perhaps New England… or in the South of France"). Critics, though (and, oh boy, there are bazoodles of 'em) deride it as "a place for poseurs", whose "churned-out, style-over substance food", "snooty service" and "joke prices" ("it makes The River Café look like a walk in the park") "mark it out as a stand-out place to avoid". / W1U 7PA; www.chilternfirehouse.com; 10.30 pm.

CHIMIS SE1 £50

132 SOUTHWARK BRIDGE RD 020 79287414 10–4B

In a no-man's-land stretch of Southwark, this Spring 2018 opening is an Argentinian/Chilean parrilla majoring in meaty and fish grills. It is brought to us by Nicolas Modad (previously head chef at Brindisa) and Federico Fugazza (founder of Porteña at Borough Market). / SE1 0DG; www.chimichurris.co.uk; @ChimichurrisUK.

CHINA TANG, DORCHESTER
HOTEL W1 £84 `4` `4` `4`

53 PARK LN   020 7629 9988   3–3A

Modelled after 1930s Shanghai by the late Sir David Tang, this opulent and gorgeous-looking Mayfair basement perennially seemed "expensive for what it is" in the food department. Scores have improved across the board in the past couple of years though, and it's winning more consistent praise for "excellent" cuisine (Peking duck the speciality) and gluggable cocktails. / W1K 1QA; www.chinatanglondon.co.uk; @ChinaTangLondon; Fri & Sat, Wed & Thu 9.30 pm.

THE CHIPPING
FORECAST £46 `3` `2` `2`

58 GREEK ST, W1   020 7851 6688 5–2A NEW | 29 ALL SAINTS RD, W11 020 7460 2745   7–1B

"Quirky and obliging" (if slightly "expensive") new-wave Notting Hill chippy on the characterful All Saints Road, that's won a reputation for its "proper fish 'n' chips" using sustainable fresh fish from Cornwall and "the friendliest staff". It started out with a stall on Berwick Market, and it's going back to its Soho roots, with the opening of a new branch in autumn 2018. /

CHISOU £63 `4` `3` `2`

4 PRINCES ST, W1   020 7629 3931   4–1A | 31 BEAUCHAMP PL, SW3   020 3155 0005 6–1D

"Classic Japanese – not trendy but lovely and with good-quality food" sums up the appeal of this pair in Mayfair (long-established) and off Knightsbridge (quite new). The "awesome sushi and very good cooked dishes" are accompanied by "great sake" ("do try the sake flights"). They're "not cheap, and like many Japanese restaurants the ambience is functional rather than funky". / www.chisourestaurant.com; Mon-Sat 10.30 pm, Sun 9.30 pm.

CHIT CHAAT CHAI
SW18 £33 `3` `3` `3`

356 OLD YORK RD   020 8480 2364   11–2B

"Deliciously different", "sensibly priced" Indian street food café near Wandsworth Town station that makes a "good addition to an increasingly foodie street". / SW18 1SS; chitchaatchai.com; @ChitChaatChai; 11 pm, Sun 10.30 pm.

CHOKHI DHANI LONDON
SW11 £57 `4` `4` `3`

UNIT 2, 2 RIVERLIGHT QUAY, NINE ELMS LANE   020 3795 9000   11–1D

A household name in India, this group of luxury hotels and resorts expands internationally for the first time with this expensively decorated newcomer on the ground floor of a block amidst the new riverside developments of Vauxhall. "It's different from a typical London offering" and fans say "the Rajasthani Royal cuisine alone justifies the trip". / SW11 8AW; www.chokhidhani.co.uk; @cdgchokhidhani; 10.30 pm, Sun 9.30 pm.

CHOTTO MATTE
W1 £60 `3` `2` `4`

11-13 FRITH ST   020 7042 7171   5–2A

"A noisy nightclub vibe" boosts the appeal of this funkily decorated (big colourful murals and architectural furniture) Japanese-Peruvian fusion joint in Soho, but for a stylish scene the food's no after thought, and on all feedback "very good". / W1D 4RB; www.chotto-matte.com; @ChottoMatteSoho; 1.30 am, Sun midnight.

CHRISKITCH N10 £48 `4` `3` `3`

7 TETHERDOWN   020 8411 0051   1–1C

"The food all looks so irresistible" at this "lovely neighbourhood spot" in Muswell Hill, serving "delicious salads, breakfasts and lunches"; "the cakes are to die for" too; its short-lived Hoxton spin-off is no more. / N10 1ND; www.chriskitch.com; @ChrisKitch_; Sun-Wed midnight, Thu-Sat 1 am; L & early evening only; may need 3+ to book.

CHRISTOPHER'S
WC2 £78 `2` `2` `3`

18 WELLINGTON ST   020 7240 4222   5–3D

The "stunning interiors", "great cocktails" and "wonderful central location" have made this smart American outfit, in a gorgeous and grand Covent Garden townhouse, a key destination for more than 25 years. Diners are divided over the quality of the food, although the "excellent sirloin steak" is recommended. Another plus: "it's never too busy at lunchtime, so good for business". / WC2E 7DD; www.christophersgrill.com; @christopherswc2; 11 pm, Sun 10.30 pm; may need 6+ to book.

CHUCS £82 `3` `3` `3`

HARRODS, 87-135 BROMPTON RD, SW1 020 7298 7552   6–1D NEW | 31 DOVER ST, W1   020 3763 2013   3–3C | 226 WESTBOURNE GROVE, W11   020 7243 9136 7–1B | SERPENTINE SACKLER GALLERY, W2   020 7298 7552   7–2D NEW

"A chic take on Italian cooking" makes these in-store deluxe cafés – run by a luxury clotheswear brand of the same name – a popular option "for a quiet and unassuming" (but fairly loaded) Mayfair, Notting Hill and Chelsea clientele, who often choose it for business. The sceptical view is that it's "perfectly nice, but why all the fuss – should they stick to frocks?" They must be doing something right though, with new branches this year in Harrods and – most notably – their takeover of Zaha Hadid's magnificent restaurant space (formerly The Magazine, RIP) at the Serpentine Sackler Gallery. / www.chucsrestaurants.com; W1 11.30 pm, Sat midnight, Sun 4.30 pm; W11 11 pm, Sun 10 pm ; W1 closed Sun D.

CHURCHILL ARMS
W8 £35 `3` `2` `5`

119 KENSINGTON CHURCH ST 020 7792 1246   7–2B

"Stunningly good-value, cheap 'n' cheerful" Thai food is served in "portions which might prove a challenge even for the very hungry" at this one-of-a-kind boozer near Notting Hill Gate. The whole set-up can seem "as mad as a box of frogs" but is "always a fun night out" – you eat in a "a cute, butterfly garden conservatory at the back of a totally normal Irish pub". "You only get an hour at the table but service is very fast." / W8 7LN; www.churchillarmskensington.co.uk; @ChurchilArmsW8; Mon-Wed 11 pm, Thu-Sat midnight; closed Sun.

CHUTNEY MARY
SW1 £87 4|4|4
73 ST JAMES'S ST 020 7629 6688 3–4D

"Top-of-the-range, expensive but memorable… nice cocktails too!"; this "beautiful and intimate" stalwart is very well-established now in its swanky St James's location, and "better all-round than when it was located in Chelsea". "A great variety of spices are used very subtly and with first class ingredients" to create some "divine" dishes. / SW1A 1PH; www.chutneymary.com; @thechutneymary; 10.30 pm; closed Sat L & Sun; Cash & cards; booking max 4 may apply.

CHUTNEYS NW1 £27 3|2|2
124 DRUMMOND ST 020 7388 0604 9–4C

"You can't beat Chutney's on taste and price" – this age-old vegetarian Indian is "a firm favourite among its Drummond Street competitors" by Euston station. "The ground-floor dining room is attractive enough – the basement less so." / NW1 2PA; www.chutneyseuston.uk; 11 pm; no Amex; may need 5+ to book.

CIAO BELLA WC1 £44 2|3|4
86-90 LAMB'S CONDUIT ST 020 7242 4119 2–1D

This "ever bustling traditional Italian" has brought an affordable taste of 'la dolce vita' to Bloomsbury for 35 years. The "standard food "is pretty good for the reasonable price", "but is not really the point": it's "very cheerful" with a "superb buzz". "Perfect for a family get-together with children." / WC1N 3LZ; www.ciaobellarestaurant.co.uk; @CiaobellaLondon; 10.30 pm, Sun 6 pm.

CIBO W14 £58 4|5|3
3 RUSSELL GDNS 020 7371 6271 8–1D

"A proper Italian restaurant, like being in Rome" – this stalwart between Olympia and Holland Park serves "consistently great food", with an emphasis on "fresh fish and seafood". A favourite of the late Michael Winner, it has fallen off the foodie radar in recent years but still scores highly, not least thanks to its "welcoming" and sympathetic staff. / W14 8EZ; www.ciborestaurant.net; 10.30 pm; closed Sat L, closed Sun.

CIGALA WC1 £65 3|2|2
54 LAMB'S CONDUIT ST 020 7405 1717 2–1D

With its "old-fashioned style" and "authentic Spanish tapas", this Iberian haunt in one of Bloomsbury's more attractive streets is a "neighbourhood favourite that's always fun to go to" – if with decor that's a little "lacking in character". / WC1N 3LW; www.cigala.co.uk; 10.45 pm, Sun 9.45 pm.

CIGALON WC2 £58 4|4|4
115 CHANCERY LANE 020 7242 8373 2–2D

Eating the "lovely fresh Provençal food in this attractive airy room on Chancery Lane" is "a very satisfying experience". Housed in a light-filled former book auction room with a huge glass rooflight, it has the "trademark quirks and innovation of the Club Gascon team" that is behind it, and "the prices are fair". / WC2A 1PP; www.cigalon.co.uk; @cigalon_london; 10 pm; closed Sat & Sun.

CINNAMON BAZAAR
WC2 £38 3|3|3
28 MAIDEN LANE 020 7395 1400 5–4D

"Fun decor" helps breathe life into this two-floor Covent Garden venture, which can get "noisy". Its Indian fusion-esque menu "is different to other Cinnamon eateries", and most reports acclaim its "fantastic dishes at a great price". / WC2E 7NA; www.cinnamon-bazaar.com; @Cinnamon_Bazaar; Tue-Thu 9 pm.

THE CINNAMON CLUB
SW1 £84 3|2|3
OLD WESTMINSTER LIBRARY, GREAT SMITH ST 020 7222 2555 2–4C

"It's been around a long time and is perhaps now overshadowed by newcomers like Gymkhana", but this posh nouvelle Indian remains one of London's most popular grand restaurants (and still features in our Top 40 most mentioned ranking) and many folks' "go-to fancy Indian". Set in Westminster's "fantastic" old Public Library it has "a lovely club-like feel, with the bookshelves reaching to the ceiling" – an incongruous but somehow fitting backdrop for Vivek Singh's "beautiful, innovative, nouvelle-Indian food" ("lots of complex flavours and some bite"). This was not a vintage year for its survey results, however, with gripes about "variable food, and service that ebbs and flows, which just isn't acceptable at these prices". / SW1P 3BU; www.cinnamonclub.com; @cinnamonclub; 11 pm, Sun 3.30 pm; closed Sun; No trainers; booking max 14 may apply; SRA-Food Made Good – 2 stars.

CINNAMON KITCHEN
EC2 £62 4|3|3
9 DEVONSHIRE SQ 020 7626 5000 10–2D

"Indian favourites imaginatively recreated" and "fusion food such as steak with masala chips" comprise a "superb menu that is hard to choose from" at the Cinnamon Club's offshoot in the City. The setting – a large atrium near Liverpool Street – is a real bonus, because "you can sit outside in a covered courtyard in virtually all weathers". / EC2M 4YL; www.cinnamon-kitchen.com; @cinnamonkitchen; 10.30 pm; closed Sat L, closed Sun.

CINNAMON KITCHEN BATTERSEA
SW11 £55 4|3|3
BATTERSEA POWER STATION 020 3955 5480 11–1C

A "new restaurant that has much promise" – this yearling in a railway arch that's part of the redevelopment of Battersea Power Station is the latest offspring of Westminster's plush Cinnamon Club, and its "refined Indian cooking under the care of Vivek Singh" is by early accounts "both interesting and delicious". / SW11 8EZ; @CinnamonKitchen.

CITY BARGE W4 £51 3|3|3
27 STRAND-ON-THE-GREEN 020 8994 2148 1–3A

"A great location on a sunny day", this riverside gastropub at Chiswick's Strand-on-the-Green (smartened up in recent times) delivers "unpretentious good food with a bit more finesse than most pubs". "The perfect end to a walk along the Thames." / W4 3PH; www.citybargechiswick.com; @citybargew4; Tue-Thu 10 pm, Fri & Sat 10.30 pm.

CITY CÀPHÊ EC2 £10 3|3|2
17 IRONMONGER ST NO TEL 10–2C

"Superb Vietnamese street food" draws a hungry City crowd to this pitstop near Bank. It's "super-busy at lunchtime – better to take away than sit at the tiny tables". / EC2V 8EY; www.citycaphe.com; @CityCaphe; closed Mon-Fri D, closed Sat & Sun; no Amex; no booking.

CITY SOCIAL EC2 £92 3|3|3
TOWER 42 25 OLD BROAD ST 020 7877 7703 10–2C

"On the 24th-floor of Tower 42, looking across at the Gherkin and Heron Tower, you enjoy some of the most spectacular views of the City" at Jason Atherton's "sleek, swish and professional" eyrie: a natural favourite for wining and dining in the Square Mile. On most accounts the "fantastic" cuisine is almost as stunning as the panorama, but there is also a school of thought that it's "average for such excessive prices". / EC2N 1HQ; www.citysociallondon.com; @CitySocial_T42; 10.30 pm; closed Sat L, closed Sun; booking max 4 may apply.

CLARETTE W1 £81 3|3|3
44 BLANDFORD ST 020 3019 7750 3–1A

This year-old Marylebone wine bar, owned in part by a scion of the family who own Château Margaux, has yet to win a huge fan base amongst reporters – those who have discovered it however award high ratings to its wine list and its menu of Mediterranean small plates. / W1U 7HS; www.clarettelondon.com; @ClaretteLondon; 10.15 pm, Sun 8.45 pm.

CLARKE'S W8   £76   4 5 4

124 KENSINGTON CHURCH ST
020 7221 9225   7–2B

"There's no messing around by chefs trying to be clever: just first class ingredients allowed to speak for themselves" alongside a "fabulous wine list" and "so-gracious" service at Sally Clarke's California-inspired institution – a Kensington stalwart that "isn't content to rest on its laurels", and whose "fresh-flavoured dishes" are "some of the best seasonal food in London". "The main room's elegant decor makes it feel more like a private dining room than a restaurant and the tables are set far enough apart to allow for quiet conversation" making it a favourite for romance (of the silver-haired variety). "A warm welcome from Sally each and every visit sets the tone for a great evening" ("she must have some clones of herself, as she always seems to be around!"). / W8 4BH; www.sallyclarke.com; @SallyClarkeLtd; 10 pm; closed Sun; booking max 14 may apply.

CLAUDE'S KITCHEN, AMUSE BOUCHE SW6   £60   3 3 4

51 PARSONS GREEN LANE   020 7371 8517
11–1B

Claude Compton has won an enthusiastic following for his "excellent and inventive" cooking, deployed in a quirky dining room above the Amuse Bouche fizz bar opposite Parsons Green station. But the food level has dropped a notch this year – "sometimes it misses, and when it does it misses badly". / SW6 4JA; www.amusebouchelondon.com/claudes-kitchen; @AmuseBoucheLDN; 11 pm; D only, closed Sun.

CLAW CARNABY W1   £40   3 3 2

21 KINGLY ST   020 7287 5742   4–2B

"Crab specialist that's a welcome addition" – that's the general verdict on this "buzzy" Soho newcomer, which is the first permanent home of a sustainable seafood pop-up, food truck and City takeaway outlet. There are caveats though – "it's sort of street food but at restaurant or pub prices…" – "couldn't taste the crab because the fries were covered in spices as well as salt". / W1B 5QA; claw.co.uk; @CLAWfood; Mon-Fri 10.30 pm, Sat 11 pm, Sun 10 pm.

CLERKENWELL CAFE   £36   3 3 3

80A MORTIMER ST, W1   020 7253 5754
10–1A | ST CHRISTOPHER'S PLACE, W1
020 7253 5754   3–1A | 27 CLERKENWELL
RD, EC1   020 7253 5754   10–1A | 60A
HOLBORN VIADUCT, EC1 NO TEL 10–2A

"Better roasted, better brewed, better poured – just better" agree fans of the coffee at this small chain with its own roastery. They also sell simple snacks, coffee-making equipment and their own beans – "so take some home!". / workshopcoffee. com; @workshopcoffee; EC1M 6 pm, Tue-Fri 7 pm; W1U & W1W 7 pm, Sat & Sun 6 pm; EC1A 6 pm; EC1 closed Sat & Sun; no bookings.

THE CLIFTON NW8   £51   3 3 5

96 CLIFTON HILL   020 7625 5010   9–3A

"Wonderful local pub", hidden-away in St John's Wood (where, back in the day, Edward VII used to conduct his affair with Lillie Langtry). Rescued from the developers, and relaunched last year, it still has yet to attract a big following amongst reporters, but food ratings are fair, and it's worth a go for its marvellous interior (enhanced by the addition of a new conservatory). / NW8 0JT; www.thecliftonnw8.com; @thecliftonnw8; 10 pm, Sun 8 pm.

CLIPSTONE W1   £82   3 3 2

5 CLIPSTONE ST   020 7637 0871   2–1B

"Still punching above its weight", Will Lander & Daniel Morgenthau's "tiny", "somewhat hipster" Fitzrovia haunt (sibling to Portland) "has dispensed with its small plates concept and now provides proper starters and main courses". Fans applaud its "imaginative take on a simple range of ingredients (with results that can be superlative)"; its "limited but intriguing wine list"; and feel that even if it's "packed" and "noisy" ("lots of hard surfaces") "that's not the point" for a "relaxed" and "lovely" place. Overall ratings are blunted, however, by a minority who feel "it's not terrible, but I hoped for more…" / W1W 6BB; www.clipstonerestaurant.co.uk; @clipstonerestaurant; 11 pm; closed Sun.

CLOS MAGGIORE WC2   £77   3 3 5

33 KING ST   020 7379 9696   5–3C

"Deserving its accolade as London's most romantic restaurant" – this "special and luxuriant" venue is an unexpected haven of "peace and tranquility", despite being bang smack in the centre of touristy Covent Garden, and "just has that certain 'je ne sais quoi' to create vibes with your significant other". "Try to get a table in the extraordinary conservatory" ("where the glass roof opens on summer days and a warming fire is lit in the winter") as "that is how the magic happens" but NB – "it needs to be booked many months in advance". The numerous other sections can be "memorable" and "cosseting" too, but there's no hiding the fact that they do play second fiddle to the "headline event". Given the emphasis on atmosphere, the surprise here has always been the high standards generally: the "professional" service, "classic and well-presented" French-inspired cuisine and the "immense wine list (you could get lost in it, look up, and find your partner gone!)". But the formerly high proportion of reports of seriously good cooking here fell off sharply this year, and a few regulars have concerns: "Once I'd have overlooked a decidedly average meal here, but two similar experiences have left me wondering: is it starting to live off a great room and stellar reputation?" / WC2E 8JD; www.closmaggiore.com; @closmaggiorewc2; 11 pm, Sun 9.30 pm.

THE CLOVE CLUB EC1   £147   4 3 3

SHOREDITCH TOWN HALL, 380 OLD ST
020 7729 6496   13–1B

"Top-end, creative dining without pretensions" has carved a global reputation for Daniel Willis, Isaac Mchale and Johnny Smith's "relaxed" blue-tiled chamber within Shoreditch's fine old town hall (whose renown is sealed by achieving the UK's highest position in the 'World's 50 Best', ranking at 33). The results from the open kitchen five a five-course or ten-course tasting menu focus on British-sourced produce and are "phenomenally good, exceptionally interesting and always innovative". As well as "inspired wine pairings", the forward-thinking approach is shown by "(surprisingly) good non-alcoholic pairings" too. "Staff have amazing knowledge of the food and wine" and their "real care" adds a lot to the experience ("my veggie boyfriend never feels like he's an inconvenience here like at so many other restaurants"). Gripes? The setting is quite "Spartan". More significantly, whereas most reports say it "exceeded our sky-high expectations", ratings here softened this year, with the chief complaint being a feeling that it's becoming "hugely overpriced": "even if the food's a wow, it's so expensive", and some feel "it's beginning to rival the River Café for non-value!". / EC1V 9LT; www.thecloveclub.com; @thecloveclub; 10.30 pm; closed Mon L, closed Sun.

CLUB GASCON EC1   £106   4 4 4

57 WEST SMITHFIELD   020 7600 6144
10–2B

Pascal Aussignac and Vincent Labyrie's "magnificent and innovative" temple to the cuisine of southwest France (and famously foie gras) has "upped its game" following a complete makeover that marked their 20 years beside Smithfield Market. There's now "more space and an expanded menu", and although one or two long-term fans are "not sure about the refurb", the ambience rating has improved dramatically and the food remains "first class". / EC1A 9DS; www.clubgascon.com; @club_gascon; Tue-Fri 10 pm; closed Mon, Sat & Sun.

THE COACH EC1   £59   4 3 3

26-28 RAY ST   020 3954 1595   10–1A

"So good to have Henry Harris back again!" – this "great revamped gastropub in Clerkenwell is under his gastronomic tutelage" (one of four, where he is collaborating with James McCulloch, including The Hero of Maida, The Three Cranes and The Harlot). "The downstairs is still recognisably a pub at the front and has a light and airy dining area at the back, while upstairs is a more formal dining area with lovely original features". Ultimately there's the risk he may move on or spread himself too thinly, but for the present "keenly priced French food" – "more fine dining than pub grub" and reminiscent of his Racine days – is the pay-off here (some dishes are "incredible", not least "knockout roasts"). / EC1R 3DJ; www.thecoachclerkenwell.co.uk; @thecoachldn; Mon & Tue 9 pm, Fri & Sat 11.30 pm, Wed 10 pm, Thu 11 pm, Sun 5 pm.

COAL OFFICE N1

2 BAGLEY WALK 020 3848 6085 9–3C

Assaf Granit, chef and co-owner of The Palomar and The Barbary, is behind this early autumn 2018 Mediterranean/Middle Eastern-inspired opening in a big, Victorian, ex-industrial brick pile by the canal in King's Cross: a 160-cover space split over three floors, with a rooftop terrace and al fresco dining area, complete with panoramic views over Granary Square. Designer Tom Dixon, whose practice is nearby, is also involved creating, for example, tableware which is for sale. / N1C 4PQ; coaloffice.com.

COAL ROOMS
SE15 £53 433

11A STATION WAY 020 7635 6699 1–4D

The tastefully restored, Grade II listed, former ticket office of Peckham Rye station is the venue for this year-old venture, named for its 'live fire' mode of cooking from the large smoker and robata grills which are central to the open kitchen. Open from breakfast on – and serving a flatbread menu at lunch – fans hail its "amazing and interesting food" ("I daren't rate it too highly for fear we won't be able to get a table!"), although other feedback say it's good but not outstanding. / SE15 4RX; www.coalrooms.com; @coalrooms; 10 pm, Sun 5 pm; closed Sun D.

THE COAL SHED
SE1 £65 333

ONE TOWER BRIDGE 020 3384 7272 10–4D

"A great addition to the SE1 restaurant scene" – this import from Brighton has a "sleek and contemporary design" within one of the new units of the development near Tower Bridge incorporating London's newest theatre, The Bridge. Although there are one or two dissenting voices for whom the venue fell short, most reports say it's a "meat-lovers dream", with "superb and personal service too". Top Menu Tips – numerous dishes are recommended: "the smoked goat is an absolute revelation", there's "exceptionally good steak", "fabulous grilled octopus" and "really pleasing sweets". / SE1 2AA; www.coalshed-restaurant.co.uk; @TheCoalShed1; 10.15 pm, Sun 8.45 pm.

CÔBA N7 £23 432

244 YORK WAY 07495 963336 9–2C

"Mouth-wateringly good" Vietnamese BBQ tucker comes with an Aussie accent at Damon Bui's former pub north of King's Cross, which is "pleasant if not that comfortable". / N7 9AG; www.cobarestaurant.co.uk; @cobafood; midnight; booking D only.

COCOTTE £51 443

95 WESTBOURNE GROVE, W2
020 3220 0076 7–1B | 8 HOXTON SQUARE, N1 020 7033 4277 13–1B

"If you like chicken this is your place" say fans of this affordable Gallic two-year-old, on the fringes of Notting Hill and Bayswater:

"simple mission (rotisserie chicken), well delivered; chicken itself good quality, tasty and wholesome". In April 2018, the French owners opened a new branch in Hoxton Square. /

COLBERT SW1 £63 113

51 SLOANE SQ 020 7730 2804 6–2D

"A magnificent location on the corner of Sloane Square" is the crown jewel feature of this "bustling" Parisian-style brasserie, whose "position right near the tube makes it so easy for a business appointment"; and where breakfasting marks "a civilised start to the day". This is still the weakest runner in the Corbin & King stable however, with Gallic brasserie fare that can be of "Cafe Rouge/airport lounge quality", and sometimes "snooty" service. Fans are un-moved though: "formulaic it may be, but it's still the best people watching site in London and a great local hangout!" / SW1W 8AX; www.colbertchelsea.com; @ColbertChelsea; Mon-Wed midnight, Thu & Fri 1 am, Sat & Sun 12 pm.

LA COLLINA NW1 £55 332

17 PRINCESS RD 020 7483 0192 9–3B

Tucked away below Primrose Hill, this "boutique Italian" specialises in "delicious, uncomplicated" Piedmontese cuisine. "Simple, quiet and sophisticated", its "unpretentious food surpasses expectations" – and is "great value". Top Tip: "the garden is a delight in the summer". / NW1 8JR; www.lacollinarestaurant.co.uk; @LacollinaR; Wed-Sat 10 pm, Tue 9.30 pm, Sun 9 pm; closed Tue L, closed Mon; booking max 8 may apply.

THE COLLINS ROOM, THE BERKELEY HOTEL
SW1 £101 234

WILTON PLACE 020 7107 8866 6–1D

"The famous Pret-a-Portea is a treat for the eyes as well as the palette" when you take tea in this refined chamber, which is part of Maybourne's super-swanky Belgravia hotel, just off Knightsbridge. The miniature cakes are inspired by catwalk creations and are a "stunning and very quirky" assortment in fab-u-lous designs. Admittedly the experience is "not exactly cheap" – "you could have a Michelin-starred lunch with wine for less money!" / SW1X 7RL; www.the-berkeley.co.uk; @TheBerkeley; 10.45 pm, Sun 10.15 pm.

LE COLOMBIER
SW3 £70 354

145 DOVEHOUSE ST 020 7351 1155 6–2C

"A little slice of France in Chelsea which never fails to please" – Didier Garnier's "tucked-away, corner-restaurant" is in the style of a "classic Gallic brasserie" and particularly benefits from its "hands-on owner" and "enthusiastic and charming" service. For its (older) "very loyal clientele", "the greatest virtue is that, as all around it changes, everything here remains the same", not least the dependable "traditional" fare. What's more "M Garnier knows his wine and has a superb list that's sensibly priced and imaginative". It's "the perfect place to take your grand aunt" – "the fact that so many regulars

keep coming back in an area where there is so much top-notch competition speaks for itself!" / SW3 6LB; www.le-colombier-restaurant.co.uk; 10.30 pm, Sun 10 pm.

COLONY GRILL ROOM, BEAUMONT HOTEL
W1 £78 234

8 BALDERTON STREET, BROWN HART GARDENS 020 7499 9499 3–2A

Corbin & King's "terrific 1920s New York-style grill room in the stunning art deco Beaumont Hotel is a stone's throw away from Selfridges, yet impossible to come across by chance". According to most reports, a visit is "a luxurious treat", on account of its "comfortable and plush" style and "typical American fare, from hot dogs to chicken pot pie". To some tastes though, the pricey food is so "straightforward" as to seem "a little uninspired." Top Tips – "the breakfast hashes are superb" and "design-your-own ice cream sundae with an amazing selection of flavours, toppings and sauces is great fun for kids and adults alike". / W1K 6TF; www.colonygrillroom.com; @ColonyGrillRoom; 10.30 pm.

THE COLTON ARMS
W14 £52 234

187 GREYHOUND RD 020 3757 8050 8–2C

"Excellent for some comfort food and a decent drink at the end of the day" – this year-old rejuvenated old tavern (nowadays owned by Hippo Inns) is set deep in the backstreets of Barons Court. A brilliant back garden is a big draw. / W14 9SD; www.thecoltonarms.co.uk; @thecoltonarms; 10 pm, Sun 8 pm.

COMPTOIR GASCON
EC1 £57 222

63 CHARTERHOUSE ST 020 7608 0851 10–1A

"The duck fat chips are worth the potential coronary", say fans of this "slightly cramped" Smithfield bistro – offshoot of nearby Club Gascon – which has some renown as "a high quality eating experience at a very reasonable price". Doubts are creeping in, though: "is this place starting to lose its flair?" – "the choices have become more limited and seem less creative", and at worse "banal". / EC1M 6HJ; www.comptoirgascon.com; @ComptoirGascon; 10 pm, Sun 9 pm; closed Mon & Sun.

COMPTOIR LIBANAIS
£39 222

As a "decent enough pit stop" (or "a great introduction to Lebanese food") these brightly decorated venues are well-located, "not bad for the price" and "a solid option for a quick bite". Expect "reliable Middle Eastern food" combined with a "nice level of hustle & bustle". / www.lecomptoir.co.uk; 10 pm (SW 8 pm), W1C & E20 Sun 8 pm; W12 closed Sun D; no bookings.

CON GUSTO
SE18 £52 344

NO 1 ST   020 8465 7452   12–2D

"A tiny (only 9 tables), really quirky restaurant in a fun, former military building" near the waterside in the historic setting of the Woolwich Arsenal. "A small menu of authentic Italian food" is served up "by genuine Italian chefs all from a tiny 300-year-old guard room which holds the open kitchen and restaurant". / SE18 6GH; www.congusto.co.uk; 9.30 pm, Sun 9 pm; closed Tue-Fri L, closed Mon.

IL CONVIVIO SW1 £76 333

143 EBURY ST   020 7730 4099   2–4A

"A real old favourite which seems to have new life with its current chef" (Cedric Neri) – this converted Georgian townhouse in Belgravia is "a secret gem", with "some very fine Italian cooking". It's "smart", "very friendly", and "the prices are fairly modest considering the quality". / SW1W 9QN; www.etruscarestaurants.com/il-convivio; 10.45 pm; closed Sun.

COOPERS RESTAURANT & BAR WC2 £49 233

49 LINCOLN'S INN FIELDS   020 7831 6211   2–2D

"The restaurant's regulars are a mix of LSE professors and barristers from Lincoln's Inn, resulting in a lively, argumentative atmosphere!" at this legal-land staple, which "hardly has any competition nearby" and which some regulars feel "could benefit from more inspiration". That said, "it's a really reliable spot where service is always welcoming and the staff attentive and helpful; and meat, sourced each day from Smithfield, is always a good choice". / WC2A 3PF; www.coopersrestaurant.co.uk; @coopers_bistro; 10.30 pm; closed Sat & Sun; no booking.

COPPA CLUB TOWER BRIDGE EC3 £44 234

THREE QUAYS WALK, LOWER THAMES ST   020 7993 3827   10–3D

There's a "lovely atmosphere and buzz" at this all-day 'club without membership' comprising a restaurant, bar and lounge, whose outside 'igloos', with stunning views of nearby Tower Bridge, have become famous for their celebratory yuletide potential. It's the first London outpost of an operation which began in gorgeous Sonning on Thames (there's now another in St Paul's) – ratings are solid the board although "the food is a bit gastropub cliché..." / EC3R 6AH; www.coppaclub.co.uk; @wearecoppaclub; Mon-Thu 11 pm, Fri & Sat midnight, Sun 10.30 pm; booking max 6 may apply.

COQ D'ARGENT
EC2 £95 233

1 POULTRY   020 7395 5000   10–2C

"Fantastic in the summer, with amazing views over the City" – D&D's London's stalwart rooftop brasserie is still, after all these years, a striking venue, complete with gardens and adjoining bar, and its classic Gallic fare is "reliable" if "not cheap". Despite its handy location right by Bank, it's perhaps "no longer the business must-do it used to be", but nevertheless still a regular choice for legions of Square Mile expense-accounters. / EC2R 8EJ; www.coqdargent.co.uk; @coqdargent1; 11 pm; closed Sun; booking max 10 may apply.

CORA PEARL WC2

30 HENRIETTA ST   020 7324 7722   5–3D

The trio behind Shepherd Market's quirky hit Kitty Fisher's (Tom Mullion, Tim Steel and Oliver Milburn) backed up their Mayfair success with this mid-Summer 2018 opening in Covent Garden, which – like its sister – is named for a well-known British-born courtesan. / WC2E 8NA; www.corapearl.co.uk; @CoraPearlCG; Mon & Tue 9 pm, Fri & Sat 11.30 pm, Wed 10 pm, Thu 11 pm, Sun 5 pm.

CORAZÓN W1 £44 243

29 POLAND ST   020 3813 1430   4–1C

"Part of a new wave finally bringing authentic Mexican cuisine to the capital", Laura Sheffield's "cosy and buzzing" taqueria off Oxford Street benefits from "friendly service" and "reasonable prices", and its tacos are "fresh and piquant" – "compares well with the Mexican food I sampled in LA recently". / W1F 8QN; www.corazonlondon.co.uk; @corazon_uk; 10 pm, Sun 9 pm.

CORE BY CLARE SMYTH W11 £115 554

92 KENSINGTON PARK RD   020 3937 5086   7–2B

"A flying start from the former head chef at Gordon Ramsay" – in this "unmissable" yearling, Clare Smyth "has finally created a fabulous restaurant on this difficult site" (most recently Notting Hill Kitchen, RIP, and in days of yore, Leith's). "If she doesn't get at least two Michelin stars this year, it will be astounding!" given the "ethereal cuisine she delivers with confidence, exuberance and pleasure". "Outstanding produce is allowed to really sing in the dishes" – with the emphasis on two tasting menu options – and "seasonal ingredients (really – not just the lip service you sometimes hear) are centre stage, with an interesting and rare focus on vegetables": "I mean, how on earth can you make a humble potato so attractive and so tasty? It's magic!" .The "light and sophisticated" room "has a relaxed feel, no tablecloths or hushed tones" and – with the "faultless", "friendly" service – the overall effect is "a pleasant, unusually relaxed and unpompous atmosphere". "Attention to detail is amazing, and watching the kitchen staff quietly gliding between stations behind the pass, overseen by Clare, is like watching a theatre production" STOP PRESS: Having won the 'Top Gastronomic' award at the Harden's London Restaurant awards, on October 1 Michelin followed suit with the award of two stars. / W11 2PN; www.corebyclaresmyth.com; @CorebyClare; 10.30 pm; closed Tue, Wed L, closed Sun & Mon.

Core W11

CORK & BOTTLE
WC2 £57 234

44-46 CRANBOURN ST   020 7734 7807   5–3B

"An eclectic mix of stunning wines from around the globe" makes this legendary 47-year-old basement wine bar "a great oasis to escape the hustle and bustle of Leicester Square". "The food is incidental", mostly "good bistro dishes from the 1980s", and they've sold nearly a million portions of the house ham & cheese pie in the past 40 years. (Nowadays owned by Will Clayton, it has a spin-off no-one's ever heard of in Bayswater and another opening in Hampstead in September 2018). Top Tip: "the cheese selection is pretty special". / WC2H 7AN; www.thecorkandbottle.co.uk; @corkbottle1971; midnight, Sun 11 pm; no booking D.

CORNERSTONE E9

3 PRINCE EDWARD ROAD,   020 8986 3922   14–1C

Tom Brown (formerly behind the stoves at Nathan Outlaw at The Capital), has branched out on his own with this minimalist Hackney Wick newcomer, where the kitchen is centre-stage in the room, putting the focus even more firmly on the predominantly fishy fare from this native Cornishman. It opened in May 2018, just too late for survey feedback – Giles Coren went overboard for it in his early press review, while our jungle telegraph says it's a brilliant addition to east London, but that the earth doesn't always move, and that it's priced for somewhere more central. / E9 5LX; cornerstonehackney.com; @Cornerstone_h_w; Mon-Wed 9 pm, Thu-Sat 9.30 pm, Sun 3.30 pm.

CORRIGAN'S MAYFAIR
W1 £102 333

28 UPPER GROSVENOR ST   020 7499 9943   3–3A

Richard Corrigan's "understated", "comfortable" and "well-spaced" Mayfair HQ is a "perfect place for business", particularly of a slightly traditionalist nature, given its high quality, luxurious British cuisine (available à la carte, or with a tasting option). To the extent that it draws criticism, it's, perhaps predictably, primarily for being "too expensive for what it is" – take the company's plastic. Top Tip: "set lunch is exceptional value". / W1K 7EH; www.corrigansmayfair.com; @CorriganMayfair; 10.30 pm; closed Sat L, closed Sun; booking max 12 may apply.

CÔTE £52 222

These "accurate imitations of a well-run French brasserie" have become the survey's most-mentioned chain, on the strength of the huge army of fans who find them an "always-dependable" standby. The "perfectly acceptable" food "is quite good when you factor in the price": "stick to their basic menus and you get a quite a good-value meal (although stray onto the more expensive dishes and you are better off going elsewhere)". The wide range of options – including breakfast and prix-fixe pre-theatre – means there's "plenty of choice for different appetites". Unlike some chains there's no effort to make outlets individual: "every branch is cut from the same cloth, but that's no bad thing". / www.cote-restaurants.co.uk; 11 pm.

COUNTER CULTURE
SW4 £54 342

16 THE PAVEMENT   020 8191 7960   11–2D

"It's cramped – 16 covers (stools) in a small space – but the food can be tremendous" at this two-year-old offshoot from Robin Gill's Dairy in Clapham Common (and even though it didn't score quite as highly as next door this year, the ability to BYO for £10 corkage can make it a very decent overall bargain). / SW4 0HY; www.countercultureclapham.co.uk; @culturesnax; no booking.

THE COW W2 £59 335

89 WESTBOURNE PARK RD   020 7221 0021   7–1B

"Fish stew and oysters to die for", washed down by a pint of Guinness, makes Tom Conran's Irish-style pub on the Notting Hill-Bayswater border an enduring favourite. "The food is always delicious, with a great emphasis on seafood". / W2 5QH; www.thecowlondon.co.uk; @TheCowLondon; Mon-Thu 11 pm, Fri & Sat midnight, Sun 10.30 pm; no Amex.

COYA £83 323

118 PICCADILLY, W1   020 7042 7118   3–4B | ANGEL COURT, 31-33 THROGMORTON ST, EC2   020 7042 7118   10–2C

"Good fun and great food is an easy mix" and it's one this Mayfair fixture carries off with its "wonderful, well-executed Peruvian fare" ("delicious ceviche"), copious Pisco sours and an "ever-buzzy" ("intolerably noisy") setting. "A decent meal is seldom enhanced by astronomical pricing" however, which can dampen enthusiasm for the experience. Comments on its year-old City sibling near Bank are in a similar vein – "a welcome addition" if a pricey one, with "crowd pleasing food that's perfect for sharing". Top Tip: Sommelier Mondays at the City branch with 50% off wine. /

CRAFT LONDON
SE10 £61 342

PENINSULA SQUARE   020 8465 5910   12–1D

"Delicious pizzas with unusual toppings, plus great coffee and salads too" win praise for the ground floor café of Stevie Parle's outpost at the

---

O2. There's also a more stylish first-floor bar and restaurant serving more ambitious, locally sourced fare. / SE10 0SQ; www.craft-london.co.uk; @CraftLDN; 10.30 pm; closed Tue-Fri L, closed Sun & Mon.

CRATE BREWERY AND
PIZZERIA E9 £24 434

7, THE WHITE BUILDING, QUEENS YARD   020 8533 3331   14–1C

"Great pizzas with a brilliant thin crispy base" reward a stroll through the Olympic Park to this engagingly grungy craft brewery and pizzeria, a short walk from Hackney Wick station: "the venue always has a great atmosphere… and lovely beer". / E9 5EN; www.cratebrewery.com; @cratebrewery; Sun-Thu 10 pm, Fri & Sat 11 pm.

CROCKER'S FOLLY
NW8 £64 324

23-24 ABERDEEN PL   020 7289 9898   9–4A

The "ornate surroundings" – "one of the country's most spectacular pub interiors", in St John's Wood – make an "eccentric" setting in which to enjoy "above average Lebanese specialities". Owned by Maroush, the group have successfully ditched the more traditional British formula they trialled initially, to focus on what they do best. Irrespective of eating, the place is worth a visit "just for the building" alone. Crocker, a Victorian entrepreneur, built his epic gin palace here – in what seems like the middle of nowhere – in the misguided expectation that it would become a major railway terminus. / NW8 8JR; www.crockersfolly.com; @Crockers_Folly; Sun-Thu 11 pm, Fri & Sat 11.30 pm.

THE CROOKED WELL
SE5 £48 323

16 GROVE LN   020 7252 7798   1–3C

Limited feedback on this elegantly updated neighbourhood pub in the heart of Camberwell, but all of it is positive regarding its gastrofare ("excellent Sunday roast"), and a setting that's "full of atmosphere". / SE5 8SY; www.thecrookedwell.com; @crookedwell; 10.30 pm; closed Mon L; no Amex; booking max 6 may apply.

THE CROSS KEYS
SW3 £60 344

1 LAWRENCE ST   020 7351 0686   6–3C

The oldest boozer in Chelsea is now a gastropub with an "awesome new chef" who turns out "great pub food". Under the same ownership as the Sands End in Fulham, it's "always welcoming" and "excellent value". / SW3 5NB; www.thecrosskeyschelsea.co.uk; @CrossKeys_PH; 9.30 pm, Sun 3.30 pm.

CUB N1 £77 443

153-155 HOXTON ST   020 3693 3202   14–2A

Feedback is limited but impressed by this offbeat Shoreditch newcomer – a collaboration between Ryan Chetiyawardana and chef Doug McMaster of Brighton's acclaimed zero-waste restaurant Silo, and with a similarly eco-zealous

---

approach. A multi-course tasting menu is served from a tiny open kitchen in an "intimate" room with a counter and yellow leather banquette seating. The Sunday Times's Marina O'Loughlin left intellectually exhilarated but hungry: our reporters describe "one of the most innovative meals in a long time" – "thoughtful, sensitive, sometimes genius food served by passionate staff" and "a wonderful way to spend a couple of hours over a tasting menu". / N1 6PJ; closed Thu-Sat L, closed Mon-Wed & Sun; Online only.

THE CULPEPER
E1 £58 334

40 COMMERCIAL ST   020 7247 5371   13–2C

"Always buzzing" Spitalfields gastropub, with the rare option to eat (in summer) "in the rooftop garden where they grow veg and herbs". Cleverly converted from an old corner boozer three years ago, it inspired mixed feedback in its second year but scores have recovered their mojo of late, with some reports of "very good" cooking. / E1 6LP; www.theculpeper.com; @TheCulpeper; 10 pm, Sun 9 pm; SRA-Food Made Good – 0 stars.

CUMBERLAND ARMS
W14 £47 333

29 NORTH END RD   020 7371 6806   8–2D

"A pub which does a first-class risotto!" – this Olympia gastroboozer is "under same ownership as The Atlas in Earl's Court, and with a similarly delicious and quick Med-inspired menu". "If you have to go to the nearby Olympia exhibition halls, it's like Medécins sans Frontières provided a nearby life-line!" / W14 8SZ; www.thecumberlandarmspub.co.uk; @thecumberland; Mon-Wed 10 pm, Thu-Sat 11 pm.

CUT, 45 PARK LANE
W1 £124 322

45 PARK LN   020 7493 4545   3–4A

"Other patrons put on a glamorous show" at this "stylish and expensive" London outpost of Los Angeles-based celeb chef, Wolfgang Puck's Cut brand, in a Park Lane hotel. For its most ardent fans, it has "the best steak in London", but it has always had such kick-in-the-crotch prices that it has never attracted a significant following amongst reporters. / W1K 1PN; www.45parklane.com; @45ParkLaneUK; 10.30 pm; closed Sun L.

CUT + GRIND N1 £33 432

THE URBANEST BUILDING, 25-27 CANAL REACH   020 3668 7683   9–3C

"Outstanding burgers" ("very tasty and not too greasy") are "served with charm and no little panache" (alongside local ale from Shoreditch brewery Redchurch) at this new operation, at the foot of a King's Cross tower block (and which won the National Burger Awards 2018). Top Tip: the vegan burger here gets a shout out. / N1C 4DD; www.cutandgrindburgers.com; @cngburgers; Mon-Fri 10 pm, Sat & Sun 9 pm.

CUT THE MUSTARD
SW16 **£24** **3 3 3**

68 MOYSER RD 07725 034101 11–2D

"Top brunch, top coffee and top sourdough bread" all win praise for this little café down Streatham way. / SW16 6SQ; cutthemustardcafe.com; @WeCutTheMustard; 5.30 pm, Sun 4 pm; closed Mon-Sun D.

CYPRUS MANGAL
SW1 **£41** **3 3 2**

45 WARWICK WAY 020 7828 5940 2–4B

Consistently rated for some of the "best kebabs around", this popular Turkish grill is a good "cheap 'n' cheerful" option in Pimlico. / SW1V 1QS; www.cyprusmangal.co.uk; Sun-Thu midnight, Fri & Sat 1 am.

DA MARIO SW7 **£45** **3 3 3**

15 GLOUCESTER RD 020 7584 9078 6–1B

"For pizza lovers", this "very friendly local Italian" near the Royal Albert Hall is "brilliant for a family meal". "The food – nice, not spectacular – is just a small part of an excellent dining experience." / SW7 4PP; www.damario.co.uk; 11.30 pm.

DA MARIO WC2 **£55** **3 4 3**

63 ENDELL ST 020 7240 3632 5–1C

"Busy, fun and great value for money" – this "typical family-run Italian" (and there aren't many of them left in Covent Garden) serves "really good classics, not just pasta"; but "the real bonus is the friendly service and buzz – when so many customers seem to be regulars, you know they must be doing something right!". / WC2H 9AJ; www.da-mario.co.uk; 10.30 pm, Mon 11 pm, Sun 3 pm; closed Sun.

DADDY BAO
SW17 **£42** **4 3 3**

113 MITCHAM RD 020 3601 3232 11–2C

"A local gem of a Taiwanese kitchen specialising in bao" (steamed buns) – this cosy Tooting spin-off from Peckham's Mr Bao opened in January 2018, and if anything is more popular than the original. Attractions include a bottomless brunch: "loving their pancakes". / SW17 9PE; www.daddybao.com; 11 pm, Sun 10.30 pm.

THE DAIRY SW4 **£50** **4 4 4**

15 THE PAVEMENT 020 7622 4165 11–2D

Irish chef Robin Gill's "really excellent and clever (but not too clever!) food" has carved a major reputation for his "vibrant" small-plates venture by Clapham Common, where the "combination of culinary skill and boundary-pushing ideas make it really special". / SW4 0HY; www.the-dairy.co.uk; @thedairyclapham; 10 pm, Sun 3.30 pm; closed Sun D, closed Mon.

DALLOWAY TERRACE, BLOOMSBURY HOTEL
WC1 **£56** **3 2 4**

16-22 GREAT RUSSELL ST 020 7347 1221 2–1C

Breakfast and brunch get top billing at this marvellous al fresco eating space, whose gorgeous greenery and attractive design (complete with retractable roof) are all the more remarkable in the un-lovely area around Centre Point. Its general food service throughout the day inspires little feedback, but this would be a great spot for a drink, coffee or light bite. / WC1B 3NN; www.dallowayterrace.com; @DallowayTerrace; 10.30 pm.

LA DAME DE PIC LONDON
EC3 **£119** **4 3 2**

10 TRINITY SQUARE 020 7297 3799 10–3D

"Amazing food with amazing attention to detail", backed up by a formidable wine list, have made this "glossy" yearling, within the palatial ex-HQ of the Port of London Authority (by the Tower of London), a "superb addition to London's top-rank restaurants" and a feather-in-the-cap for the Pic family (from Valence, in SE France) who run it. As an imposing backdrop to a business meal it's particularly well-suited, but other diners are a bit unsure about the design: "it can seem a little disjointed with different styles and spaces, one part modern with white tiles, another Art Deco with black mirrors and banquettes – this doesn't spoil the experience but could have enhanced it further". / EC3N 4AJ; ladamedepiclondon.co.uk; @FSTenTrinity; closed Sun; No shorts.

DAPHNE'S SW3 **£80** **2 2 2**

112 DRAYCOTT AVE 020 7589 4257 6–2C

To a "smart Chelsea crowd" this delightful-looking stalwart is a "perennial favourite" (as it was for Princess Di when she was alive) with Italian cooking they say is "always good". It's pricey though, and the overall value equation for those without deep pockets is questionable. It inspires less and less feedback – perhaps Richard Caring's Caprice group have forgotten they own it? / SW3 3AE; www.daphnes-restaurant.co.uk; @DaphnesLondon/; 11 pm, Sun 10 pm.

DAQUISE SW7 **£49** **2 2 2**

20 THURLOE ST 020 7589 6117 6–2C

This "old-fashioned", "homely" institution has been knocking out "huge portions of solid Polish food" washed down with "potato vodka" in "ancient surroundings" near South Ken station for 70-odd years. "Like meeting a friend from the distant past and discovering there's still something special" – "I'm just glad it's still there!" / SW7 2LT; www.daquise.co.uk; @GesslerDaquise; 10.30 pm, Mon 11 pm, Sun 3 pm; no Amex.

DARJEELING EXPRESS
W1 **£52** **5 3 3**

6-8 KINGLY ST 020 7287 2828 4–2B

"On the top floor of Kingly Court and less frantic than the more happening places below" – "Asma Khan has a winner on her hands" at this "very genuine feeling" follow-up to her former pop-up ventures. From "a well chosen menu of distinctive dishes with an authentic 'home cooked' vibe", the resulting dishes are "full of spicy flavour without being greasy or heavy". "It's so authentic even Indians can't get enough of it!" / W1B 5PW; www.darjeeling-express.com; @Darjeelingldn; Sun-Thu 11 pm, Fri & Sat midnight.

THE DARTMOUTH CASTLE
W6 **£47** **3 4 3**

26 GLENTHORNE RD 020 8748 3614 8–2C

This "excellent local pub/restaurant" near Hammersmith Broadway stands with aplomb to everyone from "the giddy lunchtime rush of the nearby office population to the more genteel folk of the 'hood dining and wining in the evening". / W6 0LS; www.thedartmouthcastle.co.uk; @DartmouthCastle; Mon-Wed 10 pm, Thu-Sat 11 pm; closed Sat L.

DARWIN BRASSERIE
EC3 **£73** **2 3 4**

1 SKY GARDEN WALK 033 3772 0020 10–3D

"The view and experience of looking across London are second to none" when you visit this all-day operation at the top of the Walkie Talkie, where a wander amongst the Sky Garden's tropical foliage is a talking point before or after either a business meal or a date. Prices are a sore subject here, though, with critics advising: "forget the food and just take in the view". / EC3M 8AF; skygarden.london/darwin; @SG_Darwin; Sun-Thu 10 pm, Fri & Sat 10.30 pm.

DASTAAN KT19 **£43** **5 4 2**

447 KINGSTON RD 020 8786 8999 1–4A

"A real diamond-in-the-rough, setting wise – why they picked this location in a most unexpected part of Ewell isn't obvious, but when you eat here all is forgotten". "Terrific and authentic Indian flavours are created by two former top chefs from Gymkhana" and even if "the shabby chic could be improved" the interior is "lively (in a good way)" and "the superb quality of food more than compensates". "Simply put: just go there!" / KT19 0DB; dastaan.co.uk; @Dastaan447; 10.30 pm, Sun 9.30 pm; closed Tue-Fri L, closed Mon; booking weekdays only.

DAYLESFORD ORGANIC
£56 **3 2 2**

44B PIMLICO RD, SW1 020 7881 8060 6–2D | 6-8 BLANDFORD ST, W1 020 3696 6500 2–1A | 76-82 SLOANE AVENUE, SW3 AWAITING TEL 6–2C NEW | 208-212 WESTBOURNE GROVE, W11 020 7313 8050 7–1B

"Lovely for a breakfast or lunch snack, and with good bread etc to buy to take home" – Lady

Bamford's faux-rustic organic cafés can make a good choice for a posh brunch, despite toppish prices and historically variable service. In October 2018, the brand arrives in its spiritual London home, with a large new 'Farmshop and Café' near chichi Brompton Cross. / www.daylesford.com; SW1 & W11 9.30 pm, Mon 7 pm, Sun 4 pm; W1 9 pm, Sun 6.15 pm; W11 no booking L.

DEAN STREET TOWNHOUSE W1 £69 2 3 5

69-71 DEAN ST 020 7434 1775 4–1D

"Soak up the superb atmosphere and enjoy!" – with a terrace in summer, and "wonderfully welcoming interior on a cold winter day, with warm fire and subdued lighting" – this slick operation (attached to a Soho House group hotel) makes a fantastic Soho rendezvous, for business or pleasure. The brasserie cooking has historically been a bit forgettable here, but it won consistent praise this year for its "honest" results. Top Tip: "Refreshing and dangerously delicious Bloody Marys" means there's "no better way to start a weekend than with brunch here". / W1D 3SE; www.deanstreettownhouse.com; @deanstreethouse; Mon-Thu midnight, Fri & Sat 1 am, Sun 11 pm.

DEFUNE W1 £84 3 2 1

34 GEORGE ST 020 7935 8311 3–1A

There are many constants in feedback over the years on this veteran Japanese in Marylebone – its small fan club swears that it serves "unquestionably the best sushi in London"; it has "no ambience"; and it's "very, very expensive". / W1U 7DP; www.defune.com; 11 pm, Sun 10.30 pm.

Department of Coffee EC1

DEHESA W1 £55 3 2 3

25 GANTON ST 020 7494 4170 4–2B

Part of the Salt Yard Group – this "lovely little dining room" off Carnaby Street has won a reputation for its "excellent quality" Spanish and Italian tapas. All reports here remain upbeat, but – while the most enthusiastic feels the cooking "never fails to impress" – since the departure of Ben Tish, the chain's chef-director, ratings have slipped and the most sceptical regulars feel the "food has fallen from delicious to mediocre". / W1F 9BP; www.saltyardgroup.co.uk/dehesa; @SaltYardGroup; 10.45 pm, Sun 9.45 pm.

DELAMINA £41 4 4 2

**56-58 MARYLEBONE LANE, W1
020 3026 6810 3–1A | 151 COMMERCIAL ST, E1 020 7078 0770 13–2B**

"Fresh Middle Eastern flavours with lots of good spice" are found on the "fairly short but tempting menu (with lots of vegetable options, but fish and meat too)" at this Marylebone venue – "a fantastic new opening" that inspires rave reviews. Its second venture from Amir and Limor Chen who run Shoreditch's Strut & Cluck – now re-branded 'Delamina East', and likewise praised (if only slightly less effusively) for its "consistently excellent and healthy" Levantine dishes. /

THE DELAUNAY WC2 £59 2 4 4

55 ALDWYCH 020 7499 8558 2–2D

"Like The Wolseley, minus the poseurs and food-tourists" – Corbin & King's "very professionally run" outpost on Aldwych is "not as hectic as its sibling" and boasts "uncramped surroundings" and "classy" comfy decor that make it particularly "perfect for business", be it at breakfast ("feels like you're being really spoilt"), lunch or dinner. It's a natural for "sophisticated pre-theatre meals" too. The "ersatz Mittel-european dishes" (schnitzel, for instance) are "satisfying" to fans, but even some supporters concede "the menu can be a little pedestrian", and a borderline-concerning number of visits were really "not very inspiring" food-wise this year. Top Tip: "marvellous Viennese afternoon tea at £19.75, with all the silverware and trimmings". / WC2B 4BB; www.thedelaunay.com; @TheDelaunayRest; midnight, Sun 11 pm; closed Sat & Sun L.

DELFINO W1 £57 3 3 2

121A MOUNT ST 020 7499 1256 3–3B

"The BEST secret in Mayfair", this "bustling and buzzing traditional Italian with the most amazing pizzas" is just a few steps from the Connaught. "The oven-fired pizza is thin, crispy and excellent". / W1K 3NW; www.finos.co.uk; 10 pm; closed Sun.

DELHI GRILL N1 £32 3 3 2

21 CHAPEL MKT 020 7278 8100 9–3D

"You can eat like a king for under £20 and every sauce is slow-cooked, all to family recipes" at this "astonishingly cheap" 'dhaba' (roadside canteen) in Islington's Chapel Market. "In a world of posh Indians, DG cuts through them all!". / N1 9EZ; www.delhigrill.com; @delhigrill; Sun-Thu 10.30 pm, Fri & Sat 11 pm; closed Sun L; cash only.

DELICATESSEN NW3 £64 3 2 2

46 ROSSLYN HILL 020 7700 5511 9–2A

"The best kosher newcomer in years" is not quite the resounding endorsement it might be given the dire state of London's kosher offerings, but this "shabby chic" Hampstead yearling is (mostly) credited to be "an excellent arrival" with "well-prepared and delicious", "kosher-fusion" dishes ("Middle Eastern inspired but including North African and central and eastern European influences"). Service can occasionally hit the wrong note here. / NW3 1NH; delicatessen.company; Sun-Thu, Sat 11 pm; closed Sat L, closed Fri.

LA DELIZIA LIMBARA SW3 £44 3 2 2

63-65 CHELSEA MANOR ST 020 7376 4111 6–3C

This "great little Italian pizza place" in a side street off the King's Road is a "best-in-class for a cheap and cheerful bite". There's a "limited menu, but what it does it does well"… and has done for yonks. / SW3 5RZ; www.ladelizia.org.uk; @ladelizia; 10 pm, Sun 3.30 pm; no Amex.

DEPARTMENT OF COFFEE EC1 £10 3 4 3

14-16 LEATHER LN 020 7419 6906 10–2A

"Leave your laptop at home and just enjoy the coffee" – "the best in town", according to many fans – at the Leather Lane original of this coffee bar group. "Good cakes, too." / EC1N 7SU; departmentofcoffee.com; @DeptOfCoffee; closed Mon-Fri D, closed Sat & Sun; no booking.

DIN TAI FUNG WC2

5-6 HENRIETTA ST AWAITING TEL 5–3D

Since launching in Taipei in 1972 – selling dumplings as a sideline from a cooking oil store that was struggling to make ends meet – this soup dumpling and noodle brand has gone global. Its first foray into the UK market was due to open at the revamped Centre Point development in Summer 2018 but will now open in 2019, preceded by this 'second' outpost in Covent Garden late in 2018; exact opening dates still TBA. / WC2E 8PT; 11 pm.

THE DINING ROOM, THE GORING HOTEL SW1 £97 3 5 4

15 BEESTON PL 020 7396 9000 2–4B

For a "quintessential English experience" in London, it's hard to beat this "wonderful family-owned and managed hotel in the heart of Victoria and its marvellous dining room". "Perfect, courteous and caring service" is at the heart of a formula which feels like "a trip back to yesteryear" and which is "class personified". As such, though not at all corporate, it's "a first-rate way to wow potential clients (especially Americans!)", backed up by luxurious traditional cuisine that's "old school and all the better for it". There's also a "fascinating wine list, with many entries chosen personally by Mr Goring on his travels". This is also the location for "the most civilised breakfast in London", and there's a "marvellous, sumptuous afternoon tea served in the opulent lounge at the Goring: enveloping cosy chairs, fine china, an extensive selection of teas, sandwiches, scones and the prettiest of cakes, plus Champagne options. A total treat best saved for special days". / SW1W 0JW; www.thegoring.com; @TheGoring; 10 pm, Sun

2.30 pm; closed Sun D; No jeans; booking max 8 may apply.

DININGS £69 532

22 HARCOURT ST, W1   020 7723 0666
9–4A | WALTON HOUSE, WALTON ST, SW3
020 7723 0666   6–2C

"Sublime fish" employed in "lots of new-style sushi" helps win nothing but adulation for Tomonari Chiba's operation, now split between two sites – both of which deliver "exquisite" Japanese cuisine. The Marylebone original suffers from being a "cramped basement", but the new Knightsbridge site makes a "great addition", with "better decor and a larger kitchen, resulting in a wider menu and a better dining experience". / dinings.co.uk.

DINNER, MANDARIN ORIENTAL SW1 £125 222

66 KNIGHTSBRIDGE   020 7201 3833   6–1D

"Heston Blumenthal would do well to pay attention and create some new ideas" at this Knightsbridge dining room, where ratings this year are continuing on their remorseless march south (and whose ongoing inclusion in William Reed's World's 50 Best awards seems to represent the worst kind of spineless kowtowing to celebrity). Undoubtedly, there are many loyalists, who "love the menu that's full of history" (being researched from medieval recipe books), and who feel Ashley Palmer-Watts and his team deliver "entertaining", "alternative" cuisine that's "so impressive". There are too many reporters however, for whom it's becoming an "overpriced nightmare" – charming "extortionate prices" for "mediocre" or even "dreadful" fare. Despite its park views, reporters are also increasingly "not sure about the dining room" either: "all dark wood and posh design looking into the kitchen, it lacks intimacy" and can seem totally "atmosphere-free". STOP PRESS – after the fire at the hotel in June 2018, the restaurant remains closed, with "partial re-opening" in late 2018 a possibility. / SW1X 7LA; www.dinnerbyheston.com; Mon-Fri 10.15 pm, Sat & Sun 10.30 pm.

DIP & FLIP £34 333

87 BATTERSEA RISE, SW11 NO TEL 11–2C |
115 TOOTING HIGH ST, SW17 NO TEL 11–2C
| 62 THE BROADWAY, SW19 NO TEL 11–2B
| 64-68 ATLANTIC RD, SW9 NO TEL 11–2C

"Delicious beef patties served with a bowl of proper gravy to dip them in – perfect!" say aficionados of this unusual twist on the burger bar, with outlets in Battersea, Brixton, Tooting and Wimbledon. "The gravy thing feels so wrong but so right at the same time – sweet potato fries on the side partially assuage that guilt." No booking, but "they'll text you when your table is ready so you can have a drink in a local bar while you wait." / 10 pm, Thu-Sat 11 pm; SW9 & SW17 booking: 8 min.

DIP IN BRILLIANT SW6 £46 333

448 FULHAM RD   020 3771 9443   6–4A

Near Stamford Bridge, this Spring 2018 newcomer is the inspiration of Dipna Anand – daughter of the founder of Southall's famous canteen Brilliant – and this new café on the site of Kishmish (RIP) offers a fast-casual concept (diners can 'dip in and out' in 30 minutes) featuring Punjabi sharing platters, thalis and tandoori dishes. Good if you're on the way to the footie, but not a substitute for a pilgrimage to the original. / SW6 1DL; www.dipinbrilliant.com; @dipnaanand; Mon-Thu 10 pm, Fri 10.30 pm, Sat 11 pm; closed Mon-Sat L, closed Sun.

DIRTY BURGER £34 222

86 THE BROADWAY, SW19   020 3859 1122
11–2B NEW | ARCH 54, 6 SOUTH LAMBETH
RD, SW8   020 7074 1444   2–4D | 13
BETHNAL GREEN RD, E1   020 7749 4525
13–1B

This hip small chain has established a solid following with its "fun" grill shacks serving "quality" burgers and "generous desserts". "Always good for families, with something for everyone", including "excellent chicken and sides". / www.eatdirtyburger.com; 10 pm-midnight, Fri & Sat 11pm-2 am, Sun 8 pm-11 pm; no bookings.

DISHOOM £44 345

22 KINGLY ST, W1   020 7420 9322   4–2B
| 12 UPPER ST MARTINS LN, WC2
020 7420 9320   5–3B | THE BARKERS
BUILDING, DERRY ST, W8   020 7420 9325
6–1A | STABLE ST, GRANARY SQ, N1
020 7420 9321   9–3C | 7 BOUNDARY ST,
E2   020 7420 9324   13–1B

"No wonder people queue out the door!" – "it feels like you are actually in Mumbai, even the smells wafting round the room", at these "terrific" and "incredibly busy" outlets, whose "distinctive" interiors generate a "vibrant atmosphere" that's reasonably faithful to the buzz in India's Irani cafés. "The bar areas with good cocktails help make the long and boring wait bearable" and, once seated, servers "are full of fun and energy" (admittedly probably with one eye on "efficiently maximising table turnover"). For most customers, any hassle is "worth it for the absolutely yum-tastic Indian street food" – special shout outs go to the "the reinvention of the bacon butty (naan with crispy cured Ginger Pig bacon) which is the perfect breakfast"; and "the black daal and Ruby Murray, which are standout dishes". But declining ratings do support the doubters who feel that "quality has declined following the brand's extraordinary rise in popularity", or that "while it's good enough, the chain definitely doesn't excite like it once did". Even most critics would acknowledge that "the glow hasn't worn off Dishoom yet", however, and if you haven't been already, you should go: it can still provide "a real revelation". / www.dishoom.com; @Dishoom; 11pm, Thu-Sat midnight; breakfast 8, Sat & Sun 9; booking: min 6 at D.

DIWANA BHEL-POORI HOUSE NW1 £28 321

121-123 DRUMMOND ST   020 7387 5556
9–4C

"Still around after nearly 50 years", this "battered-looking" south Indian veggie canteen in the 'Little India' stretch behind Euston station is "still dishing out some of the best dosas, thalis and vegetarian snacks in London" – and still at a "low, low price". Top Tip: BYO. / NW1 2HL; www.diwanabph.com; @DiwanaBhelPoori; 11.30 pm, Sun 10 pm; no Amex; may need 10+ to book.

DOKKE E1 £42 343

IVORY HOUSE, 50 ST KATHARINE'S WAY
020 7481 3954   10–3D

Feedback is limited but enthusiastic when it comes to this "small" café overlooking the water of St Katharine Docks, where healthy options and brunch are two strengths: "dishes are presented with beautiful artistry and served by friendly and helpful staff, who are up for a chat but don't intrude". / E1W 1LA; www.dokke.co.uk; @dokkelondon; Mon-Thu 11 pm, Fri & Sat midnight; booking max 10 may apply.

DOMINIQUE ANSEL BAKERY LONDON SW1 £17 322

17-21 ELIZABETH ST   020 7324 7705   2–4B

Doubts crept in this year regarding the Belgravia outpost of NYC's trendiest of bakeries. For its cronut-crazed fans, its deluxe delicacies are still the biz, but for sceptics, the performance here is "nice but not amazing", or even "losing momentum: after several visits (and numerous trips in NYC), I'm not rushing back – overrated and, I must say, overpriced". / SW1W 9RP; www.dominiqueansellondon.com; @DominiqueAnsel; 10 pm; no booking.

THE DON EC4 £63 332

THE COURTYARD, 20 ST SWITHIN'S LANE
020 7626 2606   10–3C

As "a solid choice for business entertaining", this "classy and popular" venue (which feels "slightly off-the-beaten-track", even though it's right by the Bank of England) remains one of the City's prime choices thanks to its "reliable, well-cooked French cuisine" and "huge wine list". / EC4N 8AD; www.thedonrestaurant.com; @thedonlondon; 10 pm; closed Sat & Sun; No shorts.

THE DON BISTRO AND BAR EC4 £65 344

21 ST SWITHIN'S LN   020 7626 2606   10–3C

A good City "secret" – cellars that once housed the Sandeman wine and sherry importers have been converted into a "wonderful tucked-away location" – perfect for a business meal with no mobile signal. There's a "good wine list" and it's "very buzzy at lunchtime (quiet some evenings)". "Good value" for the Square Mile, too. / EC4N 8AD; www.thedonrestaurant.com/bistro; @TheDonLondon; 10 pm; closed Sat & Sun.

DONOSTIA W1   £56   4 4 4

10 SEYMOUR PL   020 3620 1845   2–2A

"Perfect, high-quality Spanish food", "well presented by personal and engaging staff" win only the highest praise for this little but "really lively" and "fun" pintxos and tapas bar near Marble Arch (which, as well as a counter by the open kitchen, also has a couple of tables at the back). "Possibly a bit noisy" is the closest any reporter comes to a criticism. Sibling to nearby Lurra, it is named after the Basque for San Sebastian, the region's culinary mecca. / W1H 7ND; www.donostia.co.uk; @DonostiaW1; 10 pm, Sun 9 pm; closed Mon L; booking max 8 may apply.

DORCHESTER GRILL, DORCHESTER HOTEL W1   £110   3 4 4

53 PARK LANE   020 7629 8888   3–3A

Culinary mastermind Alain Ducasse is behind something of a renaissance at this "very elegant dining room" in Mayfair, which had lost its way quite badly a few years ago. With its luxurious decor and "wonderful" modern French cuisine it can be "unbeatable for a special occasion". Hardly surprisingly, it is "not cheap", but this is one of London's grander dining rooms and deserves to be more discovered again. / W1K 1QA; www.thedorchester.com; @TheDorchester; 10.30 pm, Sun 9 pm; No trainers.

DOTORI N4   £34   4 3 2

3A STROUD GREEN RD   020 7263 3562   9–1D

"Unexpectedly good" Korean and Japanese food, including "wonderful sushi", justifies submitting to the "confined" seating and inevitable wait for a table at this no-bookings outfit near Finsbury Park station. "It might be small, crowded and bustling – but that's exactly how food from the Orient should be served!". / N4 2DQ; www.dotorirestaurant.wix.com/dotorirestaurant; 10.30 pm, Sun 10 pm; closed Tue-Thu, Sun L, closed Mon; no Amex; no booking.

THE DOVE W6   £51   3 3 5

19 UPPER MALL   020 8748 5405   8–2B

History is in the air at this riverside pub, down a cute Hammersmith alley, and with fine views from the small Thames-side terrace. Feedback is enthusiastic about its "fantastic" pub scoff, but the marvellous characterful interior is the big deal here. / W6 9TA; www.fullers.co.uk; @thedovew6; Mon-Thu 11 pm, Fri & Sat midnight, Sun 10.30 pm; closed Sun D.

DOZO   £46   3 2 2

32 OLD COMPTON ST, W1   020 7434 3219   5–2A | **68 OLD BROMPTON RD, SW7**   020 7225 0505   6–2B **NEW**

"Informal Japanese" which offers "rare good value" in pricey South Kensington, near the former Christie's showroom (there's also a similar heart-of-Soho branch which inspires little feedback). Eating at "sunk-in tables" adds to the ambience. /

DRAGON CASTLE SE17   £48   3 3 3

100 WALWORTH RD   020 7277 3388   1–3C

"Hong Kong comes to the Elephant & Castle" at this "huge and bustling dim sum paradise". It's "very reliable", and "the new regional dishes are interesting and well executed". Top Tip: "don't miss the prawn & sugarcane lollipops or the turnip cake". / SE17 1JL; www.dragoncastlelondon.com; @Dragoncastle100; 10.30 pm.

DRAKES TABANCO W1   £55   2 2 4

3 WINDMILL ST   020 7637 9388   2–1C

Inspired by the sherry taverns of Andalucia, this "warm and accommodating" Fitzrovia tapas bar has "lots of interesting sherries and Spanish wines" and food of "some authenticity". / W1T 2HY; www.drakestabanco.com; @drakestabanco; Mon-Thu 11 pm, Fri & Sat midnight, Sun 10.30 pm; booking max 7 may apply.

THE DRAPERS ARMS N1   £53   3 3 4

44 BARNSBURY ST   020 7619 0348   9–3D

"Ticking the boxes for an excellent neighbourhood local" – this mega-popular Islington gastropub has a "lovely building and location", provides "solid and interesting food at quite sensible prices" and "drinkers are just as welcome as those wanting food" (with "a very good wine list if you're not into pints"). / N1 1ER; www.thedrapersarms.com; @DrapersArms; Mon & Tue, Sun 10 pm, Wed-Sat 11 pm; no Amex.

THE DROP N1

COAL DROPS YARD AWAITING TEL 9–3C

A new wine bar (with outside terrace) from the Hart Bros arrives in October 2018 at canalside retail development Coal Drops Yard (a converted Victorian coal store near King's Cross). / N1C 4AB.

THE DRUNKEN BUTLER EC1   £58   4 3 3

20 ROSEBERY AVENUE   020 7101 4020   10–1A

French cuisine with Persian influences? That's the deal at this Clerkenwell newcomer with open kitchen, the first solo effort from chef Yuma Hashemi (previously of The Chancery), serving morning coffee, and tasting menus of small plates by day and night. Standard critic Fay Maschler delivered a less-than-kind verdict, but our initial feedback is more upbeat: "a real asset to the culinary landscape with imaginative cooking beautifully presented in informal surroundings and a wine list and short cocktail list to match". / EC1R 4SX; www.thedrunkenbutler.com; @SYumaHashemi; Wed-Sat 10 pm; Online only.

THE DUCK & RICE W1   £55   3 2 4

90 BERWICK ST   020 3327 7888   4–2C

Chinese-meets-gastropub is the formula under test at this three-year-old venture on Soho's atmospheric Berwick Street Market – the brainchild of serial restaurant creator Alan Yau. The "delightful dishes" and "lovely" contemporary design do go down well with most reporters, but there's little sign just yet that he has another tearaway hit like Wagamama on his hands. / W1F 0QB; www.theduckandrice.com; @theduckandrice; Mon-Thu 11 pm, Fri & Sat 11.30 pm, Sun 10 pm.

DUCK & WAFFLE LOCAL SW1   £50   3 3 3

NO 2, ST. JAMES'S MARKET, 52 HAYMARKET   020 3900 4444   4–4D

New spin-off from the City venue, in the new St James's Market development, with its trademark duck-based menu; feedback echoes its sibling – some good, some bad, but no criticisms are grievous and breakfast is similarly recommended. / SW1Y 4RP; duckandwafflelocal.com; @duckwafflelocal; 1 am.

DUCK & WAFFLE EC2   £75   2 2 5

110 BISHOPSGATE, HERON TOWER   020 3640 7310   10–2D

"The lift up is a little scary" (in a good way), but the payoff is the "breathtaking view" from this "trendy-but-tasteful" venue on the 40th floor of the Heron Tower (adjacent to Sushisamba): a natural choice both for a business or romantic occasion. Most – but not all – reporters feel its slightly wacky menu (the restaurant being named for its signature dish) is "well conceived" and – aided by the fact that it's open 24/7 – the place is particularly popular for its "sophisticated and interesting breakfast dishes". / EC2N 4AY; www.duckandwaffle.com; @DuckandWaffle; open 24 hours.

DUCK DUCK GOOSE SW9   £41   4 4 3

49 BRIXTON STATION RD NO TEL 11–1D

"Amazing to see perfectly cooked Peking ducks and crispy pork belly coming out of a tiny shipping container!" – this "modern Chinese canteen" occupies one of the units at Pop Brixton, and the results are "super tasty!" / SW9 8PQ; www.duckduckgooselondon.com; 10 pm; Fri & Sat 11 pm; closed Sun & Mon.

THE DUCK TRUCK E1   £11   5 3 3

LAMB ST 07919 160271 13–2C

"The best street food ever" say fans of the "fab, fun, fast and delicious" dishes at this truck, permanently parked alongside Spitalfields Market. Amongst the numerous options: confit duck leg, pulled duck or duck steaks in a brioche bun, and wraps. / E1 6EA; www.theducktruck.com; @TheDuckTruck1; Mon & Tue, Sat & Sun 5 pm, Thu & Fri 6 pm, Wed 4 pm; closed Mon-Sun D.

DUCKSOUP W1 £61 **4**44

41 DEAN ST   020 7287 4599   5–2A

A "go-to spot in Soho" serving natural and biodynamic wines by the bottle or glass alongside a hybrid menu of "delectable" Italian-North African dishes "that let the high-quality ingredients sing for themselves". "Super-lively on a busy night" while also "laid back and relaxed", it's a "great place to hang out by yourself or go on a date". Top Tip: "the drinking vinegars [true] are delicious and must be tried". / W1D 4PY; www.ducksoupsoho.co.uk; @ducksoup; 10.30 pm, Sun 5 pm; closed Sun D; may need 3+ to book.

DUDDELL'S SE1 £83 **4**2**4**

6 ST THOMAS ST   020 3957 9932   10–4C

"Best Peking duck ever, other than top restaurants in Beijing!"… "and unbelievably the dim sum was even better!!" – this "great reinvention of the Michelin-starred Hong Kong favourite" occupies an "amazingly converted church" (St Thomas's in London Bridge), and even though its most ardent fans admit that it's "pricey" the "cost isn't insane, and for once the hype is right". Service, though, is "a bit chaotic at times". / SE1 9RY; www.duddells.co/london; @DuddellsLondon; 11 pm, Sun 10.30 pm.

THE DUKE OF RICHMOND E8 £49

316 QUEENSBRIDGE RD   020 7923 3990 14–1A

Chef and restaurateur, Tom Oldroyd, follows up his diminutive debut, Oldroyd in N1, with this much larger venue near London Fields, which opened in June 2018 – a pub and dining room offering a French twist on seasonal British produce; ex-Canton Arms and Winemakers Deptford chef Rory Shannon is in charge of the open fire cooking in the semi-open kitchen. Early press reviews are a tad mixed, but overall positive. / E8 3NH; www.thedukeofrichmond.com; @dukeofrichmond_; Mon-Fri 11 pm, Sat midnight, Sun 10.30 pm; closed Mon-Fri L.

DUKE OF SUSSEX W4 £52 **2**23

75 SOUTH PDE   020 8742 8801   8–1A

This handsome Victorian tavern by Acton Green Common serves "good Anglo-Spanish food in comfortable surroundings at a reasonable price". Perhaps, though, the "menu is too long" – it "looked promising, but only some of the dishes lived up to the billing". / W4 5LF; www.metropolitanpubcompany.com; @thedukew4; 10 pm, Sun 9 pm.

DUM BIRYANI W1 £53 **3**22

187 WARDOUR ST   020 3638 0974   3–1D

"It's easy to miss this Soho basement" just south of Oxford Street, housing a "really authentic" yearling Indian biryani specialist. Cooked in a heavy pot – the 'dum' – "they are available in two sizes, single or sharing, and are topped with a crisp edible topping". "The simple fit-out of the interior could be improved", though. / W1F

8ZB; dumlondon.com; Sun-Wed 10 pm, Thu-Sat 10.30 pm; may need 5+ to book.

DYNAMO £44 **3**23

200-204 PUTNEY BRIDGE RD, SW15 020 3761 2952   11–2B | 16-18 RITHERDON RD, SW17   020 8767 3197   11–2C NEW

"The best coffee stop on the way home from laps of Richmond Park!" – you don't have to arrive on two wheels to appreciate the "amazing brunch and even better pizzas" at this Putney cycle-themed café, which has recently branched out into Balham too. / www.the-dynamo.co.uk; @WeAreTheDynamo.

THE DYSART PETERSHAM TW10 £75 **3**33

135 PETERSHAM RD   020 8940 8005   1–4A

"The food is delicious, inventive and carefully sourced" at this upscale Arts & Crafts pub near Richmond Park, where "dining is so romantic with the fairy lights glittering through the leaded windows, log fire and flagstone floors". Irish chef Kenneth Culhane's cooking is "Asian-influenced and nuanced – it's not flashy, but there's a lot of thought in it". / TW10 7AA; www.thedysartarms.co.uk; @dysartpetersham; Wed-Fri 11.30 pm, Sat midnight, Sun 3.30 pm; closed Sun D, closed Mon & Tue.

E MONO NW5 £11 **4**22

285-287 KENTISH TOWN RD   020 7485 9779 9–2B

"Top kebabs" at "bargain" prices win acclaim for this small Turkish café/takeaway in Kentish Town, named for signage uncovered during its renovation (and originally brought to attention by Giles Coren over five years ago). / NW5 2JS; emono.co.uk.

E&O W11 £55 **3**4**4**

14 BLENHEIM CR   020 7229 5454   7–1A

"Still a great fusion restaurant", Will Ricker's pan-Asian tapas and cocktail hang-out in Notting Hill is "buzzing", if no longer thronged with the celebs of yesteryear. "Dependably good food, happy service, silly prices, and always very silly Notting Hill hipsters vogue-ing at the bar!" / W11 1NN; www.rickerrestaurants.com; 11 pm, Sun 10.30 pm; booking max 6 may apply.

THE EAGLE EC1 £38 **3**3**4**

159 FARRINGDON RD   020 7837 1353 10–1A

"The formula has not changed over the years" at the stripped-back pub, near Exmouth Market, that's often hailed as London's first modern-day gastropub. According to its large fan club, it's still "the original and the best", thanks to Mediterranean-inspired cooking from the blackboard that's (almost) as "tasty" as ever; and a "crowded and noisy" setting that's enjoyably rough 'n' ready. / EC1R 3AL; www.theeaglefarringdon.co.uk; @eaglefarringdon; 11 pm, Sun 5 pm; closed Sun D; no Amex; no booking.

EARL SPENCER SW18 £55 **3**2**3**

260-262 MERTON RD   020 8870 9244   11–2B

A "superb and friendly gastropub", this "large" Edwardian roadhouse in Southfields rates consistently for its "great beer" and "an ever-changing, better-than-average menu". / SW18 5JL; www.theearlspencer.com; @TheEarlSpencer; Mon & Tue, Sun 10 pm, Wed-Sat 11 pm; Mon-Thu D only, Fri-Sun open L & D.

EAT 17 £55 **3**4**3**

UNIT A 77 FULHAM PALACE RD, W6 020 8521 5279   8–2C NEW | 28-30 ORFORD RD, E17   020 8521 5279   1–1D | 64-66 BROOKSBYS WALK, E9   020 8986 6242 14–1C

The "excellent burgers and pub-type grub" at these 'Spar-supermarkets-with-kitchen-attached' in Walthamstow Village and Hackney (and also Bishop's Stortford) make them favourite local hang outs as well as "super places to go for a meal with the kids" (even if non-parents can sometimes find it "family overfriendly!"). Top Tip: the "renowned chicken burger" (and their famous bacon jam, which can be bought by the jar). In late summer 2018 a new branch opened on the opposite side of town, south of Hammersmith Broadway. / www.eat17.co.uk; @eat_17; E17 10 pm, Sun 9 pm, E9 9 pm, Fri & Sat 9.30 pm, Sun 8 pm.

EAT TOKYO £31 **3**3**2**

16 OLD COMPTON ST, W1   020 7439 9887 5–2A | 50 RED LION ST, WC1 020 7242 3490   2–1D | 27 CATHERINE ST, WC2   020 3489 1700   5–3D | 169 KING ST, W6   020 8741 7916   8–2B | 18 HILLGATE ST, W8   020 7792 9313   7–2B | 14 NORTH END RD, NW11   020 8209 0079   1–1B | 628 FINCHLEY RD, NW11   020 3609 8886   1–1B

"A go-to place for an affordable and tasty Japanese 'hit'" – this superbly consistent, "authentic" (slightly "dingy" looking) chain is "always full of Japanese diners so you know you're onto a good thing". "Prices are not the cheapest-of-the-cheap, but great value for the quality of Japanese food served" including the "real sushi, which bears no resemblance to the factory-produced, over-cooled and formulaic conveyor-belt muck you get elsewhere". "Daily specials and a wide range of lunch Bento boxes mean they're always bustling." / www.eattokyo.co.uk; Mon-Sat 11.30 pm, Sun 10.30 pm.

ECCLESTON PLACE BY TART LONDON SW1 £66

3-4 ECCLESTON YARD   020 7627 2176 2–4B

Jemima Jones and Lucy Carr-Ellison – the duo behind Tart London (the catering company favoured by London's top fashion brands) – are set to open in a very cool site in a new development near Victoria – an old Victorian space featuring the original arched roof and skylights. / SW1W 9AZ; www.eccleston-place.com; @tart_london; Tue-Sat, Mon 10.30 pm, Sun 3.30 pm.

ECO SW4 £38 323

162 CLAPHAM HIGH ST   020 7978 1108 11–2D

Sami Wasif, who helped create the Franco Manca chain, has run this "buzzy" Clapham hangout for over 20 years: "it's nothing hip or über-trendy, just serves really great pizza" (occasionally chaotically). / SW4 7UG; www.ecorestaurants.com; @ecopizzaLDN; Mon-Thu 11 pm, Fri & Sat 11.30 pm, Sun 10.30 pm.

EDERA W11 £65 343

148 HOLLAND PARK AVE   020 7221 6090 7–2A

This unusually professional neighbourhood Italian in Holland Park, boasting "attentive service and well-spaced tables", specialises in Sardinian cuisine. "Expensive for a local", it is "perfect for a business lunch or dinner" – and they know how to look after loyal regulars: "we go about 50 times a year and they treat us as family – if there's a hiccup, they're good at putting it right". / W11 4UE; www.edera.co.uk; 11 pm, Sun 10 pm.

EDWINS SE1 £57 344

202-206 BOROUGH HIGH ST   020 7403 9913 10–4B

"What a good find – a cosy room over a pub beside Borough tube station", "brimming with atmosphere and goodwill". The modern bistro food is up to scratch, too, whether an "excellent weekend breakfast" or a "lovely meal on a chilly night after Christmas". / SE1 1JX; www.edwinsborough.co.uk; @edwinsborough; 11 pm; closed Sun D.

EIGHT OVER EIGHT SW3 £56 334

392 KING'S RD   020 7349 9934   6–3B

"Always fun with a great vibe" – Will Ricker's clubby Chelsea haunt near the kink in the King's Road has a large and widespread fanclub thanks to its "always enjoyable" Asian fusion fare and yummy cocktails. / SW3 5UZ; www.rickerrestaurants.com/eight-over-eight; 11 pm, Sun 10.30 pm; closed Mon-Fri L.

ELECTRIC DINER W11 £49 223

191 PORTOBELLO RD   020 7908 9696   7–1B

In the side of one of London's oldest cinemas, this "noisy and cool brasserie" – "a great space", with comfortable US diner styling – is something of a Notting Hill classic nowadays; and as such is a prime spot for people-watching the trustafarian locals who tolerate its "sloppy service and average food". / W11 2ED; www.electricdiner.com; @ElectricDiner; 10.30 pm.

ELLA CANTA, INTERCONTINENTAL LONDON PARK LANE W1 £80 344

PARK LANE   020 7318 8715   3–4A

The Times's Giles Coren described it as "the worst restaurant he's ever reviewed", but reporters' feedback (if still a tad limited) is very much more upbeat on Martha Ortiz's London newcomer, which occupies the Intercontinental Park Lane's 'second' dining space (as made-over by David Collins Studio). Its most ardent fans say, "the heart and soul of the very best Mexico has to offer is brought to lucky London", and even those who find it "very expensive" say that "it's a fun experience, with great staff and interesting and unusual food". / W1J 7QY; www.ellacanta.com; @ellacantalondon; Mon-Thu 1 am, Fri & Sat 2 am, Sun 6 pm; closed Mon L.

ELLIOT'S CAFÉ SE1 £55 433

12 STONEY ST   020 7403 7436   10–4C

Brett Redman's "relaxed and bohemian" open-fronted venue offers "great people watching amongst the hubbub of Borough market" and is a "great place for a cheapish top-quality lunch of excellent tapas-style food" and a "wonderful list" of natural wines. / SE1 9AD; www.elliotscafe.com; @elliotscafe; 10 pm; closed Sun.

ELYSTAN STREET SW3 £107 332

43 ELYSTAN ST   020 7628 5005   6–2C

Phil Howard's "exciting", yet "unfussy" food ("at last, a top chef that has the confidence to cook a beautifully balanced meal and not hide behind another two-bite tasting menu") "pushes the boundaries, whilst feeling familiar; and always has fabulous vegetarian options that highlight the joys of the freshest in-season produce" ("roasted cabbage was my main dish of the year… and I'm no veggie!"). As a result, a massive fan club "LOVE, LOVE, LOVE" his Chelsea two-year-old, whose "restrained, light and spacious decor" and "professional" approach help set up a "thoroughly civilised and relaxed experience". But even those who consider the cuisine here "top class" can feel prices are "astronomical", and this "casual" space can also appear "canteen-like" and far too "noisy" for somewhere in this league. / SW3 3NT; www.elystanstreet.com; @elystanstreet; Mon-Thu 10 pm, Fri & Sat 10.30 pm, Sun 9.30 pm.

EMBER YARD W1 £54 334

60 BERWICK ST   020 7439 8057   3–1D

"Delicious tapas from the Salt Yard crew" – as the name suggests, this smart Soho outfit has a "focus on open-fire cooking", and ratings bounced back this year, with praise for small plates that are "often special and surprising". / W1F 8SU; www.emberyard.co.uk; @emberyard; 10 pm, Sun 9 pm; booking max 13 may apply.

EMILIA'S CRAFTED PASTA E1 £46 443

UNIT C3 IVORY HOUSE, ST KATHARINE DOCKS   020 7481 2004   10–3D

"Pasta is elevated to an art form" at this inexpensive yearling in St Katharine Docks, whose "romantic" potential on a sunny day is boosted by attractive dock-side tables. / E1W 1AT; www.emiliaspasta.com; @emiliaspasta; 11 pm, Sun 10 pm.

THE EMPRESS E9 £50 334

130 LAURISTON RD   020 8533 5123   14–2B

This landmark east London gastropub near Victoria Park is an "easy destination for a great night out or a weekend treat... always fun and welcoming". The menu "mixes conventional with more adventurous options". / E9 7LH; www.empresse9.co.uk; @elliottlidstone; 10 pm, Sun 9 pm; closed Mon L; no Amex.

ENEKO BASQUE KITCHEN & BAR WC2 £78 321

1 ALDWYCH   020 7300 0300   2–2D

Eneko Atxa's subterranean two-year-old, in the basement of No 1 Aldwych, is on numerous accounts, something of an "undiscovered gem" thanks to its "interesting Basque cooking", serving "imaginative" dishes that are "expertly cooked and presented". The main sticking point on this site, is the "below-the-streets space" which – when under-patronised – seems "echoey" and "like a bit of a mausoleum". / WC2B 4BZ; www.eneko.london; @OneAldwych; 11 pm, Sun 10 pm.

ENOTECA ROSSO W8 £69 222

276-280 KENSINGTON HIGH ST 07384 595191 8–1D

"Basically the interest is on the wine" at this Kensington newcomer, where a "well-priced" all-Italian list is showcased, stacked in triangular shelving, lining the walls. It inspires supportive but mixed feedback: "small plates are interesting and reasonably priced", but "there's a feeling of trying too hard, and not being sure what it wants to be"; still, they are "nice people". / W8 6ND; www.enotecarosso; Mon & Tue 9 pm, Fri & Sat 11.30 pm, Wed 10 pm, Thu 11 pm, Sun 5 pm.

ENOTECA TURI SW1 £78 353

87 PIMLICO RD   020 7730 3663   6–2D

"A good transplant now working seamlessly in its new home" – Giuseppi and Pamela Turi shifted after decades in Putney to a new Pimlico site a couple of years ago, and their new gig is continuing to prove "a superb addition to the SW1 scene". The "very traditional northern Italian food" is "consistently good", the setting is "simple but elegant" and the experience is "amplified by the long-standing family ownership" as the Turis are "super hosts". The big deal gastronomically speaking is the "HUGE" and "outstanding" Italian wine list "with an amazing selection of unusual and delicious vintages" – "worth a visit in its own right" and "made more interesting by the inclusion of Giuseppi's comments". / SW1W 8PH; www.enotecaturi.com; @EnotecaTuri; 11 pm; closed Sun; booking max 8 may apply.

THE ENTERPRISE
SW3   £54   2 3 4

35 WALTON ST   020 7584 3148   6–2C

"A pretty place with pretty customers" is a verdict few would contest on this "smart yet casual" Chelsea haunt – "a fun spot enjoyed by young and old" with a "great ambience and buzz". The food is "sound" with high prices reflecting the location" on gorgeous Walton Street. / SW3 2HU; www.theenterprise.co.uk; 11 pm, Sun 10.30 pm.

L'ESCARGOT W1   £76   3 4 5

48 GREEK ST   020 7439 7474   5–2A

"Thoroughly recommended, even after all these years!" – this "truly excellent" Gallic venue in the heart of Soho is marching towards its centennial in good form. A menu of "French classics, always to a high standard" is perfect "comfort food" and "combines with the lovely ambience" of the characterful dining room and "excellent service" to ensure it's "always an enjoyable experience". / W1D 4EF; www.lescargot.co.uk; @LEscargotSoho; 11.30 pm, Sun 6 pm; closed Sun D.

ESSENCE CUISINE
EC2   £36   4 3 2

94 LEONARD ST   020 7729 5678   13–1B

A fully plant-based menu (just about all of it vegan) is the draw at this sparse, health-conscious new Shoreditch venture which looks like (and is partly) a take-out, but which also has a limited amount of seating and a fuller dinner offering. The menu is 100% free of meat, dairy, gluten, and refined sugar and has been developed with US chef Matthew Kenney. Worth a go, especially if you're a raw food fan. / EC2A 4RH; www.essence-cuisine.com; @essence_cuisine; 9 pm, Mon 7 pm; closed Sun; Online only.

ESSENZA W11   £68   2 3 3

210 KENSINGTON PARK RD   020 7792 1066   7–1A

Mixed and limited feedback on this smart Notting Hill Italian. To fans it's a favourite with top class cooking (speciality black and white truffles) and a romantic interior – to the odd detractor it's not bad, merely "forgettable". / W11 1NR; www.essenza.co.uk; 11.30 pm.

EST INDIA SE1   £39   3 2 3

73-75 UNION STREET, FLAT IRON SQUARE   020 7407 2004   10–4B

"Terrific Indian food with a great range of spices, not just chilli" hits the spot at this modern outfit in a basement space of the Flat Iron Square development. / SE1 1SG; www.estindia.co.uk; @EstIndiaLondon; 11 pm, Sun 10.30 pm.

ESTIATORIO MILOS
SW1   £114   3 2 3

1 REGENT ST   020 7839 2080   4–4D

"A fabulous selection of fresh fish on display to choose from" is the dramatic hallmark of Costas Spiladis's "upscale Greek" in the West End (where you choose your fish and pay by weight). Its most ardent fans feel it "gives Scott's a run for its money", but even some who feel it has "the best fish, with the best fish chefs in town" still say it's "pricey": "bring your bank manager along with you, as they'll need to extend your overdraft after eating here!" / SW1Y 4NR; www.milos.ca/restaurants/london; @Milos_London; midnight.

EVELYNS TABLE AT THE BLUE POSTS W1   £74   4 4 4

28 RUPERT ST NO TEL   4–3D

"The guys behind The Palomar and The Barbary nailed it again", according to fans of this vibey, clandestine cellar below the characterful (Grade II listed, 275-year-old) Blue Posts pub in Chinatown, whose ground floor is now The Mulwray cocktail bar, and where here, down below, they serve funky, small plates (of Italian inspiration, with an emphasis on Cornish-sourced fish). It's even more cramped than its siblings though, with an 11-seat counter and a couple of tiny tables. / W1D 6DJ; thebluposts.co.uk; Mon-Fri 10 pm, Sat & Sun 9 pm.

EVEREST INN SE3   £41   3 2 3

41 MONTPELIER VALE   020 8852 7872   1–4D

"Great Gurkha curries" – and other Nepalese specialities (the best menu bets) – make this Blackheath curry house an "excellent local", notwithstanding that service can be "hit and miss". / SE3 0TJ; www.everestinnblackheath.co.uk; Mon-Thu 11 pm, Fri & Sat 11.30 pm, Sun 10.30 pm.

THE FALLOW DEER CAFE
TW11   £23   3 4 3

130 HIGH ST   020 8943 2578   1–4A

"A great place to bring the family on a Sunday" – this funky Teddington café is arguably the 'burb's top brunch spot. Also featured: Cocktail Fridays (the only regular evening openings, with tapas and sharing plates); and irregular evening supper clubs and events with more ambitious fare. / TW11 8JB; www.thefallowdeer.com; @FallowDeerCafe; Mon-Thu, Sat & Sun 5 pm, Fri 11 pm; closed Mon-Thu, Sat & Sun D.

LA FAMIGLIA
SW10   £63   2 2 2

7 LANGTON ST   020 7351 0761   6–3B

A datedly glamorous, "bustling" Chelsea trat' that celebrated its half centenary two years ago, and which has over the years welcomed into its delightful back garden the likes of Princess Margaret, Peter Sellers, Brigitte Bardot and Jack Nicholson. One or two diehard fans still think of it as "London's best Italian" and say "nothing changes" here; but ratings support those who feel it's "nowhere near as good as it once was years ago", "expensive" for what it is, and on its worst days, quite "poor". Top Tip: still a favourite option for Chelsea folk with kids in tow. / SW10 0JL; www.lafamiglia.co.uk; @lafamiglia_sw10; 10.30 pm, Sun 9.30 pm.

FANCY CRAB W1   £65   2 3 2

92 WIGMORE ST   020 3096 9484   3–1A

"Excellent crab" is the cornerstone offer at this year-old Marylebone concept, with a menu offering red king crab from the north Pacific in numerous guises, which is "indeed as good as lobster but larger and loads cheaper"; other items are "uneven" and "overpriced", while the venue "feels like a fast-food chain" or a "nightclub, with its noisy tables and music". / W1U 3RD; www.fancycrab.co.uk; @fancycrabuk.

FANNYS KEBABS
N16   £21

92 STOKE NEWINGTON HIGH ST   020 3302 5831   1–1C

From Claude Compton and James Morris – the duo behind Claude's Kitchen, Amuse Bouche and Tommy Tucker – this little, new, stripped-down kebab canteen on Stoke Newington High Street, opened in spring 2018 on the back of a storming crowdfunding campaign and sell-out pop-up at the Sun & 13 Cantons in Soho. No survey feedback as yet – on the short menu: 'babs (with wrap, rice or salad), bar snacks and sides. / N16 7NY; www.fannyskebabs.com; @fannyskebabs; Tue-Sat, Mon 10.30 pm, Sun 3.30 pm.

FARANG N5   £39   4 3 2

72 HIGHBURY PARK   020 7226 1609   9–1D

"Incredibly zingy Thai flavours" – "brilliant spicing and several ingredients that were new to me" – are establishing Seb Holmes's "reasonably priced" pop-up-gone-permanent (in the former premises of San Daniele, RIP) as a "foodie gem in Highbury". A few critics query "what's the fuss? The food's OK but the place is very cramped and nothing to get excited about overall". Much more numerous, though, are those who feel that "if it was located in central London it would have queues out the door every day". / N5 2XE; www.faranglondon.co.uk; @farangLDN; 10.30 pm; closed Tue-Fri L, closed Sun & Mon.

FARMACY W2   £56   2 3 4

74 WESTBOURNE GROVE   020 7221 0705   7–1B

"A fantastic vegan restaurant that your non vegan friends and kids will enjoy" is how fans proclaim Camilla Fayed's Californian-inspired Bayswater venture, which – though it does take some flak for the odd "taste-free" meal – particularly wins praise as a favoured brunch spot. / W2 5SH; www.farmacylondon.com; @farmacyuk; 10 pm, Sun 9.30 pm.

FAYRE SHARE E9 £47

**178-180 VICTORIA PARK RD 020 3960 7765
14–2C**

In Hackney's picturesque Victoria Park village, a new 'family-style' feasting joint where all menu items can be served for 1, 2 or 4 people – in particular it's "ideal for families especially where children don't eat full portions". / E9 7HD; www.fayreshare.co.uk; @FayreShare; 10 pm.

FENCHURCH RESTAURANT, SKY GARDEN EC3 £91 3 2 4

20 FENCHURCH ST 033 3772 0020 10–3D

Perched at the top of the City's 'Walkie-Talkie' tower, this 37th-floor venue has hot competition among London's recent spate of high-rise restaurant openings – but some fan feel "Iit has the best views of them all". The food is "very good", too – "delicious and well executed" – by Dan Fletcher, former head chef at The Square. "Shame it's so expensive", though. / EC3M 3BY; skygarden.london/fenchurch-restaurant; @SG_Fenchurch; 10.30 pm; booking max 7 may apply.

FERA AT CLARIDGE'S, CLARIDGE'S HOTEL W1 £122 4 4 4

49 BROOK ST 020 7107 8888 3–2B

"Seemingly doing just fine post-Simon Rogan" – this "beautiful" Art Deco chamber appears to have shrugged off the loss of the L'Enclume chef in April 2017, and although Matt Starling's ambitious cuisine is maybe a fraction less highly rated, most reports are of meals that are "perfect in every way" (even "if, like me, you were/are a Rogan fan, Fera should remain on your list!"). The "gracious and comfortable space" is "made to impress" (and "lends itself to romance or business"); "caring" service "puts you at your ease"; and where the cooking is concerned (experienced via the à la carte or the five-course and seven-course tasting menus) "you really feel the passion for the ingredients and, although stylish, there's no sacrifice of substance and flavour". Top Tip: "it can seem pricey unless set lunch is selected – £42 for an impeccably prepared three courses". / W1K 4HR; www.feraatclaridges.co.uk; @FeraAtClaridges; 10 pm.

FERDI W1 £78 1 1 2

30 SHEPHERD MARKET 07375 538309 3–4B

"Hope they can get their act together..." This year-old London outpost of a models-and-celebs hangout in Paris's 1er arrondissement (where Kim and Kanye are apparently regulars) has failed to inspire much gastronomic excitement for its international comfort food since landing in Mayfair's cute Shepherd Market. / W1J 7QN; www.ferdi-restaurant.com; @ferdi.london; midnight.

LA FERME £46 3 3 3

**154 REGENT'S PARK RD, NW1
020 7483 4492 9–3B NEW | 102-104
FARRINGDON RD, EC1 020 7837 5293
10–1A**

"Very French and lovely" – the new NW1 branch of this 'bistronomic-driven' duo of rustic-style outfits serves creative, modern Gallic cuisine; and there's solidly good ratings, too, for the cosy café/deli original, just around the corner from Exmouth Market. (Also to be seen with stalls selling French dishes and produce at numerous London food markets). /

FERNANDEZ & WELL £54 3 3 3

**43 LEXINGTON ST, W1 020 7734 1546
4–2C | 55 DUKE ST, W1 020 7042 2774
3–2A | 1-3 DENMARK ST, WC2
020 3302 9799 5–1A | SOMERSET HS,
STRAND, WC2 020 7420 9408 2–2D | 8
EXHIBITION RD, SW7 020 7589 7473 6–2C**

A small group of "appealing no-frills cafés with a rustic feel" in sought-after locations, including South Kensington and Somerset House. Already "stalwarts" on the London scene, they are "intimate" places providing "simple tapas with the best ingredients", plus "coffee or a glass of interesting wine"; and there's "no music, which aids conversation". / www.fernandezandwells.com; 11 pm, Sun 6 pm; St Anne's Court closed Sun.

FEZ MANGAL W11 £23 5 3 3

**104 LADBROKE GROVE 020 7229 3010
7–1A**

"Excellent Turkish food at cheap 'n' cheerful prices" used to guarantee queues at this "friendly" kebab house on Ladbroke Grove – "but now they've expanded you can always get a table". Top Tip: "BYO – they have no licence and don't charge corkage, so take a decent bottle of red, spend £15 per head, and eat like a king". / W11 1PY; www.fezmangal.com; @FezMangal; 11.30 pm; no Amex.

FIDDIES ITALIAN KITCHEN NW3 £38 3 3 2

**13 NEW COLLEGE PARADE 020 7586 5050
9–2A**

The "jolly owner" adds to the "very friendly" style of this "good cheap 'n' cheerful Italian" in Swiss Cottage. "The food is unpretentious, such as mix-and-match pasta/pizza with traditional fillings or toppings – nothing more, but it's good." / NW3 5EP; fiddiesitaliankitchen.com; @FiddiesItalian.

FIELDS BENEATH NW5 £11 3 2 3

**52A PRINCE OF WALES RD 020 7424 8838
9–2B**

Beneath Kentish Town station, this well-established and cosy neighbourhood café "recently went all-vegan" and the change has been a hit – "it still produces great coffee" and light dishes that are "always delicious".

"It just needs more space!" / NW5 3LN; www.thefieldsbeneath.com; Mon-Fri 4 pm, Sat & Sun 5 pm; closed Mon-Sun D.

FIFTEEN N1 £73 2 2 2

**15 WESTLAND PLACE 020 3375 1515
13–1A**

Only Jamie O's celebrity justifies the continued inclusion of this obscure Hoxton venture – in its 2002 heyday the UK's most famous restaurant by dint of the TV series of the same name. Nowadays, its once-cutting-edge Hoxton location should put it on the hipster roadmap, yet it inspires few reports, and such as do crop up continue a perennially lacklustre theme regarding its Italian fare and service. (It is a non-profit organisation, but since 2016 no longer trains the cohorts of youngsters that won it fame, although some do pass through its kitchens as part of a nationwide scheme). / N1 7LP; www.fifteen.net; @JamiesFifteen; 10.30 pm, Sun 9.30 pm; booking max 12 may apply.

FINKS SALT AND SWEET N5 £37 3 4 4

70 MOUNTGROVE RD 020 7684 7189 9–1D

Straightforward but superior deli/café on a Highbury street corner that's "fantastic any time of the day" – for the most part brunches, coffee and cakes are the orders of the day, but there's more substantial fare served on weekend evenings. / N5 2LT; finks.co.uk; @FinksLondon; Mon-Wed 7 pm, Fri & Sat 11 pm, Thu 10.30 pm, Sun 5 pm; closed Sun D.

FISCHER'S W1 £66 3 3 4

**50 MARYLEBONE HIGH ST 020 7466 5501
2–1A**

"Step into old-world Vienna" at Corbin & King's "elegant" re-creation of a "classic Austrian-themed café" (with menu to match) in Marylebone. Its strongest features are the "splendid" atmosphere – "cosy, buzzy and oozing charm" – and "very pleasant service", but its "reliable, if unadventurous dishes" (schnitzel, veal, etc) received a consistently good rep this year: "we visit Austria twice a year and when we need an Austrian food fix we always go here!" Top Tip: "great fun for a cake stop". / W1U 5HN; www.fischers.co.uk; @FischersLondon; 11 pm, Sun 10.30 pm.

FISH CENTRAL EC1 £33 3 2 2

**149-155 CENTRAL ST 020 7253 4970
13–1A**

This "unique" and "good value" Clerkenwell chippy scores well for "perfect fish, cooked simply, plus a decent set of basic wines". / EC1V 8AP; www.fishcentral.co.uk; @fishcentral1968; Mon-Thu, Sat 10.30 pm, Fri 11 pm; closed Sun.

FISH IN A TIE SW11 £38 3 3 3

105 FALCON RD 020 7924 1913 11–1C

"Good value" all round has long been the defining characteristic of this long-serving

Flat White W1

bistro, near Clapham Junction station. Despite the name, it's not just a fish and seafood place, with at least as many meat dishes as fish options featuring on the menu. / SW11 2PF; www.fishinatie.com; 11.30 pm, Sun 10.30 pm.

FISH MARKET
EC2   £60 3|2|2
16A NEW ST   020 3503 0790   10–2D

This solid performer from D&D London occupies a converted City warehouse near Liverpool Street. The "tables are slightly crowded", but the "excellent fish" lives up to its name. / EC2M 4TR; www.fishmarket-restaurant.co.uk; @FishMarketNS; 10.30 pm; closed Sun.

FISH! SE1   £59 3|2|2
CATHEDRAL ST   020 7407 3803   10–4C

"Bustling, loud and lively", "glass-enclosed" operation a two-minute step from foodie Borough Market. Its selection of fish is "a tad pricey", but generally "beautifully cooked". / SE1 9AL; www.fishkitchen.co.uk; @fishborough; 9.30 pm, Sun 3 pm.

FISHWORKS   £69 3|2|2
**7-9 SWALLOW ST, W1   020 7734 5813
4–4C | 89 MARYLEBONE HIGH ST, W1
020 7935 9796   2–1A**

"You enter through the front shop full of fresh fish" at these straightforward seafood bistros just off Piccadilly Circus and in Marylebone (surviving branches of what was once a national chain). You don't get fireworks, but you do get "excellent simple fish", "reliably prepared" at "reasonable prices" and the Swallow Street branch in particular is brilliantly located. / www.fishworks.co.uk; W1B 10.30 pm, Fri & Sat 11 pm; W1U 10.30 pm.

FIUME SW8   £56 3|4|3
**CIRCUS WEST VILLAGE, SOPWITH WAY
020 3904 9010   11–1C**

"A real asset to Battersea Power Station's restaurant scene" – this 120-cover D&D London yearling was one of the first to open in the new development and has a fine Thames-view location with copious outside tables. So long as you don't go with expectations raised too high by all the PR about input

from star chef Francesco Mazzei, it's "a very enjoyable spot" with "decent food", "friendly service" and "chic surroundings". "Handy for riverboat trips going east", too. / SW8 5BN; www.danddlondon.com/restaurant/fiume; @FiumeLondon; Tue-Sat, Mon 10 pm, Sun 9 pm; closed Mon L.

THE FIVE FIELDS
SW3   £106 5|5|4
**8-9 BLACKLANDS TER   020 7838 1082
6–2D**

"Fabulous on all levels" – Taylor Bonnyman's "utterly exceptional" dining room, "hidden in the heart of Chelsea" provides "not only a real treat, but a genuinely interesting gastronomic experience". "Beautifully crafted, creative food combinations are served with professional yet genuine charm" in "such a beautiful space". "It's difficult to find any fault" – if you tried hard you might say that the "decor is a bit 'posh restaurant'". / SW3 2SP; www.fivefieldsrestaurant.com; @The5Fields; 10 pm; closed Mon-Fri L, closed Sat & Sun; No trainers.

FIVE GUYS   £19 3|2|2

"Elevating the fast food experience" – this fast-growing US-based chain provides "a better class of quick burger" (with a good variety of toppings), plus "fries that are so savoury, and so-tasty milkshakes almost too thick to suck through a straw!" ("just don't watch the calories…"). On the downside, "the ambience leaves a lot to be desired: it feels like a less glamorous McDonalds!" / @FiveGuysUK; 11 pm, Thu-Sat midnight.

500 N19   £53 4|3|2
782 HOLLOWAY RD   020 7272 3406   9–1C

"Almost invisible from the outside", this 10-year-old local near Archway "makes you feel like you're in Italy" and serves "excellent Sardinian/Sicilian food". The name is a tribute to founder chef Mario Magli's favourite Fiat Cinquecento, and a nod to the minuscule proportions of the venue ("whose hard walls can make it noisy"). / N19 3JH; www.500restaurant.co.uk; @500restaurant; 10 pm, Sun 9 pm; Mon-Thu D only, Fri-Sun open L & D.

500 DEGREES
SE24   £23 3|2|2
**HERNE HILL, 153A DULWICH RD
020 7274 8200   11–2D**

"Cheap 'n' cheerful, and very authentic", this Herne Hill two-year-old is an "excellent neighbourhood pizzeria". The name refers to the temperature its wood-fired oven must reach to cook its pizzas: there is nothing else on the menu beyond a quartet of salads. / SE24 \N; www.500degrees.co; @500degreesuk; 11 pm, Sun 10 pm.

FLAT IRON   £32 3|4|4
**17 BEAK ST, W1   020 3019 2353   4–2B | 17
HENRIETTA ST, WC2   020 3019 4212   5–3C
| 9 DENMARK ST, WC2 NO TEL 5–1A | 46
GOLBORNE RD, W10 NO TEL 7–1A | 47-51**

CALEDONIAN RD, N1 NO TEL 9–3D NEW |
77 CURTAIN RD, EC2 NO TEL 13–1B

"If steak 'n' chips is what you want, then it's hard to beat", this "simple, yet very effective" small chain, which is "all about doing just one thing and doing it right": "superbly cooked" meat from a "limited choice" of cuts (majoring in the 'flat iron' itself) plus salad, "no starters or dessert, but a free ice cream cone as you leave". "A simple set up", it inspired "no complaints" this year, even if – with expansion, including a new King's Cross branch – ratings are not quite as exciting as once they were. / www.flatironsteak.co.uk; midnight, Sun 11.30pm; EC2 11 pm; W1F 11 pm, Thu 11.30 pm, Fri & Sat midnight, Sun 10.30 pm; no bookings.

FLAT THREE W11 £90 4|4|3
**120-122 HOLLAND PARK AVE
020 7792 8987   7–2A**

The "Nordic-Korean-Japanese fusion cooking" at this experiment-driven, "forage-style restaurant" in Holland Park is a "real surprise" and deserves wider recognition. The "top-quality ingredients" include "excellent fish and seafood", and much of the distinctive flavouring comes from fermentation processes. The venue is a well-designed basement, and there are plenty of vegan options on the tasting menus. / W11 4UA; www.flatthree.london; @infoflat3; 9.30 pm; closed Tue-Thu L, closed Sun & Mon.

FLAT WHITE W1   £10 4|4|3
17 BERWICK ST   020 7734 0370   4–2D

"London's original artisanal Kiwi coffee shop" still makes "a wonderful place to chill any day of the week" down to its "easy breezy Antipodean vibe", plus "a wide variety of music, ever-charming staff and an eclectic mix of Berwick Street locals!". All this, plus epic brews and "eggs to go with the great caffeine". / W1F 0PT; www.flatwhitesoho.co.uk; @flatwhitesoho; 6 pm; L only; cash only; no booking.

FLESH AND BUNS
WC2   £53 2|3|3
41 EARLHAM ST   020 7632 9500   5–2C

This "fun and exciting" Soho basement is a Japanese take on the Asian steamed bun phenomenon. Part of the Bone Daddies group, fans say its dishes are "always superbly cooked and presented", but ratings were dragged down this year by a significant minority who reckon it's just "overpriced and quite average". Top Tip: oft-nominated for its brunch. / WC2H 9LX; www.bonedaddies.com/restaurant/flesh-and-buns; @FleshandBuns; 10 pm, Wed-Sat 11 pm, Sun 9.30 pm; booking max 8 may apply.

FLORA INDICA
SW5   £47 4|3|3
**242 OLD BROMPTON RD   020 7370 4450
6–2A**

"Hitting the spot after a few false starts while transforming from Mr Wing (RIP)" – the former long-term occupant of this two-level (ground and basement) Earl's Court venue – this interesting yearling is decked out with distinctive steampunk flourishes to its contemporary curry house decor, and wins praise for food that's "spot on and encourages exploration of new flavours mainly from northern and central India, interpreted in a modern style". / SW5 0DE; flora-indica.com/flora03; @Flora_Indica; midnight.

FLOTSAM AND JETSAM
SW17 **£24** 3 2 3

4 BELLEVUE PARADE **020 8672 7639**
11–2C

This "phenomenally popular" cafe overlooking Wandsworth Common is a "tight ship run by a team of friendly Antipodeans" – "the only downside is that it's just not big enough". "Child and dog-friendly", naturally, it is "coffee heaven" and "great for a quick breakfast with the kids". / SW17 7EQ; www.flotsamandjetsamcafe.co.uk; @_flotsam_jetsam; Mon-Fri 3 pm, Sat & Sun 4 pm; closed Mon-Sun D; no booking.

FLOUR & GRAPE
SE1 **£47** 3 4 3

214 BERMONDSEY ST **020 7407 4682**
10–4D

Limited but enthusiastic feedback on this casual spot in Bermondsey (once known as Antico) where the focus is on fresh, handmade pasta and a selection of Italian wines. They also run the gin bar downstairs ('214 Bermondsey'). / SE1 3TQ; www.flourandgrape.com; @flourandgrape; 11 pm, Sun 10 pm; closed Mon; booking max 6 may apply.

FM MANGAL SE5 **£36** 3 3 3

54 CAMBERWELL CHURCH ST
020 7701 6677 **1–3C**

"Killer charred sumac onions, fabulously tasty grilled flatbreads and brilliant charcoal-grilled meats" win high ratings for this "cheap 'n' cheerful" Turkish grill – "a great neighbourhood gem" in Camberwell. / SE5 8QZ; midnight; no Amex; no booking.

FOLEY'S W1 **£47** 4 4 3

23 FOLEY ST **020 3137 1302** **2–1B**

"Different flavours" from an "original" menu of eclectic inspiration win enthusiastic (if slightly limited) feedback for ex-Palomar chef Mitz Vora's "warm and friendly" Fitzrovia two-year-old (which avoided a repeat of last year's uneven feedback in the current survey). / W1W 6DU; www.foleysrestaurant.co.uk; @foleyslondon; Wed-Sat 11 pm.

FOREST BAR & KITCHEN
E17 **£22**

149 FOREST RD **020 8281 4428** **1–1D**

The husband-and-wife team behind Forest Wines just a few doors down launched this neighbourhood wine bar in early 2018, providing a seasonal, modern European menu, complemented by a list of mostly organic and biodynamic vino. No survey reports yet, but looks worth a look when down Walthamstow way. / E17 6HE; forestbarandkitchen.com; @forestbarkitchn; Tue-Sat, Mon 10.30 pm, Sun 3.30 pm.

45 Jermyn St SW1

FORMAN'S E3 **£53** 4 3 2

STOUR RD, FISH ISLAND **020 8525 2365**
1–1D

Within a famous salmon smokery by the River Lea (a modern building, though the business has been on the site for over a century) – this venue "overlooks the Olympic stadium" (and offers special menus for West Ham home games). Limited feedback on its fish-based menu, but such as exists is all-round very upbeat: "I love it!". / E3 2NT; www.formans.co.uk/restaurant; @formanslondon; Thu-Sat 11 pm, Sun 5 pm; closed Thu & Fri L closed Sun D, closed Mon & Tue & Wed.

FORTNUM & MASON, THE DIAMOND JUBILEE TEA SALON W1 **£72** 3 4 4

181 PICCADILLY **020 7734 8040** **3–3D**

"Nowhere compares to the exquisite setting and experience of Fortnum & Mason high tea", according to fans of the "delicious sandwiches (made with interesting breads), excellent selection of teas and best-ever drinking chocolate" graciously served on the third floor of The Queen's favourite grocer. "A lovely place for a special occasion – it's become very expensive, but this doesn't seem to dent the enthusiasm of the hordes of family groups, ladies-who-lunch and tourists!". "It can be a bit too much food, but they offer you a doggy bag of the uneaten cakes, jam, scones…" / W1A 1ER; www.fortnumandmason.com; @Fortnums; 9.30 pm, Sun 6 pm; closed Sun D.

THE PARLOUR, FORTNUM & MASON W1 **£38** 3 3 3

181 PICCADILLY 0845 6025694 3–3D

"We treated our god-daughter to a tenth birthday ice cream (her pick of venue) accompanied by her parents and younger sister: the experience was wonderful (and delicious)!" This first floor café within the famous Piccadilly grocers is "a great place to bring the kids for a special teatime treat", where "they can have fun creating their own yummy concoctions from the wide choice of flavours and all the extra toppings". "Excellent coffee" and "delicious" light savouries too ("such as Welsh rarebit, smoked salmon etc"). / W1A 1ER; www.fortnumandmason.com; 8 pm, Sun 5 pm; closed Sun D.

45 JERMYN STREET
SW1 **£68** 3 4 4

45 JERMYN STREET, ST. JAMES'S
020 7205 4545 **3–3D**

"Slightly theatrical service" of Beef Wellington and traditional flambé dishes from trolleys adds to the retro appeal and glamorous atmosphere of Fortnum & Mason's chic, St James's restaurant (whose cocktail bar, and witty evoking of a "bygone era", contrasts sharply with the more 'maiden aunt' styling of The Fountain, RIP, which it replaced a couple of years ago). It's a useful location, nominated for business and breakfast – often at the same time! / SW1Y 6DN; www.45jermynst.com; @45JermynSt; 11.30 pm, Sun 10.30 pm; closed Sun D.

40 MALTBY STREET
SE1 **£68** 4 4 3

40 MALTBY ST **020 7237 9247** **10–4D**

"Amazing cooking in the tiniest of kitchens" – chef Steve Williams works with "great seasonal produce" at this cult foodie destination – a wine warehouse under the railway arches leading to London Bridge station, with the menu chalked up on a blackboard. "The most adventurous natural wine list is paired with great cuisine, and the knowledgeable and personable staff match them if asked." / SE1 3PA; www.40maltbystreet.com; @40maltbystreet; 9.30 pm; closed Mon, Tue, Wed L, Thu L, Sat D & Sun; no Amex; no booking.

FORZA WIN SE15 **£48** 3 4 3

UNIT 4.1, 133 COPELAND RD
020 7732 9012 **1–4D**

A "bright and airy" warehouse conversion (formerly a cash & carry) is home to this previously roving set-up – a communal-seating, vibey space, praised for its "delicious Italian food and very friendly service". / SE15 3SN; www.forzawin.com; @forzawin; Wed-Sat 11.30 pm, Sun 4 pm; closed Sun D, closed Mon & Tue.

400 RABBITS **£26** 3 3 2

143 EVELINA RD, SE15 **020 7732 4115**
1–4D | **30-32 WESTOW ST, SE19**
020 8771 6249 **1–1D**

Crystal Palace 'sodo' pizza spot which has also hopped into Nunhead (just on the border of Peckham) with its second London site – a bright canteen with hard, school-type chairs. No feedback on the original, but the food is well-rated here: wood-fired and with British rye flour sourdough bases. /

THE FOUR SEASONS £52 5️⃣1️⃣1️⃣

11 GERRARD ST, W1   020 7287 0900   5–3A
NEW | 12 GERRARD ST, W1   020 7494 0870
5–3A | 23 WARDOUR ST, W1
020 7287 9995   5–3A | 84 QUEENSWAY, W2
020 7229 4320   7–2C

"It's a bit of a dive" with "charmless" service ("you have to queue even if you've booked") but everyone raves about the "divine" duck – "the best in London" – and other "brilliant barbecued meats and roast pork" at these clattery canteens in Chinatown and Bayswater. / www.fs-restaurants.co.uk; 11pm-midnight.

FOX & GRAPES SW19 £54 3️⃣3️⃣3️⃣

9 CAMP RD   020 8619 1300   11–2A

"Wonderfully situated on the edge of Wimbledon Common", this attractive pub is ideal for recuperating "after a brisk walk" ("perfect for a boozy Sunday lunch"). "Prices are a bit punchy" for grub that's "not high end" but it delivers "high-quality pub food" that's "always decent". / SW19 4UN; www.foxandgrapeswimbledon.co.uk; @thefoxandgrapes; 11 pm, Sun 10.30 pm.

THE FOX AND ANCHOR EC1 £53 2️⃣2️⃣3️⃣

115 CHARTERHOUSE ST   020 7250 1300
10–1B

For "good, old-London pub atmosphere and straightforward food", this Victorian institution near Smithfield Market is a perennial, and – as one of the few watering holes licenced from the early hours to serve market traders – is most famous for "a quality traditional breakfast, served with a pint of Guinness". / EC1M 6AA; www.foxandanchor.com; @foxanchor; 9.30 pm, Sun 6 pm.

FOXLOW £55 2️⃣2️⃣2️⃣

LOWER JAMES ST, W1   020 7680 2710
4–3C | 15-19 BEDFORD HILL, SW12
020 7680 2700   11–2C | ST JOHN ST, EC1
020 7014 8070   10–2A

"Excellent steaks and burgers" do win a sizeable band of fans for the Hawksmoor group's budget chain of spin-offs, but – while decent enough – they seem lacklustre for a business associated with such a key brand: detractors don't say they're appalling or anything, just a bit… meh. The Chiswick branch failed to gain traction and shut up shop this year. / www.foxlow.co.uk; @FoxlowTweets; 10 pm, Fri & Sat 10.30 pm, Sun 9 pm; EC1 10.30 pm, Sun 3.30 pm ; EC1 closed Sun D; SRA-Food Made Good – 2 stars.

FRANCO MANCA £30 2️⃣2️⃣2️⃣

"Despite the ever-expanding franchise", the pizzas are "solidly enjoyable and a cut above" ("you've just got to love the sourdough bases" and "quality toppings"), according to the hordes of fans of the "buzzing, busy and rather cramped" branches of this crazily expanding chain, which nowadays is the survey's "go-to for a cheap 'n' cheerful family pizza", eclipsing the once-mighty PizzaExpress in the level of interest it generates. There's no hiding its steadily declining ratings, though, with a sentiment that "while it's still usually very reliable, standards have slipped over repeat visits"; for its harshest critics the effect is now "Frankly Manky!". / www.francomanca.co.uk; 10 pm, Wed-Sat 11 pm; no bookings.

FRANCO'S SW1 £74 3️⃣4️⃣4️⃣

61 JERMYN ST   020 7499 2211   3–3C

"Simultaneously up-to-date and old-school" – one of London's oldest Italians (dating from 1946) makes an ideal business lunch spot in St James's, with a busy, bustling atmosphere that's formal but "not too serious", and with "excellent cooking and friendly service". Perhaps unsurprisingly, it is also rather "expensive". Top Tip: "breakfast is always good here… especially if someone else is paying!". / SW1Y 6LX; www.francoslondon.com; @francoslondon; 10.30 pm, Sun 10 pm; closed Sun.

FRANKLINS SE22 £56 3️⃣2️⃣2️⃣

157 LORDSHIP LN   020 8299 9598   1–4D

"High-quality" traditional British fare has made this pub conversion an East Dulwich fixture over the past two decades; and it now has its own farm shop near the village. "A good find for lunch near Dulwich Picture Gallery". Top Tip: "quality breakfast and a great Sunday lunch too". / SE22 8HX; www.franklinsrestaurant.com; @frankinsse22; 10.30 pm, Sun 10 pm; no Amex.

FRANTOIO SW10 £68 3️⃣4️⃣4️⃣

397 KING'S RD   020 7352 4146   6–3B

Now in its 20th year, this World's End trattoria feels "like a private club" thanks to the "consistently warm welcome" extended by its charismatic owner, Bucci. It's a "family favourite" for both "fun and quality", and "if the food is not always quite perfect, the atmosphere and conviviality make up for that!". / SW10 0LR; www.frantoio.co.uk; 11 pm.

FREAK SCENE W1 £47 5️⃣3️⃣4️⃣

54 FRITH ST   07561 394 497   5–2A

Ex-Nobu head chef Scott Hallsworth and Phar Shaweewan's storming pan-Asian pop-up has found a permanent home in Soho, in the small bar premises that formerly housed the original Barrafina. Early reports suggest it's a worthy successor and award full marks to its super-freaky, tapas-y flavour-bomb dishes of Asian-Latino inspiration, washed down with a selection of cocktails. / W1D 4SL; freakscene. london; @freakscene.

FREDERICK'S N1 £66 3️⃣4️⃣5️⃣

106 CAMDEN PASSAGE   020 7359 2888
9–3D

"None of its charm has been lost over the years", say fans of this "romantic" and "spacious" Islington stalwart, where the best spot is "eating on the terrace overlooking the lovely garden". "The cooking is old school, but very enjoyable". / N1 8EG; www.fredericks.co.uk; @fredericks_n1; 11 pm; closed Sun.

FRENCHIE WC2 £79 3️⃣2️⃣2️⃣

18 HENRIETTA ST   020 7836 4422   5–3C

Perhaps the most famous alumnus of Jamie Oliver's Fifteen – Gregory Marchand (aka 'Frenchie') launched his Covent Garden operation a couple of years ago as a London spin-off to his first 'Frenchie', which opened in Paris in 2009. With its shortish menu of "quirky" Gallic dishes, "eclectic" wine list and "fun" (if "noisy") style, it was one of the hits of last year. This year, however, its ratings dipped, and – while fans still praise its "well-crafted and tasty dishes" – there are a few critics to whom it seems "totally overrated". Post-survey in July 2018, Marchand transferred the executive chef of his Parisian group, Dale Sutton, to London, presumably to help pep things up a bit? / WC2E 8QH; www.frenchiecoventgarden.com; @frenchiecoventgarden; 11 pm, Sun 10 pm.

THE FROG £71 5️⃣5️⃣4️⃣

35 SOUTHAMPTON ST, WC2   020 7199 8370
5–3D | 45-47 HOXTON SQUARE, N1
020 3813 9832   13–1B

"A new star in London's dining scene!" – Adam Handling's "outstanding" year-old Covent Garden branch is proving just as big a smash hit as his E1 original (which, in mid 2018, moved to a new, 60-cover site on the corner of Hoxton Square, together with a bar and coffee shop). His "clever and delicious" British tapas feature "brilliant taste combinations" yet "without being prissy or overly expensive"; while the "chilled" atmosphere is "that so hard-to-achieve balance of professionalism with perfect relaxation and excitement". Service, too, gets a big thumbs up: "top class and efficient but not obtrusive, and so friendly". See also Belmond Cadogan Hotel. / www.thefrogrestaurant.com; @TheFrogE1.

LA FROMAGERIE £48 3️⃣3️⃣3️⃣

2-6 MOXON ST, W1   020 7935 0341
3–1A | 52 LAMB'S CONDUIT ST, WC1
020 7242 1044   2–1D | 30 HIGHBURY
PARK, N5   020 7359 7440   9–2D

"Cheese shop by day, great little bistro by night – highly recommended" is a typically enthusiastic response to this popular and upmarket trio in Marylebone, Bloomsbury and Highbury. The quote is slightly misleading, since all three have pretty serious breakfast and brunch offerings through the day, with "delicious food and some beautiful vegetable combinations". But it is their cheese selection – from the UK, Ireland, France and Italy – that wins them renown. / www.lafromagerie.co.uk; @LaFromagerieUK.

THE FRONTLINE CLUB W2 £60 3️⃣3️⃣4️⃣

13 NORFOLK PL   020 7479 8960   7–1D

"Handy in the culinary desert that is Paddington" – this well-appointed venue is the ground floor of a club dedicated to war reporters (expect some eye-catching photoreportage on the walls). It's a "comfortable setting" for food that's "relatively simple" but "remarkably good in the context of the general quality of restaurants in the vicinity". / W2 1QJ; www.frontlineclub.com; @frontlineclub; 11 pm; closed Sat L, closed Sun; booking max 6 may apply.

FUMO WC2 £61 3️⃣3️⃣3️⃣

37 ST MARTIN'S LANE   020 3778 0430
5–4C

"A gem right next to the ENO", this two-year-old Italian cicchetti (small plates) venue from the San Carlo group is "a great addition to the theatre district". Most reporters are very happy with the food – "been twice, and both visits produced at least one truly memorable dish". / WC2N 4JS; www.sancarlofumo.co.uk/fumo-london; @sancarlo_fumo; Mon-Thu 11.30 pm, Fri & Sat midnight, Sun 10.30 pm.

GABY'S WC2 £36 3️⃣2️⃣2️⃣

30 CHARING CROSS RD   020 7836 4233
5–3B

"A staple of Theatreland", this grungy deli by Leicester Square (apparently Jeremy Corbyn's favourite restaurant) "is never going to win any awards for its decor" ("too dismal to qualify even as raffish"). The reason it's treasured by regulars, rich and poor alike, is the "ever-charming Gaby", who has been behind the counter most days since 1965, and his selection of "authentic, unmodernised Middle Eastern food", incorporating "falafel to die for", "very good value salt beef sandwiches" and "highly tasty mixed salad plates". "Thank heavens the aristocratic freeholder hasn't managed to prise it out of its premises yet – go while it's still there!". / WC2H 0DE; midnight, Sun 10 pm; no Amex.

GALLERY MESS, SAATCHI GALLERY SW3 £53 2️⃣3️⃣3️⃣

DUKE OF YORKS HQ, KINGS RD
020 7730 8135   6–2D

A "great sunny terrace" for warm weather adds to the appeal of this art-hung space – part of the impressive former barracks housing the Saatchi Gallery and a handy all-day dining (and afternoon tea) venue near Sloane Square. No-one suggests the food here will set the world on fire, however. / SW3 4RY; www.saatchigallery.com/gallerymess; @gallerymess; 11 pm, Sun 6 pm; closed Sun D.

GALLEY N1 £56 3️⃣3️⃣3️⃣

105-106 UPPER ST   020 3670 0740   9–3D

"A restaurant for a proper meal on Upper Street" – former Randall & Aubin head chef Marcel Grzyb teamed up with his sister Oriona Robb to create this welcoming yearling: "the cooking won't knock your socks off but everything is nicely done and it is a good, safe choice". / N1 1QN; www.galleylondon.co.uk; @Galleylondon; 11 pm.

GALLIPOLI £40 2️⃣3️⃣3️⃣

102 UPPER ST, N1   020 7359 0630   9–3D
120 UPPER ST, N1   020 7226 8099   9–3D

"Reliably decent Turkish food" and a "friendly, jolly atmosphere" make this pair of Ottoman-themed cafés on Upper Street in Islington a "great standby for birthday celebrations or big groups". / www.cafegallipoli.com; @CafeGallipoli; 11 pm, Fri & Sat midnight.

GALVIN AT THE ATHENAEUM W1 £66 3️⃣3️⃣2️⃣

ATHENAEUM HOTEL, 116 PICCADILLY
020 7640 3333   3–4B

Feedback is positive about the Galvin Bros' year-old revamp of this well-known Art Deco dining room, lauding its "good, mainly British cuisine", civilised location ("lovely on a sunny day, overlooking Green Park") and "high standards" generally. Its ratings are undercut, though, by incidents of "routine" cooking, and a sense that "some of its former quirkiness was lost in the (2016) makeover". Top Tip: "wonderful, luxurious afternoon tea". / W1J 7BJ; www.athenaeumhotel.com; @galvinathenaeum; midnight, Sun 11 pm.

GALVIN AT WINDOWS, PARK LANE LONDON HILTON HOTEL W1 £114 2️⃣3️⃣5️⃣

22 PARK LN   020 7208 4021   3–4A

"Truly spectacular panoramas across Buckingham Palace" (The Queen has, it is said, never forgiven them for building this place) make this 28th-floor dining room a big romantic favourite; and similarly, if on business, "clients can't help but be impressed with the outlook". With its "lovely" cooking and "excellent service" it's hard to fault generally, other than that, predictably, "it's not very competitively priced!" Top Tip: cheapskates can get all the view for the price of a cocktail in the adjoining bar. / W1K 1BE; www.galvinatwindows.com; @GalvinatWindows; Mon-Wed 10 pm, Thu-Sat 10.30 pm, Sun 3 pm; closed Sat L closed Sun D; No trainers; booking max 5 may apply.

GALVIN HOP E1 £57 2️⃣2️⃣3️⃣

35 SPITAL SQ   020 7299 0404   13–2B

"Café A Vin changed into Galvin HOP" a couple of years ago and feedback on the Galvins' posh gastropub near Spitalfields Market (and adjacent to Galvin La Chapelle) is rather limited and mixed. "The food is perhaps a notch lower than the previous incarnation", but attractions include "good steaks", and, as ever, that "you can also sit outside at the front or in the garden, which is nice in good weather". / E1 6DY; www.galvinrestaurants.com/section/62/1/galvinhop; @Galvin_brothers; 10.30 pm, Sun 9.30 pm; booking max 5 may apply.

GALVIN LA CHAPELLE E1 £85 4️⃣4️⃣5️⃣

35 SPITAL SQ   020 7299 0400   13–2B

The "exciting and gorgeous" setting (a "spectacular" conversion of a Victorian school chapel) helps create "a certain aura" – fitting both romantic dinners and power lunching – at the Galvin Bros' Spitalfields fixture. Its "fabulous standard" of modern French cuisine and "professional but easy-going service" won it more consistent praise this year as one of the best all-rounders in the City, and, some would say, in town. / E1 6DY; www.galvinlachapelle.com; @galvin_brothers; 10.30 pm, Sun 10 pm; No trainers; booking max 8 may apply.

THE GAME BIRD AT THE STAFFORD LONDON SW1 £73 3️⃣5️⃣3️⃣

16-18 ST JAMES'S PLACE   020 7518 1234
3–4C

"A great addition to this hidden gem of a hotel" in St James's – this "beautiful" dining room affords "lots of space" to diners and inspires nothing but rave reviews (and numerous nominations as a top spot for business entertaining). The "traditional British food with a twist" is "beautifully presented, with bags of taste, and the matching wines are bang on". Top Tip: as the name hints: "it's an excellent choice during the game season". / SW1A 1NJ; thestaffordlondon.com/the-game-bird; @TheGameBirdLON; 10 pm.

GANAPATI SE15 £46 4️⃣3️⃣3️⃣

38 HOLLY GROVE   020 7277 2928   1–4D

"The home-made parathas, masala dosas and pickles are the stuff of dreams" at this early pioneer of the Peckham food scene – "a favourite for many years". The "delicious South Indian regional food" comes courtesy of Claire Fisher, who was inspired to open the venue after her travels. One or two reporters, though, feel that while it's "a nice neighbourhood restaurant", it "never quite lives up to our high expectations" nowadays. / SE15 5DF; www.ganapatirestaurant.com; 10.30 pm, Sun 10 pm; closed Mon; no Amex.

GARDEN CAFE AT THE GARDEN MUSEUM SE1 £45 3️⃣2️⃣3️⃣

5 LAMBETH PALACE RD   020 7401 8865
2–4D

"Not just a museum cafe but a proper destination restaurant" – this year-old venue in a copper-and-glass pavilion at Lambeth's Garden Museum is a "really brilliant addition to what is otherwise a rather poorly served corner of London". "Fresh honest flavours are simply but interestingly prepared" by chefs Harry Kaufman (ex-St John Bread & Wine) and George Ryle (ex-Padella and Primeur). / SE1 7LB; www.gardenmuseum.org.uk; @GardenMuseumLDN; Mon, Wed & Thu, Sun 5 pm, Tue, Fri 10 pm, Sat 3.30 pm; closed Mon, Wed & Thu, Sat & Sun D; no Amex; Booking max 12 may apply.

LE GARRICK
WC2 £55 3 3 4

10-12 GARRICK ST 020 7240 7649 5–3C

"A far cry from tourist-land on its doorstep!" – this cute little bistro in Covent Garden has "a wonderful and unexpectedly intimate atmosphere" and can be "a brilliant find for pre-/post- theatre" thanks to its "lovely French dishes". / WC2E 9BH; www.legarrick.co.uk; @le_garrick; midnight, Sun 5 pm; closed Sun D.

THE GARRISON
SE1 £51 3 2 3

99 BERMONDSEY ST 020 7089 9355 10–4D

A pioneer of the Bermondsey food scene, this former pub with "quirky, fun decor" "remains a favourite, with an ever-changing menu, beautifully executed". It stays true to its prior calling with "good real ale", and "can get a bit noisy" when full. / SE1 3XB; www.thegarrison.co.uk; @TheGarrisonSE1; midnight, Sun 11 pm.

GASTRONHOME
SW11 £71 5 4 3

59 LAVENDER HILL, LONDON
020 3417 5639 11–2C

"Out-of-the-way Gallic treasure" that's worth the detour to Lavender Hill (near Clapham Junction), for Damien Fremont's traditional French cuisine 'with a modern touch'. It attracts the highest ratings and fulsome praise this year, especially for the "sublime" five-course tasting menu. Fremont and his co-founder, fellow Frenchman Christopher Nespoux, who runs the front of house, first met working at the Ritz Club 10 years ago. / SW11 \N; www.gastronhome.co.uk; @gastronhome1; 10:15 pm; closed Mon & Sun; No jeans.

THE GATE
£54 4 2 3

22-24 SEYMOUR PLACE, W1 020 7724 6656
2–2A | 51 QUEEN CAROLINE ST, W6
020 8748 6932 8–2C | 370 ST JOHN ST,
EC1 020 7278 5483 9–3D

Bravos abound for the "superb" dishes ("imaginative and ambitious conceptions whose flavours make non-vegetarians desist from any pity about a lack of meat!") at these accomplished veggies, which in recent years have added outlets in Seymour Village and Sadler's Wells to the "legendary", long-standing original (just south of Hammersmith Broadway). "However, quality of service and staff response can be variable" at all branches, and this is most particularly the case at W1, which needs to "up its game" generally, not least its cooking, as a number of regulars discern "a big drop in standards since it opened". / www.thegaterestaurants.com; @gaterestaurant; 10.30 pm; W1 Sun 9.45 pm; W6 Sun 9.30 pm; SRA-Food Made Good – 3 stars.

GAUCHO
£89 2 2 2

Steaks are "perfectly nice" but prices are "silly" at this glossy, "dimly lit" Argentinian steak house chain (whose Latino wine list is also a feature) – perhaps explaining why it went into administration in summer 2018. Under a rescue package that saw sibling brand Cau shut down, former CEO Martin Williams (who left in 2014 to set up M Restaurants) is returning to the helm. As of September 2018, it remains to be seen how many of the 12 London venues will stay open. / www.gauchorestaurants.co.uk; @gauchogroup; 11 pm, Thu-Sat midnight ; EC3 & EC1 closed Sat & Sun, WC2 & EC2 closed Sat L & Sun.

GAUTHIER SOHO
W1 £79 5 4 4

21 ROMILLY ST 020 7494 3111 5–3A

"Stepping through that front door (you ring to enter) takes you into a better world" at Alexis Gauthier's "quirky", converted townhouse in Soho, which provides "some of the best French cooking in London". "The cuisine achieves a masterful balance of traditional technique applied to the finest ingredients – flavour, intensity, plus beautiful presentation"; and the "empathic service" is "friendly but always professional". The venue's "distinctiveness continues into the maze of cosy yet elegant rooms" spread "higgledy piggledy" over a couple of floors, and "with only a few tables in each room", the style is "peaceful" going on "seductive". Why Michelin took their star away is an utter mystery. Top Tips – "the eight-course tasting menu is a fabulous foodie experience; the three-course De Luxe lunch is an absolute steal"; "the devoted vegan tasting menu is superb"; last but not least, "the truffle risotto is a 'Desert Island Dish'". / W1D 5AF; www.gauthiersoho.co.uk; @GauthierSoho; 11 pm, Sun 10.30 pm; closed Mon & Sun; booking max 7 may apply.

LE GAVROCHE
W1 £137 4 5 4

43 UPPER BROOK ST 020 7408 0881 3–2A

"When everywhere else seems forced to bow to fashion and follow the latest trend, Le Gavroche sails serenely on, delighting those who appreciate the true heart and spirit of gastronomy!!" Michel Roux Jr's Mayfair "haute cuisine temple" (here since 1982, founded by his father Albert in Chelsea in 1967) may "in some respects reflect an earlier era of fine dining", with its "fabulous" Gallic cuisine ("superb Omelette Rothschild", "soufflé Suissesse to die for!"…), but that merely reinforces its position as "an absolute favourite" for its massive following, who confirm that "every mouthful is a delight". "Very warm and welcoming staff have absolutely nailed the balance in service, friendliness and knowledge" and – especially for a basement – the very "grown up" dining room is supremely "cosy, luxurious and celebratory". "As well as top notch food, the wine list is spectacular and although there are oligarch-friendly, five-figure bottles, if you look there are some gems for those willing and able to pay more for a special wine". And "the great man's regular presence is one of the special things about Le Gavroche" – "Michel told us some of the history of the restaurant and really made us welcome!" A visit is a second-mortgage job, of course, but there's a "marvellous value set lunch (even if you do have to book it three months in advance)". / W1K 7QR; www.le-gavroche.co.uk; @michelrouxjr; 10 pm; closed Sat L, closed Sun & Mon; Jacket required.

GAYLORD W1
£60 3 3 3

79-81 MORTIMER ST 020 7580 3615 2–1B

This Fitzrovia veteran, "the ultimate traditional Indian", still cooks dishes in a tandoor oven imported in 1966, and believed to be the first in the UK. The menu has been successfully modernised in recent years, with such choices as 'paneer jalfrezi tacos' giving "an Indian twist to the Mexican street-food favourite". / W1W 7SJ; www.gaylordlondon.com; @gaylord_london; 10.45 pm, Sun 10.30 pm.

GAZELLE W1

48 ALBEMARLE ST 020 7751 5812 3–3C

Scottish chef Rob Roy Cameron (whose career includes a stint as pastry chef at the legendary El Bulli) runs the first-floor restaurant, while star-mixologist Tony Conigliaro (who started out life at Zetter before moving on to 69 Colebrooke Row and Untitled in Hackney) looks after the second-floor cocktail bar at this ambitious, two-floor Mayfair operation which set up shop in July 2018. / W1S 4DH; www.gazelle-mayfair.com; @GazelleMayfair; Tue-Sat, Mon 10.30 pm, Sun 3.30 pm.

GAZETTE
£53 3 3 3

79 SHERWOOD CT, CHATFIELD RD, SW11
020 7223 0999 11–1C | 100 BALHAM
HIGH ST, SW12 020 8772 1232 11–2C
| 147 UPPER RICHMOND RD, SW15
020 8789 6996 11–2B

"A banker for those who like traditional Gallic brasserie food", this Gallic trio in Balham, Clapham and Putney provides an "excellent-value set lunch", while the "à la carte covers all the French classics at reasonable prices". / www.gazettebrasserie.co.uk; 11 pm.

GEALES W8
£57 2 2 2

2 FARMER ST 020 7727 7528 7–2B

"If you want to eat good fish and chips" most reports still commend this pre-War Notting Hill chippie (est 1939), although its more recent Chelsea offshoot shut up shop this year. It doesn't have nearly the following it once did though, and one or two reporters feel it's now "living on the name and nothing else". / W8 7SN; www.geales.com; 10.30 pm, Sun 10 pm; closed Mon L.

GEM N1
£32 3 4 3

265 UPPER ST 020 7359 0405 9–2D

Turkish-Kurdish outfit near Angel that offers "exceptionally good value for Upper Street". "No fireworks here, simply decent portions of good food in a friendly place". Top Tip: the "set menu of mixed mezze is an especially good bargain". / N1 2UQ; www.gemrestaurant.org.uk; @Gem_restaurant; Mon-Thu 11 pm, Fri & Sat midnight, Sun 10.30 pm; no Amex.

GENESIS E1

144 COMMERCIAL ST   020 7375 2963
13–2B

When you turn your back on the family firm, you have to do it in style – in this case, the Santoro brothers moved on from their century-old family meat business and have opened this Shoreditch newcomer: a 100% plant-based restaurant with a globetrotting menu – what they call 'vegan alchemy'... It's GMO-free and organic, too (with Soil Association certification). / E1 6NU; eatgenesis.com; @EatGenesis.

GEORGE IN THE STRAND
WC2   £53 333

213 STRAND   020 7353 9638   2–2D

Opposite the Royal Courts of Justice, this traditional but updated historic hostelry is worth remembering for its "unusually interesting pub food", both in the ground floor bar and upstairs 'Pig and Goose' dining room. / WC2R 1AP; www.georgeinthestrand.com; @thegeorgestrand; Mon-Thu 10 pm, Fri & Sat 10.30 pm, Sun 9 pm.

GERMAN GYMNASIUM
N1   £72 214

1 KING'S BOULEVARD   020 7287 8000
9–3C

"The location is stunning (albeit loud when it fills with customers)", but – when evaluating this D&D London operation, housed within a "fantastic 1860s building in King's Cross" – there are just "too many missed opportunities in this grand space". "Because of the sheer size of the place (probably) the service is dreadful, which detracts from the experience", and when it comes to the "not-strictly-German cuisine" then "prices feel way too high" for an offering that's too "uninspired". As a business venue it has its fans, though, and also for the "great brunch menu with free-flowing bubbles". And "the bar's very good" too. / N1C 4BU; www.germangymnasium.com; @TheGermanGym; Tue-Sat, Mon 11 pm, Sun 3 pm; closed Mon L closed Sun D.

GIACOMO'S NW2   £38 332

428 FINCHLEY RD   020 7794 3603   1–1B

"Cosy local Italian" in Childs Hill that's "friendly", with "reliably good food" that won't break the bank. Family run, it has been established here for 16 years and "never disappoints". / NW2 2HY; www.giacomos.co.uk; 9.30 pm.

GIFTO'S LAHORE KARAHI
UB1   £27 322

162-164 THE BROADWAY   020 8813 8669
1–3A

Something of a local landmark – this large Pakistani diner on one of Southall's main routes makes an affordable choice, with top menu billing going to the "excellent grills". / UB1 1NN; www.gifto.com; @GiftosSouthall; Mon-Fri 11.30 pm, Sat & Sun midnight; booking weekdays only.

THE GILBERT SCOTT
NW1   £74 224

EUSTON RD   020 7278 3888   9–3C

A "magnificent" space, within the "spectacular neo-gothic hotel attached to St Pancras Station" provides a superb backdrop to a meal at Marcus Wareing's "impressive" dining room; and it's a good place to entertain on business ("ideally situated for the Eurostar!"). When it comes to the "very British" food however, results remain mixed: even fans can find it "a shade lacking given the ticket price" and numerous sceptics describe it as "adequate, but totally unmemorable". / NW1 2AR; www.thegilbertscott.co.uk; @Thegilbertscott; 10.30 pm, Sun 9.30 pm; booking max 7 may apply.

GINGER & WHITE   £13 333

2 ENGLAND'S LN, NW3   020 7722 9944
9–2A | 4A-5A, PERRINS CT, NW3
020 7431 9098   9–2A

These "lovely" Antipodean-style cafés in Hampstead and Belsize Park are "worth the sharp elbows to get in". The lattes and all-day breakfasts are highly rated, if a little "pricey" but – be warned – they are "often full of the activewear-clad chattering classes". / www.gingerandwhite.com; 5.30 pm; W1 closed Sun.

GINZA ONODERA
SW1   £95 442

15 BURY ST   020 7839 1101   3–3D

Aficionados of Japanese cuisine love the "wonderfully fresh and inventive yet traditional" cooking in this large, luxurious dining room below a St James's department store (which, for many years, traded as Matsuri, RIP, and is nowadays run by an international chain). It's not an inexpensive option, though, and has a peaceful style that's not everyone's cup of green tea. / SW1Y 6AL; onodera-group.com/uk; @Onodera_London; 10.30 pm, Sun 10 pm.

THE GLASSHOUSE
TW9   £82 332

14 STATION PDE   020 8940 6777   1–3A

"In the style of sister establishments Chez Bruce and La Trompette", this neighbourhood star in a parade of shops right by Kew Gardens tube station also has a fine record of "superb, well-balanced cooking with great seasonal ingredients". Its ratings sagged quite noticeably this year, though, with numerous reports that performance is "off the boil" of late, and – "with the quality seeming to have dipped" – it can seem "quiet" or "a bit lacking in atmosphere". / TW9 3PZ; www.glasshouserestaurant.co.uk; @The__Glasshouse; 11.30 pm, Sun 3.30 pm; booking max 8 may apply.

GO-VIET SW7   £56 442

53 OLD BROMPTON RD   020 7589 6432
6–2C

"Superb Vietnamese food" – "diverse, delicious and really refined" – is on the menu at this yearling from Jeff Tan, the ex-Hakkasan owner of Soho's Viet Food. One cavil: the "very plain surroundings" mean it's "lacking in atmosphere". / SW7 3JS; vietnamfood.co.uk/go-viet; Sun-Thu 10.30 pm, Sat 11 pm; closed Fri.

LA GOCCIA WC2   £52 335

FLORAL COURT, OFF FLORAL ST
020 7305 7676   5–3C

"A promising start for one of Petersham Nurseries' new openings in Floral Court" – this is the less pricey of their two new restaurants, serving pizzetti, antipasti, risotti, pasta and so on, which – on early feedback – were consistently well-rated. Well hidden, but in the heart of Covent Garden, it sits on a lovely courtyard, complete with outside tables; see also The Petersham. / WC2E 9DJ; petershamnurseries.com/dine/la-goccia; @PetershamN; Mon-Fri 10 pm, Sat & Sun 9 pm.

GODDARDS AT GREENWICH
SE10   £15 344

22 KING WILLIAM WALK   020 8305 9612
1–3D

"Traditional pie 'n' mash (but with more choice of pies these days)" and "genuine and friendly counter service" again win very positive (if limited) feedback for this Greenwich fixture (est 1890) – one of London's few surviving pie 'n' mash shops. / SE10 9HU; www.goddardsatgreenwich.co.uk; @GoddardsPieMash; Sun-Thu 7.30 pm, Fri & Sat 8 pm; L & early evening only.

GÖKYÜZÜ N4   £32 222

26-27 GRAND PDE, GREEN LANES
020 8211 8406   1–1C

"Full of noise and activity", this longstanding Green Lanes BBQ is "the most popular Turkish eatery in the area" – "with queues down the street on Sundays" – thanks to its "wonderful selection of food": "sharing platters are plentiful" ("doggy bags are happily provided") and "the quality of the grilled meat is excellent". There are now spinoffs in Chingford and Walthamstow, with Finchley opening in late 2018. Top Tip: "Turkish breakfast served till 4pm: fresh honeycomb, bread from the grill, plenty of treats – and unlimited tea". / N4 1LG; www.gokyuzurestaurant.co.uk; @Gokyuzulondon; Sun-Thu midnight, Fri & Sat 1 am.

GOLD MINE W2   £38 422

102 QUEENSWAY   020 7792 8331   7–2C

"Great roast duck" and other meats shine at this functional Bayswater Cantonese. Aficionados rate it as "better than its famous neighbour", the Four Seasons. / W2 3RR; 11 pm.

GOLDEN DRAGON
W1   £45 322

28-29 GERRARD ST   020 7734 1073   5–3A

"My go-to place for dim sum", this substantial Chinatown operation looks "rather touristy" but pleases the crowd with Cantonese favourites including "the best roast duck in town". It now has an offshoot in the new Bang Bang Oriental food hall in Colindale. / W1 6JW;

www.gdlondon.co.uk; Mon-Thu 11.30 pm, Fri & Sat midnight, Sun 11 pm.

GOLDEN HIND
W1 £39 3 3 2

73 MARYLEBONE LN 020 7486 3644 2–1A

"Brilliant, classic, old-style British fish 'n' chips – what more do you need?" That's why folk still seek out this Marylebone institution, founded in 1914. The jury is still out a bit on the new management (which changed a couple of years ago) but most reporters feel this is "still as good a chippy as you can find in Central London". / W1U 2PN; www.goldenhindrestaurant.com; 10 pm; closed Sat L, closed Sun.

GOOD EARTH £60 2 2 2

233 BROMPTON RD, SW3 020 7584 3658 6–2C | 143-145 THE BROADWAY, NW7 020 8959 7011 1–1B | 11 BELLEVUE RD, SW17 020 8682 9230 11–2C

"Reliable, good quality, pricey but satisfying" – such virtues have long attracted fans to these "old favourite", family-owned Chinese stalwarts in Knightsbridge, Balham and Mill Hill. Viewed from the other side of the coin, they serve "satisfactory but unadventurous fare that seems somewhat overpriced and lacks edginess". / www.goodearthgroup.co.uk; Mon-Sat 10.45 pm, Sun 10 pm; NW7 11.15 pm, Sun 10.45 pm.

THE GOOD EGG £57 3 3 3

UNIT G9 KINGLY COURT, W1 020 3911 2000 4–2B NEW | 93 CHURCH ST, N16 020 7682 2120 1–1C

"Exceptional breakfasts and exceptionally welcoming staff" are the two most highly praised features of this Israeli deli in Stokey, which now has a Soho offshoot too. One former fan however, complained of "corners cut" of late – hopefully just a blip. / thegoodeggn16.com; @TheGoodEgg_.

GOOD NEIGHBOUR
SE5 £39

21 CAMBERWELL CHURCH ST 07981 396 180 1–3C

Further gentrification comes to Camberwell in the form of this cute new wine bar – a late spring 2018 newcomer from Aussie chef Paul Williamson (formerly of WC in Clapham and Soho House). There's a menu of Mediterranean-inspired small plates, pizzette, cheese and charcuterie alongside a rotating range of wines. / SE5 8TR; www.goodneighbour.uk.com; @gdneighbourldn

GOODMAN £93 3 3 2

24-26 MADDOX ST, W1 020 7499 3776 3–2C | 3 SOUTH QUAY, E14 020 7531 0300 12–1C | 11 OLD JEWRY, EC2 020 7600 8220 10–2C

"A wide range of both grass-fed and grain-fed steaks from around the globe" helps fully satisfy the cravings of "those who like a good steak meal and decent bottle of red" at this "very solid" group of NYC-style steak-houses, which – amongst the more expensive

multiples – remains the "best in town". "It's not a cheap option by any means, but great for a business lunch or blow-out in the evening". / www.goodmanrestaurants.com; 10.30 pm; W1 closed Sun, EC2 closed Sat & Sun, E14 closed Sat L & Sun.

GORDON RAMSAY
SW3 £169 2 2 2

68-69 ROYAL HOSPITAL RD 020 7352 4441 6–3D

"He should concentrate on the cuisine at this price, not his celebrity!" The world-famous TV chef's original solo HQ in Chelsea continues to divide opinion and scored even lower overall marks in the survey this year. Undoubtedly it still has many advocates who feel Matt Abé (who actually does all the cooking) produces a menu that's "a total delight for the senses", and that service is "unbeatable" (under longstanding "perfectionist" maître d', Jean Claude Breton, plus "very helpful" sommelier James Lloyd). Critics, though, are more vocal than supporters, feeling the "food needs to move on", or that the ambience ("limited by the layout of the room") is "too manufactured and precious to be enjoyable". All-in-all, Michelin's continual failure to recognise the long-term slide here is baffling, and to continue to award this establishment three stars seems nothing more than cynical sucking up to the world's biggest culinary media figure. / SW3 4HP; www.gordonramsay.com; @GordonRamsay; 10.15 pm; closed Sun & Mon; No jeans; booking max 9 may apply.

GORDON'S WINE BAR
WC2 £41 2 1 5

47 VILLIERS ST 020 7930 1408 5–4D

With its ancient, dark, candle-lit cellars and the benefit of one of central London's biggest terraces (adjoining Embankment Gardens), this old wine bar (dating from the 1890s) is perpetually thronged (mostly by young professionals), and has seemingly been visited by everyone in London at some point (even if they may struggle to remember exactly what it was called). Right by Embankment tube, it's a handy rendezvous, and an affordable one too, even if the self-service food is very basic (cold cuts, cheeses, salads and simple hot platters). Queues for service, cramped seating and a general feeling of scrum are all part of the experience. / WC2N 6NE; www.gordonswinebar.com; @GordonsWineBar; 11 pm, Sun 10 pm.

GOURMET BURGER
KITCHEN £32 2 2 2

Fans of London's original upmarket burger chain still acclaim the "best patties around" but this stalwart brand is looking "a little tired and worn out" nowadays. In summer 2018, its owners Famous Brands announced they were 'considering their strategic options' after a £2m loss at the group, although many reporters feel "there's nothing really wrong with the concept". / www.gbkinfo.com; most branches close 10.30 pm; no booking.

GOURMET GOAT
SE1 £9 4 2 2

BOROUGH MARKET, UNIT 27A ROCHESTER WALK 020 8050 1973 10–4C

Nothing but positive vibes again on this Borough Market stall, which serves simple East Mediterranean dishes to take away. Top Menu Tips: kid goat or veal wrap. / SE1 9AH; www.gourmetgoat.co.uk; @gourmet_goat; Mon & Tue 4 pm, Wed & Thu, Sat 5 pm, Fri 6 pm; closed Mon-Thu, Sat D, closed Sun; no booking; SRA-Food Made Good – 3 stars.

GOYA SW1 £48 3 3 2

34 LUPUS ST 020 7976 5309 2–4C

This "reliable tapas bar" in a "desolate stretch of Pimlico" "takes some beating". "Lunch for two including a bottle of wine, sardines, lamb chops, fried potatoes, espresso and service charge for £40 is terrific value" – no wonder "it's always busy". / SW1V 3EB; www.goyarestaurant.co.uk; 10 pm, Sun 9 pm.

GRANARY SQUARE
BRASSERIE N1 £52 2 2 4

GRANARY SQUARE, 1-3 STABLE ST 020 3940 1000 9–3C

"The fantastic decor and impressive bar greet guests with a 'WOW'" at The Ivy Collection's new opening on the former site of Bruno Loubet's Grain Store (RIP), which also boasts a bar and al-fresco dining terrace. "Unfortunately all this does not translate to the average food offerings" which live up to the DNA of Richard Caring's ever-expanding stable. / N1C 4AA; www.granarysquarebrasserie.com; @granarysqbrasserie; Mon-Thu 12.30 am, Fri & Sat 1.30 am, Sun 11.30 pm; Booking max 12 may apply.

GRAND TRUNK ROAD
E18 £59 4 4 3

219 HIGH ST 020 8505 1965 1–1D

"Some amazing tastes" reward a visit to this Woodford two-year-old from the ex-manager and ex-head chef of Mayfair's Tamarind – "not your normal Indian, with a menu that showcases dishes from across the subcontinent (Afghanistan, Pakistan, North India and Bangladesh)". Even those who feel the food "is a bit pricey for its location" say "it's very good". / E18 2PB; www.gtrrestaurant.co.uk; @GT_Road; Tue-Thu 10.30 pm; closed Mon, Fri & Sat D & Sun.

GRANGER & CO £53 2 2 3

237-239 PAVILION RD, SW1 020 3848 1060 6–2D | 175 WESTBOURNE GROVE, W11 020 7229 9111 7–1B | STANLEY BUILDING, ST PANCRAS SQ, N1 020 3058 2567 9–3C | THE BUCKLEY BUILDING, 50 SEKFORDE ST, EC1 020 7251 9032 10–1A

"A great way to start the day!" – "Be prepared to wait" (particularly at the W11 original) if you want to sample the trademark funky brunch of this star Aussie chef's "cool and airy" chain. But while feedback contains lots of adulation for his "light", "fresh" and "innovative" fare, even fans can find it "a real mix in terms of quality" and those who feel it's a case of "hype and trend over taste" say "it's astonishing that people queue in the rain to eat this mediocre-at-best food!" / Mon-Sat 10 pm, Sun 5pm.

THE GREAT CHASE
EC1 £46 342

16 SAINT JOHN ST 020 7998 0640 9–3D

Chef Radoslaw Nitkowski combines high-welfare, fully halal, British ingredients with non-alcoholic drinks (mocktails, handmade cordials and rare tea) at this innovative, inclusive small restaurant, near Sadlers Wells. It doesn't inspire a huge volume of feedback, but such as exists is very positive. / EC1V 4NT; www.thegreatchase.co.uk; @thegreatchaserestaurant; Wed-Sat 10.30 pm, Sun 5 pm; closed Wed L closed Sun D, closed Mon & Tue.

GREAT NEPALESE
NW1 £40 342

48 EVERSHOLT ST 020 7388 6737 9–3C

"If you want a curry, go Nepalese", say loyal fans of this age-old (over 50 years old) small and inconspicuous-looking outfit, down the side of Euston station, where the Nepalese specials are the way to go. Very limited feedback this year, but of the 'all good' variety. / NW1 1DA; www.great-nepalese.co.uk; 11.30 pm, Sun 10 pm; closed Sun.

GREAT QUEEN STREET
WC2 £55 322

32 GREAT QUEEN ST 020 7242 0622 5–1D

"Still a great option around Covent Garden" – this "quite large" foodie gastropub (spiritually it's actually more "a restaurant that looks something like a pub") "keeps things properly seasonal" with a "rustic", "something-for-everyone" British menu "that emphasises hearty dishes like game or meat pies". "At times, service can disappear completely, but when it's there it functions well." / WC2B 5AA; www.greatqueenstreetrestaurant.co.uk; @greatqueenstreet; 10.30 pm, Mon 11 pm, Sun 3 pm; closed Sun D; no Amex.

THE GREEN EC1 £48 343

29 CLERKENWELL GRN 020 7490 8010 10–1A

Good ratings all round for this year-old modern gastropub on a corner by Clerkenwell Green, under the same ownership as The Culpeper, nearby. Top Tip: "the £15 two-course lunch menu is a steal". / EC1R 0DU; www.thegreenclerkenwell.com; 10.30 pm.

THE GREEN CAFÉ
SE10 £19 332

285 GREENWICH HIGH RD 020 8305 0799 1–3D

"Spot on for brunch at any time of the day!" – a superior "local caff" in Greenwich with "good fry-ups" and "lots of healthy options too": "bespoke English breakfast, great poached egg dishes, super sweet potato fries, good breads, waffles, fab tea and coffee; oh, and maybe a slice of cake to take home!" / SE10 8NB;

@greencafeLDN; Mon-Fri 5 pm, Sat & Sun 5.30 pm; closed Mon-Sun D.

GREEN COTTAGE
NW3 £38 322

9 NEW COLLEGE PDE 020 7722 5305 9–2A

This veteran Chinese in a Swiss Cottage parade of shops "never fails to please with its authentic food in generous portions", according to a regular who has "been going for 40 years". No huge prizes for service here, though. / NW3 5EP; 11 pm; no Amex.

THE GREEN ROOM, THE NATIONAL THEATRE
SE1 £46 232

101 UPPER GROUND 020 7452 3630 2–3D

Fans of the National Theatre's glass-walled 'neighbourhood diner' feel it's a "good pre-show venue" with "professional and helpful service" and food that's "well-prepared, albeit pretty basic". The feeling is quite widespread, however, that – for such an "interesting site" – the "disappointing menu could be so much better". / SE1 9PP; www.greenroom.london; @greenroomSE1; Wed & Thu 11 pm, Fri & Sat midnight, Sun 6 pm.

GREENBERRY CAFÉ
NW1 £56 334

101 REGENTS PARK RD 020 7483 3765 9–2B

Limited but positive feedback this year on this cute all-day café on Primrose Hill's atmospheric main drag – a top local haunt, ideal for lazy breakfasts, light lunches or coffee and a bun any time of day. / NW1 8UR; greenberrycafe.co.uk; @Greenberry_Cafe; 10.30 pm; closed Mon D & Sun D; no Amex.

THE GREENHOUSE
W1 £128 333

27A HAYS MEWS 020 7499 3331 3–3B

You feel "far from the madding crowd, but in the heart of Mayfair" at this "stylish" haunt "tucked away near Park Lane", where "a pretty entrance through a city garden leads to a calm and well-styled modern interior". It's a "spacious" and luxurious room which is "great for business, but which would also impress a date" (although it can also seem "a bit stiff" for some tastes). Having won gastronomic acclaim (not least two Michelin stars) in recent times with some "exemplary" modern cuisine, Arnaud Bignon moved on in mid-2018, perhaps explaining why ratings in this year's survey were lower across the board. New exec chef Alex Dilling (ex-Hélène Darroze) has promised to shake up the menu, with a focus on British and fresh produce. One constant, however: "one of London's best wine selections, especially if you are able to use your business credit card". / W1J 5NY; www.greenhouserestaurant.co.uk; @greenhouse27a; 10.30 pm; closed Sat L, closed Sun; booking max 12 may apply.

THE GREYHOUND CAFE
W1 £59 223

37 BERNERS ST 020 3026 3798 3–1D

"Lively and busy" first European outpost of a popular Thailand-based chain, which opened its doors in Fitzrovia in early 2018. Despite the odd adulatory newspaper review, our reporters' response is middling: it's "pleasant" (if "noisy") with somewhat fusionesque Thai cooking "of a decent standard" and "slightly chaotic service". / W1T 3NB; www.greyhoundcafe.uk; Mon-Fri 10 pm, Sat & Sun 9 pm.

GROUND COFFEE SOCIETY
SW15 £18 322

79 LOWER RICHMOND RD 0845 862 9994 11–1B

This 10-year-old Antipodean café (with an in-house roastery) in Putney serves "better coffee than many of the more self-conscious central London coffee shops". It's also a "great family breakfast/ brunch destination", and is "popular with Sunday morning cyclists". / SW15 1ET; www.groundcoffeesociety.com; @groundcoffeesociety; 6 pm; L only; no booking.

GUGLEE £40 332

7 NEW COLLEGE PDE, NW3 020 7722 8478 9–2A | 279 WEST END LN, NW6 020 7317 8555 1–1B

"A discovery" for first-timers – this duo of modern Indians in West Hampstead and Swiss Cottage win praise for their street-food-influenced dishes. / www.guglee.co.uk; 11 am.

THE GUILDFORD ARMS
SE10 £52 343

55 GUILDFORD GROVE 020 8691 6293 1–3D

"Not your typical pub food, there's real quality and great staff" at this three-storey Georgian boozer in Greenwich. "Attention to culinary detail" comes thanks to chef Guy Awford, previously of the area's "late, lamented Inside restaurant (RIP)". "Midweek lunch is exceptional value, given the quality". / SE10 8JY; www.theguildfordarms.co.uk; @GuildfordArms_; 10 pm, Sun 9 pm; closed Mon.

THE GUINEA GRILL
W1 £75 334

30 BRUTON PL 020 7409 1728 3–3B

"Old school" grill room adjacent to a tucked-away Mayfair mews pub, whose traditional British pies and steaks have grown more fashionable in recent years, and led something of a renaissance for its profile. A natural favourite for expense-accounters, the relatively grand "back dining room is the best for business", or you can grab one of their award-winning steak 'n' kidney puds in the small and cosy bar at the front. / W1J 6NL; www.theguinea.co.uk; @guineagrill; 11.30 pm, Sun 3.30 pm; closed Sat L & Sun; booking max 8 may apply.

THE GUN E14 £71 2|3|4

27 COLDHARBOUR 020 7515 5222 12–1C

A fine position by the Thames, looking over to the O2, is the draw to this 200-year-old, Grade II listed tavern in the depths of Docklands. Since its sale by ETM group to Fuller's, it doesn't attract the attention it once did as a dining destination, but feedback on eating here remains upbeat. / E14 9NS; www.thegundocklands.com; @thegundocklands; 10 pm, Sun 7 pm; closed Sun D.

GUNPOWDER £38 4|4|3

ONE TOWER BRIDGE, 4 CROWN SQUARE, SE1 AWAITING TEL 10–4D NEW | 11 WHITES ROW, E1 020 7426 0542 13–2C

"Home-style Indian tapas" – "beautifully spiced, without overpowering the flavour of the ingredients" and "each plate a unique reinvention of a traditional dish" – lures sizeable queues outside this "cosy, if slightly cramped" two-year-old "tucked away 150m from Spitalfields Market"; a second branch opened in the shiny new One Tower Bridge development at the start of September 2018. Top Menu Tip: "the spicy venison doughnut is inspired". / www.gunpowderlondon.com; @gunpowder_ldn.

GUSTOSO RISTORANTE & ENOTECA SW1 £48 2|4|3

33 WILLOW PL 020 7834 5778 2–4B

"As the years have gone by", this "enjoyable and efficient" Pimlico stalwart, "on a quiet street behind Westminster Cathedral", has won a very loyal following thanks to its "family-style atmosphere, lovely service, and well-chosen wines". Some reports say the food is a little "basic" or "variable", but most accounts describe it as "authentic" and "affordable". / SW1P 1JH; ristorantegustoso.co.uk; @GustosoRist; 10.30 pm, Sun 10 pm.

GYMKHANA W1 £70 4|3|4

42 ALBEMARLE ST 020 3011 5900 3–3C

"For high-end Indian cuisine, it's still streets ahead" – the Sethi family's epic Mayfair venture, near The Ritz, remains the survey's most-mentioned Indian, marrying "sophisticated interior design" (on an "old-style, colonial" theme), with "superbly original", "well-spiced and complex" cooking that's "so much more interesting than the huge majority of its peers". Service is "charming", but can on occasion be "erratic" too. / W1S 4JH; www.gymkhanalondon.com; @GymkhanaLondon; 10.30 pm; closed Sat & Sun.

HACHÉ £43 3|3|2

95-97 HIGH HOLBORN, WC1 020 7242 4580 2–1D | 329-331 FULHAM RD, SW10 020 7823 3515 6–3B | 24 INVERNESS ST, NW1 020 7485 9100 9–3B | 37 BEDFORD HILL, SW12 020 8772 9772 11–2C | 153 CLAPHAM HIGH ST, SW4 020 7738 8760 11–2D | 147-149 CURTAIN RD, EC2 020 7739 8396 13–1B

"Even for burgers the French do it better", say fans of this small group with a Gallic-inspired take on American fast food: "steak haché comme il faut, and les frites are also perfect". / www.hacheburgers.com; 10.30 pm, Fri-Sat 11 pm, Sun 10 pm; WC1 9 pm; WC1 Sat & Sun.

HAI CENATO SW1 £55 2|3|2

2 SIR SIMON MILTON SQUARE, 150 VICTORIA ST 020 3816 9320 2–4B

"It's pizza, Jim, but not as we know it..." say fans of Jason Atherton's large and "buzzy" pizzeria in Victoria's Nova development, who go a bundle on its "unusual toppings on good quality bases" (plus pasta and some other fare). Even some supporters acknowledge that "it's a little pricey" however, and there's quite a significant constituency that says the experience here is "reasonable" but "wouldn't leave you clamouring to return". / SW1H 0HW; haicenato. co.uk; @haicenato; 10 pm, Sun 9.30 pm; booking max 6 may apply.

HAKKASAN £99 4|2|4

17 BRUTON ST, W1 020 7907 1888 3–2C | 8 HANWAY PL, W1 020 7927 7000 5–1A

"It is everything I would expect not to like: a proven formula, a bit on the expensive side, way too trendy... but in spite of everything I can't get enough of it!" These "dark", "nightclub-style", "very noisy" Chinese/pan-Asians "haven't changed since they opened" (which, in the case of the original, was 17 years ago in 2001, with Mayfair following in 2010). They are "still at the top of their game" with "always zingy and exciting" cuisine and a "chic and moneyed aesthetic" that particularly suits those looking for "a showy-off night out". Service can be "haughty and inconsistent" – no changes there then either... Top Menu Tip: "still a go-to for quality dim sum". / www.hakkasan.com; 12.30 am, Sun 11.15 pm; W1 12.30 am, Thu-Sat 12.45 am, Sun midnight; no trainers, no sportswear.

HAM NW6 £53 3|2|3

238 WEST END LANE 020 7813 0168 1–1B

"A very welcome addition to the otherwise disappointing collection of West Hampstead eateries" is how most reporters and press reviewers judge Aussie chef Matt Osborne's new neighbourhood venture, whose brunch menu in particular "is inventive and varied, from hearty to healthy". That's the majority view anyway: to a minority, its excellence can seem a bit over-egged. / NW6 1LG; www.hamwesthampstead.com/ham; @hamwhampstead/; Wed-Sat 11 pm, Sun 6 pm; closed Mon & Tue.

HAM YARD RESTAURANT, HAM YARD HOTEL W1 £73 2|3|4

1 HAM YD 020 3642 1007 4–3D

"If you can find this hidden-away gem, it is superbly located for Theatreland" – just a short stroll from Piccadilly Circus, yet seemingly miles away, with "a great courtyard for a summer lunch", and "lovely interior" with "amazing Kit Kemp decor that makes it a particularly great lunch venue". Judged on its food alone, it can be "average" (and somewhat "let the whole meal down"), but is mostly "solid"; and the "sumptuous afternoon tea in the heart of the West End" is terrific – "somewhere to take both Granny and your hipster cousin". / W1D 7DT; www.firmdalehotels.com; @Firmdale_Hotels; 11.30 pm, Sun 10.30 pm.

THE HAMPSHIRE HOG W6 £51 3|3|3

227 KING ST 020 8748 3391 8–2B

"Attractively decorated rooms, a friendly pub ambience and good food" make it worth remembering this large pub (with big rear garden), near Hammersmith Town Hall. / W6 9JT; www.thehampshirehog.com; @TheHampshireHog; 10 pm, Sun 4 pm; closed Sun D.

HANS BAR & GRILL SW1 £78

164 PAVILION RD 020 7730 7000 6–2D

Just off Sloane Square in chichi Pavilion Road, this svelte new brasserie is run by swanky nearby boutique hotel 11 Cadogan Gardens (a stablemate of luxurious Cliveden House and Chewton Glen). It opened in May 2018, just as the survey was drawing to a close – no reports as yet on its all-day seasonal menu, but in this location, something is very wrong if it doesn't attract a hub for the Made in Chelsea crowd. / SW1X 0BP; www.hansbarandgrill.com; @HansBarGrill; 10.30pm.

THE HARCOURT W1 £59 3|3|4

32 HARCOURT ST 020 3771 8660 7–1D

This swish, five-storey gastropub (Grade II listed) on the fringes of Marylebone "is a beautiful spot in the centre of town, with a cool interior" and serving some "very good" cooking (with Nordic influences). / W1H 4HX; www.theharcourt.com; @the_harcourt; 11 pm, Sun 10.30 pm.

HARE & TORTOISE £40 3|3|2

11-13 THE BRUNSWICK, WC1 020 7278 9799 2–1D | 373 KENSINGTON HIGH ST, W14 020 7603 8887 8–1D | 156 CHISWICK HIGH RD, W4 020 8747 5966 8–2A | 38 HAVEN GRN, W5 020 8810 7066 1–2A | 296-298 UPPER RICHMOND RD, SW15 020 8394 7666 11–2B | 90 NEW BRIDGE ST, EC4 020 7651 0266 10–2A

"Tasty food in huge portions" hits the spot at this casual pan-Asian group with a "good range of dishes to please the whole family". "Consistent levels of cooking" and "well presented sushi" make it a cut above most chain rivals at a similar price and something of a quiet success story. / www.hareandtortoise-restaurants.co.uk; 11 pm; EC4 10.30, Fri 11 pm; EC4 closed Sun; W14 no bookings.

THE HARLOT W4

210 CHISWICK HIGH RD AWAITING TEL 8–2A

Henry Harris and James McCulloch (trading as Harcourt Inns) are on a roll with their pub-conversion concept; it's just been announced that a fourth venue is being developed (to join

The Coach, The Hero of Maida and Three Cranes), this time in Chiswick. The last pub of any ambition to open in downtown Chiswick was Gordon Ramsay's The Devonshire: let's hope they can do better than that: they certainly have a good start with some gorgeous premises in the shape of Chiswick's late Victorian police station (complete with charming back courtyard), which until recently traded as Carvosso's (RIP). / W4 1PD.

HARRY MORGAN'S NW8 £42 2|3|2

29-31 ST JOHN'S WOOD HIGH ST 020 7722 1869 9–3A

"Excellent salt beef", "lots of versions of chicken soup" and other Jewish deli classics are the stars of the show at this St John's Wood institution, whose overall food offer is solid rather than spectacular. "It never changes", say fans: "we love it!". Top Tip: great all-day breakfast. / NW8 7NH; www.harryms.co.uk; @morgan_hm; Sun-Thu 9 pm, Fri & Sat 9.30 pm.

HARRY'S BAR W1

30-34 JAMES ST AWAITING TEL 3–1A

A second addition to Caprice Group's new 'Harry's' brand opens in autumn 2018, with an all-day menu under the same executive chef (Diego Cardoso). With its Mayfair location and aim to "serve a slice of the 'Dolce Vita' in the heart of the West End" this is very much known territory for Richard Caring's luxury group. See also 'Harry's Dolce Vita'. / W1U 1EU; www.harrys-bar.co.uk.

HARRYS DOLCE VITA SW3 £59 3|4|5

27-31 BASIL ST 020 3940 1020 6–1D

Near the back of Harrods, "the latest addition to the Caprice Holdings group" delights Knightsbridge shoppers and other denizens of SW3 with its "glamorous" decor and very "traditional" menu of cicchetti, pasta, pizze, risotti and grills. It inspired the odd gripe ("like a crowded train carriage"), but more common are raves for its "reasonably priced" fare (for the location) and slick service ("superb coffee too… the real McCoy, oh, and did I mention the olive oil!"). A new sibling – Harry's Bar (see also) – opens in October 2018. / SW3 1BB; www.harrysdolcevita.com; Mon-Fri 10 pm, Sat & Sun 9 pm.

HARWOOD ARMS SW6 £68 4|3|3

WALHAM GROVE 020 7386 1847 6–3A

"Terrific game dishes" (not least "the best venison specials in the whole of London") are highlights of the "interesting menu" (culinary oversight comes from Brett Graham of The Ledbury and Mike Robinson of Berkshire's Pot Kiln) at this renowned hostelry, lost in the distant backstreets of Fulham, which finally seized the crown for the first time this year as the survey's No.1 gastropub (from The Anchor & Hope). "This is a pub where the food takes pride of place and drinking is incidental", but it's a "perfect mix" of the two, preserving the

"informal" approach of a traditional boozer (if with very limited space for non-diners). / SW6 1QP; www.harwoodarms.com; @HarwoodArms; Tue-Sat, Mon 9.30 pm, Sun 9 pm; closed Mon L; credit card required to book.

HASHI SW20 £37 3|3|2

54 DURHAM RD 020 8944 1888 11–2A

"Awesome sushi" and other Japanese dishes make this low-key outfit in suburban Raynes Park a "great local", "consistent year after year". ("Unfortunately they've stopped doing BYO.") / SW20 0TW; 10.30 pm, Sun 10 pm; closed Tue-Fri L, closed Mon; no Amex.

HATCHED (FORMERLY DARWIN) SW11 £69 4|4|2

189 SAINT JOHN'S HILL 020 7738 0735 11–2C

"What's not to love" about this new Battersea favourite, which inspires major love from local reporters for its "fine dining done informally and brought to the local high street". The only quibble is that its interior is "a bit Spartan", but it provides "superb top-end cooking" ("deconstructed classics, with some genuine taste sensations") from the open kitchen. / SW11 1TH; www.hatchedsw11.com; @HatchedSW11; Wed & Thu 9.30 pm, Fri & Sat 10 pm, Sun 3 pm; closed Wed & Thu L closed Sun D, closed Mon & Tue.

THE HAVELOCK TAVERN W14 £51 3|2|4

57 MASBRO RD 020 7603 5374 8–1C

This backstreet Olympia gastropub is not the major destination it once was, but locals agree it's still "at the top after all these years". "They produce different menus morning and evening, seven days a week – the cooking is imaginative, tasty and reliably so". "Amazing that they still maintain the unpretentious, high-quality food at such reasonable prices." / W14 0LS; www.havelocktavern.com; @HavelockTavern; 10.30 pm, Sun 10 pm.

HAVEN BISTRO N20 £49 3|4|3

1363 HIGH RD 020 8445 7419 1–1B

"An oasis" in Whetstone and the outer fringes of north London, which locals reckon is the best bet in the area for "good food and friendly, excellent service". / N20 9LN; www.haven-bistro.co.uk; 10.30 pm, Sun 10 pm; No shorts.

HAWKSMOOR £79 3|2|2

5A AIR ST, W1 020 7406 3980 4–4C | 11 LANGLEY ST, WC2 020 7420 9390 5–2C | 3 YEOMAN'S ROW, SW3 020 7590 9290 6–2C | 16 WINCHESTER WALK, SE1 020 7234 9940 10–4C | 157 COMMERCIAL ST, E1 020 7426 4850 13–2B | 10-12 BASINGHALL ST, EC2 020 7397 8120 10–2C

"Mouth-watering steaks at eye-watering prices" is the harsh-but-fair summary on Huw Gott and Will Beckett's famous and fashionable

steakhouse chain. To its enormous cult following: "yes, it's pricey, but – wow! – it's worth it!", thanks to its "melt-in-the-mouth" British-bred meat (some would say "the best in London"), "delicious sides", "impressive cocktail menu", and a "distinctly clubby" style that is, for a fair few expense-accounters, "perfect for business" too. With the inexorable expansion of the brand, though (next stop – NYC – with an opening in mid-2019, not far from Gramercy Park) has come an inexorable and ongoing decline in ratings, with increasing gripes about "hit-and-miss service", an atmosphere that's too "loud and busy", and a feeling that "it's not the Hawksmoor it used to be". / www.thehawksmoor.com; 10.30 pm; W1 & WC2 Fri & Sat 11 pm, Sun 9pm-10 pm; EC2 closed Sat & Sun; SRA-Food Made Good – 2 stars.

HAZ £50 2|2|2

9 CUTLER ST, E1 020 7929 7923 10–2D | 34 FOSTER LN, EC2 020 7600 4172 10–2B | 64 BISHOPSGATE, EC2 020 7628 4522 10–2D | 112 HOUNDSDITCH, EC3 020 7623 8180 10–2D | 6 MINCING LN, EC3 020 7929 3173 10–3D

"Fabulous smells, reliable cooking and rapid service" make this Turkish group a popular choice for a "self-funded lunch" in the Square Mile. On the downside, they can be "far too noisy for conversation" and sometimes the food is no more than "predictable, going on adequate". / www.hazrestaurant.co.uk; 11.30 pm; EC3 closed Sun.

HEDDON STREET KITCHEN W1 £71 2|2|2

3-9 HEDDON ST 020 7592 1212 4–3B

As "a nice option for a mid-shopping break", Gordon Ramsay's West End outfit off Regent Street improved its previously dire ratings this year, although the experience can still seem "beige". It's best with kids in tow, as under-12s eat free at any time from the menu of Tilly's Treats, designed by junior TV chef Matilda Ramsay ("and the kids love the ice cream parlour too"). / W1B 4BE; www.gordonramsay restaurants.com/heddon-street-kitc; @heddonstkitchen; midnight, Sat 1 am.

HEDONE W4 £129 4|3|2

301-303 CHISWICK HIGH RD 020 8747 0377 8–2A

Ex-solicitor, Mikael Jonsson's "idiosyncratic" passion-project in deepest Chiswick continues to inspire controversy amongst its large following. No-one is too fussed that the interior is "clinical, with harsh light": it's the hit to the wallet that elicits grief, with many critics apt to rate the food highly, but still cavil at the "outrageous prices". Its disciples, though, are "captivated" and feel "the enormous bill is entirely fair" given the "stunning" ingredients ("some not seen elsewhere"), and the "mouthwatering wonderful", "constantly evolving" and "exciting" cuisine ("only on offer as tasting menus, but with each course a surprise and delight"). In their view: "at one Michelin star this restaurant is under-rated" – "the food level sometimes touches a three-star, but is certainly two-star and way better than just the one!" Top

Menu Tip: don't miss the bread. / W4 4HH;
www.hedonerestaurant.com; @HedoneLondon; 9.30
pm; closed Tue-Thu L, closed Sun & Mon; booking
max 7 may apply.

HEIRLOOM N8 £53 3|3|3

35 PARK RD 020 8348 3565 9–1C

"A really cool neighbourhood local" up in
Crouch End, with an emphasis on seasonal
cooking and biodynamic wines. Brunch and
Sunday roast are key occasions in its week –
at other times a somewhat more ambitious,
modern British menu is served. / N8 8TE;
www.heirloomn8.co.uk; @HeirloomN8; Mon-Wed
midnight, Thu-Sat 1.30 am, Sun 11 pm.

HÉLÈNE DARROZE, THE CONNAUGHT HOTEL W1 £147 3|4|4

CARLOS PL 020 3147 7200 3–3B

"The beautiful room… the attentive,
enthusiastic and highly competent staff… the
exceptional precision of the cuisine, together
with its subtlety" – Hélène Darroze's "romantic"
operation in this most pukka of Mayfair hotels
is a fine example of "refined, effortless and
luxurious 'art de la table'" (including a notably
good wine list) and its many advocates feel you
"can't fault the place". Sceptics agree "it's very
good… just not worth the mega prices". / W1K
2AL; www.the-connaught.co.uk; @TheConnaught; 10
pm, Sun 9 pm; closed Mon & Sun; No trainers.

HELIOT STEAK HOUSE WC2 £64 3|3|3

CRANBOURN ST 020 7769 8844 5–3B

"Surprisingly tasty and well-cooked steaks
considering it's in a casino" make it worth
remembering this glitzy grill, looking down
onto the roulette tables of the UK's biggest
casino (by Leicester Square tube). Top
Tip: great pre-theatre deal. / WC2H 7AJ;
www.hippodromecasino.com; @HippodromeLDN; 1
am; closed Mon-Fri L, closed Sun.

HELIX (SEARCYS AT THE GHERKIN) EC3 £78 3|3|5

30 ST MARY AXE 033 0107 0816 10–2D

"The view – ground-level to zenith – is
breathtaking", sitting on the 39th-floor of
this London landmark: "go if you need to
impress, especially an out-of-towner". And –
though "security to enter is (understandably)
Draconian" – all-in-all performance defies
the usual rules about rooms-with-a-view: it's
"so uplifting to combine great vistas with very
competent standards". Until recent times, entry
was restricted to employees within the building,
but the caterers rebranded and relaunched the
space (fka 'Searcys at The Gherkin') in summer
2018, and it's now open to all (including the top-
floor 'Iris' bar). / EC3A 8EP; searcysatthegherkin.
co.uk/helix-restaurant; @SearcysGherkin; 9 pm, Sun
3 pm; closed Sun D.

HENRIETTA BISTRO WC2 £62

HENRIETTA ST 020 3794 5314 5–3C

Ollie Dabbous has now left this dining room
inside the new 18-room Henrietta Hotel (sibling
to Grand Pigalle in Paris), and it has been
re-christened from plain 'Henrietta'. New chef
Sylvain Roncayrol offers a menu inspired by SW
France, Basque and Corsican cuisine. / WC2E
8NA; www.henriettahotel.com; 11 pm.

HEREFORD ROAD W2 £50 4|3|3

3 HEREFORD RD 020 7727 1144 7–1B

"Excellent" seasonal British cuisine – and
"modestly priced" too, especially given the
quality of the ingredients – is complemented
by a "thoughtful wine list" at chef/patron
Tom Pemberton's "wonderful neighbourhood
restaurant" in Bayswater. The odd reporter
feels "ambience is lacking", but the majority say
"the comfortable modern design and overall
atmosphere is really conducive to a great meal".
/ W2 4AB; www.herefordroad.org; @3HerefordRoad;
10.30 pm, Sun 10 pm.

THE HERO OF MAIDA W9 £58

55 SHIRLAND RD 020 7266 9198 1–2B

Formerly popular as The Truscott Arms (RIP)
which closed after the owners tussled with the
landlords, this revivified boozer opened in
spring 2018 as part of the trio of pubs launched
by James McCulloch in partnership with the
former chef/patron of Racine. It opened too
late for significant survey feedback, but one
early report was very enthusiastic: "it seems
as if Henry Harris has worked his magic",
with some excellent dishes reported. / W9 2JD;
theheromaidavale.co.uk; @TheHeroofMaida; Mon-
Fri 11 pm, Sat & Sun 11 pm.

THE HERON W2 £39 4|3|1

1 NORFOLK CR 020 7706 9567 9–4A

"Tucked away under a grotty pub" at the foot of
a Bayswater block, you don't come here for style
points, but "Thai food, like in Thailand". Results
took a dip last year, but regulars say it's back on
form. / W2 2DN; www.theheronpaddington.com;
@theheronpaddington; 11 pm, Sun 10.30 pm.

HICCE N1

COAL DROPS YARD AWAITING TEL 9–3C

Ramsay protégée and former head chef at
Angela Hartnett's Murano, Pip Lacey will open
her first restaurant, in King's Cross's hip Coal
Drops Yard development, in late October 2018,
with friend and business partner (who will be
front-of-house) Gordy McIntyre; apparently they
have been talking about running a restaurant
together for 17 years! The focus will be on
traditional techniques (marinating, curing and
pickling) and there will (of course) be an open
wood fire for cooking. Hicce is pronounced
ee-che, by the way. / N1C 4AB; www.hicce.co.uk;
@hiccelondon; Mon & Tue 9 pm, Fri & Sat 11.30 pm,
Wed 10 pm, Thu 11 pm, Sun 5 pm.

HIDE W1 £95 5|4|5

85 PICCADILLY 020 3146 8666 3–4C

"Wow, what a debut!" – this "huge", two-floor
(plus basement bar), glass-fronted opening, on
which Russian-owned Hedonism wines have
reportedly spent £20m, is the most ambitious
new project of 2018, occupying a landmark,
250-cover site "with a great view over Green
Park", which old hands will remember from
days of yore as the home of Fahkreldine (long
RIP). On the ground floor ('Hide Below' – price
shown) is an all-day luxurious brasserie, while
this first-floor location is dedicated to even
finer dining from a six- or nine-course tasting
menu (all-in with wine from about £200, with
a lighter three-course option available at lunch).
Chef-patron "Ollie Dabbous has done it again"
with his "exquisite", "light-with-a-Nordic-touch"
cuisine, which "looks fabulous and tastes even
better"; and whose "extraordinary attention
to detail" matches that of the "stunningly
beautiful" interior (which, in an ultra-luxe
way, also appears "charming and simple").
At both locations, you can order from the
"remarkable wine list", also with the option of
dialling up any of the 6,500 wines stocked by
Hedonism's Mayfair store (keep a clear head
though – their most expensive vintages are over
£10k!). "Definitely memorable!" / W1J 8JB;
www.hide.co.uk; @hide_restaurant; Mon-Fri 10 pm,
Sat & Sun 9 pm.

HIGH ROAD BRASSERIE W4 £59 2|2|2

**162-166 CHISWICK HIGH RD 020 8742 7474
8–2A**

"A great place to watch the world go by and
for brunch on the weekend" – this Soho House
owned hang-out, complete with large outside

Hide W1

Homeslice

terrace, continues to be a top breakfasting spot for the glitterati of Chiswick (if that's not a contradiction in terms). / W4 1PR; highroadbrasserie.co.uk; @HRBrasserie; Sun-Thu 11 pm, Fri & Sat midnight; booking max 8 may apply.

HIGH TIMBER
EC4 £70 233

8 HIGH TIMBER ST 020 7248 1777 10–3B

This "reliable and accommodating" South African-owned wine bar by the Wobbly Bridge (opposite Tate Modern) has a "limited", "steak-specialist" menu – "which is good because that means it's freshly cooked". The "incredible wine cellar downstairs and decent South African list upstairs" make it a great escape from the City. "The interior is a bit spartan 1980s but the outdoor terrace on the river is great for a dreamy lunch in the summer". / EC4V 3PA; www.hightimber.com; @HTimber; 10 pm; closed Sat & Sun.

HILL & SZROK E8 £55 333

60 BROADWAY MKT 020 7254 8805 14–2B

Atmospheric Broadway Market butchers, where, by night, you perch on stools for a counter-style supper of steaks, grills and a small selection of wines. A funky set-up, but it's decidedly not cheap, and not everyone goes a bundle on the experience. / E8 4QJ; www.hillandszrok.co.uk; @hillandszrok; 10.30 pm; no Amex; no booking.

HISPANIA EC3 £66 333

72-74 LOMBARD ST 020 7621 0338 10–3C

Nothing but praise this year for the high-quality Spanish cuisine offered by this characterful two-floor restaurant right by the Bank of England, which is done out in a distinctive, comfy and plush Iberian style, teetering agreeably between the formal and informal. / EC3V 9AY; www.hispanialondon.com; @hispanialondon; Tue-Fri 10 pm, Mon 9.30 pm; closed Sat & Sun.

HIX W1 £64 122

66-70 BREWER ST 020 7292 3518 4–3C

Fans of Mark Hix's West End flagship hail its "excellent modern British food" and "terrific ambience and premier Soho location", particularly recommending it for a "lunchtime business meeting". But overall it inspires remarkably little feedback these days, far too much of it to the effect that it's too costly and can be "very disappointing". / W1F 9UP;

www.hixrestaurants.co.uk/restaurant/hix-soho; @HixRestaurants; 11.30 pm, Sun 10.30 pm.

HIX OYSTER & CHOP HOUSE
EC1 £63 322

36-37 GREENHILL RENTS, COWCROSS ST 020 7017 1930 10–1A

"Buried off Smithfield on the way to the tube", Mark Hix's original solo operation put in a strong all-round performance this year. "Business-friendly, but without compromising on quality" – "the inventive and seasonal British menu is worthwhile and there is always a decent bit of steak". Top Tip: 4pm-7pm is Happy Hour for oysters. / EC1M 6BN; www.hixrestaurants.co.uk/restaurant/hix-oyster-cho; @hixchophouse; 11 pm, Sun 10 pm; closed Sat L.

HOLBORN DINING ROOM
WC1 £75 333

252 HIGH HOLBORN 020 3747 8633 2–1D

"Pies to die for" are the ace in the Brit-food pack at this "huge dining room" of a business-friendly hotel on the edge of the City. Chef Calum Franklin is the "wizard" behind this "savoury pastry mecca", which has its own Pie Room with a dedicated take-away hatch, along with pie and Wellington masterclasses. Top Tip: "excellent choice for breakfast, too". / WC1V 7EN; www.holborndiningroom.com; @HolbornDining; 10.30 pm, Sun 10 pm.

HOLLY BUSH
NW3 £50 335

22 HOLLY MOUNT 020 7435 2892 9–1A

This "lovely, cosy, traditional pub" – an "unmodernised" 17th-century, Grade II listed building in Hampstead – is "relaxed and quiet enough for good conversation", with "a great atmosphere" and "really good food to match". "Exceptional Sunday roasts" – "but make sure you sit upstairs". / NW3 6SG; www.hollybushhampstead.co.uk; @thehollybushpub; 10 pm, Sun 8 pm.

HOME SW15
SW15 £57 333

146 UPPER RICHMOND RD 020 8780 0592 11–2B

Limited but upbeat feedback on this new neighbourhood café, bar and restaurant on the former site of BIBO (RIP) in Putney, not far from East Putney tube – run by three friends who met at west London Charlotte's Group, and serving a similarly easygoing mix of cocktails and modern bistro dishes. / SW15 2SW; www.homesw15.com; @homesw15; Mon-Fri 10 pm, Sat & Sun 9 pm.

HOMESLICE £37 333

52 WELLS ST, W1 020 3151 7488 2–1B | 13 NEAL'S YD, WC2 020 7836 4604 5–2C | 101 WOOD LANE WHITE CITY, W12 020 3034 0381 1–2B | 374-378 OLD ST,

EC1 020 3151 1121 13–1B | 69-71 QUEEN ST, EC4 020 3034 0381 10–2C

"Huge tasty pizzas" with a "very thin crust and unusual toppings" have attracted a strong following for this stripped-down concept. (The group is owned by the late Terry Wogan's sons and has a branch in his old stamping-ground, the BBC's former home at White City.) / www.homeslicepizza.co.uk; @homesliceLDN; 11 pm, EC1 & W1 Sun 10 pm; no booking.

HONEST BURGERS £28 333

"A lot of chains could learn an awful lot from Honest Burgers" which is pipped to the crown of London's best burger only narrowly by a couple of smaller groups (Patty & Bun and Bleecker). "Gloriously juicy" and "scrumptious" patties are served "with lovely buns" and – not to be forgotten – "the legendary, addictive rosemary fries to die for" (included in the price). All this plus "really helpful staff and a lively, industrial-chic vibe" make it a massive ongoing hit. "They even do gluten-free burger buns!". "No wonder it's tough times at Byron…" / www.honestburgers.co.uk; @honestburgers; 10 pm-11 pm; SW9 closed Mon D; EC3 closed Sat & Sun; no booking.

HONEY & CO W1 £47 443

25A WARREN ST 020 7388 6175 2–1B

"It's hard to get a table… and a tight fit if you do", but Sarit Packer and Itamar Srulovich's deceptively ordinary looking little Warren Street café punches well above its weight with its "amazingly friendly" service, and "exotic" and "sumptuous" Middle Eastern dishes – "a rare combination of simplicity and outstanding realisation". "A gem for any meal between breakfast (al fresco!) and late dinner." / W1T 5JZ; www.honeyandco.co.uk; @Honeyandco; Sun-Thu midnight, Fri & Sat 1 am; closed Sun; no Amex.

HONEY & SMOKE
W1 £50 432

216 GREAT PORTLAND ST 020 7388 6175 2–1B

"Delicious, copious and very original Middle Eastern cuisine" inspires nothing but praise for Honey & Co's bigger sibling, south of Great Portland Street café – a modern take on the grill house – even if ratings support those who feel "it's not quite as excellent as when it first opened". "Shame the decor is so unwelcoming", too – "it looks like a converted office" and can seem "awkward and uncomfortable", especially in comparison with the "café intimacy" of its stablemate. / W1W 5QW; www.honeyandco.co.uk/smoke; @Honeyandco; 11.30 pm; closed Sun & Mon.

HOOD SW2 £50 433

67 STREATHAM HILL 020 3601 3320 11–2D

"A small-but-changing menu of high-quality dishes using fresh, local and seasonal produce, a great selection of beers and ales plus English wines (and interesting soft drinks)" is served "promptly but without being rushed" at this "fabulous local" in Streatham. / SW2 4TX;

www.hoodrestaurants.com; @HoodStreatham; Sun-Thu midnight, Fri & Sat 1 am.

HOPPERS £61 422

49 FRITH ST, W1 NO TEL 5–2A | 77 WIGMORE ST, W1 020 3319 8110 3–1A

"Fabulous spiced dishes" based around hoppers (Sri Lankan rice pancakes) offer "a completely different experience of Indian (or akin to Indian anyway) food" at the Sethi family's "so original" and "fun" street-food cafés, in Soho and Marylebone. But while fans still find the formula "amazing… even with the wait", ratings slid badly this year due to the number of reporters who found it "didn't live up to the hype", citing issues including "pushy" or "overly swift" service and a sense it's "just a bit too pleased with its own vibe". Soho is walk-in only, except for ticketed events every other Sunday. /

THE HORSESHOE NW3 £53 334

28 HEATH ST 020 7431 7206 9–2A

This "buzzy" gastropub has a "hipper atmosphere than most in Hampstead". The "good honest local food" is a "reliable bet" to accompany "great beer" from the in-house Camden Town Brewery – founded downstairs in the cellar and now brewed nearby. / NW3 6TE; www.thehorseshoehampstead.com; @TheHorseShoeCTB; 10 pm, Fri & Sat 10.30pm, Sun 9.30 pm.

HOT STUFF SW8 £28 352

19-23 WILCOX RD 020 7720 1480 11–1D

"A simple menu of vibrant and fresh-tasting curries" is a joy at this "favourite local Indian": a "very charming" and "reasonably priced" family business in the characterful stretch of Vauxhall's Little Portugal that featured in the movie 'My Beautiful Laundrette'. / SW8 2XA; www.welovehotstuff.com; Mon-Thu, Sat, Fri 10 pm; closed Mon-Thu, Sat L, closed Sun; no Amex; no booking.

HOUSE OF HO W1 £62 344

1 PERCY ST 020 7323 9130 2–1C

Vietnam meets Japan at this "buzzy" outfit in an "attractive townhouse off Charlotte Street" in Fitzrovia. Chef Ian Pengelly's "delicious and mostly authentic food" combines with "attentive service" for "a wonderful experience that's hard not to enjoy". / W1T 1DB; www.houseofho.co.uk; @HouseOfHo; 11 pm; closed Sun.

HOUSE RESTAURANT, NATIONAL THEATRE SE1 £56 232

NATIONAL THEATRE, SOUTH BANK 020 7452 3600 2–3D

An "ideal pre-theatre venue", the National's "pleasant" dining room focuses wisely on a "small, tight menu" that satisfies most reporters – and "surprises" some. "The standard of cooking varies, but the service is always excellent": "they'll get you to your seat at the

theatre in time!". / SE1 9PX; house.nationaltheatre.org.uk; @NT_House; 10.30 pm, Sun 10 pm; D only (L served on matinee days), closed Sun.

HOVARDA W1 £68 234

36-40 RUPERT ST 020 3019 3460 4–3D

"Lovely place… shame about the ridiculous portion-sizes given the price": this good-looking winter 2017 opening, just south of Shaftesbury Avenue, is the brainchild of the folks behind Marylebone's Yosma, serving an 'Aegean-inspired' (i.e. Turkish/Greek) menu, but even those who find the "food's good, sometimes brilliant" can still on occasion feel it's "overpriced". / W1D 6DR; www.hovarda.london; Sun-Thu 11 pm, Fri & Sat 11.30 pm.

HUBBARD & BELL, HOXTON HOTEL WC1 £57 333

199-206 HIGH HOLBORN 020 7661 3030 2–1D

"A very cool place, at its best at breakfast and late at night" – this chilled hang-out in a chichi Soho House hotel (actually in Holborn, despite the name) serves superior burgers, and other "good, down-to-earth dishes". / WC1V 7BD; www.hubbardandbell.com; @HubbardandBell; Tue-Thu 9.30 pm, Fri & Sat 10 pm.

HUMBLE GRAPE £53 344

THEBERTON ST, N1 020 3904 4480 9–3D | 2 BATTERSEA RISE, SW11 020 3620 2202 11–2C | 8 DEVONSHIRE ROW, EC2 020 3887 9287 10–2D NEW | 1 SAINT BRIDE'S PASSAGE, EC4 020 7583 0688 10–2A

"Unpretentious, relaxed and with a wide choice of wines and small plates" – with the latter "nicely judged to complement wines" – plus "enthusiastic and knowledgeable service" win particular praise for the Battersea original of this small group, and also its EC4 spin-off "hidden away and almost under the crypt of St Bride's Church". Last year, a further outlet also opened in Islington (no reports yet), and in 2018 a new City branch opened near Liverpool Street. Top Tip: "Monday nights is the time to go as wine is sold at retail price". / www.humblegrape.co.uk; @humblegrape.

HUNAN SW1 £94 521

51 PIMLICO RD 020 7730 5712 6–2D

"Truly one-of-a-kind" – the Peng family's Pimlico stalwart "continues to surprise and tantalise with its amazing" cooking and is an "all-time favourite" for many reporters, as well as regularly topping the list of London's best Chinese restaurants. "Don't ask for the menu" – "let Mr Peng or his son Michael decide what you should be served with" – a never-ending stream of tapas-sized dishes (if you don't like one, you won't go hungry as plenty more will arrive). Typically results are "brilliant", and there's a "huge wine list that's amazingly well-suited to spicy food". / SW1W 8NE; www.hunanlondon.com; 11 pm; closed Sun.

HUSH W1 £86 222

8 LANCASHIRE CT 020 7659 1500 3–2B

"The best location", a courtyard off Bond Street where "you can sit when the weather is warm", makes this bar and brasserie (co-founded by Roger Moore's son Geoffrey Moore) a "perennial favourite" of the Mayfair crowd as it approaches its 20th anniversary. There's a "nice atmosphere about the place and it works equally well for business as it does for fun". "The food is lovely but so it should be at these prices – although if you're shopping in Mayfair you can probably afford it!". Branches in Holborn and St Paul's have both closed down in recent years. / W1S 1EY; www.hush.co.uk; 11 pm; closed Sun; booking max 12 may apply.

HUTONG, THE SHARD SE1 £100 224

31 ST THOMAS ST 020 3011 1257 10–4C

"On the 33rd-floor the views over London are spectacular" as you'd expect of this dramatically-located dining room – the Shard's most commented-on destination – which won more consistent praise this year for its "exciting and delicious" Chinese cuisine under chef Sifu Fei Wang. On the downside, it can still be "let down a little by the service", but there's only really one major complaint here: that it's still "grossly overpriced". / SE1 9RY; www.hutong.co.uk; @HutongShard; 10.30 pm; No shorts.

IBÉRICA £53 223

ZIG ZAG BUILDING, 70 VICTORIA ST, SW1 020 7636 8650 2–4B | 195 GREAT PORTLAND ST, W1 020 7636 8650 2–1B | 12 CABOT SQ, E14 020 7636 8650 12–1C | 89 TURNMILL ST, EC1 020 7636 8650 10–1A

"A decent Spanish option (but it won't blow your mind)" – these "welcoming and buzzy tapas bars" remain "the kind of places one can linger with friends in true Hispanic style" (but perhaps lack the pizzazz of the brand's early days), providing "cheerful" (but "uneven") service, and "reasonably priced" (but slightly "formulaic") cuisine. / 11pm, SW1 Sun 10.30 pm; W1 closed Sun D.

ICCO PIZZA £18 521

46 GOODGE ST, W1 020 7580 9688 2–1C | 21A CAMDEN HIGH ST, NW1 020 7380 0020 9–3B NEW

"Zero frills… unless you count the oil and spice shaker!" do nothing to dent the adulation for these utilitarian "pit stops" with "bare stainless steel tables and collection from the counter". Fans say its "hot, fresh, thin-based pizza" is "about the best you can get at any price anywhere", and "with a Margherita at £4 and not much more for other options, it is easy to see why there are queues out the door on busy lunchtimes". / www.icco.co.uk; @ICCO_pizza.

ICHI BUNS W1 £43 323

24 WARDOUR ST 020 3937 5888 5–3A

"Great Japanese-style decor" adds pizzazz to this energetically designed three-floor newcomer in Chinatown, complete with clubby basement (with DJs). Feedback is still quite limited, but its menu of ramen, Japanese spring rolls and wagyu beef burgers was mostly highly rated. / W1D 6QJ; www.ichibuns.co.uk; @ichibuns; Mon & Tue 11 pm, Wed & Thu midnight, Fri & Sat 2 am, Sun 10.30 pm.

IDA W10 £47 323

167 FIFTH AVE 020 8969 9853 1–2B

"Tucked away in an unfashionable corner near the Queen's Park Estate", this "genuine neighbourhood Italian" is "usually booked out by an eclectic mix of locals". "Basically this is a pasta restaurant" and – even if results are not show-stoppers – offers "well-priced, sensibly portioned home cuisine"; meanwhile, the welcome is "very friendly" (even if sometimes "the level of service could use an upgrade"), and the interior full of "rustic charm". / W10 4DT; www.idarestaurant.co.uk; 11 pm; closed Mon-Sat L, closed Sun; no Amex.

IKOYI SW1 £60 432

1 ST JAMES'S MARKET 020 3583 4660 4–4D

"Posh and West African food? I didn't think they went together" – but the "strikingly original fusion" of modern techniques and Nigerian culinary traditional has produced some of "the most interesting cooking in London" at this year-old venue in a new development behind Piccadilly Circus. "An amalgam of an African chef (Iré Hassan-Odukale) and a Heston Blumenthal chef (Canadian-Chinese Jeremy Chan, ex-Fat Duck)", it is housed in a "Scandi-chic interior". "One of the most memorable meals of the year", "it all felt new to me!" / SW1Y 4AH; www.ikoyilondon.com; closed Sun.

IL GUSCIO N5 £51 343

231 BLACKSTOCK RD 020 7354 1400 9–1D

"My local Italian and I love it!" – this tightly packed Highbury fixture serves "really tasty pizza" as well other affordable Sardinian-inspired dishes. All this plus "friendly service, and it's child-friendly too!" / N5 2LL; www.ilgusciohighbury.co.uk; Sun-Thu 10.30 pm, Fri & Sat 11 pm; closed Mon-Fri L.

IN PARMA W1 £40 432

10 CHARLOTTE PLACE 020 8127 4277 2–1C

"I hate to admit it, but the cappelletti in brodo" ("pasta filled with Parmesan cheese and beef, slowly cooked for a couple of days and served in a rich capon broth, all of which really is exceptional") "might even be better than my mother's!!" – This Fitzrovia Italian (run by the Food Roots company, and sibling to Hoxton's Via Emilia) offers "authentic Parmesan dishes, prepared by authentic Parmesans", with an emphasis on charcuterie and cheeses from Parma, and with "good Lambrusco served

in traditional crockery" (by the bowl) being something of a hallmark. "The restaurant itself is long and narrow and would be a bit of a squeeze when busy, but service is pleasant and prices reasonable. Recommended." / W1T 1SH; www.in-parma.com; 11 pm, Sun 10.30 pm.

INDIA CLUB, STRAND CONTINENTAL HOTEL WC2 £32 222

143 STRAND 020 7836 4880 2–2D

"The climb up the stairs never fails to get the taste buds revving" on arrival at this "1940s time-warp" curry house, close to the Indian High Commission in the Strand. Recently saved from redevelopment, this "iconic" venue with its "mismatched Formica-topped tables" is "still one of the best and cheapest Indians in London". Top Tip: "BYO, or buy good-value beer at the hotel bar". / WC2R 1JA; www.strand-continental.co.uk; @hostelstrandcon; 10.50 pm; booking max 6 may apply.

INDIAN ACCENT W1 £91 544

16 ALBEMARLE ST 020 7629 9802 3–3C

"Quite simply, stunning – the best sub-continental cuisine you can get anywhere outside the subcontinent!" This "addictive" newcomer (a spin-off from one of India's top restaurants, in New Delhi, with an NYC sibling) occupies the same site (and is under the same ownership) as its predecessor Chor Bizarre (RIP) and has made an "astonishingly good" debut with "very refined and skilful" fusion cuisine (blue cheese naan, for instance) that's already achieved nigh on the highest ratings in town – "slick service" and svelte decor: "it's a real joy to eat here". / W1S 4HW; indianaccent.com/london; @Indian_Accent; Sun-Thu 10 pm, Fri & Sat 10.30 pm.

INDIAN MOMENT SW11 £42 332

44 BATTERSEA RISE 020 7223 6575 11–2C

This local-favourite curry house near Clapham Junction is a "good and accessible option for all palates" – even if it "tries too hard not to be

of the after-pub variety". "The move around the corner from Northcote Road to Battersea Rise hasn't reduced its popularity, but the new dining room can get cramped and extremely noisy". / SW11 1EE; www.indianmoment.co.uk; @indianmoment; midnight, Sun 10 pm.

INDIAN OCEAN SW17 £36 342

214 TRINITY RD 020 8672 7740 11–2C

This "wonderfully friendly local curry house" with a long-established fanbase by Wandsworth Common is "quite the best Indian restaurant in the area". "Its menu is a bit different from the standard, and well executed." / SW17 7HP; www.indianoceanrestaurant.com; 11 pm, Sat 11.30 pm; closed Mon-Fri L.

INDIAN RASOI N2 £36 332

7 DENMARK TERRACE 020 8883 9093 1–1B

"Don't be fooled by the off-putting exterior" of this intimate Muswell Hill Indian, which inside you'll find "rich, tasty food with some offbeat options" – "really good, authentic grub". / N2 9HG; www.indian-rasoi.co.uk; 11 pm, Sun 10.30 pm; no Amex.

INDIAN ZING W6 £54 432

236 KING ST 020 8748 5959 8–2B

"Wonderful Indian cuisine with unusual and delicious use of spices" has generated a big name and following for Manoj Vasaikar's "varied and interesting" nouvelle Indian, a short walk from Ravenscourt Park. On the downside, its premises – while attractive – are "tightly packed" and "can be quite noisy". / W6 0RS; www.indian-zing.co.uk; @IndianZing; 10.30 pm, Sun 10 pm.

INKO NITO W1 £50

55 BROADWICK ST 020 3959 2650 4–2B

From the folks behind Zuma and Roka, comes a kind of Roka-lite aiming to capture the millennial crowd with this cheaper newcomer in Soho (designed by a Californian agency, and

Indian Accent W1

whose sibling is already open in downtown LA). As at Roka, charcoal-grill cooking on the robata (here with Korean influences) is centre stage, but prices are lower than at its swankier stablemates. Too few reviews for a rating as yet, although one early reporter does think it's "very cool". / W1F 9QS; www.inkonitorestaurant.com/london-soho; 11.30 pm, Sun 10 pm.

IPPUDO LONDON   £46   3|2|3

31A VILLIERS ST, WC2   020 3667 1877 5–4D NEW | 1 CROSSRAIL PL, E14 020 3326 9485   12–1C

"A genuine import from Japan"; lovers of "decent, authentic noodles" give the thumbs-up to the "authentic" ramen served at the three London branches of this chain originating in Fukuoka, with venues in Holborn, Embankment and Canary Wharf. One aficionado insists they're actually "better than their Japanese outlets (although twice the price!)". / @IppudoLondon; WC2 10.30 pm; E14 9.30 pm, Sun 8.30 pm; no bookings.

ISABEL W1   £77   2|4|5

26 ALBEMARLE ST   020 3096 9292   3–3C

Juan Santa Cruz's gorgeous, gold-and-ebony Mayfair yearling (on the former site of Sumosan, RIP) draws a smart, Eurotrashy crowd and is undoubtedly "beautiful, and great for people watching". "You don't mind a high-end price tag, if the food measures up" too, but whereas some fans describe "such amazing and different flavours from the tapas-style menu" there is a high proportion for whom results are "just uneventful and unexciting". / W1S 4HQ; isabelw1.london; 2.30 am, Sun 11.30 pm.

ISHTAR W1   £51   3|3|2

10-12 CRAWFORD ST   020 7224 2446   2–1A

The "high-quality Turkish cooking" at this "very welcoming" Marylebone fixture has been "remarkably consistent for a few years now". Top Tip: "exceptional grilled lamb cutlets". / W1U 6AZ; www.ishtarrestaurant.com; 10 pm, Sun 9 pm.

THE IVY WC2   £76   2|3|4

1-5 WEST ST   020 7836 4751   5–3B

"I know it's not the celeb haunt it used to be and is now a bit touristy, but they still make you feel like a king" is still a widely held view on this epic "Theatreland classic" (the original in what's an increasingly sizeable national chain); and for its many fans a visit here is still a "warm, life-affirming experience". However, it feels to some regulars like the appeal is becoming "all about the room" and its "glamorous" decor, amidst growing unease that Richard Caring's group is just "milking it" nowadays – ratings slid across the board this year, and its comfort food cuisine "is as it always was, nothing special… just now even more expensive!". / WC2H 9NQ; www.the-ivy.co.uk; @TheIvyWestSt; Mon-Wed 11.30 pm, Thu-Sat midnight, Sun 10.30 pm; No shorts; booking max 6 may apply.

THE IVY CAFÉ   £59   1|2|3

96 MARYLEBONE LN, W1   020 3301 0400 2–1A | 120 ST JOHN'S WOOD HIGH ST, NW8   020 3096 9444   9–3A | 75 HIGH ST, SW19   020 3096 9333   11–2B | 9 HILL ST, TW9   020 3146 7733   1–4A

"A dilution of the Ivy name" – the cheaper, more bistro-esque 'Café' sub-brand is "a woeful imitation of the original" that's "all style and has nothing else to recommend it". Even many of those recommending breakfast – its best feature – say the results are "very predictable", and later in the day you get "standard pub grub-type food at fine dining prices" served by "brittle" and "amateur" staff. "Avoid at all costs!" / 11 pm, Fri & Sat 11.30 pm, Sun 10.30 pm; SW19 11 pm, Sun 10.30 pm; midnight.

IVY GRILLS & BRASSERIES   £59   2|2|4

26-28 BROADWICK ST, W1   020 3301 1166 4–1C | 1 HENRIETTA ST, WC2 020 3301 0200   5–3D | 197 KING'S RD, SW3 020 3301 0300   6–3C | 96 KENSINGTON HIGH ST, W8   020 3301 0500   6–1A | ONE TOWER BRIDGE, 1 TOWER BRIDGE, SE1 020 3146 7722   10–4D | 69 OLD BROAD ST, EC2   020 3146 7744   10–2D NEW

"On a nice day in the garden, there couldn't be a better way to have lunch!" (or an "amazing brunch") than at the Chelsea Garden branch of Richard Caring's bold brand-extension – "easily the best of the Ivy offshoots". But even fans concede that "service could be better" and that "you don't come here for the food": "it's all about that warm, buzzy atmosphere in glorious surroundings (outside in summer you'll swear you are in the South of France, watching the Provencal rosé making its way around the beautifully dressed ladies-who-lunch!)" The other branches offer a similar trade-off, with the outlets in Kensington and by Tower Bridge ("incredible views from the picture windows") both scoring well for ambience, although their "comfort food" offerings are even more "memorably mediocre" than in SW3. 'Ivy in the Park' which is to open in Canary Wharf is the most recently announced arrival in the group (at 50 Canada Square Park). On the overall concept, reporters are split. For a majority "although the spin-offs are not to be compared with the original Ivy, their name does help give a certain dignity to the experience". For a significant number though, "the brand is being trashed" with these "pretentious, unimaginative, chichi and average" imitations: "Obviously I understand the need to shamelessly exploit and monetise The Ivy name, but this is taking it too far!!" / ivycollection.com.

JACKSON & RYE   £54   2|2|2

56 WARDOUR ST, W1   020 7437 8338 4–2D | 219-221 CHISWICK HIGH RD, W4 020 8747 1156   8–2A | HOTHAM HOUSE, 1 HERON SQ, TW9   020 8948 6951   1–4A

This trio of US-style diners attracts mixed reports, with the Richmond branch receiving the highest praise for a "great view of the Thames". The food is "perfectly acceptable" to some, "tasteless and insipid" to others, but there's general agreement that "breakfast is the best option". / www.jacksonrye.com; @JacksonRye; 11 pm, Sun 10.30 pm; EC2 closed Sat & Sun.

JACOB THE ANGEL WC2   £9   3|3|3

16A NEAL'S YARD NO TEL 5–2C

Zoë and Layo Paskin (the siblings behind The Palomar and The Barbary) run this tiny coffee house (just 10 covers) in Seven Dials. A few in-the-know rate it for a quick brunch, superior bun or coffee, but don't go expecting magic. / WC2H 9DP; www.jacobtheangel.co.uk; 5 pm; closed Mon-Sun D; no booking.

JAFFNA HOUSE SW17   £30   3|2|2

90 TOOTING HIGH ST   020 8672 7786 11–2C

This "no-nonsense", "authentic, family-run caff" in Tooting split opinion this year. Most reporters still approve its "wide variety of unusual Sri Lankan specialities and incredibly good value thali selection" all at "cheap prices" in "a rather 1980s time-warp dining room". Others though are more cautious: "tipped as one of the better south Indians in Tooting but very cramped and nothing out-of-the-ordinary in my experience". / SW17 0RN; 11.30 pm.

JAMAVAR W1   £83   3|4|3

8 MOUNT ST   020 7499 1800   3–3B

"Having been to Jamavar in Bangalore, I tried their London restaurant and was most impressed" – Leela Palace's "plush", colonial-style yearling ("I'm not sure the decor is very PC!") is "a great addition to Mayfair" and wins ecstatic praise from many reporters for its "super slick service" and "fabulous and spicy" dishes that "strike a balance between the traditional spicing and flavours of Indian cuisine, but with high-end presentation and gastronomic flourishes!" No hiding, however, that it was a blow when they lost founding chef Rohit Ghai in January 2018, with ratings in this year's survey at laudable levels, but miles away from the giddy heights achieved in year one. / W1K 3NF; www.jamavarrestaurants.com; @JamavarLondon; closed Sun.

JAMES COCHRAN EC3   £68

19 BEVIS MARKS, LIVERPOOL ST 020 3302 0310   10–2D

James Cochran has left his eponymous City venture which retains the right to trade under his name. (He has now re-appeared in Islington, with the opening of 1251, a few doors along from his short lived Upper Street venture). This venue, serving the small plates Cochran developed, recorded some high marks this year. That said, there were also those who, perhaps unsurprisingly, have discerned "a lack of buzz or passion" about the place in recent times and in the circumstances it seems best to leave a re-rating till next year. / EC3A 7BJ; www.jcochran.restaurant; @jcochranchef; Wed-Sat 10 pm, Sun 4.30 pm; closed Sat L & Sun.

JAMIES ITALIAN £53 1 1 1

"Just because it says Jamie Oliver on the door does not mean it is going to be good", and for the last six years his beleaguered chain has received a dire scorecard in the Harden's survey – "awful, just awful" – no wonder the TV chef had to rescue it with his own, very deep, pockets this year. With these well-publicised financial problems, media fooderati like Marina O'Loughlin in The Sunday Times have finally woken from their long slumber and begun to comment on the fact that the emperor isn't wearing any clothes (bringing new meaning to the name 'Naked Chef'!): what on earth took them so long? / www.jamiesitalian.com; @JamiesItalianUK; 11.30 pm, Sun 10.30 pm; booking: min 6.

JASHAN N8 £33 4 4 2

19 TURNPIKE LN 020 8340 9880 1–1C

"It looks like your average curry house, but is anything but" – this "low-key favourite" provides "superlative dishes and cooking amid bog-standard decor in remote Turnpike Lane" and "is so cheap too!". / N8 0EP; www.jashan.co.uk; 10.15 pm, Fri & Sat 10.30 pm; closed Mon-Sun L; no Amex; may need 6+ to book.

JEAN-GEORGES AT THE CONNAUGHT W1 £98 3 3 3

**THE CONNAUGHT, CARLOS PLACE
020 7107 8861 3–3B**

Mixed and limited feedback on this stellar NYC's chef, Jean-Georges Vongerichten's latest London foray, which occupies a light-filled conservatory at the side of this blue-blooded Mayfair hotel. Ratings are not bad for its eclectic menu – from caviar and wagyu beef to pizza and cod 'n' chips – but although results can be "really lovely", it's darn expensive and no-one is that blown away. One stand-out feature though – "superb afternoon tea". / W1K 2AL; www.the-connaught.co.uk/mayfair-restaurants/jean-georges; @TheConnaught; 11 pm.

JIDORI £23 3 3 2

**15 CATHERINE ST, WC2 020 7686 5634
5–3D | 89 KINGSLAND HIGH ST, E8
020 7686 5634 14–1A**

Well-reputed (slightly hyped) Dalston yakitori café (run by Natalie Lee-Joe & Brett Redman) which wins solid (if not spectacular) ratings for its Japanese small plates. They must be doing something right, as they opened a 50-cover Covent Garden sibling in February 2018, praised in early reports for its "good food and friendly staff". /

JIKONI W1 £68 4 4 4

21 BLANDFORD ST 020 70341988 2–1A

Ravinder Bhogal's "magic touch with flavour" helps create "wonderful and interesting dishes" at her Marylebone yearling (whose cuisine reflects the chef-patron's mixed heritage with flavours from East Africa, the Middle East, Asia and Britain). With its "informal service" and "cosy" style it's "a perfect venue for culinary exploration". / W1U 3DJ; www.jikonilondon.com;

@JikoniLondon; Wed-Fri, Tue, Sat 10.30 pm; closed Tue, Sat L, closed Sun & Mon.

JIN KICHI NW3 £47 5 4 3

73 HEATH ST 020 7794 6158 9–1A

"Like walking through a portal into Tokyo" – this "really tiny" Japanese stalwart is "one of the few Hampstead restaurants worth going to" (note: "you'll need to book"). "The stuff on the grill/ BBQ (including yakitori meat skewers) is to die for", and "the sushi remains excellent", while "a recent revamp has not dulled its charm". "Sit and watch the superb food being prepared right under your nose – amazing!". / NW3 6UG; www.jinkichi.com; 10.30 pm, Sun 10 pm; closed Mon.

JINJUU W1 £61 4 3 4

16 KINGLY ST 020 8181 8887 4–2B

Korean-American TV chef Judy Joo "puts a fun – and delicious – twist on Korean food" at her "hidden gem" – a "lively and noisy" basement off Carnaby Street. Attractions include some of "the best Korean fried chicken in town and the rest of the food is damn good too", but some feel that it's "way too small to have a DJ" – you've been warned! / W1B 5PS; www.jinjuu.com; @JinjuuSoho; Mon-Wed midnight, Thu-Sat 1.30 am, Sun 11 pm.

JOANNA'S SE19 £47 3 5 4

56 WESTOW HILL 020 8670 4052 1–4D

"A great local", this American-inspired venue in Crystal Palace has been run by two generations of the Ellner family and "celebrated its 40th anniversary this year with an excellent retro menu". "Really reliable for every occasion", from breakfast through to "taking the in-laws out for dinner". / SE19 1RX; www.joannas.uk.com; @Joannas_1978; 10 pm, Sun 9 pm.

JOE ALLEN WC2 £55 2 3 4

2 BURLEIGH ST 020 7836 0651 5–3D

"Well done!" – "The move from Exeter Street to nearby Burleigh Street looks to have paid off" for this famous and "fun" Covent Garden veteran, forced to relocate a year ago. "The iconic Joe Allen atmosphere has been almost totally recreated, with the help of most of the original fixtures and fittings from the old place". "Service has moved up a notch or two" and while "the food can still be a bit hit 'n' miss", it's actually rated as much more consistently dependable now. Top Menu Tip: the "hidden off-the-menu burger" is still the top menu choice. / WC2E 7PX; www.joeallen.co.uk; @JoeAllenWC2; 11 pm, Sun 10.30 pm.

JOE PUBLIC SW4 £15 3 4 2

4 THE PAVEMENT 020 7622 4676 11–2D

"If all you want is a quick, bite-sized tasty pizza and a glass of vino, pop in here!" – to this quirky, small, handily-located outlet (in a converted WC) by Clapham Common. / SW4 7AA; www.joepublicpizza.com; @JoepublicSW4; midnight, Sun 11 pm; no booking.

JOLENE N16

**20 NEWINGTON GREEN 020 3887 2309
1–1C**

On the former Newington Green site of Dandy (RIP), a new bakery (and evening restaurant) from the founders of Primeur and Westerns Laundry, Jeremie Cometto-Lingenheim and David Gingell. Rare and ancient grains [you can say that sort of thing with a straight face nowadays! Ed] feature in the bread and cakes, milled and baked daily on site. / N16 9PU; www.jolenen16.com.

JOLLIBEE SW5

**180-182 EARLS COURT RD AWAITING TEL
6–2A**

Fried chicken and spaghetti with sweet hot dog sauce may not sound that interesting, but when the first European branch of Filipino fast food chain Jollibee opened in Milan in early 2018, people queued for HOURS to try it. Jollibee has been 'bringing chicken joy' for over 40 years in over 750 locations – and now it's our turn with this opening, in October 2018, on the former Earl's Court Wagamama site. / SW5 9QG; www.jollibee.com.ph/international; @Jollibee.

JOLLY GARDENERS SW18 £52 3 3 3

214 GARRATT LN 020 8870 8417 11–2B

An Earlsfield gastroboozer with a dining room in a "bright extension at the back", with a "good menu", from former MasterChef winner Dhruv Baker. Top Tip: "go later in the week for more interesting food". / SW18 4EA; www.thejollygardeners.com; @Jollygardensw15; 9.30 pm.

JONES & SONS N16 £51 3 3 3

**STAMFORD WORKS, 3 GILLETT ST
020 7241 1211 14–1A**

"A weekly-changing, perfectly executed modern British menu", with plenty of steak and fish options, wins praise for this open-plan venture near Dalston station. "I'm always surprised it's not full but maybe all the local hipsters have gone vegan?" / N16 8JH; www.jonesandsonsdalston.com; @JonesSons; Mon-Thu midnight, Fri & Sat 1 am, Sun 7 pm; booking max 7 may apply.

THE JONES FAMILY KITCHEN SW1

**7-8 ECCLESTON YARD 020 7739 1740
2–4B**

This June 2018 opening near Victoria Coach Station, from the folks behind the Jones Family Project in Shoreditch, majors in steaks, with meat sourced from The Ginger Pig. Early reports suggest it's a useful newcomer in a still-underprovided area. / SW1W 9AZ; www.jonesfamilyproject.co.uk; @JonesShoreditch; Tue-Sat, Mon 10.30 pm, Sun 3.30 pm.

Jones Family Project EC2

THE JONES FAMILY PROJECT EC2 £58 344

78 GREAT EASTERN ST 020 7739 1740 13–1B

Charcoal-grilled steaks and other meaty fare are the menu mainstays at this Shoreditch basement (with cocktail bar above), and were again solidly well-rated this year. / EC2A 3JL; www.jonesfamilyproject.co.uk; @JonesShoreditch; midnight, Sun 6 pm.

JOSÉ SE1 £52 545

104 BERMONDSEY ST 020 7403 4902 10–4D

"Pretty much as good as it gets for high-end tapas, and fantastic Spanish wines" – José Pizarro's "genius" Bermondsey original is "a rare combination of delicious food" ("new twists on classic dishes" which are "exceptional in their simplicity and quality"), "plus careful service and a joyful atmosphere"… "if you can squeeze in, it's always impossibly busy". / SE1 3UB; www.josepizarro.com; @Jose_Pizarro; 10.15 pm, Sun 5.15 pm; closed Sun D; no booking.

JOSÉ PIZARRO EC2 £59 322

BROADGATE CIRCLE 020 7256 5333 13–2B

This three-year-old tapas joint in Broadgate Circle consistently rates quite well and is often deafeningly busy, but in this more corporate environment has never generated the wider interest surrounding Pizarro's original venue in Bermondsey. / EC2M 2QS; www.josepizarro.com/jose-pizarro-broadgate; @JP_Broadgate; 10.30 pm; closed Sun.

JOY KING LAU WC2 £39 322

3 LEICESTER ST 020 7437 1132 5–3A

"Old-school Cantonese" over three floors just off Leicester Square with "legendary soft shell crab and brilliant dim sum", "fabulous, flavoursome morsels that arrive hot and steaming at your table". It's "not at all glamorous, but once you start eating you won't notice!" and it's "always super busy and crowded, so you have to queue – but it's soooo worth it". / WC2H 7BL; www.joykinglau.com; 11.30 pm, Sun 10.30 pm.

JUGEMU W1 £40 523

3 WINNETT ST 020 7734 0518 4–2D

"If you know your Japanese food and you don't want high-end dining with all the associated costs, then flock here! Flock and wait for one of the precious tables" at this little Soho izakaya presided over by chef Yuya Kikuchi (the best bet is to sit at the bar and watch him in action). Stellar sushi is the star turn here, although there are other menu options. Communication is "more or less without English" and "service is fine… if you have a clue what is going on". / W1D 6JY; jugemu-uk.crayonsite.com; 10 pm, Sun 9 pm.

THE JUGGED HARE EC1 £63 422

49 CHISWELL ST 020 7614 0134 13–2A

"Fabulous olde English food" – "game, pies, Scotch eggs, jugged hares, trotters" – "in a bustling modern setting" gives this gastropub near the Barbican a real edge. "We put up with the noise and over-stretched service for the sheer variety of game in season", and "their own-brand beer is too damn good!". / EC1Y 4SA; www.thejuggedhare.com; @thejuggedhare; Mon-Wed 11 pm, Thu-Sat midnight; closed Sun.

JULIE'S W11 £55

135 PORTLAND RD 020 7229 8331 7–2A

'Coming Soon 2018' is the message on the website of this once-famous, old Holland Park classic – a famously sexy 1970s subterranean tangle of rooms, where rock stars once partied hard, and where Prince Charles had his stag night back in the day. Apparently, it's been just-about-to-reopen ever since it closed for a refurb in spring 2016 – we continue to maintain a listing in the hope rather than the expectation that this is correct. / W11 4LW; www.juliesrestaurant.com; 11 pm.

K10 £32 332

3 APPOLD ST, EC2 020 7539 9209 13–2B | MINSTER CT, MINCING LN, EC3 020 3019 2510 10–3D | 15 QUEEN ST, EC4 020 3019 9130 10–2C NEW | 78 FETTER LANE, EC4 020 3019 9140 10–2A NEW

A "lunchtime sushi favourite" in the City – the Mincing Lane branch boasts Europe's longest 'kaiten' conveyor belt of sushi, sashimi and other Japanese dishes. This and the Broadgate restaurant are only open for weekday lunch, but the chain has takeaway and delivery options in the evening. New branches opened this year in Queen Street and Fetter Lane. / www.k10.com; 3 pm; Appold 9 pm; Closed D, closed Sat & Sun; no booking at L.

KAFFEINE £13 354

15 EASTCASTLE ST, W1 020 7580 6755 3–1D | 66 GREAT TITCHFIELD ST, W1 020 7580 6755 3–1C

"Some of the best coffee shops anywhere!" – this Aussie/Kiwi-owned duo are "fabulous independents" ranking in London's very top tier, with their "delicious sarnies and salads" and addictive coffees from a regularly changing selection of suppliers. "Great vibe at both locations" too. / kaffeine.co.uk/Eastcastle; @kaffeinelondon; 6 pm, Sun 5 pm; no bookings.

KAHANI SW1

1 WILBRAHAM PLACE 020 7730 7634 6–2D

This September 2018 opening took over the 90-cover site, opposite Cadogan Hall, that was formerly Canvas (RIP). It's the brainchild of chef Peter Joseph (raised in Tamil Nadu, and ex-executive chef of Mayfair's Tamarind) and offers modern Indian cuisine, with British influences. / SW1X 9AE; www.kahanilondon.com; 10.30 pm.

KAI MAYFAIR W1 £121 222

65 SOUTH AUDLEY ST 020 7493 8988 3–3A

Not every Chinese restaurant features bottles of Chateau Pétrus on its wine list at over £8,000, and Bernard Yeoh's swish, contemporary Mayfair institution remains one of London's most ambitious Asian venues. Practically all reports agree on the high pedigree of its cuisine, but even fans can acknowledge some dishes seem very fully priced. / W1K 2QU; www.kaimayfair.co.uk; @kaimayfair; 10.45 pm; closed Sun.

KAIFENG NW4 £70 322

51 CHURCH RD 020 8203 7888 1–1B

The value equation often features in reports on this well-known Chinese stalwart in Hendon, acclaimed by fans for "wonderful kosher food that's worth paying a bit extra for". Coeliacs (also catered for) feel the same way "although pricey, it's the only place I can get a decent Chinese meal that doesn't compromise on taste". Those without special dietary requirements, though, merely find it "very overpriced". In case you're wondering, it's named after the eastern city where Jewish merchants on the Silk Road settled more than a thousand years ago. / NW4 4DU; www.kaifeng.co.uk; @KaifengKosher; 10 pm; closed Fri & Sat.

KANADA-YA £29 5③③

3 PANTON ST, SW1 020 7930 3511 5–4A |
64 ST GILES HIGH ST, WC2 020 7240 0232
5–1B | 35 UPPER ST, N1 020 7288 2787
9–3D NEW

"The best ramen in London" ("the pork broth is
wonderful – there's nought better on a cold day,
when it really hits the spot") scores nothing but
high praise for this small Japanese noodle chain
with bars in Soho, Covent Garden and now also
in Islington. Top tip – look for the "Burford eggs
done just enough with a slightly runny yolk" and
"don't miss the truffle ramen, which is absolutely
the best!" / 10.30 pm; WC2 no bookings.

KAOSARN £28 4②③

110 ST JOHNS HILL, SW11 020 7223 7888
11–2C | 181 TOOTING HIGH ST, SW17
020 8672 8811 11–2C NEW | BRIXTON
VILLAGE, COLDHARBOUR LN, SW9
020 7095 8922 11–2D

These "cheap 'n' cheerful" family-run outfits in
Brixton, Battersea and now Tooting serve "really
tasty Thai food", although "they seem to want
you in and out very quickly!" "Love that you
can BYO". / SW9 10 pm, Sun 9 pm; SW11 closed
Mon L.

KAPPACASEIN
SE16 £9 4③③

1 VOYAGER INDUSTRIAL ESTATE
07837 756852 12–2A

"Some of the best cheese toasties in London,
plus fantastic raclette" won renown for Bill
Oglethorpe's Borough Market venture – for
years a stall in the market and since 2017 with
permanent shop premises in nearby Stoney
Street. / SE16 4RP; www.kappacasein.com;
@kappacasein; closed Sat D, closed Mon-Fri & Sun;
cash only; no booking.

KASHMIR SW15 £43 4③②

18-20 LACY RD 07477 533 888 11–2B

"An upscale addition to Putney's diverse Indian
dining scene, Kashmir is the restaurant we
locals didn't know we needed!" – "a distinct cut
above a typical local cuzza", with "genuinely
delightful" service and regional Kashmiri
dishes (as well as more usual options) that
are "sensitively-spiced and freshly-cooked,
with good depth of flavour". / SW15 1NL;
www.kashmirrestaurants.co.uk; @KashmirRestUK;
Mon, Wed & Thu, Tue, Sun 10.30 pm, Fri & Sat 11
pm; closed Tue L.

KASPAR'S SEAFOOD AND
GRILL, THE SAVOY HOTEL
WC2 £92 ③③④

100 THE STRAND 020 7420 2111 5–3D

This "beautiful Art Deco dining room" – known
for decades as The Savoy River Restaurant –
puts "the emphasis on fish and seafood" with
a "very good range" realised proficiently and
"welcoming" service too. Numerous "wonderful
experiences" are reported, and it's a good venue
for business entertaining too. Top Tip: "perfect
breakfast". / WC2R 0EU; www.kaspars.co.uk;
@TheSavoyLondon; 11 pm.

KATEH W9 £70 ③②③

5 WARWICK PL 020 7289 3393 9–4A

This "lovely neighbourhood Persian" in Little
Venice serves "interesting and delicious" modern
interpretations of classic dishes with traditional
Iranian hospitality. It can be a squeeze and "the
acoustics are terrible – but it's worth it". / W9
2PX; www.katehrestaurant.co.uk; @RestaurantKateh;
11 pm; closed Mon-Fri L.

KAZAN £53 ③④③

77 WILTON RD, SW1 020 7233 8298 2–4B
| 93-94 WILTON RD, SW1 020 7233 7100
2–4B

A "local gem" a short walk from Victoria
station – this "professional and unpretentious"
Ottoman-themed outfit (with a smaller offshoot
opposite) "sets out to provide well-cooked
Turkish food to its neighbourhood, and does it
very well". "A real unexpected pleasure – quality
ingredients, treated simply and with the lightest
of touches". / www.kazan-restaurant.com; 10 pm,
Fri & Sat 10.30 pm, Sun 9.30 pm.

KAZU W1 £55

64 CHARLOTTE ST 020 3848 5777 2–1C

No reports yet on this early 2018 opening – a
'contemporary Japanese' in fairly traditional
style on Fitzrovia's 'restaurant row', majoring in
sushi. It has a good pedigree, with a head chef
formerly of Chisou (Dham Kodituwakku). /
W1T 4QD; kazurestaurants.com; @KazuRestaurants;
Mon-Fri 10 pm, Sat & Sun 9 pm.

THE KEEPER'S HOUSE,
ROYAL ACADEMY
W1 £66 ②②③

ROYAL ACADEMY OF ARTS, BURLINGTON
HOUSE, 020 7300 5881 3–3D

Tucked away in the basement of the
massively expanded Royal Academy, this
"quiet" and elegant venue (with bar, garden
and dining room) is undoubtedly "useful
if visiting an exhibition". Fans acclaim the
modern British cooking here, too, but the
odd doubter continues to feel that it "needs
to do better" on the food front. / W1J
0BD; www.royalacademy.org.uk/keepers-house;
@TheKeepersHouse; 11.30; closed Sun.

KEN LO'S MEMORIES
SW1 £60 ②②②

65-69 EBURY ST 020 7730 7734 2–4B

The late Ken Lo's Belgravia operation was
a pioneer of high-quality Oriental cuisine.
It retains a loyal fan base, but while some
regulars judge it "tried and trusted… not the
cheapest but superb", others fear it is becoming
"a shadow of its former self". / SW1W 0NZ;
www.memoriesofchina.co.uk; 11 pm, Sun 10.30 pm.

KENNINGTON TANDOORI
SE11 £54 ③③③

313 KENNINGTON RD 020 7735 9247 1–3C

For "curries a cut above the average" – and the
chance to spot MPs from nearby Westminster
– this Indian local in Kennington "is a vote
winner". There's a "buzzing ambience",
with "the owner a convivial ringmaster". Top
Tip: "avoid cricket days as it is very near The
Oval!". / SE11 4QE; www.kenningtontandoori.com;
@TheKTLondon; Mon-Thu 12.30 am, Fri 1 am; no
Amex.

KENSINGTON PLACE
W8 £60 ③②②

201-209 KENSINGTON CHURCH ST
020 7727 3184 7–2B

Top dog in the London dining scene 25
years ago – and nowadays specialising in
fish as part of the D&D London stable – this
extensively glazed, "very noisy" venue just
off Notting Hill Gate "can be patchy, but hits
the spot exactly when on form", with "lovely
fresh seafood", "cooked to perfection". /
W8 7LX; www.kensingtonplace-restaurant.co.uk;
@KPRestaurantW8; 10 pm; closed Mon L, closed
Sun.

KENSINGTON SQUARE
KITCHEN W8 £47 4④③

9 KENSINGTON SQ 020 7938 2598 6–1A

"The perfect spot for breakfast/brunch" – a
cute little café (also with basement seating)
in Kensington's oldest square, providing
"delicious coffee, cakes, soups and salads
and a nice neighbourhood feel". / W8
5EP; www.kensingtonsquarekitchen.co.uk;
@KSKRestaurant; 4.30 pm, Sun 4 pm; closed Mon-
Sun D; no Amex.

THE KENSINGTON WINE
ROOMS W8 £57 ②③③

127-129 KENSINGTON CHURCH ST
020 7727 8142 7–2B

"Lots of interesting and different wines by
the glass" ("some you would not normally
come across") is the star feature at this
modern wine bar (with stablemates in
Fulham and Hammersmith), just off Notting
Hill Gate. Most (if not quite all) reports say
"the food is pretty good too". / W8 7LP;
www.greatwinesbytheglass.com; @wine_rooms; Mon-
Wed 11 pm, Thu-Sat midnight.

KERBISHER & MALT £26 ③②②

164 SHEPHERD'S BUSH RD, W6
020 3556 0228 8–1C | 50 ABBEVILLE RD,
SW4 020 3417 4350 11–2D

This contemporary take on an "old-style fish-
and-chip shop" has won a solid following over
the past seven years, first in Brook Green and
more recently in Clapham (outposts in Ealing
and East Sheen have come and gone). Ethical
sourcing is given due prominence, and the
results are "good fresh fish, perfectly cooked"
in a "clean" environment ("a bit draughty in

winter") and giving "reliable value for money". / www.kerbisher.co.uk; 10-10.30 pm, Sun & Mon 9-9.30 pm; W6 closed Mon; no booking.

KERRIDGES BAR & GRILL SW1   £80

WHITEHALL PLACE   020 7321 3244   2–3D

Hand & Flowers chef and TV star, Tom Kerridge, launched in the capital in September 2018, taking over the magnificent chamber at this five-star hotel between Trafalgar Square and Embankment that was formerly Massimo (RIP), and which has had a makeover care of design agency The Studio. Head chef Nick Beardshaw creates, so we are told, 'refined British comfort food and reborn classics' in a brasserie-style format which aims to dispel the stultifying grandeur of its former occupant. / SW1A 2BD; www.kerridgesbarandgrill.co.uk; @kerridgesbandg; Fri-Sun, Mon-Thu 10 pm.

KETTNERS W1   £65   335

29 ROMILLY ST   020 7734 6112   5–2A

"An old treasure given the Nick Jones treatment... welcome back!" – this resurrected Soho landmark gets the thumbs-up from most who have visited after its swish revamp care of the Soho House group, certainly for its "handsome looks" (including the gorgeous bar). Its "initially underwhelming-looking" brasserie menu can "deliver real joy", even if overall ratings for the cooking are rather more middling. / W1D 5HP; www.kettners.com; 1 am, Sun midnight.

KHAN'S W2   £26   222

13-15 WESTBOURNE GROVE   020 7727 5420 7–1C

Big and busy curry house institution on Westbourne Grove, known for the distinctive palm-tree pillars in its main dining room. Its 70+ main courses number "all the standard dishes" – results are "solid if not perhaps great" but come at a cost that's "extremely cheap". Founded more than 40 years ago, it has been alcohol-free for the past 19 (no-alcohol Cobra beer is on the menu). / W2 4UA; www.khansrestaurant.com; @KhansRestaurant; Mon-Thu, Sat & Sun, Fri 11 pm.

KIKU W1   £69   332

17 HALF MOON ST   020 7499 4208   3–4B

Stalwart Mayfair Japanese near Shepherd Market, where a small but dedicated fan club continue to acclaim high quality, traditional cooking. / W1J 7BE; www.kikurestaurant.co.uk; 11 pm, Sun 10.30 pm; closed Sun L.

KILN W1   £33   434

58 BREWER ST NO TEL 4–3C

"Sit at the bar and watch with glee as dishes come towards you..." – Ben Chapman's Soho sensation instantly carved a massive reputation with its "unique menu (great for spice lovers)" that "nails Thai tastes very well", with an "original but unpretentious" selection of "excellent, hearty, modern" Thai creations ("charcoal grills, plus a speciality daily noodle dish"). Conditions are "crammed-in"

and "loud", but frickin' funky. / W1F 9TL; www.kilnsoho.com; 11 pm; closed Sun.

KIMCHEE WC1   £38   222

71 HIGH HOLBORN   020 7430 0956   2–1D

These "busy" Korean BBQ joints – a Holborn original and in the new Pancras Square development (tel 020 3907 8474) – offer a range of grilled dishes, signature hot pickles and Korean cocktails in modern settings. Reports are "slightly variable" but most feel the food is "enjoyable". / WC1V 6EA; www.kimchee.uk.com; @KIMCHEErest; 10.30 pm.

KINTAN   £35   322

21 GREAT CASTLE ST, W1   020 3890 1212 3–1C | 34-36 HIGH HOLBORN, WC1 020 7242 8076   10–2A

This Japanese tabletop BBQ is a "great place for a fun night out" in Holborn (there's also a new branch at Oxford Circus), cooking your own meat from a "good, reasonably priced set dinner selection". It is part of a Tokyo-based group with branches in eight countries. /

KIPFERL N1   £45   323

20 CAMDEN PASSAGE 020 77041 555 9–3D

"Great coffee and breakfast" are the crowd-pleasers at this Viennese café in Islington – "but it's more than a coffee house, it's a good restaurant too", say fans. "Try the dumplings and schnitzel". A second branch in Ladbroke Grove (at 95 Golborne Rd, tel 020 8969 5852) is more like a 'Heurigen' – an Austrian wine bar. / N1 8ED; www.kipferl.co.uk; @KipferlCafe; 10.30 pm, Sun 10 pm; closed Mon; booking weekdays only.

KIRAKU W5   £41   422

8 STATION PDE   020 8992 2848   1–3A

This low-profile Japanese canteen near Ealing Common tube station wins perennial high scores for its high-quality and good-value cooking – and has a loyal following from Japanese expats in the area. / W5 3LD; www.kiraku.co.uk; @kirakulondon; Tue-Thu 3 pm, Fri-Sun 11 pm; closed Tue-Thu D, closed Mon; no Amex.

KIRU SW3   £52   333

2 ELYSTAN ST   020 7584 9999   6–2D

"The food is always excellent and staff lovely" at this two-year-old contemporary take on Japanese fine dining, by Chelsea Green. The kitchen is run by Taiji Maruyama, a third-generation sushi chef with a nine-year stint at Nobu under his toque. / SW3 \N; www.kirurestaurant.com; @KiruRestaurant; 10 pm, Fri & Sat 10.30 pm.

KITCHEN TABLE AT BUBBLEDOGS W1   £166   533

70 CHARLOTTE ST   020 7637 7770   2–1C

"The most memorable meal ever, for all the right reasons!" – James Knappett's multi-course set meal, prepared in front of just 20 diners sitting around a horseshoe bar in Fitzrovia, is a "fun and fascinating spectacle", producing

"utterly astonishing", "truly superb food". "Kinda expensive... but very, very worthwhile to visit once for the experience". Arrival is equally unusual, through the hotdog-and-Champagne bar that shares the premises (see also Bubbledogs). STOP PRESS: On October 1 2018, Michelin surprised everyone by awarding Kitchen Table two stars – one of their better awards of recent times. / W1T 4QG; www.kitchentablelondon.co.uk; @bubbledogsKT; seatings only at 6 pm & 7.30 pm; closed Wed-Sat L, closed Mon & Tue & Sun.

KITCHEN W8 W8   £72   443

11-13 ABINGDON RD   020 7937 0120   6–1A

"An upmarket neighbourhood restaurant, in an upmarket part of town" – this "unpretentious" sidestreet fixture, just off High Street Ken', has a deserved reputation for "always good and sometimes exceptional cuisine" aided by input from star chef Phil Howard (who has an interest in it). If there's a weakness, it's an ambience that fans find "lovely" but which critics feel is "a touch limp" – perhaps its August 2018 revamp will add va va voom. Top Tip: "the set lunch menu is great value". / W8 6AH; www.kitchenw8.com; @KitchenW8; Sun-Thu 9.30 pm, Fri & Sat 10 pm; booking max 6 may apply.

KITTY FISHER'S W1   £75   233

10 SHEPHERD MKT   020 3302 1661   3–4B

A tsunami of press hype around its launch set the bar high for this "cute and cosy" little venture set in the "interesting and lively locale" of Shepherd Market, and now in its third year of operation. Fans do still applaud its "consistently good" British dishes and "warm and welcoming" service, but it can also seem "a touch disappointing for such a legend!", and cynics cite food "lacking oomph" as a sign that it's now "probably past its peak". / W1J 7QF; www.kittyfishers.com; @kittyfishers; 11 pm, Sun 9 pm; closed Sun.

Knife SW4

THE KITTY HAWK EC2 £49 3 3 3

11, 13 & 14 SOUTH PLACE   020 3319 9199   13–2A

Large, year-old city venue just around the corner from Finsbury Circus; no-one claims it rivals the Goodmans and Hawksmoors of the world but it provides a "very comfortable" (if slightly City-anonymous) modern environment and surprises are generally on the upside: "was expecting little but had an excellent steak and interesting starters". / EC2M 7EB; www.thekittyhawk.co.uk; @KittyHawkLdn; Mon & Tue, Fri 11 pm, Wed & Thu midnight; closed Sat & Sun.

KNIFE SW4 £57 5 5 4

160 CLAPHAM PARK RD   020 7627 6505   11–2D

"Fantastic meat" – led by "truly excellent steaks" (ethically sourced from the Lake District) – has made this tiny, "noisy" two-year-old steakhouse on the Clapham-Brixton border one of the hottest dining tickets in South London. "The Sunday lunches are legendary: homemade bread with butter, then a board of mini Yorkshire puds with unctuous dipping gravy. And that's even before the main course, where beef is best – superlatively rare". All is "served with real charm and enthusiasm" by "attentive staff who remember you when you return". / SW4 7DE; kniferestaurant.co.uk; @KnifeLondon; Wed-Sat 10 pm, Sun 4.30 pm; closed Wed-Sat L closed Sun D, closed Mon & Tue.

KOJI SW6 £84 3 3 4

58 NEW KING'S RD   020 7731 2520   11–1B

"Fantastic food and some of the best cocktails" fuels a fervent Fulham fanclub for Pat & Mark Barnett's "Asian-fusion" sushi, ceviche and robata haunt, near Parsons Green, whose "layout is nightclubby without being overbearing". / SW6 4LS; www.koji.restaurant; @koji_restaurant; D only, Sun open L & D.

KOLOSSI GRILL EC1 £38 2 3 2

56-60 ROSEBERY AVE   020 7278 5758   10–1A

"Welcoming service" in particular has helped make this prehistoric taverna a popular fixture off Exmouth Market for more than 50 years, and old-timers say "nothing has changed" over the years ("although one brother retired", apparently). But if "it's a wonder this place survives, look at the price of the set lunch" – £7 for three courses! (which fans insist is "always reliable and great value"). / EC1R 4RR; www.kolossigrill.com; 11 pm; closed Sat L, closed Sun.

KOYA £40 4 4 3

50 FRITH ST, W1   020 7434 4463   5–2A | BLOOMBERG ARCADE, QUEEN VICTORIA ST, EC2 NO TEL 10–3C

"Authentic, fresh udon" bring a real and very affordable taste of Japan to Soho and now to the City's new Bloomberg Arcade. Quite different from the ramen that has proliferated recently in London, udon are soft, fat wheat noodles

that can be eaten hot or cold – "great value for money" and "their specials change constantly and are fantastic" too. / www.koyabar.co.uk; W1 10.30 pm, Thu-Sat 11 pm, Sun 10 pm; no booking; SRA-Food Made Good – 1 star.

KRICKET W1 £48 4 4 4

12 DENMAN ST   020 7734 5612   4–3C

"A strong modern twist on Indian flavours and good vibes all round" make Rik Campbell and Will Bowlby's "hustling and fast-paced" Soho dive ("it's not a place to linger") a worthy success to their phenomenal Brixton original (in a shipping container) – "one of the most successful switches from street food to a central London restaurant in recent times, while still keeping everything well-priced". Let's hope they keep up the good work with their expansion this year, with a permanent Brixton branch, plus a new White City spin-off, which opened at TV Centre in late September 2018. / W1D 7HH; www.kricket.co.uk; @kricketlondon; 10 pm; closed Sun.

KUDU SE15 £50 3 3 3

119 QUEEN'S RD   020 3950 0226   1–4D

This somewhat South African-influenced newcomer (it's primarily trendy modern British small plates) created by chef Patrick Williams and front-of-house Amy Corbin (daughter of restaurant royalty, Chris Corbin) inspires a mix of opinions. Fans are in the majority and say "it's superb to enjoy food of this standard in the heart of Peckham", but one or two detractors feel culinary results are either "not that great" or "a bit pricey". / SE15 2EZ; www.kudu-restaurant.com; @KuduRestaurant; Mon-Fri 10 pm, Sat & Sun 9 pm.

KULU KULU £34 3 2 1

76 BREWER ST, W1   020 7734 7316   4–3C | 51-53 SHELTON ST, WC2   020 7240 5687   5–2C | 39 THURLOE PL, SW7   020 7589 2225   6–2C

"Fab for a quick and dirty sushi fix", this Soho and South Kensington duo offer "good value Japanese food". "Everything passes by on a conveyor in front of you", which makes them "non-intimidating for those not familiar with sushi and its variations". / 10 pm, SW7 10.30 pm; closed Sun; no Amex; no booking.

KUROBUTA £60 3 2 2

312 KING'S RD, SW3   020 7920 6442   6–3C | 17-20 KENDAL ST, W2   020 7920 6444   7–1D

The "mish-mash of very tasty plates" can still win praise these "fun", Japanese-inspired izakayas in Chelsea and Marble Arch. The odd fear is raised that "it's gone really downhill" since it was sold by founder, Aussie chef Scott Hallsworth, in 2017, particularly at the W2 branch, but the ratings in SW3 are pretty consistent. / www.kurobuta-london.com; @KurobutaLondon; 10.30pm; SW3 closed Mon-Thu L.

KURUMAYA EC4 £37 4 3 3

76-77 WATLING ST   020 7236 0236   10–2B

"Been going here years and love their sushi", say fans of this well-established operation near St Paul's, which has "a conveyor belt bar upstairs and a restaurant downstairs" – "the best value for money Japanese in the area, and the quality is always very good". / EC4M 9BJ; www.kurumaya.co.uk; @Kurumaya76; 9.30 pm; closed Sat & Sun.

KUTIR SW3

10 LINCOLN ST AWAITING TEL 6–2D

Ex-Jamavar chef Rohit Ghai is to launch his first solo site in November 2018, on the elegant Chelsea townhouse site that for many years housed Vineet Bhatia's excellent nouvelle Indian. As well as an à la carte option, the cuisine here will feature a tasting menu inspired by Indian hunting expeditions. / SW3 2TS; kutir.co.uk.

KYM'S BY ANDREW WONG EC4

BLOOMBERG ARCADE QUEEN VICTORIA ST AWAITING TEL 10–3C

This much-heralded venture from chef Andrew Wong opened at Bloomberg's new European HQ in the City in September 2018. (For restaurant history anoraks, Kym's was the name of Andrew's parents' Pimlico restaurant of almost three decades' standing, which he renamed A Wong in 2012; it was also one of the first ever establishments visited and reviewed for Harden's London Restaurants 1992, our very first print edition). The new venture sits alongside 10 other restaurants (including Koya, Caravan and Vinoteca) in the new Bloomberg Arcade. / EC4N 8AR; www.kymsrestaurant.com; @kymsrestaurant; Mon-Fri 10 pm, Sat & Sun 9 pm.

KYSERI W1 £57

64 GRAFTON WAY   020 7383 3717   2–1B

From Selin Kiazim and Laura Christie, the talented duo behind Shoreditch's Oklava, this small (35 cover) May 2018 newcomer, near Warren Street, showcases the cuisine of central Anatolia. It opened too late for survey feedback, but early press reviews compliment its interesting and unusual cooking and selection of wines from the eastern Mediterranean. / W1T 5DN; www.kyseri.co.uk; @kyseri_ldn; closed Sun & Mon.

THE LADBROKE ARMS W11 £54 3 3 3

54 LADBROKE RD   020 7727 6648   7–2B

"It has the feel of a pub", but this posh hostelry at the Holland Park end of Ladbroke Grove is very genteel as boozers go. It's a very consistent all-rounder, with "extremely friendly service" and "a weekly changing menu of fresh and reliable fare" that's "affordable" too. "Fun, even when crowded", its welcoming nature includes dog-owners and their pets. / W11 3NW; www.ladbrokearms.com; @ladbrokearms; Sun-Thu 11 pm, Fri & Sat midnight; no booking after 8 pm.

Lahpet E1

LADY MILDMAY
N1 £38 343

92 MILDMAY PARK 020 7241 6238 1–1C

"A better-than-average gastropub" on the corner of Newington Green, "whose properly-prepared dishes are at a level of skill which is increasingly rare in pub restaurants". Top Tip: "secret weekday lunch treat – a choice of three or four dishes from only £6!" / N1 4PR; www.ladymildmay.com; @theladymildmaypub; 11 pm; may need 6+ to book.

LAHORE KEBAB HOUSE
E1 £28 421

2-10 UMBERSTON ST 020 7481 9737 12–1A

"Kebabs and chops to die for" mean this big and famously grungy East End canteen is "still a standard bearer" for down-to-earth "full-flavoured, spicy, meaty Pakistani scoff that's always satisfying" and "at the same ultra-reasonable price-level it's maintained for the last 20 years". A Streatham offshoot never achieved traction, and has now closed. / E1 1PY; www.lahore-kebabhouse.com; 10 pm.

LAHPET E1 £50 333

58 BETHNAL GREEN RD 020 3883 5629 13–1C

If you fancy trying a still-under-represented cuisine, the latest iteration of this Burmese canteen (originally a Maltby Street stall, and then at a London Fields site which closed in March 2018) has a stylish new home in Shoreditch and "showcases some great and original dishes". Top Tip: "the Tea Leaf salad is spot on". / E1 6JW; www.lahpet.co.uk; @Lahpet.

LAMBERTS SW12 £56 555

2 STATION PARADE 020 8675 2233 11–2C

"A culinary beacon in Balham" that's been "consistently excellent for 15 years" – Joe Lambert's "outstanding local independent" provides "very seasonal" cooking of a kind that "stays current without slipping into faddishness". "The ambience is somewhat Scandi-cool" but livened up by the "engaging and lovely staff". Top Menu Tip: "outstanding Sunday roasts". / SW12 9AZ; www.lambertsrestaurant.com;

@lamberts_balham; 10 pm, Sun 4 pm; closed Tue-Fri L closed Sun D, closed Mon; no Amex.

THE LANDMARK, WINTER GARDEN NW1 £78 245

222 MARYLEBONE RD 020 7631 8000 9–4A

With its palm trees and soaring, glass-roofed atrium, it's not hard to see why this beautiful and "very relaxing" space features in lists of London's most Instagrammable locations. Its other top features include a luxurious Sunday brunch buffet with 'bottomless' champagne, and plush afternoon tea. / NW1 6JQ; www.landmarklondon.co.uk; @landmarklondon; 10.15 pm; No trainers; booking max 12 may apply.

LANGAN'S BRASSERIE W1 £67 224

STRATTON ST 020 7491 8822 3–3C

"Why change a winning formula" is the view of the many fans who "just love" this famous brasserie near The Ritz (many of whom are old enough to remember when it was opened by Peter Langan, in partnership with Michael Caine, in 1976): they say, "it's not the best, nor the coolest, nor the fanciest, but my favourite, with a brilliant atmosphere". The only dispute relates to its "retro", "classic" cuisine, which fans feel is "always predictable (in a good way)" and which critics dismiss as "churned out and very average". It's particularly recommended as being "great for business". / W1J 8LB; www.langansrestaurants.co.uk; @langanslondon; Mon-Thu 11 pm, Fri & Sat 11.30 pm; closed Sun.

PALM COURT, THE LANGHAM W1 £75 334

1C PORTLAND PLACE 020 7636 1000 2–1B

"The wonderful mirrors and damask decor and the pianist playing all make for an event" in the "very civilised" lounge of this pukka five-star, opposite Broadcasting House, which claims to be the birthplace of the sacred national ritual of afternoon tea. Options include a children's tea in conjunction with Hamley's (which includes a 'free' teddy bear): "we adults looked on enviously as the kids received jigsaw-cut sandwiches (as many as they wanted) and beautifully constructed small scones, cakes... although the adult tea was also made with marvellous attention to detail!" / W1B 1JA; www.palm-court.co.uk; @Langham_London; Sun-Thu 10.30 pm, Sat 11 pm; No trainers.

LANTANA CAFE £46 333

13-14 CHARLOTTE PL, W1 020 7323 6601 2–1C | **45 MIDDLE YD, CAMDEN LOCK PL, NW1** 020 7428 0421 9–2B | **GROUND FLOOR WEST, 44-46 SOUTHWARK ST, SE1 NO TEL** 10–4B | **UNIT 2, 1 OLIVER'S YD, 55 CITY RD, EC1** 020 7253 5273 13–1A

"Cool vibes, friendly service and an interesting menu" make this 10-year-old trio of Aussie-style cafés "favourites for brunch" in Fitzrovia, Shoreditch and London Bridge. / lantanacafe. co.uk; @lantanacafe/; EC1 9.30 pm, Sat & Sun 3 pm;

W1 3.30 pm, Sat & Sun 5 pm; NW1 5.30 pm; NW1 closed Sun; W1 no booking Sat & Sun.

LARDO £54 222

158 SANDRINGHAM RD, E8 020 3021 0747 14–1B | **197-201 RICHMOND RD, E8** 020 8533 8229 14–1B

The Arthaus building near London Fields houses the original of these East London pizza-stops, the spin-off 'Bebe' branch being in nearby Hackney Downs. Neither inspired much interest this year amongst reporters compared with previously: such as there was said the pizza is "creditable" but can seem "expensive". / 10.30 pm, Sun 9.30 pm.

THE LAUGHING HEART
E2 £64 223

277 HACKNEY RD 020 7686 9535 14–2A

As "a wine lover's choice" in particular, Charlie Mellor's stylish Hackney wine bar (above his trendy wine store), complete with brick walls, open kitchen and funky small plates menu has won a following. Feedback remains a mite variable though, with one return visitor commenting: "after a couple of excellent visits just after it opened, the shine seems to have gone off somewhat". / E2 8NA; thelaughingheartlondon. com; closed Mon-Sat L, closed Sun.

LAUNCESTON PLACE
W8 £84 344

1A LAUNCESTON PL 020 7937 6912 6–1B

This "tucked-away townhouse in Kensington" has "a unique set-up" that makes for a "romantic" ambience and – with its "attentive but unobtrusive service" – is "ideal for a relaxed, long, blow-out meal". Foodwise it's "had its ups-and-downs as chefs have changed over the last several years", but since Ben Murphy took over the stoves in early 2017, most reporters feel the "food is back on fantastic form" with "wonderful innovative dishes from this wunderkind new chef": "the little extras such as the lovely amuses bouches and petits fours lift the meal and make it a real treat". One or two reporters, though, feel it still has a way to go: "there are some wonderful flavour combinations: if the kitchen only had the level and consistency of execution to keep up with these, this place could trouble the Michelin inspectors for a visit". / W8 5RL; www.launcestonplace-restaurant.co.uk; @LauncestonPlace; 10 pm, Sun 9.30 pm; closed Mon & Tue L.

LAURENT AT CAFE ROYAL
W1

HOTEL CAFÉ ROYAL, 68 REGENT ST 020 7406 3310 4–4C

Branded for French chef Laurent Tourondel (known for his ventures in Miami, Charlotte and New York) – this May 2018 opening adds an open kitchen, grill and sushi bar to the mezzanine level of the Café Royal. / W1B 4DY; www.hotelcaferoyal.com/laurent-at-cafe-royal; @HotelCafeRoyal.

THE LEDBURY
W11 £156 5|4|4

127 LEDBURY RD   020 7792 9090   7–1B

"Phenomenal on all levels"; Brett Graham's "unfailingly impressive" Notting Hill favourite only narrowly misses 5/5 in all categories and, for very many discerning foodies, this is "the best restaurant in London", delivering food that's "sheer artistry": "original, brilliantly executed, and with a passion that shines through". Notwithstanding an interior that's "serene and upmarket, with comfortably spaced tables", the overall effect is one of "relaxed confidence throughout" and "less formal than other top-level establishments": and it's "so refreshing for a venue of this calibre to have such fun, friendly staff". "The free take-home compost is a nice touch." / W11 2AQ; www.theledbury.com; @theledbury; 9.45 pm; closed Mon & Tue L; booking max 6 may apply.

LEMONIA NW1 £49 1|4|5

89 REGENT'S PARK RD   020 7586 7454   9–3B

"Always packed to the rafters" and "buzzing, buzzing, buzzing" – this "busy cheerful hub of Primrose Hill" – a sprawling mega-taverna – has been a "warm and comforting" north London phenomenon for about as long as most folks remember. Even many fans accept the food is "tired and boring" yet "still we all love it and come back every chance we get!" The secret to its enduring (to a few sceptics "mysterious") success is that "Tony and the staff have been here for decades and a genuinely warm welcome is assured". "Our newborn son had his first restaurant experience here, followed thirty four years later by our newborn grandson's. The whole restaurant recently joined in with Happy Birthday to a 104 year old! This is a family run restaurant with a loyal family clientele." / NW1 8UY; www.lemonia.co.uk; @Lemonia_Greek; 10.30 pm, Sun 10 pm; closed Sun D; no Amex.

LEROY EC2 £50 3|4|3

18 PHIPP ST   020 7739 4443   13–1B

The team from Hackney hit Ellory (RIP) have shaken up the letters in its name in order to baptise this new venture (drawn, according to urban legend, by Shoreditch rents which are now narrower than in so-very-now E8). Occupying slightly offbeat, triangular-shaped premises opposite Oklava, "the focus is on wine and accompanying small plates" as well as some more substantial fare. Early reports are positive, praising "fab food and knowledgeable staff", but – noting that "it's not sure if it's a restaurant or a wine bar" – fall short of the gushing rapture it's inspired amongst nearly all newspaper critics. / EC2A 4NP; www.leroyshoreditch.com; @leroyshoreditch; 10.30 pm; closed Mon L, closed Sun; Credit card deposit required to book.

LEVAN SE15

3-4 BLENHEIM GROVE AWAITING TEL 1–4D

An all-day (from breakfast) restaurant and wine bar in Peckham opening in October 2018, from the team behind Brixton's Salon, featuring an offbeat wine selection and contemporary European cuisine in a casual bistro style. / SE15 4QL; levanlondon.co.uk; 10 pm, Sun 4 pm.

THE LIDO CAFÉ, BROCKWELL LIDO
SE24 £42 3|2|4

DULWICH RD   020 7737 8183   11–2D

"OK, it helps if it's a good day, but this is always an amazing location" – the all-day café, attached to Brixton's characterful old lido. It's a top brunch destination – "perfect refuelling after a swim, and I'd make a diversion for the scrambled eggs on toast!" / SE24 0PA; www.thelidocafe.co.uk; @thelidocafe; 10 pm, Sun 9 pm; closed Sun D; no Amex; booking max 8 may apply.

THE LIGHT HOUSE
SW19 £54 3|3|3

75-77 RIDGWAY   020 8944 6338   11–2B

This well-thought-of independent in Wimbledon, now entering its 20th year, is capable of producing "really outstanding food". Scores could be significantly higher but the kitchen is let down by inconsistency. "The food varies between a 5 and a 1, which means you're slightly apprehensive before you go!". / SW19 4ST; www.lighthousewimbledon.com; Sun-Thu 11 pm, Fri & Sat midnight; closed Sun D.

THE LIGHTERMAN
N1 £60 3|3|4

3 GRANARY SQUARE   020 3846 3400   9–3C

"An unbeatable location by the water in Granary Square, with lovely terrace tables for fine weather" and a "scenic, glass-walled dining room" wins a very large following for this "three-storey pub overlooking Regents Canal". On the downside, it's "very busy and noisy", but "service is efficient and personable despite what seem to be unrelenting crowds and the food's surprisingly good". / N1C 4BH; www.thelighterman.co.uk; @TheLightermanKX; Mon-Thu 10.30 pm, Fri & Sat 11 pm, Sun 9.30 pm.

LIMA £80 3|3|2

31 RATHBONE PL, W1   020 3002 2640   2–1C | 14 GARRICK ST, WC2   020 7240 5778   5–3C

"Imaginative and different" dishes, "beautifully presented" (not to mention "highly recommended pisco sours") have produced a big culinary reputation for this Peruvian duo in Fitzrovia and Covent Garden ("Floral by Lima") and "not just for the novelty factor". On the downside, they can seem "too expensive". / www.limalondongroup.com/fitzrovia; @lima_london; 10.30 pm, Sun 9.30 pm; Mon L closed.

LINA STORES W1 £36 5|3|3

51 GREEK ST   020 3929 0068   5–2A

"For what it is, this small spin-off from the well-known Italian deli is a great way to dine casually, including at the bar" – Soho institution, Lina Stores (est 1944) has opened this nearby, snappily decorated, no-reservations pit-stop, with a 12-seater kitchen counter and 50 covers over two floors. Early reports praise its "exceptional, cheap 'n' cheerful food" – the pasta is the star – and to say that the newspaper reviewers have gushed would be an understatement. / W1D 4EH; www.linastores.co.uk; @Linastores; closed Sun.

LINDEN STORES
N1 £36 4|3|3

220 SAINT PAUL'S RD   020 7226 0728   9–2D

"A brilliant new restaurant in the old Prawn on the Lawn site" (RIP) – this little spot near Highbury & Islington tube from Laura Christie (one half of Oklava) and Chris Boustead (one half of pop-up Boustead & Bidois) provides "interesting dishes (mostly small plates)" on a British tapas theme, with "friendly and professional service" and "a downstairs that's very cosy". / N1 2LL; Wed-Sat 11 pm; closed Wed-Fri L, closed Mon & Tue & Sun; Online only.

LISBOA PÂTISSERIE
W10 £8 3|2|4

57 GOLBORNE RD   020 8968 5242   7–1A

"It feels like Lisbon with the bustle and blue tiles" when you visit this long-established North Kensington café. Expect excellent coffee and "great cakes at keen prices" including "the best pastéis de natas outside (or possibly inside) Portugal". / W10 5NR; 7.30 pm, Sun 7 pm; L & early evening only; no booking.

THE LITTLE BAY
NW6 £33 3|3|4

228 BELSIZE RD   020 7372 4699   1–2B

For the cash-strapped romantic, this long-serving budget bistro off Kilburn High Road hits the right note with its intimate booths and balconies, while "under £15 for two courses represents excellent value". "I hadn't visited for ages, but nothing seems to have changed and the profiteroles were just as delicious as I remember!" / NW6 4BT; www.littlebaykilburn.co.uk; Sun-Thu 11 pm, Fri & Sat midnight.

LITTLE BIRD £59 3|2|4

1 STATION PARADE, W4   020 3145 0894   1–3A | 1 BATTERSEA RISE, SW11   020 7324 7714   11–2C

"Sumptuous sofas", "incredible cocktails", and "enjoyable Asian/European food in generous portions" win fans for Lorraine Angliss's (Annie's, Rock & Rose) neighbourhood haunts, "hidden away beside Chiswick station" and also in Battersea. / www.littlebirdrestaurants.com; @LittleBirdW4

LITTLE SOCIAL
W1 £79 4|2|3

5 POLLEN ST   020 7870 3730   3–2C

A better year for Jason Atherton's even more informal 'Social' (opposite his Pollen Street Mayfair flagship), where ratings have leapt for the "excellent, unusual, 100% more-ish food" served in a "gorgeous, cosseted ambience". Top

Tip: "pre-theatre menu is an absolute bargain". / W1S 1NE; www.littlesocial.co.uk; @_littlesocial; 10.30 pm; closed Sun; booking max 6 may apply.

LITTLE TAPERIA
SW17   £43   3 2 2

143 TOOTING HIGH ST   020 8682 3303   11–2C

"From the first taste you know that they know what they're doing" at this Hispanic three-year-old in Tooting: "a fun destination with a short list of unusual and delicious tapas". / SW17 \N; www.thelittletaperia.co.uk; @littletaperia; Mon-Fri 4 pm, Sat & Sun 4.30 pm; may need 6+ to book.

LLERENA N1   £38   4 4 2

167 UPPER ST   020 7704 9977   9–2D

Opening at the start of 2018, this Islington tapas bar is related to one of Spain's top producers of jamón ibérico (Jamón y Salud, from Extremadura) and initial feedback is enthusiastic – "a stand out for its product quality and, equally, value for money". / N1 1US; www.jamonysalud.co.uk; 11 pm, Sun 10.30 pm.

LLEWELYN'S
SE24   £54   3 2 2

293-295 RAILTON RD   020 7733 6676   11–2D

"Just the kind of restaurant you want down your street" – this all-day yearling in a former Victorian dining room opposite Herne Hill station can deliver "wonderfully judged, honest modern British food". It's by no means perfect – one or two reporters have been disappointed by the cooking, "tables are close together" and "it gets noisy when it's crowded" – but the response is mostly upbeat (and it's kid-friendly too). / SE24 0JP; www.llewelyns-restaurant.co.uk; @llewelynslondon; 9.30 pm; closed Mon; booking max 8 may apply.

LLUNA N10   £47   3 2 3

462 MUSWELL HILL BROADWAY
020 8442 2662   1–1B

This "perfect neighbourhood local" – a modern Spanish bar/restaurant on Muswell Hill's Broadway – serves a "fascinating mix of outstanding tapas dishes". It's popular in the area, and "has now expanded so you can get in at peak times". / N10 1BS; lalluna.co.uk; @lallunalondon; Sun-Thu 10.30 pm, Fri & Sat 11 pm.

LOBOS MEAT & TAPAS
SE1   £50   4 3 2

14 BOROUGH HIGH ST   020 7407 5361   10–4C

"Full of energy and zest" – the "amazing" meat-based tapas cooking wins raves for this Spanish operation, concertina-ed under a railway viaduct on the edge of Borough Market, while service is "smiling and extremely friendly". It has "a great vibe about it", but on the downside is "very squished". / SE1 9QG; www.lobostapas.co.uk; @LobosTapas; Wed-Sun 11 pm; booking max 8 may apply.

LOCANDA LOCATELLI, HYATT REGENCY
W1   £85   3 4 3

8 SEYMOUR ST   020 7935 9088   2–2A

"Always a winner" – Giorgio Locatelli's Marylebone HQ maintains a big following thanks to its "expensive but good" cuisine, fine selection of Italian wines, and "impeccable service". When it comes to the "luxurious" interior, its dim-lit and moody styling is starting to look "a little dated" to quite a few reporters, but even so the overall effect is described as "oddly agreeable" or "romantic". / W1H 7JZ; www.locandalocatelli.com; 10.30 pm; booking max 8 may apply.

LOCH FYNE   £51   0 3 3

For "consistent quality fish dishes" (and they do a good line in seafood too, particularly oysters), this national chain with its consistently "pleasant" branches "executes its staples very well". "Go off-piste, and perhaps results are more mixed" (but serious gripes are few and far between). / www.lochfyne-restaurants.com; 10 pm, WC2 Mon-Sat 10.30 pm.

LOKHANDWALA
W1   £63   3 3 3

93 CHARLOTTE ST   020 7637 7599   2–1B

"Off-the-beaten-track" Fitzrovia Indian offering, amongst other items, a range of vegan Ayurvedic shots and smoothies. Not all reporters gave it full marks, but for the most part there's praise for its "cosy interior (inspired, apparently, by an 18th century love story), fab cocktails, and originally presented (eg dosa hats) tapas dishes". / W1T 4PY; www.lokhandwala.co.uk; @lokhandwala_uk; Sun-Wed 10.30 pm, Thu-Sat 11.30 pm; closed Sun-Wed-Sat L; Credit card deposit required to book.

LONDON GRIND
SE1   £43   4 4 4

2 LONDON BRIDGE   020 7378 1928   10–3C

With its "origin coffees from the best roastery", this breakfast-to-cocktail-hour café in a stripped-down old bank above Borough Market "has inevitably become a free office space for freelancers". There "a good mix of on-trend, healthy and wholesome food" to keep them going, then "great espresso martinis" to wind down with. Top Tips – "handy for a breakfast meeting"; and "£5 cocktails on Mondays are a complete winner". / SE1 9RA; www.londongrind.com; @LondonGrind; Mon-Thu midnight, Fri & Sat 1 am, Sun 7 pm.

LONDON HOUSE
SW11   £61   2 2 2

7-9 BATTERSEA SQ   020 7592 8545   11–1C

Gordon Ramsay's Battersea venture pitches itself as a family-friendly ('kids eat free') neighbourhood local, and attracts large groups for celebratory meals. It scored some hits this year ("we had 15 folks faultlessly looked after") but those reporting misses were more vocal: "totally overpriced…", "all the atmosphere of a rail station waiting room…", "…if this is the best Gordon Ramsay can do with his spin-offs, not sure how he is keeping in business!" / SW11 3RA; www.gordonramsayrestaurants.com/london-house; @londonhouse; 11 pm, Sun 9 pm.

LONDON SHELL CO.
W2   £65   4 4 5

SHELDON SQUARE   07818 666005   7–1C

"Food tastes all the better when afloat" and fans of this "utterly delightful" canal boat, moored in the Paddington Central development, say it's "a must do!" – not just on account of the novel setting, but also the "knowledgeable staff", and "truly fresh fish and shellfish" which is exceptionally well-prepared. / W2 6EP; www.londonshellco.com; @LondonShellCo; 10.30 pm, Sun 3.30 pm; closed Sun D, closed Mon.

LONDRINO SE1   £54   2 3 3

36 SNOWSFIELDS   020 3911 4949   10–4C

Leandro Carreira has been associated with a fair few London hits (Viajante, Koya, Lyle's) and opened his first solo venture a few streets south of The Shard in November 2017. The cuisine makes a culinary nod to his native Portugal, but no more than a nod: the style is primarily experimental and cheffy, and results are very variable with reviews ranging from "not only stunning visually, but with exceptional flavour" to "up itself, lacking generosity" and "disappointing". / SE1 3SU; www.londrino.co.uk; @londrinolondon; 11 pm, Sun 3 pm; closed Sun D, closed Mon.

LORNE SW1   £60   4 5 3

76 WILTON RD   020 3327 0210   2–4B

"It arrived in a wave of critical approval and it well deserves all the praise it has received!" – Katie Exton and Peter Hall "have done an incredible job" with this "fantastic, relatively new addition to Pimlico" in the "tricky locale" near Victoria station. A "lovely little neighbourhood spot", "the kitchen produces exquisite food using market-fresh produce" from a "concise, regularly-changing menu of inventive food that's not overly fussy" but "executed delightfully, often with an unexpected twist". "Front of house is the co-owner Katie, who will guide you through the excellent wine list: her wine knowledge is superb and her advice sensible and unpretentious". (The restaurant was closed for a significant chunk of 2018 due to flooding, but has now reopened.) / SW1V 1DE; www.lornerestaurant.co.uk; 9.30 pm; closed Mon L, closed Sun.

LOUIE LOUIE
SE17   £41   3 2 3

347 WALWORTH RD   020 7450 3223   1–3C

"A welcome addition to SE17" – this popular two-year-old is a refuge from "the pollution and noise of Walworth Road" and scores well with its "fun" combination of "tasty" small plates from guest chefs, cocktails and local beers, and the soundtrack of vintage vinyl. The odd fan, though, can feel "they take advantage of being one of the only kids on the block" hereabouts, with sometimes "disinterested service". / SE17 2AL; louielouie.london; @LouieLouie_Ldn; 4.30 pm.

LUCA EC1 £80 3 3 4

88 ST JOHN ST   020 3859 3000   10–1A

"It's a joy to dine" at this "lovely" Clerkenwell yearling – a "really cool" space with bar at the front and "buzzy" conservatory restaurant to the rear. It's actually a sibling to the legendary Clove Club, although the culinary style is more traditional here, with the aim to produce Italian cuisine from British produce. Results evidence some "serious cooking" producing "consistently good" results, although fair to say it's not as earth-shattering as its stablemate and can seem a tad "pricey". Top Menu Tip: "delicious Parmesan fries". / EC1M 4EH; luca.restaurant; @LucaRestaurant; 11 pm, Sun 10 pm.

LUCE E LIMONI WC1 £59 4 4 3

91-93 GRAY'S INN RD   020 7242 3382   10–1A

"Proper, high-quality Italian cooking" backed up by an "excellent Sicilian wine list" earn consistently high ratings for Fabrizio Zafarana's "spacious and charming restaurant" on the edge of Bloomsbury. "Fabrizio is a very special host" – "it's a brilliant place for a proper catch-up meal". Top Tip: "order in advance for the best chocolate mousse in the land, made without gelatine". / WC1X 8TX; www.luceelimoni.com; @Luce_e_Limoni; Mon-Thu 10 pm, Fri & Sat 11 pm; closed Sat L, closed Sun.

LUCIANO'S SE12 £52 4 3 2

131 BURNT ASH RD   020 8852 3186   1–4D

This "great Italian" in Lee is both family-run and family-friendly, and has won high scores for its cooking this year – "what more could you want from a neighbourhood pizza and pasta restaurant?" / SE12 \N; www.lucianoslondon.co.uk; @LucianosLondon; 10.30 pm, Sun 10 pm.

LUCIO SW3 £75 3 2 2

257 FULHAM RD   020 7823 3007   6–3B

"Fab Tuscan food" ("unsurpassable homemade pasta") inspires fans of this family-run Chelsea Italian. Service can be "erratic" but regulars say if you get to know the owner it's "terrific". Top Tip: "the set lunch is fantastic value". / SW3 6HY; www.luciorestaurant.com; 10.45 pm.

LUPINS SE1 £48 4 4 3

66 UNION ST   020 3617 8819   10–4B

"Booking is essential – otherwise, be prepared to wait!" – if you want to sample Lucy Pedder and Natasha Cooke's "tiny small-plates restaurant", "in the Flat Iron complex near London Bridge" and "handy for Tate Modern and Borough Market". It's set over two floors: "a large café on the ground floor" and a "lovely", "atticy" upstairs. "The all-women staff and owners have really gotten their act together" – "friendly service enhances the whole experience" and the "unusual tapas-style dishes" are "really great sharing food with some sublime flavours"; "writing my review has reminded me to go back immediately!" / SE1 1TD; www.lupinslondon.com; 10.15 pm, Sun 8.45 pm; closed Mon D & Sun D.

LUPITA £43 3 3 2

13-15 VILLIERS ST, WC2   020 7930 5355   5–4D | 7 KENSINGTON HIGH ST, W8 020 3696 2930   6–1A | 60-62 COMMERCIAL STREET, SPITALFIELDS, E1   020 3141 6000 13–2C

"Proper enchiladas" and "amazing guacamole made at the table" are typical of the "authentic, not Tex Mex" approach at these colourful and "very friendly" budget Mexican joints in Kensington, by the side of Charing Cross station, and on the edge of the City. They also serve "good cocktails" (but the wine list is "very limited"). /

LURE NW5 £37 3 5 3

56 CHETWYND RD   020 7267 0163   9–1B

"Beautifully battered fish, great chips and a good selection of seasonal specials" make Aussie Philip Kendall's Dartmouth Park outfit more than just a top chippy – "it's a perfect local restaurant". "Lovely staff", "child-friendly", and the short list of desserts is "always worth the extra course". / NW5 1DJ; www.lurefishkitchen.co.uk; @Lurefishkitchen; Wed-Sat 10 pm, Sun 9.30 pm; closed Wed-Fri L, closed Mon & Tue; booking weekends only.

LURRA W1 £56 3 4 4

9 SEYMOUR PLACE   020 7724 4545   2–2A

"An oasis from the noise of Oxford Street" – this two-floor corner Spanish grill-house in Seymour Village is, on practically all accounts, "a wonderful tribute to Basque cuisine" – particularly its "awesome Galician steak" – and "paired with an excellent wine list". Even fans however can find the small menu selection, focussed on 2-3 main options, "too limited". Top Tip: "their courtyard is an overlooked gem in London, especially in the warmer months and on a Sunday when it's quieter". / W1H 5BA; www.lurra.co.uk; @LurraW1; 10.30 pm, Sun 3.30 pm; closed Mon L closed Sun D.

LUTYENS GRILL, THE NED EC2 £90 3 4 4

27 POULTRY   020 3828 2000   10–2C

"Quieter than the other restaurants in the building" – The Ned's steakhouse is to be found at the edge of the ground floor of the old Midland Bank HQ. Originally members-only, it's been open to all since February 2018, and its "elegant" panelled interior makes it a "perfect location for a business lunch". Most of the well-realised menu is devoted to steaks – mostly from the UK, but also with a selection from the US – and (as well as a few fish and seafood choices) there's also the option of Beef Wellington carved at the table. / EC2R 8AJ; www.thened.com; @TheNedLondon; 11 pm, Sun 5 pm; closed Sat L closed Sun D.

LYLE'S E1 £83 4 2 2

THE TEA BUILDING, 56 SHOREDITCH HIGH ST   020 3011 5911   13–1B

"Don't be put off by the hipster canteen vibe" say fans of James Lowe's venerated Shoreditch foodie-mecca, offering "always-original" small plates and "a small but really interesting wine list". But ratings here no longer scale the absolute pinnacles they once did, dragged down by a minority who find the place "too impressed by itself" for an achievement level that's good, but no more. / E1 6JJ; www.lyleslondon.com; @lyleslondon; 11 pm; closed Sat L & Sun.

M RESTAURANTS £85 2 2 2

ZIG ZAG BUILDING, VICTORIA ST, SW1   020 3327 7776   2–4B | BREWERY WHARF, LONDON RD, TW1   020 3327 7776 1–4A | 2-3 THREADNEEDLE WALK, EC2 020 3327 7770   10–2C

With their "clubby", "dark" decor, Martin Williams's Vegas-esque steakhouses can "feel like they're trying too hard to be cool". For more reporters, though, they are "an expensive but guilty pleasure" with "perfectly executed steak". Change may be afoot, because, as of September 2018, Williams is no-longer the 'ex-Gaucho CEO', but has returned back to that post to turn around the chain he headed for many years. Where this will leave this project remains to be seen. Top Tip: "excellent deal with free-flowing Prosecco". / www.mrestaurants.co.uk; @mrestaurants_; midnight; EC2 closed Sat L & Sun, SW1 closed Sun.

Lutyens Grill, The Ned EC2

MA GOA SW15 £44 443

242-244 UPPER RICHMOND RD
020 8780 1767 11–2B

"A dependable Putney stalwart now back on top form", this family-run operation serves "outstanding home cooking, Goan-style" and remains a major hit with locals, some of whom have been coming for 20 or more years. A refurb has seen the dining room modernised and reduced in size with a wine shop added next door. / SW15 6TG; www.magoaputney.co.uk; @magoarestaurant; 10.30 pm, Fri & Sat 11 pm, Sun 10pm.

MAC & WILD £54 324

65 GREAT TITCHFIELD ST, W1
020 7637 0510 3–1C | 9A DEVONSHIRE
SQUARE, EC2 020 7637 0510 10–2D

"Venison cooked in a variety of ways" sits alongside Scottish shorthorn beef, oysters and salmon at this "passionate but unpretentious" Fitzrovia three-year-old, which also has a sibling at Devonshire Square, near Liverpool Street. Owner Andy Waugh's Scottish family estate is the source for much of the produce. /

MACELLAIO RC £54 333

6 STORE ST, WC1 AWAITING TEL 2–1C
NEW | 84 OLD BROMPTON RD, SW7
020 7589 5834 6–2B | ARCH 24, 229
UNION ST, SE1 07467 307682 10–4B | 124
NORTHCOTE RD, SW11 020 3848 4800
11–2C | 38-40 EXMOUTH MARKET, EC1
020 3696 8220 10–1A

"Meat! More meat! And more meat!" is the order of the day (notwithstanding a few pasta options, and Sicilian tuna in the Exmouth Market branch) from the menu of Roberto Costa's Italian steakhouse group, which showcases "amazing cuts of beef" from Piedmont's Fassone breed of cattle, and where the arrival of the food is dramatised by the "stabbing of a steak knife into the table". "The wine list has some interesting choices" too, and some affordable ones at that. In summer 2018 it announced its fifth opening, in Bloomsbury. / www.macellaiorc.com; @macellaiorc; 11 pm.

MACHIYA SW1 £44 422

5 PANTON ST 020 7925 0333 5–4A

High-quality Japanese dishes and patisserie win strong ratings for this little two-year-old near Leicester Square, from Aaron Burgess-Smith and Tony Lam (the duo behind Kanada-Ya on the same street). It's named after the stacked wooden town houses in Kyoto, but the setting is the weakest part of the offering. / SW1Y 4DL; machi-ya.co.uk; @MachiyaLondon; 10.30 pm, Fri & Sat 11 pm, Sun 10 pm.

MADE IN ITALY £47 312

50 JAMES ST, W1 020 7224 0182 3–1A
| 249 KING'S RD, SW3 020 7352 1880
6–3C | 141 THE BROADWAY, SW19
020 8540 4330 11–2B

"Pitch-perfect pizza" with a "terrific charred flavour" emerges by the metre from the ovens at this expanding southwest London group. Occasionally "abysmal" service needs sorting out, however – "it can be really slow if they're busy". / www.madeinitalygroup.co.uk; @MADEINITALYgrp; SW3 11.30 pm; W1 11.30 pm, Sun 10.30 pm; SW19 11 pm; SW3 closed Mon L.

MADE OF DOUGH SE15 £32 443

182 BELLENDEN RD 020 7064 5288 1–4D

"From a small shop come the most divine pizzas – yes, even beating Franco Manca's original (i.e. Brixton) branch" – that's the bold claim made by fans of this year-old pop-up-turned permanent in Peckham (which also operates out of a container at Pop Brixton). / SE15 4BW; www.madeofdough.co.uk; @MadeOfDoughLDN; Mon-Thu 11 pm, Fri & Sat midnight, Sun 10 pm; no booking.

MADHU'S UB1 £41 453

39 SOUTH RD 020 8574 1897 1–3A

One of Southall's best-known Indian stalwarts – the Anand family's acclaimed central curry house has helped found a successful empire, providing catering for events at many of the capital's top venues. Those who make the pilgrimage say the food's "such good value" and "service is top-notch". / UB1 1SW; www.madhus.co.uk; Tue-Thu 3 pm, Fri-Sun 11 pm; closed Tue, Sat L & Sun L; no booking.

MAGGIE JONES'S W8 £61 224

6 OLD COURT PL 020 7937 6462 6–1A

Limited feedback this year on this "romantic" stalwart near Kensington Palace (named after the pseudonym Princess Margaret used to use when booking here). Such as there is supports the view that the main reason to visit is the date-potential of the charming, faux-rustic decor, rather than the indifferently rated Anglo-French bistro fare. / W8 4PL; www.maggie-jones.co.uk; 11 pm, Sun 10.30 pm; closed Mon-Sat & Sun.

MAGPIE W1 £72 443

10 HEDDON ST 020 3903 9096 4–3B

Just off Regent Street, the year-old West End outpost of Hackney superstar Pidgin has taken a little bit of time to settle down, and part of its original concept – the trolley service of British 'dim sum' – went by the wayside in early 2018. Now in a more conventional 'small plates' mode, at its best, it's a repeat of the "all-round brilliance" of its sibling – "really fun" and with "outstanding food you will want to go back for again and again". / W1B 4BX; www.magpie-london.com; @mgpldn; 10.30 pm, Sun 3 pm; closed Sun D.

MAGURO W9 £57 442

5 LANARK PL 020 7289 4353 9–4A

This "great little Japanese" near Little Venice is highly rated for its "tasty" dishes from a small but well thought-out menu. It's "tiny" and popular – "so be sure to book". / W9 1BT; www.maguro-restaurant.com; 11 pm, Sun 10.30 pm; no Amex.

MAISON BAB WC2

4 MERCER WALK 020 7439 9222 5–2C

A second venture from the team behind Soho's highly popular Le Bab – this latest addition to Covent Garden's new Mercers Walk development opened in September 2018. The brainchild of Stephen Tozer and Ed Brunet, the 40-cover restaurant (plus takeaway) serves the same style of modern kebabs and mezze that made its sister site such a success, but has the added benefit of a ten-seater chef's table. / WC2; www.eatlebab.com; @eatlebab; Mon-Thu 10 pm, Fri & Sat 10.30 pm.

MAISON BERTAUX W1 £8 444

28 GREEK ST 020 7437 6007 5–2A

A "Soho institution that should be experienced" – this French teahouse (est 1871) offers "wondrous pâtisserie and very good tea (in teapots) in the most charming, if somewhat ramshackle, surroundings". It's a "window on Soho", so "just sit with a delicious cake and watch the world go by". / W1D 5DQ; www.maisonbertaux.com; @Maison_Bertaux; 11 pm, Sun 9.30 pm.

MALABAR W8 £46 333

27 UXBRIDGE ST 020 7727 8800 7–2B

"A long-time favourite", this stalwart Notting Hill curry house "always delivers", even after more than 30 years, and offers a "nice mix of unusual as well as usual menu items". Ratings have tumbled from previous highs this year – perhaps just partly a reflection of the "sharp increase in competition and quality among modern Indian restaurants". / W8 7TQ; www.malabar-restaurant.co.uk; 10 pm, Sun 9 pm.

MALABAR JUNCTION WC1 £42 343

107 GT RUSSELL ST 020 7580 5230 2–1C

The "excellent South Indian menu" at this Bloomsbury stalwart includes "interesting Keralese fish specialities that distinguish it from the average curry house". The "modern colonial" décor and "especially graceful service" add to the appeal (though not everybody likes the art). "Very handy for the British Museum and a good alternative to the underwhelming chain options in Charlotte Street". / WC1B 3NA; www.malabarjunction.com; 11 pm.

MAM W11 £41 433

16 ALL SAINTS RD 020 7792 2665 7–1B

Pronounced 'mum' and meaning fermentation in Vietnamese – Colin Tu's BBQ yearling on what used to be Notting Hill's edgy frontier is well-rated as "a great new local". / W11 1HH; mamlondon.com; 11 pm; closed Mon-Fri L.

MAMAROSA EC2

SHOREDITCH VILLAGE, HOLYWELL LANE
AWAITING TEL 13–1B

A London version of Barcelona's Italian celeb-magnet is slated to open at the Shoreditch

Village development this year. It will open adjacent to the citizenM boutique hotel just off Shoreditch High Street (the original is part of Barcelona's 5-star W hotel). / EC2; 12.30 am, Sun midnight.

MAMMA DOUGH   £40   3 3 3
40 LADYWELL RD, SE13 AWAITING TEL 1–4D NEW | 179 QUEEN'S RD, SE15 020 7635 3470   1–4D | 76-78 HONOR OAK PK, SE23   020 8699 5196   1–4D | 354 COLDHARBOUR LN, SW9   020 7095 1491 11–2D

"Well-priced sourdough pizzas" served in "very basic but functional" surroundings have established a foothold in South London for this group (Brixton, Peckham, Honor Oak Park and most recently Ladywell). Fans appreciate the "small menu which makes it easy to order"; the drinks list features local craft beer, coffee roasted in Shoreditch and ginger beer brewed on site. / www.mammadough.co.uk; SE23 10 pm, SW9 11 pm, SE15 10.30 pm; Mon-Thu closed L.

MANDARIN KITCHEN W2   £40   4 3 2
14-16 QUEENSWAY   020 7727 9012   7–2C

"The best lobster noodles in London (if not the world)" is the famous signature dish of this "reliable old favourite" Chinese, opposite Queensway tube. Other standout seafood dishes include crab and razor clams. It's always full and the decor – though improved in recent years – isn't hugely inspiring, so don't come with a view to linger among elegant surroundings – "eat and leave for somewhere more salubrious!" / W2 3RX; mandarinkitchen.co.uk; 11.15 pm.

MANGAL 1 E8   £27   5 3 2
10 ARCOLA ST   020 7275 8981   14–1A

"The best shish kebabs" – "juicy", "melt-in-the-mouth tender" – all cooked in "the marble-clad pit in the middle of the room" are "the genuine article" and have won renown for this Turkish grill in Dalston. And it's "good value" too, aided by the fact that you can BYO. "After 20 years I still go here every week, and it never fails to impress!" / E8 2DJ; www.mangal1.com; @Mangalone; Mon-Fri midnight, Sat & Sun 1 am; cash only; no booking.

MANICOMIO   £75   2 2 3
85 DUKE OF YORK SQ, SW3   020 7730 3366 6–2D | 6 GUTTER LN, EC2   020 7726 5010 10–2B

"If there were such a term as Rustic Italian Fine Dining", it could be used to describe the style of these "delightful" modern Italians, located in Chelsea ("a lovely oasis just off the King's Road with outside seating"); and the City ("good for impressing business visitors"). Both locations provide "a seasonal menu with quality ingredients" that's "beautifully presented" but cost is an issue – the food seems "generally pricey for what it is". / www.manicomio.co.uk; SW3 10 pm, Sun 4 pm; EC2 10 pm; EC2 closed Sat & Sun.

MANNA NW3   £56   2 2 2
4 ERSKINE RD   020 7722 8028   9–3B

This "vegetarian and vegan place of pilgrimage" on Primrose Hill, which has logged 50 years to make it Britain's longest-serving veggie, is now "so old it's fashionable again". "The menu is enticing and quantities are vast", but when it comes to realisation, it's perennially a case of hit and miss here. / NW3 3AJ; www.mannav.com; @mannacuisine; 10 pm, Sun 7 pm; closed Mon.

MANUKA KITCHEN SW6   £53   3 4 3
510 FULHAM RD   020 7736 7588   6–4A

"They make an effort" at this nifty NZ-inspired bar/café near Fulham Broadway – a key local brunch spot with "interesting dishes and charming service". Kick off an evening in their gin bar '510 Below'. / SW6 5NJ; www.manukakitchen.com; @manukakitchen; Mon-Thu midnight, Fri & Sat 1 am, Sun 11 pm; closed Sun D; booking max 8 may apply.

MÃOS E2   £200   5 4 4
REDCHURCH ST NO TEL 13–1C

"The best food I've eaten this year!" – early reporters award the highest ratings to mould-breaking chef Nuno Mendes's "fantastic" latest project: a 16-seater that opened without fanfare in April 2018, but which is one of the most culinarily interesting arrivals of recent times. "Hidden away, up a secret staircase in Redchurch Street", it's part of Shoreditch's funky Blue Mountain School ('an interdisciplinary space dedicated to nurturing engagements and interactions between diverse practices'… and also selling really expensive stuff). This new venture is a revival of sorts of Mendes's Loft Project fine dining supper club, and it inspires ne'er a word of protest regarding the price tag – just first impressions of "an all-round excellent experience, from meeting Nuno and his brigade in the kitchen and eating snacks, to sitting down at a communal table and being served course after course of exceptional, innovative food. There is an impressive wine room too" and all-in-all it offers "a superb night out as well as a great concept". / E2 7DJ; www.maos.dinesuperb.com; Tue-Sat, Mon 10.30 pm, Sun 3.30 pm.

MAR I TERRA SE1   £42   2 2 2
14 GAMBIA ST   020 7928 7628   10–4A

"Fair value" for "authentic" scoff is to be had at this pub-turned-tapas-bar in a side street between Tate Modern and Southwark tube, which "feels like an old friend" for its many regulars, although "the experience you get slightly depends on how well you get on with the owner" (who is mostly "amiable", but on a bad day, "grumpy"). / SE1 0XH; www.mariterra.co.uk; Sun-Thu 11 pm, Fri & Sat midnight; closed Sat L & Sun.

MARCELLA SE8   £43   3 3 2
165A DEPTFORD HIGH ST   020 3903 6561 1–3D

"Another great place in burgeoning Deptford" – this "neighbourhood-style Mediterranean bistro on the increasingly-hip High Street" is a year-old sibling to Peckham's Artusi. "It's simple in style, but the food is very well executed". / SE8 3NU; www.marcella.london; @MarcellaDeptfrd; Mon-Thu 10 pm, Fri & Sat 10.30 pm; closed Mon L, closed Sun; may need 6+ to book.

MARCUS, THE BERKELEY SW1   £122   3 4 3
WILTON PL   020 7235 1200   6–1D

Marcus Wareing's "quietly luxurious" Belgravia dining room is one of London's best-known temples of gastronomy and for its very many fans it fully lives up to that reputation with its "balanced, precise and beautifully presented cuisine", "discreet and attentive service", and its "spacious and elegant" quarters ("if you want to seal a business deal, then just wow them with dinner in this place, which strikes that delicate balance between formal and relaxed!"). Not absolutely everyone is wowed though – in particular, the prices can seem plain 'silly'. STOP PRESS: Those not wowed now includes the Michelin Man who demoted Marcus from two stars to one in October 2018. / SW1X 7RL; www.marcusrestaurant.com; @marcusbelgravia; 10 pm; closed Sun; No trainers; booking max 6 may apply.

MARGOT WC2   £57   4 5 4
45 GREAT QUEEN ST   020 3409 4777   5–2D

"Very suave service" ("the staff make the meal into an occasion") adds to the polish of Pablo de Tarso and Nicolas Jaouën's "elegant" and "quite formal" ("white tablecloths, etc") Italian: one of the better options in Covent Garden "to make an evening feel special before or after a show". "Very accomplished" cooking completes the picture, although arguably "more traditional dishes work best". Top Menu Tip: "particularly excellent osso bucco". / WC2B 5AA; www.margotrestaurant.com; @MargotLDN; 11 pm, Sun 10 pm.

MARKET HALL FULHAM SW6   £22
472 FULHAM RD   020 3773 9350   6–4A

The first in a series of 'Market Halls' pitched up in Fulham Broadway's old ticket hall in 2018, transforming the fabulous space into a street food fest, with nine different, regularly changing, kitchens, which currently include Super Tacos (from Breddo's), sourdough pizzas from Yard Sale, Butchies' free-range fried chicken and hot drinks from Press Coffee. Other Market Halls will follow in Victoria (November 2018, in the former Pacha nightclub building) and London's West End (TBC). / SW6 1BY; www.markethalls.co.uk; @markethalls.

Masala Zone

THE MARKSMAN
E2   £65   4|3|4

254 HACKNEY RD   020 7739 7393   **14–2A**

"Just an East End boozer it's not" – this converted public house and dining rooms a short walk from Columbia Road has "an airy, modern and confident first-floor dining room, with food to make you smile and make you think". "It's nothing over-fancy, nothing over-priced" – "taking dishes beyond what one would describe as pub grub", although there's "no better place for a relaxed Sunday lunch". / E2 7SJ; www.marksmanpublichouse.com; @marksman_pub; 10 pm, Sun 9 pm; closed Mon-Thu L.

MAROUSH
£54   3|2|2

I) 21 EDGWARE RD, W2   020 7723 0773
7–1D | **II) 38 BEAUCHAMP PL, SW3**
020 7581 5434   **6–1C** | **V) 3-4 VERE ST, W1**
020 7493 5050   **3–1B** | **VI) 68 EDGWARE
RD, W2**   020 7224 9339   **7–1D** | **- GARDEN)**
1 CONNAUGHT ST, W2   020 7262 0222
7–1D

"The good-quality Lebanese food never disappoints" at this high-profile chain that has prospered for more than 30 years. "It's very easy to fill up on the starters, which are always delicious" – and more "affordable" than the mains. For live music and belly dancing, head to the original Edgware Road venue. Top Tip: café sections at I and II offer an excellent menu of wraps at bargain prices. / www.maroush.com; most branches close between 12.30 am-5 am.

MASALA ZONE
£43   3|3|4

"Very interesting Indian food for a chain", "professional service" and a "lovely atmosphere" have carved a strong reputation for these well-established street-food cafés. "Prices seem to be creeping up" however, and even those who praise its "fresh flavours" feel it's "not quite as good value as in the past". / www.masalazone.com; @masalazone; 11 pm, Sun 10.30 pm; W1U 9 pm, Sun 4 pm; booking: min 8.

MASH STEAKHOUSE
W1   £84   3|3|2

77 BREWER ST   020 7734 2608   **4–3C**

A stone's throw from Piccadilly Circus (next to Brasserie Zédel) this American-style steakhouse is praised by fans for its "delicious food and courteous service". Supporters similarly find the setting "wonderfully relaxed and luxurious", but it's a massive space, and – to a minority – "great steak is let down by the ambience of the huge

dining hall". / W1F 9ZN; www.mashsteak.co.uk; @mashsteaklondon; 10.30 pm; closed Sun L.

MASTERS SUPER FISH
SE1   £27   3|2|1

191 WATERLOO RD   020 7928 6924   **10–4A**

This classic chippie with table service near Waterloo station (popular with taxi drivers) may serve "only fish 'n' chips – but it's VERY GOOD fish 'n' chips!" – in "large portions and with crisp batter". / SE1 8UX; masterssuperfish.com; 10.30 pm; closed Mon L, closed Sun; no Amex; no booking, Fri D.

MATSUBA TW9
£46   3|3|2

10 RED LION ST   020 8605 3513   **1–4A**

Nothing but good feedback this year on this "excellent" Korean-run Japanese on the fringes of Richmond town centre – a low-key, café-style place, whose sushi gets top billing. / TW9 1RW; www.matsuba-restaurant.com; @matsuba; 10.30 pm, Sun 10 pm; closed Sun.

MAX'S SANDWICH SHOP
N4   £33   4|4|3

19 CROUCH HILL NO TEL 1–1C

Who knew sarnies could be so exciting? Max Halley's "fun and noisy" Crouch Hill café puts others to shame with its paper parcels of enticing stuffed-focaccia creations, washed down with some good beers. / N4 4AP; www.maxssandwichshop.com; @lunchluncheon; Wed & Thu 11 pm, Fri & Sat midnight, Sun 6 pm; closed Wed-Fri L, closed Mon & Tue; no Amex; no booking.

MAYFAIR PIZZA COMPANY
W1   £52   3|3|3

4 LANCASHIRE CT   020 7629 2889   **3–2B**

"Pizza isn't my favourite, but the truffled one here tastes better than it smells… and it smells great!" – this fun pizza stop (nowadays incorporated into the 'Mews of Mayfair' empire, to which it's a neighbour) is worth knowing about for a light, relatively affordable bite, off Bond Street. / W1S 1EY; www.mayfairpizzaco.com; @mayfairpizzaco; Wed-Sat 8.30 pm, Sun 1.30 pm.

MAZE W1
£85   1|2|1

10-13 GROSVENOR SQ   020 7107 0000
3–2A

Ratings have declined yet further this year for Gordon Ramsay's Mayfair venue, a star under long-gone founding chef Jason Atherton 10 years ago. Even fans damn it with faint praise: "food better than you expect" – "quite good, but a bit 'hotelly'". Critics don't hold back: "appalling"; "woeful food – had to send three dishes back" and "eye-watering prices". / W1K 6JP; www.gordonramsayrestaurants.com; @mazerestaurant; 9.30 pm; No trainers; booking max 9 may apply.

MAZE GRILL W1
£76   1|2|2

10-13 GROSVENOR SQ   020 7495 2211
3–2A

If it were not one of the restaurants that propelled Gordon Ramsay to fame (and also its erstwhile chef, Jason Atherton) – and if it wasn't at the heart of a posh postcode – we would have long ago dropped this hotel grill room in Mayfair: it attracts precious little feedback nowadays, all of it disappointing. / W1K 6JP; www.gordonramsay.com; @mazegrill; 11 pm; No shorts.

MAZE GRILL
SW10   £54   3|3|2

11 PARK WK   020 7255 9299   **6–3B**

The decor can seem "dreary" – a complaint that has dogged this Chelsea site ever since its heady days as 'Aubergine' (long RIP) – but this three-year-old spin-off from Gordon Ramsay's Mayfair grill puts in a better showing than the original: "dreamy burgers" and "outstanding beef" both win praise (if, as at the original, on fairly limited feedback). / SW10 0AJ; www.gordonramsay.com/mazegrill/park-walk; @GordonRamsayGRP; Mon-Thu 10 pm, Fri & Sat 11 pm, Sun 9 pm.

MAZI W8
£64   3|4|3

12-14 HILLGATE ST   020 7229 3794   **7–2B**

"Imaginative deconstructed modern Greek cooking" brings locals back to this "cramped and always crowded" taverna in the backstreets of Hillgate Village, near Notting Hill Gate tube (whose small garden is open in summer). "Once you know your way around the menu the food is excellent and at a reasonable price – the uninitiated will find it expensive." Top Tip: "fried feta and caper meringue should be a classic". / W8 7SR; www.mazi.co.uk; @mazinottinghill; Sun & Mon 10 pm, Tue-Sat 10.30 pm; closed Sun & Mon L.

MEATLIQUOR
£37   3|2|4

74 WELBECK ST, W1   020 7224 4239   **3–1B**
| **6 ST CHAD'S PLACE, WC1**   020 7837 0444
9–3C | **17 QUEENSWAY, W2**   020 7229 0172
7–2C | **133B UPPER ST, N1**   020 3711 0104
9–3D | **37 LORDSHIP LANE, SE22**
020 3066 0008   **1–4D** | **74 NORTHCOTE
RD, SW11 AWAITING TEL 11–2C NEW** |
BRIXTON MARKET, SW9   020 7924 9001
11–1D NEW

"The chilli cheeseburger and Dead Hippie are burger masterpieces", proclaim fans of this grungy, in-yer-face chain – still the go-to place for a superlative "filthy" burger ("don't go in your best jeans unless you want a dry cleaning bill afterwards"). The "delicious alcoholic milkshakes and fried onions the size of frisbees" also go down well. A new Battersea branch is opening in autumn 2018. / meatliquor.com; @MEATLiquor; W1 midnight (Fri & Sat 2 am), N1 11 pm, SE22 midnight, Sun 10.30 pm-11.30 pm; booking: min 6.

MEATMARKET
WC2 £27 322

JUBILEE MARKET HALL, 1 TAVISTOCK CT 020 7836 2139 5–3D

"Sitting above the indoor market at Covent Garden adds to the greasy-spoon vibe" of this central spin-off from the MEATliquor chain – "a good spot for a quick burger fix when out-and-about for the day in town". There's "not a worry about calories in sight" – just "burgers at their best, an excellent choice of sides (e.g. chilli cheese fries, monkey fingers and jalapeno poppaz) that add a bit of fire to the proceedings; and the milkshakes are a must-try!" / WC2E 8BD; www.themeatmarket.co.uk; @MEATmarketUK; Mon-Thu 11 pm, Fri & Sat midnight, Sun 10 pm; no Amex; no booking.

MEATMISSION N1 £31 334

14-15 HOXTON MARKET 020 7739 8212 13–1B

"Wow, what a burger (and great hot dogs too)", say fans of the trademarked 'Dead Hippie' and other mostly meaty treats at the MEATliquor group's Hoxton outlet. / N1 6HG; www.meatmission.com; @MEATmission; Sun 11 pm.

MEDITERRANEO
W11 £65 333

37 KENSINGTON PARK RD 020 7792 3131 7–1A

"A long-standing favourite" (including of actor Richard E Grant) in Notting Hill, lauded by a small but devoted fan club for its "excellent traditional Italian cooking" – "we go with the grandparents and kids at the weekend and everyone comes out happy!" / W11 2EU; www.mediterraneo-restaurant.co.uk; 11.30 pm, Sun 10.30 pm; booking max 10 may apply.

MEDLAR SW10 £81 443

438 KING'S RD 020 7349 1900 6–3B

"In an otherwise rather barren part of Chelsea", this low-profile, but immensely popular, fixture is "a great neighbourhood restaurant that's worth a journey if it's not in your neighbourhood". "Why did it lose its Michelin star" a couple of years ago? – we just don't know, as Joe Mercier-Nairne's "refined" cuisine is "very accomplished" and often "memorable"; service is "professional" and "exceptionally friendly"; and "the extent and variety of the wine list is a constant surprise, with recommendations that are spot-on every time". The weakest link is a dining room that some say is "not the most elegant", but others value its "intimate" feel. / SW10 0LJ; www.medlarrestaurant.co.uk; @MedlarChelsea; 9 pm.

MEI UME, FOUR SEASONS
HOTEL EC3 £108 334

10 TRINITY SQUARE 020 3297 3799 10–3D

"A great new restaurant addition to Four Seasons Hotel" that opened alongside the better-known Dame de Pic, which – unusually – combines dishes of Chinese and Japanese inspiration (and has one chef for each cuisine). All reports rate the food highly, but no surprises that it's no great bargain: "I went on a deal and it was absolutely delicious… not sure I'd have paid the actual price for it though!" / EC3N 4AJ; www.meiume.com; @FSTenTrinity; 10 pm; closed Sun.

MELANGE £50 322

45 TOPSFIELD PARADE, TOTTENHAM LANE, N8 020 8341 1681 9–1C | 240 HAVERSTOCK HILL, NW3 020 3759 6310 9–2A NEW

'A taste of France & Italy… in a versatile industry-vintage interior' is the promise of this modern bistro in Crouch End, which inspires limited but positive feedback. It must be doing something right, however, as this year it's spread its wings to take over the prominent Belsize Park site that was most recently The Truscott Arms (and which some still remember as the Weng Wah House, long RIP). /

MELE E PERE W1 £54 343

46 BREWER ST 020 7096 2096 4–3C

"A funky and friendly Italian in Soho that's the total opposite of all the Italian chain eateries in the area". "Staff are a joy (if sometimes overworked)" and put "real care into providing good portions of very tasty food". Top Tip: "terrific vermouth cocktails at the welcoming bar". / W1F 9TF; www.meleepere.co.uk; @meleEpere; 11 pm, Sun 10 pm.

MENIER CHOCOLATE
FACTORY SE1 £56 233

51-53 SOUTHWARK ST 020 7234 9610 10–4B

Book early for the meal-with-ticket deal at this theatre-restaurant in a converted Victorian chocolate factory opposite Borough Market: "they are such good value that they sell out early and are hard to come by". If you miss the deal, think again: there are "plenty of more attractive pre-theatre options nearby". / SE1 1RU; www.menierchocolatefactory.com; @MenChocFactory; Mon-Thu 12.30 am, Fri 1 am; closed Mon & Sun D.

MERAKI W1 £62 324

80-82 GT TITCHFIELD ST 020 7305 7686 3–1C

This "beautiful" yearling is Arjun and Peter Waney's stab at bringing their magic (Roka, Zuma, The Arts Club) to contemporary Greek cuisine, in the 100-cover Fitzrovia premises that some may remember as Efes (long RIP). Promising but a work-in-progress seems a fair summary of feedback: the vibe is "lively", and the food can be "exceptional", but reports often note it's "very expensive" and the "charming but slightly haphazard service" can "be a bit too keen on the up-sell". / W1W 7QT; www.meraki-restaurant.com; @meraki_lon; Mon-Thu 11 pm, Fri & Sat 11.30 pm, Sun 6 pm.

MERCATO METROPOLITANO
SE1 £25 533

42 NEWINGTON CAUSEWAY 020 7403 0930 1–3C

"Everyone makes their own choice and meets in the middle to eat" at this "fun" experience – a converted 45,000 square foot paper factory, which is nowadays a covered foodie market, with 25-30 stalls drawing from cuisines from all over the globe. Owned by Italian businessman Andrea Rasca (who owns two other similar centres in Italy), it has brought some much-needed life to the area north of Elephant & Castle since 2016 and is "changing and improving all the time; it's now complete with its own micro-brewery" and mushroom farm. "Perfect for a larger group of friends & family when you don't know how many of them will show up". New arrivals this year include Abel – a stall from ex-head chef of Barrafina Drury Lane, Javier Duarte Campos. STOP PRESS: a second location, Mercato Mayfair, will open in early 2019 in a Grade I former church just off Oxford Street. / SE1 6DR; www.mercatometropolitano.co.uk; @mercatometropol; 11 pm, Sun 10 pm.

THE MERCER
EC2 £63 222

34 THREADNEEDLE ST 020 7628 0001 10–2C

"Decent British cooking, competently done" keeps trade ticking over at this converted banking hall over two floors in Threadneedle Street. "Definitely a businessperson's restaurant", it also provides an "exceptional breakfast". / EC2R 8AY; www.themercer.co.uk; @TheMercerLondon; 9.30 pm; closed Sat & Sun.

MERCHANTS TAVERN
EC2 £61 334

36 CHARLOTTE RD 020 7060 5335 13–1B

"A wonderful combination of low-key style, effortlessly friendly service, and exceptionally well-crafted food" draw fans to Angela Hartnett's "buzzy", "unstuffy" and spacious pub in Shoreditch (converted from a former warehouse). A minority, though, are less wowed: it's "decent, but there's no racing of the pulse". / EC2A 3PG; www.merchantstavern.co.uk; @merchantstavern; 11 pm, Sun 9 pm.

LE MERCURY N1 £34 223

154-155 UPPER ST 020 7354 4088 9–2D

"A gem of its type" – this traditional candle-lit Islington bistro "changes surprisingly little over the years" and "you still can't beat it for value-for-money in North London". "Portions are generous and having the same price for all starters and mains makes paying as a group so much easier!" / N1 1QY; www.lemercury.co.uk; 1 am; Mon-Thu D only, Fri-Sun open L & D.

MERE W1 £89 443

74 CHARLOTTE ST 020 7268 6565 2–1B

"Monica Galetti's attention to detail shines through" and helps inspire a "stand-out total experience" at the Fitzrovia yearling that she runs with her husband David (formerly the sommelier at Le Gavroche): you start with "amazing cocktails" in the ground floor bar, and then move on to the "welcoming" downstairs restaurant. Alongside the à la carte options, it features "a very memorable tasting menu" ("exquisite flavours and textures, all perfectly cooked" and with a veggie option), and marries them with wine from the "superb" and "well-matched wine list". If there's a quibble, it's that "portions can be very small for the price". La Patronne "takes the time to visit each table"; and the "friendly and professional" service led by her hubbie adds a lot to the experience. And although "tables are perhaps a little close together", reporters generally like this "intimate" and "good-looking space". / W1T 4QH; www.mere-restaurant.com; @mererestaurant; Jacket & tie required.

Mirror Room, Rosewood London WC1

MESON DON FELIPE
SE1 £42 2 2 3

53 THE CUT 020 7928 3237 10–4A

This "fun" tapas veteran sits a minute's walk from the Old and Young Vic theatres, and is always "cramped and crowded" ("you need to arrive early to get a table"). "A very good Spanish wine list" helps buoy the "great atmosphere", and for everyone who feels the food's average or "past its sell-by", there are others who still think it's "terrific". / SE1 8LF; www.mesondonfelipe.com; 10 pm; closed Sun; no Amex; no booking after 8 pm.

MEWS OF MAYFAIR
W1 £70 3 2 3

10 LANCASHIRE COURT, NEW BOND ST
020 7518 9388 3–2B

A super-cute location – a cobbled alleyway, just off Bond Street – sets an upbeat tone to this hidden-away haunt which comprises both a bar and brasserie. Historically the former has seemed more reliable than the latter, but – while it attracts curiously few reports – such feedback as we have is all-round positive. / W1S 1EY; www.mewsofmayfair.com; @mewsofmayfair; 11 pm, Sun 4 pm; closed Sun D.

MEZA
£37 3 3 2

34 TRINITY RD, SW17 07722 111299 11–2C | 70 MITCHAM RD, SW17 020 8672 2131 11–2C

"Very fresh, bright tastes and efficient service" are the stand-out qualities in this "jolly" little pair of Lebanese cafés in Tooting and Clapham ("the Trinity Road branch buzzes a bit more than the one on Tooting Broadway"). Top Tip: "complex fried chicken livers". / www.mezarestaurant.co.uk; @MezaRestaurants; 11 pm, Fri & Sat 11.30 pm.

LA MIA MAMMA SW3 £61

257 KING'S RD 020 7351 2417 6–3C

'Food like mamma used to make' is the promise of this May 2018 opening in Chelsea, where 20 matriarchs a year are shipped over to create a rotating roster of residencies, with each chef hailing from a different region of Italy. / SW3 5EL; www.lamiamamma.co.uk; @LaMiaMamma_.

MICHAEL NADRA £60 4 3 2

6-8 ELLIOTT RD, W4 020 8742 0766 8–2A | 42 GLOUCESTER AVE, NW1 020 7722 2800 9–3B

Michael Nadra makes "a talented and charming chef/patron" and his duo of neighbourhood restaurants – in Chiswick and Camden Town (right next to the Regent's Canal) – both provide a "welcoming" venue and "surprisingly good value for sophisticated modern French cooking". On the downside, both inhabit awkward sites – NW1 is "cavernous" and slightly "remote", while W4 is low-ceilinged and tightly packed. / www.restaurant-michaelnadra.co.uk; @michaelnadra; W4 10 pm, Fri-Sat 10.30 pm, NW1 10.30 pm, Sun 9 pm; NW1 closed Mon, W4 closed Sun D.

MIEN TAY £37 3 2 2

45 FULHAM HIGH ST, SW6 020 7731 0670 11–1B NEW | 180 LAVENDER HILL, SW11 020 7350 0721 11–1C | 122 KINGSLAND RD, E2 020 7729 3074 14–2A

"Authentic, hot and spicy Vietnamese food never disappoints" at this quartet of neighbourhood restaurants in Battersea, Fulham, Shoreditch and now Wood Green. "Fabulous fresh dishes at amazing prices" can mean that they're "crowded and noisy, even on a weekday night – no wonder some of the waiters can seem grumpy…" / mientay.co.uk; @Mien_Tay; 11 pm, Sun 10 pm; E2 Sun 10.30 pm.

MILDREDS £46 3 2 2

45 LEXINGTON ST, W1 020 7494 1634 4–2C | 200 PENTONVILLE RD, N1 020 7278 9422 9–3D | 9 JAMESTOWN RD, NW1 020 7482 4200 9–3B | UPPER DALSTON SQ, E8 020 8017 1815 14–1A

"Good value vegetarian food" offering "excellent quality and choices" (including gluten-free and vegan) has driven the expansion of this 30-year-old veggie outfit from Soho into Camden, Dalston and King's Cross. The Soho original is "cramped but likeable", while the newer outposts are more "light and airy". / @mildredslondon.

MILK SW12 £16 4 3 3

20 BEDFORD HILL 020 8772 9085 11–2C

"Delicious food… as long as you don't mind queuing on weekends" continues to win many votes for this Antipodean café which is world famous down Balham way as a "fabulous breakfast and brunch" destination. / SW12 9RG; www.milk.london; @milkcoffeeldn; Mon-Wed 5 pm, Thu-Sat 10 pm, Sun 6 pm; closed Mon-Wed D; no booking.

MIN JIANG, THE
ROYAL GARDEN HOTEL
W8 £81 4 4 5

2-24 KENSINGTON HIGH ST 020 7361 1988 6–1A

"Exquisite Beijing duck" and "divine dim sum" are twin culinary highlights of this "top-class" Chinese, which occupies a "beautiful and comfortable" dining room on the eighth floor of Kensington's Royal Garden Hotel. "The rare and privileged views across the park to Kensington Palace takes this place to another level", though – "request a window seat!" / W8 4PT; www.minjiang.co.uk; @minjianglondon; 10 pm.

MINNOW SW4 £54 3 3 3

21 THE PAVEMENT 020 7720 4105 11–2D

"A strong new arrival in SW4" – "inventive modern British cooking" is "served by friendly, informal but informative, staff in a space which is larger than it appears from outside" at Jake Boyce's year-old venture, tipped for its good brunch. / SW4 0HY; minnowclapham.co.uk; @minnowclapham; Sun & Mon 5 pm, Wed & Thu 10 pm, Fri & Sat 11 pm, Tue 6 pm.

MINT LEAF £73 3 2 3

SUFFOLK PL, HAYMARKET, SW1 020 7930 9020 2–2C | ANGEL CT, LOTHBURY, EC2 020 7600 0992 10–2C

This "swanky" operation – whose slick contemporary decor has an "international feel" – serves "very different, very original Indian/ Asian fusion food" and "excellent cocktails" at its two venues, off Trafalgar Square and near Bank. / www.mintleafrestaurant.com; 10.45 pm; SW1 closed Sat L & Sun D, EC2 closed Sat & Sun.

MIRCH MASALA
SW17 £26 4 2 1

213 UPPER TOOTING RD 020 8767 8638 11–2D

"Amazing flavours at amazing prices" means it's always packed at this Pakistani canteen in Tooting – "now apparently gaining fame as Sadiq Khan's favourite restaurant". "It wins hands-down on value for money, especially with the BYO policy". Order the "wonderful slow-cooked meat specials or excellent veggie options". / SW17 7TG; www.mirchmasalarestaurant.co.uk; midnight; cash only; no booking.

MIRROR ROOM
WC1
£80 3 3 4

ROSEWOOD LONDON, 252 HIGH HOLBORN 020 3747 8620 2–1D

Pastry chef, Mark Perkins, takes inspiration from Cubism and Pop Art for the "beautiful afternoon tea" at this descriptively-named chamber within this plush Holborn hotel. It's "an interesting room" and the "exceptional cakes and pastries are truly a work of art… and taste great too!". / WC1V 7EN; www.rosewoodhotels.com; @RosewoodLondon; 11 pm, Sun 10.30 pm.

THE MODERN PANTRY
EC1
£65 2 2 2

47-48 ST JOHNS SQ 020 7553 9210 10–1A

Aussie fusion chef Anna Hansen's 10-year-old Clerkenwell flagship (the offshoot in Finsbury Square is no more) is a "perennially brilliant brunch spot" with "interesting food and great service... hence its popularity, especially on weekends". "Love the sugar-cured prawn, spring onion and sambal omelette" – a dish that has entered folklore. But some diners are not convinced, dismissing the food as merely "trendy" or "mediocre and disappointing". / EC1V 4JJ; www.themodernpantry.co.uk; @themodernpantry; 10 pm.

MOKSHA KT3
£35 5 4 3

KINGSTON RD 020 894 92211 1–4A

"First class Indian food" wins high esteem for experienced restaurateurs, Arjun Singh Rawat and Rajeev Danga's top tier North Indian two-year old, although, by dint of its New Malden location, feedback is still limited: more reports please! / KT3 3RJ; www.moksharestaurant.uk; @Mokshanewmalden; Mon & Tue 9 pm, Fri & Sat 11.30 pm, Wed 10 pm, Thu 11 pm, Sun 5 pm.

MOMO W1
£76 3 3 3

25 HEDDON ST 020 7434 4040 4–3B

Mourad Mazouz's "atmospheric" and clubby party scene first brought glamour to Moroccan cuisine – and the fast crowd to Mayfair's Heddon Street – back in the 1990s. "Tagines presented bubbling to your table" are a highlight on a menu also featuring grills, couscous and some tagine-esque North African starters (e.g. foie gras with pomegranate molasses, Scottish beef tartare with Batata harra foam). Kick off an evening with cocktails in the vibey basement bar. / W1B 4BH; www.momoresto.com; @momoresto; 1 am, Sun midnight; credit card required to book.

MON PLAISIR RESTAURANT
WC2
£53 3 3 4

19-21 MONMOUTH ST 020 7836 7243 5–2B

"Long may it survive!"; fans "never tire" of this "well-established favourite" of 70 years' standing – an "evergreen, authentic buzzing bistro" near Seven Dials, whose "charmingly eccentric", much-extended premises have "a unique, unmistakable Gallic atmosphere". The odd critic feels that its "old-fashioned French" cuisine has "seen better days", but the vast majority feel it's "no bad thing that it's predictable", praising results as "delicious" and "sensibly priced" (and loving the "fabulous cheese trolley"). Top Tip: "great pre/post theatre deals". / WC2H 9DD; www.monplaisir.co.uk; @MonPlaisir4; 11 pm; closed Sun.

MONA LISA SW10 **£39** 3 3 2

417 KING'S RD 020 7376 5447 6–3B

"No pretensions but amazing value and large portions" of "inexpensive, honest comfort food" make this Italian-run greasy spoon on the King's Road a useful option in pricey Chelsea ("workers' caff by day, restaurant by night"). Top Tip: where else can you still find a three-course set menu for £9.95? / SW10 0LR; monalisarestaurant.co.uk; 11 pm, Sun 5.30 pm; closed Sun D; no Amex.

MONKEY TEMPLE
W12
£33 3 4 2

92 ASKEW RD 020 8743 4597 8–1B

In ever-more chichi 'Askew Village' (aka deepest Shepherd's Bush) this "excellent" local curry house is a top option for a very decent curry: "nowt fancy, but reliable" and with "lovely service". / W12 9BL; monkeytempleonline.co.uk; 10.30 pm; closed Mon L; no Amex.

MONMOUTH COFFEE
COMPANY
£7 3 4 4

27 MONMOUTH ST, WC2 020 7232 3010 5–2B | 2 PARK ST, SE1 020 7232 3010 10–4C

"The best coffee on the planet" ("a fabulous diverse array complemented by very knowledgeable and friendly staff") ensure that these "caffeine-lovers' paradises" remain the survey's No.1 chain of coffee houses and are "consistently so rammed". Foodwise, there's just "a small range of good pastries, brownies and shortbreads", but at the mega-popular Borough Market branch you can "nibble on jam and butter on crusty white bread, while people watching". / www.monmouthcoffee.co.uk; WC2 6:30 pm; SE1 6 pm; SE16 Sat 1.30 pm; WC2 & SE1 closed Sun; no Amex; no booking.

MONTY'S DELI
N1
£36 4 4 3

225-227 HOXTON ST 020 7729 5737 14–1B

This "great Jewish restaurant on the fringes of Hoxton" is touted by fans as "hands-down the best place to get deli food in London". Founders Mark Ogus and Owen Barratt crowdfunded the move to a permanent site after perfecting their 'Jewish soul food' classics on a market stall. "The attention to detail is fantastic: the pickles are tiny and piquant, the spicing spot on, the potato latkes shatter crisply". Top Tip: "perfect soft and fatty salt beef and pastrami". In summer 2018, having smashed a Crowdcube fundraiser target, they have plans to expand into a national chain starting with another three London sites: the first to be in the new Victoria Market Halls development. / N1; montys-deli.com; @MontysDeli; 10 pm, Sun 4 pm; closed Sun D, closed Mon.

MORITO
£44 4 3 4

195 HACKNEY RD, E2 020 7613 0754 14–2A | 32 EXMOUTH MKT, EC1 020 7278 7007 10–1A

"An utterly brilliant tapas café, where you perch on stools, in the window or at the bar; staff are relaxed and chatty, and the food is expertly cooked, delicious and really good value". That's the low-down on Moro's first spin off, a few doors down from the mothership, on Exmouth Market. Since last year it has a "more comfortable Hackney Road version" (near Columbia Road flower market). "Lovely Mediterranean-inspired dishes here too, plus a great spacious setting", "very buzzy counter-style dining" and "you can book any time". Top Menu Tips – "yummy aubergine fritters" ("I don't know how they get them that crispy and tasty"); and a "scrumptious North African/ Mediterranean twist on brunch". / EC1 11 pm, Sun 4 pm; E2 10.30 pm, Sun 9 pm; EC1 closed Sun D; no booking.

MORO EC1
£61 4 3 3

34-36 EXMOUTH MKT 020 7833 8336 10–1A

"I've been coming for 20 years – it's yet to disappoint". Samuel & Samantha Clark's "unpretentious" ("no cheffery") Exmouth Market landmark still turns out "memorable Spanish and North African dishes, with a terrific selection of Spanish and Portuguese wines and sherries". Indeed, for its vast fan club, "the only limitation is the noise: it's not great for conversation" given how "echoey" the room can become. All this said, a small band of long-term fans do sound a warning note, feeling "the food has become a bit more variable in quality and interest" in recent years. It's still a minority view though – most reporters are just "grateful not to live nearby: otherwise I'd never go anywhere else…" / EC1R 4QE; www.moro.co.uk; @RestaurantMoro; 10.30 pm, Sun 9.30 pm; closed Sun D.

MOTCOMBS SW1 **£56** 2 3 3

26 MOTCOMB ST 020 7235 6382 6–1D

Like many of its patrons, this stalwart wine bar (upstairs) and restaurant (downstairs) has long been 'part of the furniture' in the ever-more-chichi heart of Belgravia. It's perennially been accused of somewhat "uninspired" fare, but – now under new ownership – fans feel that "even if the inimitable Mr Lawless has finally sold up, it remains good value in a top postcode". / SW1X 8JU; www.motcombs.co.uk; @Motcombs; 10 pm; closed Sun D.

MOTHER SW11 **£44** 2 2 3

2 ARCHERS LANE, BATTERSEA POWER STATION 020 7622 4386 11–1C

This dark and moodily decorated yearling – London's branch of Copenhagen's 'Italian pizza without all the nonsense' concept – occupies a railway arch at Battersea Power Station's Circus West Village. Opinion is divided on the all-important question of the pizza: "average" vying with "good value and tasty". / SW11 8AB; www.motherrestaurant.co.uk; @mother_ldn; Sun-Thu 11 pm, Fri & Sat midnight.

MR BAO SE15 £35 [4][3][3]

293 RYE LN 020 7635 0325 1–4D

Frank Yeung's "friendly and small Peckham cafe serves delectable Taiwanese street food, in particular heavenly steamed buns". In February 2018 he opened a Tooting spin-off Daddy Bao – see also. / SE15 4UA; www.mrbao.co.uk; @MrBaoUK; 11 pm; closed Sun & Mon.

MR CHOW SW1 £88 [2][3][3]

151 KNIGHTSBRIDGE 020 7589 7347 6–1D

All reporters have nice things to say about the cuisine at this datedly glamorous A-lister, near 1 Hyde Park, whose heyday was in the 1960s and 1970s. It can, however, seem "insanely expensive for what is just some nice Chinese food". / SW1X 7PA; www.mrchow.com; @mrchow; midnight; closed Mon L.

MUNAL TANDOORI SW15 £27 [3][4][2]

393 UPPER RICHMOND ROAD, PUTNEY 020 8876 3083 11–2A

"Just a great local curry" on the edge of Putney – this Nepalese has been a handy stop on the South Circular for more than 25 years. Regulars praise its "really tasty food and generous portions" – "it can't be beaten for a really inexpensive meal". / SW15 \N; Mon-Thu 11 pm, Sat midnight, Sun 10.30 pm; closed Mon-Thu L, closed Fri.

MURANO W1 £99 [4][5][3]

20-22 QUEEN ST 020 7495 1127 3–3B

Angela Hartnett's "superb" Mayfair flagship has taken Pip Lacey's 2017 departure in its stride, and although its ratings dipped fractionally year-on-year, many reporters still feel Oscar Holgado's "Italian-oriented cuisine must be amongst the best in town". When it comes to the interior, the harsh view is that these "un-flashy" premises "on a quiet street" are "a little dull", but the more common verdict is that its "restrained and elegant" style "oozes class and calm" and that "the warm welcome and graceful professional service gets any visit off to a flying start". / W1J 5PP; www.muranolondon.com; @muranolondon; 11 pm; closed Sun; credit card required to book.

MUSTARD W6 £45 [3][3][3]

98-100 SHEPHERD'S BUSH RD 020 3019 1175 8–1C

"A pleasant oasis in the desert of Shepherd's Bush Road" – this smart brasserie north of Brook Green is "a great local", offering "food that's perfectly fine, comfortable surroundings and willing service". / W6 7PD; www.mustardrestaurants.co.uk; @mustarddining; 10 pm, Sun 5 pm; closed Mon & Sun D.

NAMAASTE KITCHEN NW1 £44 [4][3][2]

64 PARKWAY 020 7485 5977 9–3B

"Creative and intelligent" cooking wins nothing but high praise for this contemporary update of the traditional curry house, in Camden Town. It has a sister venue, Salaam Namaste, in Bloomsbury. / NW1 7AH; www.namaastekitchen.co.uk; @NamaasteKitchen; midnight, Sun 6 pm.

NANASHI EC2 £62 [3][3][2]

14 RIVINGTON ST 020 7686 0010 13–2B

"First class sushi, complemented by some decent hot dishes" win a repeat thumbs-up for this Japanese yearling in Shoreditch. "The tuna sushi burger is worth a try, but the main show is the other fish". / EC2A 3DU; www.nanashi.co.uk; Tue, Wed 10.30 pm, Thu-Sat 11 pm; closed Sun & Mon.

NANBAN SW9 £44 [4][2][3]

COLDHARBOUR LN 020 7346 0098 11–2D

"Different and great flavours" are to be discovered at former MasterChef winner Tim Anderson's "fun" fixture, where he cooks up his own distinctive and very alternative 'Japanese Soul Food' (incorporating eclectic ingredients from nearby Brixton Market). / SW9 8LF; www.nanban.co.uk; @NanbanLondon; Mon-Thu 11 pm, Sat midnight, Sun 10.30 pm.

THE NARROW E14 £57 [2][2][4]

44 NARROW ST 020 7592 7950 12–1B

The "fantastic river location and views" at Gordon Ramsay's Limehouse pub have never in all the many years he's owned it been matched by its kitchen. No-one says its dire nowadays, but the reaction on the "standard gastropub food" is very middling – a "very average offering from Ramsay, this". / E14 8DP; www.gordonramsayrestaurants.com/the-narrow; @thenarrow; Mon-Thu 12.30 am, Fri 1 am.

NATIVE SE1 £56

32 SOUTHWARK ST 07943 934 375 10–4C

In its former home – "an unassuming corner of Neal's Yard" – Ivan Tisdall-Downes and Imogen Davis's on-trend venture (100% Brit produce, zero waste and, quote, 'profound respect for the natural environment') was thriving. Their lease fell through in mid-2018, but every cloud has a silver lining, as the old gaff was "rather worn and plain" and this new home is bigger, with 60 covers. A daily changing menu with a focus on game remains a feature, as do the 'Chef's Wasting Snacks' (canapés making use of leftovers others would chuck out, e.g. fish skins, potato peelings… better than it sounds anyway). It opened too late for a survey rating, but there's no reason to think its "small, exquisite, wow of a menu" and "enthusiastic and patient service" will not transfer well. / SE1 1TU; www.eatnative.co.uk; @eatnativeuk; closed Sun & Mon.

NAUGHTY PIGLETS SW2 £57 [5][5][3]

28 BRIXTON WATER LN 020 7274 7796 11–2D

"Truly the best conceptual-type restaurant I've been to in ages" – Joe and Margaux Sharratt's small French-accented outfit in a Brixton side street charms all comers with its "expert cuisine (with innovative combinations such as Devon crab, peanut and pickled cabbage)" and "love of doing it right". Opened to acclaim three years ago – and now with a sister venue at Andrew Lloyd Webber's The Other Palace theatre in Victoria – it shows no sign of flagging. Top Tip: "sit at the bar to watch the talented chefs in action". / SW2 1PE; www.naughtypiglets.co.uk; 10 pm; closed Mon-Wed L, closed Sun.

NAUTILUS NW6 £35 [4][3][1]

27-29 FORTUNE GREEN RD 020 7435 2532 1–1B

"Fish 'n' chips the way it should be!" – this classic West Hampstead chippy is reckoned by fans to be "still the best in the northwest". Nobody disputes that the fish is "fantastic", "but the restaurant needs redoing" (as it has done for decades) – "much better for take-away". Top Tip: choose matzo meal over batter. / NW6 1DU; 11 pm; closed Sun; no Amex.

NAVARRO'S W1 £39 [3][3][3]

67 CHARLOTTE ST 020 7637 7713 2–1C

This "fantastic, traditional-style tapas restaurant" in Fitzrovia was founded in 1985, well before the contemporary tapas boom. Family-run, "humble" and "down-to-earth" – it may lack the pizzazz of its more modern Iberian competitors, but is "very good value". / W1T 4PH; www.navarros.co.uk; @SpanishEchelon; 10 pm; closed Sat L, closed Sun.

NEEDOO E1 £25 [4][2][2]

87 NEW RD 020 7247 0648 13–2D

There are more famous Pakistani BYO destinations in E1, but the small-but-devoted fan club of this sizeable Whitechapel grill-house extol its "terrific curries and great value for money". / E1 1HH; www.needoogrill.co.uk; @NeedooGrill; 11.30 pm.

NEO BISTRO W1 £58 [4][4][3]

11 WOODSTOCK ST 020 7499 9427 3–1B

"In a slightly barren part of town" – just behind Bond Street tube – this "little gem" opened in summer 2017, with two young chefs (Alex Harper, ex-Harwood Arms and Mark Jarvis, ex-Anglo) inspired by the modern Parisian bistro movement. It's a "great concept" with accomplished cuisine ("a showcase of ingredients and technique"), "accommodating service" and "a thoughtful wine list". / W1C 2JF; www.neobistro.co.uk; @neo_bistro; 9.45 pm.

NEPTUNE, THE PRINCIPAL WC1 £86

THE PRINCIPAL LONDON, 8 RUSSELL SQUARE 020 7520 1806 2–1D

The setting: a dramatic late-Victorian pile (fka Hotel Russell) on the eastern flank of Russell Square which has finally received the bold revamp it's been crying out for, for decades. No expense has been spared, and this seafood temple is a superb new space. It opened just as our 2018 survey was drawing to a close,

Neptune, The Principal W1

and though we had one enthusiastic report, more muted press reviews suggest the level of achievement of the cuisine overseen by ex-Richmond-chef, Brett Redman is very fully priced. You can always poke your head around the door on a visit to one of the hotel's other venues: afternoon tea parlour Palm Court, Fitz's cocktail bar or Burr & Co coffeehouse. / WC1B 5BE; neptune.london; @Principal_Hotel; Mon-Fri 10 pm, Sat & Sun 9 pm.

NICHE EC1   £55   232

197-199 ROSEBERY AVENUE   020 7837 5048   9–3D

Only limited feedback and only reasonable ratings for this compact contemporary bistro near Sadler's Wells Theatre: London's first 100% gluten-free restaurant (motto: 'gluten-free, but you wouldn't know it'). Still, if that's your dietary ticket it has evident attractions, and they must be doing something right, as July 2018 saw them close to refurbish, and launch a new crowdsourcing campaign for a second opening, pencilled in for Ealing. / EC1R 4TJ; www.nichefoodanddrink.com; @Nichefooddrink; 11 pm, Sun 10 pm.

THE NINTH LONDON W1   £78   432

22 CHARLOTTE ST   020 3019 0880   2–1C

"It's all about the food" – you could call it "casual Michelin" – at Jun Tanaka's Fitzrovia HQ, which provides a "relaxed", "buzzing" (and quite "romantic") environment in which to enjoy his "innovative" and sometimes "amazing" culinary creations. Quibbles? – "it's quite a difficult menu to get your mind around" ("we were told it was small plates but were still asked to choose separate courses each"); and "although it's a pretty space it can feel a bit cramped". / W1T 2NB; www.theninthlondon.com; @theninthlondon; Mon-Wed 10 pm, Thu-Sat 10.30 pm; closed Sun.

NO 29 POWER STATION WEST SW8   £56   214

CIRCUS WEST, BATTERSEA POWER STATION   020 3857 9872   11–1C

"Delicious brunch in a large airy room overlooking the river" is one draw to Darwin & Wallace's latest venue, in Battersea Power Station's Circus West Village – a bar/

brasserie with a fine riverside location and small outside terrace. One bugbear: "service is friendly but can be haphazard". / SW8 5BP; www.no29powerstationwest.co.uk; @batterseapwrstn; Sun-Thu midnight, Fri & Sat 1 am.

NOBLE ROT WC1   £74   344

51 LAMB'S CONDUIT ST   020 7242 8963   2–1D

An oenophile's dream – Mark Andrew and Daniel Keeling's "jolly" Bloomsbury two-year-old is, for the second year running, in strong contention as "London's best wine option, bar none". "Old-fashioned (in a good way)", it occupies the endearingly "dingy" '70s site that for many years traded as Vats (RIP) and "aside from being a bit noisy, the place itself is wonderfully atmospheric". "Staff are friendly with an expert knowledge of the wines" and the list itself is "extensive, but even for the non-connoisseur or financially constrained customer there are quite a lot of bottles coming in at less than £30". The "well-crafted" food is "much-more-than-serviceable" too – a selection of "very tasty and reasonably priced small plates". / WC1N 3NB; www.noblerot.co.uk; @noblerotbar; 10 pm; closed Sun.

NOBU, METROPOLITAN HOTEL W1   £100   322

19 OLD PARK LN   020 7447 4747   3–4A

"The food is just as good as it always was" (if no longer as trailblazing) at this Japanese-South American fusion concept, a global operation that exploded onto the London scene 21 years ago in this minimalist (some would say boring), first-floor space, overlooking Hyde Park. "Not the destination it used to be for spotting a celeb", that's not without its benefits ("there's no problem getting a table") and though as "expensive" as it's always been (and with so-so service), it can "still impress". / W1K 1LB; www.noburestaurants.com; @NobuOldParkLane; Mon-Wed 10.30 pm, Thu-Sat 11 pm, Sun 10 pm.

NOBU BERKELEY W1   £104   322

15 BERKELEY ST   020 7290 9222   3–3C

More "brash and boisterous" than its (older) Park Lane sibling, this Mayfair venue continues to attract a steady stream of positive reviews for its "sublime sushi" and other Japanese fusion-wizardry. For how long can they keep milking the franchise as hard as they do, though? – this place seems to become ever-more "wildly overpriced" by the year. / W1J 8DY; www.noburestaurants.com; @NobuBerkeleyST; Mon-Wed 11 pm, Thu-Sat midnight, Sun 9.45 pm; closed Sun L.

NOBU SHOREDITCH EC2   £110   323

10-50 WILLOW ST   020 3818 3790   13–1B

"I can't believe there's a Nobu in Shoreditch!" – there is indeed, a 240-seater in the basement (with small courtyard garden attached) of London's first hotel from the Japanese-American superbrand, serving all "the usual fare" ("consistently great sushi", "top-notch

black cod", etc) "with a couple of Shoreditch specials". Some fans reckon it's "better than the others in the stable", especially its "buzzy, loud 'cool' dining room", but like its siblings it can seem well "overpriced": "loved it, but there were too many City-types spending the bosses' money!" / EC2A 4BH; www.nobuhotelshoreditch.com; @NobuShoreditch; Sun & Mon 10.45 pm, Tue-Sat midnight.

NOIZÉ W1   £78   454

39 WHITFIELD ST   020 7323 1310   2–1C

A particularly "excellent choice of wines both by the glass and the bottle" and "seamless and friendly service" are features of this quite small (36-seat) and agreeably "unfussily decorated" Fitzrovia newcomer (on the former site of Dabbous, RIP) – no surprises, perhaps, as its patron Mathieu Germond is a former co-owner and manager of nearby Pied à Terre. When it comes to the chef Ed Dutton's "imaginative" modern French cuisine, all reports agree results are "excellent" going on "exceptional". (There's also a basement bar.) / W1T 2SF; www.noize-restaurant.co.uk; @NoizeRestaurant; 10.30 pm; closed Sat L, closed Sun & Mon.

NOOR JAHAN   £48   333

**2A BINA GDNS, SW5   020 7373 6522   6–2B
| 26 SUSSEX PL, W2   020 7402 2332   7–1D**

An "old favourite" – this "reliable workhorse" on the Earl's Court / South Ken' borders is a proper, "old-fashioned Indian" and has everything you'd expect from a "great neighbourhood curry house", including a "loyal clientele and staff that have been there forever". There's "nothing extravagant about it, but that's its charm" and it's always "impressively busy". (It has a similar, but lesser-known Bayswater spin-off.) / W2 11.30 pm, Sun 11 pm; SW5 11.30 pm.

NOPI W1   £74   433

21-22 WARWICK ST   020 7494 9584   4–3B

The "awesome food" at influential writer-chef Yotam Ottolenghi's Soho flagship is "a treat to the tastebuds" – and his Middle Eastern small plates even make "eating out feel healthy for once". When it comes to the atmosphere, most diners experience a "happy buzz" but it's "too loud" and "busy" for some tastes. Top Tip: "delightful at breakfast". / W1B 5NE; www.nopi-restaurant.com; @ottolenghi; 10.30 pm, Sun 4 pm; closed Sun D.

NORDIC BAKERY W1   £13   322

14A GOLDEN SQ   020 3230 1077   4–3C

"Good coffee, excellent Nordic-based rye-bread sandwiches and the famous cinnamon buns" have made this café a fixture in Golden Square, Soho, for more than a decade. Its expansion plans seem to have hit the rocks, however, with the sudden closure of three satellite spin-offs all in the past year. / W1F 9JG; www.nordicbakery.com; 8 pm, Sat & Sun 7 pm; L & early evening only; no Amex; no booking.

THE NORFOLK ARMS
WC1 £49 233

28 LEIGH ST 020 7388 3937 9–4C

This King's Cross gastroboozer with an "extensive tapas menu" is a "bright, lively spot in a part of town that's otherwise a little sparse for restaurants". Food that generally exceeds expectations and "relaxed staff" make this a "good place for a party" – and there are private dining rooms upstairs. / WC1H 9EP; www.norfolkarms.co.uk; 10.30 pm, Mon 11 pm, Sun 3 pm; no Amex.

NORTH CHINA
W3 £44 342

305 UXBRIDGE RD 020 8992 9183 8–1A

"Still the stand-out Chinese" in Acton (and fans would say beyond) – this neighbourhood stalwart can pleasantly surprise with the quality of its cooking, and "the maitre d' Laurence remembers you even if you haven't been for years!". "We went three times in six days on a recent visit to town!" / W3 9QU; www.northchina.co.uk; Sun-Thu 11 pm, Fri & Sat 11.30 pm.

NORTH SEA FISH
WC1 £45 332

7-8 LEIGH ST 020 7387 5892 9–4C

A "great institution" – this "very traditional" family-run Bloomsbury chippy is one of the best around the West End, and a safe bet for "good fresh fish, grilled or battered, with proper crisp chips". "You don't come here for the ambience" – it's "had a facelift" but "never really changes… thank goodness!". / WC1H 9EW; www.northseafishrestaurant.co.uk; 10 pm; closed Sun L; no Amex.

THE NORTHALL, CORINTHIA
HOTEL WC2 £103 323

10A NORTHUMBERLAND AVE
020 7321 3100 2–3C

Overshadowed by the opening of Kerridge's Bar & Grill, opinions were more split this year on the hotel's plush 'other' dining room – an "elegant" ("slightly cavernous") space with orange leather seating and "well-spaced tables". Practically all reports are of "excellent", "traditional" cooking, but one former fan felt it "had become more noticeably overpriced since the last visit" and to another sceptic: "the food's OK, but I'm not sure how much the hotel values the place other than for serving in-house guests". / WC2N 5AE; www.thenorthall.co.uk; @CorinthiaLondon; 11 pm.

NORTHBANK EC4 £60 323

ONE PAUL'S WALK 020 7329 9299 10–3B

"It's the location that's the 'icing on the cake' – with the Thames, Tate Modern, and picture windows so that you can see it all" – at this City bar/café, beside the Wobbly Bridge. Even if it can seem "a bit pricey", the food – with "a focus on Cornwall and fish" – tries harder than that of many well-situated destinations. / EC4V 3QH; www.northbankrestaurant.co.uk; @NorthbankLondon; 10 pm; closed Sun.

NOVIKOV (ASIAN RESTAURANT)
W1 £96 324

50A BERKELEY ST 020 7399 4330 3–3C

For a "perfect, fun buzzy time", this glam Russian-owned pan-Asian near Berkeley Square is a perennial smash hit with a glossy, very Mayfair crowd. Its mix of sushi, dim sum, charcoal grill dishes and noodles is dependably delectable, but if you are at all budget-conscious, spare yourself the stress induced by the bill and head elsewhere. / W1J 8HA; www.novikovrestaurant.co.uk; @NovikovLondon; midnight.

NOVIKOV (ITALIAN RESTAURANT)
W1 £110 122

50A BERKELEY ST 020 7399 4330 3–3C

A few fans – all of whom seem to have put 'Investment Banker' in the occupation field of the survey form – feel the food is "first rate" in the Italian section of Russian restaurateur Arkady Novikov's Eurotrashy Mayfair hang-out. Those not blessed with a career in the money factories are more apt to feel the experience is "appalling all-round", with particular antipathy to the Sputnik-high prices – "bare-faced robbery!". / W1J 8HA; www.novikovrestaurant.co.uk; @NovikovLondon; Mon-Wed midnight, Thu-Sat 12.45 am, Sun 11 pm.

NUALA EC1 £57 434

70-74 CITY RD 020 3904 0462 13–1A

"Cool surroundings and diners… as befits the location" set the tone at this "interesting" (if sometimes "noisy and frantic") newcomer, just south of Silicon Roundabout, where cooking over open flames is the order of the day. Even a reporter who found results "interesting in conception but lumpy in execution", found their visit "enjoyable", and most reports are of "well presented dishes with good flavours". / EC1 2BJ; www.nualalondon.com; @nualalondon; Mon-Fri 10 pm, Sat & Sun 9 pm.

NUOVI SAPORI
SW6 £50 334

295 NEW KING'S RD 020 7736 3363 11–1B

"An old favourite" – this "welcoming neighbourhood trattoria" near Parsons Green offers a "conventional Italian menu" alongside "cheerful service and atmosphere that ensure that it's always busy". / SW6 4RE; www.nuovisaporilondon.co.uk; 11 pm; closed Sun; booking max 6 may apply.

NUSR-ET STEAKHOUSE, THE PARK TOWER KNIGHTSBRIDGE SW1

101 KNIGHTSBRIDGE AWAITING TEL 6–1D

Former incumbent on this site, One-O-One (sadly RIP), was of rare quality, but its closure wasn't too hard to fathom, given the hollow ambience that has always dogged this prime Knightsbridge site. Being too low-key shouldn't be a problem for long, however, with the announcement that in late 2018 the site's new occupant will be the London home of Turkish-butcher-turned-Instagram-sensation, Salt Bae – real name Nusret Gökçe – a new stablemate to outposts in Miami and New York, as well as in the Middle East. / SW1X 7RN; www.nusr-et.com.tr/en/home.aspx; Tue-Sat, Mon 10.30 pm, Sun 3.30 pm.

NUTBOURNE
SW11 £59 223

29 RANSOMES DOCK, 35-37 PARKGATE RD
020 7350 0555 6–4C

"There's always an interesting menu" at the Gladwin brothers' farm-to-table Battersea venture (named after the family farm and vineyard in West Sussex) in the riverside venue that for many years was Ransome's Dock (long RIP). The food's execution can vary, though – what is "excellent" in some cases only rates as "underwhelming to adequate" in others, and service is "slightly vague". / SW11 4NP; www.nutbourne-restaurant.com; @NutbourneSW11; 11 pm, Sun 5 pm; closed Sun D, closed Mon.

O'VER SE1 £51 433

44-46 SOUTHWARK ST 020 7378 9933 10–4C

This superior pizzeria near Borough Market lists pure seawater as a key ingredient in its dough. Boss Tommaso Mastromatteo is a teacher at the Associazione Verace Pizza Napoletana, which promotes and protects true Neapolitan pizza. / SE1 1UN; www.overuk.com; Wed-Sat 11 pm.

OAK £57 334

243 GOLDHAWK RD, W12 020 8741 7700 8–1B | **137 WESTBOURNE PARK RD, W2** 020 7221 3355 7–1B

"Excellent pizzas" and a vibey interior contribute to the impressive magnetism of this appealing Notting Hill pub-conversion. It has a similar (but bigger and more "comfy") Shepherd's Bush sibling, near the bottom of the Askew Road. / W12 10.30pm, Fri & Sat 11 pm Sun 9.30pm; W2 10.30pm, Fri & Sat 11 pm, Sun 10 pm.

OBLIX SE1 £102 223

LEVEL 32, THE SHARD, 31 ST. THOMAS ST
020 7268 6700 10–4C

"A table by the window overlooking the Thames and St Paul's, a glass of Champagne: ultimate romance!" – that's the impression left on some fans of this sky-high brasserie from Rainer Becker (of Zuma and Roka fame). That "the food is great, too" can seem like something of an afterthought, but on most accounts it does live up, even if prices are as steep as The Shard's glass sides! You can book for either the 'West' or 'East' sections – the former's selection of grills from the Josper (plus flatbreads, salads, and so on) is more extensive than the latter's. / SE1 9RY; www.oblixrestaurant.com; @OblixRestaurant; 11 pm; booking max 6 may apply.

ODETTE'S NW1 £70 4 3 3

130 REGENTS PARK RD 020 7586 8569 9–3B

"Surprisingly good after so many years" – star Welsh chef Bryn Williams's intimate 40-year-old Primrose Hill fixture (10 under his ownership) "has a loyal following" and under this stewardship delivers ambitious British cuisine that's "never less than delicious". / NW1 8XL; www.odettesprimrosehill.com; @Odettes_rest; 10 pm, Sun 3 pm; closed Sun D, closed Mon; no Amex.

OGNISKO RESTAURANT SW7 £50 3 4 5

55 PRINCE'S GATE, EXHIBITION RD 020 7589 0101 6–1C

The "superb" setting of this "big and airy room" – plus "a lovely terrace at the back for those warm summer days" – sets up a "special" atmosphere at this former émigrés club, occupying a wonderfully "elegant", if romantically faded, building in South Kensington. The "flavourful and varied Polish cuisine" is arguably "better than in Poland" and "you will not leave hungry"; but at least as great an attraction is the "impressive range of vodkas" and "a great long wine list including some lively, rarely seen eastern European vintages". "Ideal for the Royal Albert Hall." / SW7 2PN; www.ogniskorestaurant.co.uk; @OgniskoRest; 9 pm, Sun 3 pm; closed Mon L; No trainers.

OKA £53 3 2 2

KINGLY COURT, 1 KINGLY COURT, W1 020 7734 3556 4–2B | 251 KING'S RD, SW3 020 7349 8725 6–3C | 71 REGENTS PARK RD, NW1 020 7483 2072 9–3B

"Amazing sushi" and a "fantastic range of hot dishes" enable these "great value" Japanese cafés to stand out in the marketplace. They are "ridiculously small", though – "you might not get a table". / www.okarestaurant.co.uk; 10.30 pm.

OKLAVA EC2 £56 4 4 3

74 LUKE ST 020 7729 3032 13–1B

"Dishes bursting with flavour" from a "lively", "Turkish-with-a-twist" menu, win nothing but the highest regard for Selin Kiazim and Laura Christie's "intimate little place" in Shoreditch (across the road from Leroy). "We especially enjoyed watching an (almost) entirely female brigade of cooks working so co-operatively and well together – it feels like a really intelligently thought-through restaurant, full of people who are passionate about the food". Top Menu Tips – "really memorable pomegranate sauce lamb", "fantastic kebabs" and "don't miss out on ordering a pide, too". See also Kyseri. / EC2A 4PY; www.oklava.co.uk; @oklava_ldn; midnight; booking max 6 may apply.

OLDROYD N1 £52 3 3 2

344 UPPER ST 020 8617 9010 9–3D

That it's "very cramped" and "cheek by jowl" is the main accusation made against Tom Oldroyd's "tiny" Islington two-year-old ("basically a house made into a restaurant, where upstairs is quieter and lighter"). "As you head up the rickety staircase and cross the wonky floorboards, a hint of doubt may cross your mind – don't let it!", say fans, applauding the "unpretentious", "individual" and "full-flavoured" food from "a limited but well-put-together menu". That said, ratings were "off the boil" compared with last year – perhaps the pressure of opening the Duke of Richmond (see also)? / N1 0PD; www.oldroydlondon.com; @oldroydlondon; Mon-Thu 11 pm, Fri & Sat 11.30 pm, Sun 10 pm; booking max 4 may apply.

OLIVETO SW1 £60 4 2 1

49 ELIZABETH ST 020 7730 0074 2–4A

This popular Sardinian has provided "exceptional pasta, pizza, tuna and sweets" to the denizens of Belgravia for many years – and at reasonable prices for the locale. Any complaints? "It needs a makeover". / SW1W 9PP; www.olivorestaurants.com/oliveto; 10.30 pm, Sat 11 pm; booking max 7 may apply.

OLIVO SW1 £75 3 3 2

21 ECCLESTON ST 020 7730 2505 2–4B

"Still the go-to Belgravia Italian" – the "consistent" and "friendly" flagship of Mauro Sanna's upmarket local Sardinian group has been a fixture of the area for over 20 years and inspires more-than-local acclaim for its deft, "light and fresh" cooking alongside "some truly delicious wines" on a Sardinian list. / SW1W 9LX; www.olivorestaurants.com; 10.30 pm; closed Sat L & Sun L.

OLIVOCARNE SW1 £80 3 2 2

61 ELIZABETH ST 020 7730 7997 2–4A

"Reliably good Sardinian cooking" and "a warm welcome" greet you at this smart Belgravia outfit specialising in meat. A relatively recent addition to Mauro Sanna's established Olivo group, it is "slightly more upmarket than its sister restaurants". / SW1W 9PP; www.olivorestaurants.com; 11 pm, Sun 10.30 pm.

OLIVOMARE SW1 £79 3 3 1

10 LOWER BELGRAVE ST 020 7730 9022 2–4B

A "delightful Sardinian take on seafood and fresh fish" is the successful focus of this Belgravia venue – part of Mauro Sanna's Olivo group – whose "honest and low key" style makes it an enduring and popular destination. But while "the food speaks for itself", the interior "feels rather cramped and clinical". / SW1W 0LJ; www.olivorestaurants.com; @OlivoGroup; 11 pm, Sun 10.30 pm; booking max 10 may apply.

OLLE W1 £46 2 2 2

86-88 SHAFTESBURY AVENUE 020 7287 1979 5–3A

Limited and somewhat up-and-down reports on this two-floor Chinatown-fringe yearling, featuring traditional Korean BBQ at the table – feedback veers from total enthusiasm to the view that it is "generally disappointing". / W1D 6NH; www.ollelondon.com; 10.30 pm, Sun 10 pm.

OLLEY'S SE24 £39 3 3 2

65-69 NORWOOD RD 020 8671 8259 11–2D

"The batter is light and complements the fish well" at this thirty-year-old venue opposite Brockwell Park, themed 1980s-style with Olde Worlde flourishes. There are cheaper chippies to be found, but regulars say it "never fails to provide excellent, well-cooked fish 'n' chips". / SE24 9AA; www.olleys.info; Tue-Sun, Mon 9.30 pm; closed Mon L; no Amex.

OLYMPIC, OLYMPIC STUDIOS SW13 £49 2 2 3

117-123 CHURCH RD 020 8912 5161 11–1A

Attracting "everyone from mamas with buggies to white-haired seniors", this all-day brasserie – the ground floor of a legendary former recording studios, which is nowadays an independent local cinema and chichi members' club – has become a major social hub in Barnes. But while it's "lively and buzzy" and stylish, the food offering is "just OK", and service is "slow". / SW13 9HL; www.olympiccinema.co.uk; @Olympic_Cinema; Tue, Sat 10 pm, Wed-Fri 11 pm, Mon 9 pm.

OLYMPUS FISH N3 £34 3 3 2

140-144 BALLARDS LN 020 8371 8666 1–1B

"Super-fresh fish" "cooked on a charcoal grill", "served sizzling hot", "with plump and plentiful chips" and "in copious portions" make this "truly excellent" Turkish-run outfit in Finchley one of north London's top chippies. One or two reporters, though, fear it may be starting to "rest on its laurels". / N3 2PA; www.olympusrestaurant.co.uk; @Olympus_London; 11 pm.

OMARS PLACE SW1 £61 4 4 4

13 CAMBRIDGE ST 07881 777227 2–4B

Down a side street near Victoria station, Egyptian restaurateur Omar Shabaan has teamed up with well-known Mallorcan chef Vicente Fortea to launch this well-designed Pimlico venue – a stylishly converted former pub serving Mediterranean small plates and wine. On limited feedback to date, results are excellent. / SW1V 4PR; www.omarsplace.co.uk; @omarsplaceldn.

ON THE BAB £36 3 2 2

39 MARYLEBONE LN, W1 020 7935 2000 2–1A | 36 WELLINGTON ST, WC2 020 7240 8825 5–3D | 305 OLD ST, EC1 020 7683 0361 13–1B | 9 LUDGATE BROADWAY, EC4 020 7248 8777 10–2A

This K-pop styled, Korean street-food group has a "short and very tasty menu" of "freshly cooked and great value bites". The minimalist and buzzy outlets across central London "continue to shine": in particular the WC2 branch is "a good option in Covent Garden". / onthebab.co.uk; @onthebab; EC1 & WC2 10.30 pm,

On The Dak WC2

Sun 10 pm; W1 & EC4 4 pm; EC4 closed Sat & Sun; W1 closed Sun.

ON THE DAK
WC2   **£13**   5️⃣3️⃣1️⃣

1 MONMOUTH ST   020 7836 5619   5–2C

"It's best to eat out" ("you just have to accept the tiny interior with three tables if you eat in") at Linda Lee's (of On the Bab and Mee Market) latest creation – a simple café/take-away on the fringes of Covent Garden, serving "stunning" Korean-fried chicken. / WC2H 9DA; www.onthedak.co.uk; @OnTheDakLDN; 10 pm, Sun 9 pm.

ONE CANADA SQUARE
E14   **£62**   2️⃣3️⃣2️⃣

1 CANADA SQUARE   020 7559 5199   12–1C

In the lobby of Canary Wharf's top landmark, this is "a business restaurant primarily, so I don't really rate the atmosphere" ("it's too bland for anything else"). "However, it works perfectly for a meeting: breakfast and lunch menus are well thought out and the food well put together". For its purpose "definitely one of the best restaurants in the Wharf". / E14 5AB; www.onecanadasquarerestaurant.com; @OneCanadaSquare; 10.45 pm; closed Sun.

108 BRASSERIE
W1   **£61**   3️⃣3️⃣3️⃣

108 MARYLEBONE LN   020 7969 3900   2–1A

"Useful for the area" – this very "pleasant" and attractive hotel dining room at the top of Marylebone Lane, wins all-round praise for its brasserie fare, much of it from the Josper grill. / W1U 2QE; www.108brasserie.com; @108Marylebone; 10.30pm.

108 GARAGE W10   **£60**   2️⃣2️⃣2️⃣

108 GOLBORNE RD   020 8969 3769   7–1A

Fans still hail its "totally original cuisine" ("a total surprise to the point of mind-blowing!") at this "relaxed and laid back" venue at the top end of Portobello Market, but its ratings took a nosedive this year, reflecting the strains of expansion to Southam Street (see also) and the corresponding change of chef from Chris Denny to Greg Clarke. To the fair few who reported a bad trip, the venture can now seem "overhyped and over here, with clever food but no fireworks and too expensive to justify the clamour". Perhaps with Southam Street's opening behind them, it may now be on the up?

/ W10 5PS; www.108garage.com; 10 pm, Sun 3 pm; closed Sun D, closed Mon.

101 THAI KITCHEN
W6   **£37**   4️⃣3️⃣2️⃣

352 KING ST   020 8746 6888   8–2B

"It's like being in Thailand" – serving "real Thai fare in a real Thai setting" – according to cognoscenti of this basic and grungy caff, around the corner from Stamford Brook tube: food journos and bloggers in particular go absolutely nuts for this place. / W6 0RX; Sun-Thu 10.30 pm, Fri & Sat 11 pm; no Amex.

LES 110 DE TAILLEVENT
W1   **£72**   3️⃣2️⃣3️⃣

16 CAVENDISH SQUARE   020 3141 6016   3–1B

"If you have the money, the great indulgence of wines that are rarely served by the glass" ("where else can you buy a £500 bottle of wine in a 250ml measure") can be satiated at this London outpost of the famous Parisian venue, which occupies a converted banking hall behind Oxford Street's John Lewis – a dignified space, but one whose "small tables" make it feel more like a brasserie than a fine-dining destination. Arguably, "the wonderful wine list has put the food unfairly in the shadows", as some of the "modern French-style dishes show great skill", but – that said – while "the set lunch is excellent value, other prices seem to have crept up of late". / W1G 9DD; www.les-110-taillevent-london.com; @110London; 10.30 pm, Sun 3.30 pm; closed Sat L & Sun.

100 WARDOUR STREET
W1   **£69**

100 WARDOUR ST   020 7314 4000   4–2D

To a bizarre extent, this large D&D London venue in central Soho – home in its day to the legendary Marquee Club, and nowadays featuring entertainment with DJs, cocktails and dinner – inspires practically zero feedback. Top Tip: such commentary as we have is for what is perhaps its best feature: Saturday brunch (£25 for two courses, plus £20 for bottomless Prosecco). / W1F 0TN; www.100wardourst.com; @100WardourSt; Tue, Wed 2 am; Thu-Sat 3 am; closed Tue-Sat L & Mon.

1 LOMBARD STREET
EC3   **£78**   2️⃣2️⃣3️⃣

1 LOMBARD ST   020 7929 6611   10–3C

"With its large domed roof", "good buzz and business-like feel", Soren Jessen's converted banking hall near Bank has changed little over the years. It's "perfectly located" for Square Mile expense-accounters (who seem to make up about 99.9% of its custom), "the food is fine but nothing special", "it's spacious enough on the larger tables for confidential conversations" and does a good breakfast. / EC3V 9AA; www.1lombardstreet.com; @1LombardStreet; 10 pm; closed Sat & Sun; booking max 10 may apply.

OPERA TAVERN
WC2   **£53**   3️⃣3️⃣3️⃣

23 CATHERINE ST   020 7836 3680   5–3D

"Superior" Hispanic-inspired plates have created a major reputation over the years for this "great tapas-stop close to Covent Garden" – a "sociable" ("at times noisy") converted, two-floor pub. It was sold by its original founders Salt Yard Group in late summer 2018 to Urban Pubs and Bars – we've left the rating as is for the time being. / WC2B 5JS; www.saltyardgroup.co.uk/opera-tavern; @saltyardgroup; Mon-Wed 11 am, Thu-Sat 11.30 pm, Sun 10 pm.

OPSO W1   **£59**   3️⃣4️⃣3️⃣

10 PADDINGTON ST   020 7487 5088   2–1A

"Put aside your preconceptions of Greek food" say fans of this "buzzy and fun" Marylebone corner café, serving Greek-with-a-twist cuisine that won't break the bank, from breakfast on. / W1U 5QL; www.opso.co.uk; @OPSO_london; Mon-Thu 10 pm, Fri & Sat 11 pm, Sun 9 pm; closed Sun D.

THE ORANGE
SW1   **£60**   3️⃣3️⃣3️⃣

37 PIMLICO RD   020 7881 9844   6–2D

This "fun pub" on a pretty Pimlico square combines "traditional ambience with modern, clean premises", and there's "always something interesting on the menu", ranging from roasts to wood-fired pizza. / SW1W 8NE; www.theorange.co.uk; @theorangesw1; Mon-Thu 11.30 pm, Fri & Sat midnight, Sun 10.30 pm.

ORANGE PEKOE
SW13   **£35**   3️⃣3️⃣4️⃣

3 WHITE HART LN   020 8876 6070   11–1A

"About 30 different types of brew" further boost the civilised tone at this "always crowded" but "very pleasant" tea shop, on the fringe of Barnes, which serves "light lunches" ("interesting salads") and "sublime cakes". / SW13 0PX; www.orangepekoeteas.com; @OrangePekoeTeas; 5 pm; closed Mon-Sun D.

THE ORANGE TREE
N20   **£45**   3️⃣2️⃣3️⃣

7 TOTTERIDGE VILLAGE   020 8343 7031   1–1B

Up Totteridge way, this is the top gastropub in the village: "always buzzy" (if sometimes "very noisy") and where the modernised pub grub is consistently well rated. / N20 8NX; www.theorangetreetotteridge.co.uk; @orangetreepub; Mon-Thu 11 pm, Fri & Sat 11.30 pm, Sun 10.30 pm.

ORÉE   **£18**   3️⃣2️⃣3️⃣

275-277 FULHAM RD, SW10   020 3813 9724   6–3B | 65 KING'S RD, SW3   020 3740 4588   6–3D | 147 KENSINGTON HIGH ST, W8   020 3883 7568   6–1A

"Fabulous breads and pastries" (as well as "better coffee than some of the favourites") bring a taste of 'the boulangeries and patisseries of rural France' to the three west London sites operated by this outfit from Nantes. / www.oree.co.uk; @oreeboulangerie.

ORMER MAYFAIR
W1 £100 3|2|2

HALF MOON ST   020 7016 5601   3–4B

Somewhat more mixed feedback this year on Shaun Rankin's "smart" two-year-old tenure at this Mayfair dining room. For the most part, reports continue to extol his "extremely original and exciting cuisine" (even if it's "seriously expensive"), but service can hit the wrong note, and the "rather hotel-y" basement setting "could be more cheery". / W1J 7BH; www.ormermayfair.com; @ormermayfair; 10.30 pm; closed Sun & Mon; No shorts.

Ormer Mayfair W1

ORO DI NAPOLI
W5 £34 4|3|2

6 THE QUADRANT, LITTLE EALING LANE 020 3632 5580   1–3A

The "top-notch Neapolitan wood-fired pizza" – "beautiful, thin-crusted delights" – from this "small but perfectly formed neighbourhood joint" in South Ealing rivals those of nearby Santa Maria, "and that's saying something!". / W5 4EE; www.lorodinapoli.co.uk; 11 pm.

ORRERY W1 £90 2|3|3

55 MARYLEBONE HIGH ST   020 7616 8000 2–1A

D&D London's "pleasant light room above the Conran shop in Marylebone" has a "fantastic airy atmosphere" with attractive views, and its ambience is only limited by its "slightly corridor-like" proportions. "Dining on the roof terrace in the summer is an added bonus" too, and as a business venue it can be ideal. Fans say its Gallic cuisine is "first rate" too, although overall ratings are more middling, perhaps because it's "priced accordingly". / W1U 5RB; www.orrery-restaurant.co.uk; @The_Orrery; Sun-Thu 10 pm, Fri & Sat 10.30 pm; booking max 8 may apply.

OSCAR WILDE LOUNGE AT CAFE ROYAL W1 £82 3|3|5

68 REGENT ST   020 7406 3333   4–4C

"The most wonderful room is a beautiful backdrop to a superb afternoon tea" (the only meal the room currently supplies) in this gilded chamber (the original 'Café Royal Grill' dating back to 1865), whose "sumptuously elaborate" rococo decor is one of the finest historic restaurant spaces in town: "wonderful sandwiches, scones, cakes and pastries… and the pianist was the icing on the cake!" The hotel are permanently rumbling about re-launching the space and returning it to its former glory, so change may be afoot. / W1B \N; www.hotelcaferoyal.com/oscarwildebar; @HotelCafeRoyal; L & afternoon tea only.

OSLO COURT
NW8 £66 3|5|4

CHARLBERT ST   020 7722 8795   9–3A

"An excellent throwback, which shows that the 1970's can't have been all bad!" – this "golden oldie" ("hard to find under an apartment block" north of Regent's Park) is "unashamedly trapped in a bygone era" and everyone adores it (especially its devoted following of silver- and white-haired north Londoners). The "large menu" of retro fare is "always well-cooked", comes in "very ample portions" and is served by "the friendliest and most efficient, caring waiters on the planet" (with a special shout out to Neil, the "entertaining man in charge of the sweet trolley"; reason to visit in itself for its magnificent selection of "ridiculously indulgent desserts"). "This is not dinner, but a night out!" – "go before it disappears!" / NW8 7EN; www.oslocourtrestaurant.co.uk; 11 pm; closed Sun; No jeans.

OSTERIA, BARBICAN CENTRE EC2 £57 1|1|2

LEVEL 2 SILK ST   020 7588 3008   10–1B

The main restaurant at the Barbican arts centre is "handy for a pre-theatre supper" – ("ask for a window seat when booking") – but on its current level of performance "not a destination in its own right". A reboot by caterer Searcys with an Italian menu by chef Anthony Demetre (late of Soho's Arbutus, RIP) has failed to turn the tide, with too many complaints about the food ("style over substance") and service ("our main course never arrived, so we sat hungry through a three-hour play!"). / EC2Y 8DS; osterialondon. co.uk; @osterialondon; Wed & Thu 11 pm, Fri & Sat midnight, Sun 6 pm; closed Sun.

OSTERIA ANTICA BOLOGNA
SW11 £51 3|3|2

23 NORTHCOTE RD   020 7978 4771   11–2C

This "great neighbourhood Italian" near Clapham Junction has ticked all the boxes for "amazing pasta and allotment-fresh vegetables" for two decades. "The focus is on beautifully cooked, classic dishes rather than food presentation or stylish décor". / SW11 1NG; www.osteria.co.uk; @OsteriaAntica; Mon-Wed 11 pm, Thu-Sat 11.30 pm, Sun 10 pm.

OSTERIA BASILICO
W11 £63 4|2|2

29 KENSINGTON PARK RD   020 7727 9957 7–1A

"An all-time family favourite", this long-running Notting Hill trat is "a lovely little place, always full and lively", with "divine pizza and pasta, excellent antipasti and wonderful home-baked bread", it's "as authentic as Italian cooking gets in London". "Make friends with the manager or the service can be snooty". / W11 2EU; www.osteriabasilico.co.uk; 11.30 pm, Sun 10.30 pm; no booking, Sat L.

OSTERIA DELL'ANGOLO
SW1 £64 2|2|2

47 MARSHAM ST   020 3268 1077   2–4C

"Efficient" and "reasonably priced for Westminster", this "large" and peaceful venue serves "mainstream Italian food, all of it cooked perfectly well" – although it's "difficult to rave over any dish". Especially "useful for conference-goers at the Emmanuel Centre" nearby. / SW1P 3DR; www.osteriadellangolo.co.uk; @Osteria_Angolo; 10.30 pm; closed Sat L, closed Sun.

OSTERIA TUFO
N4 £49 3|2|2

67 FONTHILL RD   020 7272 2911   9–1D

This intimate Finsbury Park local, where proprietor Paola greets each customer, has a sensibly "limited menu" of "interesting" Neapolitan home cooking (no pizza) – "but what they do, they do well". / N4 3HZ; www.osteriatufo.co.uk; @osteriatufo; Tue-Fri 10 pm, Mon 9.30 pm; closed Mon & Sun L; no Amex.

THE OTHER NAUGHTY PIGLET SW1 £60 4|3|2

12 PALACE ST   020 7592 0322   2–4B

Andrew Lloyd Webber's import, last year, of Brixton's Naughty Piglets team to the "airy" space above his Other Palace Theatre was one of last year's better openings, and fabulous for still-dire Victoria. Its "bright-tasting" small plates are "on-trend" and "perfectly executed" and there's some "superb" wines ("Lord Lloyd Webber's bin ends at the back of the wine list make an interesting read!"). / SW1E 5JA; www.theothernaughtypiglet.co.uk; Tue-Thu 9 pm; closed Mon, Fri & Sat & Sun; booking max 10 may apply.

OTTO'S WC1 £72 4|4|4

182 GRAY'S INN RD   020 7713 0107   2–1D

"Immune to trends and setting its own agenda" – visiting this "old-fashioned" Bloomsbury parlour is a little "like stepping back a generation". "Wonderful, old-fashioned, French, classic cuisine" is served in a "delightful" dining room, overseen with "charming professionalism" by the owner Otto ("invariably there") who is "amusing and fun". Top Menu Tips – "everyone raves (rightly) about the pressed duck and Poularde de Bresse, but Otto also does the best Steak Tartare in the UK (made at the table with Otto's inevitable theatrical flourish)". / WC1X

Padella SE1

8EW; www.ottos-restaurant.com; 9.30 pm; closed Sat L, closed Sun & Mon.

OTTOLENGHI £57 322

13 MOTCOMB ST, SW1 020 7823 2707 6–1D | 63 LEDBURY RD, W11 020 7727 1121 7–1B | 287 UPPER ST, N1 020 7288 1454 9–2D | 50 ARTILLERY PAS, E1 020 7247 1999 10–2D

"Drool over the pastries" and the "exquisite" salads ("so many unusual combinations and lovely flavours, it's hard to make a decision") at Yotam Ottolenghi's "always popular", but "rather stark" cafés ("overcrowded with shared tables and yummy mummies with prams"). At its best, "the food's so fresh and creatively different, you feel you are dining on something superbly healthy", but ratings overall slipped this year, with a number of regulars noting that "while it's an excellent concept, execution's not as consistent as it should be". / www.ottolenghi.co.uk; N1 10.30pm, Sun 7 pm; W11 & SW1 8 pm, Sat 7 pm, Sun 6 pm; E1 10.30pm, Sun 6 pm; N1 closed Sun D; Holland St takeaway only; W11 & SW1 no booking.

OUTLAW'S AT THE CAPITAL SW3 £97 442

22-24 BASIL ST 020 7591 1202 6–1D

With its "perfectly prepared and delicately flavoured dishes", Nathan Outlaw's Knightsbridge outpost lives up to his renown for "truly excellent and creative fish cuisine" and ranks amongst the UK's best in that respect. The location, near the back of Harrods, is a "small" hotel dining room that has for decades divided opinion: to fans "smart" and "sophisticated", but to others "lacking some character"; although the "excellent service" from the current team helps boost its appeal. Chef Andrew Sawyer succeeded Tom Brown (who left to found Cornerstone) in late 2017, and though a small minority of reporters feel "the food has gone downhill" as a result, ratings here actually strengthened across the board this year. / SW3 1AT; www.capitalhotel.co.uk; @OUTLAWSinLondon; 10 pm; closed Sun; credit card required to book.

OVAL RESTAURANT SW1 £81

11 KNIGHTSBRIDGE 020 3668 6530 6–1D

Limited but all-round very positive feedback on this small (26 covers) oval-shaped dining room, which is part of a swish hotel right by Hyde Park Corner (which older folk will recall as Pizza on the Park). With its gold-and-light-pink colour scheme and ostrich leather walls, it's a glam location in which to enjoy some luxurious Italian cuisine (available à la carte, or with the option of five- or six-course tasting menus). / SW1X 7LY; www.thewellesley.co.uk/oval-restaurant; @WellesleyLondon; 10:30pm.

OXO TOWER, RESTAURANT SE1 £92 111

BARGE HOUSE ST 020 7803 3888 10–3A

"Same as usual – fantastic view, but grotty food at the price". The story remains the same at this South Bank landmark whose dubious achievement is invariably appearing at or near the top of the survey's lists of both most disappointing and most overpriced restaurants in London. / SE1 9PH; www.harveynichols.com/restaurant/the-oxo-tower; @OxoTowerWharf; 11 pm, Sun 10 pm; booking max 8 may apply; SRA-Food Made Good – 2 stars.

OXO TOWER, BRASSERIE SE1 £75 112

BARGE HOUSE ST 020 7803 3888 10–3A

"Fabulous views and the buzzy (perhaps too noisy) atmosphere" lure diners to the cheaper section of this South Bank landmark. But for the sky-high price they exact for its humdrum brasserie fare and so-so service, it's a perennially disappointing and overpriced experience; try to get someone else to pay… / SE1 9PH; www.harveynichols.com/restaurants/oxo-tower-london; Thu-Sat, Wed 9 pm; may need 2+ to book.

THE OYSTERMEN WC2 £58 443

32 HENRIETTA ST 020 7240 4417 5–3D

"A jewel of a find" – this "tiny", "cupboard-sized" yearling in Covent Garden receives a resounding "bravo!" from reporters for its "fun" style, "charming service" and "fabulous" seafood ("oysters are the speciality, but there's a good range of other fish dishes"). Top Tip: 'Bubbles 'n' Oysters Happy Hour – "I called in after reading a review in Harden's newsletter, and was amazed at the quality of the oysters with a glass of bubbly for £10!" STOP PRESS: just as we went to press, the Oystermen expanded into the space next door, giving them 50 covers, a walk-in-only raw bar and a bigger open kitchen. / WC2E 8NA; oystermen.co.uk; @theoystermen.

OZONE COFFEE ROASTERS EC2 £28 334

11 LEONARD ST 020 7490 1039 13–1A

Fabulous aromas from the large roasting machines in the basement hit you as you enter this hip haven for caffeine-lovers – a perfect hipster combination of cool Kiwi and chilled Shoreditch vibes, and one delivering superlative brews and dependable brunch fare. / EC2A 4AQ; ozonecoffee.co.uk; @ozonecoffeeuk; Sun-Thu 10.30 pm, Fri & Sat 11 pm; may need 8+ to book.

P FRANCO E5 £48 424

107 LOWER CLAPTON RD 020 8533 4660 14–1B

In any other 'hood, this engaging Clapton bottle shop (focused on funky 'natural' vintages) with communal central table – and serving some eclectic but interesting small dishes – would be a handy, loveable find. Sitting as it does at the very epicentre of the East End's fooderati community, it is front page news, as exemplified by its being website Eater's bizarre choice as 'London Restaurant of the Year 2017'. In September 2018 it took on a new chef for at least a 6-month residency: Anna Tobias. / E5 0NP; www.pfranco.co.uk; @pfranco_e5; Thu-Sat 10 pm, Sun 9 pm; closed Mon-Wed, Thu-Sat D only, Sun L & D; no Amex; no booking.

PADELLA SE1 £28 543

6 SOUTHWARK ST NO TEL 10–4C

"A true and glorious phenomenon… you just need to arrive very early to beat the queues!" – Tim Siadatan and Jordan Frieda's Borough Market two-year-old is the ultimate budget option in the capital thanks to serving "perfect pasta" ("the best in London"), "served quickly" and at a supremely "affordable" price, in a setting that's "cramped" but "buzzy" and "fun". And "now with a virtual queuing system in the evening, you can head off for a drink instead of waiting outside!" / SE1 1TQ; www.padella.co; @padella_pasta; 10 pm; no booking.

PALADAR SE1 £58

4-5 LONDON RD 020 7186 5555 10–4A

A stylish new restaurant, wine bar and bodega, not far from Elephant & Castle, showcasing flavours from across South America. (The name means palate in Spanish and Portuguese, and in Cuba a 'paladar' is also a privately-run restaurant with character.) Founder Charles Tyler was behind Bermondsey's once-pathbreaking Champor Champor, while chef Jose Rubio-Guevara hails from Colombia via Miami and draws on various Latino inspirations (as do the cocktails, wines and cigars). Too little feedback for a rating as yet, but for one early reporter it's already a favourite. / SE1 6JZ; www.paladarlondon.com; @paladarlondon; Tue-Sat, Mon 10.30 pm, Sun 3.30 pm.

PALATINO EC1 £59 433

71 CENTRAL ST 020 3481 5300 10–1B

"The simplicity of the dishes belies the amazing flavours that come off the plates", according to the many fans of Stevie Parle's popular yearling,

Parsons WC2

where "authentic pasta" is the highlight of its Roman-inspired menu. Arguably "being part of an office space detracts from the atmosphere" but most reporters find its setting "calm and spacious". Top Menu Tip: "divine cacio e pepe". / EC1V 8AB; palatino.london; @PalatinoLondon; 10 pm; closed Mon-Sat & Sun.

THE PALMERSTON
SE22   £57   3|3|3

91 LORDSHIP LN   020 8693 1629   1–4D

This "high class" gastropub in East Dulwich is "informal but top notch", with "consistently high-class cooking". "It's a proper restaurant operation... but in a pub." / SE22 8EP; www.thepalmerston.co.uk; @thepalmerston; 11 pm; closed Sun; no Amex.

THE PALOMAR
W1   £73   4|3|3

34 RUPERT ST   020 7439 8777   4–3D

"It is frustratingly difficult to plan to eat" at this Tel Aviv-comes-to-Theatreland venture, given its humongous popularity and limited ability to book (only possible in the relatively un-funky dining room). The main action is "sitting at the counter watching the chefs (a riot!)" and its "great range of Middle Eastern / Mediterranean tapas" delivers "small plates zinging with flavour and invention". With its "fabulous buzz", fans say "you can't say you've eaten in London till you've tried here", but there's the odd niggle too – "noisy", "cramped" and "chaotic" conditions (to fans part of the charm), and a staff attitude that can sometimes "verge on arrogant". / W1D 6DN; www.thepalomar.co.uk; @palomarsoho; 11 pm, Sun 9 pm; closed Sun L.

PAPPA CICCIA   £36   3|4|3

**105 MUNSTER RD, SW6   020 7384 1884
11–1B | 41 FULHAM HIGH ST, SW6
020 7736 0900   11–1B**

"Good, generous-sized pizzas", and a "lively" and "cheerful" atmosphere keep business ticking over at this family-owned local trio in Fulham and Putney. They are "excellent value", too, helped by BYO on beer and wine at a flat £4.50 per head. / www.pappaciccia.com; SW6 5RQ 11 pm, Sat & Sun 11.30 pm; SW6 3JJ 11 pm.

PARABOLA, DESIGN
MUSEUM W8   £60

**224-238 KENSINGTON HIGH ST
020 7940 8795   6–1A**

The food and drink operation at the new Design Museum in Kensington opened with high hopes, with Rowley Leigh at the stoves; but he quickly left, and then, following the demise of Prescott & Conran in the summer of 2018, its been taken over by caterer Searcys. The food now (e.g. 'Bassett Stilton and broccoli tart; Loch Duart salmon fillet with crushed Jersey royals') sounds monumentally unexciting, but we've left the restaurant un-rated pending feedback. / W8 6AG; www.parabola.london; @ParabolaLondon; 9.45 pm; closed Mon-Sun D.

PARADISE BY WAY
OF KENSAL GREEN
W10   £53   3|2|4

19 KILBURN LANE   020 8969 0098   1–2B

One of London's hardiest evergreen destinations – this huge and vibey Kensal Green tavern has been a magnet for cool twenty- and thirtysomethings for as long as anyone can remember (and was one of the first 'gastropubs' as such to hit the capital). The interior is gorgeous, and the menu much more "interesting" than it needs to be. / W10 4AE; www.theparadise.co.uk; @weloveparadise; 10 pm, Sun 4 pm; closed weekday L; no Amex.

PARADISE HAMPSTEAD
NW3   £41   3|5|4

49 SOUTH END RD   020 7794 6314   9–2A

"Always packed with locals" who come for the "huge portions from a menu that never changes", this "mainstay" Hampstead Heath curry house is now run by the founder's son, but the "exceptional" welcome and service "are as warm as ever". / NW3 2QB; www.paradisehampstead.co.uk; Wed & Thu 11 pm, Fri & Sat midnight, Sun 6 pm.

EL PARADOR
NW1   £40   4|4|3

245 EVERSHOLT ST   020 7387 2789   9–3C

High marks for the "wonderful", authentic tapas at this busy Hispanic, near Mornington Crescent. "Why can't the ambience match the food?" query some; but on summer days its garden provides a lovely location. / NW1 1BA; www.elparadorlondon.com; 11 pm, Fri & Sat 11.30 pm, Sun 9.30 pm; closed Sat L & Sun L; no Amex.

PARK CHINOIS
W1   £131   2|2|3

17 BERKELEY ST   020 3327 8888   3–3C

With its "sexy", "1920s-Shanghai" interior, Alan Yau's "opulent" Mayfair blow-out offers a "decadent" combination of "delicious" Chinese cuisine and regular entertainment in a "vibey" setting that's definitely "different". Sceptics dismiss it as a "ridiculously OTT" display "for people with more money than taste", but for most reporters the only downside is that "Dick Turpin turns up at the same time as the bill!" /

W1S 4NF; www.parkchinois.com; @ParkChinois; 2 am, Sun midnight; No jeans.

PARK TERRACE
RESTAURANT, ROYAL
GARDEN HOTEL
W8   £59   3|3|4

**2-24 KENSINGTON HIGH ST   020 7361 0602
6–1A**

This "comfortable and well-spaced" hotel dining room with "views over Kensington Gardens" maintains a low profile despite its mightily handy location off High Street Kensington. Worth remembering as a "reliable" standby, it mainly scores highly for its "amazing kids' afternoon tea" – "such good value" and with "plenty of space for naughty children". / W8 4PT; www.parkterracerestaurant.co.uk; 10.30 pm.

PARLOUR KENSAL
NW10   £50   3|3|4

5 REGENT ST   020 8969 2184   1–2B

Chilled Kensal Rise pub conversion that continues to inspire nothing but praise for its "good value and quality food and friendly service". Its top dish historically has been 'cow pie', but its appeal isn't limited to meat-eaters: "the vegan breakfast is great – they've really thought about it and created a real feast". / NW10 5LG; www.parlourkensal.com; @ParlourUK; 10.30 pm; closed Mon.

PARSONS WC2   £65   4|3|3

39 ENDELL ST   020 3422 0221   5–2C

"Living up to the hype despite the narrow space" – this new opening from the folks behind The 10 Cases (just across the road) is one of the most applauded arrivals of the past year and "a great addition to Covent Garden". "A short menu of the freshest fish and seafood" is served "with good wines and no faff" in a "refreshingly unpretentious", but "stylishly simple" white-tiled environment, and results are "sparkling". / WC2H 9BA; www.parsonslondon.co.uk; closed Sun.

PASSIONE E TRADIZIONE
N15   £37   3|3|2

451 WEST GREEN RD   020 8245 9491   1–1C

"A real gem in the hinterland between Wood Green and Tottenham", this "industrial-chic, trendy and hard-surfaced" Italian yearling is a sister to Mustapha Mouflih's highly rated Anima e Cuore in Kentish Town. "Yes, the pizza is brilliant" but there is also "exceptional homemade pasta" and chalkboard specials (although "don't get me wrong, quality ingredients are used, but not all the combinations are totally convincing"). Top Tip: "incredible homemade ice cream, which they now sell at the newly opened deli opposite". / N15 3PL; spinach.london; 11 pm; closed Mon & Tue L.

PASSO EC1   £50   2|2|2

80 CITY RD   020 3883 9377   13–1A

Mixed reviews for this big, all-day Italian newcomer by Old Street tube – a large, modern unit where they've spent a packet on the design. Some do praise its "imaginative" fare and say it's a good place to take business associates, but there's also a feeling that "the food doesn't live up to the prices and comes in small portions": "this is expense account grub for global biz travellers who truly believe 'Silicon Roundabout' is a really cool place". / EC1Y 2AS; www.passorestaurant.com; Tue-Thu 8.30 pm, Fri 9 pm, Sat 9.30 pm, Sun 7 pm.

PASTA REMOLI N4 £39 **3 3 3**

7 CLIFTON TERRACE   020 7263 2948   9–1D

That "the pasta is great" and that "it's an easy choice with kids" are twin strengths of this café in Finsbury Park. Top Tip: "good value for pre-theatre" (the Park Theatre being next door). / N4 3JP; www.pastaremoli.co.uk; @PastaRemoli; 11 pm, Sun 10.30 pm.

PASTAIO W1 £44 **3 2 3**

19 GANTON ST NO TEL 4–2B

As "a pasta pit-stop", Stevie Parle's "buzzy and canteen-like" Soho yearling ("well-located" in Kingly Court) wins a fair amount of praise as a "good-value-for-money" option around shopping or before a movie. On the downside, some who were "hoping for big things" given Parle's reputation felt it fell short – in particular, "amateurish" service can take the gloss off the experience. / W1F 7BU; www.pastaio.london; @pastaiolondon; Sun-Thu 10.30 pm, Fri & Sat 11 pm.

EL PASTÓR SE1 £44 **4 3 5**

7A STONEY ST NO TEL 10–4C

"Top tortillas. Amen!"… "Divine tacos"… "Wish I didn't have to share with my friend, as I could have happily hoovered the lot" – the Hart Bros' "cool and vibey" taqueria has become one of Borough Market's top destinations. "Great Mexican drinks", too, including 17 mezcals, but you can't book. / SE1 9AA; www.tacoselpastor.co.uk; @Tacos_El_Pastor; Mon-Wed 11 pm, Thu-Sat midnight; no booking.

PATARA £68 **3 3 3**

15 GREEK ST, W1   020 7437 1071   5–2A | 7 MADDOX ST, W1   020 7499 6008   4–2A | 181 FULHAM RD, SW3   020 7351 5692   6–2C | 9 BEAUCHAMP PL, SW3 020 7581 8820   6–1C | 82 HAMPSTEAD HIGH ST, NW3   020 7431 5902   9–2B | 18 HIGH ST, SW19   020 3931 6157   11–2B

"A small chain with a big reputation that's well deserved", say fans of this long-standing, "friendly and courteous" Thai group, praised for its "well-flavoured food". Ratings went into reverse this year, however, due to those who find it "a bit pricey", or "making too many concessions to western palates". Top Tip: "exceptional lunch deal". / www.pataralondon.com; @PataraLondon; 10.30 pm, Thu-Sat 11 pm; Greek St closed Sun L.

PATERNOSTER CHOP HOUSE EC4 £61 **2 2 2**

1 WARWICK COURT   020 7029 9400   10–2B

Overlooking St Paul's from the fringes of the Square Mile's Paternoster Square development, this D&D London operation caters mainly for City expense-accounters. It's best known as the location for TV show First Dates, but for romance look elsewhere – "the tables are too close together" and the food's "expensive and average". / EC4M 7DX; www.paternosterchophouse.co.uk; @paternoster1; 10.30 pm, Sun 3.30 pm; closed Sun D; booking max 12 may apply.

PATOGH W1 £17 **4 3 2**

8 CRAWFORD PL   020 7262 4015   7–1D

"Persian perfection" – "honest and straightforward" dishes offer "wonderful quality for the money" at this tiny dining room off Edgware Road. "Like I imagine being in a café in Iran" … with the addition of BYO booze! / W1H 5NE; www.patoghlondon.com; 11 pm; cash only.

PATTY AND BUN £28 **4 3 3**

18 OLD COMPTON ST, W1   020 7287 1818 5–2A | 54 JAMES ST, W1   020 7487 3188 3–1A | 14 PEMBRIDGE RD, W11 020 7229 2228   7–2B | 19 BOROUGH HIGH ST, SE1   020 7407 7994   10–4C NEW | 36 REDCHURCH ST, E2   020 7613 3335   13–1C | 2 ARTHAUS BUILDING, 205 RICHMOND RD, E8   020 8525 8250   14–1B | 22-23 LIVERPOOL ST, EC2   020 7621 1331   10–2D | 8 BROWN'S BUILDINGS, SAINT MARY AXE, EC3   020 3846 3222   10–2D

"People waiting outside in the rain for a table speaks volumes" for this expanding chain (the latest branches are in TV Centre and Borough High Street), which "really fulfils the craving for a juicy, tasty burger" (and is the equal-highest rated in town in that department). Other elements of the formula are, however, "nothing fancy". Top Menu Tip: "the Lambshank Redemption is unparalleled in the hugely contested world of burgers". / www.pattyandbun.co.uk; @pattyandbunjoe; 10 pm-11.30 pm, Sun 9 pm-10pm.

PAVILION CAFE & BAKERY E9 £9 **4 2 4**

VICTORIA PARK, OLD FORD RD 020 8980 0030   14–2C

A quaint structure in "a beautiful position on the lake" – "the cafe on the water at Victoria Park is a wonderful setting" with food that's "surprisingly excellent" – "not just exceptional English breakfast fare but also Sri Lankan and vegan options"; "superlative coffee and pastries, too". / E9 7DE; www.pavilionbakery.com; @pavilionbakery; Mon-Fri 5 pm, Sat & Sun 6 pm; closed Mon-Fri D; no Amex; no booking.

THE PEAR TREE W6 £49 **3 3 4**

14 MARGRAVINE RD   020 7381 1787   8–2C

"Awesome and very friendly" little Victorian pub, just behind Charing Cross Hospital, with a charming, small interior – the food, from a limited menu, "is lovely too". / W6 8HJ; www.thepeartreefulham.com; 10.30 pm; Mon-Thu D only, Fri-Sun open L & D.

PEARL LIANG W2 £48 **4 3 3**

8 SHELDON SQUARE   020 7289 7000   7–1C

An "uninspiring location" – a Paddington Basin basement – has not held back this large and attractively decorated Cantonese: nowadays very well-established and "always very crowded", especially at weekends, for its "amazing dim sum", of a quality "really quite different to the majority of Chinese restaurants". Top Tip: "lobster noodles also brilliant". / W2 6EZ; www.pearlliang.co.uk; @PearlLiangUK; Mon-Thu 11 pm, Fri & Sat 11.30 pm, Sun 10.30 pm.

PECKHAM BAZAAR SE15 £51 **4 3 3**

119 CONSORT RD   020 7732 2525   1–4D

Whether it's labelled "pan-Balkan" or "the best Greek-ish cooking in London", this "delightful and informal converted neighbourhood pub" "does charcoal-grilled food that's just a bit different from (and better than) the competition", and is "worth the trek" to furthest Peckham. There are also "unusual and surprisingly good wines" from the region. / SE15 3RU; www.peckhambazaar.com; @PeckhamBazaar; Sun-Thu 10.30 pm; closed Mon, Tue-Fri D only, Sat & Sun open L & D; no Amex.

PECKHAM LEVELS SE15 £16

95A RYE LANE   020 3793 7783   1–4D

This six-year project was created by the same team as Pop Brixton in response to a consultation by Southwark Council about what to do with Peckham's under-used multi storey car park. Levels five and six are home to street food traders such as Nandine (Kurdish mezze), Canard (confit duck as street food), Drums & Flats (chicken wings), Other Side Fried (fried chicken) and the splendidly named PickyWops (vegan pizza) – early feedback from reporters says it's worth a visit. / SE15 4TG; www.peckhamlevels.org; @peckhamlevels; Mon & Tue 9 pm, Fri & Sat 11.30 pm, Wed 10 pm, Thu 11 pm, Sun 5 pm; closed Sun D.

E PELLICCI E2 £16 **3 5 5**

332 BETHNAL GREEN RD   020 7739 4873 13–1D

"It never changes and that's the point" of a visit to visiting this well-preserved (hipster-free) greasy spoon in Bethnal Green, whose listed, Art Deco interior (much used in filming TV dramas) is a fine period piece. That "there's always a special welcome" confirms its position in the hearts of its fans as "one of the best places in London for breakfast" of the traditional variety.

/ E2 0AG; epellicci.com; closed Mon-Sat D, closed Sun; cash only; no booking.

PENTOLINA W14 £52 443

71 BLYTHE RD   020 3010 0091 8–1C

"Michele in the kitchen cooks up a dream and Heidi looks after the front of house beautifully" at this "very charming" backstreet Olympia favourite. The result is "delightful and imaginative Italian food" from a "short seasonal menu" served in a "lovely and low-key" setting that makes it a "perfect local", and one that folks travel for. / W14 0HP; www.pentolinarestaurant.co.uk; 10 pm; closed Sun & Mon; no Amex.

PERCY & FOUNDERS W1 £60 333

1 PEARSON SQUARE, FITZROY PLACE 020 3761 0200 2–1B

On the ground floor of a Fitzrovia development (on the site of the old Middlesex Hospital), this spacious, tucked-away bar/brasserie with terrace offers a convenient and tranquil rendezvous in the West End. Top Tip: "love their bottomless Prosecco brunch". / W1W 7EY; www.percyandfounders.co.uk; @PercyFounders; Wed & Thu 11 pm, Fri & Sat midnight, Sun 6 pm; closed Sun D.

PERILLA N16 £62 333

1-3 GREEN LANES 07467 067393 1–1C

"I cannot believe that somewhere like Perilla opened on Newington Green – what a fantastic addition to the local area!" Ben Marks and Matt Emerson's yearling, "with its "huge picture windows overlooking the green", "high ceilings, open aspect and well-spaced tables" serves some "astoundingly tasty dishes, using interesting earthy ingredients" and there's "a great local feel to the place". Not everyone who lives nearby is wowed, though: "I wanted to like this place, but found it too cool-for-skool"… "it was too quirky and elaborate and felt like a 'concept' rather than a satisfying night of food". / N16 9BS; www.perilladining.co.uk; @perilladining; 10 pm, Sun 8.30 pm; closed Mon-Fri L.

PESCATORI W1 £75 222

57 CHARLOTTE ST   020 7580 3289 2–1C

Some reporters accuse it of being too "unimaginative", but this traditional-ish West End Italian still wins an impressive number of nominations for the very "competent" quality of its fish cuisine, and "pleasant" style generally. Top Tip: "their free-flowing Prosecco deal makes this an excellent choice for a meet-up with the girls!" / W1T 4PD; www.pescatori.co.uk; @PescatoriLondon; 10.30 pm, Sun 3 pm; closed Sat L & Sun.

THE PETERSHAM WC2 £84 335

FLORAL COURT, OFF FLORAL ST 020 7305 7676 5–3C

"Enchanting decor" – very "calming and relaxing", considering it's so central – is a major highpoint of this ambitious newcomer from the Boglione family, which is part of a very attractive new development in Covent Garden. It repeats a lot of the DNA of their original venture – Richmond's famously romantic, shabby chic Petersham Nurseries – although the punchy prices for its "refined and elegant" dishes have so far inspired less controversy here. / WC2E 9DJ; petershamnurseries.com; @PetershamN; midnight.

PETERSHAM NURSERIES CAFE TW10 £78 225

CHURCH LANE (SIGNPOSTED 'ST PETER'S CHURCH') 020 8940 5230 1–4A

"It's just fab eating great food in a greenhouse in summer or on a blue-sky winter's day", say fans of this "unique and magical" destination (part of a garden centre near Ham Common), which famously "oozes Bohemian charm" and is a top "romantic" trysting spot. Even those who feel its modern British cuisine is "very good" however, concede that it's "probably not as good as it was a few years ago" (when Skye Gyngell was at the stoves, and pioneering the use of edible flowers) and more cynical souls ponder whether "seating you amongst the potted plants on rickety furniture lets them get away with the high prices and mediocre service". It now has a sibling in Covent Garden (see also). / TW10 7AB; www.petershamnurseries.com; 10.30 pm, Sun 9.30 pm; L only, closed Mon; SRA-Food Made Good – 3 stars.

THE PETERSHAM RESTAURANT TW10 £67 225

NIGHTINGALE LANE 020 8003 3602 1–4A

"The view from the restaurant is one of the best in London" – "the best tables are near the window" where you can enjoy the "splendid setting overlooking the Thames" – from the traditional dining room of this old-fashioned and "romantic" Richmond hotel. Fans (often silver-haired) acclaim its cuisine as "a safe bet", but a number of meals this year also ended up feeling "pricey" or "perfunctory". / TW10 6UZ; petershamhotel.co.uk/restaurant; @thepetersham; 9.30 pm, Sun 9 pm.

PETIT MA CUISINE TW9 £50 222

8 STATION APPROACH   020 8332 1923 1–3A

This textbook, 1950s-style "cramped" French bistro – gingham tablecloths, Toulouse-Lautrec posters and a menu of classics – is promoted by fans as a "lovely find close to Kew Gardens". "The food's decent, but prices are on the toppy side". / TW9 3QB; www.macuisinebistrot.co.uk; 10 pm, Fri & Sat 10.30 pm; no Amex.

PETIT POIS BISTRO N1 £57 423

9 HOXTON SQUARE   020 7613 3689 13–1B

"The quality is very high but the prices are not", say fans of this two-year-old Gallic bistro on Hoxton Square – "a real, cute gem" serving "lovely French fare" in a "trendy but cosy" space (and also with a small outside seating area). / N1 6NU; www.petitpoisbistro.com; @petitpoisbistro; 9.30 pm.

THE PETITE COREE NW6 £42 432

98 WEST END LANE   020 7624 9209 1–1B

"Excellent Korean/modern European fusion cooking" ensures that this "genuinely friendly" (and good value) little bistro has become a fixture on the West Hampstead culinary scene. Chef Jae worked at Nobu and Hélène Darroze (The Connaught); his wife Yeon runs the front of house. / NW6 2LU; www.thepetitecoree.com; @thepetitecoree; 9.30 pm; booking max 6 may apply.

LA PETITE MAISON W1 £97 323

54 BROOK'S MEWS   020 7495 4774 3–2B

"Always top of its game and up there with the best" is how we've customarily reviewed this glam Mayfair haunt, just around the corner from Claridges, which perennially attracts a Côte d'Azur-style crowd with its sunny, gorgeously light sharing plates and easygoing "busy and buzzy" glamour. Its ratings took a bit of a dip this year, however – it's always been "a bit too expensive" but hitherto no-one has seemed to mind. / W1K 4EG; www.lpmlondon.co.uk; @lpmlondon; 10.30 pm, Sun 9.30 pm; closed Mon.

PÉTRUS SW1 £118 444

1 KINNERTON ST   020 7592 1609 6–1D

With its "stunning" cuisine, "wine list that reads like War & Peace", "caring and attentive" staff and "beautiful" interior (arranged around a glass-walled wine vault), this luxurious Knightsbridge dining room is the only restaurant in Gordon Ramsay's stable that lives up to his name nowadays, and on practically all reports is "a joy to visit". Let's hope new chef Russell Bateman, who joined in summer 2018, can keep up the good work. / SW1X 8EA; www.gordonramsayrestaurants.com; @petrus; 10.30 pm, Sun 9.30 pm; closed Sun; No trainers.

PEYOTITO W11 £56 332

31 KENSINGTON PARK RD   020 7043 1400 7–1A

"Top-notch authentic Mexican small or sharing plates", plus "great tequila and mezcal cocktails" can add up to a "fun, noisy night out" at this two-year-old in the heart of Notting Hill, notwithstanding its "haphazard service and very cramped interior". "Low-key when empty" – maybe go "later in the evening". / W11 2EU; www.peyotitorestaurant.com; @peyotitolondon; midnight, Fri & Sat 1 am, Sun 10.30 pm.

PHAM SUSHI EC1 £41 423

159 WHITECROSS ST   020 7251 6336 13–2A

"Great sushi and sashimi", "at reasonable prices", are the draw at this "authentic" Japanese spot near the Barbican. "Flawless food without the pretentiousness of some high-end

Japanese" – no wonder it's "always packed"./_
EC1Y 8JL; www.phamsushi.com; @phamsushi;
10 pm; closed Sat L, closed Sun. / EC1Y 8JL;
www.phamsushi.com; @phamsushi; 10 pm; closed Sat
L, closed Sun.

PHAT PHUC SW3   £30   4 3 1

CHELSEA COURTYARD, 151 SYDNEY ST
020 7351 3843   6–3C

"For a simple bowl of fragrant steaming
noodles", reporters give a big thumbs up to this
basic, hilariously-named joint, in a courtyard
near Chelsea Farmers Market – about as close
as you can get to street food in SW3! / SW3 6NT;
www.phatphucnoodlebar.co.uk; @Phat_PhucNoodle.

PHO   £43   3 2 2

"Solid and tasty Vietnamese dishes are served in
a flash" at this street food chain; fans feel they've
really "nailed the concept" of "fresh", "very
decent" scoff in a "cheap 'n' cheerful" setting,
all at a "great price". / www.phocafe.co.uk; 10
pm-11pm, Sun 6.30 pm-10 pm; EC1 closed Sat L &
Sun; no booking.

PHO & BUN W1   £46   3 3 2

76 SHAFTESBURY AVE   020 7287 3528
5–3A

This straightforward Vietnamese pitstop for pho
and steamed buns, on the edge of Chinatown,
by all accounts offers "very good food and value
for money". / W1D 6ND; vieteat.co.uk/pho-bun;
@phoandbun; Sun-Thu 10.30 pm, Fri & Sat 11 pm;
booking max 8 may apply.

PHOENIX PALACE NW1   £57   3 3 3

5-9 GLENTWORTH ST   020 7486 3515   2–1A

This spacious, classic Cantonese refectory
near Baker Street scores well for "fun, good
food and great service", while fans claim it
does the "best dim sum in London". There's a
"large and varied menu, with lots of interesting
dishes" and a very "70s vibe". / NW1 5PG;
www.phoenixpalace.co.uk; 11.30 pm, Sun 10.30 pm.

PICTURE   £67   3 3 2

110 GREAT PORTLAND ST, W1
020 7637 7892   2–1B | 19 NEW CAVENDISH
ST, W1   020 7935 0058   2–1A

"Simply presented but expertly prepared taste
combinations that just make you want to come
back" from a "limited-but-seasonal menu" are
at the root of the success of this "relaxed and
reliable" duo of Fitzrovia and Marylebone
favourites. The chief gripe is that in each case
"the interior lacks atmosphere", but no-one
thinks the situation is grievous. / 10.30 pm; closed
Sun.

PIDGIN E8   £72   5 5 3

52 WILTON WAY   020 7254 8311   14–1B

"Breathtakingly inventive and excellently
executed" cooking ("best described as modern
British with a substantial Asian influence")
has won renown out of all proportion to the

"extremely small" size of this Hackney two-year-
old, which has a better claim to culinary fame
than most East End ventures. "How they keep
up such high standards with a weekly changing
tasting menu is astonishing" ("although we
have eaten there more than six times in the last
couple of years, I cannot think of any single
dish that has ever been repeated"). "And it still
feels like a cosy neighbourhood restaurant",
although on the downside "tables are very small
and crammed too close together". / E8 1BG;
www.pidginlondon.com; @PidginLondon; Wed-Sun
11 pm; closed Wed & Thu L, closed Mon & Tue.

PIEBURY CORNER   £20   3 3 3

3 CALEDONIAN RD, N1   020 7700 5441
9–3C | 209-211 HOLLOWAY RD, N7
020 7700 5441   9–2D

"A nice stop on the road to the Emirates" – this
popular 'pie deli' has won a certain notoriety
with its range of pies, whose names make most
sense if you follow The Gunners; also with a
more conventional, less Arsenal-centric caff
selling traditional scran in King's Cross. / N7 9
pm, N1 11 pm; N7 closed Mon-Wed & Sun D, N1
closed Sun D.

PIED À TERRE W1   £112   4 4 4

34 CHARLOTTE ST   020 7636 1178   2–1C

"David Moore's gastronomic home has stood
the test of time through many chefs that have
gone on to star elsewhere". All reports on this
"world-class" Fitzrovia townhouse agree that
– with the help of Asimakis Chaniotis at the
stoves (since October 2017) – "it is amazing how
standards have been maintained" with "creative
cuisine that's delicious but not fussy". "Friendly
guidance from the knowledgeable and engaging
sommelier" is another plus in navigating an
"exceptional" wine list, with "interesting and
well-priced vintages from unusual places".
Gripes about the ambience were largely absent
this year, with typical feedback describing it
as "always elegant, always stylish". Top Tip:
"the space at the front of the restaurant is
more crowded – ask for the back room when
booking". / W1T 2NH; www.pied-a-terre.co.uk;
@PiedaTerreUK; 11 pm; closed Sat L, closed Sun;
booking max 7 may apply.

PIG & BUTCHER N1   £52   4 4 4

80 LIVERPOOL RD   020 7226 8304   9–3D

"For carnivores and beer lovers", this
attractively located Islington gastroboozer
butchers its own meat on site, so "always
produces the best cuts, excellently cooked".
There's a good selection of craft ales too, "but
really it's more a restaurant than a pub", and
manages to "attract, train and keep very friendly
and knowledgeable waiting staff". / N1 0QD;
www.thepigandbutcher.co.uk; @pigandbutcher; 11
pm; Mon-Thu D only, Fri-Sun open L & D.

PILPEL   £11   3 3 2

38 BRUSHFIELD STREET, LONDON,
E1   020 7247 0146   13–2B | 60 ALIE
ST, E1   020 7952 2139   10–2D | OLD
SPITALFIELDS MKT, E1   020 7375 2282
13–2B | 146 FLEET ST, EC4   020 7583 2030
10–2A | PATERNOSTER SQ, EC4
020 7248 9281   10–2B

"Pittas of pleasure" – "Mediterranean/
Israeli street food of the best type (vegetarian,
fresh and bursting with taste)" – keep office
workers healthy and happy at these City-based
"pitstops". "No wonder there's always a queue at
lunchtime." / www.pilpel.co.uk; EC4 4 pm; E1 6
pm; Brushfield St & Alie St 9pm, Fri 4pm, Sun 6pm;
Paternoster Sq 9 pm, Fri 4 pm; EC4 branches closed
Sat & Sun; no booking.

PIQUE NIQUE SE1   £60   3 3 3

32 TANNER ST   020 7403 9549   10–4D

"Poulet de Bresse in all its glory" from the
spit roast helps earn a big thumbs-up for this
"fun sibling to neighbouring Casse-Croute",
which opened last year. "Ebullient service and
a winning, laid-back atmosphere" complete
the picture. / SE1 3LD; pique-nique.co.uk;
@piquenique32; 11 pm, Sun 6 pm.

EL PIRATA W1   £42   2 2 4

5-6 DOWN ST   020 7491 3810   3–4B

As "a reasonable option in overpriced Mayfair",
this very atmospheric, "if crowded and noisy"
tapas-haunt is "well above-average" and
"has a huge following". However, even many
reporters who view it through rose-tinted specs
would acknowledge "it needs to innovate and
generally improve its offering". / W1J 7AQ;
www.elpirata.co.uk; @elpirataw1; 10.30 pm; closed
Sat L & Sun.

PISQU W1   £56   3 2 3

23 RATHBONE PLACE   020 7436 6123   5–1A

"Very different" cuisine from the Amazon and
the Andes has carved a niche for this Peruvian
yearling off Charlotte Street in Fitzrovia. "A
good addition to the London dining scene, with
an interesting menu" and cocktails. / W1T 1HZ;
www.pisqulondon.com; @PisquLondon; Sun-Thu 11
pm, Fri & Sat midnight.

PITT CUE CO EC2   £59   4 2 2

1 THE AVE, DEVONSHIRE SQ
020 7324 7770   10–2D

"Dish after dish that will delight any carnivore
worth the name" emerges from the grill or
smoker at Tom Adams's American-inspired
operation near Liverpool Street. "Loyalists and
purist fans of 'old' Pitt Cue in Soho lament
the sterile, corporate feel of the new location,
but the food is still some of the best BBQ in
London", thanks to "utter fanaticism about the
core ingredients, combined with wonderful skill
in the kitchen". / EC2 \N; www.pittcue.co.uk;
@PittCueCo; Mon-Fri 11 pm, Sat 10.30 pm; closed
Sat L, closed Sun.

PIZARRO SE1 £60 323

194 BERMONDSEY ST 020 7256 5333 10–4D

José Pizarro's contemporary Spanish restaurant never quite matches the drama (or ratings) of his original venture – the nearby tapas bar sibling, José, on the other side of Bermondsey Street. Service here can be "a bit hit and miss", but in other respects it is a "highly competent" operation with a "warm" atmosphere and "authentic" cuisine from "a relatively short menu". / SE1 3TQ; www.josepizarro.com; @Jose_Pizarro; 10.30 pm, Sun 9.30 pm.

PIZZA DA VALTER SW17 £43 322

7 BELLEVUE RD 020 8355 7032 11–2C

"Good pasta, sides and mains as well as great pizza" win applause for this "very good local pizzeria", attractively situated by Wandsworth Common. / SW17 7EG.

PIZZA EAST £56 434

310 PORTOBELLO RD, W10 020 8969 4500 7–1A | 79 HIGHGATE RD, NW5 020 3310 2000 9–1B | 56 SHOREDITCH HIGH ST, E1 020 7729 1888 13–1B

"A really interesting take on the pizza genre" (with a focus on "original", often hearty, toppings) combined with an excitingly grungy hipster vibe ensure this successful Soho House-owned group remains "extremely popular and always busy". "Prices are reasonable too" and for such a style-conscious scene, gripes about service are notable by their absence. / www.pizzaeast.com; @PizzaEast; E1 midnight, .

PIZZA METRO SW11 £47 322

64 BATTERSEA RISE 020 7228 3812 11–2C

"Great pizza" is sold 'al metro' (it was the first place in town to serve it by length) "or as a traditional round" at this Neapolitan in Battersea, which was quite a destination back in the day. The second branch in Notting Hill closed down this year. / SW11 1EQ; www.pizzametropizza.com; @pizzametropizza; 10.30 pm, Mon 11 pm, Sun 3 pm; no Amex.

PIZZA PILGRIMS £40 333

102 BERWICK ST, W1 07780 667258 4–1D | 11-12 DEAN ST, W1 020 7287 8964 4–1D | KINGLY CT, CARNABY ST, W1 020 7287 2200 4–2B | 23 GARRICK ST, WC2 020 3019 1881 5–3C | 12 HERTSMERE RD, E14 020 3019 8020 12–1C | 136 SHOREDITCH HIGH ST, E1 020 3019 7620 13–1B | 15 EXMOUTH MKT, EC1 020 7287 8964 10–1A | SWINGERS CRAZY GOLF, SAINT MARY AXE, EC3 NO TEL 10–2D

From a tiny van named Conchetta to a bricks 'n' mortar chain – the Elliot brothers deliver a pizza hit that's still "a step-up from standard fare" at their expanding group, but their ratings are becoming more mainstream than during their heady earlier days. / pizzapilgrims.co.uk;

@pizzapilgrims; 10.30pm, Sun 9.30 pm; WC2 11 pm, Sun 10 pm; Dean St booking: min 8.

PIZZAEXPRESS £49 222

"There is a lot more competition in the chain pizza market these days"; and while this long-enduring (est 1965) feature of every high street still has a very large fan club, it is steadily losing support. Some of this may be that "it is inevitably a much less distinctive presence nowadays" and huge numbers of reporters do still see it as a "safe bet" (and most particularly "an easy choice for a meal out with a five-year old"). More rivalry doesn't really explain its steadily bombing ratings however – in particular the evaporation of the once-excellent ambience at its branches since Hony Capital took charge. In this regard, cynicism seems justified: "my favourite branch has been ruined by the greedy private equity owners cramming in small tables so that the atmosphere is as delightful as rush hour on the underground. Such a pity – as it was so good for so many years". "Generous discounting" has also seemingly become a permanent feature – "without one of their plentiful voucher deals, it can seem distinctly overpriced". / www.pizzaexpress.co.uk; 11.30 pm - midnight; most City branches closed all or part of weekend; no booking at most branches.

PIZZERIA PAPPAGONE N4 £35 343

131 STROUD GREEN RD 020 7263 2114 9–1D

"Very crowded and lively", twenty-year-old Finsbury Park stalwart featuring pizza from a wood-fired oven. "It's not for the sensitive – you will love it or overlook it as it's noisy"… adding to its appeal as a kid-friendly option! / N4 3PX; www.pizzeriapappagone.co.uk; @pizza_pappagone; midnight.

PIZZICOTTO W8 £54 443

267 KENSINGTON HIGH ST 020 7602 6777 8–1D

"So much better than the chain alternatives" – this smart three-year-old pizzeria directly opposite the new Design Museum in Kensington "specialises in on-site-produced pizzas… and what pizzas they are, the tastiest ever!". An offshoot of the family-run Il Portico five doors away, it shares the same "friendly service". / W8 6NA; www.pizzicotto.co.uk; @pizzicottow8; Mon-Thu 11 pm, Fri & Sat midnight, Sun 10.30 pm.

PLAQUEMINE LOCK N1 £46 333

139 GRAHAM ST 020 7688 1488 9–3D

This "surprising re-invention of a 'lost boozer'" done out with a "bright and colourful interior" brings "fascinating Louisiana cuisine" to Angel, right on the Regent's Canal. Opened a year ago by Jacob Kenedy (Bocca di Lupo, Gelupo and Vico), it manages to "keep the feel of a great local" while being "quite niche". Top Tip: "really first-class grilled oysters". / N1 8LB; plaqlock.com; 10 pm, Sun 9 pm.

PLATEAU E14 £74 233

4TH FLOOR, CANADA SQ 020 7715 7100 12–1C

A brilliant view, from a location convenient for Canary Wharf worker-bees, is the pull to this "reliable" business-friendly outfit from D&D London. Opinion is split on the food: some praise "Jeremy Trehout's French classicism overlaid with British-European modernism" while others find it "boring" and "expensive". Top Tip: "stick to the bar and grill and you can be in/out in an hour at a reasonable price". / E14 5ER; www.plateau-restaurant.co.uk; @plateaulondon; 11 pm; closed Sat L & Sun.

PLOT SW17 £40 444

BROADWAY MARKET, TOOTING HIGH ST 020 8767 2639 11–2C

"Yummy" food from a short but "ever-changing menu" at this two-year-old pioneer has helped put Tooting Market on the foodie map. The focus is on British small plates, and it's seasonal in more ways than one, so "you'll need to wear warm clothes" in winter because "it's under cover but still outside…". / SW17 0RL; plotkitchen.com; @plot_kitchen; midnight; closed Tue, Wed L, closed Sun & Mon.

THE PLOUGH SW14 £45 234

42 CHRIST CHURCH RD 020 8876 7833 11–1A

This 18th-century inn with a big outside terrace inhabits a leafy and lovely East Sheen conservation area, and also trades well on its proximity to Richmond Park. It wins praise from most (if not quite all) reporters for its "good, honest pub food". / SW14 \N; www.theplough.com; Mon-Thu 9.30 pm, Fri & Sat 10 pm, Sun 9 pm.

PLUM + SPILT MILK, GREAT NORTHERN HOTEL N1 £73 233

KING'S CROSS ST PANCRAS STATION, PANCRAS RD 020 3388 0818 9–3C

"Smart" railway-hotel brasserie at King's Cross (named after the livery used by the Flying Scotsman's dining carriages) that can provide "surprisingly good quality meals and attentive service". A "lovely place for lunch" – "not too businessy" – it wins particular recommendations for its "tasty and well-executed breakfast". The worst folks say about the place? – "pleasant enough but mystifyingly pricey". / N1C 4TB; plumandspiltmilk.com; @PlumSpiltMilk; 10.30 pm, Mon 11 pm, Sun 3 pm.

POLLEN STREET SOCIAL W1 £101 333

8-10 POLLEN ST 020 7290 7600 3–2C

"Well deserving its accolades" – Jason Atherton's smooth Mayfair HQ combines "consistently great quality cuisine" (in particular the "wonderful tasting menu") with an "impressively relaxed atmosphere" and "cool design" and is truly dazzling to its large and enthusiastic fan club. On the downside, "deep pockets are needed", and the service can be "slightly erratic" (although is generally "excellent"). / W1S 1NQ; www.pollenstreetsocial.com; @PollenStSocial; 10.30 pm; closed Sun; booking max 7 may apply.

POLPETTO W1　£51　3️⃣3️⃣2️⃣

11 BERWICK ST　020 7439 8627　4–2D

Russell Norman's 'bacaro' in the middle of Soho (behind what used to be called Raymond's Revue Bar) won solid ratings this year for its menu of Venetian small plates: "The food always has an extra something beyond Polpo and the price is about the same". / W1F 0PL; www.polpetto.co.uk; @polpettoW1; 11 pm, Sun 10.30 pm; booking L only.

POLPO　£52　2️⃣2️⃣2️⃣

41 BEAK ST, W1　020 7734 4479　4–2B | 6 MAIDEN LN, WC2　020 7836 8448　5–3D | DUKE OF YORK SQ, SW3　020 7730 8900 6–2D | 126-128 NOTTING HILL GATE, W11 020 7229 3283　7–2B | 2-3 COWCROSS ST, EC1　020 7250 0034　10–1A

Russell Norman's "buzzy and very casual" cicchetti cafés still have a large fan club who applaud "very tasty, tapas-style fare", "drinkable wine served in tumblers" and a "friendly atmosphere". But the feeling that it "was once original, but has now been bypassed and needs updating" captures the mood of a fair few who "expected more" of the "hit 'n' miss service" and "uninspired food". / www.polpo.co.uk; 10 pm-11.30 pm, EC1 Sun 4 pm; EC1 closed D Sun; no bookings.

POMONA'S W2　£56　3️⃣4️⃣4️⃣

47 HEREFORD RD　020 7229 1503　7–1B

La-La Land comes to W2 at this brightly converted pub, with garden – nowadays a haven of immunity-boosting, locally-sourced, charcoal-grilled, seasonal fare – "a top neighbourhood option", ideal for breakfast (including with kids in tow). It takes some flak, though, for "meagre portions priced at Notting Hill-banker levels". / W2 5AH; www.pomonas.co.uk; @PomonasLondon; Tue-Thu 10 pm, Fri & Sat 10.30 pm, Sun 9 pm; closed Mon.

LE PONT DE LA TOUR SE1　£76　2️⃣2️⃣2️⃣

36D SHAD THAMES　020 7403 8403　10–4D

"A blissful location by Thames" with "stunning views of Tower Bridge" and outside tables in summer has always been the 'crown jewel' feature of D&D London's Thames-side flagship (where, back in the day, Tony Blair memorably entertained Bill Clinton). A relaunch a couple of years ago seemed to stem its slide into obscurity, but its ratings sank again this year, with punishing pricing leaving it feeling "quite underwhelming" not helped by "very conventional" cooking and service that's "nothing like what it used to be". The wine list is "not as good as it was" either – perhaps why it receives surprisingly few expense-accounter nominations nowadays. / SE1 2YE; www.lepontdelatour.co.uk; @lepontdelatour; 10.30 pm, Sun 9.30 pm; No trainers.

POPESEYE　£63　3️⃣2️⃣2️⃣

108 BLYTHE RD, W14　020 7610 4578　8–1C | 36 HIGHGATE HILL, N19　020 3601 3830 9–1B

"Unassuming and purist" – this characterful-going-on-grotty Olympia steakhouse is little changed since opening in 1994, and serves nothing but grass-fed beef from northeast Scotland (the name comes from a thin cut of Scottish rump). The steak's very competent but some feel the plonk is better: "it's beloved of wine merchants with good reason – lots of clever bin ends". A branch in Highgate managed separately by the owners' son opened in 2015 (no recent feedback), but the Putney outpost closed earlier this year. / www.popeseye.com; W14 11.30 pm; SW15 11 pm; N19 10.30 pm, Sun 9 pm; W14 & SW15 closed Sun; N19 closed Mon.

POPOLO EC2　£52　5️⃣4️⃣3️⃣

26 RIVINGTON ST　020 7729 4299　13–1B

"Phenomenal dishes" – not least "the best pasta on the planet" – win praise from the small but very dedicated fan club of Jonathan Lawson's "friendly" little Shoreditch yearling. If you sit at the downstairs counter rather than in the small upstairs, it's "a fantastic opportunity to see the chefs working from close up". / EC2A 3DU; popoloshoreditch.com; @popolo_EC2; 2 am, Sun midnight; no booking.

POPPIES　£43　3️⃣2️⃣3️⃣

59 OLD COMPTON ST, W1　020 7482 2977 4–2D | 30 HAWLEY CR, NW1 020 7267 0440　9–2B | 6-8 HANBURY ST, E1　020 7247 0892　13–2C

Founder Pat "Pops" Newland, who started working in the East End fish trade at the age of 11, has decorated these venues (Soho, Spitalfields and Camden Town) in 1950s memorabilia, so "it feels like Poppies has been around since London's rock'n'roll days". It's not as bad as it sounds – you get "proper fish and chips": "all the classics are here, together with some welcome additions (seafood platter, lemon sole)", but "most importantly, the chips are great!". / 11 pm, Fri & Sat 11.30 pm, Sun 10.30 pm.

LA PORCHETTA PIZZERIA　£41　2️⃣3️⃣2️⃣

33 BOSWELL ST, WC1　020 7242 2434 2–1D | 147 STROUD GREEN RD, N4 020 7281 2892　9–1D | 74-77 CHALK FARM RD, NW1　020 7267 6822　9–2B | 84-86 ROSEBERY AVE, EC1　020 7837 6060 10–1A

"Pizza without the attitude" – in "large delicious portions" – along with an "exceptionally family-friendly" approach and "cheap" prices keep regulars flocking to these old-school comfort-food Italians in north London. Founded in 1990, the chain now has four branches. / www.laporchetta.net; N1, NW1 & EC1 11pm, Fri & Sat midnight, Sun 10 pm; N4 11 pm, Sun 10 pm; WC1 11 pm, Fri midnight; WC1 closed Sat & Sun; NW1, N1 & N4 closed Mon-Fri L; EC1 closed Sat L; no Amex.

IL PORTICO W8　£60　3️⃣5️⃣4️⃣

277 KENSINGTON HIGH ST　020 7602 6262 8–1D

"One of the last, good, old-fashioned Italians, churning out those dishes we love" – this "always reliable, family run Italian" has "a formula that's worked for decades, so why change?". There's a "wonderful manager, James" (the original owner's son), and "you're always welcomed like a long-lost friend". But "it's not an institution living on past glories": "the food is without pretence" but "with some newer dishes to maintain interest". / W8 6NA; www.ilportico.co.uk; 11 pm; closed Sun.

PORTLAND W1　£84　4️⃣3️⃣2️⃣

113 GREAT PORTLAND ST　020 7436 3261 2–1B

Will Lander & Daniel Morgenthau's "stark and simple" Fitzrovia three-year-old shot to fame on opening, thanks to its "clever" cuisine (for which it was quickly awarded a Michelin star); its "super choice of perfectly conditioned fine wines by the glass"; and sure-footed service that "combines professionalism with warmth and enthusiasm". Even those who feel "it's dropped off a little since its debut" feel "it's still a restaurant to go to if you like to try something new", and on most accounts a meal here remains "an exciting prospect". / W1W 6QQ; www.portlandrestaurant.co.uk; Wed & Thu 11 pm, Fri & Sat midnight, Sun 6 pm; closed Sun.

Le Pont de la Tour SE1

La Poule au Pot SW1

PORTOBELLO RISTORANTE PIZZERIA W11 £54 3 4 4

7 LADBROKE RD 020 7221 1373 7–2B

"An excellent covered terrace for summer days and evenings" is a major plus point for this "fantastic and genuine local" just off Notting Hill Gate, whose "management really make the place buzz". It serves a range of "good Italian food, especially seafood and great pizzas". / W11 3PA; www.portobellolondon.co.uk; 10 pm, Fri & Sat 11 pm, Sun 10 pm.

THE PORTRAIT, NATIONAL PORTRAIT GALLERY WC2 £67 2 3 4

ST MARTIN'S PLACE 020 7306 0055 5–4B

"Great vistas over centuries-old London rooftops to Parliament" lend a frisson to a visit to this top-floor dining room, which remains a highly popular West End destination. Even if the "pleasant", "unadventurous" food is arguably "nothing to write home about" the "other elements make up for it". Top Tip: good afternoon tea ("it looks as if Nelson could step off his pedestal and join you – who could blame him with all the goodies on offer…") / WC2H 0HE; www.npg.org.uk/visit/shop-eat-drink/restaurant.php; @NPGLondon; Sun-Wed 3 pm, Thu-Sat 8 pm; closed Sun-Wed D.

POTLI W6 £44 4 4 3

319-321 KING ST 020 8741 4328 8–2B

"Not your stereotypical curry house – the focus is on street food, with a menu that dares to be different and pulls it off superbly" at this "fun" and very popular Indian near Ravenscourt Park. For one or two sceptics, though, it's "good but hyped" – "other than the outstanding service, it wasn't as good as some of its local rivals". / W6 9NH; www.potli.co.uk; @Potlirestaurant; Sun-Thu 10 pm, Fri & Sat 10.30 pm.

LA POULE AU POT SW1 £62 2 2 5

231 EBURY ST 020 7730 7763 6–2D

"Soft lighting, snug and hidden tables" and "the whole full-on Frenchiness of it all" imbue this "dated (but that's part of the joy)" Pimlico classic with a "dark and seductive ambience" that for many years won it the survey's nomination as London's top spot for a date (and it still ranks at No. 2). "The solid French regional food has always been unspectacular" ("it's not why you come") while ultimately how much you enjoy the experience often comes down to how well you hit it off with the "colourful", very Gallic staff. / SW1W 8UT; www.pouleaupot.co.uk; 10 pm; closed Mon-Sat & Sun.

PRAWN ON THE LAWN N1 £61 3 3 2

292-294 ST PAUL'S RD 020 3302 8668 9–2D

"Top-quality fish, simply cooked" and "served tapas-style" in an "informal setting" make this fishmonger/seafood bar on Highbury Corner (with a sibling in Padstow) a "great neighbourhood place". "Can be busy and cramped, but the food is very good." / N1 2LY; prawnonthelawn.com; @PrawnOnTheLawn; 11 pm; closed Sun & Mon; no Amex.

PRIMEUR N5 £55 3 3 3

116 PETHERTON RD 020 7226 5271 1–1C

Sharing plates and unusual wines draw a steady crowd to this "lovely" if "busy" Highbury local, where seating is at communal tables in a 1920s former car garage. / N5 2RT; www.primeurN5.co.uk; @Primeurs1; 10.30 pm, Sun 5 pm; closed Mon, Tue L, Wed L, Thu L & Sun D; booking max 7 may apply.

THE PRINCESS VICTORIA W12 £48 3 3 3

217 UXBRIDGE RD 020 8749 4466 8–1B

"Back from the brink, with good, reasonably priced food and an outstanding wine list… especially for a pub in W12" – this huge gin palace (with fine, traditional interior) on the main drag out of Shepherd's Bush has survived turbulent times (due to a change of ownership) and is now back on form. / W12 9DH; www.princessvictoria.co.uk; @threecheerspubs; Mon-Thu 11 pm, Fri & Sat midnight, Sun 10.30 pm.

PRINCI W1 £37 3 2 2

135 WARDOUR ST 020 7478 8888 4–1D

This "busy coffee shop with wonderful cakes" is the Soho outpost of a smart Milanese bakery, with self-service from the counter from breakfast until late at night, providing upmarket fast food, including pizzas. / W1F 0UT; www.princi.com; midnight, Sun 10 pm; no booking.

PRIX FIXE W1 £44 3 2 2

39 DEAN ST 020 7734 5976 5–2A

"Traditional French dishes with well-integrated flavours", a "classic bistro atmosphere" and "remarkably good value" add up to a "reliable experience" at this Soho sibling to Pierre Victoire. The set lunch menu also offers an "unusually large choice". / W1D 4PU; www.prixfixe.net; @prixfixelondon; Sun-Thu 10 pm, Fri & Sat 10.30 pm.

THE PROMENADE AT THE DORCHESTER W1 £132 2 4 4

THE DORCHESTER HOTEL, 53 PARK LANE 020 7629 8888 3–3A

The "marvellous" afternoon tea in the "beautiful setting" of this grand Mayfair hotel's opulent lounge – rumoured to be as long as Nelson's Column is tall – is "a wonderful experience" – "expensive", no doubt, "but at the same time excellent value". / W1K 1QA; www.dorchestercollection.com/en/london/the-dorchester/restaurant-bars/afternoon-tea; @TheDorchester; 10.30 pm; No shorts.

PROVENDER E11 £41 3 4 4

17 HIGH ST 020 8530 3050 1–1D

Veteran Francophile restaurateur Max Renzland's "superb, neighbourhood bistro gem" is a particularly good discovery in furthest Wanstead, with "proper, traditional French cooking" that's "not flashy, over the top or over-priced" and a "relaxing and delightful atmosphere". It's "better than many restaurants I know in France… and I live there!". / E11 2AA; www.provenderlondon.co.uk; @ProvenderBistro; 10.30 pm; booking max 10 may apply.

THE PROVIDORES AND TAPA ROOM W1 £73 4 4 3

109 MARYLEBONE HIGH ST 020 7935 6175 2–1A

"Peter Gordon, the father of fusion food, still produces delicious food with great flair" – "superbly executed and with vibrant flavours" – at his Marylebone venue. There's a strong taste of his native New Zealand led by "exceptional Kiwi wines". It's quite a "cramped" place though, and some recommend "choose the bustling, atmospheric ground floor, not upstairs". / W1U 4RX; www.theprovidores.co.uk; @theprovidores; Mon-Thu 9 pm, Fri & Sat 9.30 pm, Sun 2.30 pm; SRA-Food Made Good – 2 stars.

PRUFROCK COFFEE EC1 £13 3 2 2

23-25 LEATHER LN 020 7242 0467 10–2A

A haven for City caffeine junkies for nearly 10 years, this busy café near Chancery Lane also provides good-value lunch and snacks, including "wonderful cheese scones". / EC1N 7TE; www.prufrockcoffee.com; @PrufrockCoffee; Mon-Fri 6 pm, Sat & Sun 5 pm; L only; no Amex.

THE PUNCHBOWL

W1 £61 **3 4 3**

41 FARM ST 020 7493 6841 **3–3A**

"Great pies and good crunchy vegetables" combine with "romantic booths" at this "lovely pub" in Mayfair. It's "over 300 years old" and has more recent history, under the former ownership of Madonna's ex, film director Guy Ritchie. / W1J 5RP; www.punchbowllondon.com; @ThePunchBowlLDN; 11 pm, Sun 10.30 pm; closed Sun D.

PUNJAB WC2

£41 **3 4 3**

80 NEAL ST 020 7836 9787 **5–2C**

"Long-established, traditional Indian" north of Covent Garden that's "always a pleasure". Founded in 1946 and now in the fourth generation of ownership by the same family, part of their successful formula is "very competitive prices". / WC2H 9PA; www.punjab.co.uk; 11 pm, Sun 10 pm; booking max 8 may apply.

PURE INDIAN COOKING

SW6 £50 **4 4 2**

67 FULHAM HIGH ST 020 7736 2521 **11–1B**

"Delicious and inventive Indian dishes" – "really fresh and interesting" – ensure that this unassuming little venue just off the Fulham Palace Road stands out from the curry house crowd. Chef and proprietor Shilpa Dandekar used to work for Raymond Blanc. / SW6 3JJ; www.pureindiancooking.com; @PureCooking; 10 pm, Sun 9.30 pm.

PUREZZA NW1

£45 **3 3 2**

43 PARKWAY 020 3884 0078 **9–3B**

"A welcome addition to Camden's burgeoning vegan scene" – the UK's first vegan pizzeria hit Brighton in 2015 and this "lively" London offshoot opened in March 2018, featuring sourdough, hemp or gluten-free bases, plus a smattering of other dishes. In case you were wondering, the 'artisan Mozzarella' is made from fermented brown rice milk. / NW1 7PN; www.purezza.co.uk; @purezzauk; Mon-Fri 10 pm, Sat & Sun 9 pm.

QUAGLINO'S

SW1 £76 **2 3 4**

16 BURY ST 020 7930 6767 **3–3D**

D&D London's "spectacular" Mayfair basement – dating from the 1920s but revamped in glam style by Sir Terence Conran in 1993 – put in a much better showing this year: the criticism of recent years was notable by its absence, and instead it generally "exceeded expectations" as a "buzzing and fun venue" with "delicious cocktails", lively entertainment and "OK" food. Even so, "in the evening, the very loud music and the McMafia clientele can combine to be a little oppressive!" / SW1Y 6AJ; www.quaglinos-restaurant.co.uk; @quaglinos; Sun-Thu 10.30 pm, Fri & Sat 11 pm; closed Sun; No trainers.

THE QUALITY CHOP HOUSE

EC1 £68 **3 3 3**

94 FARRINGDON RD 020 7278 1452 **10–1A**

"The wooden booths are lovely for privacy if not for comfort" (their hard benches, while "iconic", are "not really designed to be sat on for two hours or so"), at Will Lander & Daniel Morgenthau's "snug" but "bum-numbing" Grade II listed 'Working Class Caterer' (est 1869), which has been a foodie favourite since it became a trailblazer for modern British cuisine in the early '90s (and more recently its re-re-launch in 2012). Its meat-heavy menu is "innovative but not showy" and "consistently good" if a little pricey. Recent innovations include an adjacent café and wine shop. / EC1R 3EA; thequalitychophouse.com; @QualityChop; 10 pm, Sun 4 pm; closed Sun D.

QUANTUS W4

£56 **3 5 3**

38 DEVONSHIRE RD 020 8994 0488 **8–2A**

Featuring "good, Latin-influenced cuisine from a small menu", this "unpretentious" local is "one of the best in Chiswick". The experience is "made more special by owner Leo Pacarada and his staff, who could not be more obliging", and it "holds its own despite being opposite La Trompette!". / W4 2HD; www.quantus-london.com; Sun-Thu 10 pm, Fri & Sat 10.30 pm; closed Mon L, Tue L & Sun.

QUARTIERI NW6

£44 **4 3 3**

300 KILBURN HIGH RD 020 7625 8822 **1–2B**

"Traditional and new-style pizza with great flavours" from the wood-fired oven wins a consistent thumbs-up for this year-old, small-but-stylish Neapolitan-owned haunt in Kilburn. / NW6 2DB; www.quartieri.co.uk; @quartierilondon; 11 pm.

LE QUERCE SE23 £43 **3 3 2**

66-68 BROCKLEY RISE 020 8690 3761 **1–4D**

"Divine home-made pasta" and other "good Sardinian food" has made Antonello Serra's "welcoming", family-run (and "very family-friendly") neighbourhood Italian a beacon in Brockley for more than a decade. But ratings are still on the wane here, year-on-year, with some regulars expressing caution: "it's a sad thing when you find fault in something you love, but I've had two disappointing meals in a row of late – pasta was still excellent, everything else seemed rather basic". / SE23 1LN; www.lequerce.co.uk; Tue-Sun, Mon 9.30 pm; closed Mon & Tue L.

QUILON SW1

£69 **5 5 2**

41 BUCKINGHAM GATE 020 7821 1899 **2–4B**

Sriram Aylur's "amazingly light and delicate Keralan cuisine" is twinned with "impeccable service" at the Taj Group's formidably good Indian, which "maintains the great standards it's set for the last decade or so" (and which was the highest rated posh Indian in the survey this year). Even fans acknowledge the space looks "drab", which "takes away the feeling

of a special occasion", "but hey, you don't eat the decor". / SW1E 6AF; www.quilon.co.uk; @thequilon; 11 pm, Sun 10.30 pm; SRA-Food Made Good – 2 stars.

QUIRINALE SW1 £66 **3 4 3**

NORTH CT, 1 GT PETER ST 020 7222 7080 **2–4C**

One of the top culinary attractions in striking distance of the Palace of Westminster (with a clientele incorporating many MPs and senior civil servants) – this "restrained Italian" in a basement is "discreet and quiet" and serves "classic food to a high standard", alongside "an interesting and accessible wine list". / SW1P 3LL; www.quirinale.co.uk; @quirinaleresto; 10.30 pm; closed Sat L, closed Sun.

QUO VADIS W1 £60 **4 4 5**

26-29 DEAN ST 020 7437 9585 **4–1D**

This "special" Soho veteran "continues to delight and surprise", under the Hart Bros, whose sure-handed stewardship of the property is in stark contrast to when it lost its way in the Marco Pierre White years. Despite a reformatting a year ago which left its premises "somewhat truncated" (to make space for a branch of Barrafina) the dining room remains "totally charming". "When chef Jeremy Lee is at his best there is no comparison for simple excellence" and his "perfectly poised, thoughtful and considered" seasonal British comfort food is provided with "originality and flair" to create a culinary experience that's "reliable without ever being predictable"… "and you also get the best martini in town". Top Tip: breakfast: "Jeremy's golden eggs, exquisite bread, gently roasted tomatoes...there is no better way to start the day". / W1D 3LL; www.quovadissoho.co.uk; @QuoVadisSoho; 10.30 pm; closed Sun.

RABBIT SW3 £54 **3 2 3**

172 KING'S RD 020 3750 0172 **6–3C**

The Gladwin brothers' "fun", faux-rustique, four-year-old haunt on the King's Road still wins a lot of praise for its "inventive and tasty", farm-to-table "British tapas". There's a minority, though, who "go with high expectations (we were told it was amazing)", but leave finding it "overrated and overpriced". / SW3 4UP; www.rabbit-restaurant.com; @RabbitResto; 10 pm, Sun 5 pm; closed Mon L & Sun D.

RABOT 1745 SE1 £63 **2 2 2**

2-4 BEDALE ST 020 7378 8226 **10–4C**

The "quirky menu" of "unique cocoa-based cuisine" at this Borough Market venue was developed at a historic St Lucia cocoa plantation owned by Hotel Chocolat, and is rated a middling success. The big deal here? – "They serve amazing hot chocolate… well worth the calories!" It's also "a lovely place for an informal coffee", or "after work it turns into a bar, so you can have cocktails". / SE1 9AL; www.rabot1745.com; @rabot1745; 9.30 pm; closed Sun & Mon.

RADICI N1 £62 221

30 ALMEIDA ST   020 7354 4777   9–3D

"Very disappointing all round" is too often the verdict on this D&D London yearling (formerly the Almeida, RIP), where Francesco Mazzei is the figurehead for the Italian cuisine. Fans do praise it as "great for pre/post theatre" (the Almeida theatre is over the road) with "great pizza and zucchini fries" and other southern Italian fare, but numerous reporters "went expecting great things", but found "limited and not particularly well-executed" cooking, served "in a barn-like place with zero atmosphere and lacklustre service". / N1 1AD; www.radici.uk; @radici_n1; 10.30 pm, Sun 9 pm; closed Mon L.

RAGAM W1 £31 432

57 CLEVELAND ST   020 7636 9098   2–1B

"Year after year Ragam churns out delicious south Indian food, with lots of excellent vegetarian options" ("perfect dosas") – "it's not fancy but it's full of flavour and never fails!". The ambience at this basement near the Telecom Tower "doesn't get much better (despite two refurbs!), but the service is friendly" and everything comes "at a very reasonable price". / W1T 4JN; www.ragamindian.co.uk; 11 pm.

RAIL HOUSE CAFÉ SW1 £60 222

SIR SIMON MILTON SQ   020 3906 7950   2–4B

This "cool-looking venue" in Victoria's new Nova development has a "good all-round menu with lots of tasty choices", and makes "a worthy addition to the Riding House Café group". But the middling ratings indicate that Adam White's team are still struggling to meet the demands of a 300-cover operation on two floors. Top Tip: a good choice for brunch. / SW1H 0HW; www.railhouse.cafe; @railhouse_cafe; closed Mon-Sat & Sun.

RAINFOREST CAFÉ W1 £61 133

20-24 SHAFTESBURY AVE   020 7434 3111   4–3D

"You're not here for the food, but for the sake of keeping young children busy", say reports on this Piccadilly Circus fixture, complete with animatronic animals and indoor rain storms. "The food's average and overpriced, the decor's tired… but the kids love it and ask to go time and time again…" / W1V 7EU; www.therainforestcafe.co.uk; @RainforestCafe; Sun-Wed 10 pm, Thu-Sat 8.30 pm; credit card required to book.

RAMBLA W1 £52 433

64 DEAN ST   020 7734 8428   5–2A

"Big flavours (and decent-sized portions too)" help inspire only positive reviews for Victor Garvey's "superb new Catalan venture" in Soho, which delivers "accomplished" cooking and "excellent value for money". This said, numerous newspaper reviewers have gushed about the place bigtime, and there is the odd caution that "although it's above average, it's not quite as exceptional as some well-known critics might wish you to believe". / W1D 4QG; www.ramblalondon.com; @ramblasoho.

RANDALL & AUBIN W1 £60 334

14-16 BREWER ST   020 7287 4447   4–2D

"So long as you don't mind sharing a table with strangers" – this "always-fun" Soho "institution" makes a perfect way to punctuate an evening. With its "great buzz and very nice vibe, it's always full of energy", and "warm and friendly" staff deliver "outstanding fresh seafood, especially the big plateaux de fruits de mer", plus "sumptuous natives, fish 'n' chips, fish soup and lobster po'boy, all of 'em delicious". / W1F OSG; www.randallandaubin.com; @randallandaubin; Mon-Thu 11 pm, Fri & Sat midnight, Sun 10 pm; booking L only.

RANDY'S WING BAR E15 £35 333

QUEEN ELIZABETH OLYMPIC PARK 020 8555 5971   14–1C

"Very good wings, beers and cocktails" are the payoff to a trip to this unit in Hackney Wick's Here East development: feedback is limited but upbeat. / E15 2GW; www.randyswingbar.co.uk; @randyswingbar; 11 pm, Sun 10.30 pm; closed Sun D.

RAOUL'S CAFÉ W9 £42 324

13 CLIFTON RD   020 7289 7313   9–4A

"Very consistent in term of food, atmosphere (and slightly unmotivated service!)" – this popular and long-established café near Little Venice is known for its "great breakfast and brunch selection" and charming outside tables. Its other spin-offs (including in Notting Hill) are no more. / W9 1SZ; www.raoulsgourmet.com; 9 pm; no booking L.

RASA £35 332

6 DERING ST, W1   020 7629 1346   3–2B | 55 STOKE NEWINGTON CHURCH ST, N16   020 7249 0344   1–1C | 56 STOKE NEWINGTON CHURCH ST, N16 020 7249 1340   1–1C

"It's easy to over-eat" at these basic cafés, whose still-unusual Keralan menu is "still good after all these years" ("at the price it can seem quite amazing!") and "much better than 'normal' north Indians for veggies". The Stokie original is nowadays less popular than its "handy-to-know-about" offshoot "in the little patch near Oxford Circus bereft of decent options". / www.rasarestaurants.com; N16 & Travancore N16 10.45 pm, Fri & Sat 11.30 pm, W1 11 pm, Sun 9 pm; WC1 closed L, Sun L&D, N16 closed Mon-Fri L, Travancore closed L.

RAVI SHANKAR NW1 £30 322

132-135 DRUMMOND ST   020 7388 6458   9–4C

The "unbelievable value" lunchtime and weekend buffet makes this longstanding South Indian veggie a "great choice" among the Little India curry canteens near Euston station. "A bit rough around the edges", perhaps, but that is compensated by "quick and cheery service". / NW1 2HL; www.ravishankarbhelpoori.com; 10.30 pm; closed Mon-Sun L.

RED FARM WC2

9 RUSSELL ST   020 3883 9093   5–3D

A fun spin on Chinese cuisine – with an Instagrammable dim sum prawn dish that looks like the ghosts in Pac-Man – this canteen-style import from NYC (where it's famous) has quietly arrived on a three storey site in Covent Garden with very little publicity, and a recreation of its no-bookings policy. In an initial September 2018 review, The Evening Standard's Fay Maschler suggests prices are a little "ballsy", 'specially as Chinatown is only a stroll away. / WC2B 5HZ; redfarmldn.com.

RED FORT W1 £75 322

77 DEAN ST   020 7437 2525   4–1D

This once-famous Soho stalwart, modernised after a fire a few years back, is, in style, a "sort-of-posh Indian, midway between your local curry house and an upmarket place like Benares" (and the overall effect of its minimal, contemporary decor strikes some customers as a bit "dismal"). For its regulars "it's been going forever and never lets its standards slip" but more sceptical folk can just find the cooking "rather disappointing" nowadays. / W1D 3SH; redfort.co.uk; @redfortlondon; 11.30 pm; closed Sat L, closed Sun; No shorts.

THE RED LION & SUN N6 £52 323

25 NORTH RD   020 8340 1780   9–1B

This "great gastropub" in a leafy corner of Highgate "serves good, imaginative food at reasonable prices", catering for all tastes from classic Sunday roast to vegetarian and vegan. There's an "excellent wine list", "open fires", and "dogs are welcome". / N6 \N; www.theredlionandsun.com; @redlionandsun; 10 pm.

THE RED PEPPER W9 £50 322

8 FORMOSA ST   020 7266 2708   9–4A

This "tiny pizza place in Little Venice" is a popular and "friendly" local institution that is now entering its 25th year. Known for its "excellent wood-fired pizza", it also specialises in unusual dishes from Sardinia and southern Italy. / W9 1EE; www.theredpepperrestaurant.co.uk; Sun-Thu 10.30 pm, Sat, Fri 11 pm; closed Mon-Fri L; no Amex.

Regency Café SW1

three London branches of this international French-based chain. "If steak and chips tick your boxes, this will too!". "Time it wrong, and you'll have to queue". / www.relaisdevenise.com; 10.45 pm-11 pm, Sun 9 pm-10.30 pm; EC2 closed Sat & Sun; no booking.

RESTAURANT OURS
SW3 £82 [2][2][3]

264 BROMPTON RD   020 7100 2200   6–2C

As a bar, there's much to recommend this Eurotrash-friendly South Kensington two-year-old (complete with indoor foliage and fairy lights), whose current incarnation is a couple of years old. Since Tom Sellers departed this year, its food ratings have actually started to scrape off rock-bottom – whether it's that the food has improved, or folks' high expectations are now just a bit more realistic is unclear. / SW3 2AS; www.restaurant-ours.com; @restaurant_ours; midnight, Fri & Sat 1.30 am; closed Mon & Sun.

RED ROOSTER
EC2 £68 [2][2][3]

45 CURTAIN RD   020 3146 4545   13–1B

"The food is decent (the whole fried chicken with a sparkler looks impressive when it comes out) but doesn't live up to the hype" is the overall verdict on Ethiopian-Swedish chef, Marcus Samuelsson's soul-food-via-Scandinavia yearling: the London sibling to the hugely popular Harlem original, at the foot of Shoreditch's Curtain hotel. It has "a clubby (very noisy) vibe and nice live music". / EC2A 4PJ; www.thecurtain.com; @RoosterHarlem; Sun midnight; closed Sun D.

REGENCY CAFE
SW1 £16 [3][4][5]

17-19 REGENCY ST   020 7821 6596   2–4C

"I am always surprised why this great caff is never included in your guide!!" – "If you like honest-to-goodness British grub, then join the queues for a proper fry-up" at this "brilliant", "cheap 'n' cheerful" dive "caught in a 1960's time warp", whose "full English can't be beaten". "With its beautiful tiled exterior and no-nonsense service, this is surely the platonic ideal of a Greasy Spoon": "the portions are large, the service is hectic, the seats are basic, and the food is incredible". "A real SW1 institution": "everyone goes – locals from the posh flats and the council flats, taxi drivers, MPs, Channel 4 media executives, Scotland Yard detectives, über-stylish Burberry types and civil servants. We all eat here and love it!" / SW1P 4BY; regencycafe.co.uk; Mon-Fri 7.15 pm, Sat 12 pm; closed Sat D, closed Sun.

LE RELAIS DE VENISE
L'ENTRECÔTE £47 [3][3][2]

120 MARYLEBONE LN, W1   020 7486 0878 2–1A | 50 DEAN ST, W1   020 3475 4202 5–3A | 5 THROGMORTON ST, EC2 020 7638 6325   10–2C

"The simplest menu" – the only items are "great steak-frites" accompanied by their "legendary secret sauce" (though you do get a choice of dessert) – makes for a "winning formula" at the

REUBENS W1 £57 [2][2][2]

79 BAKER ST   020 7486 0035   2–1A

This age-old deli in Marylebone is one of the longest-running kosher options in the West End. "Salt beef still tops the bill", and other dishes are dependably OK, in both the café upstairs and downstairs restaurant. / W1U 6RG; www.reubensrestaurant.co.uk; 11 pm; closed Fri D & Sat; no Amex.

THE RIB MAN E1 £8 [5][3]–

BRICK LANE, BRICK LANE MARKET NO TEL 13–2C

"Unbelievably tasty ribs, worth crossing London for" and perfect pulled pork, again score high ratings from street-food star Mark Gevaux, who is to be found on Sundays on Brick Lane (and outside West Ham for home games). Delight your friends with a gift of his trademark 'Holy F**k' hot sauce. / E1 6HR; www.theribman.co.uk; @theribman; closed Sun D, closed Mon-Fri & Sat; no booking.

RIB ROOM, JUMEIRAH CARLTON TOWER HOTEL
SW1 £100 [2][2][3]

CADOGAN PL   020 7858 7250   6–1D

Lost in the Gucci-clad international black hole that is the upper end of Sloane Street, this luxurious dining room (relaunched in late 2017) has long been known for its steaks and prime beef. Feedback was limited, but conformed to the age-old theme here: good but ferociously pricey. / SW1X 9PY; www.theribroom.co.uk; @RibRoomSW1; 10.30 pm; closed Sun.

RICCARDO'S
SW3 £51 [2][2][2]

126 FULHAM RD   020 7370 6656   6–3B

This "little slice of Italy with a sunny terrace" in Chelsea "attracts a loyal clientele" despite quite a widespread feeling that it's nowadays "tired" and "without flair". But those who are more forgiving feel it's a "real antidote to the Italian-themed chains" with "always a great welcome"

perhaps from the man himself: "people say the food's hit and miss, but stick to the staples and all will be well". / SW3 6HU; www.riccardos.it; @ricardoslondon; 10 pm.

RICK STEIN
SW14 £64 [2][2][3]

TIDEWAY YARD, 125 MORTLAKE HIGH ST 020 8878 9462   11–1A

"I love Rick's TV programmes, but his Barnes restaurant is a bit of a rip off." The Stein empire "could have tried a bit harder" with their first London outpost, which even some fans say is "no better than its previous incarnation (The Depot)". You do get "lovely views of the river" from its charming riverside location, near Barnes Bridge; and the food rating is middling, not terrible; but "food-wise, this place couldn't be more different from the original in Padstow". / SW14 8SN; www.rickstein.com/eat-with-us/barnes; @SteinBarnes; 9.30 pm.

RIDING HOUSE CAFÉ
W1 £58 [2][2][3]

43-51 GREAT TITCHFIELD ST 020 7927 0840   3–1C

"Fun" Fitzrovia all-day brasserie, with vaguely Manhattan-esque undertones, where breakfast and weekend brunch are the favoured times for a visit, although it's also tipped by creative types as a good place for a business meal. But be warned: one person's "buzzy" can be another's "fiendishly noisy". / W1W 7PQ; www.ridinghousecafe.co.uk; Mon-Thu 11.30 pm, Fri & Sat midnight, Sun 10.30 pm.

THE RISING SUN
NW7 £59 [3][3][3]

137 MARSH LN   020 8959 1357   1–1B

Run by Luca and Matteo Delnevo from Parma ("who pride themselves on friendly service and great food"), this lovely old pub (circa 1600) in Mill Hill provides "delicious" Italian cooking that's "by far the best gastroboozer grub for miles". It's "exceptionally child-friendly" too and "can be very busy at weekends, so book ahead". / NW7 4EY; www.therisingsunmillhill.com; @therisingunpub; Sun-Wed 10 pm, Thu-Sat 10.30 pm; closed Mon L.

RISTORANTE FRESCOBALDI
W1 £82 [3][4][3]

15 NEW BURLINGTON PL   020 3693 3435 4–2A

The "stunning, consistently good Italian food" at this three-year-old Mayfair venture is accompanied by a wine list that reflects the ownership by a 700-year-old Florentine banking and wine dynasty. It is certainly expensive, but "I don't fully understand why it's not busier". / W1S 5HX; www.frescobaldirestaurants.com; @frescobaldi_uk; Mon-Wed midnight, Thu-Sat 1.30 am, Sun 11 pm.

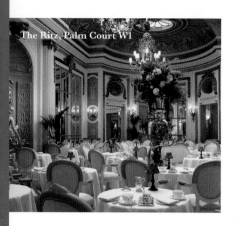

The Ritz, Palm Court W1

THE RITZ W1   £132   3 4 5

150 PICCADILLY   020 7493 8181   3–4C

"One of the best rooms in London, if not in the world!" – this "most beautiful" Louis XVI chamber provides a "glorious" riot of bronze, marble, painted ceiling and mirrors. From the kitchen overseen by John Williams, the "traditional Anglo-French dishes served from splendid silver carts" provide "an utterly magnificent and delightfully plutocratic experience… if sadly with prices to match". "Service treats you like royalty", and "for a romantic evening, you can't beat it" (especially, for older lovebirds, if combined with the evenings of music and dance). / W1J 9BR; www.theritzlondon.com; @theritzlondon; 10 pm; Jacket & tie required; SRA-Food Made Good – 3 stars.

THE RITZ, PALM COURT W1   £107   2 4 5

150 PICCADILLY   020 7493 8181   3–4C

"As a location, it's synonymous with afternoon tea", and "although it is very expensive" on practically all accounts this "gold standard" experience provides a "fantastic occasion" that's "worth it", with a drool-worthy selection of pastries, sandwiches, scones and cakes that "live up to the sumptuous surroundings", plus a choice of 18 different brews (or Champagne!) / W1J 9BR; www.theritzlondon.com; @theritzlondon; Jacket & tie required.

RIVA SW13   £64   3 3 2

169 CHURCH RD   020 8748 0434   11–1A

Tucked away in a row of Barnes shopfronts, this "soigné" North Italian is "unchanged in 20 years", during which Andreas Riva has built a devoted following, particularly amongst in-the-know foodies, with cooking that's "consistently superb, simply presented and concentrating on quality ingredients". It can feel a bit cliquey, though: "the proprietor seems to take pride in ignoring you unless you're a regular – or a celebrity". / SW13 9HR; 10 pm, Sun 9 pm; closed Sat L.

RIVEA, BULGARI HOTEL SW7   £88   3 4 3

171 KNIGHTSBRIDGE   020 7151 1025   6–1C

One of French superchef Alain Ducasse's luxury London hotel venues (the others being in the Dorchester) – this luxurious Knightsbridge basement presents his take on the cuisine of the French and Italian Riviera. While there is fulsome praise for some "delightful food" including "among the best desserts in London", some reporters expect to find more than merely "a reasonable all-rounder". / SW7 1DW; www.bulgarihotels.com; @bulgarihotels; 10.30 pm; booking max 7 may apply.

THE RIVER CAFÉ W6   £97   3 4 4

THAMES WHARF, RAINVILLE RD 020 7386 4200   8–2C

"An amazing place that's still full on a midweek winter evening after 30 years" – Hammersmith's world-famous, riverside Italian shows no sign of running out of steam: "it still feels fresh and contemporary", "Ruthie Rogers herself is still there doing some of the cooking", and it remains a standard-bearer for "the simplicity and clarity" of its Tuscan cuisine. The perennial elephant in the room here is "wallet-busting" prices, which regularly win this W6 legend the survey's booby prize as London's Most Overpriced Restaurant. Even so, most reporters are inclined to be forgiving: they "love the place despite the absurd cost", particularly those who appreciate "the very best, carefully sourced ingredients"; who adore the "helpful staff"; or who acclaim "the glorious outside terrace in summer", which "can't be matched". A sizeable minority, though, "know all the arguments as to why the place is worth it… but don't agree". A prime gripe for those who feel the most taken for a ride is the "crazy bills you get for sitting in what's basically a big canteen": while fans applaud this egalitarian set-up as "a perfect mix between formality and informality", the less charitable find it "noisy" and "crammed in" ("my chair was frequently banged into by waiters squeezing past"). / W6 9HA; www.rivercafe.co.uk; @RiverCafeLondon; Mon-Fri 9 pm, Sat 9.30 pm, Sun 3 pm; closed Sun D.

RIVINGTON GRILL SE10   £55   2 2 2

178 GREENWICH HIGH RD   020 8293 9270 1–3D

The brand that time forgot! – this Caprice Group venue is the sole survivor of a chain concept that went nowhere (and where the Rivington Street original has now gone). In direly provided Greenwich though, it's a case of 'the one-eyed man is king' – "it's fairly standard fare, but I liked the ambience and it may be your best bet if you're in SE10!"; good for "a relaxed brunch". / SE10 8NN; www.rivingtongrill.co.uk; 11 pm, Sun 10 pm; closed Mon, Tue L & Wed L.

ROAST SE1   £70   2 2 3

STONEY ST 0845 034 7300 10–4C

This Borough Market showcase for traditional British food enjoys a "great location" (incorporating a glass portico that was originally part of the Royal Opera House) with "wonderful views north to the City, east to the (bottom of the) Shard, and over the market itself". But every report of exceptional results ("best pork-and-crackling sandwich"; "amazing Chateaubriand") is matched by gripes about "very average" fare ("burnt Yorkshire pudding"; "the meat may be of a good quality but the cooking is not!"). It's also "on the expensive side". Top Tips: "excellent breakfast option – very filling"; "nab a window seat". / SE1 1TL; www.roast-restaurant.com; @roastrestaurant; 10.45 pm, Sun 6.30 pm; closed Sun D.

ROCCA DI PAPA   £43   3 4 4

73 OLD BROMPTON RD, SW7 020 7225 3413   6–2B | 75-79 DULWICH VILLAGE, SE21   020 8299 6333   1–4D

"Buzzy", "cheap 'n' cheerful" Italians in South Kensington and Dulwich Village that provide "lively service", "delicious, freshly made food" and "good pizzas with unusual toppings". "They love children and are relaxed about noise and mess", and there are "plenty of staff so you're not kept waiting". / www.roccarestaurants.com; SW7 11.30 pm; SE21 11 pm.

ROCHELLE CANTEEN E2   £64   2 2 4

ROCHELLE SCHOOL, ARNOLD CIRCUS 020 7729 5677   13–1C

The bike sheds of a former school near Spitalfields – converted by Melanie Arnold and Margot Henderson (wife of St John's Fergus) – are "a relaxed and leafy garden space, and romantic too" – "perfect for a summer lunch". It remains a favourite East End destination for those in the know on account of its simple, short menu of quality British fare but – coincidental with their opening at the ICA – ratings waned here this year, with more middling feedback and the odd "unsatisfactory meal". / E2 7ES; www.arnoldandhenderson.com; Thu-Sat 9 pm; closed Mon-Sun D; no Amex.

ROCHELLE CANTEEN AT THE ICA SW1   £45   4 4 3

THE MALL   020 7930 8619   2–3C

"I didn't think they'd do it in the arid ICA… but it's a triumph… Melanie and Margot, we love you!". Melanie Arnold and Margot Henderson have pulled off the successful opening of an offshoot to their boho Spitalfields venture in this "rather odd space" – a cultural centre near the start of The Mall – which, while "cramped and lacking comfort", is "laid back" and pepped up by "cheerful service". The main event, though, is the "simple, hearty but utterly delicious English food cooked with care and passion" – "just right, no-frills perfection!" / SW1Y 5AH; www.ica.art/visit/caf-bar; 11 pm; closed Mon.

ROGANIC W1   £93   5 4 2

5-7 BLANDFORD ST   020 3370 6260   2–1A

Simon Rogan's 2011 pop-up has been resurrected as a permanent fixture, replacing L'Autre Pied (RIP) – the most recent inhabitant of this "odd" ("cramped" and "slightly bleak")

Marylebone site – and offering either short (eight-course) or standard (over 12 courses) tasting menus. "Sometimes you want simple, delicious food, sometimes you want refinement and sophistication, and sometimes you want a meal that pushes things even further: this is a mix of sophistication and pushing-things-further, from single mouthfuls to fuller, complex, flavour-packed dishes", with "stunning presentation (every dish is a work of art) and divine tastes". Even so, there are one or two who feel that "while it's inventive and good, it's also overpriced with miniscule portions and you leave wondering what you've had". Top Menu Tip – the easiest way to dip your toe in the water here is the short, £35, business tasting menu. / W1U 3DB; www.simonrogan.co.uk; @simon_rogan; 9.15 pm; closed Sun & Mon.

RÖK £57 3|4|3

149 UPPER ST, N1 NO TEL 9–3D | 26 CURTAIN RD, EC2 020 7377 2152 13–2B

"Stripped-down ambience" and a "simple menu of interesting Nordic dishes" (many of them smoked, brined or fermented) hit the spot at this accomplished Scandi-inspired duo in Shoreditch and Islington. (There were plans for a Soho branch too, but these seem to have been backburnered for the time being). STOP PRESS: it was announced the original Shoreditch branch will close in early October 2018. / N1 midnight, EC2 11 pm, Fri & Sat 1 am; EC2 closed Sun.

ROKA £85 4|3|3

30 NORTH AUDLEY ST, W1 020 7305 5644 3–2A | 37 CHARLOTTE ST, W1 020 7580 6464 2–1C | ALDWYCH HOUSE, 71-91 ALDWYCH, WC2 020 7294 7636 2–2D | UNIT 4, PARK PAVILION, 40 CANADA SQ, E14 020 7636 5228 12–1C

"I love sitting at the counter with my partner, drinking the cocktails and sake, and having the most brilliant food!" – These "chilled" (if "noisy" and "buzzy") operations hail from the same stable as Zuma, and have carved a formidable following thanks to a Japanese-inspired array of "clean-tasting" fusion dishes, sushi and robata grills, full of "vibrant flavour". "It all adds up to a wonderful experience, but with a bill to match!" Top Tips – "fantastic weekend brunch menu, with booze included!" at all branches; and "rocking basement bar" at the Charlotte Street original. / www.rokarestaurant.com; 11.30 pm, Sun 10.30 pm; E14 11pm, Sun 8.30 pm; WC2 11 pm, Sun 8 pm; booking: max 5 online.

ROMULO CAFÉ W8 £59 3|3|3

343 KENSINGTON HIGH ST 020 3141 6390 8–1D

"You don't find many Filipino restaurants in the UK" and this two-year-old outpost of a restaurant group based in the Philippines aims to change all that. "First timers should like it" on account of its novelty; old hands may find it "a little pricier than other representatives of the cuisine… I guess you're paying for the Kensington price tag, and for food that's beautifully presented and delicious". / W8 6NW;

www.romulocafe.co.uk; @romulolondon; 10 pm; closed Sun.

ROSAS £46 3|2|2

The "cheap and tasty Thai food" at this fast-growing chain "hits a decent standard despite its many branches" and its delivered by "friendly, speedy staff" making them "a good stand-by option". Founders Saiphin and Alex Moore, who opened the original branch in 2008, have recently sold a majority stake to US investors TriSpan. / rosasthaicafe.com; @RosasThaiCafe; 10.30 pm, Fri & Sat 11 pm; E15 9 pm, Sat 10 pm, Sun 6 pm; W1F & W1D Sun 10 pm; ; E1, SW1 & SW9 6+ to book, W1 4+ to book.

THE ROSENDALE SE21 £52 3|4|3

65 ROSENDALE RD 020 8761 9008 1–4D

"Simple food but well executed (great burgers, pizzas and Sunday lunch)" has helped win a following for this fine Victorian coaching inn in West Dulwich (which has an enclosed garden for the kids). / SE21 8EZ; www.therosendale.co.uk; @threecheerspubs; 10.30 pm; no Amex.

ROSSOPOMODORO £46 2|2|2

JOHN LEWIS, 300 OXFORD ST, W1 020 7495 8409 3–1B | 50-52 MONMOUTH ST, WC2 020 7240 9095 5–3B | 214 FULHAM RD, SW10 020 7352 7677 6–3B | 1 RUFUS ST, N1 020 7739 1899 13–1B | 10 JAMESTOWN RD, NW1 020 7424 9900 9–3B | 46 GARRETT LN, SW18 020 8877 9903 11–2B

"Good Neapolitan cuisine including nice pizzas" in "huge portions (with a useful kids' menu)" is "a pleasant surprise" for most who report on this global chain, which actually originates in Naples itself. Feedback is not all bouquets, though – ratings are undercut by one or two reports of "mediocre" (e.g. "stodgy") dishes. / www.rossopomodoro.co.uk; 11 pm, Fri & Sat 11.30 pm, Sun 10 pm.

ROTI CHAI W1 £46 3|3|3

3 PORTMAN MEWS SOUTH 020 7408 0101 3–1A

"A menu inspired by street hawkers and roadside cafés" produces "delicious" and "authentic"-tasting street food at this highly popular, contemporary Indian operation, near Selfridges. The formula is essentially the same in the ground floor café or basement restaurant, and in general folks "are not sure that eating downstairs is worth the extra". / W1H 6HS; www.rotichai.com; @rotichai; 9 pm; booking D only.

ROTI KING, IAN HAMILTON HOUSE NW1 £17 5|2|1

40 DORIC WAY 020 7387 2518 9–3C

"Brought up in Singapore so the roti with curry sauce was a trip down memory lane!" – this "crazy busy" basement dive near Euston serves a "good representation of Malaysian kopitiam (coffee shop)/hawker cuisine". "The large number of SE Asian students" and "bargain

prices" result in "significant queues and the need to share the tightly packed tables" – which is "annoying… until the food arrives and all is forgiven!" / NW1 1LH; www.rotiking.in; 10.30 pm; closed Sun; no booking.

ROTORINO E8 £49 2|4|3

434 KINGSLAND RD 020 7249 9081 14–1A

Inspired by southern Italy, Stevie Parle's slick-looking venue is still capable of producing hit dishes ("gnudi worth the trip to Dalston") but a couple of poor reports this year makes it hard to give it an unqualified recommendation. / E8 4AA; www.rotorino.com; @Rotorino; 11 pm, Sun 9 pm.

ROTUNDA BAR & RESTAURANT, KINGS PLACE N1 £55 3|3|4

90 YORK WAY 020 7014 2840 9–3C

A wonderful waterside location, and "smart and buzzy" interior place this canalside dining room very much at the upper end of your typical arts centre venue, as does its 'farm to fork' ethos, with meat sourced from its own Northumberland farm. Results here – generally good – can sometimes be "run of the mill", but may see a boost from a significant summer 2018 refurb to mark its 10th year. Changes include an open-to-view kitchen (relocated from the lower level of the building), a large meat-ageing cabinet, and chef's counter heaters, enabling the terrace to be used all year round. / N1 9AG; www.rotundabarandrestaurant.co.uk; @rotundalondon; 11 pm; closed Sun.

ROUX AT PARLIAMENT SQUARE, RICS SW1 £91 5|4|3

12 GREAT GEORGE ST 020 7334 3737 2–3C

"The food is executed with such skill" at this "superb" Roux-branded operation – "a calm haven away from the Parliament Square traffic", which shines all the brighter "in the culinary wastelands of Westminster". "Warm and comforting decor from the recent revamp" softens the "very 'establishment'" decor, while service "strikes the perfect balance between being polite and informative, but willing to have a laugh". Top Tip – "at £40, the set lunch may sound expensive but this is top-class cuisine at a reasonable price" / SW1P 3AD; www.rouxatparliamentsquare.co.uk; @RouxAPS; Mon-Fri 9 pm; closed Sat & Sun; No trainers.

ROUX AT THE LANDAU, THE LANGHAM W1 £92 4|4|4

1C PORTLAND PL 020 7965 0165 2–1B

"All round 10/10!" – The re-launched Roux-branded operation in this "elegant" and "beautiful" dining room, a stone's throw from Broadcasting House, jumped up several gears this year, as a lift in ratings coincided with its February 2018 re-launch in a new more "relaxed and simple" guise, incorporating a new, central dining counter and adopting a luxurious, 'no-tablecloths' style. "Not one thing is amiss" when it comes to the "exceptional" modern French cuisine (which now takes a more ingredient-led approach), service is exemplary, and the overall experience is "one of pure indulgence" (especially for a romantic occasion). / W1B 1JA; www.rouxatthelandau.com; @Langham_Hotel; 10.30 pm, Sun 11.30 am; closed Sun D, closed Mon; No trainers.

ROVI W1 £63

59-65 WELLS ST   020 3963 8270   3–1D

This light and bright July 2018 opening from Yotam Ottolenghi is, er, Ottolenghi-like in its culinary character: that is to say, firmly rooted in eastern Mediterranean cuisine; but here with a spin that's even more veg-centred, and also now with a focus on fermentation and cooking over fire. The eco-friendly, waste-reducing, Fitzrovia site is initially open for lunch and dinner, but breakfast will follow. / W1A 3AE; www.ottolenghi.co.uk/rovi; @rovi_restaurant; 10.15 pm, Sun 3.30 pm; closed Sun D.

ROWLEY'S SW1 £74 2️⃣2️⃣2️⃣

113 JERMYN ST   020 7930 2707   4–4D

A St James's veteran from 1976, this British steakhouse inhabits some of the early premises of the Wall's meat empire (on this site from 1836). Results here have been perennially uneven over the years, and not even the promise of unlimited fries (which accompany items like entrecôte and Chateaubriand) stopped some meals this year from seeming disappointing or overpriced. / SW1Y 6HJ; www.rowleys.co.uk; @Rowleys_steak; 10.30 pm.

ROX BURGER SE13 £28 4️⃣3️⃣3️⃣

82 LEE HIGH RD   020 3372 4631   1–4D

"A great choices of amazing, fresh burgers" plus a selection of craft beers make it worth discovering this "very casual" Lewisham venture; "it's pretty small but they also do take away." / SE13 5PT; www.roxburger.com; @RoxburgerUK; 10 pm; closed Mon-Fri L.

ROYAL CHINA £56 3️⃣1️⃣2️⃣

24-26 BAKER ST, W1   020 7487 4688   2–1A | 805 FULHAM RD, SW6   020 7731 0081 11–1B | 13 QUEENSWAY, W2 020 7221 2535   7–2C | 30 WESTFERRY CIRCUS, E14   020 7719 0888   12–1B

"The only reason you would go to for the sooooo very yummy dim sum" nowadays, say loyal fans of this "super-busy and slightly chaotic" Cantonese chain, with its hallmark black-and-gold, lacquered decor. It "remains the benchmark" for many Londoners, but the "brisk (read brusque) service" seems increasingly "careless (my food arrived cold)" and the "very dated and fairly grotty environment" seems ever-more "tired". The "cavernous" Bayswater branch is best – but "you can't book at weekends, so it's first-come-first-served chaos with families and buggies". / www.royalchinagroup.co.uk; 11 pm, Sun 10 pm; W1 Fri & Sat 11.30 pm; no booking Sat & Sun L.

ROYAL CHINA CLUB W1 £68 4️⃣2️⃣2️⃣

38-42 BAKER ST   020 7486 3898   2–1A

The flagship of what many consider "the best Chinese restaurant group in London" – the China Club HQ offers "luxury twists on traditional dishes", results in "superb food, whether it's dim sum for brunch or seafood and classic Cantonese in the evening". It reopened in early August 2018 after a four-month refurb and expansion into the adjacent corner site – hopefully this will please reporters who had recommended "a facelift" (the rating above is for the former decor). / W1U 7AJ; www.royalchinagroup.co.uk; @RoyalChinaGroup; 1 am, Sun midnight; booking weekdays only.

RUCOLETTA EC2 £48 3️⃣2️⃣1️⃣

6 FOSTER LANE   020 7600 7776   10–2B

This "hidden gem" in a backstreet near St Paul's is an "old school", "cheap 'n' cheerful" Italian serving mama's cooking in the City. "The basic premises are quite crowded, but the simple food's excellent." / EC2V 6HH; www.rucoletta.co.uk; @RucolettaLondon; 9.30 pm, Thu & Fri 10 pm; closed Sat D & Sun; no Amex.

RUGOLETTA £53 3️⃣3️⃣2️⃣

308 BALLARDS LN, N12   020 8445 6742 1–1B | 59 CHURCH LN, N2   020 8815 1743 1–1B

These "excellent, cheap and reliable family Italians" in Barnet and East Finchley are popular in the area – so you "must book Friday and Saturday evenings". They are "cramped", but "don't seem to mind noisy children". / www.la-rugoletta.com; 10.30 pm; N12 Fri & Sat 11 pm; N2 closed Sun.

RULES WC2 £78 2️⃣3️⃣5️⃣

35 MAIDEN LN   020 7836 5314   5–3D

"Like stepping into a time warp" – London's oldest restaurant (in these Covent Garden premises since 1798) is a magnificent period piece, complete with a gorgeous panelled interior. Inevitably it's "very touristy", although many Londoners also harbour a very soft spot for the old place. That said, its "old-school British cooking" has been better in living memory and many reporters continue to find "prices are high for rather indifferent food": "our American friends were happy, but we were not impressed and the steak 'n' kidney pudding was not as good as we remembered!" Top Tip – "unbeatable game in season". / WC2E 7LB; www.rules.co.uk; 11.30 pm, Sun 10.30 pm; No shorts.

RUYA W1

30 UPPER GROSVENOR ST   020 3848 6710 3–3A

On swanky Park Lane, this June 2018 debut is another example of the growing number of Middle East-based restaurant empires (here Dubai) opening in prime London sites. Restaurateur Umut Özkanca and chef Colin Clague promise a fine dining take on Middle Eastern food with a nod to Özkanca's native Turkey. / W1K 7PH; ruyalondon.com; Mon & Tue

Sabor W1

9 pm, Fri & Sat 11.30 pm, Wed 10 pm, Thu 11 pm, Sun 5 pm.

SABOR W1 £60 4️⃣4️⃣4️⃣

35 HEDDON ST   020 3319 8130   4–3A

Ex-Barrafina executive head chef, Nieves Barragán Mohacho, and José Etura's yearling off Regent's Street, comprises both a downstairs floor with tapas counter and a "wonderfully buzzy" upstairs room with shared tables, which revolves around the open kitchen's asador (wood-fired oven). Both come recommended, with reporters "blown away" by the "delightful service", "outstanding" food and upstairs the "fabulous experience of cooking right in front of your eyes". But, while fans predictably say "move over Barrafina", ratings have a way to go yet to rival their former employer. Top Menu Tip – "finally, suckling pig just like you get in Spain" from the asador. / W1B 4BP; www.saborrestaurants.co.uk; @sabor_ldn; 10.30 pm, Sun 6 pm; closed Mon.

LE SACRÉ-COEUR N1 £42 2️⃣3️⃣3️⃣

18 THEBERTON ST   020 7354 2618   9–3A

"You could almost be in Paris" at this "astonishingly good-value bistro" off Upper Street – "quite the Islington institution". It has a "wide menu at an attractive fixed price, served by jolly staff who are very well led". / N1 0QX; www.lesacrecoeur.co.uk; @LeSacreCoeurUK; Sun-Thu 10.30 pm, Fri & Sat 11.30 pm.

SACRO CUORE £38 5️⃣3️⃣2️⃣

10 CROUCH END HILL, N8   020 8348 8487 1–1C | 45 CHAMBERLAYNE RD, NW10 020 8960 8558   1–2B

"The best pizza outside Italy!" (their authentic Neapolitan-style bases are "to die for") is more than enough to inspire rave reviews for this north London pair, which serve nothing else beyond a few starters and desserts. Kensal Rise came first but it could well be the case that "the Crouch End branch is even better than the original!". / www.sacrocuore.co.uk; @SacroCuorePizza.

SAGAR £36 4 3 2

**17A PERCY ST, W1 020 7631 3319 3–1D
| 31 CATHERINE ST, WC2 020 7836 6377
5–3D | 157 KING ST, W6 020 8741 8563
8–2C**

"Delicious, well-spiced, memorable" – "and really cheap!" – South Indian vegetarian food ("with most dishes also available as vegan") wins high ratings for this well-established small chain of low-key cafés, located in Covent Garden, Tottenham Court Road and Hammersmith (plus an outpost in Harrow). / www.sagarveg.co.uk; W1 10.45 pm-11pm, Sun 10 pm.

SAGARDI EC2 £70 2 3 3

**CORDY HOUSE, 95 CURTAIN RD
020 3802 0478 13–1B**

"A bit pricey but worth the splurge", say fans of this "relaxed" Basque pintxos bar and charcoal grill in Shoreditch, who praise the "fantastic, beautifully cooked" dishes (the speciality is Galician Txuleton beef). No matter the quality, others just can't get their head around the bill here: "it would have been a fine meal, but we were sold a steak that was really overpriced by a factor of 2x". / EC2A 3AH; www.sagardi.co.uk; @Sagardi_UK; 11 pm.

SAGER + WILDE £60 2 2 3

**193 HACKNEY RD, E2 020 8127 7330
14–2A | 250 PARADISE ROW, E2
020 7613 0478 14–2B**

Hackney oenophiles make a beeline for these this ambitious pair – "I love the wine list!". The Paradise Row venue, in a railway arch with a large terrace, features an Italian menu, while the Hackney Road wine bar serves snacks and charcuterie. In either case the food avoids criticism, but the liquid refreshment is the main event. /

SAIGON SAIGON
W6 £36 2 3 3

313-317 KING ST 020 8748 6887 8–2B

"Always packed", this well-established Hammersmith Vietnamese is "all round OK" at "a great price" (if arguably "nothing to get overly excited about"). There's an "extensive menu" and the "comforting and deeply flavoured pho" is always a good bet. / W6 9NH; www.saigon-saigon.co.uk; @saigonsaigonuk; 11 pm, Sun 10 pm.

ST JOHN BREAD & WINE
E1 £66 3 3 3

**94-96 COMMERCIAL ST 020 7251 0848
13–2C**

"You can't beat a great bacon sarnie and a range of other delicious breakfast specials" at this long-established spin-off from Smithfield's St John, near Spitalfields Market. At other times this utilitarian canteen serves its "very good, if sometimes overly quirky" offal-centric British menu alongside a "wine list full of vintages you've never heard of, but which are always enjoyable". / E1 6LZ; www.stjohngroup.uk.com/spitalfields; @sjrestaurant; Sun & Mon 10 pm, Tue-Sat 11 pm.

ST JOHN SMITHFIELD
EC1 £67 5 4 3

26 ST JOHN ST 020 7251 0848 10–1B

"Still managing to excel itself on a regular basis" – Trevor Gulliver and Fergus Henderson's white-walled temple near Smithfield Market coined the concept of 'nose-to-tail' eating with its "incredibly stimulating menu" featuring "all sorts of offal and cuts of meat not usually available elsewhere"; and there's "still nothing quite like it" after over two decades in operation. "Friendly and efficient service helps soften the austere interior" and, "if you want honest, seasonal British food with soul and heart", arguably "there is no better place". "We recently ate bone marrow, tripe, and pig's tongue, then watched longingly as a grouse pie was delivered to a neighbouring table." "Splendid wine" too. Top Tip – the bar and its simpler menu is a good way to dip your toe in the water. / EC1M 4AY; stjohnrestaurant.com/a/restaurants/smithfield; @SJRestaurant; 11 pm, Sun 4 pm; closed Sat L closed Sun D.

ST JOHNS N19 £55 3 4 5

91 JUNCTION RD 020 7272 1587 9–1C

"Still the top gastropub for miles around" – this Archway boozer is a "brilliant" spot throughout, both in the characterful bar, but particularly in the "spacious" and extremely atmospheric rear dining room (originally built as a ballroom). On the menu – "excellent" modern British food, provided by staff who are "cheerful even when rushed off their feet". / N19 5QU; www.stjohnstavern.com; @stjohnstavern; 10.30 pm, Sun 9.30 pm; Mon-Thu D only, Fri-Sun open L & D; no Amex; booking max 12 may apply.

ST MORITZ W1 £55 3 3 4

161 WARDOUR ST 020 7734 3324 4–1C

"Like being transported to Switzerland for the evening!" – this "unique" chalet-style, Swiss-themed "institution" in Soho may sound too kitsch to be taken seriously, but scores have been consistently strong here over many years: "the fondues are amazing", and the overall effect on a cold winter's night is "heavenly". / W1F 8WJ; www.stmoritz-restaurant.co.uk; Mon-Thu 11.30 pm, Fri & Sat midnight, Sun 10.30 pm.

SAKAGURA W1 £53 3 4 2

8 HEDDON ST 020 3405 7230 4–3B

An "enjoyable take on Japanese" – this 'steak and sake bar' in the Heddon Street foodie enclave off Regent Street invites customers to 'cook their own' meat (including "excellent wagyu beef"), fish and vegetables over a table-top BBQ or hot lava stone. There are also "exceptional sake choices", along with sake cocktails, shochu and Japanese craft beers. From the team behind Shoryu Ramen and the Japan Centre. / W1B 4BU; www.sakaguralondon.com; @sakaguraldn; Mon-Wed 11 pm, Thu-Sat midnight; closed Sun.

SAKE NO HANA
SW1 £78 3 3 3

23 ST JAMES'S ST 020 7925 8988 3–4D

Set in a very 1960s Modernist building next to The Economist, this ambitious Japanese in St James's is part of the all-conquering Hakkasan Group, but its up-and-down performance over the years means it's never achieved the high profile of its siblings. This said, "the food has moved up a level" in the last couple of years, and the place is nowadays achieving consistently good ratings all round. / SW1A 1HA; www.sakenohana.com; @sakenohana; Mon-Thu 11 pm, Fri & Sat 11.30 pm; closed Sun.

SAKONIS £28 3 2 1

**127-129 EALING RD, HA0 020 8903 9601
1–1A | 330 UXBRIDGE RD, HA5
020 8903 9601 1–1A**

"Probably the best-value buffet in London" (served through breakfast and lunch) draws fans of veggie Indian fare from far and wide to this mainstay of Wembley's Ealing Road (which at other times sells a less taste-foodish menu incorporating street food, pizza and Indo-Chinese dishes). There's also been a sibling in Hatch End since September 2017. /

SALAAM NAMASTE
WC1 £46 3 2 2

68 MILLMAN ST 020 7405 3697 2–1D

It's worth remembering this central but affordable Bloomsbury Indian – 'specialising in modern and healthy cooking' – which scores consistently solid all-round ratings. / WC1N 3EF; www.salaam-namaste.co.uk; @SalaamNamasteUK; Tue-Thu 3 pm, Fri-Sun 11 pm.

SALE E PEPE
SW1 £67 3 2 3

9-15 PAVILION RD 020 7235 0098 6–1D

Age-old trattoria near Harrods and Harvey Nichols that's "lots of fun" to a crowd who, in some cases, have been coming for decades. Don't let the "dated interior" put you off – the cuisine can be of a "very high standard". / SW1X 0HD; www.saleepepe.co.uk; @salepepe_it.

SALLOOS SW1 £67 3 2 2

62-64 KINNERTON ST 020 7235 4444 6–1D

"Very good, very authentic home-cooked Pakistani food" sums up the appeal of this veteran, tucked away in a Belgravia mews. It has always been "expensive", as might be deduced from its location a short stroll from Knightsbridge. Top Tip – legendary lamb chops. / SW1X 8ER; www.salloos.co.uk; 11 pm; closed Mon-Sat & Sun; may need 5+ to book.

SALON BRIXTON
SW9 £56 5 4 3

18 MARKET ROW 020 7501 9152 11–2D

"Capable and unshowy modern British cooking, using all sorts of influences" (plus de rigeur pickling and preserving) from a "very seasonal", if "limited" menu scores the highest praise for Nicholas Balfe's "fun" and "buzzy" fixture in Brixton Market – "one of those places where you want to eat everything on the menu" and with "a (mostly natural) wine list that's interesting, too". Top Tip: "superb vegetarian dishes". Balfe and his team are opening a bistro, Levan, in Peckham in October 2018. / SW9 8LD; www.salonbrixton.co.uk; @Salon_Brixton; 9.15 pm.

LE SALON PRIVÉ TW1 £52 343

43 CROWN RD 020 8892 0602 1–4A

Notably smart with its white tablecloths and stained-glass windows, this three-year-old St Margarets bistro is a hit with local diners for its "beautifully prepared" French classics, "friendly service and good ambience". "The new vegetarian menu is a definite winner", and for rugby fans, it's "ideal when going to Twickers!". / TW1 3EJ; lesalonprive.net; @lesalon_tweet; 11 pm, Sun 10 pm.

SALT YARD W1 £52 433

54 GOODGE ST 020 7637 0657 2–1B

"Delights such as octopus with saffron mayo" are amongst the "very appealing small plates", inspired by Spain and Italy, that put Simon Mullins's "friendly and informal" bar in Fitzrovia at the vanguard of London's "upmarket tapas" trend. Even if it no longer makes culinary waves as it did, ratings are back to a five-year high this year. Any complaints? – as ever, it's "cramped and crowded". / W1T 4NA; www.saltyard.co.uk; @SaltYardGroup; Sun-Thu 10.30 pm, Sat, Fri 11 pm; ; booking max 8 may apply.

SALUT N1 £69 322

412 ESSEX RD 020 3441 8808 9–3D

"Beautifully presented, interesting and well-cooked" modern dishes of a high level of ambition justify the trip to this Canonbury two-year-old at the 'wrong' end of the Essex Road. But it loses some points for "close tables", "small portions" and "high prices given the location". / N1 3PJ; www.salut-london.co.uk; @Salut_London; Tue-Sun 11 pm; closed Tue-Thu L, closed Mon.

SAM'S RIVERSIDE, RIVERSIDE STUDIOS W6

101 QUEEN CAROLINE ST AWAITING TEL 8–2C

Restaurateur Sam Harrison – who owned neighbourhood favourites Sam's Brasserie in Chiswick and Harrison's in Balham, until both sites were sold to Foxlow in 2015 – has announced plans to open a new restaurant and bar in February 2019 as part of the rebuilt Riverside Studios. Facing the Thames with views of Hammersmith Bridge, the all-day, 90-cover brasserie will have an outdoor terrace and private dining room, and will provide W6 with a long-needed cheaper alternative to another river café five minutes walk away… / W6 9BN; www.samsriversidelondon.com; @samsriversideW6.

SAN CARLO SW1 £64

2 REGENT STREET SAINT JAMES'S 020 3778 0768 4–4D

The glam San Carlo group's latest London fixture – and the first to carry the main brand rather than the less formal 'Cicchetti' name – is a large, 130-cover operation (most recently Norte, RIP) which opened in May 2018 on the lower half of Regent Street, plushly decked out with lots of linen, leather, marble and panelling. / SW1Y 4AU; sancarlo.co.uk/restaurants/san-carlo-london; @SanCarlo_Group.

SAN CARLO CICCHETTI £59 334

215 PICCADILLY, W1 020 7494 9435 4–4C | 30 WELLINGTON ST, WC2 020 7240 6339 5–3D

"Glitzy interiors (and customers!)" are a hallmark of these "fun and buzzy" Venetian brasseries (part of an increasingly sizeable national chain, based in Manchester). Although the locations are "a little touristic" – particularly the large branch near Piccadilly Circus – the "feel is genuinely North Italian", the food is "good for the price" , service is "warm" and "the overall experience is very good". / www.sancarlocicchetti.co.uk; @SanCarlo_Group; W1 11.30 pm; WC2 midnight; M1 11 pm, Sun 10 pm.

SAN PIETRO W8 £50 333

7 STRATFORD RD 020 7938 1805 6–1A

"A good addition to the area" – this Italian newcomer has adopted the tucked-away Kensington mews site that was for ages Chez Patrick (RIP), and although "they've spent a fortune on doing it up" bears some comparison to its predecessor: it's still "rather cramped" ("they generally seat you upstairs nowadays"); and the food (majoring in fish and pizza like its sibling Portobello Ristorante) is "good but a little pricey". / W8 6RF; www.san-pietro.co.uk; Mon & Tue 9 pm, Fri & Sat 11.30 pm, Wed 10 pm, Thu 11 pm, Sun 5 pm.

THE SANDS END SW6 £54 334

135 STEPHENDALE RD 020 7731 7823 11–1B

Prince Harry brought Meghan Markle for lunch before their engagement to this backstreet Fulham gastroboozer owned by one of his pals: a "great local spot", which fans say is "fantastically hospitable" and with consistently highly rated nosh too. / SW6 2PR; www.thesandsend.co.uk; @thesandsend; 11 pm.

SANTA MARIA £41 432

160 NEW CAVENDISH ST, W1 020 7436 9963 2–1B NEW | 92-94 WATERFORD RD, SW6 020 7384 2844 6–4A | 15 ST MARY'S RD, W5 020 8579 1462 1–3A

"The best pizza in London" is a claim that's regularly made for the "tight on space, and always crowded" Ealing original of this small group (which "has expanded into the Red Lion pub next door") – "the ingredients are painstakingly sourced and the attention to detail on the dough is second to none!" With the chain expanding constantly, however (they've just opened in Fitzrovia), overall marks support those who feel "the pizzas are good… perhaps not as good as the reputation". / www.santamariapizzeria.com; @SantaMariaPizza.

SANTA MARIA DEL SUR SW8 £54 343

129 QUEENSTOWN RD 020 7622 2088 11–1C

"One of best steaks I've had in London", reports a satisfied customer of this "off the beaten track" Argentinian steakhouse with a strong following down Battersea way. There's also a list of exclusively South American wines. / SW8 3RH; www.santamariadelsur.co.uk; @StaMariadelSur; 11 pm.

SANTINI SW1 £82 222

29 EBURY ST 020 7730 4094 2–4B

Frank Sinatra was among the notables who flocked to this sleek Belgravia Italian in its 80s heyday. Nowadays run by the founder Gino's daughter Laura, It still delivers an "imaginative menu" with Venetian specialities, a "pleasant atmosphere" and "good service", but even diehard supporters complain that it's "pricey" and sceptics say it's "gone over the hill". / SW1W 0NZ; www.santini-restaurant.com; @santinirest; 10.45 pm.

SANTO REMEDIO SE1 £63 323

152 TOOLEY ST 020 7403 3021 10–4D

"More-ish small Mexican dishes" feature at this hip new Bermondsey street food venture founded by Edson Diaz-Fuentes (ex-Wahaca) and his wife Natalie after a Kickstarter campaign (their shortlived Shoreditch site closed in 2016 after property problems). Early reports are promising: "if you enjoy Mexican food, this is the place to come". Top Tip: "hot guacamole with crickets was interesting and delicious". / SE1 2TU; www.santoremedio.co.uk; @santoremediouk; 10.30 pm; closed Sun.

SANTORE EC1 £51 332

59-61 EXMOUTH MKT 020 7812 1488 10–1A

"An antidote to Mediterranean chain restaurants", this "quite noisy" family-run Neapolitan in Exmouth Market excels for "the consistent quality of the pizzas". "We're not talking haute cuisine – just simple food, well done". Top Tip: "Try the half-and-half pizza/calzone for something a bit different and very tasty". / EC1R 4QL; www.santorerestaurant.london; @Santore_london; 10 pm.

SANXIA RENJIA £37 332

29 GOODGE ST, W1 020 7636 5886 2–1B | 36 DEPTFORD BROADWAY, SE8 020 8692 9633 1–3D

"If you can get over the location, the food is wonderful" say fans of this Chinese in "up-and-coming Deptford", blessed this year with an admiring review of its fiery Sichuanese cooking by critic Jay Rayner. But while generally upbeat, reporters don't go quite so overboard as The Observer's man did (and the sole reporter who tried its Goodge Street sibling was least impressed of all: "I was looking forward to hot, numbing food but what came out was bland and under-seasoned, even if the staff were friendly and decor, etc was fine"). /

SAPLING E8 £55
378 KINGSLAND RD 020 7870 1259 14–2A

A new wine-focused restaurant and larder on Dalston's main drag from restaurateur Bob Ritchie and sommelier Dan Whine (ace name for a sommelier, huh?). The weekly changing list of around 36 wines, including a number of grower Champagnes and other notable sparkling wines, is sustainable, organic, biodynamic or low-intervention, available by the glass and complemented by food from chef Jon Beeharry. Too little feedback for a rating as yet, but one early report says it's all-round brilliant (as does the Evening Standard's David Sexton). / E8 4AA; www.sapling-dalston.com; @saplingdalston; Mon-Fri 10 pm, Sat & Sun 9 pm.

SAPONARA N1 £27 [4][3][3]
23 PREBEND ST 020 7226 2771 9–3D

"Tucked away off Upper Street", this genuine "small" deli/restaurant "has 'Italy' sprayed all over it" – "a busy and popular" spot, featuring "lots of regional ingredients", and with "great fresh pasta" and "consistently fantastic pizza you can take away, too". / N1 8PF; saponarapizzeria.co.uk; Wed-Sat 10 pm, Tue 4.30 pm; closed Tue D, closed Sun & Mon.

SAPORI SARDI SW6 £56 [3][3][2]
786 FULHAM RD 020 7731 0755 11–1B

"Simple, well-prepared dishes" and "a real Sardinian feel" continue to inspire the small but enthusiastic fan club of this neighbourhood Italian in Fulham. / SW6 5SL; www.saporisardi.co; @saporisardi; 10.30 pm, Sun 9.30 pm; no Amex.

SARAVANAA BHAVAN HA0 £41 [4][3][2]
531-533 HIGH RD 020 8900 8526 1–1A

A "huge range of exceptional dosas" are the highlight of the menu at this Wembley branch of a South Indian-based veggie chain, billed as the world's biggest. "Great value" too, but note – "it's aimed at Indians, so not Anglo curry". / HA0 2DJ; ww12.saravanabhavanuk.com; Sun-Thu 10.30 pm, Fri & Sat 11 pm.

SARDINE N1 £58 [4][4][3]
15 MICAWBER ST 020 7490 0144 13–1A

Aptly named, this "small but perfectly formed" two-year-old, near Old Street station, is a "real find" on account of ex-Rotorino chef, Alex Jackson's, very accomplished southern French-inspired cooking – "thoughtful, without being over-prepared and foam-ridden". "Intriguing

wine list", too. / N1 7TB; www.sardine.london; @sardinelondon; 10 pm.

SARGEANTS MESS EC3 £56
TOWER OF LONDON 020 3166 6949 10–3D

Mark Sargeant's starry name helped draw attention to this May 2018 opening under Tower Bridge, with an outside terrace looking onto the wall of the Tower of London (a venture between caterers CH&Co and Historic Royal Palaces). Stylewise, the menu seems somewhat 'wrapped up in the Union Jack' – e.g. cod 'n' chips, toad in the hole, treacle tart – but early press and online reviews suggest an all-too-traditional rendering of our nation's culinary classics. / EC3N 4AB; www.sargeantsmess.com; @SargeantsMess.

SARRACINO NW6 £43 [3][3][2]
186 BROADHURST GDNS 020 7372 5889 1–1B

"Good pizzas" are the top recommendation at this "cheap 'n' cheerful" West Hampstead stalwart trattoria of long standing. / NW6 3AY; www.sarracinorestaurant.com; closed weekday L.

SARTORIA W1 £77 [3][3][3]
20 SAVILE ROW 020 7534 7000 4–3A

"Ideal for a business lunch" – D&D London's "large" and posh Italian (overseen by Francesco Mazzei) is widely seen as "a safe bet", with its combination of "well-spread-out tables", "rather formal service" and "a reliable, good quality of food". The flipside of this assessment, however, is that it can also seem "very Mayfair but nothing special" and "overpriced for what it delivers". / W1S 3PR; www.sartoria-restaurant.co.uk; @SartoriaRest; 11 pm; closed Sat L & Sun.

SAVOIR FAIRE WC1 £47 [3][4][2]
42 NEW OXFORD ST 020 7436 0707 5–1C

"Don't be put off by the funny looks" of this muralled, Gallic corner bistro (family run on this site since 1995) – "it's really good" if you're looking for a good-value meal in the environs of the British Museum. / WC1A 1EP; www.savoir.co.uk; 10.30 pm.

THE SAVOY HOTEL, SAVOY GRILL WC2 £101 [2][2][2]
STRAND 020 7592 1600 5–3D

For decades, this "atmospheric" and "impressive", "panelled chamber" just off the foyer of The Strand's famous Art Deco landmark was London's power dining scene par excellence; and with its "old-fashioned" style and menu of "solid, traditional British staples" it remains a strong business favourite to this day. Under Gordon Ramsay's management of the last 15 years, however, its performance has always been up-and-down, and this year's was one of the weakest yet, with complaints about "average food" that's "not good value for money" and a "dingy" overall ambience. /

WC2R 0EU; www.gordonramsayrestaurants.com; @savoygrill; midnight, Sun 11 pm.

THE SAVOY HOTEL, THAMES FOYER WC2 £97 [2][3][4]
THE SAVOY, THE STRAND 020 7420 2111 5–3D

For an "excellent tea in beautiful, opulent surroundings", this landmark hotel's "peaceful" lounge (set beneath a glass dome, and complete with pianist) is a "super location" providing a "classic" experience. We have no accounts of a full meal here (but prices on the all-day menu seem a tad fierce: e.g. £21 for a club sandwich with fries). / WC2R \N; www.fairmont.com/savoy-london; @fairmonthotels; 11 pm.

SCALINI SW3 £86 [3][3][3]
1-3 WALTON ST 020 7225 2301 6–2C

"If you're looking for a rock-solid, traditional Italian restaurant, then look no further", say devotees of this "loud but great fun" outfit, just "a stone's throw from Harrods". There's a "fabulous atmosphere" and the menu, which is "just what you would expect", is "executed with complete assurance". / SW3 2JD; www.scalinilondon.co.uk; 11 pm; No shorts.

SCARLETT GREEN W1 £62
4 NOEL ST 020 7723 3301 4–1C

A new opening spot from The Daisy Green Collection (Daisy Green, Timmy Green, Beans Green) on the former site of Timberyard in Soho, serving bottomless brunch and an extensive Aussie wine list. It opened in late May 2018 after the conclusion of our survey. / W1F 8JB; www.daisygreenfood.com; @daisygreenfood; midnight, Sun 10.30 pm.

SCHMALTZ TRUCK EC2 £10 [5][3][3]
EXCHANGE SQUARE NO TEL 13–2B

"An unmissable food experience in Broadgate" – this "amazingly decorated", "state-of-the-art" food truck (complete with funky floral design) offers "restaurant-grade, stylish fast food" from "a high-quality, all-chicken menu of sandwiches (using a whole breast), soups and a burger". It's "exceptional value" and "the execution of the concept is outstanding": rolls are made teardrop-shaped, better to fit the chicken breasts. The birds themselves are all French Label Rouge, and seared and roasted with the skin on. / EC2M 2QA; www.schmaltzlondon.com; @schmaltzlondon; closed Mon-Fri D, closed Sat & Sun.

SCOTT'S W1 £85 [4][4][5]
20 MOUNT ST 020 7495 7309 3–3A

"You feel like you are 'somebody' on walking in, and the gloss stays with you for a while after you leave" at Richard Caring's "legendary" Mayfair veteran (007's favourite lunch spot), whose "classically elegant" interior "oozes class", and where "every table looks like they're famous". On the menu – "sensational", "classic fish dishes" and "some of the best seafood in London" – indeed, only Sheekey's keeps it from being voted London's best in that department (although, unlike its stablemate, here "tables are far enough apart for business"). All this "glam, glam, glam" comes with a slight edge, though: in particular, the "very professional" service "can come with an attitude that matches the A-list clientele". / W1K 2HE; www.scotts-restaurant.com; 10.30 pm, Sun 10 pm; booking max 6 may apply.

SCULLY SW1 £62 **5 5 3**

SAINT JAMES'S MARKET   020 3911 6840
4–4D

"A breath of fresh air in the stuffy world of gastronomic London" – this stupendous first solo venture from former Nopi head chef Ramael Scully opened in St James's Market in early 2018, creating 'out there' fusion fare which reflects his heritage… which is Chinese/Indian/Irish/Balinese! He's assembled "a joyful, creative team of people who care and love food" and results are "exceptional in every sense": "innovative food that's a simple and pure joy" and "staff who make a visit a very special occasion". / SW1Y 4QU; www.scullyrestaurant.com; @scully_ldn; Tue-Thu 8.30 pm, Fri 9 pm, Sat 9.30 pm, Sun 7 pm.

SEA CONTAINERS, MONDRIAN LONDON SE1 £69 **1 2 2**

20 UPPER GROUND   020 3747 1063   10–3A

"Way overpriced" – this "noisy" nautical-themed dining room on the South Bank near Blackfriars Bridge has "amazing views of the river" (if from ground-floor level) but the "silly, confusing menu" of sharing plates is simply "not appropriate for a high-end hotel". The "bottomless fizz" and "burgers-and-brunch catering that masquerades as dining" are clues that it's "probably focused on the tourist wallet". / SE1 9PD; www.seacontainersrestaurant.com; @MondrianLDN; 11 pm.

SEA GARDEN & GRILL SW17 £40 **4 4 4**

BROADWAY MARKET, 29 TOOTING HIGH ST
020 8682 2995   11–2C

"Fabulous new fish restaurant in Tooting Market" with a "delicious and fresh" selection of seafood dishes, run with charm by antiques dealer, Jimmy Luttman. The set-up is very similar to that at Plot (see also) – you eat at communal tables in the covered market, or at the counter with open kitchen beyond. / SW17 0RJ; www.seagardenandgrill.co.uk; @theseagardenuk; Tue-Thu 10 pm, Fri & Sat 11 pm; closed Tue-Fri L, closed Sun & Mon.

SEAFRESH SW1 £50 **3 2 2**

80-81 WILTON RD   020 7828 0747   2–4B

This veteran Pimlico fish restaurant is "always reliable and satisfying". There are few frills, but it has "become much more upmarket" with "delicious grilled fish" – "although the set menu haddock or cod and chips remains popular",

"especially with taxi drivers". "The main problem is getting a table – it's so popular with large parties of visiting tourists." / SW1V 1DL; www.seafresh-dining.com; @SeafreshLondon; 10.30 pm; closed Sun.

SEARCYS ST PANCRAS GRAND NW1 £57 **2 1 3**

THE CONCOURSE   020 7870 9900   9–3C

The "beautiful Art Deco setting" of this modern railway dining room raises expectations which are all too often "disappointed" by the meal. There's a real sense of an opportunity missed, with Searcys' performance and "poor service" too reminiscent of the bad old days of British Rail. / NW1 2QP; www.searcys.co.uk; @SearcyStPancras; 10 pm, Sun 7.15 pm.

THE SEA SHELL NW1 £55 **3 2 2**

49 LISSON GROVE   020 7224 9000   9–4A

"An institution for decades" – this famous "fish and chippery" in Lisson Grove traces its origins back almost a century and took its current name in 1964 (but don't go expecting period decor – the interior's not unpleasant, but anodyne). "Eat in or take away, generous portions and freshly cooked". / NW1 6UH; www.seashellrestaurant.co.uk; @SeashellRestaur; 10.30 pm; closed Sun.

SEASON KITCHEN N4 £49 **3 3 2**

53 STROUD GREEN RD   020 7263 5500
9–1D

"Superlative seasonal veg" but also "great steaks" top the bill at this Finsbury Park fixture. There's a "small, changing menu" of "interesting dishes", many of which you can order in either 'starter' or 'main-course' size, and "you just know they have a passion for fine cooking". / N4 3EF; www.seasonkitchen.co.uk; @seasonkitchen; Sun-Thu 10 pm, Fri & Sat 10.30 pm; D only.

SEN VIET WC1 £20 **4 3 2**

119 KING'S CROSS RD   020 7278 2881
9–3D

"Good food in a bit of a culinary desert" makes it worth knowing about this "useful Vietnamese pit-stop" in the thinly provided southern fringes of King's Cross, which offers "freshly cooked, decent spicing and excellent value for money". / WC1X 9NH; senviet.uk; 11 pm.

SEÑOR CEVICHE W1 £51 **3 3 3**

KINGLY CT   020 7842 8540   4–2B

An "interesting attempt at Peruvian food" in Soho's thronging Kingly Court that's consistently well-rated. It's a lively spot too, if "cramped and extremely noisy". / W1B 5PW; www.senor-ceviche.com; @SenorCevicheLDN; 11 pm, Sun 10 pm; booking max 6 may apply.

SERGE ET LE PHOQUE W1 £38 **2 3 3**

THE MANDRAKE HOTEL, 20-21 NEWMAN ST
020 3146 8880   3–1D

There's a stark contrast between the vast number of newspaper column inches generated by Charles Pelletier and Frédéric Peneau's dining room, in this year-old Fitzrovia boutique-hotel dining room (whose Hong Kong sibling has a Michelin star) and the low level of reporter interest it inspires. Moreover, such feedback as we have is very mixed. / W1T 1PG; www.themandrake.com; Tue-Fri 10.30 pm, Sun & Mon ; closed Sun & Mon D, closed Sat.

SEVEN PARK PLACE SW1 £112 **4 4 3**

7-8 PARK PL   020 7316 1620   3–4C

Chef William Drabble maintains a low profile but his "expert cuisine" inspires a small but smitten fan club for this under-the-radar dining room in a swish St James's hotel – a "cosy room with enough room between tables for privacy". "He remains in the kitchen, where he belongs, and remains my favourite chef!" / SW1A 1LS; www.stjameshotelandclub.com; @SevenParkPlace; 10 pm; closed Sun & Mon.

SEXY FISH W1 £98 **1 1 2**

1-4 BERKELEY SQ   020 3764 2000   3–3B

"Crammed with people taking selfies, dodgy-looking businessmen and hapless, concierge-victim tourists", Richard Caring's "bling bling" Mayfair venture is a bad case of "too much spent on the decor and not enough concentration on the food"; and, with its huge prices and "appalling service (unless you're spending £000's)", it can end up feeling like "a horrendous rip-off and an all-round horrible experience". More upbeat reporters do find its luxurious seafood format "memorable… just best enjoyed at someone else's expense!". Top Tip – "the best ambience is at lunch, at dinner it changes quite dramatically… not in the most positive way". / W1J 6BR; www.sexyfish.com; @sexyfishlondon; 11 pm, Sun 10 pm; booking max 6 may apply.

SHACKFUYU W1 £46 **4 3 3**

14A, OLD COMPTON ST   020 7734 7492
5–2A

"Perfect Westernised Japanese food" – Bone Daddies's Soho sister has a "hip atmosphere and great staff", and provides an object lesson in "how to do fusion cuisine". "The tasting menu is a bargain at £30 as it includes all their signature dishes". Top Tip: "Kinako French toast with Matcha is a delight" – "how can bread and ice cream be this good?". / W1D 4TH; www.bonedaddies.com/restaurant/shackfuyu; @shackfuyu; 10.30 pm; no booking.

SHAHI PAKWAAN
N2   £31   5️⃣4️⃣3️⃣

**25 AYLMER PARADEAYLMER RD
020 8341 1111   1–1B**

"Authentic Hyderabadi cooking and attentive service" have helped this "great local" – a year-old shop conversion in East Finchley – "build up a very good reputation in a short time" and it's consistently rated for its excellent value. / N2 0PE; www.shahipakwaan.co.uk; Mon-Thu, Sat, Fri 11 pm, Sun 10 pm; closed Fri L.

SHAKE SHACK
       £29   3️⃣2️⃣2️⃣

**NOVA, 172 VICTORIA ST, SW1 01923 555188
2–4B | 80 NEW OXFORD ST, WC1
01925 555171 5–1B | 24 THE MARKET,
WC2 020 3598 1360 5–3D | BOXPARK
WEMBLEY, OLYMPIC WAY, HA9 NO TEL
1–1A NEW | THE STREET, WESTFIELD
STRATFORD, E20 01923 555167 14–1D | 45
CANNON ST, EC4 01923 886211 10–3B NEW**

NYC star-restaurateur Danny Meyer's global operation was founded as a hot-dog cart in a New York park in 2001 and has found success in London, as elsewhere. "Admittedly the burgers are pretty good", but ratings support those who feel "they are not that amazing versus others" and likewise that "there's nothing in the decor to make you want to hang around". Recent openings include Cannon Street and a new outlet is scheduled at Boxpark Wembley in late 2018. / WC2 & E14 11 pm, Sun 9 pm-10.30 pm; E20 9.30 pm, Fri & Sat 11 pm.

SHAMPERS W1
     £47   3️⃣4️⃣4️⃣

4 KINGLY ST   020 7437 1692   4–2B

"Still doing it right after 30 years" – "this reliable old friend ain't bust so they haven't fixed it". "They don't make them like this any more!", but if you want to see what a wine bar looked like in the 1970s, this "lively and fun" Soho venue perfectly fits the bill. It helps that "the owner, Simon, takes a personal interest" and presides over "an extensive list of wines, many of them by the glass"; plus "a varied and well-cooked menu". / W1B 5PE; www.shampers.net; @shampers_soho; 11 pm; closed Sun.

THE SHED W8
     £58   3️⃣4️⃣3️⃣

**122 PALACE GARDENS TER   020 7229 4024
7–2B**

"Unusual, intriguing and packed to the gunnels" – the Gladwin family's quirky, rustic farm-to-fork outfit just off Notting Hill Gate – on a small site which old-timers still recall as The Ark (long RIP) – can be "noisy", but the British seasonal tapas is "of good quality" and service is "good-humoured". / W8 4RT; www.theshed-restaurant.com; @theshed_resto; 10.30 pm; closed Mon L & Sun; SRA-Food Made Good – 3 stars.

J SHEEKEY WC2
     £81   3️⃣4️⃣4️⃣

**28-34 ST MARTIN'S CT   020 7240 2565
5–3B**

"A proper, old-school London tradition that never fails" – Richard Caring's "beautiful and iconic" Theatreland classic (est. 1896)

remains both the survey's No.1 most-talked-about destination and also its top choice for fish. You approach its intriguing etched-glass façade via a Dickensian alley, off St Martin's Lane, and once inside, navigate a succession of "charming", "old-fashioned small rooms" presided over by "slick" and "professional" staff. There's "a great buzz" – almost "too noisy" – and even if "tables are a little close for a private conversation", it is "particularly enjoyable for late, relaxing dinners after a show". When it comes to the "traditional" cuisine, "they are not trying to reinvent the wheel" – "dishes are not particularly delicate, creative or ambitious, but they are generous", "not overly mucked-about-with", and "showcase the quality of the produce on the plate". The wide-ranging menu of "fish and seafood galore" delivers "all you could want from the oceans!", but it's the down-to-earth "brilliant, warming, rich and comforting fish pie" that's actually its best-known option. Ratings were higher here five years ago, and the venue's ongoing "expansion has not helped standards". That said, its level of achievement has remained incredibly impressive and, on virtually all accounts, "it's a cherished, special place". / WC2N 4AL; www.j-sheekey.co.uk; @JSheekeyRest; 11.30 pm, Sun 10 pm; booking max 6 may apply.

J SHEEKEY ATLANTIC BAR
WC2   £68   3️⃣3️⃣4️⃣

**28-34 ST MARTIN'S CT   020 7240 2565
5–3B**

"Classic small plates" of "fantastic quality seafood", "served in a 1930's-style atmosphere" have evolved a separate, highly popular, identity for Sheekey's "bustling" and "beautiful" adjacent bar, which fans say is "better than the restaurant!" and whose relatively "informal" approach is particularly "great for pre-/post-theatre". Its ratings don't hit the heights they once did, however, with the odd gripe that "while the welcome was warm, the food was nothing to write home about". / WC2N 4AL; www.j-sheekey.co.uk; @JSheekeyRest; midnight, Sun 10.30 pm; booking max 3 may apply.

SHEPHERD'S SW1   £57   3️⃣3️⃣4️⃣

**MARSHAM CT, MARSHAM ST   020 7834 9552
2–4C**

"Perfect for a business lunch… and not just for politicians" – this resurrected traditional dining room is a well-known politico troughing spot, with well-spaced tables and old-school decor. One or two reporters feel "it's not up to the mark of previous years", but typically feedback is full of praise for its "charming staff" and "wonderful British dishes at reasonable prices". / SW1P 4LA; www.shepherdsrestaurant.co.uk; @shepherdsLondon; 10.30 pm; closed Sat & Sun.

SHIKUMEN, DORSETT
HOTEL W12   £55   4️⃣3️⃣2️⃣

**58 SHEPHERD'S BUSH GRN   020 8749 9978
8–1C**

"Excellent dim sum and Peking duck" backed up by a "laudably original menu" and "beautiful presentation" make this slick operation – overlooking grimy Shepherd's Bush Green – a culinary standout in West London. The

setting, in an upmarket modern hotel, is also "unexpectedly smart for SheBu". / W12 5AA; www.shikumen.co.uk; @ShikumenUK; 10.30 pm.

SHILPA W6   £34   4️⃣2️⃣1️⃣

206 KING ST   020 8741 3127   8–2B

"Skilfully blended flavours in sensational dishes" ("delicious vegetarian" and "dazzling seafood") come as a total surprise at this utterly nondescript-looking Keralan café, in an anonymous row of restaurants near Hammersmith town hall. "No 'two-pot' cooking here – clear use of fresh herbs and spices." It's also "extraordinarily good value". Any gripes? Well, the room is pretty "downbeat" and "you may have to wait while they churn out the takeaways". / W6 0RA; www.shilparestaurant.co.uk; Sun-Wed 11 pm, Thu-Sat midnight.

SHORYU RAMEN   £48   3️⃣3️⃣2️⃣

**9 REGENT ST, SW1 NO TEL 4–4D | 3
DENMAN ST, W1 NO TEL 4–3C | 5 KINGLY
CT, W1 NO TEL 4–2B | BROADGATE
CIRCLE, EC2 NO TEL 13–2B**

"Tasty (and filling) noodle dishes and decent quality sashimi" draw a steady crowd to these Japanese pit stops: a "good option in busy, trendy areas", even if "space is cramped" and "you might have to queue". / 11 pm-midnight, Sun 9.30 pm-10 pm; E14 9 pm, Sun 6 pm; no booking (except Kingly Ct).

SHU XIANGGE CHINATOWN
W1

10 GERRARD ST 07552 388888 5–1C

If you crave authenticity and offal in equal portions, this new 2018 opening on Chinatown's main drag (sibling to an existing operation in Holborn) looks like it may be the place for you. A traditional Sichuan hot-pot specialist, choose from over 80 ingredients – from assorted types of tripe, aorta and brain to wagyu beef and seafood. / W1D 5PD; www.chinatown.co.uk/en/restaurant/shu-xiangge; @chinatownlondon; Tue-Thu 10 pm, Fri & Sat 10.30 pm, Mon 9.30 pm, Sun 9 pm.

THE SICHUAN
EC1   £57   3️⃣2️⃣2️⃣

14 CITY RD   020 7588 5489   13–2A

"Reliably tasty Sichuanese food" makes it worth remembering this Sichuan two-year-old, near the entrance to the Honourable Artillery Company. / EC1Y 2AA; www.thesichuan.co.uk; Sun-Thu 10.30 pm, Fri & Sat 11 pm.

SICHUAN FOLK
E1   £45   4️⃣3️⃣2️⃣

32 HANBURY ST   020 7247 4735   13–2C

"The hot pots are exceptional… some of which are very hot!", according to fans of this "great Sichuanese". "It's not the most attractive restaurant, but the food makes a trip well worth it!" / E1 6QR; www.sichuan-folk.co.uk; 10.30 pm; no Amex.

SIGNOR SASSI
SW1   £65   2|3|3

14 KNIGHTSBRIDGE GREEN   020 7584 2277
6–1D

"You get what it says on the tin" according to fans of this classic trattoria of many years' standing near Harrods (nowadays part of the glossy San Carlo group), who acclaim its "great atmosphere" and for whom it's often a long-term favourite. Alongside strong praise, a couple of off-reports dragged down ratings this year – hopefully just a blip. / SW1X 7QL; www.signorsassi.co.uk; @SignorSassi; 11.30 pm.

SILK ROAD SE5   £23   5|2|1

49 CAMBERWELL CHURCH ST
020 7703 4832   1–3C

This "amazing Uighur canteen in the depths of Camberhell" serves "incredible" food with "punchy flavours and interesting textures" from China's northwestern Xinjiang province – "homemade noodles, dumplings, stews & lamb skewers" – "without any fanfare". It's "cash-only (and very cheap)", "noisy", with "communal benches and abrupt service" – "so don't go for a quiet romantic evening". Top Tip: "lamb and fat chunks is mind-blowing". / SE5 8TR; 11 pm; closed Mon-Sun L; cash only; no booking.

SIMPSON'S IN THE STRAND
WC2   £76   2|2|3

100 STRAND   020 7420 2111   5–3D

"The revamp seems to have done them good" at this legendary temple of traditional British cuisine (with origins back to 1828) – and most famously roast beef – which finally seems to be re-emerging after many, many years in the doldrums. Yes, it can still appear all too touristy and expensive, but "the iconic building still has a lot of atmosphere", and its "olde English staples" receive very much more consistent praise since its refurb – "it is one of the rare places in London where you can get traditional carvery on a trolley which tastes good!" Perhaps in keeping with the story of renewal, new chef Adrian Martin (who previously oversaw Annabel's and Harry's Bar) took over as chef from William Hemming in August 2018. / WC2R 0EW; www.simpsonsinthestrand.co.uk; @simpsons1828; 11 pm, Sun 8 pm; No trainers.

SIMPSON'S TAVERN
EC3   £41   1|3|5

38 1/2 BALL CT, CORNHILL   020 7626 9985
10–2C

"Olde English tradition lives on" at this ancient chophouse down a picturesque alleyway: a City institution dating from 1757. "It could be a museum of the British restaurant" with its "engaging service that treats you like one of the boys", Dickensian interior and "authentic period food", including daily roasts and house special 'stewed cheese'. / EC3V 9DR; www.simpsonstavern.co.uk; @SimpsonsTavern; Tue-Fri, Mon 3.30 pm; closed Tue-Fri, Mon D, closed Sat & Sun.

SINABRO SW11   £64   4|4|3

28 BATTERSEA RISE   020 3302 3120   11–2C

Little Battersea Rise bistro (20 covers), which receives outstanding ratings from locals for its deftly executed modern British cooking and appealing style. / SW11 1EE; www.sinabro.co.uk; @SinabroLondon; Tue-Thu 10 pm, Fri & Sat 10.30 pm; closed Tue-Thu L, closed Sun & Mon.

SINGAPORE GARDEN
NW6   £49   3|3|2

83A FAIRFAX RD   020 7624 8233   9–2A

"Utterly reliable and (even more welcome) reasonably priced", this "always packed" pan-Asian veteran in an anonymous Swiss Cottage shopping parade offers a mix of Chinese, Malaysian and Singaporean dishes. Giles Coren of The Times heads its list of admirers. / NW6 4DY; www.singaporegarden.co.uk; @SingaporeGarden; Sun-Thu 11 pm, Fri & Sat 11.30 pm.

SINGBURI ROYAL THAI
CAFÉ E11   £23   4|3|3

593 LEYTONSTONE HIGH RD   020 8281 4801
1–1D

"A 'brill' little Leytonstone local" that "feels like sitting in someone's front room". "No thrills, just great Thai food and BYO to boot!". / E11 4PA; @SingburiThaiCaf; 10.30 pm, Sun 10 pm; closed Tue-Sun L, closed Mon; cash only.

SIX PORTLAND ROAD
W11   £58   4|5|3

6 PORTLAND RD   020 7229 3130   7–2A

"An exceptional local" – this "small" modern bistro in Holland Park attracts folks from neighbouring postcodes and beyond with its "most delicious" Gallic-influenced dishes (from an ex-Terroir team) and "an interesting wine list with some unusual choices". One or two reporters discern "a lack of ambience", but for most people it's a "cosy" place with particularly "charming" service. / W11 4LA; www.sixportlandroad.com; @SixPortlandRoad; 10 pm; closed Mon & Sun D.

SKETCH, LECTURE ROOM
W1   £148   3|3|4

9 CONDUIT ST   020 7659 4500   4–2A

First timers can "look around in disbelief at the over-the-top decor" on the first floor of this huge Mayfair palazzo (and that's before the call of nature takes them to the 'Swarovski Crystal Bathrooms'), and it is a "most opulent" and "seductive" setting in which to enjoy ambitious cuisine overseen by überchef Pierre Gagnaire. Its ratings took a dive this year, however, as its vertiginous prices can seem as overblown as the interior design (it doesn't help that "sadly it looks like the Gourmet Rapide lunch has been guillotined"). / W1S 2XG; www.sketch.uk.com; @sketchlondon; 10 pm; closed Tue-Thu L, closed Sun & Mon; No trainers; booking max 6 may apply.

SKETCH, GALLERY
W1   £90   1|2|3

9 CONDUIT ST   020 7659 4500   4–2A

The "pure opulence" of this Mayfair hangout for the art and fashion crowd – with David Shrigley's "camp and ridiculous", pink-walled contemporary baroque decor – makes it many fashionista's "favourite, special place". Foodwise, it's "all very nice... but not really, at that price". Top Tip: the whole point of a meal is the chance to visit the egg-shaped toilet pods. / W1S 2XG; www.sketch.uk.com; @sketchlondon; 11 pm, Sun 8 pm; booking max 6 may apply.

SKEWD KITCHEN
EN4   £47   3|3|3

12 COCKFOSTERS PARADE   020 8449 7771
1–1C

"We eat out a lot, but finding this nearly on our doorstep made my year!" – a typically enthusiastic report on this popular modern Turkish grill in Cockfosters. / EN4 0BX; www.skewdkitchen.com; @SkewdKitchen; Mon & Tue 11 pm, Wed & Thu midnight, Fri & Sat 2 am, Sun 10.30 pm.

SKYLON, SOUTH BANK
CENTRE SE1   £76   2|2|4

BELVEDERE RD   020 7654 7800   2–3D

"Fabulous view of the Thames through huge glass windows is so romantic after a stroll along the river" in the signature dining room at the Southbank Centre. Its cooking (mostly) avoided criticism this year, but even some fans acknowledge that while "the food's fine, but it's the setting that makes the place". (See also Skylon Grill.) / SE1 8XX; www.skylon-restaurant.co.uk; @skylonsouthbank; Tue-Thu 11 pm, Fri-Sun midnight; closed Sun D; No trainers.

SKYLON GRILL
SE1   £70   2|2|4

BELVEDERE RD   020 7654 7800   2–3D

"Thank goodness for the view" – the "saving grace" at this riverside grill in the South Bank arts centre, sibling to its D&D London stablemate next door. For most reporters, the food is little better than "average" – "not so much dialling as texting it in these days. Such a shame as the space is so wonderful!". / SE1 8XX; www.skylon-restaurant.co.uk; @skylonsouthbank; 10.30 pm, Sun 4 pm; closed Sun D.

SMITH & WOLLENSKY
WC2   £102   2|2|2

THE ADELPHI BUILDING, 1-11 JOHN ADAM ST   020 7321 6007   5–4D

"Much maligned", say fans (often expense-accounters) of this outpost, near The Strand, of the famous NYC steakhouse chain, for whom its "confident cocktails", "stunning list of American wines" and "USDA cuts cooked to order make it a meat-lover's paradise – request a private booth and let the deal-making juices flow". The colossal ticket price, however, remains a major turn-off to sceptics, who say: "the steaks are ridiculously overpriced, and the wine list is designed only for oligarchs… who wouldn't be seen dead here in any case!" / WC2N 6HT; www.smithandwollensky.co.uk; @sandwollenskyuk; Mon-Thu 10.30 pm, Fri & Sat 11 pm, Sun 3.30 pm; closed Sun D; booking max 12 may apply.

SMITH'S WAPPING
E1 £71 4|4|5

22 WAPPING HIGH ST 020 7488 3456 12–1A

"If you nab a window table, you get great views" of the Thames, Tower Bridge and City at this "clean-lined, sharp and professional" fish brasserie at the foot of a Wapping development (sibling to a long-standing original, in Ongar). A superb all-rounder, it deserves to be (even) better known, given its mix of "expertly prepared" fish ("fresh ingredients handled with a light touch and the confidence not to over-egg things"), "very accommodating and unobtrusive service" and "impressive" location. / E1W 1NJ; www.smithsrestaurants.com; @smithswapping; Mon-Fri 10 pm, Sat 10.30 pm, Sun 5.30 pm; closed Sun D; No trainers.

SMITHS OF SMITHFIELD, TOP FLOOR EC1 £77 3|2|3

67-77 CHARTERHOUSE ST 020 7251 7950 10–1A

"Superb views over Smithfield meat market, St Paul's and the Square Mile" can still make a trip to this spacious top-floor restaurant special. Once upon a time it was one of the top business lunch destinations for City types, but achieves no such recommendations nowadays. But while it's "not quite as good as it used to be in its heyday, it still serves up some delicious steak". / EC1M 6HJ; www.smithsofsmithfield.co.uk; @thisissmiths; 10.30 pm, Sun 9.30 pm; closed Sat L & Sun; booking max 10 may apply.

SMITHS OF SMITHFIELD, DINING ROOM
EC1 £76 2|2|2

67-77 CHARTERHOUSE ST 020 7251 7950 10–1A

This first-floor dining room of the large (but nowadays somewhat overlooked) Smithfield venue by the meat market was one of the 1990s fave raves. As "a safe choice for an informal business lunch" it still has its fans, but even some supporters acknowledge the food "is tasty without being amazing" and harsher critics dismiss the cooking as too "colourless". / EC1M 6HJ; www.smithsofsmithfield.co.uk; @thisismiths; 10 pm; closed Sat L & Sun; booking max 12 may apply.

SMOKE & SALT
SW9 £41 5|4|3

53 BRIXTON STATION RD 07421 327556 11–1D

"Surely this is as much fun as you can have in a shipping container?" – this year-old occupant of the 20-seat unit at Pop Brixton that formerly housed Kricket (now permanent in Soho) focuses for its culinary inspirations on preserving, fermenting and smoking, and is "well

worth the trip to Brixton". All reporters acclaim the "inventive flavour combinations, perfectly seasoned with fabulous style, and served up by Remi from the tiny kitchen, plus charming bonhomie from Aaron, front of house". One issue for some customers – the background music isn't always in the background… / SW9 8PQ; www.smokeandsalt.com; @SmokeandSaltLDN; 10 pm, Sun 3 pm; closed Mon-Fri L closed Sun D; may need 4+ to book.

SMOKEHOUSE ISLINGTON
N1 £55 3|3|2

63-69 CANONBURY RD 020 7354 1144 9–2D

"Particularly good for special cuts of meat cooked to order" – a Canonbury gastropub (with garden) specialising in grills as part of a modern British menu, and "great for a winter Sunday Roast." / N1 2RG; www.smokehouseislington.co.uk; @smokehouseN1; 10 pm, Sun 9 pm; closed weekday L.

SMOKESTAK E1 £49 4|3|3

35 SCLATER ST 020 3873 1733 13–1C

"Incredible, slow-cooked smoked meats" makes David Carter's moodily designed grill-house, just off Brick Lane – arranged around a 2m width of glowing charcoal, complete with grilling paraphernalia and dudish chefs – a mecca for meat-hungry hipsters. "Good beer and cocktail selection" too. / E1 6LB; www.smokestak.co.uk; @smokestakUK; 11 pm, Sun 9.30 pm.

SMOKING GOAT
E1 £49 4|3|4

64 SHOREDITCH HIGH ST NO TEL 13–1B

"Having lived in Bangkok for 7 years I am a tough critic of Asian food, but these guys get it right every time!" – Ben Chapman's "vibey and totally unique" Thai BBQ mecca in Shoreditch delivers "such original, authentic and inventive flavour pairings and deeply satisfying plates of meat and fish" and it "feels buzzing and exciting as soon as you step through the doors". (The Soho branch closed last year.) / E1 6JJ; www.smokinggoatsoho.com; @SmokingGoatBar; Wed-Sat 11.30 pm, Sun 4 pm.

SNAPS & RYE
W10 £59 3|4|3

93 GOLBORNE RD 020 8964 3004 7–1A

"The daytime sandwiches are the prettiest creations" and the "dinner menus are incredible, with delicious seafood and beautiful flavours", say fans of this Danish diner in North Kensington, whose "fairly recent refurbishment has made it even cosier"; tipped for brunch. / W10 5NL; www.snapsandrye.com; @snapsandrye; Tue, Wed, Sun 5 pm, Thu-Sat 11 pm; closed Tue, Wed, Sun D, closed Mon.

SNOOTY FOX N5 £40 3|2|3

75 GROSVENOR AVENUE 020 7354 9532 9–2D

"Busy but very friendly pub" near Canonbury station with a fine selection of real ales, and

whose food is well-rated, in particular roasts and burgers. / N5 2NN.

SOCIAL EATING HOUSE
W1 £80 3|3|4

58-59 POLAND ST 020 7993 3251 4–1C

"It feels like it's where it's all happening … I LOVE IT!" – so say the many fans of Jason Atherton's Soho operation – who believe it "has it all… buzzing atmosphere, superb cuisine – food you really want to eat!" – wondrous cocktail bar upstairs, and staff who buzz professionally too". Its ratings were undercut this year, however, by a number of reporters who felt that "the food is good, but you do pay a lot for it". Top Tip – "excellent set lunch deal". / W1F 7NR; www.socialeatinghouse.com; @socialeathouse; 10.45 pm; closed Sun.

SOCIAL WINE & TAPAS
W1 £60 4|4|3

39 JAMES ST 020 7993 3257 3–1A

"Perfect sharing plates", "lovely staff" and a "wonderful evening atmosphere – like being on the Continent" – have made this three-year-old bar, restaurant and wine shop near Selfridges a "welcome addition" to Jason Atherton's stable of Socials. On the downside, "it can work out expensive". / W1U 1EB; www.socialwineandtapas.com; @socialwinetapas; 11 pm, Sun 9 pm; closed Sun; credit card required to book.

SOIF SW11 £59 3|3|3

27 BATTERSEA RISE 020 7223 1112 11–2C

There's "always something different and exciting to try" at this "bustling, buzzy and slightly cramped" modern bistro in Battersea, serving "tasty" small plates and with a "brilliant focus on bio/organic/orange wines that not many other places do" (it's part of Les Caves de Pyrène, which helped put natural wines on the dining map). / SW11 1HG; www.soif.co; @Soif_SW11; 11 pm, Sun 4 pm; closed Mon-Wed L closed Sun D.

SOM SAA E1 £52 5|4|4

43A COMMERCIAL ST 020 7324 7790 13–2C

"Taste explosions abound" – "a variety of flavours, with inventiveness and fun as well as staying true to authentic Thai cooking" – at this hip Spitalfields two-year-old, which also features "a spacious bar with very good cocktails". For many reporters, "it's simply the best Thai food I've had in London" ("Thai food is a favourite of mine, I've tried lots of places over the last 36 years, and this beats 'em all!") / E1 6BD; www.somsaa.com; @somsaa_london; 10.30 pm, Mon 10 pm; closed Mon L, closed Sun; may need 4+ to book.

SÔNG QUÊ E2 £35 3|3|2

134 KINGSLAND RD 020 7613 3222 14–2A

"Excellent pho, and a great buzzy atmosphere typical of the area" maintain the appeal of this long-established "cheap 'n' cheerful" Vietnamese canteen, on Shoreditch's busy

Kingsland Road. / E2 8DY; www.songque.co.uk; 11 pm, Sun 10.30 pm; no Amex.

SONNY'S KITCHEN
SW13   £56   3 3 2

94 CHURCH RD   020 8748 0393   11–1A

Rebecca Mascarenhas's long-serving "Barnes institution" (nowadays part-owned by top chef Phil Howard of Elystan Street) is, say fans, "back on form", and while ratings may still be adrift of the glory days here, most reporters feel its "consistently good" cooking and "always friendly service" equip it as a place "worthy of special occasions as well as regular lunch dates". / SW13 0DQ; www.sonnyskitchen.co.uk; @sonnyskitchen; Mon-Fri 10 pm, Sat 10.30 pm; closed Sun; booking max 5 may apply.

SOPHIES STEAKHOUSE
£63   2 2 2

42-44 GREAT WINDMILL ST, W1
020 7836 8836   4–3D | 311-313 FULHAM RD, SW10   020 7352 0088   6–3B

"For steaks and burgers, entertaining the kids, and before a match at Stamford Bridge", the original Fulham Road branch of this steakhouse duo is still "buzzing and reliable, with good, well-cooked steaks". By contrast, its new Soho outlet inspires very mixed feedback – some praise for "a good varied menu with lovely smokey flavours", but also those who feel it's become "VERY expensive…", "seems to have lost its way…", "wouldn't hurry back". / www.sophiessteakhouse.com; SW10 11.45 pm, Sun 10.45 pm; WC2 12.45 am, Sun 10.45 pm; no booking.

SORELLA SW4   £51   4 3 3

148 CLAPHAM MANOR ST   020 7720 4662
11–1D

An "excellent new Italian, with pasta to die for" – Irish chef Robin Gill's year-old relaunch of his popular The Manor, around the corner from his Clapham HQ The Dairy, takes culinary inspiration from the Amalfi coast. Reports are generally outstanding, and credit it with being a "worthy successor" on the site and "a valuable addition to the locality". There's a strong undercurrent, though, from those who were "left feeling rather underwhelmed" – they say it's OK but "not as good as it thinks it is". Top Tip – "go à la carte, the bigger portions are more suited to the cuisine than grazing on the tasting menu". / SW4 6BX; www.sorellarestaurant.co.uk; @SorellaClapham; Mon & Tue 9 pm, Fri & Sat 11.30 pm, Wed 10 pm, Thu 11 pm, Sun 5 pm.

SOUTHAM STREET
W10   £63   3 2 3

36 GOLBORNE RD   020 3903 3591   7–1A

In the un-lovely shadow of the Trellick Tower, this ambitious newcomer occupies a stylishly converted three-floor Victorian boozer, whose latest former incarnation was as West Thirty Six (RIP). The second venture from Luca Longobardi and Chris Denney of 2017's smash hit '108 Garage', it's inspired surprisingly little press attention (perhaps because of its obscure-whatever-the-trendies-may-tell-you setting), but such feedback as we have is upbeat, praising its "Asian-inspired" cuisine as "fresh, light and really great". The first floor raw bar serves Nikkei (a fusion of Peruvian and Japanese cuisines) fare, while the second floor houses a private members' tequila and mezcal bar. / W10 5PR; www.southamstreet.com; @southamstreet; Tue-Thu midnight, Fri & Sat 1 am, Sun 4 pm; closed Tue-Thu L closed Sun D, closed Mon.

SOUTINE NW8

60 SAINT JOHNS WOOD HIGH ST AWAITING TEL 9–3A

Corbin & King's latest opening takes over the prime St John's Wood site vacated as part of the retrenchment of the Carluccio's chain. An opening some time in 2019 is expected, with such limited details as are available (for example, Jeremy King's comment that it will be "Colbert meets Fischer's") suggesting a Continental, grand-café style reminiscent of the group's other ventures. / NW8 7SH; Wed-Sat midnight.

SPARROW SE13   £44   4 5 3

RENNELL ST   020 8318 6941   1–4D

"A gem in Lewisham" – and perhaps the area's first proper neighbourhood restaurant – this yearling quickly hit the sweet spot with locals, for "creative cuisine built on solid foundations" and "something that's a little different too". "Delightful" chefs Terry Blake and Yohini Nandakumar have impressive track records (St John, Bao, Merchant's Tavern, Pollen Street Social, The Square), and have put together a menu of "quirky and original sharing plates" with Sri Lankan influences. / SE13 7HD; sparrowlondon.co.uk; @sparrowlondon.

THE SPREAD EAGLE
E9   £31   3 3 3

224 HOMERTON HIGH ST   020 8985 0400
14–1C

"Vegan delight" is to be found at London's first 100%-vegan pub, occupying a prime spot in east Homerton. In most respects, it feels just like any old fun gastropub, but even the drinks and cocktails are vegan, while the Latino-slanted fare is from the folk behind Club Mexicana; "fantastic!" / E9 6AS; www.thespreadeaglelondon.co.uk; @SpreadEagleLDN.

St Leonards EC2

SPRING RESTAURANT
WC2   £85   3 3 4

NEW WING, LANCASTER PL   020 3011 0115
2–2D

Within gorgeous Somerset House, this "elegant and light-filled dining room" makes "an exceptionally civilised place to eat", and Skye Gyngell's "enticing" menu of "delicate, seasonal and delicious" dishes, plus "charming service", contribute to an "airy, fresh and delightful" experience that better fulfilled its promise this year as "one of the most impressive restaurants in this part of London". In particular, it's a romantic favourite: "I recommended it to my son for an early date, and now he's marrying the lady concerned!" / WC2R 1LA; www.springrestaurant.co.uk; @Spring_Rest; 11 pm, Sun 10.30 pm; closed Sun D; credit card required to book.

THE SQUARE W1   £131   3 3 2

6-10 BRUTON ST   020 7495 7100   3–2C

"Yet another new chef and change of design" – yet this twice-relaunched Mayfair temple of gastronomy (both times by recent buyer, Marlon Abela) nowadays bears a not-so-different set of strengths and weaknesses from its original self. Chef (since November 2017) Clement Leroy "maintains the highest standards" and fans feel it "deserves to reclaim its position as one of London's top tables" (although you can quibble as to whether the cuisine is quite as good as under Phil Howard). Despite attempts to pep up the room, it retains a "slightly downbeat ambience", but this doesn't put off the expense accounters for whom it's always been a favourite, drawn in part by its ever-formidable wine list. / W1J 6PU; www.squarerestaurant.com; @square_rest; Mon-Thu 10 pm, Fri & Sat 10.30 pm; closed Sun; booking max 8 may apply.

SRI SUWOON SW1   £34   4 4 3

44 HUGH ST   020 7828 0321   2–4B

"A backstreet Pimlico gem just off the main thoroughfare in Victoria" – this "brilliant neighbourhood Thai" wins raves from locals for its "authentic specialities with just the right amount of spice". "Service is charming and the room delightful." ("I recently revisited with two friends extremely knowledgeable about Thai food and they raved on about it!"). / SW1V 4EP; www.srisuwoon.com; @sri_suwoon; 11 pm; closed Mon & Tue, Sat L, closed Sun.

ST LEONARDS EC2 £70

70 LEONARD ST   020 7613 5346   13–1B

Formerly the site of Eyre Brothers (sadly RIP) then very briefly the very short-lived 70 Leonard St (not so sadly RIP) – now this Shoreditch venue has been taken over by Jackson Boxer (of Brunswick House/LASSCO fame) and Andrew Clarke and given a very Shoreditch makeover (lots of polished concrete), plus an ice bar for raw fish and shellfish, and open-hearth cooking for meat and vegetables. Early press reviews ("cutting edge", "vivid", "concentrated", "musky", "smokey acidity", "almost-too-pungent") suggest the cuisine is certainly not boring, and arguably an expression of "mad genius". / EC2A 4QX; stleonards.london; @stleonardsEC2.

ST LUKE'S KITCHEN, LIBRARY WC2   £64   233

112 SAINT MARTIN'S LANE   020 3302 7912   5–4C

Limited feedback this year on this "quirky" venue – "a slightly offbeat mix of clubbiness and restaurant" in a boutique guesthouse near the Coliseum, whose cuisine is "of the fusion variety". Such as there is, though, praises it as "a perfectly decent choice for a pre-theatre supper". / WC2N 4BD; www.lib-rary.com; @LibraryLondon; 1 am; closed Sun; No trainers.

STECCA SW10   £76

14 HOLLYWOOD RD   020 7460 2322   6–3B

All reports acknowledge the high quality of the cooking at this Chelsea yearling, in a posh side street near the Chelsea & Westminster Hospital (with small rear garden). Its "high prices", though, are another common theme in feedback. / SW10 9HY; www.stecca.co.uk; Sun-Wed 10 pm, Thu-Sat 10.30 pm.

STEM W1   £61   443

5 PRINCES ST   020 7629 9283   4–1A

Mark Jarvis, chef-patron of Anglo in Farringdon and Neo Bistro off Oxford Street, launched this smallish (35-cover) Mayfair newcomer in May 2018, just as the survey was closing. Early feedback is positive about the ambitious, seasonal British cuisine, from chef Sam Ashton-Booth (former head chef of Anglo) with options including a five-course tasting menu (with matching wine flight available) as well as à la carte and an express lunch. / W1J 0DW; www.stem-byneo.co.uk; @stemrestaurant; Tue-Sat, Mon 10.30 pm, Sun 3.30 pm; closed Mon L closed Sun D.

STICK & BOWL W8   £24   331

31 KENSINGTON HIGH ST   020 7937 2778   6–1A

For Chinese chow as cheap as chips and chock full of flavour, this small, 1950s-style dive on posh Kensington High Street is just the ticket – it's not a foodie fave rave, but a 'good-nosh-for-not-a-lot-of-dosh' kind of joint. / W8 5NP; 10.45 pm; cash only; no booking.

STICKS'N'SUSHI   £59   322

3 SIR SIMON MILTON SQ, VICTORIA ST, SW1   020 3141 8810   2–4B | 11 HENRIETTA ST, WC2   020 3141 8810   5–3D | 113-115 KING'S RD, SW3 AWAITING TEL 6–3C NEW | NELSON RD, SE10   020 3141 8220   1–3D | 58 WIMBLEDON HILL RD, SW19   020 3141 8800   11–2B | CROSSRAIL PL, E14   020 3141 8230   12–1C

"Scandinavian sushi… sounds odd, but it works!" This Danish chain has proved a perhaps-unlikely hit, praised as "a concept that pays off" with enjoyably "fresh" and "eclectic" food and a "lively" style. "It has gotten much more expensive", however, in recent times, and ratings have dipped accordingly. At the start of October 2018 they opened their biggest site yet on Chelsea's King's Road. / www.sticksnsushi.com; @sticksnsushi_UK; 10 pm, Wed-Sat 11 pm.

STICKY MANGO AT RSJ SE1   £47   232

33 COIN ST   020 7803 9733   10–4A

A change of direction has seen this 30-year stalwart near the South Bank arts centre modify its name (from RSJ) and adopt an "Asian-influenced menu". To some extent, it's a case of 'plus ça change' – "the key attraction here has always been its list of Loire wines and proximity to the Festival Hall – changing the cuisine hasn't affected either" (nor the ambience, which has always teetered on the "lousy"). When it comes to the cooking, views divide – what is "tasty" fare at "sensible prices" to fans is, to foes, "slightly bland and lacking kick". / SE1 9NR; www.stickymango.co.uk; @stickymangoldn; 10.30 pm; closed Sun.

STOCKWELL CONTINENTAL SW8   £43   333

169 SOUTH LAMBETH RD   020 3019 0757   11–1D

On the Stockwell site that was once popular as Rebatos (long RIP): this new venture hails from the same family as the renowned Canton Arms nearby, but in this case – a departure for this gastropub group – the focus is on Italian cooking, with a café (coffee, pastries, pizza) in the space that once was the tapas bar here, and more substantial fare in the rear restaurant. One early report captures it well: "not quite on a par with the other members of the Anchor & Hope stable yet. But the Roman style pizzas are a nice change from the heavier Neapolitans favoured by most. And the cured meats and antipasti are all good. The menu has been cleverly designed, which inevitably leads to raised eyebrows when the final bill arrives. This could become a local institution… but it's not quite there yet". / SW8 1XW; www.stockwellcontinental.com.

STORY SE1   £154   333

199 TOOLEY ST   020 7183 2117   10–4D

"Superb innovation" delivers a series of "sensational dishes" say devotees of Tom Sellers's acclaimed culinary temple, near Tower Bridge, where between eight and eleven courses of his experimental cuisine are delivered according to the evening's 'story' (with a four-course format at lunch). However, opinions diverged on the experience this year, with doubters who "don't understand the hype" and who find the concept "confused", "misjudged", or "so expensive". As the survey was concluding it emerged from a big refurb in May 2018, perhaps heralding a more consistent return to form? / SE1 2UE; www.restaurantstory.co.uk; @Rest_Story; 9.15 pm; closed Mon & Sun.

THE STRAIGHT & NARROW E14   £55   233

MOSAIC BUILDING, 45 NARROW ST   020 3745 8345   12–1B

Live music while you eat is a regular feature at this two-year-old piano bar at the foot of a new development in Limehouse. Feedback is a bit up-and-down but basically supportive: "better than expected, if a little overpriced"… "struggling to find its identity as it keeps reinventing itself…. despite which it's a great, relaxed place for Sunday lunch and mid-week dinner". / E14 8DN; www.thestraightandnarrow.co.uk; @straightNpiano; 10 pm, Sun 9 pm.

STREET PIZZA EC4   £45

10 BREAD ST   020 3030 4050   10–2B

'Bottomless' pizza (i.e. eat as much as you like for £15), plus a copious drinks menu is the concept for the latest brand in the Gordon Ramsay stable, which opened quietly on the ground floor of Bread Street Kitchen in the City's One New Change development by St Paul's. Too little feedback for a rating – online reviews are hit 'n' miss. / EC4M 9AJ; www.gordonramsayrestaurants.com/street-pizza; @GRStreetPizza; Mon-Wed midnight, Thu-Sat 3 am, Sun 10 pm.

STREET XO W1   £98   222

15 OLD BURLINGTON ST   020 3096 7555   4–3A

Superstar Spanish chef David Muñoz's nightclubby Mayfair yearling attracts only very limited feedback, and it remains mixed. Fans of the Hispanic-Asian fusion cuisine that he has concocted to great acclaim (and three Michelin stars) in Madrid say the "exceptional" cooking here is "seriously underrated". But they are not huge in number, and set against this is the view that it is "tasty and well presented but overpriced". / W1X 1RL; www.streetxo.com; @StreetXO_London; Mon-Wed 11 pm, Thu-Sat midnight, Sun 9.30 pm; closed Mon L.

SUB CULT EC2   £14   532

CONTAINER, FINSBURY AVENUE SQ NO TEL   13–2A

Gourmet US deli-style sub rolls score full marks from addicts of Ben Chancellor and Gaz Phillips's four-year-old street food brand, which, as well as weekend operations at Brockley and Maltby Street markets, can be found during the week (from 8pm to 4pm) at their container in Broadgate. / EC2M 2PP; www.sub-cult.co.uk; @SubCultSubs; Mon, Wed & Thu, Sun 5 pm, Tue, Fri 10 pm, Sat 3.30 pm.

SUKHO FINE THAI CUISINE
SW6 £52 5 5 3

855 FULHAM RD   020 7371 7600   11–1B

"The best Thai food in southwest London" – and arguably the entire capital – is found at this "lovely" if "always busy" (hence "very crowded") Fulham shop conversion. Fans travel across town attracted by its "really interesting and delicious menu" and service that's "charming and courteous". / SW6 5HJ; www.sukhogroups.com; 9.30 pm, Sun 4 pm.

SUKSAN SW10 £49 3 3 2

7 PARK WALK   020 7351 9881   6–3B

"Admirable consistency" is a virtue of this "reliable neighbourhood gem" on a Chelsea corner. Fans say it's "as good as its sibling" (Sukho Fine Thai Cuisine in Fulham), but its ratings have a little way to go to match its stellar relative. / SW10 0AJ; www.sukhogroups.com; 10.45 pm, Sun 9.45 pm.

SUMAK N8 £39 4 4 2

141 TOTTENHAM LANE   020 8341 6261   1–1C

"Seriously tasty Turkish cuisine" – "a real cut above" and "very well priced" – wins high ratings for this popular Crouch End fixture. "The welcome is warm, service is efficient, and the decor is typically Turkish (murals and slightly glitzy floor tiles)". / N8 9BJ; www.sumakrestaurants.co.uk; midnight, Sun 11.30 pm.

THE SUMMERHOUSE
W9 £71 2 2 5

60 BLOMFIELD RD   020 7286 6752   9–4A

"On a summer day you forget you're in the middle of the city" at this canalside spot in lovely Little Venice. Fans say its fish and seafood likewise "warrants a journey", but it can also feel very "expensive", and too many reporters say "it's all about the location" nowadays, citing "very average" cooking and "disappointing service", too. / W9 2PA; www.thesummerhouse.co; @FRGSummerhouse; midnight, Sun 11.30 pm; no Amex.

SUMOSAN TWIGA
SW1 £69 2 2 3

165 SLOANE ST   020 3096 0222   6–1D

"When I heard the restaurant was a fusion of Japanese and Italian, I was sceptical!" – a perhaps natural reaction to this Belgravia outpost of the 20-year-old, Moscow-based, luxury dining empire. Originally located in Mayfair – where the style was purely Japanese-fusion – when it relocated to Sloane Street a couple of years ago, it both acquired the 'Twiga' suffix to its name, and also an Italian menu (presented side-by-side). Like its predecessors on this tricky site (Monte's, Pengelley), this glossy operation inspires little feedback, as a result of a location whose primary passing trade is designer-clad Eurotrash; and, predictably, it is sometimes dismissed as "overpriced" and

mediocre all round; but some reporters do declare themselves "really surprised and pleased with the culinary results". Top Tip: dip your toe in the water with a visit to its glam second-floor cocktail bar. / SW1X 9QB; www.sumosan.com; @sumosantwiga.

SUNDAY N1 £31 4 2 3

169 HEMINGFORD RD   020 7607 3868   9–2D

"Ridiculously good breakfasts and brunch" draw big queues to this popular café, on the fringes of Islington ("if you ask how long until you're seated, be prepared for a stony stare"). / N1 1DA; @sundaybarnsbury; 10.30 pm; closed Mon, Tue D, Wed D & Sun D; no Amex.

SUPAWAN N1 £45 4 4 2

38 CALEDONIAN RD   020 7278 2888   9–3D

"A fabulous near King's Cross" offering "a busy, buzzy different take on Thai cooking". "The food takes prominence" – "real care is evident in its preparation, avoiding run-of-the-mill dishes so common elsewhere". / N1 9DT; www.supawan.co.uk; closed Sun.

SUPER TUSCAN
E1 £51 3 4 3

8A ARTILLERY PASSAGE   020 7247 8717   13–2B

This "vibrant but understated Italian", hidden down an alley in the City, is "run by two Anglo-Italian brothers who clearly have a passion for authentic food". It's "buzzy and cramped, with honest cooking using high-quality ingredients", which are "imported weekly from small specialist providers in Italy". / E1 7LJ; www.supertuscan.co.uk; 10 pm, Sun 4 pm; closed Sat & Sun.

SUSHI ATELIER
W1 £31 5 3 3

114 GREAT PORTLAND ST   020 7636 4455   2–1B

"Sit at the counter for the full experience" at this traditional-ish Japanese yearling in Fitzrovia – a new departure for the owners of the small (and well-rated) Chisou group – consistently receiving excellent ratings for its "delicious sushi and sashimi". / W1W 6PH; www.sushiatelier.co.uk; @sushiatelierlondon; 5 pm.

SUSHI BAR ATARI-YA
£46 5 2 1

20 JAMES ST, W1   020 7491 1178   3–1A | 1 STATION PDE, W5   020 8896 3175   1–3A | 75 FAIRFAX RD, NW6   020 7328 5338   9–2A

Though centrally made, the sushi is some of "the best and best-priced in London" ("not surprising as they supply many of the top restos") at this small collection of cafés, run by a Japanese food importer. "Don't expect any ambience to write home about" – decor is "very basic" – while service is "fine without being personable". Branches in N12 and W3 closed this year, which also saw the group rebrand from plain 'Atari-Ya'. / www.sushibaratariya.co.uk; W1 8

pm, NW6 & W5 9.30 pm, W9 9 pm, N12 & W3 6.30 pm, Sat & Sun 7 pm; NW6 closed Mon, W5 closed Mon & Tue.

SUSHI BAR MAKOTO
W4 £48 4 3 1

57 TURNHAM GREEN TERRACE   020 8987 3180   8–2A

"An excellent range of inexpensive sushi and sashimi is served in an unpretentious setting", at this "cheerful, local sushi café", in the foodie parade of shops near Turnham Green station. / W4 1RP; www.sushibarmakoto.co.uk; 10 pm, Sun 9 pm.

SUSHI MASA
NW2 £40 3 4 3

33B WALM LANE   020 8459 2971   1–1A

"A worthy successor to Sushi Say" – this "good neighbourhood Japanese restaurant with a tatami mat booth at the back" is doing "something not easy to achieve" by (almost) filling the boots left by its predecessor. / NW2 5SH; 10.30 pm, Sun 9 pm.

SUSHI TETSU
EC1 £89 5 5 3

12 JERUSALEM PAS   020 3217 0090   10–1A

"Like dining in Japan!" – Toru Takahashi is "the real deal" and provides an "intimate master sushi experience" at his "special" Clerkenwell 7-seater, which "is without doubt the best sushi in London at this price point" (and which, some would argue, invites comparison with The Araki, which charges about 4x the price here). The only fly in the ointment is the "ridiculous booking process" – it's just "so hard to get a seat". / EC1V 4JP; www.sushitetsu.co.uk; @SushiTetsuUK; Tue-Fri 10 pm, Sat 9.30 pm; closed Tue-Sat L, closed Sun & Mon.

SUSHISAMBA £96 2 2 3

OPERA TERRACE, 35 THE MARKET, WC2   020 3053 0000   5–3D | HERON TOWER, 110 BISHOPSGATE, EC2   020 3640 7330   10–2D

What's not to like at this "fabulous" 39th floor pan-Asian in the Heron Tower (reached by western Europe's fastest lifts!) – the interior is "very cool", "the views are to die for" and "the food just sings – punchy flavours of sweet, sour, salty deliciousness". The answer, unfortunately, is "slow and disorganised service" and "prices even higher than the skyscraper it's based in" which leave far too many reporters nowadays (including former fans) accusing it of "style over substance". Its long-awaited new Covent Garden sibling – occupying the dramatic site that has seen many chains come and go (most recently Brasserie Blanc) finally opens in November 2018. / 1.30 am, Wed-Sat 2 am.

SUTTON AND SONS £35 4|3|2

90 STOKE NEWINGTON HIGH ST, N16
020 7249 6444   1–1C | 356 ESSEX RD, N1
020 7359 1210   14–1A | 240 GRAHAM RD,
E8   020 3643 2017   14–1B

"Yummy" fresh fish and "crispy fat chips" all
in "great value, generous portions" win raves
– if from a small fanclub – for these "classy"
chippies in Stokey, Hackney Central and
Islington. October 2018 marks a first, with the
launch of London's first fully vegan chippie at
the Hackney Central branch (which is itself
moving down the road to 218 Graham Road). /
www.suttonandsons.co.uk; @sutton_and_sons; 10 pm,
Fri & Sat 10.30 pm; E8 Fri 10 pm; no bookings.

THE SWAN W4 £52 3|4|4

1 EVERSHED WALK, 119 ACTON LN
020 8994 8262   8–1A

"Everything you could want from a pub" is
to be found at this "quasi-rustic", panelled
tavern, hidden away in a backstreet on the
Chiswick/Acton borders: "unexpectedly
sophisticated food" ("from a Mediterranean/
Italian menu that delivers the classics as well as
seasonal-inspired dishes"), "seamless, jolly yet
gentle service", "terrific beer, wine and gin…
and you get hydrangeas in the kid-friendly
garden!" / W4 5HH; www.theswanchiswick.co.uk;
@SwanPubChiswick; Sun-Thu 10.30 pm, Sat, Fri 11
pm; closed weekday L.

THE SWAN AT THE GLOBE
SE1 £60 3|2|4

21 NEW GLOBE WALK   020 7928 9444
10–3B

The faux-Elizabethan tavern connected to
Shakespeare's Globe theatre (on the first floor)
has "great views over the river to St Paul's",
and food – by chef Allan Pickett – that is
"imaginative, seasonal, locally sourced and well
executed without being pretentious". Top Tip:
"gentleman's afternoon tea (beef sliders, Scotch
egg and a tankard of beer instead of bubbles) is
outstanding". / SE1 9DT; www.swanlondon.co.uk;
@swanabout; Tue-Fri 10 pm, Sat 9.30 pm.

SWEET THURSDAY
N1 £43 3|2|3

95 SOUTHGATE RD   020 7226 1727   14–1A

You'll find a "friendly welcome" (and a
good choice of wines) at this "very child-
friendly" local pizza parlour and bottle shop
in gentrified De Beauvoir Town. / N1 3JS;
www.sweetthursday.co.uk; @Pizza_and_Wine; 11 pm,
Sun 10.30 pm.

SWEETINGS EC4 £76 3|2|4

39 QUEEN VICTORIA ST   020 7248 3062
10–3B

"A throwback to 100 years ago" – this "unique",
"magnificently unchanged" Victorian relic is
"an old school experience of the best sort"
and a revered haunt for its pinstriped clientele,
attracted by "some of the finest fish and
seafood". "Sitting at the bar is lovely and you

get great attention from the waiting staff", or
sit down at the back to a full meal of "black
velvet in a tankard, followed by oysters and then
lovely fish (perfectly cooked), with splendid jam
sponge". That prices are slightly "outrageous"
has always been part of the package. Except for
private parties, it's always been a weekday lunch-
only venue, but in September 2018, they seem to
be experimenting with the odd evening service.
/ EC4N 4SA; www.sweetingsrestaurant.co.uk;
@SweetingsLondon; closed Mon-Fri D, closed Sat &
Sun; no booking.

TABERNA ETRUSCA
EC4 £58 3|2|3

9 -11 BOW CHURCHYARD   020 7248 5552
10–2C

Limited but positive praise this year for the
cooking at this long-established and traditional
City Italian. It particularly comes into its
own in summer, when you can eat on its al
fresco patio and fully enjoy its quiet location,
just off Bow Churchyard. / EC4M 9DQ;
www.etruscarestaurants.com; Tue-Fri 10 pm, Mon
3.30 pm; closed Mon D, closed Sat & Sun.

THE TABLE SE1 £48 3|2|2

83 SOUTHWARK ST   020 7401 2760   10–4B

"After a bit of culture on the South Bank", this
café-style contemporary haunt is a "go-to for
a Saturday or Sunday brunch" – "prices are
pretty fair, and they actually care about their
vegan options". / SE1 0HX; www.thetablecafe.com;
@thetablecafe; 10.30 pm; closed Mon D, Sat D & Sun
D; booking weekdays only.

TABLE DU MARCHE
N2 £55 3|3|2

111 HIGH RD   020 8883 5750   1–1B

"Onion soup, complete with toast, cheese
& plenty of onions" typifies the "tasty" and
"reasonably priced" Gallic fare at this "reliable"
bistro two-year-old in East Finchley. Top Tip:
"excellent value lunchtime prix fixe". / N2 8AG;
www.tabledumarche.co.uk; @TableDuMarche; 11
pm, Sun 10.30 pm.

TAKA W1 £59 3|3|3

18 SHEPHERD MARKET   020 3637 7677
3–4B

Limited, but positive all-round, feedback on this
small Mayfair newcomer, which aims to bring
affordably priced Japanese cooking to Shepherd
Market, with a selection of robata and sushi
(probably the way to go) dishes. / W1J 7QH;
www.takalondon.com; @takamayfair; Mon-Thu 10.30
pm, Fri & Sat 10.45 pm; closed Sun.

TAKAHASHI
SW19 £48 5|5|3

228 MERTON RD   020 8540 3041   11–2B

"An unbelievably good neighbourhood
find!" – "some of the best Japanese food
ever!" and wonderfully "caring service" can
be discovered "in a tiny room at this unlikely
location – a deeply suburban parade near South
Wimbledon tube station. The "sublime" and

"mouth-watering" cuisine – "Japanese with
a Mediterranean twist" – is freshly prepared
by chef-proprietor Taka, formerly of Nobu.
/ SW19 \N; www.takahashi-restaurant.co.uk;
@takahashi_sw19; 10 pm, Fri & Sat 10.30 pm, Sun
9 pm.

TAMARIND W1 £91 4|4|3

20 QUEEN ST   020 7629 3561   3–3B

"A consistent pleasure", this Mayfair pioneer
of Indian fine dining (in 2001, the first Indian
to bag a Michelin star) closed for six months
in early 2018 for a complete revamp – and
not before time, with reporters critical of
the "passé fit-out". The October relaunch
promises a 'private club atmosphere' with
'lighter' dishes and sharing plates under new
head chefs Karunesh Khanna (ex-Amaya) and
Manav Tuli (ex-Chutney Mary). / W1J 5PR;
www.tamarindrestaurant.com; @TamarindMayfair;
10.30 pm, Sun 10 pm; closed Sat L; No trainers.

TAMARIND KITCHEN
W1 £54 3|4|4

167-169 WARDOUR ST   020 7287 4243
4–1C

"Great Indian with food with a real vibe in the
heart of Soho" earns plaudits for this offshoot
of Mayfair's upscale Tamarind, albeit at more
"mid-level prices". The pedigree shows, though,
in its "complex spices and luxurious setting". /
W1F 8WR; tamarindkitchen.co.uk; Sun-Thu 11 pm,
Fri & Sat 11.30 pm.

TAMP COFFEE
W4 £42 3|4|4

1 DEVONSHIRE RD NO TEL 8–2A

"A bizarre combination of (superb) flat whites
and empañadas… it somehow works!" – say
devotees of this coffee bar on Chiswick's "lovely
Devonshire Road". This "quality coffee joint"
has "great snacks" and "plenty of papers to
while away a Saturday morning". / W4 \N;
www.tampcoffee.co.uk; @tampcoffee; L only; booking
max 6 may apply.

TANDOOR CHOP HOUSE
WC2 £49 4|4|3

ADELAIDE ST   020 3096 0359   5–4C

"Wow, every dish on the menu is a treat" at
this year-old modern culinary mash-up, backed
by Ennismore Capital, which combines the
trad British chophouse with northern Indian
techniques and spicing, in an atmospheric,
wood-panelled space, just behind St Martin-in-
the-Fields. / WC2N 4HW; tandoorchophouse.com;
@tandoorchop; 11 pm, Sun 10.30 pm; booking max
6 may apply.

TAPAS BRINDISA £59 3|3|2

18-20 RUPERT ST, W1   020 7478 8758   4–3D
| 46 BROADWICK ST, W1   020 7534 1690
4–2B | 18-20 SOUTHWARK ST, SE1
020 7357 8880   10–4C

"Arrive early to avoid the queue", especially
if you visit the "very busy" original Borough
Market branch of this well-known and

Texture W1

"consistently good" tapas chain, which "rarely drops the ball and is a safe bet for a swift and enjoyable meal". Of the other branches, the South Kensington one is very pleasantly located near the tube, with extensive pavement seating: "go on a summer's day and sit outside, watching the world pass by". / www.brindisakitchens.com; @Brindisa; 11 pm-11.30 pm, EC2 12.30 am, Morada Sun 4 pm; Morada closed Sun D; SE1 no booking.

TAQUERIA W11 £42 333

141-145 WESTBOURNE GROVE
020 7229 4734 7–1B

For a vivacious, "cheap 'n' cheerful" bite, this buzzy, well-established Mexican cantina on the border where Notting Hill meets Bayswater is a popular choice, with practically all reporters impressed by its authentic tacos, Latino beers and cocktails. / W11 2RS; www.taqueria.co.uk; @TaqueriaUK; 11 pm, Fri & Sat 11.30 pm, Sun 10.30 pm; no Amex.

TARANTELLA RISTORANTE PIZZERIA W4 £50 333

4 ELLIOT RD 020 8987 8877 8–2A

"Tiny family-run Italian near Turnham Green station" – "nothing flash" but a popular "cheap 'n' cheerful" local that's "a cut above the average" with "great value", "simple" home cooking ("great homemade pasta"), plus "friendly" service: "feels like you're on hols in Italia!" / W4 1PE; Mon-Fri 10.45pm, Sat & Sun 10.45 pm.

TARO £36 322

61 BREWER ST, W1 020 7734 5826
4–3C | 193 BALHAM HIGH RD, SW12
020 8675 5187 11–2C | 44A CANNON ST,
EC4 020 7236 0399 10–3B

"Fast, efficient, delicious and great value" – what more could you want from a Japanese canteen? The Soho original, now in its 20th year, is "always packed". These days there are also branches in the City and Balham. / www.tarorestaurants.co.uk; W1F 10.30 pm, Fri & Sat 11 pm, Sun 9.30 pm; W1D 10.30 pm, Fri & Sat 10.45 pm, Sun 9.30 pm, Mon 10 pm; no Amex; Brewer St only small bookings.

TAS £45 222

"Quick and cheerful", with "tasty Turkish food", this chain has a strong presence on the South Bank, and its branch adjacent to Shakespeare's Globe is especially popular (see Tas Pide). Regulars say the operation is "reliable and reasonable" – even if it has over the years "lost some of its allure". / www.tasrestaurant.com; 11.30 pm, Sun 10.30 pm; EC4 Sat 5 pm; 72 Borough High St 6 pm, Sat & Sun 4 pm; EC4 closed Sat D & Sun, cafe SE1 closed D.

TAS PIDE SE1 £37 233

20-22 NEW GLOBE WALK 020 7928 3300
10–3B

"A reliable quick meal before the Globe – never fails!" This spin-off from the Tas chain (named for its speciality of Turkish pizza, 'pide') has a cosy Anatolian interior and, although there are "no surprises here" foodwise, it's "quick and cheerful" and provides "great affordable food, in a super location with friendly staff who are patient and kind with children!" / SE1 9DR; www.tasrestaurants.co.uk; @TasRestaurants; 11.30 pm, Sun 10.30 pm.

TATE BRITAIN, WHISTLER RESTAURANT SW1 £64 234

MILLBANK 020 7887 8825 2–4C

"The joy of a wine list (an impressive worldwide selection at not-unreasonable prices) curated by Hamish Anderson, continues to be the star of the show here" in this "wonderful room" whose "murals by Rex Whistler are well worth a visit in their own right". The other aspects of the experience – not least its British fare – have traditionally played second fiddle here, but won higher ratings this year, with regulars judging both food and service to be "better than in the past". / SW1 4RG; www.tate.org.uk/visit/tate-britain/rex-whistler-restaurant; @Tate; closed Mon-Sun D; booking D only.

TATE MODERN, KITCHEN & BAR, LEVEL 6 SE1 £58 223

LEVEL 6 BOILER HOUSE, BANKSIDE
020 7887 8888 10–3B

"You come for the view, which does not disappoint" ("stunning") at Tate Modern's original upper-level perch on the South Bank of the Thames. Gastronomically, though, its seasonal British fare is something of a missed opportunity: admittedly "better than expected", but nevertheless "unexciting", from a "limited menu" and "not in the same league as the Rex Whistler" (at Tate Britain). / SE1 9TG; www.tate.org.uk; @TateFood; 9 pm; Sun-Thu L only, Fri & Sat open L & D.

TAYLOR ST BARISTAS £12 333

"Superb coffee and great cakes" make this small chain a "go-to" choice for a caffeine hit in the City or Mayfair. Service can be "slightly slow", but, "being hipster central, it's probably uncool to criticise". / www.taylor-st.com; most branches close 5 pm-5.30 pm, WC2 7 pm, Wed-Fri 9 pm; Old Broad ST, Clifton St, W1, E14 closed Sat & Sun; New St closed Sat; TW9 closed Sun.

TAYYABS E1 £28 422

83 FIELDGATE ST 020 7247 6400 10–2D

"Embrace the chaos and suck down those chops!" – this "noisy and rambunctious neighbourhood joint with 500 seats" has become "an East End institution" to rival the older Lahore. "The queues are tough" but "it's worth the wait and the hassle for fabulous Pakistani food at ridiculously cheap prices". "For Cobra, shop up the street at the Tesco Metro, as they are BYO". / E1 1JU; www.tayyabs.co.uk; @1tayyabs; 11.30 pm.

TELL YOUR FRIENDS SW6 £48

175 NEW KING'S RD 020 7731 6404 11–1B

Sisters Lucy and Tiffany Watson – best known for featuring in Made in Chelsea – are behind this vegan, spring-2018 newcomer (which is actually located in Parsons Green, not Chelsea). The aim: to 'demystify veganism and showcase how tasty it can be'. / SW6 4SW; www.tellyourfriendsldn.com.

TEMPER £48 224

25 BROADWICK ST, W1 020 3879 3834
4–1C | 5 MERCERS WALK, WC2
020 3004 6669 5–2C NEW | ANGEL
COURT, EC2 020 3004 6984 10–2C

"The theatre of the fire pits" ("grab a table at the counter to see your food cooking, and to strike up a conversation with the chefs") helps inspire fans of the "extraordinary culinary style" of Neil Rankin's "loud", "subterranean temple to everything carnivorous" in Soho, which has a spin-off in the City ("in a quiet alley by Bank") and now also in Covent Garden (where most of the cooking is in a wood-fired oven, and where they also do pizza). The verdict on the food, however, is becoming increasingly mixed – to fans the smoked BBQ fare is "brilliant and creative", featuring "dishes unlike anywhere else", but the proportion of sceptics who find the food "bland", or "over-salted" or "very over-hyped" is growing. / temperrestaurant.com; @temperldn.

THE 10 CASES
WC2 £54 3 4 3

16 ENDELL ST 020 7836 6801 5–2C

A "wonderful left-field wine list" – "a rapidly varying selection" of "different and uncommon vintages" at "sensible prices" – is what makes this highly appealing wine bar "a dark haven of happiness in the tourist wastelands of Covent Garden". There's solid support, too, for the "straightforward, well presented tapas" to accompany it. / WC2H 9BD; www.the10cases.co.uk; @10cases; 11 pm; closed Sun.

10 GREEK STREET
W1 £58 4 4 3

10 GREEK ST 020 7734 4677 5–2A

"Lovely…", "fun…", "affordable…", "…a delight!" – this "cramped" modern wine bar in Soho is "a place to go back again and again" with its "stunning and original", "locally sourced" food and its "handwritten Wine Journal with interesting entries and very reasonable mark ups". "Love sitting by the bar to watch the chefs, but does get a little smokey at times!" / W1D 4DH; www.10greekstreet.com; @10GreekStreet; 11 pm, Sun 9 pm; closed Sun; booking L only.

TENDIDO CERO
SW5 £52 3 3 4

174 OLD BROMPTON RD 020 7370 3685 6–2B

"If you want Spanish tapas, it doesn't get much better" than at this self-styled "designer tapas" and wine bar in South Kensington. It's "very noisy" when packed, which is often, but fans reckon it has "recovered from a dip a couple of years back" and now has "better tapas than you get in Spain". A warning: "be prepared for a big bill if you really go to town". / SW5 0BA; www.cambiodetercio.co.uk; @CambiodTercio; 11 pm.

TERROIRS
£53 3 2 3

5 WILLIAM IV ST, WC2 020 7036 0660 5–4C | **38 LORDSHIP LANE, SE22** 020 8693 9021 1–4D **NEW**

With its "outstanding range and quality of wines" (many of them funky, if "slightly hit-and-miss" 'biodynamique' vintages), and "limited-but-quirky menu" of rustic French fare (charcuterie, cheese, eel salad, smoked cod's roe), all at "decent prices", this well-known dive of nearly ten years' standing, near Charing Cross station, "feels like a trusty friend" to very many reporters. "Perhaps one was more excited a few years back when places like these were less common" but its ratings have softened in recent years – "dishes can be a little inconsistent" and the very "Gallic" service "has gone backwards". Still, it's "always buzzing". In October 2017, owners Cave des Pyrène rebranded its East Dulwich offshoot ToastED under the same name. / terroirswinebar.com; @TerroirsWineBar.

TEXTURE W1
£118 5 3 3

34 PORTMAN ST 020 7224 0028 2–2A

"Unbelievable… everything was magnificent!" – Aggi Sverrisson's "more-than-first-class" venture (now over ten years old) is a showcase for his truly "superb" Scandi-inspired cooking paired with an outstanding wine selection, too. "Service is occasionally hit and miss but mostly good". Top Tip – don't miss the fish tasting menu here. / W1H 7BY; www.texture-restaurant.co.uk; @TextureLondon; 11 pm; closed Tue, Wed L, closed Sun & Mon.

THALI SW5
£48 4 4 3

166 OLD BROMPTON RD 020 7373 2626 6–2B

"Why does this restaurant seem to fly under the radar?" – A "classy" contemporary Indian café on the fringes of South Kensington, decorated with Bollywood posters, which serves "lovingly prepared, fresh and aromatic dishes" (based on recipes sourced from the owner's relatives). "It should be better known." / SW5 0BA; @ThaliLondon; Sun-Thu 11 pm, Fri & Sat 11.30 pm.

THEO RANDALL
W1 £90 4 4 2

INTERCONTINENTAL HOTEL, 1 HAMILTON PL 020 7318 8747 3–4A

The home of some of "the best Italian food going" is how fans recommend this ex-River Café head chef's luxurious dining room, just off a hotel foyer by Hyde Park Corner, which also benefits from an "enormous and interesting wine list" (although the latter "can bring tears to your wallet"). The space lacks natural light, but the revamp a couple of years ago has made it more "charming". / W1J 7QY; www.theorandall.com; @theorandall; 11 pm; closed Sat L & Sun.

THEO'S SE5
£39 3 3 2

2 GROVE LN 020 3026 4224 1–3C

"Excellent charred crusts from a thin sourdough and really interesting, well-sourced toppings" inspire love for this "great neighbourhood pizzeria" in Camberwell, often praised for its "excellent value for money"; it also has a "lovely garden area at the back". / SE5 \N; www.theospizzeria.com; @theospizzaldn; Tue-Thu, Sun 10.30 pm, Fri & Sat 11 pm, Mon 10 pm; no Amex; may need 6+ to book.

THEOS SIMPLE ITALIAN
SW5 £69 3 3 2

34 - 44 BARKSTON GARDENS, KENSINGTON 020 7370 9130 6–2A

"A real mixed bag" – Theo Randall goes casual at his branded spin-off in a low-profile Earl's Court hotel. Reports generally are positive, regarding the pizza and "top pasta", but more complex dishes can be "marred by some heavy-handed treatment" and – while "staff are friendly" – "the decor is incongruous and the space feels very like the hotel restaurant that it is". / SW5 0EW; www.theossimpleitalian.co.uk; @TRSimpleItalian; 10.30 pm.

34 MAYFAIR W1
£79 2 2 3

34 GROSVENOR SQ 020 3350 3434 3–3A

Plush New York-style grill near the former US Embassy, from Richard Caring's stable, that's "perfect for a business lunch over good food" if you're willing to pay top Mayfair dollar. But ratings are down this year amid signs of resistance to such pricing: "expense accounters (and victims of hotel concierges) seem to be the mainstays". / W1K 2HD; www.34-restaurant.co.uk; @34_restaurant; 11.30 pm, Sun 10.30 pm.

THE THOMAS CUBITT
SW1 £68 3 4 4

44 ELIZABETH ST 020 7730 6060 2–4A

"A very busy, popular local in Belgravia, with excellent food and atmosphere, particularly in the first floor dining room", which – with its linen and light decor – is "more decent restaurant than good gastropub"; "genuine smiling service" too. / SW1W 9PA; www.thethomascubitt.co.uk; @TheThomasCubitt; 10 pm, Sun 9.30 pm.

THREE CRANES
EC4 £57

28 GARLICK HILL 020 3455 7437 10–2C

Historic, heart-of-the-city tavern (with two serviced apartments) that's part of the well-publicised collaboration of Henry Harris (formerly chef-patron of Racine) and founder of Harcourt Inns, James McCulloch. It's been less PR'd than the other ventures, but early reports cite "simple French food, under the guidance of Henry Harris that make this small City pub near Mansion House a very good place". / EC4V 2BA; www.threecranescity.co.uk; @threecranesldn; Mon & Tue 9 pm, Fri & Sat 11.30 pm, Wed 10 pm, Thu 11 pm, Sun 5 pm.

TIBITS
£42 3 2 3

12-14 HEDDON ST, W1 020 7758 4110 4–3B | **124 SOUTHWARK ST, SE1** 020 7202 8370 10–4B

This Swiss self-service vegetarian concept, with a flagship off Regent Street and a "welcome" branch near Tate Modern, serves "freshly prepared, global" dishes which you pay for by 100g. By West End standards, they offer "great value for money" for "lunch or dinner in relaxed surroundings" – "I've taken meat eaters and they're converted!". / www.tibits.co.uk; @tibits_uk.

TIMMY GREEN
SW1 £67 3 3 3

NOVA VICTORIA, 11 SIR SIMON MILTON SQUARE 020 3019 7404 2–4B

For "a delicious Aussie breakfast in Victoria", many reporters recommend this big (150 cover) "cheap 'n' cheerful" haunt in the huge Nova development: part of the 'Daisy Green' brasserie chain. At other times, the focus is on steaks and other grills from the Josper, plus craft beers and cocktails. / SW1E 5BH; www.daisygreenfood.com/venues/timmy-green; 11 pm, Sun 10 pm.

TING SE1 £98 ②②④

LEVEL 35, 31 ST THOMAS ST
020 7234 8108   10–4C

The Shangri-La's luxuriously appointed eyrie on the 35th floor of the Shard (named after a Chinese word for 'living room'), does win praise for its gastronomic potential, but most reports focus almost exclusively on its "excellent views" over London, 128 metres below. The other features rating mention – other than the vertiginous nature of the bill – are the memorable afternoon teas (choose from British or Oriental tea menus). / SE1 9RY; www.ting-shangri-la.com; @ShangriLaShard; 11 pm; No trainers; credit card required to book.

TISH NW3

196 HAVERSTOCK HILL   020 7431 3828
9–2A

Property developer David Levin has apparently always dreamed of opening a kosher eatery and is behind this 160-cover venture – a July 2018 opening, billed as London's 'largest and finest' kosher restaurant – an all-day brasserie in Belsize Park. Its early days – first rumbles on the bush telegraph so far suggest the fit-out is splendid, and that the cooking is still a work in progress. / NW3 2AG; www.tish.london; @tish_london; Tue-Thu 10 pm, Fri & Sat 10.30 pm, Sun 9.30 pm.

TITU W1 £61 ④⑤④

1A SHEPHERD ST   020 7493 8746   3–4B

Limited but hugely positive initial feedback on (ex-Novikov) Kiwi chef, Jeff Tyler's tiny (15-seater) newcomer in Mayfair's picturesque Shepherd Market. "It's a lovely and fun little operation, where service is by two charming young ladies who knew the food well." On the menu: handmade, non-traditional gyoza and a range of colourful Asian-inspired salads and snacks, all of which are praised for being very well-crafted. / W1J 7HJ; www.titurestaurant.com; @titulondon.

TOFFS N10 £40 ③④③

38 MUSWELL HILL BROADWAY
020 8883 8656   1–1B

"Dependably excellent" Greek Cypriot chippie in Muswell Hill, whose big fanclub extends across neighbouring postcodes and beyond – a stalwart operation, which serves "scrumptious" fish, chips and Greek salads in "portions verging on the ridiculously large". The grilled fish is particularly popular, but "battered rock and haddock are to die for", too. / N10 3RT; www.toffsfish.co.uk; @toffsfish; 10 pm; closed Sun.

TOKIMEITE W1 £109 ③②②

23 CONDUIT ST   020 3826 4411   3–2C

It has impeccable credentials – it's backed by Japan's largest agricultural co-op, ZeN-Noh, and overseen by two of Japan's more famous chefs – but this Mayfair two-year-old inspires precious little feedback. Such as there is says the food's really "quite good" but that the overall formula doesn't quite hang together – "maybe they're not quite sure what sort of restaurant this should be. Is it all about its wagyu, or is it a kappo kaiseki place [a multi-course meal, where the selection is left to the chef]… or is it just one of those bland Mayfair places for hedgies to spend obscene amounts of money…?" / W1S 2XS; www.tokimeite.com; @tokimeitelondon; 10.30 pm; closed Sun.

TOKYO DINER
WC2 £24 ③③③

2 NEWPORT PLACE   020 7287 8777   5–3B

"A huge choice of classic Japanese fast food" at "very reasonable prices for central London" make this diner a real "go-to" in Chinatown. The tastes are "authentic – just like in a Tokyo eatery", although "portions are larger". There's a "buzzy atmosphere and cheerful but slightly haphazard service". Top tip – "bento boxes definitely recommended". / WC2H 7JJ; www.tokyodiner.com; 11.30 pm; closed Tue-Sun L, closed Mon; no Amex; no booking.

TOM SIMMONS
SE1 £60 ③②②

2 STILL WALK   020 3848 2100   10–4D

"A welcome addition to the growing Tower Bridge development" – this year-old London debut of Pembrokeshire-born chef Tom Simmons (who appeared on MasterChef: The Professionals) brings a focus on Welsh ingredients to the capital, and wins praise for its "good produce, well put together", and "sensible prices". Teething issues have included gripes about staff training, and some feel "the décor could do with an uplift" but its "excellent position makes it a good choice for a business lunch" (or eating around a show at the new Bridge Theatre). Hopefully a financial restructuring (which took place in mid-summer 2018) will provide the necessary headroom to develop the site further. / SE1 2UP; tom-simmons.co.uk; @TomSimmons_TB; 11 pm; closed Sun & Mon.

TOMMI'S BURGER JOINT
£29 ③③③

30 THAYER ST, W1   020 7224 3828   3–1A |
37 BERWICK ST, W1   020 7494 9086   4–2D
| 342 KINGS RD, SW3   020 7349 0691
6–3C

"Smoky little room (in a good way), fast service, brilliant condiments and amazing burgers" – "at a decent price" – is the offer at the Soho and Marylebone outlets of Icelander Tómas Tómasson's international chain. Top Tip: "awesome sweet potato fries". / www.burgerjoint.co.uk; @BurgerJointUk; 10.30 pm, Sun 9 pm; booking: min 5.

TOMOE SW15 £37 ④②①

292 UPPER RICHMOND RD   020 3730 7884
11–2B

The "superb fresh sushi and sashimi" at this "tucked-away little place" in Putney is some of "the best no-frills Japanese food in town". "The number of Japanese customers shouts volumes" about a kitchen that has carried on where its predecessor on the site, Cho-San (RIP), left off – in the same "far-from-uplifting surroundings". / SW15 \N; 9.30 pm.

TOMS KITCHEN £67 ②②②

27 CALE ST, SW3   020 7349 0202
6–2C | 11 WESTFERRY CIRCUS, E14
020 3011 1555   12–1C | 1 COMMODITY
QUAY, E1   020 3011 5433   10–3D

These "smart" casual dining venues in Chelsea and Canary Wharf win most acclaim for their "top breakfasts" and the Somerset House outlet has "a fabulous location on the river (outside in summer)". The food is "decent" but gives no particular hints of much connection with chef Tom Aikens, who founded the group. / www.tomskitchen.co.uk; @TomsKitchens; SW3 10.30 pm, Sun 9.30 pm; WC2 10 pm; E14 9.30 pm; E1 10.30 pm; SE1 6 pm; B1 10.30 pm, Sun 5 pm; WC2, E14, B1 & E1 closed Sun D.

TONKOTSU £43 ④③③

SELFRIDGES, 400 OXFORD ST, W1
020 7437 0071   3–1A | 63 DEAN ST,
W1   020 7437 0071   5–2A | 7 BLENHEIM
CR, W11   020 7221 8300   7–1A | 4
CANVEY ST, SE1   020 7928 2228   10–4B
| BATTERSEA POWER STATION ARCHES,
SW8   020 7720 7695   11–1C NEW |
UNIT 1, ENDEAVOUR SQUARE, E20
020 8534 6809   14–1D NEW | 382 MARE ST,
E8   020 8533 1840   14–1B | ARCH 334, 1A
DUNSTON ST, E8   020 7254 2478   14–2A

"The broth is so incredibly thick and creamy, and this combined with the very generous servings make for a very good quick eat" at these cramped ramen pit-stops serving "noodles… more noodles… and some side dishes for those not wanting noodles". "As it's just a place for sustenance, you go with the flow, but staff are friendly and helpful". / www.tonkotsu.co.uk; @TonkotsuSoho; 10 pm-11 pm; Selfridges 30 mins before store closing; no bookings.

TOSA W6 £39 ③③②

332 KING ST   020 8748 0002   8–2B

"Yakitori – charcoal-grilled chicken skewers – are the real draw" at this "brilliant local" Japanese in Stamford Brook, but it has an "interesting menu" generally, which includes noodles, sashimi and sushi, and makes for "fun casual dining". / W6 0RR; 11 pm, Sun 10.30 pm.

TOZI SW1 £50 ③④③

8 GILLINGHAM ST   020 7769 9771   2–4B

"A must-try if you like Italian" – this "cheerful but noisy" specialist in Venetian cicchetti (small plates) attached to a hotel near Victoria station serves up "a lively dining experience with interesting and original dishes". / SW1V 1HN; www.tozirestaurant.co.uk; @ToziRestaurant; Tue-Thu 10 pm, Fri & Sat 10.30 pm, Mon 9.30 pm, Sun 9 pm.

THE TRAFALGAR DINING ROOMS SW1 £65 333

SPRING GARDENS 020 7870 2901 2–3C

Positive ratings (although limited feedback as yet) on the new Mediterranean-influenced restaurant and cocktail bar in the stylishly revamped foyer of the Trafalgar Hotel, whose best perches look right out onto Trafalgar Square. Don't forget to check out The Rooftop (see also) while you're there. / SW1A 2TS; www.trafalgardiningrooms.com; @DiningroomSW1; Sun-Thu 11 pm, Fri & Sat midnight.

THE TRAMSHED EC2 £60 323

32 RIVINGTON ST 020 7749 0478 13–1B

"A stuffed Damien Hirst cow dominates the dining room" at Mark Hix's big, Britart-decorated Victorian tramshed conversion in Shoreditch. Six years on from the excitement of its launch, the large space can seem "quiet", but by most accounts it's still "always a total pleasure" – if perhaps a slightly "overpriced" one – with its menu of "good steaks and impressive whole roast chicken (served upright, claws intact)". / EC2A 3LX; www.hixrestaurants.co.uk/restaurant/tramshed; @the_tramshed; 10.30 pm, Sun 4 pm.

TRANGALLAN N16 £47 443

61 NEWINGTON GRN 020 7359 4988 1–1C

"Inventive dishes that you won't find in other tapas places" distinguish this "excellent" (if "pricey") Newington Green Spaniard, with Galician specialities. / N16 9PX; www.trangallan.com; @trangallan_n16; Sat, Mon-Fri 11 pm, Sun 10 pm; closed Mon; no Amex; No trainers.

TRATRA E2 £64

2-4 BOUNDARY ST 020 7729 1051 13–1B

Limited and somewhat cautious feedback on Stéphane Reynaud's first venture outside of France, in the basement of the Conran family's stylish boutique hotel (the only bit of the Prescott & Conran empire they decided to buy back from the administrator). We've left a rating until we have more reports. / E2 7DD; boundary.london; @BoundaryLDN.

TREDWELL'S WC2 £60 222

4 UPPER ST MARTIN'S LN 020 3764 0840 5–3B

Marcus Wareing's multi-level Theatreland diner doesn't sit within any easily defined niche and continues to split opinions. At its best, this is a versatile, "buzzy and fun" destination ("especially if you can grab a booth"), suited to many occasions; and fans of its "interesting, varied menu, with amazing flavours" just "can't wait to go back". Sceptics, though, feel the food is "less inspired than expected from a Marcus Wareing venue", with "a total bill that's too much for an ultimately unsatisfying experience". Top Tip – often nominated as a kid-friendly

choice. / WC2H 9NY; www.tredwells.com; @tredwells; Mon-Thu 10 pm, Fri & Sat 11 pm, Sun 9 pm.

TREVES & HYDE E1 £54 343

15-17 LEMAN ST 020 3621 8900 10–2D

At the foot of a new aparthotel near Aldgate East tube, this year-old venture comprises a coffee shop and terrace downstairs, and a restaurant and bar upstairs, which – under seasoned chef George Tannock – tries harder than you might expect in this location: "a welcome, local, go-to business lunch place, with an excellent and varied menu and staff who are efficient but welcoming". / E1 8EN; trevesandhyde.com; @trevesandhyde; 10.30 pm, Sun 6 pm.

TRIED & TRUE SW15 £23 333

279 UPPER RICHMOND RD 020 8789 0410 11–2A

"A good local vibe", "very helpful staff" and "very good breakfasts" are key selling points of this Kiwi café in Putney. / SW15 \N; www.triedandtruecafe.co.uk; @tried_true_cafe; Mon-Fri 4 pm, Sat & Sun 4.30 pm; closed Mon-Sun D.

TRINITY SW4 £75 554

4 THE POLYGON 020 7622 1199 11–2D

"Since getting a (long-overdue) Michelin star, the team have upped their game" yet further, at Adam Byatt's ever-outstanding Clapham trailblazer – "a very slick operation", with an attractive position near Clapham Common. "In many respects it rivals Chez Bruce with the added advantages of more table space and less lead time for a table!" "Exemplary cuisine combines the familiar with interesting novelties without being outlandish or showing off". "You are made to feel very welcome" by the "unusually well-informed staff" and the setting is "delightfully calm and relaxing". See also Trinity Upstairs. / SW4 0JG; www.trinityrestaurant.co.uk; @TrinityLondon; 10 pm, Sun 9 pm; closed Mon L & Sun D.

TRINITY UPSTAIRS SW4 £50 544

4 THE POLYGON 020 3745 7227 11–2D

"Upstairs should be cloned for every city in the world" according to fans of Adam Byatt's more relaxed alternative to the main dining space below – "an informal venue" (arguably "more vibey than downstairs") with "an open kitchen, plus about 30 covers on high stools and narrow tables"; and looked after by "hard-working staff". "Adventurous, regularly changing menus" (often featuring guest chefs) use a small plates format, and results are "truly exciting". / SW4 0JG; www.trinityrestaurant.co.uk; @trinityupstairs; 10 pm.

TRISHNA W1 £83 422

15-17 BLANDFORD ST 020 7935 5624 2–1A

The Sethi family's original London venture – this "low-key"-looking, ten-year-old recreation of a famous Mumbai venue, in Marylebone, is beginning to show its age a little. Fans still tout its "exquisitely prepared and not over-spiced cuisine", as "the best in fine-end Indian dining" and on a par with its now more high-profile sibling, Gymkhana. But ratings here slid noticeably across the board in this year's survey, amidst gripes about "rather sporadic service" and food that's "starting to feel a mite unexciting nowadays". Is their empire finally showing growing pains? / W1U 3DG; www.trishnalondon.com; @TrishnaLondon; 10 pm.

LA TROMPETTE W4 £82 553

5-7 DEVONSHIRE RD 020 8747 1836 8–2A

"The kind of restaurant that sets the gold standard" – this "classy and understated" neighbourhood star has an obscure location in a Chiswick side street and echoes the "unshowy" excellence of its stablemate Chez Bruce, "delivering the goods year on year". "Novel, vibrant and exciting cooking still thrills and surprises" and service, likewise, "is outstanding – you never feel like a waiter is looking over your shoulder but the staff are attentive to everything". The persnickety feel that the interior is maybe a mite "clinical", but most reporters feel "the surroundings are lovely", "all very relaxed", cosseted by "the hum of happy diners". / W4 2EU; www.latrompette.co.uk; @LaTrompetteUK; 10.30 pm, Sun 9.30 pm.

TRULLO N1 £60 333

300-302 ST PAUL'S RD 020 7226 2733 9–2D

"It's best to book ahead at this ever-popular pit-stop, just off Highbury Corner" – a "fantastic, generous and fairly priced neighbourhood Italian", which was the survey's most commented-on destination in North London this year. "It's probably the sheer simplicity of the decor and apparently happy waiting staff – coupled with a chatty clientele who appreciate the carefully curated ingredients – which make it such a consistent pleasure to visit". "Despite the squashed and clattery interior, it manages to dish up really well-judged Italian cooking" – "simple classic dishes" ("not standard fare pasta and pizza") – "and an utterly enjoyable evening". / N1 2LH; www.trullorestaurant.com; @Trullo_LDN; 10 pm, Sun 2.30 am; closed Sun D; no Amex.

TSUNAMI SW4 £48 523

5-7 VOLTAIRE RD 020 7978 1610 11–1D

"A real gem" – "extraordinary" – this Clapham fixture has for many, many years produced some of "the best Japanese you can get, at a really reasonable price": in fact, locals feel "to be honest, it's far better than the very expensive well-known Japanese restaurants in Central London". It also mixes up "some of the most innovative cocktails in town". The catch: "it's always packed so the service lets it down... but that means nothing when you taste the food". "Pity the Fitzrovia branch closed" – but do try Yama Momo in East Dulwich. / SW4 6DQ; www.tsunamirestaurant.co.uk; 11 pm, Fri-Sun midnight; closed Sat L & Sun; no Amex.

TUYO E2 £57 3 3 3

129A PRITCHARD'S RD 020 7739 2540 14–2B

You look out from big windows at this bright contemporary café in the environs of Hackney's busy Broadway Market, where an ex-Salt Yard chef provides an eclectic menu of Mediterranean tapas, plus wine and cocktails. The food is well-rated and prices are not punishing. / E2 9AP; www.tuyo.london; @Tuyocafebistro; Sun-Thu 10.30 pm, Fri & Sat 11 pm.

1251 N1

107 UPPER ST NO TEL 9–3D

James Cochran has launched again in Islington, on the site of Chinese Laundry (RIP), just months after his James Cochran N1 closed (it has been retrospectively called a pop-up). He is also no longer cooking at the EC1 restaurant that bears his name (see also). The food here is "modern British, taking inspiration from James's Scottish and Vincentian roots" and will also feature "Asian influences". / N1 1QN; www.1251.co.uk.

28 CHURCH ROW NW3 £53 4 4 4

28 CHURCH ROW 020 7993 2062 9–2A

"Head down a modest staircase into a warm, informal space with an open kitchen to watch" at one of Hampstead's most exciting openings of recent times (for those with long memories, "the old Cellier Du Midi premises, transformed by a local couple who like to meet their customers"). On the menu "amazing contemporary tapas, with some of the more substantial offerings a meal in themselves: the pig's cheek, for example". "You can't book" and "evenings can be busy, so be prepared to wait at the pub opposite and they'll phone you when ready". / NW3 6UP; www.28churchrow.com; @28churchrow.com; 10.30 pm, Sun 9.30 pm; closed Mon-Fri L.

28-50 £68 2 2 3

15-17 MARYLEBONE LN, W1 020 7486 7922 3–1A | 17-19 MADDOX ST, W1 020 7495 1505 4–2A | 140 FETTER LN, EC4 020 7242 8877 10–2A

"Superb wines (many sold in smaller, affordable measures)" still win praise for Agnar Sverrisson's business-friendly wine bar group of bar/bistros. The food ("simple dishes" like burgers, plus cheese and charcuterie) has always been a case of "no fireworks but good value" but slipping ratings across the board this year coincided with news in June 2018 that the business is up for sale. With Fetter Lane sold off, the future for the (more successful) Marylebone and Mayfair branches is up for grabs. / www.2850.co.uk; @2850Restaurant; 9.30 pm-10.30 pm; EC4 closed Sat & Sun, W1S closed Sun.

24 THE OVAL SW9

24 CLAPHAM RD 020 7735 6111 11–1D

Now open in Oval, a May 2018 newcomer from Matt Wells (co-owner of The Dairy, Clapham) and his business partner from SW4 steakhouse Knife, Andrew Bradford. Unlike the tapas-y format which won The Dairy renown, it's full-sized plates of Modern British cuisine here which is winning upbeat initial press reviews. / SW9 0JG; www.24theoval.co.uk; @24theoval.

TWIST W1 £64 4 5 4

42 CRAWFORD ST 020 7723 3377 2–1A

"Eduardo Tuccillo's relative newcomer [it's three years old] is well-hidden in the depths of Marylebone" on a site that some reporters "date themselves" by recalling in its days as Garbo's (long RIP). As with its long-departed predecessor, the "minimalist interior" is a fraction "bare and noisy", but all reports acknowledge it as "a real winner". "Plates are designed for sharing, tapas style" and "if you are a proper foodie, you will love his phenomenally creative Italo-Spanish cooking with some Asian-fusion to surprise as well". "It's in my neighbourhood but I've only just discovered it: glad I did!" / W1H 1JW; www.twistkitchen.co.uk; @twistkitchen; closed Sun; SRA-Food Made Good – 2 stars.

TWO BROTHERS N3 £34 3 2 2

297-303 REGENT'S PARK RD 020 8346 0469 1–1B

"Authentic, high-quality fish 'n' chips" win consistently high marks for this traditional Finsbury chippy, whose high standards have made it a popular local favourite for 25 years. / N3 1DP; www.twobrothers.co.uk; 10 pm; closed Mon.

TWO LIGHTS E2

28-30 KINGSLAND RD AWAITING TEL 13–1B

From The Clove Club: the team have set up former head chef Chase Lovecky in his own restaurant, which opened in September 2018, just up the road from the mothership. We're told to expect 'a neighbourhood spot, serving modern American food', and with his track record (at momofuku in NYC and Jean Georges), it will hopefully be anything but boring. / E2 8DA; www.twolights.restaurant; 10.30 pm, Mon 11 pm, Sun 3 pm.

2 VENETI W1 £55 3 3 3

10 WIGMORE ST 020 7637 0789 3–1B

"Excellent Venetian food" is the point of difference at this "very welcoming" and "consistently good" Italian near the Wigmore Hall – a "popular (and sometimes noisy) spot for those who lunch". "The only place I've found bigoli" (a regional pasta). / W1U 2RD; www.2veneti.com; @2Veneti; 10.30 pm, Sat 11 pm; closed Sat L & Sun.

ULI W11 £47 3 4 4

5 LADBROKE RD 020 3141 5878 7–2B

"It's a surprise to find such an outstanding restaurant in such an unlikely place", say fans of Michael Lim's resurrected pan-Asian, nowadays on the more obscure fringes of Notting Hill (previously near the Portobello Road). With its "wonderful" Asian cuisine, fans feel "it's just as good as it was in All Saints Road", and even if ratings are still a tad off their historic highs, it's widely seen as "a fab addition to W11's culinary choices". / W11 3PA; www.ulilondon.com; @ulilondon; midnight, Sun 11 pm; D only, closed Sun.

UMU W1 £120 2 3 3

14-16 BRUTON PL 020 7499 8881 3–2C

"Japanese cuisine at its finest (the quality of ingredients, especially fish, is simply amazing!)" inspires respect for Marlon Abela's much-vaunted venture dedicated to Kyoto-style kaiseki cuisine, tucked away in a delightful Mayfair mews and whose sleek styling is "not typically Japanese… in a good way". Ever since it opened in 2004, it has taken flak for being "grossly overpriced", but the reason its ratings were dragged down this year related to a couple of unusually disappointing reports. / W1J 6LX; www.umurestaurant.com; 10.30 pm; closed Sun; No trainers; booking max 14 may apply.

UNION STREET CAFÉ SE1 £62 3 2 3

47-51 GREAT SUFFOLK ST 020 7592 7977 10–4B

More positive, if limited, feedback this year on this Gordon Ramsay group casual Italian in Borough: reporters award solid ratings to food that was "decent to excellent" if perhaps "not cheap" (offsetting which, there are "often good value special deals"). / SE1 0BS; www.gordonramsayrestaurants.com/union-street-cafe; @unionstreetcafe; Mon-Fri 10.30 pm, Sat midnight, Sun 5 pm; closed Sun D.

UNWINED SW17 £26 3 4 4

21-23 TOOTING HIGH ST 020 3583 9136 11–2C

"Ever-changing, themed menus" ("very global!") add pizzazz to this "delightful wine bar in the middle of Tooting market" – "a great find where guest chefs have a 6-week residency and diners squeeze round a communal table. The food's really interesting and it always leads to a fun night out". / SW17 0SN; agrapenightin.co.uk; @UnwinedSW17; Wed-Sat 11 pm, Tue 10 pm, Sun 5.30 pm; closed Tue L closed Sun D, closed Mon.

LE VACHERIN W4 £64 3 3 3

76-77 SOUTH PARADE 020 8742 2121 8–1A

"You'd think you were in a modern version of a Belle Epoque Parisian bistro" at this "classic French" outfit by Acton Green. "It specialises in delicious dishes made with Vacherin cheese – but there's much more to choose from". After 15 years, a major refurb is planned for early 2019. /

W4 5LF; www.levacherin.co.uk; @Le_Vacherin; 10.30 pm, Sun 9 pm; closed Mon L.

VAGABOND WINES
£41 2 2 3

77 BUCKINGHAM PALACE RD, SW1 020 7630 7693 2–4B NEW | 25 CHARLOTTE ST, W1 020 3441 9210 2–1C | 18-22 VANSTON PLACE, SW6 020 7381 1717 6–4A NEW | 4 NORTHCOTE RD, SW11 020 7738 0540 11–2C NEW

"A great concept" for wine tasting, accompanied by sharing plates of charcuterie, makes this chain of six bars "fun, too" ("once you've worked out how it all works!"). "Buy an Oyster-style card, top it up and sample a wide variety of different wines until you find one you just have to fill your glass with. Then repeat". On the downside, "it's easy to spend a fortune as none of the wines are cheap". The latest to open, in Battersea Power Station, is also producing its own wine on the premises. / www.vagabondwines.co.uk; @VagabondWines.

VANILLA BLACK
EC4 **£65** 4 3 3

17-18 TOOKS CT 020 7242 2622 10–2A

"Beautifully presented meat-free food" – arguably "the most adventurous vegetarian cuisine in London" (and at "incredible prices given it's so central") – inspired numerous rave reviews and much more consistently upbeat feedback this year for this ambitious operation near Chancery Lane. / EC4A 1LB; www.vanillablack.co.uk; @vanillablack1; 10 pm; closed Sun; no Amex.

VASCO & PIERO'S PAVILION
W1 **£61** 3 3 2

15 POLAND ST 020 7437 8774 4–1C

"A truly Italian venue in central London" – this "old-fashioned" Umbrian stalwart of half a century's standing has a "wonderfully understated" style, and delights its regulars with its "delicious cooking" ("superb pasta") and very characterful service. Fun fact – Gordon Brown had his engagement party here. / W1F 8QE; www.vascosfood.com; @Vasco_and_Piero; 10 pm; closed Sat L, closed Sun.

VEERASWAMY
W1 **£80** 4 4 4

VICTORY HS, 99-101 REGENT ST 020 7734 1401 4–4B

"A venerable institution that you have to visit at least once" – London's oldest Indian (est 1926) is still one of its best, having received a "calm, spacious and classy" contemporary revamp a few years ago (at the hands of its current owners, the Chutney Mary group) and serving "imaginative Indian dishes" with "original flavours". "There are probably better Indian restaurants in the West End, but for an overall experience, this takes some beating!" / W1B 4RS; www.veeraswamy.com; @theveeraswamy; Wed-Sun 9.30 pm; booking max 12 may apply.

The Wigmore, The Langham W1

VERDI'S E1
£44 3 4 3

237 MILE END RD 020 7423 9563 14–2B

"Welcoming service" and "authentic Italian food" inspired by the owner's origins in Parma (Giuseppe Verdi is the city's most famous son) make this trattoria a welcome addition to Stepney Green – "the atmosphere makes it seem long-standing". "The pizzas are worth a special mention." / E1 4AA; www.gverdi.uk; @verdislondon; Mon-Wed 5 pm, Thu-Sat 10 pm, Sun 6 pm.

VERMUTERIA N1

COAL DROPS YARD AWAITING TEL 9–3C

Anthony Demetre (he of Wild Honey and formerly Arbutus) has been announced as the latest incumbent of the Coal Drops Yard development in King's Cross. His bar and cafe will be an all-day take on the vermouth bars of Spain and Italy (vermuterias); over 50 different vermouths will be available. / N1C 4AB.

VIA EMILIA N1
£33

37A HOXTON SQUARE 020 7613 0508 13–1B

From the Food Roots company (and sibling to Fitzrovia's In Parma), this late 2017 opening in Hoxton Square obsesses over its north Italian sourcing, with home-made pasta the particular draw, served alongside charcuterie and cheeses from Parma. / N1 6NN; www.via--emilia.com; 11 pm, Sun 10.30 pm.

IL VICOLO SW1
£55 3 3 2

3-4 CROWN PASSAGE 020 7839 3960 3–4D

This "wonderful family-run restaurant" with "lovely owners" is a rarity for the heart of St James's – hidden away down an alleyway and popular for its "friendly staff and consistently good Italian food", which – considering the pukka location – is "surprisingly well priced". / SW1Y 6PP; www.ilvicolorestaurant.co.uk; 10 pm; closed Sat L & Sun.

THE VICTORIA
SW14 **£53** 2 2 3

10 WEST TEMPLE SHEEN 020 8876 4238 11–2A

"A popular Sheen gastropub near Richmond Park" with a "charming and stylish" interior, plus "a recently refurbished conservatory and play area for children". Critics feel the food is "rather ordinary" by comparison with its past best, but most reports say it's "always reliable". / SW14 7RT; victoriasheen.co.uk; @TheVictoria_Pub; 10 pm, Sun 9 pm; no Amex.

VIET FOOD W1
£32 3 2 2

34-36 WARDOUR ST 020 7494 4555 5–3A

"Just like eating in Asia", say fans of this "informal Vietnamese street food" warehouse-style operation in Chinatown, from former Hakkasan chef Jeff Tan. "Fresh and tasty – and good value for money." / W1D 6QT; www.vietnamfood.co.uk; Sun-Thu 10.30 pm, Fri & Sat 11 pm.

VIET GRILL E2
£45 3 2 2

58 KINGSLAND RD 020 7739 6686 14–2A

Long hailed as one of the better options on Kingsland Road's 'pho mile' – this "cheap 'n' cheerful" Vietnamese café only inspired limited feedback this year, but all of it positive. / E2 8DP; www.vietnamesekitchen.co.uk; @CayTreVietGrill; Tue-Fri, Mon 3.30 pm.

VIJAY NW6
£35 4 4 1

49 WILLESDEN LN 020 7328 1087 1–1B

Its decor is "old-looking" – and has been that way for about the last 30 years – but this "perennial favourite" in Kilburn continues to inspire an impressively "eclectic following (from humble local tradesmen to ladies in diamonds walking out of their limos)" with its "delicate yet pungent and flavourful South Indian dishes", and at "cheap" prices too. Top Tip – pay corkage to BYO. / NW6 7RF; www.vijayrestaurant.co.uk; Sun-Thu 10.45 pm, Fri & Sat 11.45 pm; no booking.

VILLA BIANCA
NW3 £68 222

1 PERRINS CT   020 7435 3131   9–2A

"Old-style Italian" whose popularity is underpinned by its gorgeous central Hampstead location and comfortable, retro decor. Fans acclaim it as a "top-end" destination of some accomplishment: those with less rose-tinted glasses say "it's a nice place to sit, but with overpriced and variable food that's no better than a tourist venue in Italy itself". / NW3 1QS; www.villabiancanw3.com; @VillaBiancaNW3; 11.30 pm, Sun 10.30 pm.

VILLA DI GEGGIANO
W4 £65 343

66-68 CHISWICK HIGH RD   020 3384 9442   8–2B

That it "tries hard" and "is a bit overdone on the decor" ("interesting art" on the walls) is mainly seen as a positive for this "lovely" and "upscale" Chiswick venture, operated by a 500-year-old Chianti dynasty as a showcase for Tuscan cuisine and wine. The cooking is consistently well-rated and the wine list includes "bottles from their own estate at exceptional prices". There's a 50-seater terrace for al fresco summer dining. / W4 1SY; www.villadigeggiano.co.uk; @villadigeggiano; 10.30 pm; closed Mon.

THE VINCENT ROOMS, WESTMINSTER KINGSWAY COLLEGE SW1 £38 322

76 VINCENT SQ   020 7802 8391   2–4C

"Kingsway College catering students staff this modern brasserie" in a quiet and leafy Westminster square, where customers are effectively 'guinea pigs' for training purposes. The "classic fare" is often (not always) "fully up to commercial standards" – but "service, by waiters learning their trade, can be terrible – yet the very reasonable prices make you forgive them!". / SW1P 2PD; www.westking.ac.uk/about-us/vincent-rooms-restaurant; @thevincentrooms; Mon, Fri 3 pm, Tue-Thu 9 pm; closed Mon & Fri D, closed Sat & Sun; no Amex.

VINOTECA £60 223

15 SEYMOUR PL, W1   020 7724 7288   2–2A | 18 DEVONSHIRE RD, W4   020 3701 8822   8–2A | ONE PANCRAS SQ, N1   020 3793 7210   9–3C | 7 ST JOHN ST, EC1   020 7253 8786   10–1B | BLOOMBERG ARCADE, EC2   020 3150 1292   10–3C NEW

"No surprise that the focus is on the wine" – "a huge and varied list, with loads of wines by the glass" and "many you've never heard of, to challenge your taste buds" – at these "modern/industrial" bars, of which the King's Cross and new Bloomberg branches attract most comment (Soho closed this year). "Don't forget the food though"; "it may play second fiddle" but is "simple and satisfying". / www.vinoteca.co.uk; 11 pm, W1H & W4 Sun 4 pm; W1F 10.45 pm, Sun 9.30 pm; EC1 closed Sun; W1H & W4 closed Sun D.

VIVAT BACCHUS £60 342

4 HAY'S LN, SE1   020 7234 0891   10–4C | 47 FARRINGDON ST, EC4   020 7353 2648   10–2A

"An eclectic and fascinating cellar, especially the South African options" (perhaps "the best selection of Saffa vintages in town") "scores alpha plus plus for the wines" at this very popular and "noisy" wine bar duo, and "amazingly knowledgeable and helpful staff" help with your deliberations. Though not the point, "the food is pretty good, too" with steak the top choice. / www.vivatbacchus.co.uk; 10.30 pm; closed Sun.

VIVI WC1

CENTRE POINT AWAITING TEL 5–1A

As part of the renovation of the Centre Point complex, caterers rhubarb (Sky Garden, Saatchi Gallery, Royal Albert Hall) are poised to open this new venue in autumn 2018 on the bridge link overlooking the square, featuring four separate dining areas, and with a comforting British menu: from chicken Kiev and fries to VIVI arctic roll. / WC1A 1DD; www.rhubarb.co.uk; @VIVIRestaurant; 9.30 pm.

VQ £48 233

ST GILES HOTEL, GREAT RUSSELL ST, WC1   020 7636 5888   5–1A | 325 FULHAM RD, SW10   020 7376 7224   6–3B | 24 PEMBRIDGE RD, W11   020 3745 7224   7–2B | 9 ALDGATE HIGH ST, EC3   020 3301 7224   10–2D

"Open 24/7" – the stalwart SW10 original "has been there forever, and is still the same old reliable standby at all hours": "it's a simple menu, but what they do, they do well". In recent years it's spawned a number of spin offs – WC1 in particular "has a large turnover and is reasonably priced". / www.vingtquatre.co.uk; @vqrestaurants; open 24 hours, W11 1 am, Thu-Sat 3 am, Sun midnight; booking: max 6 online.

VRISAKI N22 £42 333

73 MIDDLETON RD   020 8889 8760   1–1C

"The food just keeps coming" at this veteran Bounds Green taverna and take-away, when you go for the famous mezze special: "I've never had a bad meal and my guests ask, 'when are we going back again?'" / N22 8LZ; vrisakirestaurant.com; @vrisakiuk; 11 pm; closed Sun & Mon; no Amex.

WAGAMAMA £42 112

Fans still say "you can't go wrong for a quick noodle fix", but overall ratings are starting to crater at these ubiquitous, communal pan-Asian canteens, where "the food has gone downhill", "the quality of ingredients seems to be dropping" and service can now be very "disjointed". On the plus side "they love kids, and kids love it". / www.wagamama.com; 10 pm - 11.30 pm; EC2 Sat 9 pm; EC4 closed Sat & Sun; EC2 closed Sun; no booking.

WAHACA £39 233

For a "flavourful and fun", "dependable and quick" meal, fans of Thomasina Miers' group of street food cantinas still feel it's "one of the best chains around", citing its "decent Mexican eats" and "fab cocktails" (and that it's "great with kids", if "a bit yummy mummy at the weekends"). But while ratings for its "friendly and prompt" service and energetic vibe have proved surprisingly enduring over the years, its food score dipped this year, with some regulars noting it has felt "a tad off-the-boil" of late. / www.wahaca.com; 11 pm, Sun 10.30 pm; W12, Charlotte St, SW19 Sun 10 pm; no booking or need 6+ to book.

WAHLBURGERS WC2

JAMES ST AWAITING TEL 5–2D

If you're a Mark Wahlberg fan (aka Dirk Diggler in Boogie Nights), you only have to wait till late 2018 to visit the first of his 20 or so burger joints to be located in the UK. This first one will be opposite Covent Garden tube, with the major draw of video screens to allow 'live' FaceTime-style, video conversations with the great man himself. / WC2E; www.wahlburgersrestaurant.com; @Wahlburgers; Sun-Thu 11 pm, Fri & Sat midnight.

THE WALLACE, THE WALLACE COLLECTION
W1 £58 225

HERTFORD HS, MANCHESTER SQ   020 7563 9505   3–1A

The beautiful glass-ceilinged atrium of the Wallace Collection museum in Marylebone provides the "perfect atmosphere for tea – very civilised and respectable". "The café's food (from caterer Peyton & Byrne) is hit and miss, service not brilliant but the space is really impressive". "Always does the trick for a business meeting – so much better than sitting in a coffee shop". / W1U 3BN; www.peytonandbyrne.co.uk; 10.30 pm, Sun 4 pm; Sun-Thu closed D; no Amex; booking max 10 may apply.

WANDER N16 £48 433

214 STOKE NEWINGTON HIGH ST   020 7249 7283   1–1C

"Interesting Aussie dishes" are the reason to discover this casual small café-style venture – a Spring 2018 opening in Stokey from Australian-born chef Alexis Noble. / N16 7HU; www.wanderrestaurant.com; Tue-Thu 8.30 pm, Fri & Sat 9.30 pm, Sun 7 pm.

WATERLOO BAR & KITCHEN
SE1 £53 322

131 WATERLOO RD   020 7928 5086   10–4A

"It looks like a pretty uninspiring venue", but this busy brasserie near the Old Vic is a useful amenity – the "international menu (from crispy duck to Toulouse sausage)" can be "surprisingly good", comes "at reasonable prices" and "is served with flexibility and a smile!" / SE1 8UR; www.barandkitchen.co.uk; @BarKitchen; 11 pm, Sun 10 pm.

THE WATERWAY
W9 £52 2️⃣2️⃣3️⃣

54 FORMOSA ST 020 7266 3557 9–4A

"Great views over the canal" make this Little Venice venue – a funked-up former pub with a big terrace – an "easy-go-to local". Comments on the modern pub grub? – "nice", "solid"… / W9 2JU; www.thewaterway.co.uk; @thewaterway_; 10 pm, Sun 2.30 am.

WELLBOURNE
W12 £43 3️⃣3️⃣2️⃣

201 WOOD LANE 020 3417 4865 1–2B

This "just-opened, all-day brasserie in White City" (within the ever-more lively environs of the old Beeb commercial HQ) is a functional space whose associations with a well-known Bristol restaurant (and even a branch in Spain) might not be instantly apparent. Useful to know about though, with very competent staples produced by a duo of former Dabbous chefs. / W12 7TU; www.wellbourne.restaurant; @WellbourneWCP; 10 pm, Sun 5 pm; closed Sun D.

THE WELLS TAVERN
NW3 £56 3️⃣3️⃣4️⃣

30 WELL WALK 020 7794 3785 9–1A

"The ideal gastropub for after a walk on the Heath" – Hampstead's most popular pub (owned by Beth Coventry, Fay Maschler's sister) is one of the area's most consistent attractions, offering "a range of classic dishes alongside a well-thought-out wine list", plus "efficient and friendly service" and "a great buzz". Top Tip: "go, if possible, for the bright and airy room upstairs – it's more relaxed and spacious, and a perfect place to eat". / NW3 1BX; thewellshampstead.london; @WellsHampstead; 10 pm, Sun 9.30 pm.

WESTERNS LAUNDRY
N5 £57 3️⃣3️⃣3️⃣

34 DRAYTON PARK 020 7700 3700 9–2D

"You feel cool just knowing about this place!" – "a packed and unbelievably noisy room just off the Holloway Road", which – on its launch in 2017 – scored some of the best newspaper critic reviews of the year. With its "edgy and friendly" approach and "urban, industrial-style decor", it's indisputably "a great addition to Drayton Park" but "after all the hype" numerous reporters felt anticlimactic: "nothing really bad" but "flavours didn't always work together" and "while small plates are fashionable, these aren't small, they're tiny!" Tons of praise is recorded, too, though – "take your friends and dine on sharing plates, whose powerful and memorable tastes are so good you'll want to scoff them all and not share!" Top Tip: "It's best as a foursome, as couples may be squashed on the long sharing tables". / N5 1PB; www.westernslaundry.com; @WesternsLaundry; 10.30 pm, Sun 5 pm.

THE WET FISH CAFÉ
NW6 £50 2️⃣3️⃣4️⃣

242 WEST END LANE 020 7443 9222 1–1B

"A little corner of originality in a city plagued by uniformity" – that, to date, has been the upbeat verdict on this all-day West Hampstead bistro (named in honour of the 1930s fishmonger whose interior it inherited), still hailed by the majority as "a dream local delivering equally well for coffee, brunch and dinner". Its ratings suffered however this year on the back of several downbeat reports: "very disappointing, with a more standard and boring menu – I went back three times to check!" / NW6 1LG; www.thewetfishcafe.co.uk; @thewetfishcafe; 10 pm; no Amex; booking D only.

WHITE BEAR
SE11 £34 3️⃣3️⃣3️⃣

138 KENNINGTON PARK RD 020 7490 3535 11–1D

"A proper restaurant has recently been added to this formerly rather depressing Kennington pub, now part of the Young's chain, and with an enterprising small theatre upstairs". "Excellent for British staples: liver and bacon, Shepherd's pie, Cumberland sausage, fish 'n' chips, …" / SE11 4DJ; www.whitebearkennington.co.uk; Mon-Thu 11.30 pm; closed Fri & Sat & Sun.

THE WHITE ONION
SW19 £68 3️⃣4️⃣2️⃣

67 HIGH ST 020 8947 8278 11–2B

An offshoot of Eric and Sarah Guignard's highly rated and long-established French Table in neighbouring Surbiton, this accomplished three-year-old has proved "a great addition to the Wimbledon restaurant scene", with "complex" Gallic cuisine, "executed to a very high standard" and "swift service". / SW19 5EE; www.thewhiteonion.co.uk; @thewhiteonionSW; Tue-Thu 10 pm, Fri & Sat 10.30 pm, Sun 2.30 pm; closed Tue-Thu L closed Sun D, closed Mon.

THE WIGMORE, THE LANGHAM
W1 £50 4️⃣4️⃣4️⃣

15 LANGHAM PLACE, REGENT ST 020 7965 0198 2–1B

"Good food, good crowd, great value!" – Michel Roux's gastropub yearling makes a brilliant find near Oxford Circus, with a polished and plush (but still pub-like) interior, whose beautiful design reflects the fact that it's been carved from a corner of the luxurious Langham Hotel (of which it is part). Reports are notably upbeat on its its roster of superior pub grub, and it has "a lovely ambience, especially in winter". / W1B 3DE; www.the-wigmore.co.uk; @Langham_London; 9.30 pm, Sun 5 pm.

WILD HONEY
W1 £79 3️⃣3️⃣3️⃣

12 ST GEORGE ST 020 7758 9160 3–2C

"For dinner, it's warm and inviting", while during its busier lunchtime service, Anthony Demetre's "very comfortable" and "slightly retro" Mayfair venue is a favoured business entertaining spot. "The food is delightful (the signature rabbit dish is heavenly)" and it's also known for its "interesting and varied wine list". Top Tip: "the fixed price lunch is excellent value for money". / W1S 2FB; www.wildhoneyrestaurant.co.uk; @whrestaurant; 9.30 pm; closed Sun.

THE WILMINGTON
EC1 £54 3️⃣2️⃣3️⃣

69 ROSEBERY AVENUE 020 7837 1384 10–1A

Worth knowing about near Sadler's Wells – an "extremely busy" Clerkenwell corner pub, well-rated in all reports for its "reliably good food: from top burgers, to well-thought-out veggie options". / EC1R 4RL; www.wilmingtonclerkenwell.com; @wilmingtonec1; Mon-Thu 10 pm, Fri & Sat 10.30 pm, Sun 9 pm.

WILTONS
SW1 £95 4️⃣5️⃣4️⃣

55 JERMYN ST 020 7629 9955 3–3C

"Don't forget your jacket if you're joining the peers of the realm at this classic on Jermyn Street, which has been doing things the way they should be done for more than 270 years (!)", with "reassuringly unchanging, courteous-old school service" that "make you feel like a regular, even if you only visit annually". The "superb quality of the fare is without parallel" from an "old-fashioned, utterly untrendy menu", which particularly shines with "British seafood at its finest", but is also strong in game. "Of course it's definitely overpriced, but cheaper than joining a club and, on that basis, worth every pound!" / SW1Y 6LX; www.wiltons.co.uk; @wiltons1742; 10.30 pm; closed Sat L, closed Sun; Jacket required.

THE WINDMILL
W1 £52 2️⃣2️⃣3️⃣

6-8 MILL ST 020 7491 8050 4–2A

Not a vintage year for this classic, "slightly shabby" Mayfair boozer famous for "first-class pies, and well-kept beer to boot". Fans do still applaud "excellent English cooking", but a

Yen WC2

number of regulars filed disappointing reports: "standards dropping off…"; "didn't live up to the hype…"; "the fire alarm in the kitchen went off they burnt the pie so badly!" / W1S 2AZ; www.windmillmayfair.co.uk; @windmillpubW1; 10 pm, Sun 5 pm; closed Sat D & Sun.

THE WINE LIBRARY
EC3 £40 235

43 TRINITY SQ 020 7481 0415 10–3D

"It's the amazingly wide variety of wines sold at very good value prices" (i.e. retail) that justifies killing an afternoon in this ancient and atmospheric cellar near Tower Hill – the food, is of "good quality" but of low ambition ("pâtés, quiches, bread rolls, etc"). "If only the seats were more comfortable, I would come more often!" / EC3N 4DJ; www.winelibrary.co.uk; 7.30 pm; closed Mon D, Sat & Sun.

THE WOLSELEY
W1 £63 235

160 PICCADILLY 020 7499 6996 3–3C

"Still the best place to take friends from abroad…", "Still the best place for a business power breakfast…", "Still the absolute best buzz in London!" – Corbin & King's Grand Café near The Ritz is still at the centre of metropolitan life: a "highly tuned, effective and bustling brasserie" where the "fabulous room" means it "always feels like a glamorous treat"; and where the "interesting crowd" typically includes a few famous faces. Its "comprehensive menu" of comfort food (with some Mittel-european specials) is "not out-of-this-world" and has never aimed to be, but is generally "well executed and presented". That said, laurel-resting is an ever-present danger here, and there were one or two more "underwhelming" meals reported this year. Likewise, while on most accounts "everything is so slick", there have also been a few more reports recently of "mixed" and/or "brusque" service. Top Tip: "a good traditional afternoon tea, which (unlike so many places nowadays) doesn't cost the earth". / W1J 9EB; www.thewolseley.com; @TheWolseleyRest; midnight, Sun 11 pm.

WONG KEI W1 £32 321

41-43 WARDOUR ST 020 7437 8408 5–3A

"Always an experience… so long as you are prepared for shared tables and bordering-on-rude staff" – this "functional" multi-storey Chinatown canteen "is the perfect place for a quick, filling, tasty meal amidst a chaotic, bustling backdrop" and as you can get "unlimited free tea" and "a massive plate of food for under a tenner – you can't go wrong!" "OK, it's not for the lingering, romantic tete-a-tete… so what?" / W1D 6PY; www.wongkeilondon.com; 11.30 pm, Sun 10.30 pm; cash only.

WRIGHT BROTHERS
£64 443

13 KINGLY ST, W1 020 7434 3611 4–2B | 56 OLD BROMPTON RD, SW7 020 7581 0131 6–2B | 11 STONEY ST, SE1 020 7403 9554 10–4C | BATTERSEA

POWER STATION, SW11 020 7324 7734 11–1C | 8 LAMB ST, E1 020 7377 8706 10–2D

"An amazing selection of oysters" and other "wonderfully inventive fish and shellfish dishes" (in particular, "blackboard specials are usually excellent") have made these bustling fish bistros one of the capital's most popular chains amongst foodies, and – though relatively new – they have "an old-fashioned style, feeling like they've been there for years (in a good way…)". "The latest addition in Battersea Power Station and overlooking the Thames may be the best yet!" / SE1 10 pm, Sat 11 pm; W1 11 pm, Sun 10 pm; E1 10.30 pm, Sun 9 pm; SW7 10.30 pm, Sun 9.30 pm; booking: max 8.

WULF & LAMB
SW1 £49 322

243 PAVILION RD 020 3948 5999 6–2D

Vegan newcomer in a hyper-cute backstreet off Sloane Square, with a former Vanilla Black chef in the kitchen. Feedback is limited and a bit mixed: the food by-and-large escapes criticism, but on one visit "the ordering system didn't seem very user-friendly". Teething troubles? / SW1X 0BP; www.wulfandlamb.com; @wulfandlamb; 10 pm, Sun 9 pm; no booking.

XI'AN IMPRESSION
N7 £25 422

117 BENWELL RD 020 3441 0191 9–2D

"Out-of-this-world food" from Xi'an (the terminus of the Silk Road in central China) – "noodle-based with some street food additions, all delicious" – attracts a steady stream of Chinese diners who "pack out" this "hole-in-the-wall place literally next to the Arsenal stadium". Spurs fans will be relieved to learn that a larger sibling, Xi'an Biang Biang Noodles, opened near Spitalfields in July 2018. / N7 \N; www.xianimpression.co.uk; @xianimpression; 10 pm.

XU W1 £60 434

30 RUPERT ST 020 3319 8147 4–3D

From the team and backers behind the brilliant Bao, this "stylishly fitted-out" yearling "is a happy surprise on the edge of Chinatown", and has been smashing it since day one. "The beautiful interior gives a real air of opulence akin to 1930s, Art Deco-style, Taiwanese tea parlours in days gone by" (complete with Mahjong table); and the "excellent (Taiwanese) food, is very different to other restaurants serving 'Chinese' food" ("not every dish is a bullseye, but most are delicious and all interesting"). Top Menu Tip: shou pa chicken ("the chickeniest chicken ever"). / W1D 6DL; xulondon.com; @XU_london; Mon-Thu 11 pm; closed Fri & Sat & Sun.

YALLA YALLA £46 322

1 GREEN'S CT, W1 020 7287 7663 4–2D | 12 WINSLEY ST, W1 020 7637 4748 3–1C

Pair of Lebanese street food cafés that are "small, busy but worth queuing for!" in central London. "The original hidden in Soho is still the best", but the good-value menu of "fresh" dishes at its Fitzrovia sibling is identical. (The

Greenwich branch has bitten the dust.) / www.yalla-yalla.co.uk; Green's Court 11 pm, Sun 10 pm; Winsley Street 11.30 pm, Sat 11 pm; W1 closed Sun; booking min 10.

YAMA MOMO
SE22 £53 333

72 LORDSHIP LN 020 8299 1007 1–4D

"Consistently delicious sushi" and other "great Japanese dishes" plus "a lovely ambience and a great cocktail list" all rate well at this East Dulwich offshoot of Clapham's popular Pacific-fusion outfit, Tsunami. "Sit at the bar and watch the chefs at work." / SE22 8HF; www.yamamomo.co.uk; @YamamomoRest; 10.30 pm; closed weekday L.

YAMABAHCE W1 £41 222

26 JAMES ST 020 3905 3139 3–1A

Serial entrepreneur Alan Yau is having another crack at a Turkish pide (flatbread) concept with this white-tiled café with large central oven in a cute enclave off Oxford Street (which opened in late 2017). Early feedback is limited and not impressive – is this going to go the same way as his 2016 attempt, Babaji Pide, which started well, but has now gone down the tubes? / W1U 1EN; www.yamabahce.com; may need 6+ to book.

YARD SALE
PIZZA £38 533

54 BLACKSTOCK RD, N4 020 7226 2651 9–1D | 622 HIGH ROAD LEYTONSTONE, E11 020 8539 5333 1–1D NEW | HOE ST, E17 020 8509 0888 1–1D | 105 LOWER CLAPTON RD, E5 020 3602 9090 14–1B

"Some of the pizzas would horrify an Italian" – "try the lamb kebab-style!". "They're definitely not authentic, but they're consistently superb", say the growing legion of fans of this hip and "very self-aware" East London group, which opened a new Leytonstone branch this year (and also dug a toehold into West London in the new Market Halls development on Fulham Broadway). / 11 pm, Sun 10 pm; closed Mon-Thu L.

YASHIN W8 £87 422

1A ARGYLL RD 020 7938 1536 6–1A

'Pre-seasoned sushi' (you're not supposed to add any extra soy sauce, so as to emphasise the taste of the fish) is a speciality at this stylish modern Japanese off High Street Kensington, which opened in 2010 with high ambitions. Despite its "unique" approach and high level of achievement – fans feel its outstanding sushi is "simply the best in town" – it maintains a strangely low profile. Ditto its 'Ocean' sibling on the Old Brompton Road (not listed), where such feedback as we have says its "expensive but good". / W8 7DB; www.yashinsushi.com; @Yashinsushi; 9.30 pm; booking max 7 may apply.

YAUATCHA £81 434

BROADWICK HS, 15-17 BROADWICK ST,
W1 020 7494 8888 4–1C | BROADGATE
CIRCLE, EC2 020 3817 9888 13–2B

"Dim sum are top class – beautifully presented
and all of them delicious" – at this slick, "fun"
and hugely popular Chinese-inspired duo
(originally created by Hakkasan and Wagamama
founder, Alan Yau), whose stylish looks are
"verging on bling, but well done". Both branches
score highly, although the well-established Soho
original still has the edge over the relatively new
Broadgate Circle branch. "Great cocktails"
too – "their tea is also exquisite". Top Tip: cool
terrace in EC2. / W1 10 pm, Fri & Sat 10.30 pm;
EC2 11.30 pm; EC2 closed Sun.

THE YELLOW HOUSE SE16 £46 343

126 LOWER RD 020 7231 8777 12–2A

Good all-round ratings again this year for
this informal haunt – one of the few decent
options near Surrey Quays station. On the
menu: wood-fired pizza, plus a selection of
burgers, steaks and other grills. / SE16 2UE;
www.theyellowhouse.eu; @theyellowhousejazz; Wed-
Sat, Tue 9 pm, Sun 3 pm; closed Mon, Tue-Sat D
only, Sun open L & D.

YEN WC2 £90 444

190 STRAND, 5 ARUNDEL ST 07825 647 930
2–2D

"Vast" and high-ceilinged newcomer, south of
Aldwych, from the Japan-based fashion group
Onward, whose stark styling (featuring lots of
wood) is at odds with the more prosaic offerings
typically found in the slightly featureless environs
of Temple. On all accounts, its wide-ranging
menu (sushi and sashimi, wagyu beef steaks,
soba noodle dishes, tempura …) are "very
good" and some would say exceptional: "my
Japanese friends say this is London's best
authentic Japanese restaurant". / WC2R 3DX;
www.yen-london.co.uk; @YenRestaurant; Tue-Thu
8.30 pm, Fri 9 pm, Sat 9.30 pm, Sun 7 pm.

YI-BAN E16 £52 223

LONDON REGATTA CENTRE, ROYAL ALBERT
DOCK 020 7473 6699 12–1D

"Views of City Airport and the Albert Dock
are perhaps the best feature of this obscurely-
situated Docklands Chinese", overlooking the
water. Fans "love this place" and say its "dim
sum is second to none", but others feel "the food
quality has become average at best". / E16 2QT;
www.yi-ban.co.uk; 11 pm, Sun 10.30 pm.

YIPIN CHINA N1 £45 422

70-72 LIVERPOOL RD 020 7354 3388 9–3D

It's "hard to beat the quality of food" at
this functional Sichuan/Hunanese canteen
near Angel, which raises the bar for "deep,
savoury, deliciousness". Top Tip: "superb cold
starters: lotus root is amazing". / N1 0QD;
www.yipinchina.co.uk; 11 pm; cash only.

YMING W1 £50 342

35-36 GREEK ST 020 7734 2721 5–2A

"Ever-helpful" service is "delightful as ever at
this bright Soho stalwart" – a "quiet oasis" just
beyond Chinatown's northern borders, where
a very strong following of loyal regulars "will
come back and back for another renewal of
old acquaintance" with maitre d' William and
owner Christine. Foodwise, results are "very
reliable" and "very reasonably priced". / W1D
5DL; www.yminglondon.com; 11.45 pm; closed Sun.

YORK & ALBANY NW1 £59 112

127-129 PARKWAY 020 7592 1227 9–3B

This substantial Georgian tavern where
Camden Town meets Regent's Park is part of
Gordon Ramsay's empire, and has disappointed
most reporters this year. The owner is famous
for his tongue-lashings, and here he gets it
back in spades. "Worst meal this year: terrible
roast beef, terrible service" – "Ramsay should
get his own house in order!" / NW1 7PS;
www.gordonramsayrestaurants.com/york-and-a;
@yorkandalbany; 10.30 pm, Sun 9 pm.

YOSHI SUSHI W6 £38 342

210 KING ST 020 8748 5058 8–2B

In an anonymous row of shops near
Ravenscourt Park tube, this grungy looking
Korean/Japanese stalwart never inspires a
huge amount of feedback. Those who discover
it are delighted, however, acclaiming its
"delicious sushi, and other fantastic-value yet
high quality and flavoursome food". / W6 0RA;
www.yoshisushi.co.uk; 10.30 pm; closed Sun L.

YOSHINO W1 £48 442

3 PICCADILLY PL 020 7287 6622 4–4C

On a quiet alleyway near Piccadilly Circus, this
typically low-key (but "welcoming") Japanese,
has been an insider's secret for more than two
decades, with a simple counter downstairs and
table service up. Practically all diners agree it's
on good form again now, "after many years
of changing chefs and menus". / W1J 0DB;
www.yoshino.net; @Yoshino_London; Wed-Sat, Tue 9
pm, Sun 3 pm; closed Sun.

Zela WC2

YUM BUN EC2 £19 542

DINERAMA, 19 GREAT EASTERN ST
07919 408 221 13–2B

"Best buns in London no contest" – even
"better than Bao!" – claim fans of Lisa Meyer's
Chinese-inspired steamed buns and dumplings
(most popularly stuffed with slow-roasted
pork belly), which started as a stall in 2010 on
Broadway Market, and are now to be found
at The Kitchens, Spitalfields Market, as well
as various Street Feast locations. / EC2A 3EJ;
www.yumbun.com; @yumbun; Mon & Tue, Sun 5
pm, Wed-Fri 8 pm, Sat 6 pm; closed Mon D, Tue D,
Wed D, Sat L & Sun; no booking.

ZAFFERANO SW1 £99 333

15 LOWNDES ST 020 7235 5800 6–1D

"Still one of the top Italians in town", say fans
of this well-known Belgravian, whose heyday
was twenty years ago under founding chef
Giorgio Locatelli. But while it's still "always
busy and buzzy", survey feedback is much
more muted nowadays, and – though it avoids
damning critiques – sceptics consider it "dull
and completely overpriced". / SW1X 9EY;
www.zafferanorestaurant.com; 11 pm, Sun 10.30 pm.

ZAFFRANI N1 £48 322

47 CROSS ST 020 7226 5522 9–3D

Not a huge amount to say about this feature
of Islington's main drag, other than that it's
consistently nominated as "a good local Indian".
/ N1 2BB; www.zaffrani.co.uk; 10.30 pm.

ZAIBATSU SE10 £30 442

96 TRAFALGAR RD 020 8858 9317 1–3D

"Marvellous Japanese food" including "amazing
and well-priced sushi" brings a constant buzz
to this "deceptively unimpressive-looking
restaurant" in Greenwich, with "scruffy
Formica-topped tables". "BYO, no corkage". /
SE10 9UW; www.zaibatsufusion.co.uk; @ong_teck; 11
pm; closed Mon; cash only.

ZAIKA OF KENSINGTON W8 £65 433

1 KENSINGTON HIGH ST 020 7795 6533
6–1A

"Fine dining at its best from the sub-continent"
means this "roomy former banking hall"
beside the Kensington Gardens Hotel is a firm
"favourite Indian" for many diners – especially
since ratings have recovered well after a dip

last year. / W8 5NP; www.zaikaofkensington.com; @ZaikaLondon; 10.30 pm, Sun 9.30 pm; closed Mon L; credit card required to book.

ZELA WC2

THE STRAND   020 8089 3981   2–2D

Q: What do Cristiano Ronaldo, Enrique Iglesias, Rafael Nadal and NBC basketball star Pau Gasol have in common? A: This restaurant, and its sibling in Ibiza, plus an international chain of restaurants under the name Tatel. Who knew? This London opening (in October 2018) promises sushi and sashimi made with spanking fresh Mediterranean ingredients by chef Ricardo Sanz of Madrid's Kabuki. / WC2R 1HA; zelarestaurants.com.

ZELMAN MEATS   £62   433

HARVEY NICHOLS, 109-125 KNIGHTSBRIDGE, SW1   020 7201 8625 6–1D | 2 ST ANNE'S CT, W1   020 7437 0566 4–1D

"BBQ in excelsis!" – Misha Zelman's budget (well, by comparison to his Goodman's group, anyway) small chain of funky steakhouses inspires nothing but high praise for its "flawless" steaks from a "short-but-interesting menu of cuts", and "vibrant atmosphere". Despite such consistently positive feedback, however, its new branch near the Old Bill proved shortlived, and closed in July 2018. / W1 10.30 pm, Sun 8 pm; SW1 10 pm, Sun 7 pm; N4 midnight; W1 closed Mon L, N4 closed Mon-Fri L.

ZERET SE5   £30   443

216-218 CAMBERWELL RD   020 7701 8587 1–3C

"Hidden in an estate in Camberwell!" – it's worth discovering this "fabulous Ethiopian": a well-established, family-run operation of nearly 15 years standing, decked out with a simple, modern interior. / SE5 0ED; www.zeretkitchen.com; Sun-Thu 11 pm, Fri & Sat midnight; no Amex.

ZERO DEGREES SE3   £45   333

29-31 MONTPELIER VALE   020 8852 5619 1–4D

Since it launched in 2000, this early-wave microbrewery café (where you eat dwarfed by large steel brewing vessels) has made a fun venue for a pizza or bowl of moules frites down Blackheath way. It inspires limited feedback, but all of it positive. / SE3 0TJ; www.zerodegrees.co.uk; @Zerodegreesbeer; 10.30 pm.

ZEST, JW3 NW3   £60   332

341-351 FINCHLEY RD   020 7433 8955 1–1B

This "much-loved eatery" in West Hampstead's JW3 Jewish community centre channels the flavours of contemporary Tel Aviv. "London is very short of decent kosher restaurants... and the food here isn't bad at all." / NW3 6ET; www.zestatjw3.co.uk; @ZESTatJW3; Sun-Thu 10.30 pm; closed Fri & Sat.

ZHENG SW3   £61   432

4 SYDNEY ST   020 7352 9890   6–2C

"Very good use of spicing and heat" helps distinguish the "very good Malaysian/Chinese cooking'" at this "smart" but "fun" Chelsea yearling, which is making a good go of the tricky site that has seen restaurants come and go over the years, most recently in the form of Brasserie Gustave (RIP). / SW3 6PP; www.zhengchelsea.co.uk; 11.30 pm, Sun 10 pm; closed Tue L.

ZIA LUCIA N7   £35   433

157 HOLLOWAY RD   020 7700 3708   9–2D

"The best charcoal base ever" is just one of the four dough choices on offer (including gluten-free, all slow-fermented for 48 hours) at this "brilliant" and "welcoming" pizzeria on Holloway Road. Its popularity means "door-side queuing, but we've learned to live with it". Top Tip: "charcoal-based Andrea Pirlo (mozzarella, gorgonzola, apple, truffle and olive sauce)". / N7 8LX; www.zialucia.com; @zialuciapizza; 10.30 pm; closed Mon.

ZIANI'S SW3   £62   242

45 RADNOR WALK   020 7351 5297   6–3C

This archetypal, "very friendly" local trattoria off the King's Road is an "old favourite" of the well-heeled Chelsea crowd, and knows just how to look after them. "It's like eating in your living room!" – "a little cramped", but that's all part of the fun. / SW3 4BP; www.ziani.co.uk; 11 pm, Sun 10 pm.

ZOILO W1   £64   333

9 DUKE ST   020 7486 9699   3–1A

"Unusual but brilliant little Argentinian tapas restaurant tucked away near Selfridges." "After a day's shopping, retire to this calm oasis and you'll be transported to Buenos Aires" (well, nearly). / W1U 3EG; www.zoilo.co.uk; @Zoilo_London; Tue-Fri 10 pm, Mon 3.30 pm; closed Sun.

ZUMA SW7   £82   534

5 RAPHAEL ST   020 7584 1010   6–1C

"It takes flak for being too showy", and "can be a little over-run by glam types", but "the foundations of this fun Knightsbridge scene are as appealing as ever – fantastic, innovative cuisine, welcoming service and a wonderful, vibrant atmosphere". The Japanese-fusion dishes deliver "brilliant flavours": "superb sashimi and black cod (although all the fish is amazing)" to "steak mains to die for". "It's been a favourite for over a decade now and still feels fresh." / SW7 1DL; www.zumarestaurant.com; 10.45 pm, Sun 10.15 pm; booking max 8 may apply.

CENTRAL

SOHO, COVENT GARDEN & BLOOMSBURY (PARTS OF W1, ALL WC2 AND WC1)

Price	Name	Cuisine			
£190+	Aulis London	British, Modern	5	5	4
£110+	L'Atelier de Joel Robuchon	French	2	2	2
£100+	The Northall	British, Modern	3	2	3
	Savoy Grill	British, Traditional	2	2	2
	Smith & Wollensky	Steaks & grills	2	2	2
£90+	Kaspar's Seafood	Fish & seafood	3	3	4
	The Savoy Hotel	Afternoon tea	2	3	4
	Sushisamba Japanese	WWE			
	Yen	"	4	4	4
£80+	Bob Bob Ricard	British, Modern	3	3	5
	Mirror Room	"	3	3	4
	The Petersham	"	3	3	5
	Social Eating House	"	3	3	4
	Spring Restaurant	"	3	3	4
	Neptune, The Principal	Fish & seafood	-	-	-
	J Sheekey	"	3	4	4
	Asia de Cuba	Fusion	2	2	3
	MASH Steakhouse	Steaks & grills	3	3	2
	Oscar Wilde Lounge	Afternoon tea	3	3	5
	Lima Floral	Peruvian	3	3	2
	Yauatcha	Chinese	4	3	4
	Roka, Aldwych House	Japanese	4	3	3
£70+	Christophers	American	2	2	3
	Balthazar	British, Modern	2	2	4
	Frog by Adam Handling	"	5	5	4
	Ham Yard Restaurant	"	2	3	4
	The Ivy	"	2	3	4
	Noble Rot	"	3	4	4
	Holborn Dining Room	British, Traditional	3	3	3
	Rules	"	2	3	5
	Simpson's in the Strand	"	2	2	3
	Clos Maggiore	French	3	3	5
	L'Escargot	"	3	4	5
	Frenchie	"	3	2	2
	Gauthier Soho	"	5	4	4
	Otto's	"	4	4	4
	Evelyns Table	Italian	4	4	4
	Nopi	Mediterranean	4	3	3
	Eneko	Spanish	3	2	1
	Hawksmoor	Steaks & grills	3	2	2
	Cecconi's Pizza Bar	Pizza	2	2	3
	The Palomar	Middle Eastern	4	3	3
	Red Fort	Indian	3	2	2
£60+	Big Easy	American	2	2	3
	Scarlett Green	Australian	-	-	-
	Bryn Williams, Somerset Hs	British, Modern	4	4	3
	Dean Street Townhouse	"	2	3	5
	Ducksoup	"	4	4	4
	Heliot Steak House	"	3	3	3
	Hix	"	1	2	2
	Kettners	"	3	3	5
	The Portrait	"	2	3	4
	Quo Vadis	"	4	4	5
	St Luke's Kitchen	"	2	3	3
	Tredwell's	"	2	2	2
	Parsons	Fish & seafood	4	3	3
	Randall & Aubin	"	3	3	4
	J Sheekey Atlantic Bar	"	3	3	4
	Wright Brothers	"	4	4	3
	Café Monico	French	2	3	4
	Henrietta	"	-	-	-
	Bocca Di Lupo	Italian	4	4	3
	Café Murano	"	2	3	2
	Fumo	"	3	3	3
	Vasco & Pieros Pavilion	"	3	3	2
	100 Wardour Street	Mediterranean	-	-	-
	Aqua Nueva	Spanish	3	2	4
	Cigala	"	3	2	2
	Sophie's Steakhouse	Steaks & grills	2	2	2
	Zelman Meats	"	4	3	3
	Rainforest Café	Burgers, etc	1	3	3
	Hovarda	Turkish	2	3	4
	Hoppers	Indian, Southern	4	2	2
	aqua kyoto	Japanese	3	3	4
	Chotto Matte	"	3	2	4
	Jinjuu	Korean	4	3	4
	Patara Soho	Thai	3	3	3
	XU	Taiwanese	4	3	4
£50+	Bodeans	American	3	2	3
	Hubbard & Bell	"	3	3	3
	Jackson & Rye	"	2	2	2
	Joe Allen	"	2	3	4
	Andrew Edmunds	British, Modern	3	4	5
	Boyds Grill & Wine Bar	"	3	3	3
	Great Queen Street	"	3	2	2
	The Ivy Market Grill	"	2	2	4
	10 Greek Street	"	4	4	3
	Terroirs	"	3	2	3
	Cork & Bottle	British, Traditional	2	3	4
	George in the Strand	"	3	3	3
	The Ivy Soho Brasserie	"	2	2	4
	The Delaunay	East & Cent. European	2	4	4
	Bonnie Gull Seafood Shack	Fish & seafood	5	3	3
	The Oystermen	"	4	4	3
	Antidote Wine Bar	French	2	2	3
	Blanchette	"	2	2	3
	Bon Vivant	"	3	3	3
	Cigalon	"	4	4	4
	Le Garrick	"	3	3	4
	Mon Plaisir Restaurant	"	3	3	4
	The Good Egg	Fusion	3	3	3
	The 10 Cases	International	3	4	3
	Da Mario	Italian	3	4	3

Name	Cuisine	Rating
Dehesa	"	3 2 3
La Goccia	"	3 3 5
Luce e Limoni	"	4 4 3
Margot	"	4 5 4
Mele e Pere	"	3 4 3
Polpetto	"	3 3 2
Polpo	"	2 2 2
San Carlo Cicchetti	"	3 3 4
Barrafina	Spanish	5 5 5
Ember Yard	"	3 3 4
Morada Brindisa Asador	"	3 3 2
Opera Tavern	"	3 3 3
Rambla	"	4 3 3
Foxlow	Steaks & grills	2 2 2
Macellaio RC	"	3 3 3
St Moritz	Swiss	3 3 4
Dalloway Terrace	Afternoon tea	3 2 4
Burger & Lobster	Burgers, etc	3 3 3
Fernandez & Wells	Sandwiches, cakes, etc	3 3 3
Bodeans	BBQ	3 2 3
Cantina Laredo	Mexican/TexMex	2 2 2
Casita Andina	Peruvian	3 3 3
Ceviche Soho	"	5 3 4
Señor Ceviche	"	3 3 3
The Barbary	North African	5 5 4
Barshu	Chinese	4 2 2
The Duck & Rice	"	3 2 4
The Four Seasons	"	5 1 1
Yming	"	3 4 2
Darjeeling Express	Indian	5 3 3
Dum Biryani	"	3 2 2
Tamarind Kitchen	"	3 4 4
Flesh and Buns	Japanese	2 3 3
Inko Nito	"	– – –
Oka, Kingly Court	"	3 2 2
Sticks'n'Sushi	"	3 2 2

£40+

Name	Cuisine	Rating
Breakfast Club	American	3 3 3
Coopers Restaurant & Bar	British, Modern	2 3 3
The Norfolk Arms	"	2 3 3
Shampers	"	3 4 4
VQ, St Giles Hotel	"	2 3 3
Claw Carnaby	Fish & seafood	3 3 2
Brasserie Zédel	French	1 3 5
Prix Fixe	"	3 2 2
Relais de Venise	"	3 3 2
Savoir Faire	"	3 4 2
La Fromagerie Bloomsbury	International	3 3 3
Gordons Wine Bar	"	2 1 5
Casa Tua	Italian	4 3 3
Ciao Bella	"	2 3 4
Pastaio	"	3 2 3
La Porchetta Pizzeria	"	2 3 2
Blacklock	Steaks & grills	4 4 4
Mildreds	Vegetarian	3 2 2
Haché	Burgers, etc	3 3 2
The Chipping Forecast	Fish & chips	3 2 2
North Sea Fish	"	3 3 2
Poppies	"	3 2 3
Pizza Pilgrims	Pizza	3 3 3
Rossopomodoro	"	2 2 2

Name	Cuisine	Rating
temper Covent Garden	"	2 2 4
Bea's Cake Boutique	Sandwiches, cakes, etc	3 3 3
Chick 'n' Sours	Chicken	4 3 3
temper Soho	BBQ	2 2 4
Breddos Tacos	Mexican/TexMex	3 3 3
Corazón	"	2 4 3
Lupita	"	3 3 2
Yalla Yalla	Lebanese	3 2 2
Le Bab	Turkish	4 3 3
Golden Dragon	Chinese	3 2 2
Dishoom	Indian	3 4 5
Kricket	"	4 4 4
Malabar Junction	"	3 4 3
Punjab	"	3 4 3
Salaam Namaste	"	3 2 2
Tandoor Chop House	"	4 4 3
Bone Daddies	Japanese	3 3 4
Dozo	"	3 2 2
Ichi Buns	"	3 2 3
Ippudo London	"	3 2 3
Jugemu	"	5 2 3
Koya-Bar	"	4 4 3
Shoryu Ramen	"	3 3 2
Tonkotsu	"	4 3 3
Olle	Korean	2 2 2
Freak Scene	Pan-Asian	5 3 4
Hare & Tortoise	"	3 3 2
Cây Tre	Vietnamese	3 2 2
Pho & Bun	"	3 3 2

£35+

Name	Cuisine	Rating
Lina Stores	Italian	5 3 3
Princi	"	3 2 2
MEATliquor	Burgers, etc	3 2 4
Homeslice	Pizza	3 3 3
Gabys	Israeli	3 2 2
Joy King Lau	Chinese	3 2 2
Cinnamon Bazaar	Indian	3 3 3
Sagar	"	4 3 2
Kintan	Japanese	3 2 2
Taro	"	3 2 2
Kimchee	Korean	2 2 2
On The Bab	"	3 2 2
Bao	Taiwanese	4 3 3

£30+

Name	Cuisine	Rating
Café in the Crypt	British, Traditional	2 1 4
Bar Italia	Italian	3 3 5
Flat Iron	Steaks & grills	3 4 4
Chilli Cool	Chinese	4 2 1
Wong Kei	"	3 2 1
Beijing Dumpling	Chinese, Dim sum	4 3 2
India Club	Indian	2 2 2
Eat Tokyo	Japanese	3 3 2
Kulu Kulu	"	3 2 1
C&R Café	Malaysian	4 2 2
Kiln	Thai	4 3 4
Viet Food	Vietnamese	3 2 2

£25+

Name	Cuisine	Rating
MEATmarket	Burgers, etc	3 2 2
Patty and Bun Soho	"	4 3 3
Shake Shack	"	3 2 2
Tommi's Burger Joint	"	3 3 3

| Kanada-Ya | Japanese | 5 3 3 |

£20+
Jidori	Japanese	3 3 2
Sen Viet	"	4 3 2
Tokyo Diner	"	3 3 3
Bibimbap Soho	Korean	3 2 2

£10+
Nordic Bakery	Scandinavian	3 2 2
Bageriet	Sandwiches, cakes, etc	4 3 3
Flat White	"	4 4 3
Bun House	Chinese	4 4 4
On the Dak	Korean	5 3 1

£5+
Jacob the Angel	British, Modern	3 3 3
Maison Bertaux	Afternoon tea	4 4 4
Monmouth Coffee Company	Sandwiches, cakes, etc	3 4 4

MAYFAIR & ST JAMES'S
(PARTS OF W1 AND SW1)

£380+
| The Araki | Japanese | 5 5 3 |

£140+
| Hélène Darroze | French | 3 4 4 |
| Sketch (Lecture Rm) | " | 3 3 4 |

£130+
The Ritz	British, Traditional	3 4 5
Alain Ducasse	French	2 2 3
Le Gavroche	"	4 5 4
The Square	"	3 3 2
The Promenade	Afternoon tea	2 4 4
Park Chinois	Chinese	2 2 3

£120+
Fera at Claridge's	British, Modern	4 4 4
The Greenhouse	French	3 3 3
Cut, 45 Park Lane	Steaks & grills	3 2 2
Kai Mayfair	Chinese	2 2 2
Umu	Japanese	2 3 3

£110+
Dorchester Grill	British, Modern	3 4 4
Estiatorio Milos	Fish & seafood	3 2 3
Galvin at Windows	French	2 3 5
Seven Park Place	"	4 4 3
Novikov	Italian	1 2 2
Benares	Indian	3 2 3

£100+
Alyn Williams	British, Modern	5 5 3
Ormer Mayfair	"	3 2 2
Pollen Street Social	"	3 3 3
Corrigans Mayfair	British, Traditional	3 3 3
Ritz (Palm Court)	Afternoon tea	2 4 5
Nobu, Metropolitan Hotel	Japanese	3 2 2
Nobu Berkeley	"	3 2 2
Tokimeite	"	3 2 2

£90+
Hide	British, Modern	5 4 5
Wiltons	British, Traditional	4 5 4
Sexy Fish	Fish & seafood	1 1 2
La Petite Maison	French	3 2 3
Sketch (Gallery)	"	1 2 3
Beck at Browns	Italian	3 4 4

Bocconcino	"	3 2 2
Murano	"	4 5 3
Theo Randall	"	4 4 2
Street XO	Spanish	2 2 2
Goodman	Steaks & grills	3 3 2
Hakkasan Mayfair	Chinese	4 2 4
Indian Accent	Indian	5 4 4
Tamarind	"	4 4 3
Ginza Onodera	Japanese	4 4 2
JG at The Connaught	Pan-Asian	3 3 3
Novikov	"	3 2 4

£80+
Hush	British, Modern	2 2 2
Butlers Restaurant	British, Traditional	2 4 3
Babel House	Fish & seafood	- - -
Bentleys	"	3 4 3
Scotts	"	4 4 5
maze	French	1 2 1
Chucs Dover Street	Italian	3 3 3
Ristorante Frescobaldi	"	3 4 3
Ella Canta	Mexican/TexMex	3 4 4
Coya	Peruvian	3 2 3
China Tang	Chinese	4 4 4
Chutney Mary	Indian	4 4 4
Jamavar	"	3 4 3
Veeraswamy	"	4 4 4
Roka	Japanese	4 3 3

£70+
The Avenue	American	2 2 2
Colony Grill Room	"	2 3 4
Bonhams Restaurant	British, Modern	5 5 2
Le Caprice	"	2 4 4
Heddon Street Kitchen	"	2 2 2
Kitty Fisher's	"	2 3 3
Little Social	"	4 2 3
Magpie	"	4 4 3
Mews of Mayfair	"	3 2 3
Quaglinos	"	2 3 4
Wild Honey	"	3 3 3
English Tea Rm (Browns)	British, Traditional	3 4 4
The Game Bird	"	3 5 3
Black Roe	Fish & seafood	3 2 3
Boulestin	French	2 3 2
Ferdi	"	1 1 2
The American Bar	International	2 5 3
Isabel	"	2 4 5
Cecconis	Italian	2 2 3
Francos	"	3 4 4
Sartoria	"	3 3 3
Aquavit	Scandinavian	2 2 2
The Guinea Grill	Steaks & grills	3 3 4
Hawksmoor	"	3 2 2
maze Grill	"	1 2 2
Rowleys	"	2 2 2
34 Mayfair	"	2 2 3
Diamond Jub' Salon	Afternoon tea	3 4 4
Momo	Moroccan	3 3 3
Gymkhana	Indian	4 3 4
Mint Leaf	"	3 2 3
Sake No Hana	Japanese	3 3 3

£60+	Bellamys	British, Modern	3 4 4
	Galvin at the Athenaeum	"	3 3 2
	The Keeper's House	"	2 2 3
	Langans Brasserie	"	2 2 4
	The Punchbowl	"	3 4 3
	Stem	"	4 4 3
	The Wolseley	"	2 3 5
	Fishworks	Fish & seafood	3 2 2
	The Balcon	French	2 3 3
	Boudin Blanc	"	3 2 3
	28-50	"	2 2 3
	Café Murano	Italian	2 3 2
	Sabor	Spanish	4 4 4
	Ikoyi West African REW		
	Bombay Bustle	Indian	4 4 3
	Chisou	Japanese	4 3 2
	Kiku	"	3 3 2
	Titu	Pan-Asian	4 5 4
	Patara Mayfair	Thai	3 3 3

£50+	Duck & Waffle Local	British, Modern	3 3 3
	The Windmill	British, Traditional	2 2 3
	Neo Bistro	French	4 4 3
	Al Duca	Italian	2 2 2
	San Carlo Cicchetti	"	3 3 4
	Il Vicolo	"	3 3 2
	Burger & Lobster	Burgers, etc	3 3 3
	Delfino	Pizza	3 3 2
	Mayfair Pizza Company	"	3 3 3
	Fernandez & Wells	Sandwiches, cakes, etc	3 3 3
	Sakagura	Japanese	3 4 2
	TAKA		3 3 3

£40+	L'Artiste Musclé	French	2 2 5
	El Pirata	Spanish	2 2 4
	tibits	Vegetarian	3 2 3
	Shoryu Ramen	Japanese	3 3 2
	Yoshino	"	4 4 2

£35+	The Parlour	Ice cream	3 3 3
	Rasa	Indian, Southern	3 3 2

FITZROVIA & MARYLEBONE (PART OF W1)

£160+	Kitchen Table at Bubbledogs	Fusion	5 3 3

£110+	Pied À Te	French	4 4 4
	Texture	Scandinavian	5 3 3
	Beast	Steaks & grills	1 2 2

£90+	The Chiltern Firehouse	American	1 1 3
	Roganic	British, Modern	5 4 2
	Roux at the Landau	"	4 4 4
	Orrery	French	2 3 3
	Hakkasan	Chinese	4 2 4

£80+	Clipstone	British, Modern	3 3 2
	Portland	"	4 3 2
	Clarette	French	3 3 3

	Mere	International	4 4 3
	Locanda Locatelli	Italian	3 4 3
	Lima Fitzrovia	Peruvian	3 3 2
	Trishna	Indian	4 2 2
	Defune	Japanese	3 2 1
	Roka	"	4 3 3

£70+	The Berners Tavern	British, Modern	2 3 5
	Pescatori	Fish & seafood	2 2 2
	Noizé	French	4 5 4
	Les 110 de Taillevent	"	3 2 3
	Providores (Tapa Room)	Fusion	4 4 3
	Caffè Caldesi	Italian	3 3 2
	The Ninth London	Mediterranean	4 3 2
	Palm Court, The Langham	Afternoon tea	3 3 4

£60+	108 Brasserie	British, Modern	3 3 3
	Percy & Founders	"	3 3 3
	Picture	"	3 3 2
	Vinoteca Seymour Place	"	2 2 3
	Fischer's	East & Cent. European	3 3 4
	Fancy Crab	Fish & seafood	2 3 2
	Fishworks	"	3 2 2
	28-50	French	2 2 3
	Twist	Fusion	4 5 4
	Meraki	Greek	3 2 4
	Bernardi's	Italian	3 3 3
	Blandford Comptoir	Mediterranean	3 3 3
	ROVI	"	- - -
	Social Wine & Tapas	Spanish	4 4 3
	Zoilo	Argentinian	3 3 3
	The Bright Courtyard	Chinese	4 2 2
	Royal China Club	"	4 2 2
	Gaylord	Indian	3 3 3
	Jikoni	"	4 4 4
	Lokhandwala	"	3 3 3
	Hoppers	Indian, Southern	4 2 2
	Dinings	Japanese	5 3 2
	House of Ho	Vietnamese	3 4 4

£50+	Bubbledogs	American	3 4 4
	Caravan	British, Modern	3 3 3
	Daylesford Organic	"	3 2 2
	The Ivy Café	"	1 2 3
	The Wigmore, The Langham	British, Traditional	4 4 4
	Bonnie Gull	Fish & seafood	5 3 3
	The Wallace	French	2 2 5
	Carousel	Fusion	4 3 4
	Opso	Greek	3 4 3
	Briciole	Italian	3 2 2
	2 Veneti	"	3 3 3
	Riding House Café	Mediterranean	2 2 3
	The Harcourt	Scandinavian	3 3 4
	Mac & Wild	Scottish	3 2 4
	Barrica	Spanish	3 3 2
	Donostia	"	4 4 4
	Drakes Tabanco	"	2 2 4
	Ibérica	"	2 2 3
	Lurra	"	3 4 4
	Salt Yard	"	4 3 3
	Boxcar Butcher & Grill	Steaks & grills	4 4 3

			Rating
	The Gate	*Vegetarian*	4 2 3
	Burger & Lobster	*Burgers, etc*	3 3 3
	Pisqu	*Peruvian*	3 2 3
	Reubens	*Kosher*	2 2 2
	Maroush	*Lebanese*	3 2 2
	Honey & Smoke	*Middle Eastern*	4 3 2
	Ishtar	*Turkish*	3 3 2
	Kyseri	"	– – –
	Royal China	*Chinese*	3 1 2
	Kazu	*Japanese*	– – –
	The Greyhound Cafe	*Thai*	2 2 3
£40+	Lantana Café	*Australian*	3 3 3
	Foley's	*International*	4 4 3
	La Fromagerie Café	"	3 3 3
	In Parma	*Italian*	4 3 2
	Made in Italy James St	"	3 1 2
	Rossopomodoro, John Lewis	"	2 2 2
	Vagabond Wines	*Mediterranean*	2 2 3
	Relais de Venise	*Steaks & grills*	3 3 2
	Santa Maria	*Pizza*	4 3 2
	Yalla Yalla	*Lebanese*	3 2 2
	Delamina	*Middle Eastern*	4 4 2
	Honey & Co	"	4 4 3
	Yamabahce	*Turkish*	2 2 2
	Roti Chai	*Indian*	3 3 3
	Bone Daddies	*Japanese*	3 3 4
	Sushi Bar Atari-Ya	"	5 2 1
	Tonkotsu, Selfridges	"	4 3 3
£35+	Serge et Le Phoque	*French*	2 3 3
	Navarros	*Spanish*	3 3 3
	MEATLiquor	*Burgers, etc*	3 2 4
	Golden Hind	*Fish & chips*	3 3 2
	Buongiorno e Buonasera	*Pizza*	– – –
	Homeslice	"	3 3 3
	Workshop Coffee	*Sandwiches, cakes, etc*	3 3 3
	Chik'n	*Chicken*	3 2 2
	Sanxia Renjia	*Chinese*	3 3 2
	Chettinad	*Indian*	4 2 2
	Sagar	"	4 3 2
	Kintan	*Japanese*	3 2 2
	On The Bab Express	*Korean*	3 2 2
	Bao Fitzrovia	*Taiwanese*	4 3 3
£30+	Ragam	*Indian*	4 3 2
	Sushi Atelier	*Japanese*	5 3 3
£25+	Patty and Bun	*Burgers, etc*	4 3 3
	Tommi's Burger Joint	"	3 3 3
£20+	Bibimbap Soho	*Korean*	3 2 2
£15+	Icco Pizza	*Italian*	5 2 1
	Patogh	*Middle Eastern*	4 3 2
£10+	Kaffeine	*Sandwiches, cakes, etc*	3 5 4

BELGRAVIA, PIMLICO, VICTORIA & WESTMINSTER (SW1, EXCEPT ST JAMES'S)

			Rating
£130+	Celeste, The Lanesborough	*French*	2 2 4
£120+	Marcus, The Berkeley	*British, Modern*	3 4 3
	Dinner, Mandarin Oriental	*British, Traditional*	2 2 2
£110+	Pétrus	*French*	4 4 4
£100+	Ametsa	*Spanish*	3 4 2
	Rib Room	*Steaks & grills*	2 2 3
	The Collins Room	*Afternoon tea*	2 3 4
£90+	Roux at Parliament Square	*British, Modern*	5 4 3
	The Dining Room	*British, Traditional*	3 5 4
	Zafferano	*Italian*	3 3 3
	Hunan	*Chinese*	5 2 1
£80+	Kerridges Bar & Grill	*British, Modern*	– – –
	Chucs Harrods	*Italian*	3 3 3
	Olivocarne	"	3 2 2
	Oval Restaurant	"	– – –
	Santini	"	2 2 2
	M Restaurant	*Steaks & grills*	2 2 2
	Mr Chow	*Chinese*	2 3 3
	Amaya	*Indian*	4 2 3
	The Cinnamon Club	"	3 2 3
£70+	Hans Bar & Grill	*British, Modern*	– – –
	Olivomare	*Fish & seafood*	3 3 1
	Il Convivio	*Italian*	3 3 3
	Enoteca Turi	"	3 5 3
	Olivo	"	3 3 2
£60+	Timmy Green	*Australian*	3 3 3
	The Alfred Tennyson	*British, Modern*	2 2 3
	The Botanist	"	2 2 2
	45 Jermyn Street	"	3 4 4
	Lorne	"	4 5 3
	The Orange	"	3 3 3
	The Other Naughty Piglet	"	4 3 2
	Rail House Café	"	2 2 2
	Scully	"	5 5 3
	Tate Britain	"	2 3 4
	The Thomas Cubitt	"	3 4 4
	Bar Boulud French EWE		
	Colbert	"	1 1 3
	La Poule au Pot	"	2 2 5
	Cambridge Street Kitchen	*International*	2 3 3
	Caraffini	*Italian*	3 5 4
	Osteria DellAngolo	"	2 2 2
	Quirinale	"	3 4 3
	Sale e Pepe	"	3 2 3
	San Carlo	"	– – –
	Signor Sassi	"	2 3 3
	Omars Place	*Mediterranean*	4 4 4
	Trafalgar Dining Rooms	"	3 3 3
	Eccleston Place by Tart	*Organic*	– – –

			Rating
	Boisdale of Belgravia	Scottish	2 2 3
	Zelman Meats	Steaks & grills	4 3 3
	Oliveto	Pizza	4 2 1
	Ken Los Memories	Chinese	4 3 3
	Quilon	Indian, Southern	5 5 2
	Sumosan Twiga	Japanese	2 2 3
	Salloos	Pakistani	3 2 2
£50+	Granger & Co	Australian	2 2 3
	Aster Restaurant	British, Modern	3 2 3
	Daylesford Organic	"	3 2 2
	Shepherds	British, Traditional	3 3 4
	Motcombs	International	2 3 3
	Cacio & Pepe	Italian	3 3 2
	Hai Cenato	"	2 3 2
	Ottolenghi	"	3 2 2
	Tozi	"	3 4 3
	About Thyme	Spanish	2 3 3
	Ibérica, Zig Zag Building	"	2 2 3
	Burger & Lobster	Burgers, etc	3 3 3
	Seafresh	Fish & chips	3 2 2
	Abd El Wahab	Lebanese	3 3 3
	Kazan	Turkish	3 4 3

			Rating
	Sticks'n'Sushi	Japanese	3 2 2
£40+	Rochelle Canteen at the ICA	British, Modern	4 4 3
	Gustoso	Italian	2 4 3
	Vagabond Wines	Mediterranean	2 2 3
	Goya	Spanish	3 3 2
	Wulf & Lamb	Vegetarian	3 2 2
	Cyprus Mangal	Turkish	3 3 2
	AWong	Chinese	5 5 3
	Bone Daddies, Nova	Japanese	3 3 4
	Machiya	"	4 2 2
£35+	The Vincent Rooms	British, Modern	3 2 2
£30+	Sri Suwoon	Thai	4 4 3
£25+	Shake Shack	Burgers, etc	3 2 2
	Kanada-Ya	Japanese	5 3 3
£20+	Bleecker Burger	Burgers, etc	5 2 2
£15+	Regency Cafe	British, Traditional	3 4 5
	Domi		

WEST

CHELSEA, SOUTH KENSINGTON, KENSINGTON, EARL'S COURT & FULHAM
(SW3, SW5, SW6, SW7, SW10 & W8)

			Rating
£160+	Gordon Ramsay	French	2 2 2
£130+	Bibendum	French	3 3 4
£100+	Elystan Street	British, Modern	3 3 2
	The Five Fields	”	5 5 4
£90+	Outlaw's at The Capital	Fish & seafood	4 4 2
£80+	Launceston Place	British, Modern	3 4 4
	Medlar	”	4 4 3
	Restaurant Ours	”	2 2 3
	Rivea, Bulgari Hotel	International	3 4 3
	Daphnes	Italian	2 2 2
	Scalini	”	3 3 3
	Min Jiang	Chinese	4 4 5
	Koji	Japanese	3 3 4
	Yashin	”	4 2 2
	Zuma	”	5 3 4
£70+	Bluebird	British, Modern	2 3 3
	Clarkes	”	4 5 4
	Kitchen W8	”	4 4 3
	Le Colombier	French	3 5 4
	Lucio	Italian	3 2 2
	Manicomio	”	2 2 3
	Stecca	”	– – –

			Rating
	Cambio de Tercio	Spanish	4 3 3
	Hawksmoor Knightsbridge	Steaks & grills	3 2 2
£60+	Big Easy	American	2 2 3
	The Abingdon	British, Modern	3 3 4
	Brinkleys	”	2 2 3
	Claude's Kitchen	”	3 3 4
	The Cross Keys	”	3 4 4
	Harwood Arms	”	4 3 3
	Parabola, Design Museum	”	– – –
	Toms Kitchen	”	2 2 2
	Maggie Joness	British, Traditional	2 2 4
	Kensington Place	Fish & seafood	3 2 2
	Wright Brothers	”	4 4 3
	Belvedere Restaurant	French	3 3 5
	Mazi	Greek	3 4 3
	Enoteca Rosso	Italian	2 2 2
	La Famiglia	”	2 2 2
	Frantoio	”	3 4 4
	La Mia Mamma	”	– – –
	Il Portico	”	3 5 4
	Theos Simple Italian	”	3 3 2
	Zianis	”	2 4 2
	Sophies Steakhouse	Steaks & grills	2 2 2
	Chicama	Peruvian	4 2 4
	Good Earth	Chinese	2 2 2
	Bombay Brasserie	Indian	4 3 3
	Zaika of Kensington	Indian, Southern	4 3 3
	Chisou	Japanese	4 3 2
	Dinings	”	5 3 2
	Kurobuta	”	3 2 2
	Zheng	Malaysian	4 3 2

Patara	*Thai*	3 3 3

£50+			
Bodeans	*American*	3 2 3
The Builders Arms	*British, Modern*	2 2 4
Daylesford Organic	"	3 2 2
The Enterprise	"	2 3 4
The Ivy Chelsea Garden	"	2 2 4
Manuka Kitchen	"	3 4 3
maze Grill	"	3 3 2
Park Terrace Restaurant	"	3 3 4
Rabbit	"	3 2 3
The Sands End	"	3 3 4
The Shed	"	3 4 3
Bumpkin	*British, Traditional*	2 2 3
Bibendum Oyster Bar	*Fish & seafood*	3 3 3
Bistro Mirey	*Fusion*	4 4 3
The Admiral Codrington	*International*	3 3 4
Gallery Mess	"	2 3 3
The Kensington Wine Rooms	"	2 3 3
Aglio e Olio	*Italian*	3 3 2
Harrys Dolce Vita	"	3 4 5
Nuovi Sapori	"	3 3 4
Polpo	"	2 2 2
Riccardos	"	2 2 2
San Pietro	"	3 3 3
Sapori Sardi	"	3 3 2
The Atlas	*Mediterranean*	4 4 4
Ognisko Restaurant	*Polish*	3 4 5
Casa Brindisa	*Spanish*	3 3 2
Tendido Cero	"	3 3 4
Macellaio RC	*Steaks & grills*	3 3 3
Geales	*Fish & chips*	2 2 2
Pizzicotto	*Pizza*	4 4 3
Fernandez & Wells	*Sandwiches, cakes, etc*	3 3 3
Maroush	*Lebanese*	3 2 2
Royal China	*Chinese*	3 1 2
Romulo Café	*Filipino*	3 3 3
Pure Indian Cooking	*Indian*	4 4 2
Akira at Japan House	*Japanese*	- - -
Kiru	"	3 3 3
Oka	"	3 2 2
Sticks'n'Sushi	"	3 2 2
Eight Over Eight	*Pan-Asian*	3 3 4
Sukho Fine Thai Cuisine	*Thai*	5 5 3
Go-Viet	*Vietnamese*	4 4 2

£40+			
Kensington Square Kitchen	*British, Modern*	4 4 3
VQ	"	2 3 3
Ardiciocca	*Italian*	- - -
Chelsea Cellar	"	4 4 4
Da Mario	"	3 3 3
Made in Italy	"	3 1 2
Vagabond Wines	*Mediterranean*	2 2 3
Daquise	*Polish*	2 2 2
Haché	*Steaks & grills*	3 3 2
Tell Your Friends	*Vegetarian*	- - -
La Delizia Limbara	*Pizza*	3 2 2
Rocca Di Papa	"	3 4 4
Rossopomodoro	"	2 2 2
Santa Maria	"	4 3 2
Lupita West	*Mexican/TexMex*	3 3 2

Dip in Brilliant	*Indian*	3 3 3
Dishoom	"	3 4 5
Flora Indica	"	4 3 3
Malabar	"	3 3 3
Noor Jahan	"	3 3 3
Thali	"	4 4 3
Bone Daddies, Whole Foods	*Japanese*	3 3 4
Dozo	"	3 2 2
Suksan	*Thai*	3 3 2

£35+			
Churchill Arms	*British, Traditional*	3 2 5
Mona Lisa	*International*	3 3 2
Pappa Ciccia	*Italian*	3 4 3
Best Mangal	*Turkish*	4 3 3
Addies Thai Café	*Thai*	3 3 3
Mien Tay	*Vietnamese*	3 2 2

£30+			
Ceru	*Mediterranean*	4 3 2
Eat Tokyo	*Japanese*	3 3 2
Kulu Kulu	"	3 2 1
Phat Phuc	*Vietnamese*	4 3 1

£25+			
Tommi's Burger Joint	*Burgers, etc*	3 3 3

£20+			
Market Hall Fulham	*International*	- - -
Stick & Bowl	*Chinese*	3 3 1

£15+			
Oree	*Sandwiches, cakes, etc*	3 2 3

NOTTING HILL, HOLLAND PARK, BAYSWATER, NORTH KENSINGTON & MAIDA VALE (W2,W9,W10,W11)

£150+	The Ledbury	*British, Modern*	5 4 4
£110+	Core by Clare Smyth	*British, Modern*	5 5 4
£90+	Flat Three	*Japanese*	4 4 3
£80+	Chucs Serpentine	*Italian*	3 3 3
	Casa Cruz	*South American*	1 1 3
£70+	The Summerhouse	*Fish & seafood*	2 2 5
	Angelus	*French*	3 4 2
	Assaggi	*Italian*	3 4 2
	Kateh	*Persian*	3 2 3
£60+	The Frontline Club	*British, Modern*	3 3 4
	108 Garage	"	2 2 2
	London Shell Co.	*Fish & seafood*	4 4 5
	Assaggi Bar & Pizzeria	*Italian*	4 3 2
	Edera	"	3 4 3
	Essenza	"	2 3 3
	Mediterraneo	"	3 3 3
	Osteria Basilico	"	4 2 2
	Kurobuta	*Japanese*	3 2 2
	Southam Street	"	3 2 3
£50+	Pomona's	*American*	3 4 4

Granger & Co	Australian	2 2 3
Daylesford Organic	British, Modern	3 2 2
The Hero of Maida	"	– – –
Julies	"	– – –
The Ladbroke Arms	"	3 3 3
Paradise by way of Kensal Gn	"	3 2 4
Six Portland Road	"	4 5 3
The Waterway	"	2 2 3
Hereford Road	British, Traditional	4 3 3
Snaps & Rye	Danish	3 4 3
Cepages	French	4 3 4
The Cow	Irish	3 3 5
The Oak	Italian	3 3 4
Ottolenghi	"	3 2 2
Polpo	"	2 2 2
Portobello Ristorante	"	3 4 4
Farmacy	Vegetarian	2 3 4
Pizza East Portobello	Pizza	4 3 4
The Red Pepper	"	3 2 2
Cocotte	Chicken	4 4 3
Peyotito	Mexican/TexMex	3 3 2
Andina Picanteria	Peruvian	3 3 3
Maroush	Lebanese	3 2 2
The Four Seasons	Chinese	5 1 1
Royal	China	3 1 2
Maguro	Japanese	4 4 2
E&O	Pan-Asian	3 4 4

£40+			
Electric Diner	American	2 2 3
VQ	British, Modern	2 3 3
Bucket	Fish & seafood	– – –
The Chipping Forecast	"	3 2 2
Ida	Italian	3 2 3
Raoul's Café	Mediterranean	3 2 4
Taqueria	Mexican/TexMex	3 3 3
The Cedar Restaurant	Lebanese	3 3 2
Mandarin Kitchen	Chinese	4 3 2
Pearl Liang	"	4 3 3
Bombay Palace	Indian	4 3 2
Noor Jahan	"	3 3 3
Tonkotsu	Japanese	4 3 3
Uli	Pan-Asian	3 4 4
MAM	Vietnamese	4 3 3

£35+			
MEATliquor	Burgers, etc	3 2 4
Gold Mine	Chinese	4 2 2
The Heron	Thai	4 3 1

£30+			
Flat Iron	Steaks & grills	3 4 4
C&R Café	Malaysian	4 2 2

£25+			
Patty and Bun	Burgers, etc	4 3 3
Alounak	Persian	3 3 3
Khans	Indian	2 2 2

£20+			
Fez Mangal	Turkish	5 3 3

£5+			
Lisboa Pâtisserie	Sandwiches, cakes, etc	3 2 4

HAMMERSMITH, SHEPHERD'S BUSH, OLYMPIA, CHISWICK, BRENTFORD & EALING (W4, W5, W6, W12, W13, W14, TW8)

£120+			
Hedone	British, Modern	4 3 2

£90+			
The River Café	Italian	3 4 4

£80+			
La Trompette	French	5 5 3

£60+			
Vinoteca	British, Modern	2 2 3
Michael Nadra	French	4 3 2
Le Vacherin	"	3 3 3
Villa Di Geggiano	Italian	3 4 3
Popeseye	Steaks & grills	3 2 2
The Bird in Hand	Pizza	3 2 3

£50+			
Jackson & Rye Chiswick	American	2 2 2
The Anglesea Arms	British, Modern	4 4 4
The Brackenbury	"	4 4 4
Brackenbury Wine Rooms	"	2 2 3
Charlotte's W5	"	3 3 3
City Barge	"	3 3 3
The Colton Arms	"	2 3 4
The Dove	"	3 3 5
Duke of Sussex	"	2 2 3
Eat 17 Hammersmith	"	3 4 3
The Havelock Tavern	"	3 2 4
High Road Brasserie	"	2 2 2
The Hampshire Hog	British, Traditional	3 3 3
Albertine	French	4 4 5
The Andover Arms	International	2 3 4
Annies	"	2 3 4
L'Amorosa	Italian	4 4 3
Cibo	"	4 5 3
The Oak W12	"	3 3 4
Pentolina	"	4 4 3
Tarantella	"	3 3 3
The Swan	Mediterranean	3 4 4
The Gate	Vegetarian	4 2 3
Quantus	South American	3 5 3
Shikumen, Dorsett Hotel	Chinese	4 3 2
Brilliant	Indian	4 4 3
Indian Zing	"	4 3 2
Little Bird Chiswick	Pan-Asian	3 2 4

£40+			
Bluebird Café White City	British, Modern	– – –
The Dartmouth Castle	"	3 4 3
Mustard	"	3 3 3
The Pear Tree	"	3 3 4
The Princess Victoria	"	3 3 3
Wellbourne	"	3 3 2
Cumberland Arms	Mediterranean	3 3 3
Santa Maria	Pizza	4 3 2
Tamp Coffee	Sandwiches, cakes, etc	3 4 4
Chez Abir	Lebanese	3 4 2
North China	Chinese	3 4 2
Madhus	Indian	4 5 3
Potli	"	4 4 3
Kiraku	Japanese	4 2 2
Sushi Bar Atari-Ya	"	5 2 1

Sushi Bar Makoto	"	431
Hare & Tortoise	Pan-Asian	332

£35+			
	Homeslice	Pizza	333
	Angie's Little Food Shop	Sandwiches, cakes, etc	333
	Adams Café	Moroccan	353
	Best Mangal	Turkish	433
	Anarkali	Indian	343
	Sagar	"	432
	Tosa	Japanese	332
	Yoshi Sushi	"	342
	101 Thai Kitchen	Thai	432
	Saigon Saigon	Vietnamese	233

£30+			
	Oro Di Napoli	Pizza	432

	Monkey Temple	Indian	342
	Shilpa	Indian, Southern	421
	Eat Tokyo	Japanese	332

£25+			
	Kerbisher & Malt	Fish & chips	322
	Alounak	Persian	333
	Gifto's	Indian	322

£20+			
	Abu Zaad	Syrian	332

£5+			
	Bears Ice Cream	Ice cream	333

NORTH

HAMPSTEAD, WEST HAMPSTEAD, ST JOHN'S WOOD, REGENT'S PARK, KILBURN & CAMDEN TOWN (NW POSTCODES)

£70+			
	Landmark (Winter Gdn)	British, Modern	245
	Odettes	"	433
	The Gilbert Scott	British, Traditional	224
	Kaifeng	Chinese	322
£60+	The Booking Office	British, Modern	224
	Bradleys	"	222
	L'Aventure	French	345
	Michael Nadra	"	432
	Oslo Court	"	354
	Bull & Last	Internationa	333
	Villa Bianca	Italian	222
	Zest, JW3	Kosher	332
	Crocker's Folly	Lebanese	324
	Delicatessen	Middle Eastern	322
	Good Earth	Chinese	222
	Patara	Thai	333

£50+			
	The Clifton	British, Modern	335
	Ham	"	323
	The Horseshoe	"	334
	The Ivy Café	"	123
	Parlour Kensal	"	334
	Searcys St Pancras Grand	"	213
	The Wells Tavern	"	334
	The Wet Fish Café	"	234
	Holly Bush	British, Traditional	335
	York & Albany	"	112
	La Collina	Italian	332
	Melange	"	322
	The Rising Sun	"	333
	28 Church Row	Spanish	444
	Ceremony	Vegetarian	343
	Manna	"	222
	The Sea Shell	Fish & chips	322
	Pizza East	Pizza	434
	Greenberry Café	Sandwiches, cakes, etc	334

	Phoenix Palace	Chinese	333
	Oka	Japanese	322

£40+			
	Lantana Cafe	Australian	333
	L'Absinthe	French	233
	Authentique	"	- - -
	La Cage Imaginaire	"	234
	La Ferme	"	333
	Carob Tree	Greek	342
	Lemonia	"	145
	Anima e Cuore	Italian	531
	La Porchetta Pizzeria	"	232
	Quartieri	"	433
	Sarracino	"	332
	El Parador	Spanish	443
	Beef & Brew	Steaks & grills	343
	Haché	"	332
	Mildreds	Vegetarian	322
	Purezza	"	332
	Harry Morgans	Burgers, etc	232
	Poppies Camden	Fish & chips	323
	L'Artista	Pizza	353
	Rossopomodoro	"	222
	The Cedar Restaurant	Lebanese	332
	Skewd Kitchen	Turkish	333
	Great Nepalese	Indian	342
	Guglee	"	332
	Namaaste Kitchen	"	432
	Paradise Hampstead	"	354
	Saravanaa Bhavan	"	432
	Jin Kichi	Japanese	543
	Sushi Bar Atari-Ya	"	521
	Sushi Masa	"	343
	The Petite Coree	Korean	432
	Singapore Garden	Malaysian	332

£35+			
	Lure	Fish & seafood	353
	Fiddies Italian Kitchen	Italian	332
	Giacomos	"	332
	Nautilus	Fish & chips	431
	L'Antica Pizzeria	Pizza	453

Sacro Cuore	"	5	3	2
Green Cottage	*Chinese*	3	2	2
Bonoo	*Indian*	4	4	3
Vijay	"	4	4	1
Anjanaas	*Indian, Southern*	4	4	3
Asakusa	*Japanese*	5	2	2
Bang Bang Oriental	*Pan-Asian*	3	2	3

£30+				
The Little Bay	*Mediterranean*	3	3	4
Kenwood (Brew House)	*Sandwiches, cakes, etc*	2	2	3
Chai Thali	*Indian*	3	3	3
Ravi Shankar	"	3	2	2
Eat Tokyo	*Japanese*	3	3	2

£25+				
Shake Shack	*Burgers, etc*	3	2	2
Ali Baba	*Egyptian*	3	2	2
Chutneys	*Indian*	3	2	2
Diwana Bhel-Poori House	"	3	2	1
Sakonis	"	3	2	1

£20+				
L'Antica Pizzeria da Michele	*Pizza*	–	–	–
Ariana II	*Afghani*	3	3	2

£15+				
Icco Pizza	*Pizza*	5	2	1
Roti King	*Malaysian*	5	2	1

£10+				
Fields Beneath	*Vegetarian*	3	2	3
Ginger & White	*Sandwiches, cakes, etc*	3	3	3
E Mono	*Turkish*	4	2	2

HOXTON, ISLINGTON, HIGHGATE, CROUCH END, STOKE NEWINGTON, FINSBURY PARK, MUSWELL HILL & FINCHLEY (N POSTCODES)

£70+				
Cub	*British, Modern*	4	4	3
Fifteen	"	2	2	2
The Frog Hoxton	"	5	5	4
Plum + Spilt Milk	"	2	3	3
German Gymnasium	*East & Cent. European*	2	1	4

£60+				
Fredericks	*British, Modern*	3	4	5
The Lighterman	"	3	3	4
Perilla	"	3	3	3
Prawn on the Lawn	*Fish & seafood*	3	3	2
Bellanger	*French*	2	2	3
Salut	*International*	3	2	2
Radici	*Italian*	2	2	1
Trullo	"	3	3	3
Vinoteca	*Mediterranean*	2	2	3
Popeseye	*Steaks & grills*	3	2	2

£50+				
Granger & Co	*Australian*	2	2	3
The Bull	*British, Modern*	3	4	4
Caravan King's Cross	"	3	3	3
The Drapers Arms	"	3	3	4
Granary Square Brasserie	"	2	2	4
Heirloom	"	3	3	3
Humble Grape	"	3	4	4
Jones & Sons	"	3	3	3

Oldroyd	"	3	3	2
Pig & Butcher	"	4	4	4
The Red Lion & Sun	"	3	2	3
Rotunda Bar & Restaurant	"	3	3	4
Westerns Laundry	"	3	3	3
St Johns	*British, Traditional*	3	4	5
Galley	*Fish & seafood*	3	3	3
Bistro Aix	*French*	2	2	3
Petit Pois Bistro	"	4	2	3
Sardine	"	4	4	3
Table Du Marche	"	3	3	2
The Good Egg	*Fusion*	3	3	3
Banners	*International*	3	2	4
Primeur	"	3	3	3
500	*Italian*	4	3	2
Il Guscio	"	3	4	3
Melange	"	3	2	2
Ottolenghi	"	3	2	2
Rugoletta	"	3	3	2
Rök	*Scandinavian*	3	4	3
Barrafina	*Spanish*	5	5	5
Café del Parc	"	4	5	3
Camino King's Cross	"	3	3	2
Smokehouse Islington	*Steaks & grills*	3	3	2
Cocotte	*Chicken*	4	4	3
Bodean's	*BBQ*	3	2	3

£40+				
Breakfast Club Angel	*American*	3	3	3
Wander	*Australian*	4	3	3
Bergen House	*British, Modern*	–	–	–
Chriskitch	"	4	3	3
Haven Bistro	"	3	4	3
Season Kitchen	"	3	3	2
Snooty Fox	*British, Traditional*	3	2	3
Kipferl	*East & Cent. European*	3	2	3
Le Sacré-Coeur	*French*	2	3	3
Vrisaki	*Greek*	3	3	3
Aleion	*International*	3	3	3
Andi's	"	3	3	4
La Fromagerie	"	3	3	3
The Orange Tree	"	3	2	3
Osteria Tufo	*Italian*	3	2	2
La Porchetta Pizzeria	"	2	3	2
Alcedo	*Mediterranean*	3	4	3
Bar Esteban	*Spanish*	3	3	3
Lluna	"	3	2	3
Trangallan	"	4	4	3
Beef & Brew	*Steaks & grills*	3	4	3
Mildreds	*Vegetarian*	3	2	2
Toffs	*Fish & chips*	3	4	3
Rossopomodoro	*Pizza*	2	2	2
Sweet Thursday	"	3	2	3
Chick 'n' Sours	*Chicken*	4	3	3
Plaquemine Lock	*Cajun/creole*	3	3	3
Black Axe Mangal	*Turkish*	4	3	2
Gallipoli	"	2	3	3
Yipin China	*Chinese*	4	2	2
Dishoom	*Indian*	3	4	5
Zaffrani	"	3	2	2
Supawan	*Thai*	4	4	2

£35+	Linden Stores	British, Modern	4	3	3
	Passione e Tradizione	Italian	3	3	2
	Pasta Remoli	"	3	3	3
	Pizzeria Pappagone	"	3	4	3
	Lady Mildmay	Mediterranean	3	4	3
	Llerena	Spanish	4	4	2
	MEATLiquor Islington	Burgers, etc	3	2	4
	Sutton and Sons	Fish & chips	4	3	2
	Sacro Cuore	Pizza	5	3	2
	Yard Sale Pizza	"	5	3	3
	Zia Lucia	"	4	3	3
	Finks Salt and Sweet	Sandwiches, cakes, etc	3	4	4
	Monty's Deli	"	4	4	3
	Sumak	Turkish	4	4	2
	Indian Rasoi	Indian	3	3	2
	Rasa	Indian, Southern	3	3	2
	Farang	Thai	4	3	2
£30+	Sunday	Australian	4	2	3
	Two Brothers	Fish & seafood	3	2	2
	Le Mercury	French	2	2	3

	Via Emilia	Italian	–	–	–
	Flat Iron	Steaks & grills	3	4	4
	Cut + Grind	Burgers, etc	4	3	2
	MEATmission	"	3	3	4
	Olympus Fish	Fish & chips	3	3	2
	Max's Sandwich Shop	Sandwiches, cakes, etc	4	4	3
	Gem	Turkish	3	4	3
	Gökyüzü	"	2	2	2
	Delhi Grill	Indian	3	3	2
	Jashan	"	4	4	2
	Shahi Pakwaan	"	5	4	3
	Dotori	Korean	4	3	2
£25+	Saponara	Italian	4	3	3
	Afghan Kitchen	Afghani	4	2	2
	Xi'an Impression	Chinese	4	2	2
	Kanada-Ya	Japanese	5	3	3
£20+	Piebury Corner	British, Traditional	3	3	3
	Fannys Kebabs	Turkish	–	–	–
	CôBa	Vietnamese	4	3	2

SOUTH

SOUTH BANK (SE1)

£150+	Story	British, Modern	3	3	3
£100+	Aqua Shard	British, Modern	1	1	3
	Oblix	"	2	2	3
	Hutong, The Shard	Chinese	2	2	4
£90+	Oxo Tower (Rest')	British, Modern	1	1	1
	TING	International	2	2	4
£80+	Duddell's	Chinese, Dim sum	4	2	4
£70+	Oxo Tower (Brass')	British, Modern	1	1	2
	Le Pont de la Tour	"	2	2	2
	Skylon, South Bank Centre	"	2	2	4
	Skylon Grill	"	2	2	4
	Butlers Wharf Chop House	British, Traditional	3	2	4
	Roast	"	2	2	3
	Hawksmoor	Steaks & grills	3	2	2
	Baluchi	Indian	3	2	4
£60+	40 Maltby Street	British, Modern	4	4	3
	Sea Containers	"	1	2	2
	The Swan at the Globe	"	3	2	4
	Tom Simmons	"	3	2	2
	Union Street Café	"	3	2	3
	Applebees Fish	Fish & seafood	4	2	2
	Wright Brothers	"	4	4	3
	Arthur Hooper's	International	4	4	3
	Vivat Bacchus	"	3	4	2
	Pizarro	Spanish	3	2	3
	The Coal Shed	Steaks & grills	3	3	3
	Pique Nique	Chicken	3	3	3

	Santo Remedio	Mexican/TexMex	3	2	3
	Rabot 1745	Afro-Caribbean	2	2	2
	Bala Baya	Middle Eastern	4	2	2
£50+	The Anchor & Hope	British, Modern	4	3	3
	Caravan Bankside	"	3	3	3
	Edwins	"	3	4	4
	Elliot's Café	"	4	3	3
	The Garrison	"	3	2	3
	House Restaurant	"	2	3	2
	The Ivy Tower Bridge	"	2	2	4
	Menier Chocolate Factory	"	2	3	3
	Tate Modern (Level 7)	"	2	2	3
	Waterloo Bar & Kitchen	"	3	2	2
	fish!	Fish & seafood	3	2	2
	Native	"	–	–	–
	Casse-Croute	French	4	4	4
	Capricci	Italian	3	3	2
	Baltic	Polish	3	4	3
	Bar Douro	Portuguese	4	4	3
	Londrino	"	2	3	3
	Camino Bankside	Spanish	3	3	2
	José	"	5	4	5
	LOBOS Meat & Tapas	"	4	3	2
	Tapas Brindisa	"	3	3	2
	Macellaio RC	Steaks & grills	3	3	3
	O'ver	Pizza	4	3	3
	Chimis	Argentinian	–	–	–
	Paladar South	American	–	–	–
	Arabica Bar and Kitchen	Lebanese	3	3	3
	Champor-Champor	Thai	3	3	3
£40+	Lantana London Bridge	Australian	3	3	3
	Blueprint Café	British, Modern	2	2	4

The Garden Cafe	"	3 2 3
The Green Room	"	2 3 2
Lupins	"	4 4 3
The Table	"	3 2 2
Boro Bistro	French	3 3 3
Flour & Grape	Italian	3 4 3
Mar I Terra	Spanish	2 2 2
Meson don Felipe	"	2 2 3
tibits	Vegetarian	3 2 3
London Grind	Sandwiches, cakes, etc	4 4 4
El Pastór	Mexican/TexMex	4 3 5
Tonkotsu Bankside	Japanese	4 3 3
Sticky Mango at RSJ	Pan-Asian	2 3 2

£35+	Tas Pide	Turkish	2 3 3
	Est India	Indian	3 2 3
	Gunpowder	"	4 4 3

£25+	Mercato Metropolitano	Italian	5 3 3
	Padella	"	5 4 3
	Patty and Bun	Burgers, etc	4 3 3
	Masters Super Fish	Fish & chips	3 2 1

£5+	Monmouth Coffee Company	Sandwiches, cakes, etc	3 4 4
	Gourmet Goat	Middle Eastern	4 2 2

GREENWICH, LEWISHAM, DULWICH & BLACKHEATH (ALL SE POSTCODES, EXCEPT SE1)

£60+	Brasserie Toulouse-Lautrec	French	3 3 3
	Craft London	Pizza	3 4 2

£50+	The Camberwell Arms	British, Modern	5 3 3
	Franklins	"	3 2 2
	The Guildford Arms	"	3 4 3
	Llewelyn's	"	3 2 2
	The Palmerston	"	3 3 3
	Rivington Grill	"	2 2 2
	The Rosendale	"	3 4 3
	Terroirs	"	3 2 3
	Peckham Bazaar	Greek	4 3 3
	Brookmill	International	3 3 3
	Con Gusto	Italian	3 4 4
	Luciano's	"	4 3 2
	Coal Rooms	Steaks & grills	4 3 3
	Kudu	South African	3 3 3
	Babur	Indian	5 5 4
	Kennington Tandoori	"	3 3 3
	Sticks'n'Sushi	Japanese	3 2 2
	Yama Momo	"	3 3 3

£40+	The Crooked Well	British, Modern	3 2 3
	The Lido Café	"	3 2 4
	Louie Louie	"	3 2 3
	Sparrow	"	4 5 3
	Joannas	International	3 5 4
	The Yellow House	"	3 4 3
	Artusi	Italian	4 3 3
	Forza Win	"	3 4 3

Le Querce	"	3 3 2
Marcella	Mediterranean	3 3 2
Mamma Dough	Pizza	3 3 3
Rocca Di Papa	"	3 4 4
Zero Degrees	"	3 3 3
Dragon Castle	Chinese	3 3 3
Everest Inn	Indian	3 2 3
Ganapati	"	4 3 3
The Begging Bowl	Thai	4 2 2
Bánh Bánh	Vietnamese	3 4 3

£35+	Babette	British, Modern	3 3 4
	Black Prince	"	3 3 2
	Catford Constitutional Club	"	3 4 4
	Good Neighbour	Mediterranean	- - -
	MEATliquor ED	Burgers, etc	3 2 4
	Olleys	Fish & chips	3 3 2
	Theo's	Pizza	3 3 2
	FM Mangal	Turkish	3 3 3
	Sanxia Renjia	Chinese	3 3 2
	Mr Bao	Taiwanese	4 3 3

£30+	White Bear	British, Traditional	3 3 3
	Made of Dough	Pizza	4 4 3
	Zeret	Ethiopian	4 4 3
	Zaibatsu	Japanese	4 4 2

£25+	Rox Burger	Burgers, etc	4 3 3
	400 Rabbits	Pizza	3 3 2

£20+	500 Degrees	Pizza	3 2 2
	Silk Road	Chinese	5 2 1

£15+	Goddards At Greenwich	British, Traditional	3 4 4
	Peckham Levels	International	- - -
	The Green Café	Vegetarian	3 3 2

£5+	Kappacasein	Sandwiches, cakes, etc	4 3 3

BATTERSEA, BRIXTON, CLAPHAM, WANDSWORTH BARNES, PUTNEY & WIMBLEDON (ALL SW POSTCODES SOUTH OF THE RIVER)

£80+	Chez Bruce	British, Modern	5 5 4

£70+	Trinity	British, Modern	5 5 4
	Gastronhome	French	5 4 3

£60+	Hatched	British, Modern	4 4 2
	Rick Stein	Fish & seafood	2 2 3
	Wright Brothers	"	4 4 3
	Sinabro	French	4 4 3
	The White Onion	"	3 4 2
	London House	International	2 2 2
	Riva	Italian	3 3 2
	Good Earth	Chinese	2 2 2
	Patara	Thai	3 3 3

£50+	Bodeans	American	3 2 3

Bistro Union	British, Modern	3 3 3
Brunswick House Café	"	3 3 5
Cannizaro House	"	1 1 4
Counter Culture	"	3 4 2
The Dairy	"	4 4 4
Earl Spencer	"	3 2 3
Home SW15	"	3 3 3
Hood	"	4 3 3
Humble Grape	"	3 4 4
The Ivy Café	"	1 2 3
Lamberts	"	5 5 5
Minnow	"	3 3 3
No 29 Power Station West	"	2 1 4
Nutbourne	"	2 2 3
Salon Brixton	"	5 4 3
Sonnys Kitchen	"	3 3 2
Trinity Upstairs	"	5 4 4
The Victoria	"	2 2 3
Canton Arms	British, Traditional	4 3 4
Fox & Grapes	"	3 3 3
Jolly Gardeners	"	3 3 3
Augustine Kitchen	French	3 4 3
Bistro Vadouvan	"	4 4 3
Gazette	"	3 3 3
Soif	"	3 3 3
Annies	International	2 3 4
The Light House	"	3 3 3
Fiume	Italian	3 4 3
Osteria Antica Bologna	"	3 3 2
Sorella	"	4 3 3
Foxlow	Steaks & grills	2 2 2
Knife	"	5 5 4
Macellaio RC	"	3 3 3
Naughty Piglets	"	5 5 3
Addomme	Pizza	4 3 2
Santa Maria del Sur	Argentinian	3 4 3
Chokhi Dhani London	Indian	4 4 3
Cinnamon Kitchen	"	4 3 3
Sticks'n'Sushi	Japanese	3 2 2
Little Bird Battersea	Pan-Asian	3 2 4

£40+

The Brown Dog	British, Modern	3 3 3
Olympic Caf'	"	2 2 3
Plot	"	4 4 4
The Plough	"	2 3 4
Smoke & Salt	"	5 4 3
Sea Garden & Grill	Fish & seafood	4 4 4
Made in Italy	Italian	3 1 2
Pizza Metro	"	3 2 2
Stockwell Continental	"	3 3 3
Vagabond Wines	Mediterranean	2 2 3
Boqueria	Spanish	4 3 3
Little Taperia	"	3 2 2
Arlo's	Steaks & grills	3 2 2
Haché	Burgers, etc	3 3 2
Bradys	Fish & chips	3 4 3
Al Forno	Pizza	2 3 4
Dynamo	"	3 2 3
Mamma Dough	"	3 3 3
Mother	"	2 2 3
Pizza da Valter	"	3 2 2

Rossopomodoro	"	2 2 2
Duck Duck Goose	Chinese	4 4 3
Indian Moment	Indian	3 3 2
Kashmir	"	4 3 2
Ma Goa	"	4 4 3
Nanban	Japanese	4 2 3
Takahashi	"	5 5 3
Tonkotsu Battersea	"	4 3 3
Tsunami	"	5 2 3
Hare & Tortoise	Pan-Asian	3 3 2
Bánh Bánh	Vietnamese	3 4 3
Daddy Bao	Taiwanese	4 3 3

£35+

Fish in a Tie	Mediterranean	3 3 3
Meatliquor	Burgers, etc	3 2 4
Eco	Pizza	3 2 3
Orange Pekoe	Sandwiches, cakes, etc	3 3 4
Meza	Lebanese	3 3 2
Indian Ocean Indian	ERW	
Hashi	Japanese	3 3 2
Taro	"	3 2 2
Tomoe	"	4 2 1
Mien Tay	Vietnamese	3 2 2

£30+

Dip & Flip	Burgers, etc	3 3 3
Dirty Burger	"	2 2 2
Chicken Shop	Chicken	2 2 2
Booma	Indian	4 3 2
Chit Chaat Chai	"	3 3 3
Jaffna House	Indian, Southern	3 2 2

£25+

Unwined	British, Modern	3 4 4
Kerbisher & Malt	Fish & chips	3 2 2
Hot Stuff	Indian	3 5 2
Munal Tandoori		3 4 2
Mirch Masala	Pakistani	4 2 1
Awesome Thai	Thai	3 4 2
Kaosarn		4 2 3

£20+

Flotsam and Jetsam	Australian	3 2 3
Tried & True	British, Modern	3 3 3
Cut The Mustard	Sandwiches, cakes, etc	3 3 3

£15+

Joe Public	Pizza	3 4 2
Ground Coffee Society	Sandwiches, cakes, etc	3 2 2
Milk	"	4 3 3

OUTER WESTERN SUBURBS KEW, RICHMOND, TWICKENHAM, TEDDINGTON

£80+

| The Glasshouse | British, Modern | 3 3 2 |
| M Bar & Grill Twickenham | Steaks & grills | 2 2 2 |

£70+

| The Dysart Petersham | British, Modern | 3 3 3 |
| Petersham Nurseries Cafe | " | 2 2 5 |

£60+

The Bingham	British, Modern	3 4 5
The Petersham Restaurant	"	2 2 5
Al Boccon di'vino	Italian	4 4 5

£50+	Jackson & Rye Richmond	American	2 2 2
	The Ivy Café	British, Modern	1 2 3
	Petit Ma Cuisine	French	2 2 2
	Le Salon Privé	"	3 4 3
	A Cena	Italian	3 2 3
	Bacco	"	2 2 2
£40+	La Buvette	French	3 2 3

	Dastaan	Indian	5 4 2
	Matsuba	Japanese	3 3 2
£35+	Moksha Indian	TRE	
£20+	The Fallow Deer Cafe	International	3 4 3

EAST

SMITHFIELD & FARRINGDON (EC1)

£140+	The Clove Club	British, Modern	4 3 3
£100+	Club Gascon	French	4 4 4
£80+	Luca	Italian	3 3 4
	Sushi Tetsu	Japanese	5 5 3
£70+	Bleeding Heart Restaurant	French	3 3 5
	Smiths (Top Floor)	Steaks & grills	3 2 3
	Smiths (Dining Rm)	"	2 2 2
£60+	Anglo	British, Modern	5 4 2
	The Jugged Hare	"	4 2 2
	The Modern Pantry	"	2 2 2
	Vinoteca	"	2 2 3
	The Quality Chop House	British, Traditional	3 3 3
	St John Smithfield	"	5 4 3
	Moro	Spanish	4 3 3
	Hix Oyster & Chop House	Steaks & grills	3 2 2
£50+	Bodeans	American	3 2 3
	Granger & Co	Australian	2 2 3
	Bird of Smithfield	British, Modern	3 3 3
	Caravan	"	3 3 3
	The Coach	"	4 3 3
	The Wilmington	"	3 2 3
	The Fox and Anchor	British, Traditional	2 2 3
	Café du Marché	French	3 3 5
	Comptoir Gascon	"	2 2 2
	The Drunken Butler	"	4 3 3
	Niche	International	2 3 2
	Apulia	Italian	3 3 2
	Palatino	"	4 3 3
	Passo	"	2 2 2
	Polpo	"	2 2 2
	Ibérica	Spanish	2 2 3
	Foxlow	Steaks & grills	2 2 2
	Macellaio RC	"	3 3 3
	The Gate	Vegetarian	4 2 3
	Burger & Lobster	Burgers, etc	3 3 3
	Santore	Pizza	3 3 2
	Nuala	BBQ	4 3 4
	Ceviche Old St	Peruvian	5 3 4
	Berber & Q Shawarma Bar	Middle Eastern	4 3 3
	The Sichuan	Chinese	3 2 2

£40+	Lantana Café	Australian	3 3 3
	The Great Chase	British, Modern	3 4 2
	The Green	"	3 4 3
	La Ferme London	French	3 3 3
	La Porchetta Pizzeria	Italian	2 3 2
	Morito	Spanish	4 3 4
	Pizza Pilgrims	Pizza	3 3 3
	Breddos Tacos	Mexican/TexMex	3 3 3
	Bone Daddies, The Bower	Japanese	3 3 4
	Pham Sushi	"	4 2 3
	Cây Tre	Vietnamese	3 2 2
£35+	Kolossi Grill	Greek	2 3 2
	The Eagle	Mediterranean	3 3 4
	Homeslice	Pizza	3 3 3
	Workshop Coffee	Sandwiches, cakes, etc	3 3 3
	On The Bab	Korean	3 2 2
£30+	Fish Central	Fish & seafood	3 2 2
	Bowling Bird	International	4 4 3
£25+	Bean & Wheat	Sandwiches, cakes, etc	4 3 3
£10+	Department of Coffee	Sandwiches, cakes, etc	3 4 3
	Prufrock Coffee	"	3 2 2

THE CITY (EC2, EC3, EC4)

£110+	La Dame de Pic London	French	4 3 2
	Nobu Shoreditch	Japanese	3 2 3
£100+	Mei Ume	Japanese	3 3 4
£90+	City Social	British, Modern	3 3 3
	Fenchurch Restaurant	"	3 2 4
	Angler, South Place Hotel	Fish & seafood	4 3 3
	Coq dArgent	French	2 3 3
	Goodman City	Steaks & grills	3 3 2
	Lutyens Grill, The Ned	"	3 4 4
	Sushisamba	Japanese	2 2 3
£80+	M Restaurant	Steaks & grills	2 2 2
	Coya	Peruvian	3 2 3
	Yauatcha City	Chinese	4 3 4
£70+	Darwin Brasserie	British, Modern	2 3 4
	Duck & Waffle	"	2 2 5

Helix	"		335
High Timber	"		233
1 Lombard Street	"		223
St Leonards	"		– – –
Sweetings	Fish & seafood		324
Cecconi's at The Ned	Italian		223
Manicomio	"		223
Boisdale of Bishopsgate	Scottish		323
Sagardi	Spanish		233
Barbecoa	Steaks & grills		222
Hawksmoor	"		322
Mint Leaf Lounge	Indian		323
£60+	The Botanist	British, Modern	222
	Bread Street Kitchen	"	223
	The Don	"	332
	Sign of The Don	"	344
	James Cochran EC3	"	– – –
	The Mercer	"	222
	Merchants Tavern	"	334
	Northbank	"	323
	Vinoteca City	"	223
	Paternoster Chop House	British, Traditional	222
	Fish Market	Fish & seafood	322
	Cabotte	French	454
	28-50	"	223
	Vivat Bacchus	International	342
	Caravaggio	Italian	322
	Hispania	Spanish	333
	The Tramshed	Steaks & grills	323
	Vanilla Black	Vegetarian	433
	Red Rooster	Chicken	223
	Cinnamon Kitchen	Indian	433
	Nanashi	Japanese	332
£50+	Bodeans	American	323
	Pitt Cue Co	"	422
	The Anthologist	British, Modern	233
	Caravan	"	333
	Humble Grape	"	344
	The Ivy City Garden	"	224
	Leroy	"	343
	Sargeants Mess	"	– – –
	Osteria, Barbican Centre	Italian	112
	Popolo	"	543
	Taberna Etrusca	"	323
	Rök	Scandinavian	343
	Mac & Wild	Scottish	324
	Camino Monument	Spanish	332
	José Pizarro	"	322
	Aviary	Steaks & grills	223
	The Jones Family Project	"	344
	Three Cranes	"	
	Burger & Lobster	Burgers, etc	333
	Haz T	urkish	222
	Oklava	"	443
	Brigadiers	Indian	544
£40+	Café Below	British, Modern	322
	Coppa Club Tower Bridge	"	234
	The Kitty Hawk	"	333

VQ	"		233
Simpsons Tavern	British, Traditional		135
The Wine Library	International		235
Rucoletta	Italian		321
Blacklock	Steaks & grills		444
Relais de Venise	"		332
Haché	Burgers, etc		332
Pizza Pilgrims	Pizza		333
Street Pizza	"		– – –
temper City	BBQ		224
Koya	Japanese		443
Shoryu Ramen	"		332
Hare & Tortoise	Pan-Asian		332
£35+	Essence Cuisine	Vegetarian	432
	Homeslice	Pizza	333
	Kurumaya	Japanese	433
	Taro	"	322
	On The Bab	Korean	322
£30+	Flat Iron	Steaks & grills	344
	K10	Japanese	332
£25+	Patty and Bun	Burgers, etc	433
	Shake Shack	"	322
	Ozone Coffee Roasters	Sandwiches, cakes, etc	334
£20+	Bleecker Burger	Burgers, etc	522
	Butchies	Chicken	322
	Bibimbap	Korean	322
£15+	Yum Bun	Japanese	542
£10+	Sub Cult	Sandwiches, cakes, etc	532
	Schmaltz Truck	Chicken	533
	Pilpel	Middle Eastern	332
	City Càphê	Vietnamese	332

EAST END & DOCKLANDS (ALL E POSTCODES)

£200+	Mãos	Portuguese	544
£90+	Goodman	Steaks & grills	332
£80+	Lyle's	British, Modern	422
	Galvin La Chapelle	French	445
	Roka	Japanese	433
£70+	The Gun	British, Modern	234
	Pidgin	"	553
	Smith's Wapping	"	445
	Plateau	French	233
	Bokan	International	333
	Canto Corvino	Italian	323
	Cecconi's Shoreditch	"	223
	Hawksmoor	Steaks & grills	322
£60+	Big Easy	American	223
	Bistrotheque	British, Modern	324
	Brat	"	544

Name	Cuisine			
One Canada Square	"	2	3	2
Rochelle Canteen	"	2	2	4
Sager + Wilde	"	2	2	3
Toms Kitchen	"	2	2	2
The Marksman	British, Traditional	4	3	4
St John Bread & Wine	"	3	3	3
Wright Brothers	Fish & seafood	4	4	3
Tratra	French	–	–	–
The Laughing Heart	International	2	2	3
Il Bordello	Italian	3	4	4
Brawn	Mediterranean	4	3	3
Boisdale of Canary Wharf	Scottish	2	2	3
Buen Ayre	Argentinian	4	3	2

£50+

Name	Cuisine			
The Culpeper	British, Modern	3	3	4
Eat 17	"	3	4	3
The Empress	"	3	3	4
Galvin HOP	"	2	2	3
The Narrow	"	2	2	4
Sapling	"	–	–	–
The Straight & Narrow	"	2	3	3
Treves & Hyde	"	3	4	3
Bumpkin	British, Traditional	2	2	3
Formans	Fish & seafood	4	3	2
Blanchette East	French	2	2	3
Chez Elles	"	4	4	5
Eat 17	International	3	4	3
Lardo	Italian	2	2	2
Super	Tuscan	3	4	3
Tuyo	Mediterranean	3	3	3
Bravas	Spanish	3	4	4
Ibérica	"	2	2	3
Hill & Szrok	Steaks & grills	3	3	3
Burger & Lobster	Burgers, etc	3	3	3
Pizza East	Pizza	4	3	4
Andina	Peruvian	3	3	3
Ottolenghi	Israeli	3	2	2
Haz	Turkish	2	2	2
Lahpet	Burmese	3	3	3
Royal China	Chinese	3	1	2
Yi-Ban	"	2	2	3
Café Spice Namaste	Indian	4	4	3
Grand Trunk Road	"	4	4	3
Sticks'n'Sushi	Japanese	3	2	2
Som Saa	Thai	5	4	4

£40+

Name	Cuisine			
Breakfast Club	American	3	3	3
Duke of Richmond	British, Modern	–	–	–
Fayre Share	"	–	–	–
P Franco	"	4	2	4
L'Ami Malo	French	5	4	4
Provender	"	3	4	4
Blixen	International	3	3	3
Dokke	"	3	4	3
Emilias Crafted Pasta	Italian	4	4	3
Rotorino	"	2	4	3
Verdi's	"	3	4	3
Morito	Spanish	4	3	4
Mildreds	Vegetarian	3	2	2
Poppies	Fish & chips	3	2	3
Pizza Pilgrims	Pizza	3	3	3

Name	Cuisine			
Chick 'n' Sours	Chicken	4	3	3
Smokestak	BBQ	4	3	3
Lupita	Mexican/TexMex	3	3	2
Berber & Q	Middle Eastern	5	3	5
Delamina East	"	4	4	2
Sichuan Folk	Chinese	4	3	2
Dishoom	Indian	3	4	5
Ippudo London	Japanese	3	2	3
Tonkotsu	"	4	3	3
Smoking Goat	Thai	4	3	4
Viet Grill	Vietnamese	3	2	2

£35+

Name	Cuisine			
Sutton and Sons	Vegetarian	4	3	2
Ark Fish	Fish & chips	3	4	2
Yard Sale Pizza	Pizza	5	3	3
Randy's Wing Bar	Chicken	3	3	3
Amber	Middle Eastern	–	–	–
Gunpowder	Indian	4	4	3
Mien Tay	Vietnamese	3	2	2
Sông Quê	"	3	3	2
Bao Bar	Taiwanese	4	3	3

£30+

Name	Cuisine			
The Spread Eagle	Vegetarian	3	3	3
Dirty Burger	Shoreditch Burgers, etc	2	2	2

£25+

Name	Cuisine			
Patty and Bun	Burgers, etc	4	3	3
Shake Shack	"	3	2	2
Mangal 1	Turkish	5	3	2
Lahore Kebab House	Pakistani	4	2	1
Needoo	"	4	2	2
Tayyabs	"	4	2	2

£20+

Name	Cuisine			
Forest Bar & Kitchen	Mediterranean	–	–	–
Bleecker Burger	Burgers, etc	5	2	2
Crate	Pizza	4	3	4
Jidori	Japanese	3	3	2
Singburi Royal Thai Café	Thai	4	3	3

£15+

Name	Cuisine			
Campania & Jones	Italian	4	3	4
E Pellicci	"	3	5	5

£10+

Name	Cuisine			
The Duck Truck	Burgers, etc	5	3	3
Pilpel	Middle Eastern	3	3	2

£5+

Name	Cuisine			
The Rib Man	Burgers, etc	5	3	–
Brick Lane Beigel Bake	Sandwiches, cakes, etc	3	1	1
Pavilion Cafe & Bakery	"	4	2	4

Jamavar, London

Texture, London

Bentley's, London

MAP 1 – LONDON OVERVIEW

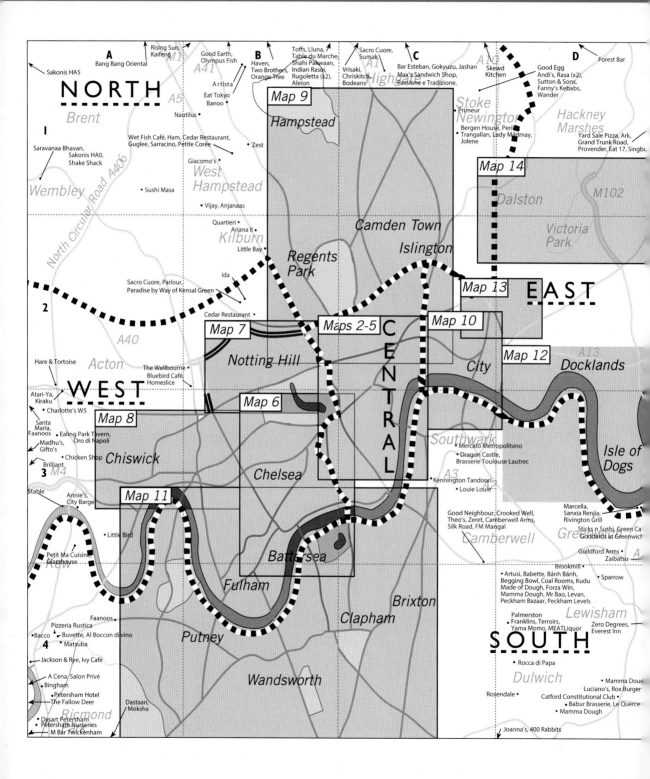

NORTH

A   Bang Bang Oriental

Sakonis HA5 •

Rising Sun, Kaifeng

Good Earth, Olympus Fish

B   Haven, Two Brothers, Orange Tree

Artista

Eat Tokyo
Banoo

Nautilus •

Brent

A41

A5

I   Saravanaa Bhavan, Sakonis HA0, Shake Shack

Wembley

North Circular Road A406

A40

Wet Fish Café, Ham, Cedar Restaurant, Guglee, Sarracino, Petite Corée

West Hampstead

• Zest

Giacomo's •

• Sushi Masa

• Vijay, Anjanaas

Kilburn

Quartieri •
• Ariana II
Little Bay •

Ida •

Sacro Cuore, Parlour, Paradise by Way of Kensal Green

Cedar Restaurant •

Toffs, Lluna, Table du Marche, Shahi Pakwaan, Indian Rasoi, Rugoletta (x2), Aleion

Sacro Cuore, Sumak

Vrisaki, Chriskitch, Bodeans

Map 9

Hampstead

Regents Park

Camden Town

Islington

Map 7

Notting Hill

Maps 2-5

CENTRAL

Bar Esteban, Gokyuzu, Jashan, Max's Sandwich Shop, Passione e Tradizione,

C

Skewd Kitchen

• Primeur

Bergen House, Perilla •
• Trangallan, Lady Mildmay, Jolene

A10

Good Egg
Andi's, Rasa (x2), Sutton & Sons, Fanny's Kebabs, Wander

D   Forest Bar

Stoke Newington

Hackney Marshes

Yard Sale Pizza, Ark, Grand Trunk Road, Provender, Eat 17, Singbu

Map 14

Dalston

M102

Victoria Park

Map 13

EAST

Map 10

Map 12

A13

Docklands

City

Isle of Dogs

Acton

Hare & Tortoise •

The Wellbourne •
Bluebird Café, Homeslice

WEST

Atari-Ya, Kiraku •

• Charlotte's W5

Santa Maria, Faanoos •

Map 8

• Ealing Park Tavern, Oro di Napoli

Madhu's, Gifto's •

• Chicken Shop

Chiswick

Brilliant •

3 M4

Stable •

Annie's, City Barge •

• Little Bird

Map 6

Chelsea

Map 11

Battersea

Fulham

Petit Ma Cuisine, Glasshouse •

Kew

Richmond

Faanoos •

Pizzeria Rustica

• Bacco • Buvette, Al Boccon divino

4 • Matsuba

Jackson & Rye, Ivy Café •

A Cena / Salon Privé •
• Bingham
• Petersham Hotel
The Fallow Deer •

• Dysart Petersham
• Petersham Nurseries
• M Bar Twickenham

Dastaan, Moksha

Putney

Wandsworth

Clapham

Brixton

Southwark

• Mercato Metropolitano

• Dragon Castle,
Brasserie Toulouse Lautrec

A3

• Kennington Tandoori

• Louie Louie

Good Neighbour, Crooked Well, Theo's, Zeret, Camberwell Arms, Silk Road, FM Mangal

Camberwell

Marcella, Sanxia Renjia, Rivington Grill

Sticks n Sushi, Green Ca
Goddards at Greenwich

Gree

Guildford Arms •
• Zaibatsu

A

Brookhill

• Artusi, Babette, Bánh Bánh, Begging Bowl, Coal Rooms, Kudu Made of Dough, Forza Win, Mamma Dough, Mr Bao, Levan, Peckham Bazaar, Peckham Levels

• Sparrow

Lewisham

Palmerston
• Franklins, Terroirs,
Yama Momo, MEATLiquor

Zero Degrees,
Everest Inn

SOUTH

• Rocca di Papa

Dulwich

Rosendale •

• Mamma Dou
Luciano's, Rox Burger
Catford Constitutional Club •
• Babur Brasserie, Le Querce
• Mamma Dough

Joanna's, 400 Rabbits

MAP 2 – WEST END OVERVIEW

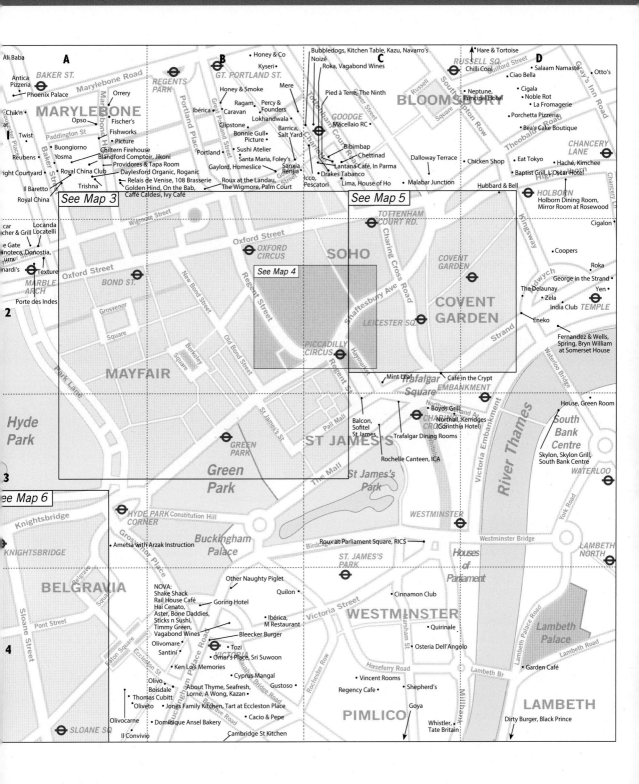

MAP 3 - MAYFAIR, ST. JAMES'S & WEST SOHO

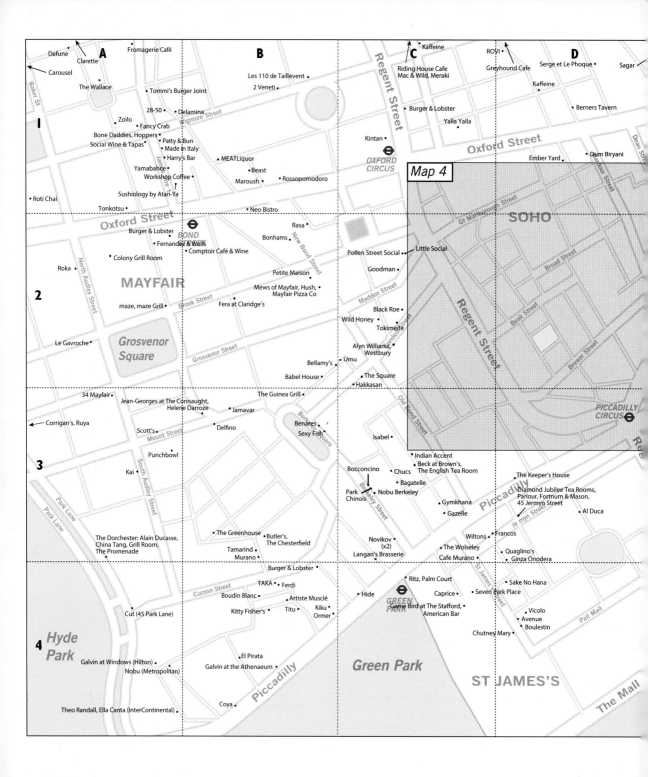

A

B

C

D

Defune
Clarette
Carousel
The Wallace

Fromagerie Café

Les 110 de Taillevent
2 Veneti

Tommi's Burger Joint

28-50 • Delamina
Zoilo
Fancy Crab
Bone Daddies, Hoppers
Social Wine & Tapas • Patty & Bun
• Made in Italy
Harry's Bar • MEATliquor
Yamabahce • Beast
Workshop Coffee
Maroush • Rossopomodoro
Sushiology by Atari-Ya
• Roti Chai
Tonkotsu • Neo Bistro

Kaffeine
Riding House Cafe
Mac & Wild, Meraki
ROVI
Greyhound Cafe
Serge et Le Phoque
Sagar
Kaffeine
Burger & Lobster
Yalla Yalla
Berners Tavern
Kintan
OXFORD
CIRCUS
Ember Yard • Dum Biryani

Map 4

SOHO

I

2

Oxford Street
BOND
Burger & Lobster
Fernandez & Wells
Colony Grill Room • Comptoir Café & Wine
Roka
MAYFAIR
maze, maze Grill
Le Gavroche
Grosvenor
Square

Rasa
Bonhams
Petite Maison
Mews of Mayfair, Hush,
Mayfair Pizza Co
Fera at Claridge's
Grosvenor Street
Bellamy's
Babel House

Pollen Street Social • Little Social
Goodman
Black Roe
Wild Honey
Tokimeite
Alyn Williams,
Westbury
Umu
• The Square
• Hakkasan

Regent Street
Beak Street
Brewer Street
Broad Street
PICCADILLY
CIRCUS

3

34 Mayfair
Jean-Georges at The Connaught,
Helene Darroze
Corrigan's, Ruya
Scott's • Jamavar
Delfino
Punchbowl
Kai

The Guinea Grill
Benares
Sexy Fish
Isabel

Indian Accent
Beck at Brown's,
The English Tea Room
Bocconcino • Chucs
Bagatelle
Park • Nobu Berkeley
Chinois
• Gymkhana
• Gazelle

The Keeper's House
Diamond Jubilee Tea Rooms,
Parlour, Fortnum & Mason,
45 Jermyn Street
• Al Duca

The Dorchester: Alain Ducasse,
China Tang, Grill Room,
The Promenade
• The Greenhouse
Butler's,
The Chesterfield
Tamarind
Murano
Burger & Lobster
TAKA • Ferdi
Boudin Blanc
• Artiste Musclé
Kitty Fisher's • Titu
Kiku
Ormer

Novikov
(x2)
Langan's Brasserie

Wiltons • Francos
• The Wolseley
Cafe Murano
Ritz, Palm Court
Hide • Caprice
Game Bird at The Stafford,
American Bar
Chutney Mary
GREEN
PARK
Quaglino's
Ginza Onodera
Sake No Hana
Seven Park Place
Vicolo
Avenue
Boulestin

4

Hyde
Park
Cut (45 Park Lane)
Galvin at Windows (Hilton)
Nobu (Metropolitan)
El Pirata
Galvin at the Athenaeum
Curzon Street
Theo Randall, Ella Canta (InterContinental)
Coya
Piccadilly

Green Park

ST JAMES'S

The Mall

Baker St
Wigmore Street
Regent Street
Oxford Street
North Audley Street
James Street
New Bond Street
Brook Street
South Audley Street
Mount Street
Park Lane
Berkeley Street
Old Bond Street
Maddox Street
Gt Marlborough Street
Piccadilly
St James Street
Pall Mall
Dean St
Harbour Street

MAP 4 — WEST SOHO & PICCADILLY

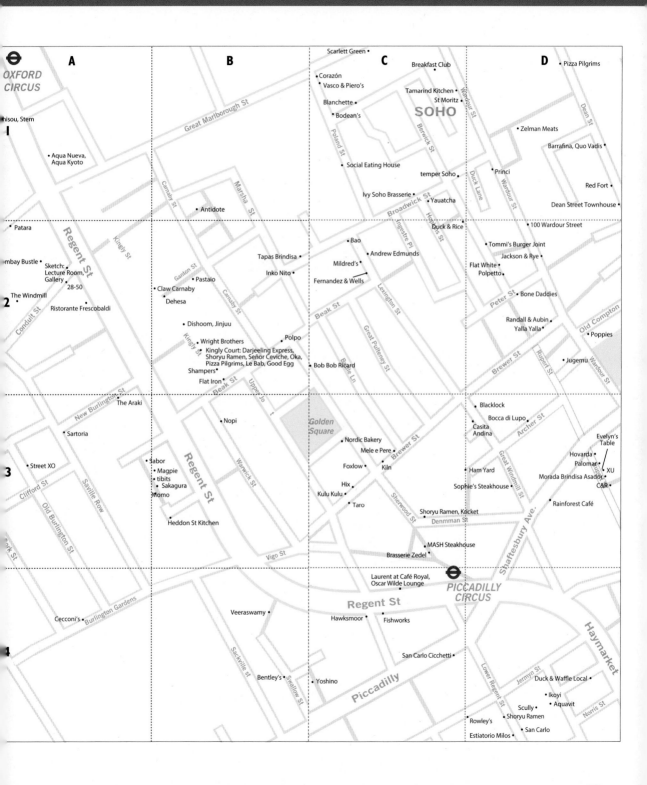

OXFORD CIRCUS

A **B** **C** **D**

Scarlett Green •

Breakfast Club • • Pizza Pilgrims

Corazón • Vasco & Piero's • Tamarind Kitchen • St Moritz •

Blanchette • • Bodean's

SOHO

Chisou, Stem •

• Zelman Meats

Barrafina, Quo Vadis •

1

Aqua Nueva, Aqua Kyoto •

• Social Eating House

temper Soho • Princi •

Ivy Soho Brasserie • • Yauatcha

Red Fort •

Dean Street Townhouse •

• Antidote

Duck & Rice • • 100 Wardour Street

• Patara

• Bao • Tommi's Burger Joint

Bombay Bustle • Tapas Brindisa • Andrew Edmunds • Jackson & Rye •

Sketch: Lecture Room, Gallery, 28-50 • Inko Nito • Mildred's • Flat White •

The Windmill • • Claw Carnaby Fernandez & Wells • Polpetto •

2 Dehesa • • Bone Daddies

Ristorante Frescobaldi •

• Dishoom, Jinjuu Randall & Aubin •
Yalla Yalla •

• Wright Brothers • Polpo • Poppies

Kingly Court: Darjeeling Express, Shoryu Ramen, Señor Ceviche, Oka, Pizza Pilgrims, Le Bab, Good Egg Bob Bob Ricard • • Jugemu

Shampers •

• Flat Iron

The Araki • • Blacklock

• Nopi • Bocca di Lupo Evelyn's Table •

Sartoria • Nordic Bakery • Casita Andina • Hovarda • Palomar • • XU

3 Street XO • Sabor • Mele e Pere • Kiln • Morada Brindisa Asador • C&R •

Magpie • Foxlow • Ham Yard • Rainforest Café •

tibits • Hix • Sophie's Steakhouse •

Sakagura • Kulu Kulu •

Momo • • Taro Shoryu Ramen, Kricket •

Heddon St Kitchen • Denmman St

• MASH Steakhouse

Brasserie Zedel •

Vigo St

Laurent at Café Royal, Oscar Wilde Lounge •

PICCADILLY CIRCUS

Regent St

Cecconi's • Veeraswamy • Hawksmoor • • Fishworks

San Carlo Cicchetti •

4 Duck & Waffle Local •

Bentley's • • Yoshino • Ikoyi • Aquavit

Scully • Shoryu Ramen •

Piccadilly Rowley's • • San Carlo

Estiatorio Milos •

MAP 5 – EAST SOHO, CHINATOWN & COVENT GARDEN

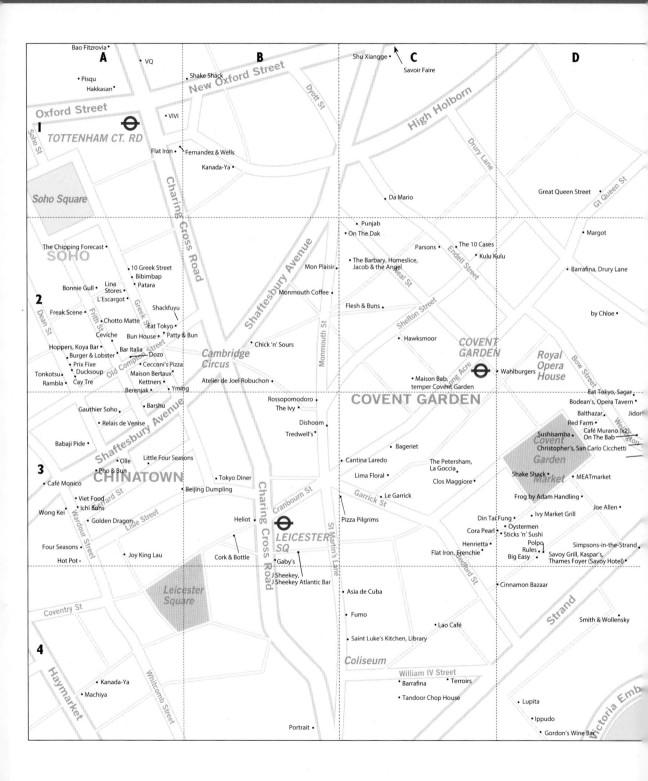

A

• Bao Fitzrovia
• VQ
• Pisqu
Hakkasan •

New Oxford Street

Dyott St

B

• Shake Shack

• VIVI

Oxford Street

I TOTTENHAM CT. RD

Soho Square

Charing Cross Road

Flat Iron • • Fernandez & Wells

Kanada-Ya •

• Da Mario

SOHO

The Chipping Forecast •

• 10 Greek Street
Bibimbap •
Lina • Patara
Stores •
L'Escargot •

Bonnie Gull •

2

Freak Scene •

Dean St

Shackfuyu •

• Chotto Matte
Ceviche • • Eat Tokyo
Bun House • • Patty & Bun

Frith Street

Hoppers, Koya Bar • • Bar Italia
• Burger & Lobster • Dozo
Prix Fixe • • Cecconi's Pizza

Greek Street

Old Compton Street

Tonkotsu • • Ducksoup
• Maison Bertaux
Rambla • • Cay Tre • Kettners
Berenjak • • Yming

Shaftesbury Avenue

Cambridge
Circus

Mon Plaisir •

Monmouth Coffee •

Chick 'n' Sours •

Atelier de Joel Robuchon •

• Shu Xiangge

C

Savoir Faire •

High Holborn

Drury Lane

• Punjab
• On The Dak
Parsons • • The 10 Cases
• Kulu Kulu
• The Barbary, Homeslice,
Jacob & the Angel

Endell Street

Flesh & Buns •

Shelton Street

• Hawksmoor

**COVENT
GARDEN**

Neal St

Long Acre

• Maison Bab, • Wahlburgers
temper Covent Garden

COVENT GARDEN

Rossopomodoro •
The Ivy •

Dishoom •

Tredwell's •

Bageriet •

Cantina Laredo •

Lima Floral •

Garrick St

• Le Garrick

Pizza Pilgrims •

Bedford St

D

• Great Queen Street

Gt. Queen St

• Margot

• Barrafina, Drury Lane

Endell Street

• by Chloe

**Royal
Opera
House**

Bow Street

Eat Tokyo, Sagar •
Bodean's, Opera Tavern •
Balthazar • Jidor
Red Farm •
Café Murano (x2)
Sushisamba • On The Bab
Christopher's, San Carlo Cicchetti

Wellington

**Covent
Garden
Market**

Shake Shack • • MEATmarket

Frog by Adam Handling •
Joe Allen •
Din Tai Fung • • Ivy Market Grill
Cora Pearl • • Oystermen
• Sticks 'n' Sushi
Henrietta • Polpo
Rules • Simpsons-in-the-Strand
Flat Iron, Frenchie • Savoy Grill, Kaspar's,
Big Easy • Thames Foyer (Savoy Hotel)

CHINATOWN

• Café Monico

Wardour Street

• Viet Food
• Ichi Buns
Wong Kei •
• Golden Dragon

Four Seasons •
Hot Pot • • Joy King Lau

Little Four Seasons •

• Pho & Bun

Newport Street

• Tokyo Diner

• Beijing Dumpling

Lisle Street

Heliot •

Cork & Bottle •

**LEICESTER
SQ**

Charing Cross Road

Cranbourn St

St Martin's Lane

Gaby's •
Sheekey, •
Sheekey Atlantic Bar •

Leicester
Square

Coventry St

The Petersham,
La Goccia •
Clos Maggiore •

Cinnamon Bazaar •

Whitcomb Street

4

Haymarket

• Kanada-Ya
• Machiya

William IV Street

• Asia de Cuba

• Fumo

• Lao Café

Saint Luke's Kitchen, Library •

Coliseum

• Barrafina
• Terroirs

• Tandoor Chop House

Portrait •

Strand

Smith & Wollensky •

• Lupita

• Ippudo

• Gordon's Wine Bar

Victoria Emb

MAP 6 – KNIGHTSBRIDGE, CHELSEA & SOUTH KENSINGTON

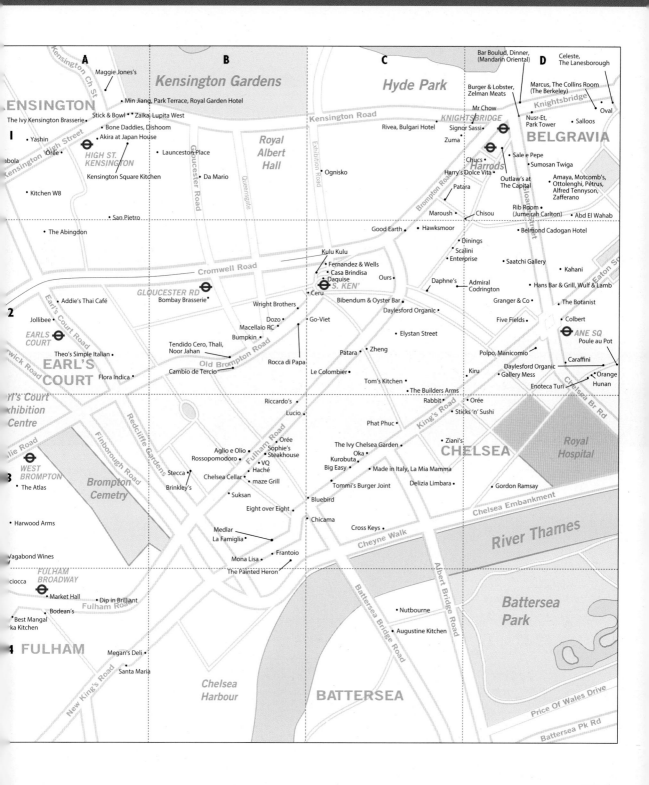

A

Maggie Jones's

Kensington Gardens

B

C

Hyde Park

Bar Boulud, Dinner, (Mandarin Oriental)

Celeste, The Lanesborough

D

Burger & Lobster, Zelman Meats

Marcus, The Collins Room (The Berkeley)

Knightsbridge

Oval

• Min Jiang, Park Terrace, Royal Garden Hotel

KENSINGTON

Mr Chow

Salloos

The Ivy Kensington Brasserie

Stick & Bowl • Zaika, Lupita West

Kensington Road

KNIGHTSBRIDGE

Nusr-Et, Park Tower

• Yashin

• Bone Daddies, Dishoom

Rivea, Bulgari Hotel

Signor Sassi

BELGRAVIA

Orée •

• Akira at Japan House

Zuma

Royal Albert Hall

• Sale e Pepe

Harrods

Chucs •

Sumosan Twiga

HIGH ST. KENSINGTON

• Launceston Place

Harry's Dolce Vita

Amaya, Motcomb's, Ottolenghi, Pétrus, Alfred Tennyson, Zafferano

Kensington Square Kitchen

• Da Mario

Ognisko •

Outlaw's at The Capital

Patara •

• Kitchen W8

Maroush •

• Chisou

Rib Room (Jumeirah Carlton)

• Abd El Wahab

• San Pietro

Good Earth •

• Hawksmoor

Belmond Cadogan Hotel •

• The Abingdon

• Dinings

Scalini •

Kulu Kulu •

• Enterprise

Saatchi Gallery •

Cromwell Road

• Fernandez & Wells

Kahani •

• Casa Brindisa

GLOUCESTER RD

Daquise •

Ours •

Daphne's •

Admiral Codrington

• Hans Bar & Grill, Wulf & Lamb

• Ceru

S. KEN'

Bombay Brasserie •

Wright Brothers •

Bibendum & Oyster Bar •

Granger & Co •

• The Botanist

• Addie's Thai Café

Daylesford Organic •

Five Fields •

• Colbert

2

Jollibee •

Dozo •

Go-Viet •

EARLS COURT

Macellaio RC •

• Elystan Street

ANE SQ

Poule au Pot •

Theo's Simple Italian •

Bumpkin •

Tendido Cero, Thali, Noor Jahan

Patara •

• Zheng

Polpo, Manicomio •

• Caraffini

Flora Indica •

Cambio de Tercio •

Rocca di Papa •

Le Colombier •

Kiru •

Daylesford Organic • Gallery Mess

• Orange Hunan

EARL'S COURT

Tom's Kitchen •

Enoteca Turi •

rl's Court xhibition Centre

• The Builders Arms

Riccardo's •

Rabbit •

• Orée

Lucio •

• Sticks 'n' Sushi

WEST BROMPTON

Phat Phuc •

Orée •

The Ivy Chelsea Garden •

• Ziani's

CHELSEA

Royal Hospital

Aglio e Olio • Sophie's

Oka •

Steakhouse

Kurobuta •

Rossopomodoro •

VQ •

Big Easy •

• Made in Italy, La Mia Mamma

• The Atlas

Stecca •

Haché •

Chelsea Cellar •

• maze Grill

Tommi's Burger Joint •

Delizia Limbara •

• Gordon Ramsay

Brinkley's •

• Harwood Arms

• Suksan

• Bluebird

Chelsea Embankment

Eight over Eight •

• Chicama

Medlar •

Cross Keys •

Vagabond Wines

La Famiglia •

River Thames

Cheyne Walk

FULHAM BROADWAY

Mona Lisa •

• Frantoio

The Painted Heron •

• Market Hall

Dip in Brilliant •

Fulham Road

Best Mangal

a Kitchen

• Bodean's

Nutbourne •

Battersea Park

FULHAM

• Megan's Deli

Augustine Kitchen •

Santa Maria •

Chelsea Harbour

BATTERSEA

Price Of Wales Drive

Battersea Pk Rd

1

Brompton Cemetery

Redcliffe Gardens

Finborough Road

Earl's Court Road

Warwick Road

Kensington High Street

Kensington Ch St

Gloucester Road

Queensgate

Exhibition Road

Brompton Road

Sloane Street

Eaton Sq

Chelsea Br Rd

King's Road

Old Brompton Road

Fulham Road

New King's Road

Battersea Bridge Road

Albert Bridge Road

MAP 7 – NOTTING HILL & BAYSWATER

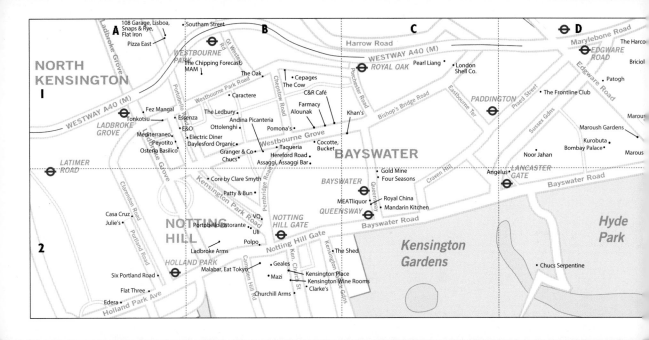

MAP 8 – HAMMERSMITH & CHISWICK

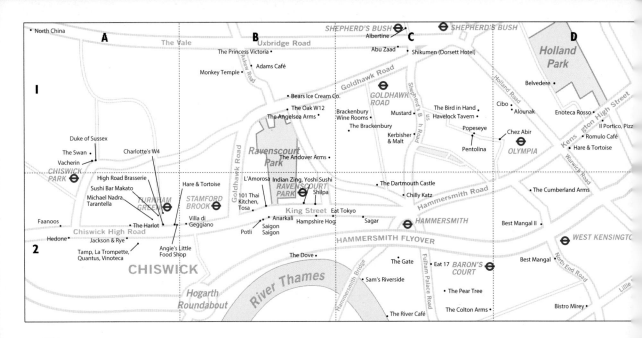

MAP 9 – HAMPSTEAD, CAMDEN TOWN & ISLINGTON

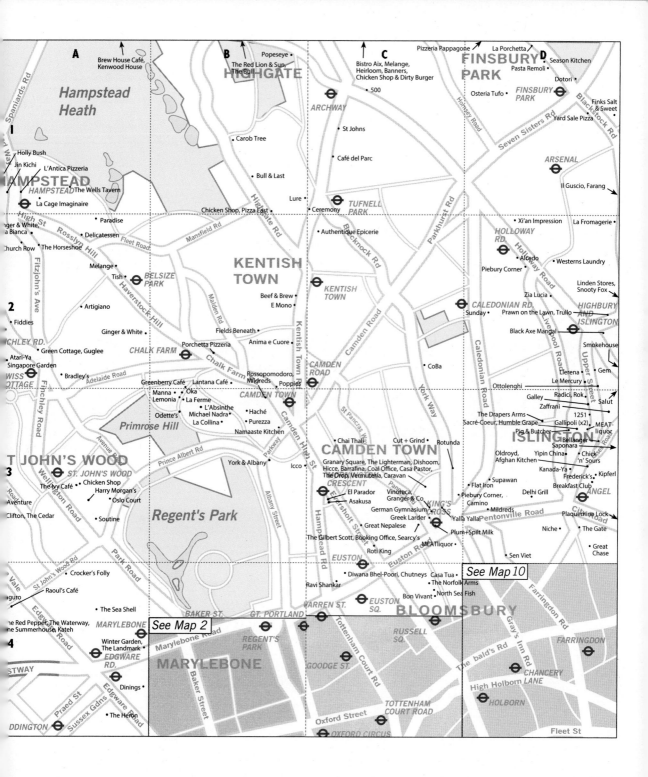

A

Brew House Café, Kenwood House

Hampstead Heath

Holly Bush
Jin Kichi
L'Antica Pizzeria
HAMPSTEAD The Wells Tavern
La Cage Imaginaire

Paradise
ger & White,
a Bianca
Delicatessen
Church Row The Horseshoe
ITCHLEY RD.
Melange
Tish BELSIZE
PARK
Artigiano
Fiddies
Ginger & White
Green Cottage, Guglee
Atari-Ya
Singapore Garden
WISS Bradley's
OTTAGE

B

Popeseye
The Red Lion & Sun,
The Bull
HIGHGATE

Carob Tree

Bull & Last

Lure

Chicken Shop, Pizza East Ceremony

KENTISH
TOWN

Beef & Brew
E Mono

Fields Beneath

Porchetta Pizzeria
CHALK FARM

Greenberry Café Lantana Café
Manna Oka
Lemonia La Ferme
Odette's
Michael Nadra
La Collina
Namaaste Kitchen

Primrose Hill

ST JOHN'S WOOD
ST. JOHN'S WOOD
The Ivy Café Chicken Shop
Harry Morgan's
Oslo Court
Soutine
Clifton, The Cedar

Regent's Park

Crocker's Folly
Raoul's Café
guro
The Sea Shell
e Red Pepper, The Waterway, MARYLEBONE
he Summerhouse, Kateh
Winter Garden, See Map 2
The Landmark
EDGWARE
RD.
MARYLEBONE
STWAY
Dinings
DDINGTON The Heron

Rossopomodoro,
Mildreds
Poppies
CAMDEN TOWN
Haché
Purezza

York & Albany
Icco

Mansfield Rd

Fleet Road

Haverstock Hill

Adelaide Road

Prince Albert Rd

Park Road

BAKER ST. GT. PORTLAND
See Map 2
Marylebone Road
REGENT'S
PARK
BAKER
Street

C

Bistro Aix, Melange,
Heirloom, Banners,
Chicken Shop & Dirty Burger

500

ARCHWAY

St Johns

Café del Parc

TUFNELL
PARK

Authentique Epicerie

KENTISH
TOWN

CAMDEN
ROAD

CoBa

Chai Thali Cut + Grind
Rotunda
Granary Square, The Lighterman, Dishoom,
Hicce, Barrafina, Coal Office, Casa Pastor,
The Drop, Vermuteria, Caravan
CRESCENT
El Parador Vinoteca,
Granger & Co
Asakusa
German Gymnasium
Greek Larder
Great Nepalese
The Gilbert Scott, Booking Office, Searcy's
Roti King
EUSTON
Diwana Bhel-Poori, Chutneys Casa Tua
Ravi Shankar
Bon Vivant
WARREN ST. EUSTON
SQ.
BLOOMSBURY

RUSSELL
SQ.

GOODGE ST.

TOTTENHAM
COURT ROAD

Oxford Street
OXFORD CIRCUS

D

Pizzeria Pappagone La Porchetta
FINSBURY Season Kitchen
PARK Pasta Remoli
Dotori
FINSBURY
PARK
Osteria Tufo
Finks Salt
& Sweet
Yard Sale Pizza

ARSENAL

Il Guscio, Farang

Xi'an Impression La Fromagerie
HOLLOWAY
RD.
Alcedo
Piebury Corner Westerns Laundry

Zia Lucia Linden Stores,
Snooty Fox
CALEDONIAN RD. HIGHBURY
Sunday Prawn on the Lawn, Trullo AND
ISLINGTON

Black Axe Mangal

Smokehouse

Ottolenghi Elerena Gem
Le Mercury
Galley Radici, Rok,
Zaffrani Salut
The Drapers Arms 1251
Sacré-Coeur, Humble Grape Gallipoli (x2)
Pig & Butcher MEAT-
Bellanger liquor
Saponara
Oldroyd, Yipin China Chick
Afghan Kitchen 'n' Sours
Kanada-Ya Frederick's,
Supawan Kipferl
Flat Iron Breakfast Club
Piebury Corner, ANGEL
Camino
Delhi Grill
Mildreds
Yalla Yalla Plaquemine Lock
Plum+Spilt Milk
Niche The Gate
MEATliquor
Great
Chase
Sen Viet

The Norfolk Arms
North Sea Fish

Farringdon Rd

Gray's Inn Rd

FARRINGDON

The. bald's Rd
High Holborn LANE
CHANCERY
LANE
HOLBORN
Fleet St

Hornsey Road
Parkhurst Rd
Blackstock Rd
Seven Sisters Rd
Holloway Road
Caledonian Road
Upper Street
Wool Road

York Way
St Pancras Way
Pancras Road
Caledonian Road
King's Cross
Pentonville Road
Euston Road
Euston Rd

Camden High St
Camden Rd
Camden Town Rd
Kentish Town Rd

Highgate Rd
Blackknock Rd

See Map 10

ISLINGTON

1

2

3

4

MAP 10 – THE CITY

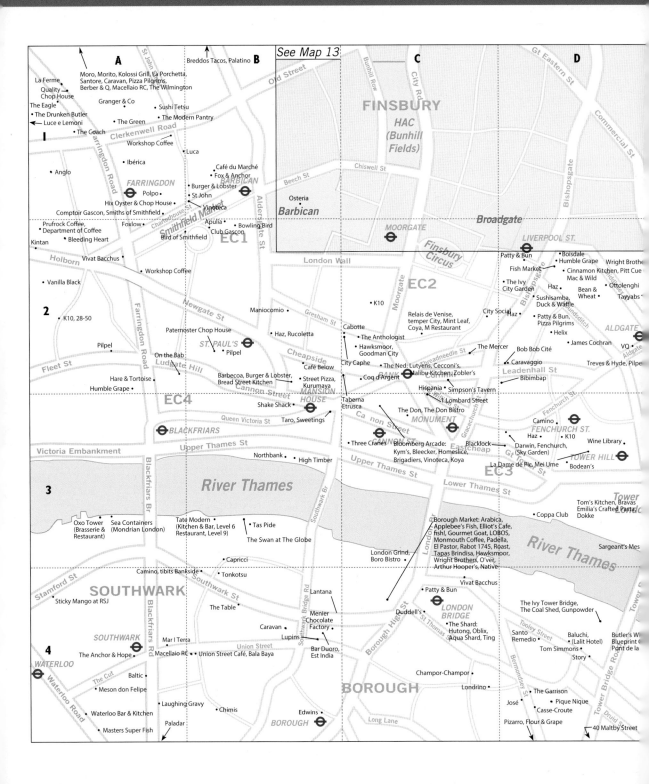

A

Breddos Tacos, Palatino **B**

See Map 13

C

D

La Ferme

Moro, Morito, Kolossi Grill, La Porchetta,
Santore, Caravan, Pizza Pilgrims,
Berber & Q, Macellaio RC, The Wilmington

Quality
Chop House

The Eagle

• The Drunken Butler

• Luce e Lemoni

Granger & Co

• Sushi Tetsu

• The Green

• The Modern Pantry

• The Coach

1

Clerkenwell Road

Workshop Coffee

• Luca

• Ibérica

FINSBURY

HAC
(Bunhill
Fields)

• Anglo

• Café du Marché

• Fox & Anchor

FARRINGDON

Polpo

• Burger & Lobster

Hix Oyster & Chop House

• St John

Comptoir Gascon, Smiths of Smithfield

• Vinoteca

BARBICAN

Osteria

Barbican

Apulia

Foxlow

• Bowling Bird

Prufrock Coffee,

Club Gascon

• Department of Coffee

• Bleeding Heart

Bird of Smithfield

Kintan

EC1

Broadgate

London Wall

MOORGATE

Vivat Bacchus

• Vanilla Black

• Workshop Coffee

LIVERPOOL ST.

Patty & Bun

• Boisdale

• Humble Grape

Wright Brothers

Fish Market

• Cinnamon Kitchen, Pitt Cue

Mac & Wild

• The Ivy
City Garden

Haz

Bean &
Wheat

• Ottolenghi

2

K10, 28-50

Newgate St

Manicomio

Gresham St

EC2

Sushisamba,
Duck & Waffle

Tayyabs

Relais de Venise,
temper City, Mint Leaf,
Coya, M Restaurant

Haz

City Social

• K10

• Patty & Bun,
Pizza Pilgrims

Pilpel

Paternoster Chop House

Haz, Rucoletta

Cabotte

ALDGATE

ST. PAUL'S

• Pilpel

• The Anthologist

Helix

• James Cochran

VQ

On the Bab

• Hawksmoor,
Goodman City

• The Mercer

Bob Bob Cité

ALDGATE

Ludgate Hill

Cheapside

Café Below

City Caphe

The Ned: Lutyens, Cecconi's,
Maliby Kitchen, Zobler's

• Caravaggio

Treves & Hyde, Pilpe

Hare & Tortoise

Barbecoa, Burger & Lobster,

• Street Pizza,

Coq d'Argent

Bibimbap

Leadenhall St

Humble Grape

Bread Street Kitchen

Kurumaya

Hispania

• Simpson's Tavern

Cannon Street

EC4

MANSION
HOUSE

Shake Shack

Taberna
Etrusca

1 Lombard Street

Camino

Taro, Sweetings

The Don, The Don Bistro

Haz

• K10

FENCHURCH ST.

Wine Library

BLACKFRIARS

Queen Victoria St

MONUMENT

• Three Cranes

Bloomberg Arcade:
Kym's, Bleecker, Homeslice,
Brigadiers, Vinoteca, Koya

Blacklock

Darwin, Fenchurch,
(Sky Garden)

TOWER HILL

Victoria Embankment

Upper Thames St

Eastcheap

EC3

La Dame de Pic, Mei Ume

Northbank

• High Timber

Upper Thames St

Lower Thames St

Bodean's

Tower

River Thames

Blackfriars Br

Tom's Kitchen, Bravas

Emilia's Crafted Pasta,
Dokke

3

Oxo Tower
(Brasserie &
Restaurant)

Sea Containers
(Mondrian London)

Tate Modern
(Kitchen & Bar, Level 6
Restaurant, Level 9)

• Tas Pide

The Swan at The Globe

Borough Market: Arabica,
Applebee's Fish, Elliot's Cafe,
fish!, Gourmet Goat, LOBOS,
Monmouth Coffee, Padella,
El Pastor, Rabot 1745, Roast,
Tapas Brindisa, Hawksmoor,
Wright Brothers, O'ver,
Arthur Hooper's, Native

• Coppa Club

River Thames

Sargeant's Mes

London Grind,
Boro Bistro

Stamford St

• Capricci

Camino, tibits Bankside

• Tonkotsu

Southwark St

SOUTHWARK

Sticky Mango at RSJ

The Table

Lantana

Vivat Bacchus

• Patty & Bun

The Ivy Tower Bridge,
The Coal Shed, Gunpowder

Menier
Chocolate
Factory

Duddell's

LONDON
BRIDGE

Santo
Remedio

Baluchi,
• (Lalit Hotel)

Butler's W
Blueprint (
Pont de la

4

SOUTHWARK

Mar I Terra

Caravan

Lupins

• The Shard:
Hutong, Oblix,
Aqua Shard, Ting

Tooley St

Tom Simmons

Story

WATERLOO

The Anchor & Hope

Macellaio RC

• Union Street Café, Bala Baya

Bar Duoro,
Est India

The Cut

Baltic

Champor-Champor

Londrino

• The Garrison

Waterloo Road

• Meson don Felipe

Union Street

José

• Pique Nique

• Casse-Croute

• Laughing Gravy

• Chimis

BOROUGH

Pizarro, Flour & Grape

Waterloo Bar & Kitchen

Edwins

Masters Super Fish

Paladar

BOROUGH

Long Lane

40 Maltby Street

MAP 11 – SOUTH LONDON (& FULHAM)

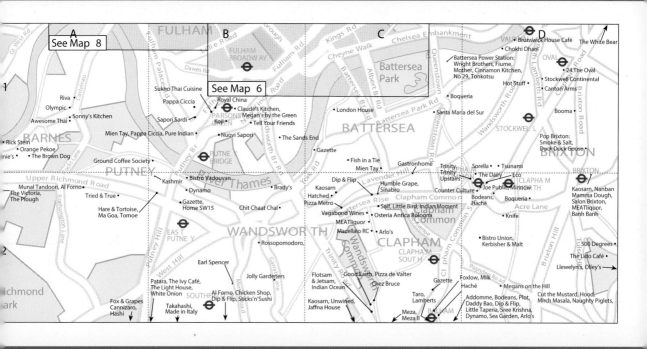

MAP 12 – EAST END & DOCKLANDS

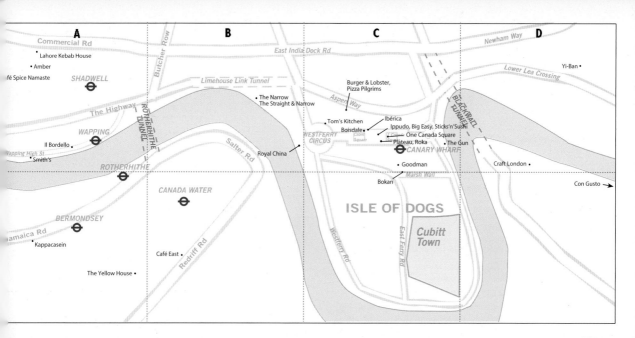

MAP 13 – SHOREDITCH & BETHNAL GREEN

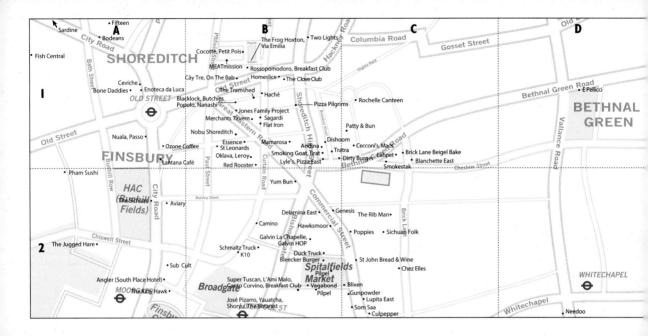

MAP 14 – EAST LONDON

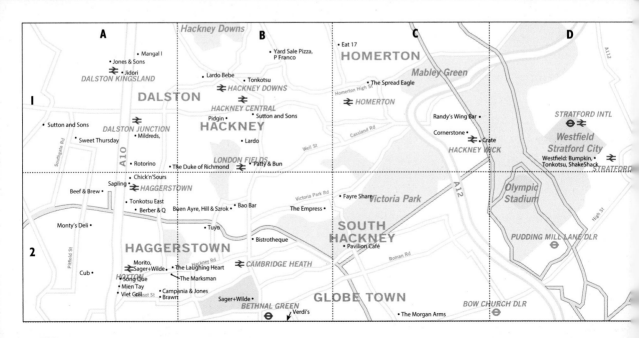

Aulis at L'Enclume, Cartmel

Belmond Le Manoir aux Quat' Saisons, Great Milton

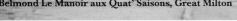

Gidleigh Park, Chagford

Northcote, Langho

Waterside Inn, Bray

TOP SCORERS

All restaurants whose food ratings is **5**; plus restaurants whose formula price is £60+ with a food rating of **4**.

£260	Aulis at L'Enclume *(Cartmel)*	5 4 4
£240	Belmond Le Manoir aux Quat' Saisons *(Great Milton)*	5 5 5
£190	L'Enclume *(Cartmel)*	5 5 4
£160	Casamia, The General *(Bristol)*	5 5 5
	Lympstone Manor *(Exmouth)*	5 5 4
	Restaurant Nathan Outlaw *(Port Isaac)*	5 5 4
	Gidleigh Park *(Chagford)*	4 4 3
£150	Waterside Inn *(Bray)*	5 5 5
	Raby Hunt *(Summerhouse)*	5 3 3
	Midsummer House *(Cambridge)*	4 4 4
	The Dining Room, Whatley Manor *(Easton Grey)*	4 3 4
£140	Andrew Fairlie, Gleneagles Hotel *(Auchterarder)*	4 4 3
£130	Black Swan *(Oldstead)*	5 5 4
	Gareth Ward at Ynyshir *(Eglwys Fach)*	5 4 4
	Restaurant Sat Bains *(Nottingham)*	5 4 3
	The Latymer, Pennyhill Park Hotel *(Bagshot)*	4 4 5
£120	The Three Chimneys *(Dunvegan)*	5 4 5
£110	Paris House *(Woburn)*	5 4 5
	Number One, Balmoral Hotel *(Edinburgh)*	5 4 4
	Restaurant Martin Wishart *(Edinburgh)*	5 4 4
	Winteringham Fields *(Winteringham)*	5 4 4
	Yorke Arms *(Ramsgill-in-Nidderdale)*	5 3 4
	Fraiche *(Oxton)*	5 4 3
	Sosban And The Old Butchers *(Menai Bridge)*	5 4 3
	The Whitebrook *(Whitebrook)*	5 4 3
	The Wilderness *(Birmingham)*	5 4 3
	Lucknam Park, Luckham Park Hotel *(Colerne)*	4 4 5
	Pale Hall Hotel Restaurant *(Bala)*	4 4 5
	The Samling *(Windermere)*	4 4 5
	The Bath Priory *(Bath)*	4 5 4
	Where The Light Gets In *(Stockport)*	4 5 4
	21212 *(Edinburgh)*	4 4 4
	The Orangery, Rockliffe Hall *(Darlington)*	4 3 3
£100	Morston Hall *(Morston)*	5 4 5
	Hambleton Hall *(Hambleton)*	5 5 4
	Moor Hall *(Aughton)*	5 5 4
	The Box Tree *(Ilkley)*	5 5 4
	Artichoke *(Amersham)*	5 4 4
	Bybrook Restaurant, Manor House *(Castle Combe)*	5 4 4
	The Moorcock Inn *(Sowerby Bridge)*	5 5 3

	Restaurant Coworth Park *(Ascot)*	4 4 5
	Sharrow Bay *(Ullswater)*	4 4 5
	Summer Lodge Country House *(Evershot)*	4 4 5
	The Castle Terrace *(Edinburgh)*	4 3 4
	Simpsons *(Birmingham)*	4 5 3
	Fischers at Baslow Hall *(Baslow)*	4 4 3
	Restaurant Tristan *(Horsham)*	4 4 3
£90	Buckland Manor *(Buckland)*	5 4 5
	Adam's *(Birmingham)*	5 5 4
	Northcote *(Langho)*	5 5 4
	The Harrow at Little Bedwyn *(Marlborough)*	5 5 4
	Driftwood Hotel *(Rosevine)*	5 4 4
	Monachyle Mhor *(Balquhidder)*	5 4 4
	Purnells *(Birmingham)*	5 4 4
	Roger Hickman's *(Norwich)*	5 4 4
	The Feathered Nest Inn *(Nether Westcote)*	5 3 4
	Bohemia, The Club Hotel & Spa *(Jersey)*	5 4 3
	Cotto *(Cambridge)*	5 4 3
	HRiSHi, Gilpin Lodge *(Windermere)*	5 4 3
	Le Champignon Sauvage *(Cheltenham)*	5 5 2
	The Forest Side *(Grasmere)*	4 5 5
	Home *(Leeds)*	4 4 5
	House of Tides *(Newcastle upon Tyne)*	4 3 5
	Hipping Hall *(Kirkby Lonsdale)*	4 4 4
	The Art School *(Liverpool)*	4 4 4
	The Barn at Moor Hall *(Aughton)*	4 4 4
	The Pompadour by Galvin, The Caledonian *(Edinburgh)*	4 4 4
	L'Ortolan *(Shinfield)*	4 3 4
	The Avenue, Lainston House Hotel *(Winchester)*	4 4 3
	The Burlington at The Devonshire Arms *(Bolton Abbey)*	4 4 3
	The Oxford Blue *(Old Windsor)*	4 4 3
	The Pass Restaurant, South Lodge Hotel *(Lower Beeding)*	4 4 3
	Restaurant James Sommerin *(Penarth)*	4 3 3
£80	Mash Inn *(Radnage)*	5 4 5
	Tyddyn Llan *(Llandrillo)*	5 4 5
	Sorrel *(Dorking)*	5 5 4
	The Clock House *(Ripley)*	5 5 4
	The Neptune *(Old Hunstanton)*	5 5 4
	Coombeshead Farm *(Lewannick)*	5 4 4
	Etch *(Brighton)*	5 4 4
	Longueville Manor *(Jersey)*	5 4 4
	The Cellar *(Anstruther)*	5 4 4
	The Peat Inn *(Cupar)*	5 4 4
	The Torridon Restaurant *(Annat)*	5 4 4
	Harry's Place *(Great Gonerby)*	5 5 3
	Lumière *(Cheltenham)*	5 5 3
	Carters of Moseley *(Birmingham)*	5 4 3
	John's House *(Mountsorrel)*	5 4 3

Restaurant		Scores
Le Cochon Aveugle (York)		5 4 3
Menu Gordon Jones (Bath)		5 4 3
Thomas Carr @ The Olive Room (Ilfracombe)		5 4 3
Samuel's, Swinton Park Hotel & Spa (Masham)		4 4 5
The Salutation Hotel & Restaurant (Sandwich)		4 4 5
Old Downton Lodge (Ludlow)		4 4 4
Paul Ainsworth at No. 6 (Padstow)		4 4 4
Read's (Faversham)		4 4 4
The Kitchen at Chewton Glen (New Milton)		4 4 4
Yorebridge House (Bainbridge)		4 4 4
Llangoed Hall (Llyswen)		4 3 4
Eat on the Green (Ellon)		4 4 3
Lake Road Kitchen (Ambleside)		4 4 3
The Nut Tree Inn (Murcott)		4 4 3
Hartnett Holder & Co (Lyndhurst)		4 3 3
Horto Restaurant at Rudding Park (Follifoot)		4 3 3

£70

Restaurant		Scores
Braidwoods (Dalry)		5 4 4
Ox (Belfast)		5 4 4
Stark (Broadstairs)		5 4 4
The Blackbird (Bagnor)		5 4 4
Thompson's (Newport)		5 4 4
Freemasons at Wiswell (Wiswell)		5 3 4
Little Fish Market (Brighton)		5 5 3
The Hare Inn Restaurant (Scawton)		5 5 3
Aizle (Edinburgh)		5 4 3
The Old Inn (Drewsteignton)		5 4 3
The Vanilla Pod (Marlow)		5 4 3
Whites (Beverley)		5 4 3
The Walnut Tree (Llandewi Skirrid)		5 3 3
Wilks (Bristol)		5 5 2
The Sir Charles Napier (Chinnor)		4 3 5
The Wild Rabbit (Kingham)		4 2 5
Little Barwick House (Barwick)		4 5 4
Mortimers (Ludlow)		4 5 4
Askham Hall (Penrith)		4 4 4
Kentisbury Grange Hotel (Kentisbury)		4 4 4
Peace & Loaf (Newcastle upon Tyne)		4 4 4
Restaurant 56 (Faringdon)		4 4 4
Stovell's (Chobham)		4 4 4
The Fordwich Arms (Fordwich)		4 4 4
The Hind's Head (Bray)		4 4 4
The Tudor Room, Great Fosters Hotel (Egham)		4 4 4
Coast (Saundersfoot)		4 3 4
The Curlew (Bodiam)		4 3 4
The Gallery Restaurant (Plympton)		4 3 4
The Star Inn (Harome)		4 3 4
63 Degrees (Manchester)		4 4 3
Isaac@ (Brighton)		4 4 3
La Rock (Sandiacre)		4 4 3
The Honours (Edinburgh)		4 4 3
Thompson (St Albans)		4 4 3
Vero Gusto (Sheffield)		4 4 3
Timberyard (Edinburgh)		4 3 3
Gamba (Glasgow)		4 4 2
Haywards Restaurant (Epping)		4 4 2
5 North Street (Winchcombe)		4 3 2
Hooked (Windermere)		4 3 2

Restaurant		Scores
The Mason's Arms (Knowstone)		4 3 2
The Olive Tree, Queensberry Hotel (Bath)		4 3 2

£60

Restaurant		Scores
Joro (Sheffield)		5 4 4
Maison Bleue (Bury St Edmunds)		5 4 4
Outlaw's Fish Kitchen (Port Isaac)		5 4 4
The Seahorse (Dartmouth)		5 4 4
The French Table (Surbiton)		5 5 3
Cail Bruich (Glasgow)		5 4 3
Le Roi Fou (Edinburgh)		5 4 3
Old Stamp House (Ambleside)		5 4 3
Orwells (Shiplake)		5 4 3
The Cross at Kenilworth (Kenilworth)		5 4 3
The Pony & Trap (Chew Magna)		5 4 3
The Royal Oak (Shipston-on-Stour)		5 4 3
The West House (Biddenden)		5 4 3
Verveine Fishmarket Restaurant (Milford-on-Sea)		5 4 3
The Old Passage Inn (Arlingham)		5 3 3
Apicius (Cranbrook)		5 4 2
Henry's Restaurant (Bath)		5 4 2
Pierhouse Hotel (Port Appin)		4 4 5
Rick Stein (Sandbanks)		4 4 5
The Pipe & Glass Inn (Beverley)		4 4 5
Ubiquitous Chip (Glasgow)		4 4 5
Pebble Beach (Barton-on-Sea)		4 3 5
Crown Inn (Bray)		4 4 4
Lickfold Inn (Lickfold)		4 4 4
Ondine (Edinburgh)		4 4 4
Rafters (Sheffield)		4 4 4
Sindhu (Marlow)		4 4 4
St Enodoc Restaurant (Rock)		4 4 4
The Butcher's Arms (Eldersfield)		4 4 4
The Dining Room (Edinburgh)		4 4 4
The Woodspeen (Newbury)		4 4 4
Beach House (Oxwich)		4 3 4
Ethicurean (Wrington)		4 3 4
Jew's House Restaurant (Lincoln)		4 3 4
The Bay Horse (Hurworth)		4 3 4
The Royal Oak (Littlefield Green)		4 3 4
The Salt Room (Brighton)		4 3 4
Darleys (Derby)		4 2 4
Arras (York)		4 4 3
Drakes of Brighton (Brighton)		4 4 3
Elderflower (Lymington)		4 4 3
Hawksmoor (Manchester)		4 4 3
Kota (Porthleven)		4 4 3
La Barbe (Reigate)		4 4 3
Lasan (Birmingham)		4 4 3
Melton's (York)		4 4 3
Rogan & Co (Cartmel)		4 4 3
Salt (Stratford upon Avon)		4 4 3
Swan (Long Melford)		4 4 3
The Beehive (White Waltham)		4 4 3
The Lighthouse Restaurant (Ashbourne)		4 4 3
The Park - by Adam Jackson (Clifton)		4 4 3
The Patricia (Newcastle upon Tyne)		4 4 3
Bronze Pig (Lincoln)		4 3 3
Eric's (Huddersfield)		4 3 3

Fish On The Green *(Bearsted)*		4 3 3
Purslane *(Cheltenham)*		4 3 3
Set *(Brighton)*		4 3 3
The Newport *(Newport On Tay)*		4 3 3
The Parsons Table *(Arundel)*		4 3 3
The Arundell Arms Hotel *(Lifton)*		4 2 3
The Cartford Inn *(Little Eccleston)*		4 2 3
The Flitch of Bacon *(Dunmow)*		4 2 3
Bottle and Glass Inn *(Binfield Heath)*		4 4 2
La Chouette *(Dinton)*		4 4 2
The Oxford Kitchen *(Oxford)*		4 3 2
Grafene Restaurant & Cocktail Bar *(Manchester)*		4 2 2

£50		
The Sportsman *(Seasalter)*		5 5 5
Benedicts *(Norwich)*		5 5 4
Pea Porridge *(Bury St Edmunds)*		5 5 4
Crab Shack *(Teignmouth)*		5 4 4
Loch Bay Restaurant *(Stein)*		5 4 4
Paco Tapas, The General *(Bristol)*		5 4 4
Prithvi *(Cheltenham)*		5 4 4
The Great House Hotel & Restaurant, Lavenham *(Lavenham)*		5 4 4
White Post *(Yeovil)*		5 4 4
Crab House Café *(Weymouth)*		5 3 4
Crabshakk *(Glasgow)*		5 3 4
Prawn on the Lawn *(Padstow)*		5 3 4
The Shore *(Penzance)*		5 3 4
Fat Olives *(Emsworth)*		5 5 3
1921 Angel Hill *(Bury St Edmunds)*		5 4 3
64 Degrees *(Brighton)*		5 4 3
Ben's Cornish Kitchen *(Marazion)*		5 4 3
Clavelshay Barn *(North Petherton)*		5 4 3
Ee-Usk (Seafood Restaurant) *(Oban)*		5 4 3
Gilpin Spice, Gilpin Lodge *(Windermere)*		5 4 3
Loch Leven Seafood Café *(Onich)*		5 4 3
No 7 Fish Bistro *(Torquay)*		5 4 3
Orchid *(Harrogate)*		5 4 3
Terre Ã Terre *(Brighton)*		5 4 3
Wilson's *(Bristol)*		5 4 3
Yu And You *(Copster Green)*		5 4 3
The Coach House Norbury *(Bishops Castle)*		5 3 3
Bosquet *(Kenilworth)*		5 4 2
Bulrush *(Bristol)*		5 4 2

£40		
Bia Bistrot *(Edinburgh)*		5 5 4
Cafe Fish Tobermory *(Tobermory)*		5 4 4
Harborne Kitchen *(Birmingham)*		5 4 4
The Parkers Arms *(Newton-in-Bowland)*		5 4 4
The Town House *(Arundel)*		5 4 4
Arbequina *(Oxford)*		5 4 3
Indian Zest *(Sunbury on Thames)*		5 4 3
Noble *(Holywood)*		5 4 3
Purslane *(Edinburgh)*		5 4 3
Pysgoty *(Aberystwyth)*		5 4 3
Skosh *(York)*		5 4 3
Trenchers *(Whitby)*		5 4 3
Wheelers Oyster Bar *(Whitstable)*		5 4 3

White Swan at Fence *(Fence)*		5 4 3
Xian *(Orpington)*		5 4 3
Butley Orford Oysterage *(Orford)*		5 3 3
Indian Essence *(Petts Wood)*		5 3 3
Sugo *(Altrincham)*		5 3 3
Umezushi *(Manchester)*		5 3 3
Yuzu *(Manchester)*		5 3 3
Seafood Shack *(Ullapool)*		5 4 2
Tharavadu *(Leeds)*		5 4 2
Ebi Sushi *(Derby)*		5 3 2

£30		
Levanter *(Ramsbottom)*		5 5 4
Applecross Inn *(Applecross)*		5 3 4
Trongs *(Ipswich)*		5 5 3
Baltzersens *(Harrogate)*		5 4 3
Colmans *(South Shields)*		5 4 3
Magpie Café *(Whitby)*		5 4 3
Oli's Thai *(Oxford)*		5 4 3
Paesano Pizza *(Glasgow)*		5 3 3
McDermotts Fish & Chips *(Croydon)*		5 4 2
Hansa's *(Leeds)*		5 3 2
Mumtaz *(Bradford)*		5 3 2
Shanghai Shanghai *(Nottingham)*		5 3 2
The Company Shed *(West Mersea)*		5 2 2

£25		
El Cartel *(Edinburgh)*		5 3 4
Rudys Pizza *(Manchester)*		5 3 3

£10		
Burger Brothers *(Brighton)*		5 4 2

The Forest Side, Grasmere

Dabbawal, Newcastle

Aizle, Edinburgh

Tattu, Leeds

ABERAERON, CEREDIGION   4–3C

HARBOURMASTER £53 3 3 4
2 QUAY PDE SA46 0BT 01545 570755

The "beautifully served (mostly sea) food in a very busy and atmospheric restaurant" justifies a trip to this modernised harbourside hotel with "stunning views towards New Quay and superb sunsets". "If you're anywhere near Ceredigion, this is the place to eat". / www.harbour-master.com; @hmaberaeron; 9 pm; no Amex. **Accommodation:** 13 rooms, from £110

ABERDEEN, ABERDEENSHIRE   9–2D

SILVER DARLING £63 3 4 3
NORTH PIER HOUSE, POCRA QUAY AB11 5DQ 01224 576229

"A change of ownership to the McGinty group has maybe slimmed down the menu" a fraction at this long-established, leading light of the Aberdeen eating scene: the conversion of a former harbour control building. It still wins consistent praise for its "lovely" fish and seafood however, and there's one definite constant – "what a view! Ships, dolphins, seals, force ten gales, and the swell of the North Sea!" / www.thesilverdarling.co.uk; Mon - Sat 9.30 pm; Sun closed; children: +16 after 8 pm.

ABERDOUR, FIFE   9–4C

ROOM WITH A VIEW £46 3 4 4
FORTH VIEW HOTEL, HAWKCRAIG POINT KY3 0TZ 01383 860 402

Albeit "located on the seashore, and only accessed by foot along the coast, or by vehicle down a very steep narrow road", the journey to this Forth estuary fish restaurant and seasonal hotel "is most certainly worth it, as you are well looked after by the husband and wife owners" and the "quality of the food is very good, with prices to match". / www.roomwithaviewrestaurant.co.uk/; Mon-Sat 5 pm, Sun 4.30 pm.

ABERGAVENNY, MONMOUTHSHIRE   2–1A

THE ANGEL HOTEL £54 3 3 3
15 CROSS ST NP7 5EN 01873 857121

This attractive and smartly refurbished town-centre hotel – sibling to the famous Walnut Tree – is "a lovely place to go either with family or on your own". The dining options – in the Oak Room or more casual Foxhunter bar – display "really good quality" from chef Wesley Hammond, while afternoon tea is popular too. / www.angelabergavenny.com/dining; @lovetheangel;

Mon-Thu 11 pm, Fri & Sat midnight, Sun 10.30 pm. **Accommodation:** 35 rooms, from £101

THE HARDWICK £54 3 2 2
OLD RAGLAN RD NP7 9AA 01873 854220

Stephen Terry's rural restaurant-with-rooms – nominally a country gastropub, but far more stylish than that implies – is one of the best-known dining destinations in Wales. Most reports applaud cuisine that "shows real finesse" ("fantastic food from local ingredients") but its ratings still suffer from one or two minority reports of a disappointing all-round experience. / www.thehardwick.co.uk; @The_Hardwick; Mon-Sat 11.30 pm, Sun 6 pm; no Amex. **Accommodation:** 8 rooms, from £150

ABERYSTWYTH, POWYS   4–3C

GWESTY CYMRU £48 2 2 4
19 MARINE TERRACE SY23 2AZ 01970 612252

"A good buzz and an excellent outdoor terrace" – "made more special when you're able to enjoy sunshine and drinks watching the movements along the promenade" – help win praise for the restaurant of this posh, contemporary hotel on the seafront. The cooking? "not bad…", "solidly reliably good, if a little unambitious". / www.gwestycymru.com; @gwestyc; Tue-Sat 10.30 pm, Sun 10 pm; no Amex; children: 5+. **Accommodation:** 8 rooms, from £85

PYSGOTY £46 5 4 3
THE HARBOUR, SOUTH PROMENADE SY23 1JY 01970 624611

"Right on the seashore, but raised above it", this "small, unique" converted Art Deco toilet has distinct California vibes; sit on the terrace eating "SUPER FRESH fish". / pysgoty.co.uk/home/; @Pysgoty; Tue-Thu 10 pm, Fri & Sat 11 pm, Sun 9 pm; no bookings.

ULTRACOMIDA £36 4 3 2
31 PIER ST SY23 2LN 01970 630686

This well-known tapas and Spanish wine merchant is a "real find", despite the "cramped" back-of-deli seating (on stools or at a shared table); the owners, who also run a Narberth sibling, launched tapas joint 'Curado Bar', in a former Burger King on Cardiff's Westgate, in 2016. / www.ultracomida.com; @ultracomida; Mon-Sat 5 pm, Sun 4 pm.

ALBOURNE, WEST SUSSEX   3–4B

THE GINGER FOX £53 3 3 3
MUDDLESWOOD ROAD BN6 9EA 01273 857 888

The country cousin in Brighton's Gingerman family is a whitewash-and-thatch gastroboozer on the edge of the South Downs which wins consistently good ratings for its well-presented menus of "delicious" dishes. / thegingerfox.com/; @GingerfoxDish; Tue-Sun .

ALDEBURGH, SUFFOLK   3–1D

ALDEBURGH FISH AND CHIPS £16 3 2 2
226 HIGH ST IP15 5DB 01728 454685

Run by the Cooney family since 1967, and with staff almost as long-serving, this is a "venerable institution and very popular"; expect to queue and "eat on the beach" amid ravenous gulls (their sibling restaurant, the Golden Galleon, has an upstairs dining room). / www.aldeburghfishandchips.co.uk; @aldefishnchips; Tue, Wed, Sun 2 pm, Thu-Sat 9 pm; cash only.

THE LIGHTHOUSE £47 3 4 5
77 HIGH STREET IP15 5AU 01728 453377

"An old favourite" (est 1995) for locals and a "place of pilgrimage" for visitors – this "really busy and buzzy" haunt "continues to deliver great food at very reasonable prices" – and "often hits the heights". "When it comes down to it, it's the service that makes the difference" under Sam Hayes, the long-time manager who bought the venue a few years ago. / www.lighthouserestaurant.co.uk; @AldeLighthouse; 10 pm.

REGATTA £43 3 3 2
171 HIGH STREET IP15 5AN 01728 452011

"Properly cooked fresh fish" – "high-quality, well presented, unpretentious and affordable" – means this popular stalwart comes "highly recommended". It's in a "lovely position with tables overlooking the sea", but it "can get noisy". / www.regattaaldeburgh.com; @AldeburghR; Sun-Fri & Sat 10 pm.

SEA SPICE, THE WHITE LION HOTEL £59 3 3 3
MARKET CROSS PLACE IP15 5BU 01728 451 800

This handsome colonial-style subcontinental in a contemporary hotel was the first ever Indian in this coastal town, and has been warmly welcomed since opening in 2016; the food is ably matched by a quaffable drinks list including craft brews by Adnams and co. / seaspice.co.uk; @SeaSpiceAlde; Mon closed; Tue - Sun 10 pm.

ALDERLEY EDGE, GREATER MANCHESTER 5–2B

YU ALDERLEY £59 3 3 4

LONDON ROAD SK9 7QD 01625 569922

Accused sometimes of "style over substance", or attracting "loud wannabes with more money than sense" – the Yu family's fashionable, pricey Asian in the heart of Cheshire's WAG-belt is something of a see-and-be-seen location, but most reports are of a "classy offering that's a cut-above". / yualderleyedge.com; @Yu_Alderleyedge; Tue-Sat 10 pm, Sun 10.30 pm; booking max 12 may apply.

ALDFORD, CHESHIRE 5–3A

THE GROSVENOR ARMS £43 3 4 4

CHESTER RD CH3 6HJ 01244 620228

"Always a real pleasure to visit", this "busy", rather fine ducal pub is on the edge of the Duke of Westminster's Cheshire estate has "lovely gardens" and serves "a decent menu, with something for everyone, and reliably good results". "It's easy to understand how the highly successful Brunning & Price chain developed from its beginnings here". / www.grosvenorarms-aldford.co.uk; @GrosArmsAldford; 6m S of Chester on B5130; Sun-Thu 9 pm, Fri & Sat 9.30 pm.

ALKHAM, KENT 3–3D

THE MARQUIS £53 3 2 3

ALKHAM VALLEY RD CT15 7DF 01304 873410

Converted into a luxe boutique hotel a decade ago, and taken over by Hythe Imperial owners the GSE Group in June 2018, this poshified village boozer "had some teething problems" – not least a divisive makeover – and is still sometimes accused of being "overpriced" or "lacking atmosphere". Most reports, though, suggest "happily it's on an even keel": go by day for the "superb" lunch deal, or by night for "the serious stuff" (with prices to match). / www.themarquisatalkham.co.uk; @marquisalkham; 9.30 pm, Sun 8.30 pm; children: 8+ at D. *Accommodation:* 10 rooms, from £95

ALRESFORD, HAMPSHIRE 2–3D

CARACOLI £21 3 3 3

15 BROAD ST SO24 9AR 01962 738730

From "cheese straws and Portuguese custard tarts to die for", to "excellent coffee" and light meals, the cookware chain's "upmarket" city-centre outpost is a hit all-round; extra marks for the "pretty prompt service". / www.caracoli.co.uk; @Caracolistore; Mon-Sun 5 pm; no Amex; no bookings.

PULPO NEGRO £40 3 3 4

28 BROAD STREET SO24 9AQ 01962 732262

For a "good weeknight buzz in rural Hants", the Alemany's "cheerful" follow-up to the Purefoy Arms is "worth a visit mos' def!"; it serves up "marvellous tapas and a good range of Lustau sherries" ("all we needed was a hot Spanish evening to complete the idyll"). / www.pulponegro.co.uk; @pulpo__negro; Mon-Sun 10.30 pm.

ALSTONEFIELD, DERBYSHIRE 5–3C

THE GEORGE £51 3 3 4

DE6 2FX 01335 310205

A new landlord at this Peak District pub "got all the locals worried but the good news so far is that nothing's changed for the worse – it's still a flower-filled elegant pub, just rooted enough that you could still come here for a pint, but with some seriously good cooking in the middle of a beautiful village…everything anyone could want!" / www.thegeorgeatalstonefield.com; Mon-Thu 9.30 pm, Fri-Sun 10 pm.

ALTRINCHAM, GREATER MANCHESTER 5–2B

THE CON CLUB £53 2 2 3

48 GREENWOOD ST WA14 1RZ 0161 696 6870

After the arrival of Salford Quays player David Vanderhook two years back, the former Altrincham Conservative Working Men's Club is now a brasserie/microbrewery, having had a "fantastic" industrial-chic makeover. The "eclectic" Japanese/grilled meat menu can seem a little "overrated", and even fans agree it's secondary to the "highly enjoyable", "loud and glamorous" atmosphere. / www.conclubuk.com; @ConClubAlty.

HONEST CRUST, MARKET HOUSE ALTRINCHAM £12 4 3 3

26 MARKET STREET WA14 1PF

"Still great" – this darling of Altrincham market hall, also lining up at the Alti crew's new Mackie Mayor market – remains the place for "really tasty sourdough pizzas with well thought-out toppings"; slight quibble: "did prices go up? Or did cheaper options come along?" / @Honest_Crust; Tue-Sat 11 pm, Sun 9 pm.

SUGO £48 5 3 3

22 SHAW'S RD, ALTRINCHAM WA14 1QU 0161 929 7706

"A superb, and authentic variety of perfectly cooked pasta dishes", using ingredients flown in weekly from Puglia, combined with the "passion" of brothers Michael and Alex Di Martiis have created a major buzz that surrounds this "basic and small" outfit near Altrincham market, which is so busy that you have to book a timed slot at a communal table. A bigger venue opened in Ancoats in summer

2018. / www.sugopastakitchen.co.uk; @Sugo_Pasta; Tue-Sat 11 pm, Sun 9 pm.

ALVESTON, WARWICKSHIRE 2–1C

BARASET BARN £49 3 4 3

PIMLICO LANE CV37 7RJ 01789 295510

"A great ladies' lunch venue" – but not just for dames, this upmarket country pub (whose original flagstone floors nod to its 200-year-pedigree) also turns out far-from-fishy seafood specials and other enjoyable fare. / www.barasetbarn.co.uk; Mon-Sat 11 pm, Sun 5 pm; lunch noon - 2.30 pm, dinner 6.30 pm - 9.30 pm; *.

AMBERLEY, WEST SUSSEX 3–4A

AMBERLEY CASTLE £98 3 1 5

BN18 9LT 01798 831992

"How wonderful to dine in the medieval hall of a castle" (nowadays a Brownsword hotel) – complete with a 12th-century barrel-vaulted ceiling (and working portcullis). It almost seems churlish to point out that the restaurant is "expensive and a bit average", but most reporters feel that it's "worth it" for the "fantastic setting". / www.amberleycastle.co.uk; @amberleycastle; N of Arundel on B2139; no jeans; booking max 6 may apply; children: 8.

AMBLE, NORTHUMBERLAND 8–1B

THE OLD BOAT HOUSE AMBLE £46 4 5 3

LEAZES STREET NE65 0AA 01665 711 232

"You can see the fishing boats bringing in the catch" from this "tiny", "unpretentious hut" on the quayside, while eating "seafood cooked 'par excellence'". There's also "sourdough pizza to change the way you think about pizza!" Founders Martin & Ruth Charlton, both chefs, have followed up their success here with three more venues on the Northumberland coast: Blyth Boathouse, La Famiglia and Fish Shack. / boathousefoodgroup.co.uk/theoldboathouse-amble.html; @TOBHFoodGroup; Mon - Thur 9 pm, Fri & Sat 9.30 pm, Sun 9 pm.

AMBLESIDE, CUMBRIA 7–3D

DRUNKEN DUCK £60 4 3 5

BARNGATES LA22 0NG 01539 436347

This "lively and lovely gastropub with rooms" has been run for more than 40 years by co-owner Staf Barton. Head chef Jonny Watson's food is "always reliably good" and staff are "friendly". Perhaps it's "more a restaurant than a pub", but it does have its own Barngates microbrewery on site. / www.drunkenduckinn.co.uk; @DrunkenDuckInn; 3m from Ambleside, towards Hawkshead; Mon-Thu midnight, Fri & Sat 1 am, Sun 11 pm; no Amex; booking evening only. *Accommodation:* 17 rooms, from £105

FELLINI'S £45 343
CHURCH ST LA22 0BT 01539 432487

A "vegetarian restaurant attached to a cinema" whose "interesting menu" and "really good" cooking make it a solid choice if you're in the market for an Italian meal – especially given that there's "no competition" locally. / www.fellinisambleside.com; Wed-Sat 10.30 pm, Sun 9.30 pm; no Amex.

LAKE ROAD KITCHEN £89 443
3 SUSSEX HOUSE, LAKE ROAD LA22 0AD 015394 22012

"Wow! What a find" – real raves for Noma grad James Cross's woodsy, Scandi-style outfit, which "focuses on foraging and extreme seasonality". It's "not just fabulous locally sourced ingredients" that impress, but the "immersive theatrical experience", featuring "knowledgeable and detailed explanations of each dish" ("double wow", the tasting menus are affordable too). Ratings, though, were depressed this year by a minority who feel the venture "never quite lives up to its promise". / www.lakeroadkitchen.co.uk; @LakeRoadKitchen; 9 pm; closed Mon & Tue.

OLD STAMP HOUSE £66 543
CHURCH ST LA22 0BU 015394 32775

Ryan Blackburn's "imaginative" cooking using "great local produce in unusual combinations" continues "to improve" and to mightily impress practically all who comment on his "pocket-sized" basement in the centre of the town. As well as an à la carte option, there's a 'signature' menu. / www.oldstamphouse.com; Wed-Sat 10 pm, Sun 9 pm.

ZEFFIRELLI'S £39 333
COMPSTON RD LA22 9AD 01539 433845

A "very popular" veggie veteran of nearly four decades' standing in the same complex as the eponymous cinema and jazz café (cue film and food deals); there's "plenty of choice for pizza lovers" and "despite being busy", service remains "efficient". / www.zeffirellis.com; @ZeffsFellinis; Sun-Thu 11 pm, Fri & Sat midnight; no Amex.

AMERSHAM, BUCKINGHAMSHIRE 3–2A

ARTICHOKE £103 544
9 MARKET SQ HP7 0DF 01494 726611

"Why no Michelin star?" Laurie Gear's "simply brilliant" fixture in a characterful part of Old Amersham espouses all the values the Tyre Man is supposed to hold so dear. "The tasting menu is a stunning experience" with "first class" cuisine and service highly "professional". "The open plan kitchen is interesting to watch too". Gripes? "It can feel a bit squeezed-in at busy times". And "try to get a table downstairs, you're more in the action: the upstairs room is a little quiet". / www.artichokerestaurant.co.uk; @ArtichokeChef; Tue-Thu 11 pm, Fri & Sat 11.30 pm; no shorts.

GILBEY'S £52 333
1 MARKET SQ HP7 0DF 01494 727242

"A local favourite" with "low beams and cosy nooks", this "gorgeous little restaurant in atmospheric Old Amersham" is "perfect for a twosome or a girly catch-up" and offers a "well presented menu of tasty food". Owned by the Gilbey gin dynasty, it includes "an altogether different wine list from their very own careful selection". / www.gilbeygroup.com/restaurants/gilbeys-old; @GilbeysAmersham; Mon-Thu 9.30 pm, Fri & Sat 10 pm, Sun 2.30 pm.

THE GREEN GROCER £12 333
91 HIGH STREET HP7 0DT 01494 724581

The green wave has come to this popular local indie – part grocer, part café, and offering "delicious coffee, salads and amazing cakes"; in early 2018, it adopted an all-vegan and -vegetarian menu, changing its name from 'The Grocer at 91', and moving the hit bacon sarnies to local sibling 'The Grocer at 15' (there's also a branch in Gerrards Cross). / www.thegrocershops.co.uk; @thegrocershops; Tue-Sat 11 pm, Sun 9 pm; no bookings.

HAWKYNS, THE CROWN INN £68 323
16 HIGH STREET HP7 0DH 01494 721541

"Has improved recently after being patchy when it first opened" – Atul Kochhar (formerly of Benares fame) is winning more acclaim for his "Indian take on British food" at the timber-framed Elizabethan coaching inn, made famous by 'Four Weddings and a Funeral'. Feedback on non-food aspects of the offering are still up-and-down however: "brilliant food is not enough – dreadful service and ambience…"; "wonderful spicing of great ingredients, only problem was how quiet it was". / www.hawkynsrestaurant.co.uk; @Hawkynsamersham; Sun-Thu 9.30 pm, Fri & Sat 10.30 pm.

TOM YUM £41 334
101 SYCAMORE ROAD HP6 5EJ 01494 728806

"A lovely and busy local Thai" – "the setting is simple", but the cooking has "fantastic flavours using always-fresh ingredients" and service is "personal". / www.tomyum.net; Mon-Sat 9.30 pm, Sun 4 pm.

ANGMERING, WEST SUSSEX 3–4A

THE LAMB AT ANGMERING £41
THE SQUARE BN16 4EQ 01903 774300

Near the South Downs and the coast – a local pub revamped in 2011 by the Norbury family. Too limited feedback as yet for a rating, but all positive. / www.thelamb-angmering.com/; @thelambangmering; Mon-Sat 9 pm, Sun 3 pm.

ANNAT, WESTER ROSS 9–2B

THE TORRIDON RESTAURANT £85 544
THE TORRIDON IV22 2EY 01445 791242

"Well off the beaten track, but well worth a long journey to visit", a stately lochside hotel (and former hunting lodge) whose food, recently under Ross Stovold of Isle of Eriska fame, is "amazing, and makes use of local produce as far as possible". "The ambience is superb and you feel as if you are in a private dining room" – another reason why you "won't want to leave". / www.thetorridon.com/restaurant; @thetorridon.

ANSTRUTHER, FIFE 9–4D

ANSTRUTHER FISH BAR £28 422
42-44 SHORE ST KY10 3AQ 01333 310518

"Putting up with the fast-food-joint interior, because of the quality of food" is all part of the experience at this "astoundingly cheap" and "warren-like" fish 'n' chippy – as is being prepared to queue ("everybody for miles around knows how good a place this is"). / www.anstrutherfishbar.co.uk; Sun-Thu 9 pm, Fri & Sat 9.30 pm; no Amex; no bookings.

THE CELLAR £88 544
24 EAST GREEN KY10 3AA 01333 310378

"Fabulously good" cooking and "very generous flights of genuinely interesting, unheard-of wines" continue to win praise for Billy Boyter's much-accoladed fixture. In October 2018, it tweaked its format in a 'new creative direction': the only option now is a nine-course taster menu, with some focus on local fish and seafood. / www.thecellaranstruther.co.uk; @The_Cellar_Fife; in the harbour area; Mon-Sat 10.30 pm; no Amex.

APPLECROSS, HIGHLAND 9–2B

APPLECROSS INN £39 534
SHORE ST IV54 8LR 01520 744262

"Super-fresh seafood amidst some of the most dramatic scenery" is the draw to this "exceptionally busy" Highlands inn. "It's a pub that does proper pub food (and I don't mean the sort of gastro-pub stuff that most pubs do now, but old-school pub grub, with red onion in the salad and sliced brown bread), but what a location" and with "seafood, in particular, that's worthy of a 'posh' dining room"; "good craic" too. / www.applecross.uk.com/inn/; off A896, S of Shieldaig; 9 pm; no Amex; may need 6+ to book. *Accommodation:* 7 rooms, from £90

APPLEDORE, DEVON 1–2C

THE COFFEE CABIN £16 343
22 THE QUAY EX39 1QS 01237 475843

"Lovely coffee and smoothies for the kids" and "excellent cakes and cream teas" are among the assets of this chilled estuary-view four-year-old, whose scale has increased with its popularity;

they also do a "great crab sandwich". / 5 pm; L only; no Amex; no bookings.

The Old Passage Inn, Arlingham

ARGYLL, ARGYLL AND BUTE   9–3B

KILBERRY INN   £57   4 4 3

KILBERRY PA29 6YD   01880 770223

Perched on the western edge of the Scottish mainland, with views across to the Inner Hebrides, Clare Johnson & David Wilson's "welcoming inn" is "a real haven for locally produced food, excellently cooked" – in particular the region's abundant seafood. / www.kilberryinn.com; @Kilberryinn; Tue-Sun 8.30 pm; no Amex. *Accommodation:* 5 rooms, from £210

ARLINGHAM, GLOUCESTERSHIRE   2–2B

THE OLD PASSAGE INN   £62   5 3 3

PASSAGE ROAD GL2 7JR   01452 740547

"The best seafood" can be enjoyed in the dining room – or better still, on the "delightful terrace" – at this venue with "fabulous views" across the Severn. In centuries past it was the site of a ford across the river. / www.theoldpassage.com; @OldPassageInn; Tue-Sat 9 pm, Sun 2.30 pm. *Accommodation:* 2 rooms, from £80

ARMAGH, COUNTY ARMAGH   10–2D

4 VICARS   £48   4 3 4

4 VICARS HILL BT61 7ED   028 3752 7772

A minimally decorated former tea-room inside part of an old Georgian building is the location for Gareth & Kasia's accomplished venture, serving a "short menu" which includes some "outstanding" dishes. / www.4vicars.com; Wed & Thu, Sun 3 pm, Fri & Sat 8.30 pm.

ARMSCOTE, WARWICKSHIRE   2–1C

THE FUZZY DUCK   £53   3 3 4

ILMINGTON ROAD CV37 8DD   01608 682293

One of the better pubs with accommodation in the Cotswolds, this cosy 18th century hostelry near Stratford-upon-Avon is also a good culinary destination, well-rated by reporters for its superior, quite traditional cuisine. / www.fuzzyduckarmscote.com; @fuzzyduckpub; 10m S of Stratford-upon-Avon on the A4300; Tue-Sat 11 pm, Sun 5 pm; no Amex; booking max 10 may apply. *Accommodation:* 4 rooms, from £75

ARUNDEL, WEST SUSSEX   3–4A

MOTTE AND BAILEY CAFE   £28   3 4 3

BN18 9AG   01903883813

"Exceptional tapas and friendly service" win plaudits for chef/patron Michael Etherington's Jekyll and Hyde establishment – tearoom by day and Spanish/Moroccan haunt from Wednesday to Saturday night. / Mon & Tue, Sun 5 pm, Wed & Thu 10.30 pm, Fri & Sat 11 pm.

THE PARSONS TABLE   £66   4 3 3

2 & 8 CASTLE MEWS, TARRANT STREET BN18 9DG   01903 883477

The "very refined cooking" at this "accomplished" and "cosy" yearling – a first venture from chef Lee Parsons, who worked under Raymond Blanc at Le Manoir, and his wife Liz – has won unanimous praise from reporters. The focus is on West Sussex produce at reasonable prices: "the set lunch is remarkable value compared with many gastropubs". / theparsonstable.co.uk; @tpt_restaurant; Sun-Thu 11 pm, Fri & Sat midnight.

THE TOWN HOUSE   £49   5 4 4

65 HIGH STREET BN18 9AJ   01903 883 847

"Chef proprietor Lee Williams produces consistently brilliant food at a reasonable price" at this "intimate and deservedly popular" restaurant-with-rooms overlooking Arundel castle – and with its own quirky history in the shape of a 16th-century dining room ceiling from Florence. "In a small town packed with eateries this 15-year-old business stands out, so it's often crammed". Top Tip: "one of very few restaurants that serve Chateaubriand for one!". / www.thetownhouse.co.uk; @thetownhousearundel; Wed-Sat 9.30 pm. *Accommodation:* 4 rooms, from £95

ASCOT, BERKSHIRE   3–3A

RESTAURANT COWORTH PARK   £102   4 4 5

BLACKNEST RD SL5 7SE   01344 876 600

"A picture-book setting" amid polo fields and parkland (albeit easily reached from the M25) is the icing on the "delicious" cake at the Dorchester Collection's ultra-plush, special occasion-friendly hotel. From tasting menus to à la carte, Adam Smith's food is all "superb"; and "yummy" afternoon teas remain a highlight. / www.coworthpark.com; @CoworthParkUK; Fri & Sat, Wed & Thu 9.30 pm, Sun 2.30 pm. *Accommodation:* 17 rooms, from £0

ASENBY, NORTH YORKSHIRE   8–4C

CRAB & LOBSTER   £70   3 3 3

DISHFORTH RD YO7 3QL   01845 577286

"In a lovely location with fantastic food and a great menu", this "old favourite" festooned with bric-a-brac has a focus on fresh seafood –

although you'd have to cross the moors to reach the closest stretch of coast. Top Tip: "stay in one of the amazing themed rooms with private hot tub". / www.crabandlobster.co.uk; @crabandlobster; at junction of Asenby Rd & Topcliffe Rd; Sun-Fri 9 pm, Sat 9.30 pm. *Accommodation:* 17 rooms, from £160

ASHBOURNE, DERBYSHIRE   5–3C

THE LIGHTHOUSE RESTAURANT   £63   4 4 3

NEW ROAD, BOYLESTONE DE6 5AA 01335 330658

As per its name, this "brilliant" fine dining room at the back of the Rose and Crown pub, and bang in the "middle of nowhere", is a real local beacon, having been voted 'Derbyshire's Restaurant of the Year' in 2018. "The tasting menu is always excellent" and "they have added the option of wine flights" now too. / www.the-lighthouse-restaurant.co.uk/; Mon & Tue closed; Wed - Sat midnight; Sun closed.

AUCHTERARDER, PERTH AND KINROSS   9–3C

ANDREW FAIRLIE, GLENEAGLES HOTEL   £148   4 4 3

PH3 1NF   01764 694267

"You are enveloped in a cocoon of luxurious decadence on arrival at this intimate room, which exudes the glamour of a previous era" – a "darkly lit, quiet space which is very romantic" (but to some tastes a tad "gloomy"). On most accounts, "the tasting menu is an ultimate culinary experience that shouldn't be missed, with each course more sublime than the last; and with superb wine pairings (which allows the sommelier to present a mini course in viniculture)". Service is generally found to be "engaged and enthused" and "very friendly". Unsurprisingly some reporters challenge the extent to which it's good value, or judge the performance to be good rather than great, but for most visitors "despite the incredible expense, for a truly memorable evening I can't think of a better place to splash out". STOP PRESS. Sad news in early November 2018 – Andrew Fairlie is to step down as he is suffering from terminal cancer. He will hand over to head chef Stevie McLaughlin, general manager Dale Dewsbury and his business partner Gregor Mathieson on February 1. / www.andrewfairlie.co.uk; @AndrewFairlie1; 10 pm; L only, closed Sun; children: 12+.

Moor Hall, Aughton

JON & FERNANDA'S £55 443

34 HIGH STREET PH3 1DB 01764 662442

"Small, family-run restaurant" where the "predominantly British menu is superb" and there's an appealing "wine list from all over the world". "It punches above its weight" and some fans are completely wowed: "far better than its neighbour, Gleneagles!" (where the owners honed their craft). / www.jonandfernandas.co.uk; Mon closed; Tue - Sat 9 pm, Sun closed; no Amex; children: 10+.

STRATHEARN RESTAURANT, GLENEAGLES HOTEL £84

AUCHTERARDER PH3 1NF 0800 731 9219

Gleneagles 'other' restaurant is less well-known than Andrew Fairlie but highly rated nevertheless as "one of the very best 'grand' dining rooms in Britain", following a traditional 'silver service' format. It will emerge in spring 2019 after a major refurbishment. / www.gleneagles.com/dine-drink/the-strathearn/; @gleneagleshotel; Tue-Sat 9.30 pm.

AUGHTON, LANCASHIRE 5–2A

THE BARN AT MOOR HALL £91 444

PRESCOT RD L39 6RT 01695 572511

"The Barn is the informal bistro alternative to the restaurant at Moor Hall: a great space, with oak beams and bare-brick walls (and with a live pianist at the weekend)". "Prices aren't that casual, but justified on the cooking front", with some "terrific" dishes – "the focus is more on simplicity and accessibility, but it still wows". / moorhall.com/the-barn/about/; @TheBarnMH; Wed-Sat 11 pm, Sun 7 pm.

MOOR HALL £102 554

PRESCOT RD L39 6RT 01695 572511

"In such a short time, what Mark Birchall has created is remarkable" at his year-old smash hit – already fêted with two Michelin stars (the second was added in October 2018). "Many restaurants at this level can become temples of gastronomy, where one has to be hushed and awestruck, but there is none of that here: staff and customers are all at their ease and it's striking just how comfortable and relaxing the set-up is". "Several of the staff have come with Mark from L'Enclume, so the service is top-notch". "The dining area is a brand new extension to the old Hall: a very modern, light

space. The kitchen is open, and behind the chefs you can see the kitchen garden that supplies some of their home-grown produce". "Freed of the Rogan stable, Mark Birchall's food has settled into his own rhythm and, arguably, has greater focus than it did at L'Enclume". "There's a selection of three-, five and eight-course tasting menus and dishes are perfection": "precise, clean, perfectly balanced flavours with a modern approach" (involving brining, curing and baking on-site). Comparisons are often made with other top kitchens: e.g. "enjoyed it more than recent meals at L'Enclume and just as good as the Clove Club". "The wine list is a fascinating collection and the sommelier team are very helpful". Complaints? "Portions are sometimes a bit small". / www.moorhall.com; @restmoorhall.

AXMINSTER, DEVON 2–4A

RIVER COTTAGE CANTEEN £44 223

TRINITY SQUARE EX13 5AN 01297 631 715

The first of Hugh Fearnley Whittingstall's family-friendly showpieces avoids the brickbats of its siblings by-and-large ("our favourite, but I've had bad reports of other branches"). There is the odd report here too of "bland and unimaginative" fare, but for the most part it's praised for its "good value". / www.rivercottage.net; @rivercottage; Tue-Sun, Mon 9.30 pm.

AYLESBURY, BUCKINGHAMSHIRE 3–2A

HARTWELL HOUSE £83 235

OXFORD ROAD HP17 8NR 01296 747444

Dinner is served by waiters in tailcoats at this Grade I-listed Jacobean and Georgian stately home, leased by the National Trust and operated as a grand spa hotel. The food may not always be a match for the magnificent Rococo interiors (or the prices!), but fans particularly tip it for lunch or afternoon tea. / www.hartwell-house.com/wine-and-dine/; @hartwellhouse; 2m W of Aylesbury on A418; 9.45 pm; no jeans; children: 4+. *Accommodation:* 50 rooms, from £290

THE KING'S HEAD £33 333

KINGS HEAD PASSAGE, MARKET SQUARE HP20 2RW 01296 718812

Run by the National Trust, this Aylesbury gastroboozer occupies a gem of a Tudor

building, with an oak-panelled dining room spearheaded by the Chiltern Brewery since 2005. Given its ties, the beers are a highlight, though it also wins praise for the "best duck" (living up to the town's mallard associations). / www.kingsheadaylesbury.co.uk; @Kings_Head; Wed-Sat 11 pm, Sun 7 pm.

BAGNOR, BERKSHIRE 2–2D

THE BLACKBIRD £78 544

HIGH STREET RG20 8AQ 01635 40005

"Who would expect to find top restaurant cuisine in a small, quaint, rural pub?" – Dom Robinson, a former head chef at Tom Aikens, returned from Dubai to imbue this village boozer with plenty of "old world charm". His "excellent, high-quality cooking" has garnered universally high ratings from our reporters – as well as a coveted star from the French tyre outfit – and it "won't break the bank". / www.theblackbird.co.uk; @BlackbirdBagnor; Wed & Thu 11 pm, Fri & Sat midnight, Sun 5 pm.

BAGSHOT, SURREY 3–3A

THE LATYMER, PENNYHILL PARK HOTEL £135 445

LONDON ROAD GU19 5EU 01276 486150

"The main restaurant really has the wow factor" at this ultra-plush country house hotel, where an architectural highlight is the superb, lavishly decorated dining room. Matt Worswick's "excellent" cuisine throws up "some really innovative dishes" which his most ardent fans feel "will earn him a second star some time soon". Even if that's too strong for other reporters, all comments on the cooking are upbeat, and there's consistent praise too for the interesting wine pairings that "really bring out the flavours of the food". Top Tip: "superb afternoon tea, with a glass of Champagne and constantly refreshed sandwiches and cakes". / www.exclusive.co.uk; @PennyHillPark; Wed-Sun 9 pm; booking max 8 may apply; children: 12+. *Accommodation:* 123 rooms, from £315

BAINBRIDGE, NORTH YORKSHIRE DALES 8–4A

YOREBRIDGE HOUSE £87 444

DL8 3EE 019 6965 2060

Dave & Charlotte Reilly opened this Victorian former school in Wensleydale as a modern boutique hotel in 2007. The kitchen has developed under chef Dan Shotton, and now "excels in fresh local North Yorkshire ingredients, combined and cooked to a very high standard". / www.yorebridgehouse.co.uk; @yorebridgehouse; Mon-Sat 11 pm, Sun 10 pm.

BAKEWELL, DERBYSHIRE 5–2C

PIEDANIELS £51 443

BATH ST DE45 1BX 01629 812687

This stalwart (est. 1994) husband-and-wife operation is an "excellent spot for a splendid relaxing lunch", where the traditional French cuisine is of an accomplished standard and "great value" to boot. / www.piedaniels-restaurant.com; Mon-Sun 11 pm.

BALA, GWYNEDD   4–2D

PALE HALL HOTEL RESTAURANT   £114   445

PALÉ ESTATE, LLANDDERFEL, LL23 7PS 01678 530 285

"The main draw is the setting (a sumptuous Victorian mansion house in beautiful grounds in the Dee valley) but the food (fine dining without pretension) comes a very close second" at this luxurious five-star property (once owned by the Duke of Westminster), near Bala. Chef Gareth Stevenson's produces a short à la carte (focussing on quality protein) as well six-course and ten-course tasting options. / www.palehall.co.uk; @palehallhotel; 2pm, 9pm.

BALLYMENA, COUNTY ANTRIM   10–1D

THE BLACKSTONE   £46   432

11 HILL ST BT43 6BH 02825 648566

"Top quality food (particularly the daily specials) from locally sourced ingredients where possible" make it worth discovering this Irish bar and restaurant (which looks nothing-to-speak-of from the outside). "Recently revisiting with visitors from England, we and they were very impressed". / Sun-Fri & Sat 9 pm.

BALQUHIDDER, PERTH AND KINROSS   9–3C

MONACHYLE MHOR   £91   544

FK19 8PQ 01877 384622

With its "very calming surroundings at the end of a 3-mile track" – a "superb setting on the side of Loch Voil" – Tom Lewis's "highly recommended" boutique hotel in the Trossachs has been a firm favourite for more than 20 years. "Fine cooking" is prepared by executive chef Marysia Paszkowska, using ingredients grown onsite or sourced and foraged in the locality, and the result is "delightful". / www.mhor.net; take the Kings House turning off the A84; 9 pm. *Accommodation:* 14 rooms, from £195

BAMBURGH, NORTHUMBERLAND   9–4D

THE POTTED LOBSTER   £47   333

3 LUCKER ROAD NE69 7BS 01668 214088

In the shadow of Bamburgh Castle, this seaside-themed two-year-old is by all accounts "a real gem and great addition to the area" (not least as it's "an area where good food is rare"); the fish and seafood is "very reliable" and servings happily "large", unlike the venue itself. / www.thepottedlobsterbamburgh.co.uk.

BAMPTON, DEVON   2–3A

THE SWAN   £43   333

STATION RD EX16 9NG 01398 332 248

Paul and Donna Berry's 60-cover gastropub inspires all-round praise, including for its quite lengthy menu, majoring in steaks. Post-survey it recruited a new head chef, Olivier Certain. / www.theswan.co; @theswanbampton; Mon-Thu 11 pm, Fri & Sat midnight, Sun 10.30 pm.

BARNET, HERTFORDSHIRE   3–2B

SAVORO   £50   332

206 HIGH STREET EN5 5SZ 020 8449 9888

Long hailed as a local beacon, an intimate hotel dining room, in a high street building that has served as both a boathouse and tearoom. "Subtle and efficient" service is matched with "quality food" (fish, speciality sourdoughs etc.) and they couldn't be more "accommodating". / www.savoro.co.uk; Mon-Sat 10 pm, Sun 7 pm. *Accommodation:* 9 rooms, from £75

BARTON-ON-SEA, HAMPSHIRE   2–4C

PEBBLE BEACH   £63   435

MARINE DRIVE BH25 7DZ 01425 627777

"Fresh and flavoursome fish" combine with "stunning sea views over the Solent to the Isle of Wight" at this "friendly" operation with a "lovely terrace" for al fresco meals. Chef Karl Wiggins took over in early 2018 from Pierre Chevillard, who had run the kitchen for more than a decade, and by all accounts the place "has kept up its very high standards". Eating here is a pleasure "that's not diminished by repeated visits". / www.pebblebeach-uk.com; @pebblebeachUK; Mon-Sat 11 pm, Sun 10.30 pm. *Accommodation:* 4 rooms, from £100

BARWICK, SOMERSET   2–3B

LITTLE BARWICK HOUSE   £72   454

BA22 9TD 01935 423902

"Our all-time favourite", say devotees of Emma & Tim Ford's "elegant" restaurant-with-rooms, which delivers "great ambience, charming service, fantastic, beautifully presented food" ("stellar cheese") and a particularly "interesting and comprehensive wine list". / www.littlebarwickhouse.co.uk; @LittleBarwick; take the A37 Yeovil to Dorchester road, turn left at the brown sign for Little Barwick House; Tue-Sat 9 pm; children: 5+. *Accommodation:* 6 rooms, from £69

BASLOW, DERBYSHIRE   5–2C

FISCHERS AT BASLOW HALL   £109   443

CALVER RD DE45 1RR 01246 583259

Susan & Max Fischer's well-known venture occupies a Edwardian property built in the style of a 17th-century manor and has a sizeable fan club for Rupert Rowley's very "consistent quality" of cuisine, "unobtrusive and slick service" and "very relaxing" style. / www.fischers-baslowhall.co.uk; @FischersBaslow; on the A623; 8.30 pm; no trainers. *Accommodation:* 11 rooms, from £180

ROWLEY'S   £56   342

CHURCH LANE DE45 1RY 01246 583880

This "brasserie-style" offshoot from Fischers of Baslow Hall, where Rupert Rowley is executive chef, wins consistent ratings for its food, and is a "great place for a family meal" for anybody visiting nearby Chatsworth House. / www.rowleysrestaurant.co.uk; @RowleysBaslow; Mon-Sun 11 pm; no Amex.

BASSENTHWAITE, CUMBRIA   7–3C

BISTRO AT THE DISTILLERY   £51   322

SETMURTHY CA13 9SJ 01768788850

On an immaculately rejigged Victorian farm, Terry Laybourne's PR-friendly three-year-old venture is one part distillery, and one part easy-going bistro, praised for its "excellent service" and venturesome drinks list; to make a day of it, you can also meet and greet their alpacas. / www.bistroatthedistillery.com; @BistroTLD; 9 pm.

BATH, SOMERSET   2–2B

ACORN VEGETARIAN KITCHEN   £55   433

2 NORTH PARADE PASSAGE BA1 1NX 01225 446059

This "fancy, upmarket" restaurant (well, by the standards of grungy veggies, anyway) in a small lane in the city-centre remains one of the UK's most distinguished non-meat destinations for its "tasty, interesting" food and "good choice of organic wines and beers". / www.acornvegetariankitchen.co.uk; @AcornVegetarian; 9.30 pm, Sat 10 pm.

THE BATH PRIORY   £118   454

WESTON RD BA1 2XT 01225 331922

"Wonderful food (and the garden provides a lot of it)" is part of the tradition at this upscale country-house hotel, whose ratings have improved this year under new executive chef Michael Nizzero (whose impressive CV includes a stint at the Waterside Inn Bray). Top Tip: "the excellent cheese trolley includes some delicious local examples". / www.thebathpriory.co.uk; @Thebathpriory; no jeans; children: 5+ L, 12+ D.

THE CIRCUS   £48   443

34 BROCK ST BA1 2LN 01225 466020

This "utterly reliable" family-run bistro near the Royal Crescent is popular for its "delightful service, delicious food, and interesting and varied menu with great fish dishes". "Professional and doesn't break the bank – what's not to like?". / www.thecircusrestaurant.co.uk; @CircusBath; Mon-Sat 10.30 pm; no Amex; children: 7+ at D.

CLAYTON'S KITCHEN £59 433

15A GEORGE ST BA1 2EN 01225 585 100

"Consistently fabulous" modern European cooking draws a steady stream of locals as well as tourists to this smart Georgian townhouse in the city centre – and it's "very good value considering the quality". Rob Clayton trained under the legendary Nico Ladenis before heading up the Bath Priory kitchen, among others. / www.claytonskitchen.com/; @PorterBath; Mon-Thu 10 pm, Fri & Sat 10.30 pm, Sun 9.30 pm.

CLIFTON SAUSAGE £55 333

5 BLADUD BUILDINGS, THE PARAGON BA1 5LS 01225 433 633

"The outside space has a lovely view over Bath" at this spin-off from a Bristol-based contemporary café, specialising in sausages (obvs) but also serving some well-rated (mostly meaty) British dishes. / www.cliftonsausage.co.uk/bath; @cliftonsausage; Wed-Sat 11 pm, Sun 7 pm.

COLONNA & SMALLS £11 444

6 CHAPEL ROW BA1 1HN 07766 808067

Thrice crowned UK Barista Champion (and up there at several World Finals) Maxwell Colonna-Dashwood runs this "very fashionable" Queen Square coffee shop. Unsurprisingly, it's hailed as "the best place for coffee" in town and the "carrot cake is also pretty damn good!" / www.colonnaandsmalls.co.uk; @colonnaandsmalls; Mon-Sat 5.30 pm, Sun 4 pm; no Amex; booking max 6 may apply.

CORKAGE £39 333

132A WALCOT STREET BA1 5BG 01225 422577

"Occupying the old Beaujolais (RIP) which many natives and visitors to Bath will fondly remember", this "very enjoyable" modern wine bar "could not be more different with its fresh approach: each plate is described by just one word and the waiter then goes on to elaborate on ingredients and how it is cooked; and there is no wine list as such, the waiter again asks your tastes and then recommends". The odd reporter finds it "annoying that things have to be explained", but for the most part there's nothing but applause for co-owner Marty Grant's "excellent and unexpected wines from across the globe" and Richard Knighting's "fresh, different and seasonal" small plates to accompany them. A second venue on Chapel Row means it has "two great locations in Bath". / corkagebath.com; @corkagebath; Tue-Sat 10 pm, Sun 2 pm.

DAN MOON AT THE GAINSBOROUGH £72 334

BEAU STREET BA1 1QY 01225358888

"Now named after the chef, Dan Moon", the "beautiful, albeit formal" dining room of this luxe Georgian city-centre hotel delivers "exceptional food", although it's "not inexpensive" outside of the "brilliant midweek lunch deals" ("no more than lunch at your local pub!"). Continue the indulgence at the celebrated on-site spa. / @GainsBathSpa; Mon-Sun 10 pm.

HARE & HOUNDS £49 334

LANSDOWN ROAD BA1 5TJ 01225 482682

"A busy and useful gastropub near the Lansdowne Park and Ride", and bolstered by chic interiors as well as ten-mile views over the countryside (walks start right from the door); "great staff" and "amazing" locally sourced food courtesy of a new chef continue to cement its appeal. / www.hareandhoundsbath.com; @HareHoundsBath; Mon-Sun 9 pm; no Amex.

HENRY'S RESTAURANT £61 542

4 SAVILLE ROW BA1 2QP 01225 780055

"Henry is well on his way to a Michelin star – or two," say fans of the "young, hardworking" chef's "ambitious, totally delicious" spot, in a bare-boards Georgian townhouse (that was once Casanis, RIP). "Lovely staff" and "well-priced" set lunches round out its charms. / www.henrysrestaurantbath.com.

INDIAN TEMPTATION £31 423

09-10 HIGH STREET (CHEAP STREET) BA1 5AQ 01225464631

The South Indian veggie cuisine is all "excellent and reasonably priced" at this elegant period venue overlooking the abbey; despite the odd service blip, it's "still definitely worth a return visit because of the quality of the food" ("typical dosas and chaat etc." but also much bolder options). / www.indiantemptation.com/; Mon-Fri 10.30 pm, Sat & Sun 11 pm.

THE IVY BATH BRASSERIE £57 234

39 MILSOM ST BA1 1DS 01225 307 100

London's Theatreland celeb hangout-turned-national chain landed in a handsome Grade II-listed former NatWest Bank plumb in the middle of Bath last year. The service is better rated here than at many in the chain, but – true to form – it's the "splendid" atmosphere "which is the main attraction – the food's adequate, but the gorgeous bar and interior makes up for it". / theivybathbrasserie.com; @ivybathbrass; Mon-Sun 12.30 am.

KOFFMANN & MR WHITE'S, ABBEY HOTEL £55

NORTH PARADE BA1 1LF 01225 461603

A collaboration between Pierre Koffmann and Marco Pierre White, located within the Abbey Hotel, which opened in October 2018. Even with six Michelin stars between them, this dim-lit, 'casual all day dining English and French Brasserie' serving 'affordable classic food' has so far inspired little in the way of national fanfare. / www.mpwrestaurants.co.uk/our-brands/koffmann-and-mr-whites/bath; @KW_Bath; Mon-Fri 10 pm, Sat 10.30 pm, Sun 9.30 pm.

MENU GORDON JONES £81 543

2 WELLSWAY BA2 3AQ 01225 480871

"Fun and full of surprises" – Gordon Jones's "quirky" operation on the edge of town provides a "top experience – up with the best". "You have no idea what's coming" as there's no menu or choice; instead, Jones decides what to cook each day, conjuring up "amazing food and drink with interesting conversation". "The absolute highlight was snails and test tubes – they serve snails along with test tubes filled with different sauces to go with them...". / www.menugordonjones.co.uk; @MenuGordonJones; Mon-Sat 11 pm, Sun 10.30 pm; no Amex.

THE MINT ROOM £46 433

LONGMEAD GOSPEL HALL, LOWER BRISTOL RD BA2 3EB 01225 446656

In a slightly utilitarian setting next to a Sainsbury's petrol station and en route to Brizzle, this swish Indian serves some "beautiful food". / www.themintroom.co.uk; @themintroom; 11 pm, Fri & Sat 11.30 pm; no shorts.

THE OLIVE TREE, QUEENSBERRY HOTEL £79 432

RUSSELL ST BA1 2QF 01225447928

"Truly outstanding" cooking from chef Chris Cleghorn continues to impress diners at this well-known venue, which won a Michelin star in October 2018 (becoming the only restaurant in town to hold one). The basement dining room doesn't please all reporters though ("a bit quiet and lacking character") and the experience is "not cheap". / www.thequeensberry.co.uk; @OliveTreeBath; Tue-Sat 10 pm; no Amex; no shorts *Accommodation:* 29 rooms, from £125

THE PUMP ROOM £49 225

STALL ST BA1 1LZ 01225 444477

This beautiful Georgian dining room, where you often eat to the strains of a live classical quartet, offers "such a lovely dining experience" (if a wholly un-foodie one). Afternoon tea is the top occasion: "gives the Savoy a run for its money!" / www.searcys.co.uk; @searcysbars; Mon-Sun 9 pm; booking weekdays only.

SCALLOP SHELL £35 433

22 MONMOUTH PLACE BA1 2AY 01225 420928

This "no-nonsense seafood restaurant" – a tasteful modern café, complete with nautical decor – has a "handy location" in the town centre, and has earned a good reputation since opening three years ago for its "always super-fresh food (wonderful scallops, great battered fish)". The centrepiece is an old Victorian bath filled with ice, with fresh fish lying on top. Top tip: "try to eat downstairs – far more atmosphere than the upper deck". / www.thescallopshell.co.uk;

@thescallopshell; Mon-Sat 5 pm, Sun 4.30 pm; no bookings.

THE WHITE HART INN £43 333

WIDCOMBE HILL BA2 6AA 01225 338053

"In the wonderful community of Widcombe" – this "down-to-earth" venue is "more a restaurant that serves drinks" than it is a pub (although they still let dogs in): "friendly and serving good hearty food". Nice 'Mediterranean Garden' for the summer. / www.whitehartbath.co.uk; Sun-Thu 11 pm, Fri & Sat midnight; no Amex. *Accommodation:* 4 rooms, from £25

THE WELLINGTON ARMS £60 434

BAUGHURST RD RG26 5LP 0118 982 0110

"Ambitious, without over-extending itself" – chef Jason King and front-of-house partner Simon Page's "relaxed and profession" operation on the Hampshire-Berkshire border is "a perfect example of what a gastropub/restaurant should be". "Great food guaranteed every time, with good use of local ingredients". / www.thewellingtonarms.com; @WellingtonArms; Mon-Thu 8.30 pm, Fri & Sat 9 pm, Sun 3 pm; no Amex. *Accommodation:* 4 rooms, from £130

THE CAPE GRAND CAFE & RESTAURANT £53 333

6A, STATION RD HP9 1NN 01494 681137

A "lovely choice for breakfast incorporating South African specialities (e.g. Boerewors sausage) as well as more standard fare" help win praise for this "light, airy and interestingly decorated" Saffa-owned café near the station – "a great coffee and lunch stop" and "something a little bit different" for the locale. / www.thecapeonline.com; @capegrandcafe; Sun-Wed 4 pm, Fri & Sat 11 pm, Thu 5 pm; no Amex.

NO.5 LONDON END £55 333

5 LONDON END HP9 2HN 01494 355500

"A small but quality establishment" – this contemporary two-year-old café aims to bring gastropub-style fare onto the high street and succeeds, serving "top burgers, and lots of other yummy offerings". / www.no5londonend.co.uk; Mon-Sat 9.30 pm, Sun 4 pm.

BRASSICA £52 443

4 THE SQUARE DT8 3AS 01308 538 100

"It's lovely to find a proper restaurant rather than another gastropub in a great position on a charming town square". Better still, Cass Titcombe's "inspired and innovative cooking" means it's an "outstanding independent restaurant", while his partner, design guru Louise Chidgey, lends it "great style" (and an interiors shop next door). /

www.brassicarestaurant.co.uk/Site/Home.html; @brassica_food; Mon-Sat 9.30 pm, Sun 2.30 pm.

FISH ON THE GREEN £68 433

CHURCH LN ME14 4EJ 01622 738 300

"Fine dining in a picturesque village" with an emphasis on "excellent fresh fish" is to be found at this "cosy" conversion on the village green, which is "one of the few top places to eat in the Maidstone area". It offers an "exciting menu of delicious dishes prepared with a combination of modern flair and traditional technique". Top Tip: "fairly priced set lunch". / www.fishonthegreen.com; Tue-Thu 9.30 pm, Fri & Sat 10 pm, Sun 4.30 pm; no Amex.

THE TERRACE, MONTAGU ARMS HOTEL £96 343

SO42 7ZL 01590 612324

In a chocolate-box village, this wisteria-clad arts and crafts hotel lost its star in 2016, and "while reviews of late appear to be mixed", fans say they're "yet to have a duff meal at this fabulous little place"; extra marks for "discreet service who anticipated our every need". / www.montaguarmshotel.co.uk; @themontaguarms; Wed-Sun, Tue 9.30 pm; no jeans; children: 11+ D. *Accommodation:* 22 rooms, from £143

THE BULL BEAUMARIS, YE OLDE BULL'S HEAD £58 334

CASTLE STREET LL58 8AP 01248 810329

The 15th-century Bull inn has been modernised in recent years, with young chef Andy Tabberner charged with producing a sophisticated modern menu. The results can be "a bit hit & miss, but more often hit than miss" – and the ratings are strong overall. (There's also "lovely decor and outside area" in the cheaper ground floor brasserie.) / www.bullsheadinn.co.uk; @bullsheadinn; on the High Street; 9.30 pm; D only, closed Mon & Sun; no jeans; children: 7+ at D. *Accommodation:* 26 rooms, from £105

CHAI NAASTO £45 433

2 - 4 FAIRFIELD ROAD BR3 3LD 020 3750 0888

"Innovative, delicious food in a great, fun setting" is the order of the day at this colourful Indian tapas spot with two siblings in the Big Smoke; "the menu changes regularly with different regions added so it is a great way to try different cuisines". / www.chai-naasto.co.uk; @ChaiNaasto.

DEVONSHIRE ARMS AT BEELEY £53 333

DEVONSHIRE SQUARE DE4 2NR 01629 733259

This classic 18th-century pub on the Duke of Devonshire's Chatsworth Estate is generally pleasing, with its "wonderful locally sourced food in a charming and lovely setting". / www.devonshirebeeley.co.uk; @DevArmsBeeley; 9.30 pm. *Accommodation:* 14 rooms, from £125

EDO £42 434

3 CAPITAL HOUSE, UNIT 2 UPPER QUEEN STREET BT1 6FB 028 9031 3054

"Really buzzing, even at 6pm" – this October 2017 newcomer, complete with kitchen on display, is achieving a strong reputation with its Spanish-influenced, modern cuisine (with an emphasis on meaty fare). "Try anything slow-cooked in 'Bertha' (their coal oven) – it melts in the mouth". / www.edorestaurant.co.uk; Mon-Sat 10.30 pm.

HOWARD STREET £39 343

56 HOWARD STREET BT1 6PG 02890 248 362

This modern brasserie is a well-known local destination and fans say that "other restaurants could learn a lot from the quality of the service". It received a boost from a revamp this year which has significantly upped its comfort levels. / www.howardstbelfast.com; Mon-Sat 9.30 pm.

JAMES STREET SOUTH £59

21 JAMES STREET SOUTH BT2 7GA 028 9043 4310

In August 2018, Niall and Joanne McKenna reformatted and refurbished their well-known local destination, converting the fine dining restaurant and its neighbouring bar and grill into a single operation to meet what they see as a growing demand for a more bistro-style rather than fine dining experience. The venture inspired mostly positive feedback this year, but we've left it un-rated as the change of format beds in. / www.jamesstreetsouth.co.uk; @jamessstsouth; Mon - Sat 10.30 pm; Sun closed.

MOURNE SEAFOOD BAR £49 433

34 - 36 BANK STREET BT1 1HL 028 9024 8544

A famous, informal dark-wood seafood joint which sources its produce direct from the owners' beds, and also has a sibling near County Down's Dundrum Bay; marks remain super-stellar, but feedback a tad limited. / www.mourneseafood.com; @msbbelfast; Mon-Thu 9.30 pm, Fri & Sat 10 pm, Sun 9 pm; no bookings at lunch.

OX £75 5|4|4

1 OXFORD ST BT1 3LA 028 9031 4121

"One of Belfast's Michelin starred restaurants
with world class and interesting food from chef
Stephen Toman and his crew" – this riverside
venue was recently acclaimed by Food & WIne
Magazine as Ireland's best and fans agree:
"definitely the most polished dining experience
in Northern Ireland". "The Ox Cave next
door is great fun too – lovely charcuterie,
cheese and wines by the glass plus live music".
/ www.oxbelfast.com; @oxbelfast; Mon-Sat 11 pm,
Sun 9 pm.

THE CRAB AND LOBSTER INN £50 3|4|4

32 FORELANDS FIELD RD PO35 5TR
01983 872244

This "lovely" and well-known spot is now
part of the IOW Character Inns group. "The
food is fresh, stylish and imaginative but
the extraordinary surroundings" – a clifftop
overlooking Bembridge Ledge – "provide the
vital ingredient X". / www.crabandlobsterinn.co.uk;
@CrabLobsterIOW; Tue-Sat 9.30 pm, Sun 2.30 pm;
no Amex. *Accommodation:* 5 rooms, from £80

ERISKA HOTEL £101 3|4|4

PA37 1SD 01631 720371

"A lovely setting in its own grounds" on a
private island in the Highlands (accessible by
bridge) means this luxurious Relais & Châteaux
property is "just made for relaxation". High
marks too for Conor Toomey's modern British
cuisine presented from a three-course prix fixe
menu. / www.eriska-hotel.co.uk; @isleoferiska; 9 pm;
D only; no shorts; children: 10. *Accommodation:* 25
rooms, from £340

THE GATSBY £59 3|3|3

97 HIGH ST HP4 2DG 01442 870403

"Perfect for the iconic Rex picturehouse",
whose foyer it occupies, this "elegant" 1930s
venue – replete with tinkling ivories and
cocktail bar – turns out "top-quality" food (not
just on pre-cinema deals). / www.thegatsby.net;
@thegatsbyathome; Mon-Sat 11 pm; no Amex;
booking max 10 may apply.

ZAZA £42 3|3|2

21-23 LOWER KINGS ROAD HP4 2AB
01442 767 055

The Berkhamsted branch of this rather superior
local chain, set around a 200-year-old living
olive tree, wins plentiful and consistently
high ratings for its classic Italian menu. /
www.zaza.co.uk; Mon-Sat 10.30 pm, Sun 10 pm.

OGINO £50 4|5|3

1ST FLOOR BEAVER HOUSE, BUTCHER
ROW HU17 0AA 01482 679500

High marks again – if from a small local
fanclub – for Julian and Rieko Ogino-Stamford's
first-floor dining room, tucked away in the town
centre, which serves accomplished Japanese
cuisine of both traditional and modern
inspiration. / ogino.co.uk/; @OGINOJAPANESE;
Tue-Sun 11 pm.

THE PIG & WHISTLE £38 4|4|4

5 SOW HILL ROAD HU17 8BG
01482 874083

Ex-Pétrus chef James Allcock's 'pint-sized bistro
and charcuterie bar' is strong on ingredient
quality (marvellous breads, cheeses, salads),
and serves funky small plates alongside sharing
platters: "a perfect lunchtime stop with friendly
and knowledgeable staff". / pigandwhistlebeverley.
co.uk; @ThePigBeverley; Tue-Sat 11 pm, Sun 10 pm.

THE PIPE & GLASS INN £68 4|4|5

WEST END HU17 7PN 01430 810246

"I like the fact that it's still the village local
despite its celebrity" – James and Kate
Mackenzie's much-accoladed inn, "tucked
away" in East Yorkshire, may "looks like a
standard country pub", but continues to inspire
little but all-round adulation from diners for its
"lovely" atmosphere, "welcoming" approach,
and food that "excels with due care and
attention". "It also has delightful rooms for
an overnight stay". / www.pipeandglass.co.uk;
@pipeandglass; Mon-Fri 10 pm.

THE WESTWOOD RESTAURANT £63 2|3|3

NEW WALK HU17 7AE 01482 881999

"The food never fails to excite", say fans of
twins Matt & Michele Barker's modern brasserie
in a Grade II listed Georgian courthouse. But
ratings have fallen this year amid reports that it's
"not as good as it was": "it's just a steakhouse
full of rich kids", grumbles one critic. /
www.thewestwood.co.uk; @The_Westwood; Mon-Sat
10 pm, Sun 2.30 am; no Amex.

WHITES £71 5|4|3

12-12A NORTH BAR WITHOUT HU17 7AB
01482 866121

"A treasure of a restaurant" (with rooms) where
locally born John Robinson is "pretty much a
one-man band producing imaginative, daily
changing tasting menus at an absurdly cheap
price". It's an "unbelievable gastronomic
experience created by the passionate
combination of fresh local foods and exquisitely
skilled cooking". Having passed the ten-year
mark last summer, Robinson plans to extend
the facilities with an upstairs 'social room' for
pre-dinner drinks. / www.whitesrestaurant.co.uk;
@Whitesbeverley; Tue-Sat 8 pm; no Amex.
Accommodation: 4 rooms, from £85

KENTISH HARE £42 4|4|3

95 BIDBOROUGH RIDGE TN3 0XB
01892 525709

The "consistently good, well-executed food"
at brothers Chris & James Tanner's "versatile"
and "welcoming" gastropub attracted nothing
but praise this year. The one mild complaint
– more of a suggestion – was that "the menu
doesn't change much". / www.thekentishhare.com;
@TheKentishHare; Tue-Sat 11 pm, Sun 6 pm.

THE WEST HOUSE £67 5|4|3

28 HIGH ST TN27 8AH 01580 291341

"Just an all-round brilliant experience" – rock
drummer-turned-chef Graham Garrett's
village restaurant in a 16th-century weaver's
cottage is "hard to beat in the Weald area
of Kent". The focus here is on "good
local ingredients" and "lovely flavours". /
www.thewesthouserestaurant.co.uk; @grahamgarrett;
Mon-Sat 11.30 pm, Sun 10.30 pm; no Amex; booking
max 6 may apply.

THE BRIDGE £48 3|3|4

HIGH ST B50 4BG 01789 773700

"A great terrace and riverside setting" is
the crown jewel feature of this riverside
eatery, on the banks of the Avon. Char-
grilled steaks are the headline attractions
of an "enjoyable" modern bistro menu. /
www.thebridgeatbidford.com/; Mon-Thu 9 pm, Fri &
Sat 9.30 pm, Sun 3 pm; no Amex.

BURGH ISLAND HOTEL £98 3|3|5

TQ7 4BG 01548 810514

"Perfect is the only word to describe Burgh
Island", with its "candle-lit dining room,
fabulous band" and "unique" atmosphere
("great for fans of Art Deco or Agatha
Christie")… all of which slightly outshine the
food; "go for the black-tie experience in the
ballroom" for full effect. / www.burghisland.com;
@burgh_island; 8.30 pm; D only, ex Sun open L & D;
no Amex; jacket & tie required; children: 12+ at D.
Accommodation: 25 rooms, from £400

THE OYSTER SHACK £51 3|3|5

MILLBURN ORCHARD FARM, STAKES HILLS
TQ7 4BE 01548 810876

This "quirky and fun" shack in a former oyster
farm overlooking the Avon estuary offers a
"warm welcome" and, in particular, "eating
on a summer's day under the outside canopies
makes for a great lunchtime". Long-term owner
Chris Yandell sold up in early 2018 to develop
his Rocktails range of no-alcohol distilled
drinks, and while praise remains solid for its
"good variety of local fish and seafood", food

ratings slipped a fraction this year (one regular notes: "they have retained much of the style of the 'old' Oyster Shack but there was some lack of attention to detail – hopefully temporary teething problems.") / www.oystershack.co.uk; @theoystershack; Wed & Thu, Sun 3 pm, Fri & Sat 9 pm.

BILDESTON, SUFFOLK 3–1C

THE BILDESTON CROWN £52 2️⃣2️⃣3️⃣

104 HIGH ST IP7 7EB 01449 740510

"Great local produce" is showcased by chef/landlord Chris Hayley on his "creative" menus at this welcoming 15th-century wood-framed former coaching inn. / www.thebildestoncrown.com; @BildestonCrown; from the A14, take the B115 to Bildeston; Mon-Sat 9.30 pm, Sun 4 pm. *Accommodation:* 12 rooms, from £100

BILLERICAY, ESSEX 3–2C

THE MAGIC MUSHROOM £58 4️⃣3️⃣3️⃣

BARLEYLANDS ROAD CM11 2UD 01268 289963

Darren Bennet's bistro has long been a beacon in these parts for relaxed modern British grub in a beamed setting; given its appeal, fans may be pleased to hear that he recently applied for a license to open 24 hours a day. / www.magicmushroomrestaurant.co.uk; next to Barleylands Farm; Tue-Sat 9.30 pm, Sun 4 pm.

BINFIELD HEATH, BERKSHIRE 2–2D

BOTTLE AND GLASS INN £65 4️⃣4️⃣2️⃣

BONES LANE RG9 4JT 01491 412 625

"Meals start with amazing bread and continue on from there" at "the latest incarnation of this slightly out-of-the-way pub near Henley" – relaunched last year by Alex Sergeant & David Holliday who "have certainly brought the standards of the Harwood Arms [London's No. 1 Pub in the Harden's survey] to South Oxfordshire". "Each dish is carefully presented with rich flavours and many lovely sauces", and the selection includes "melting venison from just around the corner". "The dining extension is very nice but still new" and "the whitewash and high ceilings can make it feel a tad sterile, but as the place fills up it becomes relaxed with the chatter of happy diners". / www.bottleandglassinn.co.uk; Mon-Thu 11 pm, Fri & Sat midnight, Sun 6 pm.

BIRMINGHAM, WEST MIDLANDS 5–4C

ADAM'S £99 5️⃣5️⃣4️⃣

16 WATERLOO ST B2 5UG 0121 643 3745

"Certainly Birmingham's No. 1 restaurant" – Adam & Natasha Stokes's "shining star of the city's dining scene" occupies a "contemporary looking, peaceful and calm" site that's "classy and comfortable, and – if lacking a picturesque view – buoyed by the happy contentment of diners". The "outstanding" food "continues to impress, with superb flavour combinations,

high quality sourcing, and real innovation – without resorting to gimmicks – to focus on letting ingredients shine". "An excellent wine list contains many top growths but also good wines at reasonable prices". "Service too hits a utopian balance of being professional but approachable and engaging". Its most dedicated fans are furthermore "amazed that it doesn't have another Michelin star" as they say "it is definitely deserving of at least two: I say that in comparison to the likes of The Fat Duck, Restaurant Gordon Ramsay and Simpson's, to name just a few!". The chef's table again comes recommended: "a magical experience of true theatre!" / www.adamsrestaurant.co.uk; @RestaurantAdams; 9.30 pm; booking max 10 may apply.

ASHA'S INDIAN BAR AND RESTAURANT £52 4️⃣4️⃣3️⃣

12-22 NEWHALL ST B3 3LX 0121 200 2767

"Still churning out excellent Indian food in Birmingham (the kebabs are particularly lovely)" – this well-liked Indian in the city-centre wins solidly good ratings all-round. It's part of the empire of well-known Indian singer and actor Asha Bhosle, which boasts 17 locations in five countries (the next of which in late 2018 is to be in Solihull's Touchwood centre). / www.ashasuk.co.uk; @ashasbirmingham; Sat & Sun 10 pm, Mon-Wed 10.30 pm, Thu & Fri 11 pm.

CARTERS OF MOSELEY £89 5️⃣4️⃣3️⃣

2C WAKE GREEN RD B13 9EZ 0121 449 8885

By all accounts "100% worth the trip to Birmingham", Carters' "pleasant informality" but "serious" 13-course tasting menus – "birch sap water", anyone? – "always make for a great night out" (kudos goes to the "charming staff"). When it comes to Brad Carter's cuisine: "so much work goes into each detail, and yet this is not style over substance: the core is original food, that works at every level. Taste, texture, visually, aroma. Course after course looks beautiful, but more importantly tastes unbelievably good!" / www.cartersofmoseley.co.uk; @cartersmoseley; 9 pm; closed Mon & Tue; children: 8+.

1847 3️⃣3️⃣3️⃣

26 GREAT WESTERN ARCADE B2 5HU 0121 236 2313

Opposite Snow Hill station, in the Great Western arcade, this bistro fixture (with a sibling in Manchester) is well worth knowing about if you're meat-free. "Mainly vegan food is attractively presented and very tasty even for non veggies". / www.by1847.com; Tue-Sat 10.30 pm, Mon 10 pm.

HARBORNE KITCHEN £45 5️⃣4️⃣4️⃣

B17 9QE 01214399150

"Fabulous, fun and inventive" meals appear from the "open-to-view kitchen" at Jamie Desogus's two-year-old in a former butcher's shop in a residential area. "It's run by a young but knowledgeable team whose enthusiasm

Adam's, Birmingham

is infectious" – and their ambition is clear in the multi-course tasting menus on offer, including an 'express' lunch consisting of a mere five courses, plus bread and snacks. / www.harbornekitchen.com; @harbornekitchen; Tue-Sat 11 pm.

JYOTI'S VEGETARIAN £24 4️⃣3️⃣2️⃣

1045 STRATFORD ROAD B28 8AS 0121 778 5501

This "lovely", humbly decorated Hall Green veggie is "a must-experience" – the sort of place "where carnivores don't miss the meat", and everyone (including TV chef Jamie Oliver) appreciates the "cheap" and "tasty" South indian victuals. / www.jyotis.co.uk; Wed-Sat 10 pm, Sun 7 pm; no Amex.

LASAN £63 4️⃣4️⃣3️⃣

3-4 DAKOTA BUILDINGS, JAMES STREET B3 1SD 0121 212 3664

"Not your typical curry house: this is fine dining Indian food!" – Jabbar Khan's contemporary Indian in the Jewellery Quarter may have lost its charismatic frontman Aktar Islam (see Opheem), but, boosted by its 2017 revamp, continues to win impressive ratings across the board. / www.lasan.co.uk; @lasan; Mon - Sat 11 pm, Sun 9 pm; no trainers.

OPHEEM £58

65 SUMMER ROW B3 1JJ 0121 201 3377

Aktar Islam left Lasan to strike out on his own at this 70-cover May 2018 newcomer. It opened too late for any survey feedback, but early reports online suggest it will rival his old gaff as Brum's foremost 'nouvelle Indian'. / opheem.com; Wed-Sat 9 pm, Sun 4 pm.

OPUS RESTAURANT £66 3️⃣4️⃣3️⃣

54 CORNWALL STREET B3 2DE 0121 200 2323

Finally liberated from the scaffolding and hoardings that had obliterated its front since 2015, this smart Colmore District brasserie is on the up; it garnered very impressive marks this year, if little in the way of commentary (beyond it being "perfect for business", and holding "very good special events"). / www.opusrestaurant.co.uk; @opuscornwallst; Mon-Sat 9 pm.

ORIGINAL PATTY MEN £29 `4` `3` `2`

9 SHAW'S PASSAGE B5 5JG 0121 643 2546

Birmingham's best burger spot, reputed not just for its pimped patties but also for its "very good" beers from local Siren Craft Brews; as of April 2018, it now has a new Scandi-style bar, 'Kilder', attached, which ups the list of brews and adds its own protein-centric British menu. / www.originalpattymen.com; @OriginalPattyM; Wed-Sat 11 pm, Sun 8 pm; no bookings.

PLOUGH £60 `3` `4` `4`

21 HIGH STREET B17 9NT 0121 427 3678

The decadent brunch (from bacon butties to tahini-topped granola) is the forte of this neighbourhood staple, though its up-to-date pub grub menu also stretches to stone-baked pizzas. "Gorgeous garden which is a gem in the summer". / www.theploughharborne.co.uk; @PloughHarborne; Mon-Sun 9.30 pm.

PURNELLS £96 `5` `4` `4`

55 CORNWALL ST B3 2DH 0121 212 9799

"Stunning…", "fantastic…", "exceptional every time…" – folks continue to be "blown away by the innovative cuisine" produced by TV-chef Glynn Purnell's luxurious 45-cover HQ, "in the smart city-centre business quarter". There are an array of menus on offer, with just tasting options available Friday lunch and Friday & Saturday evenings. / www.purnellsrestaurant.com; @purnellsrest; 9.30 pm; closed Mon, Sat L & Sun; children: 6+.

SABAI SABAI £41

8 WATERLOO STREET B2 5PG

Fourth and most ambitious of this Thai mini-chain, established in Moseley in 2003 – it occupies a large Grade II listed, city-centre property that once housed the Legal and General Assurance Society. It opened in late 2018 – limited feedback so far, but all positive. / Mon-Sun 9 pm.

SAN CARLO £54 `3` `3` `3`

4 TEMPLE STREET B2 5BN 0121 633 0251

The "busy and atmospheric" outpost of this glam national chain has been one of the city-centre's better-known destinations since it opened in the 1990s. A typical report: "it felt rather expensive for Birmingham, but the portions were generous and my seabass was very well cooked". / sancarlo.co.uk/restaurants/birmingham/; @SanCarlo_Group; Mon-Sat 10 pm, Sun 7.15 pm.

SIMPSONS £104 `4` `5` `3`

20 HIGHFIELD ROAD B15 3DU
0121 454 3434

A Midlands institution which has spent 25 years at the top of the gastronomic tree – this Edwardian villa is still the place to go for "a real treat" with "first class food" and "outstanding service" from "wonderful staff". A number of long-time customers rather regret the change to a simpler format: "the relaxed formal restaurant has been replaced by an OK Brasserie" – "…come on Simpsons, put back the white tablecloths!" / www.simpsonsrestaurant.co.uk; @simpsons_rest; Tue-Thu 9 pm, Fri & Sat 9.30 pm, Sun 2 pm. *Accommodation:* 4 rooms, from £160

TOM'S KITCHEN £57 `2` `2` `3`

53/57 WHARFSIDE STREET, THE MAILBOX B1 1RE 0121 289 5111

Mixed reviews on the first non-London outpost of this Tom Aikens-branded brasserie, bar and deli chain, at the city's Mailbox. Fans say it's a top cheap 'n' cheerful option (and tip it for breakfast) but sceptics say "it looks smart but is decent at best". / www.tomskitchen.co.uk; Mon-Fri 10 pm, Sat 10.30 pm, Sun 4 pm.

THE WILDERNESS £118 `5` `4` `3`

1 DUDLEY STREET B5 4EG 0121 643 2673

"A unique experience" – provocative chef Alex Claridge's dimly lit and theatrical two-year-old ("in a new semi-industrial venue" in the Jewellery Quarter) cold be a star in the making. "The food is absolutely stunning, and the drinks pairing innovative – not just wines, but a selection of cocktails and other beverages to create the best food/drink matches". "We had the extra course with ants... not totally convinced the ants were a great addition, but it did taste good". / wearethewilderness.co.uk; @thewildernessb5; Tue-Thu 10 pm, Fri & Sat 10.30 pm, Sun 9 pm.

EAT 17 £53

23 POTTER STREET CM23 3UH

Hackney comes to Hertfordshire at James Brundle and Chris O'Connor's November 2017 newcomer – outpost of the East London based business, blending artisan produce and a deli-vibe with a larger range provided by Spar. Early feedback is limited but all good. / www.eat17.co.uk.

THE COACH HOUSE NORBURY £53 `5` `3` `3`

NORBURY SY9 5DX 01588 650846

"A brilliant young chef is producing some incredible food: really tasty, original and beautifully presented" – Harry Bullock is said to be "a star of the future" by those who report on this restaurant-with-rooms: an eighteenth-century building in the beautiful Shropshire Hills. / www.coachhousenorbury.com; @norburycoach; Fri & Sat, Wed & Thu 8.30 pm, Sun 12 pm.

MALLORY COURT £89 `3` `2` `3`

HARBURY LANE CV33 9QB 01926 330214

"Delightful traditional dining with excellent food and certainly worthy of its awards" – so say fans of the oak-panelled dining room in this perhaps slightly sedate country house hotel (a Relais & Châteaux property) outside Leamington Spa. / www.mallory.co.uk; @mallorycourt; 2m S of Leamington Spa, off B4087; Mon-Sun 9.30 pm; no trainers. *Accommodation:* 31 rooms, from £159

HELEN BROWNING, THE ROYAL OAK £48 `4` `4` `4`

CUES LN SN6 8PP 01793 790 460

"A wonderful pub in the Wiltshire countryside, serving food from its parent farm down the road" and named for its owner, the chief exec of the Soil Association. "The menu is always changing as and when fresh produce is available and the food is always stunning": "great organic meat dishes" in particular (as you might hope!). "A pleasant outdoor eating area as well… when the sun shines!" (She also now has a Swindon chop house on Wood Street too). / www.royaloakbishopstone.co.uk; Mon-Sat 11 pm, Sun 10.30 pm.

KINLOCH HOUSE £84 `3` `4` `4`

PH10 6SG 01250 884 732

"Very smart, professional" and "well run" country-house hotel occupying a grand mansion (built in 1840), which serves "excellent", "traditional Scottish fayre" from "prime ingredients" (including famous soft fruits from nearby Blairgowrie and game bagged by shooting parties from around the world who stay in the hotel). / www.kinlochhouse.com; past the Cottage Hospital, turn L, procede 3m along A923, (signposted Dunkeld Road); 8.30 pm; no Amex; jacket required; children: 6 for dinner. *Accommodation:* 15 rooms, from £230

THE MOORINGS £49 `4` `3` `2`

HIGH STREET NR25 7NA 01263 740 054

"Incredibly fresh seafood" (plus local game and vegetables from their own garden) forms the backbone of the menu at this modest-looking bistro in a "lovely, tucked-away setting". Family-operated, it celebrates its twentieth anniversary this year. / www.blakeney-moorings.co.uk; Mon closed, Tue - Sat 10.30 pm, Sun closed; no Amex.

THE CURLEW £72 `4` `3` `4`

JUNCTION RD TN32 5UY 01580 861 394

Since a change of team, this remote coaching inn "has raised its game" winning only positive feedback this year for its "innovative menu with local ingredients": fans say it's "back to Michelin star standards". / www.thecurlewrestaurant.co.uk;

@thecurlewbodiam; 9.30 pm; closed Mon; booking max 4 may apply.

BOLLINGTON, CHESHIRE — 5–2B

THE LIME TREE £38 [3][4][4]

18-20 HIGH STREET SK10 5PH
01625 578182

Occupying two converted Victorian shops, and sourcing produce from the owner's farm in Macclesfield Forest, this appealing venue (with in-house baker) is "brilliant for Bollington". It's also "less crowded" than its more famous Didsbury sibling and "with easy parking nearby". / www.limetreebollington.co.uk; @thelimetreeres; Tue-Thu 10 pm, Fri & Sat 11 pm, Sun 6 pm.

BOLNHURST, BEDFORDSHIRE — 3–1A

THE PLOUGH AT BOLNHURST £57 [3][4][4]

MK44 2EX 01234 376274

This historic English pub with Tudor origins wins consistently high ratings for its modern European cooking, drawing a busy local crowd – "it's one of the best fusions of quality and value" hereabouts. / www.bolnhurst.com; @atBolnhurst; Mon-Sun 11 pm; no Amex.

BOLTON ABBEY, NORTH YORKSHIRE 5–1C

THE BURLINGTON AT THE DEVONSHIRE ARMS £95 [4][4][3]

BD23 6AJ 01756 718100

Another strong year for the flagship dining room of the Duke & Duchess of Devonshire's luxurious 17th century hotel, which enjoys a magnificent location "all set on the River Wharfe at Bolton Abbey". Paul Leonard's "fabulous" modern cuisine is consistently praised (be it the three-course à la carte or nine-course tasting menu) as is the "lovely" service. The cellar is of some renown here and numerous reporters nominate the wine here as the best they encountered this year. / www.thedevonshirearms.co.uk/home/dining/burlington/; @Dev_Hotels; 9pm; no trainers.

THE DEVONSHIRE BRASSERIE, THE DEVONSHIRE ARMS £49 [3][4][3]

BD23 6AJ 01756 718100

The more informal brasserie option at this pukka country retreat offers a cheaper perch from which to attack the renowned cellar here, and provides a big menu, ranging from posh daytime sandwiches to a range of steaks from the grill. Or there's the "lovely" Cocktail Lounge and Conservatory, where afternoon tea is "a great Yorkshire treat". / www.devonshirehotels.co.uk; @Dev_Hotels; on A59, 5m NE of Skipton; 9pm.

BOREHAM, ESSEX — 3–2C

THE LION INN £48 [3][3][3]

MAIN RD CM3 3JA 01245 394900

"Always busy", "very large" venue (with 23 bedrooms) serving "consistently excellent pub food". The outside area has gone recently: replaced by a 'Victorian-inspired' conservatory. / www.lioninnhotel.co.uk; Mon-Sat 9 pm; no Amex.
Accommodation: 15 rooms, from £105

BOUGHTON LEES, KENT — 3–3C

THE MANOR RESTAURANT, EASTWELL MANOR £77 [2][2][5]

EASTWELL PK TN25 4HR 01233 213000

Champneys has spent £12 million refurbishing this Elizabethan country house hotel since taking it over in 2016. Reports on the dining room were sparse this year: some suggest its standards generally "are not on a par" with the "stunning setting", but there were no serious complaints and fans declare its luxurious cuisine to be "excellent". / www.eastwellmanor.co.uk; @EastwellManor; 3m N of Ashford on A251; 9.30 pm; no jeans; booking max 8 may apply.
Accommodation: 62 rooms, from £180

BOUGHTON MONCHELSEA, KENT — 3–3C

THE MULBERRY TREE £41 [3][3][3]

HERMITAGE LN ME17 4DA 01622 749082

"It's easy to get lost when trying to find this restaurant" ("and even when you're close you may drive by mistaking it for a village house"). "But it's well worth the effort" truffling out this "hidden gem" – a "comfortable" and "friendly" location which "delivers quality food and service year after year". / www.themulberrytreekent.co.uk; @MulberryKent; 9 pm, Fri & Sat 9.30 pm; closed Mon & Sun D; no Amex.

BOURNEMOUTH, DORSET — 2–4C

ARBOR RESTAURANT, THE GREEN HOUSE HOTEL £59 [3][4][3]

4 GROVE RD BH1 3AX 01202 498900

Near the sea, this unusual hotel restaurant is a "real surprise in Bournemouth", with impeccable green credentials that span beehives on the roof, a tree mid-dining room and chairs made from recycled Playstations; despite these attractions, one reporter found the interior "rather dull", but even they thought "the food and service is compensation". / www.arbor-restaurant.co.uk; @arborrest.

CHEZ FRED £31 [4][4][2]

10 SEAMOOR RD BH4 9AN 01202 761023

"The best fish 'n' chips ever" – "fresh, moist, in a crispy batter", and served by "brisk and friendly staff" – wins adulation for Fred Capel and his team at this local legend, which "feels less claustrophobic now it's in bigger premises". / www.chezfred.co.uk; @ChezFredUK; 9 pm, Sun 8.30 pm; closed Sun L; no Amex; no bookings.

NO 34 £50

34 GERVIS ROAD BH1 3DH 01202 553737

Insufficient survey feedback so far for a rating on this dining room within a new contemporary hotel in Eastcliff. It looks as though it's a useful addition to the eating options in the area. / www.no34restaurant.co.uk/; 9; booking evening only.

WESTBEACH £56 [3][3][3]

PIER APPROACH BH2 5AA 01202 587785

A "very pleasant seaside café" a short drive from the centre of Bournemouth, with a deck right by the sand. Options range from breakfasts and light lunches, up to a £70+ seafood platter with a whole lobster. / www.west-beach.co.uk; @WestBeachBmouth; Sun & Mon 5 pm, Tue-Sat 11 pm.

BOURTON ON HILL, GLOUCESTERSHIRE — 2–1C

HORSE & GROOM £48 [3][2][2]

GL56 9AQ 01386 700413

"Handsome from the outside, and what you'd expect of a Cotswold gastropub inside" – this Georgian inn certainly looks the part. Since a 2016 takeover by the Old Amersham Hotels there's the odd fear it's "gone downhill since changing hands", but most reports continue to applaud very "decent" cooking – "all the favourites to a high standard". / www.horseandgroom.info; @thehorsegroom; Mon-Sat 11 pm; no Amex. Accommodation: 5 rooms, from £120

BOWDON, GREATER MANCHESTER — 5–2B

BORAGE £50 [4][4][3]

7 VALE VIEW, VICARAGE LANE WA14 3BD
0161 929 4775

"Innovative modern European cuisine executed to a very high standard" wins strong local praise for this mid-2017 newcomer (chef Mariusz Dobies, was formerly executive chef at Michael Caines in Manchester). "It's very reasonably priced – almost too cheap for what they do!" / www.boragebowdon.co.uk; @BorageBowdon; Wed-Sat 9 pm, Sun 8 pm.

BRACKLESHAM, WEST SUSSEX — 3–4A

BILLYS ON THE BEACH £49 [3][3][4]

BRACKLESHAM LANE PO20 8JH
01243 670373

"Right on the beach at Bracklesham Bay, with spectacular views of the Isle of Wight", this shack-like, "bustling licenced café" ("dog-friendly, child-friendly" and with a "potbelly stove that makes it cosy even in gales") is a "good family gaff". Round off "unusual" breakfasts, or a meal of local fish with a "bracing walk on the beach". / www.billysonthebeach.co.uk; @BillysontheBeach; Sun-Wed 5 pm, Thu-Sat 9 pm.

The Fat Duck, Bray

BRADFORD, WEST YORKSHIRE   5–1C

AKBAR'S   £33   4 2 3

1276 LEEDS RD BD3 8LF 01274 773311

"Outstanding and great value curry" again wins praise for this "consistently good", large outpost of a northern chain. / www.akbars.co.uk; @OfficialAkbars; Mon-Sat midnight, Sun 11.30 pm.

MUMTAZ   £31   5 3 2

**386-410 GREAT HORTON RD BD7 3HS
01274 571861**

"An institution that deserves its excellent reputation", this Kashmiri stalwart has expanded over 40 years from a Bradford street stall (on the same site) to the flagship of a curry brand with a venue in Leeds and a supermarket ready-meal factory. Fans insist: "you won't find a better Asian meal". / www.mumtaz.com; @Mumtaz; Sun-Thu midnight, Fri & Sat 1 am.

BRADWELL, DERBYSHIRE   5–2C

THE SAMUEL FOX COUNTRY INN   £54   4 3 3

STRETFIELD RD S33 9JT 01433 621 562

Chef/owner James Duckett's four-room inn is a great base for walking the Peaks – and then indulging in a "mouthwatering menu of delicious (and "reasonably priced") dishes" in the "informal" dining room. / www.samuelfox.co.uk; @SamuelFoxInn; Wed-Sat 11 pm, Sun 5.30 pm.

BRANCASTER STAITHE, NORFOLK   6–3B

THE JOLLY SAILORS   £35   3 3 3

PE31 8BJ 01485 210314

Over from the harbour and beach, this laidback 18th century boozer is "fun, fun, fun", with its "great family atmosphere" and "homemade stone-baked pizzas", washed down with their new cask beer, 'Lucky Lobster'. / www.jollysailorsbrancaster.co.uk; Mon-Thu 11 pm, Fri & Sat midnight, Sun 10.30 pm.

THE WHITE HORSE   £54   3 3 4

MAIN RD PE31 8BY 01485 210262

"What more could you ask for? The freshest of local fish cooked well and served in a lovely restaurant looking out on the best view of the north Norfolk coast". That's the appeal of this "unbeatable" and much commented-on coastal pub, with modern dining conservatory. / www.whitehorsebrancaster.co.uk; @whitehorsebranc; 9 pm.

BRAY, BERKSHIRE   3–3A

CALDESI IN CAMPAGNA   £77   3 4 4

OLD MILL LN SL6 2BG 01628 788500

"The courtyard is perfect in the summer" at Giancarlo & Katie Caldesi's "really lovely Tuscan restaurant" (which celebrated its tenth anniversary at the end of 2017 with a major revamp). "Super food is beautifully presented by attentive staff" in a setting designed "for your comfort"; "always reliable" and "very good for a celebratory meal". / www.caldesi.com; @CaldesiCampagna; Tue-Sat 11.30 pm, Sun 3.30 pm.

CROWN INN   £65   4 4 4

HIGH ST SL6 2AH 01628 621936

"Heston's concept here is 'pub food, done like you've never seen it done before', and it works, taking standard fare such as prawn cocktail, fish 'n' chips, even ploughman's lunch, and making them an experience". This beamed local in the centre of the village doesn't attract the volume of feedback of the Hind's Head, but for a more trad' experience, locals say it's "always good". / www.thecrownatbray.com; @TheCrownatBray; Mon-Thu 9.15 pm, Fri & Sat 9.45 pm, Sun 6 pm.

THE FAT DUCK   £396   3 4 3

HIGH ST SL6 2AQ 01628 580333

"How can anyone justify £325 for a tasting menu?… Without wine! But still, it's SO hard to get a booking anytime soon!". That's the conundrum in assessing Heston Blumenthal's world-famous venue, where the gulf between the 'ayes' and the 'nayes' grows ever-wider over the question of whether the "extortionate prices" are ultimately worth it for such "unmissable theatre" ("I didn't realise four hours could go by at a table with such enjoyment"). The 'ayes' still have it… if only just… reporting "an amazing adventure into a fantasy world": "an absolutely incredible and extremely personal experience" via an individual menu researched in advance around your memories that's "nothing less than magical". Many fans and foes alike, however, agree that the pricing for said trip "marks it down as a once-in-a-lifetime encounter" that's "too expensive to repeat". And amongst the growing number of sceptics – N.B. this year, for over 50% of reporters this was their vote as most overpriced meal of the year – there's some feeling that "after the latest reboot of the Fat Duck a couple of years ago, it has lost some of what made it great: dishes are avant garde purely for that purpose rather than previously when it was to make them more delicious". / www.thefatduck.co.uk; 9 pm; closed Mon & Sun.

THE HIND'S HEAD   £77   4 4 4

HIGH STREET SL6 2AB 01628 626151

"Heston B's version of pub food sets the bar high" and his "charming" Olde Englishe hostelry remains as "pleasingly professional" as ever: "it never lets you down". "It's a surprise as it's a pub" first and foremost, but the food is "fabulous", and even those who say "on paper it looked rather uninspiring" says "every dish tasted perfect". / www.hindsheadbray.com; Mon-Sat 9 pm, Sun 3.30 pm.

WATERSIDE INN   £152   5 5 5

FERRY RD SL6 2AT 01628 620691

"Heaven on earth" – Alain Roux's "superlative" institution is, for very many reporters, the country's leading temple of classic Gallic gastronomy. It helps it has a "gorgeous" Thames-side setting, with the possibility of starting off a summer meal with a glass of fizz and canapés on the beautiful outside terrace (or even a quick spin down the river in the restaurant's private launch). "The Roux chef who shuns the media produces traditional cuisine, but modernised to be lighter and healthier" [well, somewhat]. "It is a conservatively-slanted menu so there were no fireworks or innovation in terms of the dishes, but the quality of ingredients are second to none on earth" and results are "simply stunning". Unfortunately so are the prices – it is "frighteningly expensive" (and it is worth noting that the 'rapport prix/qualité' was questioned a bit more often this year). Intrinsic to the experience is the "unparalleled" service from "some of the best staff in hospitality" – a team that "has no swagger, but is all class" ("an astounding feeling of style, without being overbearing or pompous"). In May 2018 as our survey was concluding, Diego Masciaga, part of the fixtures and fittings for the last 30 years and probably the most popular maitre d' in the UK retired, leaving Frédéric Poulette the unenviable task of following in his footsteps. / www.waterside-inn.co.uk; @rouxwaterside; off A308 between Windsor & Maidenhead; 9.30 pm; closed Mon & Tue; no jeans; booking max 10 may apply; children: 9. **Accommodation:** 11 rooms, from £240

BREARTON, NORTH YORKSHIRE   5–1C

THE MALT SHOVEL   £51   3 4 3

HG3 3BX 01423 862929

A "consistently good" rustic-chic inn dating back to the 16th century; "the food is well-presented and flavoursome" and there's a "warm welcome" to go with it (backed up by the roaring fire). / www.themaltshovelbrearton.co.uk; @BleikerFamily; off A61, 6m N of Harrogate; Tue-Sat 9 pm, Sun 3 pm.

BRECON, POWYS 2–1A

THE FELIN FACH GRIFFIN £41 **4 3 4**

FELIN FACH LD3 0UB 01874 620111

"An oasis at the foot of the magnificent Brecon Beacons" – this well-known gastropub (on the site of an old cider mill) has been a foodie feature of the area for decades – a "busy venue (book ahead)", with food that's "consistently excellent". / www.eatdrinksleep.ltd.uk; @felinfachgriff; 20 mins NW of Abergavenny on A470; Mon-Sat midnight, Sun 11 pm.
Accommodation: 7 rooms, from £115

BRENTWOOD, ESSEX 3–2B

ALEC'S £76 **2 3 2**

NAVESTOCK SIDE CM14 5SD
01277 375 696

"There's plenty of room to park the white Range!", at this "very smart" (glitzy) smartened-up former pub – all white tablecloths and bright pink chairs – "a magnet for the TOWIE set". It divided views more this year as ratings declined: fans still applaud its "great seafood" and say "it's unsurprising that it's always full", but others feel "it used to be good but has gone downhill"; and are increasingly "horrified by the prices". / www.alecsrestaurant.co.uk; @Alecsrestaurant; Wed-Sat, Tue midnight, Sun 7 pm; no Amex; credit card deposit required to book; children: 12+.

BRIDPORT, DORSET 2–4B

DORSHI £25 **4 3 4**

6 CHANCERY LANE DT6 3PX 01308 423221

"The best Asian dumplings and a great night out" (with some delicious cocktails) are to be had at this buzzing haunt, discovered down a narrow alleyway, which brings a Shoreditch pop-up-turned-permanent vibe to sleepy Dorset. / dorshi.co.uk; @eatdorshi.

BRIGHTON, EAST SUSSEX 3–4B

BASKETMAKERS ARMS £43 **3 2 4**

12 GLOUCESTER RD BN1 4AD
01273 689006

This "real olde worlde", low-ceiled Victorian boozer on a corner in the North Laine area serves up some of "Brighton's best traditional pub food, year after year". / www.basket-makers-brighton.co.uk/; Mon-Thu 10 pm, Fri & Sat 10.30 pm, Sun 9 pm; no bookings.

BINCHO YAKITORI £35 **4 2 2**

63 PRESTON STREET BN1 2HE
01273 779021

"Stunning yakitori and charcoal grilled goodies" again win high praise for David Miney's izakaya (a favourite hangout for local chefs, apparently). Surroundings are "cramped" and service can be "haphazard" but "you soon forget about this when you taste the delicious Japanese BBQ". / www.binchoyakitori.com; @BinchoYakitori; Tue-Thu, Sun 10 pm, Fri & Sat 10.30 pm.

BURGER BROTHERS £13 **5 4 2**

97 NORTH RD BN1 1YE 01273 706980

"It's small, it doesn't do fries, and there are only about 5 seats," – it's mainly a take-away – but this "busy", "fun" and friendly North Laine joint "does do truly delicious amazing burgers" (they're former winners of the 'Britain's Best Burger' competition). / @BurgerBrethren; Mon-Thu 10 pm, Fri & Sat 10.30 pm, Sun 9.30 pm; no bookings.

THE CHILLI PICKLE £49 **4 3 3**

17 JUBILEE ST BN1 1GE 01273 900 383

"Excellent Indian food and sensible prices" – and with a culinary style that's "different from the usual flock wallpaper fare" ("the menu originates firmly in India instead of in the British curry house vein") – helps ensure that this "tried and tested" Arts Quarter venture remains one of the most commented-on destinations in town. That it's "a bit noisy" and "barn-like" is arguably part of its "very enjoyable" style. / www.thechillipickle.com; @TheChilliPickle; Wed-Sat 10.30 pm, Mon & Tue 10 pm, Sun 9.30 pm.

LA CHOZA HOVE £31 **4 3 3**

WESTERN ROAD BN1 2AA 01273 325444

"Fun Mexican, a notch above nearby chains" – this two-storey Hove newcomer is larger than its six-year-old sibling on Gloucester Road in North Laine, and also takes bookings (at the original it's just for larger parties). You can also just roll up for drinks here (there's an extensive mescal list). / lachoza.co.uk; @LaChozaHove.

CIN CIN £42 **4 3 3**

13-16 VINE ST BN1 4AG 01273 698813

A visit to this tiny ex-garage is "just fantastic fun"… "You sit at a bar up close and personal with other diners and enjoy the finest antipasti and pasta Brighton has to offer, prepared and cooked right in front of you". Newly sporting a Bib Gourmand, it also spawned a Hove spin-off on Western Road in January 2018, with a larger kitchen and more ambitious menu. / www.cincin.co.uk; @CinCinUK; Mon-Fri 5.30 pm, Sat 6 pm, Sun 4.30 pm.

THE COAL SHED £61 **3 3 3**

8 BOYCES ST BN1 1AN 01273 322998

"Top meat on the south coast", say fans of Dave Mothersill's original industrial-style grill operation (now with an offshoot in London as well as a fish-specialist sibling in Brighton), praised for its "superb steaks and burgers", plus "wonderful cocktails". / www.coalshed-restaurant.co.uk; @thecoalshed1; Sun-Thu 10 pm, Fri & Sat 10.30 pm.

CURRY LEAF CAFE £41 **3 4 3**

60 SHIP ST BN1 1AE 01273 207070

A "very relaxed Lanes curry house with an interesting menu" that explores south Indian cuisine, plus a good selection of craft beer. "It's not a posh joint but the smiling service helps make it a great place to visit." Launched in 2014, it now has a Kemptown offshoot and a kiosk at the station. / www.curryleafcafe.com; @curryleafcaff; 10 pm, Fri - Sat 10.30pm.

DONATELLO £32 **2 3 3**

1-3 BRIGHTON PL BN1 1HJ 01273 775477

"If you want huge portions of tasty Italian food" all at affordable prices, this stalwart of the Lanes is "hard to beat". In particular it's "a great place to take the kids" – staff are "friendly" and "families are welcome". / www.donatello.co.uk; @donatello__; Mon-Sat 11.30 pm, Sun 10 pm; no Amex.

DRAKES OF BRIGHTON £69 **4 4 3**

43 - 44 MARINE PARADE BN2 1PE
01273 696934

"For years this was Brighton's standout special occasion venue", and although this Kemptown boutique hotel has more rivals nowadays, it's "still absolutely brilliant"…"just think how lovely it would be if it weren't in a basement!" / drakesofbrighton.com/restaurant; @drakeshotel; Sat & Sun, Mon-Fri 9 pm; children: 8. *Accommodation:* 20 rooms, from £115

ENGLISH'S £54 **3 3 4**

29-31 EAST ST BN1 1HL 01273 327980

"This revered traditional fish restaurant" – a Lanes fixture in the Leigh-Jones family since 1945 (but actually established in the 1890s) wins high praise for its "gorgeous seafood" and "continued high standards". "Not as formal as it looks, and kids are well looked after" – "excellent value half lobster on the children's menu is great for promoting more adventurous eating". / www.englishs.co.uk; @englishsoB; 10 pm.

ETCH £83 **5 4 4**

216 CHURCH RD BN3 2DJ 01273 227485

"Right at the top of the vibrant Brighton food scene", chef Steven Edwards is now earning high acclaim for the tasting menus at his debut venture in Hove. "On our second visit, six courses had grown to eight for the same price – and all were very good". A former Masterchef: The Professionals winner, Edwards showcases local Sussex produce – "it's always good to hear them explain the details of the food". / www.etchfood.co.uk; @EtchFood; Sun & Mon 10.45 pm, Tue-Sat midnight.

FATTO A MANO £39 **3 3 3**

77 LONDON RD BN1 4JF 01273 600621

The superlative wood-fired Neapolitan pizzas are "good value" and "great for people with kids" at this bustling operation; in summer 2018, following a Hove spin-off, it spawned a North Laine sibling on the corner of Kensington Gardens. / www.fattoamanopizza.com/; @fattoamanopizza; Sun-Wed 5 pm, Thu-Sat 9 pm; may need 6+ to book.

FOOD FOR FRIENDS £43 442

17-18 PRINCE ALBERT ST BN1 1HF 01273 202310

"Super-busy" these days, this "closely packed" Lanes fixture has become a "veggie paradise" since opening almost 40 years ago, earning high ratings for meat-free and vegan dishes that please open-minded omnivores almost as much as its most natural audience. / foodforfriends.com; @FoodforFriends; 10 pm, Fri & Sat 10.30 pm; no booking, Sat L & Sun L.

THE GINGER DOG £50 333

12 COLLEGE PL BN2 1HN   01273 620 990

The canine-friendly (hence the name) Kemptown outpost of the local Gingerman Group continues to win solid all-round ratings; a new Ginger link, tapas bar 'Flint House', is set to open in the newest Lane – the upcoming Hannington Estate – in January 2019. / www.gingermanrestaurants.com; @GingerDogDish; off Eastern Road near Brighton College; Mon-Sat 10 pm, Sun 5 pm.

THE GINGER PIG £56 443

3 HOVE ST BN3 2TR   01273 736123

"Not overly precious, but beautiful cooking" (and in "generous portions") is the hallmark of this "always dependable", "helpful and friendly" Hove gastroboozer from the local Gingerman group. A recent "refit has made the interior more modern", as well as adding 11 boutique bedrooms upstairs. / www.thegingerpigpub.com; @gingerpigdish; 10 pm, Sun 9 pm; no trainers.

GINGERMAN £58 454

21A NORFOLK SQ BN1 2PD   01273 326688

"This tiny stalwart" just up from the sea front is "always popular and deservedly so". "Cosy but not stuffy, it has a lovely atmosphere and booking is a must" given the allure of its consistently "imaginative and skilful" cuisine. It's been "a fixture of the local food scene" for 20 years, with founders Ben and Pamela McKellar opening a series of spin-off Gingers – Dog, Pig and Fox. Scheduled to open soon are Flint House tapas in the Lanes and Ginger Fish in the new Soho House Brighton. / www.gingermanrestaurant.com; @thegingerchef; 9.45 pm; closed Mon.

INDIAN SUMMER £50 443

69 EAST ST BN1 1HQ   01273 711001

With its "fabulous-looking and gorgeous-tasting food", this "lovely" Lanes curry house is "not just a step up from the average Indian, it's a leap, hop and long-distance jump!". / www.indiansummerbrighton.co.uk; @indiansummer108; Mon-Sat 10.30 pm, Sun 10 pm.

ISAAC@ £77 443

2 GLOUCESTER STREET BN1 4EW 07765 934740

"A young team who know their stuff serve locally sourced ingredients with the utmost care, in new and exciting combinations, supported by an all British wine list" at Isaac Bartlett-Copeland's Scandi-esque North Laine "gem". "Well worth a train rip to the coast – if this place was in London, it would be utterly mobbed!" / www.isaac-at.com; @Isaac_at; Tue-Sat 10.30 pm.

IYDEA £21 332

17 KENSINGTON GARDENS BN1 4AL 01273 667 992

A "lovely" but no-frills veggie café, in North Laine, whose "huge portions" (choose a main, two sides and toppings of your choice) and "friendly staff" make it a real hit with the student population – plus others who "wish it was nearer!" / www.iydea.co.uk; @iydea; Mon-Fri 7.30 pm, Sat & Sun 10 pm; no Amex.

LITTLE FISH MARKET £72 553

10 UPPER MARKET ST BN3 1AS 01273 722213

"Fish so fresh that it's almost swimming onto the plate is treated with the utmost care, and served in beautiful combinations that show it off to its best advantage" at Duncan Ray's "intimate" 20-cover venue – "one to seek out in Hove". "First class service" too ("couldn't have been more helpful and flexible with my various food likes/dislikes and the end result was excellent"). "If this place was in London, you'd never get a table (as it is, it's tough!)" / www.thelittlefishmarket.co.uk; Tue-Sat 10.30 pm.

MURMUR £47 354

91-96 KINGS ROAD ARCHES BN1 1NB 01273 711 900

"A newcomer from the people behind 64 Degrees, whose great beach side setting makes it a favourite in good weather", when you can "sit outside, dining al fresco on the seafront, watching the world go by". "A limited modern menu" ("more approachable than that at 64 Degrees") is "well executed" – it's "slightly pricey but forgiven because of the simply fantastic service". / @Murmur_Beach; Wed & Thu 2.30 pm, Fri & Sat 9 pm, Sun 2 am.

PASCERE £65 232

8 DUKE ST BN1 1AH   01273 917 949

This "ambitious" Lanes yearling is by most accounts a "good all-rounder", with "reliable if not particularly memorable cooking". The problem is that it's "highly touted", and "though pleasant, doesn't fully live up to the hugely impressive press accolades: could the owner's role as food and drink editor of Sussex's Platinum Business Magazine have something to do with the positive press coverage…" / www.pascere.co.uk; @pascerebrighton; Tue-Sat 9.30 pm.

PETIT POIS £32 334

70 SHIP STREET BN1 1AE   01273 911211

"A busy and buzzy little spot just off the seafront" where "French bistro-style food" is served as "generous small plates" so "you can try a couple of extra dishes" all at "very fair prices". / petitpoisbrighton.co.uk; Mon-Sat 9.30 pm, Sun 4 pm.

PIKE + PINE £79 232

1D ST JAMES'S STREET BN2 1RE 01273 686668

"A coffee shop by day and a restaurant by night" – Matt Gillan has carved a major foodie reputation for this Kemptown venue, where he and his team deliver dishes across a marble-top counter. After an impressive debut, ratings have dipped however – "the café-style setting shows in the evening" and when it comes to the food, even those who acknowledge some of its virtues feel that "for £50/head it would be a good meal, but at the £150/head we paid, it was a disappointment". / www.pikeandpine.co.uk; @PikeandPine_at.

PLATEAU £73 332

1 BARTHOLOMEWS BN1 1HG 01273 733 085

An exposed-brick indie with a winning formula of social dining based on small plates and unusual natural wines; there's a focus on pescatarian eating and – for those who'd rather not tangle forks – also a range of mains. / www.plateaubrighton.co.uk; Sun-Wed 10 pm, Thu-Sat 10.30 pm.

POLPO £48 223

20 NEW RD BN1 1UF   01273 697 361

The South Coast outpost of Russell Norman's "relaxed" small plates Venetian tapas chain has outperformed sister ventures in Bristol and Exeter, which closed down quickly. Feedback here is mixed though: fans claim "every mouthful is delicious", while critics – "expecting more of Polpo" – found the food "average to good, but nothing to be wowed by". / www.polpo.co.uk; @Polpo; 11 pm, Sun 10.30 pm.

THE REGENCY RESTAURANT £41 333

131 KINGS RD BN1 2HH   01273 325014

"The freshest of fish and shellfish" are "served without fuss by friendly staff" in "the heartiest of portions" at this 1930s chippie on the seafront: to many "Brighton's best fish 'n' chips by far" (of the "classic" variety, "but not just cod and haddock: lobster, skate, oysters… you name it"). / www.theregencyrestaurant.co.uk; 10 pm. *Accommodation:* 30 rooms, from £50

RIDDLE & FINNS £53 443

12B MEETING HOUSE LN BN1 1HB 01273 821218

With its candlelit communal high tables, eating at this Lanes oyster bar is a "unique experience", combining "great decor and ambience",

The Salt Room,
Brighton

"brilliantly fresh fish and seafood" and "attentive staff". (There's nowadays a spinoff venue in the arches along the beach promenade – see also). / www.riddleandfinns.co.uk; @RiddleandFinns1; Mon-Sun 11 pm; no bookings.

RIDDLE & FINNS ON THE BEACH £54 3️⃣4️⃣4️⃣

139 KINGS ROAD ARCHES BN1 2FN 01273 721667

"A splendid selection of seafood, generous portions and good service" earn solid ratings for this offshoot of the well-established Lanes oyster bar, in a "great location" with sea views under the promenade. Although the food is good-not-stellar, there's a "huge variety" of cooking methods to choose from: "all the standard European ways, but also sashimi, Middle Eastern, bouillabaisse (maybe not 100% authentic, but really good)", and "prices are keen for what you get". / www.riddleandfinns.co.uk; @riddleandfinns1; Sun-Fri 10 pm, Sat 11 pm.

THE SALT ROOM £65 4️⃣3️⃣4️⃣

106 KINGS ROAD BN1 2FA 01273 929 488

With its "great location on the seafront, with a bank of windows overlooking the sea affording fantastic views" and outside terrace – the city's most commented-on dining destination is, say fans, "an absolute must do for any visitor", delivering "beautiful and inventive British cuisine, with an emphasis on fresh seafood". "London prices" sap some enthusiasm however, leaving to the odd accusation that it's been too "hyped", but some cognoscenti tip that "the set menus (lunch and pre theatre) are much more reasonable that the more costly à la carte". / www.saltroom-restaurant.co.uk; @TheSaltRoomUK; Mon-Sun 10 pm.

SET, UNIQUE HOTEL £65 4️⃣3️⃣3️⃣

33 REGENCY SQUARE BN1 2GG 01273 855572

Dishes at this edgy former pop-up now attached to a hip boutique hotel are "intricate but powerful constructions". There's "little choice" available – just a list of set menus (although there are more options in the adjoining Set bar) – but they have "the confidence not to over-elaborate". "Sit at the pass if you can to get a great view of the tiny kitchen and learn more from the chefs about the preparation of your dishes". / www.thesetrestaurant.com; @theset_brighton; Mon-Sun 10.30 pm.

SILO £40 3️⃣2️⃣2️⃣

39 UPPER GARDNER ST, NORTH LAINE BN1 4AN 01273 674 259

Despite publically bemoaning that he's had to 'dumb down' his food to draw locals, chef Dougie McMaster's waste-free North Laine spot continues to win warm reviews, for "amazing-looking and -tasting healthy plates" ("lovely balance of taste and texture without overdoing things") that "leave you wanting more" (…although not always in a good way). / www.silobrighton.com; @SiloBrighton; Wed & Thu 9 pm, Fri & Sat 9.30 pm, Sun 3.30 pm.

64 DEGREES £50 5️⃣4️⃣3️⃣

53 MEETING HOUSE LANE BN1 1HB 01273 770 115

"It's great sitting at the pass watching the chefs" at (Great British Menu 2017 winner) Michael Bremner's compact small-plates restaurant with open kitchen, which fans feel is "Brighton's most adventurous restaurant by quite some way". "Great combinations in sharing plate form are often classic (e.g. fettuccini with egg yolk and truffle) but the flavours are always amazing". / www.64degrees.co.uk; @chef64degrees; 9.45 pm.

SMALL BATCH COFFEE £10 3️⃣4️⃣4️⃣

17 JUBILEE ST BN1 1GE 01273 697597

Now with eight branches – plus a truck by Hove station for caffeine-craving commuters – this decade-old coffee chain remains the top dog locally for its impressive selection of beans and "welcoming" staff. The branch listed is the flagship, home to al fresco seating and their barista training lab. / www.smallbatchcoffee.co.uk; @SmallBatchCR; Mon-Sat 7 pm, Sun 6 pm; no bookings.

TERRE Ã TERRE £54 5️⃣4️⃣3️⃣

71 EAST ST BN1 1HQ 01273 729051

This "iconic vegetarian", founded 25 years ago, is "still the best veggie restaurant in the country" – its "extraordinary", "original and inventive" global-fusion cooking being "worth a special trip to Brighton", even for omnivores. Top Tip: "afternoon tea of savoury buns, muffins, sweet cakes and scones – all stunningly presented and described in extravagant tongue-in-cheek detail – tastes as good as it looks!" / www.terreaterre.co.uk; @TerreaTerre; 10.30 pm, Sat 11 pm, Sun 10 pm; booking max 8 may apply.

URCHIN £45 3️⃣3️⃣3️⃣

15-17 BELFAST ST BN3 3YS 01273 241881

Its simple, shellfish-centric menu may be "relatively unsophisticated", but this relaxed corner gastroboozer (points for the handsome rope-hung pendant lights) "never puts a foot wrong", with appealing al fresco seating and craft beers (from the new basement micro-brewery) among its assets. / www.urchinpub.wordpress.com/; @urchinpub; Mon-Thu 11 pm, Fri & Sat midnight, Sun 10.30 pm.

BRILL, BUCKINGHAMSHIRE 2–1D

POINTER £73 3️⃣4️⃣3️⃣

27 CHURCH ST HP18 9RT 01844 238339

"A warm atmosphere with comfortable seating, elegant bar and roaring fires" means this classic, quality gastropub-with-rooms in rural north Bucks "ticks all the boxes" (it even has its own farm and butcher), and it inspires a lot of feedback. Even one or two reporters who suggest it is "not quite up to all the hype" still rate the cooking as good. / www.thepointerbrill.co.uk; Tue-Thu 11 pm, Fri & Sat midnight, Sun 10 pm.

BRISTOL, CITY OF BRISTOL 2–2B

ADELINA YARD £55 4️⃣4️⃣3️⃣

QUEEN QUAY, WELSH BACK BS1 4SL 0117 911 2112

"A tiny restaurant close to Bristol Docks and Old Town", offering "really smart and imaginative cooking, which gets the best from top-quality ingredients", and which wins consistent high praise for this three-year-old from chefs Jamie Randall & Olivia Barry, who paid their dues in some of London's sharpest kitchens (Galvin Bistro Deluxe; Corrigan's). Top Tip: "if their fermented kale dish is on the menu, go for it!". / www.adelinayard.com; @AdelinaYard; Sun-Wed 11 pm, Fri & Sat 1 am, Thu midnight.

BELL'S DINER AND BAR ROOMS £52 4️⃣4️⃣4️⃣

1 YORK RD BS6 5QB 0117 924 0357

A "Bristol classic" – founded in 1976 and forerunner of the city's booming small independents gastro scene – this charmingly boho Montpelier spot is back on top form under the ownership of local mover-and-shaker Connie Coombes. It's "the absolute epitome of a neighbourhood bistro – Alice Waters (of iconic Chez Panisse in California) would feel immensely at home". / www.bellsdiner.com; Tue-Sat 10 pm.

BELLITA £45 4️⃣3️⃣2️⃣

34 COTHAM HILL BS6 6LA 0117 923 8755

The "cool" younger sister of beloved Bell's Diner – and also nodding to North Africa and Spain – steps out of its sibling's shadow with "absolutely brilliant" food and "great drinks" (perhaps the result of its unusual policy of only featuring women winemaker's on its list). A refurb' is on the cards, with Bellita set to feature on the Beeb's 'Project Interiors', a kind of GBBO for designers due in spring 2019. /

www.bellita.co.uk; @BellitaBristol; Thu-Sat, Tue, Wed 11 pm.

BIRCH £51

47 RALEIGH RD BS3 1QS 01179 028 326

Sam Leach & Beccy Massy turned this ex-office in Southville into one of the city's best-loved small plates spots – only to sell up in summer 2018 to focus on cider-making. Having reopened in August under new boss Tom Masters, its sharing ethos remains intact, but we've removed the rating for the time being. / www.birchbristol.co; Tue-Sat 10 pm, Sun 4 pm.

BOSCO PIZZERIA £42 333

96 WHITELADIES RD BS8 2QX 01179 737 978

Launched in 2014, and since joined by a sibling in Clifton Village, this Neapolitan-style pizza parlour is now a local staple, turning out puffy, chewy, scorched wood-fired pies (the main event) but also superior antipasti, polenta chips and Italian stews. / www.boscopizzeria.co.uk; @boscopizzeria; 10 pm; may need + to book.

BOX-E £46 444

UNIT 10, CARGO 1, WAPPING WHARF BS1 6WP

This "fantastic little restaurant in a shipping container overlooking the waterfront" seats 14 diners plus four at the bar, treating them to food that is "simply wonderful, deeply flavoursome and succulent". Chef Elliott Lidstone returned to his native West Country after successful stints at The Empress in Hackney and L'Ortolan in Reading. / www.boxebristol.com; @boxebristol; Wed-Sat, Tue 9.30 pm.

BRAVAS £38 344

7 COTHAM HILL BS6 6LD 0117 329 6887

"Lovely tapas" and a "buzzy" style win praise for Kieran and Imogen Waite's "busy", "cheap 'n' cheerful" tapas bar on Cotham Hill. / www.bravas.co.uk; @bravasbristol; Mon-Wed 11 pm, Thu-Sat midnight.

BULRUSH £57 542

21 COTHAM ROAD SOUTH BS6 5TZ 0117 329 0990

"Ssssh... don't tell anyone!". George Livesey and Katherine Craughwell's "real Bristolian gem" occupies a "simple and unpretentious setting" (formerly a greengrocers) which "belies the sophistication of its cooking": "exquisitely beautiful dishes" – a "clever, tasty blend of familiar ingredients mixed with foraged products" – at "astonishing value" prices; "super helpful staff" too, "all with no pretension". / www.bulrushrestaurant.co.uk; @bulrushbs6; Thu-Sat, Tue, Wed 8.30 pm.

CASAMIA, THE GENERAL £160 555

GUINEA ST BS1 6SY 0117 959 2884

"By far the best that Bristol has to offer" and still one of the country's most sought-after dining destinations; the Sanchez-Iglesias family's "beacon of creative cuisine" nowadays occupies the ground floor of the city-centre's redeveloped old General Hospital (below 200 luxury flats). The tasting menu shows "an attention to detail you don't see in other fine dining restaurants" and "watching the teamwork in the open kitchen is amazing". The cooking is intricate, with "lots of flavours on the plate". But, perhaps "it's the theatre and introduction by the chefs that really rounds off the experience". Even the establishment's most ardent fans, though, can "object to FULL payment at the time of booking". To reserve you buy a ticket: tickets are released four months in advance [!], on the first Tuesday of each month at 'noon UK time'. Drinks and other extras are then paid-for after the meal. / www.casamiarestaurant.co.uk; @casamia_; Wed-Sat 8.15 pm; no Amex.

CLIFTON SAUSAGE £55

7 PORTLAND ST BS8 4JA 0117 9731192

Est 2002 – this contemporary café majors in various types of banger, but also serves a selection of (mostly meaty) British dishes. No ratings this year as we lacked sufficient feedback, but good reports on its Bath spin-off (see also). / www.cliftonsausage.co.uk; @cliftonsausage; Mon-Thu 10 pm, Fri & Sat 10.30 pm, Sun 9.30 pm.

FLOUR & ASH £39 432

230B CHELTENHAM RD BS6 5QX 0117 908 3228

Going solo and from strength to strength after the owners closed their Westbury-on-Trym spin-off in 2017 – a "buzzy" and locally celebrated yet "down-to-earth" spot offering "brilliant pizzas cooked in the wood-fired oven and a great range of ices with unusual flavour combinations". / www.flourandash.co.uk; Tue-Sat 10 pm, Sun 5 pm.

HARI KRISHNANS KITCHEN £33 333

31A ZETLAND ROAD BS6 7AH 01179 422 299

"Very different from your usual curry house", an "excellent Southern Indian" whose Keralan dishes are "aromatic and delicately blended"; "service and ambience are all pretty standard", though. / harikrishnanskitchen.info/zetland/; Tue-Fri 11 pm, Sat & Sun midnight.

THE IVY CLIFTON BRASSERIE £56 234

42-44 CALEDONIA PLACE BS8 4DN 0117 203 4555

"An attractively spacious and opulent" former bank building in Clifton VIllage, provides the venue for this branch of the glossy London celeb-haunt. In year two of is operation, it's maintained OK ratings, with the general view being that it offers "an enjoyable experience, even if it's also an expensive one". / theivycliftonbrasserie.com; @ivycliftonbrass; Mon-Sun 12.30 am.

LIDO £55 335

OAKFIELD PL BS8 2BJ 0117 933 9533

"Stunning by night when lights twinkle on the water and swimmers glide by" – this "unique" Clifton venue occupies a Victorian Egyptian-style swimming pool whose viewing gallery is now an accomplished Spanish-North African restaurant run by ex-Moro chef Freddie Bird, with a "great tapas menu served downstairs" in the poolside bar. The outdoor heated pool is members-only, but diners can book a swim-and-eat package to work up an appetite before their meal. / www.lidobristol.com; @lidobristol; Mon-Wed 11 pm, Thu-Sat midnight; no Amex.

LOCKSIDE £42 322

NO.1 BRUNEL LOCK ROAD BS1 6XS 0117 9255 800

"Well-positioned close to the river/harbour", this "friendly and pleasant" former transport caff – a "quirky railway-carriage-shaped place" with views up to Clifton Suspension Bridge – is "definitely not your traditional greasy spoon" nowadays, and is, say fans, home to "the best breakfast in Bristol", earning good ratings for its "freshly cooked" fare. The "inviting" menu features five varieties of bubble & squeak, including smoked salmon or asparagus and accompanied by pesto or hollandaise sauce. / www.lockside.net; Mon-Sun 4 pm.

THE MINT ROOM £58 433

12-16 CLIFTON RD BS8 1AF 01173 291 300

"Indian food on another level" wins high praise for this "stylish" operation in Clifton which is "smarter than your average Indian, and, though pricey, worth every penny". The cooking is "spicy but not too hot, so all the flavours are discernible". "And they do an amazing vegetarian" option. / www.themintroom.co.uk/bristol; @TheMintRoom; Mon-Sat 11 pm, Sun 9 pm.

NO MAN'S GRACE £52

BS6 6PE 07436 588273

John Watson has established this Redland venture as another reason to visit Chandos Road with his "truly wonderful five course feasts". In August 2018, however, he put the restaurant on the market to concentrate on his young family, and its outlook is currently uncertain. / www.nomansgrace.com; @NoMansGrace; Wed & Thu 11 pm, Fri & Sat midnight, Sun 6 pm.

OTIRA & CHANDOS SOCIAL £54 544

5-7 CHANDOS ROAD BS6 6PG 0117 973 3669

"This warm and charming new venture, from a well-travelled Antipodean chef, is a fantastic addition to Redland's Chandos Road, which already boasts a few amazing venues". Stephen Gilchrist (with help from his British partner Kathryn Curtis) serves some "inspired food combinations and all are delicious and perfectly cooked". "You can eat in the restaurant or the next-door tapas bar. Both offer original ideas which are superbly executed and presented. Five visits, and everything was simply exceptional!" / www.otira.co.uk/; Mon-Sat 9.30 pm, Sun 4 pm.

PACO TAPAS, THE GENERAL £51 544

LOWER GUINEA ST BS1 6SY
0117 925 7021

"A fantastic find. We liked it so much we went straight back the next week!". Peter Sanchez-Iglesias's tapas bar – named after his dad, who is part of the team – wins extravagant praise for its "great small plates", "variety of choice", "knowledgeable staff" and "laid-back atmosphere". It's tipped as a good place to take kids too. Top Tip: "ask for a table where you can watch the chefs doing their stuff". / www.sanchez-brothers.co.uk; @PacoTapas_; Tue-Sat 10 pm.

PASTA LOCO £58 433

37A COTHAM HILL BS6 6JY 0117 973 3000

Cousins Ben Harvey & Dominic Borel have made a big impact since opening their Cotham venture two years ago (voted Best Italian in Bristol's Good Food Awards 2018): a professional operation with a "wide range of interesting and innovative" pasta options. (Their follow-up, Pasta Ripiena – Britain's first ravioli restaurant – opened a year ago to equal acclaim, with Ben's brother Joe, ex-Bell's Diner and Bellita, running the kitchen). / www.pastaloco.co.uk; @pasta_loco/; Mon-Sat 10 pm.

PASTURE £43

2 PORTWALL LANE BS1 6NB 07741 193445

On the Redcliffe site that was formerly Byzantium (RIP), chef/patron Sam Elliot's early 2018 newcomer opened too late to inspire any survey feedback. With its in-house butcher and emphasis on fire-based grills, early social media and press reports suggest that especially if you are a meat-lover, you should definitely give it a whirl. / www.pasturerestaurant.com; @pasture_bristol; Mon-Sat 10.30 pm, Sun 5 pm.

THE PUMP HOUSE £49 333

MERCHANTS ROAD BS8 4PZ
0117 927 2229

"What a lovely place" – this Victorian pumping station in Hotwells that once powered Bristol harbour's hydraulic bridges was converted into a gastropub twelve years ago by Toby Gritten, formerly of local landmark Bell's Diner. A perfect spot for a meal, a drink – or "just a cup of tea". "Downstairs is a great bar, but it can be noisy, so if you want to eat, try the upstairs restaurant". / the-pumphouse.com/; @PumpHseBristol; Mon - Sat 8 pm; Sun 4 pm.

RIVER COTTAGE CANTEEN £45 223

ST JOHNS CT, WHITELADIES RD BS8 2QY
0117 973 2458

HFW's dramatic converted church remains a bit of a Marmite affair; while fans say that its "ever-changing menu never disappoints" on the quality/quantity front, a steady stream of cynics feel that "with so much competition in Bristol they really need to up their game". / www.rivercottage.net/canteens; @plymouthcanteen; Mon-Sat 10 pm, Sun 5 pm.

RIVERSTATION £54 223

THE GROVE BS1 4RB 0117 914 4434

"A lovely harbourside location" with "good views across the old docks" is key to the appeal of this striking looking building: a former river police station. Following an extensive refit by newish owners Young's in summer 2018, there's now a huge outdoor terrace called the Pontoon. You can eat "reliable" pub classics there, with fancier fare upstairs in the restaurant (which has its own balcony). / www.riverstation.co.uk; @riverstation_; Mon-Sun 11 pm; no Amex.

ROOT £25

WAPPING WHARF BS1 6WP 0117 930 0260

A renovated cargo container in Bristol's Wapping Wharf, with views over the docks, houses this autumn 2017 newcomer, where the menu's small plates feature meat but give the veg 'star billing'. Too little feedback for a rating as yet, but the tyre man has awarded it a 'bib gourmand' and the press have raved. / www.eatdrinkbristolfashion.co.uk/root; @RootBristol; Mon-Sat 10.30 pm, Sun 9.30 pm.

SAN CARLO £42 334

44 CORN STREET BS1 1HQ 0117 922 6586

"Consistently good food", spearheaded by "superb fish & seafood dishes", wins high praise for this branch of the "glitzy" national chain established nearly 30 years ago by Brum-based Sicilian Carlo Distefano. Admirers still reckon it's "the best Italian restaurant in Bristol". / www.sancarlo.co.uk; @SanCarlo_Group; Tue-Sun, Mon 9.30 pm.

SOUK KITCHEN £37 333

277 NORTH ST BS3 1JP 0117 966 6880

Darren & Ella Lovell have raided the former Ottoman Empire to create a good-value menu of "vibrant, tasty and imaginative Middle Eastern dishes". It's opposite the Tobacco Factory, so "great for pre-theatre dining" – the only quibble is that sometimes it's "too popular for its own good: amiable but cramped". There's now a branch in Clifton that also sells hard-to-find ingredients. / www.soukkitchen.co.uk; @soukkitchenbris; Mon & Tue, Sun 9 pm, Wed & Thu 9.30 pm, Fri & Sat 10.30 pm.

SPINY LOBSTER £58 433

128-130 WHITELADIES ROAD BS8 2RS
0117 9737384

"Always excellent fresh fish" – Mitch Tonks's Bristol outpost (formerly called Rockfish Grill and sister to The Seahorse in Dartmouth) is "still great after all these years". "Our go-to place when we want a relaxing meal – you never have to worry about the quality". "The booths are fantastic, too". / www.thespinylobster.co.uk; @_SpinyLobster; Mon-Sat 11 pm, Sun 10.30 pm.

WELLBOURNE & WARFISH £46

25 THE MALL BS8 4JG 0117 239 0683

"Innovative and exciting dishes" won consistently superlative ratings for Liberty Wenham & Seldon Curry's decidedly ambitious West Country interpretation of bistro cooking. Having outgrown the original "tiny" 'Wallfish' premises, in late 2018 they announced their move into nearby Wellbourne – much to the relief of their devoted local following, who all "hoped they'd stay in Clifton". As Warfish, the team scored 5/5 for food in our survey this year, but given the changes, we've left the new venture un-rated till next year's survey. / wellbourne.restaurant; @_Wellbourne; Mon-Sat 11 pm, Sun 10.30 pm; \N.

WILKS £79 552

1 CHANDOS RD BS6 6PG 0117 9737 999

"From the unassuming shop-front style entrance, one passes into an attractive, well laid-out dining room with stylish artworks lining the walls" at James Wilkins's Redland HQ, where the "welcoming service" and "outstanding" cuisine (with a five-course tasting menu as the top option, but usually with à la carte or prix fixe alternatives) have placed it near the pinnacle of the city's culinary pecking order. "After a decor makeover, the styling now matches the brilliant food and service" according to its most ardent fans (but overall the ambience is still the least highly rated element of the operation). / www.wilksrestaurant.co.uk/; @wilksrestaurant; Wed-Sat 10 pm, Sun 9 pm; no Amex.

WILSON'S £50 543

24 CHANDOS RD BS6 6PF 0117 973 4157

"Remarkably original, with wonderful fresh ingredients" – Jan & Mary Ostle's Redlands bistro is yet another stellar independent on the Bristol gastro scene. "The food produced here in the tiny little kitchen is a revelation" – there's a "short menu of three starters, three mains, three desserts that seem to change on a daily basis", based around "taking something simple and giving it a twist, to create some exquisite dishes". / wilsonsrestaurant.co.uk; @JanWilsons; Tue-Sat 10 pm.

OLIVIER AT THE RED LION £50 433

OX49 5LG 01491 613140

"A new French landlord has brought back this lovely restaurant to the high standard of food we were used to!" – Olivier Bouet moved on from The Sweet Olive (RIP) in Aston Tirrold to take over this old pub, which has enjoyed quite a foodie reputation over the years. "Excellent food, a good wine list all at a reasonable price: a lovely French experience in South Oxfordshire". / www.theredlionbritwellsalome.co.uk; Wed-Sat 11 pm, Sun 2.30 pm.

STARK £75 544

1 OSCAR ROAD CT10 1QJ 01843 579786

"Pure magic…", "I'd pay more than double…" – "Ben Crittenden manages to conjure up dishes full of flavour bombs and surprises" in the "tiny" 12-cover venue he built with his dad. His wife Sophie serves diners, and their no-choice tasting menu (Wed-Sat only) wins universal high praise for "stunning food in one of the most quirky environments possible". / www.starkfood.co.uk; Sun & Mon 5 pm, Tue-Sat 11 pm.

WYATT & JONES £55 343

23-27 HARBOUR ST CT10 1EU
01843 865126

An "excellent" Farrow & Ball-chic indie combining superior local/seasonal dishes, "good cocktails and gin" and "superb service" (backdropped by a "lovely sunset view"); it's "a treat to go here after a day on the beach," which is just a few yards away. / www.wyattandjones.co.uk; Wed & Thu 9 pm, Fri & Sat 10 pm, Sun 4 pm.

THE LYGON ARMS £55

HIGH ST WR12 7DU 01386 852255

"The glorious dining room has been magnificently redone recently" at this famous landmark on the edge of the Cotswolds (which dates back to the fourteenth century, and which went into decline after it was sold out of the Savoy Group some years ago). Now in the same group as Cliveden and Chewton Glen, it inspired too little feedback for a rating this year, but all positive (and Giles Coren in April 2018 went a bundle on the experience). / www.lygonarmshotel.co.uk; @The_LygonArms; just off A44; 9.30 pm; D only, ex Sun open L & D; no jeans; booking max 8 may apply. *Accommodation:* 77 rooms, from £133

RUSSELL'S OF BROADWAY £56 333

20 HIGH STREET WR12 7DT 01386 853555

"Very busy", contemporary-style restaurant-with-rooms, named after – and set in – the old workshop of British furniture designer Gordon Russell. Most reporters are fans of the locally sourced British food (although for the odd diner it was "overall not a resounding success" this year). Praise too for the owners' adjoining chippy. / russellsofbroadway.co.uk/restaurant/; @russelsRandR; Mon-Sat 11 pm. *Accommodation:* 7 rooms, from £110

THE PIG £51 245

BEAULIEU ROAD SO42 7QL 01590 622354

The New Forest original of Hotel du Vin founder Robin Hutson's 'Pig' litter (there are now five, with three more opening in 2019), this country-house hotel with a shabby-chic vibe has tapped into a booming market for "quality without the fuss". Menus are built around "good local ingredients" – some from the kitchen garden, most from within 25 miles – while the "relaxed" atmosphere means both hotel and dining room are "great for families", with "plenty to encourage children to eat well". Overall, though, while it's "a delightful setting with a lovely ambience" and unimpeachable local ethos, "it's not matched by the results when it comes to the food": "the ingredients looks great in the garden but don't shine on the plate (mind you the foraged items were worse)! It just lacked flavour". / www.thepighotel.com; @The_Pig_Hotel; Mon-Fri 10 pm, Sat & Sun 10;45 pm. *Accommodation:* 26 rooms, from £139

THE GRUMPY MOLE £49 334

BROCKHAM GREEN RH3 7JS
01737 845 101

From the "quiet" setting, to the "friendly, helpful service" and "very good variety" of grub (Sunday roasts, afternoon teas, vegan menus etc.) there's "always a good time to be had at the Grumpy Mole" – a homely outpost of a five-strong Surrey chain. / www.thegrumpymole.co.uk; Mon-Sat 4.30 pm, Sun 3.30 pm; no Amex; no bookings.

THE UNRULY PIG £43 334

ORFORD RD IP12 2PU 01394 460 310

Making use of "the well-researched best of Suffolk" ingredients, "the menu will please the local clientele as well as any passing gourmet", say fans of this 16th-century inn (modernised after fire damage), and "make it a destination in this beautiful corner of the county". Some regulars, though, remain sceptical about its performance: "nice room, enthusiastic owner, but food didn't match expectations". / www.theunrulypig.co.uk; @unrulypig; Mon-Thu 9 pm, Fri & Sat 9.30 pm, Sun 8 pm.

CINNAMON CULTURE £52 333

46 PLAISTOW LN BR1 3PA 020 8289 0322

Consistently high marks this year for this plushly decorated fine dining Indian, a proud pillar of the local scene also reputed for its quaffable cocktails. / www.cinnamonculture.com; @cinnamonculture; Tue-Sat 11 pm, Sun 10.30 pm; no Amex.

SHAMPAN BROMLEY £39 322

38 CHATTERTON ROAD BR2 9QN
020 8460 7169

This sleek, veteran Indian with a pair of local satellites serves "wonderful food with a slightly modern twist" which only adds to its appeal. /

ITALIAN ORCHARD £40 344

96 WHITTINGHAM LANE PR3 5DB
01772 861240

"Considering the number of covers [300, 100 of which are in the glazed extension], even on a regular day, it's quite impressive that the kitchen maintains the quality it does" at the Braganini family's "welcoming" local landmark, which is "constantly packed and busy every day". "All the Britalian staples are to be had (you can be in and out in 20 minutes having had a pizza or pasta and a pint or a coke), or you can linger for hours enjoying a large platter of charcuterie, Fassona beef, excellent veal chops, calves' brains, osso bucco etc, and indulge in the wine list" (which boasts 200 bins). / www.italianorchard.com; Mon-Sun 10.30 pm.

BULL AT BROUGHTON £47 344

BD23 3AE 01756 792065

"Lovely seasonal and regional food" and "lots of choice for young and old" – add in quaffable real ales and there's a lot to like at this gentrified gastropub (formerly a Ribble Valley Inn, now part of Brunning & Price); it's a popular pitstop for those sampling the 'Land Rover Experience' at Broughton Hall Estate. / www.thebullatbroughton.com; @Bull_Broughton; 8.30 pm, Fri & Sat 9 pm; no bookings.

AT THE CHAPEL £46 323

28 HIGH ST BA10 0AE 01749 814070

This "bright, cheerful and lively" converted chapel-with-rooms is a "real find locally", from the "exhibitions of contemporary artists of quality on the walls" to the "surprisingly sophisticated" brasserie food (not least wood-fired pizzas) and an "excellent choice of wines from their wine shop". / www.atthechapel.co.uk; @at_the_chapel; 9.30 pm, Sun 8 pm. *Accommodation:* 8 rooms, from £100

ROTH BAR & GRILL £48 323

DURSLADE FARM, DROPPING LN BA10 0NL
01749 814060

"What a place, in the middle of the countryside!" This "hugely enjoyable" venue is the Somerset playground of Swiss contemporary art operation Hauser & Wirth, incorporating galleries, a working farm, "astonishing gardens", and a cowshed-conversion bar and grill named in honour of Swiss artist Dieter Roth. "The food is pretty good, too" particularly for brunch – "try the delicious (home cured) bacon and chocolate salami", but it's "often hard to get a table, especially at weekends". / www.rothbarandgrill.co.uk; @rothbarandgrill; Tue-Thu, Sun 5 pm, Fri & Sat 11 pm.

BUCKFASTLEIGH, DEVON　　1–3D

RIVERFORD FIELD KITCHEN　£46　433

WASH BARN　TQ11 0JU　01803 762074

This farm-based operation set in a barn "continues to delight with wonderful vegetables and salads accompanied by excellent meats", with much of the produce sourced from the surrounding fields and served at communal tables. / www.riverford.co.uk; @RiverfordFK; Mon-Sat 10 pm, Sun 7 pm; booking lunch only.

BUCKLAND, WORCESTERSHIRE　　2–2C

BUCKLAND MANOR　£99　545

WR12 7LY　01386 852626

"Top-end fine dining by long serving chef William Guthrie" helps distinguish the dining room of this "dream of a Cotswold Manor House Hotel in a gloriously isolated setting" (a Relais & Châteaux property). Both lunch and dinner have à la carte and tasting options: "splash out on the accompanying wine flight and you will remember the experience long after you forget the cost!" / www.bucklandmanor.co.uk; @Buckland_Manor; 2m SW of Broadway on B4632; jacket & tie required; booking max 8 may apply; children: 12+.

BURCOT, OXFORDSHIRE　　2–2D

THE CHEQUERS　£55　333

ABINGDON ROAD　OX14 3DP　01865 407771

"Roaring fires, good food and great atmosphere" – that's the straightforward appeal of Steven Sanderson's modernised thatched pub, in a cute Thames-side village. There's quite a wide menu, but the focus is on grass-fed, Sussex-reared steak. / www.thechequers-burcot.co.uk; @stevesanderson4; Tue-Sat 11 pm, Sun 6 pm.

BURTON BRADSTOCK, DORSET　　2–4B

HIVE BEACH CAFE　£45　434

BEACH ROAD　DT6 4RF　01308 897 070

A top location "for the freshest, no-frills seafood" – this "convivial if somewhat hectic" café right on the beach offers "unbeatable views". "Outstanding! I had mountains of crab and made a delightful mess!" / www.hivebeachcafe.co.uk; @HiveBeachCafe; Sun-Thu 5 pm, Fri & Sat 7 pm; no bookings. *Accommodation:* 2 rooms, from £95

BURTON ON TRENT, STAFFORDSHIRE　　5–3C

PASCAL AT THE OLD VICARAGE　£47　444

2 MAIN STREET　DE14 3EX　01283 533222

This redbrick vicarage restaurant is a stalwart of affordable fine dining – "the quality is still there but at a fraction of the price" – and their "sunset menu (order before 7pm) is a must". / www.pascalattheoldvicarage.co.uk/; @PascalArnoux; Mon-Thu 9 pm, Fri & Sat 10 pm, Sun 3 pm.

BURY ST EDMUNDS, SUFFOLK　　3–1C

THE ANGEL EATERIE　£53　333

THE ANGEL HOTEL, 3 ANGEL HILL, IP33 1LT　01284 714000

The relaxed ground floor brasserie of this attractive Georgian coaching inn, in the town centre, wins positive (if limited) feedback as an all-day dining destination with options from breakfast on. / www.theangel.co.uk/food-and-drink/dining-in-the-eaterie; @AngelHotelBury.

MAISON BLEUE　£64　544

30-31 CHURCHGATE ST　IP33 1RG　01284 760 623

For "an exquisite Gallic fine dining experience", Pascal & Karine Canevet's well-known and "very atmospheric" venue near the cathedral is "always a joy" (and fans "cannot understand why it does not have a Michelin star..."). Service is "knowledgeable and perfectly paced", and the food is "very French" with "everything tasting gorgeous" (fish and seafood are particularly good). Top Tip: "set lunches are magnificent value for money". / www.maisonbleue.co.uk; @Maison_Bleue; 9 pm, Sat 9.30 pm; closed Mon & Sun.

1921 ANGEL HILL　£54　543

19-21 ANGEL HILL　IP33 1UZ　01284 704870

"A real find" – "you'll be blown away" by the "chilled fine dining, exquisite flavour combinations and excellent wine list" at Zach Deakins's "quirky" venture which occupies a smartly appointed, timbered building in the heart of the town. "Where is its Michelin star?" / nineteen-twentyone.co.uk; @1921AH; 9.30 pm; closed Sun; no bookings.

THE ONE BULL　£73　333

25 ANGEL HILL　IP33 1UZ　01284 848220

Popular, modernised old pub in the heart of the town tipped as one of "the best in the area" thanks to its quality pub grub (with regularly changing specials); plus decent wine, and the fact that – being owned by the local Brewshed brewery – "they brew their own beer" just down the road. / www.theonebull.co.uk; @theonebullbury; Mon-Sat 11 pm, Sun 10.30 pm.

PEA PORRIDGE　£55　554

28-29 CANNON ST　IP33 1JR　01284 700200

Justin Sharp (chef) and his wife Jurga (front-of-house), "run a wonderful and eclectic restaurant" in a sidestreet at the heart of this lovely town, occupying a converted town house, where a meal is "akin to eating really good food at your friend's home". But there's nothing very domestic about the "seasonal and creative", 'nose-to-tail' British cuisine however ("with ingredients seldom to be found on the menus of other restaurants"): "rustic and hearty dishes" are "realised with absolute precision". "The wine list is also interesting, with excellent and informative notes". / www.peaporridge.co.uk; @peaporridge; Tue-Fri 10 pm, Sat 10.30 pm, Sun 6 pm; no Amex; no bookings.

VOUJON　£34　343

29 MUSTOW ST　IP33 1XL　01284 488122

"The best Indian restaurant in the area" pretty much ticks all the boxes: polished setting, "fantastic value" (if slightly standard) grub ("even the toilets are good!") / www.voujonburystedmunds.co.uk; 11.30 pm.

BUSHEY, HERTFORDSHIRE　　3–2A

ST JAMES　£51　332

30 HIGH ST　WD23 3HL　020 8950 2480

A "lovely restaurant" opposite the church that's become a fixture of the High Street over twenty years for its "totally decent and reliable modern European cooking, fronted by the genial Italian owner" (Alfonso); "a good option in a seriously underserved area". / www.stjamesrestaurant.co.uk; opp St James Church; Sun & Mon 10 pm, Tue-Thu 11.30 pm, Fri & Sat midnight; no Amex.

BUSHMILLS, COUNTY LONDONDERRY　　10–1D

THE FRENCH ROOMS　£45　333

45 MAIN STREET　BT57 8QA　028 2073 0033

"A delightful restaurant with an authentically Gallic flavour" – this all-day 'licensed café' offers enjoyable fare, from morning breakfasts and afternoon teas through to bistro-style cooking at lunch and dinner. / www.thefrenchrooms.com; Mon-Sat 9.30 pm.

BUXTON, DERBYSHIRE　　5–2C

SIMPLY THAI　£34　442

2-3 CAVENDISH CIRCUS　SK17 6AT　01298 24471

This "fabulous independent Thai restaurant" has been serving "gorgeous food" "in the heart of an old English spa town" for 15 years. So long as you like that kind of thing, the dining room's classic Thai decoration makes for a "lovely setting". / www.simplythaibuxton.co.uk; Mon-Sat 9.30 pm, Sun 4 pm.

CAMBER, EAST SUSSEX　　3–4C

THE GALLIVANT　£54　332

NEW LYDD RD　TN31 7RB　01797 225 057

Reporters this year "loved the whole vibe about this place" – a former 1960s motel, set back from the dunes, turned hip nautical-themed B&B. The bistro's hyper locally sourced food is mirrored by an impressively long English wine list. / www.thegallivant.co.uk; @thegallivant; Sun-Thu 11 pm, Fri & Sat 11.30 pm; children: under 12s 8.30. *Accommodation:* 20 rooms, from £115

CAMBRIDGE, CAMBRIDGESHIRE　　3–1B

AMELIE FLAMMEKUECHE　£20

GRAFTON CENTRE　CB1 1PS　07585 427545

Suffolk restaurateur Regis Crépy, who ran the Great House in Lavenham for 32 years, launched this new Alsatian venture – in a bright yellow Citroën parked in Grafton centre's funky new food court – with his son Alex in summer 2018; the headline event comes sweet or savoury, and is rounded out by tapas-style starters. / www.amelierestaurants.co.uk; @amelie_rest; Mon-Sat 9 pm, Sun 5 pm.

THE CAMBRIDGE CHOP HOUSE   £55   333

1 KINGS PARADE CB2 1SJ   01223 359506

Yards from King's, and with "lovely views" of the college chapel, this attractive, no-nonsense meat specialist continues to win enthusiastic all-round feedback; part of a nine-strong local chain, the owners are now crowdfunding to open two new sites. / www.cambscuisine.com/cambridge-chop-house; @cambscuisine; Mon-Thu 10.30 pm, Fri & Sat 11 pm, Sun 9.30 pm.

COTTO   £92   543

GONVILLE HOTEL, CB1 1LY   01223 302010

Distinguished chef Hans Schweitzer moved his "always outstanding" restaurant into new purpose-built premises in the Gonville Hotel in 2017 – a "lovely new location" for food that's "inspired, finely balanced and beautifully presented" and in a culinary style that's "interesting but grounded in established harmonies and avoiding wackiness". "It may on first look appear expensive, but it's worth every penny". / www.cottocambridge.co.uk; @cottocambridge; 9.15 pm; D only, Wed-Sat; no Amex; need + to book.

FITZBILLIES   £39   322

51 - 52 TRUMPINGTON STREET CB2 1RG   01223 352 500

Despites both its iconic status – a Cambridge landmark since 1921 – and foodie ownership (FT columnist, Tim Hayward has owned it since 2011), this Varsity café (most famous for its Chelsea buns) inspires only limited and middling feedback: "more-than-adequate if pricey comfort food in a busy environment". / www.fitzbillies.com; Mon-Sat 11.30 pm, Sun 10.30 pm.

THE IVY CAMBRIDGE BRASSERIE   £56

16 TRINITY STREET CB2 1TB   01223 344044

Too few reports as yet for a rating on this Varsity outpost of Richard Caring's facsimile of the famous star-magnet in London's Theatreland. All feedback so far is good though. / www.theivycambridgebrasserie.com; Mon-Sun 12.30 am.

MIDSUMMER HOUSE   £154   444

MIDSUMMER COMMON CB4 1HA   01223 369299

It has a very "pretty riverside setting" on the Cam in the midst of Midsummer Common, but that's not why Daniel Clifford's Victorian Villa is so often hailed as an "amazing destination".

It's the "stunning cuisine from start to finish" which creates a "seriously top-notch eating experience" with the only option in the evening being an eight-course tasting menu. However, even fans acknowledge that it is decidedly "not cheap (call your bank manager first)", and while for most diners "it's well worth every penny", there is a significant disgruntled minority for whom the final bill is "way over the top". / www.midsummerhouse.co.uk; @Midsummerhouse; Tue-Sat 9 pm.

MILLWORKS   £46   323

NEWNHAM ROAD CB3 9EY   01223 367507

"Grilled and roast meats plus plenty of other options" play a strong second fiddle to the setting at this "spacious and friendly converted mill, with operational wheel and views over water". Owners Cambscuisine recently secured £750,000 through crowdfunding to expand their nine-strong local empire. / www.themillworks.co.uk; @cambscuisine; Mon-Thu 10 pm, Fri & Sat 10.30 pm, Sun 9.30 pm.

NAVADHANYA CAMBRIDGE   £51   443

73 NEWMARKET RD CB5 8EG   01223 300583

This ex-pub is now a "civilised" dining room that's top of the local subcontinents; "subtle flavours" (it's mercifully "not English Indian food") distinguish the à la carte and seven-course tasting menu. / www.navadhanya.co.uk; @navadhanyauk; Mon-Sat 11 pm, Sun 9 pm.

OAK BISTRO   £48   242

6 LENSFIELD ROAD CB2 1EG   01223 323 361

A "very friendly" decade-old bistro that, albeit "very noisy", wins praise for its "agreeable atmosphere" (especially in the pretty walled garden); the modern Anglo/Euro food doesn't detract from a visit either. / www.theoakbistro.co.uk; @theoakbistro; Mon-Sat 11.30 pm, Sun 8 pm; no bookings.

PINT SHOP   £43   333

10 PEAS HILL CB2 3PN   01223 352 293

"Quirky" and "fun" gastroboozer – inspired by early Victorian pubs (and set in a house where EM Forster once lived) – which serves "great beer" and food that's "adequate in a city not blessed with a lot of high quality alternatives". Founded in 2014, it has spawned offshoots in Oxford and Birmingham. / www.pintshop.co.uk; @PintShop; Sun-Wed 10 pm, Thu-Sat 10.30 pm; no bookings.

THE ST JOHN'S CHOP HOUSE   £57   333

21-24 NORTHAMPTON ST CB3 0AD   01223 353 110

"Always reliable" and with a "bargain set menu", this no-nonsense eatery, over two floors of a 19th century brick building, specialises in "delicious" meaty cuisine; "staff are eager to please".

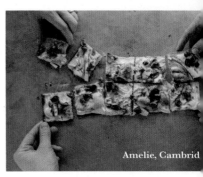

Amelie, Cambrid

/ www.cambscuisine.com/st-johns-chop-house; @cambscuisine; Tue-Sat 9.30 pm, Sun 4 pm.

STEAK & HONOUR   £17   422

4 WHEELER STREET, CAMBRIDGE, CB2 3QB CB2 3QB   07766 568430

Best known for their snub-nosed Citroën burger vans which pop up at various Cambridge locations, this two-man outfit now serves their highly rated burgers at a permanent two-storey venue beside the Corn Exchange. / www.steakandhonour.co.uk; @steakandhonour; Mon-Fri 9.30 pm, Sat 10 pm, Sun 5 pm; no bookings.

TRINITY   £53   343

15 TRINITY STREET CB2 1TB   01223 322130

"Finally a reasonable place in central Cambridge", right opposite the Great Gate of the namesake college. The interior is stylish and the menu, while "not large", offers superior seafood and meat, plus "a good choice of wines by the glass or bottle", helping it to become quite the foodie magnet since opening two years back. / www.trinitycambridge.co.uk; Sun-Thu midnight, Fri & Sat 2 am.

RESTAURANT 22   £57

22 CHESTERTON ROAD CB4 3AX   01223 351880

A well-known Victorian townhouse outside the centre, near Victoria Avenue Bridge, that opened its doors 40 years ago and, as of early 2018, is under young ex-Gordon Ramsay grad Sam Carter and his wife Alexandra (FOH). This has been one of the town's major culinary destinations for many years: feedback welcomed on his creative modern British grub – changing weekly, and running to five- or seven-course tasting menus. / www.restaurant22.co.uk; Mon-Sat 10 pm, Sun 2.30 am; children: 12+.

CANTERBURY, KENT   **3–3D**

THE AMBRETTE CANTERBURY   £43   433

14 - 15 BEER CART LANE CT1 2NY   01227 200 777

"Every mouthful is an amazing burst of flavour" at Dev Biswal's "airy" pub conversion, a spinoff from the Margate original that's "reason enough to visit Canterbury" for many fans. "Distinctly flavoured" Indian-fusion dishes give "a very interesting take on mixing British and Asian cuisines" – "beautifully prepared" and "at reasonable prices". / www.theambrette.co.uk; @The_Ambrette; Mon-Thu 9.30 pm, Fri-Sun 10 pm.

CAFÉ DES AMIS £44 3 3 4

95 ST DUNSTAN'S ST CT2 8AD
01227 464390

This "lively" Mexican in Westgate "celebrated its thirtieth anniversary in April 2018", and remains "so popular as the atmosphere is so upbeat and the food zings with joy". / www.cafedez.com; 10 pm, Fri & Sat 10.30 pm, Sun 9.30 pm; booking max 6 may apply.

CAFE MAURESQUE £42 3 4 3

8 BUTCHERY LN CT1 2JR 01227 464300

This "wonderful, atmospheric" cellar will always be a "favourite": the "decor is fantastic, with the Moroccan theme even extending into the Ladies' loo!" It has built a strong following over 15 years, helped by its "delicious Moroccan food, plus paella, tapas and other Spanish dishes". / www.cafemauresque.com; @CafeMauresque; 10 pm, Fri & Sat 10.30 pm.

COUNTY RESTAURANT, ABODE CANTERBURY £63 3 3 2

HIGH ST CT1 2RX 01227 766266

"The only place in Canterbury where you can eat an approximation of fine dining" – i.e. "delicate and flavoursome" dishes ("classics with a modern twist") and set lunches, all "at an affordable price". / www.abodecanterbury.co.uk; @ABodecanterbury; Tue-Fri 10 pm. *Accommodation:* 72 rooms, from £125

GOODS SHED £49 3 2 4

STATION ROAD WEST CT2 8AN
01227 459153

"Fantastic for breakfast, coffee, lunch, and to stock up on some foodie treats" – this "delightful informal operation (next door to Canterbury West station) overlooks the bustling farmers' market below, where most of the food is sourced", and has been a focus for local foodies since 2002. "The produce is good and the dishes are left to speak for themselves". "Every town should should have somewhere like this". / www.thegoodsshed.co.uk; Mon-Thu midnight, Fri 1 am.

ASADOR 44 £45 3 3 3

14 - 15 QUAY STREET CF10 1EA
029 2002 0039

Positive but still-limited feedback on this dim-lit Spanish yearling in the city-centre – the new flagship of Tom and Owen Morgan's '44' group – which comes complete with wine-cave and cheese room. Meats from the Asador are the main event. / asador44.co.uk/; @asador44; Mon-Fri 11.30 pm, Sat 11 pm, Sun 10.30 pm.

BAR 44 CARDIFF £35 3 3 4

15-23 WESTGATE STREET CF10 1DD
03333 44 40 49

Some feel it's "not as good as its Cowbridge sibling", but this "busy Spaniard" in the city-centre nevertheless earns praise for its "interesting selection of authentic tapas, different Spanish wines and large range of sherries". / www.bar44.co.uk; @bar44cardiff; Sun-Thu 11 pm, Fri & Sat midnight.

CAFE CITTA £35 3 4 3

4 CHURCH ST CF10 1BG 029 2022 4040

The home-cooked dishes and pizza win solid ratings at this small and unflashy family-run Italian in the city centre. It has an enthusiastic local following, so be sure to book. / www.cafecitta.com.

CASANOVA £47 3 3 2

13 QUAY ST CF10 1EA 029 2034 4044

In the "culinary wasteland" that is chain-plagued Cardiff, this authentic Italian indie has gathered quite a local following and regulars applaud its hospitable approach. Your treatment can depend on how well you're known however: one first-timer observed "the owner doted at length on certain tables while we were frequently passed by and made to wait". / www.casanovacardiff.co.uk; @CasanovaCardiff; 10 pm; closed Sun.

MINT AND MUSTARD £37 4 4 3

134 WHITCHURCH ROAD CF14 3LZ
02920 620333

It's "always a treat" to dine at this pioneer of new-wave Keralan and South Indian cuisine, whose "exciting" and "imaginative" menus include a focus on seafood. Founded in 2006, the Cardiff original wins consistently high ratings and has now spawned a small regional chain. / www.mintandmustard.com; @mintandmustard; Mon-Sun 11 pm; no shorts.

MOKSH £40 4 4 3

OCEAN BUILDING, BUTE CR CF10 5AY
029 2049 8120

"Absolutely exceptional" for the area – fourth-generation chef Stephen Gomes brings molecular gastronomy to bear on his "creative and original" take on Indian food. "Inventive and beautifully presented, the meal we had here was a work of art". / www.moksh.co.uk; @mokshcardiff; Mon-Sat 9 pm, Sun 7 pm.

PURPLE POPPADOM £41 4 4 2

185A, COWBRIDGE ROAD EAST CF11 9AJ
029 2022 0026

Ignore the drab setting next to a Cowbridge Road East butcher's shop, and take refuge in this vibrant dining room, where chef and author Anand George delivers "brilliant Keralan cooking" with nouvelle Indian flourishes; early-bird thalis are an innovation. /

purplepoppadom.com; @Purple_Poppadom; Tue-Sat 11 pm, Sun 9 pm.

VEGETARIAN FOOD STUDIO £24 3 3 2

115-117 PENARTH RD CF11 6JU
029 2023 8222

Despite the "simple surroundings" (complete with naïve wall murals) by the Taff, the vegan Indian food – ranging from northern Gujarati curries to southern dosas – at this humble spot "can be superb". / www.vegetarianfoodstudio.co.uk; @VegFoodStudio; 9.30 pm, Sun 7 pm; closed Mon; no Amex.

WALLYS £27 3 4 3

38-46 ROYAL ARCADE CF10 1AE
029 2022 9265

Royal Arcade icon with a bursting deli on the ground floor and a first-floor Viennese café turning out an "amazing selection of coffees, open sandwiches and cakes". / wallysdeli.co.uk; @wallysdeli; Mon-Fri 5.30 pm, Sat 6 pm, Sun 4.30 pm.

ALEXANDROS GREEK RESTAURANT AND DELI £39 3 4 2

68 WARWICK ROAD CA1 1DR
01228 592227

"Reliable friendly family run" Greek restaurant and deli in the city-centre, praised for its "home cooked, fresh fare" – a range of Greek classics plus more unusual weekly specials. / www.thegreek.co.uk; 9.45 pm; closed Mon L & Sun.

THE MASONS ARMS £49 3 4 5

STRAWBERRY BANK LA11 6NW
01539 568486

This "lovely Lake District pub with views over the Lyth Valley" (there are "few better places to be than on the terrace") is a "firm favourite" locally owing to its oft-changing, unpretentious menu, including game in season, and "fabulous portions". / www.strawberrybank.com; @StrawberryBank/; W from Bowland Bridge, off A5074; Mon-Sat 11 pm, Sun 10.30 pm. *Accommodation:* 7 rooms, from £75

AULIS AT L'ENCLUME £260 5 4 4

CAVENDISH ST LA11 6PZ

Billed as 'going behind the scenes' at L'Enclume – Simon Rogan's development kitchen is in a similar vein to his Soho operation of the same name, offering a first look at dishes destined for L'Enclume. Reports are relatively few, but rhapsodise over an "amazing and intimate" experience. / www.lenclume.co.uk/aulis; @AulisSimonRogan.

L'ENCLUME £198 554

CAVENDISH ST LA11 6PZ 01539 536362

"Worth the journey from Brighton to Cartmel – in fact I'd go twice as far!" Simon Rogan's "gloriously located" converted smithy "has made a sleepy Lakeland village into a foodies' delight" and reports of "magical and extraordinary" meals (e.g. "one of the best meals I've ever had") are the norm here. Even one or two who "were expecting it to be quite pretentious" are "blown away by the whole experience" – "service is good-humoured, knowledgeable, and spot-on", while the tasting menus feature a "memorable and absolutely divine" series of small plates, featuring "fascinating combinations", which "subtly exploit the best local ingredients". / www.lenclume.co.uk; @lenclume; J36 from M6, down A590 towards Cartmel; closed Mon L & Tue L. *Accommodation:* 16 rooms, from £119

ROGAN & CO £66 443

DEVONSHIRE SQUARE LA11 6QD 01539 535917

"Everything you would expect from Simon Rogan without splashing out at L'Enclume" – this spin-off brasserie near the mothership enjoys a similar "pretty and romantic village setting" and achieved much more consistent ratings this year (in which it also achieved its Michelin star). "Local ingredients are enhanced with delicate and unusual herbs" – "it's a great place to eat and be merry anytime: after a walk, after shopping, after the races or just simply because!" / www.roganandcompany.co.uk; @simon_rogan; Mon - Sat 9 pm, Sun 5 pm; no Amex; credit card deposit required to book.

BYBROOK RESTAURANT, MANOR HOUSE HOTEL £104 544

SN14 7HR 01249 782206

Chef Rob Potter (ex-Lucknam Park) delivers some "excellent" cuisine, which is "accompanied by the best of advice from the sommelier" at this welcoming luxury hotel in a famous village, now established as a top gastronomic destination for visitors to the Cotswolds. / www.exclusive.co.uk/the-manor-house/restaurants-bars/the-bybrook/; @themanorhouse; Sun-Thu 9 pm, Fri & Sat 9.30 pm; no jeans; children: 11+. *Accommodation:* 48 rooms, from £205

THE GEORGE £47 333

THE GREEN CO10 8BA 01787 280248

This "old-fashioned, smart, and welcoming" 16th-century inn overlooking a village green inspires the odd accusation of dishes showing "quantity not quality", but more commonly is well-rated for its enjoyable cooking. / www.thecavendishgeorge.co.uk; @theGeorgecav; Tue-Sun. *Accommodation:* 5 rooms, from £75

BROCKENCOTE HALL £88 324

DY10 4PY 01562 777876

Still "a lovely place to stay", the Eden Collection's swan-lake-surrounded Victorian pile is a "very relaxing" stop-off en route from North to South. Chef Tim Jenkins, elevated from sous to head chef a few years back, continues to please with his local/seasonal food, although service has dropped off a notch. / www.brockencotehall.com; on A448, outside village; Mon-Wed, Sat midnight, Thu & Fri 1 am, Sun 10 pm; no trainers. *Accommodation:* 21 rooms, from £135

GIDLEIGH PARK £165 443

TQ13 8HH 01647 432367

Chris Simpson "has made a good start" (taking over the baton from Michael Wignall) at this famous culinary Xanadu: a Tudorbethan mansion down a one-track lane on the borders of Dartmoor in gorgeous gardens that was regularly hailed by our diners' survey in Michael Caines' era, a few years ago, as the UK's top gastronomic destination. On most accounts "it's still maintaining its high standard of food and the superb wine list" and fans say that "if you're looking for an exceptional foodie experience look no further". A number of return visitors, however, this year, judged it inferior to their previous trip, especially when it came to value at the vertiginous prices. "Quibbles taking it from 5/5 to 4/5 are the wildly overpriced wine list and the sameness of some of the courses". Also, "the set of small rooms are somewhat awkward", and for style-conscious types "the 1970s-styling, with unsympathetic lighting and heavy curtains" raises the query "time for a refurb?" / www.gidleigh.co.uk; @Gidleighhotel; from village, right at Lloyds TSB, take right fork to end of lane; no jeans; children: 8. *Accommodation:* 24 rooms, from £350

COLETTE'S, THE GROVE £96

WD17 3NL 01923 296015

With the departure of Russell Bateman (chef here since 2014) to Knightsbridge's Pétrus, the future of the small main dining room of this ultra-luxurious 18th century five-star hotel is uncertain. In winter 2018, it will re-open as a pop-up (name unknown) – thereafter it will probably be a restaurant space, but no decisions seem to have been taken in this respect as yet. / www.thegrove.co.uk; @TheGroveHotel; 9.30 pm; D only, closed Mon & Sun; children: 16+. *Accommodation:* 227 rooms, from £310

THE GLASSHOUSE, THE GROVE £69 322

WD3 4TG 01923 296015

Even those who "would not usually choose a buffet restaurant" found this plush country house pile's dining room to their liking, with "lots of choice" and "above average quality" ("you won't go home hungry"); regulars meanwhile proclaim it "a great venue for a celebration". / www.thegrove.co.uk; @thegrovehotel; Mon-Sat 9.30 pm, Sun 9 pm.

PRIME STEAK & GRILL, THE CLARENDON £67 323

REDHALL LANE WD3 4LU 01923 264 580

"Excellent", "good-quality steaks" have made this "newish neighbourhood grill" (in a converted pub) a "welcome addition to the culinary desert of Beaconsfield". There's a "lovely upstairs bar for pre-dinner drinks", and "a few fish dishes and vegetarian options" to keep red-meat refuseniks happy. / www.primesteakandgrill.com/chandlers-cross; @SteakPrime.

INDIAN TIFFIN ROOM £44 433

2 CHAPEL STREET SK8 1BR 0161 491 2020

The "flavour explosions" of the South Indian street food at this "small and intimate place" (opened in 2013) have proved so popular that founders Suresh Raje Urs & Srini Sundaram have launched it as a brand, opening much larger ITRs in Manchester's First Street development and now in Leeds city centre. "You sometimes have to queue and it is very cramped when there's a full house". / www.indiantiffinroom.com; @Indtiffinroom; Mon-Sat 10.30 pm, Sun 9.30 pm.

L'ARTISAN £58 333

30 CLARENCE ST GL50 3NX 01242 571257

The Ogrodzki's properly Gallic restaurant (no franglais here) continues its successful run; even the very odd cynic praises "charming" hostess Elisabeth and some "absolutely delicious" dishes of a traditional bent. / www.lartisan-restaurant.com; Mon-Sat 10 pm, Sun 8 pm.

BHOOMI £49 444

52 SUFFOLK RD GL50 2AQ 01242 222 010

"Contemporary Indian fare – not at all your usual bog standard offerings" – earns unanimous high ratings for this modern south Indian, whose "classy decor with subtly lit, dark walls creates an air of romance". Top Tip: "try the house G&T, served with chilli and rosemary". / www.bhoomi.co.uk; @bhoomichelt.

LE CHAMPIGNON SAUVAGE £94 552

24-28 SUFFOLK RD GL50 2AQ 01242 573449

"I always visit 3-4 times a year. I'd go more often if it was not a 300 mile round trip!" – David & Helen Everitt Matthias inspire huge loyalty amongst their large fanbase, who appreciate "the hard work and support given by their teams in the kitchen and front of house" at a venture just outside the city centre where, famously, Le Patron is always at the stoves. The "unfailingly spectacular" food is "the traditional cuisine that dreams are made of", and many diners note that "the prices here still represent wonderful value for the quality offered". The cooking is complemented by "an extensive wine list (spanning a wide choice of countries, but with a particularly great variety of reasonably priced French vintages)", presided over by "Helen, who discreetly runs front of house with her young team like clockwork". When it comes to the room it's… "pleasant". Fans say: "to me, the calm space adds to the pleasure – I'm still surprised that some find it dull". STOP PRESS – in October 2018, Michelin took away their second star as they launched the Michelin 2019 guide. There's nothing in our diner survey to support this. / www.lechampignonsauvage.co.uk; @lechampsauvage; 8.45pm; closed Mon & Sun.

EAST INDIA CAFE £50 332

103 PROMENADE GL50 1NW 01242 300850

A "pretty little cellar restaurant on the Prom" combining "charming service" and "very creative and delicious 'Raj' food", from street food to tasting menus; it's "quite expensive", but then still "cheaper than Gymkhana!" Plush new sibling 'Memsahib Gin & Tea Bar' opened two minutes' walk away in November 2018. / www.eastindiacafe.com; @eastindiacafe; Mon-Sat midnight, Sun 11 pm.

THE IVY MONTPELLIER BRASSERIE £56 213

ROTUNDA TERRACE, MONTPELLIER STREET GL50 1SH 01242 894 200

"It looks beautiful but hasn't found its feet yet" – this outpost of Richard Caring's burgeoning national chain occupies the grade I listed Rotunda building, but is one of its least consistent members, with reports of "patchy" service and some "very paltry and unexciting" meals. Experiences have varied within a single meal – "how can they go so quickly from poor to perfection?" / www.theivycheltenhambrasserie.com; @ivtcheltenham; Mon-Sun 12.30 am.

KOJ £30 333

3 REGENT STREET GL50 1HE 01242 580455

MasterChef finalist Andrew Koj's "stripped back" – and crowdfunded – Asian café, long in the making, is by all accounts a "good place to know of" – the "decent (to "superb") Japanese small-plate cooking" is "unfussy", and "pretty good value" too. / kojcheltenham.co.uk; @KojCheltenham; Wed-Sat, Tue 9.30 pm.

LUMIÈRE £89 553

CLARENCE PARADE GL50 3PA 01242 222200

"Up there with experiences we've had at the country's top restaurants!" – chef Jon Howe conjures up "precise, innovative but grounded cooking" in a "small kitchen" at their "very small, intimate and calm venture", while his wife

Helen heads a "charming, unobtrusive service team". Happy customers praise what is in effect "fine dining with tailor-made tasting menus, not only for dietary requirements/allergies but also for likes and dislikes", which come "brimming over with invention and taste". / www.lumiere.cc; @LumiereChelt; Fri & Sat, Wed & Thu 8.30 pm; children: 8.

NO 131 £61 324

131 PROMENADE GL50 1NW 01242 822939

Part of the five-strong 'The Lucky Onion' chain, owned by Superdry guru Julian Dunkerton – this gorgeous Georgian house on the Prom has put the style into Cheltenham since opening five years ago; the ambience (and to some extent food) can be "great", but patchy service continues to be a drag. / theluckyonion.com/property/no-131/; @131TheProm; 9.30, Fri - Sat: 10.30.

PRITHVI £58 544

37 BATH ROAD GL53 7HG 01242 226229

"Consistently fabulous" "fine-dining food that happens to be Indian" scores consistently high marks for this "refined and stylish" outfit, where "top-quality ingredients" and "brilliant flavours" are "beautifully served". / www.prithvirestaurant.com; @37Prithvi; Tue-Sat 9.30 pm; no Amex.

PURSLANE £66 433

16 RODNEY RD GL50 1JJ 01242 321639

"What a great find!"; in the backstreets, chef/patron Gareth Fulford delivers "really interesting dishes" – notably "fish cooked à point" – and lots of "nice, foraged bits" at his stylish establishment. Another boon: it's all "very reasonably priced". / www.purslane-restaurant.co.uk; @eatatpurslane; Mon-Sun 11 pm.

TAVERN £51 333

GL50 3DN 01242 221212

"They've got a great menu of American-inspired comfort food" at this bar/bistro in the city-centre "and some real mastery at the grill. Brunches are good too". Top Menu Tip: "whole deep fried globe artichoke with greek garlic mayo". / www.thetaverncheltenham.com; Mon-Fri 9 pm, Sat 9.30 pm.

THE WHITE SPOON £58 443

WELL WALK GL50 3JX 01242 228 555

"In a quiet but central part of town, next to the museum", Chris White and Purdey Spooner's year-old venture could be classified as "fine dining in a relaxed atmosphere". The "imaginative" cuisine can hit the heights, with some best meals of the year reported, while service is "friendly and helpful". Top Tip: "set lunch is very good value". / www.thewhitespoon.co.uk; @whitespoonchelt; Mon-Sat 10.15 pm, Sun 3.30 pm.

LA BRASSERIE, CHESTER GROSVENOR £72 233

EASTGATE CH1 1LT 01244 324024

For "dependable quality" (albeit at "London prices") head to this Paris-style stalwart, which gained a glam Champagne bar during a recent refurb'. Top Tip – the "'gentleman's afternoon tea' (sliders rather than finger sandwiches)" offers an "excellent alternative" to its more traditional counterpart. / www.chestergrosvenor.com; Mon-Sun 9 pm. *Accommodation:* 80 rooms, from £230

BREWERY TAP £36 333

52-54 LOWER BRIDGE STREET CH1 1RU 01244 340999

Local brewery Spitting Feathers' real ale and real food joint is a solid performer with a winning line of cask ales, hand-pulled ciders and locally sourced grub; the location in a Jacobean great hall adds to the joys of a visit. / www.the-tap.co.uk; Mon-Sat 11 pm, Sun 10.30 pm.

THE CHEF'S TABLE £56 443

4 MUSIC HALL PAS CH1 2EU 01244403040

"A lovely compact little restaurant (albeit "not quite as tiny" after a recent refurb') serving really innovative dishes, tucked away in a passage off Northgate Street"; seasonal options use "really unusual ingredients" and "the whole experience feels special". / www.chefstablechester.co.uk; @ChefsTableCH1; closed Mon & Sun.

DOCKET NO.64 £56

64 NORTHGATE STREET CH1 2HT 01244 312158

Hot on the heels of opening Docket No. 33 in Whitchurch, this autumn 2018 newcomer opens in the heart of the city (on the site of the Ginger Wine Bar, RIP). Chester has always had a shortage of ambitious modern British ventures making this potential rival for the likes of Sticky Walnut all the more welcome. / www.docketrestaurant.com; Sun-Thu 10 pm, Fri & Sat 11 pm.

1539 £52 334

THE RACECOURSE CH1 2LY 01244 304 611

With epic views of Chester Racecourse, this stylish, decade-old restaurant is a "great place to go to the impress the clients" while "sampling some fine food". Top Tip – "best go when there is no racing otherwise you will not get in... the good lunchtime offers providing you with the perfect excuse to do lunch!" / www.restaurant1539.co.uk; @Restaurant1539; Mon-Thu 11 pm, Fri & Sat 1 am, Sun 9 pm; no bookings.

HICKORYS SMOKEHOUSE £50 333

SOUTERS LANE CH1 1SH 01244 404000

"A firm family favourite and as close to the American BBQ experience as you can get in our country" – this "lovely" and "very busy" outfit by the River Dee offers a "massive menu" featuring "great smoky burgers". The chain is obviously onto something – following the brand-new Worcester branch, their ninth outpost was due to open in Gresty Green in December 2018. / www.hickorys.co.uk/chester/; @Hickorys_; Mon-Sat 10.30 pm, Sun 9.30 pm.

JOSEPH BENJAMIN £54 333

140 NORTHGATE STREET CH1 2HT 01244 344295

Joe & Ben Wright's produce-led deli-restaurant is a "real find", close to the city walls, with every dish "tasty and well presented" (and a particularly "excellent value fixed-price lunch"); "attentive and charming service" to boot. / www.josephbenjamin.co.uk; @joseph_benjamin; Mon-Sat 11 pm, Sun 10.30 pm.

MOULES A GO GO £49 332

39 WATERGATE ROW CH1 2LE 01244 348818

"A must-go if in Chester" – a city stalwart still thriving after decamping from The Rows to the old La Tasca HQ a couple of years back; from the eponymous molluscs to the rotisserie fare it's "gorgeous" and there's a "great gin selection now too". / www.moulesagogo.co.uk; @MoulesaGoGo; Sun-Thu 9 pm, Fri & Sat 10 pm.

SIMON RADLEY, THE CHESTER GROSVENOR £99 344

56-58 EASTGATE STREET CH1 1LT 01244 324 024

"Sheer class and quality" shine through the "slightly old-fashioned setting" of the dining room at the Duke of Westminster's grand city-centre hotel, where exec chef Simon Radley celebrates 21 years at the helm in 2019. His "inventive tasting menus (including a vegetarian version) are served theatrically" and still impress all diners, even if "the price is high for this show". Baking has always been a feature here: "the pièce de resistance is not the courses themselves, but the amazing bread in between!" Notable cellar here too, which offers a heavyweight selection numbering 700 bins. / www.chestergrosvenor.com; @TheGrosvenor; Mon closed, Tue - Sat 9 pm, Sun closed; no trainers; children: 12+. *Accommodation:* 80 rooms, from £230

STICKY WALNUT £55 444

11 CHARLES ST CH2 3AZ 01244 400400

"A great sense of energy and enthusiasm for the cooking makes a visit fun and very satisfying", when you visit Gary Usher's original venture – a "cosy" and "relaxed" bistro in Hoole, "just on the outskirts of the city" (beyond the train station). Having opened in 2011, it's "still the best eatery in Chester" (unless you are determined to spend a bomb), and – to an impressive extent given the expansion of his north western empire – "standards have been maintained over several years": particularly the

"excellent modern British cuisine" ("with dishes to suit all tastes"). Top Menu Tip: "do try their signature starter of beetroot and sticky walnuts". / www.stickywalnut.com; @stickywalnut; Sun-Thu 9 pm, Fri & Sat 10 pm; credit card deposit required to book.

UPSTAIRS AT THE GRILL £50 333

70 WATERGATE ST CH1 2LA 01244 344883

The "best steakhouse" in these parts is a classy and buzzy sort of spot, spread across two floors and also featuring a cool cocktail bar. / www.upstairsatthegrill.co.uk; @UpstairsatGrill; Mon-Sat 10.30 pm, Sun 9.30 pm.

CHEW MAGNA, SOMERSET 2–2B

THE PONY & TRAP £69 543

BS40 8TQ 01275 332 627

A short drive south of Bristol, Josh & Holly Eggleton's (brother and sister) accoladed and "well-patronised" venue has "a lovely garden and amazing views" over the Chew Valley. "The 'pub' is now more of a restaurant and a fantastic one, but with many tables" (which can feel "overcrowded" in some areas) and "hardly any bar". Foodwise, there were a couple of reports of "a let down" this year, but not enough to dent the ratings, given the huge volume of reports of cooking that's "as good as it gets": "so creative, with excellent flavour and texture combinations, prepared with real skill". "Add reasonable pricing, knowledgeable service and given the stunning country setting, you have all the ingredients for a meal to relish". / www.theponyandtrap.co.uk; @theponyandtrap; Mon-Sun 9 pm; no Amex.

CHICHESTER, WEST SUSSEX 3–4A

FARMER, BUTCHER, CHEF, THE GOODWOOD HOTEL £57 423

GOODWOOD ESTATE PO18 0PX 01243 755070

Setting speed and sport to one side, Lord March's Goodwood Estate opened this new restaurant two years ago to showcase the organic Home Farm beef, lamb and pork. Visitors reckon it's now a "great part of the Goodwood experience", and former Marco Pierre White sideman Darron Bunn, the chef of the title, is winning solid ratings for his "well thought-out", "sensibly creative" cooking. Though some reporters rate the service highly, others find it "willing but clearly inexperienced". / www.goodwood.com/estate/farmer-butcher-chef/@FBCrestaurant.

FIELD & FORK £36 322

4 GUILDHALL ST PO19 1NJ 01243 789915

"Ideally placed for the Festival Theatre", Sam & Janet Mahoney's independent operation, down a side street in the town, earns consistently solid ratings for its "small but well-executed menu": "good value", especially its set deals (including pre-show). / www.fieldandfork.co.uk; @samsfork; Mon-Sat 10.30 pm.

PALLANT RESTAURANT AND CAFE £52 333

EAST PALLANT PO19 1TJ 01243 770827

"A bright, airy and elegant space" which is attached to the Pallant Art Gallery, offering "a small tapas menu, plus occasional themed lunch and evening menus". Some dishes "lack a little zing", but most reports say the food here "exhibits the virtues of simplicity, freshness, locality and someone in the kitchen who clearly knows what they are doing". / www.pallantrestaurantandcafe.co.uk; @EatAtPallant; Tue, Wed, Fri & Sat 5 pm, Thu 9 pm, Sun 8 pm.

THE RICHMOND ARMS £52 333

MILL ROAD, WEST ASHLING PO18 8EA 01243 572046

This "cheerful" and "unpretentious" Goodwood Estate gastropub has a "really interesting menu which makes good use of local ingredients", including beef from nearby Funtington. / www.therichmondarms.co.uk; Wed-Sat 9 pm, Sun 3 pm.

CHINLEY, GREATER MANCHESTER 5–2C

OLD HALL INN £48 433

WHITEHOUGH SK23 6EJ 01663 750529

It's "always buzzing and full of people – which says it all" about this "beautifully restored, atmospheric 16th-century hall", a family-run hotel that is "tucked away in the remote Peak District countryside". "Good pub food with an extra bit of imagination comes from the young chef". / www.old-hall-inn.co.uk; @oldhallinn; Mon-Sat 9.30 pm, Sun 4 pm.

CHINNOR, OXFORDSHIRE 2–2D

THE SIR CHARLES NAPIER £71 435

SPRIGGS ALLEY OX39 4BX 01494 483011

"Whether it's a cosy winter meal with lovely log fires, or a glorious summer evening under the wisteria and vines" in the "stunning garden" – Julie Griffith's "hard-to-find and charming gastropub/restaurant in the Chilterns" is "perfect for a lunch stop off the M40" (set your sat nav). Arguably it charges "stockbroker prices", but most diners feel bills are "fair" due to the "simply lovely setting" and "high standard" of "seasonal" food, plus "good real ale and an excellent wine list". / www.sircharlesnapier.co.uk; @SirCNapier; Tue-Sat 2 pm, Sun 3 pm.

CHOBHAM, SURREY 3–3A

STOVELL'S £77 444

125 WINDSOR ROAD GU24 8QS 01276 858000

"A charming location with amazing food" is the overwhelming verdict on Fernando & Kristy Stovell's attractive timbered farmhouse, just outside Chobham – although its ratings slipped just a tad this year due to a few middling reports, feedback in the survey is fundamentally very strong and supports its high accolades

Stovells, Chobham

(puzzlingly nothing from the Michelin Man, but a rare four rosettes from the AA). Alongside the à la carte, and set lunch options, there's the option of a 'Taste of Mexico' tasting menu (reflecting Fernando's homeland). / www.stovells.com; @Stovells; Mon-Sun 10 pm.

THE WHITE HART £45 334

HIGH STREET GU24 8AA 01276 857 580

Solid ratings this year for this attractive, timber-framed Brunning & Price gastropub (dating from the sixteenth century) – "what they do they do really well". / www.whitehart-chobham.co.uk; @whitehartchob; Mon-Sat 11 pm, Sun 10.30 pm.

CHRISTCHURCH, DORSET 2–4C

CAPTAIN'S CLUB HOTEL & SPA £58 344

WICK FERRY, WICK LANE BH23 1HU 01202 475111

"Eat outside here in the warm sunshine by the river… perfect" – "overlooking the Christchurch estuary is the icing on the cake" at this "modern hotel" (built twelve years ago), praised as "an always-enjoyable experience with consistently good food" in numerous reports. / www.captainsclubhotel.com.

THE JETTY, CHRISTCHURCH HARBOUR HOTEL & SPA £65 344

95 MUDEFORD BH23 3NT 01202 400950

"The views over Christchurch harbour are lovely" – "there can be few better" – at Alex Aitken's "gorgeously situated", "seafood-centric" waterside venue, in the grounds of the Christchurch Harbour Hotel, with a "vibrant (if slightly clinical) interior that works well in warmer months (but can feel more bleak in winter)". On most reports, "a wonderful range of carefully created dishes are lovingly plated" to create meals "of a consistently high standard", and – while there were a greater number of gripes about high prices here this year – for the majority it remains "expensive but worth it". / www.thejetty.co.uk; @alexatthejetty; Wed-Sat 9 pm, Sun 8 pm.

CIRENCESTER, GLOUCESTERSHIRE 2–2C

MADE BY BOB, THE CORNHALL £52 333

THE CORNHALL 26 MARKET PL GL7 2NY 01285 641818

Offering "reliably good food at decent prices" and an open kitchen that "adds to the atmosphere", reporters "love this place" – a decade-old deli and bistro with a swift trade in breakfast and lunch. / www.foodmadebybob.com; @MadeByBob; Mon-Sun 5 pm.

TIERRA & MAR £42

29 SHEEP STREET GL7 1QW 01285 642777

Limited feedback as yet on this November 2017, blue-walled newcomer, which offers a range of Hispanic and Mediterranean dishes but featuring local produce, and – from an array of menus – there are tapas options, but also sharing plates and a seven-course 'degustation' menu. / www.tierraandmar.co.uk; @TierraandMar; Mon-Sun 9 pm.

CLACHAN, ARGYLL AND BUTE 9–3B

LOCH FYNE RESTAURANT AND OYSTER BAR £51 433

LOCH FYNE PA26 8BL 01499 600264

"Exceptional seafood" is "served at the very source" at this renowned loch-side deli and restaurant, also with an in-house smoker; launched by a landowner and marine biologist, the veteran brand marked its fortieth birthday in 2018, having spawned a national empire (to which this venue is no longer linked). / www.lochfyne.com; @lochfyneoysters; 10m E of Inveraray on A83; 6 pm.

CLAUGHTON, LANCASHIRE 5–1B

THE FENWICK ARMS £44 333

LANCASTER RD LA2 9LA 01524 221250

"Convenient for exit 34 of the M6", this 250-year-old inn has "become a firm favourite" under Lancashire's Seafood Pub Company, who took over the then-ailing site in 2013; the "top-class cooking" centres on "special fish dishes" (plus steaks) and "there are now well-appointed, comfy rooms" too, chased by a breakfast "worth getting up for". / www.fenwickarms.co.uk; Mon-Sat 10.30 pm.

CLAVERING, ESSEX 3–2B

THE CRICKETERS £48 223

WICKEN RD CB11 4QT 01799 550442

This "pretty village pub" can hardly escape its association with Jamie Oliver – his folks Trevor & Sally, who still own and run it, moved in when Jamie was a baby, and he stirred his first pots in the kitchen here. Although it takes some flak for being pricey, most reporters say the food here is "surprisingly good" and can't resist a cheeky dig: "there's hype around JO, but his parents

do a much better job!" / www.thecricketers.co.uk; @CricketersThe; on B1038 between Newport & Buntingford; Mon-Sat 10 pm, Sun 5 pm; no Amex. *Accommodation:* 14 rooms, from £95

CLAYGATE, SURREY 3–3A

THE SWAN INN £51 333

2 HARE LANE KT10 9BS 01372 462 582

Owned by Claude Bosi, this old inn (with rooms) near Esher Common serves a menu bearing little resemblance to Bosi's creations at Bibendum, but its selection of 'classic pub and comfort food favourites' is "always first rate"; "smart" interior too. / www.theswanesher.co.uk; @theswan_esher; Sun-Thu 10.30 pm, Fri & Sat 11 pm.

CLEARWELL, MONMOUTHSHIRE 2–2B

TUDOR FARMHOUSE £63 443

HIGH STREET GL16 8JS 01594 833046

"A lovely boutique hotel in a quiet village in the Forest of Dean" – this small, rural venture offers "very good food with a local accent" in its beamed, stone-walled dining room. / tudorfarmhousehotel.co.uk; Mon-Sat 9.30 pm, Sun 4 pm.

CLEVEDON, NORTH SOMERSET 2–2A

TIFFIN TEA HOUSE £17 335

11 THE BEACH BS21 7QU 01275 871605

"A unique new spot on Clevedon's historic Grade I listed pier, which transforms at night into a wonderful seafood restaurant serving fresh fish caught that day". They also do coffee, cakes and cream teas. "If you are lucky you will get the added bonus of a stunning sunset". Opened in late 2017, it won best newcomer at the Somerset Food and Drink awards. / www.tiffingroup.com/the-beach-clevedon/; Mon-Sat 9.30 pm, Sun 4 pm.

CLIFTON, CUMBRIA 8–3A

GEORGE & DRAGON £51 333

CA10 2ER 01768 865381

"What a find!"; this "delightful country pub" near Penrith is "well worth seeking out" for its "locally sourced food" and "welcoming staff". If you're passing through, it makes a "great stop-off from the M6 en-route to Scotland". / www.georgeanddragonclifton.co.uk; @GeorgeDragonCli; on the A6 in the village of Clifton; Tue-Sun; no bookings. *Accommodation:* 12 rooms, from £95

CLIMPING, WEST SUSSEX 3–4A

BAILIFFSCOURT HOTEL £79 344

CLIMPING ST BN17 5RW 01903 723511

This luxurious spa hotel, in 30 acres behind Climping beach, was built in mock-medieval style for the Guinness family in 1927. Meals in the dining room, with its mullioned windows, are decently rated, although there is the odd complaint about "London prices". / www.hshotels.co.uk; Mon-Sun 11 pm; booking max 8 may apply; children: 7+. *Accommodation:* 39 rooms, from £205.

CLIPSHAM, RUTLAND   6–4A

THE OLIVE BRANCH   £47   4|4|4

MAIN ST LE15 7SH   01780 410355

One of the country's first rural 'gastropubs' when Ben Jones and Sean Hope (formerly of local luxury spot Hambleton Hall) opened it almost 20 years ago – this "relaxed and friendly" gem is currently on fine form – a "delightful country inn with a wonderful atmosphere and excellent menus sourced with local produce". Just two minutes from Stretton junction, it makes "a good stop for anyone driving on the A1". Stop Press: In November 2018, Nick Evans (formerly a top chef at Langho's Northcote Manor) joined the business as executive head chef, while Sean Hope is to take more of a backseat. / www.theolivebranchpub.com; @theolivebranch; 2m E from A1 on B664; Mon-Sat 9.30 pm, Sun 9 pm; no Amex. *Accommodation:* 6 rooms, from £135.

CLITHEROE, LANCASHIRE   5–1B

THE ASSHETON ARMS   £45   3|3|5

BB7 4BJ   01200 441227

"The pub's setting is glorious, at the top of Downham, opposite the church, looking over this completely unspoiled Ribble Valley village (no double yellow lines, no street furniture, no TV aerials)". This is the flagship in Jocelyn Neve's ever-expanding Seafood Pub Company chain. Fans say it serves "the freshest and best range of fish" hereabouts (but is there "a tendency to rely on Asian flavours rather than focusing in on what should be topnotch seafood, especially given the Neve heritage in Fleetwood?") / seafoodpubcompany.com/the-assheton-arms/; @SeafoodPubCo; Sun-Fri 11 pm, Sat midnight.

THE INN AT WHITEWELL   £57   3|3|5

FOREST OF BOWLAND BB7 3AT 01200 448222

"A staggering inn… once you've found it" – "buried in the middle of the Forest of Bowland", this "firm-favourite", olde-worlde, riverside landmark is "an absolute must for visit and ideally a stay", with its "stunning location", "consistent", traditional cooking and extensive cellar. Just one problem – "you'll never want to leave!" / www.innatwhitewell.com/; @innatwhitewell; 9:30pm.

COBHAM, SURREY   3–3A

THE CRICKETERS   £52   3|2|3

DOWNSIDE COMMON KT11 3NX 01932 862 105

'Owzat! This "cosy" and very English-sounding 17th-century inn on Downside Common now has a Gallic accent as part of Raymond Blanc's White Brasserie Company. Reporters are impressed, awarding solid marks for the "quality food". / www.cricketerscobham.com; @thecricketers1; Mon-Sat 11 pm, Sun 10 pm.

THE IVY COBHAM BRASSERIE   £56   2|3|4

48 HIGH ST KT11 3EF   01932 901777

"The Art Deco setting and conservatory garden areas are a delight" at this branch of the Ivy brand's national rollout, by all accounts an improvement on the "rather tired Italian establishment" that preceded it. As for the celebs of the West End original – well, Surrey boasts its own, and TV hosts Eamonn Holmes and Ruth Langsford have been spotted here more than once. The food splits opinion between "delicious" and "very very poor" – even from the same source, with one reporter moaning that "a great dinner" was followed by "an extremely disappointing lunch…" / theivycobhambrasserie.com; @IvyCobhamBrass; Mon-Sun 12.30 am.

COGGESHALL, ESSEX   3–2C

RANFIELDS BRASSERIE   £43   3|3|4

4 - 6 STONEHAM STREET CO6 1TT 01376 561453

"The name may have changed but not the warm ambience of this most unusual restaurant", which can count the late Peter Langan amongst its past owners, and which was previously known as Baumanns. Its modern brasserie fare is decently rated too. / www.ranfieldsbrasserie.co.uk; Mon-Sat 10.30 pm.

COLERNE, WILTSHIRE   2–2B

LUCKNAM PARK, LUCKHAM PARK HOTEL   £116   4|4|5

SN14 8AZ   01225 742777

"Superb food" in a "perfect setting" adds up to an "excellent experience" at this Palladian mansion on a Cotswolds estate, where longstanding chef Hywel Jones's "consistently excellent" cuisine is served in the elegant and formal dining room. "Would recommend it to anyone". / www.lucknampark.co.uk; @LucknamPark; 6m NE of Bath; Tue-Sat 9.45 pm, Sun 2.30 pm; jacket required; children: 5+ D & Sun L. *Accommodation:* 42 rooms, from £360.

LUCKNAM PARK (BRASSERIE)   £54   3|3|3

SN14 8AZ   01225 742777

From "lovely staff", to the "most amazing bread to start" and "super" mains (with 'Field-, Farm- and Boat-to-Plate' options), this glass-

fronted restaurant remains a pleasing, less ruinous, alternative to the main event at this famous country house pile; watch out for the excellent lunch deals. / www.lucknampark.co.uk; @lucknampark; 6m NE of Bath; 10 pm; closed Mon & Sun D.

COLNE, LANCASHIRE   5–1B

BANNY'S RESTAURANT   £29   3|2|2

1 VIVARY WAY BB8 9NW   01282 856220

"The fish, chips and mushy peas are always served piping hot and tasty" (and they "even have beer") say fans of this former Harry Ramsden's – ideal after hitting the shops at the Boundary Mill outlet. The nautical interior is pleasant, "although if you look out of the window you may think you are in a motorway service station". / www.bannys.co.uk; @Bannys; 8.45 pm; no Amex.

COLWELL BAY, ISLE OF WIGHT   2–4D

THE HUT   £53   4|3|3

COLWELL CHINE ROAD PO40 9NP 01983 898 637

"Views are excellent (across the Solent)" from the expansive terrace, "although good weather helps!", at this "unpretentious" summer-only seaside restaurant: "a top seaside venue when the sun is shining!" The order of the day – "well-cooked fish, usually with a fair selection of catch available" (plus burgers and tacos). / www.thehutcolwell.co.uk; 9 pm.

COLWYN BAY, CONWY   4–1D

BRYN WILLIAMS AT PORTH EIRIAS   £49   3|3|3

THE PROMENADE LL29 8HH   01492 577 525

This solidly-rated, modern beach-side bistro is part of a landmark development central to the new promenade in Colwyn Bay. High-achieving chef Bryn Williams (Odettes, Somerset House) comes back to his North Wales roots with a "limited but reliable" menu of gastropub-style aspiration. / www.portheirias.com; @brynportheirias; Wed-Sat 9 pm, Mon & Tue, Sun 4 pm.

CONGLETON, CHESHIRE   5–2B

PECKS   £63   2|3|4

NEWCASTLE RD CW12 4SB   01260 275 161

With its "unique 'Dinner at 8' format" – this stalwart thirty-year-old venture inspires adoration from fans for "guaranteed excellence from a menu that's constantly refreshed, contemporary and imaginative". It provoked a couple of disappointments this year, however, in part due to "overly ambitious cuisine (with too many components in most dishes)". / www.pecksrest.co.uk; @pecksrest; off A34; Tue-Sat 10.30 pm, Sun 3 pm.

MALIKS £43 4|3|4

HIGH ST SL6 9SF 01628 520085

Consistently "first-rate" Indian cuisine has earned this high street fixture a deserved reputation; Heston Blumenthal, no less, has sung its praises. It also, somewhat surprisingly, occupies "the best-looking half-timbered building in the village". Top Tip: "the Sunday buffet is amazing value". / www.maliks.co.uk/; from the M4, Junction 7 for A4 for Maidenhead; 11.30 pm, Sun 10.30 pm.

THE WHITE OAK £42 3|4|3

THE POUND SL6 9QE 01628 523043

This polished ten-year-old (more restaurant than pub) is a solid performer combining "wonderfully fresh food" and "attentive, personal service". "It's so good I'd consider selling up and moving so it could be my local!" / www.thewhiteoak.co.uk; @thewhiteoakcoo; Mon-Sat 11 pm, Sun 6 pm; no Amex.

YU AND YOU £55 5|4|3

**500 LONGSIGHT RD BB1 9EU
01254 247111**

"This former roadside (right on the busy A59) pub, looks nothing from the outside (a nondescript stone building and a somewhat windswept car park), but the interior is quite glam (like a 1990s nightclub) and it has now been turning out some of the best Chinese-ish cooking in rural Lancashire for over ten years". It's a "fun" spot and the cooking is "first rate": arguably a little "safe" ("rooted in a westernised version of Cantonese food, with no offal and not even a mention of Sichuan") but "spot-on" and "really marking it out from many Chinatown places, the ingredients are top-notch quality". www.yuandyou.com; @yuandyou; off the A59 7 miles towards Clitheroe; 11 pm; D only, closed Mon.

CORSE LAWN HOTEL £56 3|4|3

GL19 4LZ 01452 780771

Good but limited feedback on the dining room of this traditional and very comfortable country house hotel, still presided over by the Hine family who converted this Queen Anne House overlooking a duck pond 40 years ago. The cellar here is of some renown. / www.corselawn.com; @corselawn; 5m SW of Tewkesbury on B4211; Sun-Thu 10 pm, Fri & Sat 10.30 pm. *Accommodation:* 18 rooms, from £120

BAR 44 £21 4|3|3

44C HIGH ST CF71 7AG 03333 444049

Limited but upbeat feedback this year on the Morgan family's lively, sixteen-year-old Hispanic café/bar in a first-floor high street location – the original of what's now a three-strong operation in South Wales, and now with a newly opened Bristol sibling too. A selection of tapas is backed up by a wide range of wines and sherries. / www.bar44.co.uk; @bar44cowbridge; Fri & Sat midnight, Tue-Thu 11 pm, Sun 5 pm; no Amex.

HARE AND HOUNDS £46 4|3|4

ABERTHIN CF71 7LG 01446 774892

Chef Tom Watts-Jones had his first pint at this 300-year-old hostelry in the Vale of Glamorgan, whose "fresh and seasonal fare from an ever-changing menu" has won it a strong culinary reputation. The dining room serves predominantly modern bistro options, but there is also a fancier tasting option. / www.hareandhoundsaberthin.com; @Hare__Hounds; Wed-Sat 9 pm, Sun 4 pm.

APICIUS £68 5|4|2

23 STONE ST TN17 3HF 01580 714666

"Every town needs an Apicius" – a "real treat" of a village restaurant run by husband and wife team Tim Johnson & Faith Hawkins; his "confident, imaginative and skilful cooking" (you can choose to have dishes as either starters or mains) is abetted by her "charming" FOH skills. / www.restaurant-apicius.co.uk; Mon-Sat 10.30 pm, Sun 9 pm; no Amex; children: 8+.

JOLLY FISHERMAN £47 3|3|4

HAVEN HILL NE66 3TR 01665 576461

"Perched on the edge of mid-Northumberland's dramatic coastline, this former pub opposite the world-famous L Robson & Sons 'Craster Kipper' smokehouse" (as per the name, seafood features heavily on the menu) offers "great cooking" that's "excellent value" too. / www.thejollyfishermancraster.co.uk; @TheJollyCraster; near Dunstanburgh Castle; Mon-Sun 11 pm; no Amex; no bookings.

CRATHORNE ARMS £52 3|3|4

TS15 0BA 01642 961402

"Now well-established since being taken over by Eugene and Barbara McCoy" of the Cleveland Tontine some years back – a boozer off the A19 attracting everyone from "local farmers to international footballers". Its appeal – "open fires, great beer, a warm welcome and super traditional dining: from steak puddings to Lindisfarne oysters". / thecrathornearms.co.uk; 11 pm, Sun 7 pm; no bookings.

SUTOR CREEK £45 3|3|2

21 BANK ST IV11 8YE 01381 600855

Top wood-fired pizzas and "tasty" seafood dishes drawing on the Black Isle's larder make this harbour-view spot "well worth visiting" ("also try their nearby coffee shop", 'Couper's Creek'). Stop Press – from November 2018 until March 2019, as they expand the kitchen, they're relocating to Cromarty's 'The Old Brewery'. / www.sutorcreek.co.uk; 9 pm; closed Mon & Tue; no Amex.

NO. 1 £36 4|3|3

1 NEW ST NR27 9HP 01263 512316

Much-garlanded Morston Hall owner Galton Blackiston's two-storey, sea-view restaurant has a two-fold appeal: downstairs is a "very good down-to-earth fish 'n' chips spot", while the pastel-coloured "upstairs has a more interesting menu" (e.g. tacos, Korean pork belly, cockled popcorn…) / www.no1cromer.com; @no1cromer; 9 pm, sun 7pm.

THE CHEQUERS AT CROWLE £47

CROWLE GREEN WR7 4AA 01905 381772

Too limited survey feedback for a rating, but such reports as we have are very enthusiastic about this great gastropub near Droitwich; open 7 days a week serving a wide variety of food to suit all tastes. They even have beach huts out the back for outdoor summer dining. / www.thechequersatcrowle.com; @chequerscrowle1.

KARNAVAR £41 4|4|2

62 SOUTHEND CR0 1DP 020 8686 2436

"Different and novel dishes with a rare sense of adventure" inspire universal high praise for chef/owner Manoj Karnavar's "really innovative Indian" – "the exciting food helps you forget the rather drab interior and the iffy location". / Karnavar.com; @karnavarlondon; Tue-Sat 11 pm, Sun 9.30 pm; no shorts.

MCDERMOTTS FISH & CHIPS £30 5|4|2

5-7 THE FORESTDALE SHOPPING CENTRE FEATHERBED LN CR0 9AS 020 8651 1440

"Perfectly cooked skinless cod, crispy batter, excellent chips, fresh bread & butter, little dish of pickled onions and gherkins, homemade tartare sauce" – no wonder Tony and son Sean McDermott achieve outstanding ratings for their veteran New Addington chippie (est 1987). / www.mcdermottsfishandchips.co.uk; Tue-Fri 9.30 pm, Sat 9 pm.

THE POTTING SHED £47 3|3|3

THE ST SN16 9EW 01666 577833

"Owned by the Rectory Hotel on the other side of the road" – both received a "very stylish" revamp courtesy of new, music-exec owner Alex Payne in mid-2017 – this beamed gastroboozer turns out some "superb cooking" (including game) on most (if not quite all) reports. / www.thepottingshedpub.com; @pottingshedpub; 11

The Peat Inn, Cupar (Credit ZAC and ZAC)

pm; no Amex; no bookings. *Accommodation:* 12 rooms, from £95

CRUNDALE, KENT · 3–3C

THE COMPASSES INN · £54 · 434

SOLE ST CT4 7ES 01227 700 300

"The best pub restaurant we have been to in years!" – Rob and Donna Taylor's rural inn above the Downs between Canterbury and Ashford is "going from strength to strength" with "beautiful" (but not unnecessarily fancy) food that's "always consistent". / www.thecompassescrundale.co.uk; @compasses_inn; 9:3-pm.

CUCKFIELD, WEST SUSSEX · 3–4B

ROSE AND CROWN · £46 · 333

LONDON ROAD, RH17 5BS 01444 414217

"Excellent, locally prepared seasonal food" wins praise for this West Sussex pub run by father and son team Mark and Simon Dennis. The cooking's not high falutin', but too ambitious to be described as pub grub (although by day there is a sandwich menu). / www.roseandcrowncuckfield.co.uk; Wed-Sat 8.30 pm.

CULGAITH, CUMBRIA · 7–3D

MRS MILLER'S · £37 · 443

HAZEL DENE GARDEN CENTRE CA10 1QF 01768 882520

This unexpected venue, tucked away at the back of a village garden centre in the Eden Valley and open for lunch daily plus dinner on Friday and Saturday, is by all accounts both "very good and very cheap". "You can get a two-course lunch for £7", but there's "greater interest in the slightly dearer dishes, such as perfectly cooked sea bass with leeks and a good lobster sauce, or a herb-crusted pheasant breast with mash, both for a mere £11". As for desserts, "tarts are very good, with exceptional pastry". / www.mrsmillersculgaith.co.uk; @MrsMillers; Mon-Sat 9.30 pm, Sun 4 pm.

CUPAR, FIFE · 9–3D

THE PEAT INN · £83 · 544

KY15 5LH 01334 840206

"Hidden away along a narrow country road" a short drive out of St Andrews, Geoffrey & Katherine Smeddle's famous and "comfortable" country inn (which underwent a contemporary refurb a few years ago) is "the kind of establishment that creates a sense of secure well being, with moments of gastronomic grace providing the excitement!" (the cuisine is amongst the best in Scotland). Top Tip: "one of the best cheese boards ever and all Scottish cheeses". / www.thepeatinn.co.uk; @thepeatinn; at junction of B940 & B941, SW of St Andrews; 9 pm; closed Mon & Sun. *Accommodation:* 8 rooms, from £195

DALRY, NORTH AYRSHIRE · 9–4B

BRAIDWOODS · £75 · 544

DRUMASTLE MILL COTTAGE KA24 4LN 01294 833544

A "quiet, refined little haven out in the fields", this isolated conversion of an Ayrshire cottage is hosted by an accomplished husband-and-wife chef team, who celebrate their 25th anniversary here this year. "Keith and Nicola's wonderful place just never lets you down" according to all reports – "no wonder it's the only Scottish restaurant to have kept its Michelin star consistently for 19 years in a row (now 20), while others have come and gone!" It provides "very friendly and helpful service", plus "local, seasonal food, skillfully cooked and well presented from a short menu, which ensures everything is fresh and of the best possible quality". / www.braidwoods.co.uk; Wed-Sat, Tue 9 pm; children: 12+ at D.

DANEHILL, EAST SUSSEX · 3–4B

COACH AND HORSES · £48 · 333

SCHOOL LN RH17 7JF 01825 740369

This "lovely old pub" with beautiful gardens outside, and stone-walled dining room and cosy bar within, is highly rated for its "reliably good" cooking. / www.coachandhorses.co; off A275; Wed & Thu 10.30 pm, Fri & Sat 11 pm.

DARLINGTON, COUNTY DURHAM · 8–3B

THE ORANGERY, ROCKLIFFE HALL · £112 · 433

DL2 2DU 01325 729999

The stunning, glass-ceilinged dining room at Boro chairman Steve Gibson's lavish hotel and golf club, near the North Yorks border; one visitor this year – perhaps unaware of its high marks in Harden's and its AA 4-Rosette status – was "really surprised" at Richard Allen's "refined", flavoursome food (parlayed in six- or 10-course tasting menus). / www.rockliffehall.com; @rockliffehall; Wed-Sat 11 pm; jacket required.

DARSHAM, SUFFOLK · 6–4D

DARSHAM NURSERIES · £45 · 434

MAIN RD IP17 3PW 01728 667022

For "the best shakshuka you have ever eaten" to puddings "you will never forget" (or, latterly, Friday and Saturday dinners) – this converted barn café – specialising in small plates, "with plenty of vegetables, fruit and herbs grown on site", wins raves for food with "huge amounts of flavour". / www.darshamnurseries.co.uk; @DarshamNurserie; Mon-Sat 10 pm, Sun 5 pm.

DARTMOUTH, DEVON · 1–4D

ROCKFISH · £46 · 323

8 SOUTH EMBANKMENT TQ6 9BH 01803 832800

"Very fresh fish cooked with an eye on what's modern and interesting – this is how it should be done!" say fans of Mitch Tonks's original chippie, "still the best of the chain". "The daily fish list is always inviting, with sprats, gurnard and whiting". "Great value too, and they look after kids nicely". / www.therockfish.co.uk/; @therockfishuk; 9.30 pm.

THE SEAHORSE · £68 · 544

5 SOUTH EMBANKMENT TQ6 9BH 01803 835147

"A lovely spot by the harbour with real respect for the local catch" – that's the deal at Mitch Tonks's popular and well-known dining room, which serves "a great selection of top quality fish and seafood"; "still one of the best despite the expansion of the Tonks empire". / www.seahorserestaurant.co.uk; @SeahorseDevon; Tue - Sat 9.30 pm.

DATCHWORTH, HERTFORDSHIRE · 3–2B

THE TILBURY · £57 · 234

WATTON RD SG3 6TB 01438 815 550

"Calling The Tilbury a gastro-pub rather undersells it", agree fans of James & Tom Bainbridge's village green fixture – "the food is inventive and nearly always hits the spot perfectly". Scores are dragged down by a significant minority, though, who complain that the cooking ("much hyped locally") is "all show and no substance". / www.thetilbury.co.uk; @the_tilbury; 9 pm, Fri & Sat 9.30 pm; closed Mon & Sun D; no bookings.

DAVENTRY, NORTHAMPTONSHIRE · 2–1D

FAWSLEY HALL · £67 · 234

FAWSLEY NN11 3BA 01327 892000

"Pre-dinner drinks and after-dinner coffee in the beautiful old hall makes for a truly memorable trip" to this country house hotel, deep in the countryside. The food here hasn't always lived up to the surroundings, but was decently-rated this year, especially the "fantastic" afternoon tea. / www.fawsleyhall.com; @FawsleyHall; on A361 between Daventry & Banbury; Mon-Sat 10 pm. *Accommodation:* 107 rooms, from £175

DEAL, KENT   3–3D

FROG & SCOT   £47   4 3 3

86 HIGH STREET CT14 6EG 01304 379444

This "unpretentious neighbourhood bistro" features "perfectly judged cooking, from a Sportsman alumnus chef" (David Gadd) using "locally sourced ingredients including superb fish". There's an "extensive list of classics as well as organic, biodynamic and natural wines"; owners Benoit and Sarah (respectively the Frog and the Scot) also run Le Pinardier wine bar a few doors away. / www.frogandscot.co.uk; Tue-Thu 5 pm, Fri & Sat 11 pm, Sun 4 pm; no bookings.

HYTHE BAY SEAFOOD RESTAURANT   £46   3 4 3

BEACH STREET CT14 6HY 01304 365 555

"Spacious and modern seafront establishment" – part of a mini-chain of three – praised like its siblings for its "good-quality, well-priced food and decent wine". / www.hythebay.co.uk; @HytheBay.

WHITS OF WALMER   £59   4 5 3

61 THE STRAND CT14 7DP 01304 368881

"I used to go when they were off Abingdon Road in Kensington – but it's definitely worth the trip here!" says a London-based reporter who makes the 80 mile journey to Eva and Steve Whitney's "small", imaginative bistro near the sea, which rates consistently highly (as their London venture used to). / www.whits.co.uk; Mon-Sat 9.30 pm, Sun 4 pm.

DEDHAM, ESSEX   3–2C

MILSOMS   £47   3 2 3

STRATFORD RD CO7 6HW 01206 322 795

In a well-established ivy-covered Constable Country hotel, with bikes and canoes for hire, a sprawling, pubbish venture running the gamut from mezze boards to dry-aged steaks; while a solid performer, it elicited modest feedback this year (which included nominations as a good choice with kids). / www.milsomhotels.com; @milsomhotels; Mon-Sat 9 pm, Sun 7 pm; no bookings. *Accommodation:* 15 rooms, from £120

THE SUN INN   £48   3 3 4

HIGH ST CO7 6DF 01206 564325

"Better than a pub, but with all the easy cosiness of being in the relaxed countryside pub that it actually is" – this "beautiful historic inn" at the heart of a picturesque village makes a good stop-off point on the Essex/Suffolk border. / www.thesuninndedham.com; @SunInnDedham; Sun-Thu 9 pm, Fri & Sat 10 pm; no Amex. *Accommodation:* 7 rooms, from £110

LE TALBOOTH   £86   3 3 5

GUN HILL CO7 6HP 01206 323150

"The perfect setting for a perfect meal" – this half-timbered building beside the River Stour was depicted in a Constable painting. The kitchen is praised for "excellent if slightly old-fashioned cuisine", but it's the "romantic setting" (all "cosy old beams and wood fires") that most sets the pulse racing – although, having passed its 65th birthday, the restaurant was shocked to be described in The Times this year as the 'fourth sexiest' in England. / www.milsomhotels.com; @milsomhotels; 5m N of Colchester on A12, take B1029; Sun-Thu 9.30 pm, Fri & Sat 10 pm; no jeans.

DEGANWY, CONWY   4–1D

PAYSANNE   £41   3 3 2

147 STATION ROAD LL31 9EJ 01492 582079

This "long-established and popular venue" has been in the Ross family for thirty years and is now in the hands of the original founders' son. The bistro-style cooking has a strong French flavour with "fish a speciality". / www.paysannedeganwy.co.uk; @PaysanneDeganwy; Wed-Sat 9 pm, Mon & Tue, Sun 4 pm; no shorts.

DENHAM, BUCKINGHAMSHIRE   3–3A

THE SWAN INN   £53   3 3 3

VILLAGE ROAD UB9 5BH 01895 832085

Possibly the first genuine country pub off the A/M40 as you leave London, this Georgian coaching inn-turned-smart-village-gastroboozer is an understandable "favourite" for numerous reporters – "popular and crowded", with some "delicious" food and "especially lovely when sitting outside". / www.swaninndenham.co.uk; @swaninnpub9.

DERBY, DERBYSHIRE   5–3C

DARLEYS   £63   4 2 4

DARLEY ABBEY MILL DE22 1DZ 01332 364987

"Interesting and enjoyable food" of "a consistently high standard", combined with a "lovely riverside setting" have kept this venue as "leader of the Derby pack" for very many years. Set in a 19th-century former textile mill, part of the Darley Abbey Mills World Heritage site, the restaurant has a refurbished terrace overlooking the River Derwent. / www.darleys.com; @DarleysDerby; Mon-Thu 11 pm, Fri & Sat midnight, Sun 10.30 pm; no Amex; children: 10+ Sat eve.

EBI SUSHI   £42   5 3 2

59 ABBEY ST DE22 3SJ 01332 265656

"For a downbeat setting" – uninspiring façade leading to a "cramped", basic interior – "the food and service are brilliant" at this much-loved joint, akin to a "small street restaurant in Tokyo". So how exactly has it come to land in Derby? – that'll be "the Toyota factory down the road". / Tue-Sat 9.30 pm, Sun 2.30 pm; no Amex.

DINTON, BUCKINGHAMSHIRE   2–3C

LA CHOUETTE   £62   4 4 2

WESTLINGTON GRN HP17 8UW 01296 747422

"A rare gem of a restaurant!" – "Frederic the owner and chef also waits tables and is a real character" (so "don't go if you are easily offended by banter"). "Fortunately he can cook", and "whilst savouring the delicious Belgian food, you can admire his stunning wildlife photography on the walls". / www.lachouette.co.uk; off A418 between Aylesbury & Thame; Mon-Fri 11.30 pm, Sat 11 pm, Sun 10.30 pm; no Amex.

DONHEAD ST ANDREW, WILTSHIRE   2–3C

THE FORESTER INN   £50   3 4 3

LOWER STREET SP7 9EE 01747 828038

"We're so lucky to have a pub this good in the area", agree regulars at this thatched 15th-century boozer "in an idyllic village", whose kitchen uses fish from Brixham and St Mawes, rare-breed Lowlines cattle from a nearby farm, and produce from Rungis market in Paris. "OK it's pub food, but far better than average in this part of the world". / www.theforesterdonheadstandrew.co.uk; @ForesterNews; off A30; Mon-Sat 4.30 pm, Sun 3.30 pm.

DORCHESTER, DORSET   2–4B

SIENNA   £52   4 4 2

36 HIGH WEST STREET DT1 1UP 01305 250022

This "fabulous" little restaurant showcases young former MasterChef finalist Marcus Wilcox's "exquisite" modern British cooking. "There are few covers, but that helps make it so special". / www.siennadorchester.co.uk; @siennadorset; Mon-Sat midnight, Sun 10.30 pm; no Amex; children: 12+.

DORKING, SURREY   3–3A

SORREL   £84   5 5 4

77 SOUTH STREET RH4 2JU 01306 889 414

"The move from Ripley has worked" and Steve Drake is producing "phenomenal" cooking in his new 40-cover yearling – "an outstanding venture that maintains and even exceeds his former high standards". "Stunning, innovative dishes are meticulously prepared" and "he conjures up amazing flavours" (e.g. "beetroot, Douglas fir, sesame and goats' cheese packed a refreshing punch; tartare of venison with smoked egg yolk and orange purée was a rich smoky creamy mouth adventure; pre-dessert of carrot tobacco with coconut ice cream and lime gel was one of my top ten desserts; but just wait for the blackberry Waldorf!"). "Service is top-notch and the environment warm and friendly". Top Tip: "a very good value set lunch menu". Also "parking is tricky, so allow some time if you cannot get into the small adjacent car park". / www.sorrelrestaurant.co.uk; @SteveDrakeFood; credit card deposit required to book.

The Seahorse, Dartmouth

TANROAGAN £67 333

9 RIDGEWAY ST IM1 1EW 01624 612355

Those who have "struggled to find decent restaurants on the Isle of Man" amid its "chippies, takeaways and mediocre eateries" hail this "rustic-chic" sidestreet café as a "gem": the fish-centric food is abetted by "very palatable" wines and "the concept of a mini-dessert" proves popular. NB "they have a sister restaurant in Peel (the other side of the island), 'The Boatyard'". / tanroagan.co.uk/; Tue-Sat 9.30 pm.

HYTHE BAY SEAFOOD RESTAURANT £46 343

THE ESPLANADE, CT17 9FS 01304 207740

"Authentic seafood at a great price" inspires fans of this beachfront restaurant above the Seasport Centre. / www.hythebay.co.uk/our-restaurants.htm; @HytheBay.

THE OLD INN £78 543

EX6 6QR 01647 281 276

"Faultless food" from former Gidleigh Park chef Duncan Walker wins consistently high ratings for this "lovely" 17th-century village inn on the edge of Dartmoor, complete with "log fires, comfy sofas, and golden retrievers". It's a confined dining area, though, which can "leave one at the mercy of the loudly expressed opinions of the other diners". / www.old-inn.co.uk; @duncansoldinn; 9 pm; closed Sun-Tue, Wed L, Thu L.; no Amex; children: 12+. *Accommodation:* 3 rooms, from £90

THE CREEL £52 333

**25 LAMER STREET EH42 1HJ
01368 863279**

"A hidden gem of fresh cooked seafood" – this "tiny", "cosy" bistro has a "lovely setting", near the harbour, and is praised for its "creative" cooking. / Tue-Thu 9 pm, Fri & Sat 9.30 pm, Sun 4 pm.

THE ROCKS HOTEL AND RESTAURANT £33 334

MARINE ROAD EH42 1AR 01368 862287

"The atmosphere is exactly what you'd wish for" at this "unique and lively pub which exudes character"; and serves "a simple menu with large plates of tasty food from great local ingredients". / www.therockshoteldunbar.co.uk; @therocksdunbar; Mon-Sun 10.30 pm; no Amex; no bookings. *Accommodation:* 11 rooms, from £75

CROMLIX HOUSE £57 234

KINBUCK FK15 9JT 01786 825450

Dour tennis ace Andy Murray's "delightful refuge in the hills" occupies a fine Victorian building in tranquil grounds. There are fans of the glass-walled conservatory restaurant – "great cooking and a wine list to study for hours" – but also critics (for whom the "uninspired" food "did not live up to the big names behind it" – aka Albert Roux). / www.cromlix.com; @CromlixHotel; Tue-Sat midnight, Mon 11 pm, Sun 7 pm.

THE FLITCH OF BACON £68 423

THE ST CM6 3HT 01371 821 660

Some "perfect meals" have emerged from the kitchen here since owner Daniel Clifford (of Midsummer House, Cambridge fame) recruited Tim Allen (ex-Launceston Place and Wild Rabbit) as chef-partner, and took the style of the venture upmarket – "a pub it is not: no draught beer". In October 2018 it was blessed by the tyre men with a star – its survey-ratings do say it's "fantastic", but no more so than many other un-starred gastropubs around the land run by less famous names. / www.flitchofbacon.co.uk; @flitchofbaconld; Wed-Sat 9 pm, Tue 6 pm, Sun 3.30 pm; booking max 6 may apply.

THE THREE CHIMNEYS £120 545

COLBOST IV55 8ZT 01470 511258

"Worth the difficulty of getting to" – Shirley and Eddie Spear's famous, "out-of-the-way" old crofter's cottage has achieved a formidable reputation since it opened in 1984 and reports continue to say it fully lives up, with very locally-sourced food that's "pretty much perfect on every course". "Next time I'm going to stay!" / www.threechimneys.co.uk; @3_chimneys; 5m from Dunvegan Castle on B884 to Glendale; 9.30pm; children: 8+. *Accommodation:* 6 rooms, from £345

THE GARDEN HOUSE INN £48 323

FRAMWELLGATE, PETH DH1 4NQ 0191 386 3395

The head chef behind Bistro 21's success, Ruari MacKay, now runs this relaxed city-outskirts pub-with-rooms – a proper boozer backed up by an "interesting" modern British menu (from much-lauded lobster sandwiches through to chorizo and fried eggs) and drinkable real ales. / www.gardenhouseinn.com; @gardenhouseinn; Mon-Thu 11 pm, Fri & Sat 11.30 pm, Sun 10 pm.

THE GROVE - NARBERTH £89 334

MOLLESTON SA67 8BX 01834 860915

"Wonderful fusions of taste on the five-course tasting menu" and "the best afternoon tea" from chef Allister Barsby (ex-Gidleigh Park) are among the attractions at this plush 17th-century bolthole overlooking the Preseli Hills. It's a far cry from ten years ago, when owner Neil Kedward, a former civil engineer, stood in as chef after rescuing the derelict property with his wife Zoe. Now they also own Coast at Saundersfoot and the Beach House on the Gower. / www.thegrove-narberth.co.uk/; @GroveNarbeth; 9.30 pm.

JOLLY SPORTSMAN £49 444

CHAPEL LN BN7 3BA 01273 890400

"A favourite for a spot of lunch at the weekend" if you don't mind the schlep, Bruce Wass's off-the-beaten-track, humble-looking gastroboozer has notably "strong cooking" and "great service for a pub". / www.thejollysportsman.com; @JollySportsman1; NW of Lewes; Tue-Thu 9.30 pm, Fri 10 pm, Sat 9 pm, Sun 3.30 pm; no Amex.

RED LION FREEHOUSE £69 343

SN9 6AQ 01980 671124

"Off the beaten track" – a few miles from Stonehenge – "but well worth the effort" if you're in the area: this repurposed boozer has a "beautiful, thoughtful menu, warm and welcoming service" and "those little touches that make you want to return again and again". / www.redlionfreehouse.com; @redlionfreehse; Wed-Sat 9 pm, Sun 3 pm; no Amex; no bookings. *Accommodation:* 5 rooms, from £160

GRAVETYE MANOR £106 335

VOWELS LANE RH19 4LJ 01342 810567

"Perfect for a special occasion", this Elizabethan manor has a new steel-and-glass dining room overlooking one of the country's most important historic gardens, created by William Robinson in the 1880s. "The country house surroundings are luxurious, the service attentive, knowledgeable and efficient, and the food excellent from starter to dessert". Chef George Blogg's "light and balanced" meals include "delicious vegetables and fruits from arguably the best kitchen garden in England", just out of view above the famous cottage garden. Price is an issue for one or two reporters, but the majority verdict is clearly that it's "expensive but worth it". / www.gravetyemanor.co.uk; @GravetyeManor; 2m outside Turner's Hill; 9.30 pm; booking max 8 may apply; children: 7+. **Accommodation:** 17 rooms, from £250

EAST MOLESEY, SURREY — 3–3A

MEZZET £36 **4****4****3**

43 BRIDGE RD KT8 9ER 020 89794088

"What a wonderful surprise to find fresh Lebanese food so close to leafy Hampton Court" and it's "great value for money" too. The nearby Mezzet Dar offshoot serves a mix of Spanish and Lebanese tapas. / www.mezzet.co.uk; @Mezzet; 10 pm, Sun 9 pm.

MEZZET DAR £29 **3****3****3**

39 BRIDGE RD KT8 9ER 020 8783 0149

"An unusual blend of cuisines that really works" – this café a short walk across the bridge from Hampton Court mixes Spanish and Lebanese inspirations in its tapas dishes, and inspires positive (if limited) feedback. / www.mezzetdar.co.uk; @MezzetDar; Tue-Sat 10 pm, Sun 5 pm.

EASTBOURNE, EAST SUSSEX — 3–4B

THE MIRABELLE, THE GRAND HOTEL £69 **2****3****4**

KING EDWARDS PARADE BN21 4EQ 01323 412345

This 30-year veteran "hidden in the corner" of a grand seaside hotel is very much one for the traditionalists and has hitherto occupied "its own little time warp" – an approach fans see as "perfection" (but which could also seem plain dated). Change is afoot though, following the September 2017 installation of Stephanie Malvoisin to lead the kitchen, and some diehard disciples feel things could go either way: "the jury is still out on the new chef, and a potentially disastrous refurbishment (if modern influences are permitted) mean this great bastion is in greater peril than it has been for decades. I fear very greatly that modernisation may bring with it mediocrity. Cut crystal and the signature china have already sadly been downgraded to more modest standard replacements. Getting rid of the salvers, and particularly the silver cloches is also deleterious to the sense of occasion. Some things are better left as they are: the Mirabelle being a prime example!" / www.grandeastbourne.com; @Grandeastbourne; Mon closed, Tue - Sat 10 pm, Sun closed; jacket required. **Accommodation:** 152 rooms, from £199

EASTON GREY, WILTSHIRE — 2–2C

THE DINING ROOM, WHATLEY MANOR £156 **4****3****4**

SN16 0RB 01666 822888

"Highly inventive, faultlessly executed, flavour-packed fusion cooking" with French, Japanese and Korean influences – Niall Keating has fully justified his appointment at the age of 26 to succeed Martin Bruge in the kitchen of this "beautiful golden stone Cotswold manor house".

For diners, there's a real thrill in witnessing "a chef still developing his style, with some magical surprises adding up to a wonderful experience". / www.whatleymanor.com; @Whatley_Manor; 8 miles from J17 on the M4, follow A429 towards Cirencester to Malmesbury on the B4040; Mon-Thu 10 pm, Fri & Sat 10.30 pm; no jeans; children: 12+. **Accommodation:** 23 rooms, from £305

EDGEHILL, WARWICKSHIRE — 2–1D

THE CASTLE AT EDGEHILL £44 **3****3****5**

MAIN STREET OX15 6DJ 01295 670255

This cosy pub with rooms near Banbury (dating from the 18th century) looks like a fairy-tale castle and enjoys magnificent views over the Warwickshire countryside. As well as pub grub, there's a "thoughtful menu with good seasonal dishes". / castleatedgehill.co.uk; @CastleEdgehill; Mon-Sat , Sun 7 pm.

EDINBURGH, CITY OF EDINBURGH — 9–4C

AIZLE £79 **5****4****3**

107-109 ST. LEONARD'S STREET EH8 9QY 0131 662 9349

"Tasting menus can become a little tiresome" – not least when they're semi-blind, with diners only told what seasonal ingredients might feature – but this refined, country-style venture "manages it with a magical touch". / www.aizle.co.uk; @Aizle_Edinburgh; Wed-Sat 9 pm, Mon & Tue, Sun 4 pm.

ANGELS WITH BAGPIPES £61 **3****3****3**

343 HIGH ST, ROYAL MILE EH1 1PW 0131 2201111

Valvona & Crolla set up in this 16-century, bronze- and marble-adorned building – downstairs is Chanters, upstairs the dinky Halo – in 2010, and its Scotch cuisine is now a firm favourite on the otherwise touristy Royal Mile; "not a bad mouthful was had" by reporters this year, and "wine and cocktails are also excellent". / www.angelswithbagpipes.co.uk; @angelsfood; 9.45 pm.

BELL'S DINER £40 **3****3****2**

7 ST STEPHEN ST EH3 5EN 0131 225 8116

This "basic" Stockbridge institution is an "old-time favourite" (est 1972) that, bar a brief BYOB phase long ago, "hasn't changed over the years (but in a good way)"; "as always great for burger and chips", although the menu extends to haggis sides and sundaes too. / www.bellsdineredinburgh.co.uk; Mon-Sat 10 pm, Sun 3 pm; no Amex.

BIA BISTROT £44 **5****5****4**

19 COLINTON RD EH10 5DP 0131 452 8453

The "perfect neighbourhood bistro(t)" – "a lovely little place a fully way out of the centre" in Morningside "but well worth the taxi ride or walk to get there". "It's not exactly cheap 'n' cheerful but very good value, using excellent ingredients and the cooking has a

nice local feel". "Staff are brilliant and very knowledgeable" and overall this remains one of the most satisfactory places to eat in the city. / www.biabistrot.co.uk; 10 pm.

CAFÉ MARLAYNE £47 **2****2****3**

1 THISTLE STREET EH2 1EN 0131 226 2230

This "proper French" bistro with an "atmosphere to match" ("very cramped if it's full") serves "enjoyable, reliable food at very reasonable prices". A sister branch in Antigua Street closed down in June 2018. / www.cafemarlayne.com/thistle-street; Sun-Fri & Sat 10 pm; no Amex.

THE CAFÉ ROYAL BAR £53 **3****3****4**

19 WEST REGISTER ST EH2 2AA 0131 556 1884

An "always busy" operation that's been serving the good folk of Edinburgh since 1863 in its present Victorian Baroque setting – replete with Royal Doulton tiles depicting famous inventors; of the competent fish-centric cuisine, the headline event is especially "exceptional". / www.caferoyaledinburgh.co.uk/; Mon-Wed 11 pm, Thu, Sun midnight, Fri & Sat 1 am; children: 5.

CAFÉ ST-HONORÉ £55 **3****3****4**

34 NW THISTLE STREET LN EH2 1EA 0131 226 2211

"Classic Gallic charm and good French cooking" are found in spades at Neil Forbes's "small and intimate" (if perhaps "cramped") bistro "tucked away in one of Edinburgh's quieter streets". "A perfect treat" that's been a feature of the New Town for over 20 years. / www.cafesthonore.com; @CafeStHonore; Mon & Tue, Sun 10 pm, Wed-Sat 11 pm.

THE CASTLE TERRACE £109 **4****3****4**

33-35 CASTLE TER EH1 2EL 0131 229 1222

Chef Dominic Jack's "fantastic food", combining Scottish produce with French technique, wins high praise from the many fans of his chic establishment near the castle, a sister to Edinburgh's The Kitchin. Scores would have been higher but for a vociferous minority who reckon it has "lost its way" a bit this year. / www.castleterracerestaurant.com; @dominicjack; Tue-Sat 10 pm.

CHAOPHRAYA £53 **3****3****3**

33 CASTLE ST EH2 3DN 01312 267614

"The views from the conservatory are second to none" at this "eclectic" rooftop Thai – part of an eight-strong northern chain, and overlooking the castle and Firth of Forth. The food is "authentic and very good" and, while it can "sometimes be difficult to get a table", your "patience is rewarded". / www.chaophraya.co.uk; @ChaophrayaThai; On the 4th Floor; Sun-Wed 10 pm, Thu-Sat 10.30 pm.

THE DINING ROOM £63 444

28 QUEEN ST EH2 1JX 0131 220 2044

"Incredible value… the whisky was good too!" – The Scotch Malt Whisky Society's dining room occupies the first floor of a Georgian townhouse has a variety of menus (including a vegetarian option), with the blow-out option being their five-course taster menu, with the option to match each course with either wine or whiskey. / www.thediningroomedinburgh.co.uk/booking; @TheDiningRoomEd; Tue-Sat 9.30 pm, Mon 2.30 pm.

DISHOOM EDINBURGH £37 433

3A ST ANDREW SQUARE EH2 2BD 01312 026 406

"A welcome and different newcomer to the Edinburgh dining scene" – this "buzzing" yearling was the first branch outside London of the famous, Parsi-style, all-day diner chain; and its "Bombay street food" is "fantastic", provided by staff who are "lightning fast". It's "great that you can book", if only for breakfast, lunch, and groups of six or more in the evening; otherwise, "go early to avoid the queues". Top Tip: if you haven't tried it yet, "breakfast is a revelation: naan with bacon on the lightest flatbread ever tasted". / www.dishoom.com; @Dishoom; Tue-Sat 10.30 pm, Sun 8.30 pm.

DIVINO ENOTECA £59 445

5 MERCHANT ST EH1 2QD 0131 225 1770

"So unusual" and "romantic", this "very suave candlelit basement" in the Old Town serves "top-quality Italian charcuterie and cheese, excellent pasta, fish and meat dishes, and an outstanding wine and drinks selection (primarily, but not exclusively, Italian)". Opened in 2010, it is part of the local Vittoria group. / www.vittoriagroup.co.uk; @divinoed; Mon-Thu midnight, Fri 1 am.

EDUCATED FLEA £45 342

32B BROUGHTON ST EH1 3SB 01315568092

Three Birds' and Apiary's popular baby sister is a self-proclaimed 'dinky' spot. On the menu, "such a different variety of global foods (Scandi, Middle Eastern etc.) that change each season, and are locally sourced" and often pickled, smoked or of a 'nose-to-tail' bent". / educatedflea.co.uk/; @edfleaedinburgh; Mon-Sat 9 pm, Sun 3 pm.

EL CARTEL £26 534

64 THISTLE ST EH2 1EN

A "very affordable, buzzy place" in the New Town hailed by fans as "the best Mexican" in town, with "melting meats, tortillas made freshly in-house and beautiful margaritas" in a "pleasant" if basic setting. / www.elcartelmexicana.co.uk; @elcartelmexican; Tue-Sat midnight, Sun 2.30 pm; no bookings.

L'ESCARGOT BLEU £53 333

56 BROUGHTON ST EH1 3SA 0131 557 1600

In the West End, and with vibrant old-school posters lining its walls, this "bustling" and "fun" bistro delivers "good, basic French food" that's ably delivered by "great service". / www.lescargotbleu.co.uk; @Lescargot_B; 10 pm, Fri & Sat 10.30 pm; closed Sun (except Festival); no Amex.

FAVORITA £44 343

325 LEITH WALK EH6 8SA 0131 554 2430

This laid back Leith Walk staple continues to please with its wood-fired pizzas, pastas and fried treats. Owners, the Crolla family are due to expand their empire with a vast £3 million fish 'n' chippie – 'Bertie's' – in a World Heritage Site church on Victoria St, in December 2018. / www.la-favorita.com; Mon-Sat 10 pm, Sun 5 pm.

FHIOR £57

36 BROUGHTON STREET EH1 3SB 0131 477 5000

With the closure of Norn, chef Scott Smith and his wife Laura launched this minimalist summer newcomer in the city-centre too late for any survey feedback. The food focus is on ambitious experimental cuisine with a strong emphasis on local sourcing. / www.fhior.com; @FhiorRestaurant; Wed-Sat midnight.

FIELD £43 433

41 WEST NICOLSON ST EH8 9DB 01316 677010

This "tiny but excellent Southside restaurant" serves "modern Scottish food of very high quality" alongside an "interesting list" of mainly organic wines – all at "affordable prices". It's a short walk from the Queen's Hall, which makes it ideal for pre-show dining. / www.fieldrestaurant.co.uk; @Field_Edinburgh; Mon-Thu 11 pm, Fri & Sat 11.30 pm, Sun 10.30 pm.

FISHERS BISTRO £54 444

1 THE SHORE EH6 6QW 0131 554 5666

"Faultless fish" – and "first-class puddings, too" – have made this 17th-century Leith harbour watchtower a "charming" Edinburgh destination for two decades. Success at this original has brought the Shore bar/restaurant next door and a branch 'In The City'. / www.fishersrestaurants.co.uk; @FishersLeith; Wed-Sat 9.30 pm, Sun 3.30 pm.

FISHERS IN THE CITY £53 334

58 THISTLE ST EH2 1EN 0131 225 5109

"Excellent, fresh seafood is served in a pleasant manner" at this "casual bistro with a buzz" near the National Gallery – the city-centre offshoot of a Leith original that been supplying high-quality cooking in the Scottish capital since the late 1990s. / www.fishersrestaurants.co.uk; @FishersLeith; Mon-Thu 9 pm, Fri & Sat 9.30 pm, Sun 8.30 pm.

GALVIN BRASSERIE DE LUXE, THE CALEDONIAN £52 343

PRINCES ST EH1 2AB 0131 222 8988

Positive but still somewhat limited feedback on the Galvin brothers' modern hotel brasserie, complete with central bar and 'crustacea showcase', praised for its "excellent" service and "decent" cooking. / www.galvinbrasseriedeluxe.com; @galvinbrasserie; Mon-Sat 11 pm, Sun 6 pm; booking max 8 may apply.
Accommodation: 245 rooms, from £325

GARDENER'S COTTAGE £60 434

1 ROYAL TERRACE GARDENS, LONDON ROAD EH7 5DX 0131 558 1221

"Quirky, but absolutely superb", is the generally agreed verdict on Dale Mailley and Edward Murray's sustainability-minded venture: "a lovely concept" where guests eat a top-class, set menu with good wine at long friendly, communal tables in an old stone building in Royal Terrace Gardens – an experience "more casual and laid-back" than most restaurants serving food of this quality. / www.thegardenerscottage.co; @gardenersctg; Mon 10 pm, closed Tue, Wed - Sun 10 pm.

LA GARRIGUE £58 322

31 JEFFREY ST EH1 1DH 0131 557 3032

"I love traditional southwest French cuisine, and this is the real deal!". Jean-Michel Gauffre's "friendly" Old Town stalwart is "still true to its roots", serving "great recipes" including a signature cassoulet. "The extensive wine list has Languedoc and Roussillon bottles by the score that you never see in Britain". / www.lagarrigue.co.uk; @lagarrigue; Tue-Sun .

HENDERSONS THE SALAD TABLE £39 322

94 HANOVER ST EH2 1DR 0131 225 2131

Established in 1962, Scotland's longest running veggie, set beneath the deli/shop, has long been a local institution. It can get "too busy to be at its best", but even on an off-day reporters are "glad it exists" (and it has also spawned a vegan restaurant down the road, as well as a newer Holyrood spin-off). / www.hendersonsofedinburgh.co.uk; @HendersonsofEdi; Mon-Sat 9 pm, Sun 4 pm; no Amex.

THE HONOURS £75 443

58A, NORTH CASTLE STREET EH2 3LU 0131 220 2513

"Enjoyable and consistent…", "dependable and professional…" – such is the tenor of commentary on this "lovely" New Town brasserie from Martin Wishart, for 20 years one of Scotland's leading chefs. The least enthusiastic report? "pleasant enough, with some real highlights but some dishes fell a little flat, especially at the price". / www.thehonours.co.uk; @TheHonours; Tue-Sat 9.30 pm.

HOWIES £51 322

29 WATERLOO PLACE EH1 3BQ
0131 556 5766

An Edinburgh institution after nearly 30 years' service, David Howie Scott's "consistent" and "good value" (and business-friendly) Waterloo Place flagship showcases Scottish ingredients and recipes, including venison from his Perthshire estate. There are now two offshoots in Edinburgh and one in Aberdeen. / www.howies.uk.com; Mon-Sat 9.30 pm, Sun 4 pm.

THE IVY ON THE SQUARE £56 234

6 ST ANDREW SQUARE EH2 2BD
0131 526 4777

"Similar cooking and service to the London original – but don't expect to spot any celebrities" at this glass-fronted outpost of what is nowadays a national chain (which enjoys "particularly good views from the first floor"). "The Ivy is aiming at ubiquity", and generally meets expectations with its "consistent food", "linen cloths and napkins" and "stylish surroundings". "Prices seem a little steep for Edinburgh", though. / theivyedinburgh.com; @ivyedinburgh; Mon-Sun 12.30 am.

KANPAI £36 443

8 - 10 GRINDLAY STREET EH3 9AS
0131 228 1602

Sushiya's highly regarded and intimate younger sibling, near the Lyceum Theatre, is a "cute place" turning out "top Japanese food and sushi". / www.kanpaisushiedinburgh.co.uk/; Tue-Thu 10.30 pm, Fri & Sat 11 pm.

THE KITCHIN £111 334

78 COMMERCIAL STREET EH6 6LX
0131 555 1755

"Stunning and wonderful cuisine" and "superb wine" in a relatively "relaxed atmosphere" has won huge critical acclaim for Tom & Michaela Kitchin's Leith warehouse conversion, where you can eat from a range of à la carte and tasting options. Its ratings were dragged down this year, however, by quite a significant number of diners who felt that prices are becoming "excessive for what's served". / www.thekitchin.com; @TomKitchin; Tue-Thu 10 pm, Fri & Sat 10.30 pm; booking max 7 may apply; children: 5+.

MOTHER INDIA'S CAFE £36 443

3-5 INFIRMARY ST EH1 1LT 0131 524 9801

"Small plates of extremely tasty Indian treats" have made this well-known and still renowned south Asian tapas joint a highlight of the city's curry scene since its arrival from Glasgow 10 years ago. It's "great for a quick bite" – so "perfect for a nicely varied pre-theatre meal". / www.motherindiaglasgow.co.uk; @official_mindia; 10.30 pm, Fri & Sat 11 pm, Sun 10 pm; no Amex.

NAVADHANYA EDINBURGH £52 433

88 HAYMARKET TERRACE EH12 5LQ 0131 2817187

This contemporary four-year-old near Haymarket Station very consistently produces imaginative 'nouvelle Indian' cuisine of superior quality. / www.navadhanya-scotland.co.uk; @Navadhanya_Edin; Tue-Sat 11 pm, Sun 10 pm.

NEW CHAPTER £65 343

18 EYRE PL. EH3 5EP 0131 556 0006

"A super find in Edinburgh", set where New Town and Canonmills meet; from the "great deal at lunch" to the innovative use of Scottish produce, the food – by ex-Harvey Nicks Forth Floor Restaurant chef Maciek Szymij – is "always A1". / www.newchapterrestaurant.co.uk/; @newchapter18; Mon-Sat 11 pm, Sun 5 pm.

NUMBER ONE, BALMORAL HOTEL £114 544

1 PRINCES STREET EH2 2EQ
0131 557 6727

"Jeff Bland still delivers wonderful dishes in a marvellous subterranean setting" at this amazingly consistent hotel basement, which has vied for its place at the top of the city's culinary premier league for over two decades. Despite its windowless, below-ground location, its "imaginative interior design" creates "beautiful surroundings", "service is wonderful and unobtrusive" and his seasonal cuisine – be it from the three-course, or seasonal tasting menu with matching wines – is "exceptional". / www.roccofortehotels.com/hotels-and-resorts/the-balmoral-hotel/restaurants-and-bars/number-one/; @NumberOneEdin; Mon-Sun 10 pm; no trainers; booking max 5 may apply; children: 5. *Accommodation:* 188 rooms, from £360

ONDINE £66 444

2 GEORGE IV BRIDGE EH1 1AD 0131 2261888

Roy Brett's "fun" haunt is set around a stylish oyster bar (£1 a pop during 'oyster happy hour' 5.30-6.30pm) in the Old Town. A "superb choice" of "spanking fresh fish and seafood is lovingly prepared" ("the roasted seafood platter was worth the flight alone: freshest produce carefully cooked, and a genuine thing of beauty"). / www.ondinerestaurant.co.uk; @OndineEdin; Mon - Sat 10 pm, Sun closed; booking max 6 may apply.

THE OUTSIDER £41 223

15 - 16 GEORGE IV BRIDGE EH1 1EE
0131 226 3131

"Despite the name, right in the city centre near the main tourist drag" – this "decent" staple primarily trades on its "fun" ambience, and visits can be further elevated by bagging one of the castle-view tables. / www.theoutsiderrestaurant.com/; 11 pm; no Amex; booking max 12 may apply.

THE POMPADOUR BY GALVIN, THE CALEDONIAN £91 444

PRINCES STREET EH1 2AB 0131 222 8975

"Such a special place to dine" – the Waldorf Astoria's "splendid" Caledonian dining room provides a perfect setting for the Galvin Bros' "flavoursome, exciting and creative" French-based grande cuisine, which achieved the highest ratings of its seven-year tenancy this year. / www.thepompadourbygalvin.com; @Galvin_Brothers; Wed-Sun 9.30 pm.

PURSLANE £49 543

33A ST STEPHEN STREET EH3 5AH
01312 263500

"Superb, imaginative food as good as any in Edinburgh" (fish-centric and "ridiculously great value") from à la carte as well as five-course and seven-course tasting options, makes this below-stairs Stockbridge spot one of the city's top 'casual-fine-dining' choices; service will have you feeling "like a special guest". / www.purslanerestaurant.co.uk; @Purslane_1; 10 pm; closed Mon; children: 6+.

THE RABBIT HOLE £53 443

EH9 1JH 0131 229 7953

"Fabulous fish sourced from the famous Eddie's Seafood Market next door" is the prime attraction at this "lovely, small but perfect" bistro: "the chef/owner is Sicilian and Mediterranean flavours abound" and dishes come at "relatively low prices". "The wine list rates mention too". / www.therabbitholerestaurant.com; Tue-Sat midnight, Sun 2.30 pm.

RESTAURANT MARTIN WISHART £115 544

54 THE SHORE EH6 6RA 0131 553 3557

"Like the difference between travelling in a Rolls Royce and an ordinary car" – "the highest of standards are maintained year after year" at Martin Wishart's Leith HQ, which remains "one of the best restaurants in the UK". "Imaginative, flavoursome dishes, are beautifully (but not ostentatiously) presented", by "professional" staff who are "friendly and attentive, but never obtrusive". "New furnishing and decoration is an improvement" in recent times to this contemporary dining room, near the waterfront. / www.martin-wishart.co.uk; @RMWLeith; Tue-Sat 9 pm; no trainers.

RHUBARB, PRESTONFIELD HOTEL £61 334

PRIESTFIELD RD EH16 5UT 0131 225 1333

Any meal in the lavishly opulent setting of this Georgian, former private estate inside the city (the first in Scotland to grow rhubarb – hence the name) is "great for a special treat". The food is "very good", including breakfast and afternoon tea. / www.prestonfield.com; @PrestonfieldHH; Mon-Sat 10 pm, Sun 3 pm;

booking max 8 may apply; children: 12+ at D, none after 7pm. **Accommodation:** 23 rooms, from £295

LE ROI FOU   £68   5 4 3

FORTH STREET   EH1 3LE   0131 557 9346

"Up there with the likes of Kitchin" – Jérôme Henry's spring 2017 newcomer in the New Town wins high ratings across the board, including regarding its modern French cuisine, which has won it a string of awards. As well as the à la carte, there is a six-course tasting menu option. / www.leroifou.com; @LeRoiFouEdin; Mon-Thu 11 pm, Fri-Sun 12.30 am.

THE SCOTTISH CAFE & RESTAURANT, THE SCOTTISH NATIONAL GALLERY   £50   3 3 4

THE MOUND   EH2 2EL   0131 2251550

"Centrally situated on Princes Street beneath the National Art Gallery" and with great views through the big windows of the castle – the Contini family's "busy" modern brasserie makes a handy rendezvous and serves "an extremely good menu with a strong Italian influence". "Try nabbing a window table and watch the world go by between mouthfuls". / www.contini.com/scottish-cafe-and-restaurant; @continibites; Mon-Wed, Fri-Sun 5 pm, Thu 7 pm; booking lunch only.

SCRAN & SCALLIE   £56   4 4 4

1 COMELY BANK RD   EH4 1DT   0131 332 6281

"Edinburgh's leading gastropub" – Tom Kitchin's "awesome and very popular" Stockbridge venture provides "astonishing quality without any pretentiousness" – "fine cooking of fine ingredients" comes at "affordable prices" in a "pleasantly relaxed" and "upscale" environment. "I love the fact that the best of the best is available to most people!" / scranandscallie.com/; @ScranandScallie; Mon-Sun 10 pm.

THE STOCKBRIDGE   £55   4 4 4

54 ST STEPHEN'S ST   EH3 5AL   0131 226 6766

Consistently good feedback once again on this stylish and "cosy" picture-lined basement in Stockbridge, which produces quality Scottish-accented cuisine. / www.thestockbridgerestaurant.co.uk; @StockbridgeRest; Tue-Sat 9.30 pm, Sun 9 pm; children: 18+ after 8 pm.

TIMBERYARD   £76   4 3 3

10 LADY LAWSON ST   EH3 9DS   01312 211222

"Exceptional and interesting food" in the "atmospheric surroundings" of a Victorian warehouse can be a "stunning experience" at this modern, Scandi-influenced operation from the second generation of the Radford family (whose parents Andrew and Lisa ran popular Edinburgh restaurants Atrium and Blue). / www.timberyard.co; @timberyard10; 9.30 pm; closed Mon & Sun; booking max 5 may apply.

21212   £110   4 4 4

3 ROYAL TER   EH7 5AB   0845 222 1212

"An amazing experience": individualistic chef Paul Kitching serves some "exquisite" ("perhaps a tad too complicated?") cuisine and a notable wine selection, according to fans of his "cosy" Georgian townhouse, where he celebrates his tenth anniversary in 2019. The enigmatic title refers to the number of options on each of the five courses of his signature changing menu. / www.21212restaurant.co.uk; @paulk21212; Tue-Thu 9 pm, Fri & Sat 9.30 pm; children: 5+. **Accommodation:** 4 rooms, from £95

VALVONA & CROLLA   £38   2 2 3

19 ELM ROW   EH7 4AA   0131 556 6066

This famous deli (it was established in 1934) is a "Scottish institution" notable for its "strong tradition", and has a more modern, surprisingly big dining annex; though food and service can lag, it's "good fun", and "for £4 corkage, you can drink any of the (vast) selection of wines sold in the excellent shop". / www.valvonacrolla.com; Tue-Thu 7 pm, Fri & Sat 8.30 pm, Mon 5 pm, Sun 4 pm.

THE WALNUT   £34   3 4 2

9 CROALL PLACE   EH7 4LT   0131 281 1236

Now two years old, this "very good local" on the road to Leith is a superior "cheap 'n' cheerful" option, serving "fresh, home cooked food" that's a cut-above. Top Menu Tip: "the £10 lunch for two courses, with the chance to BYO, is one of Edinburgh's best bargains". / Mon-Sat 9.30 pm, Sun 4 pm.

WEDGWOOD   £59   4 5 3

267 CANONGATE   EH8 8BQ   0131 558 8737

Paul and Lisa Wedgwood's contemporary dining room halfway down the Royal Mile (much of it below ground) achieves nothing but positive feedback for its warm welcome and modern Scottish cuisine. / www.wedgwoodtherestaurant.co.uk; @chefwedgwood; Mon-Sat 10.30 pm, Sun 4 pm.

THE WHITE HORSE   £46   4 4 4

266 CANONGATE   EH8 8AA   0131 629 5300

"The new [late 2018] conversion of a grotty old pub" (one of the oldest in the city), which has been attractively modernised and has won instant acclaim for its "amazing" oysters, lobster, and shellfish plus "good value" fish dishes. / www.whitehorseoysterbar.co.uk; Mon-Sat 9.30 pm, Sun 4 pm.

THE WITCHERY BY THE CASTLE   £68   2 3 5

CASTLEHILL, THE ROYAL MILE   EH1 2NF   0131 225 5613

"Located near the approach to Edinburgh Castle", James Thomson's longstanding fixture of the Edinburgh restaurant scene offers atmosphere in abundance, with its darkly gothic original dining room, or gorgeous 'Secret Garden', although it's so well-known nowadays it "can be full of American and Japanese tourists". The food has always played second fiddle here, both to its looks and to its 500-bin wine list and extensive range of malt whiskies, Armagnacs, digestifs and liqueurs. / www.thewitchery.com; @thewitchery; 11.30 pm. **Accommodation:** 8 rooms, from £325

EGHAM, SURREY   3–3A

LEFTBANK   £42   3 3 3

WINDSOR ROAD   TW20 0AG   01784 436171

WIth great views of The Thames, this buffet-style operation is the less formal of the two eating options within The Runnymede Hotel. Limited but positive feedback for its wide array of dishes, including pizza and roasts from its wood-fired oven. / www.runnymedehotel.com; @therunnymede; Mon-Sat 10.30 pm.

THE TUDOR ROOM, GREAT FOSTERS HOTEL   £71   4 4 4

STROUDE RD   TW20 9UR   01784 433822

"That it's one of very few Michelin stars in Surrey is a sad state of affairs but this small restaurant within a 17th century manor house could easily sit shoulder to shoulder with any of its neighbouring counties' abundances!" – so say most reports on this much-accoladed and "most gorgeous" venue, where the cuisine is overseen by Douglas Balish. Top Tip: very "well-presented afternoon tea (take home what you can't eat)". / www.greatfosters.co.uk/Dining/TheTudorRoom; @GreatFosters.

EGLWYS FACH, POWYS   4–3D

GARETH WARD AT YNYSHIR   £139   5 4 4

SY20 8TA   01654 781 209

"Ynyshir is incredible: something totally unique and somewhere the whole of Wales should be proud of", according to fans (that is to say just about everyone) who report on Gareth Ward's "exquisite" cuisine at this "beautifully situated" house (next to an RSPB reserve, and whose history includes having been owned by Queen Victoria). "An exceptional 18-course tasting menu was unlike any other dining experience. Each course is presented at the table by one of the chefs and thoughtfully introduced. Each mouthful is intensely flavoured, often with nostalgic aromas of childhood seaside holidays, or rhubarb and custard boiled sweets. The cooking shows incredible skill, dedication and careful sourcing of local and foraged ingredients". / www.ynyshir.co.uk; @ynyshirrest; signposted from A487; Tue-Sat 9 pm; credit card deposit required to book; children: 9+.

THE BUTCHER'S ARMS £66 ![4][4][4]

LIME ST GL19 4NX 01452 840 381

It's all change at this well-known country inn, where owners the Winters, who held on to a Michelin star for seven years, made way for Grain Store chef Mark Block in January 2018. Despite promptly losing the accolade, early reports praise the "excellent, proper food" – and "to top it all, you can still get a decent pint". / www.thebutchersarms.net; Mon-Sat 9.30 pm, Sun 8.30 pm; children: 10+.

THE DUNCOMBE ARMS £50 ![4][4][4]

MAIN RD DE6 2GZ 01335 324 275

This "superbly renovated building in lovely countryside" in "the middle of nowhere" in particular – on the edge of the Peak District and "accessible from the culinary desert of North Staffordshire" – is "busy for good reason": from a "shortish menu" the food is of "tip top" quality. / www.duncombearms.co.uk; @DuncombeArmsPub; Mon-Sat 11 pm, Sun 10 pm.

THE BAY HORSE £49 ![4][4][3]

BAY HORSE LN LA2 0HR 01524 791204

"Off the beaten track" in the "eponymous hamlet of Bay Horse", this "smart country pub" is now into its 25th year ("it predates the railway tracks across the road"), with Wilkinson senior having ceded the reins to son Craig ("he's usually cooking, and we've never had anything that's not good"). From "skilled" terrines to an "exemplar of confit Goosnargh duck", Jr's "skilled" hand is evident – as is sourcing, with a "finger signpost outside pointing to producers around the country". "The bar is nicer than the dining room, but if you've got a warm day, the terrace overlooking the garden is a great setting". / www.bayhorseinn.com; @bayhorseinn; Wed-Sat 9 pm, Sun 8 pm; no Amex.

EAT ON THE GREEN £81 ![4][4][3]

UDNY GRN AB41 7RS 01651 842337

"Accomplished cooking" of "only the best local ingredients" sets apart 'kilted chef' Chris Wilkinson's former post office fine diner; kudos for the recent £35k donation to charity to mark its 14th birthday. / www.eatonthegreen.co.uk; @EatOnTheGreen1; 9 pm, Sun 8 pm; closed Mon & Tue.

THE DECK £47 ![3][2][4]

EMSWORTH MARINA, THORNEY ROAD PO10 8BP 01243 376161

"A lovely new restaurant serving wonderful fresh fish and almost nothing else". Ed Collison was just 22 when he took over this all-day venue at Emsworth Yacht Harbour two years ago, which enjoys "fantastic views over the marina". In early 2018 it reopened after a complete overhaul that extended it to 120 covers. (Ed will be at home in the marina, having circumnavigated the world as a sailor in the 2013-14 Clipper Round the World Race; at 18, he was the youngest crewman to complete the voyage). / thedeckcafe.co.uk; Sun-Wed 5 pm, Thu-Sat 8 pm.

FAT OLIVES £56 ![5][5][3]

30 SOUTH ST PO10 7EH 01243 377914

Lawrence & Julia Murphy have operated their "small" and "utterly charming" dining room in a 17th-century fisherman's cottage above the quay since 2000, building a "strong local following". It's "better than a neighbourhood restaurant but not posh" and its "superb cooking, local produce and attention to detail" "can't be recommended too highly". / www.fatolives.co.uk; @fat_olives; Mon-Sat midnight, Sun 11 pm; no Amex; children: 8+, except Sat L.

36 ON THE QUAY £87 ![3][3][3]

47 SOUTH ST PO10 7EG 01243 375592

This "lovely small restaurant" with rooms, a fixture on the quayside for more than 20 years, has (despite the odd 'off' review) seen its ratings revived this year as chef Gary Pearce "has found his feet" in charge of the kitchen. A local boy who trained here from the age of 17, Pearce has worked at some distinguished venues including Le Champignon Sauvage in Cheltenham. He now runs 36 with his wife Martina, with owners Ramon & Karen Farthing in the background. / www.36onthequay.co.uk; off A27 between Portsmouth & Chichester; 9 pm; closed Mon & Sun; no Amex.
Accommodation: 5 rooms, from £100

HAYWARDS RESTAURANT £71 ![4][4][2]

111 BELL COMMON CM16 4DZ 01992 577350

"At last a decent restaurant in Essex" – Amanda and Jahdre's popular five-year-old is "tucked-away behind a pub near Epping" (The Forest Gate Inn, owned by Amanda's family) and wins consistent praise for food that's "all of a very high standard" and "excellent service". / www.haywardsrestaurant.co.uk; @HaywardsRestaur; Wed & Thur 9.30 pm, Fri & Sat 10; credit card deposit required to book; children: 10.

GOOD EARTH £59 ![3][4][4]

14 - 18 HIGH STREET KT10 9RT 01372 462489

The "seriously good Chinese" – outpost of a small and up-market family-owned London chain – operates in a fairly traditional vein, but remains consistently "above average". / www.goodearthgroup.co.uk; Mon-Thu midnight, Fri 1 am; booking max 12 may apply.

THE WHEATSHEAF £52 ![3][3][3]

40 ESHER GREEN KT10 8AG 01372 464014

Refurbed and relaunched three years ago, and now rating well across the board as a "great pub with great beer, good wine list and top drawer food", "smartly served by enthusiastic, friendly staff". Close to Sandown Park so handy for pre-race lunch and post-win celebrations (or losses-drowning). / wheatsheafesher.co.uk; Mon-Sat 9.30 pm, Sun 4 pm.

GILBEY'S £52 ![2][3][3]

82 - 83 HIGH STREET SL4 6AF 01753 854921

Convivial wine bar on the High Street, just down from the famous boarding school; one reporter has "been a customer since the 1970s", and feels "it has survived well for years when others have gone bust" (having the backing of the famous gin dynasty can't harm) and "always delivers" competent food. In recent times it has added three bedrooms, plus a new 'Townhouse Restaurant' area overlooking the main drag. / www.gilbeygroup.com; @GilbeysEton; 5 min walk from Windsor Castle; Mon-Sat 4.30 pm, Sun 3.30 pm.

THE ACORN INN £55 ![3][3][2]

28 FORE ST DT2 0JW 01935 83228

A "nice old pub" – inspiration for 'The Acorn' boozer in local lad Thomas Hardy's 'Tess of the d'Urbervilles' – offering "relaxed good food", a skittles alley and "dog-friendly" hosts…what's not to like? / www.acorn-inn.co.uk; @Acorn_Inn; One mile off A37 Yeovil - Dorchester Road; 9 pm.
Accommodation: 9 rooms, from £135

SUMMER LODGE, SUMMER LODGE COUNTRY HOUSE £101 ![4][4][5]

DT2 0JR 01935 482000

"Wonderful food", "immaculate service" and a "stunning wine list" – a meal at this "beautiful" Relais & Châteaux operation (part of the Red Carnation group) is "just how dining should be in a true country hotel". Set in the heart of Wessex, elements of the building were designed by Thomas Hardy – an architect before he became a novelist [who knew? ED]. / www.summerlodgehotel.co.uk; @Summer_Lodge;

Gareth Ward
at Ynyshir

12m NW of Dorchester on A37; Mon-Sun 9.30 pm; no jeans. *Accommodation:* 24 rooms, from £235

ANGELA'S   £64   3 5 2

38 NEW BRIDGE ST   EX4 3AH   01392 499038

"Angela is front of house and husband Richard cooks" at this "little" restaurant in the town centre: "service is very friendly, and there's a core following of patrons". "There's a small menu of old-stalwart traditional French dishes" ("lots of creamy vegetables and sauces") with "everything freshly cooked to order" and delivered in "huge portions". / www.angelasrestaurant.com.

RENDEZVOUS WINE BAR   £52   3 3 3

38-40 SOUTHERNHAY EAST   EX1 1PE 01392 270 222

There's "not much choice in Exeter unfortunately" but this "business quarter stalwart" (morphing into a "night out destination on evenings and weekends") definitely merits a visit for its "super wines" and, to a slightly lesser degree, "interesting" and "good-value" menu. / www.winebar10.co.uk; @RendezvousWBar; Mon - Sat 9.15 pm, Sun closed.

LYMPSTONE MANOR   £167   5 5 4

COURTLANDS LANE   EX8 3NZ 01395 202040

"Micheal Caines back at his best: his passion and drive for his hotel are boundless!" – all of the many reports on his "flagship hotel, situated on the Exe estuary" are rapturous about "the complete package" delivered by his year-old solo venture: "foodie hotel heaven" which combines "awesome views", with "exciting food", "lovely contemporary design", "immaculate service", a "serene and beautiful environment" and a sense of "pure luxury". Some "work is needed to keep the prices in the real world" but quibbles are surprisingly few in this respect. Both Estuary (all fish) and Signature tasting menus combine exceptional flavours, textures and presentation to make them "a unique experience". / www.lympstonemanor.co.uk; @Lympstone_Manor; no shorts; children: 5.

RIVER EXE CAFE   £52   4 3 4

RIVER EXE ESTUARY   07761 116 103

"A most exciting trip on a ferry boat to get there (£5 return from Exmouth harbour) just adds to the occasion", when you pay a visit to this 'floating gastro shed' – a barge that "runs like a proper restaurant in the middle of the estuary", and which makes a "superb location" for a "delicious" meal of local seafood (with meat and veggie options for the fish-phobic). Runs April to September inclusive; you need to book. / www.riverexecafe.com/; @riverexecafe; Mon-Thu 9 pm, Fri & Sat 10 pm, Sun 3 pm.

ROCKFISH EXMOUTH   £51   3 3 3

PIER HEAD   EX8 1DU   01395 272100

Overlooking the Exe estuary (make an effort to bag a window seat), a bright, two-year old addition to Mitch Tonks's line of posh chippies that's "just about cheap but very cheerful" and offers "the freshest of fish from the heart of the coast". / www.therockfish.co.uk/restaurants/exeter/.

SHOE INN   £45   3 3 3

SHOE LN   SO32 3NT   01489 877526

This "friendly" brick dining pub by the River Meon, popular with ramblers tackling the South Downs Way, turns out "yummy" dishes from an expansive menu, and "they bake their own bread too, which is also for sale". / www.theshoeexton.co.uk; Mon-Fri 11 pm, Sat 11.30 pm, Sun 10.30 pm.

THE SQUARE AND COMPASSES   £46   3 3 3

FULLER STREET   CM3 2BB   01245 361477

Set, according to the pub's website, 'in the Bermuda Triangle of Essex between Chelmsford, Braintree and Witham' – this nicely trad 17th century inn is a solid performer turning out hearty pub classics including game sourced from the surrounding estates. / www.thesquareandcompasses.co.uk; @SCFullerStreet; Mon-Fri 11.30 pm, Sat midnight, Sun 11 pm.

THE COVE RESTAURANT & BAR   £44   3 4 5

MAENPORTH BEACH   TR11 5HN 01326 251136

The "beautiful views overlooking the breaking waves" at Maenporth Beach are the USP of this well-established outfit, with a particularly atmospheric terrace, though the "charming" staff and "lovely" fish-centric food also win reporters' approval. / www.thecovemaenporth.co.uk; @covemaenporth; Mon-Sat 9.30 pm.

OLIVER'S   £50   4 4 3

33 HIGH ST   TR11 2AD   01326 218138

A "very popular" decade-old husband-and-wife outfit on the High Street with a "wide variety of fish as you would expect in this fishing port", all "perfectly portioned", "full of flavours" and "amazing value" to boot. / www.oliversfalmouth.com; @oliversfalmouth; 9 pm; closed Mon & Sun; no Amex.

RICK STEIN'S FISH & CHIPS   £46   3 2 2

DISCOVERY QUAY   TR11 3XA   01841 532700

Mostly there's praise for the TV chef's large outlet by the Maritime Museum, where fans say the main event is superlative (albeit at a "top-end cost"). There is the odd cynic, though, who complains of "mediocre" results and thinks the bare-bones decor can feel a bit "like eating in a 1980s office block". / www.rickstein.com; @TheSeafood; 9 pm; no Amex; no bookings.

THE WHEEL HOUSE   £46   4 4 4

UPTON SLIP   TR11 3DQ   01326 318050

Feedback is limited, but remains mega-enthusiastic for this small, tucked-away bistro serving excellent seafood from its open kitchen. / 9 pm; D only, closed Sun-Tue.

RESTAURANT 56, SUDBURY HOUSE   £79   4 4 4

56 LONDON STREET   SN7 7AA 01367 245389

"A real culinary treat" is in store for diners at this elegant Georgian venue on the edge of the Cotswolds. "Chef Andrew Scott and his team have a great understanding of combining flavours; the taster menus are a genuine experience and the wine list has some excellent options". / www.restaurant56.co.uk; @56_restaurant; Wed-Sat 11.30 pm, Tue 6 pm; jacket required; booking evening only. *Accommodation:* 50 rooms, from £100

AVIATOR   £58   3 2 4

55 FARNBOROUGH RD   GU14 6EL 01252 555890

"Situated by an airfield", this Art Deco haunt (an erstwhile club house and officers' mess) "has an air of class that carries through to the brasserie from the romantically lit hotel lobby" next door. "Sublime cocktails" are its forte, but the "very reasonably priced" grub can prove "tasty" too ("it's not haute cuisine but if in the area I'd definitely go back"). / www.aviatorbytag.com; Wed-Sat 9.30 pm, Sun 2 pm.

READ'S   £84   4 4 4

MACKNADE MANOR, CANTERBURY RD ME13 8XE   01795 535344

"Reads has reliably and consistently delivered excellent food and service over three decades and it is still a treat to visit if one's budget allows!" – David and Rona Pitchford's Georgian mansion on the north Kentish coast is a "wonderful, oldy-worldy type of place (great on a winter's evening)" which provides "very stylish", but also "homely" surroundings for a culinary blow-out with the "splendid tasting menu" rating special mention. Top Tip: "The lunchtime set menu is also particularly good value for money". / www.reads.com; @READSREST; Mon closed, Tue - Sat 9.30 pm, Sun closed. *Accommodation:* 6 rooms, from £165

YARD £14 343

**10 JACOB YD, PRESTON ST ME13 8NY
01795 538265**

"Just great food time after time" makes this mill that used to turn out coffins (!) "a must visit if in Faversham"; "browse their art" before sampling the "fantastic breakfasts", "super lunches" and "occasional dinners". / @YardFaversham; Mon-Sat 5 pm, Sun 12.30 pm; no bookings.

WHITE SWAN AT FENCE £46 543

**300 WHEATLEY LANE RD BB12 9QA
01282 611773**

"Way better food than Northcote" – that's the claim by some aficionados of this "perhaps slightly unprepossessing-looking" hostelry, which vies as "the best pub restaurant in the North West" (and which was blessed with a Michelin star in October 2018). Tom Parker's "exceptional" cuisine makes "beautiful use of fresh local ingredients" and has gone from strength to strength in recent times. All this, and "as the only Timothy Taylors pub this side of the Pennines, the beer is excellent". Top Tip: "inside it's a tale of two rooms, with the welcoming bar, with open fire to the right, and a rather characterless dining room with cramped tables and a distinct lack of atmosphere to the left. Go right". / www.whiteswanatfence.co.uk; Mon-Sat 11 pm, Sun 10.30 pm.

GENERAL TARLETON £56 333

**BOROUGHBRIDGE RD HG5 0PZ
01423 340284**

"A well-looked-after and friendly pub/restaurant-with-rooms", just off the A1 (not a million miles from Harrogate), which – with its seasons devoted to seafood, truffles or game – continues to be a fair bet for a better-than-usual meal, scoring very solid ratings across the board. / www.generaltarleton.co.uk; @generaltarleton; 2m from A1, J48 towards Knaresborough; Mon-Thu midnight, Fri 1 am. *Accommodation:* 14 rooms, from £129

THE CREEL £14 433

**FIONNPHORT PIER PA66 6BL
07864 605682**

"What could be better than two huge juicy fresh scallops and Stornoway black pudding in a soft bap, looking over the water to Island of Iona. This tiny takeaway shack serves the freshest langoustines, scallops and crabs caught by the owner's father himself!" / Wed-Sat 9 pm, Sun 4 pm.

THE BRICKLAYERS ARMS £53 443

HOGPITS BOTTOM HP3 0PH   01442 833322

"Voted best dining pub in Hertfordshire (by the Good Pub Guide) and for very good reason"; from those who've "tried and tested now for over ten years", to "A-list celebs filming up the road" (at Warner Bros), this "proper" ivy-clad gastroboozer, with a trad interior and Anglo-French fusion fare, just "never disappoints". / www.bricklayersarms.com; @bricklayerspub; J18 off the M25, past Chorleywood; Mon-Thu 11.30 pm, Fri & Sat midnight, Sun 7 pm.

THE GRIFFIN INN £48 323

TN22 3SS   01825 722890

This 18th-century village inn set in beautiful countryside has a highly rated kitchen with a focus on pub classics and an extensive wine list. Fun fact: owned and run by the Pullan family since 1979, it was the childhood home of Piers Morgan when his stepdad was the landlord. / www.thegriffininn.co.uk; @GriffinInnPub; off A272; Tue-Sun. *Accommodation:* 13 rooms, from £85

ROCKSALT £52 435

4-5 FISHMARKET CT19 6AA   01303 212 070

"A superb view of the water and beautifully cooked fresh fish" – the twin key attractions of Mark Sargeant's "fabulously located" and highly popular venue on Folkestone Harbour. It's quite a "pricey" location, but for the vast majority of diners well worth it. Top Tip: "ask for a window table". / www.rocksaltfolkestone.co.uk; @rocksalt_kent; Tue-Thu 10 pm, Fri & Sat 10.30 pm, Sun 4 pm. *Accommodation:* 4 rooms, from £85

STEEP STREET COFFEE HOUSE 344

**18-24 THE OLD HIGH STREET CT20 1RL
01303 247819**

"In the heart of Folkestone's Creative Quarter", this "small independent coffee shop serves good quality coffee, and a variety of teas, as well as delicious homemade cakes, croissants, sandwiches, salads, and paninis, including gluten-free, vegan and vegetarian options". "A charming little place with shelves full of books to read or buy, comfy sofas, and big windows with views of the Old High Street, to watch the world go by". / www.steepstreet.co.uk; Mon-Sat 9.30 pm, Sun 4 pm.

HORTO RESTAURANT AT RUDDING PARK £88 433

HG3 1JH   01423 871350

"Chef Murray Wilson goes from strength to strength" at this "innovative and contemporary" two-year-old inside the new spa of a luxury hotel. Dishes and tasting menus are built around vegetables from the property's kitchen garden, with "outstanding" results produced by "experimental Japanese-influenced cooking". / www.ruddingpark.co.uk; @ruddingpark; Last Reservations Mon - Sun 20.30 pm.

BECKFORD ARMS £43 334

SP3 6PX   01747 870 385

"You'd struggle to find a better country pub" than this notably posh ivy-clad classic "in gorgeous surroundings" on the edge of the Fonthill Estate. There's a "varied menu ranging from pub food to gourmet". / www.thebeckfordarms.co.uk; @beckfordarms; 9.30 pm, Sun 9 pm; no Amex. *Accommodation:* 10 rooms, from £95

WHITE PHEASANT £50 443

21 MARKET ST CB7 5LQ   01638 720414

"To find a restaurant of this quality in Cambridge, let alone in this quiet rural village would make you jump for joy!" "Calvin Holland continues to use the best of local produce in his seasonal menus" producing cuisine that's "not exotic, but it is fantastic". / www.whitepheasant.com; @whitepheasant; Tue-Sat 9.30 pm, Sun 2.30 pm.

THE FORDWICH ARMS £73 444

KING STREET CT2 0DB   01227 710444

"Under new management and trying very hard to be exceptional" – ex-Clove Club chef, Dan Smith, Tash Norton and Guy Palmer's "idyllically located" December 2018 newcomer won instant fame and inspired an impressive volume of feedback in this year's survey, all of it very upbeat. "It's rare to find a pub that has been worked over as a restaurant but keeps a bar for locals with proper draught beers" but this "beautiful building in a perfect setting" does just that. One or two locals have "found fine dining in this local a bit incongruous" but most focus is on the "outstanding food" – "the presentation, originality and moreover the mix of ingredients blending into superlative tastes was a joy!" ("They make their own bread too – a full selection including sourdough, wholemeal, white etc along with homemade crackers"). / www.fordwicharms.co.uk; @FordwichArms; Tue-Sat 11 pm, Sun 6 pm.

CRANNOG £58 323

**TOWN CENTRE PIER PH33 6DB
01397 705589**

"A must if you are travelling to Fort William"; offering "honest" catch "with nothing to detract from the natural flavours" (not least "scallops to die for"), this red-roofed staple, on a pier overlooking Loch Linnhe, is a real "sea foodie's heaven". "Book ahead!" / www.crannog.net; @CrannogHighland; Mon-Fri 1 am, Sat & Sun 2 am; no Amex.

THE Q RESTAURANT, THE OLD QUAY HOUSE £60 334

28 FORE STREET PL23 1AQ 01726 833302

Visit on a fine day, and you can sit on the terrace adjoining the dining room, which has gorgeous views of the estuary from this 13-bedroom modern hotel. Shortish two-course and three-course prix fixe menus are served at both lunch and dinner. / theoldquayhouse. com; @theoldquayhouse; Mon-Thu 11.30 pm, Fri & Sat midnight, Sun 10.30 pm; children: 8+ at D. *Accommodation:* 11 rooms, from £190

JOLLY NICE FARM SHOP £30 433

THE OLD WHITE HORSE FILLING STATION, CIRENCESTER ROAD, GL6 8HZ 01285 760868

"Living up to its name" – "this converted petrol station on the A419 has sprawled (through its own success!) into a burger kitchen, farm shop, florist, butcher, cafe and deli with adjoining yurt and picnic field." "Straightforward food is cooked beautifully with top quality ingredients" – in particular "their burgers are superb: generous, pink, beefy, nicely grilled, and terrifically good value". / jollynicefarmshop.com; Mon-Sat 9.30 pm, Sun 4 pm.

THE FOX & GOOSE £64 334

CHURCH RD IP21 5PB 01379 586247

Paul Yaxley's "dependable" gastropub, in a listed 500-year-old former guildhall set "in a lovely part of Suffolk, well away from the coastal crowds", has provided "reliable and interesting food" for more than ten years, and the "set lunches are especially good value". / www.foxandgoose.net; @Foxygossip; off A143; 8.30 pm, Sun 8.15 pm; closed Mon; children: 9+ at D.

THE POT KILN £58 433

RG18 0XX 01635 201366

"Surrounded by lovely countryside", this red-brick boozer with a "proper, old-fashioned bar" and large garden serves excellent game and "if you are a carnivore this should be your destination restaurant". It's best-known for venison shot by the owner, foodie TV pioneer Michael Robinson (also of London's No 1 gastropub, the Harwood Arms) and other dishes rating mention this year included "great côte de boeuf" and "exceptional, gamey roast grouse". / www.potkiln.org; between J12 and J13 of the M4; Mon-Sat 11 pm.

THE ALFORD ARMS £45 344

HP1 3DD 01442 864480

This "really great country gastropub", in a hamlet in a secluded wooded valley, offers "carefully cooked food, much of it locally sourced, and a good atmosphere". Only one complaint: "it's difficult to get a table" – although drop-ins are always welcome, and the management insists nobody will go hungry. / www.alfordarmsfrithsden.co.uk; @alfordarmshp1; near Ashridge College and vineyard; Mon-Sat 11 pm, Sun 10.30 pm; booking max 12 may apply.

THE PALM £38 443

BATH RD SN8 3HT 01672 871 818

It's "easy to drive on by" this nondescript building on the A4 "but you should stop" – inside it's "a real upmarket operation", serving the "best you can get in Indian food" in a "crazy-busy and -buzzy" atmosphere. / www.thepalmindian.com; 11.30 pm.

WHITE HART £50 335

MAIN ROAD OX13 5LW 01865 390585

This beautifully preserved 15th-century chantry is now a "superior gastro-pub", serving "great food with local ingredients in a striking vaulted and panelled dining room". Top Tip: "good-value set lunch". / www.whitehart-fyfield.com; @the_whitehart; off A420; Tue-Sat 11 pm, Sun 10.30 pm.

SIX, BALTIC CENTRE FOR CONTEMPORARY ARTS £55 225

BALTIC (SIXTH FLOOR), SOUTH SHORE ROAD NE8 3BA 0191 440 4948

"Beautiful views" over the Tyne to Newcastle are the major calling card of this upscale art gallery restaurant. It's a consistently inconsistent destination though – the food can be "mediocre" and service "haphazard". / www.sixbaltic.com; @sixbaltic; Tue-Sat 9.30 pm, Sun 4 pm.

MALIKS £43 442

14 OAK END WAY SL9 8BR 01753 889634

The well-heeled baby sister to Cookham's award-winning curry house – there's also a Marlow branch – is a "super neighbourhood Indian" and "excellent takeaway" (they also have a dedicated 'express kitchen' down the road); it's singled out for its "very wide range of choices" and "very friendly service". / www.maliks.co.uk; Mon-Sat 11 pm, Sun 10.30 pm.

AUSTENWOOD LN SL9 8NL 01753 899 016

"Unusually good food for a gastropub" is the result of some "serious" cooking at this well-known destination. The interior was designed by Terry Wogan's daughter Katherine, who owns it with her husband Henry Cripps (they also own the White Oak in Cookham). / www.thethreeoaksgx.co.uk; @TheThreeOaksGX; 9.15 pm.

LA LOCANDA £49 433

MAIN STREET BB7 4HH 01200 445303

Maurizio (chef) and Cinzia (front of house) Bocchi's "fiercely Italian" venture occupies "an old weaver's cottage on the main A59 road through the village" and is "the best Italian food in this part of Lancashire". "They can't do enough to make sure you enjoy your meal, and the food is very authentically Italian, based in the Marche, but roving around other regions (there's little that you would recognise from the menu of your standard high street Britalian). The wine list – all Italian – is very special: not cheap, but good value, and full of unusual vintages. The list of Italian beers is worth a look too (even the soft drinks are largely Italian). Portions are as lavish as both agriturismo and Lancashire would expect!" / www.lalocanda.co.uk; @LaLocandaCinzia; Mon-Sun 10 pm.

ALCHEMILLA £36

1126 ARGYLE STREET G3 8TD 0141 337 6060

Limited but positive feedback (too few reports yet for a rating) on this Finnieston two-year-old: a good looking spot whose accomplished modern bistro cuisine has garnered some fantastic press reviews. / www.thisisalchemilla.com.

BATTLEFIELD REST £38 344

55 BATTLEFIELD ROAD G42 9JL 0141 636 6955

Built in 1914 (and once described as Scotland's most glamorous tram stop), Marco Giannasi's quirky-looking Southside fixture was restored in 1994; and serves a large and affordable Italian menu, also incorporating pizza and pasta. Feedback is limited but very enthusiastic. Top Tip: good pre-theatre deals. / www.battlefieldrest.co.uk.

THE BISTRO AT ONE DEVONSHIRE GARDENS £71 344

ONE DEVONSHIRE GDNS G12 0UX 0141 339 2001

Despite being one of the City's most famous culinary names (with past-chefs including Andrew Fairlie and Gordon Ramsay), this comfortable dining room deep in the West End attracts limited survey feedback nowadays, but such as there is remains positive. There is a tasting menu option, but the relatively straightforward cuisine lives up to the 'Bistro' designation of the operation nowadays. As you might hope of a Hotel du Vin property "the list is extensive and contains numerous unusual and hard-to-come-by vintages". Top Tip: affordable prix fixe menu. / www.hotelduvin.com; @HotelduVinBrand/; Mon-Thu 10 pm, Fri & Sat 10.30 pm, Sun 9.30 pm.

LA BONNE AUBERGE £53 223

161 WEST NILE ST G1 2RL 0141 352 8310

Part of the Holiday Inn, this long-established brasserie has origins dating back over 40 years and is quite well-known to locals as a city-centre standby. Limited feedback regarding its 1970s-style French bistro/brasserie staples (soupe à l'oignon, boeuf bourguignon, Pêche Melba) but it's tipped before a show at one of the nearby theatres. / www.labonneauberge.co.uk; @labonneauberge; Mon-Sat 12.30 am, Sun 10.30 pm.

CAFÉ GANDOLFI £52 335

64 ALBION ST G1 1NY 0141 552 6813

A "brilliant longstanding cafe in Merchant City – you will love the furniture and decor, especially the iconic stained-glass window" (decorated with fish) but also the "great-sized portions" of local food. / www.cafegandolfi.com; @cafegandolfi; Mon-Sun 10.30 pm; booking weekdays only.

CAIL BRUICH £63 543

725 GREAT WESTERN RD G12 8QX 01413 346265

"Top-notch in every way, and a league apart from their competitors" is the general verdict on this West End venture from brothers Paul and Chris Charalambous ("a slightly more formal setting than you'd get in, say, trendy Finnieston"). "Flavours are bright and clear, in classical combinations showing off the largely Scottish produce, and the dishes as a whole all work extremely well". It's "not much to look at from the outside", though, while the lighting inside is a bit dim "for the intricacy and delicacy of the plating, as well as for reading the menu!" / www.cailbruich.co.uk; @CailBruich; Mon-Sun 11 pm; children: 5.

CRABSHAKK £56 534

1114 ARGYLE ST, FINNESTONE G3 8TD 0141 334 6127

This "whacky little space" in Finnieston with lots of nooks and crannies, and also perches to eat up at the counter, "consistently delivers fantastic, super-fresh fish and seafood, cooked and served with real passion". Now in its tenth anniversary year, its legion of fans "absolutely love it" but be warned: it gets "really busy". / www.crabshakk.com; @CRABSHAKK; closed Mon; no Amex.

THE DHABBA £41 333

44 CANDLERIGGS G1 1LE 0141 553 1249

One of the city's best of its many Indian restaurants, this contemporary Merchant City fixture is known for "superb" north Indian

cooking with "refined and great tastes". (Nearby, it also has a sibling, Dakhin, specialising in Goan cuisine). / www.thedhabba.com; @thedhabba; Mon-Wed 11 pm, Thu-Sat midnight.

EUSEBI DELI £46 433

152 PARK ROAD G4 9HB 01416489999

"Buzzing and packed to the gills", this small deli-restaurant a short stroll from Kelvinbridge station remains one of the city's hottest foodie tickets, winning both 'Best Dining Experience' and 'Best Café' at The Scotsman's 2018 Food & Drink Awards. There are "groaning counters stuffed with delicious looking stuff to take away and a few cafe tables on the ground floor (while downstairs is a bit more restaurant-y)". Following on from breakfast and brunch options, it serves excellent antipasti, pasta and pizza at lunch and dinner. Also "good coffee as you'd expect" and an unusually tempting array of cakes. / eusebideli.com/; @eusebi_deli; Tue-Sat midnight, Sun 2.30 pm.

THE FISH PEOPLE CAFE £50 433

350 SCOTLAND STREET G5 8QF 0141 429 8787

A "great, little restaurant tucked beside the tube station" (handy if unglamorous Shields Road) and winning plaudits for its "fabulously fresh fish prepared with care and conviction". / www.thefishpeoplecafe.co.uk/; Mon-Sun 10.30 pm.

GAMBA £73 442

225A WEST GEORGE ST G2 2ND 0141 572 0899

"This is the place to come for fish in Glasgow", say fans of Derek Marshall's 21-year veteran in the city centre. The "gorgeous", "consistently fresh and yummy" dishes "based on locally caught produce" "seem to change on a daily basis". / www.gamba.co.uk; @Gamba_Glasgow; Tue-Sat 11.30 pm, Sun 3.30 pm; booking max 6 may apply.

THE GANNET £54 443

1155 ARGYLE ST G3 8TB 0141 2042081

"High-end no-nonsense food with spot-on service" have earned chefs Peter McKenna and Ivan Stein a range of accolades for their stripped-down Finnieston five-year-old (including, slightly bizarrely, being listed by Conde Nast Traveller as one of the world's top 10 restaurants). "It looks like it's going to be trendy and hipstery" (from the exterior, a bit "like a cocktail bar"), "but this is Glasgow, and it's actually a very pleasing spot a notch above a mere neighbourhood haunt: a sort of Sticky Walnut with its culinary sights set a little higher". "High end" modern bistro dishes of Scottish-sourced ingredients are served in the "very modest surroundings" of a formerly derelict building. / www.thegannetgla.com/; @TheGannetGla; Mon closed, Tue - Sat 9.30 pm, Sun 7.30 pm.

HANOI BIKE SHOP £30 332

8 RUTHVEN LN G12 9BG 0141 334 7165

A "vibrant, noisy" two-floor café where the "rickety tables are not big enough for the plates" (all part of the "real street food atmosphere"). The "pho is a sheer delight" (as of October 2018 you can 'build your own pho' bowl) and the homemade tofu, for which they're known, is "quite superb" – even to carnivores. / www.hanoibikeshop.co.uk; @hanoibikeshop; 11 pm, Fri & Sat 12.30 am.

JULIE'S KOPITIAM 532

1109 POLLOKSHAWS ROAD G41 3YG 0141 237 9560

"Brilliant and cheap Malaysian food" has won instant acclaim for this December 2017 newcomer – already inspiring a lot of feedback and buzz in the Scottish Press for a simply decorated café in Shawlands (deep in the Southside of Glasgow). / Mon-Sat 9.30 pm, Sun 4 pm.

MOTHER INDIA £40 443

28 WESTMINSTER TER G3 8AD 0141 339 9145

With its "freshly cooked food at bargain prices", this very popular West End institution has long been "a family favourite" for its tapas-sized dishes – and standards show no sign of slipping. / www.motherindiaglasgow.co.uk; @Official_Mindia; Mon-Thu 10.30 pm, Fri & Sat 11 pm, Sun 10 pm.

NIPPON KITCHEN £54 343

91 W GEORGE STREET G2 1PB 0141 328 3113

"They get the Asian-fusion thing right", turning out "quality" food, and in "hearty Glasgow rather than delicate Japanese" portions at this wood-panelled operation with oriental furniture; on the drinks front, expect "super cocktails" plus whiskeys and beers. / www.nipponrestaurant.co.uk; Sun-Thu 10 pm, Fri & Sat 11 pm.

OX AND FINCH £47 333

920 SAUCHIEHALL ST G3 7TF 0141 339 8627

"Cheery" but hip and foodie-forward Finnieston boozer offering "good value" Scottish-slanted small plates from a vast menu, alongside "interesting wines"; a Middle Eastern sibling, BABA, opened on the city's prime artery George St in November 2017. / www.oxandfinch.com; @OxAndFinch; 10 pm.

PAESANO PIZZA £33 533

94 MILLER STREET G1 1DT 0141 258 5565

"Having eaten in top Naples restaurants, I can honestly say that this wonderful restaurant in Glasgow equals the very best of the best!" – so say fans of this stunning pizzeria in the Merchant City: a busy, industrial-vibe, café-style venue, with a West End spin-off. It's all down to the hybrid yeast and sourdough, apparently. /

paesanopizza.co.uk; @paesano_pizza; Tue-Fri 11 pm, Sat & Sun midnight.

RANJITS KITCHEN £20 332

607 POLLOKSHAWS ROAD G41 2QG 0141 423 8222

"Delicious Punjabi vegetarian food is served by friendly people" in a "low-key" but "welcoming" space at this teetotal Pollokshields deli-restaurant – mainly a take-away but also offering sit-in meals from noon 'till 8.30pm (save Monday); it's "worth queuing for the fresh lemon pickle alone!" / Tue-Fri 11 pm, Sat & Sun midnight; no bookings.

ROGANO £60 334

11 EXCHANGE PLACE G1 3AN 0141 248 4055

"A Glasgow institution" – the city's oldest restaurant is an atmospheric oyster bar and dining room, treasured by some for its original 1935 Art Deco interiors, built by the craftsmen who worked on the Queen Mary. The food generally lives up to – a "good selection" of seafood (which at best is "superb"). / www.roganoglasgow.com; @roganoglagow; Tue-Sat 10 pm.

SHISH MAHAL £42 442

60-68 PARK ROAD G4 9JF 0141 334 7899

"Glasgow's oldest curry house and still one of the best"; it's now under the third generation, with the legendary Mr Ali sadly gone, but "standards have never slipped" at this local icon, which famously claims credit for inventing chicken tikka masala in the 1970s. / www.shishmahal.co.uk; Tue-Sun, Mon 9.30 pm; no bookings.

SINGL END £25 333

265 RENFREW STREET G3 6TT

This "quirky" and "delightful coffee shop" is beloved for its "top-quality" full breakfasts ("with homemade baked beans!"), muffins, sandwiches and so on, which also includes "fantastically fresh and varied bread" ("impossible to choose just one item"). In April 2018, it spawned a Merchant City sibling, at 15 St John St. / Mon-Sat 10 pm.

STRAVAIGIN £54

28 GIBSON ST G12 8NX 0141 334 2665

With its upstairs bar and downstairs dining room, this West End stalwart is celebrating its twenty fifth year of funky fare, featuring the likes of haggis 'n' neeps and burgers alongside an eclectic array of Mediterranean, Middle Eastern and Asian offerings. But despite being oft-cited as a 'founding father' of the contemporary Glaswegian food scene, it attracted too little reporter interest for a rating this year. / www.stravaigin.co.uk; @straivaiging12; 11 pm; no Amex.

TWO FAT LADIES AT THE BUTTERY £59 334

652 ARGYLE ST G3 8UF 0141 221 8188

Ryan James's business-friendly, wood-panelled, traditional-looking operation (complete with booths) can prove "hard to find if you are not local (it's in a quiet area off the M8 in the way to the SECC), but it's worth it" for the Scots seafood, and its "regular use as a film location adds to its renown". / www.twofatladiesrestaurant.com; 10 pm, Sun 9 pm.

UBIQUITOUS CHIP £62 445

12 ASHTON LN G12 8SJ 0141 334 5007

This "terrifically atmospheric" Glasgow institution in the West End is on top form: its "imaginatively presented" modern Scottish cuisine with "top-quality ingredients"; famous and "very interesting" wine list; malt selection "to die for"; and "knowledgeable staff" earning high ratings across the board. Named with irony by founder Ronnie Clydesdale in 1971, 'the Chip' is now run by his son Colin. Meals are served in the main restaurant or more casual upstairs brasserie. Tip tip: "there's the option of eating upstairs with a more informal menu". / www.ubiquitouschip.co.uk; @UbiquitousChip; 11 pm.

GLINTON, RUTLAND 6–4A

THE BLUE BELL £46 433

10 HIGH STREET PE6 7LS 01733 252285

A "friendly, easy atmosphere" adds to the charms of Will Frankgate's 18th century village pub, which added an oak-framed garden room/patio two years back, and turns out "excellent" and "reasonably" priced grub including well-sourced local meat. / www.thebluebellglinton.co.uk; @bluebellglinton; Mon-Thu 11 pm, Fri & Sat midnight, Sun 8 pm.

GOLDSBOROUGH, NORTH YORKSHIRE 8–3D

THE FOX AND HOUNDS INN £61

YO21 3RX 01947 893372

Stop Press – over a decade this remote pub went from being a secret amongst Yorkshire foodies to winning UK acclaim, but in early 2018, owner Jason Davies and his FOH wife Sue moved on. Following a brief hiatus, it has reopened again in a pubbier incarnation under new owners; we've suspended marks until feedback is in. / www.foxandhoundsgoldsborough.co.uk; @FoxGoldsborough; Mon-Sat 11 pm, Sun 10.30 pm; no Amex.

GORING-ON-THAMES, OXFORDSHIRE 2–2D

THE LEATHERNE BOTTEL £59

BRIDLE WAY RG8 0HS 01491 872667

It's been a turbulent time for this Thames Valley old-timer just outside Goring-on-Thames, which enjoys the most gorgeous riverside location, particularly in summer. Having operated as a (quite good) Italian venue since 2014 (Rossini at the Leatherne Bottel) it closed in May 2018 as our survey was ending, soon to re-open under new owners – Sally Albin with head chef Adam Hague – in June, with a new modern British tasting format. However, at the end of October 2018 they closed again, citing 'depleted capital', but with the intention to crowdfund a new venture on the site. So it's a case of watch this space. / www.leathernebottel.co.uk; @leathernebottel; Mon closed; Tue - Sat 10.30 pm; Sun 3pm; children: 10+ for D.

THE MILLER OF MANSFIELD £60 433

HIGH ST RG8 9AW 01491 872829

Elevated gastropub cuisine with a "unique twist" is on the menu at former Heston Blumenthal staffers Nick & Mary Galer's modernised 18th-century inn. The kitchen's "extraordinary attention to detail" delivers some "memorable" dishes (e.g. "a glorious clementine soup with candied citrus"). / www.millerofmansfield.com; Mon-Sat 9 pm, Sun 7 pm; 6 - 9 Sat Lunch: 12 - 2.30, Dinner 6 - 9 Sun 12 - 3, 6 - 8; 0.

GRASMERE, CUMBRIA 7–3D

THE FOREST SIDE £90 455

LA22 9RN 01539 435 250

"The food is similar in style to L'Enclume" (chef Kevin Tickle moved here from Cartmel) at this "superb" establishment, where practically all diners are "blown away by the whole experience: the interesting depth and combination of flavours, the foraged ingredients, and the different cooking techniques – all matched with some wonderful wines" (of the biodynamique variety). It's a "non-stuffy dining", Scandi-style room in a "very friendly", but "professional" and "classy" hotel, set in "gorgeous Lakeland countryside". "Costly true, but worth every penny". "We will definitely be going back even though it's a 5 hour drive away!" / www.theforestside.com; @TheForestSide; Mon-Fri 11 pm, Sat 10.30 pm.

THE JUMBLE ROOM £50 334

LANGDALE ROAD LA22 9SU 01539 435 188

Well-known and "quirky" Grasmere fixture, with "lovely, friendly service" and "delicious and different food" from an eclectic global menu – "definitely not to be missed if you're in the Lake District". / www.thejumbleroom.co.uk; Mon & Tue closed; Wed - Sun 9.30 pm. *Accommodation:* 3 rooms, from £180

GREAT BEDWYN, WILTSHIRE 2–2C

THREE TUNS FREEHOUSE £42 343

HIGH ST SN8 3NU 01672 870280

"It's the village pub: it knows it's a pub and it works like a pub, and there's nothing wrong with that". When it comes to dining chef/owner James Wilsey's cooking is "pub food plus, and staff are charming too – what's not to like?" /

GREAT GONERBY, LINCOLNSHIRE 5–3D

HARRY'S PLACE £86 553

17 HIGH STREET NG31 8JS 01476 561780

Harry & Caroline Hallam are celebrating thirty years in business at this 10-seater in their front room (which started decades before pop-ups and supper clubs entered the mainstream). Harry cooks (in a fairly traditional style), Caroline serves, and ratings all-round remain outstanding. There's no website – they write out a hand-written menu daily. Book ahead, or they won't know to buy food for you. / on B1174 1m N of Grantham; Mon closed, Tue - Sat 8.30 pm, Sun closed; no Amex; children: 5+.

GREAT MILTON, OXFORDSHIRE 2–2D

BELMOND LE MANOIR AUX QUAT' SAISONS £243 555

CHURCH ROAD OX44 7PD 01844 278881

"Any visit must include a walk through the gardens" when you visit Raymond Blanc's "enchanting" converted Elizabethan manor, and "from the moment you arrive you are hit by the peace and tranquility of the whole enterprise". "From beginning to end, the attention to detail is exceptional": "nothing is left out, nothing is too much trouble" and staff "make you feel very, very special; not in a cloying way but through sheer politesse" ("exceptional service that includes attention to young children"). On the vast majority of accounts, it's "a breathtaking, out-of-this-world gastronomic extravaganza" too, with "exquisite food (with no hint of overambitious ideas or overloading of ingredients), whose preparation is exact and whose plating is very graceful". Where reservations are expressed, the issue is usually either the absence of a certain 'je ne sais quoi' ("the food was beautiful and delicious, courses flowed perfectly, but they didn't wow"); or "the need to chat with your friendly bank manager before you open the wine list". On most accounts, though, the equation stacks up beautifully: "this was a one-off bucket-list visit, but worth it despite the vast expense". / www.manoir.com; @lemanoir; J7 take A329 towards Wallingford; Mon-Sun 9.30 pm; booking max 12 may apply. *Accommodation:* 32 rooms, from £555

GREAT WALTHAM, ESSEX 3–2C

GALVIN GREEN MAN £41 333

HOWE ST CM3 1BG 01245 408 820

Some reporters "expected more from a Galvin venture", find this two-year-old member of their highly rated stable – an ancient pub (est 1341), nowadays with a modern glass dining area – as "just average". In most feedback, though, it wins praise for bringing their "excellent food to the heart of the Essex countryside". Its multiple menus can be expensive by pub standards, but there's an "excellent-value set lunch" and a "good selection a la carte with daily fresh fish option". / www.galvinrestaurants.com;

@Galvin_brothers; Mon-Wed 5 pm, Thu-Sat 10 pm, Sun 6 pm.

GREETHAM, RUTLAND 5–3D

THE WHEATSHEAF £45 332

STRETTON RD LE15 7NP 01572 812325

"A great favourite" – this low-key pub wins plaudits for its "great pies" and "spankingly fresh" fish. "Despite the occasional waits (very popular, fresh food, small kitchen!) the result is never less than enjoyable". / www.wheatsheaf-greetham.co.uk; Tue-Sun; no Amex.

GRESFORD, WREXHAM 5–3A

PANT-YR-OCHAIN £52 334

OLD WREXHAM ROAD LL12 8TY 01978 853525

In a quaint 16th century inn with an inglenook and sizeable garden (with small lake), this Brunning & Price outfit is "one of the best gastropubs in the area"; it does, accordingly, get "busy" ("you must book"), but the "setting and atmosphere make up for that". / www.brunningandprice.co.uk/pantyrochain; 1m N of Wrexham; Mon-Sat 9.30 pm, Sun 9 pm.

GUERNSEY, CHANNEL ISLANDS –

DA NELLO £51 334

46, LE POLLET GY1 1WF 01481 721 552

Consistency is key to the success of this classic and consistently well-rated Italian fixture in the heart of St Peter Port. Tim Vidamour joined as head chef in 1979, the year after it opened, and is nowadays a partner in the business. / www.danello.gg; Mon-Thu 9 pm, Fri & Sat 9.30 pm, Sun 8.30 pm.

LE NAUTIQUE £59 333

GY1 2LE 01481 721714

On the main seafront drag, this upmarket staple "never fails to please"; both the "fish and views (through full-length picture windows onto the harbour and Castle Cornet) are superb". / lenautiquerestaurant.co.uk/; 10.30pm.

LE PETIT BISTRO £59 434

56 LOWER POLLET GY1 1WF 01481 725055

"A little piece of France" – this "quite delightful" outfit in St Peter Port serves a classic bistro menu and is consistently highly rated. / www.petitbistro.co.uk; @PetitBistroGsy; Wed & Thu, Sun 3 pm, Fri & Sat 9 pm.

LA REUNION £52 444

COBO COAST ROAD GY5 7HB

"The best restaurant on Guernsey" – this stylish venue above sister restaurant, The Rockmount, has a terrace overlooking Cobo Bay with superb sea views; and achieves impressive ratings all-round, including for its modern cuisine (with a focus on seafood). / www.lareunion.gg/; Mon-Sat 10 pm.

GUILDFORD, SURREY 3–3A

THE IVY CASTLE VIEW £56 243

TUNSGATE SQUARE, 98-100 HIGH STREET GU1 3HE

"The usual formula, but views of the castle add to the ambience" of this spin-off from the famous London Theatreland venue. As at some others in the chain, however, reports on its comfort food cooking are up-and-down. / www.theivyguildford.com; Mon-Sun 12.30 am.

RUMWONG £44 343

18-20 LONDON RD GU1 2AF 01483 536092

It's been turning out stir fries and curries for over four decades, but "the food is always incredible" at this upbeat Thai, with a low-tabled northern-Thai style 'khan tok room'; shout-outs this year for the "good-value set lunch" and "good support for gluten-free diners". "We love it!" / www.rumwong.co.uk; Mon-Sat 9.30 pm, Sun 2.30 pm; no Amex.

THE THAI TERRACE £43 334

CASTLE CAR PK, SYDENHAM RD GU1 3RW 01483 503350

"Probably as glam as lovely Guildford gets: with a rooftop view over town (improbably from the top of a multi-storey car park) and mood lighting" – this well-known venue is "great fun" and serves food that's "pricey, but so worth it". / thaiterrace.co.uk/; 10.30 pm; closed Sun; no Amex.

GULLANE, EAST LOTHIAN 9–4D

CHEZ ROUX, GREYWALLS HOTEL £65 344

EH31 2EG 01620 842144

This "beautiful" Lutyens-designed Arts & Crafts country house hotel, on the edge of a championship golf course, is reputed for its "superb" afternoon teas ("taken early not to spoil your dinner"), although the restaurant, overseen by the famous Albert, also turns out "first-class" meals. / www.greywalls.co.uk; @Greywalls_Hotel; Wed-Sat 9 pm, Sun 8 pm; jacket required. *Accommodation:* 23 rooms, from £260

HALE, GREATER MANCHESTER 5–2B

SIGIRIYA £35 443

173 ASHLEY ROAD WA15 9SD 0161 941 3025

This Hale newcomer has created a "lively buzz with its excellent food", which "combines some South Asian classics with fine Sri Lankan cuisine". Top Tip: "look out for the hoppers (Sri Lankan pancakes) on a Sunday". / sigiriya.co.uk; Mon-Sat 9.30 pm, Sun 4 pm.

Hambleton Hall, Hambleton

HAMBLETON, RUTLAND · 5–4D

FINCH'S ARMS · £47 · 2️⃣2️⃣3️⃣

OAKHAM RD LE15 8TL 01572 756575

The "location and impression from outside promise much" at this "busy old inn-with-rooms above the shores of Rutland Water". It's "a good watering hole after a stomp round the peninsula" and summer evenings on the terrace can be "a delight". Familiar criticisms are present: "some dishes wow more than others", service can be "functional rather than warm" and the whole set-up can seem like "more style than substance". On the plus-side one regular found standards "on more of an even keel" this year. / www.finchsarms.co.uk; Wed-Sat 9.30 pm, Sun 3.30 pm. *Accommodation:* 100 rooms, from £100

HAMBLETON HALL · £102 · 5️⃣5️⃣4️⃣

LE15 8TH 01572 756991

"The effortless and gracious hospitality of a country house hotel is maintained down to a tee" at Tim Hart's "magnificent" property (owned until the 1970s by part of the Hoare banking dynasty), with its "open fires, antique furnishings, and busy wallpaper"; "staff who can't do enough to help"; and "unbeatable views over Rutland Water" (which the house, in fact, pre-dates). "All of which is pointless if the food isn't great... and luckily it's brilliant". The odd critic feels Aaron Patterson's cuisine is "fairly conventional (good quality but lacking a sense of adventure)" but if you're looking for brined, pickled and foraged small plates you're missing the point here, as his "very accessible" classical cuisine delivers a "consistency and reliability" that's second to none with "wonderful attention to detail". "You do pay for it", but real complaints about value here are notable by their absence. / www.hambletonhall.com; @hambleton_hall; near Rutland Water; 9.30 pm; children: 5+. *Accommodation:* 17 rooms, from £265

HAMPTON POYLE, OXFORDSHIRE · 2–1D

THE BELL · £54 · 3️⃣3️⃣3️⃣

11 OXFORD ROAD OX5 2QD 01865 376242

"A good pub within easy reach of Oxford for lunch or dinner" and praised for its "honest and competent" cuisine. / www.thebelloxford.co.uk; Fri & Sat 9.30 pm, Sun-Thu 9 pm.

HAROME, NORTH YORKSHIRE · 8–4C

THE PHEASANT HOTEL · £58 · 4️⃣4️⃣4️⃣

YO62 5JG 01439 771241

This "idyllic hotel" with "food to die for" was part of chef Andrew Pern's Star Inn empire, and is now run by his former wife Jacquie following their split. "The cooking is interesting, and lighter than at its better-known neighbour, but still full of flavour" – and it consistently matches its ratings. / www.thepheasanthotel.com; Mon-Sun 9 pm; no Amex. *Accommodation:* 15 rooms, from £155

THE STAR INN · £75 · 4️⃣3️⃣4️⃣

HAROME YO62 5JE 01439 770397

"If Carlsberg made pubs...!" then fans of Andrew Pern's well-known destination say they would be like his thatched, 14th-century inn (which he's run for more than 20 years) with its "roaring log fire" – a perfect setting for Pern's 'modern Yorkshire' cooking, with plenty of game from the nearby moors, prepared "without pretension and yet so delicious". It doesn't wow absolutely everyone, though, with a minority of diners who say "while it's very good, I can't help feeling it's not quite what it once was". / www.thestaratharome.co.uk; @TheStaratHarome; 3m SE of Helmsley off A170; Mon - Sat 9.30 pm, Sun 6 pm; no Amex. *Accommodation:* 8 rooms, from £150

HARPENDEN, HERTFORDSHIRE · 3–2A

LUSSMANNS · £42 · 2️⃣2️⃣2️⃣

20A LEYTON ROAD AL5 2HU 01582 965393

Mixed views this year on this popular branch of a small local chain. To critics it's "overpriced for what is basically standard fare", while fans feel "you can count on a good meal every time". / www.lussmanns.com/restaurants/harpenden-restaurants/; @lussmanns; Mon & Tue, Sun 9 pm, Wed & Thu 9.30 pm, Fri & Sat 10.30 pm.

HARROGATE, NORTH YORKSHIRE · 5–1C

BALTZERSENS · £31 · 5️⃣4️⃣3️⃣

HG1 1PU 01423 202363

"Ahead of its time! In tune with the community and the world!" – Paul Rawlinson may have closed Norse (RIP) but his 'other' Harrogate spot sails on with its "fabulous coffee, incredible hot chocolate, outstanding baking and a tasty real food menu too". "The Scandi-based menu

is a great thing to have on a dank morning (we're in North Yorks, it's not unheard of!)". / www.baltzersens.co.uk; Mon-Sat 10 pm, Sun 8 pm.

BETTYS · £46 · 3️⃣4️⃣5️⃣

1 PARLIAMENT STREET HG1 2QU 01423 814070

"The most civilised hour or two you'll ever spend" could well be at this archetypal and epic English team room "institution" – "a legend that always lives up to its reputation", with "exquisite" cakes, teas and light bites that are "a fabulous treat" ("can be pricier than most, but not to be missed"). It's "always busy", though, and "the queues are not so good". / www.bettysandtaylors.co.uk; Sun-Fri & Sat 9 pm; no Amex; no bookings.

BETTYS GARDEN CAFÉ, RHS GARDENS HARLOW CARR · £39 · 4️⃣4️⃣4️⃣

CRAG LANE, BECKWITHSHAW HG3 1QB 01423 505604

"The best of the Bettys tea rooms" according to fans, "this gorgeous café in the grounds of the exceptional RHS Harlow Carr gardens never disappoints, however crowded it gets". It's "a modern building with a palm-court-style ambience" and food-wise, it's a "proper treat" (Welsh rarebit "stopped us talking for a while", and "why can't cups of tea always be as good as this?!"). / www.bettys.co.uk; @Bettys1919; Sun-Fri & Sat 9 pm.

DRUM & MONKEY · £50 · 4️⃣4️⃣4️⃣

5 MONTPELLIER GDNS HG1 2TF 01423 502650

A Montpelier institution for almost 50 years, this "old-fashioned and totally charming" family-owned seafood restaurant "just keeps on going – unchanging, and all the better for that". "Whatever fish you choose it is always fresh and well-served". / www.drumandmonkey.co.uk; @DrumAndMonkey; Mon-Sat 10 pm, Sun 5 pm; no Amex; booking max 10 may apply.

GRAVELEY'S FISH & CHIP RESTAURANT · £47 · 4️⃣3️⃣2️⃣

8-12 CHELTENHAM PARADE HG1 1DB 01423 507 093

"Consistently crispy batter" cushions the national dish at this longstanding luminary, but there's more to it than the headline event; the northern mini-chain it belongs to was founded by the Stephenson family back in 1960, and is now under son Graham after the death of patriarch Jackson-Reed in 2017. / www.graveleysofharrogate.com; @graveleys; Sun-Thu 9 pm, Fri & Sat 9.30 pm.

THE IVY HARROGATE · £56 · 3️⃣3️⃣4️⃣

7-9 PARLIAMENT STREET HG1 2QU 01423 787 100

This "real asset" to the local scene, fruit of the glam Theatreland icon's recent mega-expansion, is one of its better branches. As with other cities, the odd disappointment is not unknown, but most reports are of a suitably "buzzy" venue, with "professional" service and "good food at sensible prices". / www.theivyharrogate.com; @ivyharrogate; Mon-Sun 12.30 am.

ORCHID £51 5️⃣4️⃣3️⃣

28 SWAN ROAD HG1 2SE 01423 560 425

This "wonderful", "un-failing" Pan-Asian in the Studley Hotel was one of the first UK restaurants to combine East and Southeast Asian dishes on the same menu when it opened in 2001. "Year after year it continues to be the best all-round dining experience", with "super staff who greet you like old friends and the most sublime dishes". "Excellent value for money", too (always important in these parts…) / www.orchidrestaurant.co.uk; @orchidnstudley; Sun-Fri & Sat 10 pm. *Accommodation:* 28 rooms, from £115

RESTAURANT 92 £74 4️⃣3️⃣3️⃣

92-94 STATION PARADE HG1 1HQ 01423 503027

Michael Carr's two-year-old is "really one to watch for the future" and has won a strong local reputation. Worst complaint? "Sunday Lunch was somewhere between 'fine dining' and a more traditional big roast. Being in Yorkshire the portions did seem a little small, but my wife was very pleased to leave without feeling bloated!" / restaurant92.co.uk; Mon-Sat 9.30 pm, Sun 4 pm.

SASSO £41 4️⃣4️⃣3️⃣

8-10 PRINCES SQUARE HG1 1LX 01423 508 838

This "fantastic family-run Italian" makes for a "civilised place to meet in the business part of town". Now in its twenty first year, its "consistently varied food" takes its inspiration from Emilia Romagna, home region of chef and owner Stefano Lancellotti. / www.sassorestaurant.co.uk; @sassorestaurant; Mon-Thu 9.30 pm, Fri & Sat 10 pm, Sun 3 pm.

STUZZI £48 3️⃣4️⃣3️⃣

46B KINGS ROAD HG1 5JW 01423 705852

"Delicious and authentic Italian food" is "served with enthusiasm and knowledge in unfussy surroundings" at this hotel-brasserie. "Don't be fooled by the 'Italian tapas' idea…the servings are full-size – maybe that's the Yorkshire effect!" / @STUZZIHARROGATE; Mon-Sat 10.30 pm.

MAGGIE'S £26 3️⃣3️⃣2️⃣

ROCK-A-NORE ROAD TN34 3DW 01424 430 205

For local fans, there can be no better place to scoff a portion of "perfect fish 'n' chips with superior batter" than this "basic (plastic table cloths) but loveable first floor café on the beach with views of fishing boats and the sea" – a Hastings institution since Margaret Banfield set up shop more than twenty years ago. Top Tip: book by phone (there's no internet or wifi). /

www.towncitycards.com/locations/hastings/ma; Sun-Thu 3 pm, Fri & Sat 8 pm; cash only.

ROCK A NORE KITCHEN £34 3️⃣3️⃣2️⃣

23A ROCK-A-NORE RD TN34 3DW 01424 445425

"An intimate spot right opposite fishermen's huts" – this "welcoming" seafood restaurant is "a fab find" for most reporters, although the odd meal here was also "chaotic and disappointing" this year. / no bookings.

WEBBE'S ROCK-A-NORE £44 3️⃣3️⃣3️⃣

1 ROCK-A-NORE ROAD TN34 3DW 01424 721650

"Fantastic fish fresh from the sea just across the road" takes the lead role at Paul Webbe's "friendly and consistently good" spot opposite the Jerwood Gallery; part of his restaurant-and-cookery-school empire based on the produce of Rye Bay and East Sussex. / www.webbesrestaurants.co.uk; @WebbesRockaNore; Mon-Thu 9 pm, Fri & Sat 9.30 pm, Sun 8.30 pm.

SEA PEBBLES £32 3️⃣2️⃣3️⃣

348-352 UXBRIDGE RD HA5 4HR 020 8428 0203

"Brilliant fish" in generous portions – "more like half a whale!" – has kept the Andeou family's chippie busy since 1990. Recently expanded, it now has an offshoot in Bushey Heath. / www.seapebbles.co.uk; Tue-Fri 9.30 pm, Sat 9 pm; may need 8+ to book.

THE BLUE STRAWBERRY £49 3️⃣3️⃣3️⃣

THE STREET CM3 2DW 01245 381333

"Just off the A12", this well-known village stalwart is generally seen as "a really lovely destination that we never tire of visiting". Regulars can also find it "variable" though – "go on a good day!" / www.bluestrawberrybistrot.co.uk; @thebluestrawb; 3m E of Chelmsford; Mon-Fri 10 pm, Sat midnight, Sun 4 pm; no Amex.

JEREMY'S AT BORDE HILL £56 4️⃣4️⃣5️⃣

BORDE HILL, BORDE HILL GARDENS RH16 1XP 01444 441102

"A long-standing favourite that's always a joy" – Jeremy & Vera Ashpool's popular venue has a particularly "delightful" atmosphere, thanks to its "elegant" (although sometimes "packed") interior, and most especially due to its location in gorgeous Borde Hill Garden (200 acres of famous landscaped grounds). Service is "lovely and attentive" and the "imaginative menus are excellently delivered" and at "good value" prices. / www.jeremysrestaurant.com; @Jeremysrest; Exit 10A from the A23; Tue-Sat 9.30 pm, Sun 3 pm.

THE FEATHERS INN £49 4️⃣4️⃣2️⃣

NE43 7SW 01661 843 607

Rhian Cradock's "proper village pub with fantastic food" was "one of the originators of the local seasonal food movement" when it started-out preparing 'Northumbrian cooking' 12 years ago; and everything is presented "simply and very well", including "superb game in season". It's worth seeking out in a "difficult-to-find village overlooking the Tyne valley", and while some find it "rather cramped" or "squashy", others reckon it "cosy". / www.thefeathers.net; @thefeathersinn; Mon-Sat 4.30 pm, Sun 3.30 pm; no Amex.

SUGAR BOAT £48 3️⃣3️⃣2️⃣

30 COLQUHOUN SQUARE G84 8AQ 01436 647 522

"A lovely place that's well worth the trip out from Glasgow" – this busy wine bar made "an unexpected and welcome discovery" for a number of reporters thanks to its quality, modern bistro fare. / www.sugarboat.co.uk; @sugarboat30; 10 pm.

BLACK SWAN £90 2️⃣2️⃣2️⃣

MARKET PL YO62 5BJ 01439 770466

"A lovely afternoon tea" is a well-known feature of this attractive, traditional hotel at the centre of the town. When it comes to more substantial meals, though, the mixed themes from earlier years were again apparent: "inconsistent cooking, yet gourmet prices". / www.blackswan-helmsley.co.uk; 9.30 pm. *Accommodation:* 45 rooms, from £130

GALVIN AT CENTURION CLUB £51 3️⃣2️⃣3️⃣

CENTURION CLUB, HEMEL HEMPSTEAD ROAD HP3 8LA 01442 510520

"A modern interior, with views of the golf course" sets the scene at this Galvin Brothers yearling, which on most – if not quite all – accounts provides "a good welcome", "high quality" cooking and a "relaxing" atmosphere. It's a popular haunt for business entertaining, for which "there's a perfect setting alongside the 18th fairway and a delightful lounge that feeds into the restaurant, where you can talk shop pre-, post- or during lunch". / www.centurionclub.co.uk; Mon-Sat 9.30 pm.

CHEAL'S OF HENLEY £75 343

64 HIGH ST B95 5BX 01564 793 856

This beamed high street dining room, owned by Julie & Tony Cheal, with son Matt (ex-Simpsons) at the stove, is a "really good find"; despite "just an occasional bum note", the cooking – from six-course tasting menus to "generous" roasts – is high "quality" and "very pretty", and staff show a "real commitment to the place". / www.chealsofhenley.co.uk; @Chealshenley; Wed-Sat 9.30 pm, Sun 3 pm.

THE DUKE OF CUMBERLAND £61 324

GU27 3HQ 01428 652280

"The wonderful garden is ideal for a leisurely summer lunch" at chef/owner Simon Goodman's "cosy" 16th-century country pub, serving "hearty portions of good grub". The relatively new restaurant area "blends in well with the old building", and view of Black Down, the highest peak in Sussex, is "quintessential England". / www.thedukeofcumberland.com; @theduke_Henley; Sun-Thu 11.30 pm, Fri & Sat midnight.

THE GREYHOUND £55 333

GALLOWSTREE RD, PEPPARD COMMON RG9 5HT 0118 972 2227

Antony and Jay Worrall Thompson's operation near Henley-on-Thames is nominally a pub, but there's no beer and it's closed on Mondays and Tuesdays. It combines a "lovely candlelit ambience and discreet service", with "an extensive menu" of "well-put-together" dishes ("often a modern twist on old favourites"). / www.awtgreyhound.com/; @TheGreyhoundAWT; Mon-Sat 10.30 pm.

LUSCOMBES AT THE GOLDEN BALL £52 333

THE GOLDEN BALL, LOWER ASSENDON RG9 6AH 01491 574157

This rustic bar-restaurant – "a former pub on the outskirts of Henley" – wins consistent ratings for its assured and "unfussy" food. "Why go anywhere else?" asks one local, while a passer-by reports: "found this by accident and had a splendid lunch". / www.luscombes.co.uk; 10 pm; no Amex.

SHAUN DICKENS AT THE BOATHOUSE £68 334

THE BOATHOUSE RG9 1AZ 01491 577937

It has "a lovely setting by the river", but in other respects Shaun Dickens's contemporary-style venue again receives a split opinion. Fans applaud the "first class cuisine with exceptional service" and say it makes "a great choice for a romantic dinner or a celebration". To sceptics, though, it's merely "overpriced and

not worth the hype". / www.shaundickens.co.uk; @henleyboathouse; Sun-Thu 10 pm, Fri & Sat 11 pm.

VILLA MARINA £48 342

18 THAMESIDE RG9 1BH 01491 575262

The "formal" riverside sibling to Marlow's Villa d'Este continues to put in a "reliable" performance, with its "traditional" and not too ponced-up Italian cuisine ("including veal and liver and no pizza"), which is largely deemed "expensive but worth it". / www.villamarina-henley.com; @Villa_Marina_; opp Angel pub, nr Bridge; Mon-Thu 10.30 pm, Fri & Sat 11 pm, Sun 9 pm.

A RULE OF TUM BURGER SHOP £30 323

32 AUBREY STREET HR4 0BU 01432 351764

"Lovely burgers straight from the farm" (also "excellent veggie burgers"), plus "really good fries" and "all reasonably priced" have carved quite a name for this very popular pitstop (which has also cornered the local Deliveroo market). / www.aruleoftum.com/burger-shop; @burgershophfd; Mon-Sat 10 pm, Sun 8 pm.

BEEFY BOYS £25 443

HR4 9HU 01432 359209

An "outstanding and quirky operation" – a former pop-up that went permanent in 2015 – based, as per the name, on "great burgers", and set in the city-centre. / www.thebeefyboys.com.

CASTLE HOUSE RESTAURANT, CASTLE HOUSE HOTEL £63 334

CASTLE ST HR1 2NW 01432 356321

"'Best in Hereford' is not perhaps the highest bar to reach", but it's an accolade nevertheless due to this smart Georgian city hotel, which has "beautiful surroundings" (close to the cathedral and overlooking gardens designed by Capability Brown); and which features consistently well-rated cooking from locally born chef Claire Nicholls, with a focus on Herefordshire beef and produce from the hotel's own farm. / www.castlehse.co.uk; @castlehsehotel; 9.30 pm, Sun 9 pm. *Accommodation:* 24 rooms, from £150

A CASA MIA £38 433

160 HIGH STREET CT6 5AJ 01227 372 947

"Seriously good pizza" made "in a traditional Neapolitan style" – it was the first UK pizzeria to be certified by Naples' Associazione Verace Pizza – wins high ratings for Gennaro Esposito's casual Herne Bay spot. It "serves other very good tasty Italian dishes" too. / www.acasamia.co.uk; @AcasamiaHB; Mon-Thu 11 pm, Fri & Sat 11.30 pm, Sun 10 pm.

BURNT TRUFFLE £53 443

104-106 TELEGRAPH ROAD CH60 0AQ 0151 342 1111

Gary Usher's crowdfunded follow-up to Sticky Walnut (the first of several) "describes itself as a local bistro, but it's far better than that", offering "novel, well-prepared and VERY tasty cooking" in a "quaint and cosy cottage" in the centre of a village on the Wirral. / www.burnttruffle.net; @BuRntTruffle; Tue-Thu 9 pm, Fri & Sat 10 pm, Sun 8 pm.

THE ANGEL INN £63 333

BD23 6LT 01756 730263

In its heyday, this old Dales inn in a tiny hamlet was England's best-known dining pub. It still serves well-rated cooking both in its bar and smarter restaurant; and still attracts some attention for its wine list; but its profile generally is a little 'under the radar' nowadays. / www.angelhetton.co.uk; @angelinnhetton; 5m N of Skipton off B6265 at Rylstone; Mon-Sat 9 pm, Sun 8 pm.

BATTLESTEADS £40 344

WARK ON TYNE NE48 3LS 01434 230 209

Stone-clad old inn, beautifully situated in the country, and with an attractive garden for the summer months. The dining room provides a "good tasting menu" using a fair amount of home-grown produce. / www.battlesteads.com; @Battlesteads.

BOUCHON BISTROT £49 333

4-6 GILESGATE NE46 3NJ 01434 609943

A Gallic outpost on Gilesgate – this "favourite" local dining spot has a menu of classics from rural France – owner Greg Bureau, a second-generation restaurateur from the Loire Valley, brings a further stamp of authenticity. / www.bouchonbistrot.co.uk; @bouchonhexham; Mon-Thu 9 pm, Fri & Sat 9.30 pm; no Amex.

THE RAT INN £39 435

ANICK NE46 4LN 014 3460 2814

"No frills, no nonsense, no splodges on the plate: just good traditional food, drinks, top banter, cosy fires, gorgeous bar, nice beer" – that's the appeal of a trip to this "perfect", "old-fashioned" country gastropub, "which is still very much a pub" situated "in a hamlet, on a hillside above Hexham". "The garden has exceptional views and the hardest part to any visit is what to choose!" / www.theratinn.com; @ratales; Mon-Sat 9 pm, Sun 3 pm.

THE PARSON'S NOSE £44 **3 3 4**

**48 LISBURN STREET BT26 6AB
028 9268 3009**

"Fantastic food in a beautiful riverside setting in one of Northern Ireland's prettiest towns" is the reason to visit this destination pub – one of Ronan Sweeney's Balloo Inns. "They have a proper wood-fired pizza oven and great thin crust pizza as well as the usual pub faves and a top Sunday roast". / www.ballooinns.com/the-parsons-nose; Sun & Mon 9 pm, Tue-Sat 9.30 pm.

HINTLESHAM HALL £68 **2 2 3**

HINTLESHAM IP8 3NS 01473 652334

Dating from 1448 (although its modern history dates from 1972 when it was purchased by Robert Carrier) – this "lovely old hotel" remains a well-known destination. One or two reports feel its "attractive surroundings are let down by the restaurant (and food that's more basic than the menu would suggest)" but other feedback is more enthusiastic, particularly regarding its fine afternoon tea. / www.hintleshamhall.co.uk/; @hintlesham_hall; 4m W of Ipswich on A1071; 9 pm; jacket required; children: 12+. *Accommodation:* 33 rooms, from £99

LORD POULETT ARMS £54 **2 2 3**

TA17 8SE 01460 73149

This thatched 17th-century Somerset inn – a "lovely old, multi-roomed pub in a delightful village" – has been a haven of quality for 15 years under Steve Hill and Michelle Paynton. It has taken some flak of late for being "rather average" and pricey, in a year which saw the couple retire to France (in summer 2018). It now joins the Beckford Arms at Tisbury and the Talbot Inn at Mells under new owners, backed by Nick Jones of Soho House. / www.lordpoulettarms.com; @LordPoulettArms; 9 pm; no Amex. *Accommodation:* 4 rooms, from £85

THE FARMHOUSE AT REDCOATS £53 **4 3 3**

REDCOATS GREEN SG4 7JR 01438 729500

This 15th century hotel in rolling Herts countryside has been under the aegis of Anglian Country Inns since mid-2017, with an ongoing revamp already adding a new barn conversion juggling weddings and a vibrant bar; on the food front, the MO has changed to farm-to-fork and is gaining decent marks (more feedback please!). / www.farmhouseatredcoats.co.uk; @FarmAtRedcoats; 9.30 pm. *Accommodation:* 13 rooms, from £90

HERMITAGE RD £55 **3 3 3**

**20-21 HERMITAGE ROAD SG5 1BT
01462 433603**

It "tries to be a trendy drinks and nibbles spot" and this converted ballroom seemingly succeeds; head upstairs for all-day dining (majoring in steaks, ribs and burgers) and to the downstairs café for "the best coffee (courtesy of the legendary Faema E71) top service and delicious bagels". / www.hermitagerd.co.uk; @HermitageRd; Mon-Sat 10 pm, Sun 7 pm.

THE VICTORIA AT HOLKHAM £49 **3 2 4**

NR23 1RG 01328 711008

Down the driveway from the magnificent Palladian-style Holkham Hall, this well-known, shabby chic hotel-pub owned by the estate turns out British comfort food, with some focus on game sourced locally; "good value" for those exploring this bit of the coast. / www.holkham.co.uk; @VictoriaHolkham; on the main coast road, between Wells-next-the Sea and Burnham Overy Staithe; 9 pm; no Amex. *Accommodation:* 10 rooms, from £140

WIVETON HALL CAFE £46 **3 3 2**

1 MARSH LANE NR25 7TE 01263 740515

"Rustic cafe made famous by a TV series" ('Normal for Norfolk') and serving "all local produce" that's "reasonably priced", and largely sourced from the fruit farm where it sits, overlooking the marshes and sea. Bonus points for being "great with small children", and having "lots of room outside to run around". / www.wivetonhall.co.uk/restaurant-cafe/; @WivetonHall; 4.30 pm; closed Mon D, Tue D, Wed D, Thu D & Sun D; booking lunch only.

NOBLE £41 **5 4 3**

27A CHURCH RD BT18 9BU 028 9042 5655

"A small, first-floor restaurant" – now two years old, above a health food store in this glam town outside Belfast – "with a growing reputation for sublime food; and at reasonable prices too for the quality". It's the work of chef Pearson Morris and manager Saul McConnell. / nobleholywood.com; @nobleholywood; Wed-Sat 10 pm, Sun 7 pm.

THE PIG, COMBE HOUSE £63 **3 4 4**

GITTISHAM EX14 3AD 01404 540400

"This could be the best of the Pig group", say fans of this Elizabethan-era Otter Valley outpost of the dressed-down country-house hotel chain. "Shabby chic, with some chairs so rickety you think they're going to collapse, but once you've overcome those fears the food is wholesome and tasty". / www.combehousedevon.com;

@CombeHouseDevon; on the outskirts of Honiton; not far from the A30, A375, 303; 9.30 pm; no Amex. *Accommodation:* 15 rooms, from £215

THE HOLT £52 **3 3 2**

178 HIGH STREET EX14 1LA 01404 47707

This "very well run pub" owned and run by the family behind the nearby Otter brewery serves an "interesting and well-presented range of food" alongside "some of the best beer". "Produce is local" and the "original British menu changes every six weeks or so". / www.theholt-honiton.com; Mon closed, Tue - Thu 9 pm, Fri & Sat 9.30 pm.

THE MILL AT GORDLETON £53 **2 3 4**

SILVER STREET SO41 6DJ 01590 682219

There's no doubting the "beautiful" location of this mill-set boutique hotel, with a terrace on the river Avon, and 'Secret Garden' full of artworks; generally its food gains equally positive remarks, but – whether it's a blip, or the rise of hipper rivals like The Pig nearby – it struck a more "average" note this year. / www.themillatgordleton.co.uk; on the A337, off the M27; Mon-Sat 11 pm, Sun 9 pm; no Amex. *Accommodation:* 8 rooms, from £150

THE BELL INN £49 **4 4 5**

HIGH RD SS17 8LD 01375 642463

"The old pub oozes charm and when cold, the roaring fire near the bar is just the thing", say fans of this timber-framed 15th-century coaching inn. "Then there's the food: fantastic, but not so fancy it would put the man in the street off, and it's in generous portions". Run by the same family for 75 years, it's a place where tradition is taken seriously – a Good Friday custom of adding a new hot cross bun to a collection hanging over the bar is more than a century old. "We've been regular diners for the past 25 years and it never fails to deliver – the regularly changing menu means you never get bored". / www.bell-inn.co.uk; @Bellhorndon; signposted off B1007, off A13; Mon-Sat 11 pm, Sun 9 pm; booking max 12 may apply. *Accommodation:* 15 rooms, from £50

RESTAURANT TRISTAN £101 **4 4 3**

3 STANS WAY RH12 1HU 01403 255688

Tristan & Candy Mason have just celebrated the 10th year of their town-centre venue, which wins consistently high ratings for "really 'next-level' cuisine". "Tristan is an outstanding chef producing wonderful meals", fans agree, while "Candy ensures the high service standards". There were some minor rumblings this year about the fact that it's "not cheap", but even a reporter who felt it was "overpriced" said the food's "very good". / www.restauranttristan.co.uk; @tristanshorsham; Mon closed, Tue - Sat 9.30 pm, Sun closed.

BROWNLOW ARMS £41 3̄4̄4̄

NG32 2AZ 01400 250234

"A gem of an old stone pub tucked away on the crest of a hill in rural Lincolnshire (yet less than 5 miles from the A1)". "The panelled dining is painted a deep sea green and makes for an intimate dining experience". Dishes are "interesting, well presented and fresh-tasting and there are excellent wines by the glass". / www.brownlowarms.co.uk; on the Grantham Road; Mon-Sun 11 pm; no Amex; children: 10+. *Accommodation:* 5 rooms, from £98

KITCHEN £27 3̄3̄3̄

38 BRIDGEGATE DN14 7AB 01430 430600

"Sweet and savoury baking to tempt and delight" is the order of the day at this diminutive cafe, whose "range is magnificent and requires stern self-control". One niggle: "queuing can be frustrating" but by common consent "the wait is worthwhile". / www.kitchensnaith.co.uk; @KitchenSnaith; Mon - Sat 5 am; Sun closed.

LINO'S £40 3̄4̄3̄

**122 MARKET STREET CH47 3BH
0151 632 1408**

"An 'old reliable', yes, but the food has improved considerably over the past year or so" according to a regular at this Italian-inspired staple (est. 1983), and the "friendly service makes you feel very welcome and special every time". / www.linosrestaurant.co.uk; 3m from M53, J2; Tue-Fri 9 pm, Sat 10 pm; no Amex.

ERIC'S £68 4̄3̄3̄

73-75 LIDGET ST HD3 3JP 01484 646416

"Top-quality food and service" (the "early bird is great value for money") makes this Lindley spot a bit of a local beacon – and one that's shining brighter after a luxe revamp in September 2018. After his plans for a Mirfield burger joint were scuppered, the eponymous Eric launched lavish champagne and cocktail bar The Arborist, facing Eric's, and yards from his first burger bar, PAX, as we went to press. / www.ericsrestaurant.co.uk; @ericrestaurant; 10 pm; Sun 4pm; closed Mon, Sat L & Sun D; no Amex.

OLD HOUSE £75 3̄3̄4̄

5 SCALE LANE HU1 1LA 01482 210253

"Set in wonderful historic space" (Hull's oldest domestic building) – Chris Harrison's (ex Fat Duck) "old town gem" of a pub is part of his local street food empire (which this year added a new outlet in Trinity Market). Even those who find the "quirky" menu "confusing", and feel the "elements of the ambitious food don't always work together", feel it's an "obliging" place with a good standard of achievement. / www.shootthebull.co.uk/the-old-house-1/; @oldhousehull; Mon-Sun 9.30 pm.

TAPASYA @ MARINA £52 3̄3̄3̄

HUMBER DOCK STREET, MARINA, HU1 1TB

"Gourmet Indian food in a marina setting" wins recommendations for this glossy subcontinental. The original branch is in a less flash bit of the city, and this year has also seen the opening of an outlet in Trinity Market. / Mon-Sat 9.30 pm.

THIEVING HARRY'S £23 3̄3̄3̄

73 HUMBER PLACE HU1 1UD 01482 214141

"In Hull's thriving Humber Street": this "quirky cafe in the old part of the city with great views" makes "a great breakfast spot" in particular ("delicious!"). "It's vegetarian friendly but if you prefer a full English – no probs!" / thievingharrys. co.uk; Mon-Sat 9.30 pm, Sun 4 pm.

ELIANE OF HUNGERFORD £49 3̄3̄3̄

24 HIGH STREET RG17 0NF 01488 686100

"Gluten free, vegetarian, vegan, and other dietary requirements" are catered for at this self service café, which (promising 'food that makes your soul smile') sells "very healthy dishes, including fabulous salads, and options incorporating some strange unrecognisable ingredients". Also, since 2017, in Sunningdale. / elianesmiles.com; Mon-Sat 5 pm, Sun 4 pm.

THE FOX AND HOUNDS RESTAURANT & BAR £41 2̄2̄3̄

2 HIGH STREET SG12 8NH 01279 843 999

This village gastroboozer has become a foodie destination over the past 15 years, and it's easy to see why: chef/owner James Rix brings his Michelin restaurant background to bear on the menu, offering whole Dover sole or turbot alongside "cuts from rare-breed cattle including English Longhorn and Galloway – all grilled on a charcoal oven". / www.foxandhounds-hunsdon.co.uk; @thefoxhunsdon; off the A414, 10 min from Hertford; Mon-Sat 4.30 pm, Sun 3.30 pm; no Amex.

OLD BRIDGE HOTEL £53 2̄4̄3̄

1 HIGH ST PE29 3TQ 01480 424300

The food at Master of Wine John Hoskins's attractive ivy-sheathed townhouse hotel and bottle shop is "consistent and pleasant" enough, but it's the "impressive wine list" which continues to really stand out, being "year on year outstanding". / www.huntsbridge.com; @oldbridgehotel; off A1, off A14; Mon-Thu 9.15 pm, Fri & Sat 10 pm, Sun 9 pm. *Accommodation:* 24 rooms, from £160

GEORGE & DRAGON £49 3̄4̄3̄

THE SQUARE SP11 0AA 01264 736277

Cosy modernised sixteenth-century country pub with rooms, well-rated (if from limited feedback) for its to-the-point, restaurant-quality cooking. / www.georgeanddragon.com; @HampshirePub; Mon-Thu 9.30 pm, Fri & Sat 10 pm, Sun 9 pm.

THE BAY HORSE £64 4̄3̄4̄

45 THE GRN DL2 2AA 01325 720 663

Modernised 15th-century coaching inn in a "lovely" village setting that's "well worth the trip from Newcastle" thanks to its "excellent" cuisine: look out for the "changing specials board" and "splendid local game in season". / www.thebayhorsehurworth.com; @thebayhorse_; Mon-Sat 11.30 pm, Sun 10.30 pm.

HYTHE BAY SEAFOOD RESTAURANT £46 3̄3̄2̄

MARINE PARADE CT21 6AW 01303 233844

"If you want fish – caught yards away – this is the restaurant": an "unassuming" café-like spot on the seafront. The location is "lovely" ("sit in the window and you see the English Channel") and the food "reasonably priced" – a winning formula now exported to Dover and Deal. / www.hythebay.co.uk; 9.30 pm.

THE DUKE WILLIAM £49 3̄4̄3̄

THE ST CT3 1QP 01227 721308

There's an enthusiastic if not enormous local following for Mark Sargeant's "very enjoyable" pub in the heart of this Kent village – "so pleasant, with brilliant staff and food that's always a pleasure". / www.dukewilliam.biz; @DukeWilliamKent; Mon-Thu 11 pm, Fri & Sat midnight, Sun 10.30 pm.

THOMAS CARR @ THE OLIVE ROOM £80 5̄4̄3̄

56 FORE STREET EX34 9DJ 01271 555005

"An inspiring young chef who has a real talent with fish – never spoiling the delicate flesh of the fish itself and always accompanying the dish with exciting tasty morsels or fabulously delicate sauces" – wins high praise from the few who have visited this offbeat but competitively priced North Devon four-year-old. Its profile was helped this year by a rave review from Jay Rayner. (In February 2018, after a crowdfunding drive, Carr took over the town's Lamb Hotel, converting it into the 'Thomas Carr Seafood and Grill'.) / www.thomascarrdining.co.uk/restaurants/the-olive-room/; @ThomasCarrChef.

BETTYS   £49   **3 4 5**

32 THE GROVE LS29 9EE   01943 608029

For "a traditional afternoon tea in a venue with style" (plus "great breakfasts" and "superb" rostis) this much-loved, often oversubscribed institution is "a must if you are in Ilkley"…"long may it stay". "Compared to Harrogate or York, the parking is much better and queues less long". / www.bettys.co.uk/tea-rooms/locations/ilkle; 5.30 pm; no Amex; no bookings.

THE BOX TREE   £105   **5 5 4**

35-37 CHURCH ST LS29 9DR   01943 608484

"You have to like old-style comfort, cuisine and experience" but hitherto there's been "nowhere better" than Simon and Rena Gueller's "traditional and cosy" bastion (opened in 1962): "a proper restaurant, doing proper classical food, with proper service and a proper wine list", which on all accounts has been "on top of its game" … so we were all the more flummoxed by Michelin's decision to remove its star in October 2018! Soon thereafter, chef Kieran Smith parted ways, Simon Gueller said he was returning to the kitchen, and then immediately thereafter that came further news that Gueller had snapped up Samira Effa from Alimentum, when it was announced that the Cambridge restaurant was unexpectedly closing down. Alimentum was known for its cutting edge culinary style, whereas here it's always been "the absence of dry ice and other fripperies" that folks have loved so much, so whether the contemporary shift such a move presumably entails goes down well remains to be seen. Constants, though, are the "amazingly broad wine list" ("enviable breadth and depth, and if you look hard there are some fair prices in there"), and "one of the most knowledgeable sommeliers around", Didier da Costa. / www.theboxtree.co.uk; @boxtreeilkley; on A65 near town centre; Wed-Sat 9.30 pm, Sun 3 pm; no jeans; children: 10+.

QUINTA   £36   **3 3 2**

10 WELLS RD LS29 9JD   01943 602 670

"In a street just off the town-centre", this Mediterranean venue provides "enjoyable" cooking and "particularly great value in the Portuguese section of the wine list". "There is perhaps nothing hugely original on the menu, but it's none the worse for that when the food is well cooked as it is here". / www.quintabarandgrill.com; Mon-Sun 10.30 pm.

1900 MARINERS   £50

NEPTUNE QUAY IP4 1AX   01473 289748

At the start of October 2018, this veteran Belgian gunboat (a fine place for dining at sunset) was sold by the Crépy family (who ran it since 1994) and purchased by French chef Julien Jourdain and his wife Karine, with the aim of taking its former Gallic formula and bringing in 'a more vibrant and contemporary approach'. The Amuda (as the boat is named) will be out of action in early 2019 for a survey and repairs 'to bring the boat back to its former glory'. / www.marinersipswich.co.uk; @MarinersIpswich; Mon closed, Tue - Sat 9.30 pm, Sun closed; no Amex.

TRONGS   £36   **5 5 3**

23 ST NICHOLAS ST IP1 1TW   01473 256833

"Standards never seem to waver" at this superlative, "authentic" and "always busy" Chinese, where the "extended Vietnamese family owners" offer "exceptional, caring service". "Leave it in their capable hands" if you're not sure what to try. / www.trongs.co.uk; 10.30 pm; closed Sun.

ZAIKA   £32   **4 4 3**

17 SAINT NICHOLAS STREET IP1 1TW   01473 210110

"Probably the best Indian in a town with many curry houses" – this family-run fixture (opened in 2005) is "very popular" thanks to its "friendly" and "attentive" service and consistently good cooking. / zaikaipswich.co.uk; Mon-Sat 9.30 pm, Sun 4 pm.

BOHEMIA, THE CLUB HOTEL & SPA   £93   **5 4 3**

GREEN ST, ST HELIER JE2 4UH   01534 876500

This "truly exceptional" and much-accoladed Jersey destination provides what is by all accounts "absolute dining pleasure". "I love the atmosphere here with the bar and the sublime restaurant, where Steve Smith's cooking is outstanding". / www.bohemiajersey.com; @Bohemia_Jersey; Sun & Mon 10.30 pm, Tue-Thu 11 pm, Fri & Sat midnight; no trainers. *Accommodation:* 46 rooms, from £185

LONGUEVILLE MANOR   £83   **5 4 4**

LONGUEVILLE RD, ST SAVIOUR JE2 7WF   01534 725501

A "slightly old-fashioned" atmosphere – e.g. croquet on the lawn – does nothing to detract from the evident charms of this Relais & Châteaux stately 14th century house; "the whole experience is just spot on", with the "awesome" food (including a "cheeseboard that's not to be missed") inspiring numerous awards of top marks for its cuisine. / www.longuevillemanor.com; @longuevillemanor; head from St. Helier on the A3 towards Gorey; less than 1 mile from St. Helier; 10 pm; no jeans. *Accommodation:* 31 rooms, from £170

MARK JORDAN AT THE BEACH   £55   **3 4 3**

LA PLAGE, LA ROUTE DE LA HAULE, ST PETER JE3 7YD   01534 780180

"Well-run warm and relaxed" beach-side bistro dining with "a lovely selection of seafood and fish dishes" – from Mark Jordan, who ran the kitchen brigade at the nearby Atlantic Hotel until 2017. / www.markjordanatthebeach.com; 9.30 pm; closed Mon.

THE OYSTER BOX   £58   **3 2 4**

ST BRELADE'S BAY JE3 8EF   01534 850 888

"Top quality all round" – "you can't beat sitting down for lunch with a sea view" at this chic-casual venue with a 60-seat heated terrace on the edge of St Brelade beach. / www.oysterbox.co.uk; @JPRests; Mon-Thu 9 pm, Fri & Sat 9.30 pm, Sun 2.30 pm; no Amex.

THE MILESTONE   £56   **3 2 3**

84 GREEN LANE AT BALL STREET S3 8SE   0114 272 8327

A "lovely, friendly dining pub in a gentrifying part of Sheffield's old industrial centre"; "they're unafraid of strong, punchy flavour combinations," and the locally sourced food can be "splendid" at times. (Owners The Milestone Group launched a vast 14,000 sq ft food hall inspired by SE Asia's hawker markets, in the Rutland Cutlery Works, in November 2018). / www.the-milestone.co.uk; @TheMilestone; Mon-Sat 11.30 pm, Sun 10.30 pm; no Amex.

BOSQUET   £52   **5 4 2**

97A WARWICK RD CV8 1HP   01926 852463

"Bernard's French-regional cooking and Jane's relaxed but efficient service is a winning combination" at the Lignier's remarkably consistent southwest-French stalwart. Even the most critical reporter this year who felt the experience "lacked the ambition of past visits" said "it was still an excellent meal and good value". / www.restaurantbosquet.co.uk; 9.15 pm; closed Mon, Sat L & Sun; closed 2 weeks in Aug.

THE CROSS AT KENILWORTH   £68   **5 4 3**

16 NEW ST CV8 2EZ   01926 853840

This "good-looking" spin-off from Andreas Antona's suave Simpsons in Birmingham features "faultless food" from talented chef Adam Bennett – and it's certainly "more restaurant than pub" these days. There is one consistent grumble however: there's "an intelligent and wide-ranging wine list, but one or two less expensive bottles wouldn't go amiss". / www.thecrosskenilworth.co.uk; @TheCrossKen; Tue-Sat 9.30 pm, Sun 3.30 pm.

KENTISBURY GRANGE HOTEL   £74   **4 4 4**

EX31 4NL   01271 882 295

Part of a high-end boutique bolthole, this walnut- and marble-bedecked 17th century coaching house is a "favourite" among reporters: "the food (under Michael Caines' patronage, and spanning tasting menus to afternoon teas) is superb, and the service exemplary". / www.kentisburygrange.com/; @KentisburyG; 10pm.

FELLPACK £44

19 LAKE ROAD CA12 5BS 01768 771177

"Hearty food with an emphasis on healthy choices" and "lovely service" both win praise for this June 2017 newcomer – an upbeat modern bistro in this north Lakes town. More feedback needed for a rating however. / www.fellpack.co.uk; Wed-Sat 11 pm, Sun 4 pm.

LINGHOLM KITCHEN £39 334

PORTINSCALE CA12 5TZ 01768 771206

"You can't beat the views and service at this friendly venue" – a charming Lake District estate greenhouse café (serving brunches, afternoon teas, cakes, coffees, etc.) overlooking a reconstruction of the original, hexagonal kitchen garden that inspired Mr McGregor's garden in The Tale of Peter Rabbit. / thelingholmkitchen. co.uk.

LYZZICK HALL COUNTRY HOUSE HOTEL £59 343

UNDERSKIDDAW CA12 4PY 017687 72277

This Victorian country house on the slopes of Skiddaw, owned and run by the Fernandez family for 30 years, makes a perfect base for exploring the Lake District: "the food is good and hearty" (including from "a monthly changing tasting menu"), "the staff are well-trained" and the "very affordable" wine list is "a real treat for Iberian fans". / www.lyzzickhall.co.uk; @LyzzixkHall; Mon-Wed 11 pm, Thu-Sat midnight; no Amex. *Accommodation:* 30 rooms, from £148

THE SWAN INN £48 443

MACCLESFIELD RD SK23 7QU 01663 732943

"About as far from the sea as you can get – but fish is a speciality and it's always a treat" at this 15th-century pub in a High Peak village. There's a traditional "cosy bar serving excellent beer" as well as a modern dining room where "ultra-fresh fish and shellfish are cooked in an open kitchen with a Josper oven". / Sun-Thu 9 pm, Fri & Sat 10 pm; no Amex.

THE PHEASANT AT KEYSTON £54 323

LOOP RD PE28 0RE 01832 710241

This charming and "very reliable" thatch-and-whitewash village pub has been serving good food since 1964, and is consistently rated one of the best dining pubs in the area. / www.thepheasant-keyston.co.uk; @pheasantkeyston; 1m S of A14 between Huntingdon & Kettering, J15; Mon-Sat 11 pm; no Amex.

MARKET BISTRO £56 443

11 SATURDAY MARKET PL PE30 5DQ 01553 771483

Lucy & Richard Golding run "a wonderful little restaurant" in the town centre – "fantastic service", "lovingly prepared, inventive dishes" (if "a mite complicated") "…what more could one ask for?" The owners opened posh pub/deli Goldings, nearby, in January 2018. / www.marketbistro.co.uk; @Market_Bistro; Tue-Thu 8.30 pm, Fri & Sat 9 pm.

DAYLESFORD CAFÉ £58 223

DAYLESFORD NEAR KINGHAM GL56 0YG 01608 731700

Adjoining possibly Britain's poshest farm shop owned by Lady Bamford, this stylish café is perhaps most popular for brunch or a "casual pizza", but does also open in the evening for supper nights. / www.daylesford.com; Mon-Sat 4.30 pm, Sun 3.30 pm.

THE KINGHAM PLOUGH £57 333

THE GREEN OX7 6YD 01608 658327

A comfortable, attractive old pub-with-rooms, where chef-owner Emily Watkins, ex-of The Fat Duck, "makes an effort to present an interesting menu" of modern British grub, and by all accounts succeeds – with feedback ranging from "dependable" to "fabulous". / www.thekinghamplough.co.uk; @kinghamplough; 9 pm, Sun 8 pm; closed Sun D; no Amex. *Accommodation:* 7 rooms, from £95

THE WILD RABBIT £73 425

CHURCH ST OX7 6YA 01608 658 389

This "Cotswolds gem" – part of Lady Bamford's Daylesford organic estate – is now under the direction of chef-patron Alyn Williams, from Mayfair's acclaimed Westbury Hotel, and head chef Nathan Eades. "Sophisticated" cuisine, "several cuts above the average country pub" is served in a "spacious and stylish dining room". "There seems to be a local myth that it's horrendously expensive. We've found that it's really good value, which is quite different… I find the car park a bit daunting, though – tucking the car away between Bentleys is nerve-racking". / www.thewildrabbit.co.uk; @wildrabbitpub; Sun-Thu 11 pm, Fri & Sat 11.30 pm.

ROZ ANA £42 432

4-8 KINGSTON HILL KT2 7NH 020 8546 6388

"You can't go wrong", say the numerous local fans of chef and co-owner Deepinder Sondhi's ten-year-old on a Kingston Hill shopping parade, where "authentic Indian flavours are blended with European style". / www.roz-ana.com; @therozana; Mon-Sun 9 pm; no Amex.

THE HALF MOON £55 333

GLASSHOUSE LANE RH14 0LT 01403 820223

A restaurant run by a model – not immediately a winning formula (even if, in Jodie Kidd's case, she excelled on Celeb MasterChef); cynicism aside, this "attractively revamped" 15th century village gastroboozer, re-opened in July 2017, gains nothing but good reports for its traditional grub and "very relaxed" vibe. / www.halfmoonkirdford.co.uk; @HalfMoonKird; Wed-Fri 11 pm, Sat 11.30 pm, Sun 8 pm.

HIPPING HALL £92 444

COWAN BRIDGE LA6 2JJ 01524 271187

Cooking that's "clever without being tricksy featuring good, sometimes surprising" combinations wins ongoing acclaim for this "smooth operation" – the Wildsmith Hotels chain's original property, which has a lovely location in the Lune valley. "The wine list (in common with its sibling Forest Side) is from Buon Vino in Settle, so features lots of biodynamic and some natural wines". / www.hippinghall.com; @hippinghall; Mon-Sat 10 pm; no Amex; no trainers; children: 12+. *Accommodation:* 10 rooms, from £239

THE BLACK SWAN £49 424

FELL ROAD CA17 4NS 015396 23204

"In a lovely peaceful location in the out-of-the-way village of Ravenstonedale", nestled below the Howgills, this Cumbrian spot is a sturdy stone-built old pub with a rambling interior. Chef Scott Fairweather gives every indication of "knowing what he's doing", producing tempting, hearty but imaginative fare that's "excellent, rich and satisfying" (albeit sometimes with "MasterChef tendencies"). Service can be "hit and miss". Top Menu Tip – imaginative lunch snacks, e.g. venison hot dog. / www.blackswanhotel.com; @BlackSwanEden; Food 8:45pm every day, Bar 11pm midweek, 1am Frida.

THE SELKIRK ARMS BAR, BISTRO AND RESTAURANT £54 323

HIGH STREET DG6 4JG 01557 330402

Some feel the bar (which has the same menu as the restaurant) has the best atmosphere at this townhouse hotel with garden, near the harbour. Even a reporter who didn't enjoy their trip said it's a "friendly" place and "obviously the place to go" locally. / www.selkirkarmshotel.co.uk; @selkirkarms; 9pm.

THE MASON'S ARMS £77 432

SOUTH MOLTON EX36 4RY 01398 341231

"Mark Dodson's previous experience at the Waterside Inn is evident in the refined cuisine offered at this delightful country inn", on the edge of Exmoor. The hand-painted Renaissance-style ceiling in the dining room is certainly not what you might expect to find in a 13th-century thatched cottage. / www.masonsarmsdevon.co.uk; @masonsknowstone; Tue-Sat 9 pm, Sun 2 pm; booking max 4 may apply; children: 5+ after 6pm.

BELLE ÉPOQUE £51

60 KING ST WA16 6DT 01565 633060

"The location is beautiful" – a gorgeous Art Nouveau building dating from 1907 – but this well-known landmark is too often said to be "overpriced and living on very faded past glories". Nowadays marketed as a 'Wedding Venue, Restaurant and Boutique B&B', its food events seem to offer very limited dining possibilities nowadays, so for the time being we've left it unrated. / www.thebelleepoque.com; @TheBelleEpoque; 1.5m from M6, J19; Mon-Sat 11.30 pm, Sun 10.30 pm; booking max 6 may apply. *Accommodation:* 7 rooms, from £110

KYLESKU HOTEL £52 435

IV27 4HW 01971 502231

In a "fantastic remote Highlands setting", this 17th-century inn beside a slipway onto Lock Glendhu serves "fabulous meals", with "seafood that is quite different". "Views over the bay are outstanding, even when the rain is falling". / www.kyleskuhotel.co.uk; on A894, S of Scourie, N of Lochinver; Sun-Thu 10.30 pm, Sat 11 pm. *Accommodation:* 8 rooms, from £55

FALCONDALE HOTEL £53 343

FALCONDALE DRIVE SA48 7RX 01570 422910

Five minutes out of town, down its own long drive, this attractive manor house hotel and wedding venue sits in its own 14 acre grounds. Good reports (if not hugely numerous) on its "romantic" dining room which provides "well executed dishes from local produce that's hard to better at the price" in these parts. / www.thefalcondale.co.uk; Mon-Thu midnight, Fri 1 am. *Accommodation:* 19 rooms, from £149

LANGAR HALL £62 335

CHURCH LN NG13 9HG 01949 860559

This grand Belvoir Valley family home-turned-country-house hotel "oozes charm", and its "reliable restaurant" produces some "beautifully executed meals". Charismatic founder Imogen Skirving (who died in a car crash in 2016) was one of a kind, and was always going to be an impossible act to follow, so inevitably the enterprise "has lost some edge", but by most accounts her granddaughter Lila has made a very good fist of taking over: "the food is still delicious and the overall atmosphere still wonderful in the post-Imogen era". / www.langarhall.com; @Langarhallhotel; off A52 between Nottingham & Grantham; Sun-Thu 8.30 pm, Fri & Sat 9 pm; no Amex; no trainers. *Accommodation:* 12 rooms, from £100

THE BELL INN £49 333

GL7 3LF 01367 860249

"A welcome addition to the Cotswolds scene" – this rescued "quaint" village gastroboozer provides "great pub food in a fantastic setting". Opened in late 2017 by chef Tom Noest and manager Peter Creed, it got off to a flying start when Giles Coren gushed hyperbolically in The Times that he eaten the "best mouthful of my life" here (roast dry-aged sirloin, since you ask). One or two reports do say it "justifies such hype" but those "left bitterly disappointed having read such a glittering review" say it's merely "good all-round". / thebelllangford.com; Mon-Sun 9.30 pm.

NORTHCOTE £92 554

NORTHCOTE RD BB6 8BE 01254 240555

"Lisa Goodwin Allen carries on the excellent tradition" at the North West's best-known country house hotel, which – since Nigel Haworth stepped back a little from the stoves – is "going from strength to strength", with cuisine that's "inventive but not outlandish" ("clever dishes that are incredible on the palate, deeply satisfying in both form and function"). There's a "hugely varied and interesting wine list too, introduced wonderfully knowledgeably, and giving opportunities for great wine recommendations and 'flights'". The location is an old manor house in the picturesque Ribble Valley, which has been much-extended over the years, whose "professional-without-being-overbearing" staff create "a friendly and welcoming experience" (although some longtime visitors feel it's a "pity they have extended the cosy buildings leaving them less characterful"). "A beautiful experience in a beautiful part of the country". / www.northcote.com; @NorthcoteUK; M6, J31 then A59; Mon-Thu 9.30 pm, Fri & Sat 10 pm, Sun 9 pm; no trainers. *Accommodation:* 18 rooms, from £280

BRITANNIA INN £45 333

LLANMADOC SA3 1DB 01792 386624

A characterful, stone-walled interior and big garden with views (plus kids' play area) set the scene at this attractive pub on the Gower Peninsula, which achieves all-round good scores for pub grub served in the bar and more ambitious cuisine in its restaurant. / www.britanniainngower.co.uk.

THE EARL OF MARCH £40 333

LAVANT RD P018 0BQ 01243 533993

"In a picturesque location" ("with a nice garden/terrace with fine views of the South Downs looking towards Goodwood"), this "elegant" 18th-century former coaching inn is owned and run by Giles Thompson, ex-executive chef at The Ritz, and wins good ratings for its high-quality food. Fun fact: the poet William Blake was apparently inspired by the view to write the alternative English national anthem, Jerusalem, during his stay here in 1803. / www.theearlofmarch.com; Mon-Thu midnight, Fri 1 am.

THE GREAT HOUSE HOTEL & RESTAURANT, LAVENHAM £58 544

MARKET PL CO10 9QZ 01787 247431

"An old time favourite that's recently changed hands with no obvious downside": this "very special" landmark – "magically situated" in an old inn dating from the 14th century on "a beautiful town square" – was sold by the Crépy family this year after their 32 years at the helm, but "the staff have all stayed on"

Northcote, Langho

and "everything has continued seamlessly". It delivers an "outstanding all-round" and "very French" experience, with "excellent classical French cooking plus a wine list to match" and "special mention going to the sublime cheese (selected from a large trolley with a superb variety of options)". / www.greathouse.co.uk; @GreatHouseHotel; follow directions to Guildhall; Mon-Sat 11 pm; no Amex. *Accommodation:* 5 rooms, from £95

LAVENHAM GREYHOUND £52 2|3|3

97 HIGH STREET CO10 9PZ 01787 249553

"A very good addition to the Stuart Inns portfolio" that's riding high after a "smart" 2017 expansion and refurb'. There's definitely the odd gripe (the menu seems "all jumbled together" and prices high) but most praise the "very different" menu ("much better than just pub food"). / www.lavenhamgreyhound.com; @LavenhamGH/; 10 pm.

NUMBER TEN £41 3|4|3

10 LADY ST CO10 9RA 01787 249438

A "great relaxing wine bar/restaurant" in a rustic-chic 15th century house; the pizza ("served on Sundays only") really hits the mark, but the seasonal food is "wonderful" on any given day. If you want to indulge, just follow the hand-carved spiral staircase to the upstairs 'Crown Post Suite', complete with patio. / www.ten-lavenham.co.uk; Mon-Sun 10 pm.

SWAN HOTEL £57 2|3|5

HIGH ST CO10 9QA 01787 247477

"Romantic beams and log fires in a quirky building" provide a "fine, period setting" at this 15th-century hotel. A full meal in the restaurant gets second billing to the "fabulous afternoon tea", which "includes a Gentlemen's option for anyone not wanting a sweet meal". / www.theswanatlavenham.co.uk; @SwanLavenham; Mon-Sun 10 pm; no jeans; children: 12+ at D. *Accommodation:* 45 rooms, from £195

LEAMINGTON SPA, WARWICKSHIRE 5–4C

LA COPPOLA £49 3|4|3

86 REGENT ST CV32 4NS 01926 888 873

A "fantastic", dramatically decorated Italian, with two local siblings, that continues to win raves for its "excellent" food (including "fish done the Italian way"); sadly, the trio went into administration in 2017 – subsequently extended to spring 2019 – so the future looks uncertain. / www.lacoppola.co.uk; Sun-Thu 10 pm, Fri & Sat 10.30 pm; no Amex.

OSCARS FRENCH BISTRO £57 3|3|3

39 CHANDOS STREET CV32 4RL 01926 452807

"A real gem" – "it really feels like you've walked into a restaurant in rural France" when you step inside this popular and "consistently excellent" local ("a superb replica of a warm and cosy bistro of twenty years

ago") – a "cramped and busy" operation with "fantastic food and knowledgeable staff". / www.oscarsfrenchbistro.co.uk; @oscars_bistro; 9.30 pm; closed Mon & Sun.

TAME HARE £71 3|4|4

97 WARWICK STREET CV32 4RJ 01926 316191

An ambitious three-year-old "slightly off the main drag in town, but worth seeking out" for the "best (British with a twist) cooking in Leamington"; in autumn 2018 they launched a new tapas-style menu, and prices are apparently "a total steal for food this good". / www.thetamehare.co.uk/; @thetamehare; Wed & Thu 9 pm, Fri & Sat 9.30 pm, Sun 3 pm.

LECHLADE, GLOUCESTERSHIRE 2–2C

THE FIVE ALLS £51 4|4|4

FILKINS GL7 3JQ 01367 860875

A "terrific modern boho inn" – this 18th-century village pub excels for its "perfect, good-value food, great ambience, good wines and the really lovely people running the place". STOP PRESS: Change may be afoot: it was acquired in summer 2018 by a Cardiff-based business called the Barkby Group, with Sebastian Snow – who created the small 'Turf to Table' chain of which it was part – departing in October 2018. / www.thefiveallsfilkins.co.uk; @fivealllsfilkins; 9.30 pm, Fri & Sat 10 pm; closed Sun D; no Amex.

LEEDS, WEST YORKSHIRE 5–1C

AAGRAH £37 3|4|3

ABERFORD RD LS25 2HF 0113 2455 667

The high-riding northern Kashmiri chain remains a remarkably solid and "good value" performer, combining an "amazing choice of fish and shellfish" and a "super atmosphere". If you're not a fan of Tiger, they've just launched their first craft beer in tandem with Yorkshire's Kirkstall Brewery. / www.aagrah.com; @Aagrahgroup; from A1 take A642 Aberford Rd to Garforth; Mon-Thu 10.30 pm, Fri & Sat 11 pm, Sun 9 pm.

ART'S £40 3|4|3

42 CALL LANE LS1 6DT 0113 243 8243

Proudly billing itself as Leeds's original café/bar (it dates from the 1990s), this "relaxed" and "friendly" hangout, close to the Corn Exchange, "hits all the right spots"; the Med- and Asian-accented small or large plates are "as good as ever" and "service has improved" of late. / www.artscafebar.com; @artscafeleeds; Mon-Fri 11 pm, Sat midnight, Sun 9 pm.

BUNDOBUST £30 4|3|3

6 MILL HILL LS1 5DQ 0113 243 1248

"Delicious vegetarian Indian street food" combines with "tasty craft beers" at this "chilled-out place" with a "great vibe" – a collaboration between local restaurant Prashad and Bradford craft beer specialist The Sparrow. Dishes are "very basic, but isn't that part of the point with street food?", and "it's fun, unusual

and delicious" – "even card-carrying carnivores forget it's veggie!" / www.bundobust.com; @Bundobust; Mon-Thu 9.30 pm, Fri & Sat 10 pm, Sun 8 pm; booking weekdays only.

CRAFTHOUSE, TRINITY LEEDS £63 2|2|4

LEVEL 5 LS1 6HW 0113 897 0444

D&D London's smart venue on top of Trinity Leeds shopping centre wins praise for its "great views over the city", but finds reporters sharply divided over the quality of its cuisine. To some, it's a "top-class restaurant where just about everything is right, and the food full of flavour". Others see "good ingredients" let down by "unimaginative", "uninspired" or "pretentious preparation". / www.crafthouse-restaurant.com; @CrafthouseLeeds; Tue-Sat midnight, Mon 11 pm, Sun 7 pm; booking max 8 may apply.

FAZENDA, WATERMAN'S PLACE £48 3|4|2

3 WHARF APPROACH, GRANARY WHF LS1 4GL 0113 400 1183

"Meat, meat and more meat" is the "best thing" at this central branch of a chain featuring Brazilian 'rodizio' (a buffet, where you eat as much as you like for a fixed price). "If your definition of a good deal is more grilled meat than you can comfortably stomach, this is the place for you!". "Nice views over the wharf" too "(it doesn't feel like it's just past the train station!)". / www.fazenda.co.uk/leeds/; @FazendaGroup; Mon-Sat 10 pm, Sun 9 pm.

FUJI HIRO £28 4|3|2

45 WADE LN LS2 8NJ 0113 243 9184

For "noodles at their best", this no-frills ramen, gyoza and curry Japanese in the Merrion Centre is a prized feature of the city-centre. "Big servings of tasty food make it an excellent pit-stop". / merrioncentre.co.uk/units/fuji-hiro; Sun-Thu 9 pm, Fri & Sat 9.30 pm; may need 5+ to book.

HANSA'S £34 5|3|2

72-74 NORTH ST LS2 7PN 0113 244 4408

A veggie stalwart of more than 30 years' standing, Hansa Dabhi's smart Gujarati operation in the city-centre "never lets you down". "I'm not vegetarian, but the food is SO good". / www.hansasrestaurant.com; @HansasLeeds; Mon-Fri 10 pm, Sat 11 pm, Sun 2 pm.

HOME £96 4|4|5

16/17 KIRKGATE LS1 6BY 0113 430 0161

"A brilliant new addition to Leed's food scene" – Mark Owens and Elizabeth Cottam's stylishly retro newcomer on Leeds oldest street wins nothing but positive feedback. From a seasonal, British, ten-course tasting menu (you can opt for the standard, vegetarian, or pescatarian version), "the food is imaginatively produced very well cooked and sensibly priced" (with a few reporters mentioning the 'M'-word) but top billing goes to the "wonderful, well-spaced dining room which is classy and stylish" and

The Man Behind The Curtain, Leeds

has a superb atmosphere. / www.homeleeds.co.uk;
Wed-Sat 8 pm, Sun 3 pm.

IBERICA £27 344

**HEPPER HOUSE, 17A EAST PARADE LS1
2BH 01134 037 007**

Limited but upbeat feedback on the London-
born and mostly -based tapas chain's seventh
outpost. Its main draw: the ultra-glam converted
auction house setting, replete with lightwell,
cocktail bar and wine bar/deli. / www.ibericares
taurants.com/restaurants/iberica-leeds/; Mon-Sat 11
pm, Sun 10 pm.

ISSHO £62 344

**VICTORIA GATE, GEORGE ST LS2 7AU
0113 426 5000**

"I must confess I thought it was going to be a
classic style-over-substance place – actually it has
style AND substance!" – D&D London's sexy
looking yearling on the rooftop of the Trinity
shopping centre with terrace and sleek Kori
Bar for cocktails wins nothing but praise for its
"great Japanese small-plate dining possibilities"
which encompass tempura, sushi, robatayaki,
and so on. / www.issho-restaurant.com; Mon-Sat
11.30 pm, Sun 6 pm.

KENDELLS
BISTRO £52 444

**ST PETERS SQUARE LS9 8AH 0113
2436553**

"Well known on the Leeds dining circuit" – this
"brilliant bustling and always busy" favourite
is "top notch for romance" and serves "well-
prepared, classic dishes all sensibly priced (as
is the wine list)". / www.kendellsbistro.co.uk;
@KendellsBistro; Wed-Sat 9 pm, Sun 3.30 pm; no
Amex.

THE MAN BEHIND THE
CURTAIN £129 332

**TOP FLOOR FLANNELS, 68-78 VICAR LN
LS1 7JH 0113 2432376**

"Takes all your prejudices and chucks 'em out
of the window" – Michael O'Hare's wild and
wacky city-centre four-year-old continues to
astound and delight its large fan base with multi-
course extravaganzas that are a total wow: "pure
theatre", with "sensational" dishes ("beautifully
artistic presentations, without losing any balance
of texture or flavour") delivered by "great
northern servers who cut through the potential
pretension". There's no hiding, however, that
it has put in a more mixed performance since
it moved in October 2017 from the quirky
rooftop space over the Flannels department
store to the newly-converted basement below

it, with a vocal minority of refuseniks now
dragging ratings down: "not as good as it used
to be…", "more style over substance now…",
"chef seems to be playing the 'superstar',
but the food can be disappointing". /
www.themanbehindthecurtain.co.uk; @hairmetalchef;
Tue-Sat 8.30 pm.

MUSTARD POT £40 332

20 STAINBECK LN LS7 3QY 0113 269 5699

A Georgian-style Chapel Allerton gastroboozer
with a garden; the pubby fare is "delicious",
with "especially good homemade pies" regularly
drawing special praise. / themustardpot.com/;
@Mustardpot; Sun-Wed 11 pm, Fri & Sat 1 am, Thu
midnight.

OX CLUB £57 433

19A THE HEADROW LS1 6PU 07470 359961

"Nestled within the popular Headrow House
bar complex", the Belgrave Music Hall team's
"warm" restaurant ("not just thanks to the
smoky wafts from the Grillworks charcoal grill!")
should not be "underestimated"; from the
"unusual" seasonal food to the "spot-on" service,
"everything about the place is great" (though it
did leave the odd cynic cold). / www.oxclub.co.uk;
Tue-Sat 10 pm, Sun 3 pm.

PATTY SMITHS, BELGRAVE
MUSIC HALL £26 423

**1 CROSS BELGRAVE ST LS2 8JP
0113 234 6160**

"Small, almost pop-up feeding station in the
Belgrave Music Hall", which shares the ground
floor with a pizza pitstop; on the menu, the "best
burgers anywhere" and other "food to die for"
("the Session Fries are a meal in themselves). /
www.belgravemusichall.com; @pattysmithsUK; Mon-
Fri 10.30 pm, Sat 11 pm.

PRASHAD £46 432

**137 WHITEHALL RD BD11 1AT
0113 285 2037**

"Still ahead of the game" – this stalwart
Gujarati achieves very consistent acclaim for
its "wonderful, innovative Indian vegetarian
food" (that's "not just for veggies"). /
www.prashad.co.uk; @prashad_veggie/; 10pm, 9pm
(Bank Holidays/Sundays); closed Mon, Tue L, Wed L
& Thu L; no Amex.

RED CHILLI £42 433

**6 GREAT GEORGE STREET LS1 3DW
01132 429688**

"Consistently good food" arrives "in enormous
portions" at this four-strong northern chain's
city-centre basement venue, kitted out with
1920s Shanghai décor and specialising
in palette-tingling Sichuanese cuisine. /
redchillirestaurant.co.uk/leeds/; Tue-Sun, Mon 9.30
pm.

THE RELIANCE £40 344

76-78 NORTH ST LS2 7PN 0113 295 6060

This sprawling bar and dining venue – a
favourite of critic Marina O'Loughlin,
apparently – serves "exceptional food" from a
"varied specials menu", including "home-cured
bacon and black pudding" from the on-site
charcuterie curing room. It also has its own
small cinema, where you might eat ramen while
watching 'Tampopo'! / www.the-reliance.co.uk;
@The_Reliance; Mon-Sat 9.30 pm, Sun 2.30 pm; no
bookings.

SALVO'S £44 443

**115 & 107 OTLEY ROAD LS6 3PX
0113 275 2752**

The Dammone family's Headingley stalwart,
founded by Salvatore in 1976, is by many
accounts "still the best Italian in Leeds".
Known for its "delicious" pasta and pizza, it has
developed under sons Gip & John to incorporate
a café/salumeria and offer ambitious 'alter ego'
tasting menus. "They never rest on their laurels,
the tastes and flavours are always developing". /
www.salvos.co.uk; @salvosleeds; Mon-Sun 9 pm.

SOUS LE NEZ EN
VILLE £51 332

**QUEBEC HS, QUEBEC ST LS1 2HA
0113 244 0108**

A "Leeds institution" of three decades'
standing – this city-centre cellar is the perfect
place to celebrate a business milestone over a
beef-heavy French menu and a bottle or two
from the 40-page wine list ("it has to be one of
the best lists ever"), navigated with the help of
"very approachable and knowledgeable staff". /
www.souslenez.com; @SousLeNezLeeds; 9.45 pm, Sat
10.30 pm; closed Sun.

SUKHOTHAI £37 443

8 REGENT ST LS7 4PE 0113 237 0141

Since its launch in 2002, Ban Kaewkraikhot's
lavishly decorated Thai venture in Chapel
Allerton has become one of the best known
destinations in the city, and spawned a number
of offshoots. Ratings remain high here for
its high quality all-round performance. /
www.sukhothai.co.uk; @Sukhothai_; 10.45pm; Mon-
Thu D only, Fri-Sun open L & D; no Amex.

TATTU £35 334

29 EAST PARADE, MINERVA HOUSE LS1 5PS 0113 245 1080

"I thought it would be all about the bling. It's actually rather good… with the bling!" That's the majority view on this sleek Asian haunt. "It can be a bit noisy when full" but it doesn't detract from the enjoyable "Chinese-influenced small plates and fusion cooking", and even a reporter who said "it's too expensive for what it is" rated the food as good. / www.tattu.co.uk; @tatturestaurant; Sun-Thu 1 am, Fri & Sat 2 am.

THARAVADU £41 542

7- 8 MILL HILL LS1 5DQ 0113 244 0500

"If you judged it just from the outside, you might not go in" but you'd miss out on this very popular South Indian near the railway station. "Exceptional", "fresh and different" Keralan dishes ("the fish curries are outstanding") are served in a "very friendly" manner. "It's incredibly busy so book". / www.tharavadurestaurants.com; @TharavaduRestau; Mon-Thu 10 pm, Fri & Sat 10.30 pm.

ZAAP £29 334

16 GRAND ARCADE LS1 6PG 0113 243 2586

"Great value authentic Thai street food is served in tin trays whilst you dine in a tuk tuk" – the "crazy" (by design) formula at this bright, "buzzing" and, nevertheless, "characterful" outlet in the city-centre's Grand Arcade. / www.zaapthai.co.uk/zaap-leeds; @ZaapThai; Sun-Thu 11 pm, Fri & Sat midnight; no bookings.

ZUCCO £45 433

603 MEANWOOD ROAD LS6 4AY 01132 249679

A "fantastic Italian restaurant serving small plates of gorgeous regional food and a really interesting wine list"; "you get the feeling the (Venetian) owners really care" and "that's why it is always full even though it's a trip out of town". / www.zucco.co.uk; @Zuccouk; Tue-Thu 10 pm, Fri & Sat 10.30 pm, Sun 8.30 pm.

LEICESTER, LEICESTERSHIRE 5–4D

BOBBY'S £25 322

154-156 BELGRAVE RD LE4 5AT 0116 266 0106

Since 1976 this Indian sweet shop and canteen has been one of the best-liked landmarks of the Golden Mile, known for its filling and cheap, veggie Gujarati and Indo-Chinese fare. With its smart and modern refurb however (and the introduction of a 'healthy dishes' section to its menu), fans now say it's an all-round winner. / www.eatatbobbys.com; @bobbysleicester; Mon, Wed-Sun 10 pm; no Amex.

KAYAL £38 433

153 GRANBY ST LE1 6FE 0116 255 4667

"Fabulous South Indian food" including "dosas to die for" has long since earned respect for this family-run outfit – an early ambassador of Keralan cuisine in England – as possibly the best Indian restaurant in Leicester. / www.kayalrestaurant.com/; @kayalrestaurant; Mon-Sat 11 pm.

LEINTWARDINE, SHROPSHIRE 5–4A

JOLLY FROG £51 444

THE TODDINGS SY7 0LX 01547 540298

"The 'new' Jolly Frog has an even more 'bistro'-ish atmosphere" – "newly refurbished" after a change in ownership in spring 2018, this long standing Gallic fixture in the middle of nowhere in particular but not too far from Ludlow "has maintained its quality with very good fish dishes" and other fare. / www.jollyfrogpub.co.uk; Wed-Sat 9.30 pm, Sun 2.30 pm; may need 6+ to book.

LEWANNICK, CORNWALL 1–3C

COOMBESHEAD FARM £87 544

COOMBESHEAD FARM PL15 7QQ 01566 782 009

"Tucked away in the Cornish countryside" – an "all-round fabulous experience" awaits diners at the "stunning", "tremendously friendly" country brainchild of NYC's Spotted Pig's April Bloomfield and Pitt Cue Co.'s Tom Adams – "as long as you like communal dining" (often with "industry professionals finding out how it's done"). Seasonal 5-course set menus "come mostly from the working dairy farm" (e.g. "home cured charcuterie from their own rare breed pigs") supplemented by "fine produce from local suppliers". "Such care is taken in the food preparation and you can stand in the kitchen watching the cooking take place… but it's worth going just for the bread". / www.coombesheadfarm.co.uk.

LEYBURN, NORTH YORKSHIRE 8–4B

THE BLUE LION £50 323

EAST WHITTON DL8 4SN 01969 624273

This "lovely" old coaching inn – stone floors, wood fires, celeb guests ranging from Daniel Craig to Prince Charles – rates well for its cooking. There are some "interesting choices on its traditional pub menu" and "it's a stand out-place for game (perfect grouse, for which I happily drive 45 miles)". / www.thebluelion.co.uk; @bluelioninn.

LICHFIELD, STAFFORDSHIRE 5–4C

THE BOAT INN £57

WALSALL ROAD WS14 0BU 01543361692

The greige exterior hints at the contemporary and high culinary ambitions of this modishly converted pub. Too little feedback for a rating as yet, but chef Liam Dillon was the winner of this year's Best Chef Award at the Midlands Food, Drink & Hospitality Awards. There are four-course and seven-course tasting menu options as well as the à la carte. / www.theboatinnlichfield.com; Tue-Sat 9.30 pm.

MCKENZIE'S £46 344

THE CORN EXCHANGE, CONDUIT STREET WS13 6JU 01543 417371

"The great atmosphere of this historic building" – the town's former corn exchange – provides a dramatic location for this large modern brasserie. In the evening, meat and steak-lovers are particularly well catered for, but there's a wide variety of choice here from breakfast on (including sandwich options during the day). / mckenziesrestaurant.com; @Mck_Lichfield; Tue-Thu 10 pm, Fri & Sat 11 pm, Sun 9 pm.

LICKFOLD, WEST SUSSEX 3–4A

LICKFOLD INN £69 444

HIGHSTEAD LN GU28 9EY 01798 861285

"Even the bar snacks are exceptional" at star London chef (of restaurant Story) Tom Sellers's smart country pub, which has a "very welcoming bar and delightful, elegant dining room" as well as, by all accounts, "superb, top-quality food". A few miles north of Petworth, it's "a bit off the beaten track but well worth the effort to visit". / www.thelickfoldinn.co.uk; @LickfoldInn; 3m N of A272 between Midhurst & Petworth; Mon-Sat 10.30 pm; no Amex.

LIFTON, DEVON 1–3C

THE ARUNDELL ARMS HOTEL £64 423

PL16 0AA 01566 784666

A "serene and timeless oasis" – this "old fashioned" country inn near Dartmoor has been a centre for fly fishing since the 1930s, with 20 miles of private riverbank on the Tamar and its tributaries at the disposal of overnight guests. There's "excellent cooking", too – with "locally sourced ingredients" that "never disappoint". / www.arundellarms.com; 0.5m off A30, Lifton Down exit; Mon-Sat 1.30 am, Sun 11.30 pm; no Amex; no jeans. *Accommodation:* 21 rooms, from £179

LINCOLN, LINCOLNSHIRE 6–3A

BRONZE PIG £61 433

4 BURTON ROAD LN1 3LB 01522 524817

A vividly decorated, upscale restaurant-with-rooms, near the castle, whose winning formula includes MasterChef grad Eamon Hunt at the pass, and Sicilian owner Pompeo Siracusa as FOH. Five years in, quibbles over service and prices have stilled, with praise of late for the "good cooking" of "fresh local ingredients". / www.thebronzepig.co.uk; @thebronzepig; Wed-Sat 10 pm, Sun 2.30 pm.

JEW'S HOUSE RESTAURANT £65 434

15 THE STRAIT LN2 1JD 01522 524851

"Very historic surroundings" – it's set in a 12th century stone house that's one of Lincoln's oldest buildings – certainly ramp up the drama of a visit to this well-reputed establishment, though the food is also reliably "imaginative" too, with a "great lunch option" to boot. / www.jewshouserestaurant.co.uk; @JewsHouselincs; Wed-Sat, Tue 9 pm; no Amex.

THE OLD BAKERY £58 334

26-28 BURTON ROAD LN1 3LB
01522 576057

"The food is always cooked to perfection" at this cute city-centre restaurant-with-rooms. Chef-owner Ivano de Serio's "menu changes frequently and it's always interesting, with a nice little twist or different interpretation of the dish". / www.theold-bakery.co.uk; @theoldbakeryrestaurant; Tue-Sat 8.30 pm, Sun 1.30 pm; no jeans. *Accommodation:* 4 rooms, from £65

LINLITHGOW, WEST LOTHIAN 9–4C

CHAMPANY INN £81 334

EH49 7LU 01506 834532

Reporters just "love it here", whether visiting the famed steak house ("utter perfection") or "informal" chop house ("the only thing on this planet that I will actually queue for"). Downside? "Prices seem to be related to their (celeb-magnet) reputation" rather than the "essentially simple cooking" – "however, if you stay, the value of the accommodation makes up for it". / www.champany.com; 2m NE of Linlithgow on junction of A904 & A803; Mon-Sat 10 pm; no jeans; children: 8+. *Accommodation:* 16 rooms, from £125

LITTLE ECCLESTON, LANCASHIRE 5–1A

THE CARTFORD INN £63 423

CARTFORD LANE PR3 0YP 01995 670 166

"The view over the curve of the River Wyre really makes it in terms of setting" at Patrick & Julie Beaume's "quirky riverside inn" ("if you get a table with a river view, you often get to see the river change direction as the tide comes in several miles down-river. If you're very, very lucky, you may even see the Wyre bore"). "The menu is an enticing combination, including pub classics, sharing boards, and mouthwatering à la carte dishes and daily specials focusing on locally-sourced ingredients with a French twist" ("breadcrumbed snails with nduja mayonnaise makes a great nibble, French Onion Soup is a paragon of its type, excellent moules frites comes in a surfeit of delicious cream sauce"). "The young team are genuinely friendly" but service can be "indifferent". Top Menu Tip: "The oxtail suet pudding is a fixture on the menu, and deservedly so". / www.thecartfordinn.co.uk; @Cartfordinn; Sun-Fri & Sat 10 pm.

LITTLEFIELD GREEN, BERKSHIRE 3–3A

THE ROYAL OAK £67 434

PALEY STREET SL6 3JN 01628 620541

"Delicious cooking in a lovely atmosphere" ensure that veteran broadcaster Parky and his son Nick Parkinson's gastropub is rated "one of the best in the county". It also manages to impress as a "great local". / www.theroyaloakpaleystreet.com; @royaloakpaleystreet; Tue-Sun 9 pm; booking max 4 may apply; children: 3+.

LITTLEHAMPTON, WEST SUSSEX 3–4A

EAST BEACH CAFE £45 324

SEA ROAD BN17 5GB 01903 731 903

"Simple but delicious food right on the beach" – the formula at this "family-friendly" spot, designed to resemble driftwood by Thomas Heatherwick; the "fish 'n' chips are excellent, and even better eaten outside on a sunny day". / www.eastbeachcafe.co.uk; @EastBeachCafe; Wed-Sat 9.30 pm, Sun 3.30 pm.

LIVERPOOL, MERSEYSIDE 5–2A

THE ART SCHOOL £94 444

SUGNALL ST L7 7DX 0151 230 8600

Paul Askew's "seriously good" open-kitchen four-year-old with large skylight ("attractive if slightly Spartan"), near the Liverpool Philharmonic – is the most commented-on European restaurant in town, and many diners consider it "the star of the Liverpool food scene" thanks to his "excellent" tasting menus (there's quite an array, and also a cheaper lunch and earlybird prix fixe alternative); and with the sourcing of high-quality local ingredients often commended. For a minority, though, the scoff seems more middling, and service – while "top quality" to most reporters – at times comes over as "a bit stuffy" or "inflexible". / www.theartschoolrestaurant.co.uk; @ArtSchoolLpool; Tue-Thu midnight, Fri & Sat 2 am.

BELZAN £35

371 SMITHDOWN ROAD L15 3JJ
0151 733 8595

No survey feedback yet, but some in the press (notably The Guardian's Grace Dent) have waxed lyrical regarding this December 2017 opening – the result of a successful Kickstarter campaign – serving fairly funky fare in a busy modern bistro environment. / belzan.co.uk; @belzan_lpl; Mon-Sat midnight, Sun 11 pm.

ETSU £42 343

25 THE STRAND, OFF BRUNSWICK STREET L2 0XJ 0151 236 7530

"A warm little gem hidden in an unlikely corner of central Liverpool", a short hop from The Strand, and offering "always good" Japanese cuisine and "lovely service without trying to be too chic". In September 2018 they announced plans to take over the neighbouring property, gaining a new deli section. / www.etsu-restaurant.co.uk; @EtsuRestaurant; off Brunswick street; Fri-Sun-Wed & Thu 10.30 pm.

FAZENDA £48 342

UNIT B, HORTON HS L2 3YL 01516591183

"The meat's good quality, and there's no limits to what you can select" at this branch of a Brazilian buffet chain, where you eat as much as you like for a fixed price; by its nature, it's "good for groups". / www.fazenda.co.uk/liverpool; @FazendaGroup; Mon-Sun 10.30 pm; no shorts.

FONSECA'S £38 332

12 STANLEY ST L1 6AF 0151 255 0808

The original Delifonseca (re-named to avoid confusion with its spin-off), now with vintage cocktail bar, wins praise for its "really good food and interesting choices" from a daily-changing blackboard menu. Change may be afoot, however, with the owner eyeing a vast, Kickstarter-funded expansion of its dockside spin-off (home to a famed market hall), with plans to eventually operate from one base. / www.delifonseca.co.uk; @Delifonseca; 9 pm, Fri & Sat 10 pm; closed Mon & Sun.

HANOVER STREET SOCIAL £47 344

16-20 HANOVER ST L1 4AA 0151 709 8764

"An excellent set menu along with a central location pulls in the punters" and ensures this modern brasserie and bar near the docks is "always busy". / www.hanoverstreetsocial.co.uk; @hanoversocial; Mon-Sat , Sun 10.30 pm.

HOST £35 342

31 HOPE ST L1 9XH 0151 708 5831

"Whether for a quick pre-show bite or a meal with friends", 60 Hope Street's bright and "buzzy" sibling near the Phil – with "bright-eyed and bushy-tailed staff" to match – is a "highly enjoyable" choice. The style of cooking here is Pan-Asian, "fusion-style tapas": "fresh-tasting", "eclectic" and "delicious". / www.ho-st.co.uk; @HOST_Liverpool; Wed-Sat 10.30 pm, Sun 9.30 pm.

THE ITALIAN CLUB FISH £45 433

128 BOLD ST L1 4JA 0151 707 2110

The Italian Club's bright baby sister "transforms from standard café-style during the day" (plus deli) to a "busy, authentic" restaurant by night, serving "classic" fish, great pizza and other staples. / www.theitalianclubfish.co.uk; @italianclubnews; Mon-Sat 11 pm, Sun 10.30 pm; no Amex.

THE LONDON CARRIAGE WORKS, HOPE STREET HOTEL £64 222

40 HOPE STREET L1 9DA 0151 705 2222

For a "really good breakfast" or "fab afternoon tea", this boutique hotel dining room does still win recommendations. Feedback is much more limited nowadays, though, compared with the heady days of its opening in 2003, when it was the hottest ticket in town. / www.thelondoncarriageworks.co.uk; @LdnCarriageWrks; Sun-Thu 8.30 pm, Fri & Sat 9 pm; no shorts; booking max 8 may apply. *Accommodation:* 89 rooms, from £150

LUNYA £47 433

18-20 COLLEGE LN L1 3DS 0151 706 9770

"Tapas with style… and it never disappoints" – that's the appeal of Peter and Elaine Kinsella's re-located operation: "a brilliant and buzzing bar/restaurant" (plus in-house deli) that "continues the high quality of the original" having moved a short distance from the first site, in Liverpool One. In summer 2018, the couple opened a spin-off, Lunyalita – one of a number of new openings in Albert Dock, with the arched ceilings and brickwork typical of the location. / www.lunya.co.uk; @Lunya; Mon & Tue 9 pm, Wed & Thu 9.30 pm, Fri & Sat 10 pm, Sun 8.30 pm.

MARAY £46 444
91 BOLD STREET L1 4HF 0151 709 5820

This "excellent, innovative independent on trendy Bold Street" is inspired by the North African/Middle Eastern cuisine found in the Marais district of Paris and "trying hard to be trendy like Ottolenghi". The place is "very buzzy", with "fantastic small plates", "great wine and cocktails" – and it's "brilliant value". "Good idea to book as it gets very busy". / www.maray.co.uk; @marayliverpool; Sun-Thu 10 pm, Fri & Sat 11 pm.

MOWGLI £40 344
69 BOLD ST L1 4EZ 0151 708 9356

"I have not met anyone who has been who hasn't raved!" – ex-barrister, Nisha Katona's "trendily located" street food venture is "a really good new wave Indian" and has "succeeded in spades" in 'The Pool', providing "fresh", "punchy" dishes that are "incredibly varied in flavour, and variety" in an environment that's "always full and buzzing", alongside some "very interesting cocktails". "No booking, so in the evenings you need to put your name on the list and go for a drink until your table is ready". Top Tip: "take pot luck and order the tiffin box where the chef chooses what you get". (This was her initial branch – she's expanded her "Dishoom of the North West" to other sites and cities now). / www.mowglistreetfood.com; @Mowglistfood; Sun-Wed 9.30 pm, Thu-Sat 10.30 pm.

OKTOPUS £30 323
HARDMAN YARD, 24 HARDMAN ST L1 9AX 07565 299879

"A fantastic new restaurant of delightful small plates", say fans of this yearling, whose "interesting and tasty dishes" make it one of the stars of Liverpool's gastro boom. Foes beg to differ, complaining that it's "difficult to put together a balanced meal" from plates which are in fact "medium-sized" – or, more bluntly: "starters after starters. Uninspiring!". / www.oktopus-restaurant.com; @Hello_Oktopus; Mon-Sat 9.45 pm.

PANORAMIC 34, WEST TOWER £69 345
BROOK STREET L3 9PJ 0151 236 5534

"On the 34th floor of West Tower, right in the heart of Liverpool – the 360 degree vista over the city's waterfront here is simply quite stunning!" It's "a treat on many levels", though, generally confounding those cynical about rooms with a view, with its "amazing food"

and "sharp and efficient service". Top tip: try it for afternoon tea. / www.panoramic34.com/; @Panoramic34; Tue-Sat 11 pm, Sun 10 pm; no Amex; no trainers.

PEN FACTORY £38 333
13 HOPE ST L1 9BQ 0151 709 7887

"A magic place that just gets better" – Paddy Byrne and chef Tom Gill's two-year-old factory conversion is a reincarnation of their landmark former venture, the Everyman Bistro next door – so is almost as handy for the theatre. There's "cheap and tasty" Med-based food, "charming staff", and "a lovely garden too". / www.pen-factory.co.uk/; @ThePenFactory; Sun-Thu midnight, Fri & Sat 1 am.

ROSKI £66 223
16 RODNEY STREET L1 2TE 0151 708 8698

Somewhat mixed feedback on this "ambitious" city-centre newcomer, opened in late 2017 by BBC MasterChef: The Professionals winner Anton Piotrowski (on the site that was Puschka, RIP). Fans hail its "delightful and intimate" style and "outstanding" cuisine from the five-course and seven-course tasting menus. Some early visitors, though, have also left "disappointed" (an echo of Marina O'Loughlin in The Sunday Times, who reported "hit after hit" but a culinary style she found "tortured"). / www.roskirestaurant.com; @roskirestaurant; Tue-Sat 9.30 pm.

SALT HOUSE £46 323
1 HANOVER STREET L1 3DW 0151 706 0092

A "relaxed" urban-chic charcuterie and tapas bar, extending across two floors, and turning out "interesting plates full of flavour" (plus "reasonable" wines); those who regularly visit "have never been disappointed with any of the dishes served". / www.salthousetapas.co.uk; @salthousetapas; 10.30 pm.

SALT HOUSE BACARO £40 333
47 CASTLE ST L2 9UB 01516650047

The business district "sister to Salt House Tapas" is "always a local favourite", with an Italian "small plates menu that means you can take your time and graze over a leisurely glass of wine". Owners Red and Blue Restaurants launched a fourth city-centre joint, 'Rocket and Ruby', on Castle St in late 2018, with a Bacaro expansion also in the pipeline. / www.salthousebacaro.co.uk/; @salthousebacaro; 10.30 pm.

SAN CARLO £59 334
41 CASTLE ST L2 9SH 0151 236 0073

A business district branch of the ever-growing ultra-glam Italian chain; though the sceney vibe and high prices can attract criticism, it impressed reporters this year, with "top seafood" a highlight. / www.sancarlo.co.uk; @SanCarlo_Group; 11 pm.

60 HOPE STREET £60 343
60 HOPE ST L1 9BZ 0151 707 6060

"Still one of my favourite places to eat in Liverpool"; "it never fails to deliver", say fans, who reckon this Georgian townhouse, near the Anglican cathedral (opened by Gary and Colin Manning in 1999), compares favourably with many of the city's newer venues: the menu is "interesting" and "standards all-round are high and delivered at an excellent price". / www.60hopestreet.com; @60HopeSt; Mon-Sat 10.30 pm, Sun 6 pm.

SPIRE £50 442
1 CHURCH ROAD L15 9EA 0151 734 5040

"A neighbourhood gem" with a modern British menu, around the corner from Penny Lane, where Matt & Adam Locke have provided "delicious cooking that's beautifully presented and fantastic value" for more than a decade. / www.spirerestaurant.co.uk; @spirerestaurant; Mon - Thu 9 pm, Fri & Sat 9.30 pm, Sun closed.

WRECKFISH £46 444
60 SEEL STREET L1 4BE 01244 400400

"The Latest (and flagship) branch of Gary Usher's small but perfectly formed bistro chain" – this November 2017 newcomer (at the time of opening, the product of Kickstarter UK's biggest ever restaurant campaign) has created more of a splash than any Liverpool opening of the last decade: an "impressively refurbished" workshop in the city's old merchant quarter that's now a "buzzy" and "lovely" space (where some of the seating is communal) and with "charming" staff. "Recognisably following his rewarding general formula" – it "serves quality produce in a fresh and interesting way, and delivers great value". Quibbles are minor: e.g. "many things to love about this place, with some great cooking and brilliant ideas, but some dishes just need better balance to counteract the riot of flavours". Top Tip: "Early bird dinner menu (two courses for £17) is a no-brainer". / wreckfish.co; @WreckfishBistro; Mon-Sun 10 pm.

LLANARTHNE, CARMARTHENSHIRE 4–4C

WRIGHTS FOOD EMPORIUM £37 434
GOLDEN GROVE ARMS SA32 8JU 01558 668929

"A great place for lunch" of a relatively "cheap and cheerful" variety – former AA chief inspector and Y Polyn owner Simon Wright's three-year-old café/deli is also the perfect place to stock up after a tasty bite. There are "interesting wines" from small, low-intervention producers, own-label nibbles, and even a couple of rooms if you want to stay overnight. / maryann@wrightsfood.co.uk; @WrightsFood; Sun & Mon 5 pm, Wed & Thu 7 pm, Fri & Sat 9 pm; no bookings.

THE WALNUT
TREE   £74 5 3 3

**LLANDDEWI SKIRRID NP7 8AW
01873 852797**

"We revisited after thirty years – the quality is as high as ever". Shaun Hill has, for the last ten years, continued the excellence pioneered back-in-the-day by Franco & Ann Taruschio, and this rural pub is to this day "arguably the best restaurant in Wales". "Consistently delicious seasonal food is perfectly cooked and conceived" and prices are "good value" given the "seamless standard that's a delight for the taste buds". / www.thewalnuttreeinn.com; @lovewalnuttree; 3m NE of Abergavenny on B4521; 9.30 pm; closed Mon & Sun. *Accommodation:* 5 rooms, from £300

TYDDYN LLAN   £89 5 4 5

LL21 0ST 01490 440264

Bryan Webb's "always brilliant" cuisine is "simple yet elegant" in style, and a good match for its "beautiful setting" – a comfortable Victorian former hunting lodge "tucked away in rural Wales". There's also an "eclectic wine list with some gems and real bargains". "You're looked after from the moment you arrive" at this "fabulous romantic destination" by his wife Susan and her team. / www.tyddynllan.co.uk; @BryanWWebb; on B4401 between Corwen and Bala; Mon-Sun 9 pm; credit card deposit required to book. *Accommodation:* 12 rooms, from £180

BODYSGALLEN HALL,
DINING ROOM   £75 3 4 4

**THE ROYAL WELSH WAY LL30 1RS
01492 584466**

The National Trust's imposing Elizabethan hotel, set in spectacular parkland and with rare 17th century features, is "ideal for romantics", with "the food matching the elegance of the setting" ("we have been going for over thirty years and have never had a bad meal"). / www.bodysgallen.com; @BodysgallenHall; 2m off A55 on A470; Sun-Thu 9 pm, Fri & Sat 9.30 pm; no trainers; children: 6+. *Accommodation:* 31 rooms, from £179

SOSBAN   £50

NORTH DOCK SA15 2LF 01554 270 020

Promising if limited feedback on this modern brasserie in a town about 10 miles outside Swansea, which occupies a very attractively converted old pump-house on the old docks. / www.sosban.wales; @sosbanllanelli; Wed-Sat 11 pm, Tue 3 pm.

CORN MILL   £50 3 3 4

DEE LN LL20 8PN 01978 869555

"An amazing setting overlooking the River Dee" – "with decking overhanging the river and the water wheel, it's spectacular" – makes this "excellent" Brunning & Price gastropub "a very good place to head for" in this picturesque town, with "an extensive and varied menu". "It's at its pinnacle in the winter months when the river is at its fullest and all the flows seem to collide in a cauldron of spray!" / www.cornmill-llangollen.co.uk; Mon-Sat 10.30 pm.

CARLTON
RIVERSIDE   £56 3 2 2

IRFON CR LD5 4SP 01591 610248

Though "quiet and quite slow" – well, it does sit in Britain's smallest town – this relaxed restaurant-with-rooms of some renown still turns out "excellent cooking" that's "worth supporting"; even a regular who felt it "lacks the creative inspiration of old" said "the food is still perfectly cooked". / www.carltonriverside.com; Mon-Thu 11.30 pm, Fri & Sat midnight, Sun 7 pm; no Amex. *Accommodation:* 4 rooms, from £60

LLANGOED HALL   £88 4 3 4

LD3 0YP 01874 754525

"Nick Brodie's honest hard work" produces some "stunning" results at this impressive-looking and well-regarded country house hotel – a "lovely" property handy for Hay Festival goers. In the evening, the choice is from either a six-course or nine-course tasting menu. / www.llangoedhall.com; @TheLlangoedHall; 11m NW of Brecon on A470; 8.45 pm; no Amex; jacket required. *Accommodation:* 23 rooms, from £210

CABERFEIDH   4 3 3

MAIN STREET IV27 4JZ 01571 844321

"A more relaxed outlet of the wonderful Albannach on the hill above. This dining room behind the bar near the harbour offers great casual dining, beers and wines". Now that Colin Craig and Lesley Crosfield only do B&B at their original venture (which had its Michelin star removed this year as a result), their spin-off pub is the focus of their culinary activities. / www.thecaberfeidh.co.uk; Mon-Sun 8.30 pm.

CHAPTER ONE   £60 4 3 2

**FARNBOROUGH COMMON BR6 8NF
01689 854848**

This "superb" stalwart fixture of the outer London fringes has made a "welcome return to form" this year with long-time chef Andy McLeish back in the kitchen full-time, having bought the premises in late 2017 from the business that formerly employed him as group executive chef. "Although it has an unprepossessing exterior, once through the doors it's a worthwhile experience" – "picture perfect plating and great tastes" all "at fair prices". / www.chaptersrestaurants.com; @chapter1kent; Mon-Fri 11.30 pm, Sat 11 pm, Sun 10.30 pm; no trainers; booking max 12 may apply.

THE ANGEL   £53 3 2 3

47 BICESTER RD HP18 9EE 01844 208268

A 16th century country inn with a cosy bar, bright conservatory and dining room bearing a striking wattle-and-daub feature wall; the food is "super reliable, especially fish" and comes accompanied by a "well-chosen wine list". / www.angelrestaurant.co.uk; @theangeluk; 2m NW of Thames, off B4011; Mon-Sat 9.30 pm, Sun 3 pm. *Accommodation:* 4 rooms, from £110

Llangoed Hall,
Llyswen

THE MOLE &
CHICKEN   £58 3 4 4

EASINGTON LANE HP18 9EY 01844 208387

"Sitting outside on a fine summer day is a joy" at this rustic and ivy-clad country pub-with-rooms whose "lovely garden" has super views overlooking the Oxon-Bucks borders. It delivers straightforward cooking from breakfast on: "nothing fancy but a good meal". / www.themoleandchicken.co.uk; @moleandchicken; follow signs from B4011 at Long Crendon; 9.30 pm, Sun 9 pm. *Accommodation:* 5 rooms, from £110

MELFORD VALLEY
TANDOORI   £28 4 3 3

HALL ST CO10 9JT 01787 311 518

On Long Melford's main drag, and widely regarded as the best subcontinental in the area, this "recently refurbished" spot now "looks really good", and can pack in 100 diners. Top Tip: "they have an all-you-can-eat Sunday buffet for £7.95". / www.melfordvalley.com; @MelfordValley; Mon-Sat 10.30 pm, Sun 10 pm.

SWAN £62 443

HALL ST CO10 9JQ 01787 464545

Now in its sixth year, the Macmillans' superior Tudor pub in an "amazing village" has "got the recipe just right" – the formula now spanning a private dining room, deli counter and growing clutch of bedrooms. "Try the fabulous tasting menu at the new Chef's Table", or afternoon tea ("a must with a glass of Champagne!"). / www.longmelfordswan.co.uk; Mon-Sun 10 pm; 6pm - 9pm, Fri & Sat 6pm - 10pm, Sun 7pm - 9pm.

LOSTWITHIEL, CORNWALL 1–3B

ASQUITHS £56 443

19 NORTH STREET PL22 0EF 01208 871714

Graham Cuthbertson provided some reporters' best meals of the year with "outstanding presentation and taste" at his simply decorated restaurant opposite the town's church. / asquithsrestaurant.co.uk.

LOUGHBOROUGH, LEICESTERSHIRE 5–3D

THE HAMMER & PINCERS £44 443

5 EAST RD LE12 6ST 01509 880735

In a picturesque village ten minutes from Loughborough, this beamed gastroboozer has built up a real foodie following over the past fifteen years for its ambitious cuisine, spanning ten-course grazing menus and haute Sunday lunch; marks remain stellar but it attracted little commentary this year. / www.hammerandpincers.co.uk; 9.30 pm, 4pm Sun; closed Mon & Sun D; no Amex.

LOWER BEEDING, WEST SUSSEX 3–4B

THE PASS RESTAURANT, SOUTH LODGE HOTEL £99 443

BRIGHTON ROAD RH13 6PS 01403 891711

"OK – it's a bit of a gimmick, but I liked it". You eat in a theatrical open-kitchen set-up at this 28-cover country house hotel restaurant. Feedback is thinner than in some past years, but lauds "beautiful, inventive and story-filled food and joyous, unpompous service". / www.exclusive.co.uk/south-lodge/restaurants-bars/the-pass; @southlodgehotel; Wed-Sun 8.30 pm; children: 12+. *Accommodation:* 89 rooms, from £235

LOWER BOCKHAMPTON, DORSET 2–4B

YALBURY COTTAGE £55 443

DT2 8PZ 01305 262382

This "lovely" thatched restaurant with rooms, set in prime Hardy land, has a slight time-capsule vibe and the superior homemade food is "excellent"; "go with an appetite" – "portions and number of courses are generous". / www.yalburycottage.com; @YalburyDorset; Mon-Sat 11 pm, Sun 10.30 pm; no Amex. *Accommodation:* 8 rooms, from £120

LOWER FROYLE, HAMPSHIRE 2–3D

THE ANCHOR INN £48 323

GU34 4NA 01420 23261

This well turned-out and hospitable country pub-with-rooms achieves consistently good ratings for its "above average food" – and especially "one of the best Sunday lunches in the area". / www.anchorinnatlowerfroyle.co.uk; @anchorinnfroyle; Mon-Thu 11 pm, Fri & Sat midnight, Sun 10.30 pm. *Accommodation:* 5 rooms, from £120

LOWER SLAUGHTER, GLOUCESTERSHIRE 2–1C

THE SLAUGHTERS MANOR HOUSE £99 333

COPSEHILL RD GL54 2HP 01451 820456

"Set in beautiful grounds and in one of the UK's most beautiful villages" – locations don't come more picturebook than this well-known hotel (nowadays in the hands of the Brownsword group), which – on limited feedback – provides an "impeccable all round experience". Afternoon tea here is also recommended: "croquet on the lawn anyone?" / www.slaughtersmanor.co.uk; @SlaughtersManor; 2m from Burton-on-the-Water on A429; no jeans; children: 8.

LOWER SWELL, SOMERSET 2–1C

THE LANGFORD £60 444

LANGFORD FIVEHEAD TA3 6PH 01460 282020

"Charming old Manor House" (15th century) run by owners Olly & Rebecca Jackson where "a drink in the garden in summer, or in front of the log fire in winter, precedes a marvellous meal". The menu is prix-fixe for three courses with four options per course. / www.langfordfivehead.co.uk/; @Langford5head; Tue-Sat 10.30 pm.

LUDLOW, SHROPSHIRE 5–4A

THE CHARLTON ARMS, CHARLTON ARMS HOTEL £44 334

LUDFORD BRIDGE SY8 1PJ 01584 872813

Cedric Bosi's attractive stone inn near the bridge has fine views of the River Teme from its dining room. "The cooking is of a high standard from a small but regularly changing menu" (and was blessed in October 2018 with a Bib Gourmand from the tyre men). / www.thecharltonarms.co.uk; @Charlton_Ludlow

CSONS AT THE GREEN CAFE £38 334

DINHAM MILLENNIUM GREEN SY8 1EG 01584 879872

What was formerly Clive Davis' local staple (and FKA Green Café), is now "under new ownership (CSons – Shrewsbury)", aka four brothers with deep roots in the Ludlow scene. Fans "didn't think it could be any better, but it is", with an "extended menu including breakfast" and, of late, Fri/Sat dinners. In particular "it's a fabulous spot for al fresco breakfast or lunch overlooking the River Teme". / csons-ludlow.co.uk; @greencafeludlow; Fri-Sun-Wed & Thu 10.30 pm.

GOLDEN MOMENTS £33 443

50 BROAD STREET SY8 1NH 01584 878 488

"One of the best anywhere" – a polished and "constantly excellent" Indian, on the best-known street in a well-known foodie town; "you may have to wait as it's all freshly cooked, but it's worth the wait". / www.goldenmomentsofludlow.co.uk/; Mon-Sat 11 pm, Sun 10 pm.

MORTIMERS £71 454

17 CORVE ST SY8 1DA 01584 872 325

"Thankfully serious cooking and professional service have returned to Ludlow" – and, aptly, to the "convivial" old locale of La Bécasse (RIP) and Hibiscus (pre-London move) – at this rising star from Wayne Smith, the bluff northern protégé of Hibiscus's former boss Claude Bosi. All reports are strong, and the best say his cuisine here is "inspired and unique". / www.mortimersludlow.co.uk; @MortimersLudlow; Wed & Thu 9.30 pm, Fri & Sat 10 pm, Sun 3 pm.

OLD DOWNTON LODGE £86 444

DOWNTON ON THE ROCK SY8 2HU 01568 771826

"The big investment in all aspects of the operation backed up by a really friendly team is now paying off" at this attractive hotel (converted from ancient barns and a former cider mill) where the dining room feels positively baronial. As well as six-course and nine-course tasting menus, chef Karl Martin also provides a simpler 'Market Menu' option. / www.olddowntonlodge.com; @olddowntonlodge; Sun & Mon 5 pm, Wed & Thu 10 pm, Fri & Sat 11 pm, Tue 6 pm; children: 11.

PIZZA TEN £49 443

2B QUALITY SQUARE SY8 1AR 01584 879450

"Simple, fresh and so, so tasty pasta and pizza – perfect in all ways", say fans of this independent pizzeria in foodie Ludlow, whose toppings show an unusual level of sophistication. "They just do everything right". / www.pizzaten.co.uk; Mon-Sat 9.30 pm, Sun 4 pm.

LUTON, BEDFORDSHIRE 3–2A

LUTON HOO, LUTON HOO HOTEL £51 234

THE MANSION HOUSE, LUTON HOO ESTATE LU1 3TQ 01582 734437

The "lovely afternoon tea" ("with lots of food and very good quality" sips) remains the highlight of this "elegant" country house hotel and spa, featured in 'Four Weddings', and handily just ten minutes' drive from the airport, but it also houses the smart 'Wernher' restaurant, dripping with chandeliers. / www.lutonhoo.co.uk; @lutonhoo; Tue-Sat 9.30 pm, Sun 2.30 pm; online only.

THE WHITE HART   £55   443

51 STOCKPORT RD OL4 4JJ   01457 872566

"Always a great experience both in the restaurant and the brasserie" – this much-expanded 18th-century hilltop inn, set in a hamlet near Saddleworth, has wonderful views over the Pennines and provides consistently highly-rated cooking. Owner Charles Brierley found it semi-derelict 25 years ago, and has transformed it into a real crowd-pleaser. / www.thewhitehart.co.uk; @whitehartlydgte; 2m E of Oldham on A669, then A6050; Sun-Thu 11 pm, Fri & Sat midnight. *Accommodation:* 12 rooms, from £120

HIX OYSTER & FISH HOUSE   £52   444

COBB RD DT7 3JP   01297 446910

"Fabulous views over Lyme Regis Harbour" plus "consistently delicious, fresh, local seafood" and "always-helpful service" win this cliff-top venue comfortably the highest ratings this year amongst the upmarket group owned by influential chef-turned-restaurateur Mark Hix – who grew up nearby and regularly lunches here. / www.restaurantsetcltd.co.uk; @hixlymeregis; 10 pm.

ELDERFLOWER   £66   443

QUAY ST SO41 3AS   01590 676908

"A key attraction in delightful Lymington" with "a good location on the quay side" (opposite the pier). Andrew & Marjolaine Du Bourg's restaurant-with-rooms provides "superbly presented" and "innovative" French-accented cuisine and makes "a great choice for a special occasion". / www.elderflowerrestaurant.co.uk; @TheElderflower1; Wed & Thu 9.30 pm, Fri & Sat 10 pm, Sun 4 pm. *Accommodation:* 95 rooms, from £0

MONKEY HOUSE   £46   343

167 SOUTHAMPTON ROAD SO41 9HA   01590 676754

"A quirky little pub" – "a free house with a great range of beers" – which provides "first class food served by very friendly staff"; large outside terrace for warm days. / www.themonkeyhouse.co.uk; Mon-Sat 9.30 pm, Sun 4 pm.

LA BOHEME   £52   443

3 MILL LANE WA13 9SD   01925 753657

"A rare high quality, traditional French-style restaurant", set on the plush suburban fringes of South Manchester. No-one (of the very many who report) has a bad word to say about the place: Olivier Troalen's cuisine is "sensational,

with exquisite presentation" and "the service is second to none". It all comes "at fair prices too". Top Tip: "best at lunchtime: ridiculously underpriced!" / laboheme.co.uk; Mon-Sat 10 pm, Sun 9 pm.

HARTNETT HOLDER & CO, LIME WOOD HOTEL   £83   433

BEAULIEU RD SO43 7FZ   02380 287177

"Smart casual in approach": chef-turned-restaurateur Angela Hartnett's rural hideaway – an "uber-stylish country house" in the New Forest – is somewhere "you could take the kids for lunch and eat well, and also good for a relaxed, grown-up dinner", serving "very good", "Italian-style" cooking. / www.limewoodhotel.co.uk/food/hh-and-co; @limewoodhotel; Mon-Sat midnight, Sun 5 pm; booking max 4 may apply.

THE PUNCH BOWL INN   £54   445

LA8 8HR   01539 568237

"Yet to find a more impressive pub in the Lake District" – this "simply outstanding" inn, set in a tiny village, caters for every taste from "local beers around the open fire" to "well-executed restaurant-style meals": "the food is homegrown, seasonal and full of flavour" and "served in a friendly, efficient manner". / www.the-punchbowl.co.uk; @PunchbowlInn; off A5074 towards Bowness, turn right after Lyth Hotel; 8.45 pm. *Accommodation:* 9 rooms, from £105

NOVELLO   £54   432

11A CLIFTON ST FY8 5EP   01253 730278

"Ostensibly an Italian restaurant" – the Lioveri family's fifteen-year-old fixture cooks "more in a modern British idiom" (although "there is a bit too much sous vide work, gels, foams and spherification to be really cutting edge"). "Apart from unnecessary modernist touches", the "execution is excellent" and a meal far more "refined" than its unassuming exterior might suggest. / www.thenovello.co.uk; @novello_lytham; Tue-Sat 10 pm.

THREE HORSESHOES   £51   334

HIGH ST CB23 8AB   01954 210221

With its fortunes revived under the Huntsbridge Group of late, this "lovely old thatched building with sunny conservatory" joined the local, ever-growing Cambscuisine empire in January 2018; fans say it's "back in business", turning out "interesting and well-prepared" food. / www.threehorseshoesmadingley.co.uk; @3hs_restaurant; 2m W of Cambridge, off A14 or M11; Mon-Thu 9 pm, Fri & Sat 9.30 pm, Sun 8 pm.

THE CROWN   £52   444

BURCHETTS GREEN SL6 6QZ   01628 824079

Simon Bonwick has earned rave reviews (and a Michelin star) for his "excellent cooking" at this "perfect – and very friendly – family business", where son Dean runs front-of-house and other children help out. Simon cooks solo, knocking out dishes inspired by classical gastronomy. / thecrownburchettsgreen.com; Wed-Sat 9 pm, Sun 1.30 pm.

FREDERIC BISTRO   £43   343

MARKET BUILDINGS, EARL ST ME14 1HP   01622 297414

"A bit of France in the middle of Maidstone", serving "huge portions of wholesome food" (e.g. cassoulet, chicken chasseur, …) and "an excellent choice of (350+) wines" (plus gins) in the new bar next door. The only low point? It's "very busy" since the expansion and "does get noisy". / www.fredericbistro.com; Mon-Sun 9.30 pm.

THE OLD BELL HOTEL   £61   333

ABBEY ROW SN16 0AG   01666 822344

England's oldest hotel, with "multiple rooms" for drinking, dining and unwinding in, has been given a new lease of life, with a refurb' and new chef, Frederic Fetiveau, as of early 2018; initial reports suggest both are positive developments. / www.oldbellhotel.com; @oldesthotel; Mon-Sat 9.30 pm, Sun 9 pm. *Accommodation:* 33 rooms, from £115

ADAM REID AT THE FRENCH , MIDLAND HOTEL   £119   343

PETER ST M60 2DS   01612354780

This "superb, very elegant space" put in a stronger performance in the survey this year, perhaps aided by "a recent change of style and presentation" that has seen it "dispense with white tablecloths to pursue a more informal approach". Adam Reid's cuisine is "very enjoyable" and his four-, six- and nine-course menus deliver some "beautifully balanced dishes". Perhaps unfairly, however, there remains an air of promise unfulfilled over this famous chamber. It's not just that it still carries the weight of being the last Manchester restaurant to hold a Michelin star back in the distant days of 1974. But in the present day, it's by no means as much commented-on in the survey as one might expect for such a big name, and amongst those reports we do receive, some still talk of the odd "terrible" trip, or a meal with "patchy service, and dishes where some, but not all, were interesting". In October 2018 the £115m sale of the hotel was announced – renovation is planned but whether change

is afoot for The French remains to be seen. / www.the-french.co.uk; @thefrenchmcr; 9.30 pm; closed Mon, Tue L & Sun; no trainers; children: 9+.
Accommodation: 312 rooms, from £145

AKBAR'S £33 `4` `2` `2`
73-83 LIVERPOOL RD M3 4NQ
0161 834 8444

This much-loved curry house is perennially busy ("you have to queue") for good reasons: the food is both "delicious" and "cheap 'n' cheerful" – £14.95 buys a 'meat feast balti, gigantic naan and pilau rice', and if you can clear your plate dessert comes free. / www.akbars.co.uk; Sun-Thu 11 pm, Fri & Sat 11.30 pm; may need 10+ to book.

ALBATROSS & ARNOLD £55 `3` `3` `2`
LEFTBANK M3 3AN 0161 325 4444

"A bit weird and not easy to find from ground-level" – this bar and lounge on the first floor of an indoor golf driving-range in Spinningfields (complete with 'a suspended light installation featuring over 1000 beautifully lit golf balls') "doesn't immediately scream fine-dining". The focus is on a trendy, meat-focussed small-plates menu and early reports suggest that, unlikely as it sounds, there's "some proper high-end cooking going on here". / www.albatrossandarnold.uk.com; @AlbatrossArnold; Mon-Thu 11 pm.

ALBERT SQUARE CHOP HOUSE £47 `3` `3` `4`
THE MEMORIAL HALL, ALBERT SQ M2 5PF
0161 834 1866

An "always vibrant" spot, in Thomas Worthington's iconic Gothic Revival Memorial Hall, run by the people behind Sam's and Mr Thomas's, aka the Victorian Chop Houses; the British pub grub hits the spot and there's "very good service" to match. / www.albertsquarechophouse.com; @chophouseAlbert; Mon-Thu 9.30 pm, Fri & Sat 10 pm, Sun 8.30 pm.

ALBERT'S SCHLOSS £51 `3` `3` `4`
27 PETER STREET M2 5QR 0161 833 4040

"My go-to for a night out with friends: epic fun at very reasonable prices" – this Germanic-theme bar "is loud (very loud), it's kitsch and it's full of people drinking too much. However, these people are drinking very good beer; that music is an oompah covers band; the service is friendly and efficient; and the food is about 500% better than it needs to be. If the idea is to capture the spirit of a German beerhaus i.e. massive, borderline-rowdy but warm and convivial, crammed, with good beer and good food, this very much hits the spot!". They do brunch now too (and have just raised £10m to take the concept to other cities). / albertsschloss.co.uk; @AlbertsSchloss; Mon-Sun 2 am.

ALBERT'S SHED £46 `4` `3` `3`
20 CASTLE ST M3 4LZ 0161 839 9818

The eponymous Albert's old tool shed (he's the uncle of the owner) is now a stylish,

contemporary haunt with a popular canalside terrace – hence why it's "best in summer" – plus reasonably priced, mostly English grub. (Part of a three-strong local empire, which recently announced plans to add a Standish branch.) / www.albertsshed.com; @alberts_shed; Mon-Thu 10 pm, Fri 10.30 pm, Sat 11 pm, Sun 9.30 pm; no Amex.

ALMOST FAMOUS £29 `4` `3` `3`
100-102 HIGH ST M4 1HP 0161 244 9422

"If you want dirty do Almost Famous, because it'll be properly filthy", say fans of the original branch of what is now a four-strong regional burger group. "Becoming a mini-chain may have taken the edge off the too-cool-for-school-ness, but its burgers remain a clear cut above the Byrons/GBKs of this world". / www.almostfamousburgers.com; @AlmostFamousNQ; Mon-Thu 9.30 pm, Fri-Sun 10 pm; no bookings.

ARTISAN CAFE BAR, ARTISAN KITCHEN & BAR £44 `3` `4` `3`
AVENUE NORTH, 18-22 BRIDGE ST M3 3BZ
0161 832 4181

A "bustling, dark" warehouse-style operation, whose menu of "accurately cooked" pizzas and bistro staples is "popular with both couples and groups out for dinner and a good time" or post-browsing the shops at 'The Avenue'. A sleek two-year-old café-bar sibling is located on the ground floor. / www.artisan.uk.com; @Artisan_MCR; 10.45pm .

AUSTRALASIA £63 `3` `3` `4`
1 THE AVENUE SPINNINGFIELDS M3 3AP
0161 831 0288

This "uber-trendy" subterranean venue off Deansgate serves an "interesting fusion menu" of "Australian tapas" with Indonesian and Japanese influences. Fans love "trying different food via sharing plates here", but a significant minority reckon it's "nice but overhyped and overpriced". / www.australasia.uk.com; @AustralasiaMcr; 10.45 pm.

BAR SAN JUAN £33 `4` `3` `5`
56 BEECH RD M21 9EG 0161 881 9259

"Tiny, cramped and you always have to queue but that's all part of the fun" at this "brilliant" tapas joint on Chorlton's back streets, which feels "like being in Spain". "Unusual" specials are "worth looking out for" – it's all good and "very affordable" too. / barsanjuan.com; Tue-Thu 11.30 pm, Fri & Sat midnight, Sun 11 pm.

BUNDOBUST £30 `4` `2` `3`
61 PICCADILLY M1 2AQ 0161 359 6757

"Wow! Fresh, cheap and tasty as hell!"; the Indian street food menu is full of character and "they have a large list of craft ales and ciders" – "what a combo!" – at this "unmissable" if "basic" vegetarian treat: "a fantastic addition to the curry scene in Manchester", and one that's quickly become one of the city's foremost destinations. "No table service and queues at the bar to order can be lengthy at busy times". /

www.bundobust.com; @BundobustMCR; Mon-Thu 9.30 pm, Fri & Sat 10 pm, Sun 8 pm.

CANTO £36
FAIRBAIRN HOUSE, HENRY STREET M4 5DH 0161 870 5904

The team behind El Gato Negro have opened a second 110-cover site in the Fairbairn building in Ancoats. The tiled (partly with cork!) space serves 'modern Portuguese' cuisine inspired by chef/patron Simon Shaw's travels to Lisbon, as well as head chef Carlos Gomes' upbringing in Porto. / www.cantorestaurant.com; Tue-Thu 11 pm, Fri & Sat midnight.

CHAOPHRAYA £51 `3` `3` `4`
19 CHAPEL WALKS, OFF CROSS STREET M2 1HN 0161 832 8342

A strikingly smart outpost of the UK-wide Thai Leisure Group, which makes "an ideal setting to relax and talk – and you can hear yourself, with not too much background chatter"; the ever-growing Midlands-and-up chain spawned a Liverpool cocktail joint, Thaikhun Street Bar, in October 2018. / www.chaophraya.co.uk; @ChaophrayaThai; Mon-Thu 10.30 pm, Fri & Sat 11 pm, Sun 9.30 pm.

THE CREAMERIES £42
406 WILBRAHAM ROAD, CHORLTON M21 0SD 0161 312 8328

This minimal-looking, spring 2018 newcomer in Chorlton in a converted Edwardian creamery – a crowd-funded venture from former Aumbry owner Mary Ellen McTague and baker Sophie Yeoman – opened too late for survey feedback, but has set Manc's foodie media abuzz, winning best newcomer at Manchester's Food & Drink Awards. Although there are a few 'proper' dishes on the minimal menu and there's more ambitious cooking in the evenings, its prime strengths especially by day seem to be its baked goods (cakes, breads, pastries, etc), cheeses and coffee. / www.thecreameries.co.uk; @hellocreameries; Wed-Sat 9 pm, Sun 4 pm.

CROMA £38 `3` `3` `4`
1-3 CLARENCE ST M2 4DE 0161 237 9799

"Reliable and good quality" pizzas are the hallmark of this flagship of a small Manchester chain – "think Pizza Express ++", especially as the distinct modern interiors are by Enzo Apicella, the veteran Pizza Express design guru. / www.cromapizza.co.uk; @cromapizza; Mon-Wed 11 pm, Thu-Sat midnight.

DISHOOM
MANCHESTER HALL, 36 BRIDGE STREET, SPINNINGFIELDS M3 3BT AWAITING TEL

The famous bacon naan will finally hit Manchester in early December 2018 as this Mumbai-inspired chain opens in the grade II-listed Manchester Hall. This new addition has gone down a storm in Edinburgh – it will be bizarre if it doesn't here too. / www.dishoom.com; @Dishoom; Wed-Sat 11 pm, Sun 7 pm.

Tast Cuina Catalana, Manchester

1847 VEGETARIAN RESTAURANT £36 3|3|3

CHAPEL WALKS M2 1HN 0161 832 8994

"Fresh, creative and warming" – the beautifully presented cuisine at Damien Davenport's veggie indie (with a sibling in Brum) near the Exchange Theatre is well worth discovering, and not only if you try to eat meat-free. "Is this the best veggie in Manchester"? / www.by1847.com/manchester/; Sun-Thu 9 pm, Fri & Sat 9.30 pm.

EVUNA £45 3|3|3

277 - 279 DEANSGATE M3 4EW 0161 819 2752

"It may not be the best place for tapas in Manchester any more (that crown's been stolen by El Gato Negro)", but this fifteen-year-old Deansgate bar and wine merchant is still "way above" many other "much-hyped" local pretenders, certainly amongst oenophiles. A fourth branch is due to open in Altrincham on the old site of EAT:kaizen in January 2019. / www.evuna.com; @evunamanchester; Wed-Sat 9.30 pm, Sun 3.30 pm.

EL GATO NEGRO £47 4|3|4

52 KING STREET M2 4LY 0161 694 8585

"Still smashing it" – this "throbbing and bustling" operation remains the most commented-on place in town, and "feels like it's been around for years" even though it only made the move from Ripponden two years ago. The "stylish and splendid" interior "shows what a big budget will deliver, and the buzzy atmosphere is ensured by the droves of customers". On the menu: "Spanish small plates with a North African influence", which provide "an excellent tapas feast – not quite the magical heights that modern tapas can sometimes soar too, but terrifically good nevertheless". "If you're lucky enough to get a table on the open-roofed top floor on a pleasant evening you're in for a treat". / www.elgatonegrotapas.com; @ElGatoNegroFood; Mon - Thur 10 pm, Fri & Sat 11 pm, Sun 9.30 pm.

GLAMOROUS £42 3|2|2

WING YIP BUS' CENTRE, OLDHAM RD M4 5HU 0161 839 3312

"The trolley service dim sum (good, if nothing exceptional) is the draw to this Cantonese barn" which sits "above a cash and carry" and has "oh-so glamorous (ho ho) views of a multi-storey car park"; "be prepared to queue in a slightly disorganised way", and "don't miss your number being called or you'll be at the back of the queue again". / www.glamorous-restaurant.co.uk; @glamorous_uk; Wed-Sat 10.30 pm, Sun 9.30 pm.

GRAFENE RESTAURANT & COCKTAIL BAR £63 4|2|2

55 KING STREET M2 4LQ 0161 696 9700

First the caveats – critics says "it feels like it's trying too hard with service that doesn't match the heights the food is trying to reach, and with an atmosphere that's a bit flat". Moving on, though, esteem is growing for Paul and Kathryn Roden's modernistic two-year-old, looking onto Chapel Walks, which recently recruited an ex-Fraiche chef: it's increasingly seen as "a good addition to Manchester" with ever-more accomplished modern cuisine. / @grafenemcr; Mon-Sat 10 pm, Sun 8 pm.

HAWKSMOOR £66 4|4|3

184-186 DEANSGATE M3 3WB 0161 836 6980

"Now established as one of Manchester's best restaurants", the northern outpost of this epic modern steakhouse group has recreated much of the special aura it has established 'darn sarf' with its formula of "first class" British steaks, well-crafted cocktails, and "slick service", all provided in an impressively converted Victorian space. "It's not a cheap day out… but blimey it's worth it!" according to (nearly all) reporters. Top Tip: "despite the meat focus, the seafood here is a hidden gem – it's stellar, as is the wine list". / www.thehawksmoor.com; @HawksmoorLondon; Tue-Thu 11.30 pm, Fri & Sat midnight, Sun 11 pm.

HISPI BISTRO £53 4|3|3

1C SCHOOL LANE M20 6RD 0161 445 3996

"Part of the slick Gary Usher machine", his Didsbury operation "is the classic neighbourhood bistro" which on all accounts is "genuinely what every local restaurant should be". "It serves lots of things you want to eat. There are no fireworks, but it's all so very good". / www.hispi.net/; @HispiBistro; Sun-Thu 9 pm, Fri & Sat 10 pm.

HOME £42 3|2|2

2 TONY WILSON PLACE M15 4FN 0161 212 3500

This "good quality arts centre café" inhabits "a great building" (with five on-site cinemas) and wins solid ratings for its "good pizza (with some unusual toppings)" and other dishes – "perfect before or after an art-house film". / homemcr.org; @HOME_mcr; Wed-Sat 8 pm, Sun 3 pm.

IBÉRICA, SPINNINGFIELDS £48 3|2|3

14-15 THE AVENUE M3 3HF 01613 581 350

This vivid Spinningfields spin-off of the hit national chain continues to garner mixed feedback, not least because Manchester has a fiesta of Spanish competitors; but, despite the odd criticism of food and service (less since portions grew), there continue to be fans, for whom the oft-changing menu is "always excellent". / www.ibericarestaurants.com; Mon-Sat 11 pm, Sun 10 pm.

INDIAN TIFFIN ROOM £47 3|2|2

2 ISABELLA BANKS STREET, FIRST STREET, M15 4RL 0161 228 1000

"Fresh and exciting little taste bombs, with no evidence of gloopy sauce" sums up the appeal of the Indian street-food-style dishes at this jazzy First Street operation, which has "a quirky design, with the bar and kitchen being housed in old shipping containers, and with the best seats in the booths by the window". Having taken Cheadle by storm, this new unit opened a couple of years ago – it can seem "a bit chaotic" but mostly wins praise for its tasty and affordable options (and the "great selection of dosas and thalis include much that will suit vegetarians or vegans"). / www.indiantiffinroom.com/manchester-restaur; @Indtiffinroom; Wed-Sat 8 pm, Sun 3 pm.

INDIQUE £44 4|3|3

110-112 BURTON ROAD M20 1LP 0161 438 0241

"Wonderful Indian food, extremely well presented" again wins praise for this contemporary four year old in West Didsbury. / www.indiquerestaurant.co.uk/; @IndiqueDidsbury; Mon-Fri 10.30 pm, Sat 11 pm.

JAMES MARTIN £53 4|4|2

2 WATSON ST M3 4LP 0161 828 0345

"Based in Manchester235 ['a Las Vegas-style casino'] this is an unlikely place for a restaurant like this" ("not ideal for fine dining", or even "terrible"), but fans feel it's "a real, somewhat forgotten, gem in the centre of Manchester" and say "once you're in you forget where you are". All reports agree, however, on the "fantastic value": the food is "refined, very well cooked and very tasty" and "the cost of the wine flight is amazingly cheap, considering the quality". / www.jamesmartinmanchester.co.uk; @JamesMartinMCR; Mon - Thur 10 pm, Fri & Sat 11 pm, Sun 5 pm.

KALA

KING STREET M2 7AT

Never a man to stand still, Gary Usher will open the sixth outpost of his growing, crowd-funded north western empire in the heart of the city-centre. Opening in February 2019, the venue will be open from breakfast onwards, and incorporate a 70-cover restaurant, plus a bar set out 'Barrafina-style' where up to 15 people can eat. Rather than feeling rustic, the site is apparently a massive glass-fronted building with polished floors, hence Usher plans to use marble and lots of black to suit the glass feel. / @kala_manchester.

KATSOURIS DELI £15 3|3|2

113 DEANSGATE M3 2BQ 0161 937 0010

With its eat-in or take-away menu of hearty ciabatta sandwiches and help-yourself carvery, this famous and "great value" pitstop caters to those in need of a refuel in the city-centre. "Top breakfasts", too. / www.katsourisdeli.co.uk; Mon-Sat 4.30 pm, Sun; no Amex.

THE LIME TREE £40 4 5 4

8 LAPWING LN M20 2WS 0161 445 1217

Patrick Hannity's "top-notch" Didsbury brasserie has been "the model of consistency" for more than 30 years. "It retains the perfect combination of great food with fantastic wine and brilliant service in a vibrant atmosphere" and – though somewhat overshadowed nowadays by flashier openings elsewhere in the city – still has a fan club who consider it "Manchester's best": "a bit of a schlep so we only go on my birthday, but I wouldn't go anywhere else". / www.thelimetreerestaurant.co.uk; @thelimetreeres; Tue-Fri 10 pm, Sat 10.30 pm, Sun 6 pm.

LUNYA £46 3 3 2

BARTON ARCADE, DEANSGATE M3 2BW 0161 413 3317

"Wonderful tapas" ("pleasant, but not on the same level as El Gato Negro, etc") is the main attraction at this "very busy" Manc branch of Liverpool's successful Spanish/Catalan outfit. Downstairs is a bar and "beautiful deli, well-stocked with tempting delicacies", while the main restaurant is on the first floor. / www.lunya.co.uk/manchester; @lunyaMCR; Mon-Wed 9.30 pm, Thu 10 pm, Fri 10.30 pm, Sat 11 pm, Sun 9 pm.

MACKIE MAYOR 3 3 5

1 EAGLE STREET M4 5JY

"A truly brilliant addition to the Manchester dining scene, Altrincham Market's bigger, better sibling" arrives in "a beautifully converted market in Manchester's Northern Quarter" (a former meat market, empty for decades), providing a "fantastic selection of street food vendors all under one roof". "It's a little pricey, but choose from any of a number of cuisine stalls, from Asian buns to fish 'n' chips, washed down with good wines or Manchester's own Blackjack craft beers". It's "always buzzing". / www.mackiemayor.co.uk; Mon-Sat 9.30 pm, Sun 4 pm.

MEI DIM £21 4 2 2

M1 4EE 0161 236 6868

"Chinatown as it should be" (not least if you're looking for dim sum): a basement outfit providing "good food, low prices, energetic service and clean but unpretentious décor". It draws "mostly Chinese customers" and others "who know what the dishes should taste like". / Mon-Thu 11.30 pm, Fri & Sat midnight, Sun 10 pm.

MI AND PHO £26 4 3 3

M22 4FZ 0161 312 3290

Despite its out-on-a-limb location (in Northenden), this south Manchester Vietnamese café is one of the city's better-known cheap eats currently – locals fans say that in their experience it's "the best Vietnamese scoff outside London!" / www.miandpho.com; @MiandPho; Tue-Fri, Sun 9 pm, Sat 10 pm.

MR COOPER'S, THE MIDLAND HOTEL £54 3 3 3

PETER ST M60 2DS 0161 235 4781

"The casual option at The Midland" provides "a beautiful setting in this magnificent, historic hotel" complete with a pretty, garden-style interior (with its own tree!) and is a more "solid" destination than The French, with "strong, straightforward cooking". "You wouldn't necessarily make a special journey, but if you were staying you wouldn't be at all disappointed to find this downstairs". Following the sale of the hotel in late 2018 to a Swedish-Israeli partnership change may be afoot. / www.mrcoopers.co.uk; @mrcoopersmcr; Mon-Sat 10 pm, Sun 8 pm.

MUGHLI £33 4 3 3

30 WILMSLOW RD M14 5TQ 0161 248 0900

"Miles ahead of your average curry", this veteran (est. 1991) on Rusholme's Curry Mile attracts extravagant praise for its "street food and charcoal pit dishes". "The menu changes subtly at regular (as yet unidentified) intervals, but pani puri are always excellent" and the "gunpowder fries are positively addictive". / www.mughli.com; @mughli; Mon-Thu midnight, Fri & Sat 12.30 am, Sun 10.30 pm.

PETER STREET KITCHEN, RADISSON BLU £48

FREE TRADE HALL, PETER STREET M2 5GP 0161 835 8941

Japanese and Mexican 'small plates' is the unusual offering from this late 2018 newcomer on Deansgate, which is open all day for a bewildering range of meals, from breakfast and afternoon tea to elegant weekend 'Rikyu' brunches; sake is a particular feature. Sibling to three London 'Kitchens' (Mayfair, Monmouth and Leicester Square). / www.peterstreetkitchen.co.uk; @peterst_kitchen; Mon-Fri 10 pm, Sat 10.30 pm, Sun 9.30 pm.

RANDALL & AUBIN £59 3 3 4

64 BRIDGE STREET M3 3BN 0161 711 1007

"So pleased R&A have expanded to Manchester, bringing their Soho class, ambience and quality of food here" – "wonderfully fresh seafood" is "served professionally in a very chilled bar and dining room" at this "Cosmopolitan-feeling" venture in Spinningfields: the spin-off from the well-known London foodie hotspot. A franchise, though it attracted lots of 'bums on seats', it hit well-publicised financial problems in mid-2018, and was bought out of receivership by the original founders Ed Baines & Jamie Poulton, with a view to turning it around commercially. / www.randallandaubin.com; @randallandaubinmcr; Mon-Sun 11 pm; booking lunch only.

RED CHILLI £42 3 3 2

70-72 PORTLAND STREET M1 4GU 0161 236 2888

A "nicely authentic" Chinatown establishment – part of a four-strong northern chain – where they don't damp down the Beijing and Sichuanese food, be it red-hot gong bao chicken or using more adventurous cuts; add in "extremely efficient" staff and it's reliably "busy". / www.redchillirestaurant.co.uk; 11pm, Fri & Sat midnight; closed Mon.

REFUGE BY VOLTA £37 2 3 4

OXFORD STREET M60 7HA 0161 223 5151

"Probably Manchester's grandest dining room (and bar)", this (sometimes "very noisy") venue in a refurbished Victorian office building is run by DJ partners Luke Cowdrey and Justin Crawford, aka The Unabombers (and owners of Volta in West Didsbury). The menu of eclectic small plates mostly earns a solid rep from reporters, but results can also be "workmanlike"; "nice Negronis" though. / www.refugemcr.co.uk; @TheRefugeMcr; Tue-Sat 10.30 pm, Sun 8.30 pm.

ROSSO £79 3 3 3

43 SPRING GARDENS M2 2BG 0161 8321400

Nearing its first decade, Rio Ferdinand's glitzy Italian-and-cocktails venue, in a smartly converted grade II listed building, is as big a hit with its foodie fans as it is with local celebs, winning solid ratings all-round. / www.rossorestaurants.com; @rossorestaurants; Sun-Thu 10 pm, Fri & Sat 11 pm.

RUDYS PIZZA £25 5 3 3

9 COTTON STREET, ANCOATS, M4 5BF 07931 162059

"The best pizza in Manchester" ("as good as you'll find anywhere outside Naples!") with authentic thin crusts and delicious toppings ("their margherita con mozzarella di bufala makes me drool just thinking about it") – this Ancoats legend is "worthy of its reputation" inspiring many reports, all positive. It's "as basic as the most basic space you can imagine", "really busy but totally worth it". "The original one is still going strong, but the new one on Peter Street is also very good" and "with two branches in the city now you're never too far away from pizza heaven". / www.rudyspizza.co.uk; @RudysPizzaMcr; Wed-Sat 8 pm, Sun 3 pm; no bookings.

SALVIS £50 3 3 2

UNIT 22B, THE CORN EXCHANGE M4 3TR 0161 222 8021

An "Italian with a bias towards Naples" which "also functions as a very good deli"; "not at all glam" like most of the local competition, the "cosy" basement spot "has the feel of a friendly little family-run trattoria, despite being in the new, multi-million-pound Corn Exchange". / www.salvismanchester.co.uk/.

SAM'S CHOP HOUSE £47 443

BACK POOL FOLD OFF CROSS STREET M2 1HN 0161 834 3210

With a menu of "great-tasting British classics" ("corned beef hash is my absolute favourite"), this Manchester institution (est 1872) is a place of pilgrimage for those of the city's trenchermen who like their traditional scoff with no fancy, poncey, modern nonsense. It was a regular haunt of the city's great artist, LS Lowry; his life-size statue in bronze is by the bar. / www.samschophouse.com; @chophousesams; Sun & Mon 10 pm, Tue-Thu 11.30 pm, Fri & Sat midnight.

SAN CARLO £59 335

40 KING STREET WEST M3 2WY 0161 834 6226

"Big and always buzzy, San Carlo sails on as ever" – this traditional city-centre Italian is "a celeb-magnet" in these parts, and its "bustling", see-and-be-seen style carries much of its appeal. The food is by no means incidental though – "choose well from the menu, and it can be excellent, and it's never less than pretty good". Service takes different people different ways: one or two reports say service can "leave much to be desired" seeming "over-attentive" or even "insincere", but most reports are of professional staff with "great front of house skills" ("helpful and always on hand"). / www.sancarlo.co.uk; @SanCarlo_Group; Tue-Thu 10 pm, Fri & Sat 10.30 pm, Mon 9.30 pm, Sun 9 pm.

SAN CARLO CICCHETTI £49 334

42 KING STREET WEST M3 2QG 0161 839 2233

On the ground floor of Kendal's (and with its own entrance), this "light and bright and airy" city-centre branch of San Carlo's more informal brand is "always packed", thanks to its "terrific, rip-roaring Italian small plates for sharing"; good for breakfasts too. / www.sancarlocicchetti.co.uk; @SC_Cicchetti; Mon-Sat 11 pm, Sun 10 pm; booking evening only.

63 DEGREES £70 443

20 CHURCH ST M4 1PN 0161 832 5438

"A taste of France in Manchester's Northern Quarter" and thus sticking out a touch amid the burger and pizza joints, the Moreau family's classy brasserie relocated to this larger, more prominent site two years back; by all accounts it offers Gallic cooking "at its best" and ably accompanied by "fine wines". / www.63degrees.co.uk; @63DegreesNQ; Tue-Thu 11 pm, Fri-Sun midnight.

SOLITA £40 423

37 TURNER ST M4 1DW 0161 839 2200

"Burger heaven" for hungry hipsters is hailed by fans of this ongoing Northern Quarter smash-hit (with spin-offs in Didsbury and Prestwich; Preston is no more), where the "massive Big Manc" and other "gorgeous burgers" are just part of an extensive and "interesting menu of meaty delights" – in fact one or two reporters feel the burgers are bettered by the other options. That's a minor quibble though – on practically all accounts this "upbeat" and "creatively decorated" venue is "the best burger joint around". Top Men Tip: "the secret here are the steaks, which are both very good, and good value". / www.solita.co.uk; @SolitaNQ; Sun-Thu 10 pm, Fri & Sat 11 pm.

TAMPOPO £36 322

16 ALBERT SQ M2 5PF 0161 819 1966

"Better than Wagamama etc." – if you're in the market for a quick city-centre lunch, this "consistent" and "authentic" Pan-Asian continues to be a real local favourite; in summer 2018 they added a third Manc outpost in Piccadilly Gardens, but "the original branch on Albert Square in still a cut above the rest". / www.tampopo.co.uk; @TampopoEats; Mon-Wed 10.30 pm, Thu-Sat 11 pm, Sun 10 pm; may need 7+ to book.

TAPEO & WINE £48 333

209 DEANSGATE M3 3NW 0161 832 2770

"Fantastic small Spanish plates and a brilliant wine list" are on the team sheet at this Deansgate two-year-old which has a following among Manchester's Iberian football elite, led by Pep Guardiola and Jose Mourinho, managers of City and United. (Hardly surprising: the place is owned by former United (now Arsenal) star Juan Mata and his father, Juan Manuel.) But it's fair to say that while it's "good, however it's not up to the super-high standards of some other tapas-joints in the city". / tapeoandwine.com; Mon-Sat 9.30 pm, Sun 4 pm.

TATTU £66 334

3 HARDMAN SQ, GARTSIDE ST M3 3EB 0161 819 2060

Everyone agrees there's an "absolutely stunning ambience" at this glam outfit, which is a magnet for a well groomed, Instagram-conscious crowd. There's the odd gripe that it's too pricey, but most reports are of "excellent" Asian cuisine. Next stop Birmingham, where a big opening was announced in October 2018. / www.tattu.co.uk; @tatturestaurant; 10:45pm; no trainers.

THIS & THAT £24 422

3 SOAP ST M4 1EW 0161 832 4971

"Although it's in a seedy part of town" and "looks a bit worn" (even after a refurb'), this "cheap and cheerful" curry café elicits only raves. Expect a "massive whack of flavour for very little cash" ("no menu, just point at the dish and you get a dollop") – "a fiver gets you a plateful, three curries rice and naan". Top Tip – "go there before the office crowd". / www.thisandthatcafe.co.uk; Mon-Thu 4.30 pm, Fri & Sat 8 pm, Sun 4 pm; cash only.

TNQ RESTAURANT & BAR £54 442

108 HIGH ST M4 1HQ 0161 832 7115

"Reliable" and "improving" – this Northern Quarter mainstay remains a safe bet locally for its "excellent and assured", "seasonal and local" British cuisine "at very reasonable prices". "Been going for years and never been disappointed." / www.tnq.co.uk; @TNQrestaurant; Tue-Sat 11 pm.

TRY THAI £34 433

52-54 FAULKNER ST M1 4FH 0161 228 1822

This Chinatown joint was once a "great little secret" but, post-expansion (adding a Thai-style canopy bar and lavish velvet curtains), it now "gets very busy", so "book way in advance"; the lunch and early evening deals are "excellent value, but don't showcase the best of their food". / www.try-thai.co.uk; Sun-Thu 10.30 pm, Fri & Sat midnight.

20 STORIES £59 445

NO 1 SPINNINGFIELDS, 1 HARDMAN SQUARE M3 3JE 0161 204 3333

"A beautiful space filled with beautiful people (yes, Manchester has them too!)" – D&D London's 19th-floor newcomer at the top of No 1 Spinningfields, "has stunning views of the city and a soundtrack to match" (and also a "fabulous outside terrace"). But "as well as being a see-and-be-seen destination, it's a genuinely great restaurant", and although the odd doubter feels "it's not sure what it's trying to be, top class restaurant or destination bar" or says "its London backers have brought London prices to Manchester" – on most accounts Aiden Byrne's "very accessible" cuisine is repeating the success he found at Manchester House. STOP PRESS: In November 2018, just as it was all going so well, it was announced that Aiden Byrne has stepped down, for reasons that are not yet clear. / 20stories.co.uk; @20StoriesMCR; Sun-Thu midnight, Fri & Sat 2 am.

UMEZUSHI £44 533

UNIT 4, MIRABEL STREET M3 1PJ 0871 811 8877

"Tucked away, but highly worth hunting out" – this "minuscule restaurant (17 covers) built into railway arches" below Victoria station again wins rave reviews for its "amazing Japanese food" – including "incredible quality sushi and sashimi" and "stunning wagyu beef". "If you're not sure what to order, ask the waiters to build a meal for you"; better still, go for the day's tasting menu – but you'll have to book and pay in advance. / www.umezushi.co.uk; @Umezushi_M31PJ; Wed & Thu 9.30 pm, Fri & Sat 10.30 pm, Sun 9 pm; booking max 10 may apply.

WHITWORTH ART GALLERY £30 225

THE UNIVERSITY OF MANCHESTER, OXFORD RD M15 6ER 0161 275 7511

With a "pleasant outlook through the glass walls… even if you are in Moss Side", the Whitworth's "very friendly, well-run" café addendum makes a "wonderful setting for a tasty lunch or late breakfast". / www.whitworth.manchester.ac.uk; @WhitworthArt; Mon-Wed, Fri-Sun 5 pm, Thu 9 pm; booking evening only.

WING'S £48 454

1 LINCOLN SQ M2 5LN 0161 834 9000

"Daintier dishes than in more traditional Chinese restaurants, but of superb quality" help draw the smart crowd to Wing Shing Chu's "elegant" city-centre Cantonese, praised in particular for its "immaculate service". It's "certainly not a cheap choice", but there are no complaints about the prices. "We alternate the banquets and are never disappointed". / www.wingsrestaurant.co.uk; Mon-Sat midnight, Sun 11 pm; children: 11+ after 8 pm Mon-Fri.

WOOD RESTAURANT £66

JACK ROSENTHAL STREET M15 4RA 0161 236 5211

MasterChef winner, Simon Wood's newcomer is to be found a short walk from Home Manchester – a glass-fronted open-kitchen style operation in the up-and-coming First Street development. Too limited feedback as yet for a rating, but its hearty modern British fare won it one of six nominations as 'Top Newcomer' as part of the Manchester Food and Drink Festival Awards 2018. / www.woodmanchester.com/; @woodrestaurants.

YANG SING £42 423

34 PRINCESS STREET M1 4JY 0161 236 2200

Many of Manchester's most discerning foodies "still reckon this is the best Chinese in town", but Harry & Bonnie Yeung's famous Chinatown destination suffers from bouts of "inconsistency" nowadays. Some reporters have experienced this up-and-down quality first hand ("can be very good, but can also be like a bog-standard takeaway"). Some just sense it ("I personally have had very few even slightly disappointing meals here, but you do hear a few too many reports of unsatisfactory visits to recommend it with absolute confidence"). But actually most feedback is still just unconditionally in favour of its cuisine ("still the best…", "back on top form…", "an old favourite that never fails…") even if there's an acknowledgement that when it comes to the setting, "it seems nowhere near as busy as it used to be, so, certainly at dim

Buoy & Oyster, Margate

sum times it lacks the buzzy atmosphere it used to have". A fair final summary from one aficionado runs as follows: "I do know that Yang Sing is much better than its critics make out. It strikes a better balance between serving authentic Chinese food and catering to English tastes than its local competitors; and while it is more expensive than some the food is in my experience still worth it". / www.yang-sing.com; @yangsingmcr; Mon - Thur 11.30 pm, Fri 11.45 pm, Sat 12.15 am, S.

YUZU £41 533

39 FAULKNER ST M1 4EE 0161 236 4159

"Accomplished and delicious Japanese cuisine at very sensible prices" isn't easy to find – especially in Chinatown – but this "little gem" of a corner spot on the edge of this area is the exception, seeming to "set itself apart from the humdrum"; "there's no sushi, but the rice in the don bowls is better than all the sushi restaurants I've been to in the UK". / www.yuzumanchester.co.uk; @yuzumanchester; 9.30 pm; closed Mon & Sun.

MANNINGTREE, ESSEX 3–2C

LUCCA ENOTECA £34 343

39-43 HIGH ST CO11 1AH 01206 390044

"Manningtree is spoilt to have such a well run, genuine pizzeria" according to a Shepherds Bush-based fan of this local Italian, from the owners of the nearby Mistley Thorn: an "absolute gem" that's achieved consistently good ratings for five years now. / www.luccafoods.co.uk; @LuccaEnoteca; Mon-Sun 11 pm.

MARAZION, CORNWALL 1–4A

BEN'S CORNISH KITCHEN £54 543

WEST END TR17 0EL 01736 719200

Ben and Jayne Prior's "top quality" seaside bistro again won a hymn of praise this year on all fronts – not least for its "first-rate" cooking ("brilliant fish" in particular) and for its "unbeatable value". / www.benscornishkitchen.com; @cornishkitchen; Tue-Sat 10.30 pm.

MARGATE, KENT 3–3D

THE AMBRETTE £58 433

10 FORT HILL CT9 1QE 01843 231 504

"Simply amazing", agree fans of Dev Biswal's Margate flagship: "the best Indian/Asian fusion restaurant ever", which has now moved from King Street into roomier premises on Fort Hill, near the Turner Contemporary gallery. The "beautifully crafted, quality spiced food is not at all like a bog-standard Indian" – and represents "astonishing value", especially for lunch. Founded in 2010, it now has offshoots in Canterbury and Rye. / www.theambrette.co.uk; @the_ambrette; Mon-Thu 9.30 pm, Fri & Sat 10 pm, Sun 8.30 pm.

BAY AT SANDS, SANDS HOTEL £57 344

CT9 1DH 01843 228228

Despite some teething problems after chef Eddy Seys' 2017 arrival, all is now well at this "sophisticated" hotel restaurant "brightening up the almost derelict" high street, and with "a grandstand view of the lovely beach and sunset"; readers will be happy to know that the lunch menu is "now reinstated". / www.sandshotelmargate.co.uk; @SandsHotelMarga; Mon-Sun 9 pm.

BUOY & OYSTER £53 443

44 HIGH STREET CT9 1DS 01843 446631

"A lovely new addition to Margate", "this light and airy bistro tucked off the High Street has wonderful views out over the Sands and out to sea (and a great balcony terrace for fine-weather dining)". It's family-run by the "passionate owners", who use "high-quality ingredients" – "go for the deceptively simple-sounding fish dishes". / www.buoyandoyster.com; @BuoyandOyster.

GB PIZZA £33 442

14A MARINE DRIVE CT9 1DH 01843 297 700

"Inventive toppings on a super crust" result in "expertly created pizzas" at this "superb" small operation on the sea-front. It's not super-comfy though: "amenities are basic" and some of the seating is "cramped and awkward". / www.greatbritishpizza.com; @gbPizzaCo; Tue-Sat 10.30 pm, Sun 10 pm.

HANTVERK & FOUND £43 343

18 KING STREET CT9 1DA 01843 280 454

"Tiny" and "quirky" this cupboard-sized eatery and gallery may be, but no one doubts its "delicious food", not least the "terrific fresh fish" it specialises in. / www.hantverk-found.co.uk; @Hantverk_found; Fri & Sat 10 pm, Thu 9.30 pm, Sun 4 pm.

POST OFFICE £33

22-23 CECIL SQUARE CT9 1BA 01843 210116

It's hard not to admire the ambition of this swanky newcomer – the conversion of the town's former, listed post office into a glossy, contemporary brasserie that's at odds with the slightly downbeat milieu of the location. It got off to a rocky start ("a beautiful room let down by poor cooking, indifferent service and outrageous prices"); post-survey, they dropped the 'Old' from the name (i.e. it was formerly 'The Old Post Office') and simplified the formula. / postofficemargate.com; @TOPOMargate; Wed-Sat 11 pm, Sun 4 pm.

ASCOUGH'S
BISTRO   £41   3 3 2

**24 ST MARY'S ROAD LE16 7DU
01858 466 966**

"A bit of an oasis in this town" – this contemporary town-centre brasserie offers "tasty and well-cooked food from a wide and reasonably priced menu". Its "barn like premises can seem a bit cold at times", but mostly they appear "busy and friendly". / www.ascoughsbistro.co.uk/; 9.00pm.

THE HARROW AT LITTLE
BEDWYN   £92   5 5 4

LITTLE BEDWYN SN8 3JP 01672 870871

"A beautiful selection of wines complement the cuisine" at Sue & Roger's "converted pub in the middle of nowhere" (he is a well-known wine expert), but the "glorious" cooking is far from incidental and the whole set-up has a "lovely, very welcoming and friendly atmosphere". Why Michelin decided to take their star away in October 2018 is anyone's guess, but is not borne out to any extent by the "brilliant" rep it receives in our diners' survey. Top Tip: "the food and wine pairing events, which showcase Roger's skills with some standout pairings". / www.theharrowatlittlebedwyn.co.uk; @littlebedwyn; 9 pm; closed Mon, Tue & Sun; no trainers; credit card deposit required to book.

RICK STEIN   £59   3 4 3

**LLORAN HOUSE, 42A HIGH STREET SN8
1HQ 01672 233333**

"It's now a regular favourite", say fans of this two-year-old in the high street from the globe-trotting TV chef, who feel his "elegant, upmarket brasserie" is proving "a splendid addition to Marlborough's eateries". But while fans say "the food is always good, and the staff young and excellent" some support is more nuanced: "reasonably priced, food was good but not memorable". / www.rickstein.com/eat-with-us/marlborough/; @SteinMarlb; Mon-Sat 10 pm, Sun 9 pm.

THE COACH   £50   4 4 4

3 WEST STREET SL7 2LS 01628 483013

"Turn up early as there's no booking" at Tom Kerridge's 'other' place in town. Spared the Michelin-fuelled expectations of its older sibling perhaps allows its virtues to shine all the brighter: "the food is well thought-out and well executed", service is "friendly" and although it can become "hectic" it "is well worth the wait". Top Tip: "they also do fantastic breakfasts, especially the Kedgeree". / www.thecoachmarlow.co.uk; @TheCoachMarlow; Tue-Sat 9.30 pm; no bookings.

HAND &
FLOWERS   £89   3 2 3

WEST STREET SL7 2BP 01628 482277

"Two stars????" – Tom Kerridge's renowned (because of Michelin) destination is "a nice pub with very good food but it's not up to the incredibly high standards that the French tyre company seem to think it merits" and consequently can appear "way over-hyped". A fair number of reporters do indeed experience "magnificent cooking" ("so many things on the menu that you're dying to eat") delivered with "warm-heartedness, of a kind not given in most London eateries"; and in an "atmospheric setting, which remains like a gastropub despite the awards". But, perhaps because TK has been distracted by his launch in the capital, the gulf between expectations and reality grew noticeably this year, and for a significant proportion of diners it now merely seems like "an adequate but unexceptional meal at a very inflated price"; or at worse "tremendously disappointing and truly bad". / www.thehandandflowers.co.uk; @HandFMarlow; Mon-Sat 9.30 pm, Sun 2.30 pm. *Accommodation:* 4 rooms, from £140

THE IVY MARLOW
GARDEN   £56   2 1 4

66-68 HIGH ST SL7 1AH 01628 902 777

"A touch of London glamour in the Thames Valley" – this "convivial" and "always busy" outpost of Richard Caring's brand is one of the most commented-on in the survey, and many reporters do see it as a "lovely" spot ("you'd never believe that it used to be a shoe shop from the stylish interior"); and "a good addition to the ever-increasing Marlow foodie scene". Characteristically for this brand extension however, there are also many who report "such a disappointing experience: I've persevered four times and each time the service was as bad as the first (which I first put down to teething problems) – shame as it is indeed a beautiful spot". There are also a worrying number of reports where the food experience was plain "poor"… "uneatable" even. / www.theivymarlowgarden.com; @iymarlowgarden; Mon-Sun 12.30 am.

SINDHU, MACDONALD
COMPLEAT ANGLER
HOTEL   £68   4 4 4

**THE COMPLEAT ANGLER SL7 1RG
01628 405 405**

"It's almost worth going for lunch (or in summer) just so you can see the view" at this "gloriously situated venue, overlooking the Thames at Marlow". In defiance of its uninspired culinary history, though, Atul Kochhar's nouvelle Indian operation is about much more than merely the picturesque landscape – "just brilliant", with "subtle layered flavours, beautifully presented". / www.sindhurestaurant.co.uk; @SindhuMarlow; Mon-Sat 10 pm, Sun 9.30 pm.

THE VANILLA
POD   £73   5 4 3

31 WEST ST SL7 2LS 01628 898101

"A model of consistency, value and great taste" – Michael Macdonald's "small and beautifully formed hidden gem" – "a quiet, old timbered room, looking onto a garden" – wins practically nothing but rapturous feedback: "a most wonderful experience" providing "fine dining at reasonable prices" where "everything is outstanding". Top Tip: "good value for lunch with a choice of well-balanced set menus". / www.thevanillapod.co.uk; 10 pm; closed Mon & Sun.

ANGKOR SOUL   £36   4 4 3

**12 STOCKPORT RD SK6 6BJ
0161 222 0707**

"Amazing Cambodian food", "delicately flavoured in generous portions" means that "booking is essential, even at lunchtime" at this "small cafe-style room next to an independent cinema", in a leafy, small town outside Manchester (named for the stack of vinyl in the basement, which you can peruse if you're a fan). "Traditional lunchtime pub grub of soup and a sandwich is transformed by Cambodian flavours into spicy soup and well-filled baguettes (with coconut reigning supreme)". The evening menu is a little longer. If you're over Altrincham way they opened a new branch there in late summer 2018. Top Menu Tip: "try the amazing black rice pudding". / www.angkorsoul.co.uk; @angkor_soul; Wed-Sat 11 pm, Tue 3 pm.

LA POPOTE   £59   4 5 3

**CHURCH FARM, MANCHESTER ROAD SK11
9HF 01260 224785**

This "French-style bistro" is a "real find in a small Cheshire village", with a "varied menu of high-quality dishes" backed up by "wonderful and very professional silver service". Proprietors Victor Janssen, a Dutch-born chef, and his Scottish wife Lynne ran award-winning restaurants in South Africa for decades, and are now cooking what they like best. Top Tip: "go on a themed evening with live (but not intrusive) music". / la-popote.co.uk; Mon-Sat 9.30 pm, Sun 4 pm.

SAMUEL'S, SWINTON PARK
HOTEL & SPA   £87   4 4 5

SWINTON PARK HG4 4JH 01765 680900

"A lovely, spacious dining room in a lovely hotel" – a spectacular country pile, which added an £8m country club and spa in June 2018, and is just the spot for "old-fashioned luxury" – "proper fine food with polite but not subservient service". New chef (since mid 2017) Mehdi Amiri has maintained the "exceptional" standards; only quibble: dainty portion sizes means one or two "leave hungry". (There's also a new dining option here at the club: The Terrace). / www.swintonestate.com/eating; @swintonestate; Wed-Sun 9.30 pm; no jeans;

children: 8+ at D. *Accommodation:* 31 rooms, from £31

THE POET　　£50　443

MAIDSTONE RD TN12 7JH 01892 722416

This "fantastic gem" – a "beautiful 17th-century Kentish village pub", complete with wooden beams – "features some pretty stellar cooking for such an informal venue". Petrus Madutlela is a "South African chef who brings some twists and fresh ideas" to the kitchen, and his "relatively limited, gradually evolving menu provides wonderfully accomplished cuisine". "Well worth a detour". / @poetatmatfield; Tue-Thu 9 pm, Fri & Sat 9.30 pm, Sun 4 pm.

STONES　　£53　454

1C DALE RD DE4 3LT 01629 56061

The Stone family's stalwart "exudes class", from its "lovely setting" on the coursing River Derwent ("the terrace is ideal for warm summer days"), to its "just brilliant" and "very well thought-out" food – coming "at a fraction of the cost of top-end restaurants". / www.stones-restaurant.co.uk; @stonesmatlock; Tue-Thu 10 pm, Fri & Sat 10.30 pm, Sun 4 pm; no Amex; no shorts.

THE SCARLET HOTEL　　£69　345

TREDRAGON RD TR8 4DQ 01637 861800

"Romance personified" – the restaurant at a beach-side spa hotel "takes some beating on a summer's evening at sunset". The cooking is well above-par, and "the chef caters for specialised diets with flair and imagination". / www.scarlethotel.co.uk; Mon-Sat 9.30 pm, Sun 4 pm.

MIDDLE HOUSE　　£45　333

HIGH STREET TN20 6AB 01435 872146

You'll find "excellent food" – much of it locally sourced pub classics at surprisingly good "value for money" – at this Grade 1-listed, wood-framed Elizabethan inn dominating the high street of a historic village (built as a private house for Sir Thomas Gresham, Elizabeth I's banker). In 2018 they added a new extension: "a welcome addition with a London feel to the cooler section of the established restaurant". / www.themiddlehousemayfield.co.uk; Mon-Sat 9.30 pm, Sun 4 pm.

DYLAN'S RESTAURANT　　£50　334

ST GEORGE'S ROAD LL59 5EY 01248 716 714

A "beautiful setting" with "excellent views" of the Menai Straits is the backdrop to a meal at this "busy and reliable" wine-bar style operation: a "friendly" venue with "competent cooking" (burgers, pizzas, salads, plus more ambitious dishes). Also now with spin-offs in Criccieth, and, most recently, Llandudno. / www.dylansrestaurant.co.uk; @dylanspizzeria; 10 pm .

SOSBAN AND THE OLD BUTCHERS　　£115　543

1 HIGH ST, MENAI BRIDGE LL59 5EE 01248 208 131

"Perfection on a plate" – Stephen and Bethan Stevens's converted old butchers shop on the Isle of Anglesey has won culinary fame (including from the Tyre Men) for its menus created based on availability on any given day: "a fantastic 'surprise' using ingredients married together that you wouldn't always expect but work perfectly. Steve and Bethan work wonderfully together – one of the highlights is to see Steve putting together the dishes on the pass". / www.sosbanandtheoldbutchers.com; @The_oldbutchers; Mon-Sun 10.30 pm.

VERVEINE FISHMARKET RESTAURANT　　£64　543

98 HIGH ST SO41 0QE 01590 642 176

Chef David Wykes has earned a glowing reputation for his "calm" dining room with open kitchen behind a fishmonger – "one of those restaurants you're continually looking for an excuse or reason to return to" with "outstanding" preparation of fish. / www.verveine.co.uk; @98verveine; 9.30 pm; closed Mon & Sun; no Amex.

HARE　　£49　344

3 HIGH STREET OX7 6LA 01993 835 763

On a continuing upswing since turnaround queen Sue Hawkins (of Bar Humbug fame) took it over in 2016, a stone Cotswold pub where chef Matt Dare delivers daily changing marine cuisine. The piano-turned-cutlery sideboard was such a hit that they now sell it. / www.themiltonhare.co.uk; @themiltonhare; Mon-Sat 11 pm, Sun 10.30 pm.

THE MISTLEY THORN RESTAURANT & ROOMS　　£42　333

HIGH ST CO11 1HE 01206 392 821

This "beautifully restored" coastal gastroboozer-with-rooms is "a cool place to visit" with a history "worth investigating" (revolving around the Witchfinder General). "Superb local produce, especially fish and seafood, are accurately and unfussily cooked" by chef-patron Sherri Singleton, who also runs a cookery school. / www.mistleythorn.com; @mistleythorn; 9.30 pm. *Accommodation:* 11 rooms, from £100

WINE AND BRINE　　£58　443

59 MAIN ST BT67 0LQ 028 9261 0500

Great British Menu star Chris McGowan has brought a bit of glitter (and a slew of awards) to the main street of town with this three-year-old operation. The local food, often brined or fermented (hence the name) is "great quality"; the other headline event – "very drinkable". / www.wineandbrine.co.uk; @wine_brine; Wed-Sat 9.30 pm, Sun 6 pm.

CHECKERS　　£88

BROAD ST, POWYS SY15 6PN 01686 669 822

After eighteen years, the Shropshire and Mid-Wales region has lost its last star – or handed it back, after Checkers chef Stéphane Borie opted to focus on private clients. Under the aegis of his wife Sarah Francis and her co-owner sister Kathryn, a more casual breakfast and lunch spot, Checkers Pantry, was due to open in November 2018; it was too early for a rating as we went to press. / www.checkerswales.co.uk; @checkerswales; 9 pm; closed Mon, Tue L, Wed L, Thu L & Sun; no Amex; children: 8+ at D. *Accommodation:* 5 rooms, from £125

MIDLAND HOTEL　　£52　445

MARINE ROAD WEST LA4 4BU 01524 424000

The "stunning view across Morecambe Bay" certainly adds to the magic of this "real gem" of an art deco hotel – "well worth a detour from the motorway" (the A863). Unusually, the food actually lives up to the backdrop, and it remains particularly reputed for its "superb, well balanced afternoon tea". / www.englishlakes.co.uk; @englishlakes; Mon-Sat 9.30 pm, Sun 9 pm. *Accommodation:* 44 rooms, from £94

THE FOX INN　　£45　323

LOWER ODDINGTON GL56 0UR 01451 870 862

"A lovely quintessential pub" – this smartly refurbished Cotswold stone inn sits three miles from Stow-on-the-Wold. "Reliable" cooking ("not your normal pub grub, so nice to see things like rabbit on the menu") and "decent real ales" complete the picture. / www.thefoxinnbroadwell.com; @foxinn; on A436 near Stow-on-the-Wold; Mon-Thu 9 pm, Fri & Sat 9.30 pm, Sun 8.30 pm; no Amex. *Accommodation:* 3 rooms, from £85

ANCHOR INN　　£48　433

THE STREET NR25 7AA 01263 741392

"Fresh fine fish and local food served in a cosy yet efficient old building", which is popular with bird-watchers and other visitors to the north

Norfolk coast. "It's exceptional every time", say fans of the pub, which was gutted and refurbished when the current owners took over a few years ago. / www.morstonanchor.co.uk; @morstonanchor.

MORSTON HALL £109 5 4 5

MAIN COAST RD NR25 7AA 01263 741041

A "magical" hideaway in rural Norfolk – Galton Blackiston's "elegant" country house hotel, in a marvellous location near the coast, seemingly "just gets better and better", delivering "very special" cuisine ("balanced, fresh, clean-tasting and flavoursome"), served in a single sitting nightly from "an immaculate, set seven-course menu that changes daily". Many who report were staying over too, and certainly don't tire of the experience of eating in: "four wonderful dinners over four consecutive nights that didn't put a foot wrong". "There's a large wine list at all prices. Service is classy. It's excellent in every way". / www.morstonhall.com; @MorstonHall; between Blakeney & Wells on A149; Sun-Thu 9 pm, Fri & Sat 9.30 pm. *Accommodation:* 13 rooms, from £330

MOSELEY, WEST MIDLANDS 5–4C

DAMASCENA £17 4 3 3

133 ALCESTER ROAD B13 8JP
0121 449 9245

"Delicious Middle Eastern food at incredibly reasonable prices" will "lift your spirits with the fresh tastes of mint, lemon and pomegranate" at this four-year-old, which has already sprouted two branches. "Don't be fooled into thinking it's just a coffee house" – although "the spiced Arabian coffee with dates and tahini is very moreish!". / damascena.co.uk; @Damascena_UK; Mon-Thu 9 pm, Fri & Sat 10 pm, Sun 6 pm.

SABAI SABAI £48 3 3 3

25 WOODBRIDGE ROAD B13 8EH
0121 449 4498

Torquil and Juree Chidwick's original restaurant and wine bar of their local mini-chain – this Moseley fifteen-year-old provides a simple but effective Thai formula. / sabaisabai-restaurant.co.uk; @SabaiSabai1; Mon-Sat 10 pm, Sun 9 pm.

MOULTON, CAMBRIDGESHIRE 3–1C

THE PACKHORSE INN £55 3 2 3

BRIDGE ST CB8 8SP 01638 751818

A "little gem in a quiet village", this "great traditional inn has a wide choice of home-cooked food and bar snacks", which most (if not quite all) reporters rate as "interesting" and "delicious". / www.thepackhorseinn.com; @Moultopackhorse; Sun-Thu 11 pm, Fri & Sat midnight.

MOUNTSORREL, LEICESTERSHIRE 5–3D

JOHN'S HOUSE £83 5 4 3

139-141 LOUGHBOROUGH ROAD LE12 7AA
01509 415569

"A real treat!". Chef John Duffin returned to the family farm five years ago to open his widely acclaimed first restaurant, producing "brilliant accessible food in a house attached to a farm shop and petting zoo in an unprepossessing village". "The taster menu is worth every penny – a must do", while "lunch is a steal". / www.johnshouse.co.uk; @JohnsHouseRest; Mon closed; Tue - Sat 9 pm; Sun closed.

MOUSEHOLE, CORNWALL 1–4A

THE OLD COASTGUARD £35 4 3 4

THE PARADE TR19 6PR 01736 731222

In a "simply perfect spot" gazing out to sea and St Michael's Mount, this hotel dining room "has gone through many variations", but has clearly settled into its stride under the Gurnard's Head team. The "mainly locally sourced" (fish-slanted) food is "melt in the mouth". / www.oldcoastguardhotel.co.uk; @leroundhouse; Mon-Sun 9 pm. *Accommodation:* 20 rooms, from £170

2 FORE STREET RESTAURANT £46 4 4 3

2 FORE ST TR19 6PF 01736 731164

"What a find!" – a relaxed cottage-bound establishment offering "excellent food at very reasonable prices" ("no wonder it's so busy!") – as you'd expect the focus is strongly on fish. / www.2forestreet.co.uk; Wed-Sat, Tue 9 pm, Sun 3 pm. *Accommodation:* 2 rooms, from £250

MUDEFORD, DORSET 2–4C

NOISY LOBSTER £51 3 3 3

BH23 4AN 01425 272162

"Part of a small South Coast chain", and enjoying a stellar beachfront position, this unassuming red-brick eatery elicits praise for its "consistent cooking" (with seafood unsurprisingly in the star role); a first-floor extension with a bar is currently in the works. / avon-beach.noisylobster.co.uk/; @thenoisylobster; Mon-Sat 11 pm, Sun 5 pm.

MURCOTT, OXFORDSHIRE 2–1D

THE NUT TREE INN £82 4 4 3

MAIN STREET OX5 2RE 01865 331253

Local boy Michael North and his wife Imogen's "cosy thatched pub" has made a real name for itself in the past dozen years for its "consistently great food for a reasonable price". Still a real pub, serving the house Nut Tree ale, it serves everything from bar snacks to a "fantastic tasting menu paired with exciting wine choices" – while "a candlelit dinner by the open fire makes for romance". Set in a small village, it's hardly remote: the M40 – and Bicester shopping village – are just a few minutes away by car. /

Morston Hall, Morston

www.nuttreeinn.co.uk; @nuttreeinn/; Mon-Sat 9 pm, Sun 3 pm; booking max 4 may apply.

MUTHILL, PERTH AND KINROSS 9–3C

BARLEY BREE £67 3 3 2

6 WILLOUGHBY ST PH5 2AB 01764 681451

Just down the road from Gleneagles, Fabrice & Alison Bouteloup's smart-rustic restaurant-with-rooms serves "delicious and comforting" Gallic food; "Fabrice is also a very good baker", hence the "amazing" bread. / www.barleybree.com; @barleybree6; Mon-Sat 9.30 pm, Sun 3 pm; no Amex. *Accommodation:* 6 rooms, from £110

NAILSWORTH, GLOUCESTERSHIRE 2–2B

WILD GARLIC £51 4 4 2

3 COSSACKS SQ GL6 0DB 01453 832615

Matthew Bearshall's bistro with five rooms is "a wonderful place with interesting, skilled cooking and seasonal, locally sourced ingredients". There remains the odd sceptic for whom it's lost some impetus since the launch of nearby spin-off Wilder, with its surprise 8-course tasting menus, but that's not reflected in its high overall marks. / www.wild-garlic.co.uk; @TheWildGarlic; Wed-Sat 9.30 pm, Sun 2.30 pm; no Amex. *Accommodation:* 3 rooms, from £90

NANTGAREDIG, CARMARTHENSHIRE 4–4C

Y POLYN £58 4 3 4

CAPEL DEWI SA32 7LH 01267 290000

"People are prepared to drive miles to visit this very popular (and deservedly so) rural Welsh restaurant". It "never disappoints": the "excellent" cooking is ambitious but without pretension; and the service "professional" but relaxed ("you get to pour your own wine"). / www.ypolyn.co.uk; @PolyNation; Tue-Thu 9 pm, Fri & Sat 9.30 pm, Sun 2.30 pm.

NETHER BURROW, CUMBRIA 7–4D

THE HIGHWAYMAN £48 3 3 3

BURROW LA6 2RJ 01524 273 338

The ever-growing Brunning & Price empire snapped up this "favourite pub in the Lune Valley area" in spring 2018 (as well as three other Ribble Valley Inns), with ex-owners Northcote opting to focus on the rest of their portfolio, including the famous hotel. /

www.highwaymaninn.co.uk; @highwayman_inn;
Mon & Tue, Thu-Sat 11 pm, Sun 10.30 pm, Wed
11.30 pm.

THE FEATHERED NEST INN £96 5 3 4

OX7 6SD 01993 833 030

"Sublime food" in the "breathtaking
surroundings" of an "exceptional inn in idyllic
Cotswold countryside". Polish-born Kuba
Winkowski, the Craft Guild of Chefs 2018
'chef of the year', wins universal praise for his
"wonderful" repertoire of dishes, which includes
sturgeon with caviar and fennel. It is, though,
"eye-wateringly pricey" – "perhaps even more
expensive than London, but worth it if you're
feeling flush". / www.thefeatherednestinn.co.uk;
@FeatheredNestIn; Thu-Sun 9.30 pm.
Accommodation: 4 rooms, from £150

CHEWTON GLEN £84 3 3 4

**CHEWTON GLEN RD BH23 5QL
01425 282212**

A "great and stately environment" is provided in
spades by this famously luxurious country hotel,
set in 130 acres on the fringes of Bournemouth.
Culinarily speaking, it's best known for its
"unbeatable" wine list "to match the setting",
but Luke Matthews's cuisine is solidly supported
too, even if there is a perennial complaint in
some quarters that it is "hugely overpriced".
/ www.chewtonglen.com; @chewtonglen; on A337
between New Milton & Highcliffe; 10 pm; no trainers.
Accommodation: 70 rooms, from £325

THE KITCHEN AT CHEWTON GLEN £86 4 4 4

**CHEWTON FARM ROAD BH23 5QL
01425 275341**

"Surprisingly fab burgers" are a highlight at
the year-old, casual dining destination of this
famously luxurious country house hotel, which
is part of a purpose-built cookery school run in
association with James Martin. Other items on
the menu branded with the name of the former
'Saturday Kitchen' chef include pizza, chargrills
and salads. / www.chewtonglen.com/thekitchen/;
@TheKitchenatCG; Mon-Sat 9.30 pm.

THE MARRAM GRASS £49 4 3 3

WHITE LODGE LL61 6RS 01248 440 077

"In a lovely Anglesey setting", this nowadays
well-known conversion of a potting shed
(on the family's caravan park) is a "quirky
set-up" but one well worth discovering for its
"wonderful, locally sourced tasting menu"
(with eight courses, although there is also a
three-course option). Next Stop for owners Liam
and Ellis Barrie is a new venture in the Albert
Dock, Liverpool. / www.themarramgrass.com;
@TheMarramGrass; Fri-Sun, Mon-Thu 9 pm.

ARIGATO £44 4 3 4

**1 BRIDGE STREET RG14 5BE
01635 580015**

"Delightful Japanese food in the centre of
Newbury" is the prospect offered by this
2017 newcomer in a Georgian building next
to the river, where an ex-Nobu chef serves
"freshly made sushi and sashimi and a wide
variety of mainly Japanese main courses". /
www.arigatodining.co.uk; @ArigatoDining; Tue-Sat
9.30 pm, Sun 4 pm.

THE WOODSPEEN £63 4 4 4

LAMBOURN RD RG20 8BN 01635 265 070

John Campbell's "open and airy" modernised
ex-pub not far from Newbury "has great
interior design", sits in a "delightful countryside
location" and is establishing itself as a major
destination, especially considering that "it's
in the middle of nowhere". It offers "an
excellent all-round experience" with "clever,
but not too clever food that's skilfully cooked
and good value"; "outstanding cocktails (both
alcoholic and non-alcoholic)"; and "superb
wine (with "unusual options from countries
such as Turkey"). / www.thewoodspeen.com;
@thewoodspeen; Mon-Sat 10 pm, Sun 5 pm.

ADRIANOS £46 3 3 3

90 HIGH STREET NE3 1HB 0191 284 6464

This "superb local Italian" is "a lovely
restaurant off the High Street", well-rated for
its "authentic" Sardinian-influenced food and
"staff who look as if they enjoy working here".
/ www.adrianos.co.uk; Mon-Wed 9 pm, Fri & Sat 10
pm, Thu 9.30 pm, Sun 6 pm.

ARTISAN, THE BISCUIT FACTORY £56 3 3 2

STODDARD ST NE2 1AN 0191 260 5411

"Andrew Wilkinson consistently produces meals
bursting with flavour from first rate, locally
sourced, ingredients" in the "unique setting"
of this converted Victorian warehouse (part of
the UK's largest arts and crafts galleries): "a
banker of a restaurant, with interesting monthly
tasting menus and 'fish Friday' options". /
www.artisannewcastle.com; @artisan_NE; Wed-Sat
9.30 pm, Sun 3.30 pm.

BLACKFRIARS RESTAURANT £60 3 3 3

FRIARS ST NE1 4XN 0191 261 5945

"Reliable food, locally sourced served in
an ancient setting" (a 13th-century friary
refectory that claims to be the oldest
dining room in the UK) wins praise for
Andy Hook's "recently refurbished" (last
year) 'Restaurant & Banqueting Hall'. /
www.blackfriarsrestaurant.co.uk; @BlackfriarsRest;
Mon-Sat 10 pm, Sun 4 pm.

BROAD CHARE £49 3 3 3

25 BROAD CHARE NE1 3DQ 019 1211 2144

This brilliant pub is "small but just what is
needed" on the Quayside, and is one of the
most commented-on destinations in town.
"There's a great choice of cask ales and
interesting bar food during the day" (top
quality small dishes supplemented by daily
specials). "Upstairs the bustling restaurant
serves clientele from surrounding businesses
and the law courts (or visiting Live Theatre next
door)". "Simple pub grub is done with love". /
www.thebroadchare.co.uk; @_thebroadchare; Mon-
Sat 10 pm, Sun 5 pm; no Amex.

CAFÉ ROYAL £49 3 2 3

8 NELSON ST NE1 5AW 0191 231 3000

With its "wonderfully elegant" Georgian
architecture and tall windows, this "very
popular" café bistro is a "nice spot to read the
paper and have breakfast" (the former provided
on Sundays), but also to sample the "delicious"
Mediterranean food or splash out on an
afternoon tea. / www.sjf.co.uk; @caferoyalsjf; Mon-
Sat 10 pm, Sun 5 pm; booking weekdays only.

CAL'S OWN £36 4 4 3

**1-2 HOLLY AVENUE WEST NE2 2AR
0191 281 5522**

Jesmond-born Calvin Kitchin and his brother
Kerry have achieved cult status amongst fans
for their "authentic Neapolitan pizza, with no
frills", which has earned Associazione Verace
Pizza Napoletana accreditation – one of only
two awarded in Britain. / www.calsown.co.uk;
@cals_own; Wed & Thu 10.30 pm, Fri & Sat 9.30 pm,
Sun 9 pm.

CHILLI PADI £27 4 3 3

**8-10 LEAZES PARK ROAD NE1 4PF
0191 230 1133**

"Top Malaysian food" plus the ability to BYO,
both win praise for this simple, "cheap 'n'
cheerful" city-centre spot, which makes a feature
of a selection of clay pot dishes. / www.chilli-padi.
co.uk.

DABBAWAL £36 4 3 3

**1 BRENTWOOD MEWS NE2 3DG
0191 281 3434**

The home-style Indian street food can be "out
of this world" at this quirky, colourful Jesmond
sibling to the city-centre HQ, and preferred to
the original by some; fans can't get enough –
and "even get take-outs from here now" (well it
is named after Bombay's proto-Deliveroo lunch-
delivery men). / www.dabbawal.com; @Dabbawal.

DABBAWAL £38 4 3 3

**69-75 HIGH BRIDGE NE1 6BX
0191 232 5133**

"Head and shoulders above your ordinary curry
house" – with "palate-zinging" but also "delicate
and original" dishes – this eleven-year-old street
food pioneer near the Theatre Royal (with an
offshoot in Jesmond) is a "perfect location for

a night on the Toon". "Even the mocktails are fantastic!". / www.dabbawal.com; @dabbawal; Fri-Sun-Wed & Thu 10.30 pm.

DOBSON AND PARNELL £57 434

21 QUEEN ST NE1 3UG 0191 221 0904

On the former site of Café 21 and Pan Haggerty, chef Troy Terrington is turning out contemporary food comparable to owner Andy Hook's other two restaurants – Blackfriars and Hinnies. Service is willing, friendly and not stuffy and matches the ambience of the dining room and the pricing – which, given the quality of cooking, is excellent'. / www.dobsonandparnell.co.uk; @DobsonParnell; Mon-Sat 10 pm.

DOSA KITCHEN £29 433

7 OSBORNE ROAD (REAR) NE2 2AE

"Tucked away in a quiet corner of Jesmond" down an alleyway, this "small" venture is "the new-this-year, permanent home for a very successful former pop-up, specializing in South Indian food". "Fabulous dosas" are the highlight of an "excellent menu". Top Tip: "Sunday Sapaad (Buffet) menu is especially good". / www.dosakitchen.co.uk; @DosaKitchenUK; Tue-Sat 10.30 pm, Sun 9 pm.

FRANCESCA'S £38 344

134 MANOR HOUSE RD NE2 2NE 0191 281 6586

"It's always busy but that only adds to experience" at this "cheap 'n' cheerful", "fantastically buzzy" Italian diner in Jesmond (where there are often queues). "Lovely food and fantastic value for money" ensure high loyalty amongst fans ("I'm still eating here 30 years later"). / www.francesca.com; Mon-Thu 11 pm, Fri & Sat 11.30 pm, Sun 10.30 pm; no Amex; no bookings.

HOUSE OF TIDES £99 435

28-30 THE CLOSE NE1 3RN 0191 2303720

For "an outstanding all-round gastronomic experience" most reporters continue to acclaim Kenny Atkinson's converted sixteenth-century former merchant's townhouse on the Quayside as Newcastle's No. 1 dining destination. / www.houseoftides.co.uk; @houseoftides; Fri, Tue-Thu 3.30 pm, Sat 9 pm; booking max 4 may apply.

JESMOND DENE HOUSE £72 234

JESMOND DENE RD NE2 2EY 0191 212 6066

"A gorgeous spot for a great afternoon selection of treats" or "great-value breakfast": Terry Laybourne's boutique hotel makes a top destination, boosted by its "lovely setting" – "a grand dining room with spectacular views of Jesmond Dene". For a more substantial meal it's recommendable but with reservations: "good, sometimes great, but also often disappointing". / www.jesmonddenehouse.co.uk; @jesmonddenehous;

Mon-Sun 9.30 pm; booking max 7 may apply.
Accommodation: 40 rooms, from £120

PANI'S £31 345

61-65 HIGH BRIDGE NE1 6BX 0191 232 4366

Brothers Roberto & Walter Pani opened their "lovely" and "buzzy" favourite in 1995 – "a great-value Italian venue which rarely disappoints", offering a "varied menu of high-standard" Sardinian and Italian classics. "Staff are very motivated", while last year's "successful refurbishment makes it brighter inside". / www.paniscafe.co.uk; @PanisCafe; 10 pm; closed Sun; no Amex; no bookings at lunch.

PARADISO £43 353

1 MARKET LN NE1 6QQ 0191 221 1240

"You're always welcomed back like long-lost friends" at this "reliable and fun" three-storey operation tucked away in the centre of town. The food is "consistently good" from a predominantly Italo-Mediterranean menu (although there's the odd Thai or North African dish), but the stars of the show are the "wonderful staff" – "and children are adored, especially if they're good eaters!". / www.paradiso.co.uk; @ParadisoNE1; Mon-Thu 10.30 pm, Fri & Sat 10.45 pm.

THE PATRICIA £62 443

139 JESMOND ROAD NE2 1JY 0191 2814443

"Simplicity disguises outstanding cooking" at Nick Grieve's stylish modern bistro in Jesmond, where the menu is pretty short and to the point, but brilliantly well-realised. / @thepatricianci.

PEACE & LOAF £75 444

217 JESMOND ROAD NE2 1LA 0191 281 5222

"Fun and delicious amuse bouche" accompany the "top class taster menu (unpredictable and beautifully prepared)" at Dave Coulson's stylish venue in Jesmond, but there are also a wide variety of à la carte and prix fixe offerings from which to enjoy his deft modern British cuisine. / www.peaceandloaf.co.uk; @peaceandloafjes; Mon-Wed 9 pm, Thu-Sat 9.30 pm, Sun 3.30 pm.

SACHINS £40 333

FORTH BANKS NE1 3SG 0191 261 9035

"The food is always amazing", say fans of this well-known Punjabi curry house near Central Station, run for nearly 20 years by Bob & Neeta Arora. / www.sachins.co.uk; @Sachins_NCL; Mon-Sat 9.30 pm, Sun 2.30 pm.

A TASTE OF PERSIA £31 443

14 MARLBOROUGH CR NE1 4EE 0191 221 0088

Eat like a king amid carpets, cushions and multi-coloured lamps at this "consistently terrific" suburban staple (also with Jesmond sibling); it delivers Persian dishes "full of flavour" in a "very convivial atmosphere". / www.atasteofpersia.com; 10 pm; closed Sun.

21 £57 444

TRINITY GDNS NE1 2HH 0191 222 0755

"Still ranking as the best overall restaurant in town" for many reporters – Terry Laybourne's "consistently excellent" flagship – in several guises and at different addresses since 1988, and still one of the most commented-on destinations in town – "delivers every time", with "exciting and appealing" brasserie-style cuisine and "staff who take a personal interest in customers". "It's as good for a business lunch, as an evening dinner or Sunday lunch". / www.cafetwentyone.co.uk; @21Newcastle; Mon-Sat 10.30 pm, Sun 8 pm.

TYNESIDE COFFEE ROOMS, TYNESIDE CINEMA £31 235

10 PILGRIM ST NE1 6QG 0191 227 5520

A slice of Art Deco history – this "fantastic" café at the UK's last surviving newsreel theatre has been a Newcastle institution for 80 years. It's a "happy place, with a cheerful atmosphere and homely food" – "sometimes just tea and toast is ideal before a film". / www.tynesidecinema.co.uk; Mon-Sat 10 pm, Sun 7 pm; no Amex.

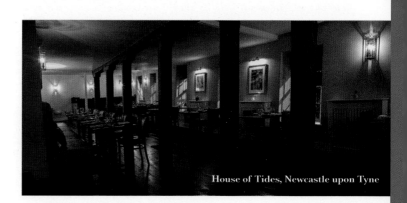

House of Tides, Newcastle upon Tyne

URY £34 `4` `3` `2`

27 QUEEN STREET NE1 3UG
0191 232 7799

Near the iconic bridge, this "authentic" venture (rebranded from popular haunt Rasa in 2015) is "miles apart from the typical provincial curry house", featuring "excellent South Indian food with welcoming, knowledgeable and attentive staff" (many from the old Rasa days). / www.uryrestaurants.com; @UryRestaurants; Sun-Thu 10.30 pm, Fri & Sat 11 pm.

VALLEY JUNCTION 397 £30 `3` `3` `3`

OLD JESMOND STN, ARCHBOLD TER NE2 1DB 0191 281 6397

"In an old signal box joined with an old carriage" – this quirkily located Indian comes heartily recommended by a small but enthusiastic fan club. / www.valleyrestaurants.co.uk; @ValleyRestaura1; near Civic Centre, off Sandyford Rd; 10.30; closed Mon, Fri L & Sun L.

BRUNEL'S £49 `3` `4` `3`

32 DOWNS ROAD BT33 0SG 028 4372 3951

"Since moving to a fab larger premises this wee gem has gone from strength to strength". That's the early feedback on Paul Cunningham's recently relocated rural venue (which moved from being above the nearby Anchor Bar last year): "delicious seasonal cooking from an award-winning chef. One to watch". / www.brunelsrestaurant.co.uk; Mon & Tue, Sun 8 pm, Wed-Sat 9.30 pm.

THE NEWPORT £61 `4` `3` `3`

1 HIGH STREET DD6 8AA 01382 541 449

"I am normally suspicious of places with a magnificent view. However, Jamie Scott's food is tremendous: small plates with a lot of very local ingredients and well worth a visit, even when the Tay is completely fogbound!" – A typically upbeat report on this beautifully situated inn: the AA's Scottish Restaurant of the Year 2018/9. / www.thenewport.co.uk/; Tue-Sat 11.30 pm, Sun 3.30 pm.

THOMPSON'S £72 `5` `4` `4`

11 TOWN LANE PO30 1JU 01983 526118

An "experience not to be missed"; star-strewn young chef Robert Thompson is "really starting to shine through" at his brick-fronted Newport three-year-old – a "warm but chic" open-kitchen concept (upstairs is less cramped) with tasting menus showcasing "an extensive use of fresh, local ingredients" and an "excellent wine list" to match. / www.robertthompson.co.uk; @RThompsonIOW; 11pm.

LLYS MEDDYG £52 `4` `3` `3`

EAST STREET SA42 0SY 01239 820008

"Always a highlight of our trips to the delightful little market town of Newport" – a polished Georgian coaching house in Pembrokeshire Coast National Park, and drawing impressively on the rich local larder. It offers several eating options, from a seasonal al fresco area, to a cellar bar and "romantic" dining room. / www.llysmeddyg.com; @llysmeddyg; 9 pm; D only, closed Sun; no Amex. *Accommodation:* 8 rooms, from £100

BEACHED LAMB £29 `3` `3` `4`

72 FORE STREET TR7 1EY 01637 872297

"Delicious breakfasts" and lunches come "in very cool surroundings" at this chilled, ultra-vibrant café, handy for Fistral and Towan beaches, and they "also do great cake and coffee!" /

THE DAWNAY ARMS £50 `4` `4` `3`

YO30 2BR 01347 848345

Laidback, beamed gastroboozer built in 1779, with a garden stretching down to the River Ouse; chef/owner Martel Smith (an MPW grad) turns out an "interesting" and "consistently delicious" menu (from classics to more adventurous fare) that makes the most of local sourcing. / www.thedawnayatnewton.co.uk; @thedawnayarms; Tue-Sat 9 pm, Sun 4 pm.

THE PARKERS ARMS £44 `5` `4` `4`

HALL GATE HILL BB7 3DY 01200 446236

"Stosie Madi continues to turn out some of the most exciting, most accomplished food in the North" at "this lovely, well-run pub in a pretty village at the edge of the Forest of Bowland", which is "very much worth the trip". There is "superb use of local produce in tasty and often unique ways" (reflecting her half-French, half-Lebanese heritage), and "behind it all, she has a deep understanding of classical (and less classical) techniques, ingredients and how to combine flavours". Top Menu Tips: "game in season is a highlight", as are pies and "anything cooked on the charcoal grill, whether meat or veg". / www.parkersarms.co.uk; @parkersarms; Sun-Fri & Sat 10 pm. *Accommodation:* 4 rooms, from £77

LES MIRABELLES £49 `4` `5` `4`

FOREST EDGE RD SP5 2BN 01794 390205

"Splendid French cuisine using local produce" is on the menu at this well-known Gallic classic with "lovely views across the New Forest". There's also "an interesting wine list selected by the proprietor, Claude – take his advice and you won't be disappointed". / www.lesmirabelles.co.uk; off A36 between Southampton & Salisbury; Mon closed, Tue - Sat 10 pm, Sun closed; no Amex.

NUTTER'S £54 `4` `4` `4`

EDENFIELD ROAD OL12 7TT 01706 650167

"Andrew Nutter is in the kitchen with Mum front of house" at the TV chef's dining room, part of an "imposing" manor house inside "well-tended grounds": "a reliable culinary experience with an exceptional wine list". / www.nuttersrestaurant.com; @nuttersofficial; between Edenfield & Norden on A680; Tue-Thu 9 pm, Fri & Sat 9.30 pm, Sun 8 pm.

CLAVELSHAY BARN £51 `5` `4` `3`

LOWER CLAVELSHAY FARM TA6 6PJ 01278 662629

"A real find tucked away in a fold of the Quantock Hills in darkest Somerset" – "Owner, Sue, makes sure everyone has a great experience" and "serves really excellent food at very reasonable prices" at this venture in a traditional stone barn on her family's dairy farm. / clavelshaybarn.co.uk; Thu-Sat 9 pm, Sun 2.30 pm.

STAITH HOUSE £51 `4` `3` `2`

57 LOW LIGHTS NE30 1JA 0191 270 8441

A "cheerful" nautical-chic pub, "right on the North Shields fish quay" and with predictably "excellent" catch ("but also game sourced locally"). Owner and MasterChef: The Professionals finalist John Calton is on a high, having opened a new bistro, Route, on the Quayside in May 2018. / www.thestaithhouse.co.uk; @Thestaithhouse; Mon-Thu 9 pm, Fri & Sat 9.30 pm, Sun 5 pm; credit card deposit required to book.

WHEATSHEAF INN £60 `2` `3` `4`

WEST END GL54 3EZ 01451 860244

"Very popular" Cotswolds pub in a "pretty village location" that fans say offers a "perfect balance between warm atmosphere and good food", and which has been recently "refurbished and the restaurant extended" as part of the Lucky Onion group, owned by Julian Dunkerton of the Superdry fashion empire. Sceptics feel it's "perfectly pleasant, but fail to see what all the hype is about". / www.cotswoldswheatsheaf.com; @wheatsheafgl54; Mon-Sat 10 pm, Sun 9.30 pm. *Accommodation:* 14 rooms, from £140

BENEDICTS £59 554

**9 ST BENEDICTS ST NR2 4PE
01603 926 080**

With more of a "neighbourhood" vibe than nearby rival Roger Hickman's – Richard Bainbridge's very accomplished venture (which opened in 2015) is likewise extolled by its fan club (which is slightly bigger than its close rival) as "the best restaurant in Norwich by miles, and really deserving of a Michelin star". "Richard and his wife, Katja, have attracted a kitchen brigade and front of house team which oozes slickly-professional but utterly-natural hospitality". Be it from the à la carte, six-course or eight-course tasting menus, "the challenge and interest which comes with each dish is stunning". / www.restaurantbenedicts.com/home; @restbenedicts; just off the city centre (2 doors up from Pizza Express); Tue-Sat 9.15 pm.

FARMYARD £45 444

NR2 4PF 01603733188

"Everything about Farmyard works" – so say fans of Hannah Springham and chef Andrew Jones's popular modern bistro. "The food is always just a little different" with some "slightly odd combinations" but works, and the venue "punches way above its weight". (The couple also now run the Dial House hotel in Reepham). / www.farmyardrestaurant.com; Tues-Thurs 9pm; Fri-Sat 10pm.

THE GUNTON ARMS £52 345

**CROMER RD, THORPE MKT NR11 8TZ
01263 832010**

"A magnificent open fire" – where "steak to die for" and venison from the surrounding Gunton deer park are grilled to order – is the centrepiece of dining at this highly styled 'country pub', hung with paintings by YBAs and other artists. Fans love its "delicious hearty food", "superb gardens" and "gorgeous rooms if you're able to stay over", but a few dissenting voices suggest it is "resting on its laurels", or is "more show than substance". / www.theguntonarms.co.uk; Mon-Sat 11 pm, Sun 10.30 pm. *Accommodation:* 8 rooms, from £95

LAST WINE BAR & RESTAURANT £54 334

**70 - 76 ST GEORGES STREET NR3 1AB
01603 626 626**

Nearing its thirtieth, this Victorian shoe factory 'remains a Norwich institution where loyal regulars feel like family" – and which is "much more cosy" since a ground-floor refurb'. "Fine wines", many by the glass or carafe, remain the draw but, as of 2017, new (ex-Gingerman Group) "chef Iain McCarten has really made his mark" with some "very tasty" cooking. / www.thelastwinebar.co.uk; @LastWineBar; Mon - Sat 10.30 pm, Sun closed.

NAMASTE INDIA £26 442

2A OPIE STREET NR1 3DN 01603 662016

"Astonishingly tasty vegan food (light, nutritious and spiced with a deft hand)" make it worth discovering this "tiny restaurant on a backstreet in central Norwich", where "prices are low for the quality achieved". / namasteindiannorwich.com; Mon-Sat 9.30 pm, Sun 4 pm.

ROGER HICKMAN'S £91 544

**79 UPPER ST. GILES ST NR2 1AB
01603 633522**

"If anything the food and service have upped a gear here over the past 12 months, perhaps in response to increased local competition?" Roger Hickman's 'fine dining establishment' is, according to its fans "still the best fine dining in town", with very assured cooking and service that's "efficient without being too formal". It occupies the premises which traded for many years as Adlards (where Roger was head chef, before taking it over himself), and so the site has quite a history as the top venue locally. / www.rogerhickmansrestaurant.com; @rogerhickmans; 10 pm; closed Mon & Sun.

ALCHEMILLA £32 434

192 DERBY ROAD NG7 1NF 0115 941 3515

"A fantastic and innovative addition to the Nottingham restaurant scene" – Alex Bond's summer 2017 newcomer occupies a "spacious, historic coach house" a mile or two north east of the city-centre on the borders of The Park Estate. "The only offer is of a five-, seven- or ten-course tasting menu" (everyone at the table is requested to go for the same one). "It's pushing for excellence" in an ambitious, pushing-the-outside-of-the-envelope kind of way, and "getting better each time" providing some "outstanding combinations of flavours and textures". / alchemillarestaurant.uk; @alchemillaresto; Tue-Sat 9.30 pm.

ANNIE'S BURGER SHACK £24 433

5 BROADWAY NG1 1PR 01156849920

This Lace Market venue "does what it does very well" – namely "exceptional" burgers, with a "great, great choice" of options taking in veggie and vegan versions and (as of late) new Micky D's-style takeaway breakfast muffins; a second branch opened in a Grade II-listed church in Derby in Autumn 2018. / www.anniesburgershack.com; @original_annies; Sun-Thu 11 pm, Fri & Sat midnight.

BARESCA £35 333

9 BYARD LN NG1 2GJ 0115 948 3900

Escabeche's lively city-centre sibling serves up superior tapas that's "always delicious", albeit "featuring more carbs than might be appropriate". It's particularly recommended for the set lunch or "pre-theatre menú del dia – always delicious and amazing how much you get for the very modest price". / www.baresca.co.uk;

@barescanotts; Sun & Mon 10.30 pm, Tue-Thu 11 pm, Fri & Sat midnight.

CAFE ROYA £42 343

**130 WOLLATON RD NG9 2PE
0115 922 1902**

A popular and "interesting" two-floor veggie "just out of town" in Beeston, with a "small but select wine list" and decent lunch deals; by all accounts it's "well worth a try" (even for carnivores). / caferoya.restaurantwebx.com/; @CafeRoya; Tue-Sat 9.30 pm, Sun 2.30 pm.

CALCUTTA CLUB £45 433

**8-10 MAID MARIAN WAY NG1 6HS
0115 941 4441**

A relative newcomer to Nottingham's 'curry corner', John & Barry Dhaliwal's ("the original owners of Memsaab next door") polo-themed operation is inspired by the lavish banquets thrown by sporting maharajas and: "a smart traditional curry restaurant, with a good range of dishes, all of which are tasty with a tendency to be hearty rather than delicate, but none the worse for that!" and delivering some "super flavours". / www.calcutta-club.co.uk; @TheCalcuttaClub; Mon-Thu 10.30 pm, Fri & Sat 11 pm, Sun 10 pm.

CHINO LATINO, PARK PLAZA HOTEL £60 422

**41 MAID MARIAN WAY NG1 6GD
0115 947 7444**

"Not your average Asian venue" and totally not what you would expect off the foyer of a boring-looking business hotel – "amazing" fusion cuisine and "sushi to die for" have earned consistently high ratings for a number of years at this unexpected modern Pan-Asian mashup. Unfortunately there is another constant: service is often "hit and miss". / www.chinolatino.eu; @chinilatinoeu; 10.30 pm; closed Sun.

THE CUMIN £37 452

**62-64 MAID MARIAN WAY NG1 6BQ
0115 941 9941**

"Monika and Sunny are always welcoming and professional" at their subcontinental staple, on the curry strip, and they still serve the "best biryani ever" (plus other "very flavourful food with bold use of spicing"). / www.thecumin.co.uk; @Thecumin; Mon-Thu 11 pm, Fri & Sat 11.30 pm.

Restaurant Sat Bains, Nottingham
(Credit John Scott Blackwell)

FRENCH LIVING £43 3 3 3

27 KING ST NG1 2AY 0115 958 5885

"Good honest French cooking" has been the approach at this "lovely" homage to all things Gallic for 25 years: a restaurant, café, deli and boutique in the heart of the city-centre run by Corsica-born owner Stéphane Luiggi; "very swillable wine by the carafe, helps keep things more affordable". / www.frenchliving.co.uk; 10 pm; closed Mon & Sun; no Amex.

THE FRUSTRATED CHEF £35 3 3 2

**90-94 CHILWELL ROAD, BEESTON NG9 1ES
0115 922 8300**

"There's always an interesting choice of modern dishes" at this "always busy" Beeston 'world tapas' restaurant – a "welcoming" fixture that's "very good value for money". / thefrustratedchef.co.uk; Mon-Sat 9.30 pm, Sun 4 pm.

HART'S £66 3 4 3

**STANDARD HILL, PARK ROW NG1 6GN
0115 988 1900**

"Utterly reliable in every way: year in and year out, it's always a real pleasure to visit" – few restaurants have the longevity of Paul Hart's modern brasserie "favourite" near the Castle: an "attractive and airy" (and business-friendly) environment, with a "calm and quiet" ("slightly bland") atmosphere, a "well-run" air, and very dependable modern British cuisine. "What's not to like?" / www.hartsnottingham.co.uk; 10 pm, Sun 9 pm. *Accommodation:* 139 rooms, from £125

IBERICO £42 4 4 4

**THE SHIRE HALL, HIGH PAVEMENT NG1
1HN 01159 410410**

"Exciting" tapas, that's "true to its Spanish heritage" helps make this "intimate" ("murky but characterful") cellar "in a historic building in the Lace Market" an "outstanding" option for dinner (for all-day tapas, head to the Bar Iberico spinoff on Carlton Street). Top Tip "pre-theatre menu under £13 remains a top value option". / www.ibericotapas.com; @ibericotapas; Tue-Sat 10 pm; children: 12+ D.

MASALA JUNCTION £48 4 4 3

**301-303 MANSFIELD ROAD, CARRINGTON
NG5 2DA 0115 9622366**

In a "beautiful" former NatWest bank a mile out of town, this newish arrival is well "worth the trip" for its "high-quality Indian fare" and "very personable proprietor" (Naj Aziz, ex-of the award-winning MemSaab on Maid Marian Way, aka Madras Mile). / masalajunction.co.uk/; @masalajct; Mon-Thu 10.30 pm, Fri & Sat 11 pm.

MEMSAAB £44 4 3 4

**12-14 MAID MARIAN WAY NG1 6HS
0115 957 0009**

"The food is definitely a cut-above your average Indian" (e.g. "the Tandoori Ostrich starter was out of this world") and "never disappoints" at

this city-centre legend. "Service and ambience are good but if the former in particular were fine-tuned more it would make this an exceptional destination". / www.mem-saab.co.uk; @MemSaabNotts; near Castle, opposite Park Plaza Hotel; Mon-Thu 10.30 pm, Fri & Sat 11 pm, Sun 10 pm; no shorts.

RESTAURANT SAT BAINS £130 5 4 3

LENTON LANE NG7 2SA 0115 986 6566

"Like escaping down the rabbit hole in Alice in Wonderland into a new world, albeit a world more relaxed than Alice's": when you arrive at Sat Bains's famous foodie Shangri-la, bizarrely situated on the fringes of an industrial estate next to the A52, "a concrete and pylon forest gives way to the most exquisite and wonderful place". Once inside the humble looking building: "a magical experience kicks in" – "staff are knowledgeable and approachable, and the food is out of this world". There are seven-course and ten-course tasting menu options in the restaurant, and you can also book at a chef's table (for up to eight diners) or at 'Nucleus' (his development kitchen) which can take up to six diners at night. / www.restaurantsatbains.com; @satbains1; Wed & Thu 9 pm, Fri & Sat 9.30 pm; no Amex; children: 8+. *Accommodation:* 8 rooms, from £129

SHANGHAI SHANGHAI £33 5 3 2

15 GOOSE GATE NG1 1FE 0115 958 4688

Offering "excellent and authentic Sichuan cooking in a basic, student-friendly setting", this Lace Market outfit, always buzzing with "lots of Chinese customers" (good sign), is "worth a visit...no, I mean several visits". / www.shanghai-shanghai.co.uk; @ShanghaiShang; Sun-Thu 10 pm, Fri & Sat 11 pm.

THE TAILORS ARMS £49

WILFORD LANE NG11 7AX 01159 144487

Formerly known as the Wilford Green, this May 2018 newcomer has received a major revamp to re-open as a contemporary gastropub, with steaks and burgers topping the menu. / www.thetailorsarms.com; @thetailorsarms; Mon-Thu 11 pm, Fri & Sat 11.30 pm, Sun 10.30 pm.

THEA CAFFEA £21 3 3 3

**ENFIELD CHAMBERS, 14A LOW PAVEMENT
NG1 7DL 0115 941 2110**

This six-year-old tearoom in "lovely surroundings" (a cute brick building with a terrace, chequered tiles and vintage china cups) is "an oasis of calm", with "always a tasty quiche or Welsh rarebit to be recommended". / @TheaCaffea; Mon-Fri 5.30 pm, Sat 6 pm, Sun 4.30 pm.

200 DEGREES £12 3 3 4

HESTON HS, MEADOW LANE NG2 3HE

This "excellent", "hipster" Nottingham "indie" and "brilliant barista school" (with seven

UK branches) recently received a £3m cash injection, with its sights set on becoming a national staple. The MO: "delicious coffee and quality savoury and sweet foods" – and "they bring it to your table". / www.200degs.com; @200degreescafe; Tue-Fri 9 pm, Mon 9.30 pm, Sun 3 pm; no bookings.

VICTORIA HOTEL £38 3 3 3

DOVECOTE LN NG9 1JG 0115 925 4049

With a menu that "offers something for everyone" (from "sausages to curry, with plenty of choices for vegetarians") – this "jolly", "old-fashioned" late-Victorian red-brick freehouse by Beeston station, is "well worth a visit". "The food is simple and tasty – not what you'd call a top restaurant experience but reliable and seemingly using good ingredients". Fun fact: it was mentioned in Notts local boy DH Lawrence's first novel, The White Peacock. / www.victoriabeeston.co.uk; @TheVicBeeston; Sun-Thu 11 pm, Fri & Sat midnight; no Amex; children: 18+ after 8 pm.

THE WOLLATON £50 3 3 2

**LAMBOURNE DRIVE NG8 1GR 0115
9288610**

"Ideal for a family", with Wollaton Hall's deer park just over the road, this convivial gastroboozer is an "always reliable" spot where the "menu changes monthly, is varied, and sometimes quite original". / www.thewollaton.co.uk; 9 pm, Sun 5 pm; closed Sun D.

WORLD SERVICE £58 4 4 4

**NEWDIGATE HS, CASTLEGATE NG1 6AF
0115 847 5587**

This "quirky" venue (very popular locally), which shares a 17th-century townhouse and its courtyard garden with The Nottingham Club (and has something of an old-fashioned sports pavilion vibe), scores consistently well for its "fantastic food" – much of it inspired by Far Eastern flavours – "excellent cocktails and a varied wine list". / www.worldservicerestaurant.com; @ws_restaurant; Tue-Fri 10 pm, Sat 9.30 pm; children: 10+ at D.

ZAAP £34 3 3 3

**UNIT B, BROMLEY PLACE NG1 6JG
0115 947 0204**

Decked out with tuk-tuks and other exotic paraphernalia, this Thai street-food operation is one of a number of spin-offs from the Leeds original, and wins positive feedback for its "authentic" dishes from a long menu. / www.zaapthai.co.uk; @ZaapNottingham; Sun-Thu 11 pm, Fri & Sat midnight.

OARE, KENT 3-3C

THE THREE MARINERS £45 2 3 3

2 CHURCH RD ME13 0QA 01795 533633

This "secluded" 18th-century inn on the corner of a steep hill near Faversham inspired more mixed opinions since a change of ownership in late 2017: most reporters still see it as a "a

The Neptune, Old Hunstanton

quintessential pub" with "sound" cooking, but others say "it's lost lots of what made it special and has become very ordinary". / www.thethreemarinersoare.co.uk; Mon-Sat 11 pm, Sun 10.30 pm; no Amex.

OBAN, ARGYLL AND BUTE   9–3B

EE-USK (SEAFOOD RESTAURANT)   £52   543

NORTH PIER PA34 5QD 01631 565666

"In a glass box by the edge of the harbour" and "overlooking the sea and islands" – you encounter "fabulous fresh fish (including the best seafood platter ever)" at this seafront venue. The name means 'fish' in Gaelic. / www.eeusk.com; @eeuskoban; 9-9.30 pm; no Amex; children: 12+ at D.

ETIVE   £58   442

43 STEVENSON STREET PA34 5NA
01631 564899

Named for the nearby loch where John McNulty (chef) and David Lapsley (sommelier) previously operated, this "comfortable" restaurant inspires high praise: "top quality local produce sourced by a great young chef, while David the sommelier knows his stuff and explains everything you're eating and drinking with the utmost knowledge – great value for money". / www.etiverestaurant.co.uk; @EtiveRestaurant.

THE OBAN FISH & CHIP SHOP   £23   542

116 GEORGE STREET PA34 5NT
01631 567000

"Outstandingly good fish and chips, but also a varied menu of other delights" have made this 40-cover chippy and take-away a local institution: "great for families, kids, everyone". / obanfishandchipshop.co.uk; Mon-Sat 9.30 pm, Sun 4 pm.

OLD HUNSTANTON, NORFOLK   6–3B

THE NEPTUNE   £87   554

85 OLD HUNSTANTON RD PE36 6HZ
01485 532122

"We go once or twice a year and it never disappoints" – Kevin Mangeolle's "smart" and "characterful" converted coaching inn (which he runs with wife Jacki) delivers "heaven on a plate" for the good number who report on it. It's a "tiny", "very intimate" dining room, and

the cuisine – be it from the prix fixe menus or tasting option – "continues to grow in quality, providing real food to taste and savour". "You are looked after in a really friendly informed way too, which allows everyone to thoroughly enjoy the experience in their own way". / www.theneptune.co.uk; @NeptuneChef; Tue-Sun 9 pm; may need + to book; children: 10+. *Accommodation:* 6 rooms, from £120

OLD WINDSOR, BERKSHIRE   3–3A

THE OXFORD BLUE   £90   443

10 CRIMP HILL SL4 2QY 01753 861954

"Great British pub food" of a distinctly superior stamp is served in the "fantastic environment" of this 19th-century inn on the edge of Windsor Great Park, a two-year-old venture from chef-proprietor Steven Ellis, who spent a decade working with Clare Smyth. His wife Ami, the "amazing pastry chef" here, is also a graduate of some pretty serious kitchens. "Highlights are the extras and the attention to detail", of a level that comes as a "real surprise" outside a fine-dining venue. / www.oxfordbluepub.co.uk; @OxfordBluePub; Wed-Sat 10 pm, Sun 5 pm.

OLDSTEAD, NORTH YORKSHIRE   5–1D

BLACK SWAN   £132   554

YO61 4BL 01347 868 387

"Deserving its reputation – a place to go if you really enjoy experiencing a chef at the top of his game": Tommy Banks and his family's "old pub with no fancy frills" is "set in the isolated depths of the North Yorks countryside" and, while "really not easy to get to, is really really worth it when you do". This Great British Chef winner's food is "a revelation" that "really pushes the boundaries" and with "real flair for finding interesting ways to bring flavour from their extensive garden and local country into their menu" (they own a nearby farm), including by "featuring locally foraged ingredients such as wild garlic and fir". And while "each course is a delight", it's "the feeling of welcome and sheer enthusiasm you get from the parents and his brother James that make this a fabulous experience". "You either love or hate the set-menu format, but The Black Swan certainly should be on every restaurant-goers bucket list". Top Menu Tip: "the heritage beetroot confit in beef dripping should, if there's any justice, become the new 'snail porridge' of Fat Duck fame". / www.blackswanoldstead.co.uk;

@BlkSwanOldstead; Sat & Sun-Fri 8.30 pm; no Amex. *Accommodation:* 4 rooms, from £270

OMBERSLEY, WORCESTERSHIRE   2–1B

VENTURE IN   £58   433

MAIN ROAD WR9 0EW 01905 620552

A "very traditional", half-timbered 15th century house with a "lot of atmosphere" (fire, beams, slouchable sofas). Chef-owner Toby Fletcher "never fails to deliver great food" of the Anglo-French mould, and has a particular "passion for seafood". / www.theventurein.co.uk; Tue-Sat 9.30 pm, Sun 2 pm.

ONGAR, ESSEX   3–2B

SMITH'S BRASSERIE   £52   443

FYFIELD RD CM5 0AL 01277 365578

"Not the most original fayre, but always top quality fish, and a guaranteed good experience!" – this very competent and well-established, contemporary operation (now also with a Docklands offshoot) "can be noisy and crowded but is always reliable". / www.smithsrestaurants.com; @SmithsOfOngar; left off A414 towards Fyfield; Mon-Fri 10 pm, Sat 10.30 pm, Sun 10 pm; no trainers; children: 12+.

ONICH, HIGHLAND   9–3B

LOCH LEVEN SEAFOOD CAFÉ   £51   543

PH33 6SA 01855 821 048

This "rather crowded" seasonal spot (plus fish shop) remains "well worth the diversion" en route to Fort William for its "usually amazing" catch. The decor (which now includes a glass-walled coffee room) is "basic", so best take refuge on the terrace, enjoying prime views of the namesake loch. / www.lochlevenseafoodcafe.co.uk; 9 pm; no Amex.

ORFORD, SUFFOLK   3–1D

BUTLEY ORFORD OYSTERAGE   £47   533

MARKET HILL IP12 2LH 01394 450277

"OK, the ambience is a bit noisy when it's full, and it can be chilly on a winter's day", but the Pinney family's "no-nonsense and basic" canteen just "goes on and on producing beautiful, honest fish dishes": a short menu of "top fish cooked in a very simple way so that the flavour of the fish shines through". "Much of it is from their own boats" – "the oysters are tops (and the other shellfish)" and "their fish pie is the best on the planet". "You can walk it off by the sea or climbing the castle". / www.butleyorfordoysterage.co.uk; @Pinneysoforford; on the B1078, off the A12 from Ipswich; 9 pm; no Amex.

Black Swan, Oldstead

THE CROWN & CASTLE £59 [4][3][4]

IP12 2LJ 01394 450205

"Superb cooking, using local supplies of divine smoked fish and shellfish, pork and lamb", makes eating a "real treat" at this "delightful and quirky hotel" in an attractive village. Longstanding owner Ruth Watson, a TV 'Hotel Inspector', has sold up but remains involved – and regulars report that "nothing has changed". / www.crownandcastle.co.uk; @CrownandCOrford; on main road to Orford, near Woodbridge; Tue-Sat 11 pm, Sun 10.30 pm; no Amex; booking max 10 may apply; children: 8+ at D. *Accommodation:* 21 rooms, from £135

ORPINGTON, KENT	3–3B

XIAN £40 [5][4][3]

324 HIGH ST BR6 0NG 01689 871881

"Amazing as ever", agree the many fans of this family-run Chinese in the outer suburbs, which for years has been a "model of consistency" – "you'd never be embarrassed to bring friends here because the food is always exceptional". / Tue-Sun 10.30 pm.

OSWESTRY, SHROPSHIRE	5–3A

SEBASTIAN'S £65 [3][4][3]

**45 WILLOW STREET SY11 1AQ
01691 655 444**

In "a town that has too many chains", this "very reliable", oak-beamed restaurant-with-rooms with delicious modern British cuisine is still going strong after three decades, and is a bit of a local star – no wonder it's always "packed". / www.sebastians-hotel.com; Sun & Mon 10 pm, Tue-Sat 11 pm; no Amex. *Accommodation:* 5 rooms, from £75

OTLEY, WEST YORKSHIRE	5–1C

BUON APPS £56 [3][5][4]

WHARFEBANK BUSINESS CENTRE, ILKLEY RD LS21 3JP 01943 468 458

On the banks of the River Wharfe in an attractive former paper mill with outside terrace, Alessandro and Elena Sofia's fifteen-year-old venture is that rare creature: a rural, traditional Italian, with a menu running from pizza and pasta to more substantial dishes. It's consistently well-rated in reports for all aspects of its operation, but most of all its "friendly" staff ("they even treat children as if they matter"). / www.buonappsotley.co.uk; @Buonapps; Sun-Thu 11 pm, Fri & Sat midnight.

OTTERSHAW, SURREY	3–3A

THE MANOR AT FOXHILLS £106 [3][4][4]

STONEHILL RD KT16 0EL 01932 872050

Boasting one of the South's best golf courses and one of England's first natural swimming pools, this swish Victorian manor house is "an amazing place" to visit. Diners can choose between the casual 'Nineteen' eatery or beamed restaurant 'The Manor', offering "very good", pretty-as-a-picture cuisine, not least afternoon tea. / www.foxhills.co.uk; @FoxhillsSurrey; J11 on M25, A320 to Ottershaw at 2nd roundabout turn right, turn right again, then left; Mon-Sun 9.30 pm; no jeans. *Accommodation:* 36 rooms, from £135

OUNDLE, RUTLAND	3–1A

TAP & KITCHEN £47 [3][2][4]

STATION ROAD PE8 4DE 01832 275069

Run by the local Nene Valley Brewers, this attractive, industrial-style bar/restaurant wins solid ratings for its excellent beers and locally sourced modern brasserie fare. / www.tapandkitchen.com; @tapandkitchen; Mon-Sat 11 pm, Sun 9 pm.

OXFORD, OXFORDSHIRE	2–2D

AL-SHAMI £29 [4][3][3]

25 WALTON CR OX1 2JG 01865 310066

A Jericho institution for more than 30 years – "the food remains excellent" at this "charming" Lebanese. To newcomers it's still "a real find" – "so many small dishes to choose from that I never got to the mains, although my friends were impressed with those". "Pleasing and original choice of vegetarian offerings", too. / www.al-shami.co.uk; midnight; no Amex. *Accommodation:* 12 rooms, from £60

ARBEQUINA £40 [5][4][3]

74 COWLEY RD OX4 1JB 01865 792777

"Fabulous" tapas has made an instant hit of this small, year-old bar in an old chemist's shop (from Rufus Thurston, owner of Oxford legend Oli's Thai, and Ben Whyles of east Oxford's Door 74): "yet another independent to liven up the Oxford food scene". "Enthusiastic, knowledgeable and friendly staff" add to the "brilliant experience". / arbequina.co.uk; @arbequinaoxford; Mon-Sat 10.30 pm.

ASHMOLEAN DINING ROOM £54 [2][2][4]

BEAUMONT ST OX1 2PH 01865 553 823

"A good place to escape from the tourist hordes of central Oxford" (although it can get pretty crowded itself), this roof-top spot is "excellent for afternoon tea" and has an open cocktail bar complete with fake grass and deckchairs to while away summer days. When it comes to the "straightforward" (perhaps rather "unadventurous") main menu results are "fine". / www.ashmoleandiningroom.com; 10 pm; closed Mon, Tue D, Thu D & Sun D.

ATOMIC BURGER £36 [3][3][3]

92 COWLEY RD OX4 1JE 01865 790 855

"A real step above the 'usual' burger joint with great product, excellent energetic staff and an entertaining environment" enlivened by retro memorabilia. "The only downside is that booking is an absolute must and there can be a wait for your table" (if it's full, they have a diner just down the road). / www.atomicburger.co.uk; @atomicburgers; 10.30 pm; no Amex.

BRANCA £48 [3][3][3]

111 WALTON ST OX2 6AJ 01865 556111

This well-established Italian in Jericho has expanded over the years to incorporate a deli, while retaining the qualities that made it popular. "I'm always so impressed" by the "faultless food, even when serving a very large group". / www.branca.co.uk; 11 pm; no Amex.

BRASSERIE BLANC £49 [2][3][3]

71-72 WALTON ST OX2 6AG 01865 510999

A fixture in pretty Jericho for two decades, Raymond Blanc's brasserie (on the site where he first made his name) is the template for the twenty branches he has rolled out across the country. Regulars reckon it's "the original and the best" and certainly consistently reviewed as a "reliable" and "good value" option. / www.brasserieblanc.com; @brasserieblanc; Mon-Sat 10 pm, Sun 9 pm.

CHERWELL BOATHOUSE £48 [3][2][5]

BARDWELL ROAD OX2 6ST 01865 552746

A legend for its "wonderful wine list" since the 1960s – this "delightful and unique" north Oxford venue is "a reliable old favourite" set in a working boathouse on a tributary of the Thames – so you can work up an appetite with an afternoon of punting. The solidly rated food doesn't aim to set the world on fire, but is "good value and well-cooked – something that is quite hard to find in this overpriced city". Top Tip: "The occasional set dinners with chosen wines are a highlight". / www.cherwellboathouse.co.uk; @Cherwell_Boat; Mon-Sat 10 pm, Sun 5 pm.

CHIANG MAI £47 [3][3][4]

KEMP HALL PASSAGE, 130A HIGH STREET OX1 4DH 01865 202233

"A real find down a side alley off the High in Oxford", and occupying a slightly unexpected venue for a Thai – a wood-panelled Tudor-style room in an ancient medieval building; "not quite what it used to be" perhaps (given greater competition in the town nowadays), but it's "still good". / www.chiangmaikitchen.co.uk; Mon-Sat 11.30 pm, Sun 10.30 pm; no Amex.

CINNAMON KITCHEN OXFORD £54 4|3|3

309 THE WESTGATE, QUEEN STREET OX1 1NZ 01865 951670

"Situated in the new Westgate centre – an offshoot of the London's Cinnamon Club which opened in late 2017, and which inspires a strong amount of feedback: all positive. "Better than most Oxford restaurants", "the menu is interesting and the cooking up to scratch": "not a patch on the Cinnamon Club original, but for Oxford this is an astounding addition". / www.cinnamon-kitchen.com/; @CinnamonKitchen; Tue-Thu 9.30 pm, Fri & Sat 10 pm.

GEE'S £55 2|3|4

61 BANBURY RD OX2 6PE 01865 553540

A "lovely" Grade II listed Victorian conservatory provides a very "attractive setting" at this well-known and highly popular venue. But despite some reports of "fine" meals, most feedback suggests it's "living on past glories" – including a stint as Raymond Blanc's original Petit Blanc – while "Oxford has improved overall" ("humdrum menu and humdrum cooking"). / www.gees-restaurant.co.uk; @geesrestaurant; Mon-Sat 11 pm, Sun 10.30 pm.

JOLLY POST BOY £47 3|4|3

22 FLORENCE PARK ROAD OX4 3PH

The new regime (as of 2016) has "turned this tired and old venue into a local treat", whose "good small menu" features "great daily specials", slap-up Sunday roasts and ten taps with sought-after craft beers. / Tue-Sat 11 pm, Sun 10 pm.

THE MAGDALEN ARMS £49 3|2|3

243 IFFLEY ROAD OX4 1SJ 01865 243 159

The oxblood-walled country cousin to the capital's celebrated Anchor & Hope, turning out pleasingly hearty and creative British gasto fare, which elicits solid marks but little in the way of commentary; the pretty terrace to the rear hosts a flea market every first Saturday of the month. / www.magdalenarms.com; @magdalen_arms; Mon-Sat 11 pm, Sun 10.30 pm; no Amex; no bookings.

MY SICHUAN £45 4|2|2

THE OLD SCHOOL, GLOUCESTER GRN OX1 2DA 01865 236 899

"Exactly what dining in an authentic restaurant in a town in Sichuan would be like" – down to the "cheap furniture and cheap tableware, and service of the silent just-point-at-the-menu variety". On the food front it's "really exciting"..."expect lots of garlic and chilli and offal (plus "squishy textures") and enjoy!" / www.mysichuan.co.uk; Mon-Sun 10.30 pm.

NO.1 SHIP STREET £52 3|3|3

1 SHIP STREET OX1 3DA 01865 806637

"A stylish new venue in Oxford" with "green walls and copper tables" – this "hard-surfaced" modern British brasserie is praised as a useful addition with "excellent" standards in the city-centre. / www.no1shipstreet.com; Mon-Sat 9.30 pm, Sun 4 pm.

OLI'S THAI £39 5|4|3

38 MAGDALEN RD OX4 1RB 01865 790223

"A taste sensation! – every dish is a masterpiece" at this cult Thai café. Despite being permanently crammed, "they maintain phenomenal standards, with beautiful, exotic flavours" – and "the best of the best" is still "exceptional value for money". There's just one complaint: "you have to book three months in advance!" / www.olisthai.com; @olisthai; Tue-Fri 9 pm, Sat 2.30 pm.

THE OXFORD KITCHEN £66 4|3|2

215 BANBURY RD OX2 7HQ 01865 511 149

Chef Paul Welburn's "excellent and beautifully presented" dishes from an "interesting" menu are winning accolades for a venue whose modest Summertown shopping-drag setting belies its ambition. Top Tip: sit upstairs, where the atmosphere is more "pleasant and relaxed". / www.theoxfordkitchen.co.uk; @Kitchenoxford; Mon-Wed 11 pm, Thu-Sat midnight, Sun 9.30 pm.

THE PERCH £56 3|3|3

BINSEY LN OX2 0NG 01865 7228891

Claiming to be 'as old as the university', this thatched 17th-century building, a short stroll across Port Meadow from the city-centre has a "delightful" garden on the river, and was "nicely renovated" when experienced local licensee Jon Ellse took it over a few years ago. The 'gastropub grub' is "certainly not shabby" although quite "old skool". / www.the-perch.co.uk; @theperchoxford; Mon-Sat 9.30 pm, Sun 9 pm.

PIERRE VICTOIRE £46 3|3|3

LITTLE CLARENDON ST OX1 2HP 01865 316616

"No-nonsense French cuisine, done well" ensures that this city-centre bistro is "always busy"; and with its "small scuffed tables and chairs packed close together" somehow it "manages to feel intimate, while being crowded and buzzing". Open for more than 20 years, it's a survivor from a franchised 90s chain that went belly-up. "Absolutely love it here, the prices are amazing for delicious, classic food". / www.pierrevictoire.co.uk; 11 pm, Sun 10 pm; no Amex.

QUOD, OLD BANK HOTEL £51 2|3|4

92-94 HIGH ST OX1 4BJ 01865 202505

"Reliable cooking in a fun atmosphere" – "nothing too fancy (but all the better for that)" – and a "lovely garden for the summer" make this "Oxford institution" an "excellent venue for entertaining hungry young students", with a menu that has "something for everyone". / www.oldbank-hotel.co.uk; @QuodBrasserie; Mon-Sun 9 pm; booking max 10 may apply. *Accommodation:* 42 rooms, from £140

SOJO £42 4|3|2

6-9 HYTHE BRIDGE ST OX1 2EW 01865 202888

"Busy as ever… good as ever" – fans again hail this "exceptional" operation near the station for its "brilliant Chinese food at reasonable prices". "The heat of the dishes echoes what you'd be served in China – and the number of Asian patrons supports this". / www.sojooxford.co.uk; Mon-Fri 11 pm, Sat 11.30 pm, Sun 10.30 pm; no bookings.

TURL STREET KITCHEN £47 3|3|3

16 TURL ST OX1 3DH 01865 264 171

With a "limited" but "flavoursome" menu of local/seasonal food, this "rustic" non-profit provides a "respite from the cacophony of Oxford", and prices are "very reasonable" too. / www.turlstreetkitchen.co.uk; @turlstkitchen; 10 pm, Fri & Sat 10.30 pm, .

THE VAULTS AND GARDEN CAFE £21 3|2|3

UNIVERSITY CHURCH OF ST MARY THE VIRGIN, RADCLIFFE SQ OX1 4AH 01865 279112

"A great location in central Oxford" is a unique selling point of this quirky café – part of the University church on the High, with a medieval vaulted interior, and gorgeous outside seating in the churchyard. "The choice of fare is limited" (breakfasts; plus simple dishes such as curry, tagine, and soup) but adequately nourishes its clientele of students, clerics and tourists. / www.thevaultsandgarden.com; @VaultsandGarden; 6 pm; L only.

ZHENG £38 3|3|2

82 WALTON ST OX2 6EA 01865 51 11 88

"The menu might put you off by covering three different Chinese cuisines (Sichuan, Shanghai, Canton) along with Malaysia and Singapore" – but stick with it: the food is "classy", "portions are generous and the prices reasonable" at this "somewhat crowded but reliable" Pan-Asian in Jericho. It now also has a smart sibling in Chelsea. / www.zhengoxford.co.uk; Mon, Wed-Sun, Tue 11 pm.

THE HAYCUTTER £45 334

TANHOUSE ROAD RH8 9PE 01883 776955

This "wonderful addition to the east Surrey scene" has achieved excellent ratings in the year since it reopened after a £2 million, two-year head-to-toe refurb by successful, Chester-based pub group Brunning & Price. / www.brunningandprice.co.uk/haycutter; Mon-Sat 9.30 pm, Sun 4 pm.

FRAICHE £115 543

11 ROSE MOUNT CH43 5SG 0151 652 2914

"Year on year Marc Williamson keeps providing a sublime experience that I happily travel up from London for!" – that's the level of enthusiasm provoked by this 12-seater on the fringe of Birkenhead which is now acknowledged as one of the UK's foremost destinations: "a must-do, with a warm welcome, fabulous relaxing atmosphere and exceptional food and wine". / www.restaurantfraiche.com; @marcatfraiche; Wed-Sun 9.30 pm; no Amex.

BEACH HOUSE £61 434

OXWICH BEACH SA3 1LS 01792 390965

"A totally unexpected find, with sensational food" – this descriptively named two-year-old is "a fine modern building with spectacular views of the beach", and the cooking from chef Hywel Griffith is "first class". / www.beachhouseoxwich.co.uk; @beachhouseoxwich.

APPLETONS AT THE VINEYARD £68 334

DARK LANE PL27 7SE 01841 541413

"Tricky to find, tucked away down a quiet lane, at the centre (New Zealand-style) of a working vineyard" – "this restaurant is run by Andy Appleton (formerly of Jamie Oliver's Fifteen Cornwall)" serving varied modern British cuisine with a strong Mediterranean slant. / www.appletonsatthevineyard.com; @_Appletons; Wed & Thu 2.30 pm, Fri & Sat 9 pm, Sun 2 am.

PAUL AINSWORTH AT NO. 6 £86 444

6 MIDDLE ST PL28 8AP 01841 532093

"We have been visiting this restaurant since Paul took over around ten years ago and it's now difficult to find words for how wonderful the experience is" – such is the typical view we have published year in, year out on Paul Ainsworth's "small", "intimate" and "atmospheric" townhouse, which often beats more famous names locally in our diner survey. This year, however, it inspired an unusual amount of flak for "pushing it" with "sky high prices" and portion sizes that are "a joke" (although even some such critics acknowledge that the "set lunch is a bargain"). / www.number6inpadstow.co.uk; @no6padstow; Mon-Fri 6 pm, Sat 5 pm, Sun 3 pm; no Amex; children: 4+.

PRAWN ON THE LAWN £59 534

11 DUKE STREET PL28 8AB 01841 532223

"A little gem!" – Rick & Katie Toogood's "exceptional" seafood specialist, an offshoot of their Islington original, serves "the freshest of fish cooked simply but superbly". It's "very small (24 covers), so booking is essential", but worth it as a "good laid back alternative to The Seafood Restaurant and Paul Ainsworth at No 6" (and more enthusiastic fans this year feel it "beats its more famous Padstow neighbours by a country mile"). "There's an on-site fishmongers, which you can choose from if you don't fancy anything on the small menu". / prawnonthelawn.com; @PrawnOnTheLawn; Mon-Sat 10 pm.

RICK STEIN'S CAFÉ £49 342

10 MIDDLE STREET PL28 8AP 01841 532700

"Very good value for money" – perhaps the best of the 'Padstein' restaurants – is to be found at this casual operation, serving "a limited but high quality" array of fish and seafood. / www.rickstein.com; Sun-Fri & Sat 10 pm; no Amex; booking evening only. *Accommodation:* 3 rooms, from £100

ROJANOS IN THE SQUARE £51 432

9 MILL SQ PL28 8AE 01841 532 796

"Paul Ainsworth's casual option in beautiful Padstow" – the No. 6 chef provides "interesting competition to Rick Stein" at his café-style venue, with "good quality Italian food, freshly prepared and cooked to order" (particularly top pizza). / www.paul-ainsworth.co.uk/rojanos-in-the-square; @rojanos; Sun & Mon 10 pm, Tue-Thu 11.30 pm, Fri & Sat midnight.

SEAFOOD RESTAURANT £77 333

RIVERSIDE PL28 8BY 01841 532700

"We've been coming for many years and still it ticks all the boxes", according to fans of TV Rick's original HQ, who say this "brightly-lit and buzzy room" near the harbour (but without views to speak of) "continues to be the jewel in the crown of his empire and is a must-try if you're in the area": "not cheap, but delivering well-cooked, top-class seafood, including all the classics", plus some more "interesting flavour combinations" (with lots of Indian and Asian tastes). Rapturous reports are relatively few, though, and the overall verdict is a little more middling: "Love Rick but they cram in punters at very high prices". / www.rickstein.com/eat-with-us/the-seafood-restaurant; @TheSeafood; Sun-Fri & Sat 9.30 pm; no Amex; booking max 14 may apply; children: 3+. *Accommodation:* 16 rooms, from £150

1 MOSTYN SQUARE £44 333

MOSTYN SQUARE CH64 6SL 0151 336 1963

In a "quaint" Wirral village with "extensive views over the River Dee marshes to North Wales", this venue (formerly the Marsh Cat) has been re-named after renovations and switching to a modern British menu. Ratings are now solid, with regulars reporting that "it's now back to its best". / www.1mostynsq.co.uk; @1MostynSquare; Mon-Sat 9.30 pm, Sun 5 pm.

HURTWOOD INN £56 332

WALKING BOTTOM GU5 9RR 01306 731769

The relatively new Italian owners of this village pub/hotel, attractively sited in the Surrey Hills, used to run restaurants in nearby Guildford. Pizza is a mainstay of the Italian-slanted menu, which wins respectable praise from local reporters. / hurtwoodinn.com; Mon-Sat 9.30 pm, Sun 4 pm.

CRINGLETIE HOUSE £48 333

EDINBURGH RD EH45 8PL 01721 725750

"A beautiful castle setting with fine Scottish dining": that's the appealing prospect offered by this "very relaxed country house hotel" – a "romantic" Scots-Baronial mansion with walled garden less than an hour's drive from Edinburgh. / www.cringletie.com; @CringletieHouse; between Peebles and Eddleston on A703, 20m S of Edinburgh; Mon-Sat 10.30 pm; children: 4. *Accommodation:* 15 rooms, from £99

OSSO £45 343

INNERLEITHEN RD EH45 8BA 01721 724477

"Ally and his team provide a warm and welcome" at this family-run venture. By day

Fraiche, Oxton

they serve coffee and cakes, but there are fancier lunchtime and dinner menus also which come well-rated. / www.ossorestaurant.com; @ossorestaurant; Tue-Sun, Mon 9.30 pm.

INN AT PENALLT £43 3|3|3

NP25 4SE 01600 772765

"Good pub food with nice views and good walking" – all are amongst the attractions of this friendly country pub in the Wye Valley. The menu focuses on meat, and there's also a tasting option (although it's an extended traditional meal rather than much in the way of small-plates frippery). / www.theinnatpenallt.co.uk; @InnPenallt; Wed-Sat 9 pm, Sun 3.30 pm. *Accommodation:* 4 rooms, from £75.

RESTAURANT JAMES SOMMERIN £94 4|3|3

THE ESPLANADE CF64 3AU 07722 216 727

"James Sommerin lets the ingredients do the talking with clever twists, and the seasonality of sourcing is evident in his choice of dishes", say the many fans of his Beach Cliff HQ "overlooking the sea and pier", applauding his "exceptional" and "inventive" cuisine. Ratings came off the boil slightly this year, however, due to one or two "disappointing" meals. / www.jamessommerinrestaurant.co.uk; @RestaurantJS; Mon closed Tue - Sun 9.30 pm.

ASKHAM HALL £71 4|4|4

ASKHAM CA10 2PF 01931 712350

"A beautiful setting and melt in the mouth food" – that's the appeal in a nutshell of this gorgeous Cumbrian manor house, in a Lakeland village. Chef Richard Swale's seasonal cuisine is available via a short à la carte menu or seven-course tasting option. / www.askhamhall.co.uk; @AskhamHall; Tue-Sat 11 pm, Sun 9 pm; children: 10.

THE PIG, HUNSTRETE HOUSE £53 3|5|5

HUNSTRETE BS39 4NS 01761 490 490

Part of the growing national chain – this "very accommodating", shabby-chic country-house hotel in a Grade II-listed Mendips mansion serves "delicious, locally-sourced food". But it's the setting which really elevates it above the average: "wonderful views across the fields (and sometimes even deer)", "lovely gardens", "a conservatory to dine in and terrific ambience". / www.thepighotel.com/near-bath; @The_Pig_Hotel; 9.30 pm.

THE CORNISH HEN £15 3|3|2

27 MARKET PLACE TR18 2JD 01736 350223

"The sign says the best coffee in Penzance and the sign is not wrong". "Generally described as a deli but it's really a café selling food on the side. A pleasant place to eat, drink and watch the world passing by". / Mon-Fri 6 pm, Sat 5 pm.

THE SHORE £53 5|3|4

13-14 ALVERTON STREET TR18 2QP 01736 362444

"Bruce Rennie is a wizard with local Cornish fish" and produces "the most amazing taster menus with fish and flavours that zing with freshness" at this cheerfully decorated, small modern bistro. / www.theshorerestaurant.uk/; @The_Shore_Pz; Mon closed; Tue - Sat 9 pm; Sun closed; no Amex.

TOLCARNE INN £48 4|3|3

TOLCARNE PL TR18 5PR 01736 363074

Ben Tunnicliffe took over this 300-year-old harbourside inn in 2012, and its "fresh, innovative and fun" ethos continues to please; the food is "straightforward, carefully cooked" and fish-centric – no surprise given Newlyn Fish Market just round the corner. / www.tolcarneinn.co.uk; 10 pm.

VICTORIA INN £47 3|3|4

TR20 9NP 01736 710309

Just east of Marazion (home to St. Michael's Mount), this ancient (12th century) inn has a "wonderful setting", and receives nothing but praise for its "superior-end-of-pub-food" cuisine. / www.victoriainn-penzance.co.uk/; @victoriainn_pz; Tue-Fri 9 pm, Mon 9.30 pm, Sun 3 pm.

ECKINGTON MANOR £72 3|3|3

HAMMOCK ROAD WR10 3BJ 01386 751600

A country house hotel and cookery school in a "beautiful setting in attractive timbered buildings", with an "almost conservatory-like" first-floor dining room; perhaps owing to high expectations – "the chef (Mark Stinchcombe) won MasterChef: The Professionals a few years back" – reports continue to waver, but the consensus is that it's overall "worth a visit". / @EckingtonManor; Wed-Sat 9 pm, Sun 3.30 pm. *Accommodation:* 17 rooms, from £169.

CAFE TABOU £56 4|3|2

4 ST JOHN'S PL PH1 5SZ 01738 446698

"A little bit of Paris come to Scotland" – or Polish, technically, given the pedigree of chef Marek Michalak – at this city-centre bistro, which has been a "favourite for many years"; ("gourmet evenings are great but even on a run-of-the-mill day the food is always of a very high standard"). / www.cafetabou.com; @CafeTabouPerth; Sun, Mon 8 pm, Tue-Sat 9 pm; no Amex.

63 TAY STREET £65 3|4|3

63 TAY ST PH2 8NN 01738 441451

Graeme Pallister's elegant Scottish dining room, on the Tay, is a "great place for a special occasion or just to enjoy some amazing food" – locally sourced and served in an airy space by "attentive" and "knowledgeable" staff. / www.63taystreet.com; @63TayStreet; on city side of River Tay, 1m from Dundee Rd; Mon-Sun 11 pm; no Amex.

PREVOST £60 4|4|2

20 PRIESTGATE PE1 1JA

"Great cooking in a bit of a culinary desert" is the prospect at Lee Clarke's minimalist Prestgate yearling, where "really good, innovative food is well-presented, and served well". "Great value – I loved it!" / @foodleeclarke; Mon-Sat 10 pm; no trainers; credit card deposit required to book.

JSW £77 3|2|3

20 DRAGON STREET GU31 4JJ 01730 262030

"The perfect spot for an occasion", Jake Saul Watkins's muted former coaching inn provides "a different take on delicious ingredients without being pretentious" in "an area otherwise lacking any great food", and "with a consistency established over more than ten years". Some find the experience "very quiet"; to others, that means it's "mercifully free of muzak". / www.jswrestaurant.com; on the old A3; 8 min walk from the railway station; Thu-Sat, Wed 9 pm; children: 5+ D. *Accommodation:* 4 rooms, from £95

INDIAN ESSENCE £49 5|3|3

176-178 PETTS WOOD RD BR5 1LG 01689 838 700

"I have been to most of the 'top end' Indians in London – Jamavar, Benares, Cinnamon Club, Gymkhana and Café Spice Namaste. In 'darkest' Petts Wood (surprisingly) this gem of a restaurant sits in an ordinary suburban row of shops with a self-effacing exterior. I have dined there in parties of 4 up to 24 and the standard of food is unvaryingly exemplary." Atul Kochhar's surprising suburban venture "shows his flair just as much as Benares did" with "sophisticated" cuisine that's "amazing... even better considering the location!" / www.indianessence.co.uk; @IndianEssence1; Tue-Sat 11 pm, Sun 10.30 pm; no trainers.

NEW STREET BAR & GRILL £50

NEW STREET GU28 0AS 01798 345 111

Steaks and grilled fish top the wide menu of this modern brasserie, which opened in May 2018 in this sleepy market town near the South Downs (which was formerly known as The Leconfield). / www.newstreetbarandgrill.co.uk; Wed-Sat 11 pm, Sun 9 pm.

THE NOAHS ARK INN £47 345

LURGASHALL GU28 9ET 01428 707 346

"On a picture-perfect village green", this 16th century inn is "as welcoming in the winter in its cosy interior as it is in the summer watching the cricket outside". A "good restaurant as well as being a good local pub", the "food is always excellently presented and of the highest quality". / www.noahsarkinn.co.uk; @TheNoahsArkInn; Mon-Sat 11.30 pm, Sun 8 pm.

THE FOX HOLE £49 323

DL2 3SJ 01325 374286

"The best pub food in Piercebridge! (not that there's a lot of competition…)" – Jack Bowles and Ellie Richmond have created "a very buzzy spot" at their four-year-old pub conversion. Most reports praise "superb locally sourced ingredients cooked by an enthusiastic chef". The worst review? – "enjoyed it, but wouldn't hurry back". / the-foxhole.co.uk; @TheFoxHolePub; Mon-Sat 9.30 pm, Sun 4 pm.

FRIENDS £59 334

11 HIGH ST HA5 5PJ 020 8866 0286

Savoy-trained Terry Farr's "lovely small restaurant" has been a half-timbered fixture on this deeply suburban high street for 25 years. "It can be a bit pricey, but for special occasions is worth it". / www.friendsrestaurant.co.uk; Mon-Sat 11 pm, Sun 10.30 pm.

CLOG & BILLYCOCK £45 333

BILLINGE END RD BB2 6QB 01254 201163

"Back on form and deservedly popular" – this well-known, "comfortable" gastropub on the 'Yellow Hills' achieved more consistent ratings this year for it's "mixture of pub classics, sharing boards and seasonal specials". As our survey was concluding in May 2018, it was sold, along with its Ribble Valley Inn stablemates, to the Brunning & Price group. / www.theclogandbillycock.com; @CloganBillycock; Mon-Sat 10.30 pm.

PERKINS £59 233

OLD RAILWAY STATION NG12 5NA 0115 937 3695

Opened in 1982, this "lovely", family-run venture has a quirky location – an old railway station in the countryside. Feedback remains a little mixed however: even those reporting an essentially good experience can find the cooking "unexciting" or "expensive for what it is". / www.perkinsrestaurant.co.uk; @PerkinsNotts; off A606 between Nottingham & Melton Mowbray; Mon-Sun 11 pm.

THE GREEDY GOOSE £37 234

PRYSTEN HOUSE FINEWELL ST PL1 2AE 01494 863566

Ben Palmer and his partner Francesca's attractive venue occupies a 15th century building complete with cute courtyard. There's an affordable à la carte menu, although options run to an eleven-course tasting offer. Feedback is upbeat on the whole, although one reporter found "a poor experience relative to all the vox pop praise online". Top Tip: £13 for three courses weekday lunches and early evening. / www.thegreedygoose.co.uk; @greedygooseplym; 11pm; children: 4.

ROCK SALT £46 444

31 STONEHOUSE ST PL1 3PE 01752 225522

This ex-pub turned "romantic" leading light of Millbay's dining scene "continues to produce excitingly different dishes to your average brasserie" (with options such as a seven-course tasting menu), and "to a consistently high level". A "really good choice of breakfast dishes" also makes it "a perfect spot for a lazy brunch". / www.rocksaltcafe.co.uk; @rocksaltcafeuk; Mon-Sun 11 pm; booking max 6 may apply.

THE GALLERY RESTAURANT £78 434

BORINGDON HILL PL7 4DP 01752 344455

"The Gallery in Boringdon has risen up the ranks of local Plymouth eateries" and "must be one of the best in the south west" nowadays. "Chef Scott Paton has worked wonders" in the dining room of this 40-room five-star hotel: "the setting is wonderful" and the cooking "memorable". / www.boringdonhall.co.uk/food-drink/gallery-restaurant/; @BoringdonHall.

SAMS ON THE BEACH £48 334

PL24 2TL 01726 812255

A "magnificent position on the beach provides the opportunity to enjoy a convivial lunch without losing sight of the children" at this converted lifeboat station (with three other Cornish branches) which serves a "hearty range of pizzas whilst not forgetting to offer wonderfully fresh fish". / www.samscornwall.co.uk; @samscornwall; Mon-Sun 9 pm; no Amex.

BRANKSOME BEACH £55 334

PINECLIFF RD BH13 6LP 01202 767235

Bang on the beach and with prime views of Poole Bay (especially from the upstairs terrace bar), this 1930s gastropub was once home to the UK's first solarium; these days it turns out "good food that's value for money" (a feature "not always associated with Sandbanks" just up the road). / www.branksomebeach.co.uk; @branksome_beach; Mon-Sun 5 pm.

GUILDHALL TAVERN £52 444

15 MARKET STREET BH15 1NB 01202 671717

"French owners produce fish that is simply but superbly cooked" at this "popular (booking essential)" and "welcoming" little seafood specialist tucked away near the harbour. "Always a pleasure to eat there: must have had 50 dinners in the last five years and all were up to a very high standard". / www.guildhalltavern.co.uk; Mon closed, Tue - Sat 10 pm, Sun closed; no Amex.

1863 BAR BISTRO ROOMS £57 344

ELM HOUSE, HIGH STREET CA10 2NH 017684 86334

"We were staying at Sharrow Bay and were told rather sniffily that there was nowhere else decent to eat locally. Well there is!" – This small Lakeland bar-bistro with rooms inspires relatively limited feedback, but fans say its modern-ish fare (there's also a tasting option) comes "thoroughly recommended". / www.1863ullswater.co.uk; @1863Ullswater; Last food orders at 9pm; children: 10.

AIRDS HOTEL £78 333

PA38 4DF 01631 730236

A romantic Relais & Châteaux property in an old ferry inn, and surrounded by prime walking and cycling country; the victuals (including local seafood and game, parlayed in the à la carte or seven-course tasting menus) are not cheap, but what feedback there is on the remote spot remains very respectable. / www.airds-hotel.com; @AirdsHotel; 20m N of Oban; 9.30 pm; no jeans; children: 8+ at D. **Accommodation:** 11 rooms, from £290

PIERHOUSE HOTEL £63 445

PA38 4DE 01631 730302

"Fab shellfish" and the "best view in Scotland" encapsulate the appeal of this "friendly family-run hotel" in a former West Coast piermaster's house. The "stunning views from the dining room over Loch Linnhe to Lismore and beyond" are complemented by "really helpful and obliging staff". / www.pierhousehotel.co.uk; @pierhousehotel; just off A828, follow signs for Port Appin & Lismore Ferry; Mon-Sat 11.30 pm, Sun 10.30 pm. *Accommodation:* 12 rooms, from £100

PORT ISAAC, CORNWALL   1–3B

FRESH FROM THE SEA   £22   432

18 NEW ROAD PL29 3SB   01208 880849

"Fresh and lovely seafood" is the hallmark of this wee fisherman's cottage on the harbour just near where the boats land the catch – mostly a fishmonger's, but also featuring a cosy café. "There are Michelin stars down the road but a crab sandwich here takes some beating". / www.freshfromthesea.co.uk; Wed-Sat 9 pm, Sun 3.30 pm; no bookings.

OUTLAW'S FISH KITCHEN   £63   544

1 MIDDLE ST PL29 3RH   01208 881138

"A delightful tiny restaurant with a tiny kitchen serving tiny plates of deliciousness" – Nathan Outlaw's "casual", more affordable spin-off provides "an exciting and appetising tasting menu" of "extremely good" fish and seafood "tapas". / www.nathan-outlaw.com/restaurants/ outlaws-fish-kitchen; @outlawsgrubclub; 9 pm; closed Mon & Sun.

PORT GAVERNE HOTEL   £51   343

PL29 3SQ   01208 880244

"One thing Port Isaac itself lacks is decent pub food – walk in to the next bay, and this is what the Port Gaverne provides", with its "delicious seafood and local beer overlooking the beach" – no wonder it's a firm favourite with Martin Clunes, who films Doc Martin hereabouts. / www.portgavernehotel.co.uk; N of Port Isaac on coast road (B3314); Mon-Thu 10.30 pm, Fri & Sat 10.45 pm; no Amex; children: 7+. *Accommodation:* 15 rooms, from £53

RESTAURANT NATHAN OUTLAW   £167   554

6 NEW RD PL29 3SB   01208 880 896

"Well worth the drive to Cornwall…" – the famous Cornish chef's flagship occupies "a romantic clifftop setting, overlooking the sea" in a beautiful village "on the stunningly beautiful North Cornish coast", and numerous reporters acclaim it for "the best fish and seafood in the UK". "It really really does live up to the hype. The simplified, choice-free menu means you just need to sit back and let the chef's brilliant creations work their magic". Dishes are "so exquisitely prepared, with such clean and pure but striking flavours". "Service led by Stephi Little is so friendly, yet it retains a level of easy expertise, and the wine flight, concocted by sommelier Damon Little, supplies perfect matches with sometimes unfamiliar labels". (And it's not just good for fish: "Nathan was cooking.

I'm a veggie and the vegetarian menu was the best I've ever eaten!") / www.nathan-outlaw.com; @ResNathanOutlaw; Fri & Sat, Wed & Thu 9 pm.

PORTHGAIN, PEMBROKESHIRE   4–4B

THE SHED   £39   433

SA62 5BN   01348 831518

"Idyllically located, right on the harbour at Porthgain, this "very rustic but charmingly so" bistro is "always friendly" and has a "simple and relaxed atmosphere". It serves "fish as fresh as you'll find: everything from traditional, wonderfully crisp and crunchy fish 'n' chips to imaginatively prepared and delicious dishes" (e.g. "the best monkfish stew ever"). Sit outside in the summer overlooking the water". / www.theshedporthgain.co.uk; @ShedPorthgain; Tue-Sun, Mon 9.30 pm; no Amex; no bookings.

PORTHLEVEN, CORNWALL   1–4A

KOTA   £62   443

HARBOUR HEAD TR13 9JA   01326 562407

"Accomplished and memorably inventive", Kiwi chef Jude Kereama wins high praise for the cooking at the harbourside restaurant he runs with his wife Jane, which "uses fresh local seafood and adds a twist of Japan and Asia". "The wine list is advanced for the area, with very well chosen bottles, particularly from New Zealand". / www.kotarestaurant.co.uk; @KotaRestaurant; Mon-Sat 11 pm, Sun 10.30 pm; no Amex. *Accommodation:* 2 rooms, from £70

KOTA KAI   £37   333

CELTIC HOUSE, HARBOUR HEAD TR13 9JY 01326 574411

An "idyllic setting" with "fab views over Porthleven harbour" elevates a visit to Kota's "very child-friendly" and "relaxed" sibling (both run by Great British Menu chef Jude Kereama); particular shout-outs for the "tasty burgers and steak with an Asian twist". / www.kotakai.co.uk; @Kota_Kai; Mon & Tue, Thu-Sat 9 pm.

RICK STEIN'S SEAFOOD RESTAURANT   £89   324

MOUNT PLEASANT TR13 9JS 01841 532700

"With its lovely location, overlooking the harbour in a nicely refurbished old warehouse, the Porthleven Stein has more charm and character than the nearby Falmouth branch" and there's "a great buzz about the place". When it comes to the range of fish and seafood, reports are generally upbeat (with some "exceptionally good" meals noted), but overall food scores are middling with gripes about high prices in particular. Service likewise seemed more 'hit 'n' miss' this year ("either efficient and friendly or forgetful and impersonal"). / www.rickstein.com; @TheSeafood; children: 3.

THE SQUARE AT PORTHLEVEN   £35   333

7 FORE STREET TR13 9HQ   01326 573 911

Attractively situated modern brasserie with outside tables near the harbour, which "uses lots of local produce and produces its own ice cream". "Book if you want to guarantee a table". / www.thesquareatporthleven.co.uk; @thesquarepl; Wed-Sat 9 pm, Sun 3.30 pm.

PORTMEIRION, GWYNEDD   4–2C

PORTMEIRION HOTEL   £76   335

LL48 6ET   01766 772440

For "location, location and location" it is tough to beat this very "romantic" hotel dining room with "beautiful views over the estuary" at the heart of the famous Mediterranean-style village (and gardens), developed from 1925 on by Sir Clough Williams-Ellis. When it comes to the cuisine, some reporters feel "they could do better" or that service "can be a little haphazard", but on all accounts it's "definitely one to try". / www.portmeirion-village.com/eat/ the-hotel-dining-room/; off A487 at Minffordd; Mon-Sat 1 am, Sun midnight. *Accommodation:* 14 rooms, from £185

PORTRUSH, COUNTY ANTRIM   10–1D

PORTRUSH DELI CO   £11   444

7 BATH STREET BT56 8AN   02870822871

"Cara O'Donovan continues to serve up amazing degustation menus" (featuring "the most delicious quail" ever) at this dinky (eight-seat) deli and cafe, which also has a line in gourmet sandwiches and salads; refreshingly, it's BYOB with no corkage charge. / www.portrushdeli.com; Mon-Sat 11 pm, Sun 10 pm.

PORTSMOUTH, HAMPSHIRE   2–4D

ABARBISTRO   £44   322

58 WHITE HART RD PO1 2JA   02392 811585

"Okay, so it doesn't command brilliant views" but "on a sunny day, sitting in the courtyard" at this Old Portsmouth bistro is "delightful". From a menu that's "quite adventurous" results are "better than average", and they serve "out-of-the-way wines" from their upstairs bottle shop. / www.abarbistro.co.uk; @abarbistro; 10 pm.

PORTSTEWART, COUNTY LONDONDERRY   10–1D

HARRY'S SHACK   £39   434

118 STRAND ROAD BT55 7PG 028 7083 1783

"Fabulously fresh fish" is "imaginatively prepared, in the perfect location" at this "great spot on the beach at Portstewart". Sadly it's now the last link in the Harry's chain, with both its long running 'Harry's' Bridgend predecessor and younger offshoot, 'Harry's Derry', shutting in recent times. / www.facebook.com/HarrysShack; @Harrys_Shack; Sun & Mon 8.30 pm, Tue-Thu 9 pm, Fri & Sat 9.30 pm.

Yorke Arms, Ramsgill-in-Nidderdale

PRESTON BAGOT, WARWICKSHIRE   5–4C

THE CRABMILL   £48   322

B95 5EE   01926 843342

Not far from the M40, this "deservedly popular" gastropub beckons with its "always reliable" grub (including "excellent fish 'n' chips"); the classy, beamed interior is appealing, but al fresco dining can be "very pleasant" in sunshine too. / www.thecrabmill.co.uk; @lvlycrabmill; on main road between Warwick & Henley-in-Arden; Mon-Thu 9 pm, Fri & Sat 9.30 pm, Sun 8.30 pm; no Amex.

PRESTON, LANCASHIRE   5–1A

BUKHARA   £37   442

**154 PRESTON NEW RD   PR5 0UP
01772 877710**

"A must visit when in the Blackburn/Preston area for a really authentic curry experience" – this roadside destination is among the "best in Lancashire" for "great Indian cooking with a twist" ("never over-spiced but always interesting"). "It doesn't sell alcohol, if that bothers you". / www.bukharasamlesbury.co.uk; Mon-Sun 11 pm.

PWLLHELI, GWYNEDD   4–2C

PLAS BODEGROES £64

NEFYN RD LL53 5TH   01758 612363

Our feedback is stellar, as it often has been regarding Chris and Gunna Chown's wonderful retreat – a Grade II listed restaurant-with-rooms outside Pwllheli, which they took back from a management company that they felt had made a poor fist of running it after they retired. We've left it un-rated however as change is again afoot – having recently failed to sell the business as a going concern, in October 2018 they announced they are now applying for planning permission to sell it as a residence as they no longer feel it is viable as a restaurant. / www.bodegroes.co.uk; @plasbodegroes; on A497 1m W of Pwllheli; Tue-Sat 10 pm; no Amex; children: 12+ at D.
Accommodation: 10 rooms, from £130

QUEENSBURY, MIDDLESEX   3–3A

REGENCY CLUB   £40   332

**19-21 QUEENSBURY STATION PDE HA8 5NR
020 8952 6300**

Beloved by Lily Allen (if that's an incentive!) this ultra-buzzy, wood-panelled curry club – perked up by a recent refurb' – has a winning line in Kenyan-slanted Indian cuisine, including especially "great starters". / www.regencyclub.co.uk; @RegencyClubUK; Mon-Sat 11 pm, Sun 10.30 pm; children: 18+.

RADNAGE, BUCKINGHAMSHIRE   3–2A

MASH INN   £84   545

**HORSESHOE RD, BENNETT END HP14 4EB
01494 482 440**

"Everything exceeds expectation" at Nick Mash's "totally relaxing", two-year-old conversion of an 18th-century inn (FKA The Three Horseshoes), "remotely located in beautiful Chilterns countryside". "Every dish has an unusual twist, from foraged salads to meat cooked over the rustic charcoal grill in the fantastic adjoining open kitchen". "This is exciting dining not often found outside London". / www.themashinn.com; Mon-Fri 10.30 pm, Sat 11 pm.

RAMSBOTTOM, LANCASHIRE   5–1B

BARATXURI   £46   443

1 SMITHY ST BL0 9AT   01706 559090

"What was a fabulous pintxo bar in the rather incongruous setting of Ramsbottom has added an impressive wood-fired Pereruela oven" and expanded into the next-door shop, adding a dining room (or 'comedor') for "super", mostly roasted things ("especially meat"). The bar still turns out "fabulous" pintxos, but seems to have "lost its former focus", although "the wine list (shared with nearby sibling Levanter) remains interesting and fairly priced". / www.levanterfinefoods.co.uk/baratxuri; @BaratxuriBar; Wed-Sat , Sun 7 pm.

EAGLE & CHILD   £51   333

3 WHALLEY ROAD BL0 0DL   01706 557181

"Beautifully renovated", traditional pub on the village green (with an extensive garden for the summer months) that wins praise for its "high quality food" and "great selection of cask ales". / eagle-and-child.com; @EagleChildRammy; M6, J27; Tue-Sat 9.30 pm, Sun 2.30 pm; no Amex.

THE HUNGRY DUCK £46

**76 BRIDGE STREET BL0 9AG
01706 550899**

This little five-year-old venture was revamped about a year ago. Feedback is still too limited for a rating, but it's a promising option, serving hearty bistro fare. / www.hungry-duck.co.uk; @HungryDuckUK; Mon-Sat 5 pm.

LEVANTER   £37   554

10 SQUARE ST BL0 9BE   01706 551530

"True Andalusian cooking in Lancashire" – Joe & Fiona Botham's "excellent" tapas joint has a "fantastic selection of tasty morsels, reasonably priced" ("mostly made with high quality, Spanish ingredients"), plus an "interesting" wine list shared with sibling Baratxuri, round the corner. "It was pretty perfect to start with, but now you can book!" / www.levanterfinefoods.co.uk; @levanterfoods; Wed 11 pm.

RAMSGATE, KENT   3–3D

THE EMPIRE ROOM, ROYAL HARBOUR HOTEL £44   444

**10-12 NELSON CRESCENT CT11 9JF
01843 582511**

"Chef Craig Mather showcases the best local produce with great finesse in his short seasonal menus" at this "eccentric (in a good way) local gem", "tucked away in the basement of the Royal Harbour Hotel" – "a cosy, club-like space, with warm red walls, and with original Empire magazine covers on display". "His light touch allows the ingredients to speak for themselves", while "the fish dishes have no rival in this part of Kent". "There's a garden for summertime with dogs welcome to dine alongside their humans in the sun". / theempireroom.co.uk/; @EmpRoom; Mon-Sat 10 pm.

FLAVOURS BY KUMAR   £38   442

2 EFFINGHAM ST CT11 9AT   01843 852631

"Although located in a rather dated former pub, in a Ramsgate backstreet", this "startling" place is a "brilliant find". It may look like a "basic curry house", but fans say the cuisine is "on a par with some of London's top Indian restaurants, at a fifth of the price" ("close to matching the meals I've had at Gymkhana"). Indian-born Anil Kumar, formerly head chef at Ambrette, has opened a second branch in Margate. / www.flavoursbykumar.co.uk/; @flavoursbykumar; Tue-Fri 9 pm, Mon 9.30 pm, Sun 3 pm.

RAMSGILL-IN-NIDDERDALE, NORTH YORKSHIRE   8–4B

YORKE ARMS   £115   534

HG3 5RL   01423 755243

Famous for the "sheer excellence" of its food for more than 20 years, this old moorland coaching inn was put on the gastronomic map by self-taught cook Frances Atkins, one of the leading British chefs of her generation. Having sold the business a year ago so her husband Bill could retire, Frances agreed to stay on board, working with new owner Jonathan Turner – to a chorus of cheers from grateful foodies. The restaurant reopened after renovations in summer 2018 , with regulars hoping "the new owner runs it in the same way" (and we've rated it on the assumption that he does). Top tip: "make sure you see the kitchen garden". / www.theyorkearms.co.uk; @theyorkearms; 4m W of Pateley Bridge; 8.45 pm; closed Mon & Sun.
Accommodation: 16 rooms, from £200

RASCILLS   £67   4|4|3

**VILLAGE FARM, HOWKER LN YO61 3LF
01347 822031**

"A 20-cover operation where the chef cooks and his wife serves" – Lindsey and Richard Johns "have a good pedigree having owned the Artisan in Hessle" and their small, high-ceilinged two-year-old venture north of York is likewise proving "a worthy addition to the area" thanks to its "grown-up and assured cuisine". / rascillsrestaurant.co.uk; Mon-Sat 9.30 pm, Sun 4 pm.

BRIDGE INN   £44   3|3|4

27 BAIRD ROAD EH28 8RA   0131 333 1320

"Sit next to the canal and watch the world go by" on a sunny day at this "excellently situated" and well-known pub (which you can cycle to, down the towpath), where chef Ben Watson delivers "very pleasant well-cooked food" with produce from the pub's own walled garden and pork from their own pigs. / www.bridgeinn.com; Sun-Thu 11 pm, Fri & Sat midnight.

FORBURY'S   £66   3|3|2

1 FORBURY SQ RG1 3BB   0118 957 4044

A smart, roomy and well-established hotel dining room, handy for the station. Popular for business entertaining: it remains worthy of investigation principally on account of its superb wine list, though the food is "good quality" too. / www.forburys.co.uk; @forburys; Tue-Sat 9.30 pm.

LONDON STREET BRASSERIE   £64   3|2|3

RIVERSIDE ORACLE, 2 - 4 LONDON STREET RG1 4PN   0118 950 5036

In a "fab location for the busy shopper or night out in town" (and with "outside tables beside the canal for warm summer evenings"), this 18th-century tollhouse combines "lovely brasserie food and friendly service". / www.londonstbrasserie.co.uk; @lsb_reading; 10.30 pm, Fri & Sat 11 pm.

THAMES LIDO   £18   3|4|4

NAPIER ROAD RG1 8FR   0118 207 0640

"Who knew there was something this nice in READING?" This conversion of an Edwardian Lido (by the same folks behind the restoration of Bristol's Lido) opened in October 2017 and is a brilliant addition to the area. The café serves food from breakfast on, and for meals later in the day there's "an ever-changing menu that keeps you coming back for more". / @ThamesLido.

THE DIAL HOUSE   £50

MARKET PLACE NR10 4JJ   01603 879900

Limited but positive all-round feedback on the dining room at this small (8-room) but handsome Georgian building, overlooking the market square of an unspoilt rural market town. And that was before it was purchased by Hannah Springham and Andrew Jones, the owners of Norwich's Farmyard, who aim to improve the food offering here. / www.thedialhouse.org.uk/; @thedialhouse.

LA BARBE   £66   4|4|3

71 BELL ST RH2 7AN   01737 241966

Having just celebrated its 35th anniversary, Serge Tassi's veteran "continues to up its game"; "it still keeps its French brasserie heart", with "authentic" cooking that "takes advantage of the seasons". It's "not cheap but reasonably priced". / www.labarbe.co.uk; @LaBarbeReigate; Mon-Sat 11 pm, Sun 10.30 pm.

MARKHAM MOOR INN   £37   3|3|3

**OLD GREAT NORTH ROAD DN22 0QU
01777 838229**

"It looks like a pub from the outside" (and does provide an extensive pub menu), "but the great quality restaurant is far away from pub grub" at this old inn – "worth considering if you're travelling along the A1" with accommodation and a garden (complete with kids' play area). / www.markhammoorinn.co.uk; Mon-Sat 9.30 pm, Sun 4 pm.

CHEZ LINDSAY   £53   3|4|3

11 HILL RISE TW10 6UQ   020 8948 7473

"Delicious" galettes (traditional buckwheat savoury pancakes) and plenty of seafood are cooked to order at this "typical" Breton bistro near Richmond Bridge. "Jolly waiters make for a great evening here", and there's a list of sparkling ciders as well as wine. / www.chez-lindsay.co.uk; @Chez_Lindsay; Mon-Sat 11 pm, Sun 10 pm; no Amex.

THE DUKE   £47   3|4|3

2 DUKE ST TW9 1HP   020 8940 4067

This 'Food and Fuel' gastroboozer with a Victorian bar remains a local staple for its "nice friendly ambience" and – amongst other things – "great steak, every time!" Stop Press: The Duke was acquired by Brunning & Price in August 2018, so perhaps change is afoot. / www.foodandfuel.co.uk/our-pubs/the-duke-richmond/; @TheDukePub; Mon-Thu 10 pm, Fri & Sat 10.30 pm, Sun 9 pm.

THE RETREAT KITCHEN   £23   3|4|3

16 HILL RISE TW10 6UA   020 8127 0700

"A vegan surprise" not far from Richmond Bridge – this "fantastic", simple, little café has a "lovely atmosphere" and provides food that's "all healthy and cooked on-site" – "tasty and you feel good!" / www.theretreatkitchen.co.uk; Mon-Sat 9.30 pm, Sun 4 pm.

ANCHOR   £67   3|3|3

HIGH ST GU23 6AE   01483 211866

This handsome old brick-and-beams pub serves "ambitious but very consistent" meals, prepared by an enthusiastic team led by "an excellent young chef" – Mike Wall-Palmer – "ably guided by Steve Drake", the owner, whose main operation is now Sorrel in Dorking. / www.ripleyanchor.co.uk; @RipleyAnchor; Mon-Sat 11 pm, Sun 9 pm.

THE CLOCK HOUSE   £86   5|5|4

**THE CLOCK HOUSE, HIGH ST GU23 6AQ
01483 224777**

"Maybe even better than when it was Drakes" – there's certainly been no dive in quality at Serina Drake's "delightful" property (renamed after the split from her husband, who is now at Sorrel in Dorking). "You are made to feel like you are the only guests in the restaurant by the very friendly staff" and Fred Clapperton's cuisine is "sensational and very good value". / www.theclockhouserestaurant.co.uk; @tchripley; 9.15 pm; closed Mon, Tue L & Sun.

PINNOCKS   £13   3|3|4

HIGH ST GU23 6AF   01483 222419

"If you like large, delicious mugs of coffee served in a listed building crammed with books and comfy chairs, Pinnocks is the place for you" – a "lovely, quirky" café also reputed for its "great sausage rolls". / www.pinnockscoffeehouse.com; @pinnockscoffee; Wed-Sat , Sun 7 pm.

DINING ROOM   £59   4|4|2

**PAVILION BUILDINGS, ROCK RD PL27 6JS
01208 862622**

Fred & Donna Beedle's comfortable, classy operation turns out some "exceptional" classical food, all homemade and strong on local produce, in a slightly less exceptional setting amid a parade of shops. / www.thediningroomrock.co.uk; @TheDiningRmRock; Mon-Thu midnight, Fri & Sat 1 am, Sun 11 pm; no Amex; children: 10+.

MARINERS   £53   3|2|3

PL27 6LD   01208 863 679

"Nathan Outlaw + Pub food = A Great Combination", according to most reports on this Sharp's Brewery pub, with Camel estuary views from its terrace and balcony. Not everyone's wowed though: "why he gives his name to this place I don't know: couldn't eat my steak, and how can you get smoked salmon wrong?" / www.themarinersrock.com/; @TheMarinersRock; 9.30 pm Sun 4.30 pm.

ST ENODOC RESTAURANT, ST ENODOC HOTEL £68 444

ROCK ROAD PL27 6LA 01208 863394

"Top-class", "well-crafted seafood in a perfect location with views across the Camel estuary" remain the key features of this hotel venue which has seen two Nathans – first Nathan Outlaw, then MasterChef winner James Nathan – come and go in recent times (the latter departing in summer 2017 leaving Felix Craft at the stoves). Fans say he "maintains the same very high standard" of his predecessor, and the most critical review is still pretty measured: "the food's gone from outstanding to good". / www.enodoc-hotel.co.uk/food.html; 9 pm.

ROCKBEARE, DEVON 1-3D

THE JACK IN THE GREEN INN £48 322

EX5 2EE 01404 822240

Five minutes from Junction 29 of the M5, this flagstone-floored, surprisingly roomy gastroboozer is the ultimate anti-service-station, turning out quality pub grub and a particularly good-value 'Totally Devon' menu showcasing the best of the West Country. / www.jackinthegreen.uk.com; @JackGreenInn; On the old A30, 3 miles east of junction 29 of M5; Mon-Thu 12.30 am, Fri 1 am; no Amex.

ROSEVINE, CORNWALL 1-4B

DRIFTWOOD HOTEL £91 544

TR2 5EW 01872 580644

Cornish-born Chris Eden is "a chef who knows how to please", and his "fabulous food" is perfectly showcased in the "idyllic setting" of a clifftop boutique hotel with its own private beach on the Roseland Peninsula. Top Tip: "the lobster is truly wonderful". / www.driftwoodhotel.co.uk; @DriftwoodHotel; off the A30 to Truro, towards St Mawes; 9.30pm; D only; children: 7. *Accommodation:* 15 rooms, from £185

ROWSLEY, DERBYSHIRE 5-2C

THE PEACOCK AT ROWSLEY £78 333

BAKEWELL RD DE4 2EB 01629 733518

A rather traditionally decorated country house hotel in the Peak District (dating from 1652, and with gardens bordering the River Derwent) with both a bar and ambitious (if pricey) restaurant, where Dan Smith's cooking continues to win very solid ratings. There's a range of menus, running up to a 10-course tasting option. / www.thepeacockatrowsley.com; @peacockrowsley; 9 pm, Sun 8.30 pm; booking max 8 may apply; children: 10+ at D. *Accommodation:* 15 rooms, from £160

RUTHIN, DENBIGHSHIRE 4-1D

ON THE HILL £44 443

1 UPPER CLWYD STREET LL15 1HY 01824 707736

Long-established and "unpretentious" bistro in a "quirky, comfortable" 16th century building; for "quality and quantity", the "friendly" operation is "probably the best in Ruthin!" – so "book (you'll need to, for lunch and dinner)" and "be delighted". / onthehillrestaurant.co.uk/; Mon-Sat 9 pm.

RYE, EAST SUSSEX 3-4C

LANDGATE BISTRO £41 432

5 - 6 LANDGATE TN31 7LH 01797 222829

Longstanding chef-proprietor Martin Peacock serves up "delicious food" with "interesting and perfectly balanced flavours on his locally sourced menus", including fish, game and notably Romney Marsh lamb. The bistro is small, with a "trendy but nicely atmospheric dining room". / www.landgatebistro.co.uk; Wed-Sat 11 pm, Sun 3.30 pm; no Amex.

TUSCAN RYE £40 333

8 LION ST TN31 7LB 01797 223269

Owners Franco (chef) & Jen (front-of-house) returned to the fold of this "very popular" beamed dining room in October 2015 after two years' absence; by all accounts, it's again turning out "interesting dishes from Tuscany" and "wines to match" (watch out for tasting events, or pop in for a pre-cinema drink). / www.tuscankitchenrye.co.uk; Thu-Sat 11 pm, Sun 4 pm.

WEBBE'S AT THE FISH CAFE £52 322

17 TOWER STREET TN31 7AT 01797 222 226

"A jewel of a piscine experience", say fans of the "fresh" and "creative fish dishes" – using the catch landed at Rye and Hastings – at this "fuss-free", "café-style" venue; an Edwardian warehouse conversion that's one of chef Paul Webbe's four East Sussex venues. / www.webbesrestaurants.co.uk/the-fish-cafe/; @webbesrye; 9.30 pm.

SALISBURY, WILTSHIRE 2-3C

ANOKAA £50 332

60 FISHERTON ST SP2 7RB 01722 414142

Halfway between Salisbury station and the Marketplace, this local favourite skips the usual Indian fare for adventurous, beautifully presented fusion dishes; the buffet lunch is particularly good value. / www.anokaa.com; @eatatanokaa; 10.30 pm; no shorts.

SALTAIRE, WEST YORKSHIRE 5-1C

SALTS DINER, SALTS MILL £37 323

SALTS MILL, VICTORIA ROAD BD18 3LA 01274 530 533

A very "competent" (if sometimes "extremely noisy") gallery café in the "interesting" setting of the UNESCO-listed Salts Mill complex, and with arty David Hockney napkins to match. / www.saltsmill.org.uk; 2m from Bradford on A650; Mon-Sat midnight, Sun 10 pm; no Amex; no bookings.

SALTBURN, COUNTY DURHAM 8-3C

THE SEAVIEW £44 444

THE FORESHORE BUILDING, LOWER PROMENADE TS12 1HQ 01287 236015

"Terrific views over Saltburn pier and the seafront from a first floor banquette" further boost the appeal of "this airy and modern fish 'n' chip café", set over two floors and with an outside terrace. "Prices are very reasonable and the food's great" and "while there's always a long queue it's worth the wait". "A 'fine dining' menu was introduced recently giving a lovely contrast to the typical (though very good) chippie fare: all beautifully cooked and presented". / theseaviewrestaurant.co.uk; Mon-Sat 9.30 pm, Sun 4 pm.

SALTHOUSE, NORFOLK 6-3C

DUN COW £43 333

PURDY ST NR25 7XA 01263 740467

"A great pub on the North Norfolk coast with a casual feel" (beams, brick fireplace) and "nice staff", plus a garden overlooking the marshes; on the food front, the fish pie elicits special mention. / www.salthouseduncow.com; @salthouseduncow; 9pm.

SANCTON, EAST YORKSHIRE 5-1D

STAR £41 222

KING ST YO43 4QP 01430 827269

Ben and Lindsey Cox's well-known destination pub in the East Ridings attracted plentiful but uneven commentary this year. "Massively extended" a couple of years ago, "you can feel like a headcount rather than a welcome guest" nowadays and "some areas are better and more comfortable than others". The food can be "first class", but can also "fail to live up to the hype" or seem "good, but nothing like as special as it once was". / www.thestarsancton.co.uk; Tue-Sat 9.30 pm, Sun 8 pm.

SANDBANKS, DORSET 2-4C

RICK STEIN £61 445

10-14 BANKS RD BH13 7QB 01202 283 000

"Fabulous seafood in a friendly and casual environment, and with a gorgeous setting overlooking Poole Harbour" is the prospect at this two-year-old outpost of the Stein empire which is "not quite as much of a 'dining experience' as Stein's Seafood Restaurant in Padstow, but thoroughly enjoyable nevertheless".

Spicier dishes are often the ones singled out for praise here ("Goan fish curry alone is worth the drive down from London…"; "order the extremely messy Singapore chilli crab and pig out"; "Indonesian seafood curry was bursting with flavour"). Some of the praise is caveated by concerns over its prices though ("£28 for fish 'n' chips which was nothing special"). / www.rickstein.com/eat-with-us/rick-stein-sandbanks; @SteinSandbanks; Mon-Thu 9.30 pm, Fri & Sat 10 pm, Sun 9 pm; children: 3.

LA ROCK   £75   4|4|3

4 BRIDGE STREET   NG10 5QT   0115 9399 833

"Consistently impressive" cooking "served by attentive and knowledgeable staff" has garnered uniformly high ratings this year for this "high-quality" outfit just off the M1. It's "excellent value" too, especially when you take into consideration extras such as the "superb amuse bouche". / www.larockrestaurant.co.uk; @laRock_NG10; Wed-Sat 8.30 pm, Sun 1.30 pm.

THE SALUTATION HOTEL & RESTAURANT   £80   4|4|5

KNIGHTRIDER ST   CT13 9EW   01304 619919

"A welcome addition to the east Kent dining scene", the restaurant opened in 2017 following a makeover of this Grade I-listed Lutyens-designed boutique hotel, "famed for its gardens". First-year ratings for food are excellent, and it seems to be "settling down as a top gastronomic destination after a shaky start". Chef Shane Hughes (ex-Connaught, Whatley Manor, Ynyshir Hall) offers a range of meal options, including a "delicious and playful afternoon tea" and a 'blind' menu served in the Tasting Room. / www.the-salutation.com; @Salut_Sandwich; 9pm; may need + to book. *Accommodation:* 17 rooms, from £233

THE BELL AT SAPPERTON   £47   3|3|4

GL7 6LE   01285 760298

"With a new chef and a new menu, things are really looking up at the Bell", according to fans of this country pub – in true rustic style, "you can arrive on your trusty steed and tether him up at his own appointed rail". / www.bellsapperton.co.uk; @bellsapperton; from Cirencester take the A419 towards Stroud, turn right to Sapperton; Mon-Sat 11 pm, Sun 9 pm.

COAST   £73   4|3|4

COPPET HALL BEACH   SA69 9AJ   01834 810800

"Ambitious and exceptional" cooking, "focused on fish and seafood", is reason enough to seek out this sleek-looking and modern, timber-clad operation – "unless it's for the wonderful seaside views", which make it a "perfect romantic spot at sunset". Regular diners report that there's

been "no decline in standards" in the year since new chef Tom Hine, "Padstow-born and trained", took over from Will Holland. / coastsaundersfoot.co.uk; @CoastRestaurant; 8.45 pm; closed Mon & Tue.

LANTERNA   £55   4|5|3

33 QUEEN STREET   YO11 1HQ   01723 363616

A local institution for four decades, "this family-run restaurant is a must when in Scarborough". Giorgio Alessio's "unfailingly delicious" cooking is a wonderful marriage of Piedmontese skill with Yorkshire produce. The opening dish on his menu sets the tone: 'stufato di pesce di Scarborough' (local fish stew) – "book early!". / www.lanterna-ristorante.co.uk; Mon closed, Tue - Sat 9.30 pm, Sun closed; no Amex.

THE HARE INN RESTAURANT   £74   5|5|3

YO7 2HG   01845 597 769

"A husband and wife labour of love" – Paul and Liz Jackson's ancient inn (thirteenth century) overlooking the North York Moors offers a "feast for all the senses" with its six-course and eight-course tasting menus (there's no à la carte). "Service is exceptional with a really personal touch". / www.thehare-inn.com; @harescawton; off A170; closed Mon, Tue & Sun D.

SAN PIETRO RESTAURANT   £59   3|3|3

11 HIGH STREET EAST   DN15 6UH   01724 277774

Limited but positive feedback on this restaurant-with-rooms – one of North Lincolnshire's few foodie bright sparks, set in converted windmill. There is a Mediterranean slant on the modern British cuisine and also a 'Taste of Sicily' menu, reflecting the heritage of the owner Pietro Catalano. / www.sanpietro.uk.com/; @SanPietroNLincs; 21:00. *Accommodation:* 14 rooms, from £105

THE SPORTSMAN   £57   5|5|5

FAVERSHAM ROAD   CT5 4BP   01227 273370

"From the outside, it really is a scruffy, rundown-looking pub in a bleak landscape" ("with views over fields … the sea is out over the back"), but "it's worth the long haul to find Stephen Harris's uninviting-looking old place as it offers inspiring cuisine" that many consider "the best 'pub' food in the UK". "The decor has been tidied up a bit recently, but happily not enough to jeopardise its second most attractive feature: it is unforgettably ordinary! That there's zero pretension contrasts spectacularly with the peerless kitchen". "The culinary approach is not fussy or arty but the straightforward route produces something sublime (dab and smear practitioners take

The Sportsman, Seasalter (Credit Philip Harris)

note!)": "simple, unpretentious and fantastically flavoursome" dishes using "good local produce (including lamb)" and with "fish cooking a highlight, as are the oysters, both natives and poached rocks". "The tasting menu is a real 'tour de force'" with "every dish spot-on" (you have to order it in advance, but there's now also a shorter one you can have on the day). "Good wine too at even better prices". "Everything just seems to work together perfectly". / www.thesportsmanseasalter.co.uk; @sportsmankent; Mon-Sat 11 pm, Sun 10 pm; no Amex; children: 18+ in main bar.

THE JOLLY CRICKETERS   £51   3|3|3

24 CHALFONT RD   HP9 2YG   01494 676308

A "quintessential English country pub in the Chilterns" ("cosy, welcoming, in a beautiful village, and only 20 miles from London") with an "interesting gastropub menu". It was a rundown local boozer destined for closure when former Soho House chef Chris Lillitou and his wife Amanda rescued it 10 years ago. / www.thejollycricketers.co.uk; @jollycricketers; 11.15 pm, Fri & Sat 11.30, Sun 10.30.

LITTLE GARDEN   £41   3|4|3

1-2 WELL COURT, BANK STREET   TN13 1UN   01732 469397

"Fresh, contemporary food" – including burgers and steaks singed under the Josper grill – is "pleasantly served" at this two-floor pitstop, run by Benjamin James of Chipstead's George & Dragon, and featuring a pretty decked courtyard with fairy lights (plus gingerbread house pop-up bar at Christmas). / www.littlegardensevenoaks.com/; @Littlegarden7; Mon-Thu 11 pm.

THE CRICKET INN   £46   3|3|3

PENNY LN   S17 3AZ   0114 236 5256

"Window seats have interesting views" at this pub on the edge of the Peak District. Run in part by local food hero Richard Smith, the food ranges between hearty classic dishes and more imaginative options. / www.cricketinn.co.uk; @cricketinnshef; Mon & Tue, Sun 10 pm, Wed-Sat 11 pm; no Amex.

JORO £65 544

294 SHALESMOOR S3 8US 0114 299 1539

"The best thing to happen in Sheffield in the last 20 years!" – This "exciting", Nordic-inspired venture "in a (comfortable) shipping container" is "one of those places you go and find yourself talking about a lot… because it's amazing!". Service from a "passionate young team" is "thoughtful but relaxed", and Luke French's "fantastically innovative, fairly priced tasting menus" of small plates deliver "some very advanced and clever cooking". / www.jororestaurant.co.uk; @JoroRestaurant; Tue-Sat 10 pm.

NONNA'S £48 433

535 - 541 ECCLESHALL ROAD S11 8PR 0114 268 6166

Maurizio Mori's much-loved Eccleshall operation (est. 1996) offers "the full, noisy Italian experience – home-style cooking, wonderful wine list and frenetic staff". / www.nonnas.co.uk/sheffield; @NonnasCucina; Mon-Sat 11 pm, Sun 10.30 pm; no Amex.

RAFTERS £65 444

220 OAKBROOK RD, NETHER GRN S11 7ED 0114 230 4819

Tom Lawson and Alistair Myers's "quiet and intimate upstairs dining room in an unlikely neighbourhood" hosts arguably "the top restaurant in Sheffield" and it "goes from strength to strength with new tasting menus: its weekend 'Experience' menus may sound a bit naff but they're excellent" (Experience One is an enhancement of the regular three-course menu, Experience Two is a longer tasting menu). "This is a stunning venue at the top of its game, with stunning, well-thought-out food and service, and staff who know what they're serving". / www.raftersrestaurant.co.uk; @rafterss11; Mon-Sat 10.30 pm; children: 8.

SILVERSMITHS £51 333

111 ARUNDEL ST S1 2NT 0114 270 6160

"One of Sheffield's old industrial spaces, converted into a comfortable restaurant with quirky style", and going like a dream since the then 'Runaway Girl' featured on Ramsay's Kitchen Nightmares in 2008; "they have a nicely considered menu with some interesting (Yorks-centric) choices", and the fishcakes are a "classic well worth trying". / www.silversmiths-restaurant.com; @Silversmiths; Mon-Sun 10.30 pm.

STREET FOOD CHEF £12 433

90 ARUNDEL ST S1 4RE 0114 275 2390

This popular, "cheap 'n' cheerful" Mexican cantina has been pumping out high-quality burritos, tacos, nachos and quesadillas for almost ten years. Eat in or take-away either here or at the Sharrow Vale Road sibling. /

www.streetfoodchef.co.uk; @streetfoodchef; Mon-Sat 5 pm, Sun 4.30 pm; no Amex; no bookings.

TAMPER COFFEE £18 444

149 ARUNDEL STREET S1 2NU 0114 275 7970

This striking, Kiwi-owned former industrial space, with vaulted red-brick ceiling in the Cultural Industries Quarter provides a "quirky, original and an all-round excellent experience" incorporating "very good coffee" (it has ties with Shoreditch's excellent Ozone coffee) and "good food that's out of the ordinary". "It's a top place for brunch". / tampercoffee.co.uk; Mon-Sat 9.30 pm, Sun 4 pm.

VERO GUSTO £77 443

12 NORFOLK ROW S1 2PA 0114 276 0004

"One of the best Italian restaurants in the North of England" is "run by a young couple with children, and unusually, of the two, the chef is the woman". The "rare" and "excellent" wine list shares honours with the "brilliant cooking". / www.verogusto.com; 10 pm; closed Mon & Sun.

THREE ACRES £63 334

ROYDHOUSE HD8 8LR 01484 602606

Fresh from celebrating its 50th anniversary, this hill-top institution (near the Emley TV transmitter) is "just how a traditional pub should be" according to most reports. It's become "so much more than just a pub with food" over the years, though, and – while "still a great favourite" – "it's not the cheapest" and can also appear a little "glitzy" or "corporate". / www.3acres.com; @3AcresInn; Mon-Sat 10.30 pm, Sun 4 pm; no Amex. *Accommodation:* 16 rooms, from £125

THE GREEN £65 333

3 THE GREEN DT9 3HY 01935 813821

"Very popular with the local smart crowd" – this "delightful" local, picturesquely located in the town, provides "well-presented and good quality" cooking from Russian chef/owner Sasha Matkevich. / www.greenrestaurant.co.uk; @greensherborne; Tue - Sat 9.30 pm; closed Mon & Sun.

KINGHAMS £54 344

GOMSHALL LN GU5 9HE 01483 202168

This beamed 17th-century house is set in "a pretty village" and has a "lovely garden seating area" for al fresco meals in the summer. "Consistently good" cooking and "excellent service" completes a package that has kept diners happy at Paul Barker's Surrey Hills stalwart for more than twenty five years. / www.kinghams-restaurant.co.uk; @KinghamsShere; off A25 between Dorking & Guildford; Mon-Wed 11 pm, Thu-Sat midnight.

L'ORTOLAN £99 434

CHURCH LN RG2 9BY 0118 988 8500

"A drink in the conservatory" has been a precursor to any meal at this bastion of fine dining for 35 years – in a converted village rectory near Reading – that "keeps up standards", with chef Tom Clarke's "absolutely superb" cooking: "a perfect balance of flavours, portion size and excitement on the plate, from the amuse bouche to the pudding". One or two reporters find the ambience a tad "hushed", but more commonly it's thought to be "lovely". / www.lortolan.com; @lortolan; 8.30 pm; closed Mon & Sun.

ORWELLS £63 543

SHIPLAKE ROW RG9 4DP 0118 940 3673

Ryan Simpson and Liam Trotman's smartly converted old pub – "beautifully situated" in the woods between Reading and Henley – has "grown in stature since it opened" a couple of years ago "and has not rested on its laurels". One or two reporters accuse it of "trying too hard", but the overwhelming picture is of "superb cooking matched by the quirky and superb selection of wines available from their Coravin". "Surely Michelin must give it a star soon – it's already a cut above many who have that honour!" / www.orwellsatshiplake.co.uk; @Orwells_Rest; 9.30 pm; closed Mon, Tue & Sun D.

AAGRAH £33 332

4 SALTAIRE RD BD18 3HN 01274 530880

A Shipley institution since 1977, this Kashmiri operation "continues to deliver great quality" in two formats – full menu and an upstairs carvery with a "brilliant buffet". There are now 12 branches and a catering division spread across Yorkshire, each of them managed by a member of chairman Mohammed Aslam's extended family. / www.aagrah.com; @Aagrahgroup; Mon-Thu 10.30 pm, Fri & Sat 11 pm, Sun 9 pm.

THE ROYAL OAK £61 543

2 UPPER FARM BARN, WHATCOTE CV36 5EF 01295 688 100

"The Cravens, previously at The Chef's Dozen in Chipping Campden, have moved to this small village near Shipston on Stour" and occupy this "comfortable" and "airy" conversion of one of England's oldest pubs (est. 1168). "Richard is still the best chef in the area" according to a number of reports, with a heavy focus on seasonal game bartered with locals or shipped in from Scotland. His South African-born wife Solanche is responsible for an SA-heavy wine list (there's also pigeon biltong). / www.theroyaloakwhatcote.co.uk; Wed-Sat 9 pm, Sun 2.30 pm.

SHIRLEY, DERBYSHIRE 5–3C

THE SARACEN'S HEAD £37 3 3 3

CHURCH LANE DE6 3AS 01335 360 330

A "beautifully furnished", long-established Derby Dale gastroboozer with "fab views" opposite the village church, and where the pub-style classics, rounded out by blackboard specials, make it something of a local favourite. / www.saracens-head-shirley.co.uk; Mon-Sun 9 pm; no Amex.

SHREWSBURY, SHROPSHIRE 5–4A

CSONS £39 4 3 3

8 MILK STREET SY1 1SZ 01743 272709

"A tremendous coffee shop and café run by the four Crouch brothers: they do what they say, producing fresh locally sourced food but with a globally-inspired menu changing daily". It provides "superb coffee and bright vibrant tasty street food." ("I had spicy Lebanese potatoes followed by their own succulent pressed beef burger and then a Japanese bean bun based dessert.") / www.csons-shrewsbury.co.uk; @CSonsShrewsbury; Mon & Tue 3.30 pm, Wed-Sat 10 pm, Sun 3 pm.

NUMBER FOUR £35 3 3 3

4 BUTCHER ROW SY1 1UW 01743 366691

This "very busy" but slickly run town-centre operation, a pleasingly light and airy space with a vaulted roof, has a winning line in unpretentious light bites, with the "lovely" full English and "best eggs Benedict" around perennial highlights. / www.number-four.com; @numberfourSY1; Tue-Thu 9 pm, Fri & Sat 9.30 pm, Mon 4 pm.

SLAD, GLOUCESTERSHIRE 2–2B

WOOLPACK 3 3 3

GL6 7QA 01452 813429

In the picturesque Slad valley, this "lovely, traditional pub" has won more attention of late thanks to Adam Glover's "excellent" food from a regularly changing menu. Alongside some more ambitious fare, there's pizza on Monday night, plus more traditional pub grub ("couldn't fault the ham sandwich: properly home-cooked thick-cut ham, nicely seasoned"). / Sun & Mon 11 pm, Tue-Thu midnight, Fri & Sat 1 am.

SLEAT, HIGHLAND 9–2B

KINLOCH LODGE £114 3 3 4

SLEAT IV43 8QY 01471 833333

"Situated on the shore of Loch na Daal with superb views across the Sound of Sleat to Knoydart" – the Macdonald of Macdonalds (Lord Godfrey, 34th hereditary chief of the clan, and food-writer wife, Claire) – have created an "ideal bolthole" at this well-known culinary destination. There are some reports of food that's "OK, but not really worth the price", but most reports of are of "being really well looked-after, with fantastic tasting menus using lots of local produce". / www.kinloch-lodge.co.uk; @kinloch_lodge; 9 pm; no Amex. **Accommodation:** 19 rooms, from £99

SNAPE, SUFFOLK 3–1D

THE CROWN INN £43 3 3 4

BRIDGE RD IP17 1SL 01728 688324

This 15th-century smugglers' tavern "in a delightful Suffolk village" has a "high standard of cooking", thanks to landlord-chef Garry Cook and his wife Teresa, whose smallholding produces vegetables and meat for the kitchen, including prize-winning rare-breed pork. "Take in the summer air here, or snuggle by the open fire on a cold winter's day". / www.snape-crown.co.uk; off A12 towards Aldeburgh; 9.30 pm, Sat 10 pm, Sun 9.30 pm; no Amex. **Accommodation:** 2 rooms, from £90

THE PLOUGH AND SAIL £36 3 3 2

SNAPE BRIDGE IP17 1SR 01728 688413

Twins Alex & Oliver Burnside's "very welcoming and efficient" pub offers a "good range of light lunch dishes" (extending to formal dinners) in a spacious setting that's ideally placed for the concert hall, art-browsing and shops at Snape Maltings. / www.theploughandsailsnape.com/; @PloughandSail; 10 pm.

SOLIHULL, WEST MIDLANDS 5–4C

PEEL'S, HAMPTON MANOR £80 3 4 5

SHADOWBROOK LANE B92 0EN 01675 446080

Afternoon tea is much-recommended at this "fabulous oasis of excellence" – the Hill family's stately restaurant with rooms, set in 45 acres on the outskirts of Birmingham. Still less feedback than we would like – but all very positive – on dining here, with options including a four-course or seven-course set menu. / www.hamptonmanor.com/; @HamptonManor; 9pm.

SONNING-ON-THAMES, BERKSHIRE 2–2D

THE FRENCH HORN £90 3 4 5

RG4 6TN 0118 969 2204

This "archetypal English restaurant" in a "very romantic setting" has been run "to the highest standards" by two generations of the Emmanuel family for almost 50 years. Distinguished by its "roaring log fires" (used to roast the signature dish of duck), it sits on the Thames "with sweeping lawns down to the river", just over the bridge from the desirable village of Sonning, home to the Clooneys and Theresa May. There's a "phenomenal and extensive wine list", and "the food is pretty good too" – although it tends to be rather overshadowed by this very traditional operation's other virtues. / www.thefrenchhorn.co.uk; @The_French_Horn; Mon-Sat 10.45 pm, Sun 9.45 pm; booking max 10 may apply. **Accommodation:** 21 rooms, from £160

SOUTH FERRIBY, LINCOLNSHIRE 6–2A

HOPE AND ANCHOR £49 3 4 3

SLUICE ROAD DN18 6JQ 01652 635334

In a "great setting" right on the Humber Estuary, and now Lincolnshire's only Bib Gourmand, this four-year-old in a 19th-century building combines "exceptional food and atmosphere", the former from chef Slawomir Mikolajczyk, who trained under Big Sweary, and is a steak maestro abetted by a fancy MaturMeat cabinet. / www.thehopeandanchorpub.co.uk; @hopeandanchorsf; Mon closed; Tue - Thu 9 pm, Fri & Sat 10 pm; Sun 6.

HOPE AND ANCHOR £45 4 4 4

SLUICE RD DN18 6JQ 01652 635 334

"On a beautiful spring day, amidst uplifting views of the river and the northern Wolds (which just go on and on and…), there are worse places to sit out and take in the afternoon sun than this posh boozer" in an isolated position on the banks of the Humber. "Slawek and his team combine the coziness of a country pub, with a menu with something for everyone and most attentive service". / www.thehopeandanchorpub.co.uk; @hopeandanchorsf; Tue-Thu, Sun 11 pm, Fri & Sat midnight.

SOUTH MILTON SANDS, DEVON 1–4C

BEACHHOUSE £53 3 3 3

TQ7 3JY 01548 561144

"It may only be a shack, but the seafood is super-fresh and tasty, and far more than fish 'n' chips" at this "warm and cosy" hut – a "rustic" joint a "stone's throw from the beach" and reachable via footpath from the car parks at both Milton and Thurlestone Sands. / www.beachhousedevon.com; Mon-Sat 11 pm, Sun 5 pm.

SOUTH SHIELDS, TYNE AND WEAR 8–2B

COLMANS £35 5 4 3

182-186 OCEAN RD NE33 2JQ 0191 456 1202

"Famous for fish for nearly 100 years" – fans hail this family-run veteran as "the top fish 'n' chip shop and restaurant in the North East": "super-motivated staff are welcoming and friendly", there's a "busy and exciting buzz" and the main event is "always well appreciated". "The new seafood palace nearby is fine, but you can't beat the old original!" (See also Colman's Seafood Temple). / www.colmansfishandchips.co.uk; @ColmansSeafood; 6.00pm; L only; no Amex; no bookings.

COLMANS SEAFOOD TEMPLE £34 4 4 3

SEA ROAD NE33 2LD

"Magnificent views over the North Sea" accompany a trip to this year-old new venture from the nearby fish 'n' chip supremo, which occupies a converted landmark on the seafront.

"Top fish 'n' chips" as you'd hope, plus "local coastal cuisine as well as a cocktail and oyster bar". /

SOUTHAMPTON, HAMPSHIRE   2–3D

LAKAZ MAMAN   £26   4 3 3

22 BEDFORD PLACE   SO15 2DB
023 8063 9217

MasterChef winner Shelina Permalloo's dinky Mauritian street food spot is "an oasis in the culinary desert that is Southampton", replete with tropical decor; "BYO with offie opposite" for a small corkage fee. / www.lakazmaman.com; @lakazmaman; Mon-Sun 10 pm.

SOUTHBOURNE, DORSET   2–4C

RESTAURANT ROOTS   4 2 3

141 BELLE VUE ROAD   BH6 3EN
01202 430005

A choice of tasting menus including two vegetarian options enhances a visit to this ambitious, 26-cover Southbourne venture, tucked away in Southbourne. Even a reporter who found it "pretentious, expensive, with some odd food combinations" rated the food as good, and more commonly it's described as "fabulous and excellent value". Service, though, can on occasion seem "overbearing" to fans and foes alike. / restaurantroots.co.uk; Mon-Sat 9.30 pm, Sun 4 pm.

SOUTHEND-ON-SEA, ESSEX   3–3C

THE PIPE OF PORT   £52   3 3 3

84 HIGH ST   SS1 1JN   01702 614606

This veteran basement wine bar and dining room (a former Davy's) near Southend station wins solid ratings for its traditional home-produced cooking, including classic pies, backed up by a list of 150 wines. / www.pipeofport.co.uk; @ThePipeofPort; basement just off High Street; Mon-Sat 9.50 pm, Sun 2.30 pm; no Amex; children: 16+.

SOUTHPORT, MERSEYSIDE   5–1A

BISTROT VÉRITÉ   £51   4 4 3

7 LIVERPOOL ROAD   PR8 4AR
01704 564 199

"This cosy Birkdale French bistro is deservedly popular for its consistently very good food,

Sole Bay Fish Company, Southwold

much of it locally sourced" (and "very reasonably priced" to boot); add in "welcoming, timely and professional" service and locals feel "lucky to live near this gem!" / www.bistrotverite.co.uk; Tue-Sat.

SOUTHSEA, HAMPSHIRE   2–4D

THE VINCENT HOTEL V-CAFE   £51   3 4 3

98 LORD STREET   PR8 1JR   0843 509 4586

The swish boutique hotel café/restaurant is "worth a visit at any time of day", but is "particularly good for people-watching at weekends". "The sushi dishes are worth trying as an alternative to the main menu" ("so clean, so careful") and the "open kitchen helps you see exactly how it's being prepared". / www.thevincenthotel.com; @vincenthotel; 10 pm. *Accommodation:* 60 rooms, from £93

RESTAURANT 27   £65   3 4 4

27A SOUTHSEA PARADE   PO5 2JF
023 9287 6272

With "high ambition" and a "limited menu (but this is no disadvantage)", this unassuming 'global French' hotspot, just off the seafront, is a bright spark in Portsmouth's still-emerging food scene. / www.restaurant27.com; @R27_southsea; Mon-Sat 10.30 pm.

SOUTHWOLD, SUFFOLK   3–1D

THE CROWN, ADNAMS HOTEL   £57   1 2 3

90 HIGH ST   IP18 6DP   01502 722275

This popular and handsome Adnams inn has attracted sparse feedback this year, but the ratings indicate there has been little or no improvement in a food offering that "varies from tasty to heavy and uninspired". / www.adnams.co.uk/stay-with-us/the-crown; @CrownSouthwold; Mon-Thu 11 pm, Fri & Sat midnight, Sun 10.30 pm; no Amex. *Accommodation:* 14 rooms, from £160

SOLE BAY FISH COMPANY   £32   4 3 4

22E BLACKSHORE   IP18 6ND   01502 724241

"Fish and shellfish fresh off their own boats" is the trump card at this quirky-looking harbour shack with "their own smokehouse". "Sticking with the local ethos" they now have a licence with "drinks from the local Adnams brewery/wine merchant/distillery", but it's all still pretty rough and ready by the standards of chichi Southwold. / www.solebayfishco.co.uk; Mon-Sun 5 pm.

SUTHERLAND HOUSE   £53   3 2 3

56 HIGH ST   IP18 6DN   01502 724544

"If it's Southwold it has to be fish, and this is the place to get it intelligently and excellently cooked" – a period-charm-packed B&B now run by former GM Andy Rudd and his wife Kinga – "always a pleasure to visit". / www.sutherlandhouse.co.uk;

@SH_Southwold; Mon-Fri 10 pm, Sat 10.30 pm. *Accommodation:* 3 rooms, from £150

THE SWAN   £56   2 3 3

THE MARKET PL   IP18 6EG   01502 722186

All agree that the "peaceful and genteel" Adnams brewery's flagship 17th-century hotel "on Southwold's bijou market place" was "in definite need of a facelift hotel-wise and a thorough kick-up-the-behind cooking-wise", and it reopened in October 2017 after a year-long re-fit. It's been a mixed success though. Fans feel "it could have only improved (which it has)"; and feel the new Still Room restaurant looks great". More common, however, are those who say: "oh dear! they misjudged with a more-Shoreditch-than-Southwold refit and threw the baby out with the bathwater". It doesn't help that "bills seem to have increased to reflect the massive cost of the refurb", so despite the fact that most reports actually do applaud "charming staff who are trying their best" and "good and inventive cooking", being charged "the upper end of London prices" contributes to an impression that "the whole concept just isn't working". (Those who are most enthusiastic ate in the old bar: "it's now named the Tap Room and ticks all the boxes"). / www.adnams.co.uk/stay-with-us/the-swan; @swansouthwold; Mon-Sat 11.30 pm, Sun 7 pm; no Amex; no jeans; children: 5+ at D. *Accommodation:* 42 rooms, from £185

SOWERBY BRIDGE, WEST YORKSHIRE   5–1C

GIMBALS   £39   3 3 3

76 WHARF ST   HX6 2AF   01422 839329

Janet & Simon Baker's eccentrically named (after a compass stabiliser) and oddly decorated stalwart (est. 1995) remains "very welcome in a surprisingly underserved area" owing to its good-value seasonal food. / www.gimbals.co.uk; @gimbalsworld; Mon-Sun 9.30 pm; no Amex.

THE MOORCOCK INN   £101   5 5 3

MOORBOTTOM LANE   HX6 3RP
01422 832103

"It came out of nowhere!" – "You will need your satnav" to find this lonely pub that feels marooned on't moors (but is actually quite near the M62). "From the outside, it's a bare, unadorned building, and is pretty much the same inside, with a distinct lack of frills and ornamentation". Under new ownership since February 2018, it's immediately making a major name for itself (including in the national press) – "just hope it doesn't get too busy now the secret is out!". "A former sous-chef from respected Belgian restaurant, 'In De Wulf', has arrived in Calderdale and is doing extraordinary food". "They make their own charcuterie and sourdough bread and cultured butter" and "with two repurposed pizza ovens they make their own charcoal and have an impressive charcoal stove-BBQ contraption". "When it comes to the resulting food, it's a sort of Basque Etxebarri meets Nordic on the Pennine moors, or maybe a sort of Rogan-style for people who like to eat heartily rather than be merely titillated". "Exquisite!" Service is "really friendly and knowledgeable" too. "The wine list is apparently largely natural, but I had one of the best pints of bitter I've had in a long time". "It's a complete gem – I've now been nine times since it opened!" / www.themoorcock.co.uk; @norlandmoorcock; Wed-Sat 11 pm, Sun 4 pm.

THE PLOUGH INN £42 222

WOODMAN LANE SO21 2NW 01962 776353

"Standard pub fayre that's probably not too bad" is the lukewarm verdict from some regulars at this popular rural gastroboozer, who say that while it's still a "reliable" culinary choice, "it's gone downhill" since brewery Wadworth imposed more "standardisation", which "has reduced the menu, and its originality". / www.ploughinnsparsholt.co.uk; Mon-Sat 9.30 pm, Sun 9 pm; no Amex.

BARRISSIMO £12 343

28 ST PETERS ST AL1 3NA 01727 869999

"A welcome change from the chain coffee shops that are all too evident in town", this "busy" and "good value" family-run cafe offers "great-value homemade Italian food and fantastic coffee" (all "freshly made each day and served with a smile"). / @Barrissimo; Mon-Sat 7 pm, Sun 6 pm; cash only.

DYLANS KINGS ARMS £49 333

7 GEORGE STREET AL3 4ER 01727530332

"What a find": "a small restaurant behind an even smaller pub front – both excellent" from local luminary Sean Hughes and chef Drew Knight. From the snacks (up front) to the 'Bill of Fayre' (out back), the seasonal food is "very close to the quality of Auberge du Lac (Knight's old gaffe) at a quarter of the cost". In summer 2018, Hughes opened The Plough, a scenic 45-minute walk away in the hamlet of Sleapshyde. / www.dylanskingsarms.com; Mon-Thu 9 pm, Fri & Sat 10 pm, Sun 3 pm.

LUSSMANNS £52 334

WAXHOUSE GATE, HIGH ST AL3 4EW 01727 851941

"Always buzzy from the set lunch to late-night dinners", Andrei Lussmann's flagship has an enthusiastic local following for its "consistent" menu of MSC-labelled sustainable fish and "reasonable prices". The former PizzaExpress executive has another four 'casual dining' venues under the same name in Hertfordshire, with investment from Luke Johnson. / www.lussmanns.com/restaurants/st-albans-restaurants/; @lussmanns; Mon & Tue, Sun 9 pm, Wed & Thu 9.30 pm, Fri & Sat 10.30 pm.

THE PRAE WOOD ARMS £42 234

GARDEN HOUSE LANE AL3 6JZ 01727 229090

A "beautiful location" – this "large, rambling and well-spaced" Georgian private home was opened as a gastropub by the Chester-based Brunning & Price chain in 2016, and has quickly built a solid reputation for a "pleasant" menu "full of excellent choices", "allied with good service". / www.brunningandprice.co.uk/praewoodarms/; Mon-Sat 9.30 pm, Sun 4 pm.

PRIME STEAK & GRILL £65 343

83 - 85 LONDON ROAD AL1 1LN 01727 840 309

Opposite art deco cinema The Odyssey, this slick banquette-lined venue wins solid feedback for the main event – grass-fed, 21-day aged and sourced from the Queen's own butcher; now with two siblings in Chandler's Cross and (as of late) Beaconsfield. / www.primesteakandgrill.com; Mon-Wed 11 pm, Thu-Sat midnight.

TABURE £43 343

6 SPENCER STREET AL3 5EG 01727 569068

With its "interesting" and "beautifully flavoured" dishes to share or hog, and "using only organic meat and poultry", this "noisy" Turkish dining room is "really unexpected for a not particularly amazing location (off the High St) and in an otherwise culinary desert". (There's a sibling Tabure on Berkhamsted's High Street.) / www.tabure.co.uk/; @Tabure_Kitchen; Tue-Sat 11 pm, Sun 10 pm.

THOMPSON £73 443

2 HATFIELD RD AL1 3RP 01727 730 777

"A great local restaurant for that special occasion" – chef Phil Thompson, formerly of Auberge du Lac, has built a loyal following in the area for his town-centre operation (which changed its name from Thompson@Darcy's in January 2018). "The kitchen is adaptable and everything is freshly cooked on the premises"; "it's very exciting to find food this good in St Albans". / www.thompsonstalbans.co.uk; @ThompsonDining; Wed-Sat, Tue 9 pm, Sun 3 pm.

SEAFOOD RESTAURANT £75 335

THE SCORES, BRUCE EMBANKMENT KY16 9AB 01334 479475

"The views here from the big glass windows over the beach are unmatchable" at this superbly located, stylishly decorated restaurant, situated near to the British Golf Museum and looking over the West Sands. The fish and seafood menu "is not particularly unusual but solidly well-realised". / www.theseafoodrestaurant.com; @seafoodrestau; Mon-Sun 9.30 pm; children: 12+ at D.

BLAS RESTAURANT, TWR Y FELIN HOTEL £61 433

ST DAVIDS SA62 6QT 01437 725 555

Down a narrow street in the town centre, this funkily decorated pitstop has built a formidable name for its "great burgers", and puts a strong emphasis on ethical sourcing; "it's good for children and adults alike". / www.twryfelinhotel.com/dining; @twryfelin; Mon-Sat 10 pm, Sun 9 pm; children: 12.

PORTHMEOR BEACH CAFE £42 335

PORTHMEOR BEACH TR26 1JZ 01736 793366

"Inventive tapas-style dishes from an open-plan kitchen" and a "buzzy atmosphere" "in the shadow of Tate St Ives" make this café "an unbeatable place to watch the sun go down". Earlier in the day, it's equally "good for afternoon tea looking out to sea"; breakfast and lunch, too. / www.porthmeor-beach.co.uk; @PorthmeorStIves; Mon-Sat 9.50 pm, Sun 2.30 pm; no Amex.

PORTHMINSTER CAFÉ £62 335

PORTHMINSTER BEACH TR26 2EB 01736 795352

A "fabulous setting", with a "sublime view if you get a window table", is the trump card of this famous venue overlooking Porthminster Beach. The ratings for food have revived a little this year after a slump, and while there are still the odd reports of "mediocre" results, there were more reports of "stunning fish dishes" from a kitchen which is "never short of ideas". / www.porthminstercafe.co.uk; @PorthBCafe; Mon-Sun 11 pm; no Amex.

PORTHMINSTER KITCHEN £52 333

WHARF RD TR26 1LG

"A breathtaking view of the beach" is a highpoint at this three-year-old in the centre of town, which is consistently well-rated for its modern brasserie fare (and is open from breakfast). / Mon-Sat 9.30 pm, Sun 4 pm.

HALF MAN HALF BURGER £30 432

7 MARINE COURT TN38 0DX 01424 552332

This burger bar in a swish Art Deco seafront complex inspired by the Queen Mary recently celebrated its third birthday (an Eastbourne sibling is a year younger); "there's a reason for the queues!": its 100% Sussex beef patties, served two at a time, and "simply the best". / www.halfmanhalfburger.com; @HalfManHalfBrgr; Tue-Sat 11 pm, Sun 10 pm; no bookings.

3 MERCATORIA TN38 0EB 01424 200355

"Helpful staff" contribute to the good vibes at this backstreet fixture, a little way away from the seafront, serving a modern bistro menu (with regularly changing specials). Top Tip – there's a prix fixe deal, but not on the busiest weekend evenings. / www.stclementsrestaurant.co.uk; @StClementsRest; Mon-Sun 9 pm.

ST MARGARETS, GREATER LONDON 1–4A

THE CROWN £54 3 3 3

TW1 2NH 020 8892 5896

This smartly turned-out Georgian tavern wins solid ratings for its "high-standard" meals, and is a regular match-day rendezvous for rugby fans visiting Twickenham stadium, less than a mile away. / www.crowntwickenham.co.uk; @crowntwickenham; booking max 7 may apply.

ST MAWES, CORNWALL 1–4B

HOTEL TRESANTON £72 2 4 5

27 LOWER CASTLE ROAD TR2 5DR 01326 270055

Olga Polizzi's La Dolce Vita-worthy destination hotel has a "superb position in a lovely village" ("what a view") and "they organise everything very professionally with great charm… except the weather!" The food has always slightly played second fiddle here, but won more praise this year, especially for "marvellous, simply prepared fish". / www.tresanton.com; @hoteltresanton; 9 pm; booking max 10 may apply; children: 6+ at dinner. *Accommodation:* 40 rooms, from £250

ST MERRYN, CORNWALL 1–3B

THE CORNISH ARMS £43 3 2 3

CHURCHTOWN PL28 8ND 01841 520288

Rick Stein's large, "lively" village gastropub feels very much like the "relaxed" local watering hole it is, rather than a more fancy, foodie destination; and wins solid ratings for its "delicious", straightforward cooking, "well conditioned beers" and "decent wine list". / www.rickstein.com/eat-with-us/the-cornish-arm; @rick_stein; Mon-Sat 9 pm, Sun 8 pm; no Amex; online only.

ST TUDY, CORNWALL 1–3B

ST TUDY INN £47 3 2 4

BODMIN PL30 3NN 01208 850 656

"Run by one of Cornwall's most talented chefs, Emily Scott" – "she manages to achieve a great balance between keeping it as a good village pub for residents alongside being a fantastic place to eat" (or stay). New feature: the existing choice of bottles is "now complemented by a fine-wine list". / www.sttudyinn.com; @sttudyinn; Mon-Sun 10.30 pm; no Amex.

STADHAMPTON, OXFORDSHIRE 2–2D

THE CRAZY BEAR £66 3 3 4

BEAR LN OX44 7UR 01865 890714

Funky decor is part of the offbeat package that originally won a name for this rural inn of over 25 years' standing, which has both English and Thai restaurants under the same roof. Feedback was much more consistent this year regarding the cooking and also the "very friendly service". / www.crazybeargroup.co.uk; @CrazyBearGroup; Mon-Fri 1 am, Sat & Sun 2 am; children: 12+ at Fri & Sat D. *Accommodation:* 16 rooms, from £169

STAMFORD, LINCOLNSHIRE 6–4A

THE GEORGE HOTEL £85 2 3 4

71 ST MARTINS PE9 2LB 01780 750750

"The atmosphere is pure history and romance" in the "traditional oak-lined dining room with silver-domed trolleys" of this "beautifully preserved Georgian coaching inn". "All credit to owner Laurence Hoskins for maintaining the traditional values of this "truly magnificent establishment" – a "treasure of an institution" which sits "at the heart of the fine stone town of Stamford". "There is a price to pay for dining here" though – prices are rather OTT – and it's "best to avoid the clever dishes and stick to basics: oysters, smoked salmon (even the hysterically expensive Dover sole) and above all the beef" – "a taste of what life should always be like" if you have a taste for all things old school. Top Tip: if you want to dip your toe in the water, try the cheaper (but less exciting) Garden Room bistro. / www.georgehotelofstamford.com; @GeorgeStamford; 9.30 pm; jacket required; children: 8+ at D. *Accommodation:* 47 rooms, from £190

STANHOE, NORFOLK 6–3B

THE DUCK INN £52 4 4 3

BURNHAM RD PE31 8QD 01485 518 330

"Unusual food combinations" from an "appealing menu with brilliant choices" keep diners happy at this "cosy pub" by a village duck pond. Chef/owner Ben Handley was brought up in a pub at Hunstanton, and has also taken over the Hunworth Bell near Holt. / www.duckinn.co.uk; @duckinnstanhoe; Mon-Sat 10 pm, Sun 9 pm.

STANTON, SUFFOLK 3–1C

LEAPING HARE VINEYARD £56 3 3 5

WYKEN VINEYARDS IP31 2DW 01359 250287

A 400-year-old oak-framed barn provides an "elegant setting" for the restaurant of the Wyken vineyard. "Nearly everything on the menu is sourced locally and freshness is key". "It's a lovely place, with great dining and atmosphere, surrounded by excellent gardens". / www.wykenvineyards.co.uk; 9m NE of Bury St Edmunds; follow tourist signs off A143; Sun-Thu 3 pm, Fri & Sat.

STEIN, HIGHLAND 9–2A

LOCH BAY RESTAURANT £50 5 4 4

1 MACLEODS TERRACE IV55 8GA 01470 592235

Michael Smith's "very intimate and cosy" three-year-old lacks the formality of its ambitious peers in this part of the world, yet wins similar praise for his accomplished and "excellent" cuisine – "predominantly fish-related from a five-course taster menu" (and also with a simpler three-course option). / www.lochbay-seafood-restaurant.co.uk; @lochbayskye/; 22m from Portree via A87 and B886; 8m from Dunvegan; Tue-Sat 9 pm, Sun 1.30 pm; no Amex; children: 8+ at D.

STOCKBRIDGE, HAMPSHIRE 2–3D

CLOS DU MARQUIS £56 4 4 3

LONDON RD SO20 6DE 01264 810738

"This South African-run former pub produces first-rate French cuisine" – somewhat surprisingly, especially adding in the setting right on the A30. The "lovely" dishes tend towards the rustic (as does the appealing auberge-esque room) and service is "superb". / www.closdumarquis.co.uk; 2m E on A30 from Stockbridge; Sun-Wed 4 pm, Fri & Sat 11 pm, Thu 5 pm.

GREYHOUND £66 3 2 4

31 HIGH STREET SO20 6EY 01264 810833

"A lovely setting in the rear garden and welcoming atmosphere throughout" helps earn solid ratings for this 19th-century pub-with-rooms on the River Test, at the epicentre of Hampshire's world-class fly fishing territory. Culinary highpoints include its "no-choice set lunch that's excellent value". / www.thegreyhoundonthetest.co.uk; @GHStockbridge; Wed-Sat 9 pm, Sun 8 pm; booking max 12 may apply. *Accommodation:* 7 rooms, from £100

THYME & TIDES £34 3 2 2

THE HIGH ST SO20 6HE 01264 810101

"Posh brunch nosh is served cheerfully in this busy and slightly chaotic deli" – "an inexpensive, and light-hearted venue catering to a genteel and upmarket clientele". If you're shopping, the "fish counter is out of this world", and it's also open on Friday nights for fish 'n' chips. Garden for warm days. / www.thymeandtidesdeli.co.uk; @thymeandtides; Mon-Sat 5 pm, Sun 4 pm; no Amex; booking weekends only.

STOCKCROSS, BERKSHIRE 2–2D

THE VINEYARD AT STOCKCROSS £103 3 4 3

RG20 8JU 01635 528770

It's the "sumptuous wine list" – an amazing selection, with "a great North American range" – which is the undisputed 'crown jewel' feature of Sir Peter Michael's luxurious hotel. But the liquid refreshment is ably "supported by unfussy modern cuisine" from chef Robby Jenks, available in the evenings through a seven-course tasting menu, with appropriate wine matches, or the à la carte. The interior is "pleasant", perhaps a little "old-fashioned". Top Tip: "interesting double (US/European) wine pairings". / www.the-vineyard.co.uk; @VineyardNewbury; from M4, J13 take A34 towards Hungerford; Tue-Sat 9 pm, Sun 1.30 pm; no jeans. *Accommodation:* 49 rooms, from £194

STOCKPORT, GREATER MANCHESTER — 5–2B

EASY FISH COMPANY — £42 — 4 3 3

117 HEATON MOOR ROAD SK4 4HY 0161 442 0823

"They know what to do with a fish at this restaurant behind a fishmonger" in this Victorian suburb of Stockport (which was upgraded from a more deli-style offering a couple of years ago). / www.theeasyfishco.com; Tue-Sat 11 pm, Sun 10 pm.

WHERE THE LIGHT GETS IN — £110 — 4 5 4

7 ROSTRON ROW SK1 1JY 016 1477 5744

"Yes I know, it's Stockport but… WOW!" Sam Buckley's "splendidly hipster" bare-brick-walled converted Victorian warehouse with open kitchen and a tasting-menu-only format has taken the foodie world by storm since it opened in late 2016. On most accounts it fully lives up: "the hipster foodie intensity might be a turn-off for some people but the warmth and enthusiasm of the staff and sheer quality of the food make it a wonderful experience". "The pace is leisured and slow, focused on the kitchen and with the chance to chat and absorb; there's great music; plenty of chef-based action, and without a doubt it has killer appeal to anyone wanting to be immersed in food and watch a talented team". And "you leave feeling sated, but in a really good way, from the beautifully judged surprise menu". Well, that's the unqualified version anyway. But there are also a number of reports which are supportive but with reservations: e.g. "there's a lot of ambition on show at WTLGI, and I think their determination to pare back to the basics and tell a story with their food means that their regularly changing menu will sometimes hit, sometimes miss; for us it mostly missed, but I can see the potential; we were no doubt unlucky in attending on one of the coldest days in the year, and our expectations were sky-high because of stellar reviews and travelling specially from London, but this was just too austere and worthy" (or as another reporters said: "so pure you have to be an expert to appreciate the subtlety and get joy from it"). Still, everyone agrees that although it's a little "earnest", "they try very hard to look after you well". And even most critics feel: "I wish them well, because they are outstanding in some aspects and genuinely different". / wtlgi.co; @wtlgi; 9 pm.

STOKE HOLY CROSS, NORFOLK — 6–4C

STOKE MILL — £58 — 3 2 3

MILL ROAD NR14 8PA 01508 493 337

"The setting and building are incredible" at this 700-year-old mill on the River Tas (once home to the business that grew into Colman's Mustard). "The interior is not quite as picturesque as the outside" but "the food is the main thing, and usually it's excellent". / www.stokemill.co.uk; @StokeMill; Mon-Sat 11 pm, Sun 10 pm.

STOKE ROW, OXFORDSHIRE — 2–2D

THE CROOKED BILLET — £59 — 4 4 5

NEWLANDS LN RG9 5PU 01491 681048

"Wonderful out-of-the-way" gastropub "down the end of a winding lane" and with "an amazing indoors with a dining room plastered with intriguing old photos", which still "sets standards others struggle to meet" (listen up pop pickers, it's owned by ex-Sweet and John Otway rock guitarist Paul Clerehugh, who set up here in 1989). "Never had a bad meal, course or service: it always delivers with taste, charm and pizzazz". "A handwritten daily changing menu is always a joy to hold – other pretenders take note". / www.thecrookedbillet.co.uk; @Crooked_Billet; off the A4130; Mon-Thu 11 pm, Fri & Sat midnight, Sun 10.30 pm.

STOKE-BY-NAYLAND, SUFFOLK — 3–2C

THE CROWN — £51 — 3 3 4

PARK STREET CO6 4SE 01206 262 001

Well-known Constable Country gastropub with rooms, which has a good number of outside tables for summer dining. The brasserie-style cooking remains well-rated: a wide range incorporating steak, fish and vegetarian options. / www.crowninn.net; @crowninnsuffolk; on B1068; Tue-Sat. *Accommodation:* 11 rooms, from £11

STOW ON THE WOLD, GLOUCESTERSHIRE — 2–1C

THE OLD BUTCHERS — £53 — 4 3 3

PARK ST GL54 1AQ 01451 831700

Peter & Louise Robinson's "lovely" and "slick" (but higgledy-piggledy) restaurant in the centre of Stow is well worth a butcher's (geddit?) for its "wonderfully fresh" and "well-executed" seafood and steaks, with occasional nods to Japan or the USA. / www.theoldbutchers.squarespace.com; @Theoldbutcher; on the main road heading out of Stow on the Wold towards Oddington; Mon-Fri 9.30 pm, Sat 10 pm, Sun 9 pm; booking max 12 may apply.

STRACHUR, ARGYLL AND BUTE — 9–4B

INVER RESTAURANT — £55 — 4 5 4

STRACTHLACHLAN PA27 8BU 01369 860 537

In a fisherman's croft on Loch Fyne, this "idyllic" Nordic-inflected dining room is "a Scottish hidden gem", its "clever" food drawing on the local larder. "Now with (luxe) overnight bothies", the odd cynic feels that it's become "just another destination place", but others will love the excuse to stay on for the fabulous breakfast baskets. / www.inverrestaurant.co.uk; @inverrestaurant; Mon-Sat 10.30 pm, Sun 10 pm.

STRATFORD UPON AVON, WARWICKSHIRE — 2–1C

LAMBS — £48 — 2 2 3

12 SHEEP STREET CV37 6EF 01789 292554

Reviews on this cosy, wood-beamed venue in one of the town's oldest houses are positive, if focused on the practical: "always reliable" most particularly its "good value pre-theatre set". / www.lambsrestaurant.co.uk; @lambsrestaurant; Mon-Sun 9 pm; no Amex.

LOXLEYS — £47 — 2 2 3

3 SHEEP ST CV37 6EF 01789 292128

In the "epicentre of restaurants for the hungry tourist or theatregoer", this ex-clothes shop "deserves your serious consideration", say fans. There were also reports of "average" or "poor value" food this year, but those "habitually choosing the pre-theatre set menu before a visit to the RSC" seem to find it "well cooked and attractively presented". / loxleysrestaurant.co.uk/; @twitter.com/Loxleys; Mon-Sat 11 pm, Sun 10.30 pm.

NO. 9 — £49 — 3 3 2

9 CHURCH STREET CV37 6HB 01789 415 522

Wayne Thomson serves everything from well-priced pre-theatre meals to ambitious nine-course tasting menus at his "superb" neighbourhood spot. Open since 2010, it "gets better every year", according to most regulars. / no9churchst.com; @dineno9; Mon closed, Tue - Sat 9.30 pm, Sun closed.

THE OPPO — £47 — 2 3 3

13 SHEEP STREET CV37 6EF 01789 269980

Just around the corner from the RSC, this long-serving bistro with "Tudor-type" decor is "THE place to eat in Stratford if you're going to the theatre – they put you through with speed (but don't make you feel hassled)", the food is "reliable (if not exciting)", while "staff are helpful (but not obsequious)". "What more does anyone want before a dollop of Shakespeare?" / www.theoppo.co.uk; @OppoStratford; Mon-Thu 9 pm, Fri & Sat 10.30 pm; no Amex; booking max 12 may apply.

ROOFTOP RESTAURANT, ROYAL SHAKESPEARE THEATRE — £43 — 2 2 4

WATERSIDE CV37 6BB 01789 403449

A "nice setting" – especially if you can nab "a window seat to enjoy the view" – boosts a visit to the RSC's large and airy rooftop bar/restaurant, with outside terrace overlooking the swans gliding along the Avon. The food is not really the point, but by most accounts it's "perfectly decent – especially for an institutional restaurant". / www.rsc.org.uk/eat; Mon-Sun 9 pm; no Amex; online only.

SALT £63 443

8 CHURCH ST CV37 6HB 01789 263566

"Just what Stratford needed" – this "very promising", crowdsource-funded yearling opened in one of the town's half-timbered houses in March 2017 "and quickly became a favourite". "I've dined there 16 times in first 12 months, and chef Paul Foster has produced excellent food time after time by simply focusing on flavour and the best seasonal ingredients". In October 2018, his hard work was rewarded with a Michelin star. / www.salt-restaurant.co.uk; @salt_dining; Wed-Sat 11 pm, Tue 3 pm.

STUCKTON, HAMPSHIRE   2-3C

THE THREE LIONS £62 332

STUCKTON RD SP6 2HF 01425 652489

"The decor (homely & 1980s) and the staff (friendly & helpful) haven't changed at all in years" at the Womersley's time-capsule New Forest inn. "The menu also rarely changes" but, thanks to former Lucknam Park chef Mike, that means the "same delicious result" every time, which absolutely no one seems to mind. / www.thethreelionsrestaurant.co.uk; off the A338; Mon-Sat 10 pm, Sun 9.30 pm; no Amex. *Accommodation:* 7 rooms, from £105

STUDLAND, DORSET   2-4C

PIG ON THE BEACH £52 335

MANOR HOUSE, MANOR ROAD BH19 3AU 01929 450 288

This "idyllic" shabby-chic clifftop hotel "is a wonderful, very quirky experience, (almost) on the beach" and overlooking Studland Bay, and "with cooking based around their garden and local produce". On most accounts the resulting dishes are "delicious", although the less rose-tinted view is that "there's nothing wrong with them, but the cuisine is hardly groundbreaking stuff, and a little overpriced". Meals are served in the 'greenhouse dining room', and come complete with "Pig Hut wines, supplied by Chapoutier". Part of a boutique-y chain which is booming across southern England, three Pigs are scheduled to open in 2019 alone. / www.thepighotel.com/on-the-beach/; Mon & Tue, Sun 9 pm, Wed & Thu 9.30 pm, Fri & Sat 10.30 pm.

Raby Hunt, Summerhouse

SHELLBAY £49 345

FERRY ROAD BH19 3BA 01929 450363

"Location, location, location! – but the fish and seafood is also very good" at this seafront outfit, which has "fantastic views of the sunset over Poole Harbour towards Brownsea Island". "It looks like an unassuming shack from the outside, but don't be put off": inside, "it's not exactly white table cloths but it has a nice rustic feel". / www.shellbay.net; near the Sandbanks to Swanage ferry; 9 pm.

SUDBURY, SUFFOLK   3-2C

SECRET GARDEN £39 444

17 - 21 FRIARS STREET CO10 2AA 01787 372030

"What a difference a new venue makes" – this two-year-old spin-off of the neighbouring café, set in the fine surrounds of beamed, 400-year-old Buzzards Hall is praised for French-influenced food which "gets better and better" and "the wine list is carefully chosen and not expensive". / www.tsg.uk.net; Tue-Sat 11 pm, Sun 10 pm.

SHILLINGFORDS, THE QUAY THEATRE £41 443

QUAY LANE CO10 2AN 01787 374745

In arts venue The Quay, Carl Shillingford's unusual Thursday to Saturday night wild food pop-up delivers "foraged food where the dishes taste even better than their description" ('White Cloud' salad, 'Seagrass Sushi' etc.) plus "interesting, reasonable wines"; it's "an experience to really enjoy and remember". / www.quaysudbury.com/shillingfords-quay; @thequaytheatre; Tue-Sat 11 pm, Sun 10 pm.

SUMMERHOUSE, COUNTY DURHAM   8-3B

RABY HUNT £151 533

DL2 3UD 01325 374 237

"One of the most memorable meals I have ever had...", "an out-of-this-world experience...", "just magical..." – folks don't hold back in their praise for the Close family's restaurant-with-rooms, set in an off-the-beaten-track village in County Durham, which "balances a modern kitchen and a clubby old-school dining room of dark wood panelling very effectively" and serves a "15-course menu of superb cooking coupled with great invention (to leave us gushing over a 'salad of winter vegetables' is deeply impressive!)". Some resistance crept in regarding the level of expense however this year: even those who rate the cuisine highly can find the overall experience "overpriced". / www.rabyhuntrestaurant.co.uk; @therabyhunt; Fri & Sat, Wed & Thu 9.30 pm. *Accommodation:* 2 rooms, from £125

SUNBURY ON THAMES, SURREY   3-3A

INDIAN ZEST £42 543

21 THAMES STREET TW16 5QF 01932 765 000

"The best Indian in the area... no... one of the best full stop!", say fan of Manoj Vasaikar's

well-established colonial-style villa (sibling to his Indian Zing near Hammersmith), on the south west outer-fringes of the capital. / www.indianzest.co.uk; @Indian_Zest; midnight.

SUNNINGHILL, BERKSHIRE   3-3A

CARPENTER'S ARMS £58 344

78 UPPER VILLAGE RD SL5 7AQ 01344 622763

A "hidden gem" – a "good-looking" pub hosting dining room 'La Cloche', serving "interesting" Gallic food, to the left, and a cosy lounge for watching the footie to the right; "once you get to know the lovely owners you'll find they're NOT grumpy at all, just very French!" / www.laclochepub.com; Mon-Thu 9.30 pm, Fri-Sun 10 pm.

SURBITON, GREATER LONDON   3-3A

DOOSRA £19 453

282 EWELL ROAD KT6 7AQ 020 8241 2288

"We are very lucky to have such a great restaurant start up just around the corner here in Surbiton!" – This "friendly" January 2018 newcomer offers "very interesting street food" that's "a fantastic modern take on Indian cuisine". "It's starting to expand the menu – if the new dishes are as good as the amazing samosas, we're in for a treat!" / doosra.kitchen.

THE FRENCH TABLE £65 553

85 MAPLE RD KT6 4AW 020 8399 2365

"An unexpected find for such a modest suburban location" – Sarah & Eric Guignard's well-known bright spark in a shopping parade "consistently maintains a high standard" and is "still providing memorably good food after all these years in its slightly poky setting". The cuisine has a discernible French accent but comes with "creative touches" ("there's always something that's exciting to try!"). "The attentive service is just right" too – "helpful without being distracting". / www.thefrenchtable.co.uk; @thefrenchtable; Wed-Sat 9 pm, Sun 8 pm.

NO 97 £55 344

97 MAPLE ROAD KT6 4AW 020 3411 9797

Sam Berry's "buzzy", "sophisticated" and "beautifully designed" two-year-old in the outer suburbs has won a strong following for its modern European cuisine and basement gin bar. This year he opened One One Four with a similar vibe, in the former premises of Retro Bistrot in Teddington. / no-97.co.uk; @no_ninetyseven; Tue-Sat midnight, Sun 2.30 pm.

SUTTON GAULT, CAMBRIDGESHIRE   3-1B

THE ANCHOR £47 323

BURY LN CB6 2BD 01353 778537

This food-led 18th-century Fenland inn has earned solid ratings since the return two years ago of long-term owners Adam Pickup and Carlene Bunten, who has leased the premises out for a few years. "Simple dishes with interesting flavours are cooked perfectly, and service is warm, friendly and efficient". / www.anchorsuttongault.co.uk; @TheanchorinnSG; 7m W of Ely, signposted off B1381 in Sutton; Mon-Thu 10 pm, Fri 10.30 pm, Sat 11 pm, Sun 9.30 pm; no Amex. *Accommodation:* 4 rooms, from £80

PATRICKS WITH ROOMS £58 333

638 MUMBLES RD SA3 4EA 01792 360199

A Mumbles restaurant-with-rooms featuring a handsome colonial-style bar and a pleasant dining room overlooking Swansea Bay. The menu abounds with "excellent, good-value" options – be it decadent afternoon teas or local speciality laverbread. / www.patrickswithrooms.com; @PatricksMumbles; in Mumbles, 1m before pier; Mon-Sat 9.50 pm, Sun 2.30 pm. *Accommodation:* 10 rooms, from £110

THE WHEATSHEAF AT SWINTON £49

MAIN ST TD11 3JJ 01890 860257

Overlooking the village green of a small Borders village – the attractive, contemporary dining room of a good-looking pub with rooms; too limited feedback for a rating this year, but it serves a quality menu majoring in steak using 28-day aged Scottish Borders beef. / www.wheatsheaf-swinton.co.uk; @Wheat_sheaf; between Kelso & Berwick-upon-Tweed, by village green; 9 pm; Closed Sun D Jan & Feb; children: 8+. *Accommodation:* 124 rooms, from £112

ANDRÉ GARRETT AT CLIVEDEN, CLIVEDEN HOUSE £92 334

CLIVEDEN RD SL6 0JF 01628 668561

"A great experience, especially if you're flying in by helicopter…". The stunning dining room of the scandal-drenched former Astor country pile, where Christine Keeler met defence minister John Profumo in 1961, makes a "sublime setting" for "fantastic food". "The tasting menu dishes are all very good" – "perhaps not outstanding at this price" – but generally thought to be "worth it". In October 2018, chef André Garrett announced that he was leaving the restaurant to join London's Corinthia hotel. / www.clivedenhouse.co.uk; @Cliveden_House; 9.45 pm; no trainers. *Accommodation:* 48 rooms, from £445

THE PHEASANT INN £48 334

HIGHER BURWARDSLEY CH3 9PF 01829 770434

"Beautiful views over the Cheshire Plain" set the scene at this "very busy", cosy rural pub (with rooms) between Beeston and Peckforton, whose long menu comes well-rated. /

www.thepheasantinn.co.uk; @pheasant_inn; Mon - Thur 9.30 pm, Fri & Sat 10 pm, Sun 9 pm.

AUGUSTUS £54 343

3 THE COURTYARD, ST JAMES ST TA1 1JR 01823 324 354

"A gem" of a neighbourhood restaurant tucked away in a quiet courtyard but well-known locally; albeit "short", the daily-changing menu is "always beautifully done". The (ex-Castle Hotel) duo behind it, Richard Guest and Cedric Chirrosel, launched fish spot 'Albatross', a minute away in Riverside Place, in summer 2018. / www.augustustaunton.co.uk; @augustustaunton; Tue - Sat 9.30 pm; no Amex.

CORNISH ARMS £43 333

15 WEST STREET PL19 8AN

"A world apart from the rough and ready boozer it was in the 1990s" – this "excellent rural-style pub (but in the town)" is nowadays "a warm and welcoming local with restaurant standard food to boot. Chef patron [for the last five years] John Hooker has truly stamped his mark here, and whilst not doing anything too fashionably clever ensures that dishes really do taste their best". / www.thecornisharmstavistock.co.uk; Mon-Thu 11 pm, Fri & Sat midnight, Sun 10.30 pm.

THE KING'S HEAD £49 333

TW11 8HG

The original White Brasserie Co. gastroboozer, in attractive Victorian premises – snugs, fires, walled patio etc. – is a "great easy local" praised for its "friendly and nice atmosphere". On the food front it's more "sensible" than sensational but reporters have "nothing to complain about" overall. / kingsheadteddington.com/; Mon-Sat 11 pm, Sun 10 pm.

CRAB SHACK £50 544

3 QUEEN ST TQ14 9HN 01626 777956

"Seafood served as it should be: it couldn't be fresher coming off the boat on the Back Beach", wins universal acclaim for this "fun, if not particularly smart place". A change of ownership has brought "a wider choice of fish" but thankfully no compromise on quality – and "it's still as difficult as ever to get a table without booking 2 weeks ahead…". / www.crabshackonthebeach.co.uk/; @@CrabShack3; 9 pm; closed Mon & Tue; no Amex.

GUMSTOOL INN, CALCOT MANOR £53 223

GL8 8YJ 01666 890391

A flagstone-floored English boozer set within a posh hotel and spa complex, and less formal

than the conservatory restaurant on site; its superior pub food continues to win approval and the garden is "perfect for a lovely al fresco lunch surrounded by birdsong". / www.calcotmanor.co.uk; @Calcot_Manor; crossroads of A46 & A41345; Mon-Sat 10 pm, Sun 5 pm; no jeans; no bookings; children: 12+ at dinner in Conservatory. *Accommodation:* 35 rooms, from £240

ERIC'S FISH & CHIPS £24 433

DROVE ORCHARD, THORNHAM RD PE36 6LS 01485 472 025

Titchwell Manor chef Eric Snaith's bright, tiled village fish 'n' chippy is a North Norfolk coast staple, having been shortlisted for the National Fish and Chip Awards for two years straight. / www.ericsfishandchips.com; @ericsFandC; Mon-Sat 10 pm, Sun 8 pm; no bookings.

TWELVE RESTAURANT & LOUNGE BAR £54 333

MARSH MILL VILLAGE, FLEETWOOD ROAD NORTH FY5 4JZ 01253 821212

Funkily decorated contemporary bar/restaurant on the Lancashire coast near Blackpool that's a "consistent" destination of nearly two decades' standing. One regular visitor was less impressed this year, but even so says it's "still the best place in the Fylde". / www.twelve-restaurant.co.uk; Tue-Sat 1 am, Sun 8.30 pm.

LAWNS RESTAURANT, THORNTON HALL HOTEL & SPA £87 343

NESTON RD CH63 1JF 0151 336 3938

"Love the option for a savoury as well as a sweet afternoon tea!" (for which it won a national award this year) – this grand country house on the Wirral provides a "lovely" setting. When it comes to a fuller meal, its "elegant nouvelle-type cuisine" is also well-rated. / www.thorntonhallhotel.com; @thelawnsrest; Tue-Sat 10.30 pm; booking max 8 may apply.

THE RED FOX £43 333

LIVERPOOL ROAD CH64 7TL 0151 353 2920

Added to the ever-growing chain three years ago, and turning out "good pub food" and an excellent whisky list, this is now a "top-of-the-range Brunning & Price outlet set in glorious grounds" – an ex-country club whose raised rear terraces overlook landscaped lawns. / www.brunningandprice.co.uk/redfox; @redfoxpub; Mon-Sun 10.30 pm.

THE HORSE GUARDS
INN   £47 4 5 5

UPPERTON RD GU28 9AF   01798 342 332

"A relaxed rural delight", this "convivial" 17th-century inn on the edge of Petworth Park has won high ratings for several years now, and "just can't be faulted". There's "an interesting menu" of "beautifully executed, adventurous dishes", many of them using "excellent locally sourced ingredients" ("suppliers are listed on a blackboard"), plus "hyper-local sparkling wine". / www.thehorseguardsinn.co.uk; 9 pm, Fri & Sat 9.30 pm; no Amex.

PYTHOUSE KITCHEN
GARDEN   £47 3 3 5

WEST HATCH SP3 6PA   01747 870444

"Dining in a walled kitchen garden off the very local fresh produce" can be a "magical" experience at this bucolic South Wiltshire venture (part of an estate which also operates as a wedding venue, glamping destination and fruit picking centre). The short menu of simple fare has options from breakfast onwards. / www.pythousekitchengarden.co.uk; Mon-Sat 9.30 pm, Sun 4 pm.

TITCHWELL
MANOR   £61 3 3 3

**TITCHWELL MANOR PE31 8BB
01485 210 221**

The Snaith family's red-brick Victorian hotel is the "ideal destination for lovers of seafood and bird watchers" exploring the Norfolk coast; the light-filled, jazzily decorated 'Eating Rooms' may be preferred to the more formal conservatory, which can feel "awkwardly quiet" at times. / www.titchwellmanor.com; @TitchwellManor; 9:30pm. *Accommodation:* 29 rooms, from £27

STAGG INN   £57 3 4 3

HR5 3RL   01544 230221

"Consistently good and well priced food, with a great cheese board, a very comprehensive wine list (mostly from Tanners), and my favourite bread and butter pudding in all the world!" – such are the attractions of Steve and Nicola Reynolds's pub with rooms (which they have run for the last 20 years). / www.thestagg.co.uk; @thestagginn; on B4355, NE of Kington; Mon-Sat 11 pm, Sun 10 pm; credit card deposit required to book. *Accommodation:* 7 rooms, from £100

CAFE FISH
TOBERMORY   £41 5 4 4

THE PIER PA75 6NU   01688 301253

"Nothing could be better than sitting on the quayside in Tobermory in the sunshine, feasting on their hot seafood platter with butter dribbling down your chin"; "everything is cooked à point, and it's hard not asking for seconds of their malty soda bread". Stop Press – in August 2018 it went on the market; hopefully the new owners won't mess with the winning formula. / www.thecafefish.com; 10 pm; Closed Nov-Mar; no Amex; children: 14+ after 8 pm.

THE SALUTATION
INN   £38 4 4 3

68 FORE STREET EX3 0HL   01392 873060

"Really excellent cooking, with quality ingredients at a fair price" wins very enthusiastic reviews (if from a smallish fanclub) for the dining room at this handsome eighteenth century inn, which nowadays operates as a restaurant-with-rooms. There's also a cheaper eating option – The Glasshouse, set in a glazed-in courtyard. / www.salutationtopsham.co.uk; Mon-Sat 9.30 pm, Sun 4 pm.

ELEPHANT RESTAURANT &
BRASSERIE   £64 3 2 2

**3-4 BEACON TER, HARBOURSIDE TQ1 2BH
01803 200044**

"Simon Hulstone's sensational food is all about delivering flavour by showcasing ingredients, which he does wonderfully", according to most reports on the TV-chef's accolaled venture, in a Georgian terrace, which they applaud as "an intimate hideaway with great views". "It lacks that special feel" to some diners, though, and ratings have slipped noticeably in the past couple of years, with gripes about food which, especially at the high prices, is "good but not mind-blowing" ("I don't have a clue as to how it got a Michelin star"). / www.elephantrestaurant.co.uk; @elephantrest; Mon-Sat 10 pm; children: 14+ at bar.

NO 7 FISH
BISTRO   £50 5 4 3

**7 BEACON TERRACE TQ1 2BH
01803 295055**

"Brilliant for fish-lovers" – the Stacey family's "warm and casual" (but rather unsung) operation (with a wine bar upstairs) has served up the pick of Tor Bay's seafood (most of it landed at Brixham harbour at the other end of the bay) for 25 years. Daily specials are listed on a "series of blackboards, with a separate board advertising tempura, and a tray of fish samples is also brought round". / www.no7-fish.com; @no7fishbistro; Mon-Thu 10 pm, Fri & Sat midnight.

THE GURNARD'S
HEAD   £51 3 2 3

TR26 3DE   01736 796928

"Right on the coast miles from anywhere, but worth the journey (or better still the walk)" – this bright yellow gastropub-with-rooms is a beacon of hospitality for hungry visitors to England's wild west, a short drive from St Ives. Service is "well-meaning" but can be "wayward", while the cooking is "consistent" and can be "excellent" ("as you might expect, the fish is to be recommended"). / www.gurnardshead.co.uk; @gurnardshead; on coastal road between Land's End & St Ives, near Zennor B3306; Mon-Sat 11 pm, Sun 10.30 pm; no Amex. *Accommodation:* 7 rooms, from £7

CROCKER'S TABLE £58

74 HIGH STREET HP23 4AF   01442 767 877

MasterChef: The Professionals 2015 runner-up, Scott Barnard's quirky (especially for beyond the M25) newcomer features 14 seats around the counter of an open kitchen. It opened in May 2018 shortly before our survey came to a conclusion, so no feedback for a rating as yet, but early press and blog reports suggests its funky small plates make it well worth a try. / www.crockerstring.co.uk; @crockers_ct; Mon-Sat 11 pm, Sun 4 pm.

HIDDEN HUT   £14 4 3 5

PORTSCATHO BEACH TR2 5EW

Much-loved beach shack on a National Trust coastal path on the Roseland Peninsula; from Cornish pasties to clotted cream ice-cream, it's all brilliant, but their 'feast nights' (diners bring plates and booze and, well, feast under the stars) are a legend, selling out in minutes. / www.hiddenhut.co.uk; @TheHiddenHut; cash only; no bookings.

HUBBOX   £31 3 3 3

**116 KENWYN STREET TR1 3DJ
01872 240700**

A fun and funky burger, dogs and beer chain, now with seven South-West England branches, in an airy converted church; it received uniformly solid marks this year, but more feedback wouldn't go amiss! / www.hubbox.co.uk; @TheHubBox; Mon-Thu 9 pm, Fri & Sat 9.30 pm, Sun 8 pm.

TABB'S   £55 4 4 4

85 KENWYN ST TR1 3BZ   01872 262110

"An intimate fine dining establishment a little out of the centre" that's "head and shoulders above anything else in Truro" owing to its "brilliant" classical cuisine and "excellently chosen" wines. Top Tip: "Nigel's monthly Sunday roasts are always special and allow him to show off more of his flair". / www.tabbs.co.uk/; @Nigeltabb; Tue-Sat 9 pm; no Amex.

TUDDENHAM MILL,
TUDDENHAM MILL
HOTEL   £60 2 2 3

HIGH ST IP28 6SQ   01638 713 552

The "attractive dining room" of a boutique hotel in an old water mill provides a "gorgeous setting" with "serene views". Results from the kitchen can be "delicious" too, but it suffered from inconsistent reports again this year, including of sometimes "confused" service. / www.tuddenhammill.co.uk; @Tuddenham_Mill; 9 pm. *Accommodation:* 165 rooms, from £205

THE BEACON KITCHEN   £57   444

TEA GARDEN LANE   TN3 9JH   01892 524252

This distinctive wedding venue in an Arts & Crafts country house set in 17 acres (part of Pete Cornwell's 'I'll be Mother' group) also functions as a restaurant which attracts consistently high ratings for its "great food and service in a beautiful setting". There's a "fabulous outdoor terrace and oh! the views". / www.the-beacon.co.uk; @Thebeacon_tw; Wed-Sat 11 pm, Sun 6 pm. *Accommodation:* 3 rooms, from £97

HOTEL DU VIN & BISTRO   £47   223

CRESCENT ROAD   TN1 2LY   01892 320 749

A Grade II-listed mansion hosts this branch of the national chain, with a dining room that serves decent Gallic bistro fare. As usual with HDV, a big plus is "my sort of wine at a reasonable price". / www.hotelduvin.com/locations/tunbridge-wel; @HotelduVinBrand; Mon-Fri 9.30 pm, Sun 10 pm, Sat 10.30 pm; booking max 10 may apply. *Accommodation:* 34 rooms, from £120

THE IVY ROYAL TUNBRIDGE WELLS   £56   334

46-50 HIGH STREET   TN1 1XF
01892 240 700

"An Ivy outpost somewhere between 'Ivy Cafe' Marylebone and the original in style" – this new spin-off from the famous Theatreland icon wins a better rep than some others: "the whole family enjoyed it and ambience was great". / www.theivytunbridgewells.com; @ivytunbridge; Mon-Sun 12.30 am.

SANKEY'S THE OLD FISHMARKET   £46   333

19 THE UPPER PANTILES   TN2 5TN
01892511422

"Slip in for some no-nonsense fish staples and a decent wine list", at this diminutive jewel of the local Sankey's empire, which occupies the Old Fishmarket building in the Pantiles. Al fresco seating makes it "an ideal place for a lazy sunny afternoon" – perhaps fuelled by the weekday oyster happy hour, with molluscs at £1 a pop! / www.sankeys.co.uk; @sankeysrtw; Tue-Sat 9 pm.

THACKERAY'S   £92   222

85 LONDON RD   TN1 1EA   01892 511921

"A treat, every time", say fans of this long-established Regency villa, which is well supported for its "beautiful, locally sourced food and a formal but charming atmosphere". However ratings are dragged down by a sizeable minority who are "disappointed" by its performance generally: "Like Marmite: you love it or you hate it… we are in the latter category…" / www.thackerays-restaurant.co.uk; @Thackeraysrest; Tue-Sat 10.30 pm, Sun 2.30 pm.

THE TWENTY SIX   £54   444

15A CHURCH ROAD   TN4 0RX   01892 544607

"In an oasis for food", this cosy branch of the Kent-based 'I'll be Mother' group is the epitome of a "great local" serving some "genuinely exceptional cooking". Chef Simon Ulph moved to Jackson Boxer's new London venture, St Leonards, in June 2018, with Megs Buchanan stepping in at the stoves. / thetwenty-six.co.uk; @thetwenty_six; Wed-Sat 9 pm.

UMI   £27   442

30 YORK STREET   TW1 3LJ   020 8892 2976

"Super sushi and other Japanese dishes" – including ramen, tempura and gyoza – have helped this fairly basic two-year-old establish an enthusiastic local fan base. / Tue-Sat 11 pm, Sun 10 pm.

LONGSANDS FISH KITCHEN   £43   433

27 FRONT STREET   NE30 4DZ
0191 272 8552

"A real find in this lovely Geordie coastal resort", this "bustling and very busy" seafood restaurant has "good choices, from basic takeaway fish 'n' chips to delicious and more sophisticated fish dishes" which vary depending on the local North Sea catch. / www.longsandsfishkitchen.com; @LongsandsFish; Mon-Thu 1 am, Fri & Sat 2 am, Sun 6 pm.

RILEY'S FISH SHACK   £34   434

KING EDWARD'S BAY   NE30 4BY
0191 257 1371

"Hats off to Jay Rayner: this foodie pilgrimage was every bit as rewarding as he promised it would be!" The Observer's man helped drive the renown of this "unique experience literally on the beach, with warm fire, warm blankets and delicious food"; and "on a good day it's hard to imagine anything better that the stonkingly fresh fish served from this shack [a converted shipping container] looking at the sea". There are drawbacks: "a) you have to wait so long to be served; and b) you either eat in the cold (let's be real here) or take it home, by which time it's a bit lukewarm". And also, "it's not ideal if your wife likes comfortable chairs and good loos". But "for brilliant nosh in a brilliant location" it's the dog's. / www.rileysfishshack.com; @rileysfishshack; Mon-Thu 10.30 pm, Fri-Sun 11 pm; no bookings.

TYTHERLEIGH ARMS   £48   343

EX13 7BE   01460 220214

Regulars are "so lucky to have this as a local" – a 16th century inn, near the Devon-Dorset border, that wins plaudits for its "beautiful food" and "very fair" prices; it's also a "nice place to stay" (in a tastefully converted stable). / www.tytherleigharms.com; @TytherleighArms; Mon-Thu 9 pm, Fri & Sat 9.30 pm, Sun 8 pm; children: 5.

SEAFOOD SHACK   £46   542

WEST ARGYLE STREET   IV26 2TY

"The best food in Ullapool" – "fresh fish every day" – is the secret behind the success of this BBC Food Awards laureate, a lunchtime-only truck run by 'lassies' Kirsty and Fenella, yards from the harbour. / Mon-Sat 10 pm; no bookings.

SHARROW BAY   £101   445

CA10 2LZ   01768 486301

This 70-year-old institution – England's original country-house hotel – occupies a "lovely setting by Lake Ullswater" with "views to die for". It might seem "rather stuffy and old-fashioned" these days, but for many silver-haired reporters that equates to seeming the epitome of romance, and a meal here is "still worth the journey", aided by its "quality cooking and wonderful wines". / www.sharrowbay.co.uk; @sharrowbay; on Pooley Bridge Rd towards Howtown; 9 pm; no jeans; children: 8+. *Accommodation:* 17 rooms, from £355

NORTHCOTE MANOR   £96   344

BURRINGTON   EX37 9LZ   01769 560501

"Well worth searching out in the Devon countryside – a grand, old hotel, with a very interesting dining room (with murals of the history of the manor) and extensive grounds with good views for wandering around to walk off the meal". "A lovely place with superb food": there's a three-course menu in the evening or a blow-out 'gourmet' option. / www.northcotemanor.co.uk; @NorthcoteDevon; Mon-Thu 9.30 pm, Fri & Sat 10 pm, Sun 9 pm; no jeans. *Accommodation:* 11 rooms, from £155

THE BAITING HOUSE AT UPPER SAPEY   £49   433

STOURPORT ROAD   WR6 6XT   01886 853201

"Charles and Scott in the kitchen used to work for Underhills and that influence is evident in a number of the dishes" at this three-year-old gastropub: the original of an expanding local group (now up to four). "The lunch menu is more classic pub (the fish 'n' chips, with a chunky piece of fish in a wafer thin batter and equally excellent chips, set an unbeatable standard"). At dinner the cuisine is more "memorable" – "a short menu but with more than enough to tempt". / www.baitinghouse.co.uk/; @TheBaitingHouse; Tue-Thu 11 pm, Fri & Sat midnight, Mon 10.30 pm, Sun 10 pm; children: 1.

UPPER SLAUGHTER, GLOUCESTERSHIRE | 2–1C

LORDS OF THE MANOR £96 224

STOW-ON-THE-WOLD GL54 2JD
01451 820243

This "awesome" honey-coloured 17th-century former rectory with stunning gardens has long been a leading gastronomic destination in the Cotswolds, although its food ratings reflect divided feedback this year. While some felt "each dish was uniquely exquisite – it's rare to find such seamless and consistent excellence" – others were "disappointed" by "tasteless" and "overpriced" meals. / www.lordsofthemanor.com; @CotswoldLords; 4m W of Stow on the Wold; Mon-Sat 9.30 pm, Sun 2 pm; no jeans; children: 7+ at D in restaurant. *Accommodation:* 26 rooms, from £199

USK VALLEY, NEWPORT | 2–2A

STEAK ON SIX £57

CELTIC MANOR RESORT, COLDRA WOODS
NP18 1HQ 01633 410262

"Amazing views of the valley" reward a trip to this "relaxing", contemporary venue on the sixth floor of this monumental resort. Too few reports for a rating, but such feedback as we have is positive on its steak house menu. / www.celtic-manor.com/dining/restaurants/steak-on-six; @TheCelticManor; Sun-Thu 10 pm, Fri & Sat 11 pm.

WADDESDON, BUCKINGHAMSHIRE | 3–2A

THE FIVE ARROWS £56 333

HIGH ST HP18 0JE 01296 651727

Built as a Victorian coaching inn at the gate of Waddesdon Manor – the Rothschild family seat – this "lovely, little hotel" is well rated for its "fabulous food", and benefits from a well-stocked cellar featuring wines from Rothschild family wineries. / www.thefivearrows.co.uk; @WaddesdonManor; on A41; Mon-Thu 9 pm, Fri & Sat 9.30 pm, Sun 8.30 pm. *Accommodation:* 11 rooms, from £95

WADDINGTON, LANCASHIRE | 5–1B

THE HIGHER BUCK £49 443

THE SQUARE BB7 3HZ 01200 423226

Chef-landlord Michael Heathcote's "brilliant village pub" is "always a great place to finish a walk" in the gorgeous Ribble Valley, thanks to its "classy, above-par pub food" chosen from a "blackboard menu full of locally sourced food" – "hearty" fare "all about flavour and ingredients", with "great in-season specials". /

www.higherbuck.com; @thehigherbuck; Mon-Thu 9 pm, Fri & Sat 9.30 pm, Sun 8 pm.

WADEBRIDGE, CORNWALL | 1–3B

BRIDGE BISTRO £44 332

4 MOLESWORTH ST PL27 7DA
01208 815342

Those who have "watched Bridge Bistro go from strength to strength" over the years – and expand next door, doubling in size – proclaim the husband-and-wife team's "amazing knack for finding brilliant staff" and "great menu options" that are "simple and quite delicious"… "long may they continue!" / www.bridgebistro.co.uk/; @Bridge_Bistro; 9 pm; closed Sun D; no Amex.

WARLINGHAM, SURREY | 3–3B

CHEZ VOUS £63 322

432 LIMPSFIELD RD CR6 9LA
01883 620451

"In a locality which is a desert for good food, this restaurant (with rooms) stands out like an oasis" – albeit one that still draws the odd quibble – "the quality of the cooking is sometimes let down by the haphazard service". / www.chezvous.co.uk; @ChezVousLtd; 9.30 pm, Fri & Sat 10 pm; closed Mon & Sun D.

WARWICK, WARWICKSHIRE | 5–4C

TAILORS £57 443

22 MARKET PLACE CV34 4SL
01926 410590

Fishmonger, butcher, casino and tailor (hence the name), this "small and personal" venue has had many lives, and in its ten-year-old restaurant incarnation now turns out "lovely" and "attractive" food of a fine, seasonal bent. / www.tailorsrestaurant.co.uk; 9 pm; closed Mon & Sun; no Amex; no bookings; children: 12+ for dinner.

WASS, NORTH YORKSHIRE | 8–4C

THE STAPYLTON ARMS £46 344

YO61 4BE 01347 868280

An "utterly delightful" North York Moors pub – now with three rooms – taken over by Robert & Gillian Thompson of the White Swan in Ampleforth two years back, and FKA The Wombwell Arms; "the menu is humble" but "very good, and also good value by local standards". / www.stapyltonarms.co.uk/; Mon-Sat 9.30 pm, Sun 4 pm.

WATERGATE BAY, CORNWALL | 1–3B

FIFTEEN CORNWALL, WATERGATE BAY HOTEL £88 335

TR8 4AA 01637 861000

"Spectacular Atlantic views" help win plenty of praise for this social enterprise (with links to Jamie Oliver, but run locally with profits to the Cornwall Food Foundation). The "fabulous" beachside location can create a "top dining

experience", although "prices are high" and results don't always justify them. It's a natural brunch spot, and they're nice to kids too. / www.fifteencornwall.co.uk; @fifteencornwall; on the Atlantic coast between Padstow and Newquay; 9.15 pm; children: 4+ at D.

WATH-IN-NIDDERDALE, NORTH YORKSHIRE | 8–4B

SPORTSMAN'S ARMS £54 322

THE SPORTSMANS ARMS HG3 5PP
01423 711306

This remote 17th-century inn near Pateley Bridge has been run along traditional lines by Ray & Jane Carter for more than 30 years. The "sensible down-to earth-cooking" – notable for an abundance of game, often shot within a mile – is "cracking good value" (but "book a long time ahead"). / www.sportsmans-arms.co.uk; take Wath Road from Pateley Bridge; Tue-Sat 9.30 pm, Sun 4 pm; no Amex. *Accommodation:* 11 rooms, from £120

WEALD SEVENOAKS, KENT | 3–3B

GIACOMO £53 333

MORLEYS ROAD TN14 6QR 01732 746200

"Authentic Italian cooking… authentic Italian staff" – there's no doubting the provenance of this "old-fashioned, family-run Italian"; Top Tip – it can get "very noisy (not least during sporadic Elvis or Michael Bublé tribute nights) so ask for a window table in the conservatory". / www.giacomos.uk.com; Thu & Fri 1 pm, Tue, Wed, Sat .

WELL, HAMPSHIRE | 2–3D

THE CHEQUERS INN 322

WHITE HILL RG29 1TL 01256 862605

"A rejuvenated country inn" in "a lovely rural setting"; "slightly cluttered and traditionally old fashioned" – it "serves generous portions of well-prepared food from a short daily menu" in its restaurant and "local ales" in the bar. / www.chequers-well.com; Mon-Sat 9 pm, Sun 8 pm.

WELLAND, WORCESTERSHIRE | 2–1B

INN AT WELLAND £47 323

HOOK BANK, DRAKE ST WR13 6LN
01684 592317

In Hook Bank, a "really good gastropub" with designer touches and a menu encompassing both classics and more adventurous grub; it has split opinion in the past but, with "attentive" staff and an "overall relaxing" vibe, the majority "cannot really ask for much more". / www.theinnatwelland.co.uk/; @innatwelland; Tue-Sat 9.30 pm, Sun 2.30 pm.

SHAMPAN 3 - WELLING £42 3|2|3

8 FALCONWOOD PARADE, THE GREEN DA16 2PL 020 8304 9569

Relaxed branch of a three-strong southern Indian chain offering "wonderful food with a slightly modern twist which doesn't detract from its deliciousness"; service can be a tad "brash" for some tastes. / www.shampangroup.com; @ShampanGroup; Mon-Sat 11 pm, Sun 9 pm.

WELLS CRAB HOUSE £49 4|4|3

38 FREEMAN ST NR23 1BA 013 2871 0456

Kelly & Scott Dougal took over this "small" venue near the quay two years ago, and quickly established its reputation as a top East Anglian destination for "excellent and imaginative seafood", sourced directly from local fishermen every morning. / wellscrabhouse.co.uk; @wellscrabhouse; Mon-Sat 9 pm, Sun 3 pm.

GOODFELLOWS £58 4|3|3

5 - 5 B SADLER STREET BA5 2RR 01749 673866

Adam Fellows's "delightful" venture has a "small but thoughtful menu majoring on fish, simply but creatively cooked and served". "The wine list includes some decent half-bottles, which is a rare treat". / www.goodfellowswells.co.uk; @goodfellowswest; Mon-Sat 11.30 pm, Sun 6 pm.

AUBERGE DU LAC, BROCKET HALL £90

AL8 7XG 01707 368888

Still too little feedback for a rating at this Lakeside converted hunting lodge on Lord Palmerston's former estate, which in the early 2000s – with JC Novelli at the stoves – was one of the country's better-known, rural, romantic dining spots. Such reports as we have, though, are of the 'all good' variety. / www.brocket-hall.co.uk; @AubergeBrocket; on B653 towards Harpenden; Wed-Sat 9.30 pm, Sun 2 pm; no jeans; children: 12+. *Accommodation:* 16 rooms, from £175

THE WAGGONERS £48 4|4|3

BRICKWALL CLOSE, AYOT GRN AL6 9AA 01707 324241

You'll find a "very warm welcome from the French owner, Laurent Brydniak, and very good food" at this little-changed 400-year-old boozer. In fact, the Gallic cuisine is "much finer than you might expect from a pub meal" – and there's a "superb cheese trolley" to boot. / www.thewaggoners.co.uk.

LONDON HOUSE £55 4|3|3

30 STATION APPROACH KT14 6NF 01932 482026

With "superb food, excellent service and a great atmosphere", MasterChef semi-finalist Ben Piette's two-year-old spot is "a brilliant find" in West Byfleet; in early 2018 they "opened Camouflage next door for pre-or -post dinner drinks" (their 'The Pantry' deli on the other side makes for a real foodie sandwich). / www.restaurantlondonhouse.co.uk; @_londonhouse; Tue-Sat 9.30 pm, Sun 2.30 pm.

THE CAT INN £51 4|3|3

NORTH LANE RH19 4PP 01342 810369

"The Cat looks and feels like an archetypal village pub" ("it retains a proper bar with a good range of ales and craft beers, but also has a large well-designed restaurant extension"). "In truth, it's mostly about the food" – "a cut above the average gastropub fare", which "at its best, it's the best". / www.catinn.co.uk; @TheCatInn; Mon-Thu 9 pm, Fri & Sat 9.30 pm, Sun 8.30 pm; no Amex; children: 7+. *Accommodation:* 4 rooms, from £110

RAJDANI 3|4|3

17-20 LONDON ROAD TN15 6ES 01474 853501

"Family-run Indian, just a few hundred yards from Brands Hatch, celebrating its twentieth anniversary, offering a short, changing, contemporary menu to appeal to all tastes (and a new gourmet menu, with a greater choice of fish, gluten-free, vegetarian and vegan dishes)." / www.rajdani.co.uk; Mon-Sat 9.30 pm, Sun 4 pm.

THE SWAN £54 3|3|2

35 SWAN ST ME19 6JU 01732 521910

A "comfortable, attractive" 15th-century inn offering "enjoyable" brasserie fare and cocktails, and hailed for its "good menu of excellent choices". / www.theswanwestmalling.co.uk; @swanwm; Mon-Sat 11.30 pm, Sun 7 pm.

THE COMPANY SHED £38 5|2|2

129 COAST RD CO5 8PA 01206 382700

"A must try" – "take your own bread and wine (glasses are provided)" if you want to eat some of "the best, freshest seafood you'll find anywhere, in this somewhat off-putting wooden shed". "The setting is basic but you always have to queue to get in, and no wonder". / www.thecompanyshed.co; Tue-Fri 11 pm, Sat midnight, Sun 10.30 pm; no bookings.

COAST RD CO5 8LT 01206 381600

"Oysters to die for (cultivated within eyesight) and wonderful fish options" mean that it's worth braving the crowds and "very basic dining conditions" to eat at this seafront diner. It's "consistently good value", with "interesting specials to encourage new experiences". / www.westmerseaoysterbar.co.uk; Mon-Sat 10 pm, Sun 5 pm; no Amex; no shorts.

THE WENSLEYDALE HEIFER £65 3|2|3

MAIN ST DL8 4LS 01969 622322

This family-run village restaurant-with-rooms wins consistent ratings for its "lovely food", including (despite its distinctly beefy name) a menu of "super fish" specialities. / www.wensleydaleheifer.co.uk; @wensleyheifer; Mon-Sat 10.30 pm, Sun 4 pm; booking max 6 may apply. *Accommodation:* 13 rooms, from £130

SEVERN & WYE SMOKERY £42 3|3|3

CHAXHILL GL14 1QW 01452 760191

Richard & Shirley Cook's veteran smokery reopened doors in October 2017 after a three-year revamp, adding new food hall/café/shop and fish counter 'The Barn'. "The ambience is a bit clinical", but largely compensated for by "perfect views over the Severn, Bristol Channel and Welsh Hills" – plus "delicious fresh" fishy food. / severnandwye.co.uk/restaurant; @severnwye; Mon-Wed 6 pm, Thu-Sat 9 pm, Sun 4 pm.

THE WILD MUSHROOM £50 3|3|3

WOODGATE HOUSE, WESTFIELD LANE TN35 4SB 01424 751137

Established a decade ago, and with three other local spin-offs as well as a cookery school, Paul Webbe's relaxed farmhouse venture remains a brilliant spot for local/seasonal foraged and fished ingredients. / www.webbesrestaurants.co.uk; @WebbesGroup; Wed-Sat 9.30 pm, Sun 2 pm.

THE WESTLETON CROWN £49 3|3|3

THE ST IP17 3AD 01728 648777

This dog-friendly 12th century inn, with pleasant patio seating and log fires, was taken over by the East-Anglian Chestnut Group, which is expanding its reach to the coast, in mid-2018; rooms are a mite "cluttered", but it makes for a "lovely weekend away with good cooking and friendly staff". / www.westletoncrown.co.uk; @Westleton_Crown; 9.30 pm.

The Whitebrook, Whitebrook

TRENCHERS £48 `543`

NEW QUAY RD YO21 1DH 01947 603212

"Superb posh fish 'n' chips" ("they told me the boat which caught my meal!") are to be found at this "classic and timeless chippy" – a Whitby institution for more than 30 years. Its first spin-off opened in summer 2018 at the newly restored Whitley Bay Spanish City dome. / www.trenchersrestaurant.co.uk; 8.30 pm; may need 7+ to book.

CRAB HOUSE CAFÉ £50 `534`

FERRYMANS WAY, PORTLAND ROAD DT4 9YU 01305 788 867

"The essence of summer eating" – "select the simplest dishes" (go for the "very fresh fish and crab" – one or two more complex options are "mucked about with unnecessarily") and they are "guaranteed to be good" at this "fun and interesting" beachside café (behind Chesil Beach and owned by local oyster farmers). / www.crabhousecafe.co.uk; @crabhousecafe; overlooking the Fleet Lagoon, on the road to Portland; Mon-Sat 10 pm, Sun 5 pm; no Amex; 8+ deposit of £10 per head.

AL MOLO £51 `333`

PIER BANDSTAND, THE ESPLANADE DT4 7RN 01305 839 888

Fine views accompany a trip to this Art Deco landmark, which occupies the former bandstand of the town's pier. The food is traditional Italian, and particularly strong on pasta and seafood – fans say it's "fantastic". / www.almolo.co.uk; @AlMoloWeymouth; Fri-Sun, Mon-Thu 9 pm.

BENEDICTS OF WHALLEY £37 `333`

1 GEORGE ST BB7 9TH 01254 824 468

Stop Press – after 40 years dressing local ladies, Hilary Cookson, owner of the Whalley department store (which this spot is attached to), announced she was selling up in autumn 2018. On a positive note, the café will remain in business under new owners, and hopefully keep up the good work (the full English through to epic cakes). / www.benedictsofwhalley.co.uk; @BenedictsDeli; 7.30 pm, Sun 4 pm.

BREDA MURPHY RESTAURANT £51 `434`

41 STATION RD BB7 9RH 01254 823446

"Really fresh food and the warmest Irish hospitality" has made this Anglo-Irish café, "conveniently located opposite the train station" a firm favourite in the Ribble Valley. A major refurb in 2017 doubled its capacity and added an Irish gin bar, enabling more ambitious cooking and Fri/Sat evening opening. Top Tip: "the signature fish pie is never off the menu". / www.bredamurphy.co.uk/; @Breda_Murphy; Wed-Sat 10.30 pm, Sun 9.30 pm.

THE THREE FISHES £44 `333`

MITTON RD BB7 9PQ 01254 826888

The cradle of the Ribble Valley Inns chain and, to some, "still the best" – this converted old village pub has a very solid reputation for its "seasonal produce and classic Lancashire dishes". In May 2018 it ceased its connections to Northcote, as the group was swallowed by Chester-based pub chain Brunning & Price. / www.thethreefishes.com; @the_threefishes; Mon-Sat 11 pm, Sun 10.30 pm.

MAGPIE CAFÉ £38 `543`

14 PIER RD YO21 3PU 01947 602058

"Our regular fish 'n' chip fix for years… despite living 150 miles away!" This "epic" Harbourside "stalwart" is often hailed for "the best fish 'n' chips in the UK" and "nothing seems to have changed since before the fire" last year: the frying is "expertly done, with moist fish, crisp batter; and there are also more adventurous items on the menu, which can be really good (e.g. the seafood stew)". "Basically, it's everything you could want from a seaside chippy… and with big portions" ("portion control seems utterly missing!"). "Only drawback is that it can get crowded, but then you're in Whitby". Top Tip: "if you can get a window seat then the view over Whitby can be glorious" (but taking away and enjoying your tucker on the harbour wall also comes recommended). / www.magpiecafe.co.uk; @themagpiecafe; 9 pm; no Amex; no bookings at lunch.

THE STAR INN THE HARBOUR £49 `224`

LANGBORNE ROAD YO21 1YN 01947 821 900

This fish-based venture is the latest from North Yorkshire star-chef Andrew Pern (of Harome fame), in the former tourist information centre of his home town, by the harbour-side. He's created a "marvellous", "very buzzy" space in a "cracking location", but as with his other recent openings, food and service receive a more mixed scorecard – to fans "well-cooked and extremely fresh fish and seafood", but to foes "woeful and bigged up beyond belief by sycophantic food hacks". A fair middle view? – "None of the food was bad, and some was great. However, it feels like a franchise; it does not feel like the proprietor is around, or cares". / www.starinntheharbour.co.uk; @HarbourStarInn; Mon-Wed 9.30 pm, Thu 10 pm, Fri 10.30 pm, Sat 11 pm, Sun 9 pm; may need + to book.

DOCKET NO.33 £49

33 HIGH STREET SY13 1AZ 01948 665553

It opened barely a year ago, and we still lack sufficient feedback for a rating on Stuart Collins's modern British venture in the heart of an attractive and ancient market town near the Welsh border (with no culinary oppo to speak of). The word on the street, though, is that its ambitious cuisine makes it well worth a visit: you can eat à la carte, and there's also a 5-course tasting menu (for £37, with a very reasonably priced £20 drinks pairing option). / docketrestaurant.com.

THE BEEHIVE £62 `443`

WALTHAM RD SL6 3SH 01628822877

"A lovely location overlooking the village cricket pitch" contributes to the winning recipe for Dom Chapman's "brilliant" former pub (he was previously a Heston Blumenthal lieutenant at the Fat Duck and Hind's Head). "Some stunning dishes are delivered very competently" (e.g. "the wild rabbit lasagne was divine, and the sea bream with tarka dhal inspired"). Top Tip: if you're flying via Heathrow, "a 15-minute detour takes you here". / www.thebeehivewhitewaltham.com; @thebeehivetweet; 2.30pm for lunch and 9.30pm for dinner Mon-Fri, 9..

THE WHITEBROOK, RESTAURANT WITH ROOMS £114 `543`

NP25 4TX 01600 860254

"Top chef, outstanding food, a great fine dining experience": Great British Menu chef, Chris Harrod continues to inspire high acclaim at this stylish restaurant-with-rooms in the Wye Valley, with his "Noma-esque" cuisine. "Vaut le détour!". / www.thewhitebrook.co.uk; @TheWhitebrook; 2m W of A466, 5m S of Monmouth; 9 pm; closed Mon; children: 12+ for D. *Accommodation:* 8 rooms, from £145

HINNIES £44 `343`

10 EAST PARADE NE26 1AP 0191 447 0500

"Excellent local dishes, presented in a novel style" win praise for this seafront fixture, which has a "fantastic view over the promenade". "It caters really well for children of all ages with a fantastic menu with make-your-own pizza and build-your-own ice-cream". / www.hinnies.co.uk/; @hinniesrest; Tue-Sat 10 pm, Sun 5 pm.

WHITSTABLE, KENT   3–4D

CRAB & WINKLE   £53   3 3 3

SOUTH QUAY, WHITSTABLE HARBOUR CT5 1AB 01227 779377

A "lovely seafood restaurant, with views of Whitstable Harbour" and "great locally sourced seafood" that's "not too expensive" – the MO at this simply decorated café with a pleasing terrace. / www.crabandwinklerestaurant.co.uk; @Crab_Winkle; Mon-Sat 10.30 pm; no Amex; children: 6.

HARBOUR STREET TAPAS   £35   4 3 2

48 HARBOUR STREET CT5 1AQ 01227 273373

This "very buzzy" two-year-old serves "great, fresh-flavoured" tapas and charcuterie from a menu which "changes frequently". The "very friendly owners" are both well-known industry veterans – food supplier Lee Murray from the Goods Shed in Canterbury and chef Tim Wilson, ex-The Ivy and Groucho Club. / www.harbourstreettapas.com; @harbourttapas; Mon-Sat 9.30 pm, Sun 4 pm.

JOJO   £38   3 4 3

2 HERNE BAY RD CT5 2LQ 01227 274591

"Our local go-to restaurant for a quality meal" – this well-established Med-inspired joint has terrific views over Whitstable from Tankerton Slopes. "The tapas-style menu's based on seasonal ingredients and fish, so everything's always really fresh". / www.jojosrestaurant.co.uk; @jojostankerton; Thu-Sat 11 pm, Sun 3 pm; cash only.

THE LOBSTER SHACK RESTAURANT   £24   4 2 3

EAST QUAY CT5 1AB 01227 771923

"Nothing fancy, just wonderfully fresh seafood cooked perfectly" is a typical endorsement of this "terrific value" beachside haunt "tucked away behind the harbour" in foodie Whitstable. "Excellent lobster and line-caught fish, simply served" along with "plateau de fruits de mer" lead the wine, best enjoyed at an outside table. / www.eqvenue.com/restaurant; @brewerybarwhits; 9 pm.

PEARSON'S ARMS   £46   3 3 4

THE HORSEBRIDGE, SEA WALL CT5 1BT 01227 773133

"In a superb position (especially with a table in the window) overlooking the Thames estuary" – "this excellent pub (downstairs) and restaurant ("tucked away upstairs") on the front" stands out for its "very good fish". Chef/patron Richard Phillips offers a wide range from a "superb-value set lunch" to his five-course tasting menu. / www.pearsonsarmsbyrichardphillips.co.uk; @pearsonsarms; Mon-Sun 11 pm.

SAMPHIRE   £50   3 3 3

4 HIGH STREET CT5 1BQ 01227 770075

A "lovely, little" fixture on the High Street for more than a decade – this "friendly" independent bistro makes "interesting" use of local produce to create some "fantastic" flavours and is "always busy" as a result. / www.samphirewhitstable.co.uk; @samphirewhit; Mon-Sun 9 pm; no Amex.

THAI ORCHID   £24   3 4 2

82 MIDDLE WALL CT5 1BN 01227 262165

"A new and welcome addition to the dining scene in Whitstable" – this bright and airy modern café provides "great tasting food and very friendly service" and is "excellent value". / thaiorchidwhitstable.com; Mon-Sat 9.30 pm, Sun 4 pm.

WHEELERS OYSTER BAR   £48   5 4 3

8 HIGH STREET CT5 1BQ 01227 273311

"You could be forgiven if you thought you were eating in someone's living room" at this "quirky", "casual and basic" institution (est. 1856), where you eat "in a tiny back parlour that maybe seats 14-16 people"; and which "serves superbly fresh seafood" with "oysters a speciality". "It's not licensed, but there's a good selection of wines offered in the off-licence opposite". / www.wheelersoysterbar.com; @WheelersOB; Mon & Tue, Thu, Sun 9 pm, Fri 9.30 pm, Sat 10 pm; cash only.

WHITSTABLE OYSTER FISHERY CO.   £62   3 2 4

ROYAL NATIVE OYSTER STORES, HORSEBRIDGE CT5 1BU 01227 276856

"A converted warehouse on the Whitstable shoreline overlooking the oyster beds" provides a "fantastic beach-side location" for this very well-known day-tripper destination. "It's not innovative cooking but they use lovely fresh produce and portions are generous", while the overall "relaxing" vibe is "lively and uplifting". On the downside "prices are a bit steep" and service can be "unenthusiastic" especially at peak times when it can seem "overstretched". / www.whitstableoystercompany.com; Tue-Sat 8 pm.

WILLIAN, HERTFORDSHIRE   3–2B

THE FOX   £49   2 2 3

SG6 2AE 01462 480233

Regulars disagree this year on this well-appointed gastropub-with-rooms just off the A1 in a pretty village with a duck pond: some feel "it seems more over-extended of late with cooking that's not what it was", but others praise "very superior" food and continue to rate it highly. / www.foxatwillian.co.uk; @FoxAtWillian; 1 mile from junction 9 off A1M; Mon-Thu 9 pm, Fri & Sat 9.30 pm, Sun 8.30 pm.

WINCHCOMBE, GLOUCESTERSHIRE 2–1C

5 NORTH STREET   £77   4 3 2

5 NORTH ST GL54 5LH 01242 604566

Losing a star in 2018 has done little to dent enthusiasm for Marcus & Kate Ashenford's "brilliant" gem occupying a beamed ex-tearoom in a pretty Cotswold village. The "reassuringly small menu reflects the fact that everything is cooked to order", with "utterly delicious" and "interesting" results. / www.5northstreetrestaurant.co.uk; Tue-Sun 9 pm; no Amex.

WINCHESTER, HAMPSHIRE   2–3D

THE BLACK RAT   £60   3 3 4

88 CHESIL ST SO23 0HX 01962 844465

"The most innovative restaurant for miles around", say fans of this acclaimed pub conversion on the edge of town, which has built a formidable reputation since it opened more than 10 years ago. But while most reports are of "beautifully presented and well-executed" cuisine, ratings are sapped slightly by reports of dishes that "try too hard", or "read well on the menu, but don't meet expectations". Top Tip: "the excellent and very reasonably priced lunch menu". / www.theblackrat.co.uk; @the_black_rat; Mon-Sat 10.30 pm, Sun 9 pm; children: 18+ except weekend L.

THE CHESIL RECTORY   £66   3 4 5

1 CHESIL ST SO23 0HU 01962 851555

With its "medieval exposed beams and stripped, creaky flooring", this "cosy restaurant" in a 600-year-old merchant's house is "one of the most romantic places, with lots of small, quirkily decorated rooms". Staff are "chilled but attentive" and the food – although it may struggle to match the unique surroundings – is, on practically all accounts, "more than accomplished". / www.chesilrectory.co.uk; @ChesilRectory; 9 pm, Fri & Sat 9.30 pm, Sun 8.30 pm; children: 12+ at D.

GANDHI RESTAURANT   £34   4 4 2

163-164 HIGH ST SO23 9BA 01962863940

"Some of the best fine Indian dining away from gourmet restaurants in London" can be found at this "upmarket" family-run operation, founded more than 30 years ago. "Chef Amnart Ubonrat's menu featuring such delights as wood pigeon, beef ox cheeks and spice-crusted venison sets it apart from its rivals". / www.gandhirestaurant.com/; 11.30pm.

HOTEL DU VIN & BISTRO   £47   2 2 4

SOUTHGATE STREET SO23 9EF 01962 896 329

"Whilst the elegant dining room continues to impress", and the cellar remains a strong point, both "food and service can be hit and miss" at this attractive Georgian red-brick – the first link in the HdV chain; perennially up and down, when it comes to a decent meal it's one "for risk-takers only". / www.hotelduvin.com; @HdV_Winchester; Mon-Thu 10 pm, Fri & Sat 10.30 pm, Sun 9.30 pm; booking max 12 may apply. *Accommodation:* 24 rooms, from £145

KYOTO KITCHEN   £42   **4 4 3**

70 PARCHMENT STREET   SO23 8AT 01962 890895

Strong ratings (if on somewhat limited feedback) on Miff Kayum's well-appointed Japanese, where the focus is on sushi and sashimi (plus tempura and a selection of 'large plates'). / www.kyotokitchen.co.uk; @Kyoto_Kitchen; Tue-Thu 3 pm, Fri-Sun 11 pm.

THE AVENUE, LAINSTON HOUSE HOTEL   £94   **4 4 3**

WOODMAN LN   SO21 2LT   01962 776088

The dining room of this plush country-house hotel – "a classic five-star" in an 18th-century mansion – serves an "imaginative menu of innovative food, much of it local produce". Exec chef Andrew Birch, who took over the kitchen in June 2017, is "definitely one to watch". / www.lainstonhouse.com; @lainstonhouse; Sun-Thu 9.30 pm, Fri & Sat 10 pm. *Accommodation:* 50 rooms, from £245

PALM PAN ASIA   £43   **4 4 3**

166-167 HIGH ST   SO23 9BA   01962 864 040

"As good as being there – from someone who lived there", is one reporter's verdict on this "impressive pan-Asian gourmet experience, that builds on classic Thai dishes with interesting taste combinations". / www.palmpanasia.co.uk/; @palm_panasia.

RICK STEIN   £62   **3 4 3**

7 HIGH STREET   SO23 9JX   01962 353535

"Excellent seafood (I'd say better than Padstow)" makes this venue "in the heart of town" – Stein's first outside Cornwall when it opened five years ago – "the perfect place to entertain and impress a client". Ratings have edged up this year: "although it can be a bit pricey, it's very enjoyable". / www.rickstein.com; @SteinWinchester; Mon-Sat 10.30 pm, Sun 10 pm.

RIVER COTTAGE CANTEEN   £50   **2 1 2**

ABBEY MILL, ABBEY MILL GARDENS   SO23 9GH   01962457747

An "impressive and interesting mill conversion" ("a bit noisy, though") – Hugh Fearnley-Whittingstall's well-known operation puts in a mixed performance. It's praised for its use of "good ingredients", but "the food combinations can be a bit strange", preparation "can lack attention to detail" and "service is poor at times". / www.rivercottage.net/canteens/winchester; @WinCanteen; Tue - Sat 9.15 pm, Sun 4 pm.

WYKEHAM ARMS   £56   **2 2 4**

75 KINGSGATE ST   SO23 9PE   01962 853834

A "very unusual" interior is the highpoint of this ancient pub near the cathedral (nowadays run by Fuller's), where drinkers sit at disused desks from the town's posh boys' boarding school (after whose 14th-century founder it is named). It's a highly atmospheric haunt, although popularity means it can be "overcrowded, cramped and noisy". Foodwise "quality has been all over the place" in recent years, but fans say "it's the best it's been since the good old days of late". / www.wykehamarmswinchester.co.uk; @WykehmarmsLL; between Cathedral and College; Mon-Sat 11 pm, Sun 10.30 pm; children: 14+. *Accommodation:* 14 rooms, from £139

CEDAR MANOR   £68   **3 3 3**

AMBLESIDE ROAD   LA23 1AX   015394 43192

Small boutique hotel a short walk from Windermere with an attractive, traditional dining room serving a good-value, prix fixe menu of straightforward, enjoyable dishes. / www.cedarmanor.co.uk; @CedarManorHotel; Wed-Sat 11 pm, Sun 7 pm.

GILPIN SPICE, GILPIN LODGE   £52   **5 4 3**

CROOK ROAD   LA23 3NE   01539 488818

"Love this new addition to The Gilpin" – the hotel's second restaurant is also run by Hrishikesh Desai – "a funky space" with "an open kitchen, and a counter for more casual dining" in "a separate building (handily nearer the car park) that's also open for lunch". It serves "a splendid selection of food with a spicy (mild or otherwise) twist" ("the word is Spice, not chilli, and it's the first time I've had a meal like that that hasn't left my digestive system complaining the next day"). On all accounts, results are "superb" with "outstanding, bright, fresh flavours. Just wow!" / www.thegilpin.co.uk; Wed-Sat 9 pm, Sun 4 pm.

HOLBECK GHYLL   £104   **3 3 5**

HOLBECK LANE   LA23 1LU   01539 432375

"Lovely food and highly professional service in a beautiful Lakeland setting" have carved a big reputation for this luxurious old hunting lodge, which has "brilliant views" over Lake Windermere. Even the author of an 'off report', who considered the experience "pricey" and "not as impressive as hitherto" says the cooking is "competent to good". / www.holbeckghyll.com; @HolbeckGhyll; 3m N of Windermere, towards Troutbeck; 9.30 pm; no jeans; children: 7+ at D. *Accommodation:* 33 rooms, from £190

HOMEGROUND   £18   **3 4 3**

LA23 1DX   015394 44863

"The best cafe in Windermere with the best brunches" (both the hash browns and huevos rancheros come recommended). "There is usually a queue to get a table but it's well worth the wait". / www.homegroundcafe.co.uk; @Homegroundcafe; no bookings.

HOOKED   £75   **4 3 2**

ELLERTHWAITE SQUARE   LA23 1DP 015394 48443

"Lovely fresh fish cooked to perfection" remains the considerable draw to this diminutive eight-year-old, occasionally "a little lacking in atmosphere" and "expensive, but worth it!" / www.hookedwindermere.co.uk/; Mon closed, Tue - Sun 10.30pm; no Amex; booking max 6 may apply.

HRISHI, GILPIN LODGE   £93   **5 4 3**

CROOK RD   LA23 3NE   01539 488818

Hrishikesh Desai's outstanding Asian-fusion cuisine inspires extremely high ratings for the main dining room of this boutique-ified Lakeland Hotel (which occupies a Georgian-style building, dating from 1901): "spread across several rooms of the main building, it's open for dinner only". See also 'Gilpin Spice' (which actually inspired more interest this year). / www.thegilpin.co.uk; @chef_keller; Tue-Sat 10 pm; no jeans; children: 7+. *Accommodation:* 20 rooms, from £255

LANGDALE CHASE   £67

AMBLESIDE ROAD   LA23 1LW   015394 32201

Few venues enjoy as stunning a location as this hotel within a Victorian mansion, overlooking Lake Windermere (which for a year now has been part of the House of Daniel Thwaites hotel and pub portfolio). Feedback was too limited for a rating this year, but such as we had was all positive, including for afternoon tea. / www.langdalechase.co.uk; @Langdale_Chase; Wed-Sat 9 pm, Sun 2.30 pm.

LINTHWAITE HOUSE   £82

CROOK ROAD   LA23 3JA   015394 88600

In June 2018, this well-known and beautifully positioned Lakeland hotel (nowadays part of the Leeu Collection) re-opened after a £10 million refit, complete with a new restaurant, bar and conservatory. The menu designed by chef Ritu Dalmia is now predominantly Italian in style – a rating will have to await feedback in next year's survey. / www.linthwaite.com; @LinthwaiteHouse; near Windermere golf club; 9 pm; no jeans; children: 7+ at D. *Accommodation:* 30 rooms, from £180

THE SAMLING   £110   **4 4 5**

AMBLESIDE ROAD   LA23 1LR   01539 431922

"The food and ambience have been raised to a different level" at this acclaimed country hotel, which unveiled a new glass-walled restaurant, wine cellar, chef's table and chef (Peter Howarth, ex-of Gidleigh Park) in October 2017. It won real paeans this year for its "wonderful" food (taking in "superb" tasting menus) and "the perfect setting overlooking Lake Windermere" ("the best view of any restaurant I've ever been to"). / www.thesamlinghotel.co.uk; @theSamlingHotel; take A591 from town; 9.30 pm. *Accommodation:* 11 rooms, from £300

AL FASSIA £45 443

27 ST LEONARDS RD SL4 3BP
01753 855370

This twenty-year-old Moroccan remains one of the town's leading culinary lights, serving a range of tagines, couscous, kebabs and mezze, and with "a great choice of vegetarian options". / www.alfassiarestaurant.com; @AlfassiaWindsor; Mon-Thu 10 pm, Fri & Sat 10.30 pm, Sun 9 pm.

MEIMO £34 343

69-70 PEASCOD ST SL4 1DE
01753 862 222

"Very friendly service" won particular praise this year for this affordable café, serving Moroccan mezze and brochettes, alongside a selection of 'Meimo Burgers'. / www.meimo.co.uk; @MeimoWindsor; Sun-Thu 10 pm, Fri & Sat 10.30 pm.

BRIDGEWATER ARMS £50 433

THE BRIDGEWATER ARMS DL2 3RN
01325 730 302

Veteran East Coast fishmongers "Hodgsons' local Hartlepool catch features on the eclectic and imaginative menu" ("so many delicious dishes it's hard to choose!", also including "meat and game in season") at this posh one-time school; "nor is the eventual bill too fishy either". / www.thebridgewaterarms.com; 9 pm.

WINTERINGHAM FIELDS £117 544

1 SILVER ST DN15 9ND 01724 733096

"It is about time that Michelin acknowledged this as one of England's finest restaurants" said diners in our annual survey, and the tyre man did just that in October 2018, finally rewarding Colin McGurran's revitalisation of this "romantic" rural restaurant with rooms, near the banks of the Humber, which in the 1990s perennially featured in listings of the country's Top 10 culinary destinations. "The seven-course tasting menu is superb, the service excellent throughout and the deal to include overnight accommodation is very good value". / www.winteringhamfields.co.uk; @winteringhamf; 4m SW of Humber Bridge; Tue-Sat 9 pm; no Amex; no trainers. *Accommodation:* 11 rooms, from £180

FREEMASONS AT WISWELL £77 534

8 VICARAGE FOLD CLITHEROE BB7 9DF
01254 822218

"Situated in a tiny village" in the Ribble Valley, this is a "delightful old pub" and Steve Smith's cuisine has established it as one of Lancashire's top dining destinations (bearing comparison with Northcote down the road). "The juxtaposition of some classical ideas (sauce grand veneur with game, for example), modern techniques and a hint of the Orient" produces some truly "excellent" dishes (although quite a few fans fear that "over complication" can be an issue: "the amount of sauces and colours on the plate can be OTT"). "Interesting wine list" too. Service is mostly "friendly and helpful" but can be "patchy" ("sometimes they're good; sometimes they're pleasant, but below par"). / www.freemasonswiswell.co.uk; @Wiswellman; Wed-Sat 9 pm, Sun 8 pm; no Amex; booking max 6 may apply.

WIVETON BELL £49 333

BLAKENEY RD NR25 7TL 01263 740 101

Handy for the North Norfolk salt marshes, "a very popular gastropub/restaurant" (the former a "bit busy") with "great views" of the local green. At lunch expect "the standard fish 'n' chips" and other gastro classics; dinner is bolder. / www.wivetonbell.co.uk; @wivetonbell; 9 pm; no Amex; booking evening only.

PARIS HOUSE £111 545

WOBURN PARK MK17 9QP 01525 290692

"A beautiful restaurant in the grounds of Woburn Abbey, with a big sweeping drive" – this well-known old Tudor building was revamped in spring 2017 and "the makeover has improved the dining room immensely: the cold old decor is now light and bright…" matching standards generally, with "superb food from Phil Fanning's brigade". How long will Michelin make him wait before giving him his star back? / www.parishouse.co.uk; @ParisHousechef; on A4012; Thu-Sat 8.30 pm, Sun 1.30 pm.

THE INN WEST END £48 434

42 GUILDFORD RD GU24 9PW
01276 858652

This poshified village gastropub-with-rooms, handy for Ascot Racecourse, was taken over by Barons Pub Company in October 2018, joining their seven-strong Surrey and Berks portfolio. Here's hoping it retains its character – "what a real gastropub should be", from the fine food to the "well-kept real ales". / www.the-inn.co.uk; @InnWestEnd; Mon-Sat 11 pm, Sun 10.30 pm; no trainers; children: 5+.

THE COD'S SCALLOPS £27 442

170 BRAMCOTE LN NG8 2QP
0115 985 4107

"Delicious and deeply satisfying 'posh' fish 'n' chips (probably something to do with the fact they are battered in beef dripping!)" again wins strong local praise for this booth-lined spot (also with wet fish counter). / www.codsscallops.com; @TheCodsScallops; 9 pm, Fri & Sat 9.30 pm; closed Sun; no Amex; no bookings.

BILASH £54 443

2 CHEAPSIDE WV1 1TU 01902 427762

"The restaurant equivalent to Man City in the Premiership" – Sitab Khan's family-run operation has built a formidable reputation for his "efficient" and "very personal" curry house (which celebrated its 35th anniversary with a £100k refurb completed in early 2018). "Depending on where you sit, you can watch the consistently high quality food prepared in front of you and it's good value in a town that lacks good places to eat". "May Wolverhampton Wanderers one day emulate them…" / www.thebilash.co.uk; @thebilash; 10.30 pm; closed Sun.

THE TABLE £39 344

QUAY ST IP12 1BX 01394 382428

Cheerful, modern "bistro-style" venue that's a local favourite, serving cakes and salads from the counter, as well as a menu of more ambitious fare. It's five years old in its current guise, but there's been a restaurant on the site for the last fifty years. / www.thetablewoodbridge.co.uk; Mon-Fri 9 pm, Sat 9.30 pm.

SPOT IN THE WOODS £71 343

174 WOODLANDS RD, NETLEY MARSH, NEW FOREST SO40 7GL 023 8029 3784

With acclaimed wine expert Gerard Basset fighting illness, he and his wife Nina transformed their hotel Terravina from March 2018 into this new, much less formal boutique B&B, complete with a 'Kitchen Café' open seven days a week from 8am to 4pm, serving "very good quality" all-day breakfasts, sandwiches and wraps alongside specials of the day. It's "an excellent location for exploration of the New Forest". / www.hotelterravina.co.uk; @Hotel_TerraVina; 9.30 pm. *Accommodation:* 11 rooms, from £165

CRABSHACK £46 433

2 MARINE PARADE BN11 3PN
01903 215070

"Great fresh crab.........and other seafood as well" can make for a "terrific, informal meal" at this three-year-old café with large terrace near the seafront. / www.crabshackworthing.co.uk; @CrabShack10; Tue-Thu 9 pm, Fri & Sat 9.30 pm, Sun 4 pm.

THE HAND & TRUMPET £46 223

MAIN RD CW3 9BJ 01270 820048

Pub belonging to the Brunning & Price empire – and showcasing their usual "dependable food and service in a relaxed atmosphere" ("the menu choice is increasing", and there's an "excellent variety" of beers); the pleasant vintage-style interior leads out to a deck overlooking a pond. / www.brunningandprice.co.uk/hand; Tue-Sun .

ETHICUREAN £65 4|3|4

BARLEY WOOD WALLED GARDEN, LONG LN BS40 5SA 01934 863713

A "really different" ethical venture whose veggie-friendly food is "inventive and delicious" (à la carte by day, set menu by night). Set among art studios and a cider barn in a Victorian walled garden minutes from the airport, it can feel "too greenhouse-y" for some, but sitting outside in summer it's the "perfect location". / www.theethicurean.com; @TheEthicurean; Tue-Sun.

THE WIFE OF BATH RESTAURANT, ROOMS AND TAPAS BAR £56 4|3|3

4 UPPER BRIDGE ST TN25 5AF 01233 812232

"Authentic northern Spanish cooking" featuring tapas and Galician beef has transformed this veteran Kent restaurant (est 1962) under the ownership of Mark Sargeant, of Rock Salt in Folkestone – it's "reached new heights since the takeover" in 2016. / www.thewifeofbath.com; @TheWifeofBath2; off A28 between Ashford & Canterbury; Wed-Sat, Tue 9.30 pm, Sun 5 pm; no Amex. *Accommodation:* 5 rooms, from £95

BILLY WINTERS BAR & DINER £35 2|3|4

FERRY BRIDGE BOATYARD, PORTLAND ROAD, DT4 9JZ 01305 774954

"You go for the wonderful location" – "a splendid vantagepoint with views over Portland Harbour" – if you seek out this brightly-decorated prefab, near the water, with outside seating. It's not a foodie locale however: it serves fish 'n' chips, baps, burgers, pizzas and other beachy snacks. / Wed & Thu, Sun 6 pm, Fri & Sat 10 pm; no bookings.

Le Cochon Aveugle, York

THE BERKELEY ARMS £42 4|4|3

59 MAIN ST LE14 2AG 01572 787 587

"A perfect country pub experience" – Beil & Louise Hitchen's "lively and welcoming" gastroboozer is "a fine place" that's "always packed out". "The food is seasonal, the ingredients local (brilliant game in season – quail, grouse, partridge, venison, pigeon and so much more) and the cooking inventive and beautifully executed". / www.theberkeleyarms.co.uk; @TheBekeleyArms; Tue-Sat 11 pm, Sun 5 pm; no Amex.

WHITE POST £57 5|4|4

RIMPTON HILL BA22 8AR 019 3585 1525

"High class food without the price tag" again wins high praise for Brett & Kelly Sutton's restaurant-with-rooms. "You it could be excused for thinking you're in a high end restaurant in London instead of a Top 50 gastropub in the country, and there are wonderful tasting courses". Top Tip: "their 'pudding club' is a very good way to sample many delicious options from the dessert menu after a light main course". / thewhitepost.com; @thewhitepost; Tue-Sat 10 pm, Sun 2 pm.

AMBIENTE £24 3|3|3

31 FOSSGATE YO1 9TA 01904 638 252

"You are transported to Spain" at this buzzing, industrial-style spin-off to the four-strong York-born chain (also with branches in Hull and Leeds); on the menu, "yummy" and "authentic" tapas plus "superb sherry" delivered by "all Spanish staff". / www.ambiente-tapas.co.uk; 10 pm.

ARRAS £66 4|4|3

THE OLD COACH HOUSE, PEASHOLME GREEN YO1 7PW 01904 633 737

Not everyone vibes with the decor, or often, by extension, the overall experience of this ambitious yearling "occupying the premises of the much lamented La Langhe" (RIP). What is

"a lovely, very peaceful setting with abstract art on the walls" to some tastes is plain "strange" to others. But "even if it's bonkers decor, what matters is the food", and – be if from the à la carte or the tasting menu – "blimey does it deliver ("the styling's a bit cold, but the cooking's red hot!")"… or at least that's the majority verdict. The downbeat view is that the dishes are "bland" and "don't stand out", but even critics concede that the "excellent cheese 'chariot' with a unique selection of side, is exceptional" – "described at the table by Chef/Patron Adam Humphrey for whom it is a genuine passion. Save a space for the huge selection of petit fours that Willy Wonka himself would be proud of". / www.arrasrestaurant.co.uk; @ArrasRestaurant; Tue-Sat 9.30 pm.

BARBARKAN £38 3|3|4

58 WALMGATE YO1 9TL 01904 672474

"A lovely, cheap 'n' cheerful Polish restaurant serving all day, five minutes walk from the centre of York. The Polish and Eastern European specialities such as pierogi, schnitzel and borscht are particularly fine. Leave room for pudding: the cakes are epic!" / www.deli-barbakan.co.uk; @TheBarbakan; Tue-Sat 10 pm, Mon 3 pm, Sun 9 pm.

BETTYS £39 3|4|4

6-8 ST HELEN'S SQUARE YO1 8QP 01904 659142

"Everyone who visits York goes to the iconic Betty's" – so "be prepared to queue" – but everyone also agrees that it's "always worth the wait", with its "lovely baked goods and treats to buy in the shop and a fabulous afternoon tea with a good selection of cakes and speciality brews. Highly recommend!" Or "proper leaf tea and a fat rascal completes a memorable brunch". / www.bettys.co.uk/tea-rooms/locations/york; @Bettys1919; Sun-Fri & Sat 9 pm; no Amex; booking lunch only.

CAFE NO. 8 BISTRO £52 3|3|3

8 GILLYGATE YO31 7EQ 01904 653074

"Simple, no-fuss good cooking" is rustled up in a tiny kitchen at this small bistro, using "excellent ingredients, and prepared with some imagination". It can feel a "little cramped", but there's a secluded garden at the back adjoining the medieval city walls. / www.cafeno8.co.uk; @cafeno8; Mon-Sun 10 pm; no Amex.

LE COCHON AVEUGLE £84 5|4|3

37 WALMGATE YO1 9TX 01904 640222

A "great concept, expertly executed" – Josh & Victoria Overington's "superb" venture provides some of "the best high-end dining in York". "Josh is rightly lauded for his food" – "unique, experimental, fun, complicated, very intelligent" – and the format is that you get what you are given (which changes between days, and even between tables on the same sitting) from a four-course or eight-course menu. To accompany, there is an "exciting", "fairly priced wine list with huge number of wines by the glass" presided over by Vicky. "It's limited by its small space, but they try hard" and the whole experience is "ungimmicky" and shows "remarkable attention to detail". / www.lecochonaveugle.uk; @lecochonaveugle; Wed-Fri, Sun 9 pm.

IL PARADISO DEL CIBO £38 3 3 4

40 WALMGATE YO1 9TJ 0190 461 1444

"A great find" – behind an unprepossessing exterior, Sardinian Paolo Silesu's "jolly and buzzing" outfit serves "excellent and imaginative dishes" including the Italian classics (and is "paradise for pizza lovers"). He recently opened an out-of-town branch at Sutton-on-the-Forest. / www.ilparadisodelciboyork.com; 10pm; closed Mon D, Tue D, Wed D, Thu D & Fri D.

THE IVY ST HELEN'S SQUARE £56 2 2 4

2 SAINT HELEN'S SQUARE YO1 8QP 01904 403888

The Ivy's provincial roll-out landed in York amid reports of a "packed"120-seat dining room. It also generated a familiar split of opinion: some see it as a "fun and delicious addition" to the city's dining scene, while to others it is "pure commercial exploitation – almost London prices for something akin to cook-chill food". Adding insult to injury, there's "not a celebrity in sight…" / www.theivyyork.com; @theivyyork; Mon-Sat 12.30 am.

MANNION & CO £36 3 2 2

1 BLAKE ST YO1 8QJ 01904 631030

Andrew Burton's rustic-chic former greengrocer's turned café, deli and artisan bakery, with a two-year-old spin-off in Helmsley. You "can be cheek by jowl" with your neighbours, but the victuals (grazing platters, sausage rolls, stuffed sandwiches) make it "far better than the chains". Top Tip: much-nominated for its excellent breakfasts. / www.mannionandco.co.uk; @MannionsofYork; Mon-Sat 5 pm, Sun 4.30 pm; no bookings.

MELTON'S £65 4 4 3

7 SCARCROFT RD YO23 1ND 01904 634 341

This "utterly reliable destination in a terrace house just outside the city walls" (towards the racecourse) has been a "local restaurant of choice" for almost 30 years. "Often forgotten amongst the new openings in York, it remains one of the best addresses in the city, with great food and intelligent wines". Chef-proprietor Michael Hjort trained with the Roux Brothers in the 1980s before returning to his home city; he is now part of the gastronomic establishment as director of York Food Festival and owner of the Walmgate Ale House and, most recently, the Chopping Block above it. / www.meltonsrestaurant.co.uk; @meltons1; Wed-Sat, Tue 9.30 pm; no Amex.

MIDDLETHORPE HALL £106 3 3 4

BISHOPTHORPE ROAD YO23 2GB 01904 641241

The "ultra-traditional" wood-panelled dining room of this handsome William & Mary country pile, now owned by the National Trust and operated as a hotel, is the perfect setting for a "civilized lunch", with "food and service that match the splendid surroundings". "A must for dining when visiting York", or just drop in for afternoon tea. / www.middlethorpe.com; 9.30 pm; no shorts; children: 6+. **Accommodation:** 29 rooms, from £199

LOS MOROS £21 4 4 2

SHAMBLES FOOD COURT, SHAMBLES MARKET YO1 7LA 07758 210621

"Brilliant Moroccan street food" makes this stall in Shambles Market "a must visit" say fans, perhaps mindful of its No 1 position on TripAdvisor last year. Owner Tarik Abdeladim is cleary doing something right as he opened his first permanent venture in Grape Lane in October 2018 . / restaurantsnapshot.com/LosMoros; Mon-Sat 9.30 pm, Sun 4 pm.

MR PS CURIOUS TAVERN £44 3 3 3

71 LOW PETERGATE YO1 7HY 01904 521177

"Lively, interesting and fun" – Andrew Pern's wilfully wild and wacky venue serves "unusual plates of Yorkshire food in eclectic surroundings" and, though it can seem pricey, it was generally well-rated this year. / mrpscurioustavern.co.uk/; @MrPsTavern; Tue-Fri 10 pm, Sat 11 pm, Sun 6 pm.

MUMBAI LOUNGE £40 3 2 3

47 FOSSGATE YO1 9TF 01904 654 155

One of York's better Indians; there's "plenty of atmosphere" at this vividly decorated venue, and its wide-ranging menu, covering multiple regions of the subcontinent, continues to impress, even those "not particularly enthusiastic" about the genre. / www.mumbailoungeyork.co.uk; Sun-Thu 11.30 pm, Fri & Sat midnight.

PAIRINGS £33 4 4 4

28 CASTLEGATE YO1 9RP 01904 848909

A "great little wine bar with exceptional wines, personal service and tasty nibbles" – this three-year-old venture offers simple food (sharing platters, charcuterie, cheeses) to help soak up its vinous offerings. Top Tip: "the 'Pairing Wine Flights' matching food with wine are a fab concept and fun to experiment with". / pairings.co.uk; Mon-Sat 9.30 pm, Sun 4 pm.

THE PARK - BY ADAM JACKSON £66 4 4 3

4 - 5 SAINT PETER'S GROVE YO30 6AQ 01904 640101

"A wonderful dining experience" is trumpeted by fans of Adam Jackson's flavour-packed cuisine at this town house hotel dining room. À la carte is available on an 'earlybird' basis, but the main event is a seven-course tasting menu. / www.marmadukestownhousehotelyork.com/the-park/; @theparkrestaura; Sun-Thu 11 pm, Fri & Sat midnight; children: 14.

PARTISAN £24 4 4 3

112 MICKLEGATE YO1 6JX 01904 629866

"Housed in beautiful, old premises with stunning period decor" – this "relaxed" yearling provides "a lovely choice of coffees, breakfast dishes and cakes to die for" plus counter salads and some more interesting options; on Thursday and Friday nights, the menu steps up a further gear. / www.partisanuk.com; @YorkPartisan; Mon-Sat 9.30 pm, Sun 4 pm.

PIG AND PASTRY £15 3 4 3

35 BISHOPTHORPE ROAD YO23 1NA 01904 675115

"A little cafe, and it's often a bit of a squash" at this "proper local spot" outside the city walls. "Steve and his staff always have a smile on their faces even when the place is busy… which is to say often". "The food is freshly prepared from local ingredients and is usually really, really good". Breakfasts in particular here inspire queues, and – despite the name – include "fabulous veggie options". / thepigandpastry.com/; @Thepigandpastry; Mon - Sat 5.00pm.

RATTLE OWL £43 4 4 2

104 MICKLEGATE YO1 6JX 01904 658 658

"The food is lovely" at Clarrie O'Callaghan's diminutive, "bistro-style" three-year-old in a grade II-listed former bookshop on Micklegate, although one or two diners feel "the setting lets it down a bit" – "it's like a cafe serving top-class meals". Top Tip: "their lunch including wine and coffee for £20 is one of the best offers in town". / www.rattleowl.co.uk; @TheRattleOwl; Mon closed; Tue - Sat 9.30 pm; Sun 4 pm.

ROOTS £51

68 MARYGATE YO30 7BH

'Great British Menu' winner Tommy Banks and family, who run legendary country-inn-with-rooms The Black Swan at Oldstead, have opened this newcomer in central York: a converted Tudorbethan pub near the river. Early press reviews says the menu features dishes of similar obscure inspiration to those at The Black Swan, and are by-and-large ecstatic. / www.rootsyork.com; @RootsYork; Tue-Sat 10 pm, Mon 3 pm, Sun 9 pm.

SKOSH £45 5 4 3

98 MICKLEGATE YO1 6JX 01904 634 849

"Highly originally, generally awesome" – Neil
Bentinck's "effortlessly friendly" two-year-old
venture in the middle of the city achieves a
seldom-seen level of diner-satisfaction. "It's
tapas-y small plates, and it's not cheap, but it's
also really clever and really delicious". "Every
single dish is so exciting and different" with "big
flavours on the plate" – "remarkable, intelligent,
technically brilliant cooking with a nod to India
[and elsewhere in Asia]". Its "very buzzy",
"tables are a bit close together, and the chairs
aren't the most comfortable": "so if you want a
nice quiet restaurant for a tête à téte then this
is possibly not the place for you". But for some
accessible theatre, "sit on the stools and you
can see into the kitchen". / www.skoshyork.co.uk;
@skoshyork; Sun-Fri 11 pm, Sat 11.30 pm; credit card
deposit required to book.

STAR INN THE
CITY £63 1 1 4

**LENDAL ENGINE HOUSE, MUSEUM STREET
YO1 7DR 01904 619208**

"Set in a lovely location next to the river",
Andrew Pern's "posh gastropub" – a city
offshoot from the Star Inn at Harome – is
certainly capable of fine meals, and fans applaud
its "proper ingredients, cooked well" that
"celebrate British food". But its ratings continue
to be dragged down by "inconsistent cooking
and sketchy service": "dining here really is a
rollercoaster: they need to get a grip and ensure
some consistency in both food and service". /
www.starinnthecity.co.uk; @Starinnthecity; Mon-Thu
9 pm, Fri & Sat 9.30 pm, Sun 5 pm.

31 CASTLEGATE
RESTAURANT £47 3 3 4

31 CASTLEGATE YO1 9RN 01904 621404

"Housed in an old Georgian architects drawing
office" – this "consistently good" venture in the
centre of the city wins all-round praise. Top Tip:
"very reasonably priced early bird menu". /
www.31castlegate.co.uk; @31castlegate; 9.30pm.

THE WHIPPET
INN £50 3 3 3

15 NORTH ST YO1 6JD 01904 500660

"Handy for the station", this glam, brick-walled
steak and ale house turns out "competent
cooking" (spanning blackboard offers and
particularly "outstanding steaks") plus a "fab
G&T range"; NB – it's adults (14+) only, so leave
the nippers at home. / www.thewhippetinn.co.uk;
@WhippetWhere; Sun-Thu 11 pm, Fri & Sat
midnight.

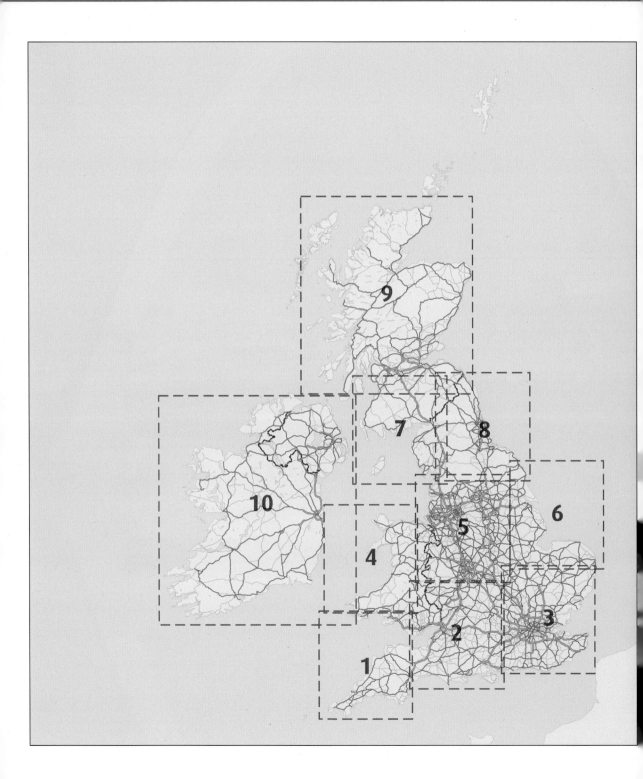

MAP 1

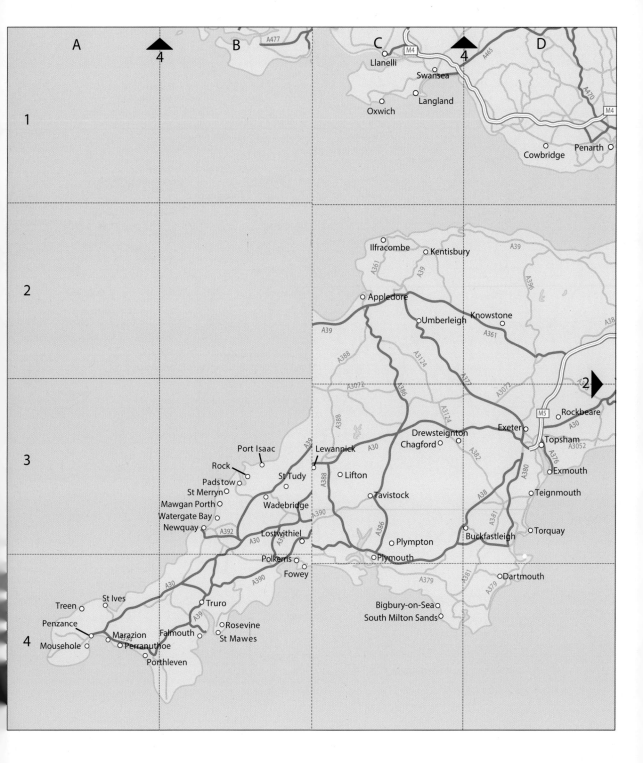

A   B   C   D

A477

4

M4

4

A465

Llanelli

Swansea

A470

M4

Langland

Oxwich

Penarth

Cowbridge

1

2

Ilfracombe

Kentisbury

A39

A361

A39

A39

A396

Appledore

A38

Umberleigh

Knowstone

A39

A361

A388

A3124

A37

2

A3072

A386

A3072

A388

M5

Rockbeare

A3124

Drewsteignton

Exeter

A30

Port Isaac

A39

Lewannick

Chagford

Topsham

A3052

Rock

St Tudy

A30

Lifton

A392

A376

Padstow

A388

Exmouth

3

St Merryn

Wadebridge

Tavistock

A38

Teignmouth

Mawgan Porth

A390

A381

Watergate Bay

A386

Newquay

A392

Lostwithiel

A380

Torquay

A30

A390

Plympton

Buckfastleigh

Polkerris

Plymouth

Fowey

A30

A379

A361

Dartmouth

A379

Treen

St Ives

Truro

Bigbury-on-Sea

A390

A39

South Milton Sands

Penzance

Rosevine

Mousehole

Marazion

Falmouth

St Mawes

Perranuthoe

Porthleven

4

MAP 2

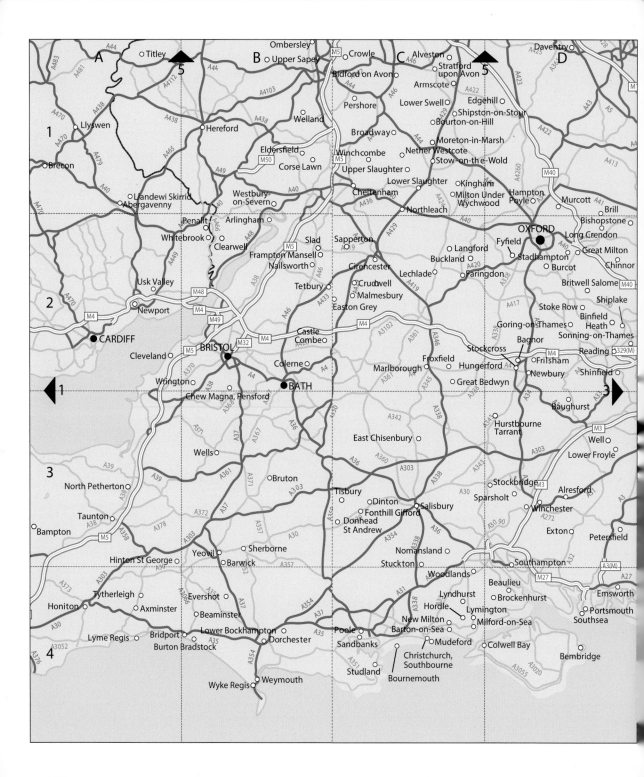

MAP 3

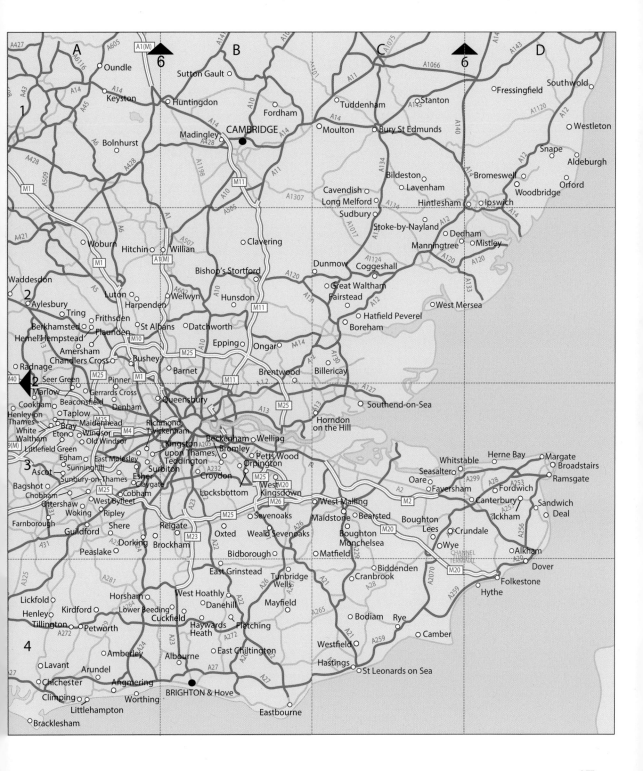

MAP 4

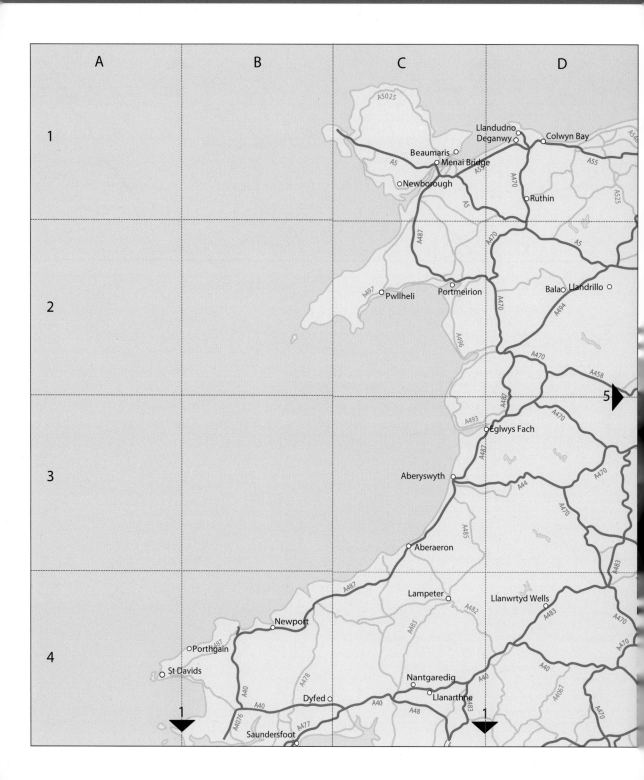

MAP 5

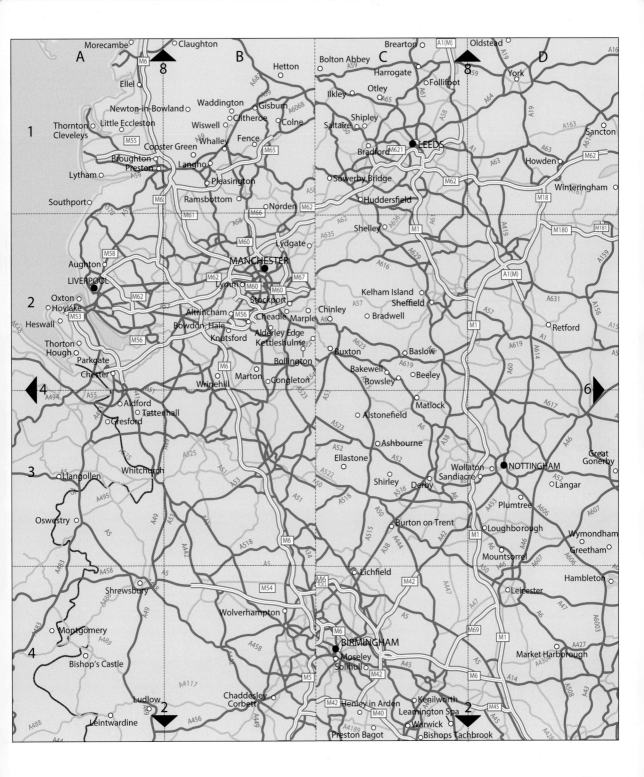

MAP 6

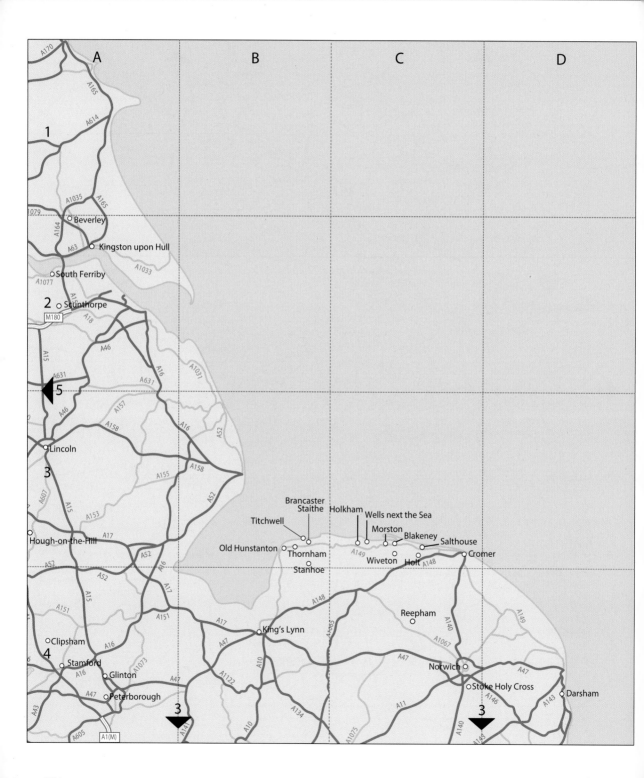

A   B   C   D

1

A170
A165
A614
A1035
A165
1079
A164
Beverley
A63
Kingston upon Hull
A1033
South Ferriby
A1077

2   Scunthorpe
A1
M180
A18
A46
A16
A1031
A15
A631

5
A46
A157
A631
A16
A158
A52
Lincoln

3
A607
A158
A16
A155
A158
A15
A153
A52
Hough-on-the-Hill
A17
A52

Brancaster
Staithe   Holkham
Titchwell   Wells next the Sea
Morston
Old Hunstanton   Thornham   Blakeney   Salthouse
A149
Wiveton   Holt   Cromer
Stanhoe   *A148*

A52
A52
A151
A17
A148
Reepham
A149
A1067
A140
Clipsham   *A16*   King's Lynn
A17
A47
4   Stamford
A10
A1073
A47
Glinton   *A16*
Norwich   *A47*
A47
A1122
Stoke Holy Cross
Peterborough   *A134*
A11
A146   Darsham
A143
A43
3
A10
A1075
A140
3
A605
A1(M)

MAP 7

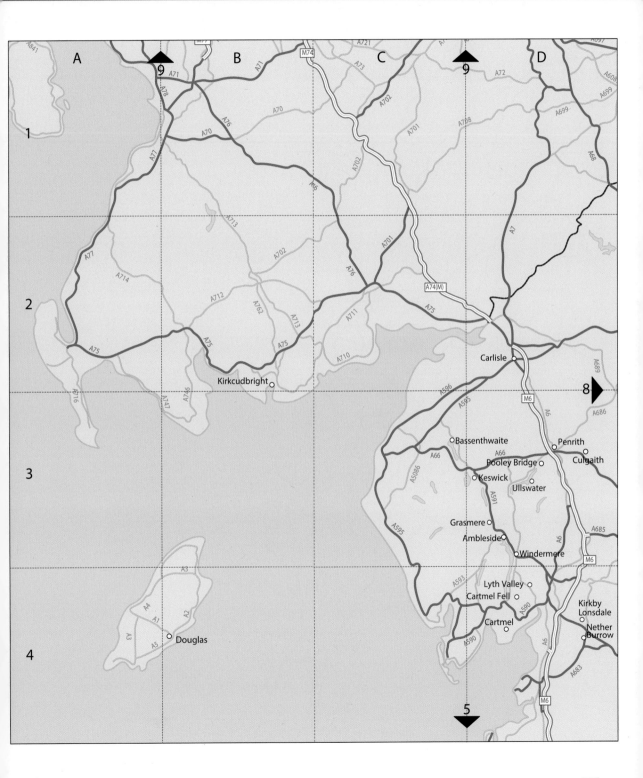

A

B

C

D

1

2

3

4

9

9

8

5

A841

M77

A74

A721

A73

A697

A72

A608

A699

A71

A702

A701

A708

A699

A68

A71

A78

A70

A76

A70

A46

A702

A701

A7

A713

A702

A76

A701

A74(M)

A77

A75

A714

A712

A762

A713

A711

A75

A716

A747

A746

A75

A710

A75

A75

Kirkcudbright

Carlisle

A596

A689

A595

M6

A6

A686

Bassenthwaite

A66

Penrith

A5086

Pooley Bridge

Culgaith

Keswick

A66

Ullswater

A591

A685

Grasmere

A6

A595

Ambleside

Windermere

M6

A593

Lyth Valley

Cartmel Fell

A590

Kirkby
Lonsdale

A3

Cartmel

Nether
Burrow

A4

A1

A2

A590

A6

A3

A5

Douglas

A683

M6

275

MAP 8

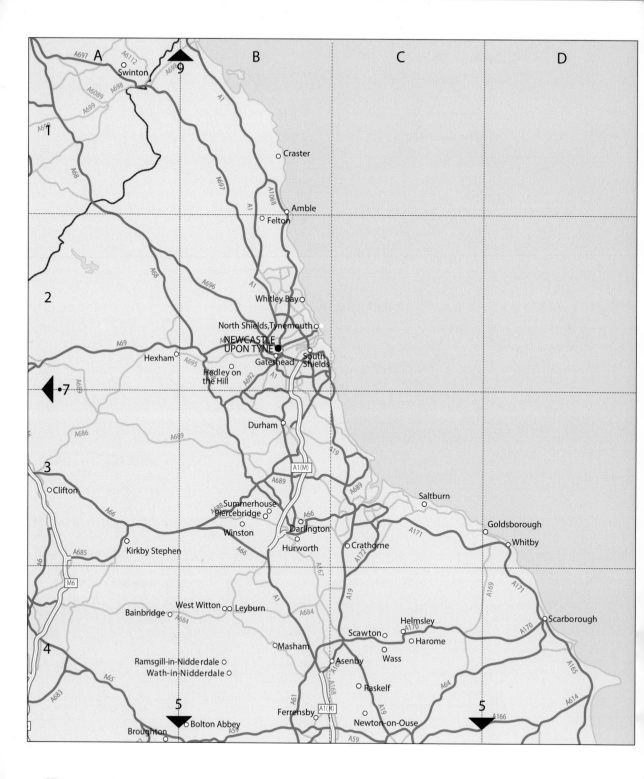

MAP 9

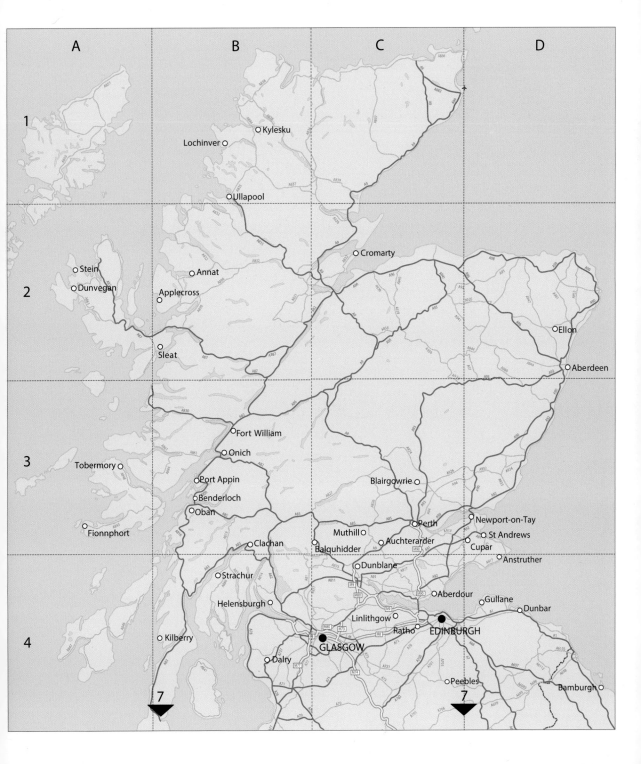

A B C D

1

Kylesku

Lochinver

Ullapool

2

Stein
Dunvegan
Applecross
Annat
Cromarty
Ellon
Aberdeen

Sleat

3

Tobermory
Fort William
Onich
Port Appin
Benderloch
Oban
Fionnphort
Blairgowrie
Perth
Newport-on-Tay
St Andrews
Clachan
Muthill
Auchterarder
Cupar
Balquhidder
Anstruther
Dunblane
Strachur
Aberdour
Gullane
Helensburgh
Dunbar
Linlithgow
Ratho
EDINBURGH
GLASGOW
4

Kilberry
Dalry
Peebles
Bamburgh

7 7

MAP 10

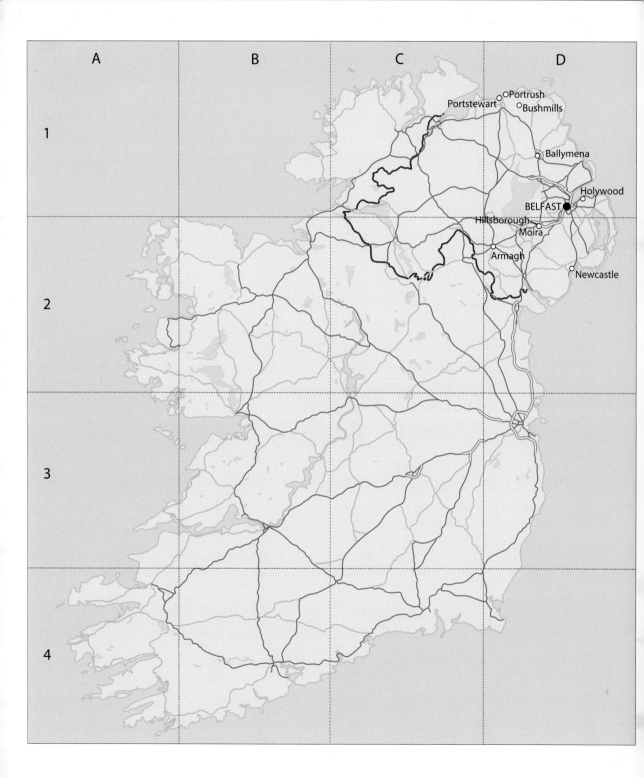

A B C D

1

2

3

4

Portstewart Portrush
Bushmills

Ballymena

Holywood

BELFAST

Hillsborough
Moira

Armagh

Newcastle

ALPHABETICAL INDEX

Melford Valley Tandoori *Long Melford* 221

Melton's *York* 265

MemSaab *Nottingham* 236

Menier Chocolate Factory *London* 84

Menu Gordon Jones *Bath* 172

Meraki *London* 84

Mercato Metropolitano *London* 84

The Mercer *London* 84

Merchants Tavern *London* 84

Le Mercury *London* 84

Mere *London* 84

Meson don Felipe *London* 85

Mews of Mayfair *London* 85

Meza 85

Mezzet *East Molesey* 197

Mezzet Dar *East Molesey* 197

Mi And Pho *Manchester* 226

La Mia Mamma *London* 85

Michael Nadra 85

Middle House *Mayfield* 230

Middlethorpe Hall *York* 265

Midland Hotel *Morecambe* 230

Midsummer House *Cambridge* 186

Mien Tay 85

Mildreds 85

The Milestone *Kelham Island* 213

Milk *London* 85

The Mill at Gordleton *Hordle* 211

The Miller of Mansfield *Goring-on-Thames* 206

Millworks *Cambridge* 186

Milsoms *Dedham* 195

Min Jiang, The Royal Garden Hotel *London* 85

Minnow *London* 85

Mint and Mustard *Cardiff* 187

Mint Leaf 85

The Mint Room *Bath* 172

The Mint Room *Bristol* 182

The Mirabelle, The Grand Hotel *Eastbourne* 197

Les Mirabelles *Nomansland* 234

Mirch Masala *London* 85

Mirror Room *London* 86

The Mistley Thorn Restaurant & Rooms *Mistley* 230

The Modern Pantry *London* 86

Moksh *Cardiff* 187

Moksha *London* 86

The Mole & Chicken *Long Crendon* 221

Al Molo *Weymouth* 260

Momo *London* 86

Mon Plaisir Restaurant *London* 86

Mona Lisa *London* 86

Monachyle Mhor *Balquhidder* 171

Monkey House *Lymington* 223

Monkey Temple *London* 86

Monmouth Coffee Company 86

Monty's Deli *London* 86

Moor Hall *Aughton* 170

The Moorcock Inn *Sowerby Bridge* 250

The Moorings *Blakeney* 176

Morito 86

Moro *London* 86

Los Moros *York* 265

Morston Hall *Morston* 231

Mortimers *Ludlow* 222

Motcombs *London* 86

Mother *London* 86

Mother India *Glasgow* 205

Mother India's Cafe *Edinburgh* 199

Motte And Bailey Cafe *Arundel* 169

Moules A Go Go *Chester* 190

Mourne Seafood Bar *Belfast* 173

Mowgli *Liverpool* 220

Mr Bao *London* 87

Mr Chow *London* 87

Mr Cooper's, The Midland Hotel *Manchester* 226

Mr Ps Curious Tavern *York* 265

Mrs Miller's *Culgaith* 194

Mughli *Manchester* 226

The Mulberry Tree *Boughton Monchelsea* 177

Mumbai Lounge *York* 265

Mumtaz *Bradford* 178

Munal Tandoori *London* 87

Murano *London* 87

Murmur *Brighton* 180

Mustard *London* 87

Mustard Pot *Leeds* 217

My Sichuan *Oxford* 239

Namaaste Kitchen *London* 87

Namaste India *Norwich* 235

Nanashi *London* 87

Nanban *London* 87

The Narrow *London* 87

Native *London* 87

Naughty Piglets *London* 87

Nautilus *London* 87

Le Nautique *Guernsey* 207

Navadhanya Cambridge *Cambridge* 186

Navadhanya Edinburgh *Edinburgh* 199

Navarro's *London* 87

Needoo *London* 87

Neo Bistro *London* 87

The Neptune *Old Hunstanton* 237

Neptune, The Principal *London* 87

New Chapter *Edinburgh* 199

New Street Bar & Grill *Petworth* 241

The Newport *Newport On Tay* 234

Niche *London* 88

1900 Mariners *Ipswich* 213

1921 Angel Hill *Bury St Edmunds* 185

The Ninth London *London* 88

Nippon Kitchen *Glasgow* 205

No 131 *Cheltenham* 189

No 29 Power Station West *London* 88

No 34 *Bournemouth* 177

No 7 Fish Bistro *Torquay* 256

No 97 *Surbiton* 254

No Man's Grace *Bristol* 182

No. 1 *Cromer* 193

No. 9 *Stratford upon Avon* 253

No.1 Ship Street *Oxford* 239

No.5 London End *Beaconsfield* 173

The Noahs Ark Inn *Petworth* 241

Noble *Holywood* 211

Noble Rot *London* 88

Nobu, Metropolitan Hotel *London* 88

Nobu Berkeley *London* 88

Nobu Shoreditch *London* 88

Noisy Lobster *Mudeford* 231

Noizé *London* 88

Nonna's *Sheffield* 248

Noor Jahan 88

Nopi *London* 88

Nordic Bakery *London* 88

The Norfolk Arms *London* 89

North China *London* 89

North Sea Fish *London* 89

The Northall, Corinthia Hotel *London* 89

Northbank *London* 89

Northcote *Langho* 215

Northcote Manor *Umberleigh* 257

Novello *Lytham* 223

Novikov (Asian restaurant) *London* 89

Novikov (Italian restaurant) *London* 89

Nuala *London* 89

Number Four *Shrewsbury* 249

Number One, Balmoral Hotel *Edinburgh* 199

Number Ten *Lavenham* 216

Nuovi Sapori *London* 89

Nusr-Et Steakhouse *London* 89

The Nut Tree Inn *Murcott* 231

Nutbourne *London* 89

Nutter's *Norden* 234

O'ver *London* 89

Oak 89

Oak Bistro *Cambridge* 186

The Oban Fish & Chip Shop *Oban* 237

Oblix *London* 89

Odette's *London* 90

Ogino *Beverley* 174

Ognisko Restaurant *London* 90

Oka 90

Oklava *London* 90

Oktopus *Liverpool* 220

The Old Bakery *Lincoln* 219

The Old Bell Hotel *Malmesbury* 223

The Old Boat House Amble *Amble* 167

Old Bridge Hotel *Huntingdon* 212

The Old Butchers *Stow on the Wold* 253

The Old Coastguard *Mousehole* 231

Old Downton Lodge *Ludlow* 222

Old Hall Inn *Chinley* 190

Old House *Hull* 212

The Old Inn *Drewsteignton* 196

The Old Passage Inn *Arlingham* 169

Old Stamp House *Ambleside* 168

Oldroyd *London* 90

Oli's Thai *Oxford* 239

The Olive Branch *Clipsham* 192

The Olive Tree, Queensberry Hotel *Bath* 172

Oliver's *Falmouth* 202

Oliveto *London* 90

Olivier at the Red Lion *Britwell Salome* 183

Olivo *London* 90

Olivocarne *London* 90

Olivomare *London* 90

Olle *London* 90

Olley's *London* 90

Olympic, Olympic Studios *London* 90

Olympus Fish *London* 90

Omar's Place *London* 90

On The Bab (GROUP) 90

On the Dak *London* 91

On The Hill *Ruthin* 246

Ondine *Edinburgh* 199

The One Bull *Bury St Edmunds* 185

One Canada Square *London* 91

108 Brasserie *London* 91

108 Garage *London* 91

101 Thai Kitchen *London* 91

100 Wardour Street *London* 91

1 Lombard Street *London* 91

1 Mostyn Square *Parkgate* 240

Les 110 de Taillevent *London* 91

Opera Tavern *London* 91

Opheem *Birmingham* 175

The Oppo *Stratford upon Avon* 253

Opso *London* 91

Opus Restaurant *Birmingham* 175

Indian Accent, London